Wetlands Regulation

Case Law, Interpretation, and Commentary

Theda Braddock Fowler

ABS Consulting

Government Institutes
Rockville, Maryland

ABS Consulting
4 Research Place, Rockville, Maryland 20850, USA
Phone: (301) 921-2300
Fax: (301) 921-0373
Email: giinfo@govinst.com
Internet: http://www.govinst.com

06 05 04 03 4 3 2 1

Library of Congress Cataloging-in-Publication Data

Fowler, Theda Braddock.
Wetlands regulation : case law, interpretation, and commentary / Theda Braddock Fowler.
p. cm.
Includes index.
ISBN 0-86587-968-0
1. Wetlands--Law and legislation--United States. 2. Wetlands--Law and legislation--United States--Cases. I. Title.

KF5624.F69 2003
346.7304'6918--dc21

2003052416

Printed in the United States of America

For Alan

Summary Contents

Contents

Introduction

This text started out as an update of *Wetlands: An Introduction to Ecology, the Law, and Permitting*, which was published in 1995 and has become an international seller. People interested in wetlands regulation in Italy, Brazil, and China, to name a few, bought the book. In this country, it sold to law schools, libraries, as well as to many, many individuals. At its core, this book is a much enlarged and updated version.

In the course of that updating procedure, two guiding principles were adhered to. One, there is no wetlands regulation casebook for law school classes in existence, so this text will satisfy that need. Two, in telling the story of the "how" and "why" of wetland regulation, it became apparent that the federal wetlands cases themselves tell the story the best. The reader can follow the logic of the courts and thus gain a better understanding of why the law is the way it is. Particularly in the area of regulatory takings, where none of the cases seem to have a predictable outcome, the reader can observe the courts' thought processes as they struggle with ancient concepts and modern uses. Jurisdiction, too, is a constantly evolving area, especially when an assertion of jurisdiction may mean that someone goes to jail or pays a hefty fine.

Not every wetlands case, however, is a gem. Some are so convoluted as to have almost no value to the reader. Others are long—too long—and seem to take forever to make their point. Choosing and excerpting what has been included in this text was a daunting task. Not every case is represented in this text. The reader is encouraged to visit a law library or download from the Internet the other cases cited in the text and read them.

Wetlands law changes constantly. As population pressures militate in favor of development in wetlands, the courts will be strained to justify allowing that development (thus enraging environmentalists), or denying development (thus enraging developers and property owners). Wetland science is also forcing changes in the law through its new-found recognition of the different values of wetlands. Other legal theories, statutes, and treaties alter the course of wetlands regulation.

The book is divided into five sections covering jurisdiction, the permit requirement, permitting procedures, enforcement, and regulatory takings. Included in each section are representative cases, some of them the classic exposition of the law. Each section builds on itself with the more basic cases first, and ending with the most modern explanation of the law in that area.

Not included in this text are any chapters on wetland ecology. Although the chapters in *Wetlands: An Introduction to Ecology, the Law, and Permitting* are still valid, there are so many, much more authoritative texts on wetlands ecology that it was felt this text, focusing as it does on the law of wetland regulation, should not try to serve two masters.

It is hoped that this new, more complete exposition of federal wetlands law will be useful to students, developers, and ecologists in every country with wetlands.

About the Author

Theda Braddock Fowler is a member of the California, Maryland, Massachusetts, and Washington State Bars. She is admitted to the Bars of the Federal District Courts for the Northern District of California, the District of Maryland, the District of Massachusetts, and the Western District of Washington, as well as the Federal Courts of Appeal for the Fourth and Ninth Circuits. She is also admitted to practice before the United States Court of Federal Claims and the United States Supreme Court.

Her interest in wetlands began at an early age with sailing at her parents' summer home on Cape Cod. Law school took her to San Francisco. She practiced there for several years before moving back to Annapolis, Maryland, where she had gone to college. She continued her sailing on Chesapeake Bay and met her husband. When the U.S. Army transferred him to Ft. Lewis, Washington, she moved to Steilacoom on the shore of Puget Sound. She has always practiced law where wetlands abound.

Part One

JURISDICTION

The basic source of power by which the federal government regulates wetlands is Article I, §8, Clause 3 of the United States Constitution, the "Commerce Clause." The Commerce Clause requires that before the federal government can regulate an activity, it must have a substantial effect on interstate commerce. Initially, under the power to regulate the navigability of interstate waters, an obvious exercise of federal power under the Commerce Clause, cases began to find that discharges of pollutants in suspension (which then settled out and obstructed navigability) could be prohibited under the Rivers and Harbors Act of 1899. Then, but still prior to enactment of the Clean Water Act, the Supreme Court held that a discharge of aviation fuel could also be prohibited under the same Act.

In 1972 Congress enacted the Clean Water Act which prohibited the discharge of dredge or fill materials in "waters of the United States." Wetlands adjacent to navigable waters came to be included in the definition of "waters of the United States." As time went by, the Court discarded the concept of adjacency and held that a wetland was subject to regulation under the Commerce Clause if it was used by migratory birds.

In very recent decisions, however, the Supreme Court has begun limiting the formerly expansive jurisdiction under the Commerce Clause, particularly of isolated wetlands, i.e., those that are not hydrologically connected to navigable waters, even if they are visited by migratory birds.

Chapter 1

THE COMMERCE CLAUSE

Usually the Commerce Clause is broadly construed because so many activities either have an actual, immediate effect of interstate commerce or could have an effect, particularly if the activity or conduct is considered in the aggregate rather than in individual instances. Recently, however, the Supreme Court, in the following sharply divided opinion, indicated that such power is not necessarily unlimited. Although not a wetland case at all, the first case in this book contains an excellent exposition of the history of the Commerce Clause, the understanding of which is a necessary first principle in understanding how Congress believed it could use the Commerce Clause to establish jurisdiction over wetlands.

UNITED STATES v. LOPEZ

514 U.S. 549, 115 S.Ct. 1624, 131 L.Ed. 2d 626 (1995)

In the Gun-Free School Zones Act of 1990, Congress made it a federal offense "for any individual knowingly to possess a firearm at a place that the individual knows, or has reasonable cause to believe, is a school zone." 18 U.S.C.§922(q)(1)(A) (1988 ed, Supp V) [18 U.S.C.A.§922(q)(1)(A)]. The Act neither regulates a commercial activity nor contains a requirement that the possession be connected in any way to interstate commerce. We hold that the Act exceeds the authority of Congress "[t]o regulate Commerce... among the several States...." U.S. Const, Art I, §8, cl 3.

On March 10, 1992, respondent, who was then a 12th-grade student, arrived at Edison High School in San Antonio, Texas, carrying a concealed .38-caliber handgun and five bullets. Acting upon an anonymous tip, school authorities confronted respondent, who admitted that he was carrying the weapon. He was arrested and charged under Texas law with firearm possession on school premises. See Tex Penal Code Ann §46.03(a)(1) (Supp 1994). The next day, the state charges were dismissed after federal agents charged respondent by complaint with violating the Gun-Free School Zones Act of 1990. 18 U.S.C.§922(q)(1)(A) (1988 ed, Supp V) [18 U.S.C.A.§922(q)(1)(A)].

A federal grand jury indicted respondent on one count of knowing possession of a firearm at a school zone, in violation of §922(q). Respondent moved to dismiss his federal indictment on the ground that §922(q) "is unconstitutional as it is beyond the power of Congress to legislate control over our public schools." The District Court denied the motion, concluding that §922(q) "is a constitutional exercise of Congress' well-defined power to regulate activities in and affecting commerce, and the 'business' of elementary, middle and high schools ... affects interstate commerce." App to Pet for Cert 55a. Respondent waived his right to a jury trial. The District Court conducted a bench trial, found him guilty of violating §922(q), and sentenced him to six months' imprisonment and two years' supervised release.

On appeal, respondent challenged his conviction based on his claim that §922(q) exceeded Congress' power to legislate under the Commerce Clause. The Court of Appeals for the Fifth Circuit agreed and reversed respondent's conviction. It held that, in light of what it characterized as insufficient congressional findings and legislative history, "section 922(q), in the full reach of its terms, is invalid as beyond the power of Congress under the Commerce Clause." 2 F.3d 1342, 1367-1368 (1993). Because of the importance of the issue, we granted certiorari, 511 U.S. 1029, 128 L.Ed. 2d 189, 114 S.Ct. 1536 (1994), and we now affirm.

We start with first principles. The Constitution creates a Federal Government of enumerated powers. See Art I, §8. As James Madison wrote: "The powers delegated by the proposed Constitution to the federal government are few and defined. Those which are to remain in the State governments are numerous and indefinite." The Federalist No. 45, pp 292-293 (C. Rossiter ed 1961). This constitutionally mandated division of authority "was adopted by the Framers to ensure protection of our fundamental liberties." *Gregory v. Ashcroft*, 501 U.S. 452, 458, 115 L.Ed.2d 410, 111 S.Ct. 2395 (1991) (internal quotation marks omitted). "Just as the separation and independence of the coordinate branches of the Federal Government serve to prevent the accumulation of excessive power in any one branch, a healthy balance of power between the States and the Federal Government will reduce the risk of tyranny and abuse from either front." *Ibid.*

The Constitution delegates to Congress the power "[t]o regulate Commerce with foreign Nations, and among the several States, and with the Indian Tribes." Art I, §8, cl 3. The Court, through Chief Justice Marshall, first defined the nature of Congress' commerce power in *Gibbons v. Ogden*, 9 Wheat 1, 189-190, 6 L.Ed. 23 (1824):

> "Commerce, undoubtedly, is traffic, but it is something more: it is intercourse. It describes the commercial intercourse between nations, and parts of nations, in all its branches, and is regulated by prescribing rules for carrying on that intercourse."

> The commerce power "is the power to regulate; that is, to prescribe the rule by which commerce is to be governed. This power, like all others vested in congress, is complete in itself, may be exercised to its utmost extent, and acknowledges no limitations, other than are prescribed in the Constitution." *Id.*, at 196, 6 L.Ed. 23. The *Gibbons* Court, however, acknowledged that limitations on the commerce power are inherent in the very language of the Commerce Clause.
>
> "It is not intended to say that these words comprehend that commerce, which is completely internal, which is carried on between man and man in a State, or between different parts of the same State, and which does not extend to or affect other States. Such a power would be inconvenient, and is certainly unnecessary.
>
> "Comprehensive as the word 'among' is, it may very properly be restricted to that commerce which concerns more States than one. . . . The enumeration presupposes something not enumerated; and that something, if we regard the language or the subject of the sentence, must be the exclusively internal commerce of a State." *Id.*, at 194-195, 6 L.Ed. 23.

For nearly a century thereafter, the Court's Commerce Clause decisions dealt but rarely with the extent of Congress' power, and almost entirely with the Commerce Clause as a limit on state legislation that discriminated against interstate commerce. See, *e.g., Veazie v. Moor*, 14 How 568, 573-575, 14 L.Ed. 545 (1853) (upholding a state-created steamboat monopoly because it involved regulation of wholly internal commerce); *Kidd v. Pearson*, 128 U.S. 1, 17, 20-22, 32 L.Ed. 346, 9 S.Ct. 6 (1888) (upholding a state prohibition on the manufacture of intoxicating liquor because the commerce power "does not comprehend the purely internal domestic commerce of a State which is carried on between man and man within a State or between different parts of the same State"); see also L. Tribe, *American Constitutional Law* 306 (2d ed 1988). Under this line of precedent, the Court held that certain categories of activity such as "production," "manufacturing," and "mining" were within the province of state governments, and thus were beyond the power of Congress under the Commerce Clause. See *Wickard v. Filburn*, 317 U.S. 111, 121, 87 L.Ed. 122, 63 S.Ct. 82 (1942) (describing development of Commerce Clause jurisprudence).

In 1887, Congress enacted the Interstate Commerce Act, 24 Stat 379, and in 1890, Congress enacted the Sherman Antitrust Act, 26 Stat 209, as amended, 15 U.S.C. §1 *et seq.* [15 U.S.C. §§1 *et seq.*]. These laws ushered in a new era of federal regulation under the commerce power. When cases involving these laws first reached this Court, we imported from our negative Commerce Clause cases the approach that Congress could not regulate activities such as "production," "manufacturing," and "mining." See, *e.g., United States v. E. C. Knight Co.*, 156 U.S. 1, 12, 39 L.Ed. 325, 15 S.Ct. 249 (1895) ("Commerce succeeds to manufacture, and is not part of it"); *Carter v. Carter Coal Co.*, 298 U.S. 238, 304, 80 L.Ed. 1160, 56 S.Ct. 855 (1936) ("Mining brings the subject matter of commerce into existence. Commerce disposes of it"). Simultaneously, however, the Court held that, where the interstate and intrastate aspects of commerce were so mingled together that full regulation of interstate commerce required incidental regulation of intrastate commerce, the Commerce Clause authorized such regulation. See, *e.g., Shreveport Rate Cases*, 234 U.S. 342, 58 L.Ed. 1341, 34 S.Ct. 833 (1914).

In *A.L.A. Schechter Poultry Corp. v. United States*, 295 U.S. 495, 550, 79 L.Ed. 1570, 55 S.Ct. 837, 97 ALR 947 (1935), the Court struck down regulations that fixed the hours and wages of individuals employed by an intrastate business because the activity being regulated related to interstate commerce only indirectly. In doing so, the Court characterized the distinction between direct and indirect effects of intrastate transactions upon interstate commerce as "a fundamental one, essential to the maintenance of our constitutional system." *Id.*, at 548, 79 L.Ed. 1570, 55 S.Ct. 837. Activities that affected interstate commerce directly were within Congress' power; activities that affected interstate commerce indirectly were beyond Congress' reach. *Id.*, at 546, 79 L.Ed. 1570, 55 S.Ct. 837. The justification for this formal distinction was rooted in the fear that otherwise "there would be virtually no limit to the federal power and for all practical purposes we should have a completely centralized government." *Id.*, at 548, 79 L.Ed. 1570, 55 S.Ct. 837.

Two years later, in the watershed case of *NLRB v. Jones & Laughlin Steel Corp.*, 301 U.S. 1, 81 L.Ed. 893, 57 S.Ct. 615 (1937), the Court upheld the National Labor Relations Act against a Commerce Clause challenge, and in the process, departed from the distinction between "direct" and "indirect" effects on interstate commerce. *Id.*, at 36-38, 81 L.Ed. 893, 57 S.Ct. 615 ("The question [of the scope of Congress' power] is necessarily one of degree"). The Court held that intrastate activities that "have such a close and substantial relation to interstate commerce that their control is essential or appropriate to protect that commerce from burdens and obstructions" are within Congress' power to regulate. *Id.*, at 37, 81 L.Ed. 893, 57 S.Ct. 615.

In *United States v. Darby*, 312 U.S. 100, 85 L.Ed. 609, 61 S.Ct. 451, 132 ALR 1430 (1941), the Court upheld the Fair Labor Standards Act, stating:

> The power of Congress over interstate commerce is not confined to the regulation of commerce among the states. It extends to those activities intrastate which so affect interstate commerce or the exercise of the power of Congress over it as to make regulation of them appropriate means to the attainment of a legitimate end, the exercise of the granted power of Congress to regulate interstate commerce. *Id.*, at 118, 85 L.Ed. 609, 61 S.Ct. 451, 132 ALR 1430.

See also *United States v. Wrightwood Dairy Co.*, 315 U.S. 110, 119, 86 L.Ed. 726, 62 S.Ct. 523 (1942) (the commerce power "extends to those intrastate activities which in a substantial way interfere with or obstruct the exercise of the granted power").

In *Wickard v. Filburn*, the Court upheld the application of amendments to the Agricultural Adjustment Act of 1938 to the production and consumption of homegrown wheat. 317 U.S., at 128-129, 87 L.Ed. 122, 63 S.Ct. 82. The *Wickard* Court explicitly rejected earlier distinctions between direct and indirect effects on interstate commerce, stating:

> [E]ven if appellee's activity be local and though it may not be regarded as commerce, it may still, whatever its nature, be reached by Congress if it exerts a substantial economic effect on interstate commerce, and this irrespective of whether such effect is what might at some earlier time have been defined as 'direct' or 'indirect.' *Id.*, at 125, 87 L.Ed. 122, 63 S.Ct. 82.

The *Wickard* Court emphasized that although Filburn's own contribution to the demand for wheat may have been trivial by itself, that was not "enough to remove him from the scope of federal regulation where, as here, his contribution, taken together with that of many others similarly situated, is far from trivial." *Id.*, at 127-128, 87 L.Ed. 122, 63 S.Ct. 82.

Jones & Laughlin Steel, Darby, and *Wickard* ushered in an era of Commerce Clause jurisprudence that greatly expanded the previously defined authority of Congress under that Clause. In part, this was a recognition of the great changes that had occurred in the way business was carried on in this country. Enterprises that had once been local or at most regional in nature had become national in scope. But the doctrinal change also reflected a view that earlier Commerce Clause cases artificially had constrained the authority of Congress to regulate interstate commerce.

But even these modern-era precedents which have expanded congressional power under the Commerce Clause confirm that this power is subject to outer limits. In *Jones & Laughlin Steel*, the Court warned that the scope of the interstate commerce power "must be considered in the light of our dual system of government and may not be extended so as to embrace effects upon interstate commerce so indirect and remote that to embrace them, in view of our complex society, would effectually obliterate the distinction between what is national and what is local and create a completely centralized government." 301 U.S., at 37, 81 L.Ed. 893, 57 S.Ct. 615; see also *Darby, supra*, at 119-120, 85 L.Ed. 609, 61 S.Ct. 451, 132 ALR 1430 (Congress may regulate intrastate activity that has a "substantial effect" on interstate commerce); *Wickard, supra*, at 125, 121, 87 L.Ed. 122, 63 S.Ct. 82 (Congress may regulate activity that "exerts a substantial economic effect on interstate commerce"). Since that time, the Court has heeded that warning and undertaken to decide whether a rational basis existed for concluding that a regulated activity sufficiently affected interstate commerce. See, *e.g.*, *Hodel v. Virginia Surface Mining & Reclamation Assn., Inc.*, 452 U.S. 264, 276-280, 69 L.Ed. 2d 1, 101 S.Ct. 2352 (1981); *Perez v. United States*, 402 U.S. 146, 155-156, 28 L.Ed. 2d 686, 91 S.Ct. 1357 (1971); *Katzenbach v. McClung*, 379 U.S. 294, 299-301, 13 L.Ed. 2d 290, 85 S.Ct. 377 (1964); *Heart of Atlanta Motel, Inc. v. United States*, 379 U.S. 241, 252-253, 13 L.Ed. 2d 258, 85 S.Ct. 348 (1964).

Similarly, in *Maryland v. Wirtz*, 392 U.S. 183, 20 L.Ed. 2d 1020, 88 S.Ct. 2017 (1968), the Court reaffirmed that "the power to regulate commerce, though broad indeed, has limits" that "[t]he Court has ample power" to enforce. *Id.*, at 196, 20 L.Ed. 2d 1020, 88 S.Ct. 2017, overruled on other grounds, *National League of Cities v. Usery*, 426 U.S. 833, 49 L.Ed. 2d 245, 96 S.Ct. 2465 (1976), overruled by *Garcia v. San Antonio Metropolitan Transit Authority*, 469 U.S. 528, 83 L.Ed. 2d 1016, 105 S.Ct. 1005 (1985). In response to the dissent's warnings that the Court was powerless to enforce the limitations on Congress' commerce powers because "[a]ll activities affecting commerce, even in the minutest degree, *[Wickard]*, may be regulated and controlled by Congress," 392 U.S., at 204, 20 L.Ed. 2d 1020, 88 S.Ct. 2017 (Douglas, J., dissenting), the *Wirtz* Court replied that the dissent had misread precedent as "[n]either here nor in *Wickard* has the Court declared that Congress may use a relatively trivial impact on commerce as an excuse for broad general regulation of state or private activities," *id.*, at 197, n 27, 20 L.Ed. 2d 1020, 88 S.Ct. 2017. Rather, "[t]he Court has said only that where *a general regulatory statute bears a substantial relation to commerce*, the *de minimis* character of individual instances arising under that statute is of no consequence." *Ibid.* (first emphasis added).

Consistent with this structure, we have identified three broad categories of activity that Congress may regulate under its commerce power. *Perez, supra*, at 150, 28 L.Ed. 2d 686, 91 S.Ct. 1357; see also *Hodel, supra*, at 276-277, 276-280, 69 L.Ed. 2d 1, 101 S.Ct. 2352. First, Congress may regulate the use of the channels of interstate commerce. See, *e.g.*, *Darby*, 312 U.S., at 114, 85 L.Ed. 609, 61 S.Ct. 451, 132 ALR 1430; *Heart of Atlanta Motel, supra*, at 256, 13 L.Ed. 2d 258, 85 S.Ct. 348 ("'[T]he authority of Congress to keep the channels of interstate commerce free from immoral and injurious uses has been frequently sustained, and is no longer open to question.'" (quoting *Caminetti v. United States*, 242 U.S. 470, 491, 61 L.Ed. 442, 37 S.Ct. 192 (1917)). Second, Congress is empowered to regulate and protect the instrumentalities of interstate commerce, or persons or things in interstate commerce, even though the threat may come only from intrastate activities. *See, e.g., Shreveport Rate Cases*, 234 U.S. 342 (1914); *Southern R. Co. v. United States*, 222 U.S. 20,

56 L.Ed. 72, 32 S.Ct. 2 (1911) (upholding amendments to Safety Appliance Act as applied to vehicles used in intrastate commerce); *Perez, supra*, at 150, 28 L.Ed. 2d 686, 91 S.Ct. 1357 ("[F]or example, the destruction of an aircraft (18 U.S.C. §32 [18 U.S.C.A. §32]), or ... thefts from interstate shipments (18 U.S.C. §659 [18 U.S.C.A. §659])"). Finally, Congress' commerce authority includes the power to regulate those activities having a substantial relation to interstate commerce, *Jones & Laughlin Steel*, 301 U.S., at 37, 81 L.Ed. 893, 57 S.Ct. 615, *i.e.,* those activities that substantially affect interstate commerce, *Wirtz, supra*, at 196, n 27, 20 L.Ed. 2d 1020, 88 S.Ct. 2017.

Within this final category, admittedly, our case law has not been clear whether an activity must "affect" or "substantially affect" interstate commerce in order to be within Congress' power to regulate it under the Commerce Clause. Compare *Preseault v. ICC*, 494 U.S. 1, 17, 108 L.Ed. 2d 1, 110 S.Ct. 914 (1990), with *Wirtz, supra*, at 196, n 27, 20 L.Ed. 2d 1020, 88 S.Ct. 2017 (the Court has never declared that "Congress may use a relatively trivial impact on commerce as an excuse for broad general regulation of state or private activities"). We conclude, consistent with the great weight of our case law, that the proper test requires an analysis of whether the regulated activity "substantially affects" interstate commerce.

We now turn to consider the power of Congress, in the light of this framework, to enact §922(q). The first two categories of authority may be quickly disposed of: §922(q) is not a regulation of the use of the channels of interstate commerce, nor is it an attempt to prohibit the interstate transportation of a commodity through the channels of commerce; nor can §922(q) be justified as a regulation by which Congress has sought to protect an instrumentality of interstate commerce or a thing in interstate commerce. Thus, if §922(q) is to be sustained, it must be under the third category as a regulation of an activity that substantially affects interstate commerce.

First, we have upheld a wide variety of congressional Acts regulating intrastate economic activity where we have concluded that the activity substantially affected interstate commerce. Examples include the regulation of intrastate coal mining; *Hodel, supra*, intrastate extortionate credit transactions; *Perez, supra*, restaurants utilizing substantial interstate supplies; *McClung, supra*, inns and hotels catering to interstate guests, *Heart of Atlanta Motel, supra*; and production and consumption of homegrown wheat, *Wickard v. Filburn*, 317 U.S. 111, 87 L.Ed. 122, 63 S.Ct. 82 (1942). These examples are by no means exhaustive, but the pattern is clear. Where economic activity substantially affects interstate commerce, legislation regulating that activity will be sustained.

Even *Wickard*, which is perhaps the most far reaching example of Commerce Clause authority over intrastate activity, involved economic activity in a way that the possession of a gun in a school zone does not. Roscoe Filburn operated a small farm in Ohio, on which, in the year involved, he raised 23 acres of wheat. It was his practice to sow winter wheat in the fall, and after harvesting it in July to sell a portion of the crop, to feed part of it to poultry and livestock on the farm, to use some in making flour for home consumption, and to keep the remainder for seeding future crops. The Secretary of Agriculture assessed a penalty against him under the Agricultural Adjustment Act of 1938 because he harvested about 12 acres more wheat than his allotment under the Act permitted. The Act was designed to regulate the volume of wheat moving in interstate and foreign commerce in order to avoid surpluses and shortages, and concomitant fluctuation in wheat prices, which had previously obtained. The Court said, in an opinion sustaining the application of the Act to Filburn's activity:

> One of the primary purposes of the Act in question was to increase the market price of wheat and to that end to limit the volume thereof that could affect the market. It can hardly be denied that a factor of such volume and variability as home-consumed wheat would have a substantial influence on price and market conditions. This may arise because being in marketable condition such wheat overhangs the market and, if induced by rising prices, tends to flow into the market and check price increases. But if we assume that it is never marketed, it supplies a need of the man who grew it which would otherwise be reflected by purchases in the open market. Home-grown wheat in this sense competes with wheat in commerce. 317 U.S., at 128, 87 L.Ed. 122, 63 S.Ct. 82.

Section 922(q) is a criminal statute that by its terms has nothing to do with "commerce" or any sort of economic enterprise, however broadly one might define those terms. Section 922(q) is not an essential part of a larger regulation of economic activity, in which the regulatory scheme could be undercut unless the intrastate activity were regulated. It cannot, therefore, be sustained under our cases upholding regulations of activities that arise out of or are connected with a commercial transaction, which viewed in the aggregate, substantially affects interstate commerce.

Second, §922(q) contains no jurisdictional element which would ensure, through case-by-case inquiry, that the firearm possession in question affects interstate commerce. For example, in *United States v. Bass*, 404 U.S. 336, 30 L.Ed. 2d 488, 92 S.Ct. 515 (1971), the Court interpreted former 18 U.S.C. §1202(a) [18 U.S.C.A. §1202(a)], which made it a crime for a felon to "receiv[e], posses[s], or transpor[t] in commerce or affecting commerce ... any firearm." 404 U.S., at 337, 30 L.Ed. 2d 488, 92 S.Ct. 515. The Court interpreted the possession component of §1202(a) to require an additional nexus to interstate commerce both because the statute was ambiguous, and because "unless Congress conveys its purpose clearly, it will not be deemed to have significantly changed the federal-state balance." *Id.*, at 349, 30 L.Ed. 2d 488, 92 S.Ct. 515. The *Bass* Court set aside the conviction because, although the Government had demonstrated that Bass had possessed a firearm, it had failed "to show the requisite nexus with interstate commerce." *Id.*, at 347, 30 L.Ed. 2d 488, 92 S.Ct. 515. The Court thus interpreted the statute to reserve the constitutional question whether Congress could regulate, without more, the "mere possession" of firearms. See *id.*, at 339, n 4, 30 L.Ed. 2d 488, 92 S.Ct. 515; see also *United States v. Five Gambling Devices*, 346 U.S. 441, 448, 98 L.Ed. 179, 74 S.Ct. 190 (1953) (plurality opinion) ("The principle is old and deeply imbedded in our jurisprudence that this Court will construe a statute in a manner that requires decision of serious constitutional questions only if the statutory language leaves no reasonable alternative"). Unlike the statute in *Bass*, §922(q) has no express jurisdictional element which might limit its reach to a discrete set of firearm possessions that additionally have an explicit connection with or effect on interstate commerce.

Although as part of our independent evaluation of constitutionality under the Commerce Clause we of course consider legislative findings, and indeed even congressional committee findings, regarding effect on interstate commerce, see, *e.g., Preseault v. ICC*, 494 U.S., at 17, 108 L.Ed. 2d 1, 110 S.Ct. 914 (1990), the Government concedes that "[n]either the statute nor its legislative history contain[s] express congressional findings regarding the effects upon interstate commerce of gun possession in a school zone." Brief for United States 5-6. We agree with the Government that Congress normally is not required to make formal findings as to the substantial burdens that an activity has on interstate commerce. See *McClung*, 379 U.S., at 304, 13 L.Ed. 2d 290, 85 S.Ct. 377; see also *Perez*, 402 U.S., at 156, 28 L.Ed. 2d 686, 91 S.Ct. 1357 ("Congress need [not] make particularized findings in order to legislate"). But to the extent that congressional findings would enable us to evaluate the legislative judgment that the activity in question substantially affected interstate commerce, even though no such substantial effect was visible to the naked eye, they are lacking here.

The Government argues that Congress has accumulated institutional expertise regarding the regulation of firearms through previous enactments. Cf. *Fullilove v. Klutznick*, 448 U.S. 448, 503, 65 L.Ed. 2d 902, 100 S.Ct. 2758 (1980) (Powell, J., concurring). We agree, however, with the Fifth Circuit that importation of previous findings to justify §922(q) is especially inappropriate here because the "prior federal enactments or Congressional findings [do not] speak to the subject matter of section 922(q) or its relationship to interstate commerce. Indeed, section 922(q) plows thoroughly new ground and represents a sharp break with the long-standing pattern of federal firearms legislation." 2 F.3d at 1366.

The Government's essential contention, *in fine,* is that we may determine here that §922(q) is valid because possession of a firearm in a local school zone does indeed substantially affect interstate commerce. Brief for United States 17. The Government argues that possession of a firearm in a school zone may result in violent crime and that violent crime can be expected to affect the functioning of the national economy in two ways. First, the costs of violent crime are substantial, and, through the mechanism of insurance, those costs are spread throughout the population. See *United States v. Evans*, 928 F.2d 858, 862 (CA9 1991). Second, violent crime reduces the willingness of individuals to travel to areas within the country that are perceived to be unsafe. Cf. *Heart of Atlanta Motel*, 379 U.S., at 253, 13 L.Ed. 2d 258, 85 S.Ct. 348. The Government also argues that the presence of guns in schools poses a substantial threat to the educational process by threatening the learning environment. A handicapped educational process, in turn, will result in a less productive citizenry. That, in turn, would have an adverse effect on the Nation's economic well-being. As a result, the Government argues that Congress could rationally have concluded that §922(q) substantially affects interstate commerce.

We pause to consider the implications of the Government's arguments. The Government admits, under its "costs of crime" reasoning, that Congress could regulate not only all violent crime, but all activities that might lead to violent crime, regardless of how tenuously they relate to interstate commerce. See Tr. of Oral Arg. 8-9. Similarly, under the Government's "national productivity" reasoning, Congress could regulate any activity that it found was related to the economic productivity of individual citizens: family law (including marriage, divorce, and child custody), for example. Under the theories that the Government presents in support of §922(q), it is difficult to perceive any limitation on federal power, even in areas such as criminal law enforcement or education where States historically have been sovereign. Thus, if we were to accept the Government's arguments, we are hard pressed to posit any activity by an individual that Congress is without power to regulate....

Admittedly, a determination whether an intrastate activity is commercial or noncommercial may in some cases result in legal uncertainty. But, so long as Congress' authority is limited to those powers enumerated in the Constitution, and so long as those enumerated powers are interpreted as having judicially enforceable outer limits, congressional legislation under the Commerce Clause always will engender "legal uncertainty." *Post*, at 17, 131 L.Ed. 2d, at 683. As Chief Justice Marshall stated in *McCulloch v. Maryland*, 4 Wheat 316, 4 L.Ed. 579 (1819):

> "Th[e] [federal] government is acknowledged by all to be one of enumerated powers. The principle, that it can exercise only the powers granted to it ... is now universally admitted. But the question respecting the extent of the powers actually granted, is perpetually

> arising, and will probably continue to arise, as long as our system shall exist." *Id.*, at 405, 4 L.Ed. 579. See also *Gibbons v. Ogden*, 9 Wheat, at 195, 6 L.Ed. 23 ("The enumeration presupposes something not enumerated"). The Constitution mandates this uncertainty by withholding from Congress a plenary police power that would authorize enactment of every type of legislation. See Art I, §8. Congress has operated within this framework of legal uncertainty ever since this Court determined that it was the judiciary's duty "to say what the law is." *Marbury v. Madison*, 1 Cranch 137, 177, 2 L.Ed. 60 (1803) (Marshall, C. J.). Any possible benefit from eliminating this "legal uncertainty" would be at the expense of the Constitution's system of enumerated powers.

In *Jones & Laughlin Steel*, 301 U.S., at 37, 81 L.Ed. 893, 57 S.Ct. 615, we held that the question of congressional power under the Commerce Clause "is necessarily one of degree." To the same effect is the concurring opinion of Justice Cardozo in *Schechter Poultry:*

> "There is a view of causation that would obliterate the distinction between what is national and what is local in the activities of commerce. Motion at the outer rim is communicated perceptibly, though minutely, to recording instruments at the center. A society such as ours 'is an elastic medium which transmits all tremors throughout its territory; the only question is of their size.'" 295 U.S., at 554, 79 L.Ed. 1570, 55 S.Ct. 837, 97 ALR 947 (quoting *United States v. A.L.A. Schechter Poultry Corp.*, 76 F.2d 617, 624 (CA2 1935) (L. Hand, J., concurring)).

These are not precise formulations, and in the nature of things they cannot be. But we think they point the way to a correct decision of this case. The possession of a gun in a local school zone is in no sense an economic activity that might, through repetition elsewhere, substantially affect any sort of interstate commerce. Respondent was a local student at a local school; there is no indication that he had recently moved in interstate commerce, and there is no requirement that his possession of the firearm have any concrete tie to interstate commerce.

To uphold the Government's contentions here, we would have to pile inference upon inference in a manner that would bid fair to convert congressional authority under the Commerce Clause to a general police power of the sort retained by the States. Admittedly, some of our prior cases have taken long steps down that road, giving great deference to congressional action. See *supra*, at 556-558, 131 L.Ed. 2d, at 636-637. The broad language in these opinions has suggested the possibility of additional expansion, but we decline here to proceed any further. To do so would require us to conclude that the Constitution's enumeration of powers does not presuppose something not enumerated, cf. *Gibbons v. Ogden, supra*, at 195, 6 L.Ed. 23, and that there never will be a distinction between what is truly national and what is truly local, cf. *Jones & Laughlin Steel, supra*, at 30, 81 L.Ed. 893, 57 S.Ct. 615. This we are unwilling to do.

For the foregoing reasons the judgment of the Court of Appeals is *affirmed.*

[Footnotes omitted]

In another recent opinion, *U.S. v. Morrison*, No. 99-5, decided May 16, 2000, the Supreme Court found that the federal Violence Against Women Act, which gave the victims of crimes motivated by gender a civil remedy against the perpetrator, was an invalid regulation of interstate commerce because a gender-motivated crime is not an economic activity regardless of the aggregate effect on interstate commerce. But see *U.S. v. Moon*, 178 F.3d 1297 (6th Cir. 1999) (drug trafficking is clearly commercial activity that has long been within federal power to regulate, citing *U.S. v. Tucker*, 90 F.3d 1135 (6th Cir. 1999)).

UNITED STATES v. WILSON

133 F.3d 251 (4th Cir. 1997)

The defendants in this case were convicted of felony violations of the Clean Water Act for knowingly discharging fill and excavated material into wetlands of the United States without a permit. On this appeal they challenge: (1) the validity of federal regulations purporting to regulate activities that "could affect" interstate commerce....

Because we conclude that 33 C.F.R. §328.3(a)(3) (1993) (defining waters of the United States to include those waters whose degradation "could affect" interstate commerce) is unauthorized by the Clean Water Act as limited by the Commerce Clause and therefore is invalid... we reverse and remand for a new trial.

I

In February 1996, after a seven-week trial, a jury convicted James J. Wilson, Interstate General Co., L.P., and St. Charles Associates, L.P., on four felony counts charging them with knowingly discharging fill material and excavated dirt into wetlands on four separate parcels without a permit, in violation of the Clean Water Act, 33 U.S.C. §§1319(c)(2)(A) & 1311(a). The district court sentenced Wilson to 21 months imprisonment and 1 year supervised release and fined him $1 million. It fined the other two defendants $3 million and placed them on 5 years probation. The court also ordered the defendants to implement a wetlands restoration and mitigation plan proposed by the government....

At trial, the government introduced evidence that during the period from 1988 to 1993, the defendants attempted to drain at least three of the four parcels of land involved in this case by digging ditches. The excavated dirt was deposited next to the ditches—a process known as "sidecasting." The government also introduced evidence that the defendants transported a substantial amount of fill dirt and gravel and deposited it on three of the parcels; only one parcel involved sidecasting without the addition of fill. The government presented evidence that all four of these parcels contained wetlands and that the defendants failed to obtain permits from the Army Corps of Engineers, the agency charged with issuing permits under the relevant section of the Act, 33 U.S.C. §1344, prior to making efforts to drain and fill the parcels.

Although the parcels in question were not, because of neighboring development, located in pristine wilderness areas, the government presented substantial evidence about the physical characteristics which identified them as wetlands, including testimonial and photographic evidence of significant standing water, reports of vegetation typical to hydrologic soils, and infrared aerial photographs showing a pattern of stream courses visible under the vegetation. Evidence also showed that the properties were identified as containing wetlands on public documents including the National Wetlands Inventory Map and topographical maps of Charles County and the State of Maryland. The government demonstrated that water from these lands flowed in a drainage pattern through ditches, intermittent streams, and creeks, ultimately joining the Potomac River, a tributary of the Chesapeake Bay.

The government also produced evidence of the defendants' awareness of the physical conditions of their land. The very development work underlying the present prosecution involved efforts to improve the drainage of the areas to make building feasible. Substantial fill was later added in an attempt to raise the ground level of the parcels. Some construction work involved repeated reshoring efforts because of wetness-induced ground shifting and collapse. Evidence was introduced that bids for work at one of the parcels actually contained different price quotations for wet and dry work because of the level of moisture on parts of the property. And witnesses gave testimony that despite the attempts at drying the property through ditching and draining or through the pumping off of standing water, and even after hundreds of truck loads of stone, gravel and other fill had been added to three of the parcels, wetland-loving plants continued to sprout through the fill.

Witnesses also testified at trial that a private consulting firm retained by the defendants informed the defendants that its observations of conditions on the parcels led it to conclude that the parcels contained wetlands. The firm recommended seeking permits from the Army Corps of Engineers before beginning development. The defendants were also contacted by Charles County zoning authorities concerned about the possible presence of wetlands in the vicinity of the new construction projects. Finally, the government presented evidence that even as the defendants complied with an Army Corps of Engineers order to cease construction on one of the parcels and remove fill dirt that had already been added, they continued to develop the other parcels without notifying the Corps or making an effort to ascertain whether a permit was necessary.

The defendants introduced contradictory evidence suggesting that whether the four parcels were wetlands under the Clean Water Act was unclear. They offered evidence which they claim showed that the Army Corps of Engineers was inconsistent in asserting jurisdiction over the parcels in question, claiming that the Corps took action on only one parcel, even though it had been aware for years of the ongoing development. Defendants also introduced an internal Corps memorandum that stated that while the areas in the St. Charles community have the "necessary parameters ... to be considered wetlands when using the Corps Wetland Delineation Manual, it is not clear to me that these areas can be interpreted as 'waters of the United States' within the meaning or purview of Section 404." That memo suggested obtaining guidance from higher authority as to what constitutes "waters of the United States." The defendants also introduced evidence indicating their belief that they had legally drained three parcels prior to introducing fill, and that no fill was discharged into the fourth which was being drained by the digging of ditches.

Following 15 hours of deliberation, the jury convicted all defendants of the four felony counts. Because of the felony convictions, the defendants were not convicted of four misdemeanor counts for the "negligent" violations of the Clean Water Act involving the same parcels.

II

The defendants challenge the authority of regulation 33 C.F.R. §328.3(a)(3) (1993) (defining waters of the United States to include those waters whose degradation "could affect" interstate commerce) to extend jurisdiction of the Clean Water Act to the four parcels in question. They also challenge the district court's instructions to the jury which were based on that regulation. They argue that the regulation and instructions exceed not only the authority of the Clean Water Act (which regulates "waters of the United States" without defining them), but also the Commerce Clause, U.S. Const. art. I, §8, cl. 3. They maintain that in allowing the jury to find a nexus with interstate commerce based on whether activities "could affect" interstate commerce, the court authorized a "limitless view of federal jurisdiction," far more expansive than the standard recently summarized in *United States v. Lopez*, 514 U.S. 549, 131 L. Ed. 2d 626, 115 S. Ct. 1624 (1995).

While the defendants argue that the regulation and jury instructions are fatally flawed under *Lopez* because of their invocation of "potential" uses and effects on commerce, they do not challenge the constitutionality of the Clean Water Act itself.

In instructing the jury based upon 33 C.F.R. §328.3(a)(3) (1993), the district court in this case said:

> The government must prove that these waters have some potential connection with interstate commerce. If you find, ladies and gentlemen, beyond a reasonable doubt that these waters were or could be used by visitors from other states for recreational or other purposes, or that fish or shellfish are or could be taken from these waters and sold in interstate or foreign commerce, or that these waters were used or could have been used for industrial purposes by industries in interstate commerce, or that these waters were subject to the ebb and flow of the tide or that the use, degradation or construction [sic] [destruction?] of such waters could affect interstate commerce, then I instruct you as a matter of law that the government has established such connection with interstate commerce and that these waters, including wetlands, are waters of [the] United States.

The Clean Water Act prohibits the discharge, without a permit, of pollutants into "navigable waters." 33 U.S.C. §§1311(a), 1362(12)(A). While the regulatory power of Congress over waters that are navigable in fact is well established, *see, e.g., United States v. Rands*, 389 U.S. 121, 122-23, 19 L.Ed. 2d 329, 88 S.Ct. 265 (1967) ("The Commerce Clause confers a unique position upon the Government in connection with navigable waters. 'The power to regulate commerce comprehends the control for that purpose, and to the extent necessary, of all the navigable waters of the United States ....'" (*quoting Gilman v. Philadelphia*, 70 U.S. (3 Wall.) 713, 724-25, 18 L. Ed. 96 (1866)), the Clean Water Act defines "navigable waters" as "the waters of the United States," 33 U.S.C. §1362(7). Construing the Clean Water Act, the Supreme Court has indicated that in defining "navigable waters" as "waters of the United States," Congress intended "to exercise its powers under the Commerce Clause to regulate at least some waters that would not be deemed 'navigable' under the classical understanding of that term." *United States v. Riverside Bayview Homes, Inc.*, 474 U.S. 121, 133, 88 L.Ed.2d 419, 106 S.Ct. 455 (1985). Accordingly, the power of Congress to regulate the discharge of pollutants into at least some nonnavigable waters is indisputable, but the limits of this power are far from clear. As explained in *Lopez*, Congress can clearly regulate discharges of pollutants that substantially affect interstate commerce. *See* 514 U.S. 549, 558-59, 115 S.Ct. 1624, 131 L.Ed.2d 626 (1995). Presumably, Congress may also regulate the discharge of pollutants into *nonnavigable* waters to the extent necessary to protect the use or potential use of *navigable* waters as channels or instrumentalities of interstate commerce, although the extent of that power is not entirely clear. Finally, it is arguable that Congress has the power to regulate the discharge of pollutants into any waters that themselves flow across state lines, or connect to waters that do so, regardless of whether such waters are navigable in fact, merely because of the interstate nature of such waters, although the existence of such a far reaching power could be drawn into question by the Court's recent federalism jurisprudence. *See, e.g., Printz v. United States*, 138 L.Ed.2d 914, 117 S.Ct. 2365 (1997); *Seminole Tribe v. Florida*, 517 U.S. 44, 116 S.Ct. 1114, 134 L.Ed.2d 252 (1996); *Lopez*, 514 U.S. 549, 131 L.Ed.2d 626, 115 S.Ct. 1624; *New York v. United States*, 505 U.S. 144, 120 L.Ed.2d 120, 112 S.Ct. 2408 (1992).

However, we need not resolve these difficult questions about the extent and limits of congressional power to regulate nonnavigable waters to resolve the issue before us. The regulation challenged here, 33 C.F.R. §328.3(a)(3) (1993), defines "waters of the United States" to include:

> All other waters such as intrastate lakes, rivers, streams (including intermittent streams), mud flats, sand flats, wetlands, sloughs, prairie potholes, wet meadows, playa lakes, or natural ponds, the use, degradation or destruction of which *could affect interstate or foreign commerce* .... (Emphasis added).

This regulation purports to extend the coverage of the Clean Water Act to a variety of waters that are intrastate, nonnavigable, or both, solely on the basis that the use, degradation, or destruction of such waters *could* affect interstate commerce. The regulation requires neither that the regulated activity have a *substantial* affect on interstate commerce, nor that the covered waters have any sort of nexus with navigable, or even interstate, waters. Were this regulation a statute, duly enacted by Congress, it would present serious constitutional difficulties, because, at least at first blush, it would appear to exceed congressional authority under the Commerce Clause. This regulation is not, however, a statute. Absent a clear indication to the contrary, we should not lightly presume that merely by defining "navigable waters" as "the waters of the United States," 33 U.S.C. §1362(7), Congress authorized the Army Corps of Engineers to assert its jurisdiction in such a sweeping and constitutionally troubling manner. Even as a matter of statutory construction, one would expect that the phrase "waters of the United States" when used to define the phrase "navigable waters" refers to waters which, if not navigable in fact, are at least interstate or closely related to navigable or interstate waters. When viewed in light of its statutory authority, 33 C.F.R. §328.3(a)(3) (1993), which defines "waters of the United States" to include intrastate waters that need have nothing to do with navigable or interstate waters, expands the statutory phrase "waters of the United States" beyond its definitional limit.

Accordingly, we believe that in promulgating 33 C.F.R. §328.3(a)(3) (1993), the Army Corps of Engineers exceeded its congressional authorization under the Clean Water Act, and that, for this reason, 33 C.F.R. §328.3(a)(3) (1993) is invalid. For the same reason, the district court's instruction based upon this regulation is also erroneous....

For cases disagreeing with *Wilson,* see *U.S. v. Hallmark Construction Co.*, 14 F.Supp.2d 1069 (N.D.Ill. 1998); *Solid Waste Agency of Northern Cook County v. U.S. Army Corps of Engineers*, 998 F.Supp. 946 (N.D.Ill. 1998). For cases which cite *Wilson* positively, see *U.S. v. Deaton*, 2000 WL 359755 (4th Cir. April 7, 2000); *National Ass'n. of Homebuilders v. U.S. Army Corps of Engineers*, 2000 WL 433072 (E.D.Va. March 9, 2000); *U.S. v. Sartori*, 62 F.Supp.2d 1362 (S.D.Fla. June 29, 1999); *U.S. v. Ellis*, 172 F.3d 864 (4th Cir. 1999).

Chapter 2
THE RIVERS AND HARBORS ACT OF 1899

Prior to the enactment of the Clean Water Act in 1972, the Rivers and Harbors Act of 1899 was the only statutory source of federal power to regulate dredging and filling albeit only in navigable waters. As the following cases demonstrate, in tortured but nonetheless results-oriented readings of its plain language, in later years, the Rivers and Harbors Act of 1899 was also used to attempt to regulate the discharge of industrial pollution, originally because it actually did interfere with navigability, but later because there was no other statute to address such an obvious wrong as water pollution. These cases also reveal a sharply divided Court; the first case is a 5-4 decision. Over time, but still prior to the 1972 enactment of the Clean Water Act, either the dissenters softened their views or the majority hardened its stance, but the definition of words such as "obstruction" actually became "pollution," and "obstruct" came to mean "pollute."

UNITED STATES v. REPUBLIC STEEL CORP.

362 U.S. 482, 80 S.Ct. 884, 4 L.Ed. 2d 903 (1960)

This is a suit by the United States to enjoin respondent companies from depositing industrial solids in the Calumet River (which flows out of Lake Michigan and connects eventually with the Mississippi) without first obtaining a permit from the Chief of Engineers of the Army providing conditions for the removal of the deposits and to order and direct them to restore the depth of the channel to 21 feet by removing portions of existing deposits.

The District Court found that the Calumet was used by vessels requiring a 21-foot draft, and that depth has been maintained by the Corps of Engineers. Respondents, who operate mills on the banks of the river for the production of iron and related products, use large quantities of the water from the river, returning it through numerous sewers. The processes they use create industrial waste containing various solids. A substantial quantity of these solids is recovered in settling basins but, according to the findings, many fine particles are discharged into the river and they flocculate into larger units and are deposited in the river bottom. Soundings show a progressive decrease in the depth of the river in the vicinity of respondents' mills. But respondents have refused, since 1951, the demand of the Corps of Engineers that they dredge that portion of the river. The shoaling conditions being created in the vicinity of these plants were found by the District Court to be created by the waste discharged from the mills of respondents. This shoaling was found to have reduced the depth of the channel to 17 feet in some places and to 12 feet in others. The District Court made findings which credited respondents with 81.5% of the waste deposited in the channel, and it allocated that in various proportions among the three respondents. See 155 F.Supp. 442.

The Court of Appeals did not review the sufficiency of evidence. It dealt only with questions of law and directed that the complaint be dismissed. 264 F.2d 289. The case is here on a petition for a writ of certiorari which we granted because of the public importance of the questions tendered. 359 U.S. 1010, 3 L.Ed. 2d 1035, 79 S.Ct. 1150.

Section 10 of the Rivers and Harbors Act of 1899, 30 Stat. 1121, 1151, as amended, 33 U.S.C. §403, provides in part:

"That the creation of *any obstruction* not affirmatively authorized by Congress, *to the navigable capacity* of any of the waters of the United States is hereby prohibited; ...." (Italics added.)

The section goes on to outlaw various structures "in" any navigable waters except those initiated by plans recommended by the Chief of Engineers and authorized by the Secretary of the Army. Section 10 then states that "it shall not be lawful to excavate or fill, or in any manner to alter or modify the ... capacity of ... the channel of any navigable water of the United States, unless the work has been recommended by the Chief of Engineers and authorized by the Secretary of the Army prior to beginning the same."

A criminal penalty is added by §12; and §12 further provides that the United States may sue to have "any structures or parts of structures erected" in violation of the Act removed. Section 17 directs the Department of Justice to "conduct the legal proceedings necessary to enforce" the provisions of the Act, including §10.

Section 13 forbids the discharge of "any refuse matter of any kind or description whatever other than that flowing from streets and sewers and passing therefrom in a liquid state, into any navigable water of the United States"; but §13 grants authority to the Secretary of the Army to permit such deposits under conditions prescribed by him.

Our conclusions are that the industrial deposits placed by respondents in the Calumet have, on the findings of the District Court, created an "obstruction" within the meaning of §10 of the Act and are discharges not exempt under §13. We also conclude that the District Court was authorized to grant the relief.

The history of federal control over obstructions to the navigable capacity of our rivers and harbors goes back to *Willamette Iron Bridge Co. v. Hatch*, 125 U.S. 1, 8, 31 L.Ed. 629, 632, 8 S.Ct. 811, where the Court held "there is no common law of the United States" which prohibits "obstructions" in our navigable rivers. Congress acted promptly, forbidding by §10 of the Rivers and Harbors Act of 1890, 26 Stat. 426, 454, "the creation of any obstruction, not affirmatively authorized by law, to the navigable capacity" of any waters of the United States. The 1899 Act followed a report to Congress by the Secretary of War, which at the direction of Congress, 29 Stat. 234, contained a compilation and revision of existing laws relating to navigable waters. The 1899 Act was said to contain "no essential changes in the existing law." Certainly so far as outlawry of any "obstructions" in navigable rivers is concerned there was no change relevant to our present problem.

It is argued that "obstruction" means some kind of structure. The design of §10 should be enough to refute that argument, since the ban of "any obstruction," unless approved by Congress, appears in the first part of §10, followed by a semi-colon and another provision which bans various kinds of structures unless authorized by the Secretary of the Army.

The reach of §10 seems plain. Certain types of structures, enumerated in the second clause, may not be erected "in" any navigable river without approval by the Secretary of the Army. Nor may excavations or fills, described in the third clause, that alter or modify "the course, location, condition, or capacity of" a navigable river be made unless "the work" has been approved by the Secretary of the Army. There is, apart from these invasions of navigable rivers, which the

Secretary of the Army may approve, the generalized first clause which prohibits "the creation of any obstruction not affirmatively authorized by Congress, to the navigable capacity" of such rivers. We can only conclude that Congress planned to ban any type of "obstruction," not merely those specifically made subject to approval by the Secretary of the Army. It seems, moreover, that the first clause being specifically aimed at "navigable capacity" serves an end that may at times be broader than those served by the other clauses. Some structures mentioned in the second clause may only deter movements in commerce, falling short of adversely affecting navigable capacity. And navigable capacity of a waterway may conceivably be affected by means other than the excavations and fills mentioned in the third clause. We would need to strain hard to conclude that the only obstructions banned by §10 are those enumerated in the second and third clauses. In short, the first clause is aimed at protecting "navigable capacity," though it is adversely affected in ways other than those specified in the other clauses.

There is an argument that §10 of the 1890 Act, 26 Stat. 454, which was the predecessor of the section with which we are now concerned, used the words "any obstruction" in the narrow sense, embracing only the prior enumeration of obstructions in the preceding sections of the Act. The argument is a labored one which we do not stop to refute step by step. It is unnecessary to do so, for the Court in *United States v. Rio Grande Dam & Irrig. Co.*, 174 U.S. 690, 708, 43 L.Ed. 1136, 1143, 19 S.Ct. 770, decided not long after the 1890 Act became effective, gave the concept of "obstruction," as used in §10, a broad sweep: "It is not a prohibition of any obstruction to the navigation, but any obstruction to the navigable capacity, and anything, wherever done or however done, within the limits of the jurisdiction of the United States which tends to destroy the navigable capacity of one of the navigable waters of the United States, is within the terms of the prohibition." This broad construction given §10 of the 1890 Act was carried over to §10 of the 1899 Act in *Sanitary Dist. v. United States,* 266 U.S. 405, 429, 69 L.Ed. 352, 364, 45 S.Ct. 176, the Court citing *United States v. Rio Grande Dam & Irrig. Co. (U.S.) supra*, with approval and saying that §10 of the 1899 Act was "a broad expression of policy in unmistakable terms, advancing upon" §10 of the 1890 Act.

The decision in *Sanitary Dist. v. United States (U.S.) supra*, seems us to be decisive. There the Court affirmed a decree enjoining the diversion of water from Lake Michigan through this same river. Mr. Justice Holmes, writing for the Court, did not read §10 narrowly but in the spirit in which Congress moved to fill the gap created by *Willamette Iron Bridge Co. v Hatch*, 125 U.S. 1, 31 L.Ed. 629, 8 S.Ct. 811, *supra*. That which effects the water level may, he said, amount to an "obstruction" within the meaning of §10:

"Evidence is sufficient, if evidence is necessary, to show that a withdrawal of water on the scale directed by the statute of Illinois threatens and will affect the level of the Lakes, and that is a matter which cannot be done without the consent of the United States, even were there no international covenant in the case." *Sanitary Dist. v. United States*, *supra* (266 U.S. 426) ...

"There is neither reason nor opportunity for a construction that would not cover the present case. As now applied it concerns a change in the condition of the Lakes and the Chicago River, admitted to be navigable, and, if that be necessary, an obstruction to their navigable capacity...." *Id.* 266 U.S. at 429.

It is said that that case is distinguishable because it involved the erections of "structures," prohibited by the second clause of §10. The "structures" erected, however, were not "in" navigable waters. The Sanitary District had reversed the flow of the Chicago River, "formerly a little stream flowing into Lake Michigan," 266 U.S. at 424, and used it as a sluiceway to draw down the waters of the Great Lakes to a dangerous degree. Moreover, the Court did not rely on the second clause of §10 but on the first and the third. *Id.* 266 U.S. at 428. The decree in that case did not run against any "structure"; it merely enjoined the diversion of water from Lake Michigan in excess of 250,000 cubic feet per minute.

That broad construction of §10 was reaffirmed in *Wisconsin v. Illinois*, 278 U.S. 367, 414, 73 L.Ed. 426, 433, 49 S.Ct. 163, another case involving the reduction of the water level of the Great Lakes by means of withdrawals through the Chicago River. And the Court, speaking through Chief Justice Taft (*Id.* 278 U.S. at 406, 414, 417), made clear that it adhered to what Mr. Justice Holmes had earlier said, "This withdrawal is prohibited by Congress, except so far as it may be authorized by the Secretary of War." *Sanitary Dist. v. United States, supra* (266 U.S. at 429).

The teaching of those cases is that the term "obstruction" as used in §10 is broad enough to include diminution of the navigable capacity of a waterway by means not included in the second or third clauses. In the *Sanitary Dist.* case it was caused by lowering the water level. Here it is caused by clogging the channel with deposits of inorganic solids. Each affected the navigable "capacity" of the river. The concept of "obstruction" which was broad enough to include the former seems to us plainly adequate to include the latter.

As noted, §13 bans the discharge in any navigable water of "any refuse matter of any kind or description whatever other than that flowing from streets and sewers and passing therefrom in a liquid state." The materials carried here are "industrial solids," as the District Court found. The particles creating the present obstruction were in suspension, not in solution. Articles in suspension, such as organic matter in sewage, may undergo chemical change. Others settle out. All matter in suspension is not saved by the exception clause in §13. Refuse flowing from "sewers" in a "liquid state" means to us "sewage." Any doubts are resolved by a consistent administrative construction which refused to give immunity to industrial wastes resulting in the deposit of solids in the very river in question. The fact that discharges from streets and sewers may contain some articles in suspension that settle out and potentially impair navigability is no reason for us to enlarge the group to include these industrial discharges. We follow the line Congress has drawn and cannot accept the invitation to broaden the exception in §13 because other matters "in a liquid state" might logically have been treated as favorably as sewage is treated. We read the 1899 Act charitably in light of the purpose to be served. The philosophy of the statement of Mr. Justice Holmes in *New Jersey v. New York*, 283 U.S. 336, 342, 75 L.Ed. 1104, 1106, 51 S.Ct. 478, that "A river is more than an amenity, it is a treasure," forbids a narrow, cramped reading either of §13 or of §10. [Footnotes omitted.]

Six years later, and perhaps somewhat chastened by the intricate legislative history analyzed by the dissent in *Republic Steel*, Justice Douglas engaged in his own legislative history analysis and made his frustration obvious in the following, very strongly worded opinion concerning the discharge of pollutants of any kind into navigable waters, whether or not navigability is obstructed. The dissenters are left to bleat that they do not mean to condone pollution by their grindingly literal reading of the Rivers and Harbors Act of 1899.

UNITED STATES v. STANDARD OIL COMPANY

384 U.S. 224, 86 S.Ct. 1427, 16 L.Ed.2d 492 (1966)

The question presented for decision is whether the statutory ban on depositing "any refuse matter" of any "kind or description" in a navigable water covers the discharge of commercially valuable aviation gasoline.

Section 13 of the Rivers and Harbors Act provides:

> "It shall not be lawful to throw, discharge, or deposit ... any refuse matter of any kind or description whatever other than that flowing from streets and sewers and passing therefrom in a liquid state, into any navigable water of the United States ...." 33 U.S.C §407 (1964 ed).

The indictment charged appellee, Standard Oil (Kentucky), with violating §13 by allowing to be discharged into the St. Johns River "refuse matter" consisting of 100-octane aviation gasoline. Appellee moved to dismiss the indictment, and, for the purposes of the motion, the parties entered into a stipulation of fact. It states that the gasoline was commercially valuable and that it was discharged into the St. Johns only because a shut-off valve at dockside had been "accidentally" left open.

The District Court dismissed the indictment because it was of the view that the statutory phrase "refuse matter" does not include commercially valuable oil. The United States appealed directly to this Court under the Criminal Appeals Act (18 U.S.C §3731 (1964 ed)). We noted probable jurisdiction. 382 U.S. 807, 15 L.Ed. 2d 57, 86 S.Ct. 68.

This case comes to us at a time in the Nation's history when there is greater concern than ever over pollution—one of the main threats to our free-flowing rivers and to our lakes as well. The crisis that we face in this respect would not, of course, warrant us in manufacturing offenses where Congress has not acted nor in stretching statutory language in a criminal field to meet strange conditions. But whatever may be said of the rule of strict construction, it cannot provide a substitute for common sense, precedent, and legislative history. We cannot construe §13 of the Rivers and Harbors Act in a vacuum. Nor can we read it as Baron Parke would read a pleading.

The statutory words are "any refuse matter of any kind or description." We said *in United States v. Republic Steel Corp.*, 362 U.S. 482, 491, 4 L.Ed. 2d 903, 909, 80 S.Ct. 884, that the history of this provision and of related legislation dealing with our free-flowing rivers "forbids a narrow, cramped reading" of §13. The District Court recognized that if this were waste oil it would be "refuse matter" within the meaning of §13 but concluded that it was not within the statute because it was "valuable" oil. That is "a narrow, cramped reading" of §13 in partial defeat of its purpose.

Oil is oil and whether usable or not by industrial standards it has the same deleterious effect on waterways. In either case, its presence in our rivers and harbors is both a menace to navigation and a pollutant. This seems to be the administrative construction of §13, the Solicitor General advising us that it is the basis of prosecution in approximately one-third of the oil pollution cases reported to the Department of Justice by the Office of the Chief of Engineers.

Section 13 codified pre-existing statutes: An 1886 Act (24 Stat 329) made it unlawful to empty "any ballast, stone, slate, gravel, earth, slack, rubbish, wreck, filth, slabs, edgings, sawdust, slag, or cinders, or other refuse or mill-waste of any kind into New York Harbor"—which plainly includes valuable pre-discharge material.

An 1888 Act (25 Stat 209) "to prevent obstructive and injurious deposits" within the Harbor of New York and adjacent waters banned the discharge of "refuse, dirt, ashes, cinders, mud, sand, dredgings, sludge, acid, *or any other matter of any kind,* other than that flowing from streets, sewers, and passing therefrom in a liquid state"—which also plainly includes valuable pre-discharge discharge material. (Emphasis added.)

The 1890 Act (26 Stat 453) made unlawful emptying into navigable waters "any ballast, stone, slate, gravel, earth, rubbish, wreck, filth, slabs, edgings, sawdust, slag, cinders, ashes, refuse, or other waste of any kind ... which shall tend to impede or obstruct navigation." Here also valuable pre-discharge materials were included.

The 1894 Act (28 Stat 363) prohibited deposits in harbors and rivers for which Congress had appropriated money for improvements, of "ballast, refuse, dirt, ashes, cinders, mud, sand, dredgings, sludge, acid, *or any other matter of any kind* other than that flowing from streets, sewers, and passing therefrom in a liquid state." (Emphasis added.) This Act also included valuable pre-discharge material.

The Acts of 1886 and 1888, then, dealt specifically with the New York Harbor; the scope of the latter was considerably broader, covering as it did the deposit of "any other matter of any kind." The Acts of 1890 and 1894 paralleled the earlier enactments pertaining to New York, applying their terms to waterways throughout the Nation.

The 1899 Act now before us was no more than an attempt to consolidate these prior Acts into one. It was indeed stated by the sponsor in the Senate to be "in accord with the statutes now in existence, only scattered ... from the beginning of the statutes down through to the end" (32 Cong Rec 2296), and reflecting merely "[v]ery slight changes to remove ambiguities." *Id.,* p. 2297.

From an examination of these statutes, several points are clear. *First,* the 1894 Act and its antecedent, the 1888 Act applicable to the New York Harbor, drew on their face no distinction between valuable and valueless substances. *Second,* of the enumerated substances, some may well have had commercial or industrial value prior to discharge into the covered waterways. To be more specific, ashes and acids were banned whether or not they had any remaining commercial or industrial value. *Third,* these Acts applied not only to the enumerated substances but also to the discharge of "any other matter of any kind." Since the enumerated substances included those with a pre-discharge value, the rule of *ejusdem generis* does not require limiting this latter category to substances lacking a pre-discharge value. *Fourth,* the coverage of these Acts was not diminished by the codification of 1899. The use of the term "refuse" in the codification serves in the place of the lengthy list of enumerated substances found in the earlier Acts and the catch-all provision found in the Act of 1890. The legislative history demonstrates without contradiction that Congress intended to codify without substantive change the earlier Acts.

The philosophy of those antecedent laws seems to us to be clearly embodied in the present law. It is plain from its legislative history that the "serious injury" to our water-courses (S Rep No. 224, 50th Cong, 1st Sess, p. 2) sought to be remedied was caused in part by obstacles that impeded navigation and in part by pollution—"the discharge of sawmill waste into streams" (*ibid.*) and the injury of channels by "deposits of ballast, steam-boat ashes, oysters, and rubbish from passing vessels" (*ibid*). The list is obviously not an exhaustive list of pollutants. The words of the Act are broad and inclusive: "any refuse matter of any kind or description whatever." Only one exception is stated: "other than that flowing from streets and sewers and passing therefrom in a liquid state, into any navigable water of the United States." More comprehensive language would be difficult to select. The word "refuse" does not stand alone; the "refuse" banned is "of any kind or description whatever," apart from the one exception noted. And, for the reasons already stated, the meaning we must give the term "refuse" must reflect the present codification's statutory antecedents.

The Court of Appeals for the Second Circuit in *United States v. Ballard Oil Co.*, 195 F.2d 369 (L. Hand, Augustus Hand, and Harrie Chase, JJ.) held that causing good oil to spill into a watercourse violated §13. The word "refuse" in that setting, said the court, "is satisfied by anything which has become waste, however useful it may earlier have been." *Id.*, p. 371. There is nothing more deserving of the label "refuse" than oil spilled into a river.

That seems to us to be the common sense of the matter. The word "refuse" includes all foreign substances and pollutants apart from those "flowing from streets and sewers and passing therefrom in a liquid state" into the watercourse. That reading of §13 is in keeping with the teaching of Mr. Justice Holmes that a "river is more than an amenity, it is a treasure." *New Jersey v. New York*, 283 U.S. 336, 342, 75 L. Ed. 1104, 1106, 51 S.Ct. 478. It reads §13 charitably as *United States v. Republic Steel Corp., supra*, admonished.

We pass only on the quality of the pollutant, not on the quantity of proof necessary to support a conviction nor on the question as to what scienter requirement the Act imposes, as those questions are not before us in this restricted appeal.

Reversed [Footnotes omitted].

Gradually, the Corps' permitting function under the Rivers and Harbors Act of 1899 evolved by the enactment of new statutes and agreements with other federal departments to include the Corps' consideration of other impacts besides simple navigability. Ultimately, this authority included consideration of environmental impacts among other factors when the Corps was deciding whether to issue a Rivers and Harbors Act permit.

ZABEL v. TABB

430 F.2d 199 (5th Cir. 1970)

It is the destiny of the Fifth Circuit to be in the middle of great, oftentimes explosive issues of spectacular public importance. So it is here as we enter in depth the contemporary interest in the preservation of our environment. By an injunction requiring the issuance of a permit to fill in eleven acres of tidelands in the beautiful Boca Ciega Bay in the St. Petersburg–Tampa,

Florida, area for use as a commercial mobile trailer park, the District Judge held that the Secretary of the Army and his functionary, the Chief of Engineers, had no power to consider anything except interference with navigation. There being no such obstruction to navigation, they were ordered to issue a permit even though the permittees acknowledge that "there was evidence before the Corps of Engineers sufficient to justify an administrative agency finding that [the] fill would do damage to the ecology or marine life on the bottom." We hold that nothing in the statutory structure compels the Secretary to close his eyes to all that others see or think they see. The establishment was entitled, if not required, to consider ecological factors and, being persuaded by them, to deny that which might have been granted routinely five, ten, or fifteen years ago before man's explosive increase made all, including Congress, aware of civilization's potential destruction from breathing its own polluted air and drinking its own infected water and the immeasurable loss from a *Silent Spring*-like disturbance of nature's economy. We reverse.

I. GENESIS: THE BEGINNING

In setting the stage we draw freely on the Government's brief. This suit was instituted by Landholders, Zabel and Russell, on May 10, 1967, to compel the Secretary of the Army to issue a permit to dredge and fill in the navigable waters of Boca Ciega Bay, in Pinellas County near St. Petersburg, Florida....

Landholders own land riparian to Boca Ciega Bay and adjacent land underlying the Bay. It is navigable water of the United States on the Gulf side of Pinellas Peninsula, its length being traversed by the Intracoastal Waterway, which enters Tampa Bay from Boca Ciega Bay and is thus an arm of the Gulf of Mexico. The Zabel and Russell property is located about one mile from the Intracoastal Waterway.

Landholders desire to dredge and fill on their property in the Bay for a trailer park, with a bridge or culvert to their adjoining upland. To this purpose they first applied to the state and local authorities for permission to perform the work and obtained the consent or approval of all such agencies having jurisdiction to prohibit the work.... Landholders then applied to the Corps of Engineers for a federal permit to perform the dredging and filling.... The United States Fish and Wildlife Service, Department of the Interior, also opposed the dredging and filling because it "would have a distinctly harmful effect on the fish and wildlife resources of Boca Ciega Bay."

A public hearing was held in St. Petersburg in November, 1966, and on December 30, 1966, the District Engineer at Jacksonville, Florida, Colonel Tabb, recommended to his superiors that the application be denied. He said that "The proposed work would have no material adverse effect on navigation," but that:

> Careful consideration has been given to the general public interest in this case. The virtually unanimous opposition to the proposed work as expressed in the protests which were received and as exhaustively presented at the public hearing have convinced me that approval of the application would not be in the public interest. The continued opposition of the U.S. Fish & Wildlife Service despite efforts on the part of the applicants to reduce the extent of damage leads me to the conclusion that approval of the work would not be consistent with the intent of Congress as expressed in the Fish & Wildlife Coordination Act, as amended, 12 August 1958. Further, the opposition of the State of Florida and of county authorities as described in paragraph 5 above gives additional support to my conclusion that the work should not be authorized.

The Division Engineer, South Atlantic Division, Atlanta, Georgia, concurred in that recommendation stating: "In view of the wide-spread opposition to the proposed work, it is apparent that approval of the application would not be in the public interest." The Chief of Engineers concurred for the same reasons. Finally, the Secretary of the Army denied the application on February 28, 1967, because issuance of the requested permit:

> 1. Would result in a distinctly harmful effect on the fish and wildlife resources in Boca Ciega Bay,
>
> 2. Would be inconsistent with the purposes of the Fish and Wildlife Coordination Act of 1958, as amended (16 U.S.C. 662),
>
> 3. Is opposed by the Florida Board of Conservation on behalf of the State of Florida, and by the County Health Board of Pinellas County and the Board of County Commissioners of Pinellas County, and
>
> 4. Would be contrary to the public interest.

Landholders then instituted this suit to review the Secretary's determination and for an order compelling him to issue a permit. They urged that the proposed work would not hinder navigation and that the Secretary had no authority to refuse the permit on other grounds. They acknowledged that "there was evidence before the Corps of Engineers sufficient to justify an administrative agency finding that our fill would do damage to the ecology or marine life on the bottom." The Government urged lack of jurisdiction and supported the denial of the permit on authority of §10 of the Rivers and Harbors Act of March 3, 1899, 30 Stat. 1121, 1151, 33 U.S.C.A. §403, giving the Secretary discretion to issue permits and on the Fish and Wildlife Coordination Act of March 10, 1934, 48 Stat. 401, as amended, 16 U.S.C.A. §§661 and 662(a), requiring the Secretary to consult with the Fish and Wildlife Service and state conservation agencies before issuing a permit to dredge and fill....

The question presented to us is whether the Secretary of the Army can refuse to authorize a dredge and fill project in navigable waters for factually substantial ecological reasons even though the project would not interfere with navigation, flood control, or the production of power. To answer this question in the affirmative, we must answer two intermediate questions affirmatively. (1) Does Congress for ecological reasons have the power to prohibit a project on private riparian submerged land in navigable waters? (2) If it does, has Congress committed the power to prohibit to the Secretary of the Army?

II. CONSTITUTIONAL POWER

The starting point here is the Commerce Clause and its expansive reach. The test for determining whether Congress has the power to protect wildlife in navigable waters and thereby to regulate the use of private property for this reason is whether there is a basis for the Congressional judgment that the activity regulated has a substantial effect on interstate commerce. *Wickard v. Filburn*, 1942, 317 U.S. 111, 125, 63 S.Ct. 82, 87 L.Ed. 122, 135. That this activity meets this test is hardly questioned. In this time of awakening to the reality that we cannot continue to despoil our environment and yet exist, the nation knows, if Courts do not, that the destruction of fish and wildlife in our estuarine waters does have a substantial, and in some areas a devastating, effect on interstate commerce. Landholders do not contend otherwise. Nor is it challenged that dredge and fill projects are activities which may tend to destroy the ecological balance and thereby affect commerce substantially. Because of these potential effects Congress has the power to regulate such projects.

III. RELINQUISHMENT OF THE POWER

Landholders do not challenge the existence of power. They argue that Congress in the historic compromise over the oil rich tidelands controversy abandoned its power over other natural resources by the relinquishment to the states in the Submerged Lands Act. By it they urge the Government stripped itself of the power to regulate tidelands property except for purposes relating to (i) navigation, (ii) flood control, and (iii) hydroelectric power. This rests on the expressed Congressional reservation of control for these three purposes over the submerged lands, title to and power over which Congress relinquished to the states.

The argument assumes that when Congress relinquished title to the land and the right and power to manage and use the land, it relinquished its power under the Commerce clause except in particulars (i), (ii), and (iii). It also assumes that reservation of these three enumerated aspects of the commerce power implied that Congress gave up its plenary power over the myriad other aspects of commerce. See, *e.g., Heart of Atlanta Motel, Inc. v. United States*, 1964, 379 U.S. 241, 85 S.Ct. 348, 13 L.Ed. 2d. 258; *Katzenbach v. McClung*, 1964, 379 U.S. 294, 85 S.Ct. 377, 13 L.Ed. 2d 290.

A nice argument can be contrived that the net effect of these provisions was to vest in the adjacent states [1] title in these tidelands and their natural resources and [2] [a] the exclusive power to use, exploit and manage these lands [b] only subject to the reserved power of the Federal Government regarding (i) navigation, (ii) flood control, and (iii) production of power. Certainly, this brief synopsis of (1) and (2) (a) is the literal import of §1311 (a) (1) (2). Likewise, the reservation summarized as (2) (b) is literally specified in §1311 (d). On this approach, the Federal Government turned over to adjacent states the full management and use of the tidelands reserving only those limited powers over commerce comprehended within the three particulars.

But this argument ignores both language found elsewhere and the legislative purpose of the Act. The controversy, often pressed with emotional overtones, was over oil and gas and whether the states were to reap the economic benefits of development royalties and to regulate the exploration and development or whether these benefits and these controls were to be exercised by the Federal Government as an adjunct of then newly declared "paramount rights," *United States v. California*, 1947, 332 U.S. 804, 805, 68 S.Ct. 20, 92 L.Ed. 382, 383. The Act and this relinquishment reflect the legislative compromise found in the combination of the Submerged Lands Act and the Outer Continental Shelf Act. The adjacent states were to be the "owner" of the resources and reap exclusively the economic benefits of resources in the tidelands and have full control over management and exploitation. The Federal Government, on the other hand, was given exclusive ownership and control *vis-a-vis* the states in the Outer Continental Shelf.

Although it was easy to make this division, the nature of the physical area of the controversy presented immediate operational problems growing out of the water. The Federal Government's traditional concern with navigation, especially on the high seas, its later but then quite extensive concern in flood control, hydroelectric power production, and the frequent combination of both under grandiose projects of a Corps of Engineers, raised specific problems calling for accommodation of the (i) sweeping Federal divestiture and (ii) the continued fulfillment of the

Federal Government's role in these activities. Thus, for example, the states, exclusive right to grant exploration privileges, determine the location and spacing of development wells or drilling platforms posed prospects of maritime hazards. Without imposing its own notions of how development ought to be conducted, restricted, expanded, or controlled, the Federal Government had to have, and reserved expressly this power even to prohibit a drilling rig platform at a particular location. These specific reservations eliminated these frequent and extensive activities as a source of further state versus national controversy.

Whatever remaining doubt there might be on this reading was expressly eliminated by language in §1314 (a) which specifically retains in the Federal Government "all of its ... rights in and powers of regulation and control of said lands and ... waters for the constitutional purposes of commerce.... " 43 U.S.C.A. §1314 (a). This section, which encompasses and pervades the entire Act, makes it clear that Congress intended to and did retain all its constitutional powers over commerce and did not relinquish certain portions of the power by specifically reserving others.

All of this is additionally borne out by the legislative history and *United States v. Rands*, 1967, 389 U.S. 121, 127, 88 S.Ct. 265, 19 L.Ed. 2d 329, 335:

> Finally, respondent urge that the Government's position subverts the policy of the Submerged Lands Act, which confirmed and vested in the States title to the lands beneath navigable waters within their boundaries and to natural resources within such lands and waters, together with the right and power to manage, develop, and use such lands and natural resources. However, reliance on that Act is misplaced, for it expressly recognized that the United States retained all its navigational servitude and rights in and powers of regulation and control of said lands and navigable waters for the constitutional purposes of commerce, navigation, national defense, and international affairs, all of which shall be paramount to, but shall not be deemed to include, proprietary rights of ownership.... Nothing in the Act was to be construed as the release or relinquishment of any rights of the United States arising under the constitutional authority of Congress to regulate or improve navigation, or to provide for flood control, or the production of power. The Act left congressional power over commerce and the dominant navigational servitude of the United States precisely where it found them.

Congress clearly has the power under the Commerce Clause to regulate the use of Landholders' submerged riparian property for conservation purposes and has not given up this power in the Submerged Lands Act.

IV. PROHIBITING OBSTRUCTIONS TO NAVIGATION

The action of the Chief of Engineers and the Secretary of the Army under attack rests immediately on the Rivers and Harbors Act, 33 U.S.C.A. §403, which declares that "the creation of any obstruction ... to the navigable capacity of any of the waters of the United States is prohibited." The Act covers both building of structures and the excavating and filling in navigable waters. It is structured as a flat prohibition *unless*—the unless being the issuance of approval by the Secretary after recommendation of the Chief of Engineers. The Act itself does not put any restrictions on denial of a permit or the reasons why the Secretary may refuse to grant a permit to one seeking to build structures on or dredge and fill his own property. Although the Act has always been read as tempering the outright prohibition by the rule of reason against arbitrary action, the Act does flatly forbid the obstruction. The administrator may grant permission on conditions and conversely deny permission when the situation does not allow for those conditions.

But the statute does not prescribe either generally or specifically what those conditions may be. The question for us is whether under the Act the Secretary may include conservation considerations as conditions to be met to make the proposed project acceptable. Until now there has been no absolute answer to this question. In fact, in most cases under the Rivers and Harbors Act the Courts have been faced only with navigation problems. See, *e.g., Sanitary Dist. v. United States*, 1925, 266 U.S. 405, 45 S.Ct. 176, 69 L.Ed. 352; *Wisconsin v. Illinois*, 1929, 278 U.S. 367, 49 S.Ct. 163, 73 L.Ed. 426; *United States v. Republic Steel Corp.*, 1960, 362 U.S. 482, 80 S.Ct. 884, 4 L.Ed. 2d 903.

One very big exception is *United States ex rel. Greathouse v. Dern*, 1933, 289 U.S. 352, 53 S.Ct. 614, 77 L.Ed. 1250. There petitioners sought a writ of mandamus to compel the Secretary of War and the Chief of Engineers to issue a permit to build a wharf in navigable waters. The Secretary, specifically finding that it would not interfere with navigation, denied the permit. The Supreme Court held that mandamus would not issue because the allowance of mandamus "is controlled by equitable principles ... and it may be refused for reasons comparable to those which would lead a Court of equity, in the exercise of a sound discretion, to withhold its protection of an undoubted legal right." The reason was that the United States had plans to condemn petitioners' land for use as a means of access to a proposed parkway. Allowing a wharf to be built would increase the expense to the government since it would increase the market value of the land and would require the government to pay for tearing down the wharf. The importance of *Greathouse* is that it recognized that the Corps of Engineers does not have to wear navigational blinders when it considers a permit request. That there must be a reason does not mean that the reason has to be navigability.

Another case holds that the Corps has a duty to consider factors other than navigational. *Citizens Committee for the Hudson Valley v. Volpe,* S.D.N.Y., 1969, 302 F.Supp. 1083, *aff'd.*, 2 Cir. 1970, 425 F.2d 97 [1970]. There the District Court held that the Corps must consider a fill project in the context of the entire expressway project of which it was a part rather than just considering the fill and its effect on navigation. The reasoning was that the approval of the Secretary of Transportation was necessary before a proposed causeway could be constructed. The causeway, along with the fill, was an integral part of the expressway project. However, if the Corps and Secretary of the Army approved the fill and the State completed it, the Secretary of Transportation, considering the enormous expense of the fill, would have no choice, other than approving the causeway. The Army thus had exceeded its authority in approving the fill on only navigational considerations since approval of the fill was effectually approval of the causeway.

But such circuity is not necessary. Governmental agencies in executing a particular statutory responsibility ordinarily are required to take heed of, sometimes effectuate and other times not thwart other valid statutory governmental policies. And here the government-wide policy of environmental conservation is spectacularly revealed in at least two statutes, The Fish and Wildlife Coordination Act and the National Environmental Policy Act of 1969.

The Fish and Wildlife Coordination Act clearly requires the dredging and filling agency (under a governmental permit), whether public or private, to consult with the Fish and Wildlife Service, with a view of conservation of wildlife resources. If there be any question as to whether the statute directs the licensing agency (the Corps) to so consult it can quickly be dispelled. Common sense and reason dictate that it would be incongruous for Congress, in light of the fact that it intends conservation to be considered in private dredge and fill operations (as evidenced by the clear wording of the statute), not to direct the only federal agency concerned with licensing such projects both to consult and to take such factors into account.

The second proof that the Secretary is directed and authorized by the Fish and Wildlife Coordination Act to consider conservation is found in the legislative history. The Senate Report on the Fish and Wildlife Coordination Act states:

> Finally, the nursery and feeding grounds of valuable crustaceans, such as shrimp, as well as the young of valuable marine fishes, may be affected by dredging, filling, and diking operations often carried out to improve navigation and provide new industrial or residential land.... Existing law has questionable application to projects of the Corps of Engineers for the dredging of bays and estuaries for navigation and filling purposes. More seriously, existing law has no application whatsoever to the dredging and filling of bays and estuaries by private interests or other non-Federal entities in navigable waters under permit from the Corps of Engineers. This is a particularly serious deficiency from the standpoint of commercial fishing interests. The dredging of these bays and estuaries along the coastlines to aid navigation and also to provide land fills for real estate and similar developments, both by Federal agencies or other agencies under permit from the Corps of Engineers, has increased tremendously in the last 5 years. Obviously, dredging activity of this sort has a profound disturbing effect on aquatic life, including shrimp and other species of tremendous significance to the commercial fishing industry. The bays, estuaries, and related marsh areas are highly important as spawning and nursery grounds for many commercial species of fish and shellfish. S. Rep. No. 1981, 85th Cong. 2d Sess. (July 28, 1958). 1958 U.S.C.C. & A.N. pp. 3446, 3448, 3450.

This Report clearly shows that Congress intended the Chief of Engineers and Secretary of the Army to consult with the Fish and Wildlife Service before issuing a permit for a private dredge and fill operation.

This interpretation was judicially accepted in *Udall v. FPC*:

> Section 2(a), 16 U.S.C §662(a), provides that an agency evaluating a license under which 'the waters of any stream or other body of water are proposed ... to be impounded first shall consult with the United States Fish and Wildlife Service, Department of the Interior ... with a view to the conservation of wildlife resources by preventing loss of and damage to such resources ....' Certainly the wildlife conservation aspect of the project must be explored and evaluated. 1967, 387 U.S. 428, 443-44, 87 S.Ct. 1712, 18 L.Ed. 2d 869, 879.

The meaning and application of the Act are also reflected by the actions of the Executive that show the statute authorizes and directs the Secretary to consult with the Fish and Wildlife Service in deciding whether to grant a dredge and fill permit. In a Memorandum of Understanding between the Secretary of the Army and the Secretary of the Interior, it is provided that, upon receipt of an application for a permit to dredge or fill in navigable waters, the District Engineer of the Corps of Engineers concerned is required to send notices to all interested parties, including the appropriate Regional Directors of the Federal Water Pollution Control Administration, the Fish and Wildlife Service, the National Park Service and the appropriate state conservation, resources, and water pollution agencies. The District Engineer is given the initial responsibility of evaluating all relevant factors in reaching a decision as to whether the particular permit involved should be granted or denied. The Memorandum also provides that in case of conflicting views the ultimate decision shall be made by the Secretary of the Army after consultation with the Secretary of the Interior....

The intent of the three branches has been unequivocally expressed: The Secretary must weigh the effect a dredge and fill project will have on conservation before he issues a permit lifting the Congressional ban....

VII. CONCLUSION

Landholders' contentions fail on all grounds. The case is reversed and since there are no questions remaining to be resolved by the District Court, judgment is rendered for the Government and the associated agent-defendants.

[Footnotes omitted.]

Not all cases under the Rivers and Harbors Act of 1899 have supported continued expansion of jurisdiction. There are some limits beyond which even the most activist court will not go to force environmental regulation on Congress.

UNITED STATES v. DEXTER CORPORATION

507 F.2d 1038 (7th Cir. 1974)

In this case an information charged that Dexter Corporation, a manufacturer, and appellant North Shore Sanitary District, a municipal corporation, "did cause ... to be discharged and deposited from out of The Dexter Corporation's Midland Division plant facility and ... The North Shore Sanitary District sewer system, refuse matter, to wit: phenolic resin, into Lake Michigan ...; in violation of Title 33, United States Code, Sections 407 and 411."

Section 407, originally Section 13 of the Rivers and Harbors Act of 1899, declares that "it shall not be lawful to ... cause ... to be ... discharged, or deposited either from ... the shore, wharf, manufacturing establishment, or mill of any kind, any refuse matter of any kind or description whatever other than that flowing from streets and sewers and passing therefrom in a liquid state, into any navigable water ...." Section 411 makes a violation of Section 407 a misdemeanor.

Dexter Corporation pleaded *nolo contendere*, was fined $500 and is not before us now. North Shore Sanitary District went to trial before the district court, sitting without a jury. The essential facts were stipulated.

North Shore Sanitary District is a municipal corporation of the State of Illinois and, as duly authorized, operates a sanitary sewer system in Lake County. Dexter Corporation's manufacturing plant connects with and utilizes this municipal system for the discharge of waste and storm water.

In its manufacturing operation Dexter uses phenolic resin, a toxic and to some extent corrosive liquid that is lighter than water. During a rainstorm, an employee at the Dexter plant accidentally caused a substantial quantity of phenolic resin to be discharged into the sanitary sewer system where its subsequent course was diverted through a by-pass, which the Sanitary District Used at times of heavy rainfall, and thence into Lake Michigan. Under normal conditions the Sanitary District's processing of sewerage would have prevented the phenolic resin from reaching the lake. But in this case the rainy weather by-pass had been opened and the toxic liquid flowed untreated from the sewer into the lake. There, being lighter than water, it was discovered on the surface.

On these facts the district court found the Sanitary District guilty of violating Section 407 and imposed a $500 fine. This appeal followed.

We now consider whether the exception stated in Section 407 makes the section's general prohibitory language inapplicable here. Certainly, the phenolic resin in this case comes within the comprehensive statutory designation of "any refuse matter of any kind or description whatever" discharged from a "manufacturing establishment." But the statute proceeds to exclude from its coverage refuse matter "flowing from streets and sewers and passing therefrom in a liquid state." On its face this exclusionary language seems applicable to the effluent in this case. The parties have stipulated and the government concedes that the Sanitary District caused the refuse in question to pass through its sewers into the lake and that the refuse was at all times a liquid.

There was a rational basis for this explicit exception in the circumstances of the statute's enactment. Concern to eliminate immediate and potential hazards to navigation moved Congress to enact late Nineteenth Century legislation that culminated in the Rivers and Harbors Act of 1899. Thus, though Section 13 of the 1899 Act has also served in more recent times to provide some protection for the quality of bodies of water, its essential design was to safeguard their navigability. In this historic context, the statutory exception that governs this case is understandable. Although the statutory prohibition of the deposit or discharge of refuse into streams covered liquids as well as solids, an influx of liquid, free of solids in suspension, posed no significant immediate or potential hazard to navigability. At the same time local communities were progressively developing sanitary and storm sewerage systems and regulating their effluent. It is not surprising, therefore, that Congress in 1899 should see fit to leave the treatment and disposition of all liquid waste handled by local public sewerage systems to local regulation, exercising federal control thereover only to the extent necessary to prevent public sewers from becoming conduits for solids that might accumulate in and eventually impair the navigability of adjacent waters. In any event, the language of the statutory exception is clear and unambiguous.

At argument, the appellee predicated a contrary interpretation of the controlling statutory language upon *United States v. Republic Steel Corp.*, 1960, 362 U.S. 482, 4 L.Ed. 2d 903, 80 S.Ct. 884. However, that case involved only "industrial solids" and held that such matter, discharged through a sewerage system in the form of particles suspended in water, is not within the Section 407 exception. It is true that, in this context, the opinion of the Court spoke of two categories of "articles in suspension," namely, "organic matter in sewage" and "industrial solids." The significance of these categories is not clear, particularly since no such breakdown is undertaken in the statute. In any event, the case was concerned only with industrial solids and decided merely that under Section 407 such solids in suspension were not refuse in a liquid state.

Subsequently, a few courts, incorrectly we think, have relied on *United States v. Republic Steel Corp.*, as authority for making the Section 407 exception inapplicable to liquid waste of industrial origin that is passed through public sewers. But the *Republic Steel* holding does not require and rational reading of the simple language of Section 407 does not permit that interpretation.

In a single sentence the statute prohibits the deposit or discharge in navigable water of "refuse matter of any kind or description whatever," except for "that flowing from ... sewers ... in a liquid state." The quoted pronoun "that" must refer to the subject phrase, "refuse matter of any kind." Thus, the exception is not limited to refuse of domestic origin. We will not substitute for what the statute says our notions of what might preferably have been said.

The judgment is reversed. [Footnotes omitted.]

The Courts are similarly indisposed to allow the Rivers and Harbors Act of 1899 to be used to invent the novel concept of a "regulatory obstruction." A physical obstruction is still required.

LAKE TAHOE WATERCRAFT RECREATION ASSOC. v. TAHOE REGIONAL PLANNING AGENCY

24 F.Supp. 2d 1062 (E.D.Ca. 1998)

The Lake Tahoe Watercraft Recreation Association and various watercraft manufacturers, retailers and users bring this action challenging the legality of Tahoe Regional Planning Agency ("TRPA") Ordinance No. 97-12 ("Ordinance"). In particular, plaintiffs challenge the portion of the Ordinance prohibiting the discharge of unburned fuel and oil from the operation of watercraft propelled by carbureted two-stroke engines commencing June 1, 1999.

Plaintiffs' complaint alleges: violations of the equal protection, due process, and commerce clauses of the United States Constitution; an illegal taking; violation of the Federal Aid in Sport Fish Restoration Act; the Ordinance obstructs access to a navigable waterway; failure to comply with various provisions of the Compact; the Ordinance is void for vagueness; and violations of the California and Nevada Constitutions and laws. Defendant TRPA moves for judgment on the pleadings as to the first through fifth and ninth through eighteenth causes of action. Fed.R.Civ.P. 12(c). Intervenor-defendant The League to Save Lake Tahoe ("League") moves to dismiss the first through eighteenth causes of action. Fed. R. Civ. P. 12(b)(6). The League also contends the entire action is barred by the applicable statute of limitations. Defendants' motions are granted; plaintiffs are given leave to file an amended complaint as to certain causes of action.

BACKGROUND

In 1968, California and Nevada entered into the Tahoe Regional Planning Compact ("Compact") to create a regional agency with extensive powers to regulate and control development within the Lake Tahoe Basin in order to protect the natural resources and ecological balance of the area. *League to Save Lake Tahoe v. Tahoe Regional Planning Agency*, 507 F.2d 517, 518 (1974), *cert. denied*, 420 U.S. 974, 95 S.Ct. 1398, 43 L.Ed. 2d 654 (1975). *See also* Cal.Gov.Code §§66800, 66801; Nev.Rev.Stat. §§277.190–277.220. In 1969, Congress consented to the Compact, pursuant to Article I, §10, cl. 3 of the United States Constitution. Tahoe Regional Planning Compact, Pub. L. No. 91-148, 82 Stat. 360 (1969).

In 1980, California and Nevada extensively amended the Compact to impose numerous specific mandates on TRPA. Congress consented to the Compact that same year. Tahoe Regional Planning Compact—Consent of Congress, Pub.L. 96-551, 94 Stat. 3233 (1980). The Compact, as amended, directed TRPA to adopt environmental threshold carrying capacities for the region, including standards for water quality, and to implement these environmental standards through agency ordinances rules and regulations. Compact, Art. V(c) & (d), Art. VI(a).

On June 25, 1997, TRPA adopted Ordinance No. 97-12 which, among other things, prohibits "the discharge of unburned fuel and oil from the operation of watercraft propelled by carbureted two-stroke engines [in Lake Tahoe and certain other lakes and waterways] ... commencing June 1, 1999." The Ordinance amended an existing TRPA ordinance prohibiting the discharge of toxic or hazardous waste to Lake Tahoe and the Tahoe Region. TRPA Code of Ordinances 81.2.D....

8. ACCESS TO NAVIGABLE WATERWAY

Plaintiffs contend that the Ordinance violates 33 U.S.C. §403 because it "obstructs access" to a navigable waterway. Complaint, P. 81. Section 403 prohibits "the creation of any obstruction not affirmatively authorized by Congress, to the navigable capacity of any of the waters of the United States." By its own terms section 403 contemplates physical obstructions. Plaintiffs cite no authority for their position that section 403 also applies to "regulatory" obstructions, nor has the court found any such authority. Plaintiffs rely on *United States v. Republic Steel Corp.*, 362 U.S. 482, 486-87, 4 L.Ed. 2d 903, 80 S.Ct. 884 (1960) for their contention that an "obstruction ... does not need to be a 'physical' obstruction or structure." There, however, the Supreme Court held only that "obstructions" for purposes of section 403 were not limited to structures generally or those specifically enumerated in the second clause of the section 403. *Id.* Significantly, that case involved a physical obstruction—industrial deposits placed in a river and found to have reduced the depth of the channel of the river—and the Court found the deposits constituted an "obstruction" for purposes of section 403. *Id.* at 489.[11] Contrary to plaintiffs' assertion, a physical obstruction is required under the case law interpreting the statute; a "regulatory" obstruction does not suffice. Accordingly, plaintiffs' fifth cause of action is dismissed with prejudice....

Chapter 3

THE CLEAN WATER ACT

The evolutionary judicial process finally led Congress to the enactment of the Federal Water Pollution Control Act Amendments of 1972 (known popularly as the Clean Water Act), including §404, 33 U.S.C. §1344, which is used to regulate activities in wetlands. "Pollutants" are now expansively defined to include "dredged spoil, solid waste, incinerator residue, sewage, garbage, sewage sludge, munitions, chemical wastes, biological materials, radioactive materials, heat, wrecked or discarded equipment, rock, sand, cellar dirt and industrial, municipal, and agricultural waste discharged into water ...." 33 U.S.C. §1362(6).

The stated goal of the Clean Water Act is "...to restore and maintain the chemical, physical, and biological integrity of waters of the United States through the control of discharges of dredged or fill material." 40 C.F.R. §230.1(a). The Clean Water Act prohibits discharging pollutants from a point source into "waters of the United States" without a permit, the purpose of the permit being to control pollution. 33 U.S.C. §1311. Generally, the Environmental Protection Agency is empowered to grant pollutant discharge permits. 33 U.S.C. §1342. See also *Orange Environment, Inc. v. County of Orange*, 817 F.Supp. 1051 (S.D.N.Y. 1993), *aff'd. sub nom. Orange Env't. v. Orange County Legislature*, 2 F.3d 1235 (2d Cir. 1993). The Corps, however, because of its historic role in dredging and fill activities under the Rivers and Harbors Act, has been given a special duty under the Clean Water Act: the Corps may grant the permits to discharge "dredged and fill material into the navigable waters at specified disposal sites," wetlands among them. Although the Corps actually grants the permits, the Environmental Protection Agency retains an oversight function and may, in certain circumstances, overrule the Corps's permit decision. See *Memorandum of Agreement Between the Department of the Army and the Environmental Protection Agency Concerning Determination of the Geographic Jurisdiction of the Section 404 Program and the Application of Exceptions Under Section 404(f) of the Clean Water Act* (January 19, 1989). Thus, if it is determined that the area in question is a wetland, a permit to discharge dredged or fill material will be necessary unless one of the exempt activities is contemplated or the activity fits either a general or nationwide permit.

Even though the Clean Water Act never uses the word "wetlands," their inclusion in the regulatory scheme as "waters of the United States" is found in the regulations and case law. The Corps initially took the position that the extent of its permitting authority under the Clean Water Act was coterminous with its traditional authority under the Rivers and Harbors Act, namely navigable waters, including waters subject to the ebb and flow of the tides, waters which are or have been used to transport interstate commerce, tidal flats under navigable waters, and the natural meandering of rivers. A citizens suit forced the expansion of the Corps's regulatory definition of "waters of the United States" to include wetlands.

NATURAL RESOURCES DEFENSE COUNCIL, INC. v. CALLAWAY

392 F. Supp. 685 (D.C.D.C. 1975)

... it is DECLARED that:

1. Congress by defining the term "navigable waters" in Section 502(7) of the Federal Water Pollution Control Act Amendments of 1972, 86 Stat. 816, 33 U.S.C. §1251 et seq. (the "Water Act") to mean "the waters of the United States, including the territorial seas," asserted federal jurisdiction over the nation's waters to the maximum extent permissible under the Commerce Clause of the Constitution. Accordingly, as used in the Water Act, the term is not limited to the traditional tests of navigability.

2. Defendants Howard H. Callaway, Secretary of the Army, and Lt. Gen. William C. Gribble, Chief, Army Corps of Engineers, are without authority to amend or change the statutory definition of navigable waters and they are hereby declared to have acted unlawfully and in derogation of their responsibilities under Section 404 of the Water Act by the adoption of the definition of navigability described at 33 C.F.R. §209.210(d)(1), 39 Federal Register 12119 (April 3, 1974) and 33 C.F.R. 209.260; and it is ORDERED that Defendants Callaway and Gribble:

> 1. Revoke and rescind so much of 39 Federal Register 12115, et seq. (April 3, 1974) as limits the permit jurisdiction of the Corps of Engineers by definition or otherwise to other than "the waters of the United States."
>
> 2. Publish within forty (40) days of the date of this Order proposed regulations clearly recognizing the full regulatory mandate of the Water Act.
>
> 3. Publish within forty (40) days of the date of this Order final regulations clearly recognizing the full regulatory mandate of the Water Act; and it is

FURTHER ORDERED that the Clerk of this Court shall enter a final Judgment upon this Order Granting Plaintiffs' Motion for Partial Summary Judgment, the Court expressly having determined that there is no just reason for delay in the entry of final Judgment on this Order; and it is

FURTHER ORDERED that Defendants' Motion to Dismiss be and hereby is DENIED.

UNITED STATES v. RIVERSIDE BAYVIEW HOMES, INC.

474 U.S. 121, 106 S.Ct. 455, 88 L.Ed. 2d 419 (1985)

This case presents the question whether the Clean Water Act (CWA), 33 U.S.C. §1251 et seq. [33 U.S.C.A. §§1251 et seq.], together with certain regulations promulgated under its authority by the Army Corps of Engineers, authorizes the Corps to require landowners to obtain permits from the Corps before discharging fill material into wetlands adjacent to navigable bodies of water and their tributaries.

I

The relevant provisions of the Clean Water Act originated in the Federal Water Pollution Control Act Amendments of 1972, 86 Stat. 816, and have remained essentially unchanged since that time. Under §§301 and 502 of the Act, 33 U.S.C. §§1311 and 1362 [33 U.S.C.A. §§1311 and 1362], any discharge of dredged or fill materials into "navigable waters"—defined as the "waters of the United States"—is forbidden unless authorized by a permit issued by the Corps of Engineers pursuant to §404, 33 U.S.C. §1344 [33 U.S.C.A. §1344]. After initially construing the Act to cover only waters navigable in fact, in 1975 the Corps issued interim final regulations redefining "the waters of the United States" to include not only actually navigable waters but also tributaries of such waters, interstate waters and their tributaries, and nonnavigable intrastate waters whose use or misuse could affect interstate commerce. 40 Fed. Reg. 31320 (1975). More importantly for present purposes, the Corps construed the Act to cover all "freshwater wetlands" that were adjacent to other covered waters. A "freshwater wetland" was defined as an area that is "periodically inundated" and is "normally characterized by the prevalence of vegetation that requires saturated soil conditions for growth and reproduction." 33 C.F.R. §209.120(d)(2)(h) (1976). In 1977, the Corps refined its definition of wetlands by eliminating the reference to periodic inundation and making other minor changes. The 1977 definition read as follows:

> The term 'wetlands' means those areas that are inundated or saturated by surface or ground water at a frequency and duration sufficient to support, and that under normal circumstances do support, a prevalance of vegetation typically adapted for life in saturated soil conditions. Wetlands generally include swamps, marshes, bogs and similar areas. 33 C.F.R. §323.2(c) (1978).

In 1982, the 1977 regulations were replaced by substantively identical regulations that remain in force today. See 33 C.F.R. §323.2 (1985).

Respondent Riverside Bayview Homes, Inc. (hereafter respondent), owns 80 acres of low-lying, marshy land near the shores of Lake St. Clair in Macomb County, Michigan. In 1976, respondent began to place fill materials on its property as part of its preparations for construction of a housing development. The Corps of Engineers, believing that the property was an "adjacent wetland" under the 1975 regulation defining "waters of the United States," filed suit in the United States District Court for the Eastern District of Michigan, seeking to enjoin respondent from filling the property without the permission of the Corps.

The District Court held that the portion of respondent's property lying below 575.5 feet above sea level was a covered wetland and enjoined respondent from filling it without a permit. Civ No. 77-70041 (Feb. 24, 1977) (App to Pet for Cert 22a); Civ No. 77-70041 (June 21, 1979) (App to Pet for Cert 32a). Respondent appealed, and the Court of Appeals remanded for consideration of the effect of the intervening 1977 amendments to the regulation. 615 F.2d 1363 (1980). On remand, the District Court again held the property to be a wetland subject to the Corps' permit authority. Civ No. 77-70041 (May 10, 1981) (App to Pet for Cert 42a).

Respondent again appealed, and the Sixth Circuit reversed. 729 F.2d 391 (1984). The court construed the Corps' regulation to exclude from the category of adjacent wetlands—and hence from that of "waters of the United States"—wetlands that were not subject to flooding by adjacent navigable waters at a frequency sufficient to support the growth of aquatic vegetation. The court adopted this construction of the regulation because, in its view, a broader definition of wetlands might result in the taking of private property without just compensation. The court also expressed its doubt that Congress, in granting the Corps jurisdiction to regulate the filling of "navigable waters," intended to allow regulation of wetlands that were not the result of flooding by navigable waters. Under the court's reading of the regulation, respondent's property was not within the Corps' jurisdiction, because its semiaquatic characteristics were not the result of frequent flooding by the nearby navigable waters. Respondent was therefore free to fill the property without obtaining a permit.

We granted certiorari to consider the proper interpretation of the Corps' regulation defining "waters of the United States" and the scope of the Corps' jurisdiction under the Clean Water Act, both of which were called into question by the Sixth Circuit's ruling. 469 U.S. 1206, 84 L.Ed. 2d 318, 105 S.Ct 1166 (1985). We now reverse....

III

Purged of its spurious constitutional overtones, the question whether the regulation at issue requires respondent to obtain a permit before filling its property is an easy one. The regulation extends the Corps' authority under §404 to all wetlands adjacent to navigable or interstate waters and their tributaries. Wetlands, in turn, are defined as lands that are "inundated *or saturated* by surface *or ground water* at a frequency and duration sufficient to support, and that under normal circumstances do support, a prevalence of vegetation typically adapted for life in saturated soil conditions." 33 C.F.R. §323.2(c) (1985) (emphasis added). The plain language of the regulation refutes the Court of Appeals' conclusion that inundation or "frequent flooding" by the adjacent body of water is a *sine qua non* of a wetland under the regulation. Indeed, the regulation could hardly state more clearly that saturation by either surface or ground water is sufficient to bring an area within the category of wetlands, provided that the saturation is sufficient to and does support wetland vegetation.

The history of the regulation underscores the absence of any requirement of inundation. The interim final regulation that the current regulation replaced explicitly included a requirement of "periodi[c] inundation." 33 C.F.R. §209.120(d)(2)(h) (1976). In deleting the reference to "periodic inundation" from the regulation as finally promulgated, the Corps explained that it was repudiating the interpretation of that language "as requiring inundation over a record period of years." 42 Fed. Reg. 37128 (1977). In fashioning its own requirement of "frequent flooding" the Court of Appeals improperly reintroduced into the regulation precisely what the Corps had excised.

Without the nonexistent requirement of frequent flooding, the regulatory definition of adjacent wetlands covers the property here. The District Court found that respondent's property was "characterized by the presence of vegetation that requires saturated soil conditions for growth and reproduction," (App to Pet for Cert 24a), and that the source of the saturated soil conditions on the property was ground water. There is no plausible suggestion that these findings are clearly erroneous, and they plainly bring the property within the category of wetlands as defined by the current regulation. In addition, the court found that the wetland located on respondent's property was adjacent to a body of navigable water, since the area characterized by saturated soil conditions and wetland vegetation extended beyond the boundary of respondent's property to Black Creek, a navigable waterway. Again, the court's finding is not clearly erroneous. Together, these findings establish that respondent's property is a wetland adjacent to a navigable waterway. Hence, it is part of the "waters of the United States" as defined by 33 C.F.R. §323.2 (1985), and if the regulation itself is valid as a construction of the term "waters of the United States" as used in the Clean Water Act, a question which we now address, the property falls within the scope of the Corps' jurisdiction over "navigable waters" under §404 of the Act.

IV

A

An agency's construction of a statute it is charged with enforcing is entitled to deference if it is reasonable and not in conflict with the expressed intent of Congress. *Chemical Manufacturers Assn. v. Natural Resources Defense Council, Inc.*, 470 U.S. 116, 125, 84 L. Ed. 2d 90, 105 S.Ct. 1102 (1985); *Chevron U. S. A. Inc. v. Natural Resources Defense Council, Inc.*, 467 U.S. 837, 842-845, 81 L.Ed. 2d 694, 104 S.Ct. 2778 (1984). Accordingly, our review is limited to the question whether it is reasonable, in light of the language, policies, and legislative history of the Act for the Corps to exercise jurisdiction over wetlands adjacent to but not regularly flooded by rivers, streams, and other hydrographic features more conventionally identifiable as "waters."

On a purely linguistic level, it may appear unreasonable to classify "lands," wet or otherwise, as "waters." Such a simplistic response, however, does justice neither to the problem faced by the Corps in defining the scope of its authority under §404(a) nor to the realities of the problem of water pollution that the Clean Water Act was intended to combat. In determining the limits of its power to regulate discharges under the Act, the Corps must necessarily choose some point at which water ends and land begins. Our common experience tells us that this is often no easy task: the transition from water to solid ground is not necessarily or even typically an abrupt one. Rather, between open waters and dry land may lie shallows, marshes, mudflats, swamps, bogs- in short, a huge array of areas that are not wholly aquatic but nevertheless fall far short of being dry land. Where on this continuum to find the limit of "waters" is far from obvious.

Faced with such a problem of defining the bounds of its regulatory authority, an agency may appropriately look to the legislative history and underlying policies of its statutory grants of authority. Neither of these sources provides unambiguous guidance for the Corps in this case, but together they do support the reasonableness of the Corps' approach of defining adjacent wetlands as "waters" within the meaning of §404(a). Section 404 originated as part of the Federal Water Pollution Control Act Amendments of 1972, which constituted a comprehensive legislative attempt "to restore and maintain the chemical, physical, and biological integrity of the Nation's waters." CWA §101, 33 U.S.C. §1251 [33 U.S.C.A. §1251]. This objective incorporated a broad, systemic view of the goal of maintaining and improving water quality: as the House Report on the legislation put it, "the word 'integrity' ... refers to a condition in which the natural structure and function of ecosystems [are] maintained." HR Rep No. 92-911, p 76 (1972). Protection of aquatic ecosystems, Congress recognized, demanded broad federal authority to control pollution, for "[w]ater moves in hydrologic cycles and it is essential that discharge of pollutants be controlled at the source." S Rep No. 92-414, p 77 (1972).

In keeping with these views, Congress chose to define the waters covered by the Act broadly. Although the Act prohibits discharges into "navigable waters," see CWA §§301(a), 404(a), 502(12), 33 U.S.C. §§1311(a), 1344(a), 1362(12) [33 U.S.C.A. §§1311(a), 1344(a), 1362(12)], the Act's definition of "navigable waters" as "the waters of the United States" makes it clear that the term "navigable" as used in the Act is of limited import. In adopting this definition of "navigable waters," Congress evidently intended to repudiate limits that had been placed on federal regulation by earlier water pollution control statutes and to exercise its powers under the Commerce Clause to regulate at least some waters that would not be deemed "navigable" under the classical understanding of that term. See S Conf Rep No. 92-1236, p 144 (1972); 118 Cong Rec 33756-33757 (1972) (statement of Rep. Dingell).

Of course, it is one thing to recognize that Congress intended to allow regulation of waters that might not satisfy traditional tests of navigability; it is another to assert that Congress intended to abandon traditional notions of "waters" and include in that term "wetlands" as well. Nonetheless, the evident breadth of congressional concern for protection of water quality and aquatic ecosystems suggests that it is reasonable for the Corps to interpret the term "waters" to encompass wetlands adjacent to waters as more conventionally defined. Following the lead of the Environmental Protection Agency, see 38 Fed. Reg. 10834 (1973), the Corps has determined that wetlands adjacent to navigable waters do as a general matter play a key role in protecting and enhancing water quality:

> The regulation of activities that cause water pollution cannot rely on ... artificial lines ... but must focus on all waters that together form the entire aquatic system. Water moves in hydrologic cycles, and the pollution of this part of the aquatic system, regardless of whether it is above or below an ordinary high water mark, or mean high tide line, will affect the water quality of the other waters within that aquatic system.
>
> For this reason, the landward limit of Federal jurisdiction under Section 404 must include any adjacent wetlands that form the border of or are in reasonable proximity to other waters of the United States, as these wetlands are part of this aquatic system. 42 Fed. Reg. 37128 (1977).

We cannot say that the Corps' conclusion that adjacent wetlands are inseparably bound up with the "waters" of the United States—based as it is on the Corps' and EPA's technical expertise—is unreasonable. In view of the breadth of federal regulatory authority contemplated by the Act itself and the inherent difficulties of defining precise bounds to regulable waters, the Corps' ecological judgment about the relationship between waters and their adjacent wetlands provides an adequate basis for a legal judgment that adjacent wetlands may be defined as waters under the Act.

This holds true even for wetlands that are not the result of flooding or permeation by water having its source in adjacent bodies of open water. The Corps has concluded that wetlands may affect the water quality of adjacent lakes, rivers, and streams even when the waters of those bodies do not actually inundate the wetlands. For example, wetlands that are not flooded by adjacent waters may still tend to drain into those waters. In such circumstances, the Corps has concluded that wetlands may serve to filter and purify water draining into adjacent bodies of water, see 33 C.F.R. §320.4(b)(2)(vii) (1985), and to slow the flow of surface runoff into lakes, rivers, and streams and thus prevent flooding and erosion, see §§320.4(b)(2)(iv) and (v). In addition, adjacent wetlands may "serve significant natural biological functions, including food chain production, general habitat, and nesting, spawning, rearing and resting sites for aquatic ... species." §320.4(b)(2)(i). In short, the Corps has concluded that wetlands adjacent to lakes, rivers, streams, and other bodies of water may function as integral parts of the aquatic environment even when the moisture creating the wetlands does not find its source in the adjacent bodies of water. Again, we cannot say that the Corps' judgment on these matters is unreasonable, and we therefore conclude that a definition of "waters of the United States" encompassing all wetlands adjacent to other bodies of water over which the Corps has jurisdiction is a permissible interpretation of the Act. Because respondent's property is part of a wetland that actually abuts on a navigable waterway, respondent was required to have a permit in this case....

The significance of Congress' treatment of the Corps' §404 jurisdiction in its consideration of the Clean Water Act of 1977 is twofold. First, the scope of the Corps' asserted jurisdiction over wetlands was specifically brought to Congress' attention, and Congress rejected measures designed to curb the Corps' jurisdiction in large part because of its concern that protection of wetlands would be unduly hampered by a narrowed definition of "navigable waters." Although we are chary of attributing significance to Congress' failure to act, a refusal by Congress to overrule an agency's construction of legislation is at least some evidence of the reasonableness of that construction, particularly where the administrative construction has been brought to Congress' attention through legislation specifically designed to supplant it. See *Bob Jones University v. United States,* 461 U.S. 574, 599-601, 76 L.Ed. 2d 157, 103 S.Ct. 2017 (1983*); United States v. Rutherford*, 442 U.S. 544, 554, and n. 10, 61 L.Ed. 2d 68, 99 S.Ct. 2470 (1979).

Second, it is notable that even those who would have restricted the reach of the Corps' jurisdiction would have done so not by removing wetlands altogether from the definition of "waters of the United States," but only by restricting the scope of "navigable waters" under §404 to waters navigable in fact *and their adjacent wetlands.* In amending the definition of "navigable waters" for purposes of §404 only, the backers of the House bill would have left intact the existing definition of "navigable waters" for purposes of §301 of the Act, which generally prohibits discharges of pollutants into navigable waters. As the House Report explained: "'Navigable waters' as used in section 301 includes all of the waters of the United States including their adjacent wetlands." HR Rep No. 95-139, p 24 (1977). Thus, even those who thought that the Corps' existing authority under §404 was too broad recognized (1) that the definition of "navigable waters" then in force for both §301 and §404 was reasonably interpreted to include adjacent wetlands, (2) that the water quality concerns of the Clean Water Act demanded regulation of at least some discharges into wetlands, and (3) that whatever jurisdiction the Corps would retain over discharges of fill material after passage of the 1977 legislation should extend to discharges into wetlands adjacent to any waters over which the Corps retained jurisdiction. These views provide additional support for a conclusion that Congress in 1977 acquiesced in the Corps' definition of waters as including adjacent wetlands.

Two features actually included in the legislation that Congress enacted in 1977 also support the view that the Act authorizes the Corps to regulate discharges into wetlands. First, in amending §404 to allow federally approved state permit programs to supplant regulation by the Corps of certain discharges of fill material, Congress provided that the States would not be permitted to supersede the Corps' jurisdiction to regulate discharges into actually navigable waters and waters subject to the ebb and flow of the tide, "including wetlands adjacent thereto." CWA §404(g)(1), 33 U.S.C. §1344(g)(1) [33 U.S.C.A. §1344(g)(1)]. Here, then, Congress expressly stated that the term "waters" included adjacent wetlands. Second, the 1977 Act authorized an appropriation of $6 million for completion by the Department of Interior of a "National Wetlands Inventory" to assist the States "in the development and operation of programs under this Act." CWA §208(i)(2), 33 U.S.C. §1288(i)(2) [33 U.S.C.A. §1288(i)(2)]. The enactment of this provision reflects congressional recognition that wetlands are a concern of the Clean Water Act and supports the conclusion that in defining the waters covered by the Act to include wetlands, the Corps is "implementing congressional policy rather than embarking on a frolic of its own." *Red Lion Broadcasting Co. v. FCC*, 395 U.S. 367, 375, 23 L.Ed. 2d 371, 89 S.Ct. 1794 (1969).

C

We are thus persuaded that the language, policies, and history of the Clean Water Act compel a finding that the Corps has acted reasonably in interpreting the Act to require permits for the discharge of fill material into wetlands adjacent to the "waters of the United States." The regulation in which the Corps has embodied this interpretation by its terms includes the wetlands on respondent's property within the class of waters that may not be filled without a permit; and, as we have seen, there is no reason to interpret the regulation more narrowly than its terms would indicate. Accordingly, the judgment of the Court of Appeals is reversed.

[Footnotes omitted.]

Chapter 4

PROOF OF THE PRESENCE OF WETLANDS

Usually the property owner conducts the wetland delineation, most likely using a consultant with specialized knowledge in this area. The Corps has issued detailed information concerning the proper delineation of wetlands:

> Increasingly, potential applicants for Department of the Army permits are hiring environmental consultants to do wetlands determinations and delineations for them. (A list of consultants who have asked to be listed is available online.) In addition, because of Federal budgetary and work force constraints, we are requesting that many potential applicants have wetlands delineations done by consultants. Under existing constraints, the Corps of Engineers will field verify as many wetlands delineations as possible. We recommend that wetlands delineations performed by consultants be submitted for review and verification at least one month in advance of a submittal of a Department of the Army permit application.
>
> All wetlands delineations will be reviewed to ensure compliance with the methodology contained in the Corps of Engineers Wetlands Delineation Manual dated January 1987 and that sufficient information is provided to justify the wetland/upland boundaries as shown on the delineation map(s). To obtain a jurisdictional determination letter, all consultant-prepared wetlands delineations shall contain:
>
>> A wetlands delineation map depicting a point to point survey of the wetlands boundary as flagged by the consultant in the field. The consultant should review the survey for accuracy before submittal to this office. We prefer topographic maps with contour intervals of one or two feet and at a scale of one inch equals 100 feet. However, these specifications may vary depending upon the scope of the delineation and the nature of the project. In certain situations, a point to point survey of the wetlands boundary may not be required. However, the boundary must be reproducible in some manner. The consultant should contact this office for approval before submitting a delineation without a point to point survey. In all cases, the wetlands boundary must be marked with survey flagging or stakes in the field before this office will conduct a site inspection to verify the delineation. The flags or stakes must be sequentially numbered and those numbers shall appear on the survey for each point;
>>
>> The type(s) of wetlands present, such as riparian willow, wet meadow, marsh, vernal pool, etc., should be shown on the delineation map. The respective sizes in acres of each type should be included either on the map or in a report;
>>
>> The location of all sample sites should be shown on the delineation map(s);
>>
>> Wetlands delineation data forms, or similar data sheets, for each sample site, cross-referenced to the sites should be shown on the delineation map(s). The data for each sample site shall clearly list the indicators or lack of indicators for soils, vegetation, and hydrology, and shall include the basis for determining whether the sample site is wetland or upland. The number of sample sites will vary depending upon the

size and shape of the wetlands, the degree of difficulty in differentiating wetland and upland, width of transition zones, etc.;

A site location map, preferably a 7.5-minute USGS quadrangle, shall be included and any other pertinent maps of the site; and

A brief written report shall be included with the submittal. This report should list the property owner(s) and/or the developer(s) requesting the delineation. The report shall also describe the nature of the proposed development, and when a permit application will be submitted for the project. Your report should explain the basis for the wetlands boundary location and any problems or questionable areas. The dates of the actual field work should also be included in this narrative.

Wetlands delineations that are complete and accurate will be acknowledged in writing by the Corps of Engineers.

A wetlands delineation field data sheet is available for field use. This form should be used for wetland delineations subject to Corps of Engineers verification. If you and/or your consultants have questions regarding wetlands delineation procedures, please contact the U.S. Army, Corps of Engineers, Sacramento District Regulatory Branch.

If a property owner disagrees with a Corps delineation of wetlands on the property, there can be extensive expert testimony at the ensuing trial.

UNITED STATES v. LAMBERT

589 F.Supp. 366 (M.D.Fla. 1984)

Subsequent to the filing of the complaint in this case (18 May 1981) Dr. Arnold Banner, a Ph.D. in marine biology employed by the Fish and Wildlife Service, conducted an extensive investigation into the boundaries of suspected wetlands on the defendants' property, the nature of the wetlands, and the loss to the surrounding ecology caused by filling operations on the property by the defendant William Lambert. Dr. Banner studied the aerial photographs in evidence as Government's exhibits 4A, B, C, and D. He studied topographical surveys of the property, compared measurements of water levels at the culvert south of the defendants' southwest corner with water levels in the Banana River at the Port Canaveral locks. He examined the vegetation on the defendants' property. For that purpose he made several site visits before the litigation commenced and a total of nineteen between 1980 and 1984.

Government exhibit 6 shows a transect line along which Dr. Banner caused elevations to be measured. Overlays to Government exhibit 6 contain photographs taken by Dr. Banner during his site inspections from 1980 to 1982. Many of these photographs show various species of plants relied upon by Dr. Banner as indicators of wetlands. Such plants are listed by the Army Corps manual in evidence as Government exhibit 110 as indicators of wetlands because of their tolerance for life in saturated soil. The plants found by Dr. Banner through his photographic and on site investigations are listed on Government exhibit 12. These plants were, according to Dr. Banner, prevalent in the areas which he ultimately concluded to be wetlands. Based on Government exhibit 5, 8A and 8B, he concluded that the elevation in the suspected wetlands before the filling operation began ranged from .75 feet to 1.5 feet above mean sea level or an average of .9 feet above mean sea level (NGVD).

Dr. Banner testified to a salinity gradient as follows: sea water—35 parts per 1000; Banana River water—30 parts per 1000; tidal creek south of Lambert property—22 parts per 1000; station 10 in western wetlands (Government exhibit 5)—14 parts per 1000. He stated this gradient is typical of an estuary. Dr. Banner personally observed on numerous occasions that when water was measured at 1.5 feet NGVD at the culvert southwest of the property, the water would flow north through the culvert and along the ditch across the south side of the defendants' property all the way to the southeastern end of the property.

The average water level in the Banana River according to the evidence in this case is .57 feet above NGVD. Based on a study of annual changes in water levels of the Banana River, Dr. Banner concluded the river should cause inundation on the property in its unfilled state at least 100 days a year. This was grounded in part on water level readings gathered at the Port Canaveral locks during a ten-year period. The record of water levels during the study period indicated that water levels at the Port Canaveral locks which are less than two miles from the defendants' property equalled or exceeded .9 feet NGVD 96 days a year and equalled 1.1 feet NGVD 57 days a year (see Government exhibit 13). Based on visual observations of the soil on the defendants' wetlands, Dr. Banner testified that it was saturated throughout the year—as opposed to inundated.

The Government's hydrologist, Michael Lofton, corroborated Dr. Banner's findings. He testified that in a typical year water levels at the Port Canaveral locks would equal or exceed .9 feet NGVD 125 days per year. He further testified that when the water level in the Banana River equalled or exceeded 1.0 foot NGVD, the culvert southwest of the property provided a "good hydraulic connection" to the Banana River. He also testified, however, that the culvert would be an obstruction to the northward flow of the water from the river at river stages less than 1.0 foot NGVD. His study of the water data taken from the Port Canaveral locks showed that over the study period, the river on an average annual basis was at or above 1.0 foot NGVD 73 days a year. Finally, Mr. Lofton, using water level data gathered over a period of 17 months at the culvert and the water level data gathered at the Port Canaveral locks, performed a regression analysis. See Government exhibit 56. This analysis purported to show a strong correlation between the water level at the locks and the culvert.

The hydrologist's conclusions, however, are not viewed by the court as conclusive evidence that water levels at or above .9 feet NGVD at the Port Canaveral locks cause inundation on the defendants' wetlands. The regression analysis did not take into account independent factors contributing to the water level at the site such as well water flowing from the defendants' property into the culvert or surface water flowing across the defendants' property from the north from a disposal site which the evidence indicates exists to the north and west of the defendants' property. Furthermore, water levels at the culvert do not necessarily predict an equal water level on the defendants' wetlands. Mr. Lofton admitted that a higher water level in the culvert was required to connect the water to the eastern wetland than to the central or western wetland. He testified that it would require a water level between 1.0 foot and 1.1 feet NGVD to connect water in the culvert with the eastern wetland.

As part of his investigation, Dr. Banner studied soil samples from the wetlands areas. He determined that soils in the wetland areas had three to six inches of organic material at the surface.

Based on his studies, Dr. Banner concluded that the defendants' property contained prior to filling operations three "wetland areas" as that term is defined by the Army Corps of Engineers regulation found in 33 C.F.R. 323.2(c) (1980). The factors considered by Dr. Banner were summarized for the court's benefit on plaintiff's exhibit 10. The wetlands found by Dr. Banner were delineated on a survey map in evidence as Government exhibit 20. Although Dr. Banner's wetland determination is contradicted in some aspects by respectable expert witnesses presented by the defendants, it is also corroborated in some respects by those and by other witnesses, particularly Conrad White, Irene Sadowski, and William Kruczynski. On the basis of Dr. Banner's testimony, the court finds that the Government has proved by a preponderance of the evidence that the defendants' property before the filling operations of Mr. Lambert, contained three wetland fingers and a wetland bridge between the western wetland and the central wetland as depicted on Government exhibit 20.

In reaching this finding the court has concluded that proof by a preponderance of the evidence is the burden of persuasion upon the Government. See *United States v. Ward*, 448 U.S. 242, 248, 65 L.Ed. 2d 742, 100 S.Ct. 2636 (1980), and *United States v. Regan*, 232 U.S. 37, 47, 58 L.Ed. 494, 34 S.Ct. 213 (1914). The court, however, has also concluded that in assessing the weight to be given the testimony of the various witnesses, the court must give substantial deference to the well reasoned conclusions of those Government witnesses who are officials charged by law with administering the provisions of the Clean Water Act. See *National Wildlife Federation v. Marsh*, 721 F.2d 767 (11th Cir. 1983), and *Avoyelles Sportsmen's League, Inc. v. Marsh*, 715 F.2d 897 (5th Cir. 1983).

In *Avoyelles*, the case was before the district court in a different posture than is the present. In *Avoyelles*, the trial judge had before him a formal agency determination of wetland boundaries before he was called upon to rule on that same issue. In that circumstance, the trial court was limited in its role to determination of whether or not the agency finding was arbitrary and capricious. In the present case, no formal agency record was established and presented to this court for review; therefore, this court has assumed a broader latitude in dealing with the position of the Government, although it is still bound as stated above to give significant deference to the testimony of responsible Government officials.

There are other reasons why the court has determined to accept as reliable the conclusion of Dr. Banner as to the extent of wetlands on defendants' property. The defendants' principal expert witness, Dr. George Cornwell, conceded that the defendants' property had a central and western wetland and, to that extent, he corroborated the testimony of Dr. Banner. Dr. Cornwell's main objection to the characterization of the eastern finger as wetland was to the use of plants tolerant to life in saturated soil as indicators of wetland. He testified that such vegetation was not "typically adapted" to life in saturated soil. He testified that if a plant lives in wetlands, but also lives in dry areas, it is "a lousy indicator" of wetlands. Regardless of the logic of this conclusion, it has been held that the Corps regulations may encompass plants which in fact are tolerant to life in saturated soil even though they may not live out an entire life cycle in such soil. *Avoyelles Sportsmen's League, Inc. v. Marsh*, *supra*, at 913.

The evidence before the court indicates that there is a close physical proximity between the defendants' wetlands as defined by Dr. Banner and the Banana River. The parties agree that the Banana River is a navigable water. Additionally, both defense and Government witnesses agree that there is a ground water connection between the Banana River and the defendants' property. A ground water connection to navigable water causing saturation has been held sufficient to bring property within the Corps' wetlands definition provided the other elements of the definition are present. See *United States v. Tilton,* 705 F.2d 429 (11th Cir. 1983), note 1 (but for an apparently contrary holding *see United States v. Riverside Bayview Homes Inc. et al.*, 729 F.2d 391 (6th Cir. 1984)).

Although the extent of surface water intrusion on defendants' property from the Banana River is in sharp dispute, it is clear from the evidence that the culvert through Banana River Drive provides a means for such intrusion. It is also indisputable that on some occasions water from the river flows through the culvert and onto defendants' wetlands. Further evidence of the adjacency of defendants' wetlands to the Banana River was provided by the testimony of Dr. William Kruczynski, a Ph.D. employed by the Environmental Protection Agency. He characterized the upland areas on defendants' property and the road lying east of the property as "relic dunes" separating the wetlands from the Banana River. Based on the foregoing evidence, the court finds that the defendants' wetlands are "adjacent" for purposes of Section 323.2(a)(2), 33 C.F.R. (1980).

There is no substantial dispute that the fill placed in the wetlands was a "discharge of a pollutant" within the purview of 33 U.S.C. §1311(a) and 1362(12). The defendant argues that his filling operations were permitted under Section 323.4-2 of the Corps regulations as they existed in 1980. 33 C.F.R. §323.4-2(a)(1) (1980) reads as follows:

(a) Discharges of dredged or fill material into the following waters of the United States are hereby permitted for purposes of Section 404, provided the conditions in paragraph (b) below are met:

(1) Non-tidal rivers, streams and their impoundments including adjacent wetlands that are located above the headwaters;

It is, however, inapplicable. The defendants' wetlands are adjacent to the Banana River which even if non-tidal has not been shown to have a flow less than five cubic feet per minute. The fill, therefore, was not placed above "headwaters" as defined in 33 C.F.R. §323.2(i) (1980). Hence the court concludes that the placing of fill in the wetlands as depicted on Government Exhibit 21 by the defendant William Lambert constituted a series of violations of Section 1311(a) of Title 33, United States Code. These violations began in or about 1977 and ended in or about March 1982.

Restoration

Under Section 1319(b) and (d), Title 33, United States Code, the court has the authority to compel restoration and impose a civil penalty as a means of enforcing compliance with Section 1311 of Title 33. A violation of Section 1311, however, does not automatically require restoration. *See United States v. Context-Marks Corp.*, 729 F.2d 1294 (11th Cir. 1984). In considering the restoration issue, the three wetlands fingers should be considered separately.

The eastern wetland was shown by the evidence to have been a transitional area, that is, an area transitioning to upland status. Mr. White characterized the eastern wetland as a "stressed" wetland producing a number of plants not indicative of a wetland. William Kruczynski, a Government rebuttal witness, testified that the construction of State Road 528 (shown on Government exhibit 112) has contributed to the drying out process on the eastern wetland. One of the defendants' experts, Mr. J. B. Butler, testified that the natural watershed to the defendants' property was severely truncated by the construction of State Road 528 (also referred to as Bennett Causeway). Mr. Butler testified that 75 to 80 percent of the eastern wetland was over one foot NGVD before the defendants' filling commenced. It was not until after the present litigation commenced that any Government agent classified the north half of the eastern wetland as a wetland area within the Corps jurisdiction. The foregoing evidence and the lack of a significant and clearly demonstrated surface water connection between the eastern wetland and the Banana River lead the court to conclude that restoration of the eastern wetland would be an unduly burdensome and inequitable application of injunctive power.

The Government has urged the court to order restoration of the eastern wetland to prevent Mr. Lambert from profiting through the fill operation in violation of the Clean Water Act. The Government's factual basis for this argument is the testimony of Philip Pickens, a real estate appraiser. Mr. Pickens testified that Mr. Lambert had considerably enhanced the value of his property by the filling. There are two reasons why the Government's position should be rejected. First, Mr. Pickens' testimony dealing with enhancement is subject to question on a competency basis. Mr. Pickens, although a qualified appraiser, made certain assumptions which render the probative value of his opinion questionable. He testified that nine acres on Mr. Lambert's property were filled and assumed that the fill would permit commercial use of the land. There was, however, no factual predicate for this assumption. Furthermore, he admitted that he did not go on the property for purposes of a site examination and did not know if the filled areas had a sufficient configuration to permit use for anything. Given these limitations on Mr. Pickens' testimony, the court cannot determine the extent to which, if at all, the fill enhanced the value of the Lambert site. Additionally, the injunctive power possessed by the court under the Clean Water Act is not designed to penalize a landowner for improving his property. It is designed to permit the court to restore favorable environmental factors which have been disrupted by unlawful filling activities. This court concludes that the evidence is not sufficiently clear that the filling of the eastern wetland so significantly disrupted the navigable body of water to which it is adjacent that an order of restoration would be consistent with the burden which would thereby be imposed on the landowner.

The court has also not overlooked the testimony of Dr. William Kruczynski to the effect that he saw highly organic water coming from the fill on the eastern wetland at a location on the southeast corner of the defendants' property and moving from there into the roadside ditch which leads to the culvert and ultimately to the Banana River. This testimony, however, is not sufficiently strong to require the court to order restoration of the entire eastern wetland. The probative value of this testimony was significantly undermined on cross-examination which elicited an admission from the witness that in previous deposition testimony he placed the site of the leachate on the east side of the defendants' property near a gate which is north of the defendants' southeast corner and not proximately related to the ditch. The testimony of Mr. Delbert Hicks, an expert in aquatic biology with the EPA, also suggests that un-ionized ammonia may be forming in the fill area and could move thence to the Banana River via the culvert. However, the amount of such ammonia was not quantified and a conclusion on the present record that it presents a threat to the ecology of the Banana River is too speculative to justify removal of the fill from the eastern wetland.

With regard to the central wetland, the evidence shows that the defendant by excavation created a six-acre lake. The excavation of the lake was not a violation of the Clean Water Act as was earlier noted by this court's opinion in this case in connection with the denial of the preliminary injunction. In connection with the excavation of the lake, fill pads were placed in the central wetland in violation of the Act. These fill pads, however, have now been removed. The only other violation of the Act which occurred in connection with the excavation of the lake was a *de minimis* addition of fill to the areas adjacent to the excavation site by drippings from the dragline as the excavated materials were extracted and placed in trucks. The court, therefore, concludes that there is no justifiable basis under the law for requiring the landowner to fill the excavation which has been referred to in the testimony variously as "Lake Lambert" or "the pit," depending on one's point of view.

Mr. Delbert Hicks testified that ammonia from the pit "might" move out of the pit and into the roadside ditch and thence, via the culvert, to the Banana River. The ammonia is forming by a combination of water in the pit with organic nitrogen leaching into the pit from the filled areas.

Mr. Hicks could not say how long the leachate will continue to produce ammonia in the pit. He testified that only ammonia in un-ionized form is harmful to marine life. At concentrations of .34 to 3.2 milligrams per liter, un-ionized ammonia is lethal and at .03 to .12 milligrams per liter, un-ionized ammonia is debilitating to certain marine species. His testimony with regard to the ammonia was based in part upon a measurement of ammonia level at the culvert in September of 1983. The measurement at that time produced a finding of .4 milligrams per liter of un-ionized ammonia. Mr. Hicks, however, was totally unaware when giving this testimony of any source producing ammonia at the culvert other than the Lambert pit. Specifically he was unaware of a source of ammonia northwest of the Lambert site. Later testimony by Mr. Lambert indicated that a fill area exists northwest of his property where scallop shells are being used for fill. Mr. Hicks admitted on rebuttal that water coming from that fill area northwest of the Lambert property is a source of ammonia to the culvert. Furthermore, Mr. Hicks admitted that the ammonia forming in Lake Lambert is forming only at depths where there is no oxygen. In the area of the lake nearest to the mechanical connection provided by two PVC pipes running from the south end of the lake, no anoxic condition was found. In other areas of the lake to the north of its southern extreme, anoxic conditions were found at depths between 8 and 11 feet.

Dr. Joseph Delfino, a water quality expert for the defendants, testified that it was not possible that the site could be affecting the ammonia and nitrogen content of the Banana River. He testified that the source of ammonia northwest of the Lamberts' property could account for some of the un-ionized ammonia found by the EPA at the culvert. He further testified that the Government data on the quantity of hydrogen sulfide and ammonia was insufficient to quantify either the un-ionized hydrogen sulfide or ammonia in the lake. He also testified that the water quality in Lake Lambert is typical of that in the surrounding areas.

Because the excavation of the lake with minor exceptions did not involve an illegal fill and the water of the lake has not been proved by a preponderance of the evidence to be itself a pollutant of the Banana River, the court concludes there is no justifiable basis for ordering a fill of the lake. As an incidental matter, it should be noted the pit on the Lambert property was not alleged in the complaint to be a point source of pollution and its status as such is actually beyond the issues framed by the complaint.

With regard to the western wetland which all parties conclude is the wettest of the areas on the defendants' property, the court finds that removal of the fill, including the fill placed in the bridge area, would not be unduly burdensome to the defendants and would significantly protect and preserve the value of the western wetland as a contributing factor in the environment surrounding the Banana River. The parties are, therefore, directed to submit to the court within 30 days from the filing of this opinion a proposed final judgment and a stipulated plan for the restoration of the western wetland. If the parties are not able to stipulate on a restoration plan, they shall within the 30-day period submit separate plans for restoration. Any such plan shall specify a time for the commencement of the restoration work and also a maximum time within which the work is to be concluded. The plan shall also provide for periodic and final inspection of the restoration by a representative of the Environmental Protection Agency.

The court concludes that a civil penalty should be imposed on the defendant William Lambert for the filling of the three wetland fingers in violation of the Clean Water Act. The court will, however, reserve ruling on the amount of the penalty until the court has examined and approved a proposed restoration plan. Additionally the final judgment shall permanently enjoin the defendants from further filling or otherwise discharging a pollutant into the remaining and restored wetlands.

The evidence will not support a finding that Mrs. Lucille H. Lambert actively directed or caused the illegal fill. The court, therefore, concludes that it would be inappropriate to impose a civil penalty on Mrs. Lambert. The evidence does indicate, however, that she was aware that the fill activities were progressing, was aware that they were progressing in areas claimed by the United States Army Corps of Engineers to be wetlands without a permit, and was aware that her husband was responsible for the activities on property jointly owned by her with her husband. The court, therefore, concludes that the fine which will hereafter be imposed shall constitute a lien on the joint interest of Mr. and Mrs. Lambert in the property and as a joint owner of the property, Mrs. Lambert shall be equally subject to the court's permanent injunction.

DONE AND ORDERED in Chambers at Orlando, Florida, this 11th day of June, 1984.

If the Corps or the Environmental Protection Agency determines that a wetland is present, there is not much chance that a court will overturn the decision, particularly if a permit is also issued, but, if they decide that a wetland is not present, judicial review is available.

NATIONAL WILDLIFE FEDERATION v. HANSON

623 F. Supp. 1539 (E.D.N.C. 1985)

This action was brought under §505 (citizens' suit provision) of the Clean Water Act (CWA) to challenge a determination by the United States Army Corps of Engineers (Corps) that a particular tract of land in eastern North Carolina was not a "wetland" under §404 of the CWA and, therefore, not subject to the regulatory authority of the Corps. 33 U.S.C. §1365 and §1344....

I. FACTS AND PRIOR PROCEEDINGS

The allegations of Count I of the amended complaint concern a tract of land containing approximately 32,750 acres located in Tyrell, Hyde, and Washington Counties in North Carolina (Tract I). Tract I is a part of a large expanse of land lying in a peninsula formed by Albemarle Sound, Pamlico Sound, and the Alligator River. These large sounds—bodies of water separated from the Atlantic Ocean by the thin finger of land known as North Carolina's famous "Outer Banks"—provide drainage for Tract I and other similar lands in the eastern part of the state.

Tract I itself lies south of Phelps Lake and east of New Lake. Historically, the area was considered a forested swamp, useful solely for timber production. Periodic efforts have been made over the years—beginning as early as 1787—to utilize the property for other purposes, such as cattle and row-crop farming. These efforts have centered around the use of drainage canals to lower the natural water table. New Lake Canal and Pungo Lake Canal were completed in 1843, but most of the canals now in place were apparently constructed after 1970. Just how successful these previous farming ventures were is uncertain. It does appear, however, that when those efforts were abandoned the property quickly reverted to its former character.

Tract I is owned by FCF. PMA is a general partnership organized for the primary purpose of constructing and operating a peat-to-methanol synthetic fuel plant on Tract I. Peat for this process will be provided from the large deposits appearing on Tract I. Although FCF originally sought to mine peat from the entire tract, a permit issued by the North Carolina Department of Natural and Economic Resources on 21 February 1980 only allows FCF to mine peat on a 15,000-acre site on Tract I.

In order to mine peat on Tract I, excess water from the property must be drained through the construction of further drainage ditches and the use of pumps. In order to accomplish this task, PMA has applied for a state permit to pump three million gallons of ground water per day from the mining site. Once the soil is adequately drained, the vegetation will be removed and the surface tilled and sloped, to facilitate further drainage. The peat will then be removed through the use of sod machines and squeezed through a tube to create long cylindrical shapes. The peat, when formed into these cylindrical shapes, will be laid on the land surface to dry until ready for use in the peat-to-methanol plant to be built on Tract I.

The Corps consulted with FCF about its peat mining operations in late 1974, when FCF's plans were still confined to an upland area, not the subject of this litigation. In 1976, and again in April of 1978, the Corps advised FCF that expansion of its operations into new areas would necessitate a permit under §404 since the proposed areas were probably wetlands within the Corps' jurisdiction.

During the spring of 1979, FCF began to solidify its plans to expand its peat mining into Tract I. In April of 1979, a member of the Corps inspected the proposed site on Tract I and advised FCF that some parts of its operations would "definitely" require a §404 permit while a determination as to whether the whole operation would necessitate a permit required "further in-depth study" of the mining operations and "aerial photography possibly of the vegetation currently existing." FCF was further advised to request in writing a wetlands determination and to provide the Corps with further information about its operations.

On 3 July 1979, FCF formally asked the Corps to determine whether a §404 permit was required for its proposed expanded operations. Following this request, the Corps visited Tract I on 15 July 1979, observed a small mining operation in progress, and took a "cross-country tour" of the proposed mining site. The actual extent of this tour is unclear. The document memorializing this visit notes that the vegetation included "shrubs" typically "pocosin" on the easternmost portion and that the large drainage ditches which bisect the area indicate "that the ground water level is considerably below the surface."

On 15 August 1979, the Corps again visited the proposed mining site on Tract I and took another cross-country tour of uncertain detail. The Corps concluded that "vegetation typically found on a bog or pocosin area was prevalent and dominant throughout the majority of the mining area." Nevertheless, the Corps determined that the vegetation alone was not a "sufficient indicator of wetlands that would fall under the Corps' jurisdiction" since the drainage network "most likely" had lowered the water table and dried the upper layers of soil. The Corps further stated:

> This determination that the area is a non-404 wetland carries one stipulation—that the site should be revisited during the late winter or early spring after a significant rainfall to determine then if the soils were saturated to the point of possibly reclassifying the area. It should be stressed that in an area with similar vegetation but without the extensive drainage that this area exhibits would be a very good candidate for inclusion under the Corps' jurisdiction.

The Corps did not appear to be fully satisfied with this preliminary conclusion, however. On 15 August 1980, Colonel Robert K. Hughes, then District Engineer of the Corps' Wilmington District, wrote a memorandum to Corps Headquarters in Washington, D.C., discussing problems the Corps was having in determining which areas of FCF's landholdings were "wetlands" under §404. Colonel Hughes gave particular emphasis to the difficulties involved in making these determinations because of the extensive canals present on the property. He noted that the Wilmington office had requested the Division Engineer and the Regional Administrator of EPA to initiate a joint technical review board pursuant to "Memorandum of Understanding: Geographical Jurisdiction of the §404 Program." 45 Fed. Reg. 45,018 (1980).

Subsequently, on 26 August 1980, a meeting was held in Washington, D.C., at which time a decision was made not to convene a technical review board since there was apparently "not (sic) CorpsEPA technical disagreement." Further, a decision was made that the Corps would send a letter to FCF advising it that Tract I did not constitute "wetlands" under the §404 permit program. This letter was sent to FCF on 15 September 1980.

Although the record is sketchy, it appears that the Corps made at least two visits to Tract I following this wetlands determination. On 13 March 1982, a Corps staff member visited the property primarily to determine whether a methanol pipeline could be constructed on Tract I under an applicable nationwide permit. During May of 1983, a Corps member also visited the site for an undisclosed purpose. No notes or memoranda were prepared on this visit.

Sometime after the Corps' determination, in a letter dated 2 August 1983, the United States Fish and Wildlife Service requested the Corps to reconsider its position and exercise jurisdiction over Tract I. The Fish and Wildlife Service based this request, in part, upon the high water table on Tract I and the presence of wetland vegetation. It also contended that the drainage system had not caused Tract I to lose its wetland characteristics based upon the fact that PMA was required to obtain a state permit to allow it to pump three million gallons of water a day off the property. The Corps replied on 26 August 1983 stating, in essence, that it could not give a full response to the Fish and Wildlife Service's request since it had already received plaintiffs' statutory notice of their intention to sue over the matter.

After proper notice, this action was filed by plaintiffs challenging the wetlands determination. The private defendants filed a motion for summary judgment based upon the six-volume administrative record collected by the Corps and purporting to contain all materials relevant to the Corps' determination. The plaintiffs filed a cross-motion for summary judgment, and the federal defendants subsequently filed their own motion for summary judgment. The plaintiffs requested, and were granted by the court, permission to file supplemental materials designated as Volumes

7 through 10 in further support of their motion. All parties were given an opportunity to respond to these additional materials.

II. CWA AND WETLANDS RESPONSIBILITY

Wetlands, in a non-legal sense, are areas characterized by vegetation growing in soils that are periodically or normally saturated with water. Council on Environmental Quality, Our Nation's Wetlands, an Interagency Task Force Report (1978) (Our Nation's Wetlands), pp. 5–7. Marshes, swamps, and bogs are typical types of wetlands. Wetlands occur between upland areas and deep water areas, such as oceans, bays, rivers, or lakes. Water levels in wetlands rise and recede in part according to rainfall, so that at times they may be quite dry. *Id.*, see also *Avoyelles Sportsmen's League, Inc. v. Marsh*, 715 F.2d 897, 913 (5th Cir. 1983).

Wetlands are believed to perform important and unique ecological functions. For example, wetlands purify water by holding nutrients and recycling pollutants; they provide flood protection by retarding surface runoff from rainwater and shielding upland areas from storm damage; and they provide vital food resources and habitat for fish and wildlife. *United States v. Riverside Bayview Homes,* 474 U.S. 121, 88 L.Ed. 2d 419, 106 S.Ct. 455, 54 U.S.L.W. 4027, 4031 (1985), reversing 729 F.2d 391 (6th Cir. 1984); 33 C.F.R. §320.4(b)(2)(iv), (v) and (vii) (1985); Our Nation's Wetlands, 19-27. This is true even when the source of the moisture creating the wetlands is from ground or rain water, and not from the adjacent bodies of water. *United States v. Riverside Bayview Homes, supra,* at 4031.

The CWA is a comprehensive statute designed to "restore and maintain the chemical, physical and biological integrity of the Nation's waters." 33 U.S.C. §1251(a). Section 301(a) of the CWA contains an absolute prohibition against the discharge of pollutants into the Nation's waters, except those discharges made in compliance with standards promulgated or permits issued under the Act. 33 U.S.C. §1311(a). The Administrator of EPA and the Secretary of the Army, acting through the Chief of Engineers of the Army Corps of Engineers, share responsibility for issuance of permits under the CWA and enforcement of their terms. 33 U.S.C. §1342 and §1344.

Under §404 the Corps is responsible for the administration of a permit program for the discharge of dredged and fill materials into "navigable waters." 33 U.S.C. §1344(a). The EPA continues to carry ultimate responsibility for the overall concerns of the CWA, including determinations of what constitutes "navigable waters" for purposes of §404. See *Avoyelles Sportsmen's League, Inc. v. Marsh, supra* at 903 n.12; 43 Op. Att'y Gen. No. 15 (September 5, 1979). "Navigable waters" are defined as "waters of the United States including the territorial seas." 33 U.S.C. §1362(7). Although at one time the Corps adopted the traditional, but narrow view of "navigable waters," its 1977 regulations substantially broadened the definition. Navigable waters are now specifically defined to include "all waters of the United States," which are further defined to include "wetlands." 33 C.F.R. §323.2(a) and (b). For purposes of the §404 permit program, "wetlands" are:

> "those areas that are inundated or saturated by surface or ground water at a frequency and duration sufficient to support, and that under normal circumstances do support, a prevalence of vegetation typically adapted for life in saturated soil conditions. Wetlands generally include swamps, marshes, bogs, and similar areas." 33 C.F.R. §323.2(c).

Congress recognized the importance of protecting wetlands in order to achieve its statutory goal of restoring the chemical and biological integrity of our Nation's waters. As expressed by Congress at the time of the 1977 amendments to the CWA:

> "... The wetlands and bays, estuaries and deltas are the Nation's most biologically active areas. They represent a principal source of food supply. They are the spawning grounds for much of the fish and shellfish which populate the oceans, and they are passages for numerous upland game fish. They also provide nesting areas for a myriad of species of birds and wildlife. The unregulated destruction of these areas is a matter which needs to be corrected and which implementation of section 404 has attempted to achieve." 1977 U.S. Code Cong. & Ad. News 4326, 4336.

There seems to be no serious dispute that the proposed peat mining efforts and construction of the peat-to-methanol plant are "[dredge] and fill" activities within the meaning of §404. Thus, if Tract I is considered to be "wetlands," as defined in 33 C.F.R. §323.2(c), a §404 permit is required to proceed with these development plans.

III. CONTENTIONS OF THE PARTIES

The plaintiffs contend, in essence, that the Corps abdicated its mandatory duty under §404 to regulate dredge and fill activities on wetlands by declaring Tract I not to be "wetlands" within the meaning of the CWA. They also assert that the EPA violated the CWA by failing to prevent the Corps from so abdicating its duties and by failing to take appropriate action to prohibit PMA from discharging pollutants without a §404 permit. Plaintiffs request the court to find that Tract I constitutes a "wetland" within the meaning of §404, to require the private defendants to obtain a permit to continue their peat mining activities, and to issue other appropriate injunctive relief. In the alternative, they argue that the Corps' determination is arbitrary and capricious, and that the court should set it aside and remand the matter to the Corps for a wetlands redetermination.

The federal and private defendants contend that the court must defer to the Corps' determination unless it finds it to be arbitrary and capricious under the Administrative Procedure Act (APA), 5 U.S.C. §§701 et seq. (1977). As might be expected, all defendants assert that the Corps' determination was not arbitrary and capricious, but entirely appropriate based upon the six-volume administrative record. Specifically, they contend the Corps made numerous visual inspections of Tract I and correctly concluded that the drainage canals had altered the hydrology of the land so that Tract I could no longer be considered to be "wetlands" within the meaning of §404. The defendants contend that the Corps' administrative record is adequate to support its determination and urge the court not to rely upon the supplemental materials filed by the plaintiffs.

IV. STANDARD OF REVIEW

Judicial review of the Corps' decision is governed by the APA. The APA provides in relevant part that a court shall set aside agency "findings, conclusions, and actions" that are "arbitrary, capricious, or an abuse of discretion, or otherwise not in accordance with law." 5 U.S.C. § 706(2)(A). In *Citizens to Preserve Overton Park v. Volpe*, 401 U.S. 402, 415, 28 L.Ed. 2d 136, 91 S.Ct. 814 (1971), the Supreme Court made clear that this standard of review is highly deferential and that final agency action is "entitled to a presumption of regularity." But, although the "ultimate standard of review is a narrow one," the Supreme Court also made clear that the reviewing court must carefully "consider whether the decision was based on a consideration of the relevant factors and whether there has been a clear error in judgment." *Id.* at 416. The reviewing court is not "empowered to substitute its judgment for that of the agency." *Id.* Rather, a reviewing court's duty is to hold the agency to "certain minimal standards of rationality" and not to inject its opinion in place of that of the agency who, because of its particular expertise, has been entrusted with the decision-making power. *Ethyl Corp. v. EPA,* 176 U.S. App. D.C. 373, 541 F.2d 1, 36 (D.C. Cir.), *cert. denied,* 426 U.S. 941, 96 S.Ct. 2662, 49 L.Ed. 2d 394 (1976).

This review is also limited in scope to the materials before the agency at the time it made this decision, and a court must view critically any *"post hoc rationalizations." Citizens to Preserve Overton Park v. Volpe, supra,* at 419–20. If the agency's determination cannot be sustained based upon the record, then it must be remanded for further consideration. *Camp v. Pitts*, 411 U.S. 138, 143, 36 L.Ed. 2d 106, 93 S.Ct. 1241 (1973). The court may, however, under limited circumstances, consider matters outside of the record for background information. See, *e.g., Asarco, Inc. v. EPA*, 616 F.2d 1153, 1160 (9th Cir. 1980).

The plaintiffs contend, in essence, that the court should substitute its judgment in this case for that of the Corps. In *Avoyelles Sportsmen's League, Inc. v. Marsh, supra*, the Fifth Circuit was similarly asked to substitute its judgment for that of the Corps and EPA on the ground that a wetlands determination involves a question of the Corps' basic jurisdiction. In rejecting that contention the court noted that jurisdictional decisions often require the use of a particular agency's expertise, and the wetlands determination is no exception. *Id.* The wetlands determination "which requires analysis of the types of vegetation, soil, and water conditions that would indicate the existence of wetlands, is the kind of scientific decision normally accorded significant deference by the courts." *Avoyelles Sportsmen's League, Inc. v. Marsh, supra* at 906; see also *FPC v. Transcontinental Gas Pipe Line*, 423 U.S. 326, 331, 46 L.Ed. 2d 533, 96 S.Ct. 579, (1976) (noting that agency was required to make decision concerning the factual predicates necessary to assert its statutory authority); *Deltona Corp. v. Alexander*, 682 F.2d 888, 893-94 (11th Cir. 1982) (holding that Corps itself must first make determination on jurisdiction under §404). Although a few courts have not applied this deferential standard to wetlands determinations, they have done so without discussing what is the appropriate standard of review and are, therefore, unpersuasive. See, *e.g., Bayou Des Familles Dev. v. United States Corps of Engineers*, 541 F.Supp. 1025 (E.D. La. 1982) (upholding Corps wetlands determination); *United States v. Lee Wood Contracting, Inc.*, 529 F.Supp. 119 (E.D. Mich. 1981) (enforcement action holding that land is "neighboring wetlands" within Corps' jurisdiction); *Parkview Corp. v. Dept. of Army Corps of Engineers*, 469 F.Supp. 217 (E.D. Wis. 1979) (granting Corps' summary judgment motion that the land is a wetland under 1974 definition within Corps' jurisdiction); *P.F.Z. Properties, Inc. v. Train,* 393 F. Supp. 1370 (D.D.C. 1975) (holding that Corps had jurisdiction over proposed site). Thus, the Corps' wetland determination will be subject to the same limited judicial review employed to review other agency decisions.

V. METHODOLOGY

The language of the Corps' 1977 regulations makes clear that aquatic vegetation is a primary indicator of wetlands, although its presence or absence will not always be determinative. As explained in the preamble to the regulations, an area is a wetland within the Corps' statutory jurisdiction if it is:

> "inundated or saturated by water at a frequency and duration sufficient to support aquatic vegetation. This inundation or saturation may be caused by either surface water, ground water, or a combination of both." 42 Fed. Reg. 37,122, 37,128 (1977).

Thus, in addition to vegetation, the Corps must consider the water conditions (hydrology) and soils in order to make a wetlands determination. *Avoyelles Sportsmen's League, Inc. v. Marsh, supra* at 906.

Neither the CWA nor the enabling regulations specify the precise methodology to be used by the Corps in analyzing the vegetation, hydrology, and soils. The defendants argue that the Corps was able to adequately consider these factors by visually inspecting Tract I prior to its determination, and that it was unnecessary to perform any more in-depth studies or tests. The plaintiffs contend, on the other hand, that failing to more thoroughly study the soils, hydrology and vegetation amounted, in essence, to a failure to meaningfully consider these factors. The issue in this case is, then, whether the methods employed by the Corps meet the minimal degree of rationality necessary to uphold its decision under the APA.

Certainly there will be cases where the Corps will be able to determine the character of an area from one or two visual inspections. In obvious wetland areas, it will be abundantly clear that aquatic vegetation is prevalent and that the necessary inundation and saturation is present. In other cases, the complete absence of these characteristics will be readily apparent and no further visits, tests, or studies will be required. To require more in-depth investigation under these circumstances will unnecessarily burden the Corps with meaningless tasks.

In a third class of cases, however, the peculiar environmental characteristics of a particular tract of land may make it much more difficult for the Corps to determine whether wetlands are present. The Corps must then use its scientific expertise to analyze the nature of the land to determine what methods are reasonably necessary to make an accurate decision. Under these circumstances the burden necessarily will be greater on the Corps to study the property in order to make a jurisdictional determination. See, *e.g., City Fed. Sav. & Loan Ass'n v. Fed. Home Loan Bank Board,* 600 F.2d 681, 689 (7th Cir. 1979) (holding that agency must provide more in-depth explanation for issues subject to vigorous controversy).

Because its environmental character is not readily apparent, Tract I falls into this third class of cases. Although the Corps recognized that Tract I may have been a wetland at one time, it ultimately concluded that the drainage system had altered its character. The preamble to the 1977 regulations makes clear that lawful development may, in fact, change an area's character. 42 Fed. Reg. 37,122, 37,128. But whether development has progressed that far in any given case may present a difficult question. This is especially true in this case since the Corps seems to acknowledge that one main wetland indicator—aquatic vegetation—remains present on the property. Moreover, in spite of the questions concerning the altered conditions, the Corps failed to conduct an in-depth investigation to determine exactly when the canals were constructed and the vegetation removed. There is nothing in the record, then, which indicates whether the Corps believes that the canals were built and the vegetation removed before or after enactment of the CWA.

Although the Corps initially leaned towards a finding that Tract I was, at least in part, a wetland, it ultimately seemed quite uncertain over its proper characterization. As early as 1976, a Corps investigator indicated his belief that Tract I contained at least some wetlands. Later, in 1979, this belief was affirmed preliminarily, but the investigator recommended "aerial photography possibly" of the vegetation. During August of 1979, a Corps investigator noted that Tract I contained a prevalence of "vegetation typically found in a bog or pocosin (types of wetlands)." For the first time, however, the Corps investigator noted that Tract I might not be a wetland because of a "likely" change in the water table as a result of the drainage network. This tentative conclusion was explicitly conditioned on at least one further visit to the property in late winter or early spring after a significant rainfall. This trip was never made. The Corps' failure to make this trip is particularly significant since the regulatory definition of wetlands makes clear that wetlands are not limited to areas that are permanently inundated. *Avoyelles Sportsmen's League, Inc. v. Marsh, supra* at 913. Thus, the level of inundation may not be apparent from one or two visits during a single season of the year.

Moreover, just one month before the Corps finally resolved the jurisdictional issue the then District Engineer for the Wilmington District wrote to Corps Headquarters in Washington, D.C., to discuss the difficulties the Corps was experiencing in making a final jurisdictional determination on Tract I as a result of, in part, the effects of the drainage system. The District Engineer noted that the Corps had requested EPA to convene a joint technical review board pursuant to a "Memorandum of Understanding: Geographical Jurisdiction of the §404 Program." 45 Fed. Reg. 45,018. This board, had it been convened, would have consisted of experts from relevant fields who would have assisted the Corps in making its final decision. In spite of the obvious difficulties with the characterization of Tract I, a mere week and a half after the District Engineer sent the letter to Corps Headquarters, the Corps withdrew its request for a technical review board and determined that Tract I was not a wetland under its jurisdiction. The Corps arrived at this final decision without performing any further studies or tests, including the aerial photography or the revisit recommended by its own staff.

This procedure can hardly suffice to meet the Corps' obligation under the CWA to make a reasoned decision. *Sierra Club v. United States Army Corps of Engineers*, 701 F.2d 1011, 1032-33 (2d Cir. 1983) (holding that failure of the Corps to conduct an independent investigation and its reliance on an obviously questionable EIS in issuing a §404 permit is arbitrary and capricious). *Buttrey v. United States*, 690 F.2d 1170, 1185 (5th Cir. 1982), cert. denied, 461 U.S. 927, 103 S.Ct. 2087, 77 L.Ed.2d 298 (1983) (although the Corps did not conduct its own investigation, it relied upon credible information and reports supplied by other individuals and agencies including the Fish & Wildlife Service, the Environmental Protection Agency and the National Marine Fisheries Service). There is no evidence in the administrative record that the Corps gathered any information about the level of inundation during any time other than July and August of 1979. Similarly, there is no indication that the soils were ever analyzed or the vegetation meaningfully evaluated. Since it is clear that Tract I presented a difficult jurisdictional question for the Corps, its determination cannot stand without some scientific basis disclosed in the record.

The defendants also contend, in essence, that if the Corps' pre-determination methodology is lacking, any defect was cured by its post-determination visits to the property in March of 1982 and May of 1983. As noted above, this court must view "critically" any such "*post hoc* rationalizations." *Citizens to Preserve Overton Park v. Volpe, supra,* at 419–20. The March 1982 visit appears to have been a limited visit made primarily for the narrow purpose of determining the propriety of constructing a methanol pipeline under a nationwide permit. Moreover, there is no discussion in the record of any relevant observations made during the May 1983 visit. Thus, these visits do not provide any further reasoning to cure the defects in the Corps' methodology.

Finally, as an alternative theory, the private defendants urge the court to apply the Sixth Circuit's decision in *United States v. Riverside Bayview Homes, Inc,* 729 F.2d 391 (6th Cir. 1984), *rev'd,* 474 U.S. 121, 88 L.Ed. 2d 419, 106 S.Ct. 455, 54 U.S.L.W. 4027 (1985). In *Riverside,* the Sixth Circuit interpreted the inundation requirement of the Corps' regulations to mandate frequent flooding from adjacent navigable waters. That decision has recently been reversed by a unanimous Supreme Court. *United States v. Riverside Bayview Homes, Inc.*, 474 U.S. 121, 88 L.Ed. 2d 419, 106 S. Ct. 455, 54 U.S.L.W. 4027 (1985).

In short, there is no scientific basis in the record supporting the Corps' final determination, or its sudden ability to resolve a question it previously found so difficult. Given the apparently ambiguous character of Tract I, minimum rationality suggests that the Corps' investigation must be more in-depth than the casual visual observations disclosed in this record. The Corps' determination must be based on sound scientific analysis of the vegetation, hydrology, and soils employed after actual investigation into those factors. Since that analysis is lacking, the determination of the Corps cannot be upheld and will be set aside as arbitrary and capricious.

The court is aware of the efforts of PMA and FCF to comply with the numerous state and federal regulatory requirements. In addition to providing all information requested of them, PMA voluntarily commissioned numerous studies to assess the environmental impacts the peat mining operations, even though these studies were not required by law. On the other hand they apparently pressured the Corps into a hasty wetlands jurisdictional determination. Unfortunately, the delicate environmental problems presented by the proposed development of Tract I are not capable of quick and easy solutions. And, despite PMA and FCF's efforts, this court is required to ensure that the federal defendants comply with their statutory responsibilities in addressing the difficult problems, like the ones presented here, that often arise when business interests and the environment conflict.

VI. RELIEF

The plaintiffs contend that, upon remand, the court should give the Corps specific instructions on how to properly proceed in making its wetlands determination. Although this court is empowered to review jurisdictional decisions to determine whether they are arbitrary or capricious, the ultimate responsibility rests with the Corps to employ its scientific expertise to develop an appropriate methodology. *FPC v. Transcontinental Gas Pipe Line, supra* at 333–34.

The motions of defendants for summary judgment are denied, and the motion of plaintiffs for summary judgment is allowed. An appropriate order will issue.

ORDER

For the reasons set forth in a Memorandum Opinion of even date herewith, it is hereby ORDERED that:

1. This matter be, and it is hereby, remanded to the Corps for a redetermination, consistent with the Memorandum Opinion, as to whether Tract I, or any part thereof, is a wetland within the Corps' §404 jurisdiction.

2. The private defendants be, and they are hereby, restrained from engaging in any dredge and fill activities until such time as a proper wetlands determination is made and all necessary permits, if any, are obtained.

[Footnotes omitted.]

CHAPTER 5

ARTIFICIAL WETLANDS

Some assertions of jurisdiction over wetlands with less conspicuous connections either to navigable waters or interstate commerce have been upheld by the courts. In particular, so-called "artificially created wetlands," those which were not naturally present before but resulted from some man-made activity, are subject to Clean Water Act jurisdiction. *See also United States v. DeFelice*, 641 F.2d 1169 (5th Cir. La, 1981), *cert. denied*, 454 U.S. 940, 70 L.Ed.2d 247, 102 S.Ct. 474 (1981); *Swanson v. United States*, 789 F.2d 1368 (9th Cir. Idaho 1986); *United States v. Ft. Pierre*, 747 F.2d 464 (8th Cir. S.D. 1984); *Weiszmann v. District Engineer, U.S. Army Corps of Engineers*, 526 F.2d 1302 (5th Cir. Fla. 1976); *Track 12, Inc. v. District Engineer*, 618 F.Supp. 448 (D.Minn. 1985); *United States v. Bradshaw*, 541 F.Supp. 880 (D.Md. 1981).

LESLIE SALT CO. v. UNITED STATES

896 F.2d 354 (9th Cir. 1990)

This is an appeal from a district court decision denying the Army Corps of Engineers jurisdiction under the Clean Water Act, 33 U.S.C. §1251 et seq., over a parcel of land near the San Francisco Bay. 700 F. Supp. 476. The Corps had sought to require the landowner to obtain a permit before draining and filling the land, which over many years had acquired some aquatic characteristics. The district court found that because these conditions were artificial and were in part caused by the government, the Corps lacked jurisdiction. We reverse and remand.

BACKGROUND

This dispute revolves around a 153-acre tract of undeveloped land south of San Francisco, called the Newark Coyote Property, owned by Leslie Salt. A road separates the property into two parcels, one of 143 acres ("parcel 143") and one of 10 acres ("parcel 10"). The property abuts the San Francisco National Wildlife Refuge and lies approximately one-quarter mile from the Newark Slough, a tidal arm of the San Francisco Bay.

The present condition of the property, or rather its condition in late 1985 through 1986 when the Corps claimed jurisdiction, is the result of many artificial changes to the property over the last 100 years. Originally the property was pasture land. The first change occurred early in this century, when Leslie's predecessors in interest constructed facilities for the manufacture of salt. They excavated pits on the eastern one-third of parcel 143 for depositing calcium chloride, and created large, shallow, water-tight basins on the western two-thirds for crystallizing salt. Salt production on the property effectively stopped in 1959. The calcium chloride pits and the crystallizers remained however, and each year they temporarily filled with water during the winter rainy season. The extent of ponding is limited, but standing water did form on the property and remain long enough for fish to live in the ponds. Plant life, which had been nonexistent due to the high salinity and compaction of the soil, formed in the crystallizers after Leslie plowed the property in 1983 to combat a dust problem.

The property was also substantially affected by construction of a sewer line and public roads on and around the property. This construction created ditches, road beds, and most importantly, culverts which hydrologically connected the property to the Newark Slough. Caltrans, the state highway authority, also breached a levy on the wildlife refuge adjacent to the property and destroyed a tidegate which had prevented the tidal backflow from reaching Leslie's property.

The effect of all this human activity was to foster natural, ecological developments: tidewater reached the edges of Leslie's property and caused the creation of some wetland features on the southern fringes. Migratory birds used the crystallizers and calcium chloride pits as habitat during the winter and spring when they were flooded. In addition, an endangered species, the salt marsh harvest mouse, used the property as habitat.

The controversy over this property arose in late 1985 when Leslie started to dig a feeder ditch and siltation pond on parcel 143 in order to drain the land. The Corps soon became aware of this activity and responded by issuing a cease and desist order pursuant to its authority under Section 404 of the Clean Water Act. In that Act Congress directed the Corps, through the Secretary of the Army, to "restore and maintain the chemical, physical, and biological integrity of the Nation's waters." 33 U.S.C. §1251(a). The Corps claimed that Leslie was discharging a pollutant (fill) into waters of the United States in violation of section 301 of the Act. The Corps also claimed that Leslie's activities were obstructing the navigable waters of the United States in violation of section 10 of the Rivers and Harbors Appropriations Act. The Corps issued a second cease and desist order in early 1987 to stop Leslie from placing fill on parcel 10. The Corps issued that order in response to Leslie's attempts to block a culvert that connected its property to the Newark Slough.

In sum, the Corps claimed jurisdiction over the majority of the property. Leslie challenged that claim of jurisdiction and filed suit; the Corps countersued. The district court found in favor of Leslie on all grounds, holding that the property was not subject to the Corps' jurisdiction. The United States appealed that decision. Save San Francisco Bay Association and the National Audubon Society intervened on behalf of the United States.

The Corps now asserts jurisdiction over the property based on two separate theories which apply to two distinct portions of Leslie's land. First, the Corps argues that most of parcel 10 and the southern tip of parcel 143 are adjacent wetlands that are part of the Corps' Clean Water Act jurisdiction. To resolve this dispute we must first determine whether Congress intended that Clean Water Act jurisdiction should extend to property which government actions helped make aquatic. Because we find that it did, we then look to the Corps' regulations interpreting the Act, to determine whether they allow Corps jurisdiction. The Corps' second theory relates to the former crystallizers and calcium chloride pits. The Corps claims that these features are "other waters," as defined by Corps' regulations, that are subject to its jurisdiction....

THE SOUTHERN PORTIONS OF THE PROPERTY

The Corps claims that the southern portions of the property are wetlands within its jurisdiction. The district court denied the Corps jurisdiction for three reasons: (1) the wetland conditions were caused by the government, (2) the conditions were not "normal," as required by 33 C.F.R. §328.3(b), and (3) the property was not adjacent to waters of the United States, as required by 33 C.F.R. §328.3(a)(7)....

THE CRYSTALLIZERS AND PITS

The Corps determined that the former crystallizers and calcium chloride pits qualified as "other waters" that were under Corps jurisdiction according to 33 C.F.R. §328.3(a)(3). That section defines "waters of the United States" to include:

> "All other waters such as intrastate lakes, rivers, streams (including intermittent streams), mudflats, sandflats, wetlands, sloughs, prairie potholes, wet meadows, playa lakes, or natural ponds, the use, degradation or destruction of which could affect interstate or foreign commerce...."

The district court held that the crystallizers and pits were not described by this section for two reasons. First, because they are artificial structures and the regulation lists only natural formations. Second, the court concluded that the ponding was too temporary to qualify as other waters. The district court also addressed but did not decide the question of whether the property has a sufficient connection to interstate commerce.

A. ARTIFICIAL VS. NATURAL FORMATIONS

The district court applied the doctrine of *ejusdem generis* to construe the regulations to exclude artificially created waters. The court noted that all the waters listed as "other waters" in section 328.3(a)(3) were naturally created, and concluded that the artificially created crystallizers and calcium chloride pits could not be covered by that section. The *ejusdem generis* rule of statutory construction is used to illuminate the intent of the drafters; when the rule conflicts with other, clearer indications of intent, its results should be ignored. *See Weyerhaeuser S.S. Co. v. United States,* 372 U.S. 597, 601, 10 L.Ed. 2d 1, 83 S.Ct. 926 (1963); *Black's Law Dictionary,* 464 (5th ed. 1979). Reliance on the rule is inappropriate in this case.

First, the district court's interpretation conflicts with other parts of the Corps' regulations which assert that the Corps generally has jurisdiction over man-made waters under both the Clean Water Act and the Rivers and Harbors Act. *See* 33 C.F.R. §§328.5, 329.8. The Corps also defines at least one of the features listed in section 328.3(a)(3) to include artificial waters. *See* 33 C.F.R. §323.2(b) ("lake" includes "a standing body of open water created by artificially blocking or restricting the flow of a river, stream or tidal area"). In addition, the Corps' comments to the final regulations support the power of the Corps to assert jurisdiction over artificially created waters:

> "[We] generally do not consider the following waters to be "waters of the United States." However, the Corps reserves the right on a case-by-case basis to determine that a particular waterbody within these categories of waters is a water of the United States....
>
> (c) Artificial lakes or ponds created by excavating and/or diking dry land to collect and retain water and which *are used* exclusively for such purposes as stock watering, irrigation, settling basins, or rice growing....
>
> (e) Waterfilled depressions created in dry land incidental to construction activity and pits excavated in dry land for the purpose of obtaining fill, sand or *gravel unless and until the construction or excavation operation is abandoned* and the resulting body of water meets the definitions of waters of the United States (see 33 C.F.R. 328.3(a)). 51 Fed. Reg. 41206, 41217 (1986) (emphasis added).

These comments show that the Corps intends to exempt from its jurisdiction only those artificially created waters which are currently being used for commercial purposes, and that even those waters are subject to such jurisdiction on a "case-by-case" basis of review. The crystallizers and calcium chloride pits have not been used for commercial purposes for decades and so are not subject to even this limited exemption. Finally, courts have uniformly included artificially created waters in the Corps' jurisdiction under the Clean Water Act and the Rivers and Harbors Act. *See, e.g., Tull,* 769 F.2d 182 (mosquito-control ditch); *Stoeco Dev. Ltd. v. Dept. of the Army Corps of Eng'rs,* 701 F. Supp. 1075, 1078 (D.N.J. 1988) (artificially created wetland), *appeal dismissed,* 879 F.2d 860 (3rd Cir. 1989); *United States v. Akers,* 651 F. Supp. 320 (E.D.Cal. 1987) (same); *Track 12,* 618 F. Supp. 448 (same); *United States v. Ciampitti,* 583 F. Supp. 483 (D.N.J. 1984) (same), *affirmed,* 772 F.2d 893 (3rd Cir. 1985), *cert. denied,* 475 U.S. 1014, 89 L. Ed. 2d 307, 106 S. Ct. 1192 (1986). We reject the district court's interpretation of the regulations as creating a distinction between artificial and natural waters....

CONCLUSION

The southern portions of Leslie's property meet both the statutory and regulatory requirements for the Corps to exert Clean Water Act jurisdiction over them. The fact that the government in part caused the inundation of the property is not of consequence. Similarly, the government's actions do not affect the normalcy or adjacency requirements of the regulations. As to the crystallizers and calcium chloride pits, their artificiality and temporary wetness pose no obstacle to Corps jurisdiction. We remand to the district court for a factual determination of the sufficiency of the property's connections to interstate commerce. Because the record reflects that the Corps' jurisdiction does not extend to the total property, we also remand to determine over which portion of the property the Corps has valid jurisdiction in light of this opinion's legal conclusions. Costs will abide the final determination.

Chapter 6

SEASONAL WETLANDS

In another example of an assertion of jurisdiction over wetlands with a less-than-conspicuous hydrologic connection to navigable waters or interstate commerce, the Corps has successfully asserted jurisdiction over wetlands that are only present at certain times of the year.

QUIVIRA MINING COMPANY v. UNITED STATES ENVIRONMENTAL PROTECTION AGENCY

765 F.2d 126 (10th Cir. 1985)

Petitioners in these consolidated cases challenge the authority of the Environmental Protection Agency [hereinafter EPA] under the Clean Water Act, as amended, 33 U.S.C. §1251, *et seq.*, to regulate the discharge of pollutants from uranium mining and milling facilities into gullies or "arroyos."

Quivira Mining Company [formerly Kerr-McGee Nuclear Corp.] is contesting EPA permits (National Pollution Discharge Elimination System Permits) to two of its uranium milling or mining facilities near Grants, New Mexico. Those facilities are referred to as Ambrosia Lake, which discharges pollutants into Arroyo del Puerto under Permit No. NM0020532, and Lee Mines, which discharges pollutants into San Mateo Creek under Permit No. NM0028207. Homestake Mining Company [formerly United Nuclear Homestake Partners] contests Permit No. NM0020389 regulating its discharges into Arroyo del Puerto. The companies contend that Arroyo del Puerto and San Mateo Creek are not "waters of the United States," and therefore the EPA has no jurisdiction under the Clean Water Act to require permits authorizing discharges into these waters.

This appeal is from two written determinations of the EPA Administrator [hereinafter Administrator] to deny review, which are embodied in orders dated August 5, 1983. There are two issues before the court. First, the court must determine how much deference, if any, to give to the findings of the Administrator. Petitioners contend that the court should evaluate the record independently, giving no special weight to the factual determinations of the agency, because the agency's determinations of the facts are "jurisdictional." The EPA contends that the record is the product of an adjudicatory hearing and the court must find the agency action to be "unsupported by substantial evidence" before such action can be set aside. The second issue is whether the discharges are subject to regulation as discharges into the waters of the United States.

The Clean Water Act does not set forth standards for reviewing the EPA's decision, so this court must look to the Administrative Procedure Act for guidance. 5 U.S.C. §701, *et seq.; Avoyelles Sportsmen's League, Inc. v. Marsh*, 715 F.2d 897, 904 (5th Cir. 1983). When agency action is based upon an adjudicatory hearing, the court may not set aside the agency decision unless it is unsupported by substantial evidence. 5 U.S.C. §706(2) (E). Substantial evidence is "such relevant evidence as a reasonable mind would accept to support a conclusion." *Richardson v. Perales*, 402 U.S. 389, 401, 28 L.Ed. 2d 842, 91 S.Ct. 1420 (1971), quoting *Consolidated Edison Co. v. N.L.R.B.*, 305 U.S. 197, 229, 83 L.Ed. 126, 59 S.Ct. 206 (1938); *Consolo v. Federal Maritime Commission*, 383 U.S. 607, 16 L.Ed. 2d 131, 86 S.Ct. 1018 (1966). It is something less than the weight of the evidence, and the possibility of drawing two inconsistent conclusions from the evidence does not prevent an administrative agency's finding from being supported by substantial evidence. *Consolo, supra,* at 620.

Petitioners contend that when the agency's determinations of fact are "jurisdictional," the court must independently assess the record, giving no special weight to the determinations of the agency. See *Crowell v. Benson,* 285 U.S. 22, 76 L.Ed. 598, 52 S.Ct. 285 (1932).

We agree that the court must engage in a substantial inquiry and an in-depth review of the record. *Chrysler Corp. v. Dept. of Transportation,* 472 F.2d 659 (6th Cir. 1972). Such an inquiry is required by the "substantial evidence" test. *Id.* We disagree, however, that this court may engage in independent or *de novo* review without giving weight to the determination of the Administrator. *Crowell v. Benson, supra,* to the extent that it retains its validity, does not apply to this case. The standards set forth in the Administrative Procedure Act govern.

Petitioners' argument would require that in every case involving the issuance of an EPA permit to discharge pollutants the adjudicatory hearings and special findings of the Administrator would be entitled to no special weight. Such a result would contradict the clear meaning of the Administrative Procedure Act and would deprive the appellate courts of the expertise of the agency in determining such matters.

Viewed in the light of the substantial evidence test, the court finds that both the Arroyo del Puerto and the San Mateo Creek flow for short distances from the discharge points. Although neither the Arroyo del Puerto nor the San Mateo Creek is navigable-in-fact, surface flow occasionally occurs, at times of heavy rainfall, providing a surface connection with navigable waters independent of the underground flow. Additionally, the waters of the Arroyo del Puerto and the San Mateo Creek soak into the earth's surface, become part of the underground aquifers, and after a lengthy period, perhaps centuries, the underground water moves toward eventual discharge at Horace Springs or the Rio San Jose.

It is the national goal of the Clean Water Act to eliminate the discharge of pollutants into navigable waters. 33 U.S.C. §1251(a) (1). The term "navigable waters" means "the waters of the United States, including the territorial seas." *United States v. Earth Sciences, Inc.,* 599 F.2d 368 (10th Cir. 1979), this court noted the Clean Water Act is designed to regulate to the fullest extent possible sources emitting pollution into rivers, streams and lakes. *Id.* at 373. "The touchstone of the regulatory scheme is that those needing to use the waters for waste distribution must seek and obtain a permit to discharge that waste, with the quantity and quality of the discharge regulated." *Id.* It is the intent of the Clean Water Act to cover, as much as possible, all waters of the United States instead of just some. *Deltona Corp. v. United States,* 228 Ct. Cl. 476, 657 F.2d 1184, 1186 (1981).

The extent of the Clean Water Act's coverage of discharges of pollution is illustrated by a review of some of the cases which have been before the United States Court of Appeals for the Tenth Circuit. In *Ward v. Coleman,* 598 F.2d 1187 (10th Cir. 1979), *reversed on other grounds* 448 U.S. 242, 65 L.Ed.2d 742, 100 S.Ct. 2636 (1980), the court found that Boggie Creek, a tributary of the Arkansas River, is a navigable water of the United States for purposes of the Clean Water Act because the Arkansas River is navigable in fact. *Id.,* 598 F.2d at 1188, n.1. In *United States v. Earth Sciences, Inc., supra,* the court found the Rito Seco to be a "water of the United States," although it is not navigable in fact nor does it transport any goods or materials, and although it is located entirely in Costilla County, Colorado. Although the Rito Seco did not provide a very significant link in the chain of interstate commerce, the court found that the stipulation of facts indicated at least some interstate impact from the stream and that was all that was necessary under the act. There the facts were that the stream supported trout and some beaver, the water collected in the reservoirs was used for agricultural irrigation, and the resulting products were sold into interstate commerce. The court stated, "It seems clear Congress intended to regulate discharges made into every creek, stream, river, or body of water that in any way may affect interstate commerce. Every court to discuss the issue has used a commerce power approach and agreed upon that interpretation." *Id.* at 375. In *United States v. Texas Pipe Line Co.,* 611 F.2d 345 (10th Cir. 1979), the court found that the Clean Water Act covered oil spilled into an unnamed tributary of Caney Creek, which discharges into Clear Boggie Creek, itself a tributary of the Red River. The record reflected that there was a small flow of water in the unnamed tributary at the time of the spill, but there was no evidence that the other streams were or were not flowing. The court stated, "Congress did not in this Act use the term 'navigable waters' in the traditional sense; Congress intended to extend the coverage of the act as far as permissible under the commerce clause." *Id.* at 347. Even though nothing in the record supported an interstate commerce effect of this unnamed tributary, the court found that it was "without question" within the intended coverage of the Clean Water Act. The result was based substantially on the fact that the tributary was flowing a small amount of water at the time of the spill. "It makes no difference that a stream was or was not at the time of the spill discharging water continuously into a river navigable in the traditional sense." *Id.*

This court's findings in *Earth Sciences* and *Texas Pipe Line* compel a finding herein affirming the decision of the EPA. Substantial evidence here supports the Administrator's findings that both the Arroyo del Puerto and San Mateo Creek are waters of the United States. Substantial evidence before the Administrator supports his finding that during times of intense rainfall, there can be a surface connection between the Arroyo del Puerto, San Mateo Creek and navigable-in-fact streams. Further, the record supports the finding that both the Arroyo del Puerto and San Mateo Creek flow for a period after the time of discharge of pollutants into the waters. Further, the flow continues regularly through underground aquifers fed by the surface flow of the San Mateo Creek and Arroyo del Puerto into navigable-in-fact streams. The court finds that the impact on interstate commerce is sufficient enough to satisfy the commerce clause. And, as noted above, it was the clear intent of Congress to regulate waters of the United States to the fullest extent possible under the commerce clause.

The decision of the Administrator is AFFIRMED. [Footnotes omitted.]

See also *Friends of Santa Fe County v. LAC Minerals, Inc.*, 892 F.Supp. 1333 (D.N.M. 1995); *United States v. Phelps Dodge Corp.*, 391 F.Supp. 1181 (D.Ariz. 1975).

CHAPTER 7
ISOLATED WETLANDS

The courts do not view isolated wetlands jurisdiction with particular favor, especially when the government argues that its basis of jurisdiction is the Commerce Clause because the isolated wetland may be used as bird or wildlife habitat. But see *Utah by Division of Parks & Recreation v. Marsh*, 740 F.2d 799 (10th Cir. Utah 1984); *Palila v. Hawaii Department of Land & Natural Resources*, 471 F.Supp. 985 (D.Haw. 1979), *aff'd*, 639 F.2d 495 (9th Cir. Haw. 1981).

TABB LAKES, LTD. v. UNITED STATES

715 F. Supp. 726 (E.D.Va. 1988)

This matter is before the Court on the plaintiff's and defendants' cross Motions for Summary Judgment. The issue is whether the Army Corps of Engineers (Corps) has jurisdiction to require a permit in this case.

Originally plaintiff, Tabb Lakes, Ltd. (Tabb Lakes), sought a permit under section 404 of the Clean Water Act (CWA), in October, 1986, requesting permission to fill portions of its property for development purposes. 33 U.S.C. §1344. While a decision was pending, Tabb Lakes withdrew its permit application in August 1987 on grounds that it had determined that the property in question was not subject to the Corps' jurisdiction. After Tabb Lakes had commenced this declaratory judgment action, the Corps, in July, 1988, completed its Quantitative Wetlands Jurisdictional Determination which it alleges is the basis for the Corps' asserted jurisdiction over Tabb Lakes' property.

Tabb Lakes filed this complaint on September 21, 1987, seeking a declaratory judgment that its property did not fall within the jurisdictional parameters of section 404 of the CWA. In January 1988 the United States filed its Motion to Dismiss or for Partial Summary Judgment and in March and May 1988 Tabb Lakes filed its own Motion to Dismiss and for Summary Judgment (Amended).

In its Motion for Summary Judgment, Tabb Lakes challenges, among other things, the failure of the Corps to comply with proper notice and comment procedures under the Administrative Procedures Act (APA) before it issued a memorandum, in effect, rule making, which was subsequently the basis for making the jurisdictional determination in this case, claiming that Corps' jurisdiction stems from the regulations implementing section 404 of the CWA. 33 C.F.R. §§320, *et seq.*

The specific regulations set out at 33 C.F.R. §328.3 (a)(3) provide the definition of waters subject to Corps regulation:

"For the purpose of this regulation these terms are defined as follows:

(a) The term 'waters of the United States' means

(1) [NA]

(2) [NA]

(3) All other waters such as intrastate lakes, rivers, streams (including intermittent streams), mudflats, sandflats, wetlands, sloughs, prairie potholes, wet meadows, playa lakes, or natural ponds, the use, degradation or destruction of which 'could affect interstate or foreign commerce including any such waters;

(i) Which are or could be used by interstate or foreign travelers for recreational or other purposes, or

(ii) From which fish or shellfish are or could be taken and sold in interstate or foreign commerce; or

(iii) Which are used or could be used for industrial purpose[s] by industries in interstate commerce; ..."

On November 8, 1985, Brigadier General Patrick J. Kelly, the Deputy Director of Civil Works for the U. S. Army Corps of Engineers in Washington, D.C., issued a memorandum to all district Corps offices listing the seven [7] standards which would indicate a sufficient interstate commerce connection to warrant exercise of jurisdiction by the Corps over isolated waters and wetlands. Specifically, number 5 is the indicator relied on by the Corps in this case and it reads, "Waters which are used or could be used as habitat by other migratory birds which cross state lines."

Before a rule is promulgated or amended, section 553 of the APA requires agencies to afford notice of such impending action and to provide an opportunity for public comment. However, an exemption applies:

"(A) to interpretative rules, general statements of policy, or rules of agency organization, or procedure, or practice; ..." 5 U.S.C. §553(b)(3)(A).

The threshold issue here is whether Brigadier General Kelly's November 8, 1985, Memorandum falls within this exception, which exception, according to *Batterton v. Marshall,* 208 U.S. App. D.C. 321, 648 F.2d 694, 703 (D.C. Cir. 1980), is a "narrow one" and to be "only reluctantly countenanced." The United States urges that these are merely interpretive rule changes, or at most policy statements.

The APA's §553 notice and comment provisions seek to insure public participation and fairness to affected parties where agencies hold governmental authority, and to provide for an input of all relevant facts and alternatives. *American Hospital Association v. Bowen,* 640 F. Supp. 453 (D.C. Cir. 1986), *rev'd,* 266 U.S. App. D.C. 190, 834 F.2d 1037, 1044 (D.C. Cir. 1987). Although the distinction between a substantive and interpretive rule is a gray area, the Courts generally differentiate cases "in which an agency is merely explicating Congress' desires from those cases in which the agency is adding substantive content of its own." *Id.* at 1045.

"Substantive rules are ones which grant rights, impose obligations, or produce other significant effects on public interests, or which effect a change in existing law or policy. *Id.* Interpretive rules, by contrast, are those which merely clarify or explain existing law or regulations, are essentially ... instructional, and do not have the full force and effect of a substantive rule but are in the form of an explanation of particular terms." *Id.* The task is very fact specific, however the

Court in *American Hospital Association*, 834 F.2d at 1046, noted that a typical example of a substantive rule was a parole board's use of guidelines that established factors for determining parole eligibility and were thus critical to the ultimate parole decision. *Id.* (citing *Pickus v. United States Board of Parole,* 507 F.2d 1110, 1112-13 (D.C. Cir. 1974)).

Beyond any doubt, the memorandum produced a "significant effect on public interests" in a 38-acre tract at Tabb Lakes, most of which is a wetland, but not water, and which is brought into Corps jurisdiction as "water which is used or could be used as habitat by other migratory birds which cross state lines." Incidentally, not ducks or geese, but woodpeckers, songbirds, etc. In this case it is clear that Brigadier General Kelly's Memorandum affected a change in Corps policy intended to have the full force and effect of a substantive rule, and that the Corps relied on the memorandum in reaching its jurisdiction determination. Deposition of W. H. Poore, Jr., pp. 50-51; Memorandum of Brigadier General Patrick J. Kelly, November 8, 1985. Additionally, on February 11, 1986, General Kelly issued a second memorandum in which he noted that his November 8, 1985, memorandum "clarified for the first time the factors which are indicative of a connection to interstate commerce for purposes of the CWA." Kelly Memorandum, February 11, 1986. He further noted that "... you should notify your districts that, effective immediately, all waterbodies which are or reasonably could be used by migratory birds are waters of the United States and should be regulated as such for all *ongoing* and future discharges of dredged or fill material." *Id.* General Kelly implies in that memorandum that he disagreed with the Corps' Galveston District Office determination denying jurisdiction in the Pond 12 case and that the District should have asserted jurisdiction if it followed his 1985 Memorandum. *Id.*; see *National Wildlife Federation v. Laubscher*, 662 F. Supp. 548 (S.D. Tex. 1987).

Accordingly, we find that General Kelly's November 8, 1985, far-reaching Memorandum did not fall within any exceptions but instead required appropriate notice and comment under the APA.

The United States also asserts that, at most, the Kelly Memorandum is a general statement of policy expressly exempted from the informal rulemaking requirements of the APA. This Court first notes that while a substantive rule establishes a standard of conduct which has the force of law in subsequent proceedings, "a general statement of policy, on the other hand, does not establish a binding norm. It is not finally determinative of the uses or rights to which it is addressed. The agency cannot apply or rely upon a general statement of policy as law because a general statement of policy only announces what the agency seeks to establish as policy." *American Hospital Association,* 834 F.2d at 1046 (citing *Pacific Gas and Electric Co. v. Federal Power Commission,* 164 U.S. App. D.C. 371, 506 F.2d 33, 38 (D.C. Cir. 1974)). In distinguishing between legislative rules and policy statements some Courts have followed the test set out in *American Bus Association v. United States,* 201 U.S. App. D.C. 66, 627 F.2d 525, 529 (D.C. Cir. 1980).

> "First, courts have said that, unless a pronouncement acts prospectively, it is a binding norm. Thus, a statement of policy may not have a present effect.
>
> The second criterion is whether a purported policy statement genuinely leaves the agency and its decisionmakers free to exercise discretion."

Again, the Corps intended the November 8, 1985, Kelly Memorandum binding and intended that it take effect immediately. The subsequent February 11, 1986, Kelly Memorandum clearly indicates that the Corps did not intend to leave its district personnel with discretion in this area.

Accordingly, the November 8, 1985, Kelly Memorandum was not excepted from notice and comment requirements under the APA as a policy statement.

The Kelly Memorandum does not fall within any of the exceptions to §553 of the APA. This Court must, therefore, set aside any agency action found to be without observance of procedure required by law. 5 U.S.C. §706(2) (D); *Natural Resources Defense Council, Inc. v. U. S. Environmental Protention Agency,* 683 F.2d 752 (3rd Cir. 1982); *Brown Express, Inc. v. United States,* 607 F.2d 695, 703 (5th Cir. 1979).

Although this Court has grave doubts that a property now so used, or seen as an expectant habitat for some migratory birds, can be declared to be such a nexus to interstate commerce as to warrant Army Corps of Engineers jurisdiction, we do not here decide that issue. Further, it is unnecessary for the Court to make a decision as to Counts II, III and IV.

Determining that the Army Corps of Engineers does not have jurisdiction in this particular case, we enter judgment for the plaintiff. Each side shall bear its own costs and attorneys fees.

An Order will be entered contemporaneously herewith declaring that the Army Corps of Engineers does not have jurisdiction in this particular case.

ORDER.

The motion of plaintiff for summary judgment on Count I is GRANTED, on grounds that the Army Corps of Engineers has no jurisdiction to require a permit. Each side shall bear its own costs and attorneys fees.

It is so ORDERED.

HOFFMAN HOMES, INC. v. UNITED STATES ENVIRONMENTAL PROTECTION AGENCY

999 F.2d 256 (7th Cir. 1993)

A tremendous amount of effort has gone into trying to determine whether a small wetland near Chicago may be regulated under the Clean Water Act. After having issued, then vacated, one opinion on this subject, we hope now to resolve this difficult question.

I. BACKGROUND

On March 26, 1986, an employee of the Army Corps of Engineers was driving through the Village of Hoffman Estates, Illinois. The employee happened to see that work had begun in a former soybean field on a new subdivision called "Victoria Crossings." The subdivision would occupy a 43-acre square parcel which is bordered on the west by the Schaumburg Branch of Poplar Creek, on the east by a road, on the north by another subdivision, and on the south by a wetland and a road.

The Corps investigated the site; it determined that the subdivision's owner, Hoffman Homes, Inc. ("Hoffman"), had violated the Clean Water Act ("CWA" or "Act"), 33 U.S.C. §1251 *et seq.,* when it filled and graded parts of the site in preparation for construction. Specifically, the Corps felt Hoffman illegally filled two wetlands, "Area A" and "Area B."

Area A was a bowl-shaped depression at the northeast border of the tract that covered approximately one-acre. The basin was lined with relatively impermeable clay; before being filled by Hoffman, Area A collected rain water and snow melt and frequently ponded or saturated during wet weather. Area A contained at least four different types of wetland vegetation, including cattails. Area A was not directly connected to any body of water, either on the surface or by groundwater, and lay approximately 750 feet from Poplar Creek. Area B ran along the entire western and most of the southern borders of the tract. This wetland covered 13.3 acres, of which Hoffman had filled 5.9 acres. Area B is part of a 50-acre wetland area adjacent to the Poplar Creek. The creek flows into the Fox River which is a tributary of the Illinois River which empties into the Mississippi River.

Having been designated as wetlands pursuant to 33 C.F.R. §328.3(b), the sites could not legally be filled unless Hoffman obtained a permit pursuant to 33 U.S.C. §1342 or §1344. On May 30, 1986, the Corps issued a cease and desist order to Hoffman. This order instructed Hoffman to stop filling wetlands at the site and to apply for an after-the-fact permit to fill the areas. Hoffman did so. The Environmental Protection Agency ("EPA" or "Agency"), which shares responsibility with the Corps for administering and enforcing the CWA, then objected to Hoffman's plans for mitigating the damage to the wetlands. Consequently, on November 20, 1987, the Corps denied Hoffman's permit application and referred the matter to the EPA.

The EPA on December 22, 1987, issued a compliance order pursuant to 33 U.S.C. §1319(a). The order stated that Hoffman had filled wetlands without a permit, thereby violating 33 U.S.C. §1311. The compliance order directed Hoffman to cease its filling activities and to submit and carry out a plan to restore the wetlands to their original condition. On January 12, 1988, the EPA also issued an administrative complaint against Hoffman, pursuant to 33 U.S.C. §1319(g), seeking a $125,000 penalty for Hoffman's filling activities. Hoffman answered the complaint, admitting it had filled the two areas but denying they were waters subject to the CWA. On October 24, 1988, hearings commenced before an EPA Administrative Law Judge ("ALJ"). The hearings lasted a total of 21 days but did not run consecutively. The final hearing was held January 19, 1989.

On August 4, 1988, while the hearings before the ALJ were still proceeding, Hoffman brought an action in district court seeking a declaration of the compliance order's invalidity and an injunction against its enforcement. At that time the EPA had not yet decided whether to enforce its compliance order by bringing an action in a federal court pursuant to 33 U.S.C. §1319(b). Consequently, the district court dismissed Hoffman's action in January 1989. The district court held that the CWA precluded pre-enforcement review of the EPA's compliance order. *See Hoffman Group, Inc. v. United States E.P.A.*, No. 88 C 6695, 1989 U.S. Dist. Decision, 599, at *2 (N.D. Ill. Jan. 23, 1989). Hoffman appealed the district court's decision and we affirmed. We explained that Hoffman was not entitled to judicial review unless the EPA either assessed administrative penalties against Hoffman or sought judicial enforcement of its compliance order. Until such time, Hoffman was not subject to penalties or an injunction for not obeying the EPA's compliance order. *See Hoffman Group, Inc. v. E.P.A.*, 902 F.2d 567, 568 (7th Cir. 1990).

Shortly after our decision Hoffman became entitled to judicial review. On November 19, 1990, the EPA's Chief Judicial Officer ("CJO") assessed a $50,000 fine against Hoffman for having discharged "dredged or fill material" into Area A without a permit in violation of 33 U.S.C. §1311 and §1314 and affirmed another $50,000 penalty against Hoffman for filling Area B.

In fining Hoffman for filling Area A, the CJO was reversing the ALJ. On September 14, 1989, in the ALJ's "Initial Decision," the ALJ had found that although Area A was a wetland it was not subject to the CWA's permit requirements. The ALJ characterized Area A as being "isolated." Initial Decision at 48. The EPA had not shown, the ALJ found, that Area A had any surface or groundwater connection with Poplar Creek. In the ALJ's opinion, the Agency also failed to show that Area A performed flood control or sediment trapping in connection with drainage into or the possible flooding of the creek. *Id.* at 45. Instead, the ALJ found that water drained into Area A from the immediately surrounding area, collected there, and then slowly evaporated or dissipated. *Id.* at 47. "There is also no basis for determining if Area A has any effect on the Schaumburg Branch [of Poplar Creek], because it simply cannot be determined what the drainage or flow of water would be if Area A were not there." *Id.*

The ALJ recognized that under EPA and Corps regulations, Area A would be subject to the CWA permit requirements if the wetland affected interstate commerce, *see* 40 C.F.R. §30.3(s)(3), 33 C.F.R. §328.3(a)(3), and further noted that the EPA and Corps consider a wetland to affect interstate commerce if, for instance, the wetland serves as habitat for migratory birds. Initial Decision at 48. The ALJ, however, found the EPA had not presented evidence of actual use by migratory birds of Area A nor of any special characteristics that would attract migratory birds to Area A.

Since there was nothing more "than the theoretical possibility" Area A would be used by migratory birds, the ALJ found the regulations did not apply. *Id.* at 49. The EPA appealed the ALJ's decision to the CJO. The EPA, however, did not challenge the ALJ's findings regarding Area A's hydrological isolation; the Agency only challenged the ALJ's conclusion that given those findings the regulations were inapplicable to Area A.

The CJO held that the EPA could not assert jurisdiction over "an isolated, intrastate water body" unless it could demonstrate "that the destruction of that water body will have an effect on interstate commerce." Final Decision at 9. To satisfy its burden of proof, the CJO required the EPA to "show some minimal, potential effect on interstate commerce." *Id.* This effect was shown, the CJO concluded, when the EPA demonstrated Area A provided "a suitable habitat for migratory birds before it was filled in." *Id.* at 2. The CJO noted that Area B supported migratory bird habitat and by its proximity Area A could as well. *Id.* at 30.

Hoffman appealed the CJO's decision regarding Area A, but not Area B, to this court. We exercised jurisdiction pursuant to 33 U.S.C. §1319(g)(8)(B). The developer contended the CWA did not give the EPA regulatory authority over Area A. The EPA maintained it had jurisdiction due to the potential use of Area A by migratory birds. We held the EPA's regulations went beyond the limits of the Clean Water Act and the commerce clause, U.S. Const. art. 1, §8, cl. 3. Accordingly, on April 22, 1992, we vacated the EPA's $50,000 penalty against Hoffman for filling Area A. *See Hoffman Homes, Inc. v. Administrator, United States E.P.A.*, 961 F.2d 1310, 1321-23 (7th Cir. 1992).

The EPA then filed a petition for rehearing and suggested the rehearing be conducted *en banc.* On September 4, 1992, we granted the petition for rehearing and vacated our opinion and order. We further ordered that the matter be referred to our senior staff attorney, Donald J. Wall, for the purpose of conducting settlement negotiations between the parties pursuant to Federal Rule of Appellate Procedure 33 and Circuit Rule 33. *See Hoffman Homes, Inc. v. Administrator, United States E.P.A.*, 975 F.2d 1554, 1554 (7th Cir. 1992). Since that time, Mr. Wall has conferred with counsel to the parties on numerous occasions. On March 25, 1993, he informed the court that the parties were unable to reach a settlement and further negotiations would be futile. The matter is thus back in the hands of the original panel which heard the oral arguments on this case nearly two years ago.

II. DISCUSSION

Hoffman Homes does not dispute that the EPA and the Corps have correctly characterized Area A as a wetland pursuant to 33 C.F.R. §328.3(b) and 40 C.F.R. §230.3(t). Nor does Hoffman deny having filled Area A. Hoffman disputes only that the small wetland can be regulated under the Clean Water Act.

Congress's objective in enacting the Clean Water Act was "to restore and maintain the chemical, physical, and biological integrity of the Nation's waters." 33 U.S.C. §1251(a). To that end, the CWA prohibits "the discharge of dredged or fill material into the navigable waters" without a permit. *Id.* §1344(a). The CWA defines "navigable waters" as meaning "the waters of the United States, including the territorial seas." *Id.* §1362(7).

The CWA, though, does not define the term "waters of the United States." The EPA and the Corps have done so in two identically worded regulations. According to the EPA and the Corps, "waters of the United States" includes, among other things, bodies of water wholly within a state whose use or misuse could affect interstate commerce:

> (s) The term *waters of the United States* means: ...
>
> > (3) All other waters such as intrastate lakes, rivers, streams (including intermittent streams), mudflats, sandflats, wetlands, sloughs, prairie potholes, wet meadows, playa lakes, or natural ponds, the use, degradation or destruction of which could affect interstate or foreign commerce including any such waters:
> >
> > > (i) Which are or could be used by interstate or foreign travelers for recreational or other purposes; or
> > >
> > > (ii) From which fish or shellfish are or could be taken and sold in interstate or foreign commerce; or
> > >
> > > (iii) Which are used or could be used for industrial purpose by industries in interstate commerce; ...

40 C.F.R. §230.3(s)(3) (EPA's definition); 33 C.F.R. §328.3(a)(3) (Corps' definition).

The EPA's Chief Judicial Officer ruled that the regulation extended to Area A by virtue of the wetland's potential effect on interstate commerce. It was not necessary under the regulation, the CJO held, that the EPA show an actual effect on interstate commerce. The CJO noted the EPA's regulation explicitly forbids the "degradation or destruction" of intrastate wetlands when such actions "could affect" interstate commerce: "The use of the word 'could' means that EPA need not show *an actual effect on interstate commerce. Showing a potential effect will suffice."* Final Decision at 11.

Our job is to determine whether (i) the EPA properly interpreted 40 C.F.R. §230.3(s)(3) and (ii) whether the CJO's finding of a violation of the CWA is supported by "substantial evidence." See

33 U.S.C. §1319(g)(8) (mandating standard of review); *Arkansas v. Oklahoma,* 117 L. Ed. 2d 239, 112 S. Ct. 1046, 1060 (1992).

Regarding the first question, we have stated that "an agency's construction of its own regulation binds a court in all but extraordinary cases." *Homemakers N. Shore, Inc. v. Bowen,* 832 F.2d 408, 411 (7th Cir. 1987); *accord United States v. Baxter Healthcare Corp.,* 901 F.2d 1401, 1407 (7th Cir. 1990) (court gives great deference to agency's interpretations of its own regulations). We must uphold the EPA's interpretation of 40 C.F.R. §230.3(s)(3) "unless it is plainly erroneous or inconsistent with the regulation." *United States v. Larionoff,* 431 U.S. 864, 872, 53 L. Ed. 2d 48, 97 S. Ct. 2150 (1977) (citation omitted); *accord Wisconsin Elec. Power Co. v. Reilly,* 893 F.2d 901, 907 (7th Cir. 1990).

Hoffman Homes has failed to persuade us the EPA has misread 40 C.F.R §230.3(s)(3). The regulation speaks of regulating wetlands and other bodies of water whose use, degradation, or destruction "could" affect interstate commerce. This includes waters "which are or *could* be" used by interstate travellers, "from which fish or shellfish are or *could* be taken," and which "are used or *could* be used" for industrial purposes. *Id.* (emphasis added). We agree with the CJO that the use of the word "could" indicates the regulation covers waters whose connection to interstate commerce may be potential rather than actual, minimal rather than substantial.

We also agree with the CJO that it is reasonable to interpret the regulation as allowing migratory birds to be that connection between a wetland and interstate commerce. Throughout North America, millions of people annually spend more than a billion dollars on hunting, trapping, and observing migratory birds. Yet the cumulative loss of wetlands has reduced populations of many bird species and consequently the ability of people to hunt, trap, and observe those birds. *See North American Waterfowl Management Plan 1* (1985); *cf. Palila v. Hawaii Dep't of Land & Natural Resources,* 471 F. Supp. 985 (D. Haw. 1979) (protecting endangered bird preserves interstate commerce in species and interstate movement of persons wishing to study species), *aff'd,* 639 F.2d 495 (9th Cir. 1981). *See generally United States v. Byrd,* 609 F.2d 1204, 1209 (7th Cir. 1979) (Congress's commerce clause power "has come to mean that Congress may regulate activities which affect interstate commerce").

Next we must determine whether the CJO's finding of a violation of the regulation is supported by "substantial evidence." The Supreme Court recently emphasized in *Arkansas v. Oklahoma,* 117 L. Ed. 2d 239, 112 S. Ct. 1046 (1992), that a "court reviewing an agency's adjudicative action should accept the agency's factual findings if those findings are supported by substantial evidence on the record as a whole." *Id.* at 1060. "Substantial evidence is more than a mere scintilla. It means such relevant evidence as a reasonable mind might accept as adequate to support a conclusion." *Consolidated Edison Co. v. National Labor Relations Board,* 305 U.S. 197, 229, 83 L. Ed. 126, 59 S. Ct. 206 (1938).

We obviously do not need to examine the EPA's finding that Hoffman filled Area A; Hoffman has admitted this act. We must ask, however, if the EPA's finding that Area A, before being filled, was a suitable or potential habitat for migratory birds is supported by substantial evidence. The ALJ, as noted earlier, found there was no evidence that any migratory birds actually used Area A. The witnesses the EPA presented only testified as to seeing migratory birds at Area B. The ALJ also found the EPA had failed to present any evidence "that Area A contains any characteristic that would render it any more attractive to birds than any other land that at one time or another contains water." Initial Decision at 48. The ALJ concluded: "It has not been shown by the preponderance of the evidence that Area A has characteristics whose use by and value to migratory birds is well established and that it is likely that it will be used by migratory birds." *Id.* at 50.

Despite the ALJ's findings, the CJO concluded that on the same evidence Area A was a site suitable to migratory birds. Final Decision at 26. First, the CJO noted that Area A was located relatively close to Area B which itself was part of a 50-acre wetland area and bordered Poplar Creek. Five witnesses testified before the ALJ as to the numerous migratory bird species they had spotted at Area B, including white egrets, blue herons, green herons, Canada geese, mallard ducks, red-winged blackbirds, and mourning doves. *Id.* at 27 n.25. The CJO reasoned that if Area B would support those migratory birds then Area A would as well.

The CJO based this conclusion in part on the transcripts of testimony of two witnesses, Gerald Bade, a fish and wildlife biologist with the United States Fish and Wildlife Service, and Douglas Ehorn, an EPA water quality specialist. In the CJO's words, "Bade ... testified that the value of Wetland B as a suitable habitat for migratory birds would be replicated at Area A." Ehorn stated it was a "good possibility" migratory birds would use Area A.

Based on our examination of the record, "we find the CJO's conclusion that Area A was suitable for migratory bird habitat to be unsupported by substantial evidence on the record as a whole. Bade, for example, testified as to what he had seen at Area B and not Area A. His testimony as to the suitability of Area A was merely speculation based on the assumption that Area A was a wetland similar to Area B. In contrast to Area B, Area A does not border a stream, it does not adjoin a large wetland, its only source of moisture is rainfall, it is only wet part of the year, and it covers approximately one acre instead of 50.

Bade, moreover, admitted that Victoria Crossing would have a low waterfowl value because of the lack of open water. Similarly, Ehorn said he never observed any large waterfowl at the site. Dana Sanders, a plant ecologist associated with the Corps, also testified and characterized Area A as having only "moderate" suitability as a resting place for migratory birds.

It is true, of course, that migratory birds can alight most anywhere. As Gerald Bade testified, he has seen mallards in parking lot puddles. The ALJ, however, was in the unique position to view the evidence, to hear the testimony, and to judge the credibility of the witnesses. He concluded that the evidence did not support the conclusion that Area A had characteristics whose use by and value to migratory birds is well established. We agree. The migratory birds are better judges of what is suitable for their welfare than are we, the ALJ or the CJO. Having avoided Area A the migratory birds have thus spoken and submitted their own evidence. We see no need to argue with them. No justification whatsoever is seen from the evidence to interfere with private ownership based on what appears to be no more than a well intentioned effort in these particular factual circumstances to expand government control beyond reasonable or practical limits. After April showers not every temporary wet spot necessarily becomes subject to government control.

III. CONCLUSION

Almost 100 years ago the Supreme Court characterized wetlands as "the cause of malarial and malignant fevers" and opined that "the police power is never more legitimately exercised than in removing such nuisances." *Leovy v. United States,* 177 U.S. 621, 636, 44 L. Ed. 914, 20 S. Ct. 797 (1900). We know now that wetlands are not nuisances but instead are vital to the well-being of both humans and wildlife. Nonetheless, it is our conclusion based on the particular facts and findings below that Area A is not subject to regulation under the Clean Water Act. For this reason we vacate the EPA's order requiring Hoffman Homes, Inc. to pay a $50,000 administrative penalty for the filling of Area A.

VACATED

MANION, Circuit Judge, concurring in the judgment. I agree with the court's conclusion that the EPA has no authority to regulate Area A, but for different reasons. I would vacate the EPA's order in this case for the reasons set out in *Hoffman Homes, Inc. v. EPA,* 961 F.2d 1310 (7th Cir. 1992) (since vacated). I incorporate by reference that previously published opinion as my concurrence, subject to the following additional comments.

I agree with the court's holding that the CJO did not misconstrue the EPA's permit regulation, 40 C.F.R. §230.3(s)(3). That regulation provides that the EPA has jurisdiction over all wetlands "the use, degradation, or destruction of which could affect interstate or foreign commerce." The CJO interpreted this regulation to give the EPA jurisdiction over any wetland that could have a "minimal, potential effect" on interstate commerce. This construction is reasonable, given that it is consistent with the regulation's assertion of jurisdiction over wetlands that "*could* affect interstate commerce." To overturn the CJO's interpretation of the regulation would be inconsistent with the great deference we give to an agency's interpretation of its own regulations.

The regulation reflects the EPA's position that the Clean Water Act gives it jurisdiction over all "waters"—including wetlands within reach of the Commerce Clause. Does the Clean Water Act give the EPA jurisdiction over Area A? Area A is an "isolated wetland," and isolated wetlands by definition have no effect on the waters of the United States. That definition is not pulled from thin air; rather, it is the EPA's own definition. The ALJ found that Area A has no surface or ground water connection to any other body of water, does not perform any water quality functions as to any other body of water, and is not actually used as a wildlife habitat. The EPA has never challenged these findings, and the CJO did not alter or discard them. Thus, the ALJ's findings are the EPA's findings; in other words, the ALJ's definition of "isolated wetlands" is the EPA's definition.

It follows from the EPA's own definition of "isolated wetlands" that regulating Area A does not further the Clean Water Act's purpose to "restore and maintain the chemical, physical, and biological integrity of the Nation's waters." See 33 U.S.C. §1251. Therefore, the Clean Water Act does not give the EPA authority to regulate Area A, even if the Commerce Clause allows Congress to regulate isolated wetlands. See 961 F.2d at 1312-16 for a fuller discussion of the Clean Water Act's construction.

But even if the EPA were correct that the Clean Water Act authorizes regulation of isolated wetlands, I would still vacate the EPA's order in this case. For reasons stated in the previous panel opinion in this case, I would hold that the Commerce Clause does not empower Congress to regulate isolated wetlands such as Area A. See 961 F.2d at 1316-23. To hold otherwise would be, in effect, to hold that Congress' power under the Commerce Clause is virtually limitless. The commerce power as construed by the courts is indeed expansive, but not so expansive as to authorize regulation of puddles merely because a bird traveling interstate might decide to stop for a drink. [Footnotes omitted.]

UNITED STATES v. WILSON

133 F.3d 251 (4th Cir. 1997)

The defendants in this case were convicted of felony violations of the Clean Water Act for knowingly discharging fill and excavated material into wetlands of the United States without a permit. On this appeal they challenge: … the district court's application of the Clean Water Act to wetlands that do not have a "direct or indirect surface connection to other waters of the United States…."

The defendants also contend that the district court, in instructing the jury on the relationship between wetlands and interstate waters, gratuitously and improperly extended the jurisdiction of the Clean Water Act beyond its stated limits to any wetland "even without a direct or indirect surface connection" with interstate waters. They claim that their property was not adjacent to waters of the United States and that any wetlands that may have been involved were too remote from navigable waters to be under the jurisdiction of the Clean Water Act. They observe that the wetlands involved here were "more than ten miles from the Chesapeake Bay, more than six miles from the Potomac River, and hundreds of yards from the nearest creeks." They add that the district court's interpretation of the nexus between wetlands and interstate waters also exceeds the Commerce Clause's limitation of governmental power.

The government argues, without addressing the district court's instruction, that the wetlands involved in this case "were [as a factual matter] clearly adjacent to streams which flow into the Chesapeake Bay" and therefore "were properly regulated pursuant to the Commerce Clause."

Because of the divergence of these contentions and the presentation of conflicting evidence at trial, the question of whether the jury was properly instructed with respect to the scope of the Clean Water Act is material to whether the jury's factual findings were properly informed by the law. Although the Clean Water Act itself authorizes the regulation of only "navigable waters," which are defined as "waters of the United States," *see* 33 U.S.C. §§1311(a), 1362(12)(A), 1362(7), the Army Corps of Engineers has defined "waters of the United States" to include wetlands *adjacent* to waters that otherwise constitute waters of the United States. 33 C.F.R. §328.3(7) (1993). Although the Supreme Court has upheld the validity of 33 C.F.R. §328.3(7) as a reasonable construction of the Clean Water Act, it did so explicitly in the context of a wetland "that *actually abuts* on a *navigable* waterway." *Riverside Bayview Homes,* 474 U.S. at 135 (emphasis added).

In instructing the jury in this case, the district court extended the application of the Clean Water Act substantially beyond the regulations that had been approved in *Riverside Bayview Homes*, instructing the jury that waters of the United States included adjacent wetlands "*even without a direct or indirect surface connection to other waters of the United States.*" (Emphasis added). This instruction intolerably stretches the ordinary meaning of the word "adjacent" and the phrase "waters of the United States" to include wetlands remote from any interstate or navigable waters. The magnitude of this extension is particularly highlighted when recognizing that the Army Corps of Engineers' statutory mandate extends not to the regulation of "wetlands adjacent to waters of the United States," but only to the regulation of "waters of the United States," and that the Corps' regulation of such wetlands is based solely on its definition of wetlands as "waters of the United States." Furthermore, as noted above, we should interpret the Clean Water Act in light of the constitutional difficulties that would arise by extending the Act's coverage to *waters* that are connected closely to neither interstate nor navigable waters, and which do not otherwise substantially affect interstate commerce. It was thus error for the district court to have instructed the jury to extend the jurisdiction of the Clean Water Act to wetlands that lack any "direct or indirect surface connection" to interstate waters, navigable waters, or interstate commerce.

Because we cannot determine as a result of this error whether the jury properly exercised the jurisdiction of the Clean Water Act, a new trial is necessary....

CHAPTER 8

MIGRATORY BIRDS

Until quite recently, many courts had found federal jurisdiction in wetlands inhabited by migratory birds. The following Seventh Circuit opinion, although overruled by a sharply-divided United States Supreme Court on January 9, 2001, is included in this text, in part, for the discussion of this issue as it pertains to jurisdictions other than Illinois. The controlling Supreme Court opinion immediately follows.

SOLID WASTE AGENCY OF NORTHERN COOK COUNTY v. U.S. ARMY CORPS OF ENGINEERS

998 F. Supp. 946 (N.D.Ill. 1998)

This action concerns the future of a 533-acre parcel of real estate owned by plaintiff Solid Waste Agency of Northern Cook County. Defendant United States Army Corps of Engineers asserted regulatory jurisdiction over the property after determining that it contained approximately 55 acres of navigable waters as defined by the Clean Water Act. 33 U.S.C. §1262(7). It then denied plaintiff a permit to develop the property under section 404 of that statute. 33 U.S.C. §1344(a). Plaintiff sought judicial review of these actions under the Administrative Procedure Act, 5 U.S.C. §§701 *et seq.* ("APA"), and the parties filed cross-motions for summary judgment on the issue of jurisdiction. For the reasons below, plaintiff's motion for summary judgment will be denied and defendant's motion for summary judgment will be granted....

Plaintiff contends that the waters of the proposed balefill site are not subject to federal regulatory jurisdiction under the commerce clause. It argues that the migratory birds on the balefill site do not have any relationship with interstate commerce because they do not support any human commercial activity on the site itself. Noting that the balefill area is closed to the public and is not visible from adjacent properties, plaintiff reasons that it cannot be subject to federal jurisdiction because "birds do not conduct commerce, people do." (Pl.'s S.J. Mem. at 3.) The court must therefore decide whether the commerce clause authorizes the federal government to exercise regulatory jurisdiction over isolated intrastate waters that serve as a habitat for migratory birds.

The Seventh Circuit addressed this very issue in *Hoffman Homes, Inc. v. EPA*, 961 F.2d 1310 (7th Cir. 1992) ("*Hoffman Homes I*"). In that case, a residential developer was fined after it filled a one-acre pond on its property without a permit. *Id.* at 1311. The EPA had asserted jurisdiction over the pond pursuant to 40 C.F.R. §230.3(s)(3) after finding that it could be used as a habitat by migratory birds. *Id.* at 1311-1312. The Seventh Circuit held that the EPA had exceeded its authority under the commerce clause by extending jurisdiction over the pond based solely on its potential use as a habitat for migratory birds. *Id.* at 1321-1322. Reasoning that birds do not affect commerce until they are "watched, photographed, shot at or otherwise impacted by the people who do," *id.* at 1320, the court explained that:

> The EPA has provided evidence of only one interstate connection: [The pond] is a potential landing site for migratory birds. Although we recognize that the Commerce Clause power is broad, it has never been extended to reach all areas in (much less those only potentially in) migratory bird flyways. Such an extension, we believe, would effectually

> obliterate the distinction between what is national and what is local and create a completely centralized government. After all, what area of the United States is not a potential landing spot for migratory birds? The Commerce Clause, at the very least, requires some connection to human commercial activity.

Id. at 1321-1322 (citations omitted). In addition to holding that 40 C.F.R. §230.3(s)(3) was unconstitutional, the court concluded that the regulation went beyond its statutory mandate because the Clean Water Act did not authorize the regulation of isolated intrastate wetlands. *Id.* at 1316.

On rehearing, the court vacated its first opinion and held that 40 C.F.R. §230.3(s)(3) did not violate the commerce clause. *Hoffman Homes, Inc. v. EPA*, 999 F.2d 256, 260-261 (7th Cir. 1993) ("*Hoffman Homes II*"). The court explained that it was reasonable for the EPA to interpret the regulation as extending its jurisdiction to waters whose connection with interstate commerce was "potential rather than actual, minimal rather than substantial." *Id.* at 261. It further explained that the potential use of wetlands by migratory birds was sufficient to invoke commerce clause jurisdiction because "millions of people annually spend more than a billion dollars on hunting, trapping, and observing migratory birds" and "the cumulative loss of wetlands has reduced populations of many bird species." *Id.* at 261. The court nevertheless ruled in favor of the developer because the EPA had not presented substantial evidence that the water site was a suitable or potential habitat for migratory birds. *Id.* at 261–262.

The Seventh Circuit has not been alone in suggesting that the migratory bird rule is a valid application of federal commerce clause power. In *Leslie Salt Co. v. United States*, 896 F.2d 354 (9th Cir. 1990), a company sought to develop a property that contained surface depressions as a result of previous industrial usage. *Id.* at 355–356. The Army Corps of Engineers asserted jurisdiction over the site under 33 C.F.R. §328.3(a) because the excavations collected water on a seasonal basis and could be used as a habitat for migratory birds. *Id.* at 357, 360. The district court held that the ponds were not "other waters" under 33 C.F.R. §328.3(a) because they were not of a natural origin and were only seasonally filled. *Leslie Salt Co. v. United States*, 700 F. Supp. 476 (N.D. Cal. 1988) ("*Leslie Salt I*"). The Ninth Circuit reversed, explaining that the "commerce clause power, and thus the Clean Water Act, is broad enough to extend the Corps' jurisdiction to local waters which may provide habitat to migratory birds and endangered species." *Leslie Salt Co. v. United States*, 896 F.2d 354, 360 (9th Cir. 1990) ("*Leslie Salt II*"). When the Court of Appeals remanded the case to the district court to determine whether the ponds could be used as a habitat by migratory birds, the district court found that the property was a seasonal home to more than 50 species of migratory birds and was thus subject to federal commerce clause jurisdiction. *Leslie Salt Co. v. United States*, 820 F. Supp. 478, 480 (N.D. Cal. 1992) ("*Leslie Salt III*"). On a second appeal, the Ninth Circuit affirmed this finding and reiterated that the migratory bird rule was a valid exercise of the federal commerce clause power. *Leslie Salt Co. v. United States*, 55 F.3d 1388, 1392 (9th Cir. 1995) ("*Leslie Salt IV*").

The Tenth Circuit reached a similar result in *Utah v. Marsh*, 740 F.2d 799 (10th Cir. 1984). In that case, the Army Corps of Engineers asserted regulatory jurisdiction over an intrastate lake pursuant to a regulation which, like 33 C.F.R. §328.3(a), conferred administrative authority over isolated wetlands whose degradation or destruction could affect interstate commerce. *Id.* at 802 & n.4, 803. Plaintiff argued that the lake had no effect on interstate commerce because it was located entirely within the borders of the state. *Id.* at 803. The court explained that the lake was subject to federal commerce clause jurisdiction because, among other things, it was "on the flyway of several species of migratory waterfowl which are protected under international treaties." *Id.* at 804.

These cases establish that the commerce clause authorizes the federal government to regulate isolated intrastate waters that serve as a habitat for migratory birds. The reason for this rule, it seems, is that the cumulative degradation of intrastate waters could have a substantial effect on interstate commercial interests relating to those birds. *See Hoffman Homes II*, 999 F.2d at 261 ("cumulative loss of wetlands has reduced populations of many bird species and consequently the ability of people to hunt, trap, and observe those birds"). Under this rule, a federal agency may assert jurisdiction over intrastate waters even if the destruction of those particular waters will not have a substantial effect on interstate commerce and there is no evidence that migratory birds support human commercial activity there.

There is reason to consider whether this rule remains valid after the recent decision in *United States v. Lopez*, 514 U.S. 549, 131 L.Ed. 2d 626, 115 S.Ct. 1624 (1995). In that case, the Supreme Court held that Congress exceeded its commerce clause powers by imposing criminal sanctions on the possession of handguns in local school zones. *Id.* at 551, discussing 18 U.S.C. §922(q). The government argued that the prevention of violent crime in local school zones was related to interstate commerce because education promotes a sound national economy, the threat of violence deters interstate travel, and the cost of violent crime is spread to the population as a whole through insurance. *Id.* at 563–564. After surveying the history of commerce clause jurisprudence, the Court explained that the commerce clause authorizes Congress to regulate (1) the use of the channels of interstate commerce, (2) the instrumentalities of interstate commerce, or the persons or things in interstate commerce, and (3) activities that substantially affect interstate commerce. *Id.* at 558–559. Deciding that only the last category applied to the statute in question, the Court held that the possession of a gun in a local school zone is not "an economic activity that might, through repetition elsewhere, substantially affect any sort of interstate commerce." *Id.* at 567. It further explained that the statute could not be sustained under case law upholding the regulation of activities "that arise out of or are connected with a commercial transaction, which viewed in the aggregate, substantially affects interstate commerce." *Id.* at 561. The statute was therefore declared unconstitutional.

The Fourth Circuit has recently suggested that the migratory bird rule is unconstitutional under *Lopez*. In *United States v. Wilson*, 133 F.3d 251 (4th Cir. 1997), the appellant was convicted of filling intrastate wetlands without a permit in violation of the Clean Water Act, 33 U.S.C. §§1319(c)(2)(A) and 1311(a). *Id.* at 254. The Army Corps of Engineers had asserted jurisdiction over the fill areas pursuant to 33 C.F.R. §328.3(a)(3), and the appellant challenged the validity of this regulation under both the Clean Water Act and the commerce clause. Writing for the majority, Judge Niemeyer stated in dicta and without explanation that the regulation presented "serious constitutional difficulties, because, at least at first blush, it would appear to exceed congressional authority under the Commerce Clause." *Id.* at 257. Writing separately, Judge Luttig declined to adopt this portion of the majority opinion on the grounds that it was based on an overly expansive reading of the commerce clause. *See Wilson*, 133 F.3d at 266 (Luttig, J., dis.).

Respectfully, this court does not agree that *Lopez* places the regulation of intrastate migratory bird habitats beyond the reach of federal commerce clause jurisdiction. It is well established that the commerce clause authorizes the federal government to regulate activities whose effect on interstate commerce is substantial only in the aggregate. *See, e.g., Wickard v. Filburn*, 317 U.S. 111, 127-128, 87 L.Ed. 122, 63 S.Ct. 82 (1942) (commerce clause allows regulation of private commercial transactions that have a substantial effect on interstate commerce when "taken together with that of many others" but are otherwise trivial); *Maryland v. Wirtz*, 392 U.S. 183, 197 n.27, 20 L.Ed. 2d 1020, 88 S.Ct. 2017 (1968) ("where a general regulatory statute bears a substantial relation to commerce, the *de minimis* character of individual instances arising under that statute is of no consequence"); *Fry v. United States*, 421 U.S. 542, 547, 44 L.Ed. 2d 363, 95 S.Ct. 1792 (1975) (purely intrastate activity may be regulated "where the activity, combined with like conduct by others similarly situated, affects commerce among the States or with foreign nations"). The Supreme Court expressly affirmed this line of cases in *Lopez,* 514 U.S. at 557, *quoting Wirtz*, 392 U.S. at 197 n.27. Distinguishing *Wickard* on the facts, the *Lopez* Court held that the criminal statute at issue did not concern activities which might substantially affect interstate commerce through "repetition" or when "viewed in the aggregate." 514 U.S. at 560-561, 567. Thus, while the *Lopez* decision may help to define the outer limits of federal commerce clause jurisdiction, it does not signal a retreat from the constitutional principles set forth in *Wickard* and its progeny.

The migratory bird rule finds ample support in this line of cases. Migratory birds have long been regarded as a proper subject for federal commerce clause regulation. *See Andrus v. Allard,* 444 U.S. 51, 63 n.19, 62 L.Ed. 2d 210, 100 S.Ct. 318 (1979) ("assumption that the national commerce power does not reach migratory wildlife is clearly flawed"); *Hoffman Homes II*, 999 F.2d at 261 ("millions of people annually spend more than a billion dollars on hunting, trapping, and observing migratory birds"); *Cochrane v. United States*, 92 F.2d 623, 627 (7th Cir. 1937) (commerce clause allows federal government "to protect the game, nongame, and insectivorous birds which migrate with the changing seasons"). By implication, the power to protect migratory birds extends to the habitats in which they live. While the destruction of a single habitat is unlikely to affect the viability of migratory bird populations, the destruction of numerous such habitats may, in the aggregate, have a substantial affect on their livelihood. *See Hoffman Homes II*, 999 F.2d at 261 (cumulative loss of habitat has reduced the population of many bird species and has impaired the ability of people to hunt, trap, and observe them). On this point, the following analysis is persuasive:

> Isolated wetlands provide habitat to migratory birds whose continued existence supports billions of dollars in interstate commerce. The incremental destruction of migratory bird habitat directly and negatively impacts migratory bird populations and, thereby interstate commerce. Isolated wetlands are a crucial link in the direct chain of causation between healthy migratory bird populations and interstate commerce. It should, therefore, be irrelevant whether a migratory bird is ever observed, photographed, or hunted at the particular isolated wetland in question. Unlike in *Lopez*, the connection of isolated wetlands to interstate commerce is well-documented and does not require the court to "pile inference upon inference" in a manner that gives rise to a general federal police power. Lori J. Warner, "The Potential Impact of United States v. Lopez on Environmental Regulations," 7 *Duke Environmental Law & Policy Forum* 321, 354-355 (1997) (citations omitted).

For these reasons, the commerce clause authorizes the federal government to regulate isolated intrastate waters that provide a habitat for migratory birds even if the particular birds on the site do not substantially affect interstate commerce....

C. CLEAN WATER ACT

Plaintiff contends that the migratory bird rule goes beyond its statutory mandate because the Clean Water Act only authorizes federal regulations that deal strictly with water quality. The court must defer to an agency's interpretation of its own authorizing statute so long as that interpretation is reasonable and not in conflict with the expressed intent of Congress. *United States v. Riverside Bayview Homes, Inc.*, 474 U.S. 121, 131, 88 L. Ed. 2d 419, 106 S. Ct. 455 (1985); *Chevron U.S.A. Inc. v. Natural Resources Defense Council, Inc.*, 467 U.S. 837, 842-845, 81 L. Ed. 2d 694, 104 S. Ct. 2778 (1984). Accordingly, the court must decide whether it was reasonable for the Army Corps of Engineers to interpret the statutory term "waters of the United States" to include intrastate waters that provide a habitat for migratory birds.

The Seventh Circuit arguably resolved this question in *Hoffman Homes II*, 999 F.2d 256. The issue in that case, as defined by the court, was whether it was reasonable for the EPA to construe the term "other waters" in 40 C.F.R. §230.3(s)(3) to include waters that serve as a habitat for migratory birds. *Id.* at 260. Although the court did not expressly consider whether the regulation was within the scope of the Clean Water Act, it arguably reached the issue by implication. Vacating an earlier decision in which it held that the regulation was beyond its statutory mandate, the court explained that the EPA's interpretation of the regulation was both reasonable and authorized by the commerce clause. *Id.* at 260-261. In light of the fact that the Clean Water Act extends federal jurisdiction to the limits of the commerce clause, this holding virtually implied that the migratory bird rule was consistent with its authorizing statute. *Id.* at 261. It is also apparent that the court could not have reached its decision in the case if the regulation at issue were illegal. Because the Seventh Circuit did not address the issue directly, however, the court will discuss it here.

Both the language and the legislative history of the Clean Water Act suggest that it authorizes the regulation of intrastate migratory bird habitats. The purpose of the statute is "to restore and maintain the chemical, physical, and biological integrity of the Nation's waters." 33 U.S.C. §1251(a). In part, this is necessary to achieve "the protection and propagation of fish, shellfish, and wildlife." 33 U.S.C. §1251(a)(2). Moreover, the statute authorizes the EPA to promulgate regulations in order to protect fish and wildlife. 33 U.S.C. §1343(c)(1). To the extent that the actual language of the Clean Water Act reveals that Congress intended to protect wildlife, the migratory bird rule would appear to be a permissible construction of that statute.

The legislative history of the Clean Water Act leads to the same conclusion. That history reveals that Congress intended "to extend Clean Water Act jurisdiction over waters of the United States to the maximum extent possible under the Commerce Clause." S.Rep. No. 1236, 92nd Cong., 2d Sess. 144 (1972), U.S.C.C.A.N. 1972, at pp. 3668, 3776. The Seventh Circuit has long recognized that Congress intended to make the Clean Water Act as far-reaching as the commerce clause permits. *See Rueth v. EPA*, 13 F.3d 227, 231 (7th Cir. 1993); *United States v. Huebner*, 752 F.2d 1235, 1239 (7th Cir. 1985); *United States v. Byrd*, 609 F.2d 1204, 1209 (7th Cir. 1979). To the extent that the commerce clause authorizes the federal government to regulate intrastate migratory bird habitats, then, the Clean Water Act must as well. For these reasons, the court finds that 33 C.F.R. §328.3(a)(3), as applied to intrastate migratory bird habitats, is a reasonable construction of the Clean Water Act.

Notably, the Fourth Circuit reached the opposite conclusion in *United States v. Wilson*, 133 F.3d 251 (4th Cir. 1997). In that case, the court explained that 33 C.F.R. §328.3(a)(3) went beyond its statutory mandate because the term "waters of the United States" cannot include intrastate or nonnavigable waters whose degradation or destruction could affect interstate commerce. *Id.* at 256-257. Relying generally on the Supreme Court's decision in *Lopez,* 514 U.S. 549, 131 L. Ed. 2d 626, 115 S. Ct. 1624, the majority explained that the phrase "waters of the United States" must refer "to waters which, if not navigable in fact, are at least interstate or closely related to navigable or interstate waters." 133 F.3d at 257. In a separate opinion, Judge Luttig declined to adopt this portion of the majority opinion on the grounds that it was based on an overly expansive reading of *Lopez. Id.* at 266.

This court respectfully declines to follow the majority in *Wilson.* Because the scope of federal regulatory jurisdiction under the Clean Water Act is coextensive with that of the commerce clause, and because the commerce clause authorizes the federal regulation of intrastate migratory bird habitats, the migratory bird rule must be a valid application of the Clean Water Act. For the reasons discussed in Part II.A. of this opinion, the court does not believe that *Lopez* requires a contrary result. On this point, then, the court agrees with the Ninth Circuit that "the commerce clause power, and thus the Clean Water Act, is broad enough to extend the Corps' jurisdiction to local waters which may provide habitat to migratory birds and endangered species." *Leslie Salt II,* 896 F.2d at 360....

III. CONCLUSION

For the reasons stated above, the court finds that defendant Army Corps of Engineers did not exceed its authority under the commerce clause by extending regulatory jurisdiction over the waters of plaintiff's proposed balefill site pursuant to 33 C.F.R. §328.3(a)(3); as applied in this case, 33 C.F.R. §328.3(a)(3) does not exceed its mandate under the Clean Water Act; the extension of regulatory jurisdiction over the proposed balefill Site was not arbitrary and capricious under the APA, 5 U.S.C. §706(1)(A); and the migratory bird rule set forth at 51 Fed. Reg. 41,217 was exempt from the notice and comment requirements of the APA, 5 U.S.C. §553.

ORDERED: Defendant's motion for summary judgment is granted; plaintiff's motion for summary judgment is denied.

SOLID WASTE AGENCY OF NORTHERN COOK COUNTY v. ARMY CORPS OF ENGINEERS

531 U.S. 159, 121 S.Ct. 675, 148 L.Ed.2d 576 (2001)

Section 404(a) of the Clean Water Act (CWA or Act), 86 Stat. 884, as amended, 33 U.S.C. §1344(a), regulates the discharge of dredged or fill material into "navigable waters." The United States Army Corps of Engineers (Corps), has interpreted §404(a) to confer federal authority over an abandoned sand and gravel pit in northern Illinois which provides habitat for migratory birds. We are asked to decide whether the provisions of §404(a) may be fairly extended to these waters, and, if so, whether Congress could exercise such authority consistent with the Commerce Clause, U.S. Const., Art. I, §8, cl. 3. We answer the first question in the negative and therefore do not reach the second.

Petitioner, the Solid Waste Agency of Northern Cook County (SWANCC), is a consortium of 23 suburban Chicago cities and villages that united in an effort to locate and develop a disposal site for baled nonhazardous solid waste. The Chicago Gravel Company informed the municipalities of the availability of a 533-acre parcel, bestriding the Illinois counties Cook and Kane, which had been the site of a sand and gravel pit mining operation for three decades up until about 1960. Long since abandoned, the old mining site eventually gave way to a successional stage forest, with its remnant excavation trenches evolving into a scattering of permanent and seasonal ponds of varying size (from under one-tenth of an acre to several acres) and depth (from several inches to several feet).

The municipalities decided to purchase the site for disposal of their baled nonhazardous solid waste. By law, SWANCC was required to file for various permits from Cook County and the State of Illinois before it could begin operation of its balefill project. In addition, because the operation called for the filling of some of the permanent and seasonal ponds, SWANCC contacted federal respondents (hereinafter respondents), including the Corps, to determine if a federal landfill permit was required under §404(a) of the CWA, 33 U.S.C. §1344(a).

Section 404(a) grants the Corps authority to issue permits "for the discharge of dredged or fill material into the navigable waters at specified disposal sites." Ibid. The term "navigable waters" is defined under the Act as "the waters of the United States, including the territorial seas." §1362(7). The Corps has issued regulations defining the term "waters of the United States" to include "waters such as intrastate lakes, rivers, streams (including intermittent streams), mudflats, sandflats, wetlands, sloughs, prairie potholes, wet meadows, playa lakes, or natural ponds, the use, degradation or destruction of which could affect interstate or foreign commerce ...." 33 CFR §328.3(a)(3) (1999).

In 1986, in an attempt to "clarify" the reach of its jurisdiction, the Corps stated that §404(a) extends to instrastate waters:

a. Which are or would be used as habitat by birds protected by Migratory Bird Treaties; or

b. Which are or would be used as habitat by other migratory birds which cross state lines; or

c. Which are or would be used as habitat for endangered species; or

d. Used to irrigate crops sold in interstate commerce." 51 Fed. Reg. 41217.

This last promulgation has been dubbed the "Migratory Bird Rule.

The Corps initially concluded that it had no jurisdiction over the site because it contained no "wetlands," or areas which support "vegetation typically adapted for life in saturated soil conditions," 33 CFR §328.3(b)(1999). However, after the Illinois Nature Preserves Commission informed the Corps that a number of migratory bird species had been observed at the site, the Corps reconsidered and ultimately asserted jurisdiction over the balefill site pursuant to subpart (b) of the "Migratory Bird Rule." The Corps found that approximately 121 bird species had been observed at the site, including several known to depend upon aquatic environments for a significant portion of their life requirements. Thus, on November 16, 1987, the Corps formally "determined that the seasonally ponded, abandoned gravel mining depressions located on the project site, while not wetlands, did qualify as 'waters of the United States' ... based upon the following criteria: (1) the proposed site had been abandoned as a gravel mining operation; (2) the water areas and spoil piles had developed a natural character; and (3) the water areas are used as habitat by migratory bird [sic] which cross state lines." U.S. Army Corps of Engineers, Chicago District, Dept. of Army Permit Evaluation and Decision Document, Lodging of Petitioner, Tab No. 1, p. 6.

During the application process, SWANCC made several proposals to mitigate the likely displacement of the migratory birds and to preserve a great blue heron rookery located on the site. Its balefill project ultimately received the necessary local and state approval. By 1993, SWANCC had received a special use planned development permit from the Cook County Board of Appeals, a landfill development permit from the Illinois Environmental Protection Agency, and approval from the Illinois Department of Conservation.

Despite SWANCC's securing the required water quality certification from the Illinois Environmental Protection Agency, the Corps refused to issue a §404(a) permit. The Corps found that SWANCC had not established that its proposal was the "least environmentally damaging, most practicable alternative" for disposal of nonhazardous solid waste; that SWANCC's failure to set aside sufficient funds to remediate leaks posed an "unacceptable risk to the public's drinking water supply"; and that the impact of the project upon area-sensitive species was "unmitigatable since a landfill surface cannot be redeveloped into a forested habitat." *Id.*, at 87.

Petitioner filed suit under the Administrative Procedure Act, 5 U.S.C. §701 et seq., in the Northern District of Illinois challenging both the Corps' jurisdiction over the site and the merits of its denial of the §404(a) permit. The District Court granted summary judgment to respondents on the jurisdictional issue, and petitioner abandoned its challenge to the Corps' permit decision. On appeal to the Court of Appeals for the Seventh Circuit, petitioner renewed its attack on respondents' use of the "Migratory Bird Rule" to assert jurisdiction over the site. Petitioner argued that respondents had exceeded their statutory authority in interpreting the CWA to cover nonnavigable, isolated, intrastate waters based upon the presence of migratory birds and, in the alternative, that Congress lacked the power under the Commerce Clause to grant such regulatory jurisdiction.

The Court of Appeals began its analysis with the constitutional question, holding that Congress has the authority to regulate such waters based upon "the cumulative impact doctrine, under which a single activity that itself has no discernible effect on interstate commerce may still be regulated if the aggregate effect of that class of activity has a substantial impact on interstate commerce." 191 F.3d 845, 850 (CA7 1999). The aggregate effect of the "destruction of the natural habitat of migratory birds" on interstate commerce, the court held, was substantial because each year millions of Americans cross state lines and spend over a billion dollars to hunt and observe migratory birds. *Ibid.* The Court of Appeals then turned to the regulatory question. The court held that the CWA reaches as many waters as the Commerce Clause allows and, given its earlier Commerce Clause ruling, it therefore followed that respondents' "Migratory Bird Rule" was a reasonable interpretation of the Act. *See id.*, at 851–852. We granted certiorari, 529 U.S. 1129 (2000), and now reverse.

Congress passed the CWA for the stated purpose of "restor[ing] and maintain[ing] the chemical, physical, and biological integrity of the Nation's waters." 33 U.S.C. §1251(a). In so doing, Congress chose to "recognize, preserve, and protect the primary responsibilities and rights of States to prevent, reduce, and eliminate pollution, to plan the development and use (including restoration, preservation, and enhancement) of land and water resources, and to consult with the Administrator in the exercise of his authority under this chapter." §1251(b). Relevant here, §404(a) authorizes respondents to regulate the discharge of fill material into "navigable waters," 33

U.S.C. §1344(a), which the statute defines as "the waters of the United States, including the territorial seas," §1362(7). Respondents have interpreted these words to cover the abandoned gravel pit at issue here because it is used as habitat for migratory birds. We conclude that the "Migratory Bird Rule" is not fairly supported by the CWA.

This is not the first time we have been called upon to evaluate the meaning of §404(a). In *United States v. Riverside Bayview Homes, Inc.*, 474 U.S. 121 (1985), we held that the Corps had §404(a) jurisdiction over wetlands that actually abutted on a navigable waterway. In so doing, we noted that the term "navigable" is of "limited import" and that Congress evidenced its intent to "regulate at least some waters that would not be deemed 'navigable' under the classical understanding of that term." *Id.*, at 133. But our holding was based in large measure upon Congress' unequivocal acquiescence to, and approval of, the Corps' regulations interpreting the CWA to cover wetlands adjacent to navigable waters. See *id.*, at 135—139. We found that Congress' concern for the protection of water quality and aquatic ecosystems indicated its intent to regulate wetlands "inseparably bound up with the 'waters' of the United States." *Id.*, at 134.

It was the significant nexus between the wetlands and "navigable waters" that informed our reading of the CWA in *Riverside Bayview Homes*. Indeed, we did not "express any opinion" on the "question of the authority of the Corps to regulate discharges of fill material into wetlands that are not adjacent to bodies of open water ... ." *Id.*, at 131–132, n. 8. In order to rule for respondents here, we would have to hold that the jurisdiction of the Corps extends to ponds that are not adjacent to open water. But we conclude that the text of the statute will not allow this.

Indeed, the Corps' original interpretation of the CWA, promulgated two years after its enactment, is inconsistent with that which it espouses here. Its 1974 regulations defined §404(a)'s "navigable waters" to mean "those waters of the United States which are subject to the ebb and flow of the tide, and/or are presently, or have been in the past, or may be in the future susceptible for use for purposes of interstate or foreign commerce." 33 CFR §209.120(d)(1). The Corps emphasized that "[i]t is the water body's capability of use by the public for purposes of transportation or commerce which is the determinative factor." §209.260(e)(1). Respondents put forward no persuasive evidence that the Corps mistook Congress' intent in 1974.

Respondents next contend that whatever its original aim in 1972, Congress charted a new course five years later when it approved the more expansive definition of "navigable waters" found in the Corps' 1977 regulations. In July 1977, the Corps formally adopted 33 CFR §323.2(a)(5) (1978), which defined "waters of the United States" to include "isolated wetlands and lakes, intermittent streams, prairie potholes, and other waters that are not part of a tributary system to interstate waters or to navigable waters of the United States, the degradation or destruction of which could affect interstate commerce." Respondents argue that Congress was aware of this more expansive interpretation during its 1977 amendments to the CWA. Specifically, respondents point to a failed House bill, H.R. 3199, that would have defined "navigable waters" as "all waters which are presently used, or are susceptible to use in their natural condition or by reasonable improvement as a means to transport interstate or foreign commerce." 123 Cong. Rec. 10420, 10434 (1977). They also point to the passage in §404(g)(1) that authorizes a State to apply to the Environmental Protection Agency for permission "to administer its own individual and general permit program for the discharge of dredged or fill material into the navigable waters (other than those waters which are presently used, or are susceptible to use in their natural condition or by reasonable improvement as a means to transport interstate or foreign commerce ... including wetlands adjacent thereto) within its jurisdiction ...." 33 U.S.C. §1344(g)(1). The failure to pass legislation that would have overturned the Corps' 1977 regulations and the extension of jurisdiction in §404(g) to waters "other than" traditional "navigable waters," respondents submit, indicate that Congress recognized and accepted a broad definition of "navigable waters" that includes nonnavigable, isolated, intrastate waters.

Although we have recognized congressional acquiescence to administrative interpretations of a statute in some situations, we have done so with extreme care. "[F]ailed legislative proposals are 'a particularly dangerous ground on which to rest an interpretation of a prior statute.'" *Central Bank of Denver, N. A. v. First Interstate Bank of Denver, N. A.*, 511 U.S. 164, 187 (1994) (quoting *Pension Benefit Guaranty Corporation v. LTV Corp.*, 496 U.S. 633, 650 (1990)). A bill can be proposed for any number of reasons, and it can be rejected for just as many others. The relationship between the actions and inactions of the 95th Congress and the intent of the 92d Congress in passing §404(a) is also considerably attenuated. Because "subsequent history is less illuminating than the contemporaneous evidence," Hagen v. Utah, 510 U.S. 399, 420 (1994), respondents face a difficult task in overcoming the plain text and import of §404(a).

We conclude that respondents have failed to make the necessary showing that the failure of the 1977 House bill demonstrates Congress' acquiescence to the Corps' regulations or the "Migratory Bird Rule," which, of course, did not first appear until 1986. Although respondents cite some legislative history showing Congress' recognition of the Corps' assertion of jurisdiction over "isolated waters," as we explained in *Riverside Bayview Homes*, "[i]n both Chambers, debate on the proposals to narrow the definition of navigable waters centered largely on the issue of wetlands preservation." 474 U.S., at 136. Beyond Congress' desire to regulate wetlands adjacent to "navigable waters," respondents point us to no persuasive evidence that the House bill was proposed in response to the Corps' claim of jurisdiction over nonnavigable, isolated, intrastate waters or that its failure indicated congressional acquiescence to such jurisdiction.

Section 404(g) is equally unenlightening. In Riverside Bayview Homes we recognized that Congress intended the phrase "navigable waters" to include "at least some waters that would not be deemed 'navigable' under the classical understanding of that term." *Id.*, at 133. But §404(g) gives no intimation of what those waters might be; it simply refers to them as "other ... waters." Respondents conjecture that "other ... waters" must incorporate the Corps' 1977 regulations, but it is also plausible, as petitioner contends, that Congress simply wanted to include all waters adjacent to "navigable waters," such as nonnavigable tributaries and streams. The exact meaning of §404(g) is not before us and we express no opinion on it, but for present purposes it is sufficient to say, as we did in *Riverside Bayview Homes*, that "§404(g)(1) does not conclusively determine the construction to be placed on the use of the term 'waters' elsewhere in the Act (particularly in §502(7), which contains the relevant definition of 'navigable waters') ...." *Id.*, at 138, n. 11.

We thus decline respondents' invitation to take what they see as the next ineluctable step after *Riverside Bayview Homes*: holding that isolated ponds, some only seasonal, wholly located within two Illinois counties, fall under §404(a)'s definition of "navigable waters" because they serve as habitat for migratory birds. As counsel for respondents conceded at oral argument, such a ruling would assume that "the use of the word navigable in the statute ... does not have any independent significance." Tr. of Oral Arg. 28. We cannot agree that Congress' separate definitional use of the phrase "waters of the United States" constitutes a basis for reading the term "navigable waters" out of the statute. We said in Riverside Bayview Homes that the word "navigable" in the statute was of "limited effect" and went on to hold that §404(a) extended to nonnavigable wetlands adjacent to open waters. But it is one thing to give a word limited effect and quite another to give it no effect whatever. The term "navigable" has at least the import of showing us what Congress had in mind as its authority for enacting the CWA: its traditional jurisdiction over waters that were or had been navigable in fact or which could reasonably be so made. See, *e.g.*, *United States v. Appalachian Elec. Power Co.*, 311 U.S. 377, 407–408 (1940).

Respondents—relying upon all of the arguments addressed above—contend that, at the very least, it must be said that Congress did not address the precise question of §404(a)'s scope with regard to nonnavigable, isolated, intrastate waters, and that, therefore, we should give deference to the "Migratory Bird Rule." See, *e.g.*, *Chevron U.S. A. Inc. v. Natural Resources Defense Council, Inc.*, 467 U.S. 837 (1984). We find §404(a) to be clear, but even were we to agree with respondents, we would not extend Chevron deference here.

Where an administrative interpretation of a statute invokes the outer limits of Congress' power, we expect a clear indication that Congress intended that result. See *Edward J. DeBartolo Corp. v. Florida Gulf Coast Building & Constr. Trades Council*, 485 U.S. 568, 575 (1988). This requirement stems from our prudential desire not to needlessly reach constitutional issues and our assumption that Congress does not casually authorize administrative agencies to interpret a statute to push the limit of congressional authority. *See ibid.* This concern is heightened where the administrative interpretation alters the federal-state framework by permitting federal encroachment upon a traditional state power. See *United States v. Bass*, 404 U.S. 336, 349 (1971)("[U]nless Congress conveys its purpose clearly, it will not be deemed to have significantly changed the federal-state balance"). Thus, "where an otherwise acceptable construction of a statute would raise serious constitutional problems, the Court will construe the statute to avoid such problems unless such construction is plainly contrary to the intent of Congress." *DeBartolo*, supra, at 575.

Twice in the past six years we have reaffirmed the proposition that the grant of authority to Congress under the Commerce Clause, though broad, is not unlimited. See *United States v. Morrison*, 529 U.S. 598 (2000); *United States v. Lopez*, 514 U.S. 549 (1995). Respondents argue that the "Migratory Bird Rule" falls within Congress' power to regulate intrastate activities that "substantially affect" interstate commerce. They note that the protection of migratory birds is a "national interest of very nearly the first magnitude," *Missouri v. Holland*, 252 U.S. 416, 435 (1920), and that, as the Court of Appeals found, millions of people spend over a billion dollars annually on recreational pursuits relating to migratory birds. These arguments raise significant constitutional questions. For example, we would have to evaluate the precise object or activity that, in the aggregate, substantially affects interstate commerce. This is not clear, for although the Corps has claimed jurisdiction over petitioner's land because it contains water areas used as habitat by migratory birds, respondents now, *post litem motam*, focus upon the fact that the regulated activity is petitioner's municipal landfill, which is "plainly of a commercial nature." Brief for Federal Respondents 43. But this is a far cry, indeed, from the "navigable waters" and "waters of the United States" to which the statute by its terms extends.

These are significant constitutional questions raised by respondents' application of their regulations, and yet we find nothing approaching a clear statement from Congress that it intended §404(a) to reach an abandoned sand and gravel pit such as we have here. Permitting respondents to claim federal jurisdiction over ponds and mudflats falling within the "Migratory Bird Rule" would result in a significant impingement of the States' traditional and primary power over land and water use. See, *e.g.*, *Hess v. Port Authority Trans-Hudson Corporation*, 513 U.S. 30, 44 (1994) ("[R]egulation of land use [is] a function traditionally performed by local governments"). Rather than expressing a desire to readjust the federal-state balance in this manner, Congress chose to "recognize, preserve, and protect the primary responsibilities and rights of States ... to plan the development and use ... of land and water resources ...." 33 U.S.C. §1251(b). We thus read the statute as written to avoid the significant constitutional and federalism questions raised by respondents' interpretation, and therefore reject the request for administrative deference.

We hold that 33 CFR §328.3(a)(3) (1999), as clarified and applied to petitioner's balefill site pursuant to the "Migratory Bird Rule," 51 Fed. Reg. 41217 (1986), exceeds the authority granted to respondents under §404(a) of the CWA. The judgment of the Court of Appeals for the Seventh Circuit is therefore

REVERSED.

Justice Stevens, with whom Justice Souter, Justice Ginsburg, and Justice

Breyer join, dissenting.

In 1969, the Cuyahoga River in Cleveland, Ohio, coated with a slick of industrial waste, caught fire. Congress responded to that dramatic event, and to others like it, by enacting the Federal Water Pollution Control Act (FWPCA) Amendments of 1972, 86 Stat. 817, as amended 33 U.S.C. §1251 *et seq.*, commonly known as the Clean Water Act (Clean Water Act, CWA, or Act). The Act proclaimed the ambitious goal of ending water pollution by 1985. §1251(a). The Court's past interpretations of the CWA have been fully consistent with that goal. Although Congress' vision of zero pollution remains unfulfilled, its pursuit has unquestionably retarded the destruction of the aquatic environment. Our Nation's waters no longer burn. Today, however, the Court takes an unfortunate step that needlessly weakens our principal safeguard against toxic water.

It is fair to characterize the Clean Water Act as "watershed" legislation. The statute endorsed fundamental changes in both the purpose and the scope of federal regulation of the Nation's waters. In §13 of the Rivers and Harbors Appropriation Act of 1899 (RHA), 30 Stat. 1152, as amended, 33 U.S.C. §407 Congress had assigned to the Army Corps of Engineers (Corps) the mission of regulating discharges into certain waters in order to protect their use as highways for the transportation of interstate and foreign commerce; the scope of the Corps' jurisdiction under the RHA accordingly extended only to waters that were "navigable." In the CWA, however, Congress broadened the Corps' mission to include the purpose of protecting the quality of our Nation's waters for esthetic, health, recreational, and environmental uses. The scope of its jurisdiction was therefore redefined to encompass all of "the waters of the United States, including the territorial seas." §1362(7). That definition requires neither actual nor potential navigability.

The Court has previously held that the Corps' broadened jurisdiction under the CWA properly included an 80-acre parcel of low-lying marshy land that was not itself navigable, directly adjacent to navigable water, or even hydrologically connected to navigable water, but which was part of a larger area, characterized by poor drainage, that ultimately abutted a navigable creek. *United States v. Riverside Bayview Homes, Inc.*, 474 U.S. 121 (1985). Our broad finding in *Riverside Bayview* that the 1977 Congress had acquiesced in the Corps' understanding of its jurisdiction applies equally to the 410-acre parcel at issue here. Moreover, once Congress crossed the legal watershed that separates navigable streams of commerce from marshes and inland lakes, there is no principled reason for limiting the statute's protection to those waters or wetlands that happen to lie near a navigable stream.

In its decision today, the Court draws a new jurisdictional line, one that invalidates the 1986 migratory bird regulation as well as the Corps' assertion of jurisdiction over all waters except for actually navigable waters, their tributaries, and wetlands adjacent to each. Its holding rests on two equally untenable premises: (1) that when Congress passed the 1972 CWA, it did not intend "to exert anything more than its commerce power over navigation," *ante*, at 7, n.3; and (2) that in 1972 Congress drew the boundary defining the Corps' jurisdiction at the odd line on which the Court today settles.

As I shall explain, the text of the 1972 amendments affords no support for the Court's holding, and amendments Congress adopted in 1977 do support the Corps' present interpretation of its mission as extending to so-called "isolated" waters. Indeed, simple common sense cuts against the particular definition of the Corps' jurisdiction favored by the majority.

I

The significance of the FWPCA Amendments of 1972 is illuminated by a reference to the history of federal water regulation, a history that the majority largely ignores. Federal regulation of the Nation's waters began in the 19th century with efforts targeted exclusively at "promot[ing] water transportation and commerce." Kalen, *Commerce to Conservation: The Call for a National Water Policy and the Evolution of Federal Jurisdiction Over Wetlands*, 69 N.D.L.Rev. 873, 877 (1993). This goal was pursued through the various Rivers and Harbors Acts, the most comprehensive of which was the RHA of 1899. Section 13 of the 1899 RHA, commonly known as the Refuse Act, prohibited the discharge of "refuse" into any "navigable water" or its tributaries, as well as the deposit of "refuse" on the bank of a navigable water "whereby navigation shall or may be impeded or obstructed" without first obtaining a permit from the Secretary of the Army. 30 Stat. 1152.

During the middle of the 20th century, the goals of federal water regulation began to shift away from an exclusive focus on protecting navigability and toward a concern for preventing environmental degradation. Kalen, 69 N.D.L.Rev., at 877–879, and n.30. This awakening of interest in the use of federal power to protect the aquatic environment was helped along by efforts to reinterpret §13 of the RHA in order to apply its permit requirement to industrial discharges into navigable waters, even when such discharges did nothing to impede navigability. *See, e.g., United States v. Republic Steel Corp.*, 362 U.S. 482, 490–491 (1960) (noting that the term "refuse" in §13 was broad enough to include industrial waste). Seeds of this nascent concern with pollution control can also be found in the FWPCA, which was first enacted in 1948 and then incrementally expanded in the following years.

The shift in the focus of federal water regulation from protecting navigability toward environmental protection reached a dramatic climax in 1972, with the passage of the CWA. The Act, which was passed as an amendment to the existing FWPCA, was universally described by its supporters as the first truly comprehensive federal water pollution legislation. The "major purpose" of the CWA was "to establish a comprehensive long-range policy for the elimination of water pollution." S.Rep.No. 92–414, p. 95 (1971), reprinted in 2 Legislative History of the Water Pollution Control Act Amendments of 1972 (Committee Print compiled for the Senate Committee on Public Works by the Library of Congress), Ser. No. 93–1, p. 1511 (1971) (hereinafter Leg. Hist.) (emphasis added). And "[n]o Congressman's remarks on the legislation were complete without reference to [its] 'comprehensive' nature ...." *Milwaukee v. Illinois*, 451 U.S. 304, 318 (1981) (Rehnquist, J.). A House sponsor described the bill as "the most comprehensive and far-reaching water pollution bill we have ever drafted," 1 Leg. Hist. 369 (Rep. Mizell), and Senator Randolph, Chairman of the Committee on Public Works, stated: "It is perhaps the most comprehensive legislation that the Congress of the United States has ever developed in this particular field of the environment." 2 *id.*, at 1269. This Court was therefore undoubtedly correct when it described the 1972 amendments as establishing "a comprehensive program for controlling and abating water pollution." *Train v. City of New York*, 420 U.S. 35, 37 (1975).

Section 404 of the CWA resembles §13 of the RHA, but, unlike the earlier statute, the primary purpose of which is the maintenance of navigability, §404 was principally intended as a pollution control measure. A comparison of the contents of the RHA and the 1972 Act vividly illustrates the fundamental difference between the purposes of the two provisions. The earlier statute contains pages of detailed appropriations for improvements in specific navigation facilities, 30 Stat. 1121–1149, for studies concerning the feasibility of a canal across the Isthmus of Panama, *id.*, at 1150, and for surveys of the advisability of harbor improvements at numerous other locations, *id.*, at 1155–1161. Tellingly, §13, which broadly prohibits the discharge of refuse into navigable waters, contains an exception for refuse "flowing from streets and sewers ... in a liquid state." *Id.*, at 1152.

The 1972 Act, in contrast, appropriated large sums of money for research and related programs for water pollution control, 86 Stat. 816–833, and for the construction of water treatment works, *id.*, at 833–844. Strikingly absent from its declaration of "goals and policy" is any reference to avoiding or removing obstructions to navigation. Instead, the principal objective of the Act, as stated by Congress in §101, was "to restore and maintain the chemical, physical, and biological integrity of the Nation's waters." 33 U.S.C. §1251. Congress therefore directed federal agencies in §102 to "develop comprehensive programs for preventing, reducing, or eliminating the pollution of the navigable waters and ground waters and improving the sanitary condition of surface and underground waters." 33 U.S.C. §1252. The CWA commands federal agencies to give "due regard," not to the interest of unobstructed navigation, but rather to "improvements which are necessary to conserve such waters for the protection and propagation of fish and aquatic life and wildlife [and] recreational purposes." *Ibid.*

Because of the statute's ambitious and comprehensive goals, it was, of course, necessary to expand its jurisdictional scope. Thus, although Congress opted to carry over the traditional jurisdictional term "navigable waters" from the RHA and prior versions of the FWPCA, it broadened the definition of that term to encompass all "waters of the United States." §1362(7). Indeed, the 1972 conferees arrived at the final formulation by specifically deleting the word "navigable" from the definition that had originally appeared in the House version of the Act. The majority today undoes that deletion.

The Conference Report explained that the definition in §502(7) was intended to "be given the broadest possible constitutional interpretation." S.Conf. Rep. No. 92–1236, p. 144 (1972), reprinted in 1 Leg. Hist. 327. The Court dismisses this clear assertion of legislative intent with the back of its hand. *Ante*, at 7, n.3. The statement, it claims, "signifies that Congress intended to exert [nothing] more than its commerce power over navigation." *Ibid.*

The majority's reading drains all meaning from the conference amendment. By 1972, Congress' Commerce Clause power over "navigation" had long since been established. *The Daniel Ball*, 10 Wall. 557 (1871); *Gilman v. Philadelphia*, 3 Wall. 713 (1866); *Gibbons v. Ogden*, 9 Wheat. 1 (1824). Why should Congress intend that its assertion of federal jurisdiction be given the "broadest possible constitutional interpretation" if it did not intend to reach beyond the very heartland of its commerce power? The activities regulated by the CWA have nothing to do with Congress' "commerce power over navigation." Indeed, the goals of the 1972 statute have nothing to do with navigation at all.

As we recognized in *Riverside Bayview*, the interests served by the statute embrace the protection of "'significant natural biological functions, including food chain production, general habitat, and nesting, spawning, rearing and resting sites'" for various species of aquatic wildlife. 474 U.S., at 134–135. For wetlands and "isolated" inland lakes, that interest is equally powerful, regardless of the proximity of the swamp or the water to a navigable stream. Nothing in the text, the stated purposes, or the legislative history of the CWA supports the conclusion that in 1972 Congress contemplated—much less commanded—the odd jurisdictional line that the Court has drawn today.

The majority accuses respondents of reading the term "navigable" out of the statute. *Ante*, at 11. But that was accomplished by Congress when it deleted the word from the §502(7) definition. After all, it is the definition that is the appropriate focus of our attention. *Babbitt v. Sweet Home Chapter, Communities for Great Ore.*, 515 U.S. 687, 697–698, n.10 (1995) (refusing to be guided by the common-law definition of the term "take" when construing that term within the Endangered Species Act of 1973 and looking instead to the meaning of the terms contained in the definition of "take" supplied by the statute). Moreover, a proper understanding of the history of federal water pollution regulation makes clear that—even on respondents' broad reading—the presence of the word "navigable" in the statute is not inexplicable. The term was initially used in the various Rivers and Harbors Acts because (1) at the time those statutes were first enacted, Congress' power over the Nation's waters was viewed as extending only to "water bodies that were deemed 'navigable' and therefore suitable for moving goods to or from markets," Power 513; and (2) those statutes had the primary purpose of protecting navigation. Congress' choice to employ the term "navigable waters" in the 1972 Clean Water Act simply continued nearly a century of usage. Viewed in light of the history of federal water regulation, the broad §502(7) definition, and Congress' unambiguous instructions in the Conference Report, it is clear that the term "navigable waters" operates in the statute as a shorthand for "waters over which federal authority may properly be asserted."

II

As the majority correctly notes, *ante*, at 7, when the Corps first promulgated regulations pursuant to §404 of the 1972 Act, it construed its authority as being essentially the same as it had been under the 1899 RHA. The reaction to those regulations in the federal courts, in the environmental Protection Agency (EPA), and in Congress, convinced the Corps that the statute required it "to protect water quality to the full extent of the [C]ommerce [C]lause" and to extend federal regulation over discharges "to many areas that have never before been subject to Federal permits or to this form of water quality protection." 40 Fed. Reg. 31320 (1975).

In 1975, the Corps therefore adopted the interim regulations that we upheld in *Riverside Bayview*. As we noted in that case, the new regulations understood "the waters of the United States" to include, not only navigable waters and their tributaries, but also "nonnavigable intrastate waters whose use or misuse could affect interstate commerce." 474 U.S., at 123. The 1975 regulations provided that the new program would become effective in three phases: phase 1, which became effective immediately, encompassed the navigable waters covered by the 1974 regulation and the RHA; phase 2, effective after July 1, 1976, extended Corps jurisdiction to nonnavigable tributaries, freshwater wetlands adjacent to primary navigable waters, and lakes; and phase 3, effective after July 1, 1977, extended Corps jurisdiction to all other waters covered under the statute, including any waters not covered by phases 1 and 2 (such as "intermittent rivers, streams, tributaries, and perched wetlands that are not contiguous or adjacent to navigable waters") that "the District Engineer determines necessitate regulation for the protection of water quality." 40 Fed. Reg. 31325–31326 (1975). The final version of these regulations, adopted in 1977, made clear that the covered waters included "isolated lakes and wetlands, intermittent streams, prairie potholes, and other waters that are not part of a tributary system to interstate waters or to navigable waters of the United States, the degradation or destruction of which could affect interstate commerce."

The Corps' broadened reading of its jurisdiction provoked opposition among some members of Congress. As a result, in 1977, Congress considered a proposal that would have limited the Corps' jurisdiction under §404 to waters that are used, or by reasonable improvement could be used, as a means to transport interstate or foreign commerce and their adjacent wetlands. H.R. 3199, 95th Cong., 1st Sess., §16(f) (1977). A bill embodying that proposal passed the House but was defeated in the Senate. The debates demonstrate that Congress was fully aware of the Corps' understanding of the scope of its jurisdiction under the 1972 Act. We summarized these debates in our opinion in *Riverside Bayview*:

> In both Chambers, debate on the proposals to narrow the definition of navigable waters centered largely on the issue of wetlands reservation. See [123 Cong. Rec.], at 10426–10432 (House debate); *id.*, at 26710–26729 (Senate debate). Proponents of a more limited §404 jurisdiction contended that the Corps' assertion of jurisdiction over wetlands and other nonnavigable 'waters' had far exceeded what Congress had intended in enacting §404. Opponents of the proposed changes argued that a narrower definition of 'navigable waters' for purposes of §404 would exclude vast stretches of crucial wetlands from the Corps' jurisdiction, with detrimental effects on wetlands ecosystems, water quality, and the aquatic environment generally. The debate, particularly in the Senate, was lengthy. In the House, the debate ended with the adoption of a narrowed definition of 'waters'; but in the Senate the limiting amendment was defeated and the old definition retained. The Conference Committee adopted the Senate's approach: efforts to narrow the definition of 'waters' were abandoned; the legislation as ultimately passed, in the words of Senator Baker, 'retain[ed] the comprehensive jurisdiction over the Nation's waters exercised in the 1972 Federal Water Pollution Control Act.' 474 U.S., at 136–137.

The net result of that extensive debate was a congressional endorsement of the position that the Corps maintains today. We explained in Riverside Bayview:

> [T]he scope of the Corps' asserted jurisdiction over wetlands was specifically brought to Congress' attention, and Congress rejected measures designed to curb the Corps' jurisdiction in large part because of its concern that protection of wetlands would be unduly

> hampered by a narrowed definition of 'navigable waters.' Although we are chary of attributing significance to Congress' failure to act, a refusal by Congress to overrule an agency's construction of legislation is at least some evidence of the reasonableness of that construction, particularly where the administrative construction has been brought to Congress' attention through legislation specifically designed to supplant it. *Id.*, at 137.

Even if the majority were correct that Congress did not extend the Corps' jurisdiction in the 1972 CWA to reach beyond navigable waters and their nonnavigable tributaries, Congress' rejection of the House's efforts in 1977 to cut back on the Corps' 1975 assertion of jurisdiction clearly indicates congressional acquiescence in that assertion. Indeed, our broad determination in *Riverside Bayview* that the 1977 Congress acquiesced in the very regulations at issue in this case should foreclose petitioner's present urgings to the contrary. The majority's refusal in today's decision to acknowledge the scope of our prior decision is troubling. Compare *id.*, at 136 ("Congress acquiesced in the [1975] administrative construction [of the Corps' jurisdiction]"), with *ante*, at 9 ("We conclude that respondents have failed to make the necessary showing that the failure of the 1977 House bill demonstrates Congress' acquiescence to the Corps' regulations..."). Having already concluded that Congress acquiesced in the Corps' regulatory definition of its jurisdiction, the Court is wrong to reverse course today. See *Dickerson v. United States*, 530 U.S. 428, 443 (2000) (Rehnquist, C. J.)("'[T]he doctrine [of stare decisis] carries such persuasive force that we have always required a departure from precedent to be supported by some "special justification"'").

More important than the 1977 bill that did not become law are the provisions that actually were included in the 1977 revisions. Instead of agreeing with those who sought to withdraw the Corps' jurisdiction over "isolated" waters, Congress opted to exempt several classes of such waters from federal control. §67, 91 Stat. 1601, 33 U.S.C. §1344(f). For example, the 1977 amendments expressly exclude from the Corps' regulatory power the discharge of fill material "for the purpose of construction or maintenance of farm or stock ponds or irrigation ditches, or the maintenance of drainage ditches," and "for the purpose of construction of temporary sedimentation basins on a construction site which does not include placement of fill material into the navigable waters." *Ibid.* The specific exemption of these waters from the Corps' jurisdiction indicates that the 1977 Congress recognized that similarly "isolated" waters not covered by the exceptions would fall within the statute's outer limits.

In addition to the enumerated exceptions, the 1977 amendments included a new section, §404(g), which authorized the States to administer their own permit programs over certain nonnavigable waters. Section 404(g)(1) provides, in relevant part:

> The Governor of any State desiring to administer its own individual and general permit program for the discharge of dredged or fill material into the navigable waters (other than those waters which are presently used, or are susceptible to use in their natural condition or by reasonable improvement as a means to transport interstate or foreign commerce ..., including wetlands adjacent thereto) within its jurisdiction may submit to the Administrator a full and complete description of the program it proposes to establish and administer under State law or under an interstate compact. 33 U.S.C. §1344(g)(1).

Section 404(g)(1)'s reference to navigable waters "other than those waters which are presently used, or are susceptible to use" for transporting commerce and their adjacent wetlands appears to suggest that Congress viewed (and accepted) the Act's regulations as covering more than navigable waters in the traditional sense. The majority correctly points out that §404(g)(1) is itself ambiguous because it does not indicate precisely how far Congress considered federal jurisdiction to extend. *Ante*, at 10. But the Court ignores the provision's legislative history, which makes clear that Congress understood §404(g)(1)—and therefore federal jurisdiction—to extend, not only to navigable waters and nonnavigable tributaries, but also to "isolated" waters, such as those at issue in this case.

The Conference Report discussing the 1977 amendments, for example, states that §404(g) "establish[es] a process to allow the Governor of any State to administer an individual and general permit program for the discharge of dredged or fill material into phase 2 and 3 waters after the approval of a program by the Administrator." H.R.Conf.Rep. No. 95–830, p. 101 (1977), reprinted in 3 Legislative History of the Clean Water Act of 1977 (Committee Print Compiled for the Committee on Environment and Public Works by the Library of Congress), Ser. No. 95–14, p. 285 (emphasis added) (hereinafter Leg. Hist. of CWA). Similarly, a Senate Report discussing the 1977 amendments explains that, under §404(g), "the [C]orps will continue to administer the section 404 permit program in all navigable waters for a discharge of dredge or fill material until the approval of a State program for phase 2 and 3 waters." S.Rep.No. 95–370, p. 75 (1977), reprinted in 4 Leg. Hist. of CWA 708 (emphases added).

Of course, as I have already discussed, "phase 1" waters are navigable waters and their contiguous wetlands, "phase 2" waters are the "primary tributaries" of navigable waters and their adjacent wetlands, and "phase 3" waters are all other waters covered by the statute, and can include such "isolated" waters as "intermittent rivers, streams, tributaries, and perched wetlands that are not contiguous or adjacent to navigable waters." The legislative history of the 1977 amendments therefore plainly establishes that, when it enacted §404(g), Congress believed—and desired—the Corps' jurisdiction to extend beyond just navigable waters, their tributaries, and the wetlands adjacent to each.

In dismissing the significance of §404(g)(1), the majority quotes out of context language in the very same 1977 Senate Report that I have quoted above. *Ante*, at 10, n. 6. It is true that the Report states that "[t]he committee amendment does not redefine navigable waters." S. Rep. No. 95–370, at 75, reprinted in 4 Leg. Hist. of CWA 708 (emphasis added). But the majority fails to point out that the quoted language appears in the course of an explanation of the Senate's refusal to go along with House efforts to narrow the scope of the Corps' CWA jurisdiction to traditionally navigable waters. Thus, the immediately preceding sentence warns that "[t]o limit the jurisdiction of the [FWPCA] with reference to discharges of the pollutants of dredged or fill material would cripple efforts to achieve the act's objectives." *Ibid.* The Court would do well to heed that warning.

The majority also places great weight, *ante*, at 10, on our statement in *Riverside Bayview* that §404(g) "does not conclusively determine the construction to be placed on the use of the term 'waters' elsewhere in the Act," 474 U.S., at 138, n.11 (emphasis added). This is simply more selective reading. In that case, we also went on to say with respect to the significance of §404(g) that "the various provisions of the Act should be read *in pari materia*." *Ibid.* More-over, our ultimate conclusion in *Riverside Bayview* was that §404(g) "suggest[s] strongly that the term 'waters' as used in the Act" supports the Corps' reading. *Ibid.*

III

Although it might have appeared problematic on a "linguistic" level for the Corps to classify "lands" as "waters" in *Riverside Bayview*, 474 U.S., at 131–132, we squarely held that the agency's construction of the statute that it was charged with enforcing was entitled to deference under *Chevron U.S. A. Inc. v. Natural Resources Defense Council, Inc.*, 467 U.S. 837 (1984). Today, however, the majority refuses to extend such deference to the same agency's construction of the same statute, *see ante*, at 11–13. This refusal is unfaithful to both *Riverside Bayview* and *Chevron*. For it is the majority's reading, not the agency's, that does violence to the scheme Congress chose to put into place.

Contrary to the Court's suggestion, the Corps' interpretation of the statute does not "encroac[h]" upon "traditional state power" over land use. *Ante*, at 12. "Land use planning in essence chooses particular uses for the land; environmental regulation, at its core, does not mandate particular uses of the land but requires only that, however the land is used, damage to the environment is kept within prescribed limits." *California Coastal Comm'n v. Granite Rock Co.*, 480 U.S. 572, 587 (1987). The CWA is not a land-use code; it is a paradigm of environmental regulation. Such regulation is an accepted exercise of federal power. *Hodel v. Virginia Surface Mining & Reclamation Assn.*, Inc., 452 U.S. 264, 282 (1981).

It is particularly ironic for the Court to raise the specter of federalism while construing a statute that makes explicit efforts to foster local control over water regulation. Faced with calls to cut back on federal jurisdiction over water pollution, Congress rejected attempts to narrow the scope of that jurisdiction and, by incorporating §404(g), opted instead for a scheme that encouraged States to supplant federal control with their own regulatory programs. S.Rep.No. 95–370, at 75, reprinted in 4 Leg. Hist. of CWA 708 ("The committee amendment does not redefine navigable waters. Instead, the committee amendment intends to assure continued protection of all the Nation's waters, but allows States to assume the primary responsibility for protecting those lakes, rivers, streams, swamps, marshes, and other portions of the navigable waters outside the [C]orps program in the so-called phase I waters" (emphasis added)).

Because Illinois could have taken advantage of the opportunities offered to it through §404(g), the federalism concerns to which the majority adverts are misplaced. The Corps' interpretation of the statute as extending beyond navigable waters, tributaries of navigable waters, and wetlands adjacent to each is manifestly reasonable and therefore entitled to deference.

IV

Because I am convinced that the Court's miserly construction of the statute is incorrect, I shall comment briefly on petitioner's argument that Congress is without power to prohibit it from filling any part of the 31 acres of ponds on its property in Cook County, Illinois. The Corps' exercise of its §404 permitting power over "isolated" waters that serve as habitat for migratory birds falls well within the boundaries set by this Court's Commerce Clause jurisprudence.

In *United States v. Lopez*, 514 U.S. 549, 558–559 (1995), this Court identified "three broad categories of activity that Congress may regulate under its commerce power": (1) channels of interstate commerce; (2) instrumentalities of interstate commerce, or persons and things in interstate commerce; and (3) activities that "substantially affect" interstate commerce. *Ibid.* The migratory bird rule at issue here is properly analyzed under the third category. In order to constitute a proper exercise of Congress' power over intrastate activities that "substantially affect" interstate commerce, it is not necessary that each individual instance of the activity substantially affect commerce; it is enough that, taken in the aggregate, the class of activities in question has such an effect. *Perez v. United States*, 402 U.S. 146 (1971) (noting that it is the "class" of regulated activities, not the individual instance, that is to be considered in the "affects" commerce analysis); see also *Hodel*, 452 U.S., at 277; *Wickard v. Filburn*, 317 U.S. 111, 127–128 (1942).

The activity being regulated in this case (and by the Corps' §404 regulations in general) is the discharge of fill material into water. The Corps did not assert jurisdiction over petitioner's land simply because the waters were "used as habitat by migratory birds." It asserted jurisdiction because petitioner planned to discharge fill into waters "used as habitat by migratory birds." Had petitioner intended to engage in some other activity besides discharging fill (*i.e.*, had there been no activity to regulate), or, conversely, had the waters not been habitat for migratory birds (*i.e.*, had there been no basis for federal jurisdiction), the Corps would never have become involved in petitioner's use of its land. There can be no doubt that, unlike the class of activities Congress was attempting to regulate in *United States v. Morrison*, 529 U.S. 598, 613 (2000) ("[g]ender-motivated crimes"), and *Lopez*, 514 U.S., at 561 (possession of guns near school property), the discharge of fill material into the Nation's waters is almost always undertaken for economic reasons. See V. Albrecht & B. Goode, *Wetland Regulation in the Real World*, Exh. 3 (Feb. 1994) demonstrating that the overwhelming majority of acreage for which §404 permits are sought is intended for commercial, industrial, or other economic use).

Moreover, no one disputes that the discharge of fill into "isolated" waters that serve as migratory bird habitat will, in the aggregate, adversely affect migratory bird populations. See, *e.g.*, 1 Secretary of the Interior, Report to Congress, *The Impact of Federal Programs on Wetlands: The Lower Mississippi Alluvial Plain and the Prairie Pothole Region 79–80* (Oct. 1988) (noting that "isolated," phase 3 waters "are among [the] most important and also the most threatened ecosystems in the United States" because "[t]hey are prime nesting grounds for many species of North American waterfowl ..." and provide "[u]p to 50 percent of the [U.S.] production of migratory waterfowl"). Nor does petitioner dispute that the particular waters it seeks to fill are home to many important species of migratory birds, including the second-largest breeding colony of Great Blue Herons in northeastern Illinois, App. to Pet. for Cert. 3a, and several species of waterfowl protected by international treaty and Illinois endangered species laws, Brief for Federal Respondents 7.

In addition to the intrinsic value of migratory birds, *see Missouri v.Holland*, 252 U.S. 416, 435 (1920) (noting the importance of migratory birds as "protectors of our forests and our crops" and as "a food supply"), it is undisputed that literally millions of people regularly participate in birdwatching and hunting and that those activities generate a host of commercial activities of great value. The causal connection between the filling of wetlands and the decline of commercial activities associated with migratory birds is not "attenuated," *Morrison*, 529 U.S., at 612; it is direct and concrete. *Cf. Gibbs v. Babbitt*, 214 F.3d 483, 492–493 (CA4 2000) ("The relationship between red wolf takings and interstate commerce is quite direct—with no red wolves, there will be no red wolf related tourism ...").

Finally, the migratory bird rule does not blur the "distinction between what is truly national and what is truly local." *Morrison*, 529 U.S., at 617–618. Justice Holmes cogently observed in *Missouri v. Holland* that the protection of migratory birds is a textbook example of a national problem. 252 U.S., at 435 ("It is not sufficient to rely upon the States [to protect migratory birds].

The reliance is vain ..."). The destruction of aquatic migratory bird habitat, like so many other environmental problems, is an action in which the benefits (*e.g.*, a new landfill) are disproportionately local, while many of the costs (*e.g.*, fewer migratory birds) are widely dispersed and often borne by citizens living in other States. In such situations, described by economists as involving "externalities," federal regulation is both appropriate and necessary. Revesz, *Rehabilitating Interstate Competition: Rethinking the "Race-to-the-Bottom" Rationale for Federal Environmental Regulation*, 67 N.Y.U.L.Rev. 1210, 1222 (1992) ("The presence of interstate externalities is a powerful reason for intervention at the federal level"); *cf. Hodel*, 452 U.S., at 281–282 (deferring to Congress' finding that nationwide standards were "essential" in order to avoid "destructive interstate competition" that might undermine environmental standards). Identifying the Corps' jurisdiction by reference to waters that serve as habitat for birds that migrate over state lines also satisfies this Court's expressed desire for some "jurisdictional element" that limits federal activity to its proper scope. *Morrison*, 529 U.S., at 612.

The power to regulate commerce among the several States necessarily and properly includes the power to preserve the natural resources that generate such commerce. Cf. *Sporhase v. Nebraska ex rel. Douglas*, 458 U.S. 941, 953 (1982) (holding water to be an "article of commerce"). Migratory birds, and the waters on which they rely, are such resources. Moreover, the protection of migratory birds is a well-established federal responsibility. As Justice Holmes noted in *Missouri v. Holland*, the federal interest in protecting these birds is of "the first magnitude." 252 U.S., at 435. Because of their transitory nature, they "can be protected only by national action." *Ibid.*

Whether it is necessary or appropriate to refuse to allow petitioner to fill those ponds is a question on which we have no voice. Whether the Federal Government has the power to require such permission, however, is a question that is easily answered. If, as it does, the Commerce Clause empowers Congress to regulate particular "activities causing air or water pollution, or other environmental hazards that may have effects in more than one State," *Hodel*, 452 U.S., at 282, it also empowers Congress to control individual actions that, in the aggregate, would have the same effect. *Perez*, 402 U.S., at 154; *Wickard*, 317 U.S., at 127–128. There is no merit in petitioner's constitutional argument.

Because I would affirm the judgment of the Court of Appeals, I respectfully dissent.

In early 2003, the Corps embarked on its rule-making procedure, publishing the following for public comment:

SUMMARY: The U.S. Army Corps of Engineers (Corps) and the Environmental Protection Agency (EPA) are today issuing an Advance Notice of Proposed Rulemaking (ANPRM) in order to obtain early comment on issues associated with the scope of waters that are subject to the Clean Water Act (CWA), in light of the U.S. Supreme Court decision in *Solid Waste Agency of Northern Cook County v. U.S. Army Corps of Engineers*, 531 U.S. 159 (2001) (*SWANCC*).

Today's ANPRM requests public input on issues associated with the definition of "waters of the United States" and also solicits information or data from the general public, the scientific community, and Federal and State resource agencies on the implications of the *SWANCC* decision for jurisdictional decisions under the CWA. The goal of the agencies is to develop proposed regulations that will further the public interest by clarifying what waters are subject to CWA jurisdiction and affording full protection to these waters through an appropriate focus of Federal and State resources consistent with the CWA. The input received from the public in response to today's ANPRM will be used by the agencies to determine the issues to be addressed and the substantive approach for a future proposed rulemaking addressing the scope of CWA jurisdiction.

Pending this rulemaking, should questions arise, the regulated community should seek assistance from the Corps and EPA, in accordance with the joint memorandum attached as Appendix A....

Persons or entities that discharge pollutants (including dredged or fill material) to "waters of the U.S." could be regulated by a rulemaking based on this ANPRM. The CWA generally prohibits the discharge of pollutants into "waters of the U.S." without a permit issued by EPA or a State or Tribe approved by EPA under section 402 of the Act, or, in the case of dredged or fill material, by the Corps or an approved State or Tribe under section 404 of the Act. In addition, under the CWA, States or approved Tribes establish water quality standards for "waters of the U.S.", and also may assume responsibility for issuance of CWA permits for discharges into waters and wetlands subject to the Act....

Today's ANPRM seeks public input on what, if any, revisions in light of *SWANCC* might be appropriate to the regulations that define "waters of the U.S.," and today's ANPRM thus would be of interest to all entities discharging to, or regulating, such waters. In addition, because the Oil Pollution Act (OPA) is applicable to waters and wetlands subject to the CWA, today's ANPRM may have implications for persons or entities subject to the OPA. Examples of entities potentially regulated include: ...

II. THE IMPORTANCE OF UPDATING THE REGULATIONS

The agencies have not engaged in a review of the regulations with the public concerning CWA jurisdiction for some time. This ANPRM will help ensure that the regulations are consistent with the CWA and the public understands what waters are subject to CWA jurisdiction. The goal of the agencies is to develop proposed regulations that will further the public interest by clarifying what waters are subject to CWA jurisdiction and affording full protection to these waters through an appropriate focus of Federal and State resources consistent with the CWA. It is appropriate to review the regulations to ensure that they are consistent with the *SWANCC* decision. *SWANCC* eliminates CWA jurisdiction over isolated waters that are intrastate and non-navigable, where the sole basis for asserting CWA jurisdiction is the actual or potential use of the waters as habitat for migratory birds that cross State lines in their migrations. *SWANCC* also calls into question whether CWA jurisdiction over isolated, intrastate, non-navigable waters could now be predicated on the other factors listed in the "Migratory Bird Rule" or the other rationales of 33 CFR 328.3(a)(3)(i)-(iii).

Although the *SWANCC* case itself specifically involves section 404 of the CWA, the Court's decision may also affect the scope of regulatory jurisdiction under other provisions of the CWA, including programs under sections 303, 311, 401, and 402. Under each of these sections, the relevant agencies have jurisdiction over "waters of the United States." The agencies will consider the potential implications of the rulemaking for these other sections.

- Section 404 dredged and fill material permit program. This program establishes a permitting system to regulate discharges of dredged or fill material into waters of the United States.

- Section 303 water quality standards program. Under this program, States and authorized Indian Tribes establish water quality standards for navigable waters to "protect the public health or welfare" and "enhance the quality of water," "taking into consideration their use and value for public water supplies, propagation of fish and wildlife, recreational purposes, and agriculture, industrial, and other purposes, and also taking into consideration their use and value for navigation."

- Section 311 spill program and the Oil Pollution Act (OPA). Section 311 of the CWA addresses pollution from both oil and hazardous substance releases. Together with the Oil Pollution Act, it provides EPA and the U.S. Coast Guard with the authority to establish a program for preventing, preparing for, and responding to spills that occur in navigable waters of the United States.

- Section 401 State water-quality certification program. Section 401 provides that no Federal permit or license for activities that might result in a discharge to navigable waters may be issued unless a section 401 water-quality certification is obtained from or waived by States or authorized Tribes.

- Section 402 National Pollutant Discharge Elimination System (NPDES) permitting program. This program establishes a permitting system to regulate point source discharges of pollutants (other than dredged or fill material) into waters of the United States.

III. LEGISLATIVE AND REGULATORY CONTEXT

The Federal Water Pollution Control Act Amendments, now known as the Clean Water Act (CWA), was enacted in 1972. In the years since its enactment, the scope of waters regulated under the CWA has been discussed in regulations, legislation, and judicial decisions.

The CWA was intended to "restore and maintain the chemical, physical, and biological integrity of the Nation's waters." 33 U.S.C. section 1251(a). Its specific provisions were designed to improve upon the protection of the Nation's waters provided under earlier statutory schemes such as the Rivers and Harbors Act of 1899 ("RHA") (33 U.S.C. sections 403, 407, 411) and the Federal Water Pollution Control Act of 1948 (62 Stat. 1155) and its subsequent amendments through 1970. In doing so, Congress recognized "the primary responsibilities and rights of States to prevent, reduce, and eliminate pollution, to plan the development and use (including restoration, preservation, and enhancement) of land and water resources ...." 33 U.S.C. section 1251(b).

The jurisdictional scope of the CWA is "navigable waters," defined in the statute as "waters of the United States, including the territorial seas." CWA section 502(7), 33 U.S.C. section 1362(7). The existing CWA section 404 regulations define "waters of the United States" as follows:

> (1) All waters which are currently used, or were used in the past, or may be susceptible to use in interstate or foreign commerce, including all waters which are subject to ebb and flow of the tide;
>
> (2) All interstate waters including interstate wetlands;
>
> (3) All other waters such as intrastate lakes, rivers, streams (including intermittent streams), mudflats, sandflats, wetlands, sloughs, prairie potholes, wet meadows, playa lakes, or

natural ponds, the use, degradation or destruction of which could affect interstate or foreign commerce including any such waters:

(i) which are or could be used by interstate or foreign travelers for recreational or other purposes; or

(ii) from which fish or shellfish are or could be taken and sold in interstate or foreign commerce; or

(iii) which are used or could be used for industrial purposes by industries in interstate commerce.

(4) All impoundments of waters otherwise defined as waters of the United States under the definition;

(5) Tributaries of waters identified in paragraphs (a)(1)-(4) of this section;

(6) The territorial seas;

(7) Wetlands adjacent to waters (other than waters that are themselves wetlands) identified in paragraphs (a)(1)-(6) of this section.

(8) Waters of the United States do not include prior converted cropland ... Waste treatment systems, including treatment ponds or lagoons designed to meet the requirements of CWA (other than cooling ponds ...) are not waters of the United States.

40 CFR.230.3(s); 33 CFR 328.3(a).

Counterpart and substantively similar regulatory definitions appear at 40 CFR 110.1, 112.2, 116.3, 117.1, 122.2, 232.2, 300.5, part 300 App. E, 302.3 and 401.11 (hereafter referred to as "the counterpart definitions").

In regulatory preambles, both the Corps and EPA provided examples of additional types of links to interstate commerce which might serve as a basis under 40 CFR 230.3(a)(3) and 33 CFR 328.3(a)(3) for establishing CWA jurisdiction over intrastate waters which were not part of the tributary system or their adjacent wetlands. These included use of waters (1) as habitat by birds protected by Migratory Bird Treaties or which cross State lines, (2) as habitat for endangered species, or (3) to irrigate crops sold in commerce. 51 FR 41217 (November 13, 1986), 53 FR 20765 (June 6, 1988). These examples became known as the "Migratory Bird Rule," even though the examples were neither a rule nor entirely about birds. The Migratory Bird Rule later became the focus of the *SWANCC* case....

There is an extensive body of knowledge about the functions and values of wetlands, which include flood risk reduction, water quality improvement, fish and wildlife habitat, and maintenance of the hydrologic integrity of aquatic ecosystems. The ANPRM seeks information regarding the functions and values of wetlands and other waters that may be affected by the issues discussed in this ANPRM.

V. SOLICITATION OF COMMENTS

The agencies are seeking comment on issues related to the jurisdictional status of isolated waters under the CWA which the public wishes to call to our attention. To assist the public in considering these issues, the following discussion and specific questions are presented. The agencies will carefully consider the responses received to this ANPRM in determining what regulatory changes may be appropriate and the issues to be addressed in a proposed rulemaking to clarify CWA jurisdiction.

The *SWANCC* holding eliminates CWA jurisdiction over isolated, intrastate, non-navigable waters where the sole basis for asserting CWA jurisdiction is the actual or potential use of the waters as habitat for migratory birds that cross State lines in their migrations. 531 U.S. at 174 ("We hold that 33 CFR § 328.3(a)(3) (1999), as clarified and applied to petitioner's balefill site pursuant to the 'Migratory Bird Rule,' 51 Fed. Reg. 41217 (1986), exceeds the authority granted to respondents under §404(a) of the CWA"). The agencies seek comment on the use of the factors in 33 CFR 328.3(a)(3)(i)-(iii) or the counterpart regulations in determining CWA jurisdiction over isolated, intrastate, non-navigable waters.

The agencies solicit comment from the public on the following issues:

1) Whether, and, if so, under what circumstances, the factors listed in 33 CFR 328.3(a)(3)(i)-(iii) (*i.e.*, use of the water by interstate or foreign travelers for recreational or other purposes, the presence of fish or shellfish that could be taken and sold in interstate commerce, the use of the water for industrial purposes by industries in interstate commerce) or any other factors provide a basis for determining CWA jurisdiction over isolated, intrastate, non-navigable waters?

2) Whether the regulations should define "isolated waters," and if so, what factors should be considered in determining whether a water is or is not isolated for jurisdictional purposes?

SOLICITATION OF INFORMATION

In answering the questions set forth above, please provide, as appropriate, any information (*e.g.*, scientific and technical studies and data, analysis of environmental impacts, effects on interstate commerce, other impacts, etc.) supporting your views, and specific recommendations on how to implement such views. Additionally, we invite your views as to whether any other revisions are needed to the existing regulations on which waters are jurisdictional under the CWA. As noted elsewhere in this document, the agencies are also soliciting data and information on the availability and effectiveness of other Federal or State programs for the protection of aquatic resources, and on the functions and values of wetlands and other waters that may be affected by the issues discussed in this ANPRM.

VI. RELATED FEDERAL AND STATE AUTHORITIES

The *SWANCC* decision addresses CWA jurisdiction, and other Federal or State laws and programs may still protect a water and related ecosystem even if that water is no longer jurisdictional under the CWA following *SWANCC*. The Federal government remains committed to wetlands protection through the Food Security Act's Swampbuster requirements and Federal agricultural program benefits and restoration through such Federal programs as the Wetlands Reserve Program (administered by the U.S. Department of Agriculture), grant making programs such as Partners in Wildlife (administered by the Fish and Wildlife Service), the Coastal Wetlands Restoration Program (administered by the National Marine Fisheries Service), the State Grant, Five Star Restoration, and National Estuary Programs (administered by EPA), and the Migratory Bird Conservation Commission (composed of the Secretaries of Interior and Agriculture, the Administrator of EPA and Members of Congress).

The *SWANCC* decision also highlights the role of States in protecting waters not addressed by Federal law. Prior to *SWANCC,* fifteen States had programs that addressed isolated wetlands. Since *SWANCC,* additional States have considered, and two have adopted, legislation to protect isolated waters. The Federal agencies have a number of initiatives to assist States in these efforts to protect wetlands. For example, EPA's Wetland Program Development Grants are available to assist States, Tribes, and local governments for building their wetland program capacities. In addition, the U.S. Department of Justice and other Federal agencies co-sponsored a national wetlands conference with the National Governors Association Center for Best Practices, National Conference of State Legislatures, the Association of State Wetlands Managers, and the National Association of Attorneys General. This conference and the dialogue that has ensued will promote close collaboration between Federal agencies and States in developing, implementing, and enforcing wetlands protection programs. EPA also is providing funding to the National Governors Association Center for Best Practices to assist States in developing appropriate policies and actions to protect intrastate isolated waters.

In light of this, the agencies solicit information and data from the general public, the scientific community, and Federal and State resource agencies on the availability and effectiveness of other Federal or State programs for the protection of aquatic resources and practical experience with their implementation. The agencies are also interested in data and comments from State and local agencies on the effect of no longer asserting jurisdiction over some of the waters (and discharges to those waters) in a watershed on the implementation of Total Maximum Daily Loads (TMDLs) and attainment of water quality standards....

APPENDIX A

The following guidance document will not appear in the Code of Federal Regulations.

JOINT MEMORANDUM INTRODUCTION

This document provides clarifying guidance regarding the Supreme Court's decision in *Solid Waste Agency of Northern Cook County v. United States Army Corps of Engineers*, 531 U.S. 159 (2001) ("*SWANCC*") and addresses several legal issues concerning Clean Water Act ("CWA") jurisdiction that have arisen since *SWANCC* in various factual scenarios involving federal regulation of "navigable waters." Because the case law interpreting *SWANCC* has developed over the last two years, the Agencies are issuing this updated guidance, which supersedes prior guidance on this issue. The Corps and EPA are also initiating a rulemaking process to collect information and to consider jurisdictional issues as set forth in the attached ANPRM. Jurisdictional decisions will be based on Supreme Court cases including *United States v. Riverside Bayview Homes*, 474 U.S. 121 (1985) and *SWANCC*, regulations, and applicable case law in each jurisdiction.

BACKGROUND

In *SWANCC*, the Supreme Court held that the Army Corps of Engineers had exceeded its authority in asserting CWA jurisdiction pursuant to § 404(a) over isolated, intrastate, non-navigable waters under 33 C.F.R. §328.3(a)(3), based on their use as habitat for migratory birds pursuant to preamble language commonly referred to as the "Migratory Bird Rule," 51 Fed. Reg. 41217 (1986). "Navigable waters" are defined in §502 of the CWA to mean "waters of the United States, including the territorial seas." In *SWANCC*, the Court determined that the term "navigable" had significance in indicating the authority Congress intended to exercise in asserting CWA jurisdiction. 531 U.S. at 172. After reviewing the jurisdictional scope of the statutory definition of "navigable waters" in §502, the Court concluded that neither the text of the statute nor its legislative history supported the Corps' assertion of jurisdiction over the waters involved in SWANCC. *Id.* at 170–171.

In *SWANCC*, the Supreme Court recognized that "Congress passed the CWA for the stated purpose of 'restoring and maintaining the chemical, physical, and biological integrity of the Nation's waters'" and also noted that "Congress chose to 'recognize, preserve, and protect the primary responsibilities and rights of States to prevent, reduce, and eliminate pollution, to plan the development and use (including restoration, preservation, and enhancement) of land and water resources.'" *Id.* at 166–67 (citing 33 U.S.C. §1251(a) and (b)). However, expressing "serious constitutional and federalism questions" raised by the Corps' interpretation of the CWA, the Court stated that "where an administrative interpretation of a statute invokes the outer limits of Congress' power, we expect a clear indication that Congress intended that result." *Id.* at 174, 172. Finding "nothing approaching a clear statement from Congress that it intended § 404(a) to reach an abandoned sand and gravel pit" (id. at 174), the Court held that the Migratory Bird Rule, as applied to petitioners' property, exceeded the agencies' authority under §404(a). *Id.* at 174.

THE SCOPE OF CWA JURISDICTION AFTER SWANCC

Because *SWANCC* limited use of 33 C.F.R. §328.3(a)(3) as a basis of jurisdiction over certain isolated waters, it has focused greater attention on CWA jurisdiction generally, and specifically over tributaries to jurisdictional waters and over wetlands that are "adjacent wetlands" for CWA purposes.

As indicated, §502 of the CWA defines the term navigable waters to mean "waters of the United States, including the territorial seas." The Supreme Court has recognized that this definition clearly includes those waters that are considered traditional navigable waters. In SWANCC, the Court noted that while "the word 'navigable' in the statute was of 'limited import'" (quoting Riverside, 474 U.S. 121 (1985)), "the term 'navigable' has at least the import of showing us what Congress had in mind as its authority for enacting the CWA: its traditional jurisdiction over waters that were or had been navigable in fact or which could reasonably be so made." 531 U.S. at 172. In addition, the Court reiterated in *SWANCC* that Congress evidenced its intent to regulate "at least some waters that would not be deemed 'navigable' under the classical understanding of that term." *SWANCC* at 171 (quoting Riverside, 474 U.S. at 133). Relying on that intent, for many years, EPA and the Corps have interpreted their regulations to assert CWA jurisdiction over non-navigable tributaries of navigable waters and their adjacent wetlands. Courts have upheld the view that traditional navigable waters and, generally speaking, their tributary systems (and their adjacent wetlands) remain subject to CWA jurisdiction.

Several federal district and appellate courts have addressed the effect of *SWANCC* on CWA jurisdiction, and the case law on the precise scope of federal CWA jurisdiction in light of *SWANCC* is still developing. While a majority of cases hold that *SWANCC* applies only to waters that are isolated, intrastate and non-navigable, several courts have interpreted *SWANCC's* reasoning to apply to waters other than the isolated waters at issue in that case. This memorandum attempts to add greater clarity concerning federal CWA jurisdiction following *SWANCC* by identifying specific categories of waters, explaining which categories of waters are jurisdictional or non-jurisdictional, and pointing out where more refined factual and legal analysis will be required to make a jurisdictional determination.

Although the *SWANCC* case itself specifically involved Section 404 of the CWA, the Court's decision may affect the scope of regulatory jurisdiction under other provisions of the CWA as well, including the Section 402 NPDES program, the Section 311 oil spill program, water quality standards under Section 303, and Section 401 water quality certification. Under each of these sections, the relevant agencies have jurisdiction over "waters of the United States." CWA §502(7).

This memorandum does not discuss the exact factual predicates that are necessary to establish jurisdiction in individual cases. We recognize that the field staff and the public could benefit from additional guidance on how to apply the applicable legal principles to individual cases.[1] Should questions arise concerning CWA jurisdiction, the regulated community should seek assistance from the Corps and EPA.

A. ISOLATED, INTRASTATE WATERS THAT ARE NON-NAVIGABLE

SWANCC squarely eliminates CWA jurisdiction over isolated waters that are intrastate and non-navigable, where the sole basis for asserting CWA jurisdiction is the actual or potential use of the waters as habitat for migratory birds that cross state lines in their migrations. 531 U.S. at 174 ("We hold that 33 C.F.R. §328.3(a)(3) (1999), as clarified and applied to petitioner's balefill site pursuant to the 'Migratory Bird Rule,' 51 Fed. Reg. 41217 (1986), exceeds the authority granted to respondents under §404(a) of the CWA"). The EPA and the Corps are now precluded from asserting CWA jurisdiction in such situations, including over waters such as isolated, non-navigable, intrastate vernal pools, playa lakes and pocosins. *SWANCC* also calls into question whether CWA jurisdiction over isolated, intrastate, non-navigable waters could now be predicated on the other factors listed in the Migratory Bird Rule, 51 Fed. Reg. 41217 (*i.e.*, use of the water as habitat for birds protected by Migratory Bird Treaties; use of the water as habitat for Federally protected endangered or threatened species; or use of the water to irrigate crops sold in interstate commerce).

---

[1] The CWA provisions and regulations described in this document contain legally binding requirements. This document does not substitute for those provisions or regulations, nor is it a regulation itself. It does not impose legally binding requirements on EPA, the Corps, or the regulated community, and may not apply to a particular situation depending on the circumstances. Any decisions regarding a particular water will be based on the applicable statutes, regulations, and case law. Therefore, interested persons are free to raise questions and objections about the appropriateness of the application of this guidance to a particular situation, and EPA and/or the Corps will consider whether or not the recommendations or interpretations of this guidance are appropriate in that situation based on the law and regulations.

By the same token, in light of *SWANCC*, it is uncertain whether there remains any basis for jurisdiction under the other rationales of §328.3(a)(3)(i)-(iii) over isolated, non-navigable, intrastate waters (*i.e.*, use of the water by interstate or foreign travelers for recreational or other purposes; the presence of fish or shellfish that could be taken and sold in interstate commerce; use of the water for industrial purposes by industries in interstate commerce). Furthermore, within the states comprising the Fourth Circuit, CWA jurisdiction under 33 C.F.R. §328.3(a)(3) in its entirety has been precluded since 1997 by the Fourth Circuit's ruling in *United States v. Wilson*, 133 F. 3d 251, 257 (Cir. 1997) (invalidating 33 C.F.R. §328.3(a)(3)).

In view of *SWANCC*, neither agency will assert CWA jurisdiction over isolated waters that are both intrastate and non-navigable, where the sole basis available for asserting CWA jurisdiction rests on any of the factors listed in the "Migratory Bird Rule." In addition, in view of the uncertainties after SWANCC concerning jurisdiction over isolated waters that are both intrastate and non-navigable based on other grounds listed in 33 C.F.R. §328.3(a)(3)(i)-(iii), field staff should seek formal project-specific Headquarters approval prior to asserting jurisdiction over such waters, including permitting and enforcement actions.

B. TRADITIONAL NAVIGABLE WATERS

As noted, traditional navigable waters are jurisdictional. Traditional navigable waters are waters that are subject to the ebb and flow of the tide, or waters that are presently used, or have been used in the past, or may be susceptible for use to transport interstate or foreign commerce. 33 C.F.R. §328.3(a)(1); *United States v. Appalachian Elec. Power Co.*, 311 U.S. 377, 407-408 (1940) (water considered navigable, although not navigable at present but could be made navigable with reasonable improvements); *Economy Light & Power Co. v. United States*, 256 U.S. 113 (1911) (dams and other structures do not eliminate navigability); *SWANCC*, 531 U.S. at 172 (referring to traditional jurisdiction over waters that were or had been navigable in fact or which could reasonably be so made).[2]

In accord with the analysis in *SWANCC*, waters that fall within the definition of traditional navigable waters remain jurisdictional under the CWA. Thus, isolated, intrastate waters that are capable of supporting navigation by watercraft remain subject to CWA jurisdiction after SWANCC if they are traditional navigable waters, *i.e.*, if they meet any of the tests for being navigable-in-fact. See, *e.g.*, *Colvin v. United States,* 181 F. Supp. 2d 1050 (C.D. Cal. 2001) (isolated man-made water body capable of boating found to be "water of the United States").

C. ADJACENT WETLANDS

(1) WETLANDS ADJACENT TO TRADITIONAL NAVIGABLE WATERS

CWA jurisdiction also extends to wetlands that are adjacent to traditional navigable waters. The Supreme Court did not disturb its earlier holding in *Riverside* when it rendered its decision in *SWANCC*. *Riverside* dealt with a wetland adjacent to Black Creek, a traditional navigable water. 474 U.S. 121 (1985); *see also SWANCC*, 531 U.S. at 167 ("[i]n *Riverside*, we held that the Corps had

---

2 These traditional navigable waters are not limited to those regulated under Section 10 of the Rivers and Harbors Act of 1899; traditional navigable waters include waters which, although used, susceptible to use, or historically used, to transport goods or people in commerce, do not form part of a continuous waterborne highway.

§404(a) jurisdiction over wetlands that actually abutted on a navigable waterway"). The Court in Riverside found that "Congress' concern for the protection of water quality and aquatic ecosystems indicated its intent to regulate wetlands 'inseparably bound up with'" jurisdictional waters. 474 U.S. at 134. Thus, wetlands adjacent to traditional navigable waters clearly remain jurisdictional after *SWANCC.* The Corps and EPA currently define "adjacent" as "bordering, contiguous, or neighboring. Wetlands separated from other waters of the United States by man-made dikes or barriers, natural river berms, beach dunes, and the like are 'adjacent wetlands.'" 33 C.F.R. §328.3(b); 40 C.F.R. §230.3(b). The Supreme Court has not itself defined the term "adjacent," nor stated whether the basis for adjacency is geographic proximity or hydrology.

(2) WETLANDS ADJACENT TO NON-NAVIGABLE WATERS

The reasoning in *Riverside*, as followed by a number of post-*SWANCC* courts, supports jurisdiction over wetlands adjacent to non-navigable waters that are tributaries to navigable waters. Since *SWANCC,* some courts have expressed the view that *SWANCC* raised questions about adjacency jurisdiction, so that wetlands are jurisdictional only if they are adjacent to navigable waters. See, *e.g.*, *Rice v. Harken*, discussed infra.

D. TRIBUTARIES

A number of court decisions have held that *SWANCC* does not change the principle that CWA jurisdiction extends to tributaries of navigable waters. See, *e.g.*, *Headwaters v. Talent Irrigation Dist.*, 243 F.3d 526, 534 (9th Cir. 2001) ("Even tributaries that flow intermittently are 'waters of the United States'"); *United States v. Interstate Gen. Co.,* No. 01-4513, slip op. at 7, 2002 WL 1421411 (4th Cir. July 2, 2002), aff'ing 152 F. Supp. 2d 843 (D.Md. 2001) (refusing to grant writ of *coram nobis*; rejecting argument that SWANCC eliminated jurisdiction over wetlands adjacent to non-navigable tributaries); *United States v. Krilich*, 393F.3d 784 (7th Cir. 2002) (rejecting motion to vacate consent decree, finding that *SWANCC* did not alter regulations interpreting "waters of the U.S." other than 33 C.F.R. §328.3(a)(3)); *Community Ass. for Restoration of the Env't v. Henry Bosma Dairy,* 305 F.3d 953 (9th Cir. 2002) (drain that flowed into a canal that flows into a river is jurisdictional); *Idaho Rural Council v. Bosma*, 143 F. Supp. 2d 1169, 1178 (D.Idaho 2001) ("waters of the United States include waters that are tributary to navigable waters"); *Aiello v. Town of Brookhaven*, 136 F. Supp. 2d 81, 118 (E.D. N.Y. 2001) (non-navigable pond and creek determined to be tributaries of navigable waters, and therefore "waters of the United States under the CWA"). Jurisdiction has been recognized even when the tributaries in question flow for a significant distance before reaching a navigable water or are several times removed from the navigable waters (*i.e.*, "tributaries of tributaries"). *See, e.g., United States v. Lamplight Equestrian Ctr.,* No. 00 C 6486, 2002 WL 360652, at *8 (ND. Ill. Mar. 8, 2002) ("Even where the distance from the tributary to the navigable water is significant, the quality of the tributary is still vital to the quality of navigable waters"); *United States v. Buday,* 138 F. Supp. 2d 1282, 1291-92 (D.Mont. 2001) ("water quality of tributaries ... distant though the tributaries may be from navigable streams, is vital to the quality of navigable waters"); *United States v. Rueth Dev. Co.*, No. 2:96CV540, 2001 WL 17580078 (N.D.Ind. Sept. 26, 2001) (refusing to reopen a consent decree in a CWA case and determining that jurisdiction remained over wetlands adjacent to a non-navigable (man-made) waterway that flows into a navigable water).

Some courts have interpreted the reasoning in *SWANCC* to potentially circumscribe CWA jurisdiction over tributaries by finding CWA jurisdiction attaches only where navigable waters and waters immediately adjacent to navigable waters are involved. *Rice v. Harken* is the leading case taking the narrowest view of CWA jurisdiction after *SWANCC*. 250 F.3d 264 (5th Cir. 2001) (rehearing denied). *Harken* interpreted the scope of "navigable waters" under the Oil Pollution Act (OPA). The Fifth Circuit relied on *SWANCC* to conclude "it appears that a body of water is subject to regulation under the CWA if the body of water is actually navigable or is adjacent to an open body of navigable water." 250 F.3d at 269. The analysis in *Harken* implies that the Fifth Circuit might limit CWA jurisdiction to only those tributaries that are traditionally navigable or immediately adjacent to a navigable water.

A few post-*SWANCC* district court opinions have relied on *Harken* or reasoning similar to that employed by the Harken court to limit jurisdiction. See, *e.g.*, *United States v. Rapanos*, 190 F. Supp. 2d 1011(E.D.Mich. 2002) (government appeal pending) ("the Court finds as a matter of law that the wetlands on Defendant's property were not directly adjacent to navigable waters, and therefore, the government cannot regulate Defendant's property."); *United States v. Needham*, No. 6:01-CV-01897, 2002 WL 1162790 (W.D.La. Jan. 23, 2002) (government appeal pending) (district court affirmed finding of no liability by bankruptcy court for debtors under OPA for discharge of oil since drainage ditch into which oil was discharged was found to be neither a navigable water nor adjacent to an open body of navigable water). See also *United States v. Newdunn*, 195 F. Supp. 2d 751 (E.D.Va. 2002) (government appeal pending) (wetlands and tributaries not contiguous or adjacent to navigable waters are outside CWA jurisdiction); *United States v. RGM Corp.*, 222 F. Supp. 2d 780 (E.D.Va. 2002) (government appeal pending) (wetlands on property not contiguous to navigable river and, thus, jurisdiction not established based upon adjacency to navigable water).

Another question that has arisen is whether CWA jurisdiction is affected when a surface tributary to jurisdictional waters flows for some of its length through ditches, culverts, pipes, storm sewers, or similar manmade conveyances. A number of courts have held that waters with manmade features are jurisdictional. For example, in *Headwaters Inc. v. Talent Irrigation District*, the Ninth Circuit held that manmade irrigation canals that diverted water from one set of natural streams and lakes to other streams and creeks were connected as tributaries to waters of the United States, and consequently fell within the purview of CWA jurisdiction. 243 F.3d at 533-34. However, some courts have taken a different view of the circumstances under which man-made conveyances satisfy the requirements for CWA jurisdiction. See, *e.g.*, *Newdunn*, 195 F. Supp.2d at 765 (government appeal pending) (court determined that Corps had failed to carry its burden of establishing CWA jurisdiction over wetlands from which surface water had to pass through a spur ditch, a series of man-made ditches and culverts as well as non-navigable portions of a creek before finally reaching navigable waters).

A number of courts have held that waters connected to traditional navigable waters only intermittently or ephemerally are subject to CWA jurisdiction. The language and reasoning in the Ninth Circuit's decision in *Headwaters Inc. v. Talent Irrigation District* indicates that the intermittent flow of waters does not affect CWA jurisdiction. 243 F.3d at 534 ("Even tributaries that flow intermittently are 'waters of the United States.'"). Other cases, however, have suggested that SWANCC eliminated from CWA jurisdiction some waters that flow only intermittently. *See, e.g., Newdunn*, 195 F. Supp. 2d at 764, 767-68 (government appeal pending) (ditches and culverts with intermittent flow not jurisdictional).

A factor in determining jurisdiction over waters with intermittent flows is the presence or absence of an ordinary high water mark (OHWM). Corps regulations provide that, in the absence of adjacent wetlands, the lateral limits of non-tidal waters extend to the OHWM (33 C.F.R. § 328.4(c)(1)). One court has interpreted this regulation to require the presence of a continuous OHWM. *United States v. RGM*, 222 F. Supp.2d 780 (E.D.Va. 2002) (government appeal pending).

CONCLUSION

In light of *SWANCC*, field staff should not assert CWA jurisdiction over isolated waters that are both intrastate and non-navigable, where the sole basis available for asserting CWA jurisdiction rests on any of the factors listed in the "Migratory Bird Rule." In addition, field staff should seek formal project-specific HQ approval prior to asserting jurisdiction over waters based on other factors listed in 33 C.F.R. §328.3(a)(3)(i)-(iii).

Field staff should continue to assert jurisdiction over traditional navigable waters (and adjacent wetlands) and, generally speaking, their tributary systems (and adjacent wetlands). Field staff should make jurisdictional and permitting decisions on a case-by-case basis considering this guidance, applicable regulations, and any additional relevant court decisions. Where questions remain, the regulated community should seek assistance from the agencies on questions of jurisdiction.

Part 2

The permit requirement

Having determined that our land is a "wetland," and having determined that there is, therefore, federal jurisdiction to regulate certain activities in our wetland, the U.S. Army Corps of Engineers ("Corps") and the U.S. Environmental Protection Agency ("EPA") may or may not grant us a permit under §404 if our activity in one which requires a permit.

Why is a permit required? The EPA specifies several reasons why activities involving a discharge of dredged or fill material may constitute a "loss of values" in wetlands in that the discharge is likely to destroy habitat and adversely affect biological productivity by smothering, dewatering, permanently flooding, or altering substrate elevation or periodicity of water movement. The discharge may also destroy wetland vegetation or result in the advancement of succession to dry land species. The discharge may obstruct circulation patterns that flush large expanses of wetland systems such that an apparently minor loss may result in major losses through secondary impacts. The discharge may also modify the capacity of wetlands to retain and store floodwaters and to serve as a buffer zone shielding upland areas from wave actions, storm damage, and erosion. 40 C.F.R. §230.41(b).

In dealing with the Corps, we are instructed that it is a "highly decentralized organization" in which most of the permitting authority has been delegated to 36 district engineers and 11 division engineers. 33 C.F.R. §320.1(a)(2). While the Corps has authorized its district engineers to "issue formal determinations concerning the applicability of the Clean Water Act or the Rivers and Harbors Act of 1899 to activities or tracts of land," the EPA shares oversight authority and retains a veto power. 33 C.F.R. §320.1(a)(6).

Chapter 9

General regulatory policies

In addition to the Clean Water Act and the Rivers and Harbors Act of 1899, in making a wetland permit decision, the district engineers must also comply with a number of other federal statutes similarly intended to protect the environment: the Coastal Zone Management Act of 1972 (which requires a permit applicant to furnish a certification that the proposed activity will comply the state's coastal zone management program); the Marine Protection, Research and Sanctuaries Act of 1972 (which authorizes the Secretary of Commerce to issue regulations controlling activities in certain designated areas in order to preserve or restore conservation, recreational, ecological, or aesthetic values); the National Environmental Policy Act of 1969 (which requires federal agencies to interpret and administer regulations in such a manner as to encourage a productive and enjoyable harmony between Man and his environment, and to ensure that presently unquantified environmental amenities are given appropriate consideration in decision-making); the Fish and Wildlife Act of 1956, the Migratory Marine Game-Fish Act, and the Fish and Wildlife Coordination Act (which requires that any federal agency that proposes to control or modify any body of water to first consult with the U.S. Fish and Wildlife Service or the National Marine Fisheries Service); the National Historic Preservation Act of 1966 (which authorizes the Advisory Council on Historic Preservation to review and comment upon activities licensed by the Federal Government which will have an effect upon properties listed or eligible for listing in the National Register of Historic Places); the Preservation of Historical and Archeological Data Act of

1974 (which permits the Secretary of Interior to take necessary action to recover and preserve data prior to commencement of an activity which alters any terrain such that significant historical or archeological data is threatened); the Interstate Land Sales Full Disclosure Act (which prohibits any developer or agent from selling or leasing any lot in a subdivision unless the purchaser is furnished in advance with a report stating whether or not a permit has been applied for, issued, or denied by the Corps, or whether any enforcement action has been taken as a consequence of non-application for or denial of a permit); and the Endangered Species Act (which requires the Corps, in consultation with the U.S. Fish and Wildlife Service and the National Marine Fisheries Service, to ensure that any activity is not likely to jeopardize the continued existence of threatened or endangered species or result in the destruction or adverse modification of habitat).

In 1992, the Corps signed memoranda of agreement with the EPA, the Department of Commerce, and the Department of Interior requiring that, if there is a dispute between the Corps and them, the dispute will be "elevated" to a higher level within each agency so as to avoid delay in individual permit decisions when there is a policy dispute.

The Clean Water Act and the regulations also require that any applicant for a §404 permit "that may result in a discharge of a pollutant into waters of the United States" also obtain a certification from the discharge-originating state or the interstate water pollution control agency which has jurisdiction over the point source of the pollution that the discharge will comply with the "applicable effluent limitations and water quality standards." 33 U.S.C. §1341; 33 C.F.R. §§320.3(a), 320.4(d), and 325(b)(1). State certification of water quality will be conclusive evidence of compliance unless the EPA intervenes. Although technically no permit will be granted until the certification has been obtained, a waiver by the certifying agency may be deemed to have occurred if the agency fails to act within 60 days of the request. 33 C.F.R. §325.2(b)(1)(ii). The Corps has the authority to notify the agency that a shorter period of time than 60 days may be required, and, conversely, the Corps may determine that a longer period will be necessary based on information provided by the agency. In no event will this time enlargement last longer than one year.

Once the certification has been issued prior to the permit decision, any subsequent denial or modification of the certification will not affect ordinarily a §404 permit but the Corps may consider the subsequent denial or modification as part of the public interest review and may respond accordingly. Regulatory Guidance Letter, *Section 401 Water Quality Certification*, 87-3. However, if the Corps finds that there has been a "sufficient change" in the project such then the Corps may require that a new water quality certification be applied for. An exception to this process is when a state court voids a certification prior to the §404 permit issuance. There is no review of state water quality certificates in federal court. *Roosevelt Campobello International Park Commission v. U.S. Environmental Protection Agency*, 684 F.2d 1041 (1st Cir. 1982). In that case, the Corps cannot issue the §404 permit until the certification is "legally revived," *i.e.*, by the appellate process, re-issuance, or waiver. After the §404 permit has been issued, a subsequent denial or modification of a certification or the certification is voided by a court, will not necessarily affect the terms of the §404 permit but the Corps may consider modification, suspension, or revocation of the §404 permit.

In addition to the foregoing long list of other applicable statutes, the Corps has its own set of general policies for evaluating permit applications (33 C.F.R. §320.4.) and must also follow the EPA's Guidelines for Specification of Disposal Sites for Dredged or Fill Material (the "Guidelines") (40 C.F.R. §230). Under the Guidelines, the over-arching rule is that no discharge of dredged or fill material will be permitted if there is a practicable alternative which would have a less adverse impact on the aquatic ecosystem. 40 C.F.R. §230.10. An alternative is "practicable" if it is "available and capable of being done after taking into consideration cost, existing technology, and logistics in light of overall project purposes" and, if it is otherwise a practicable alternative 'an area not presently owned by the applicant which could reasonably be obtained, utilized, expanded or managed in order to fulfill that basic purpose of the proposed activity may be considered." 40 C.F.R. §230.10(a)(2). *See Bersani v. U.S. Environmental Protection Agency,* 850 F.2d 36 (2d Cir. N.Y. 1988), *cert denied,* 489 U.S. 1089, 103 L.Ed.2d 859, 109 S.Ct. 1556 (1989). Of course, the first "practicable alternative" is an activity which does not involve the discharge of dredged or fill material into a wetland. 40 C.F.R. §230.10(a)(1)(i). In addition, if the project is not "water dependent," *i.e.*, does not require access or proximity to or siting within the wetland to fulfill its basic purpose, then practicable alternatives are presumed to be available unless clearly demonstrated otherwise. 40 C.F.R. §230.10(a)(3).

Nonetheless, even if there are no practicable alternatives, no discharge will be permitted if it causes or contributes to violations of any State water quality standard, violates any toxic effluent standard, jeopardizes endangered species (unless exempted), or violates any requirement concerning any marine sanctuary. 40 C.F.R. §230.10(b). And no permit will issue if the activity causes or contributes to significant degradation of waters of the United States, including effects on human health or welfare (which includes effects on municipal water supplies, plankton, fish, shellfish, wildlife, and special aquatic species); effects on the life stages of aquatic life and other wildlife dependent on aquatic ecosystems; effects on aquatic ecosystem diversity, productivity, and stability (including loss of fish and wildlife habitat or loss of a wetland to assimilate nutrients, purify water, or reduce wave energy); and effects on recreational, aesthetic, and economic values. 40 C.F.R. §230.10(c).

EPA requires the Corps to certify that disposal sites for the discharge of dredged or fill material either comply with the Guidelines, will comply with the inclusion of appropriate conditions, or do not comply. The Corps' finding of compliance or non-compliance constitute a formal factual determination. In making this determination in the case of wetlands, the Corps applies a series of "reviews" starting with a "public interest review." 33 C.F.R. §§320.4(a). The general rule is that unnecessary alteration or destruction of wetlands is contrary to the public interest unless, after applying the EPA's Guidelines, the Corps nonetheless concludes that the benefits of the proposed alteration outweigh the damage to the wetland resource, either considered individually or as the wetland fits into a larger interrelated wetland area. The Corps will also consider specifically the effect of the discharge on wetlands. 33 C.F.R. §320.4(b). The Corps believes that "most wetlands constitute a productive and valuable public resource, the unnecessary alteration or destruction of which should be discouraged as contrary to the public interest." The Corps considers that some wetlands are more important than others. They are: "wetlands which serve significant natural biological functions, including food chain production, general habitat and nesting, spawning, rearing and resting sites for aquatic or land species; wetlands set aside for study of the aquatic environment or as sanctuaries or refuges; wetlands the destruction or alteration of which would affect detrimentally natural drainage characteristics, sedimentation patterns, salinity distribution, flushing characteristics, current patterns, or other environmental characteristics; wetlands which are significant in shielding other areas from wave action, erosion, or storm damage. Such wetlands are often associated with barrier beaches, islands, reefs and bars; wetlands which serve as valuable storage areas for storm and flood waters; wetlands which are ground water discharge areas that maintain minimum baseflows important to aquatic resources and those which are prime natural recharge areas; wetlands which serve significant water purification functions; and wetlands which are unique in nature or scarce in quantity to the region or local area." *Id.*

In addition, the Corps cautions that "although a particular alteration of a wetland may constitute a minor change, the cumulative effect of numerous piecemeal changes can result in a major impairment of wetland resources. Thus, the particular wetland site for which an application is made will be evaluated with the recognition that it may be part of a complete and interrelated wetland area. In addition, the district engineer may undertake, where appropriate, reviews of particular wetland areas in consultation with the Regional Director of the U. S. Fish and Wildlife Service, the Regional Director of the National Marine Fisheries Service of the National Oceanic and Atmospheric Administration, the Regional Administrator of the Environmental Protection Agency, the local representative of the Soil Conservation Service of the Department of Agriculture, and the head of the appropriate state agency to assess the cumulative effect of activities in such areas." *Id.* The Corps is concerned about the conservation of wildlife resources by prevention of their direct and indirect loss and damage due to the activity proposed in a permit application. The Corps is required to give full consideration to the views of those agencies on fish and wildlife matters in deciding on the issuance, denial, or conditioning of individual or general permits.

If the Corps has identified the wetland as an "important" one, no permit will be granted which involves the alteration of the wetland unless the Corps district engineer concludes that the benefits of the proposed alteration outweigh the damage to the wetlands resource. In evaluating whether a particular discharge activity should be permitted, the Corps will apply the EPA Guidelines

During the Corps' public interest review, it will also consider the effect which the proposed structure or activity may have on wild and scenic rivers, historic properties and National Landmarks, National Rivers, National Wilderness Areas, National Seashores, National Recreation Areas, National Lakeshores, National Parks, National Monuments, estuarine and marine sanctuaries, archeological resources, including Indian religious or cultural sites, and such other areas as may be established under federal or state law for similar and related purposes. Recognition of those values is often reflected by state, regional, or local land use classifications, or by similar federal controls or policies. Action on permit applications should, insofar as possible, be consistent with, and avoid significant adverse effects on the values or purposes for which those classifications, controls, or policies were established. The Corps, however, is not controlled by local zoning limitations.

If the permit application involves erosion protection, it will usually receive favorable consideration. However, if the protective structure may cause damage to the property of others, adversely affect public health and safety, adversely impact floodplain or wetland values, or otherwise appears contrary to the public interest, the Corps will so advise the applicant and inform him of possible alternative methods of protecting his property. A riparian landowner's general right of access to navigable waters of the United States is subject to the similar rights of access held by nearby riparian landowners and to the general public's right of navigation on the water surface. In the case of proposals which create undue interference with access to, or use of, navigable waters, the authorization will generally be denied.

A Corps permit does not convey any property rights or any exclusive privileges. The applicant's signature on an application is an affirmation that the applicant possesses or will possess the requisite property interest to undertake the activity proposed in the application. The Corps will not enter into disputes but will remind the applicant of the above. The dispute over property ownership will not be a factor in the Corps public interest decision.

Permit applications for activities in a marine sanctuary will be evaluated for impact on the marine sanctuary. No permit will be issued until the applicant provides a certification from the Secretary of Commerce that the proposed activity is consistent with the purposes of Title III of the Marine Protection, Research and Sanctuaries Act of 1972, as amended, and can be carried out within the regulations to control activities within the marine sanctuary.

Processing of an application for a permit normally will proceed concurrently with the processing of other required Federal, state, and/or local authorizations or certifications. However, where the other required authorization and/or certification has been denied for activities which also require a §404 permit before final action has been taken on the §404 permit application, the Corps will, after considering the likelihood of subsequent approval of the other authorization and/or certification and the time and effort remaining to complete processing the §404 permit application, either immediately deny the §404 permit without prejudice or continue processing the application to a conclusion. If the Corps continues processing the application, it will conclude by either denying the permit as contrary to the public interest, or denying it without prejudice indicating that except for the other Federal, state or local denial the §404 permit could, under appropriate conditions, be issued. Denial without prejudice means that there is no prejudice to the right of the applicant to reinstate processing of the §404 permit application if subsequent approval is received from the appropriate Federal, state and/or local agency on a previously denied authorization and/or certification.

The Corps will give due consideration to the official views of state, local, and tribal governments as a reflection of local factors of the public interest. unless there are significant issues of overriding national importance. Such issues would include but are not necessarily limited to national security, navigation, national economic development, water quality, preservation of special aquatic areas, including wetlands, with significant interstate importance, and national energy needs. If a §404 permit application draws conflicting comments from several agencies within the same state, the Corps will ask the Governor to express his views or to designate one state agency to represent the official state position in the particular case. The district engineer shall develop operating procedures for establishing official communications with Indian Tribes within the district through the appointment of a tribal representative who will receive all pertinent public notices, and respond to such notices with the official tribal position on the proposed activity.

Many wetlands are located in floodplains, which themselves possess significant natural values and carry out numerous functions important to the public interest. These include: water resources values (natural moderation of floods, water quality maintenance, and groundwater recharge); living resource values (fish, wildlife, and plant resources); cultural resource values (open space, natural beauty, scientific study, outdoor education, and recreation); and cultivated resource values (agriculture, aquaculture, and forestry). Although a particular alteration to a floodplain may constitute a minor change, the cumulative impact of such changes may result in a significant degradation of floodplain values and functions and in increased potential for harm to upstream and downstream activities. In accordance with the requirements of Executive Order 11988, the Corps, as part of its public interest review, avoid authorizing floodplain developments whenever practicable alternatives exist outside the floodplain. If there are no such practicable alternatives, the district engineer shall consider, as a means of mitigation, alternatives within the floodplain which will lessen any significant adverse impact to the floodplain.

The Corps and EPA consider mitigation to be an important aspect of the review and balancing process on many §404 permit applications. Consideration of mitigation will occur throughout the permit application review process and includes avoiding, minimizing, rectifying, reducing, or compensating for resource losses. Losses will be avoided to the extent practicable. Compensation may occur on-site or at an off-site location. The Corps may require minor project modifications, *i.e.*, those that are considered feasible (cost, constructability, etc.) to the applicant and that, if adopted, will result in a project that generally meets the applicant's purpose and need. Such modifications can include reductions in scope and size; changes in construction methods, materials or timing; and operation and maintenance practices or other similar modifications that reflect a sensitivity to environmental quality within the context of the work proposed.

Further mitigation measures may be required to satisfy legal requirements. For Section 404 applications, mitigation shall be required to ensure that the project complies with the 404(b)(1) Guidelines, but only those measures required to ensure that the project is not contrary to the public interest may be required under this subparagraph.

All compensatory mitigation will be for significant resource losses which are specifically identifiable, reasonably likely to occur, and of importance to the human or aquatic environment. Also, all mitigation will be directly related to the impacts of the proposal, appropriate to the scope and degree of those impacts, and reasonably enforceable.

Chapter 10

ACTIVITIES REQUIRING A PERMIT

While most activity occurring in a wetland, one which, at a minimum, places solid matter in the wetland, will be subject to the permit requirement, it is important to remember that the §404 does not apply to prohibit all activities which may occur in a wetland, but only to the "discharge of dredged or fill material" from a "point source." "Dredged material" is defined as any "material that is excavated or dredged from waters of the United States." 33 C.F.R. §323.2(c). Discharges of material or liquids from a "non-point source" are regulated by the individual States, not the Corps or EPA.

AVOYELLES SPORTSMEN'S LEAGUE, INC. v. MARSH

715 F.2d 897 (5th Cir. 1983)

This is an appeal from a district court judgment that enjoined the private defendants. from any additional clearing, except by permit under 33 U.S.C. §1344 (Supp. V 1981), of certain lands determined by the district court to be wetlands. The federal defendants contend that the district court should have reviewed the Environmental Protection Agency's ("EPA") final wetlands determination (attached as an appendix to this opinion) on the basis of the administrative record, and that the court erred in adopting its own wetlands determination instead of reviewing the agency's determination under the arbitrary and capricious standard. The federal defendants also dispute the district court's conclusion that the mere removal of vegetation from wetlands constitutes a discharge of a pollutant under section 301(a) of the Clean Water Act ("CWA"), 33 U.S.C. §1311(a) (1976). The private defendants contest the validity of the district court's determination that approximately 90 percent of their land is a wetland, as well as the court's conclusion that their landclearing activities fall under the CWA's prohibition on the discharge of pollutants into waters of the United States.

For the reasons set forth below, to the extent that the district court's decision that 90 percent of the Lake Long Tract is a wetland is inconsistent with the EPA's determination, the decision of the district court is reversed. The court's determination that the private defendants' actual landclearing activities require permits is affirmed.

I. FACTUAL AND PROCEDURAL BACKGROUND

This case concerns an approximately 20,000-acre tract of land (the "Lake Long Tract") in Avoyelles Parish, Louisiana. The tract lies within the Bayou Natchitoches basin, an area of approximately 140,000 acres, which, along with the Ouachita, Black and Tensas river basins, makes up the Red River backwater area. The Bayou Natchitoches basin is subject to flooding during the spring months, and it experiences an average rainfall of 60 inches per year.

Much of the basin had been cleared of forest before the private defendants began their landclearing activities, but 80,000 acres were still forested. The Lake Long Tract made up a quarter of this forested area. The topography of the tract itself is uneven, resulting in some areas with permanent water impoundments and other drier areas that support a variety of plant species.

The private defendants own the Lake Long Tract. They decided that the land could be put to agricultural use, specifically soybean production. Consequently, they began a program of large-scale deforestation in June of 1978. Using bulldozers with shearing blades that "floated" along the ground, the defendants cut the timber and vegetation at or just above ground level. The trees were then raked into windrows, burned, and the stumps and ashes were disced into the ground by other machinery. The shearing and raking caused some leveling of the tract, and the defendants dug one drainage ditch.

On August 25, 1978, the Vicksburg District of the Army Corps of Engineers ordered defendant Prevot to halt his activities pending a wetlands determination by the Corps. Thereafter, Dr. Donald G. Rhodes, an expert consultant employed by the Corps, undertook a comprehensive vegetative mapping of the Lake Long Tract and determined that 35 percent of it was a wetland. In October, 1978, the Fish and Wildlife Service wrote a letter to the Corps stating that the Service believed that the entire tract was a wetland. After Dr. Rhodes had made his determination, the landowners resumed their activities on the portion of the tract that the Corps had not designated as a wetland.

On November 8, 1978, the plaintiffs brought this citizens' suit against a number of Corps and EPA officials, as well as against the private landowners. The plaintiffs claimed, *inter alia*, that the landclearing activities would result in the discharge of dredged and fill material into the waters of the United States in violation of sections 301(a) and 404 of the CWA, 33 U.S.C. §§1311, 1344 (1976 & Supp. V 1981), and also result in the discharge of pollutants into the waters of the United States in violation of section 402 of the CWA, 33 U.S.C. §1342 (1976 & Supp. V 1981). The plaintiffs requested a declaration that the tract was a wetland within the scope of the CWA, that the private defendants could not engage in their landclearing activities without obtaining a permit from the EPA or the Corps, and that the federal defendants had failed to exercise their "mandatory duty" to designate the tract a wetland and to order the private defendants to cease and desist from discharging pollutants and dredged materials. The plaintiffs also sought injunctive relief against the federal defendants to require them to exercise their jurisdiction over the property and to issue cease-and-desist orders until the private defendants obtained the requisite permits. The district court immediately issued a temporary restraining order, preventing the private defendants from engaging in landclearing activities pending the court's action on the plaintiffs' motion for a preliminary injunction.

On January 17, 1979, the district court granted the plaintiffs' motion for a preliminary injunction and ordered the federal defendants to prepare a final wetlands determination within 60 days. All of the private parties were to have the opportunity to participate in the administrative proceedings, and the federal defendants were to file a preliminary report within 45 days. The court allowed the private defendants to engage in normal cultivation on the more than 10,000 acres that had been cleared, but ordered them to apply for a permit with respect to the area already designated by the government as a wetland and enjoined them for 60 days from engaging in landclearing activities on the remainder of the tract.

The parties complied with the court's preliminary order, and the EPA submitted its final wetlands determination on March 26, 1979. After examining the vegetation, soil conditions, and hydrology of the tract, the EPA concluded that approximately 80 percent of the land was a wetland. In a brief final paragraph, the EPA also offered its views of the types of activities that would require a section 404 permit.

At the private defendants' request, the district court agreed to bifurcate the consideration of the two major issues in the case: (1) how much of the Lake Long Tract was a wetland, and (2) which activities required a section 404 permit. After extensive trials on both issues, the court decided that a section 404 permit was required for the landclearing activities and that over 90 percent of the Lake Long Tract was a wetland. The court then enjoined the private defendants from engaging in any additional landclearing activities, without a section 404 permit, on the land that the court had determined to be a wetland, other than the land already cleared. The defendants timely appealed....

We turn then to our consideration of whether the district court's conclusion that the private defendants' landclearing activities required a section 404 permit was correct. In reviewing the trial court's decision, we are bound by the traditional standard requiring us to uphold a trial court's factual findings unless they are clearly erroneous. Fed.R.Civ.P. 52(a). Of course, we are free to make our own independent assessment of the court's legal conclusions. *Sierra Club v. Sigler,* 695 F.2d 957, 967-68 (5th Cir.1983)....

The private defendants are the only parties who challenge the district court's factual findings. While they have indicated portions of the record that support their contention that the landclearing activities did not result in any significant digging up of the earth or leveling of the land, the plaintiffs presented their own eyewitness testimony to the effect that large chunks of earth had been torn up, holes dug, and sloughs filed in. Resolution of this conflict in the evidence is properly left to the district court, who has had an opportunity to hear and observe the witnesses. We cannot say on the basis of this record that the trial court's factual findings were clearly erroneous....

The district court held that the private defendants' landclearing activities constituted a "discharge of a pollutant" into the waters of the United States, and that engaging in those activities without a section 404 dredge-and-fill permit was a violation of section 301(a) of the CWA. 33 U.S.C. §1311(a). As the district court did, we must look beyond section 301(a) itself, to the statutory and regulatory definitions, in order to determine whether the district court's holding was correct.

Section 502(12) defines the term "discharge of a pollutant" as "(a) any addition of any pollutant to navigable waters from any point source ...." 33 U.S.C. §1362(12). A "point source" is defined in section 502(14) as "any discernible, confined and discrete conveyance, including but not limited to any ... container, rolling stock, concentrated animal feeding operation, or vessel ... from which pollutants are or may be discharged ...." 33 U.S.C. §1362(14). Section 502(6) defines the term "pollutant" to mean "dredged spoil, solid waste, incinerator residue, sewage, garbage, sewage sludge, munitions, chemical wastes, biological materials, radioactive materials, heat, wrecked or discarded equipment, rock, sand, cellar dirt and industrial, municipal and agricultural waste discharged into water." 33 U.S.C. §1362(6). The question in this case is whether the landclearing activities were (1) a discharge (2) of a pollutant (3) from a point source (4) into navigable waters. Further, we must determine whether the activities were "normal agricultural activities" exempted from the permit requirements by 33 U.S.C. §1344(f).

As discussed in Part II, these activities did occur in navigable waters, as that term is defined in the statute. Further, we agree with the district court that the bulldozers and backhoes were "point sources," since they collected into windrows and piles material that may ultimately have found its way back into the waters. *See Sierra Club v. Abston Construction Co.,* 620 F.2d 41 (5th Cir.1980) (mining scrap piles may be point sources even though material may not be carried directly to waters from the piles); *United States v. Holland,* 373 F. Supp. 665, 668 (M.D.Fla. 1974) (bulldozers are point sources). The question then is whether these activities constituted a "discharge" of a "pollutant."

Emphasizing that the removal of all of the vegetation would destroy the vital ecological function of the wetlands, the district court concluded that the landclearing activities constituted a "discharge" within the meaning of the CWA. Both the federal and private defendants argue that the "mere removal" of wetlands vegetation was not a discharge because the term discharge is defined as the "addition" of pollutants, not the removal of materials. The district court rejected this argument as "untenable" because it believed that the federal defendants' interpretation would frustrate the ecological purposes of the CWA. 473 F. Supp. at 536. In the court's view, the federal defendants' argument implied that "the excavation of [a] ditch six feet deep and 100 feet long requires a §404 permit (is destructive of wetlands) but that the clearing of 20,000 acres of forest wetlands by methods involving only *de minimis* movement of earth does not (is not destructive of wetlands)." *Id.*

The District of Columbia Circuit recently reversed a district court's decision where the lower court had rejected the EPA's view that section 402 of the CWA only covered the *addition* of pollutants. *National Wildlife Federation v. Gorsuch,* 224 U.S. App. D.C. 41, 693 F.2d 156 (D.C.Cir.1982). Like the district court here, the trial court in *National Wildlife* found that the EPA's "'overly literal and technical' construction was the 'more tortured' and ... less consonant with Congress' zero-discharge goal." 693 F.2d at 166. As an initial matter, the court of appeals held that the district court had failed to give enough deference to the EPA's construction of the Act. 693 F.2d at 166-67 (citing *EPA v. National Crushed Stone Association,* 449 U.S. 64, 83, 101 S.Ct. 295, 307, 66 L.Ed.2d 268 (1980)). Besides the fact that Congress had "given the EPA substantial discretion in administering" the CWA, the court of appeals noted that the agency's construction had been "made contemporaneously with the passage of the Act, and ha[d] been consistently adhered to since." 693 F.2d at 107. The court of appeals then went on to note that the district court had "paid too much attention to the broad stated purposes of the Act, and too little attention to the legislative history that must inform its view of those purpose." *Id.* at 171. Finally, noting that regulation by the states of dam-induced pollution was provided for in section 208, 33 U.S.C. §1218, the *National Wildlife* court concluded that the EPA's interpretation of the statute was reasonable and therefore it must be respected. *See also Missouri ex rel. Ashcroft v. Department of the Army,* 672 F.2d 1297, 1304 (8th Cir.1982) (district court did not err in holding that operation of dam did not result in discharge of pollutant as discharge requires "addition" of pollutant from "point source" and neither term applied to soil erosion or oxygen content of water).

A brief analysis of the district court's factual findings indicates that the dispute about whether the CWA covers the mere removal of vegetation is a false issue in this case. The EPA has explained on appeal that it agrees with the district court that "if vegetation or other materials are redeposited in the wetland, that activity is a discharge. [Their] point of disagreement with the district court was with its apparent conclusion that removal activities [were] covered by the Act even when nothing is redeposited on the land." Federal Defendants' Reply Brief at 2 n. 1. The district court's factual findings demonstrate that this is not a "mere removal" case. The court found that "during the clearing process small sloughs were filled in and larger ones partially filled thereby levelling the land." 473 F. Supp. at 536. The landowners' own witness admitted to burying logs in holes that he had dug, and the plaintiffs' witnesses testified that material that would not burn was buried. Since the landclearing activities involved the redeposit of materials, rather than their mere removal, we need not determine today whether mere removal may constitute a discharge under the CWA. Any suggestion made by the district court that the term "discharge" does cover removal is pure dicta.

The word "addition," as used in the definition of the term "discharge," may reasonably be understood to include "redeposit." As the district court recognized, this reading of the definition is consistent with both the purposes and legislative history of the statute. The CWA was designed to "restore and maintain the chemical, physical, and biological integrity of the Nation's waters," 33 U.S.C. §1251(a), and as discussed in Part II, the legislative history indicates that Congress recognized the importance of protecting wetlands as a means of reaching the statutory goals. *See, e.g., 3 Legislative History,* at 869 (remarks of Sen. Muskie) (quoted by the district court, 473 F. Supp. at 536). There is ample evidence in the record to support the district court's conclusion that the landowners' redepositing activities would significantly alter the character of the wetlands and limit the vital ecological functions served by the tract. Since we have concluded that the term "discharge" covers the redepositing of materials taken from the wetlands, we hold that the district court correctly decided that the landclearing activities on the Lake Long Tract constituted a discharge within the meaning of the Act.

Similarly, we agree with the district court, the plaintiffs and the federal defendants that the material discharged in this case was "fill," if not "dredged," material and hence subject to the Corps' regulation under section 404, as long as the activities did not fall within the section 404(f) exemption. The term "fill material" is defined in the Corps' regulations as

> any material used for the primary purpose of replacing an aquatic area with dry land or of changing the bottom elevation of a waterbody. The term does not include any pollutant discharged into the water primarily to dispose of waste, as that activity is regulated under Section 402 of the Federal Water Pollution Control Act Amendments of 1972.

33 C.F.R. §323.2(m). The regulations define the "discharge of fill material" as

> the addition of fill material into waters of the United States. The term generally includes, without limitation, the following activities: Placement of fill that is necessary to the construction of any structure in a water of the United States; the building of any structure or impoundment requiring rock, sand, dirt, or other material for its construction; site-development fills for recreational, industrial, commercial, residential, and other uses; causeways or road fills; dams and dikes; artificial islands; property protection and/or reclamation devices such as rip-rap, groins, seawalls, breakwaters, and revetments; beach nourishment; levees; fill for structures such as sewage treatment facilities, intake and outfall pipes associated with power plants and subaqueous utility lines; and artificial reefs. The term does not include plowing, cultivating, seeding and harvesting for the production of food, fiber, and forest products.

33 C.F.R. §323.2(n).

As discussed above, the burying of the unburned material, as well as the discing, had the effect of filling in the sloughs on the tract and leveling the land. The landowners insist that any leveling was "incidental" to their clearing activities and therefore the material was not deposited for the "primary purpose" of changing the character of the land. The district court found, however, that there had been significant leveling. The plaintiffs' witnesses testified that sloughs that had contained rainwater in the past had been filled in; thus, the activities were "changing the bottom elevation of the waterbody." Certainly, the activities were designed to "replace the area with dry land." Accordingly, we hold that the district court correctly concluded that the landowners were discharging "fill material" into the wetlands.

The district court also found that removal of the vegetation constituted dredging. The regulations define "dredged material" as "material that is excavated or dredged from waters of the United States." 33 C.F.R. §323.2(k). The district court reasoned that since the vegetation was part of the wetlands, it was also part of the "waters of the United States;" therefore, removal of the vegetation constituted dredging.

The landowners emphasize that dredging is "excavation." They argue that the vegetation is a wetland indicator, not a part of the wetland itself; therefore, the removal of the vegetation from the surface of the wetland is not "dredging." The federal defendants agree with the landowners that the removal of vegetation from above ground is not dredging, but they do not view this as a crucial issue in this case because they agree with the district court that the landowners were discharging "fill material." Federal Defendants' Brief at 19 n. 17. We note that there was testimony that the landowners' activities included the digging of ditches and holes, which would constitute "dredging" even under the landowners' interpretation of the regulation. Like the federal defendants, however, we do not believe that a decision whether there was a discharge of dredged material is necessary here, since we have concluded that there was a discharge of fill material.

C. STATUTORY EXEMPTIONS

Finally, the private defendants argue that their activities are normal farming activities exempt under section 404(f) of the Act. 33 U.S.C. §1344(f) (Supp. V 1981). Section 404(f)(1) exempts from the permit requirements:

> (f)(1) Except as provided in paragraph (2) of this subsection, the discharge of dredged or fill material—
>
> > (A) from normal farming, silviculture, and ranching activities such as plowing, seeding, cultivating, minor drainage, harvesting for the production of food, fiber, and forest products, or upland soil and water conservation practices.

33 U.S.C. §1344(f)(1)(A). The Corps' regulations further implement this limitation by excluding "plowing, cultivating, feeding and harvesting for the production of food, fiber, and forest products" while the private defendants' landclearing activities are not those specified in the Act, the defendants insist that the activities are nonetheless "normal" farming practices that should fall within the exemption.

The district court believed that the section 404(f)(1) exemptions were limited to "ongoing" agricultural activities. It reasoned that the word "'normal' connote[d] an established and continuing activity," and that the activities set out as examples in section 404(f)(1)(A) were the kinds of activities that would "only occur on a continuing basis as part of an ongoing farming or forestry operation." *Avoyelles I,* 473 F. Supp. at 535. Because "no farming operation was or could have been contemplated [on the Lake Long Tract] until after the acreage had been cleared," the district court concluded that the activities in this case were not "normal farming activities." *Id.* It added that this conclusion was "buttressed" by the fact that "section 404(f)(2) specifically takes away the exemption for activities that involve changing the use of the land." *Id.* Since we agree with the district court that section 404(f)(2) precludes applying the "normal farming activities" exemption in this case, we affirm the district court's decision on that basis.

Section 404(f)(2) takes away at least some of the exemptions arguably provided by section 404(f)(1):

> (2) Any discharge of dredged or fill material into the navigable waters incidental to any activity having as its purpose bringing an area of the navigable waters into a use to which it was not previously subject, where the flow or circulation of navigable waters may be impaired or the reach of such waters be reduced, shall be required to have a permit under this section.

33 U.S.C. §1344(f)(2). Read together, the two parts of section 404(f) provide a narrow exemption for agricultural and silvicultural activities that have little or no adverse effect on the nation's waters. This is precisely what Congress intended in enacting the amendment. During the Senate debates on the 1977 amendments, Senator Muskie, one of the primary sponsors of the CWA, explained:

> New subsection 404(f) provides that Federal permits will not be required for those narrowly defined activities that cause little or no adverse effects either individually or cumulatively. While it is understood that some of these activities may necessarily result in incidental filling and minor harm to aquatic resources, the exemptions do not apply to discharges that convert extensive areas of water into dry land or impede circulation or reduce the reach or size of the water body.

3 Legislative History, at 474. As the district court opinion ably demonstrates, the purpose and effect of the landclearing activities on the Lake Long Tract was to bring "an area of the navigable waters into a use to which it was not previously subject." 33 U.S.C. §1344(f)(2). All of the vegetation was cut down, the land leveled, and at least one ditch dug to increase drainage so that the property could be *changed* from a forest to a soybean field. These changes can hardly be viewed as having a minimal adverse effect on the wetlands.[46] Accordingly, we hold that the district court was correct in concluding that the landclearing activities in this case were not exempt farming activities under section 404(f)(1).

Since, as we have observed, additional litigation could ensue from the Corps' section 404 permit determinations, however, a word of caution seems appropriate. Our partial affirmance of the district court's decisions on permanent injunction is based upon the same total activities approach used by the district court. That court did not make a tract-by-tract determination of what precise activities were observed in each area of the lands involved, nor does the district court's opinion disclose the precise location of the lands previously cleared, on which permits are required only for construction of dikes, levees or major drainage projects. If a section 404 permit application is filed on any part of the lands covered by the district court's injunction, the Corps should be free to apply its expertise to that permit determination without any constraint from the district court's injunctive determinations except those we have expressly affirmed, *i.e.*, (1) that the bulldozers and backhoes are "point sources" within the meaning of the CWA; (2) that the filling in of the sloughs and leveling of the land resulted in the redepositing of fill material into the waters of the United States and was therefore a "discharge of a pollutant;" and (3) that the landclearing activities observed on the land thus far were not exempt from the Corps' section 404 permit requirements because those activities constituted a change in use of the wetlands....

V CONCLUSION

(1) that the bulldozers and backhoes were "point sources" within the meaning of the Clean Water Act;

(2) that in filling in the sloughs and leveling the land, the landowners were redepositing fill material into waters of the United States, and that therefore, these activities constituted a "discharge of a pollutant";

(3) that the landclearing activities were not exempt from the Corps' permit requirements under section 404(f)(1) of the CWA because those activities constituted a change in use of wetlands under section 404(f)(2).

Accordingly, we affirm the district court's judgment that these landclearing activities may not be carried out without a section 404 dredge-and-fill permit; however, we note that should a section 404 permit application be filed, the Corps will be free to apply its expertise to that permit determination without any constraint from the district court's injunctive determinations except those we have expressly affirmed.

AFFIRMED in part and REVERSED in part. ...

See also *National Min. Ass'n. v. U.S. Army Corps of Engineers*, 145 F.3d 1399 (C.A.D.C. 1998) ("A requirement that all pollutants must come from outside sources would effectively remove the dredge-and-fill provisions from the statute.... We only hold that by asserting jurisdiction over '*any* redeposit,' including incidental fall back, the *Tulloch* Rule outruns the Corps's statutory authority. Since the [Clean Water] Act sets out no bright line between incidental fallback on the one hand and regulable redeposits on the other, a reasoned attempt by the agencies to draw such a line would merit considerable deference."); *Save Our Wetlands v. Sands*, 711 F.2d 634 (5th Cir. 1983); Regulatory Guidance Letter 90–5, *Landclearing Activities Subject to Section 404 Jurisdiction*, July 18, 1990.

In May 1999, the regulatory definition of a "discharge of dredged material" was amended. Now the definition reads "the addition of dredged material into, including any redeposit of dredged material *other than incidental fallback* within, the waters of the United States including, but not limited to, the addition of dredged material to a specified disposal site, the runoff or overflow from a contained land or water disposal area, and any addition, including redeposit *other than incidental fall back*, of dredged material, including excavated material, into waters of the United States which is incidental to any activity, including mechanized landclearing, ditching, channelization, or other excavation." 33 C.F.R. §323.3(d). (Emphasis added.)

Specifically excluded from this definition are discharges of pollutants into waters of the United States resulting from the onshore subsequent processing of dredged materials that is extracted for any commercial use (other than fill). These discharges are subject to §402 of the Clean Water Act even though the extraction and deposit of such material may require a permit under §404. Also excluded from the definition of a "discharge of dredged material" are activities that involve only the cutting or removing of vegetation above the ground (*e.g.*, mowing, rotary cutting, and chainsawing) where the activity neither substantially disturbs the root system, nor involves mechanized pushing, dragging, or other similar activities that redeposit excavated soil material. *Id.* "Incidental fallback" is now specifically excluded from the definition of a "discharge of dredged material". *Id.* But be aware that, in the case of pile driving, the Corps will assert jurisdiction over pilings on a site-specific basis when they are placed so close together that they effectively replace an aquatic area with dry land or change the bottom elevation of the waterbody, especially if they are placed so close together as to encourage sedimentation. Regulatory Guidance Letter 90-8, *Applicability of Section 404 to Pilings*, December 14, 1990.

"Fill material" is now defined as "any material used for the primary purpose of replacing an aquatic area with dry land or of changing the bottom elevation of a waterbody" but does not include "any pollutant discharged into water primarily to dispose of waste, as that activity is regulated under §402 of the Clean Water Act. 33 C.F.R. §323.2(e). The definition of a "discharge of fill material" is "the addition of fill material into waters of the United States … [including] without limitation, the following activities: [p]lacement of fill that is necessary for the construction of any structure in a water of the United States; the building of any structure or impoundment requiring rock, sand, dirt, or other material for its construction; site-development fills for recreational, industrial, commercial, residential, and other uses; causeways or road fills; dams and dikes; artificial islands; property protection and/or reclamation devices such as riprap, groins, seawalls, breakwaters, and revetments; beach nourishment; levees; fill for structures such as sewage treatment facilities, intake and outfall pipes associated with power plants and subaqueous utility lines; and artificial reefs … [but] does not include plowing, cultivating, seeding and harvesting for the production of food, fiber, and forest products." 33 C.F.R. §323.2(f).

The definition of "point source" is "any discernible, confined, and discrete conveyance, including but not limited to any pipe, ditch, channel, tunnel, conduit, well, discrete fissure, container, rolling stock, concentrated animal feeding operation, or vessel or other floating craft, from which pollutants may be discharged" (but not agricultural stormwater discharges and return flows from irrigated agriculture). 33 U.S.C. §1362(14). It has evoked some controversy. Even the exclusion of agricultural stormwater discharges is subject to doubt given new knowledge of the source of nitrates in confined lakes and bays. Stormwater drainage has traditionally been considered a "non-point source," however, if fill material is placed in such a manner as to increase the likelihood than rainwater will carry the fill into a wetland, then jurisdiction has been asserted successfully. *Sierra Club v. Abston Construction Co.*, 620 F.2d 41 (5th Cir. Ala. 1980). Such other unprohibited activities might include the dredging activity itself (so long as there is no discharge of the excavated material). But see the following case:

SALT POND ASSOCIATES v. UNITED STATES ARMY CORPS OF ENGINEERS

815 F. Supp. 766 D.Del. 1993)

I. BACKGROUND

This dispute stems from Plaintiff's efforts to develop a piece of land for resale as waterfront lots. On November 29, 1988, the Plaintiff paid 5.5 million dollars for property located along the Town of Bethany Beach known as the Salt Pond property.... In an effort to ensure that any and all federal, environmental wetlands requirements were being satisfied under the Clean Water Act (hereinafter "CWA") and other environmental protection laws,... the Plaintiff ("Salt Pond") apparently engaged in extensive consultation with the United States Army Corp of Engineers ("the Government"), as well as their own environmental experts.... However, despite efforts by both sides to protect the "developing" interests of Salt Pond and the "environmental" interests that the Government is legally required to protect, irreconcilable disputes have arisen between the parties. These disputes, leading to Plaintiff's request to this Court for relief, center around the breadth of the Government's regulatory jurisdiction under the circumstances presented by this case as well as the allegedly adverse impact this land development will have on the environment.

On January 25, 1989, the Plaintiff submitted to the Government a wetlands delineation report requesting verification by the Government of its proposed section 404 wetlands delineation.... On April 4, 1991, after Plaintiff had spent over two years towards the development of the property, the Government informed the Plaintiff that a 12-acre area of the total land was in fact under the jurisdictional control of the Government. *Id.* On August 12, 1991, during an on-site inspection by the Government's investigators, the Government determined that ten ponds (hereinafter "the ponds") had been excavated in wetlands by the Plaintiff and that the Plaintiff had engaged in regulated land clearing in wetlands....

On October 5, 1991, the Government issued a Cease and Desist letter which required the Plaintiff to discontinue any and all development of the land because of numerous environmental violations discovered during the latest on-site investigation by the Government.... As a follow-up to that order, the Government directed the Plaintiff to apply for an "after-the-fact" permit ... for work already undertaken and work still to be undertaken in connection with the development of the Salt Pond property.... After significant correspondence regarding the appropriate procedural mechanisms, Salt Pond submitted to this after-the-fact permit process under full reservation of its rights in the hope that any and all environmental violations could be remedied so that the development of the land could proceed to completion.... Plaintiff further implored the Government to sever from the permit application consideration of Plaintiff's application for a water and sewer utility crossing permit (hereinafter "the Loop canal permit") pleading that the issuance of this permit under Section 10 of the Rivers and Harbors Act (hereinafter "RHA") was completely unrelated to matters pertaining to section 404 wetlands jurisdiction and the excavation of the ponds. The Government by informing the Plaintiff that its request for the Loop Canal permit would only be processed in conjunction with the required "after-the-fact" permit.... After giving public notice of Salt Pond's permit application on March 25, 1992, and receiving extensive commentary on the project from environmental agencies and individual environmentalists, the Government ultimately denied Salt Pond's application on September 24, 1992, finding the project in its entirety "contrary to the general public interest." ... The Government offered the Plaintiff an opportunity to receive an alternative permit which would include the Loop Canal permit if Salt Pond satisfied 31 "special conditions." ... The Government indicated that if this alternative permit was not accepted by the Plaintiff, then Plaintiff would have 60 days in which to initiate action for environmental restoration including the complete restoration of the excavated ponds.... Additionally, subsequent efforts by Salt Pond to have the Loop Canal permit determination severed from the denial of the after-the-fact permit decision were once again rejected by the Government....

It is the Government's "conditional" grant of the Loop Canal permit which is at the heart of the present dispute. Particularly significant are those special conditions associated with the Plaintiff's filling in or otherwise restoring the ponds and the fact that the Loop Canal permit decision was linked to and dependent upon the pond restoration conditions. Specifically, the Plaintiff posits that the Government's environmental findings fail to establish a "sufficient causal connection between the alleged violations and the mandated corrective action." ...

Plaintiff contends that the Government has no section 404 jurisdiction over the excavation of these ponds because excavation is an unregulated activity for which no Government permit is required and, that by conditioning the grant of the after-the-fact permit, including the Loop Canal permit request, upon these pond restoration conditions, the Government is attempting to improperly regulate the excavation of these ponds through some sort of "back-door" approach to the permit application process.... It is the Plaintiff's ultimate position that any and all conditions relating to the restoration or filling of the excavated ponds are improper and that the withholding of the Loop Canal permit pending the restoration of the ponds is an improper use of the Government's authority.

II. NATURE AND STAGE OF PROCEEDING

The Plaintiff has filed a motion for a preliminary injunction setting forth various demands for relief (hereinafter "Plaintiff's Motion").... Specifically, the Plaintiff seeks ... an injunction preventing the Government from taking any enforcement action for the alleged environmental violations....

Defendant opposes the motion and counters in a motion to dismiss (hereinafter "Defendant's Motion"),... that the Court is without proper jurisdiction to grant any of this relief sought by the Plaintiff. Specifically, the Government asserts that Salt Pond's demands that (1) this Court delete all the special conditions requiring restoration of the ponds to wetlands and (2) order the Government to issue the Loop Canal permit are beyond the scope of relief this Court may grant to the Plaintiff.... Additionally, the Government contends that Plaintiff's request for an injunction prohibiting the Government from taking any enforcement action is barred as impermissible "pre-enforcement" judicial review.... Lastly, the Government argues that even if the Court finds that it has jurisdiction to entertain Plaintiff's demands for relief, the Plaintiff has not satisfied its burdens under the appropriate standards upon which a preliminary injunction may be granted....

B. PRELIMINARY INJUNCTION

The conventional standards for the issuance of a preliminary injunction in this Circuit have recently been described as follows:

> A preliminary injunction is an "extraordinary remedy" which will be granted only if the moving party can demonstrate: (1) the reasonable probability of eventual success in the litigation and (2) that the movant will be irreparably injured *pendente lite* if relief is not granted. Moreover, while the burden rests upon the moving party to make these two requisite showings, the district court should take into account, when they are relevant, (3) the possibility of harm to interested persons from the grant or denial cafe the injunction, and (4) the public interest (citations omitted).

Chez Sez III Corp. v. Township of Union, 945 F.2d 628, 634 (3rd Cir. 1991), *cert. denied,* U.S. , 117 L.Ed. 2d 493, 112 S.Ct. 1265 (1992).

Additionally, in some instances, this Circuit has seemingly required that the moving party demonstrate a *strong probability* of success on the merits when seeking a stay of an administrative agency action in the form of a preliminary injunction as authorized by section 705. See *A.O. Smith Corp. v. FTC,* 530 F.2d 515, 525 (3rd Cir. 1976) (did movant make a strong showing that it is likely to prevail on the merits); *Commonwealth of Pennsylvania ex rel. Creamer v. United States Dep't of Agriculture,* 469 F.2d 1387, 1388 n.1 (3rd Cir. 1972) (same); *Penn Central Transp. Co.,* 457 F.2d 381 (3rd Cir. 1972) (same*); accord, Virginia Petroleum Jobbers Ass'n v. Fed. Power Comm'n,* 104 U.S. App. D.C. 106, 259 F.2d 921, 925 (D.C. Cir. 1958) (movant must make a "strong showing that it is likely to prevail on the merits of its case"). This potential tension is of no consequence here, however, because the Court finds that the Plaintiff meets both the "heightened" and "conventional" standards for the granting of a preliminary injunction.

1. PROBABILITY OF SUCCESS ON THE MERITS: POND RESTORATION AND THE AFTER-THE-FACT PERMIT

Plaintiff raises a number of arguments in order to support its "strong probability of success on the merits" position that the Government was without ample and statutory authority to require the Plaintiff to restore the ponds.... First, Plaintiff contends that under the statutory framework of the CWA and the regulations adopted under it, no permit is required for the excavation or dredging of a pond located in section 404 wetlands. Secondly, Plaintiff contends that the Government impermissibly relied on a Regulatory Guidance Letter (hereinafter "RGL") as the basis for requiring a permit for excavation. Lastly, the Plaintiff contends that the Government has improperly expanded its authority through a misapplication of a procedural regulation.... Plaintiff's arguments are compelling. Presently, the reach of the CWA extends only to the *discharge* of pollutants into navigable waters and not the excavation or dredging activities that occur in section 404 wetlands.... Furthermore, the current regulatory standards promulgated under the CWA support Plaintiff's position that pond excavation is not a "discharge of dredged material" subject to CWA Jurisdiction.... From both the statutory and regulatory framework, the Court easily concludes that absent some affirmative change from the legislature itself ... or a validly promulgated regulatory revision which observes all the necessary procedures required by law,... the Government was apparently without jurisdiction to require the Plaintiff to submit to the after-the-fact permit process for excavation activities and accordingly could not legally compel the Plaintiff to restore the excavated ponds.

The Government does not pretend to rely on the express language of the CWA or the regulatory standards cited by the Plaintiff as the source of its authority to require pond restoration in the case at bar. Rather, "in compelling Plaintiff to seek permit approval for the dredging or excavation of ponds in wetlands",... the Government deviates from the present legal standards indicating that RGL 90-5 provides the basis for requiring a permit for land clearing activities associated with the excavation or dredging that took place in the pond's area....

RGL 90-5 provides in pertinent part: "... It is our position that mechanized land clearing activities in jurisdictional wetlands result in a redeposition of soil that is subject to regulation under section 404...." ... The Government contends that under this provision it was indeed authorized to require that the Plaintiff apply for an after-the-fact permit for certain pond excavation activities in the first instance and then subsequently require the Plaintiff to restore the ponds when the permit application was denied.

While the Government's decision to adopt the policy put forth by 90-5 is arguably beneficial for the protection of the environment,... the Government's profound reliance on it in lieu of its own validly promulgated regulations is fatal to its after-the-fact permit decision here. *Accord, Frisby*, 755 F.2d at 1055 (failure of an agency to act in compliance with its own regulations is fatal to the action) (citation omitted). The Government has essentially adopted the substantive change in current policy called for by this RGL without observing the procedures required by law. *See* 5 U.S.C. §706 (2)(D). Those procedures require that when a rule is to be used by a governmental agency in a manner having the force of law, to have any effect, it must have been issued in accordance with the appropriate notice-and-comment requirements of section 553 of the APA....

Here, the record plainly demonstrates that the Government relied on RGL 90-5 without satisfying any of the requisite procedures. *See* 5 U.S.C. §553 (b-e) (notice, participation, comment period, advance publication and a right to petition for redress not satisfied);... In fact, the Government does not contend that it met any of these prerequisites. Rather, the Government seemingly claims that 90-5 was merely used for "guidance" as an "interpretive rule" or "general statement of policy" not subject to the notice and comment requirements of the APA.... *See* 5 U.S.C. §553(b)(3)(A) (exceptions).... The Plaintiff counters that the Government employed RGL 90-5 as a substantive legislative rule requiring the appropriate APA procedures.... The distinction between interpretive and substantive rules is best defined as follows:

> Interpretive rules are those which merely clarify existing law or regulations. They express the agency's intended course of action, its tentative view of the meaning of a particular statutory term, or internal house-keeping measures organizing agency activities,.... By contrast, substantive rules grant rights, impose obligations, or produce other significant effects on private interests ....

American Ambulance, 911 F.2d at 907 (citations omitted).... When a rule is "substantive" as compared to "interpretive", it must be issued by the Government agency pursuant to the notice-and-comment procedures of the APA. *Bailey v. Sullivan*, 885 F.2d 52, 62 (3rd Cir. 1989); *First State Bank of Hudson County v. United States*, 599 F.2d 558, 564 (3rd Cir. 1979), *cert. denied,* 444 U.S. 1013, 62 L. Ed. 2d 642, 100 S. Ct. 662 (1980); *Rosetti v. Sullivan,* 788 F. Supp. 1380, 1387 (E.D.Pa. 1992) (citing *Bailey* and *First State*).

There is little doubt that in this preliminary instance the Government used RGL 90-5 as a *substantive* rule having the force of law in that it modifies existing law or policy. In particular, this RGL alters existing rights by superimposing a permit requirement for activities that under the current statutory and regulatory framework (*see* 33 C.F.R. §323.2(d)) are not subject to CWA jurisdiction. *Accord, Tabb Lakes, Ltd. v. United States,* 715 F. Supp. 726 (E.D.Va. 1988) (court rejected Government's exercise of CWA Jurisdiction requiring developer to obtain a permit where Government exercised said jurisdiction via memorandum and not in accordance with the notice-and-procedure requirements of the APA), *aff'd,* 885 F.2d 866 (4th Cir. 1989).

Furthermore, because the Government's reliance on this rule imposes extreme additional obligations for Salt Pond and has significant effects on the private interests of the residents in the development ... the Government cannot rightfully claim that it is an interpretive rule that "merely clarifies existing law." *American Ambulance,* 911 F.2d at 907. Because this interim review of the record indicates that the Plaintiff would eventually succeed in proving that the Government did not comply with the notice-and-comment procedures of the APA, the Court finds that the Plaintiff would undoubtedly prove that the Government was not authorized in the first instance to employ 90-5 as a basis for requiring the Plaintiff to seek an after-the-fact permit for landscaping activities associated with the excavation or dredging of the ponds in wetlands. Furthermore, because no permit requirement can be imposed for such work, the Government cannot compel the plaintiff to restore the ponds.

Perhaps recognizing the patent impropriety of relying on 90-5 as the key ground to support the pond filling requirements of its permit decision, the Government has attempted to minimize its reliance on RGL 90-5,... by emphasizing a new-found theory of regulatory authority whereby the Government can apparently under a procedural regulation take whatever steps it deems necessary to protect the public interest.... In particular, the Government claims that pursuant to its duties to protect the overall public interest, to protect the particular values of wetlands and to apply the EPA's guidelines, it is empowered to include any and all "special conditions" as part of a permit decision for regulated activities over which it does have jurisdiction.... It indicates that in this instance "[its] authority arises from the fact there were extensive activities at the site which required a permit from the [Government]." ...

As a source of this "extensive activities special conditions" authority, the Government points to 33 C.F.R. §325.4(a), which provides that:

> District Engineers will add special conditions to the Department of the Army permits when such conditions are necessary to satisfy legal requirements or to otherwise satisfy the public interest requirement. *Permit conditions will directly relate to the impacts of the proposal, appropriate to the scope and degree of those impacts and reasonably enforceable.*

Id. (emphasis added).

In essence, the Government claims that under this regulation, even though Plaintiff is entitled to engage in the unregulated excavation of ponds by focusing on certain pond excavation and land clearing activities that it views as jurisdictional, it necessarily acquires CWA jurisdiction over pond excavation itself and, as a result, can require the Plaintiff to restore the ponds.

For numerous reasons, the court finds the Government's reliance on this regulation to be extremely unpersuasive. First, in issuing its Cease and Desist letter and subsequently requiring the Plaintiff to submit to an after-the-fact permit, the Government incorrectly presumed that it had statutory and regulatory jurisdiction over certain land clearing activities.... As has been demonstrated, this presumption of CWA jurisdiction is belied by any reasonable interpretation of the relevant statutes and regulations at issue here or the record presently before this Court....

Second, the Court concurs with the Plaintiff in that such an expansive reading of this regulation is manifestly inconsistent with the jurisdictional limits of the CWA's grant of authority for Government regulation of fill activities (and not excavation activities), as well as 33 C.F.R. §323.2(d), which provides that excavation of ponds is an unregulated activity.... To date, no Court has ever given this regulation such an extensive construction....

Lastly, the fact that the legislative and executive branches, as well as countless administrative agencies, are presently debating the issue of whether pond excavation and land clearing activities are to be considered regulated discharges under the CWA repudiates the Government's expansive view of this special conditions provision....

Accordingly, for all of the above stated reasons, the Court finds that the Plaintiff has demonstrated a strong probability that the exercise of CWA jurisdiction over pond excavation activities and the subsequent pond filling requirements associated with the Government's permit decision was arbitrary and capricious, in excess of the Governments statutory authority under the CWA, was issued without observance of the procedures required by law and, in toto, constituted an abuse of discretion. *See* 5 U.S.C. §§706(A), (C) and (D).... Therefore, as relates to the pond restoration requirements, the Court is satisfied that the Plaintiff has met the probability of success on the merits prong necessary for the issuance of a preliminary injunction.

2. PROBABILITY OF SUCCESS ON THE MERITS: LINKING THE CANAL PERMIT TO SECTION 404 WETLANDS ISSUES

In support of its motion for a preliminary injunction Plaintiff also raises the separate and distinct argument that the Government was without authority to mandate that the Loop Canal permit be part of an application for all other permit activities, nor was it authorized to require that issuance of that permit be conditioned upon pond restoration.... The Government counters that pursuant to its regulations, it was well within its authority to require that the Loop Canal permit request be included with all other activities in one application....

The Government relies on 33 C.F.R. §325.1(d)(2). That section provides in pertinent part:

> All activities which the applicant plans to undertake which are *reasonably related to the same project and for which a DA permit would be required* should be included in the same permit application. District engineers should reject, as incomplete, any permit application which fails to comply with this requirement. For example, a permit application for a marina will include dredging required for access as well as any fill associated with construction of the marina.

Id. (emphasis added).

Notwithstanding the impassioned arguments from the Plaintiff, ... the Court agrees with the theory espoused by the Government. The plain language of this provision suggests that all activities reasonably related to one project that require a permit should be included in one permit application. Here, the "project" is the housing development and all its concomitant and necessary incidental processes. It is beyond dispute that the request for the Loop Canal permit is "reasonably related" to the project. Indeed, the Plaintiff itself has consistently dramatized how important its issuance is for the viability of the development. Thus, the Government is authorized to require that the request for the Loop Canal permit be included with any other activities requiring a permit "reasonably related" to the housing development.

3. IRREPARABLE INJURY

Having found that the Plaintiff has demonstrated a probability of success regarding the Government's permit decision, the Court must assess whether plaintiff has demonstrated that, in the absence of preliminary relief, it will suffer irreparable harm. In support of its plea for injunctive relief the Plaintiff is essentially alleging that if a preliminary injunction is not issued staying the Government's requirement that the Plaintiff initiate pond restoration, it will suffer immediate and catastrophic economic consequences.

Where the moving party is asserting what amounts to be purely economic injury, that party must meet a stringent standard. *Drabbant Enterprises, Inc. v. Great Atlantic & Pacific Tea Company, Inc.,* 688 F. Supp. 1567, 1573 (D.Del. 1988). In particular, the moving party must demonstrate a clear showing of immediate irreparable harm and must show that the harm is peculiar, going beyond pure economic injuries which are generally compensable. *Id.*

Here, Plaintiff undoubtedly satisfies these standards. The immediate irreparable injury that Salt Pond is subject to if the Court does not stay the pond restoration requirements imposed by the Government extends well beyond the significant cost of actually restoring the ponds. *Cf. A.O. Smith*, 530 F.2d at 527 (mere economic burden resulting from government agency's regulation not sufficient to establish irreparable injury). Rather, as a result of the Government's probably improper permit decision, the irreparable injury that will be suffered in the absence of this stay is the immediate termination of the development project and an *overall loss* of millions of dollars to the Plaintiff.... In particular, the Court is satisfied that unless Salt Pond can indicate to lot owners, home owners, prospective buyers and builders and lending institutions that the ponds need not be filled "there is a strong probability that the development project will fail and the Partnership will lose millions of dollars." *Id.* at 198....

Numerous courts have held that this kind of showing satisfies the "irreparable injury" element of a preliminary injunction application. *See, e.g., Stephen D. Devito, Trucking Inc. v. RISWMC*, 770 F. Supp. 775, 778 (D.R.I.) (irreparable injury shown and preliminary injunction granted where a government action effectively precluded the party from conducting its primary business activity and where the potential economic loss was so great as to threaten the very existence of the moving party's business), *aff'd*, 947 F.2d 1004 (per curium) (1st Cir. 1991); *Baltimore and Ohio R. Co. v. Oberly*, 606 F. Supp. 1340, 1347-49 (D.Del. 1985) (in reliance on the affidavit of the moving party's general manager, court issued preliminary injunction finding that irreparable injury existed where Plaintiff would likely have to shut down if forced to comply with the State's regulation and was faced with the heavy loss of revenue and their competitive position in a specific market); *Northern Natural Gas v. U.S. Dept. of Energy*, 464 F. Supp. 1145, 1155-58 (D.Del. 1979) (millions of dollars in overall loss to the Plaintiff held sufficient to constitute irreparable injury, *even though plaintiff's solvency not threatened)*.

Furthermore, the Court finds Plaintiff's injuries "peculiar" because, in the absence of this preliminary relief, the Plaintiff is without a viable means of compensation for its business related economic injuries. First, Plaintiff's irreparable injuries are not merely a loss of profits for which they can recover through other business ventures. *Cf. Instant Air Freight Co. v. CF Air Freight Inc.*, 882 F.2d 797, 802 (3rd Cir. 1989) (no showing of irreparable injury where moving party was free to secure other business); *Norfolk Southern Corp. v. Oberly*, 594 F. Supp. 514, 520-21 (D.Del. 1984) (loss of profits not recoverable immediately but potentially recoverable by the moving party after a hearing on the merits are not "peculiar" and thus do not constitute a showing of irreparable injury by the moving party). Plaintiff is a single enterprise entity, ... who as indicated faces complete devastation if the pond restoration requirements are not stayed. Moreover, as Plaintiff aptly points out, ... unlike a dispute between private commercial litigants, the Plaintiff has no means of recovering for its economic damages because the Government retains sovereign immunity for its conduct. Thus, Plaintiff has demonstrated that the alleged injuries it will suffer if a preliminary injunction does not issue are "peculiar" in that they are not generally compensable. *Accord, Drabbant*, 688 F. Supp. at 1574. As a result, the Plaintiff has made the requisite showing of irreparable injury in the absence of injunctive relief.

4. HARMS TO INTERESTED PARTIES AND THE PUBLIC INTEREST

In the absence of injunctive relief, the Court also finds that the harm to interested persons such as the lot owners far outweighs any harm to either party if the injunction is issued. In this consideration, the Court weighs heavily the fact that without the injunction staying the requirement that the Plaintiff restore the ponds, Plaintiff would likely be subject to a multiplicity of lawsuits from residents of the development who purchased their lots with the expectation of receiving waterfront property.... Also, in the absence of this injunction, the development will likely collapse, leaving many of the owners without permanent water and utility service. Such a scenario would devastate those who have purchased lots because, without these vital services being offered on a permanent basis, their purchases would effectively be rendered meaningless. On the contrary, the public interest is not harmed by delaying this pond restoration as the ponds have already been excavated and there exists no continuing damage to the environment. Thus, the Court finds that these equitable concerns favor issuing the injunction.

5. PRELIMINARY INJUNCTION CONCLUSIONS

For the reasons contained herein, the Court finds that the standards for a preliminary injunction have been met in this case. Accordingly, pending a full review of the administrative record prepared in connection with the Government's after-the-fact permit process and decision, the Government action requiring the Plaintiff to completely restore the ponds is postponed. In issuing the preliminary injunction, the Court also declares that (1) the Government was probably without CWA jurisdiction to require an after-the-fact permit for pond excavation activities in the first place and (2) that it was probably without CWA authority to require the restoration of the ponds. Further, the Court cautions that to the extent that the Plaintiff has engaged in activities over which the Government may in fact exercise CWA jurisdiction, the Plaintiff's Loop Canal permit request is properly included as part of one permit application....

V. SUMMARY

The Government's requirement that the Plaintiff initiate plans to restore the ponds is postponed pending a full review of the administrative record. The Court dismisses the Plaintiff's requests that this Court enjoin the Government from future enforcement actions and that the Court direct the Government to issue Plaintiff the Loop Canal permit on the grounds that they are beyond the scope of relief available to the Plaintiff at this stage of the proceedings.

Vegetation destruction, even if no mechanized equipment is used in wetlands, also may require a permit. *Save Our Wetlands, Inc. v. Sands*, 711 F.2d 634 (5th Cir. 1983). See also 52 ALR Fed. 788, Supp. §5.

Drainage activities may trigger the permit requirement. A drained area may still be considered a wetland because of the "normal circumstances" provision of the definition, i.e., if the area under normal circumstances is a wetland, then any drainage will not destroy jurisdiction over it. A further caution remains that discharges of fill material into drained wetlands may require a §404 permit. The Corps will look to the effect on the wetland of the fill so as to exclude minor discharges as part of a dredging operation, which do not necessarily affect a wetland, and discharges, no matter how small, which do affect the wetland. *Save Our Community v. U.S.*

Environmental Protection Agency, 971 F.2d 1155 (5th Cir. Tex. 1992); *Orleans Audubon Society v. Lee*, 742 F.2d 901 (5th Cir. La. 1984), *reh'g. denied en banc*, 750 F.2d 69 (5th Cir. La. 1984).

Pile driving, if it goes too far, may trigger the permit requirement.. The Corps will assert §404 jurisdiction over pilings on a site-specific basis when they are placed so close together that they effectively replace "an aquatic area with dry land or [change] the bottom elevation of the waterbody. Pilings may have this function or effect when they are placed so as to facilitate sedimentation, or are placed so densely that they in effect displace a substantial percentage of the water in the project area." Regulatory Guidance Letter, *Applicability of Section 404 to Pilings*, No. 90-8.

Initially there was some disagreement between the Corps and the Environmental Protection Agency over what constituted a discharge of "fill material" as defined in the Corps' Clean Water Act regulations at 33 C.F.R. §323.2(k). The Corps took the position that its jurisdiction extended over discharges of fill material which are intended to replace an aquatic area or change the bottom elevation of a water body. The Environmental Protection Agency took the position that all solid waste discharges, regardless of their intent or effect, were covered by §404.

To resolve their conflict, the Corps and the Environmental Protection Agency entered into a "*Memorandum of Agreement ... Concerning Regulation of Discharges of Solid Waste Under the Clean Water Act*." 51 Fed.Reg. 8871 (March 14, 1986). Under the *Memorandum*, a discharge will be considered "fill material," and thus subject to Corps jurisdiction, if (1) "[t]he discharge has as its primary purpose or has as one principle purpose of multi-purposes to replace a portion of the waters of the United States with dry land or to raise the bottom elevation," or (2) "[t]he discharge results from activities such as road construction or other activities where the material to be discharged is generally identified with construction-type activities," or (3) "[a] principal effect of the discharge is physical loss or physical modification of waters of the United States, including smothering of aquatic life or habitat," or (4) "[t]he discharge is heterogeneous in nature and of the type normally associated with sanitary landfill discharges." The Environmental Protection Agency retained jurisdiction over a discharge "in a liquid, semi-liquid, or suspended form or if it is a discharge of solid material of a homogeneous nature normally associated with single industry wastes ... including placer mining wastes, phosphate mining wastes, titanium mining wastes, sand and gravel wastes, fly ash, and drilling muds." *Id.*

CHAPTER 11

GENERAL PERMITS

Section 404(e) of the Clean Water Act authorizes the Corps "after notice and opportunity for public hearing" to issue "general permits on a state, regional, or nationwide basis for any category of activities involving discharges of dredged or fill material if (the Corps) determines that such activities in such category are (1) similar in nature and similar in their impact on water quality and the aquatic environment; (2) will cause only minimal cumulative adverse effects when performed separately; and, (3) will have only minimal cumulative adverse effect on water quality and the aquatic environment." 33 U.S.C. §1344(e)(1). See also 40 C.F.R. §230.7(a).

ABENAKI NATION v. HUGHES

805 F. Supp. 234 (D.Vt. 1992)

I. INTRODUCTION

Plaintiffs moved for a temporary restraining order and preliminary injunction to enjoin defendants from all actions associated with raising the Spillway elevation of the Orman Croft Generating Station, a hydroelectric facility in Highgate, Vermont. The parties agreed to a hearing on the merits and plaintiffs withdrew their temporary restraining order in early September, 1992. The parties understood and agreed that a decision on the merits would obviate the need for a preliminary injunction.

The litigation stems from the authorization granted to the Village of Swanton (hereafter "the Village") to raise the Spillway elevation of the Orman Croft Generating Station (hereafter "the Project") by the Army Corps of Engineers (hereafter "the Corps") on July 15, 1992. Pursuant to Section 404 of the Federal Water Pollution Control Act, 33 U.S.C. §1344(e), this authorization was granted under a general permit, General Permit 38, first issued by the Corps in 1982 and reissued in 1987.

Plaintiffs claim that General Permit 38 (hereafter "GP 38") is invalid because of procedural violations. Even if valid, plaintiffs claim that the Project is not eligible for authorization under GP 38. Plaintiffs also allege that the authorization granted by the Corps under GP 38 violates a variety of federal statutes, specifically (1) The National Environmental Policy Act, 42 U.S.C. §§4321-4370 (1992) (hereafter "NEPA"); (2) the federal Water Pollution Control Act, 33 U.S.C. §§1251-1387 (1992) (popularly known as the Clean Water Act) (hereafter "CWA"); (3) the National Historic Preservation Act, 16 U.S.C. §470 (1992) (hereafter "NHPA"); and (4) the Native American Graves Protection and Repatriation Act 25 U.S.C. §§3001-3013 (1992) (hereafter "NAGPRA"). For these reasons plaintiffs claim that the authorization by the Corps is void and that until the Project is properly permitted all activity connected with it must cease.

II. BACKGROUND

The Village has operated a hydroelectric facility at Highgate Falls since 1928. It has upgraded the facility twice before, in 1930 and 1954, and in 1979 decided to upgrade it again.

In order to proceed with this proposed Project, the Village was required to apply for a license from the Federal Energy Regulatory Commission (hereafter "FERC") pursuant to the Federal Power Act, 16 U.S.C. §§791-828 (1992). It also needed a permit from the Corps for the discharge of dredged or fill material into the Mississquoi River pursuant to the Corps' responsibilities under the CWA, 33 U.S.C. §1344.

... For its part, the Corps may issue individual permits on a project by project basis (otherwise known as individual §404 permits) or general permits, if activities involved "will cause only minimal adverse environmental effects when performed separately and will have only minimal cumulative adverse effects on the environment," on a State, regional or nationwide basis. 33 U.S.C. §1344(e)(1).

On October 22, 1982 the Corps issued GP 38 ... for certain hydroelectric development activities in the New England region. The public notice of the proposed GP 38 declared that

> To avoid duplicating the regulatory control exercised by the Federal Energy Regulatory Commission (FERC) for hydropower development or expansion projects which cause minimal or no adverse environmental effects, the New England Division of the US Army Corps of Engineers proposes to issue a general permit that, subject to certain conditions, would eliminate the need for Corps of Engineers approval of fills associated with such work at existing dams or at new or existing run-of-river projects throughout New England....

GP 38 was subject to six Special Conditions ("SC") and 24 General Conditions.... The second SC states that the "activity which includes the discharge must be licensed or formally exempted by the [FERC]. No discharge is allowed unless and until the [FERC] license or formal exemption, as well as all other required local, State and Federal licenses and permits have been obtained." ...

In short, GP 38 provided for FERC to be the lead agency in regulating hydroelectric projects in the New England Region and ensuring that they complied with applicable regulations, including NEPA and NHPA. While the Corps was still responsible for ensuring compliance with the dictates of the CWA, GP 38 called for the Corps to utilize the information gathered by the FERC and issue authorization if the discharge "caused minimal or no adverse environmental effects." If FERC concluded that there would be more than minimal adverse effects, or if the Corps determined on its own that a proposed action was outside the realm of GP 38, permit applicants would not be eligible for authorization under GP 38 and would have to proceed with an individual §404 permit application.

Some time after the Corps issued GP 38 the Village commenced efforts to obtain the necessary permits for the envisioned improvements to the Highgate facility. Pursuant to the FPA and NEPA, the FERC conducted an Environmental Assessment ("EA") of the Project and made a Finding of No Significant Impact ("FONSI").... Specifically it found that the project would result in only "short-term minor [environmental] impacts" and concluded that "issuance of a license, as conditioned herein, for the project will not constitute a major Federal action significantly affecting the quality of the human environment." ...

Prior to issuance of the FERC license, the Corps determined that the project was eligible under GP 38 and issued the authorization to proceed on January 24, 1984. The Corps based its determination on the Village's application for a permit, its FERC license application and the EA conducted by FERC.... On May 24, 1984 FERC issued a license for the Project....

In 1987 GP 38 was reissued for another five years with several changes and amendments after public notice was given ... and a supplement to the 1982 Statement of Findings was made. (AR 188). In the meantime, work on the Project remained in the initial stages. On January 22, 1990, the Village filed a request with FERC for the amendment of its license, proposing to reduce the overall height of the project. In considering this request, FERC found that the amended project would "reduce the adverse effects of the project, most significantly those impacts on cultural resources and wetlands." ... On March 14, 1991, FERC issued an order amending the original license to conform with the Village's proposed changes....

On September 5, 1991, the Village submitted a request to the Corps for authorization under GP 38 for the reduced Project. The Village initially believed that the authorization granted by the Corps in 1984 was suitable ground to grant authorization in 1991.... In informal meetings and discussions as early as mid-September 1991 ... and as late as February, 1992,... Corps personnel from the New England Division informed the Village that the Project was not eligible for authorization under GP 38 and that an individual §404 permit would be necessary. This conclusion was based upon an expressed concern regarding the adverse impact of the Project on wetlands and the inadequacy of proposed mitigation plans.

Corps Headquarters agreed with the New England Division that an individual §404 permit would be required if mitigation plans were not adequate but also stated that a conditioned general permit assuring adequate mitigation would allow authorization under GP 38.... It advised the New England Division that adequate mitigation could be considered to remain below the minimal impact threshold for the general permit just as under NEPA it can be considered to reach a finding of no significant impact....

After consultation with the Vermont state archeologist concerning historical resources at the mitigation sites,... the Village,... and Corps Headquarters,... the Corps issued a conditioned authorization under GP 38 on July 15, 1992.... This conditioned authorization imposed 23 Special Conditions ("SC") which the Corps believes ensures that the Project will cause minimal or no adverse impact making it eligible for authorization under GP 38. It is this authorization to which plaintiffs object.

III. DISCUSSION

A. BASIS OF REVIEW

1. JURISDICTION

Plaintiffs allege violations of the Administrative Procedure Act, 5 U.S.C. §§500-590 (1992) (hereafter "APA"), NEPA, CWA, NHPA and NAGPRA. The court has jurisdiction under 28 U.S.C. §1331 to hear these claims.

2. STANDARD OF REVIEW

Courts traditionally afford the decisions of administrative agencies due deference in reviewing agency action. *See, Citizens to Preserve Overton Park v. Volpe*, 401 U.S. 402, 415, 28 L.Ed. 2d 136, 91 S.Ct. 814 (1971).

The Second Circuit has stated the appropriate standard of review when reviewing actions and decisions by the Corps to issue permits. "In reviewing the validity of a decision by the Corps to issue a permit under the [CWA], a court should, as provided by the [APA], uphold the decision unless it is 'arbitrary, capricious, an abuse of discretion, or otherwise not in accordance with law.'" *Sierra Club v. United States Army Corps of Eng.*, 701 F.2d 1011, 1032 (2d Cir. 1983) (quoting 5 U.S.C. §706(2)(A)). In defining arbitrary and capricious, the Second Circuit has stated that

An agency's decision is held to be arbitrary and capricious when it relies on factors Congress did not want considered, or utterly fails to analyze an important aspect of the problem, or offers an explanation contrary to the evidence before it, or its explanation ... is so implausible that it cannot be ascribed to differing views or agency expertise. *Sierra Club v. United States Army Corps of Eng.*, 772 F.2d 1043, 1051 (2d Cir. 1985).

Accordingly, any review of the decision by the Corps to authorize the Project under GP 38 is limited to the arbitrary and capricious standard as established by statute and defined by relevant case law.

B. PLAINTIFFS' CLAIMS

1. CLAIM I—GENERAL PERMIT 38 IS INVALID

Plaintiffs assert that General Permit 38, first issued in 1982 and reissued in 1987, is invalid because it fails to comply with the requirements of the APA, NEPA and the Corps' own regulations.

A. APA

Plaintiffs claim that GP 38 is a "rule" under the APA because it is an agency statement of general applicability designed to implement the CWA. As a "rule" the APA requires it to be published in the Federal Register. 5 U.S.C. §553. Plaintiffs claim that because GP 38 is a rule and the Corps failed to publish it in the Federal Register, it is invalid and any authorization stemming from it is void.

While facially attractive, this claim is unsupported by both the APA and case law. The APA defines "rule" as the "whole or part of an agency statement of general or particular applicability and future effect designed to implement law." 5 U.S.C. §551(4). It defines adjudication as the "agency process for formulation of an order." 5 U.S.C. §551(7). An order is defined in turn as "the whole or part of a final disposition, whether affirmative, negative, injunctive or declaratory in form, of an agency in a matter other than rule making but including licensing." 5 U.S.C. §551(6). License is defined to "include the whole or part of an agency permit...." 5 U.S.C. §551(8).

From these definitions a general permit is more appropriately classified as an adjudication rather than a rule. Such a conclusion was reached in *National Wildlife Federation v. Marsh,* 568 F. Supp. 985, 992 n.12 (D.C. 1983), which stated that a "permit decision-making proceeding is clearly adjudication rather than rule making." As an "adjudication" and not a "rule," publication of GP 38 in the Federal Register was unnecessary. GP 38 was not issued in violation of the APA.

B. NEPA

Plaintiffs claim that the issuance of GP 38 was a major federal action significantly affecting the environment and that prior to issuing GP 38 the Corps prepared neither an EIS nor an EA and therefore violated the dictates of NEPA.

NEPA requires that

> All agencies of the Federal Government shall—...
>
> (C) include in every recommendation or report on proposals for legislation and other major Federal actions significantly affecting the quality of the human environment, a detailed statement by the responsible official on —
>
> > (i) the environmental impact of the proposed action,
> >
> > (ii) any adverse environmental effects which cannot be avoided should the proposal be implemented,
> >
> > (iii) alternatives to the proposed action....

42 U.S.C. §4332(2)(C)(i), (ii) and (iii) (1992).

The Council on Environmental Quality ("CEQ") is responsible for interpreting and administering NEPA. 42 U.S.C. §§4342–44. The regulations promulgated by the CEQ are found in 40 C.F.R. §§1500–1517 The regulations establish that this "detailed statement," known as an environmental impact study ("EIS"), is unnecessary if an agency finds through an environment assessment ("EA") that a major federal action will not have a significant impact on the quality of human life, generally known as a finding of no significant impact ("FONSI"). 33 C.F.R. §1501.4(a)(2). The CEQ defined an EA at §1508.9, but specifically left the procedures by which an EA is prepared to the individual agencies. §1501.3. The Corps has promulgated such procedures and they are found at 33 C.F.R. part 230.

The Corps procedures for implementing NEPA state that "most permits will normally require only an EA." 33 C.F.R. §230.7(a). The procedures define an EA as a "brief document which provides sufficient information to a [Corps] district commander on potential environmental effects of the proposed action, and, if appropriate, its alternatives for determining whether to prepare an EIS or a FONSI." §230.10(a). No specific format is required, §230.10(b), but an EA should include a brief discussion of the need for the proposed action, the environmental impacts of the proposed action and a list of agencies and interested parties consulted.

As to the initial issuance of GP 38, plaintiffs' claim is factually incorrect. The administrative record contains an EA conducted by the Corps in 1982 prior to the issuance of GP 38 ... as well as a statement of findings.... Both of these documents satisfy the procedural requirements of NEPA as set out in 33 C.F.R. §325.2(a)(4) and (6). The FONSI reached by the Corps in 1982 rendered the requirement for an EIS unnecessary.

Plaintiffs assert that the 1987 version of GP 38 was a new permit and at the least a new EA should have been conducted by the Corps. It is not clear from the statute or the regulations whether reissuing GP 38 in 1987 served to make it a "new" general permit and hence subject to a new round of scrutiny under NEPA or whether reissuing only required an updated statement of findings. The Corps obviously believed the latter was the correct course as it only prepared a supplement to the 1982 statement of findings....

The regulations promulgated by the Corps concerning the processing of permits, 33 C.F.R. Part 325, do shed light on this issue indirectly. Section 325.3(b) requires that public notice be published for reissuance of existing regional permits within their area of jurisdiction It is clear that the Corps complied with this regulation.... Section 325.7(a) directs that modifications which result in "significant increases in scope of a permitted activity will be processed as new applications for permits." Such modifications would clearly be "new permits" for NEPA purposes and require a new EA. But a proposal to reissue a permit which is not significantly different in scope from its predecessor is not a "new permit" and need not be subjected to the scrutiny attended its forebear. Indeed, reissuing a permit seems more akin to extending an existing permit than issuing a new one. The Corps treats extensions of permits due to expire as follows:

Requests for extensions will be processed in accordance with the regular procedures of §325.2 of this part, except that such processing is not required where the district engineer determines that there have been no significant changes in the attendant circumstances since the authorization was issued. 33 C.F.R. §325.6(d).

GP 38 was reissued in essentially the same form in 1987.... It neither increased the scope of activities eligible for authorization under it nor decreased the regulation of those activities. In fact, it added reporting requirements for permit applicants and limited its geographic scope.... After publishing public notice and considering comments received from the public, the Corps issued a supplemental statement of findings that the activities authorized under GP 38 caused minimal acceptable environmental impacts.... Although there is no explicit regulation stating that this was all the procedure required, related regulations suggest that it is.

Based on the administrative record and this analysis, it was not necessary for the Corps to conduct a new EA in 1987 in order to reissue GP 38. By conducting the original BA in 1982, making two statements of findings and complying with the notice provisions, the Corps met the requirements of NEPA when it issued and reissued GP 38.

C. CORPS REGULATIONS

Plaintiffs contend that the Corps violated its own regulations governing the issuance of permits under the CWA by not providing notice and the chance to comment on impending general permits to the public, 33 C.F.R. §325.3(a), and more specifically, to Indian tribes, §325.3(d), and by not preparing either an EA or an EIS prior to issuance. This latter claim was addressed above and need not be repeated.

Plaintiffs claim that the Corps failed to notify anyone in Vermont of the proposed GP 38. Factually this is incorrect. The Corps provided notice of the proposed GP 38 to municipalities, state agencies and officials, private organizations and some individuals....

The Corps did not directly notify plaintiffs and would thus be in violation of 33 C.F.R. §325.3(d) if any of the plaintiffs qualified as an Indian tribe. However, neither the Abenaki Nation of Mississquoi, the Abenaki Tribal Council nor the Abenaki people are recognized by the Bureau of Indian Affairs as a federal Indian tribe. Section 325.3(d) requires the Corps to provide notice to "appropriate Indian Tribes or tribal representatives." The Corps' failure to provide notice to the plaintiff was reasonable in light of the plaintiffs absence from the list of federally recognized tribes and the extensive notice it provided to other public forums and groups. Because the Corps did not violate its own regulations or those imposed by NEPA or the APA in issuing GP 38, plaintiff's claim that GP 38 is invalid fails.

2. CLAIM II—THE JULY 15, 1992 AUTHORIZATION VIOLATED NEPA

In the early stages of the permit process reinitiated by the Village in its September 9, 1991 permit application, Corps personnel indicated that the Project would not be eligible for authorization under GP 38 because of its impact on wetlands.... Corps personnel also indicated that an EIS might be necessary because of significant impact on the human environment.... Corps personnel maintained these positions until as late as February 27, 1992.... In early March of 1992 the Corps modified its position,... holding out the possibility that with upfront mitigation which had reasonable assurance of success, the Project would become eligible under GP 38.... The Village capitalized on this possibility, preparing mitigation plans and agreeing to the conditions imposed by the Corps, leading to the authorization under GP 38 for the Project....

Plaintiffs claim that this chain of events was in violation of NEPA. Specifically, they allege defendants violated NEPA by not preparing an EIS, by failing to give adequate consideration to historic resources at the Project site, improperly relying on the FERC EA and failing to provide proper notice of its intent not to conduct an EIS.

A. FAILURE TO PERFORM AN EIS

Plaintiffs' contention that the Corps was required to conduct an EIS before authorizing the Project under GP 38 apparently stems (1) from the informal statements from Corps personnel that an EIS would be necessary and (2) from the Corps decision that the Project could be authorized under GP 38 if adequate mitigation was reasonably assured.

As to the informal statements made by Corps personnel regarding the need for an EIS, it would hardly make sense to hold the Corps, or any other agency, bound by the informal statements of its employees. *See, e.g., American Trucking Assns. v. Atchison, T. & S.F.R. Co.*, 387 U.S. 397, 416, 18 L.Ed.2d 847, 87 S.Ct. 1608 (1967) (agency "faced with new developments or in light of reconsideration of the relevant facts and its mandate, may alter its past interpretation"). Plaintiffs do not contest this but rather argue that the Corps has failed to articulate a rational connection between the facts found and the choice made.

The administrative record indicates that once the Corps reached the position that it was possible that the Project could be permitted under GP 38 if the authorization was conditioned upon an adequate mitigation plan for cultural and biological impacts, the Corps gave great consideration to whether or not the mitigation plan proposed by the Village was adequate.... Moreover, the mitigation plan is mandated by the authorization and the Project cannot proceed unless the plan is followed.... Based on these facts, the Corps' decision to authorize the Project under GP 38 was rationally related to the facts found and the decision cannot be said to be arbitrary and capricious.

Even with a mitigation plan reducing the impacts of the Project to "minimal," plaintiffs maintain that the requirements of NEPA apply and defendants were required to conduct an EIS before granting authorization.

The authorization granted on July 15, 1992 was conditioned upon the satisfaction of 23 specific conditions concerning the creation of 30 acres of wetlands to compensate for the loss of wetlands caused by the Project and the impact on any historical or cultural resources.... These conditions were imposed in order to cause the Project to remain below the minimal impact threshold for GP 38. Implicitly, it also avoided the need to prepare an EIS. Plaintiffs rely on a memorandum prepared by the CEQ to support their claim that the mitigation plan does not obviate the need for an EIS under NEPA.

In its memorandum, "Forty Most Asked Questions Concerning CEQ's National Environmental Policy Act Regulations," 46 Fed. Reg. 18,026 (1981), the CEQ said:

> Mitigation measures may be relied upon to make a finding of no significant impact only if they are imposed by statute or regulation, or submitted by an applicant or agency as part of the original proposal. As a general rule, the regulations contemplate that agencies should use a broad approach in defining significance and should not rely on the possibility of mitigation as an excuse to avoid the EIS requirement.

Id. at 18,038. Because the mitigation plan was not part of the original proposal nor imposed by statute or regulation, plaintiffs contend that the Corps' reliance on the mitigation plan to avoid the EIS requirement was unjustified

The Supreme Court has held that CEQ *regulations* are entitled to substantial deference. *Robertson v. Methow Valley Citizens Council,* 490 U.S. 332, 354, 104 L.Ed. 2d 351, 109 S.Ct. 1835 (1989). However, in considering the weight of this CEQ memorandum, the D.C. Circuit has stated that "[CEQ] interpretations are generally entitled to deference ... the 'Forty Questions' publication, however, is merely an informal statement, not a regulation, and we do not find it to be persuasive authority." *Cabinet Mountains Wilderness v. Peterson*, 222 U.S. App. D.C. 228, 685 F.2d 678, 682 (D.C.Cir. 1982) (citations omitted). *See also, Friends of the Earth v. Hintz,* 800 F.2d 822, 837 n.15 (9th Cir. 1986) (courts have uniformly held that "Forty Questions" is not controlling authority, citing decisions in the 5th, 9th and D.C. Circuits). While other circuits (including this one) have referenced the memorandum in reaching a decision, *see, Sierra Club v. Marsh,* 769 F.2d

868, 877 (1st Cir. 1985) (reversing Corps decision based on promised mitigation plan); *Sierra Club v. United States Army Corps of Engineers,* 772 F.2d 1043, 1059 (2d Cir. 1985) (Mansfield, concurring), none have held that the memorandum is binding or entitled to substantial deference as CEQ regulations are.

Not only have courts given the "Forty Questions" document slight deference, but the majority of them have specifically held that mitigation measures are appropriately considered in determining whether a federal action will have a significant impact or not. *See generally, C.A.R.E. Now, Inc. v. FAA,* 844 F.2d 1569 (11th Cir. 1988); *Sierra Club v. United States Dept. of Transportation,* 243 U.S. App. D.C. 302, 753 F.2d 120 (D.C. Cir. 1985). As the D.C. Circuit has explained:

NEPA's EIS requirement is governed by the rule of reason, and an EIS must be prepared only when significant environmental impacts will occur as a result of the proposed action. If, however the proposal is modified prior to implementation by adding specific mitigation measures which completely compensate for any possible adverse environmental impacts stemming from the original proposal, the statutory threshold of significant environmental effects is not crossed and an EIS is not required. To require an EIS in such circumstances would trivialize NEPA and would "diminish its utility in providing useful environmental analysis for major federal actions that truly affect the environment."

Cabinet Mountain, supra at 682 (citations omitted).

The Second Circuit, in reviewing a challenge to another hydroelectric project, recently discussed the role of mitigation measures in supporting an agency's FONSI:

"We conclude that FERC took the requisite 'hard look' at the environmental impact of the [project]. It examined the Project's impact on the aesthetic, cultural, historical, and recreational aspects of the site; it considered inconsistencies with state environmental plans; and it proposed measures to minimize certain unavoidable environmental impacts. Under these circumstances, given that FERC's findings regarding the adequacy of mitigation measures are supported by substantial evidence, FERC has 'convincingly documented' its finding of no significant impact."

Friends of the Ompompanoosuc v. FERC, 968 F.2d 1549, 1556-67 (2d Cir. 1992). As long as the adequacy of mitigation measures are clearly supported, *Ompompanoosuc* strongly suggests that the Second Circuit joins the majority of courts in finding it proper for an agency to consider mitigation plans in determining the significance of the environmental impact of an action.

In the present case, the Corps was not engaged in the process of determining whether or not the Project would significantly impact the human environment. Rather, it was engaged in determining whether the Project was below the threshold imposed by GP 38, i.e., whether it caused minimal or no adverse impact. In either case, the use of mitigation plans to reach such a finding is acceptable, even though the CEQ recommends against it. As in *Ompompanoosuc,* there is substantial evidence that the mitigation plans will adequately minimize any adverse environmental impacts. *See, supra* n.9. As such, the authorization and its mandatory conditions were properly issued under GP 38. While a court may disagree with the final result, its review under NEPA is to insure that its procedural requirements have been followed and that the agency involved has taken the requisite "hard look" at the environmental impact of the action. *See, Ompompanoosuc, supra* at 1556-57 (*supra* at 1556-57 ("Once an agency has made a decision subject to NEPA's procedural requirements, the only role for a court is to ensure that the agency has considered the environmental consequences.") (quoting *Strycker's Bay Neighborhood Council,*

Inc. v. Karlen, 444 U.S. 223, 227, 62 L.Ed. 2d 433, 100 S.Ct. 497 (1980). The record here is replete with indications that the Corps did in fact take the necessary "hard look." ... For these reasons, the Corps' finding that the Project, as conditioned by the mitigation plan, caused minimal adverse environmental effect was not arbitrary or capricious nor an abuse of discretion and an EIS under NEPA was not necessary.

B. HISTORIC RESOURCES

Plaintiffs claim that in making its determination of only minimal adverse impact the Corps did not give adequate consideration to the impact on historical resources at the Project site as required by NEPA, 40 C.F.R. §1508.27(b)(3), (8). Plaintiffs recognize that the FERC license and the mitigation plan provide for consultation about the future of any historic sites but Plaintiffs take issue with them because they make no explicit commitment to avoiding losses. Because any losses of historic resources would be significant, plaintiffs argue that an EIS is required before the Project can continue.

Again, the court would point to the administrative record in finding that the Corps did consider the impact of the Project on any historic sites in making its determination and giving its approval under GP 38 to the Village.... Moreover, the authorization was conditioned to mitigate the impact on historical and cultural resources. Condition 7 of the authorization provides:

> Upon completion of the monitoring of the mitigation area, a determination shall be made by the Corps as to whether or not any manipulation (i.e. grading or excavation) or inundation/flooding of the site will be required to accomplish the mitigation. Should site manipulation or inundation/flooding be necessary, a Phase I archaeological study (and, if determined necessary by the Corps and the Vt. [State Historical Preservation Officer] SHPO, a Phase II study) shall be conducted to determine if the area contains any resources of cultural significance. These studies shall be commenced within two months after a determination that manipulation or inundation/flooding is necessary. A report documenting the results of these studies shall be submitted to the Corps and the Vt. SHPO so that a determination of the effect may be made within three months after completion of the studies. Should the Corps, the Vt. SHPO and the Advisory Council on Historic Preservation determine that mitigation in way of avoidance or data recovery be necessary, this shall be accomplished before work can commence on the site....

Accordingly the Corps addressed the issue of potential losses of historic resources by requiring participation of the appropriate state and federal agencies and also requiring avoidance or data recovery as necessary. The mitigation plan addresses the impact on historical sites adequately and therefore, as concluded above, the Corps did not act arbitrarily or capriciously in deciding an EIS was not necessary.

C. FERC ENVIRONMENTAL ASSESSMENT

Plaintiffs assert that the Corps improperly relied on the FERC EA in granting authorization under GP 38 and was required to conduct its own EA and EIS. FERC is the lead agency for the Project Pursuant to NEPA, it conducted an EA and subsequently reached a FONSI in regards to the Village's original application.... When the Village applied to amend its license, the FERC found that the impacts of the Project would be diminished by the reduction in size of the Project and granted an amended license.... As discussed previously, in accordance with NEPA the Corps has promulgated their own regulations for implementing NEPA. *See*, 33 C.F.R. §§230, 325. Both those regulations and the regulations promulgated by the CEQ allow for the adoption of another agency's EIS or EAFONSI by the Corps. See, 33 C.F.R. §230.21; 40 C.F.R. §1506.3(a). The Corps may consider another agency's EIS or EAFONSI adequate "unless the district commander finds substantial doubt as to technical or procedural adequacy or omission of factors important to the Corps decision." 33 C.F.R. §230.21.

Plaintiffs' claim is contrary to the regulations and again seems to be based on the preliminary statements of Corps employees who implied that the FERC EA was inadequate.... Plaintiffs do not challenge the FERC EA, only the Corps' reliance on it. But the regulations specifically allow the Corps to rely on another agency's EAFONSI. Where the district commander found no substantial doubt as to the FERC EAFONSI nor omission of important factors, the Corps has not violated the procedure of NEPA by relying on it to authorize the Project under GP 38.

D. NOTICE

Plaintiffs' final NEPA related claim alleges that the Corps was required to provide public notice of its intent not to perform an EIS prior to issuance of the July 15, 1992 authorization. Plaintiffs cite several Second Circuit decisions—*Hanly v. Kleindienst,* 471 F.2d 823 (2d Cir. 1972), *Cross-Sound Ferry Service, Inc. v. United States*, 573 F.2d 725 (2d Cir. 1978) and *WATCH v. Harris*, 603 F.2d 310 (2d Cir. 1979)—to support their claim However, these cases held "that the agency 'must give notice to the public of the proposed major federal action and an opportunity to submit relevant facts which might bear upon the agency's threshold decision'" as to whether an EIS was required. *WATCH, supra* at 326 n.36, *supra* at 326 n.36, quoting *Hanly, supra* at 836.

As discussed above, the Corps *did* provide the required notice and opportunity to be heard prior to its initial issuance of GP 38 in 1982 and to its reissue in 1987.... It also published an EA and a statement of findings explaining its decision that GP 38 did not have a significant impact on the human environment.

As for the recent authorization granted the Project, Corps regulations provide that after a regional permit is issued in "compliance with the other procedures of this regulation ... individual activities falling within those categories that are authorized by such regional permits do not have to be further authorized by the procedures of this regulation." 33 C.F.R. §325.2(e)(2). Therefore, once the Corps determined that the Project was within the scope of GP 38, the Project was no longer subject to the Corps regulations implementing NEPA. Thus, notice of the Project's authorization under GP 38 was not necessary.

It is only when an agency is required to conduct an EA or an EIS that it is required to give public notice of the proposed action and provide an opportunity for public comment. The Corps was not required to conduct an EA or an EIS for the Village's permit application and so the notice obligation discussed in WATCH never attached. Plaintiffs' claim fails.

3. CLAIM III—THE MITIGATION PLAN REQUIRES AN INDIVIDUAL §404 PERMIT

Plaintiffs claim that the creation of the compensatory wetlands required by the Special Conditions attached to the authorization granted the Project will encompass a "discharge" into "navigable waters" within the meaning of section 404 of the CWA, 33 U.S.C. §1344 and requires the Corps to issue a permit. *See, U.S. v. Riverside Bayview Homes, Inc.*, 474 U.S. 121, 123, 88 L.Ed.2d

419, 106 S.Ct. 455 (1985). Because the Corps' own regulations require that all permits reasonably related to the same activity be applied for in the same application, plaintiffs assert that until the alleged "discharge" created by the mitigation plan is permitted under section 404, the Project application for authorization under GP 38 is incomplete and the Project should be enjoined until the application is completed.

Section 404 of the CWA, 33 U.S.C. §1344, requires a permit to be issued for "the discharge of dredged or fill material into the navigable waters at specified disposal sites." "Navigable waters" is defined as "the waters of the United States, including the territorial seas," 33 U.S.C. §1362(7), which in turn are defined by Corps regulations to include wetlands, 33 C.F.R. §328.3(a). The courts have interpreted the CWA as including both natural and artificial wetlands. *See, Leslie Salt Co. v. U.S.*, 896 F.2d 354 (9th Cir. 1990), *cert. denied,* U.S. , 111 S. Ct. 1089, 112 L. Ed. 2d 1194 (1991); *U.S. v. Akers,* 651 F. Supp. 320 (E.D.Cal. 1987). Thus, discharge of dredged or fill material into a river or wetland, natural or man-made, would require a permit under Section 404.

Plaintiffs' argument rests on several faulty assumptions. The first is that manipulation or flooding will be necessary to create the wetlands. As mentioned above, it is quite possible that the mitigation sites will revert to their original form as wetlands once farming activities cease. If this is the case, the Corps would have no procedural responsibilities to fulfill under the CWA.

If it does become necessary to successfully complete the mitigation by flooding it is not contemplated that this will result in a "discharge" into the Mississquoi within the meaning of section 404 of the CWA. Rather, mitigation will likely be accomplished by diverting water from the river itself to the sites (a fact plaintiffs acknowledge in their pretrial brief). The definition of "discharge" is defined to include "discharge of pollutants," 33 U.S.C. §1362(16), which is in turn defined to include dredged spoil, solid waste, sewage, rock, sand and agricultural waste, among other things. 33 U.S.C. §1362(6). Thus if creation of the wetlands occurs by flooding the mitigation sites with waters from the Mississquoi, nothing included in the definition of pollutants will be discharged into the Mississquoi as a result.

Plaintiffs also mistakenly assume that the mitigation sites currently proposed constitute "waters of the United States" and that any flooding of the mitigation sites will therefore constitute a discharge into "waters of the United States," requiring a section 404 permit. At present the mitigation sites do not constitute "waters of the United States" under the definitions of the CWA, 33 U.S.C. §1362, or those of the Corps regulations, 33 C.F.R. §328.3. Until the mitigation sites are determined to constitute "waters of the United States," the provisions of section 404 cannot apply and no permit is required.

Plaintiffs' final flawed assumption is that the regulation requires the Corps to issue a permit for a discharge of which might occur at some future date at the same time as issuing authorization under GP 38. It does not. The regulation requires that all "activities that the applicant *plans to undertake*" be included in the same permit application. 33 C.F.R. §325.1(d)(2). There are no current plans to discharge any fill or dredged material into "waters of the United States" because no such discharges appear necessary. Should such plans arise, the Village will be required to obtain a permit, or failing that, provide alternate mitigation. An individual section 404 permit is accordingly not required and plaintiffs' claim fails.

4. CLAIM IV—PROJECT IS OUTSIDE THE SCOPE OF GP 38

Plaintiffs claim that the Project is ineligible for authorization under GP 38 because it entails adverse impacts to the natural and cultural environment which are more than the minimal impacts allowed under GP 38. They also allege that the Project is likely to require the filling of wetlands in violation of GP 38.

The substance of plaintiffs' claim here is the same as that addressed earlier in connection with NEPA and the Corps determination that the Project caused minimal or no adverse impacts. The Corps has addressed the cultural and environmental impacts of the Project and determined that, as conditioned, the Project will cause minimal adverse environmental and cultural impacts and authorization under GP 38 is appropriate. That determination was not arbitrary or capricious nor was it an abuse of discretion.

When GP 38 was extended in 1987 in contained 6 Special Conditions. Special condition 4 declared that "no permanent or temporary fill shall be deposited in wetlands under this permit." If plaintiffs' claim is correct that wetlands will be filled as a result of the Corps' authorization, and it's not clear that it is, the Project would clearly be in violation of the terms of GP 38. This possibility does not place the Project outside the scope of GP 38 but subjects its permit to possible revocation. Plaintiffs' claim fails.

5. CLAIM V—THE JULY 15 AUTHORIZATION VIOLATED THE NHPA

Plaintiffs claim that the Corps committed two violations of the NHPA by 1) failing to determine the effects of the approval on any historic property as required by Section 106 of the NHPA and 2) failing to give notice to interested parties prior to granting authorization for the Project. Plaintiffs request that all action at the Project be enjoined until the Corps complies with these provisions of the NHPA.

The "NHPA requires only that agencies acquire information before acting." *Connecticut Trust for Historic Preservation v. I.C.C.,* 841 F.2d 479 (2d Cir. 1988). Section 106 of the NHPA seeks to implement this by requiring that all agencies "having authority to license any undertaking shall... prior to the issuance of any license ... take into account the effect of the undertaking on any district, site, building, structure, or object that is included in or is eligible for inclusion in the National Register." 16 U.S.C. §470f.

Regulations describe the methods by which Section 106 review is to be conducted. *See generally,* 36 C.F.R. §800. When the effect of the proposed action is adverse, the agency is required to notify the Advisory Council on Historic Preservation ("Council") and consult with the SHPO "to seek ways to avoid or reduce the effects on historic properties." 36 C.F.R. §800.5(e). The agency is also required to involve "interested persons" as consulting parties when they so request. §800.5(e)(1). Interested persons include "the representative of an Indian tribe." §800.5(e)(1)(ii). The NHPA defines Indian tribe as "the governing body of any Indian tribe, band, nation, or other group that is recognized as an Indian tribe by the Secretary of the Interior...." §800.2(g).

As an initial matter, under the terms of the statute, none of the plaintiffs qualify as "interested persons." It is undisputed that no plaintiff is formally recognized by the Secretary of the Interior as an Indian Tribe. A list of recognized tribes was published in the 1988 Federal Register, 53 Fed. Reg. no. 250, p. 52829, et seq. (122988) and plaintiffs were not included. Nor have they been added to the list since that time. Declaration of Holly Reckord, Acting Chief, Branch of Acknowledgment and Research, Bureau of Indian Affairs. Whether plaintiffs are an "Indian tribe" for other purposes (such as the receipt of benefits from other federal or state agencies) does not bear on their rights under the NHPA. As such, the plaintiffs are not "interested parties" by the terms of the statute and were not entitled to participate as consulting parties, §800.5(e)(1), nor were they entitled to receive documents produced under a Section 106 review. §800.5(e)(2).

As members of the public though, the plaintiffs were entitled to "an adequate opportunity to receive information and express their views." §800.5(e)(3). The record shows that the Corps met with the plaintiffs Hilda Robtoy and Dee Brightstar on November 6, 1991,... and with Robtoy, Brightstar and John Moody on December 17, 1991,... in their representative capacity for the Abenaki Nation of the Mississquoi to discuss their concerns and the Project's impact on prehistoric cultural resources. The Corps provided "adequate opportunity" for the plaintiffs to receive information and express their views and as such did not violate any of the notice provisions of the NHPA.

As to whether or not the Corps adequately considered the effects of the Project on any historical sites, the analysis is not so straightforward. In issuing a license to the Village for the Project, the FERC was required to insure that the NHPA requirements were met. FERC made a finding of no adverse effect on the inundation site based on a mitigation plan that mandated avoidance and mitigation of impacts to the area.... Both the SHPO and the Council concurred. As to this finding, the Corps was obligated to accept the lead agency's finding. 33 C.F.R. Part 325 App. C(2)(c). Moreover, it appears that Plaintiffs are not challenging this finding, as FERC is not named as a defendant in this action.

Where the analysis becomes more involved is in relation to the mitigation site. The plaintiffs claim that the historic resources at the mitigation site were not adequately considered by the FERC license nor by the Corps authorization. Review here is limited to whether the Corps complied with the procedural requirements of the CPA and acquired adequate information concerning the historic resources at the site and sought "ways to avoid or reduce the effects" of the Project.

The record and the conditions attached to the authorization make it clear that the Corps did indeed satisfy these requirements. In addition to meeting with plaintiffs several times, the Corps consulted with the SHPO concerning the Project's impact on historical resources,... and both are in agreement as to how the possible adverse effects should be mitigated if any historic properties are discovered. Moreover, the conditions attached to the authorization adopt the recommendations of the SHPO, *see,* Affidavit of Martha Abair, Corps Project manager, Defendant's Exhibit A, and set out concrete steps to be followed if any historical resources are discovered at the mitigation site....

Procedurally the Corps is in technical violation of the CPA due to its failure to prepare a Memorandum of Agreement ("MoA") between the SHPO and itself concerning how the effects of the Project will be taken into account. 36 C.F.R. §800.5(e)(4). However, this violation is not fatal, given the NHPA's permission that its regulations "may be implemented in a flexible manner." §800.3(b). While the NHPA requires mutual agreements between the CORPS and SHPO to be executed in a MoA, the Corps' regulations require such agreements to be formalized either through an MoA or through permit conditioning. 33 C.F.R. Part 325 App. C(9). The Corps and the SHPO have taken this latter path and given the flexibility allowed by the NHPA itself and that the conditioned permit fulfills the goals of the NHPA, the Corp's failure to execute an MoA is insufficient to hold it has violated the NHPA.

6. CLAIM VI—NAGPRA VIOLATION

Plaintiffs' final claim is made under NAGPRA, 25 U.S.C. §3005(4). Plaintiffs claim that because the mitigation plan leaves the fate of the remains and artifacts which may be unearthed in the hands of the Corps, the State and the Village, it violates NAGPRA and is unlawful. Prior to reaching the merits of plaintiffs' claim, several definitional hurdles must be cleared.

NAGPRA defines Indian tribe as follows:

> "Indian tribe" means any tribe, band, nation, or other organized group or community of Indians, including any Alaska Native village ... which is recognized as eligible for the special programs and services by the United States to Indians because of their status as Indians.

25 U.S.C. §3001(7). As discussed earlier, it is undisputed that the Abenaki Nation of Mississquoi is not an "Indian tribe" recognized by the Secretary of the Interior. Nonetheless, that plaintiff contends that for purposes of NAGPRA it does constitute an Indian tribe, citing its receipt of federal funds and a recent decision by the Vermont Supreme Court.

Plaintiff's argument that it does indeed constitute an Indian tribe may have practical merit as to the receipt of federal funds but appears to be stretching the *Elliot* decision rather thin. In any event, the merits of those arguments need not be addressed here because the language of NAGPRA includes "organized group or community of Indians ... eligible for the special programs and services provided by the United States to Indians because of their status as Indians." The regulation which sets out the procedures for establishing that an American Indian group exists as an Indian tribe, 25 C.F.R. §83 (1992), defines Indian group or group to mean "any Indian aggregation within the continental United States that the Secretary of the Interior does not acknowledge to be an Indian tribe." The Abenaki Nation of Mississquoi falls squarely within this definition and the fact that it receives funds and assistance from the United States because of its members status as Indians includes it within the class protected by NAGPRA.

NAGPRA applies to the disposition of Native American cultural items that are "excavated or discovered on federal or tribal lands." 25 U.S.C. §3002(a). Federal lands are defined in relevant part as "land other than tribal lands which are controlled or owned by the United States." §3001(5). Plaintiffs urge a broad construction of "control" to include the Corps' regulatory powers under the CWA and its involvement in devising and supervising the mitigation plan.

Such a broad reading is not consistent with the statute, which exhibits no intent to apply the Act to situations where federal involvement is limited as it is here to the issuance of a permit. To adopt such a broad reading of the Act would invoke its provisions whenever the government issued permits or provided federal funding pursuant to statutory obligations.

As yet there have been no cultural or funerary items discovered at the mitigation Site, though the possibility of their existence is extremely high. However, NAGPRA applies to cultural and funerary objects already possessed or under the control of a Federal agency or museum, §3003 and §3004, or those already discovered or excavated, §3002. As to plaintiffs' claim, the court must hold that even if NAGPRA were to apply, which it does not, the claim is premature.

IV. CONCLUSION

On the basis of the foregoing discussion the court holds that the Plaintiffs have failed to sustain any of the claims pled and accordingly the Defendants are entitled to judgement as a matter of law. The July 15, 1992, conditioned authorization of the Corps of Engineers to the Village of Swanton to raise the spillway of the Orman Croft Generating Station is affirmed. [Footnotes omitted.]

In the Corps' regulations the purpose of these "general permits," like "nationwide permits" discussed below, is "to allow certain activities to occur with little, if any, delay or paperwork" by eliminating the need for a permit application if the activity is one covered by the general permit. 33 C.F.R. §320.1(a)(3). In a *Section 404 Enforcement Memorandum of Agreement Procedures Regarding the Applicability of Previously-Issued Corps Permits*, the Corps and the EPA agreed that "the Corps will be responsible for determining whether an alleged illegal discharge of dredged or fill material is authorized under an individual or general permit" When the EPA becomes aware of an alleged illegal discharge, it has agreed to "contact the appropriate Corps district and request a determination as to whether the discharge is authorized by an individual or general permit." A Corps determination, which must be made within either two or ten working days depending upon how much information the EPA gives it, that the discharge is authorized or unauthorized is a final enforcement decision. Nonetheless, if the EPA either does not receive a timely Corps determination or "reasonably believes that such discharge is not authorized," the EPA may take "immediate enforcement action against the discharger when necessary to minimize impacts to the environment." The EPA still has to contact the Corps in any event and, if the Corps finds that the discharge was authorized, that, too, is a "final determination." In order to find out what kinds of activities in wetlands have been authorized in which states or regions, it is necessary to contact the local Corps division or district office directly.

CHAPTER 12

NATIONWIDE PERMITS

The Corps' regulations, 33 C.F.R. §330.6, authorize it to issue, reissue, modify, suspend, revoke, either in whole or for specific geographical areas, classes of activities, or classes of waters, or propose regional conditions to "Nationwide Permits" (hereinafter "NWPs") as long as a number of "General," and a handful of "Section 404 Only," conditions are met. This program is so generous in its coverage that only a few of the NWPs require a special notice procedure before commencing the activity. The remainder of the NWPs are technically self-executing though wisdom and practice teach that the Corps should be contacted whenever any activity will be conducted in a wetland just to make certain that a NWP applies. 33 C.F.R. §330.6(a)(1) allows a landowner to request and receive a confirmation from the Corps that the proposed activity complies with an NWP. There are, however, so many regional variations to the NWPs that one hoping to escape the individual permit process should *always* check with the local Corps office before commencing any activity in a wetland. Further, NWPs must be modified or reissued every five years so it is important to check the date of any document describing an NWP.

Coastal zone management consistency determinations and state water quality certifications remain necessary though that procedure may itself by eliminated by the applicability of the NWP in the individual state. 33 C.F.R. §330.4. If the state issues a water quality certification with conditions on a state-wide or regional basis, then under the Corps's regulations, the conditions will become part of the NWP in that particular state or region, unless the Corps determines that the conditions do not comply with other Corps regulations, in which case the water quality certification is deemed denied until the state issues a certification or waives its right to do so. Other federal statutes, such as the Endangered Species Act and the National Historic Preservation Act, remain applicable.

VIEUX CARRE PROPERTY OWNERS, RESIDENTS & ASSOCIATES, INC. v. BROWN

875 F.2d 453 (5th Cir. 1989)

This dispute focuses the Court's attention on a private plaintiff's enforcement of the National Historic Preservation Act of (NHPA) against the United States Army Corps of Engineers (the Corps). Vieux Carre Property Owners, Residents & Associates, Inc. (the Vieux Carre), the plaintiffs-appellants in this case, is made up of landowners within the Vieux Carre National Historic Landmark District—popularly referred to as the French Quarter—on the Mississippi River in New Orleans, Louisiana. The Vieux Carre ultimately seeks to arrest the construction of an aquarium and riverfront park currently being erected on and just landward of the Bienville Street Wharf at the foot of Bienville Street. This appeal comes from the district court's summary dismissal of the Vieux Carre's suit on jurisdictional grounds.

The Vieux Carre first claims that the Rivers and Harbors Act, 33 U.S.C. §403 (RHA) and the Corps' regulations found in 33 C.F.R. §§320 through 330 (1987), require the Corps to issue a permit for the aquarium phase of the project, and that such permitting in turn requires the Corps to submit the project to the NHPA historic impact review process dictated by 16 U.S.C. §§470f and 470h-

2(f). The Vieux Carre then claims that the park phase required an individual permit, but that even if it complied with the Corps' nationwide permit that itself triggered section 470f and required the Corps to follow the historic impact review procedures detailed in 36 C.F.R. §§800 *et seq*. The Corps failed to submit any of the project to the NHPA review process. Thus, the Vieux Carre sued for a declaratory judgment against the Corps and an injunction against those developing or otherwise authorizing the project, namely, the Audubon Park Commission, the City of New Orleans, the Board of Commissioners of the Port of New Orleans, and the Board of Commissioners of the Orleans Levee District. We find that the dismissal of the Vieux Carre's aquarium phase claim was proper, though for different reasons than those stated by the district court. We reverse the court's dismissal of the Vieux Carre's riverfront park claim against the Corps and remand for further legal and factual findings in relation to that claim. We affirm the court's dismissal of the Vieux Carre's request to enjoin the other appellees from proceeding with the project.

FACTS AND PROCEEDINGS BELOW

In July 1986, the Louisiana Legislature authorized the Audubon Park Commission—a local governmental entity then in charge of operating a New Orleans park and zoo—to acquire riverfront property for a world-class aquarium and riverfront park. As authorized by this legislation, in November 1986, an election was held in which New Orleans voters approved a millage tax necessary to fund bonds for construction of the project. No federal funds will be involved. Following local governmental approvals—including those by the City of New Orleans' Vieux Carre Commission, the New Orleans Planning Commission, and the New Orleans City Council—of the proposed site at the foot of Bienville Street, in April 1987, the Audubon Park Commission submitted tentative plans to the Corps to determine whether permitting would be required. The plans describe the project in two phases: Phase A involves construction of the aquarium just landward of and overlapping slightly onto the Bienville Street Wharf; Phase B shows a park on top of the wharf, reserving the riverward face of the wharf for continued maritime use.

Near its landward edge, the Bienville Street Wharf sits atop a three-sided box levee that runs alongside the Mississippi River. The riverward vertical of the levee currently serves as the Ordinary High Water Line (OHWL) of the river, and as such is the Corps' benchmark for determining its jurisdiction under the RHA. This riverward vertical of the levee consists of a concrete and steel bulkhead. In order to achieve a desirable factor of safety against enbankment failure, the foundation piles of the aquarium must be augmented by a new bulkhead, consisting of piles and sheet pile, installed just landward of the existing bulkhead. The new bulkhead admittedly will achieve the desired factor of safety. Though the existing bulkhead will be undisturbed, it appears that the primary available post-construction bulkhead support will be attributable to the new bulkhead.

The second, riverfront park phase of the project calls for removal of large metal sheds atop the wharf and the placement of sod, trees, and benches.

After reviewing the plans, the Corps concluded in May 1987 that its regulations did not require a permit for the aquarium because the entire project is to be built landward of the OHWL. Thus, the project is not within the navigable waterways of the United States and is therefore outside the Corps' RHA jurisdiction. The Corps found that the park, which will be located atop the wharf completely riverward of the OHWL and therefore indisputably within the Corps' jurisdiction, is already within a nationwide Corps permit promulgated under the RHA. It falls within this permit, the Corps asserts, because the plan submitted for review does not involve modifications that would change the dimensions of the wharf and because the riverward edge of the wharf would still be dedicated to maritime use.

The Corps informed the Audubon Park Commission of its conclusions by letter dated May 14, 1987. The Corps did not submit the project to the NHPA review process. The Vieux Carre filed this suit on August 6, 1987. Following an evidentiary hearing, the district court dismissed the suit, finding that the Vieux Carre had no direct right of action under the RHA, sections 10 and 14, 33 U.S.C. §§403, 408, to compel the Corps to require permitting, and that the Administrative Procedure Act (APA) does not provide for federal court review of these specific Corps decisions because they are committed to the Corps' discretion. 5 U.S.C. §701(a)(2). As of May 1988, the plans for the aquarium had been finalized and the foundation had been poured.

We affirm the district court's dismissal of the Vieux Carre's requested injunction, finding that neither the APA nor the NHPA give a private plaintiff a right of action against any of the defendants other than the Corps. We reverse the district court on both of its findings as they pertain to the Vieux Carre's claims against the Corps, but we approve the Corps' determination that the aquarium phase of the project did not require a permit. We remand to the district court to determine whether the riverside park in fact falls within the claimed nationwide Corps permit, and, if so, whether, *inter alia,* the nationwide permitting of the park triggers the NHPA procedures....

STANDING AGAINST THE CORPS

The APA, 5 U.S.C. §702, grants federal court standing to any "person suffering legal wrong because of agency action, or adversely affected or aggrieved by agency action within the meaning of a relevant statute." The Supreme Court has interpreted this to require that the interest the plaintiff seeks to protect or advance in his complaint "is arguably within the zone of interests to be protected or regulated by the statute or constitutional guarantee in question." *Association of Data Processing Service Organizations, Inc. v. Camp,* 397 U.S. 150, 90 S.Ct. 827, 830, 25 L.Ed. 2d 184 (1970). This Court generally applies this zone of interests test for standing. *See, e.g., Baker v. Bell,* 630 F.2d 1046, 1051 (5th Cir. 1980).

It is perhaps arguable that if the Vieux Carre sought review of the Corps' actions as they relate only to the RHA, it would not have APA standing because appellant's concern is historic preservation rather than the navigability of the Mississippi River. We need not and do not decide that issue. Even if the Vieux Carre is not within the RHA's zone of interests, however, it may have standing if the NHPA is one of the "relevant statutes" implicated by the Corps' complained of inaction. The D.C. Circuit, in *Committee for Auto Responsibility v. Solomon,* 195 U.S. App. D.C. 410, 603 F.2d 992, 997 (D.C.Cir. 1979), *cert. denied,* 445 U.S. 915, 100 S.Ct. 1274, 63 L.Ed. 2d 599 (1980), noted that the Supreme Court has defined a section 702 "relevant statute" as a statute plaintiff alleges was violated. The *Solomon* court ruled that the National Environmental Policy Act (NEPA) was the statute allegedly violated where the parties did not dispute that an action of the General Services Administration had triggered the NEPA requirement to prepare an environmental impact statement.

Similarly, in its complaint, the Vieux Carre alleges the Corps' violations of the NHPA undiluted by any claimed prerequisite violations of the RHA, asserting that the Corps violated 16 U.S.C.

§470f because "the Corps' review of preliminary plans and reservation of final approval for this project constitute the requisite federal assistance to compel application of the NHPA," and because it did not submit the park phase to the section 470f process when it determined that the project fell under the nationwide permit created by 33 C.F.R. 330.5(a)(3). The Vieux Carre also asserts that the Corps violated its own regulation, 33 C.F.R. 330.5(b)(9), which directs it to evaluate the historic impact of certain projects that fall under nationwide permits. The Vieux Carre is arguably within the zone of interests sought to be protected by both the NHPA and this particular Corps regulation. *Cf. United States v. SCRAP,* 412 U.S. 669, 93 S. Ct. 2405, 2415 n. 13, 37 L. Ed. 2d 254 (1973) ("zone-of-interests" test satisfied because environmental group plaintiffs have an environmental interest that the NEPA seeks to protect); *Cady v. Morton,* 527 F.2d 786, 791 (9th Cir. 1975) (an interest in widely shared aesthetic and environmental concerns falls within the zone of interests to be protected by NEPA); *Citizens Committee for Hudson Valley v. Volpe,* 425 F.2d 97, 105 (2d Cir.), *cert. denied* 400 U.S. 949, 91 S.Ct. 237, 27 L.Ed. 2d 256 (1970).

We therefore hold that the Vieux Carre's historic preservation concerns are arguably within the zone of interests Congress sought to protect through the interrelation of the various statutes and regulations that the Vieux Carre has claimed were violated in this action. The Second Circuit made a similar finding in *Volpe,* in which it ruled that a resident citizens' committee had standing to challenge the Corps' issuance, without prior approval of the Secretary of Transportation or consent from Congress, of a permit to the State of New York to dredge and fill the Hudson River for construction of a proposed expressway. The *Volpe* court found that the plaintiffs were aggrieved within the meaning of at least three relevant statutes. *Id.* at 104. First, because part of the project was a causeway, the Corps should have secured consent for the project from the Secretary of Transportation as required by the Department of Transportation Act. Plaintiff's environmental interests were within the zone of interests sought to be protected by this statute because the Act required the Secretary to consider historical values before approving a project under its jurisdiction. The *Volpe* court also found other, more directly relevant statutes that provided those plaintiffs with standing. These included the Hudson River Basin Compact Act, which instructed all agencies to consider the immense economic, natural, scenic, historic, and recreational value of Hudson River Basin resources before approving activities affecting the area. Finally, the court found that the plaintiffs had standing under the Corps' own regulations, which directed it to evaluate factors such as environmental effects before issuing such permits. *Id.* at 105.

In summary, although the Vieux Carre cannot enjoin the Audubon Park Commission's project, it has standing to assert its claim for a declaratory judgment against the Corps....

PERMITTING THE RIVERSIDE PARK

The Corps admits that the park phase of the project comes under a nationwide permit, but maintains that such a permit is not subject to the historical impact review procedures of 16 U.S.C. §§470f and 470h-2(f). The Vieux Carre contends that (1) the park is not permitted by a nationwide permit and therefore requires an individual permit; (2) if a nationwide permit covers the park, making an individual permit unnecessary, that nationwide permit unnecessary, that nationwide permit is a "license" triggering section 470f's historic impact review procedures.

The original Bienville Street Wharf, permitted by the Corps in 1930, could itself come within only one nationwide permit, that under the provisions of 33 C.F.R. §330.3(b) for "structures or work completed before December 18, 1968, or in waterbodies over which the district engineer had not asserted jurisdiction at the time the activity occurred provided, in both instances, there is no interference with navigation." The Corps stipulated that the reconstruction of the wharf pursuant to the 1930 permit affected the navigability of the Mississippi River. Thus, the original wharf structure does not fall under a nationwide permit.

That does not mean, however, that the park phase cannot fall under such a permit. Section 330.5(a)(3) grants nationwide permits for:

> The repair, rehabilitation, or replacement of any previously authorized, currently serviceable, structure or fill, or of any currently serviceable structure or fill constructed prior to the requirement for authorization, provided such repair, rehabilitation, or replacement does not result in a deviation from the plans of the original structure or fill, and further provided that the structure or fill has not been put to uses differing from uses specified for it in any permit authorizing its original construction. Minor deviations due to changes in materials or construction techniques and which are necessary to make repair, rehabilitation, or replacement are permitted.

This nationwide permit is subject to the section 330.5(b)(9) requirement that the district engineer give the advisory council an opportunity to comment if he determines that historic properties may be adversely affected by the repair, rehabilitation, or replacement.

If the riverfront park does not fit within this section 330.5(a)(3) nationwide permit, it must be individually permitted because its location riverward of the box levee—the OHWL—places it within the navigable waters of the United States and the Corps' jurisdiction under the second clause of RHA section 10. If an individual permit is necessary, the NHPA section 470f historic impact review procedures would concededly be triggered. Before discussing whether the park falls within the section 330.5(a)(3) permit, however, we address the relationship between nationwide permits and section 470f.

The Vieux Carre asserts that even if we find that the park project is covered by the section 330.5(a)(3) nationwide permit, "a permit is a permit," and nothing in the wording of section 470f indicates that some federal agency licensing is exempt from its requirements. The Corps' regulations in fact state that permits are either "in the form of individual permits or general permits." 33 C.F.R. §325.5(a). A "nationwide permit" is simply "a type of general permit." *See* 33 C.F.R. §§325.5(c)(2) and 330.1.

Interpreting the Clean Water Act (CWA), similar in relevant part to the NHPA, the Tenth Circuit, in *Andrews,* 758 F.2d at 512-13, held that by allowing a party to proceed under a nationwide permit the Corps had triggered provisions of the CWA requiring agencies to issue environmental impact statements. In so holding, the court distinguished the CWA from the NEPA, which explicitly states that it is triggered by "major federal actions." As noted above, however, the Eighth Circuit recently approved the parties' treatment of the NHPA's section 470f "undertaking" requirement as "coterminous" with the NEPA's "major Federal actions" triggering event. *Ringsred,* 828 F.2d at 1309; *cf. Lee,* 742 F.2d at 901 (referring throughout to activities falling under a nationwide permit as "exempt" from permitting requirements).

The Tenth Circuit's *Andrews* interpretation, if adopted for the NHPA, reflects the NHPA's statutory purpose, which contemplates widespread agency responsibility for the protection of historic interests. *See, e.g.,* 16 U.S.C. §470(b)(4); H.R.Rep. No. 1916, 89th Cong., 2d Sess. 7, *reprinted in* 1966 U.S.Code Cong. & Admin. News 3307, 3309. It is also true to the NHPA statutory language itself.

Section 330.5(b)'s incorporation of an accelerated historic review procedure as a precondition to a project falling under a section 330.5(a)(3) nationwide permit does not seem to help the Corps' case. In addition to the fact that the Corps concedes that it did not evaluate the historic impact of either phase of the project, we note that through correspondence the Advisory Council has warned the Corps that section 330.5(b)(9) does not satisfy section 470f requirements. Indeed, regulations promulgated under the NHPA provide for counterpart regulations only under specific circumstances:

> In consultation with the Council, agencies may develop counterpart regulations to carry out the section 106 process. When concurred in by the Council, such counterpart regulations shall stand in place of these regulations for the purposes of the agency's compliance with section 106. 36 C.F.R. §800.15 (1987).

The Corps' position that nationwide permits do not trigger section 470f, however, has great practical appeal, especially in relation to the nationwide permit described in 33 C.F.R. §330.5(a)(3), which unquestionably covers such activities as repainting and reroofing original structures. Congress clearly did not intend to require the Corps to subject such truly inconsequential projects to the procedural complexities of section 470f. *See* National Historic Preservation Act Amendments of 1980, H.R. No. 96-1457, 1980 U.S. Code Cong. & Admin. News 6378, 6408; *cf. 162.20 Acres of Land,* 639 F.2d at 302 n. 3. Such a literal construction of section 470f is unreasonable and unintended, and as such is a result we must endeavor to avoid. *See, e.g., United States v. Mendoza,* 565 F.2d 1285, 1288, *on reh'g,* 581 F.2d 89 (5th Cir. 1978) (citing "the celebrated" *Rector of Holy Trinity Church v. United States,* 143 U.S. 457, 12 S. Ct. 511, 36 L. Ed. 226 (1892), as the seminal case approving judicial avoidance of absurd but literal statutory constructions). Moreover, the applicability of section 470f should not be at the whim of the Corps' subsequent "permit" label; such labeling does not alter congressional intent.

And, as pointed out by the Corps, the nationwide permits of 33 C.F.R. §330 are specifically designed to expedite activities with inconsequential effects on the RHA concerns. *See* 33 C.F.R. §330.1 (stating that nationwide permits "are designed to allow certain activities to occur with little, if any, delay or paperwork"). Indeed, "the purpose of the nationwide permit system is to allow certain types of [activities to go forward] without prior Corps approval." *Lee,* 742 F.2d at 909; *see also Andrews,* 758 F.2d at 511. Consequently, 33 C.F.R. §330.1 notes that some of its chapter's nationwide permits require notification to the district engineer prior to commencement of the activity in question. Presumably, these are the more significant projects — those more likely to have measurable impacts on navigation. We hold that nationwide permits authorizing truly inconsequential activities are not triggering "licenses" under section 470f.

We now turn to whether section 330.5(a)(3) authorizes such inconsequential activities, for we find that the regulation's failure to require notification by the "permittee" to the Corps is not dispositive of the issue. This nationwide permit has not previously been interpreted by a federal court in a published opinion. The Corps apparently determined that the park constitutes a "rehabilitation" or "replacement" of the wharf, that the park plans do not deviate from the 1930 plans of the wharf except for minor deviations due to changes in materials or construction techniques that are necessary for the rehabilitation or replacement, and that the park is not a use differing from uses specified in the 1930 wharf permit. The reviewing court must determine whether the Corps' interpretation of its own regulation is reasonable and consistent with the regulations themselves. *Lyng v. Payne,* 476 U.S. 926, 106 S.Ct. 2333, 90 L.Ed.2d 921 (1986). Because the district court did not address this issue, we remand for an interpretation of the scope of section 330.5(a)(3); a determination of whether the Corps' finding that the riverfront park is covered by this nationwide permit (as the district court defines it) was arbitrary or capricious; and if the park is covered by section 330.5(a)(3), a ruling on whether the project is so inconsequential that it escapes section 470f's historic impact review requirements.

Finally, if the district court finds that the riverfront park does fall under section 330.5(a)(3) and is inconsequential, it must also address the Vieux Carre's argument that this nationwide permit is invalid because the Corps did not evaluate the park's impact on historic properties as is required by the Corps' own regulation—section 330.5(b)(9). The Audubon Park Commission notified the Corps (so as to apparently trigger that regulation) when it submitted plans for the project and asked whether permits would be necessary.

CONCLUSION

Because we find that the Vieux Carre has no private right of action under the RHA, and that the APA grants judicial review only of federal agency actions, we affirm the district court's dismissal of the Vieux Carre's claims against all defendants except the Corps. We further hold that the Corps' determination that the aquarium phase of the project was outside its RHA section 10 permitting jurisdiction reflects a reasonable interpretation of the statute and an evaluation of these specific facts that is neither arbitrary nor capricious. Finally, we remand to the district court for a ruling on whether the park phase falls within the nationwide permit in 33 C.F.R. §330.5(a)(3). If the district court determines that the Corps' interpretation of this nationwide permit regulation, or its finding that the park is within the regulation, is arbitrary and capricious, the project must be individually permitted because it is within the Corps' RHA jurisdiction, and thus is subject to section 470f review. If, however, the district court sustains the Corps' determination that the park phase does fall within this nationwide permit regulation, the court is to go on to determine whether the project is so inconsequential that it nevertheless escapes the historic preservation review requirements of NHPA section 470f; and if it does thus escape section 470f, the district court must address section 330.5(b)(9).

Accordingly, the judgment of the district court is AFFIRMED in part and REVERSED in part, and the cause is REMANDED for further proceedings consistent herewith. [Footnotes omitted.]

NWPs frequently provide a safe harbor in violation cases since the Corps is authorized to terminate an enforcement proceeding with an after-the-fact NWP if all of the terms and conditions of the NWP have been satisfied either before or after the activity has been accomplished. Nonetheless, the Corps retains discretionary authority, even in cases in which an NWP would appear to apply, to suspend, modify, or revoke an NWP authorization if the Corps determines that the activity would have more than a minimal individual or cumulative net adverse effect on the environment, or that the activity is contrary to the public interest. In these instances, the Corps must instruct the landowner to apply for an individual permit. Another useful regulation is that two or more different NWPs may be applied to a single and complete project (but the same NWP may not be applied more than once to a single and complete project). In addition, under certain conditions, an NWP may be applied to a portion of a larger project while the individual permit is being evaluated on a different portion.

Some of the NWPs require a delineation. In these cases, if the Corps determines that the adverse effects are more than minimal, the Corps may either require an individual permit or allow the landowner to propose mitigation measures. If the landowner bites the bullet and proposes mitigation along with the original notification, the Corps may consider the mitigation proposal at the same time it is deciding whether the adverse effects are minimal, thus enhancing the chances of permit issuance. Nonetheless, the Corps is supposed to consider the availability of NWPs in reviewing all permit applications, and thus may contact a landowner that an activity could comply with an NWP after reasonable project modifications and/or activity-specific conditions.

Effective in March, 2002, are the following Nationwide Permits, excerpted from the *Federal Register*, Vol. 67, No. 10 (January 15, 2002).

Summary**:** The Corps of Engineers is reissuing all the existing Nationwide Permits (NWPs), General Conditions, and definitions with some modifications, and one new General Condition. These final NWPs will be effective on March 18, 2002. All NWPs except NWPs 7, 12, 14, 27, 31, 40, 41, 42, 43, and 44 expire on February 11, 2002. Existing NWPs 7, 12, 14, 27, 31, 40, 41, 42, 43, and 44 expire on March 18, 2002. In order to reduce the confusion regarding the expiration of the NWPs and the administrative burden of reissuing NWPs at different times, we are issuing all NWPs on the same date so that they expire on the same date. Thus, all issued, reissued and modified NWPs, and General Conditions contained within this notice will become effective on March 18, 2002, and expire on March 19, 2007.

NATIONWIDE PERMITS

NATIONWIDE PERMIT GENERAL CONDITIONS

NATIONWIDE PERMITS

1. *Aids to Navigation*. The placement of aids to navigation and Regulatory markers which are approved by and installed in accordance with the requirements of the U.S. Coast Guard (USCG) (See 33 C.F.R., chapter I, subchapter C part 66). (Section 10)

2. *Structures in Artificial Canals*. Structures constructed in artificial canals within principally residential developments where the connection of the canal to navigable water of the U.S. has been previously authorized (see 33 C.F.R. 322.5(g)). (Section 10)

3. *Maintenance*. Activities related to:

(i) The repair, rehabilitation, or replacement of any previously authorized, currently serviceable, structure, or fill, or of any currently serviceable structure or fill authorized by 33

C.F.R. 330.3, provided that the structure or fill is not to be put to uses differing from those uses specified or contemplated for it in the original permit or the most recently authorized modification. Minor deviations in the structure's configuration or filled area including those due to changes in materials, construction techniques, or current construction codes or safety standards which are necessary to make repair, rehabilitation, or replacement are permitted, provided the adverse environmental effects resulting from such repair, rehabilitation, or replacement are minimal. Currently serviceable means useable as is or with some maintenance, but not so degraded as to essentially require reconstruction. This NWP authorizes the repair, rehabilitation, or replacement of those structures or fills destroyed or damaged by storms, floods, fire or other discrete events, provided the repair, rehabilitation, or replacement is commenced, or is under contract to commence, within two years of the date of their destruction or damage. In cases of catastrophic events, such as hurricanes or tornadoes, this two-year limit may be waived by the District Engineer, provided the permittee can demonstrate funding, contract, or other similar delays.

(ii) Discharges of dredged or fill material, including excavation, into all waters of the U.S. to remove accumulated sediments and debris in the vicinity of, and within, existing structures (*e.g.*, bridges, culverted road crossings, water intake structures, etc.) and the placement of new or additional riprap to protect the structure, provided the permittee notifies the District Engineer in accordance with General Condition 13. The removal of sediment is limited to the minimum necessary to restore the waterway in the immediate vicinity of the structure to the approximate dimensions that existed when the structure was built, but cannot extend further than 200 feet in any direction from the structure. The placement of rip rap must be the minimum necessary to protect the structure or to ensure the safety of the structure. All excavated materials must be deposited and retained in an upland area unless otherwise specifically approved by the District Engineer under separate authorization. Any bank stabilization measures not directly associated with the structure will require a separate authorization from the District Engineer.

(iii) Discharges of dredged or fill material, including excavation, into all waters of the U.S. for activities associated with the restoration of upland areas damaged by a storm, flood, or other discrete event, including the construction, placement, or installation of upland protection structures and minor dredging to remove obstructions in a water of the U.S. (Uplands lost as a result of a storm, flood, or other discrete event can be replaced without a Section 404 permit provided the uplands are restored to their original pre-event location.

This NWP is for the activities in waters of the U.S. associated with the replacement of the uplands.) The permittee must notify the District Engineer, in accordance with General Condition 13, within 12-months of the date of the damage and the work must commence, or be under contract to commence, within two years of the date of the damage. The permittee should provide evidence, such as a recent topographic survey or photographs, to justify the extent of the proposed restoration. The restoration of the damaged areas cannot exceed the contours, or ordinary high water mark, that existed before the damage. The District Engineer retains the right to determine the extent of the pre-existing conditions and the extent of any restoration work authorized by this permit. Minor dredging to remove obstructions from the adjacent waterbody is limited to 50 cubic yards below the plane of the ordinary high water mark, and is limited to the amount necessary to restore the preexisting bottom contours of the waterbody. The dredging may not be done primarily to obtain fill for any restoration activities. The discharge of dredged or fill material and all related work needed to restore the upland must be part of a single and complete project. This permit cannot be used in conjunction with NWP 18 or NWP 19 to restore damaged upland areas. This permit cannot be used to reclaim historic lands lost, over an extended period, to normal erosion processes. This permit does not authorize maintenance dredging for the primary purpose of navigation and beach restoration. This permit does not authorize new stream channelization or stream relocation projects. Any work authorized by this permit must not cause more than minimal degradation of water quality, more than minimal changes to the flow characteristics of the stream, or increase flooding (See General Conditions 9 and 21). (Sections 10 and 404)

Note: This NWP authorizes the repair, rehabilitation, or replacement of any previously authorized structure or fill that does not qualify for the Section 404(f) exemption for maintenance.

4. *Fish and Wildlife Harvesting, Enhancement, and Attraction Devices and Activities*. Fish and wildlife harvesting devices and activities such as pound nets, crab traps, crab dredging, eel pots, lobster traps, duck blinds, clam and oyster digging; and small fish attraction devices such as open water fish concentrators (sea kites, etc.). This NWP authorizes shellfish seeding provided this activity does not occur in wetlands or sites that support submerged aquatic vegetation (including sites where submerged aquatic vegetation is documented to exist, but may not be present in a given year). This NWP does not authorize artificial reefs or impoundments and semi-impoundments of waters of the U.S. for the culture or holding of motile species such as lobster or the use of covered oyster trays or clam racks. (Sections 10 and 404)

5. *Scientific Measurement Devices*. Devices, whose purpose is to measure and record scientific data such as staff gages, tide gages, water recording devices, water quality testing and improvement devices and similar structures. Small weirs and flumes constructed primarily to record water quantity and velocity are also authorized provided the discharge is limited to 25 cubic yards and further for discharges of 10 to 25 cubic yards provided the permittee notifies the District Engineer in accordance with the "Notification" General Condition. (Sections 10 and 404)

6. *Survey Activities*. Survey activities including core sampling, seismic exploratory operations, plugging of seismic shot holes and other exploratory-type bore holes, soil survey, sampling, and historic resources surveys. Discharges and structures associated with the recovery of historic resources are not authorized by this NWP. Drilling and the discharge of excavated material from test wells for oil and gas exploration is not authorized by this NWP; the plugging of such wells is authorized. Fill placed for roads, pads and other similar activities is not authorized by this NWP. The NWP does not authorize any permanent structures. The discharge of drilling mud and cuttings may require a permit under section 402 of the CWA. (Sections 10 and 404)

7. *Outfall Structures and Maintenance*. Activities related to: (i) Construction of outfall structures and associated intake structures where the effluent from the outfall is authorized, conditionally authorized, or specifically exempted, or are otherwise in compliance with regulations issued under the National Pollutant Discharge Elimination System Program (Section 402 of the CWA), and (ii) Maintenance excavation, including dredging, to remove accumulated sediments blocking or restricting outfall and intake structures, accumulated sediments from small impoundments associated with outfall and intake structures, and accumulated sediments from canals associated with outfall and intake structures, provided that the activity meets all of the following criteria:

a. The permittee notifies the District Engineer in accordance with General Condition 13;

b. The amount of excavated or dredged material must be the minimum necessary to restore the outfalls, intakes, small impoundments, and canals to original design capacities and design configurations (*i.e.,* depth and width);

c. The excavated or dredged material is deposited and retained at an upland site, unless otherwise approved by the District Engineer under separate authorization; and

d. Proper soil erosion and sediment control measures are used to minimize reentry of sediments into waters of the U.S. The construction of intake structures is not authorized by this NWP, unless they are directly associated with an authorized outfall structure. For maintenance excavation and dredging to remove accumulated sediments, the notification must include information regarding the original design capacities and configurations of the facility and the presence of special aquatic sites (*e.g.,* vegetated shallows) in the vicinity of the proposed work. (Sections 10 and 404)

8. *Oil and Gas Structures*. Structures for the exploration, production, and transportation of oil, gas, and minerals on the outer continental shelf within areas leased for such purposes by the DOI, Minerals Management Service (MMS). Such structures shall not be placed within the limits of any designated shipping safety fairway or traffic separation scheme, except temporary anchors that comply with the fairway regulations in 33 C.F.R. 322.5(l). (Where such limits have not been designated, or where changes are anticipated, District Engineers will consider asserting discretionary authority in accordance with 33 C.F.R. 330.4(e) and will also review such proposals to ensure they comply with the provisions of the fairway regulations in 33 C.F.R. 322.5(l). Any Corps review under this permit will be limited to the effects on navigation and national security in accordance with 33 C.F.R. 322.5(f)). Such structures will not be placed in established danger zones or restricted areas as designated in 33 C.F.R. part 334: nor will such structures be permitted in EPA or Corps designated dredged material disposal areas. (Section 10)

9. *Structures in Fleeting and Anchorage Areas*. Structures, buoys, floats and other devices placed within anchorage or fleeting areas to facilitate moorage of vessels where the USCG has established such areas for that purpose. (Section 10)

10. *Mooring Buoys*. Non-commercial, single-boat, mooring buoys. (Section 10)

11. *Temporary Recreational Structures*. Temporary buoys, markers, small floating docks, and similar structures placed for recreational use during specific events such as water skiing competitions and boat races or seasonal use provided that such structures are removed within 30 days after use has been discontinued. At Corps of Engineers reservoirs, the reservoir manager must approve each buoy or marker individually. (Section 10)

12. *Utility Line Activities*. Activities required for the construction, maintenance and repair of utility lines and associated facilities in waters of the U.S. as follows:

(i) Utility lines: The construction, maintenance, or repair of utility lines, including outfall and intake structures and the associated excavation, backfill, or bedding for the utility lines, in all waters of the U.S., provided there is no change in preconstruction contours. A "utility line" is defined as any pipe or pipeline for the transportation of any gaseous, liquid, liquescent, or slurry substance, for any purpose, and any cable, line, or wire for the transmission for any purpose of electrical energy, telephone, and telegraph messages, and radio and television communication (see Note 1, below). Material resulting from trench excavation may be temporarily sidecast (up to three months) into waters of the U.S., provided that the material is not placed in such a manner that it is dispersed by currents or other forces. The District Engineer may extend the period of temporary side casting not to exceed a total of 180 days, where appropriate. In wetlands, the top 6" to 12" of the trench should normally be backfilled with topsoil from the trench. Furthermore, the trench cannot be constructed in such a manner as to drain waters of the U.S. (*e.g.,* backfilling with extensive gravel layers, creating a french drain effect). For example, utility line trenches can be backfilled with clay blocks to ensure that the trench does not drain the waters of the U.S. through which the utility line is installed. Any exposed slopes and stream banks must be stabilized immediately upon completion of the utility line crossing of each waterbody.

(ii) Utility line substations: The construction, maintenance, or expansion of a substation facility associated with a power line or utility line in non-tidal waters of the U.S., excluding non-tidal wetlands adjacent to tidal waters, provided the activity does not result in the loss of greater than 1/2-acre of non-tidal waters of the U.S.

(iii) Foundations for overhead utility line towers, poles, and anchors: The construction or maintenance of foundations for overhead utility line towers, poles, and anchors in all waters of the U.S., provided the foundations are the minimum size necessary and separate footings for each tower leg (rather than a larger single pad) are used where feasible.

(iv) Access roads: The construction of access roads for the construction and maintenance of utility lines, including overhead power lines and utility line substations, in non-tidal waters of the U.S., excluding non-tidal wetlands adjacent to tidal waters, provided the discharges do not cause the loss of greater than 1/2-acre of non-tidal waters of the U.S. Access roads shall be the minimum width necessary (see Note 2, below). Access roads must be constructed so that the length of the road minimizes the adverse effects on waters of the U.S. and as near as possible to preconstruction contours and elevations (*e.g.,* at grade corduroy roads or geotextile/gravel roads). Access roads constructed above preconstruction contours and elevations in waters of the U.S. must be properly bridged or culverted to maintain surface flows. The term "utility line" does not include activities which drain a water of the U.S., such as drainage tile, or French drains; however, it does apply to pipes conveying drainage from another area. For the purposes of this NWP, the loss of waters of the U.S. includes the filled area plus waters of the U.S. that are adversely affected by flooding, excavation, or drainage as a result of the project. Activities authorized by paragraph (i) through (iv) may not exceed a total of 1/2-acre loss of waters of the U.S. Waters of the U.S. temporarily affected by filling, flooding, excavation, or drainage, where the project area is restored to preconstruction contours and elevation, is not included in the calculation of permanent loss of waters of the U.S. This includes temporary construction mats (*e.g.,* timber, steel, geotextile) used during construction and removed upon completion of the work. Where certain functions and values of waters of the U.S. are permanently adversely affected, such as the conversion of a forested wetland to a herbaceous wetland in the permanently maintained utility line right-of-way, mitigation will be required to reduce the adverse effects of the project to the minimal level. Mechanized land clearing necessary for the construction, maintenance, or repair of utility lines and the construction, maintenance and expansion of utility line substations, foundations for overhead utility lines, and access roads is authorized, provided the cleared area is kept to the minimum necessary and preconstruction contours are maintained as near as possible. The area of waters of the U.S. that is filled, excavated, or flooded must be limited to the minimum necessary to construct the utility line, substations, foundations, and access roads. Excess material must be removed to upland areas immediately upon completion of construction. This NWP may authorize utility lines in or affecting navigable waters of the U.S. even if there is no associated discharge of dredged or fill material (See 33 C.F.R. part 322).

Notification: The permittee must notify the District Engineer in accordance with General Condition 13, if any of the following criteria are met:

(a) Mechanized land clearing in a forested wetland for the utility line right-of-way;

(b) A Section 10 permit is required;

(c) The utility line in waters of the U.S., excluding overhead lines, exceeds 500 feet;

(d) The utility line is placed within a jurisdictional area (*i.e.,* water of the U.S.), and it runs parallel to a stream bed that is within that jurisdictional area;

(e) Discharges associated with the construction of utility line substations that result in the loss of greater than 1/10-acre of waters of the U.S.; or

(f) Permanent access roads constructed above grade in waters of the U.S. for a distance of more than 500 feet.

(g) Permanent access roads constructed in waters of the U.S. with impervious materials. (Sections 10 and 404)

Note 1: Overhead utility lines constructed over Section 10 waters and utility lines that are routed in or under Section 10 waters without a discharge of dredged or fill material require a Section 10 permit; except for pipes or pipelines used to transport gaseous, liquid, liquescent, or slurry substances over navigable waters of the U.S., which are considered to be bridges, not utility lines, and may require a permit from the USCG pursuant to section 9 of the Rivers and Harbors Act of 1899. However, any discharges of dredged or fill material associated with such pipelines will require a Corps permit under Section 404.

Note 2: Access roads used for both construction and maintenance may be authorized, provided they meet the terms and conditions of this NWP. Access roads used solely for construction of the utility line must be removed upon completion of the work and the area restored to preconstruction contours, elevations, and wetland conditions. Temporary access roads for construction may be authorized by NWP 33.

Note 3: Where the proposed utility line is constructed or installed in navigable waters of the U.S. (*i.e.,* Section 10 waters), copies of the PCN and NWP verification will be sent by the Corps to the National Oceanic and Atmospheric Administration (NOAA), National Ocean Service (NOS), for charting the utility line to protect navigation.

13. *Bank Stabilization*. Bank stabilization activities necessary for erosion prevention provided the activity meets all of the following criteria:

a. No material is placed more than the minimum needed for erosion protection;

b. The bank stabilization activity is less than 500 feet in length;

c. The activity will not exceed an average of one cubic yard per running foot placed along the bank below the plane of the ordinary high water mark or the high tide line;

d. No material is placed in any special aquatic site, including wetlands;

e. No material is of the type, or is placed in any location, or in any manner, to impair surface water flow into or out of any wetland area;

f. No material is placed in a manner that will be eroded by normal or expected high flows (properly anchored trees and treetops may be used in low energy areas); and,

g. The activity is part of a single and complete project.

Bank stabilization activities in excess of 500 feet in length or greater than an average of one cubic yard per running foot may be authorized if the permittee notifies the District Engineer in accordance with the "*Notification*" General Condition 13 and the District Engineer determines the activity complies with the other terms and conditions of the NWP and the adverse environmental effects are minimal both individually and cumulatively. This NWP may not be used for the channelization of waters of the U.S. (Sections 10 and 404)

14. *Linear Transportation Projects*.

Activities required for the construction, expansion, modification, or improvement of linear transportation crossings (*e.g.,* highways, railways, trails, airport runways, and taxiways) in waters of the U.S., including wetlands, if the activity meets the following criteria:

a. This NWP is subject to the following acreage limits:

(1) For linear transportation projects in non-tidal waters, provided the discharge does not cause the loss of greater than 1/2-acre of waters of the U.S.;

(2) For linear transportation projects in tidal waters, provided the discharge does not cause the loss of greater than 1/3-acre of waters of the U.S.

b. The permittee must notify the District Engineer in accordance with General Condition 13 if any of the following criteria are met:

(1) The discharge causes the loss of greater than 1/10-acre of waters of the U.S.; or

(2) There is a discharge in a special aquatic site, including wetlands;

c. The *notification* must include a compensatory mitigation proposal to offset permanent losses of waters of the U.S. to ensure that those losses result only in minimal adverse effects to the aquatic environment and a statement describing how temporary losses will be minimized to the maximum extent practicable;

d. For discharges in special aquatic sites, including wetlands, and stream riffle and pool complexes, the *notification* must include a delineation of the affected special aquatic sites;

e. The width of the fill is limited to the minimum necessary for the crossing;

f. This permit does not authorize stream channelization, and the authorized activities must not cause more than minimal changes to the hydraulic flow characteristics of the stream, increase flooding, or cause more than minimal degradation of water quality of any stream (see General Conditions 9 and 21);

g. This permit cannot be used to authorize non-linear features commonly associated with transportation projects, such as vehicle maintenance or storage buildings, parking lots, train stations, or aircraft hangars; and

h. The crossing is a single and complete project for crossing waters of the U.S. Where a road segment (*i.e.*, the shortest segment of a road with independent utility that is part of a larger project) has multiple crossings of streams (several single and complete projects) the Corps will consider whether it should use its discretionary authority to require an Individual Permit. (Sections 10 and 404)

Note: Some discharges for the construction of farm roads, forest roads, or temporary roads for moving mining equipment may be eligible for an exemption from the need for a Section 404 permit (see 33 C.F.R. 323.4).

15. *U.S. Coast Guard Approved Bridges*. Discharges of dredged or fill material incidental to the construction of bridges across navigable waters of the U.S., including cofferdams, abutments, foundation seals, piers, and temporary construction and access fills provided such discharges have been authorized by the USCG as part of the bridge permit. Causeways and approach fills are not included in this NWP and will require an individual or regional Section 404 permit. (Section 404)

16. *Return Water From Upland Contained Disposal Areas*. Return water from upland, contained dredged material disposal area. The dredging itself may require a Section 404 permit (33 C.F.R. 323.2(d)), but will require a Section 10 permit if located in navigable waters of the U.S. The return water from a contained disposal area is administratively defined as a discharge of dredged material by 33 C.F.R. 323.2(d), even though the disposal itself occurs on the upland and does not require a Section 404 permit. This NWP satisfies the technical requirement for a Section 404 permit for the return water where the quality of the return water is controlled by the state through the Section 401 certification procedures. (Section 404)

17. *Hydropower Projects*. Discharges of dredged or fill material associated with (a) small hydropower projects at existing reservoirs where the project, which includes the fill, are licensed by the Federal Energy Regulatory Commission (FERC) under the Federal Power Act of 1920, as amended; and has a total generating capacity of not more than 5000 kW; and the permittee notifies the District Engineer in accordance with the "Notification" General Condition; or (b) hydropower projects for which the FERC has granted an exemption from licensing pursuant to section 408 of the Energy Security Act of 1980 (16 U.S.C. 2705 and 2708) and section 30 of the Federal Power Act, as amended; provided the permittee notifies the District Engineer in accordance with the "Notification" General Condition. (Section 404)

18. *Minor Discharges*. Minor discharges of dredged or fill material into all waters of the U.S. if the activity meets all of the following criteria:

a. The quantity of discharged material and the volume of area excavated do not exceed 25 cubic yards below the plane of the ordinary high water mark or the high tide line;

b. The discharge, including any excavated area, will not cause the loss of more than 110-acre of a special aquatic site, including wetlands. For the purposes of this NWP, the acreage limitation includes the filled area and excavated area plus special aquatic sites that are adversely affected by flooding and special aquatic sites that are drained so that they would no longer be a water of the U.S. as a result of the project;

c. If the discharge, including any excavated area, exceeds 10 cubic yards below the plane of the ordinary high water mark or the high tide line or if the discharge is in a special aquatic site, including wetlands, the permittee notifies the District Engineer in accordance with the "Notification" General Condition. For discharges in special aquatic sites, including wetlands, the notification must also include a delineation of affected special aquatic sites, including wetlands (also see 33 C.F.R. 330.1(e)); and

d. The discharge, including all attendant features, both temporary and permanent, is part of a single and complete project and is not placed for the purpose of a stream diversion. (Sections 10 and 404)

19. *Minor Dredging*. Dredging of no more than 25 cubic yards below the plane of the ordinary high water mark or the mean high water mark from navigable waters of the U.S. (*i.e.,* Section 10 waters) as part of a single and complete project. This NWP does not authorize the dredging or degradation through siltation of coral reefs, sites that support submerged aquatic vegetation (including sites where submerged aquatic vegetation is documented to exist, but may not be present in a given year), anadromous fish spawning areas, or wetlands, or the connection of canals or other artificial waterways to navigable waters of the U.S. (see 33 C.F.R. 322.5(g)). (Sections 10 and 404)

20. *Oil Spill Cleanup*. Activities required for the containment and cleanup of oil and hazardous substances which are subject to the National Oil and Hazardous Substances Pollution Contingency Plan (40 C.F.R. part 300) provided that the work is done in accordance with the Spill Control and Countermeasure Plan required by 40 C.F.R. 112.3 and any existing state contingency plan and provided that the Regional Response Team (if one exists in the area) concurs with the proposed containment and cleanup action. (Sections 10 and 404)

21. *Surface Coal Mining Activities*. Discharges of dredged or fill material into waters of the U.S. associated with surface coal mining and reclamation operations provided the coal mining activities are authorized by the DOI, Office of Surface Mining (OSM), or by states with approved programs under Title V of the Surface Mining Control and Reclamation Act of 1977 and provided the permittee notifies the District Engineer in accordance with the "Notification" General Condition. In addition, to be authorized by this NWP, the District Engineer must determine that the activity complies with the terms and conditions of the NWP and that the adverse environmental effects are minimal both individually and cumulatively and must notify the project sponsor of this determination in writing. The Corps, at the discretion of the District Engineer, may require a bond to ensure success of the mitigation, if no other Federal or state agency has required one. For discharges in special aquatic sites, including wetlands, and stream riffle and pool complexes, the notification must also include a delineation of affected special aquatic sites, including wetlands. (also, see 33 C.F.R. 330.1(e))

Mitigation: In determining the need for as well as the level and type of mitigation, the District Engineer will ensure no more than minimal adverse effects to the aquatic environment occur. As such, District Engineers will determine on a case-by-case basis the requirement for adequate mitigation to ensure the effects to aquatic systems are minimal. In cases where OSM or the state has required mitigation for the loss of aquatic habitat, the Corps may consider this in determining appropriate mitigation under Section 404. (Sections 10 and 404)

22. *Removal of Vessels*. Temporary structures or minor discharges of dredged or fill material required for the removal of wrecked, abandoned, or disabled vessels, or the removal of man-made obstructions to navigation. This NWP does not authorize the removal of vessels listed or determined eligible for listing on the National Register of Historic Places unless the District Engineer is notified and indicates that there is compliance with the "Historic Properties" General Condition. This NWP does not authorize maintenance dredging, shoal removal, or riverbank snagging. Vessel disposal in waters of the U.S. may need a permit from EPA (see 40 C.F.R. 229.3). (Sections 10 and 404)

23. *Approved Categorical Exclusions*. Activities undertaken, assisted, authorized, regulated, funded, or financed, in whole or in part, by another Federal agency or department where that agency or department has determined, pursuant to the Council on Environmental Quality Regulation for Implementing the Procedural Provisions of the National Environmental Policy Act (NEPA) (40 C.F.R. part 1500 *et seq.*), that the activity, work, or discharge is categorically excluded from environmental documentation, because it is included within a category of actions which neither individually nor cumulatively have a significant effect on the human environment, and the Office of the Chief of Engineers (ATTN: CECWOR) has been furnished notice of the agency's or department's application for the categorical exclusion and concurs with that determination. Before approval for purposes of this NWP of any agency's categorical exclusions, the Chief of Engineers will solicit public comment. In addressing these comments, the Chief of Engineers may require certain conditions for authorization of an agency's categorical exclusions under this NWP. (Sections 10 and 404)

24. *State Administered Section 404 Program*. Any activity permitted by a state administering its own Section 404 permit program pursuant to 33 U.S.C. 1344(g)–(l) is permitted pursuant to section 10 of the Rivers and Harbors Act of 1899. Those activities that do not involve a Section 404 state permit are not included in this NWP, but certain structures will be exempted by section 154 of Pub. L. 94–587, 90 Stat. 2917 (33 U.S.C. 591) (see 33 C.F.R. 322.3(a)(2)). (Section 10)

25. *Structural Discharges*. Discharges of material such as concrete, sand, rock, etc., into tightly sealed forms or cells where the material will be used as a structural member for standard pile supported structures, such as bridges, transmission line footings, and walkways or for general navigation, such as mooring cells, including the excavation of bottom material from within the form prior to the discharge of concrete, sand, rock, etc. This NWP does not authorize filled structural members that would support buildings, building pads, homes, house pads, parking areas, storage areas and other such structures. The structure itself may require a Section 10 permit if located in navigable waters of the U.S. (Section 404)

26. [Reserved]

27. *Stream and Wetland Restoration Activities*. Activities in waters of the U.S. associated with the restoration of former waters, the enhancement of degraded tidal and non-tidal wetlands and riparian areas, the creation of tidal and non-tidal wetlands and riparian areas, and the restoration and enhancement of non-tidal streams and non-tidal open water areas as follows:

(a) *The activity is conducted on:*

(1) Non-Federal public lands and private lands, in accordance with the terms and conditions of a binding wetland enhancement, restoration, or creation agreement between the landowner and the U.S. Fish and Wildlife Service (FWS) or the Natural Resources Conservation Service (NRCS), the National Marine Fisheries Service, the National Ocean Service, or voluntary wetland restoration, enhancement, and creation actions documented by the NRCS pursuant to NRCS regulations; or

(2) Reclaimed surface coal mine lands, in accordance with a Surface Mining Control and Reclamation Act permit issued by the OSM or the applicable state agency (the future reversion does not apply to streams or wetlands created, restored, or enhanced as mitigation for the mining impacts, nor naturally due to hydrologic or topographic features, nor for a mitigation bank); or

(3) Any other public, private or tribal lands;

(b) *Notification:* For activities on any public or private land that are not described by paragraphs (a)(1) or (a)(2) above, the permittee must notify the District Engineer in accordance with General Condition 13; and

(c) Planting of only native species should occur on the site.

Activities authorized by this NWP include, to the extent that a Corps permit is required, but are not limited to: the removal of accumulated sediments; the installation, removal, and maintenance of small water control structures, dikes, and berms; the installation of current deflectors; the enhancement, restoration, or creation of riffle and pool stream structure; the placement of in-stream habitat structures; modifications of the stream bed and/or banks to restore or create stream meanders; the backfilling of artificial channels and drainage ditches; the removal of existing drainage structures; the construction of small nesting islands; the construction of open water areas; the construction of oyster habitat over unvegetated bottom in tidal waters; activities needed to reestablish vegetation, including plowing or discing for seed bed preparation and the planting of appropriate wetland species; mechanized land clearing to remove non-native invasive, exotic or nuisance vegetation; and other related activities. This NWP does not authorize the conversion of a stream to another aquatic use, such as the creation of an impoundment for waterfowl habitat. This NWP does not authorize stream channelization. This NWP does not authorize the conversion of natural wetlands to another aquatic use, such as creation of waterfowl impoundments where a forested wetland previously existed. However, this NWP authorizes the relocation of non-tidal waters, including non-tidal wetlands, on the project site provided there are net gains in aquatic resource functions and values. For example, this NWP may authorize the creation of an open water impoundment in a non-tidal emergent wetland, provided the non-tidal emergent wetland is replaced by creating that wetland type on the project site. This NWP does not authorize the relocation of tidal waters or the conversion of tidal waters, including tidal wetlands, to other aquatic uses, such as the conversion of tidal wetlands into open water impoundments. *Reversion.* For enhancement, restoration, and creation projects conducted under paragraphs (a)(3), this NWP does not authorize any future discharge of dredged or fill material associated with the reversion of the area to its prior condition. In such cases a separate permit would be required for any reversion. For restoration, enhancement, and creation projects conducted under paragraphs (a)(1) and (a)(2), this NWP also authorizes any future discharge of dredged or fill material associated with the reversion of the area to its documented prior condition and use (*i.e.,* prior to the restoration, enhancement, or creation activities). The reversion must occur within five years after expiration of a limited term wetland restoration or creation agreement or permit, even if the discharge occurs after this NWP expires. This NWP also authorizes the reversion of wetlands that were restored, enhanced, or created on prior-converted cropland that has not been abandoned, in accordance with a binding agreement between the landowner and NRCS or FWS (even though the restoration, enhancement, or creation activity did not require a Section 404 permit). The five-year reversion limit does not apply to agreements without time limits reached under paragraph (a)(1). The prior condition will be documented in the original agreement or permit, and the determination of return to prior conditions will be made by the Federal agency or appropriate state agency executing the agreement or permit. Before any reversion activity the permittee or the appropriate Federal or state agency must notify the District Engineer and include the documentation of the prior condition. Once an area has reverted to its prior physical condition, it will be subject to whatever the Corps Regulatory requirements will be at that future date. (Sections 10 and 404)

Note: Compensatory mitigation is not required for activities authorized by this NWP, provided the authorized work results in a net increase in aquatic resource functions and values in the project area. This NWP can be used to authorize compensatory mitigation projects, including mitigation banks, provided the permittee notifies the District Engineer in accordance with General Condition 13, and the project includes compensatory mitigation for impacts to waters of the U.S. caused by the authorized work. However, this NWP does not authorize the reversion of an area used for a compensatory mitigation project to its prior condition. NWP 27 can be used to authorize impacts at a mitigation bank, but only in circumstances where it has been approved under the Interagency Federal Mitigation Bank Guidelines.

28. *Modifications of Existing Marinas*. Reconfiguration of existing docking facilities within an authorized marina area. No dredging, additional slips, dock spaces, or expansion of any kind within waters of the U.S. is authorized by this NWP. (Section 10)

29. *Single-family Housing*. Discharges of dredged or fill material into non-tidal waters of the U.S., including non-tidal wetlands for the construction or expansion of a single-family home and attendant features (such as a garage, driveway, storage shed, and/or septic field) for an Individual Permittee provided that the activity meets all of the following criteria:

a. The discharge does not cause the loss of more than 14-acre of non-tidal waters of the U.S., including non-tidal wetlands;

b. The permittee notifies the District Engineer in accordance with the "Notification" General Condition;

c. The permittee has taken all practicable actions to minimize the onsite and off-site impacts of the discharge. For example, the location of the home may need to be adjusted onsite to avoid flooding of adjacent property owners;

d. The discharge is part of a single and complete project; furthermore, that for any subdivision created on or after November 22, 1991, the discharges authorized under this NWP may not exceed an aggregate total loss of waters of the U.S. of 14-acre for the entire subdivision;

e. An individual may use this NWP only for a single-family home for a personal residence;

f. This NWP may be used only once per parcel;

g. This NWP may not be used in conjunction with NWP 14 or NWP 18, for any parcel; and,

h. Sufficient vegetated buffers must be maintained adjacent to all open water bodies, streams, etc., to preclude water quality degradation due to erosion and sedimentation. For the purposes of this NWP, the acreage of loss of waters of the U.S. includes the filled area previously permitted, the proposed filled area, and any other waters of the U.S. that are adversely affected by flooding, excavation, or drainage as a result of the project. This NWP authorizes activities only by individuals; for this purpose, the term "individual" refers to a natural person and/or a married couple, but does not include a corporation, partnership, or similar entity. For the purposes of this NWP, a parcel of land is defined as "the entire contiguous quantity of land in possession of, recorded as property of, or owned (in any form of ownership, including land owned as a partner, corporation, joint tenant, etc.) by the same individual (and/or that individual's spouse), and comprises not only the area of wetlands sought to be filled, but also all land contiguous to those wetlands, owned by the individual (and/or that individual's spouse) in any form of ownership." (Sections 10 and 404)

30. *Moist Soil Management for Wildlife*. Discharges of dredged or fill material and maintenance activities that are associated with moist soil management for wildlife performed on non-tidal Federally-owned or managed, state-owned or managed property, and local government agency-owned or managed property, for the purpose of continuing ongoing, site-specific, wildlife management activities where soil manipulation is used to manage habitat and feeding areas for wildlife. Such activities include, but are not limited to: The repair, maintenance or replacement of existing water control structures; the repair or maintenance of dikes; and plowing or discing to impede succession, prepare seed beds, or establish fire breaks. Sufficient vegetated buffers must be maintained adjacent to all open water bodies, streams, etc., to preclude water quality degradation due to erosion and sedimentation. This NWP does not authorize the construction of new dikes, roads, water control structures, etc. associated with the management areas. This NWP does not authorize converting wetlands to uplands, impoundments or other open water bodies. (Section 404)

31. *Maintenance of Existing Flood Control Facilities*. Discharge of dredge or fill material resulting from activities associated with the maintenance of existing flood control facilities, including debris basins, retention/detention basins, and channels that

(i) were previously authorized by the Corps by Individual Permit, General Permit, by 33 C.F.R. 330.3, or did not require a permit at the time it was constructed, or

(ii) were constructed by the Corps and transferred to a non-Federal sponsor for operation and maintenance. Activities authorized by this NWP are limited to those resulting from maintenance activities that are conducted within the "maintenance baseline," as described in the definition below. Activities including the discharges of dredged or fill materials, associated with maintenance activities in flood control facilities in any watercourse that has previously been determined to be within the maintenance baseline, are authorized under this NWP. The NWP does not authorize the removal of sediment and associated vegetation from the natural water courses except to the extent that these have been included in the maintenance baseline. All dredged material must be placed in an upland site or an authorized disposal site in waters of the U.S., and proper siltation controls must be used. (Activities of any kind that result in only incidental fallback, or only the cutting and removing of vegetation above the ground, *e.g.,* mowing, rotary cutting, and chainsawing, where the activity neither substantially disturbs the root system nor involves mechanized pushing, dragging, or other similar activities that redeposit excavated soil material, do not require a Section 404 permit in accordance with 33 C.F.R. 323.2(d)(2)).

Notification: After the maintenance baseline is established, and before any maintenance work is conducted, the permittee must notify the District Engineer in accordance with the "Notification" General Condition. The notification may be for activity-specific maintenance or for maintenance of the entire flood control facility by submitting a five year (or less) maintenance plan.

Maintenance Baseline: The maintenance baseline is a description of the physical characteristics (*e.g.,* depth, width, length, location, configuration, or design flood capacity, etc.) of a flood control project within which maintenance activities are normally authorized by NWP 31, subject to any case-specific conditions required by the District Engineer. The District Engineer will approve the maintenance baseline based on the approved or constructed capacity of the flood control facility, whichever is smaller, including any areas where there are no constructed channels, but which are part of the facility. If no evidence of the constructed capacity exist, the approved constructed capacity will be used. The prospective permittee will provide documentation of the physical characteristics of the flood control facility (which will normally consist of as-built or approved drawings) and documentation of the design capacities of the flood control facility. The documentation will also include BMPs to ensure that the impacts to the aquatic environment are minimal, especially in maintenance areas where there are no constructed channels. (The Corps may request maintenance records in areas where there has not been recent maintenance.) Revocation or modification of the final determination of the maintenance baseline can only be done in accordance with 33 C.F.R. 330.5. Except in emergencies as described below, this NWP can not be used until the District Engineer approves the maintenance baseline and determines the need for mitigation and any regional or activity-specific conditions. Once determined, the maintenance baseline will remain valid for any subsequent reissuance of this NWP. This permit does not authorize maintenance of a flood control facility that has been abandoned. A flood control facility will be considered abandoned if it has operated at a significantly reduced capacity without needed maintenance being accomplished in a timely manner. *Mitigation:* The District Engineer will determine any required mitigation onetime only for impacts associated with maintenance work at the same time that the maintenance baseline is approved. Such one-time mitigation will be required when necessary to ensure that adverse environmental impacts are no more than minimal, both individually and cumulatively. Such mitigation will only be required once for any specific reach of a flood control project. However, if one-time mitigation is required for impacts associated with maintenance activities, the District Engineer will not delay needed maintenance, provided the District Engineer and the permittee establish a schedule for identification, approval, development, construction and completion of any such required mitigation. Once the one-time mitigation described above has been completed, or a determination made that mitigation is not required, no further mitigation will be required for maintenance activities within the maintenance baseline. In determining appropriate mitigation, the District

Engineer will give special consideration to natural water courses that have been included in the maintenance baseline and require compensatory mitigation and/or BMPs as appropriate.

Emergency Situations: In emergency situations, this NWP may be used to authorize maintenance activities in flood control facilities for which no maintenance baseline has been approved. Emergency situations are those which would result in an unacceptable hazard to life, a significant loss of property, or an immediate, unforeseen, and significant economic hardship if action is not taken before a maintenance baseline can be approved. In such situations, the determination of mitigation requirements, if any, may be deferred until the emergency has been resolved. Once the emergency has ended, a maintenance baseline must be established expeditiously, and mitigation, including mitigation for maintenance conducted during the emergency, must be required as appropriate. (Sections 10 and 404)

32. *Completed Enforcement Actions*. Any structure, work or discharge of dredged or fill material, remaining in place, or undertaken for mitigation, restoration, or environmental benefit in compliance with either:

(i) The terms of a final written Corps non-judicial settlement agreement resolving a violation of section 404 of the CWA and/or section 10 of the Rivers and Harbors Act of 1899; or the terms of an EPA 309(a) order on consent resolving a violation of section 404 of the CWA, provided that:

a. The unauthorized activity affected no more than 5 acres of non-tidal wetlands or 1 acre of tidal wetlands;

b. The settlement agreement provides for environmental benefits, to an equal or greater degree, than the environmental detriments caused by the unauthorized activity that is authorized by this NWP; and

c. The District Engineer issues a verification letter authorizing the activity subject to the terms and conditions of this NWP and the settlement agreement, including a specified completion date; or

(ii) The terms of a final Federal court decision, consent decree, or settlement agreement resulting from an enforcement action brought by the U.S. under section 404 of the CWA and/or section 10 of the Rivers and Harbors Act of 1899; or

(iii) The terms of a final court decision, consent decree, settlement agreement, or non-judicial settlement agreement resulting from a natural resource damage claim brought by a trustee or trustees for natural resources (as defined by the National Contingency Plan at 40 C.F.R. subpart G) under section 311 of the Clean Water Act (CWA), section 107 of the Comprehensive Environmental Response, Compensation and Liability Act (CERCLA or Superfund), section 312 of the National Marine Sanctuaries Act (NMSA), section 1002 of the Oil Pollution Act of 1990 (OPA), or the Park System Resource Protection Act at 16 U.S.C. '19jj, to the extent that a Corps permit is required.

For either (i), (ii) or (iii) above, compliance is a condition of the NWP itself. Any authorization under this NWP is automatically revoked if the permittee does not comply with the terms of this NWP or the terms of the court decision, consent decree, or judicial/non-judicial settlement agreement or fails to complete the work by the specified completion date. This NWP does not apply to any activities occurring after the date of the decision, decree, or agreement that are not for the purpose of mitigation, restoration, or environmental benefit. Before reaching any settlement agreement, the Corps will ensure compliance with the provisions of 33 C.F.R. part 326 and 33 C.F.R. 330.6 (d)(2) and (e). (Sections 10 and 404)

33. *Temporary Construction, Access and Dewatering*. Temporary structures, work and discharges, including cofferdams, necessary for construction activities or access fills or dewatering of construction sites; provided that the associated primary activity is authorized by the Corps of Engineers or the USCG, or for other construction activities not subject to the Corps or USCG regulations. Appropriate measures must be taken to maintain near normal downstream flows and to minimize flooding. Fill must be of materials, and placed in a manner, that will not be eroded by expected high flows. The use of dredged material may be allowed if it is determined by the District Engineer that it will not cause more than minimal adverse effects on aquatic resources. Temporary fill must be entirely removed to upland areas, or dredged material returned to its original location, following completion of the construction activity, and the affected areas must be restored to the pre-project conditions. Cofferdams cannot be used to dewater wetlands or other aquatic areas to change their use. Structures left in place after cofferdams are removed require a Section 10 permit if located in navigable waters of the U.S. (See 33 C.F.R. part 322). The permittee must notify the District Engineer in accordance with the "Notification" General Condition. The notification must also include a restoration plan of reasonable measures to avoid and minimize adverse effects to aquatic resources. The District Engineer will add Special Conditions, where necessary, to ensure environmental adverse effects is minimal. Such conditions may include: limiting the temporary work to the minimum necessary; requiring seasonal restrictions; modifying the restoration plan; and requiring alternative construction methods (e.g. construction mats in wetlands where practicable.). (Sections 10 and 404)

34. *Cranberry Production Activities*. Discharges of dredged or fill material for dikes, berms, pumps, water control structures or leveling of cranberry beds associated with expansion, enhancement, or modification activities at existing cranberry production operations provided that the activity meets all of the following criteria:

a. The cumulative total acreage of disturbance per cranberry production operation, including but not limited to, filling, flooding, ditching, or clearing, does not exceed 10 acres of waters of the U.S., including wetlands;

b. The permittee notifies the District Engineer in accordance with the "Notification" General Condition. The notification must include a delineation of affected special aquatic sites, including wetlands; and,

c. The activity does not result in a net loss of wetland acreage. This NWP does not authorize any discharge of dredged or fill material related to other cranberry production activities such as warehouses, processing facilities, or parking areas. For the purposes of this NWP, the cumulative total of 10 acres will be measured over the period that this NWP is valid. (Section 404)

35. *Maintenance Dredging of Existing Basins*. Excavation and removal of accumulated sediment for maintenance of existing marina basins, access channels to marinas or boat slips, and boat slips to previously authorized depths or controlling depths for ingress/egress, whichever is less, provided the dredged material is disposed of at an upland site and proper siltation controls are used. (Section 10)

36. *Boat Ramps*. Activities required for the construction of boat ramps provided:

a. The discharge into waters of the U.S. does not exceed 50 cubic yards of concrete, rock, crushed stone or gravel into forms, or placement of pre-cast concrete planks or slabs. (Unsuitable material that causes unacceptable chemical pollution or is structurally unstable is not authorized);

b. The boat ramp does not exceed 20 feet in width;

c. The base material is crushed stone, gravel or other suitable material;

d. The excavation is limited to the area necessary for site preparation and all excavated material is removed to the upland; and,

e. No material is placed in special aquatic sites, including wetlands.

Another NWP, Regional General Permit, or Individual Permit may authorize dredging to provide access to the boat ramp after obtaining a Section 10 if located in navigable waters of the U.S. (Sections 10 and 404)

37. *Emergency Watershed Protection and Rehabilitation*. Work done by or funded by:

a. The NRCS which is a situation requiring immediate action under its emergency Watershed Protection Program (7 C.F.R. part 624); or

b. The USFS under its Burned-Area Emergency Rehabilitation Handbook (FSH 509.13); or

c. The DOI for wildland fire management burned area emergency stabilization and rehabilitation (DOI Manual part 620, Ch. 3).

For all of the above provisions, the District Engineer must be notified in accordance with the General Condition 13. (Also, see 33 C.F.R. 330.1(e)). (Sections 10 and 404)

38. *Cleanup of Hazardous and Toxic Waste*. Specific activities required to effect the containment, stabilization, or removal of hazardous or toxic waste materials that are performed, ordered, or sponsored by a government agency with established legal or regulatory authority provided the permittee notifies the District Engineer in accordance with the "Notification" General Condition. For discharges in special aquatic sites, including wetlands, the notification must also include a delineation of affected special aquatic sites, including wetlands. Court ordered remedial action plans or related settlements are also authorized by this NWP. This NWP does not authorize the establishment of new disposal sites or the expansion of existing sites used for the disposal of hazardous or toxic waste. Activities undertaken entirely on a Comprehensive Environmental Response, Compensation, and Liability Act (CERCLA) site by authority of CERCLA as approved or required by EPA, are not required to obtain permits under section 404 of the CWA or section 10 of the Rivers and Harbors Act. (Sections 10 and 404)

39. *Residential, Commercial, and Institutional Developments*. Discharges of dredged or fill material into non-tidal waters of the U.S., excluding non-tidal wetlands adjacent to tidal waters, for the construction or expansion of residential, commercial, and institutional building foundations and building pads and attendant features that are necessary for the use and maintenance of the structures. Attendant features may include, but are not limited to, roads, parking lots, garages, yards, utility lines, stormwater management facilities, and recreation facilities such as playgrounds, playing fields, and golf courses (provided the golf course is an integral part of the residential development). The construction of new ski areas or oil and gas wells is not authorized by this NWP. Residential developments include multiple and single unit developments. Examples of commercial developments include retail stores, industrial facilities, restaurants, business parks, and shopping centers. Examples of institutional developments include schools, fire stations, government office buildings, judicial buildings, public works buildings, libraries, hospitals, and places of worship. The activities listed above are authorized, provided the activities meet all of the following criteria:

a. The discharge does not cause the loss of greater than 12-acre of non-tidal waters of the U.S., excluding non-tidal wetlands adjacent to tidal waters;

b. The discharge does not cause the loss of greater than 300 linear-feet of a stream bed, unless for intermittent stream beds this criterion is waived in writing pursuant to a determination by the District Engineer, as specified below, that the project complies with all terms and conditions of this NWP and that any adverse impacts of the project on the aquatic environment are minimal, both individually and cumulatively;

c. The permittee must notify the District Engineer in accordance with General Condition 13, if any of the following criteria are met:

(1) The discharge causes the loss of greater than 1/10-acre of non-tidal waters of the U.S., excluding non-tidal wetlands adjacent to tidal waters; or

(2) The discharge causes the loss of any open waters, including perennial or intermittent streams, below the ordinary high water mark (see Note, below); or

(3) The discharge causes the loss of greater than 300 linear feet of intermittent stream bed. In such case, to be authorized the District Engineer must determine that the activity complies with the other terms and conditions of the NWP, determine adverse environmental effects are minimal both individually and cumulatively, and waive the limitation on stream impacts in writing before the permittee may proceed;

d. For discharges in special aquatic sites, including wetlands, the notification must include a delineation of affected special aquatic sites;

e. The discharge is part of a single and complete project;

f. The permittee must avoid and minimize discharges into waters of the U.S. at the project site to the maximum extent practicable. The notification, when required, must include a written statement explaining how avoidance and minimization of losses of waters of the U.S. were achieved on the project site. Compensatory mitigation will normally be required to offset the losses of waters of the U.S. (See General Condition 19.) The notification must also include a compensatory mitigation proposal for offsetting unavoidable losses of waters of the U.S. If an applicant asserts that the adverse effects of the project are minimal without mitigation, then the applicant may submit justification explaining why compensatory mitigation should not be required for the District Engineer's consideration;

g. When this NWP is used in conjunction with any other NWP, any combined total permanent loss of waters of the U.S. exceeding 110-acre requires that the permittee notify the District Engineer in accordance with General Condition 13;

h. Any work authorized by this NWP must not cause more than minimal degradation of water quality or more than minimal changes to the flow characteristics of any stream (see General Conditions 9 and 21);

i. For discharges causing the loss of 1/10-acre or less of waters of the U.S., the permittee must submit a report, within 30 days of completion of the work, to the District Engineer that contains the following information:

(1) The name, address, and telephone number of the permittee;

(2) The location of the work;

(3) A description of the work;

(4) The type and acreage of the loss of waters of the U.S. (*e.g.*, 1/12-acre of emergent wetlands); and

(5) The type and acreage of any compensatory mitigation used to offset the loss of waters of the U.S. (*e.g.*, 1/12-acre of emergent wetlands created on-site);

j. If there are any open waters or streams within the project area, the permittee will establish and maintain, to the maximum extent practicable, wetland or upland vegetated buffers next to those open waters or streams consistent with General Condition 19. Deed restrictions, conservation easements, protective covenants, or other means of land conservation and preservation are required to protect and maintain the vegetated buffers established on the project site. Only residential, commercial, and institutional activities with structures on the foundation(s) or building pad(s), as well as the attendant features, are authorized by this NWP. The compensatory mitigation proposal that is required in paragraph (e) of this NWP may be either conceptual or detailed. The wetland or upland vegetated buffer required in paragraph (i) of this NWP will be determined on a case-by-case basis by the District Engineer for addressing water quality concerns. The required wetland or upland vegetated buffer is part of the overall compensatory mitigation requirement for this NWP. If the project site was previously used for agricultural purposes and the farm owner/operator used NWP 40 to authorize activities in waters of the U.S. to increase production or construct farm buildings, NWP 39 cannot be used by the developer to authorize additional activities. This is more than the acreage limit for NWP 39 impacts to waters of the U.S. (*i.e.*, the combined acreage loss authorized under NWPs 39 and 40 cannot exceed 1/2-acre, see General Condition 15).

Subdivisions: For residential subdivisions, the aggregate total loss of waters of U.S. authorized by NWP 39 can not exceed 1/2-acre. This includes any loss of waters associated with development of individual subdivision lots. (Sections 10 and 404)

Note: Areas where wetland vegetation is not present should be determined by the presence or absence of an ordinary high water mark or bed and bank. Areas that are waters of the U.S.

based on this criterion would require a PCN although water is infrequently present in the stream channel (except for ephemeral waters, which do not require PCNs).

40. *Agricultural Activities*. Discharges of dredged or fill material into non-tidal waters of the U.S., excluding non-tidal wetlands adjacent to tidal waters, for improving agricultural production and the construction of building pads for farm buildings. Authorized activities include the installation, placement, or construction of drainage tiles, ditches, or levees; mechanized land clearing; land leveling; the relocation of existing serviceable drainage ditches constructed in waters of the U.S.; and similar activities, provided the permittee complies with the following terms and conditions:

a. For discharges into non-tidal wetlands to improve agricultural production, the following criteria must be met if the permittee is an United States Department of Agriculture (USDA) Program participant:

(1) The permittee must obtain a categorical minimal effects exemption, minimal effect exemption, or mitigation exemption from NRCS in accordance with the provisions of the Food Security Act of 1985, as amended (16 U.S.C. 3801 et seq.);

(2) The discharge into non-tidal wetlands does not result in the loss of greater than 1/2-acre of non-tidal wetlands on a farm tract;

(3) The permittee must have NRCS certified wetland delineation;

(4) The permittee must implement an NRCS-approved compensatory mitigation plan that fully offsets wetland losses, if required; and

(5) The permittee must submit a report, within 30 days of completion of the authorized work, to the District Engineer that contains the following information:

(a) The name, address, and telephone number of the permittee;

(b) The location of the work;

(c) A description of the work;

(d) The type and acreage (or square feet) of the loss of wetlands (*e.g.*, 13-acre of emergent wetlands); and

(e) The type, acreage (or square feet), and location of compensatory mitigation (e.g. 1/3-acre of emergent wetland on a farm tract; credits purchased from a mitigation bank); or

b. For discharges into non-tidal wetlands to improve agricultural production, the following criteria must be met if the permittee is not a USDA Program participant (or a USDA Program participant for which the proposed work does not qualify for authorization under paragraph (a) of this NWP):

(1) The discharge into non-tidal wetlands does not result in the loss of greater than 1/2-acre of non-tidal wetlands on a farm tract;

(2) The permittee must notify the District Engineer in accordance with General Condition 13, if the discharge results in the loss of greater than 1/10-acre of non-tidal wetlands;

(3) The notification must include a delineation of affected wetlands; and

(4) The notification must include a compensatory mitigation proposal to offset losses of waters of the U.S.; or

c. For the construction of building pads for farm buildings, the discharge does not cause the loss of greater than 1/2-acre of non-tidal wetlands that were in agricultural production prior to December 23, 1985, (*i.e.,* farmed wetlands) and the permittee must notify the District Engineer in accordance with General Condition 13; and

d. Any activity in other waters of the U.S. is limited to the relocation of existing serviceable drainage ditches constructed in non-tidal streams. This NWP does not authorize the relocation of greater than 300 linear-feet of existing serviceable drainage ditches constructed in non-tidal streams unless, for drainage ditches constructed in intermittent nontidal streams, the District Engineer waives this criterion in writing, and the District Engineer has determined that the project complies with all terms and conditions of this NWP, and that any adverse impacts of the project on the aquatic environment are minimal, both individually and cumulatively. For impacts exceeding 300-linear feet of impacts to existing serviceable ditches constructed in intermittent non-tidal streams, the permittee must notify the District Engineer in accordance with the "Notification" General Condition 13; and

e. The term "farm tract" refers to a parcel of land identified by the Farm Service Agency. The Corps will identify other waters of the U.S. on the farm tract. NRCS will determine if a proposed agricultural activity meets the terms and conditions of paragraph a. of this NWP, except as provided below. For those activities that require notification, the District Engineer will determine if a proposed agricultural activity is authorized by paragraphs b., c., and/or d. of this NWP. USDA Program participants requesting authorization for discharges of dredged or fill material into waters of the U.S. authorized by paragraphs (c) or (d) of this NWP, in addition to paragraph (a), must notify the District Engineer in accordance with General Condition 13 and the District Engineer will determine if the entire single and complete project is authorized by this NWP. Discharges of dredged or fill material into waters of the U.S. associated with completing required compensatory mitigation are authorized by this NWP. However, total impacts, including other authorized impacts under this NWP, may not exceed the 1/2-acre limit of this NWP.

This NWP does not affect, or otherwise regulate, discharges associated with agricultural activities when the discharge qualifies for an exemption under section 404(f) of the CWA, even though a categorical minimal effects exemption, minimal effect exemption, or mitigation exemption from NRCS pursuant to the Food Security Act of 1985, as amended, may be required. Activities authorized by paragraphs a. through d. may not exceed a total of 1/2-acre on a single farm tract. If the site was used for agricultural purposes and the farm owner/operator used either paragraphs a., b., or c. of this NWP to authorize activities in waters of the U.S. to increase agricultural production or construct farm buildings, and the current landowner wants to use NWP 39 to authorize residential, commercial, or industrial development activities in waters of the U.S. on the site, the combined acreage loss authorized by NWPs 39 and 40 cannot exceed 1/2-acre (see General Condition 15). (Section 404)

41. *Reshaping Existing Drainage Ditches*. Discharges of dredged or fill material into non-tidal waters of the U.S., excluding non-tidal wetlands adjacent to tidal waters, to modify the cross-sectional configuration of currently serviceable drainage ditches constructed in waters of the U.S. The reshaping of the ditch cannot increase drainage capacity beyond the original design capacity. Nor can it expand the area drained by the ditch as originally designed (*i.e.,* the capacity of the ditch must be the same as originally designed and it cannot drain additional wetlands or other waters of the U.S.). Compensatory mitigation is not required because the work is designed to improve water quality (*e.g.,* by regrading the drainage ditch with gentler slopes, which can reduce erosion, increase growth of vegetation, increase uptake of nutrients and other substances by vegetation, etc.).

Notification: The permittee must notify the District Engineer in accordance with General Condition 13 if greater than 500 linear feet of drainage ditch will be reshaped. Material resulting from excavation may not be permanently sidecast into waters but may be temporarily sidecast (up to three months) into waters of the U.S., provided the material is not placed in such a manner that it is dispersed by currents or other forces. The District Engineer may extend the period of temporary sidecasting not to exceed a total of 180 days, where appropriate. In general, this NWP does not apply to reshaping drainage ditches constructed in uplands, since these areas are generally not waters of the U.S., and thus no permit from the Corps is required, or to the maintenance of existing drainage ditches to their original dimensions and configuration, which does not require a Section 404 permit (see 33 C.F.R. 323.4(a)(3)). This NWP does not authorize the relocation of drainage ditches constructed in waters of the U.S.; the location of the centerline of the reshaped drainage ditch must be approximately the same as the location of the centerline of the original drainage ditch. This NWP does not authorize stream channelization or stream relocation projects. (Section 404)

42. *Recreational Facilities*. Discharges of dredged or fill material into non-tidal waters of the U.S., excluding non-tidal wetlands adjacent to tidal waters, for the construction or expansion of recreational facilities, provided the activity meets all of the following criteria:

a. The discharge does not cause the loss of greater than 1/2-acre of non-tidal waters of the U.S., excluding non-tidal wetlands adjacent to tidal waters;

b. The discharge does not cause the loss of greater than 300 linear-feet of a stream bed, unless for intermittent stream beds this criterion is waived in writing pursuant to a determination by the District Engineer, as specified below, that the project complies with all terms and conditions of this NWP and that any adverse impacts of the project on the aquatic environment are minimal, both individually and cumulatively;

c. The permittee notifies the District Engineer in accordance with the "Notification" General Condition 13 for discharges exceeding 300 linear feet of impact of intermittent stream beds. In such cases, to be authorized the District Engineer must determine that the activity complies with the other terms and conditions of the NWP, determine the adverse environmental effects are minimal both individually and cumulatively, and waive this limitation in writing before the permittee may proceed;

d. For discharges causing the loss of greater than 1/10-acre of non-tidal waters of the U.S., the permittee notifies the District Engineer in accordance with General Condition 13;

e. For discharges in special aquatic sites, including wetlands, the notification must include a delineation of affected special aquatic sites;

f. The discharge is part of a single and complete project; and

g. Compensatory mitigation will normally be required to offset the losses of waters of the U.S.

The notification must also include a compensatory mitigation proposal to offset authorized losses of waters of the U.S. For the purposes of this NWP, the term "recreational facility" is defined as a recreational activity that is integrated into the natural landscape and does not substantially change preconstruction grades or deviate from natural landscape contours. For the purpose of this permit, the primary function of recreational facilities does not include the use of motor vehicles, buildings, or impervious surfaces. Examples of recreational facilities that may be authorized by this NWP include hiking trails, bike paths, horse paths, nature centers, and campgrounds (excluding trailer parks). This NWP may authorize the construction or expansion of golf courses and the expansion of ski areas, provided the golf course or ski area does not substantially deviate from natural landscape contours. Additionally, these activities are designed to minimize adverse effects to waters of the U.S. and riparian areas through the use of such practices as integrated pest management, adequate stormwater management facilities, vegetated buffers, reduced fertilizer use, etc. The facility must have an adequate water quality management plan in accordance with General Condition 9, such as a stormwater management facility, to ensure that the recreational facility results in no substantial adverse effects to water quality. This NWP also authorizes the construction or expansion of small support facilities, such as maintenance and storage buildings and stables that are directly related to the recreational activity. This NWP does not authorize other buildings, such as hotels, restaurants, etc. The construction or expansion of playing fields (*e.g.,* baseball, soccer, or football fields), basketball and tennis courts, racetracks, stadiums, arenas, and the construction of new ski areas are not authorized by this NWP. (Section 404)

43. *Stormwater Management Facilities*. Discharges of dredged or fill material into non-tidal waters of the U.S., excluding non-tidal wetlands adjacent to tidal waters, for the construction and maintenance of stormwater management facilities, including activities for the excavation of stormwater ponds/facilities, detention basins, and retention basins; the installation and maintenance of water control structures, outfall structures and emergency spillways; and the maintenance dredging of existing stormwater management ponds/facilities and detention and retention basins, provided the activity meets all of the following criteria:

a. The discharge for the construction of new stormwater management facilities does not cause the loss of greater than 1/2-acre of non-tidal waters of the U.S., excluding non-tidal wetlands adjacent to tidal waters;

b. The discharge does not cause the loss of greater than 300 linear-feet of a stream bed, unless for intermittent stream beds this criterion is waived in writing pursuant to a determination by the District Engineer, as specified below, that the project complies with all terms and conditions of this NWP and that any adverse impacts of the project on the aquatic environment are minimal, both individually and cumulatively;

c. For discharges causing the loss of greater than 300 linear feet of intermittent stream beds, the permittee notifies the District Engineer in accordance with the "Notification"

General Condition 13. In such cases, to be authorized the District Engineer must determine that the activity complies with the other terms and conditions of the NWP, determine the adverse environmental effects are minimal both individually and cumulatively, and waive this limitation in writing before the permittee may proceed;

d. The discharges of dredged or fill material for the construction of new stormwater management facilities in perennial streams is not authorized;

e. For discharges or excavation for the construction of new stormwater management facilities or for the maintenance of existing stormwater management facilities causing the loss of greater than 1/10-acre of non-tidal waters, excluding non-tidal wetlands adjacent to tidal waters, provided the permittee notifies the District Engineer in accordance with the "Notification" General Condition 13. In addition, the notification must include:

(1) A maintenance plan. The maintenance plan should be in accordance with state and local requirements, if any such requirements exist;

(2) For discharges in special aquatic sites, including wetlands and submerged aquatic vegetation, the notification must include a delineation of affected areas; and

(3) A compensatory mitigation proposal that offsets the loss of waters of the U.S. Maintenance in constructed areas will not require mitigation provided such maintenance is accomplished in designated maintenance areas and not within compensatory mitigation areas (*i.e.,* District Engineers may designate nonmaintenance areas, normally at the downstream end of the stormwater management facility, in existing stormwater management facilities). (No mitigation will be required for activities that are exempt from Section 404 permit requirements);

f. The permittee must avoid and minimize discharges into waters of the U.S. at the project site to the maximum extent practicable, and the notification must include a written statement to the District Engineer detailing compliance with this condition (i.e. why the discharge must occur in waters of the U.S. and why additional minimization cannot be achieved);

g. The stormwater management facility must comply with General Condition 21 and be designed using BMPs and watershed protection techniques. Examples may include forebays (deeper areas at the upstream end of the stormwater management facility that would be maintained through excavation), vegetated buffers, and siting considerations to minimize adverse effects to aquatic resources. Another example of a BMP would be bioengineering methods incorporated into the facility design to benefit water quality and minimize adverse effects to aquatic resources from storm flows, especially downstream of the facility, that provide, to the maximum extent practicable, for long term aquatic resource protection and enhancement;

h. Maintenance excavation will be in accordance with an approved maintenance plan and will not exceed the original contours of the facility as approved and constructed; and

i. The discharge is part of a single and complete project. (Section 404)

44. *Mining Activities*. Discharges of dredged or fill material into:

(i) Isolated waters; streams where the annual average flow is 1 cubic foot per second or less, and non-tidal wetlands adjacent to headwater streams, for aggregate mining (*i.e.*, sand, gravel, and crushed and broken stone) and associated support activities;

(ii) Lower perennial streams, excluding wetlands adjacent to lower perennial streams, for aggregate mining activities (support activities in lower perennial streams or adjacent wetlands are not authorized by this NWP); and/or

(iii) Isolated waters and non-tidal wetlands adjacent to headwater streams, for hard rock/mineral mining activities (*i.e.*, extraction of metalliferous ores from subsurface locations) and associated support activities, provided the discharge meets the following criteria:

a. The mined area within waters of the U.S., plus the acreage loss of waters of the U.S. resulting from support activities, cannot exceed 1/2-acre;

b. The permittee must avoid and minimize discharges into waters of the U.S. at the project site to the maximum extent practicable, and the notification must include a written statement detailing compliance with this condition (*i.e.*, why the discharge must occur in waters of the U.S. and why additional minimization cannot be achieved);

c. In addition to General Conditions 17 and 20, activities authorized by this permit must not substantially alter the sediment characteristics of areas of concentrated shellfish beds or fish spawning areas. Normally, the mandated water quality management plan should address these impacts;

d. The permittee must implement necessary measures to prevent increases in stream gradient and water velocities and to prevent adverse effects (*e.g.*, head cutting, bank erosion) to upstream and downstream channel conditions;

e. Activities authorized by this permit must not result in adverse effects on the course, capacity, or condition of navigable waters of the U.S.;

f. The permittee must use measures to minimize downstream turbidity;

g. Wetland impacts must be compensated through mitigation approved by the Corps;

h. Beneficiation and mineral processing for hard rock/mineral mining activities may not occur within 200 feet of the ordinary high water mark of any open waterbody. Although the Corps does not regulate discharges from these activities, a CWA section 402 permit may be required;

i. All activities authorized must comply with General Conditions 9 and 21. Further, the District Engineer may require modifications to the required water quality management plan to ensure that the authorized work results in minimal adverse effects to water quality;

j. Except for aggregate mining activities in lower perennial streams, no aggregate mining can occur within stream beds where the average annual flow is greater than 1 cubic foot per second or in waters of the U.S. within 100 feet of the ordinary high water mark of headwater stream segments where the average annual flow of the stream is greater than 1 cubic foot per second (aggregate mining can occur in areas immediately adjacent to the ordinary high water mark of a stream where the average annual flow is 1 cubic foot per second or less);

k. Single and complete project: The discharge must be for a single and complete project, including support activities. Discharges of dredged or fill material into waters of the U.S. for multiple mining activities on several designated parcels of a single and complete mining operation can be authorized by this NWP provided the 12-acre limit is not exceeded; and

Notification: The permittee must notify the District Engineer in accordance with General Condition 13. The notification must include: (1) A description of waters of the U.S. adversely affected by the project; (2) A written statement to the District Engineer detailing compliance with paragraph (b), above (*i.e.,* why the discharge must occur in waters of the U.S. and why additional minimization cannot be achieved); (3) A description of measures taken to ensure that the proposed work complies with paragraphs (c) through (f), above; and (4) A reclamation plan (for aggregate mining in isolated waters and non-tidal wetlands adjacent to headwaters and hard rock/mineral mining only). This NWP does not authorize hard rock/mineral mining, including placer mining, in streams. No hard rock/mineral mining can occur in waters of the U.S. within 100 feet of the ordinary high water mark of headwater streams. The term's "headwaters" and "isolated waters" are defined at 33 C.F.R. 330.2(d) and (e), respectively. For the purposes of this NWP, the term "lower perennial stream" is defined as follows: "A stream in which the gradient is low and water velocity is slow, there is no tidal influence, some water flows throughout the year, and the substrate consists mainly of sand and mud." (Sections 10 and 404)

NATIONWIDE PERMIT GENERAL CONDITIONS

The following General Conditions must be followed in order for any authorization by an NWP to be valid:

1. *Navigation*. No activity may cause more than a minimal adverse effect on navigation.

2. *Proper Maintenance*. Any structure or fill authorized shall be properly maintained, including maintenance to ensure public safety.

3. *Soil Erosion and Sediment Controls*. Appropriate soil erosion and sediment controls must be used and maintained in effective operating condition during construction, and all exposed soil and other fills, as well as any work below the ordinary high water mark or high tide line, must be permanently stabilized at the earliest practicable date. Permittees are encouraged to perform work within waters of the United States during periods of low-flow or no-flow.

4. *Aquatic Life Movements*. No activity may substantially disrupt the necessary life-cycle movements of those species of aquatic life indigenous to the waterbody, including those species that normally migrate through the area, unless the activity's primary purpose is to impound water. Culverts placed in streams must be installed to maintain low flow conditions.

5. *Equipment*. Heavy equipment working in wetlands must be placed on mats, or other measures must be taken to minimize soil disturbance.

6. *Regional and Case-By-Case Conditions*. The activity must comply with any regional conditions that may have been added by the Division Engineer (see 33 C.F.R. 330.4(e)). Additionally, any case specific conditions added by the Corps or by the state or tribe in its Section 401 Water Quality Certification and Coastal Zone Management Act consistency determination.

7. *Wild and Scenic Rivers*. No activity may occur in a component of the National Wild and Scenic River System; or in a river officially designated by Congress as a "study river" for possible inclusion in the system, while the river is in an official study status; unless the appropriate Federal agency, with direct management responsibility for such river, has determined in writing that the proposed activity will not adversely affect the Wild and Scenic River designation, or study status. Information on Wild and Scenic Rivers may be obtained from the appropriate Federal land management agency in the area (*e.g.,* National Park Service, U.S. Forest Service, Bureau of Land Management, U.S. Fish and Wildlife Service).

8. *Tribal Rights*. No activity or its operation may impair reserved tribal rights, including, but not limited to, reserved water rights and treaty fishing and hunting rights.

9. *Water Quality*. (a) In certain states and tribal lands an individual 401 Water Quality Certification must be obtained or waived (See 33 C.F.R. 330.4(c)). (b) For NWPs 12, 14, 17, 18, 32, 39, 40, 42, 43, and 44, where the state or tribal 401 certification (either generically or individually) does not require or approve water quality management measures, the permittee must provide water quality management measures that will ensure that the authorized work does not result in more than minimal degradation of water quality (or the Corps determines that compliance with state or local standards, where applicable, will ensure no more than minimal adverse effect on water quality). An important component of water quality management includes stormwater management that minimizes degradation of the downstream aquatic system, including water quality (refer to General Condition 21 for stormwater management requirements). Another important component of water quality management is the establishment and maintenance of vegetated buffers next to open waters, including streams (refer to General Condition 19 for vegetated buffer requirements for the NWPs). This condition is only applicable to projects that have the potential to affect water quality. While appropriate measures must be taken, in most cases it is not necessary to conduct detailed studies to identify such measures or to require monitoring.

10. *Coastal Zone Management*. In certain states, an individual state coastal zone management consistency concurrence must be obtained or waived (see Section 330.4(d)).

11. *Endangered Species*. (a) No activity is authorized under any NWP which is likely to jeopardize the continued existence of a threatened or endangered species or a species proposed for such designation, as identified under the Federal Endangered Species Act (ESA), or which will destroy or adversely modify the critical habitat of such species. Non-federal permittees shall notify the District Engineer if any listed species or designated critical habitat might be affected or is in the vicinity of the project, or is located in the designated critical habitat and shall not begin work on the activity until notified by the District Engineer that the requirements of the ESA have been satisfied and that the activity is authorized. For activities that may affect Federally-listed endangered or threatened species or designated critical habitat, the notification must include the name(s) of the endangered or threatened species that may be affected by the proposed work or that utilize the designated critical habitat that may be affected by the proposed work. As a result of formal or informal consultation with the FWS or NMFS the District Engineer may add species-specific regional endangered species conditions to the NWPs. (b) Authorization of an activity by a NWP does not authorize the "take" of a threatened or endangered species as defined under the ESA. In the absence of separate authorization (*e.g.,* an ESA Section 10 Permit, a Biological Opinion with "incidental take" provisions, etc.) From the USFWS or the NMFS, both lethal and non-lethal "takes" of protected species are in violation of the ESA. Information on the location of threatened and endangered species and their critical habitat can be obtained directly from the offices of the USFWS and NMFS or their world wide web pages at *http://www.fws.gov/r9endspp/endspp.html* and *http://www.nfms.gov/prot_res/esahome.html* respectively.

12. *Historic Properties*. No activity which may affect historic properties listed, or eligible for listing, in the National Register of Historic Places is authorized, until the District Engineer has complied with the provisions of 33 C.F.R. part 325, Appendix C. The prospective permittee must notify the District Engineer if the authorized activity may affect any historic properties listed, determined to be eligible, or which the prospective permittee has reason to believe may be eligible for listing on the National Register of Historic Places, and shall not begin the activity until notified by the District Engineer that the requirements of the National Historic Preservation Act have been satisfied and that the activity is authorized. Information on the location and existence of historic resources can be obtained from the State

Historic Preservation Office and the National Register of Historic Places (see 33 C.F.R. 330.4(g)). For activities that may affect historic properties listed in, or eligible for listing in, the National Register of Historic Places, the notification must state which historic property may be affected by the proposed work or include a vicinity map indicating the location of the historic property.

13. *Notification.*

(a) *Timing;* where required by the terms of the NWP, the prospective permittee must notify the District Engineer with a preconstruction notification (PCN) as early as possible. The District Engineer must determine if the notification is complete within 30 days of the date of receipt and can request additional information necessary to make the PCN complete only once. However, if the prospective permittee does not provide all of the requested information, then the District Engineer will notify the prospective permittee that the notification is still incomplete and the PCN review process will not commence until all of the requested information has been received by the District Engineer. The prospective permittee shall not begin the activity:

(1) Until notified in writing by the District Engineer that the activity may proceed under the NWP with any special conditions imposed by the District or Division Engineer; or

(2) If notified in writing by the District or Division Engineer that an Individual Permit is required; or

(3) Unless 45 days have passed from the District Engineer's receipt of the complete notification and the prospective permittee has not received written notice from the District or Division Engineer. Subsequently, the permittee's right to proceed under the NWP may be modified, suspended, or revoked only in accordance with the procedure set forth in 33 C.F.R. 330.5(d)(2).

(b) *Contents of Notification:* The notification must be in writing and include the following information:

(1) Name, address and telephone numbers of the prospective permittee;

(2) Location of the proposed project;

(3) Brief description of the proposed project; the project's purpose; direct and indirect adverse environmental effects the project would cause; any other NWP(s), Regional General Permit(s), or Individual Permit(s) used or intended to be used to authorize any part of the proposed project or any related activity. Sketches should be provided when necessary to show that the activity complies with the terms of the NWP (Sketches usually clarify the project and when provided result in a quicker decision.);

(4) For NWPs 7, 12, 14, 18, 21, 34, 38, 39, 41, 42, and 43, the PCN must also include a delineation of affected special aquatic sites, including wetlands, vegetated shallows (*e.g.,* submerged aquatic vegetation, seagrass beds), and riffle and pool complexes (see paragraph 13(f));

(5) For NWP 7 (Outfall Structures and Maintenance), the PCN must include information regarding the original design capacities and configurations of those areas of the facility where maintenance dredging or excavation is proposed;

(6) For NWP 14 (Linear Transportation Crossings), the PCN must include a compensatory mitigation proposal to offset permanent losses of waters of the U.S. and a statement describing how temporary losses of waters of the U.S. will be minimized to the maximum extent practicable;

(7) For NWP 21 (Surface Coal Mining Activities), the PCN must include an Office of Surface Mining (OSM) or state-approved mitigation plan, if applicable. To be authorized by this NWP, the District Engineer must determine that the activity complies with the terms and conditions of the NWP and that the adverse environmental effects are minimal both individually and cumulatively and must notify the project sponsor of this determination in writing;

(8) For NWP 27 (Stream and Wetland Restoration), the PCN must include documentation of the prior condition of the site that will be reverted by the permittee;

(9) For NWP 29 (Single-Family Housing), the PCN must also include:

(i) Any past use of this NWP by the Individual Permittee and/or the permittee's spouse;

(ii) A statement that the single-family housing activity is for a personal residence of the permittee;

(iii) A description of the entire parcel, including its size, and a delineation of wetlands. For the purpose of this NWP, parcels of land measuring 14-acre or less will not require a formal on-site delineation. However, the applicant shall provide an indication of where the wetlands are and the amount of wetlands that exists on the property. For parcels greater than 14-acre in size, formal wetland delineation must be prepared in accordance with the current method required by the Corps. (See paragraph 13(f));

(iv) A written description of all land (including, if available, legal descriptions) owned by the prospective permittee and/or the prospective permittee's spouse, within a one mile radius of the parcel, in any form of ownership (including any land owned as a partner, corporation, joint tenant, co-tenant, or as a tenant-by-the-entirety) and any land on which a purchase and sale agreement or other contract for sale or purchase has been executed;

(10) For NWP 31 (Maintenance of Existing Flood Control Projects), the prospective permittee must either notify the District Engineer with a PCN prior to each maintenance activity or submit a five year (or less) maintenance plan. In addition, the PCN must include all of the following:

(i) Sufficient baseline information identifying the approved channel depths and configurations and existing facilities. Minor deviations are authorized, provided the approved flood control protection or drainage is not increased;

(ii) A delineation of any affected special aquatic sites, including wetlands; and,

(iii) Location of the dredged material disposal site;

(11) For NWP 33 (Temporary Construction, Access, and Dewatering), the PCN must also include a restoration plan of reasonable measures to avoid and minimize adverse effects to aquatic resources;

(12) For NWPs 39, 43 and 44, the PCN must also include a written statement to the District Engineer explaining how avoidance and minimization for losses of waters of the U.S. were achieved on the project site;

(13) For NWP 39 and NWP 42, the PCN must include a compensatory mitigation proposal to offset losses of waters of the U.S. or justification explaining why compensatory mitigation should not be required. For discharges that cause the loss of greater than 300 linear feet of an intermittent stream bed, to be authorized, the District Engineer must determine that the activity complies with the other terms and conditions of the NWP, determine adverse environmental effects are minimal both individually and cumulatively, and waive the limitation on stream impacts in writing before the permittee may proceed;

(14) For NWP 40 (Agricultural Activities), the PCN must include a compensatory mitigation proposal to offset losses of waters of the U.S. This NWP does not authorize the relocation of greater than 300 linear-feet of existing serviceable drainage ditches constructed in non-tidal streams unless, for drainage ditches constructed in intermittent nontidal streams, the District Engineer waives this criterion in writing, and the District Engineer has determined that the project complies with all terms and conditions of this NWP, and that any adverse impacts of the project on the aquatic environment are minimal, both individually and cumulatively;

(15) For NWP 43 (Stormwater Management Facilities), the PCN must include, for the construction of new stormwater management facilities, a maintenance plan (in accordance with state and local requirements, if applicable) and a compensatory miti-

gation proposal to offset losses of waters of the U.S. For discharges that cause the loss of greater than 300 linear feet of an intermittent stream bed, to be authorized, the District Engineer must determine that the activity complies with the other terms and conditions of the NWP, determine adverse environmental effects are minimal both individually and cumulatively, and waive the limitation on stream impacts in writing before the permittee may proceed;

(16) For NWP 44 (Mining Activities), the PCN must include a description of all waters of the U.S. adversely affected by the project, a description of measures taken to minimize adverse effects to waters of the U.S., a description of measures taken to comply with the criteria of the NWP, and a reclamation plan (for all aggregate mining activities in isolated waters and non-tidal wetlands adjacent to headwaters and any hard rock/mineral mining activities);

(17) For activities that may adversely affect Federally-listed endangered or threatened species, the PCN must include the name(s) of those endangered or threatened species that may be affected by the proposed work or utilize the designated critical habitat that may be affected by the proposed work; and

(18) For activities that may affect historic properties listed in, or eligible for listing in, the National Register of Historic Places, the PCN must state which historic property may be affected by the proposed work or include a vicinity map indicating the location of the historic property.

(c) *Form of Notification:* The standard Individual Permit application form (Form ENG 4345) may be used as the notification but must clearly indicate that it is a PCN and must include all of the information required in (b) (1)–(18) of General Condition 13. A letter containing the requisite information may also be used.

(d) *District Engineer's Decision:* In reviewing the PCN for the proposed activity, the District Engineer will determine whether the activity authorized by the NWP will result in more than minimal individual or cumulative adverse environmental effects or may be contrary to the public interest. The prospective permittee may submit a proposed mitigation plan with the PCN to expedite the process. The District Engineer will consider any proposed compensatory mitigation the applicant has included in the proposal in determining whether the net adverse environmental effects to the aquatic environment of the proposed work are minimal. If the District Engineer determines that the activity complies with the terms and conditions of the NWP and that the adverse effects on the aquatic environment are minimal, after considering mitigation, the District Engineer will notify the permittee and include any conditions the District Engineer deems necessary. The District Engineer must approve any compensatory mitigation proposal before the permittee commences work. If the prospective permittee is required to submit a compensatory mitigation proposal with the PCN, the proposal may be either conceptual or detailed. If the prospective permittee elects to submit a compensatory mitigation plan with the PCN, the District Engineer will expeditiously review the proposed compensatory mitigation plan. The District Engineer must review the plan within 45 days of receiving a complete PCN and determine whether the conceptual or specific proposed mitigation would ensure no more than minimal adverse effects on the aquatic environment. If the net adverse effects of the project on the aquatic environment (after consideration of the compensatory mitigation proposal) are determined by the District Engineer to be minimal, the District Engineer will provide a timely written response to the applicant. The response will state that the project can proceed under the terms and conditions of the NWP. If the District Engineer determines that the adverse effects of the proposed work are more than minimal, then the District Engineer will notify the applicant either:

(1) That the project does not qualify for authorization under the NWP and instruct the applicant on the procedures to seek authorization under an Individual Permit;

(2) that the project is authorized under the NWP subject to the applicant's submission of a mitigation proposal that would reduce the adverse effects on the aquatic environment to the minimal level; or

(3) that the project is authorized under the NWP with specific modifications or conditions. Where the District Engineer determines that mitigation is required to ensure no more than minimal adverse effects occur to the aquatic environment, the activity will be authorized within the 45-day PCN period. The authorization will include the necessary conceptual or specific mitigation or a requirement that the applicant submit a mitigation proposal that would reduce the adverse effects on the aquatic environment to the minimal level. When conceptual mitigation is included, or a mitigation plan is required under item (2) above, no work in waters of the U.S. will occur until the District Engineer has approved a specific mitigation plan.

(e) *Agency Coordination:* The District Engineer will consider any comments from Federal and state agencies concerning the proposed activity's compliance with the terms and conditions of the NWPs and the need for mitigation to reduce the project's adverse environmental effects to a minimal level. For activities requiring notification to the District Engineer that result in the loss of greater than 1/2-acre of waters of the U.S., the District Engineer will provide immediately (*e.g.,* via facsimile transmission, overnight mail, or other expeditious manner) a copy to the appropriate Federal or state offices (USFWS, state natural resource or water quality agency, EPA, State Historic Preservation Officer (SHPO), and, if appropriate, the NMFS). With the exception of NWP 37, these agencies will then have 10 calendar days from the date the material is transmitted to telephone or fax the District Engineer notice that they intend to provide substantive, site-specific comments. If so contacted by an agency, the District Engineer will wait an additional 15 calendar days before making a decision on the notification. The District Engineer will fully consider agency comments received within the specified time frame, but will provide no response to the resource agency, except as provided below. The District Engineer will indicate in the administrative record associated with each notification that the resource agencies' concerns were considered. As required by section 305(b)(4)(B) of the Magnuson-Stevens Fishery Conservation and Management Act, the District Engineer will provide a response to NMFS within 30 days of receipt of any Essential Fish Habitat conservation recommendations. Applicants are encouraged to provide the Corps multiple copies of notifications to expedite agency notification.

(f) *Wetland Delineations:* Wetland delineations must be prepared in accordance with the current method required by the Corps (For NWP 29 see paragraph (b)(9)(iii) for parcels less than (1/4-acre in size). The permittee may ask the Corps to delineate the special aquatic site. There may be some delay if the Corps does the delineation. Furthermore, the 45-day period will not start until the wetland delineation has been completed and submitted to the Corps, where appropriate.

14. *Compliance Certification*. Every permittee who has received NWP verification from the Corps will submit signed certification regarding the completed work and any required mitigation. The certification will be forwarded by the Corps with the authorization letter and will include:

(a) A statement that the authorized work was done in accordance with the Corps authorization, including any general or specific conditions;

(b) A statement that any required mitigation was completed in accordance with the permit conditions; and

(c) The signature of the permittee certifying the completion of the work and mitigation.

15. *Use of Multiple Nationwide Permits*. The use of more than one NWP for a single and complete project is prohibited, except when the acreage loss of waters of the U.S. authorized by the NWPs does not exceed the acreage limit of the NWP with the highest specified acreage limit (e.g. if a road crossing over tidal waters is constructed under NWP 14, with associated bank stabilization authorized by NWP 13, the maximum acreage loss of waters of the U.S. for the total project cannot exceed 1/3-acre).

16. *Water Supply Intakes*. No activity, including structures and work in navigable waters of the U.S. or discharges of dredged or fill material, may occur in the proximity of a public water supply intake except where the activity is for repair of the public water supply intake structures or adjacent bank stabilization.

17. *Shellfish Beds*. No activity, including structures and work in navigable waters of the U.S. or discharges of dredged or fill material, may occur in areas of concentrated shellfish populations, unless the activity is directly related to a shellfish harvesting activity authorized by NWP 4.

18. *Suitable Material*. No activity, including structures and work in navigable waters of the U.S. or discharges of dredged or fill material, may consist of unsuitable material (*e.g.,* trash, debris, car bodies, asphalt, etc.) and material used for construction or discharged must be free from toxic pollutants in toxic amounts (see section 307 of the CWA).

19. *Mitigation*. The District Engineer will consider the factors discussed below when determining the acceptability of appropriate and practicable mitigation necessary to offset adverse effects on the aquatic environment that are more than minimal.

(a) The project must be designed and constructed to avoid and minimize adverse effects to waters of the U.S. to the maximum extent practicable at the project site (*i.e.,* on site).

(b) Mitigation in all its forms (avoiding, minimizing, rectifying, reducing or compensating) will be required to the extent necessary to ensure that the adverse effects to the aquatic environment are minimal.

(c) Compensatory mitigation at a minimum one-for-one ratio will be required for all wetland impacts requiring a PCN, unless the District Engineer determines in writing that some other form of mitigation would be more environmentally appropriate and provides a project-specific waiver of this requirement. Consistent with National policy, the District Engineer will establish a preference for restoration of wetlands as compensatory mitigation, with preservation used only in exceptional circumstances.

(d) Compensatory mitigation (*i.e.*, replacement or substitution of aquatic resources for those impacted) will not be used to increase the acreage losses allowed by the acreage limits of some of the NWPs. For example, 1/4-acre of wetlands cannot be created to change a 3/4-acre loss of wetlands to a 1/2-acre loss associated with NWP 39 verification. However, 1/2-acre of created wetlands can be used to reduce the impacts of a 1/2-acre loss of wetlands to the minimum impact level in order to meet the minimal impact requirement associated with NWPs.

(e) To be practicable, the mitigation must be available and capable of being done considering costs, existing technology, and logistics in light of the overall project purposes. Examples of mitigation that may be appropriate and practicable include, but are not limited to: reducing the size of the project; establishing and maintaining wetland or upland vegetated buffers to protect open waters such as streams; and replacing losses of aquatic resource functions and values by creating, restoring, enhancing, or preserving similar functions and values, preferably in the same watershed.

(f) Compensatory mitigation plans for projects in or near streams or other open waters will normally include a requirement for the establishment, maintenance, and legal protection (*e.g.*, easements, deed restrictions) of vegetated buffers to open waters. In many cases, vegetated buffers will be the only compensatory mitigation required. Vegetated buffers should consist of native species. The width of the vegetated buffers required will address documented water quality or aquatic habitat loss concerns. Normally, the vegetated buffer will be 25 to 50 feet wide on each side of the stream, but the District Engineers may require slightly wider vegetated buffers to address documented water quality or habitat loss concerns. Where both wetlands and open waters exist on the project site, the Corps will determine the appropriate compensatory mitigation (*e.g.*, stream buffers or wetlands compensation) based on what is best for the aquatic environment on a watershed basis. In cases where vegetated buffers are determined to be the most appropriate form of compensatory mitigation, the District Engineer may waive or reduce the requirement to provide wetland compensatory mitigation for wetland impacts.

(g) Compensatory mitigation proposals submitted with the "notification" may be either conceptual or detailed. If conceptual plans are approved under the verification, then the Corps will condition the verification to require detailed plans be submitted and approved by the Corps prior to construction of the authorized activity in waters of the U.S.

(h) Permittees may propose the use of mitigation banks, in-lieu fee arrangements or separate activity-specific compensatory mitigation. In all cases that require compensatory mitigation, the mitigation provisions will specify the party responsible for accomplishing and/or complying with the mitigation plan.

20. *Spawning Areas*. Activities, including structures and work in navigable waters of the U.S. or discharges of dredged or fill material, in spawning areas during spawning seasons must be avoided to the maximum extent practicable. Activities that result in the physical destruction (*e.g.*, excavate, fill, or smother downstream by substantial turbidity) of an important spawning area are not authorized.

21. *Management of Water Flows*. To the maximum extent practicable, the activity must be designed to maintain preconstruction downstream flow conditions (*e.g.*, location, capacity, and flow rates). Furthermore, the activity must not permanently restrict or impede the passage of normal or expected high flows (unless the primary purpose of the fill is to impound waters) and the structure or discharge of dredged or fill material must withstand expected high flows. The activity must, to the maximum extent practicable, provide for retaining excess flows from the site, provide for maintaining surface flow rates from the site similar to preconstruction conditions, and provide for not increasing water flows from the project site, relocating water, or redirecting water flow beyond preconstruction conditions. Stream channelizing will be reduced to the minimal amount necessary, and the activity must, to the maximum extent practicable, reduce adverse effects such as flooding or erosion downstream and upstream of the project site, unless the activity is part of a larger system designed to manage water flows. In most cases, it will not be a requirement to conduct detailed studies and monitoring of water flow. This condition is only applicable to projects that have the potential to affect waterflows. While appropriate measures must be taken, it is not necessary to conduct detailed studies to identify such measures or require monitoring to ensure their effectiveness. Normally, the Corps will defer to state and local authorities regarding management of water flow.

22. *Adverse Effects From Impoundments*. If the activity creates an impoundment of water, adverse effects to the aquatic system due to the acceleration of the passage of water, and/or the restricting its flow shall be minimized to the maximum extent practicable. This includes structures and work in navigable waters of the U.S., or discharges of dredged or fill material.

23. *Waterfowl Breeding Areas*. Activities, including structures and work in navigable waters of the U.S. or discharges of dredged or fill material, into breeding areas for migratory waterfowl must be avoided to the maximum extent practicable.

24. *Removal of Temporary Fills*. Any temporary fills must be removed in their entirety and the affected areas returned to their preexisting elevation.

25. *Designated Critical Resource Waters*. Critical resource waters include, NOAA-designated marine sanctuaries, National Estuarine Research Reserves, National Wild and Scenic Rivers, critical habitat for Federally listed threatened and endangered species, coral reefs, state natural heritage sites, and outstanding national resource waters or other waters officially designated by a state as having particular environmental or ecological significance and identified by the District Engineer after notice and opportunity for public comment. The District Engineer may also designate additional critical resource waters after notice and opportunity for comment. (a) Except as noted below, discharges of dredged or fill material into waters of the U.S. are not authorized by NWPs 7, 12, 14, 16, 17, 21, 29, 31, 35, 39, 40, 42, 43, and 44 for any activity within, or directly affecting, critical resource waters, including wetlands adjacent to such waters. Discharges of dredged or fill materials into waters of the U.S. may be authorized by the above NWPs in National Wild and Scenic Rivers if the activity complies with General Condition 7. Further, such discharges may be authorized in designated critical habitat for Federally listed threatened or endangered species if the activity complies with General Condition 11 and the USFWS or the NMFS has concurred in a determination of compliance with this condition. (b) For NWPs 3, 8, 10, 13, 15, 18, 19, 22, 23, 25, 27, 28, 30, 33, 34, 36, 37, and 38, notification is required in accordance with General Condition 13,for any activity proposed in the designated critical resource waters including wetlands adjacent to those waters. The District Engineer may authorize activities under these NWPs only after it is determined that the impacts to the critical resource waters will be no more than minimal.

26. *Fills Within 100-Year Floodplains*. For purposes of this General Condition, 100-year floodplains will be identified through the existing Federal Emergency Management Agency's

(FEMA) Flood Insurance Rate Maps or FEMA-approved local floodplain maps.

(a) *Discharges in Floodplain; Below Headwaters.* Discharges of dredged or fill material into waters of the U.S. within the mapped 100-year floodplain, below headwaters (i.e. five cfs), resulting in permanent above-grade fills, are not authorized by NWPs 39, 40, 42, 43, and 44.

(b) *Discharges in Floodway; Above Headwaters.* Discharges of dredged or fill material into waters of the U.S. within the FEMA or locally mapped floodway, resulting in permanent above-grade fills, are not authorized by NWPs 39, 40, 42, and 44.

(c) The permittee must comply with any applicable FEMA-approved state or local floodplain management requirements.

27. *Construction Period*. For activities that have not been verified by the Corps and the project was commenced or under contract to commence by the expiration date of the NWP (or modification or revocation date), the work must be completed within 12-months after such date (including any modification that affects the project). For activities that have been verified and the project was commenced or under contract to commence within the verification period, the work must be completed by the date determined by the Corps. For projects that have been verified by the Corps, an extension of a Corps approved completion date maybe requested. This request must be submitted at least one month before the previously approved completion date.

Further Information

1. District Engineers have authority to determine if an activity complies with the terms and conditions of an NWP.

2. NWPs do not obviate the need to obtain other Federal, state, or local permits, approvals, or authorizations required by law.

3. NWPs do not grant any property rights or exclusive privileges.

4. NWPs do not authorize any injury to the property or rights of others.

5. NWPs do not authorize interference with any existing or proposed Federal project.

DEFINITIONS

Best Management Practices (BMPs):BMPs are policies, practices, procedures, or structures implemented to mitigate the adverse environmental effects on surface water quality resulting from development. BMPs are categorized as structural or nonstructural. A BMP policy may affect the limits on a development.

Compensatory Mitigation: For purposes of Section 10/404, compensatory mitigation is the restoration, creation, enhancement, or in exceptional circumstances, preservation of wetlands and/or other aquatic resources for the purpose of compensating for unavoidable adverse impacts which remain after all appropriate and practicable avoidance and minimization has been achieved.

Creation: The establishment of a wetland or other aquatic resource where one did not formerly exist.

Enhancement: Activities conducted in existing wetlands or other aquatic resources that increase one or more aquatic functions.

Ephemeral Stream: An ephemeral stream has flowing water only during and for a short duration after, precipitation events in a typical year. Ephemeral stream beds are located above the water table year-round. Groundwater is not a source of water for the stream. Runoff from rainfall is the primary source of water for stream flow.

Farm Tract: A unit of contiguous land under one ownership that is operated as a farm or part of a farm.

Flood Fringe: That portion of the 100-year floodplain outside of the floodway (often referred to as "floodway fringe").

Floodway: The area regulated by Federal, state, or local requirements to provide for the discharge of the base flood so the cumulative increase in water surface elevation is no more than a designated amount (not to exceed one foot as set by the National Flood Insurance Program) within the 100-year floodplain.

Independent Utility: A test to determine what constitutes a single and complete project in the Corps regulatory program. A project is considered to have independent utility if it would be constructed absent the construction of other projects in the project area. Portions of a multi-phase project that depend upon other phases of the project do not have independent utility. Phases of a project that would be constructed even if the other phases were not built can be considered as separate single and complete projects with independent utility.

Intermittent Stream: An intermittent stream has flowing water during certain times of the year, when groundwater provides water for stream flow. During dry periods, intermittent streams may not have flowing water. Runoff from rainfall is a supplemental source of water for stream flow.

Loss of Waters of the U.S.: Waters of the U.S. that include the filled area and other waters that are permanently adversely affected by flooding, excavation, or drainage because of the regulated activity. Permanent adverse effects include permanent above-grade, at-grade, or below-grade fills that change an aquatic area to dry land, increase the bottom elevation of a waterbody, or change the use of a waterbody. The acreage of loss of waters of the U.S. is the threshold measurement of the impact to existing waters for determining whether a project may qualify for an NWP; it is not a net threshold that is calculated after considering compensatory mitigation that may be used to offset losses of aquatic functions and values. The loss of stream bed includes the linear feet of stream bed that is filled or excavated. Waters of the U.S. temporarily filled, flooded, excavated, or drained, but restored to preconstruction contours and elevations after construction, are not included in the measurement of loss of waters of the U.S. Impacts to ephemeral waters are only not included in the acreage or linear foot measurements of loss of waters of the U.S. or loss of stream bed, for the purpose of determining compliance with the threshold limits of the NWPs.

Non-tidal Wetland: A non-tidal wetland is a wetland (*i.e.*, a water of the U.S.) that is not subject to the ebb and flow of tidal waters. The definition of a wetland can be found at 33 C.F.R. 328.3(b). Non-tidal wetlands contiguous to tidal waters are located landward of the high tide line (*i.e.*, spring high tide line).

Open Water: An area that, during a year with normal patterns of precipitation, has standing or flowing water for sufficient duration to establish an ordinary high water mark. Aquatic vegetation within the area of standing or flowing water is either non-emergent, sparse, or absent. Vegetated shallows are considered to be open waters. The term "open water" includes rivers, streams, lakes, and ponds. For the purposes of the NWPs, this term does not include ephemeral waters.

Perennial Stream: A perennial stream has flowing water year-round during a typical year. The water table is located above the stream bed for most of the year. Groundwater is the primary source of water for stream flow. Runoff from rainfall is a supplemental source of water for stream flow.

Permanent Above-grade Fill: A discharge of dredged or fill material into waters of the U.S., including wetlands, that results in a substantial increase in ground elevation and permanently converts part or all of the waterbody to dry land. Structural fills authorized by NWPs 3, 25, 36, etc. are not included.

Preservation: The protection of ecologically important wetlands or other aquatic resources in perpetuity through the implementation of appropriate legal and physical mechanisms. Preservation may include protection of upland areas adjacent to wetlands as necessary to ensure protection and/or enhancement of the overall aquatic ecosystem.

Restoration: Re-establishment of wetland and/or other aquatic resource characteristics and function(s) at a site where they have ceased to exist, or exist in a substantially degraded state.

Riffle and Pool Complex: Riffle and pool complexes are special aquatic sites under the 404(b)(1) Guidelines. Riffle and pool complexes sometimes characterize steep gradient sections of streams. Such stream sections are recognizable by their hydraulic characteristics. The rapid movement of water over a course substrate in riffles results in a rough flow, a turbulent surface, and high dissolved oxygen levels in the water. Pools are deeper areas associated with riffles. A slower stream velocity, a streaming flow, a smooth surface, and a finer substrate characterize pools.

Single and Complete Project: The term "single and complete project" is defined at 33 C.F.R. 330.2(i) as the total project proposed or accomplished by one owner/developer or partnership or other association of owners/developers (see definition of independent utility). For linear projects, the "single and complete project" (*i.e.*, a single and complete crossing) will apply to each crossing of a separate water of the U.S. (*i.e.*, a single waterbody) at that location. An exception is for linear projects crossing a single waterbody several times at separate and distant locations: each crossing is considered a single and complete project. However, individual channels in a braided stream or river, or individual arms of a large, irregularly shaped wetland or lake, etc., are not separate waterbodies.

Stormwater Management: Stormwater management is the mechanism for controlling stormwater runoff for the urposes of reducing downstream erosion, water quality degradation, and flooding and mitigating the adverse effects of changes in land use on the aquatic environment.

Stormwater Management Facilities: Stormwater management facilities are those facilities, including but not limited to, stormwater retention and detention ponds and BMPs, which retain water for a period of time to control runoff and/or improve the quality (*i.e.,* by reducing the concentration of nutrients, sediments, hazardous substances and other pollutants) of stormwater runoff.

Stream Bed: The substrate of the stream channel between the ordinary high water marks. The substrate may be bedrock or inorganic particles that range in size from clay to boulders. Wetlands contiguous to the stream bed, but outside of the ordinary high water marks, are not considered part of the stream bed.

Stream Channelization: The manipulation of a stream channel to increase the rate of water flow through the stream channel. Manipulation may include deepening, widening, straightening, armoring, or other activities that change the stream crosssection or other aspects of stream channel geometry to increase the rate of water flow through the stream channel. A channelized stream remains a water of the U.S., despite the modifications to increase the rate of water flow.

Tidal Wetland: A tidal wetland is a wetland (*i.e.,* water of the U.S.) that is inundated by tidal waters. The definitions of a wetland and tidal waters can be found at 33 C.F.R. 328.3(b) and 33 C.F.R. 328.3(f), respectively. Tidal waters rise and fall in a predictable and measurable rhythm or cycle due to the gravitational pulls of the moon and sun. Tidal waters end where the rise and fall of the water surface can no longer be practically measured in a predictable rhythm due to masking by other waters, wind, or other effects. Tidal wetlands are located channelward of the high tide line (*i.e.,* spring high tide line) and are inundated by tidal waters two times per lunar month, during spring high tides.

Vegetated Buffer: A vegetated upland or wetland area next to rivers, streams, lakes, or other open waters which separates the open water from developed areas, including agricultural land. Vegetated buffers provide a variety of aquatic habitat functions and values (*e.g.,* aquatic habitat for fish and other aquatic organisms, moderation of water temperature changes, and detritus for aquatic food webs) and help improve or maintain local water quality. A vegetated buffer can be established by maintaining an existing vegetated area or planting native trees, shrubs, and herbaceous plants on land next to openwaters. Mowed lawns are not considered vegetated buffers because they provide little or no aquatic habitat functions and values. The establishment and maintenance of vegetated buffers is a method of compensatory mitigation that can be used in conjunction with the restoration, creation, enhancement, or preservation of aquatic habitats to ensure that activities authorized by NWPs result in minimal adverse effects to the aquatic environment. (See General Condition 19.)

Vegetated Shallows: Vegetated shallows are special aquatic sites under the 404(b)(1) Guidelines. They are areas that are permanently inundated and under normal circumstances have rooted aquatic vegetation, such as seagrasses in marine and estuarine systems and a variety of vascular rooted plants in freshwater systems.

Waterbody: A waterbody is any area that in a normal year has water flowing or standing above ground to the extent that evidence of an ordinary high water mark is established. Wetlands contiguous to the waterbody are considered part of the waterbody.

Chapter 13

EXEMPT ACTIVITIES

After considering the regulatory exemptions by nationwide permit discussed above, there are still six more statutory exemptions to §404's coverage, all of them designed to exclude from jurisdiction routine, essentially commercial activities so long as the activities have minor impacts on wetlands:

(1) For discharges of dredged and fill material into wetlands and minor drainage (but not a gradual conversion from wetland to non-wetland) which occur during normal farming, silviculture, and ranching activities (plowing, seeding, cultivating, minor drainage, and harvesting for the production of food, fiber, and forest products, or upland soil and water conservation practices) so long as the discharge occurred only in an area which was, at the time of the discharge, part of a legitimate, continuously-operated farming operation. If the farm field has lain fallow long enough that it now requires modification of its evolved hydrologic regime to convert it back to farmland, then the exemption will be lost. *See also* Regulatory Guidance Letter 90-7, *Clarification of the Phrase "Normal Circumstances" as it Pertains to Cropped Wetlands*, September 26, 1990; *Memorandum for the Field: Clean Water Act Section 404 Regulatory Program and Agricultural Activities*, May 3, 1990; *U.S. v. Cumberland Farms of Connecticut*, 647 F.Supp. 1166 (D.Mass.), *aff'd*, 826 F.2d 1151 (1st Cir. 1987), *cert. denied*, 489 U.S. 1061, 98 L.Ed.2d 981, 108 S.Ct. 1016 (1988).

(2) For the purpose of maintenance of currently serviceable dikes, dams, levees, groins, riprap, breakwaters, causeways, bridge abutments or approaches, and transportation structures;

(3) For the purpose of construction or maintenance of farm or stock ponds or irrigation ditches (*see also* Regulatory Guidance Letter No. 87-7, *Section 404(f)(1)(C) Statutory Exemption for Drainage Ditch Maintenance*, August 17, 1987);

(4) For the purpose of construction of temporary sedimentation basins on a construction site (but not the placement of fill material into navigable waters);

(5) For the purpose of construction or maintenance of farm, forest, or temporary mining roads so long as these roads are constructed and maintained in such a way as to assure compliance with §404(f)(2) (*see also* Regulatory Guidance Letter No. 86-3, *Section 404(f)(1) Exemption of Farm and Forest Roads (33 CFR Part 323.4(a)(6))*; and,

(6) Certain state programs.

CHAPTER 14

THE RECAPTURE PROVISION

Even though there are five specific topics of exempt activities, these activities will lose their exempt status if the purpose of the activity is to bring "... an area of navigable waters into a use to which it was not previously subject, where the flow or circulation of navigable waters may be impaired, or the reach of such waters is reduced." The essential inquiry is whether the activity is "normal and ongoing" or whether it is truly a "new use," which the Corps concedes requires a "judgment call." A "new use" can readily be found if the activity causes some significant alteration to the area's hydrology. *See also Bayou Marcus Livestock & Agricultural Co. v. E.P.A.*, 20 Envt'l.L.Rep. 20445 (N.D.Fla. 1989); Regulatory Guidance Letter No. 87-9, *Section 404 (1)(C) Exemption for Construction or Maintenance of Farm or Stock Ponds,* August 27, 1987.

UNITED STATES v. HUEBNER

752 F.2d 1235 (7th Cir. 1985), *cert. denied* 474 U.S. 817, 106 S.Ct. 62, 88 L.Ed.2d 50 (1985)

In 1978, pursuant to litigation commenced under the Clean Water Act (CWA), 33 U.S.C. §1251 *et seq.* (1978), by the United States Army Corps of Engineers (Corps), defendants Roland G. Huebner, William Huebner, and the Petenwell Potato Farms (Huebners), entered into a consent decree with the Corps regarding the maintenance of the wetlands on their property. In 1983, following a six-day hearing, the district court found the Huebners in contempt of the 1978 order and ordered them to comply with a restoration plan developed by the Corps. The Huebners appeal the lower court's contempt order and restoration plan. We affirm the district court's finding of contempt, reverse the district court's restoration order and remand with instructions.

I. FACTS

In 1977, the Huebners, owners of a 4,000-acre vegetable farm, acquired "Bear Bluff Farms," a 5,000 acre property in Jackson County, Wisconsin, the largest continuous area of wetlands in Wisconsin. The wetlands on Bear Bluff provide a habitat for wetland foliage and wildlife, and moderate the flow of water to surrounding wildlife refuges by absorbing excess stream flow in periods of high water and releasing water during the dry season.

Since the turn of the century Bear Bluff has been used intermittently for a variety of agricultural purposes, including the production of dryland crops, such as corn and oats. For the 20 years preceding the Huebners' ownership, however, only cranberries have been grown on the land. Cranberry cultivation requires a constant supply of water to protect against frost, to flood the berries for harvesting, to mulch them in the winter, and to irrigate them in the growing season. When the Huebners acquired Bear Bluff, the farm included three cranberry beds, including a 57-acre cranberry bed called the Staege bed on the southern part of the property. The Staege bed was served by three diked reservoirs: the Hunter's Peak, Juleane, and Unnamed Reservoirs.

The record indicates that the Huebners intended to expand the cranberry operations of Bear Bluff Farms and to use a portion of the farm for growing vegetables and other upland crops.

In 1977, the Huebners began to plow sections of the farm to clear out existing ditches and dig new ones. On September 2, 1977, the St. Paul District of the United States Army Crops [Corps] of Engineers issued several cease and desist orders to the Huebners, alleging that their ditching activities constituted a permitless "discharge of dredged or fill material" into the Bear Bluff wetlands in violation of section 301 of the Federal Water Pollution Control Act, 33 U.S.C. §1311 (1976), renamed the "Clean Water Act" in 1977. On November 10, 1977 the Corps filed a complaint in the district court seeking a permanent injunction and a financial penalty against the Huebners. In June, 1978 the parties settled the action by entering into a consent decree approved by District Judge James E. Doyle.

Paragraphs 1 and 2 of the ten paragraph order are most significant for purposes of this appeal. Paragraph 1 permanently enjoins the Huebners "from any and all operations which constitute the discharge of dredged or fill material into waters of the United States, including wetlands within the ... described area of Jackson County, Wisconsin ... except as in accordance with a Department of Army permit and other lawful authority." Paragraph 2 requires that the Huebners notify the Corps "in writing, twenty (20) days prior to the commencement of any discharge of dredged or fill material on any portion or portions of the land described in paragraph 1," so that the Corps could "notify the defendants, in writing, of the need for the Department of Army permit as to the stated sites."

Paragraphs 4, 5, and 7 relate principally to the restoration and continued maintenance of wetlands in the Hunters Peak, Juleane, and Unnamed Reservoirs. Paragraphs 4 and 5 describe certain restoration and maintenance activities to be performed by the Huebners on culverts, embankments, and ditches, which activities would restore the ditches and dikes to the dimensions existing prior to the dredging that prompted the order. Paragraph 7 requires the Huebners to "maintain and operate the control structures and reservoirs referred to in paragraph 4 above in a safe manner, for maximum drainage control, and to protect the integrity of the dikes and the structures therein."

The Huebners complied with the immediate restoration provisions of the consent order. On November 16, 1982, however, the government moved for an order to show cause why the Huebners should not be held in contempt for violating the 1978 order. The government, through its affidavits, charged that dredged material had been placed on the sides of Beaver Creek and was sliding into the adjacent wetlands, that a portion of the wetland had been plowed and furrowed by a marsh plow, and that the dikes of the Hunter's Peak, Julane [Juleane], and Unnamed Reservoirs had been leveled and scraped by a bulldozer without notice to the Corps and without any Corps permit allowing such activity. The Huebners had planted barley in a plowed portion of the Hunter's Peak, and stated that they intended to plant corn.

The district court adopted the government's "proposed finding of fact" as "preliminary findings of fact" on January 17, 1983, and held evidentiary hearings for six days, in April and May of 1983. On August 4, 1983 the district court entered an order holding the Huebners in civil contempt of the court's 1978 consent order on the grounds that the government had proved by "clear and convincing evidence" that the Huebners had made permitless discharges of dredged and fill material into the Bear Bluff wetlands in violation of the 1978 order. The Huebners allege that they are not in contempt of the district court's 1978 order because the activities in which they engaged in on their land did not require a Corps permit. They allege that the district court erred in its interpretation of the agricultural exemptions of the CWA, as relevant to the 1978 consent order, in determining when permits are required. The Huebners also argue that the district court denied them due process by improperly excluding certain evidence during the contempt hearing, and that the court abused its discretion in refusing to amend the 1983 restoration plan.

II. THE CLEAN WATER ACT

Congress enacted the CWA "to restore and maintain the chemical, physical and biological integrity of the Nation's waters." 33 U.S.C. §1251(a) (1978). The goal of the CWA is to eliminate by 1985 "the discharge of pollutants into navigable waters." 33 U.S.C. §1251(a)(1) (1978).

The "navigable waters" subject to Corps authority under the Act include wetlands, which have been defined as

> those areas that are inundated or saturated by surface or ground water at a frequency and duration sufficient to support, and that under normal circumstances do support, a prevalence of vegetation typically adapted for life in saturated soil conditions. Wetlands generally include swamps, marshes, bogs and similar areas.

33 C.F.R. §323.2(a)(7)(c) (1983). The term "navigable waters" has been given "the broadest constitutional interpretation," 1 LEGISLATIVE HISTORY at 178 (Senate Consideration of the Conference Report on S. 2770, Oct. 4, 1972), in recognition of the fact that

> the regulation of activities that cause water pollution ... must focus on all waters that together form the entire aquatic system. Water moves in hydrologic cycles, and the pollution of [a] part of the aquatic system ... will affect the water quality of the other waters within that aquatic system.

42 Fed. Reg. 37,128 (1977). *See also* 2 LEGISLATIVE HISTORY at 1495 (Report of Senate Committee on Public Works).

The CWA defines "pollutant" to include "dredged soil ... rock, sand, [and] cellar dirt," 33 U.S.C. §1362(6) (1978), and establishes a permit system to control discharges of dredged material. Section 1344 of the Act authorizes the Secretary of the Army to act through the Corps to issue such permits under certain conditions and procedures. The permit process is "the cornerstone of the ... scheme for cleaning up the nation's waters." *United States Steel Corp. v. Train,* 556 F.2d 822, 829 (7th Cir. 1977). *See also Mobil Oil Corp. v. United States E.P.A.,* 716 F.2d 1187, 1189 (7th Cir. 1983), *cert. denied,* 466 U.S. 980, 104 S.Ct. 2363, 80 L.Ed. 2d 835 (1984); *Citizens for a Better Environment v. Environmental Protection Agency,* 596 F.2d 720, 721-22 (7th Cir. 1979); *United States v. Byrd,* 609 F.2d 1204, 1206 (7th Cir. 1979); *American Meat Institute v. Environmental Protection Agency,* 526 F.2d 442, 444-45 (7th Cir. 1975).

The Huebners did not challenge the authority of the Corps to regulate parts of Bear Bluff Farms as wetlands in the district court, but argued that their activities were exempt from the CWA's permit process under Section 1344(f)(1). The district court held that the phrase "discharge of dredged or fill material" in the 1978 consent order incorporated the legal meaning of those terms under the CWA and therefore the question of whether the Huebners' permitless activities violated the terms of the 1978 consent decree hinged on the court's interpretation of the scope of Section 1344(f)(1)'s exemptions. The district court held that "it is clear that the amendments that created the subsection (f) exceptions on which defendants rely were not intended to exempt all farming operations from the permit requirements, but only those whose effect upon wetlands or other waters was so minimal as not to warrant federal review and supervision." R. 118, Order at 17-18. The court then analyzed the defendants' actions in light of the purposes of the Clean Water Act, the intent of Congress in enacting the farming exceptions, and the terms of the 1978 order. Our review of the legislative history confirms the conclusion reached by the lower court.

Section 1344(f)(1) provides exemptions from the permit process for discharges into wetlands caused by agricultural activities, such as plowing and the maintenance of dikes, ponds, and farm roads. The exceptions of Section 1344(f)(1) are subject to section 1344(f)(2), however, which provides that discharges are not exempt from the permit process if they bring "an area of the navigable waters into a use to which it was not previously subject, where the flow or circulation of navigable waters may be impaired or the reach of such waters be reduced."

Our review of the legislative history of the agricultural exemptions convinces us that because of the significance of inland wetlands, which make up 85 percent of the nation's wetlands, Congress intended that Section 1344(f)(1) exempt from the permit process only "narrowly defined activities ... that cause little or no adverse effects either individually or cumulatively [and which do not] convert more extensive areas of water into dry land or impede circulation or reduce the reach and size of the water body." 3 LEGISLATIVE HISTORY at 420 (statement of Rep. Harsha, member of the conference committee, during House debates). *See also id.* at 474. The Fifth Circuit also has held that §1344(f)(1) was designed to be a "narrow exemption." *Avoyelles Sportsmen's League, Inc. v. Marsh,* 715 F.2d 897, 925 n.44 (5th Cir. 1983).

Recognizing that "there has been widespread concern that many activities that are normally considered routine would be prohibited or made extremely difficult because of the complex regulatory procedures," 4 LEGISLATIVE HISTORY 897 (statement of Sen. Randolph), Congress enacted in the 1977 amendments a delicate balance of exceptions that protected wetlands while permitting routine activities to go on unimpeded.

> The drainages exemption is very clearly intended to put to rest, once and for all, the fears that permits are required for draining poorly drained farm or forest land of which millions of acres exist. No permits are required for such drainage. Permits are required only where ditches or channels are dredged in a swamp, marsh, bog or other truly aquatic area.

4 LEGISLATIVE HISTORY 1042 (statement of Sen. Muskie). We therefore affirm the district court's narrow interpretation of the agricultural exemptions and its incorporation of the purpose of those exemptions into the finding of contempt against the Huebners for violation of the 1978 consent decree.

III. FINDINGS AS TO SPECIFIC ACTIVITIES ON BEAR BLUFF FARMS

In civil contempt proceedings for violations of a consent decree, plaintiffs must prove the violations by clear and convincing evidence in the trial court. *Squillacote v. Local 248, Meat & Allied Food Wkrs.,* 534 F.2d 735, 747 (7th Cir. 1976). The court's factual determinations are accorded great weight on appeal when they depend on credibility determinations based on the demeanor of witnesses at trial. *Cf. NLRB v. Cutting, Inc.,* 701 F.2d 659, 663 (7th Cir. 1983). Moreover, the remedy chosen by the trial court in a contempt proceeding on a consent decree is "discretionary in character and is not to be reversed except for abuse of such discretion or unless clearly erroneous." *Walaschek & Associates, Inc. v. Crow,* 733 F.2d 51, 53 (7th Cir. 1984), *quoting Jewel Tea Co. v. Kraus,* 204 F.2d 549, 551 (7th Cir. 1953). Our review of the lower court's findings of fact and conclusions of law as to the particular challenged activities is guided therefore by these standards.

A. PLOWING THE RESERVOIRS

The lower court found that the Huebners used a marsh plow to plow and remove wetland vegetation from the three reservoirs at sites 10, 11, and 12, and leveled the dikes in these reservoirs. The court found that the Huebners plowed the reservoirs to decrease the capacity of the soil to store water in preparation for the immediate planting of barley and for the future planting of corn and other dryland crops. The court held that in doing so the Huebners failed "to protect the integrity of the dikes" and to guarantee "maximum drainage control" in direct violation of paragraph 7 of the 1978 consent decree.

The Huebners do not deny these activities but argue that they were not required to notify the Corps or obtain a permit for the plowing of the reservoirs because the "nonfunctional and nonproductive" nature of the reservoirs required that they cease to be used as reservoirs. The Huebners claim that their activity will make the reservoirs "more effective land," and argue on appeal that "the so-called reservoirs had been cropped for decades before the unsuccessful attempt to convert this land into reservoirs in 1956." The Huebners stated purpose, however, is in direct opposition not only to the purposes of the Clean Water Act, but, more importantly, to the terms of the consent decree, which required a return to the status of the land as it had existed prior to the discharge activities which had initially prompted the 1978 order. We therefore affirm the court's finding that the Huebners were in violation of the 1978 order when they plowed the reservoirs.

B. CLEANING, DEEPENING AND DIGGING DITCHES

In conjunction with the plowing of the reservoirs, the district court found that the Huebners had used backhoes to clean and deepen existing ditches at sites 1, 2, and 14 and used a dragline to excavate an approximately 400 foot long new ditch at site 3. The court found that the result of the deepening activities at sites 2 and 14 was to drain the reservoirs. The court also found that at sites 1, 2, 3, and 14 the Huebners had sidecast materials onto the wetlands, used bulldozers to spread the discharge over several acres, and formed the materials into farm roads which were broader than necessary according to best management practices.

The Huebners argue that the evidence showed that their ditches were used solely for irrigation purposes, and therefore they were exempt from the permit procedure under Section 1344(f)(1)(c), which exempts discharges related to the "construction or maintenance of irrigation ditches." The Huebners also argued that the water level in the ditches had been raised, indicating that the groundwater level surrounding the ditch was higher than it had been prior to the 1978 decree. The Huebners argued that the evidence of a higher groundwater level showed a compliance with the purposes of the 1978 order.

The district court rejected the Huebners' focus on ditch water level and looked instead to the results of Huebners' dredging activity as it affected the surrounding wetlands. We think this interpretation of the purpose of the 1978 consent order was proper. We think the government succinctly stated the fallacy of the Huebners' argument at oral argument when counsel stated that "the Clean Water Act is not a Full Ditch Act:" the water level of the ditches is not the key to compliance with the purposes of the 1978 order.

The district court correctly reasoned that even if the ditches at issue were irrigation ditches, the restrictions of Section 1344(f)(2) still applied. Under Section 1344(f)(2), the discharge of dredged materials from the construction of irrigation ditches requires a permit where such discharges "bring an area of navigable waters into a use to which it was not previously subject and where the flow of the waters is impaired and their reach reduced." The district court reasoned that the sidecasting and spreading activity reduced the reach of the wetlands surrounding the ditches at issue. The court therefore concluded that the defendants had violated the 1978 order by not giving notice of such activity and by not obtaining a permit. We affirm the court's conclusion that the Huebners' ditching activity, whether it involved irrigation or drainage ditches, ran afoul of the provisions of Section 1344(f)(2). The Huebners' activity constituted a discharge of dredged material onto a wetland, thereby disturbing the reach of its waters. Such activity required notice and application for a permit under the 1978 consent decree.

C. MAINTENANCE OF FARM ROADS

The district court found that at sites 1, 5, and 6 the Huebners bulldozed excess road fill into adjacent wetlands and maintained the roads at a greater width than necessary. The Huebners argued that discharges made in connection with the maintenance of farm roads are exempt from permit requirements under Section 1344(f)(1)(E). The court concluded, however, that the Huebners' bulldozing activities violated Section 1344(f)(1)(E)'s requirement that the "best management practices" be used in the maintenance of farm roads, and reasoned therefore that the Huebners should have given notice and obtained a permit if necessary before widening the roads. We find nothing clearly erroneous in the court's conclusion and affirm the lower court's ruling that Section 1344(f)(1)(E) exemptions for discharges made in the construction and maintenance of farm roads does not apply to the Huebners' activities. The Huebners' failure to give notice and apply for a permit for these activities was a violation of the 1978 order.

D. EXPANSION OF CRANBERRY BEDS

The court below held that the Huebners' expansion of the Staege cranberry beds at site 9 without a permit violated both paragraphs 1 and 2 of the consent order because it found that the conversion of the adjacent wetlands into cranberry beds was a "use" of the wetlands to which they had not been previously subject, therefore requiring a permit under Section 1344(f)(2). 33 C.F.R. §323.4(a)(1)(ii) provides:

an operation ceases to be established when the area on which it is conducted has been converted to another use or has lain idle so long that modifications to the hydrological regime are necessary to resume operations.

Relying on this definition, the district court found that since the Huebners had had to drain the surrounding area in order to expand the bed, this conversion brought it within the terms of the regulation. We affirm the court's ruling.

E. SCRAPING ACTIVITY

Finally, the district court found that the defendants used a bulldozer to move large mounds of dirt and level a 10 to 12 acre area at site 13 in violation of paragraphs 1 and 2, which prohibit discharges without a permit. The court reasoned that the scraping of materials from a wetland constitutes a discharge, because wetlands are defined by the presence of aquatic vegetation. *See* 33 C.F.R. §323.2(a)(7)(c) (1983). Moreover, the regulations also provide that Section 1344(f)(1)'s exemption for plowing "does not include the redistribution of soil, rock, sand, or other surficial materials in a manner which changes any of area of the waters of the United States to dry land. For example, the redistribution of surface materials by blading, grading, or other means to fill in wetland areas is not plowing." 33 C.F.R. §323.4(D) (1983). *See also Avoyelles Sportsmen's League v. Alexander,* 473 F. Supp. 525, 533 (W.D.La 1979), 715 F.2d 897 (5th Cir. 1983). We find nothing erroneous in the court's conclusion, and affirm the court's ruling that the Huebners violated the 1978 order by not giving notice and applying for a permit for this scraping activity....

IV. RESTORATION PLAN

A lower court's remedy for civil contempt is reviewable only under the limited "abuse of discretion" standard. *Sportmart, Inc. v. Wolverine World Wide, Inc.,* 601 F.2d 313 (7th Cir. 1979). The court below exercised its discretion in ordering particular restoration activities to be performed by the Huebners after considering whether the plan: (1) is achievable as a practical matter; (2) confers maximum environmental benefits; and (3) bears an equitable relationship to the degree and kind of wrong. R. 137, Order at 1. *See United States v. Sexton Cove Estates, Inc.,* 526 F.2d 1293, 1301 (5th Cir. 1976). Upon review we find one portion of the district court's order to have been an abuse of discretion. The majority of the court's order, however, was within the court's discretion.

The district court's remedial order requiring the Huebners to maintain certain water levels and to conduct other restoration activities withstands our review under the abuse of discretion standard. The record presents sufficient evidence to support the practicability of the maintenance of specified water levels at the reservoirs and other locations. The district court relied heavily on assessments of the credibility of the experts who testified as to the practicability of the water level aspect of the plan, noting that the achievability of such levels was "not a matter of common sense." R. 137 at 4. We must accord great weight to lower courts' factual determinations when they depend on the assessment of a witness' credibility, *cf. NLRB v. Cutting, Inc.,* 701 F.2d 659, 663 (7th Cir. 1983), and thus we affirm that portion of the district court's order.

The Huebners complain bitterly about the ordered destruction of their permitless ten-acre expansion of the Staege cranberry beds, alleging that the beds are worth $400,000 and that their destruction is neither "cost-effective nor environmentally warranted." We agree with the Huebners and find the district court's order to destroy the ten-acre bed to have been an abuse of discretion. The district court found that the Huebners' cranberry bed expansion "would not achieve maximum environmental benefits for the land at issue," and that, given the nature of the Huebners' repeated violations, the destruction of this bed bore an equitable relationship to the harm to the land caused by the Huebners.

Expert testimony in the record indicates however, that cranberry beds are compatible with wetlands, although they do not perform the same water filtration and storage functions as an undisturbed wetland. The district court also noted that the Huebners might have been able to expand the Staege bed had they applied for an expansion permit in the first instance. R. 137 at 8. Moreover, evidence in the record reveals that some representatives of the Corps were cognizant of the Huebners' expansion of the cranberry beds. While this Corps conduct was insufficient to meet the exacting requirements necessary for the government to be estopped from seeking a contempt citation against the Huebners, it should have been a factor to be given considerable weight by the trial court in fashioning a restoration order. Given this evidence, we think that it was an abuse of discretion for the district court to find that the destruction of the cranberry expansion bed bore an equitable relationship to the degree and kind of wrong committed by the Huebners. The Huebners did not follow the rules of the consent decree, admittedly, but it is a draconian exercise of judicial discretion to order undone a ten-acre expansion of cranberry beds which it took the Huebners several years to develop and which beds are not inherently incompatible with the surrounding wetlands. Therefore, we reverse the district court's remedial order and remand with instructions to strike that portion of the order decreeing the destruction of the ten-acre cranberry bed.

V. CONCLUSION

It must be emphasized that any perceived severity in the findings and the remedy of the district court which we affirm in part and reverse in part here were brought on the Huebners by their own failure to comply to the terms of the 1978 consent order into which they had voluntarily entered. While the Huebners and amicus, the Wisconsin Cranberry Growers Association, voice concern over the ability of cranberry farming to continue in Wisconsin should we affirm the district court's orders, we decline to be persuaded by these highly speculative prophecies of doom. The Huebners may continue to farm their land. The district court recognized in ordering the restoration plan that the Huebners may still plant corn on parts of their property. R. 137 at 3. The Huebners may continue to farm cranberries or other crops, as long as they comply with the terms of the 1978 order which requires notice and application for permits. Other cranberry farmers or owners of wetlands property are also not prohibited from making a productive use of their property; proper compliance with the permit process is all that is required under the Clean Water Act to ensure that the use of the nation's wetlands proceeds with care. In conclusion then, the district court's finding of contempt is affirmed and its remedial restoration order is reversed and remanded with instructions to the district court to strike that portion of the order ordering the destruction of the ten-acre cranberry bed.

AFFIRMED in part, REVERSED and REMANDED in part

See also *U.S. v. Brace*, 41 F.3d 117 (3d Cir. 1994), *cert. denied* 515 U.S. 1158, 115 S.Ct. 2610, 132 L.Ed.2d 854 (1995).

UNITED STATES v. AKERS

785 F.2d 814 (9th Cir. 1986), *cert. denied* 479 U.S. 828, 017 S.Ct. 107, 93 L.Ed.2d 56 (1986)

This litigation is the unfortunate result of a standoff between a California farmer who seeks to farm his wetlands more productively and the Army Corps of Engineers which regulates wetland use under the Clean Water Act ("Act"), 33 U.S.C. §§1251-1376 (1982 & Supp. I 1984). The Corps succeeded in enjoining dredge and fill activities for which a permit had not been sought. We are asked to construe the Act's exemptions and review the scope of the preliminary injunction awarded to the government. We have jurisdiction under 28 U.S.C. §1292(a)(1), and we affirm.

BACKGROUND

In January 1984, Robert W. Akers purchased approximately 9,600 acres in Lassen and Modoc counties, near Bieber, California. The property includes 2,889 acres of wetlands, known locally as the "Big Swamp." Ash Creek, a tributary to the Pit River, flows across the property. The Pit River, Ash Creek, and their channels and adjacent wetlands are subject to the Corps's jurisdiction under Section 404 of the Act, 33 U.S.C. §1344 (1982).

Big Swamp is an important wildlife habitat. It provides seasonal refuge for numerous species, including the bald eagle and peregrine falcon, both endangered species, the greater sandhill crane, listed as rare by California authorities, and the cackling Canada goose, whose numbers have decreased sharply in recent years. Less threatened species, including Canada geese, snow geese, and mallard, pintail, shoveler and cinnamon teal ducks, also inhabit the area.

The following chronology summarizes Akers' battle with the Corps over Big Swamp farming:

> March 1984: Corps learned of Akers' "farming plan" to carry out extensive grading, leveling, drainage and water diversion to convert the wetlands to farm land suitable for growing upland crops. After a preliminary investigation, the Corps determined that its jurisdiction extended to roughly one-third of Akers' property and that a Section 404 permit would be required.
>
> May 4: Akers sued the government for declaratory and injunctive relief under the Act alleging that the Corps's assertion of regulatory jurisdiction was improper and illegal. TRO issued enjoining Corps from asserting regulatory jurisdiction over Akers until hearing on motion for preliminary injunction. The order also enjoined Akers from construction activities.
>
> May 15: Akers' motion for preliminary injunction was denied.
>
> July 16: Akers voluntarily dismissed his lawsuit. He began the first of three phases of earthmoving activity. Along the western border of his property, he built a dike 3,500 feet long, two to three feet high and six feet wide. He first told the Corps he was ditch cleaning, but later said he was repairing a pre-existing temporary irrigation structure. Late

July early Corps determined that August Akers needed a permit and issued a cease and desist order. By that time, the project was finished.

August 13: Corps withdrew cease and desist order based on assurances that the dike would be used only for the purposes that the previous structure had served (although new dike was longer and in a different location).

August 30: Akers was informed by the Corps's District Engineer ("DE") that 2,889 acres of his farm contained wetlands within the Corps's jurisdiction.

September 2: Corps learned of work in central portion of wetlands.

September 13: Corps's aerial survey revealed two-mile long dike had been constructed east-to-west through the wetlands. On the west end, the dike connected perpendicularly to the other recently-constructed dike on he western property line. A grader and tractor (pulling discs) were seen along the dike. Some wetlands south of the dike had been leveled. Corps issued a cease and desist order.

September 17: Fly-over showed that sometime after September 13, the dike had been lengthened from two to three miles.

September 26: Fly-over revealed large north-south ditch on the eastern edge of the property, possibly 50 feet wide. While the ditch was mostly on non-wetlands, it filled two natural channels of Ash Creek. Corps also observed roads being constructed in the north-west section of the property. These roads blocked several overflow channels of the Pit River.

October 3: The U.S. sued Akers seeking declaratory and injunctive relief, civil penalties and restoration.

October 5: District court granted TRO forbidding Akers from depositing dredged or fill material in waters on his property, except in certain channels with Corps's permission. October 24: Court orally granted government's motion for preliminary injunction. October 31: Written TRO entered.

January 14, 1985: Oral argument on actions for reconsideration, and intervention of the California Cattlemen's Association, Agricultural Council of California, National Cattlemen's Association, and California Farm Bureau ("Cattlemen") on behalf of Akers and the National Audubon Society and National Wildlife Federation ("Audubon") on behalf of the government.

January 15: Court issued written findings of fact, conclusions of law and order reconfirming the earlier oral preliminary injunction. The order prohibited Akers from depositing dredged or fill material into the waters, channels or wetlands previously delineated by the Corps unless he: (1) obtains a permit from the Corps, or (2) submits a proposal for dredge or fill activities, which he asserts are not within the Corps's jurisdiction, and (a) is informed in writing by the DE that a permit is not necessary; or (b) is not informed in writing by the DE whether a permit is necessary within 15 days of receipt of his proposal. The court also ordered that Akers must comply in good faith with Corps' cease and desist orders regarding dredge and fill activities on his property.

January 31: Court granted permissive intervention of the Cattlemen and Audubon groups.

This appeal followed. Akers has not applied for a §404 permit from the Corps.

STANDARD OF REVIEW

A preliminary injunction will be reversed "only if the lower court abused its discretion or based its decision on an erroneous legal standard or clearly erroneous findings of fact." *Flynt Distributing Co., Inc. v. Harvey,* 734 F.2d 1389, 1394 (9th Cir. 1984). The injunction will be upheld if the court correctly found that the government demonstrated either (1) probable success on the merits and the possibility of irreparable injury, or (2) that serious questions are raised and the balance of the hardships tips sharply in its favor. *Goldie's Bookstore, Inc. v. Superior Court,* 739 F.2d 466, 470 (9th Cir. 1984). These are not separate tests, but rather, "extremes of a single continuum." *Benda v. Grand Lodge of the International Association of Machinists & Aerospace Workers,* 584 F.2d 308, 315 (9th Cir. 1978), *cert. dismissed,* 441 U.S. 937, 99 S.Ct. 2065, 60 L.Ed. 2d 667 (1979).

STATUTORY FRAMEWORK

The Act aims "to restore and maintain the chemical, physical, and biological integrity of the Nation's waters." 33 U.S.C. §1251(a) (1982). "This purpose is to be achieved by compliance with the Act, including compliance with the permit requirements." *Weinberger v. Romero-Barcelo,* 456 U.S. 305, 315, 72 L.Ed.2d 91, 102 S.Ct. 1798 (1982) [Footnote omitted.]

The Act prohibits the discharge of dredged or fill materials into "navigable waters"—defined as "waters of the United States"—unless authorized by a permit issued by the Corps pursuant to §404. *See generally* 33 U.S.C. §§1311, 1344 (1982). "Waters of the United States" is broken down into seven categories, including wetlands. *See* 33 C.F.R. §323.2(a) (1985).

Recently, a unanimous Supreme Court upheld the Corps's wetlands definition in *United States v. Riverside Bayview Homes, Inc.,* 474 U.S. 121, 106 S.Ct. 455, 88 L.Ed.2d 419 (1985). The lands in question are wetlands under the Corps's definition; hence, the Corps had authority, absent an applicable exception, to require Akers to obtain a permit before engaging in dredge and fill activities.

Limited exemptions from the permit requirement are found in Section 1344(f), which provides in pertinent part:

> (f) Non-prohibited discharge of dredged or fill material (1) Except as provided in paragraph (2) of this subsection, the discharge of dredged or fill material—
>
> > (A) from normal farming, silviculture, and ranching activities such as plowing, seeding, cultivating, minor drainage, harvesting for the production of food, fiber, and forest products, or upland soil and water conservation practices;...
> >
> > (C) for the purpose of construction or maintenance of farm or stock ponds or irrigation ditches, or the maintenance of drainage ditches;...
> >
> > (E) for the purpose of construction or maintenance of farm roads or forest roads, or temporary roads for moving mining equipment, where such roads are constructed

> and maintained, in accordance with best management practices, to assure that flow and circulation patterns and chemical and biological characteristics of the navigable waters are not impaired, that the reach of the navigable waters is not reduced, and that any adverse effect on the aquatic environment will be otherwise minimized;...is not prohibited by or otherwise subject to regulation under this section....
>
> (2) Any discharge of dredged or fill material into the navigable waters incidental to any activity having as its purpose bringing an area of the navigable waters into a use to which it was not previously subject, where the flow or circulation of navigable waters may be impaired or the reach of such waters be reduced, shall be required to have a permit under this section.

Akers' activities must be analyzed in light of the Act's purposes and the intended scope of its exemptions. The Fifth and Seventh Circuits have construed the §1344(f)(1) exemptions narrowly. *See United States v. Huebner,* 752 F.2d 1235, 1240-41 (7th Cir.), *cert. denied,* 474 U.S. 817, 106 S.Ct. 62, 88 L.Ed.2d 50 (1985); *Avoyelles Sportsmen's League, Inc. v. Marsh,* 715 F.2d 897, 925 n.44 (5th Cir. 1983).

This construction is consistent with the legislative history. Senator Muskie described the exemptions during Senate debate:

> New subsection 404(f) provides that Federal permits will not be required for those narrowly defined activities that cause little or no adverse effects either individually or cumulatively. While it is understood that some of these activities may necessarily result in incidental filling and minor harm to aquatic resources, the exemptions do not apply to discharges that convert extensive areas of water into dry land or impede circulation or reduce the reach or size of the water body.

3 Legislative History of the Clean Water Act of 1977 ("Leg. Hist.") at 474 (Senate Debate, Dec. 15, 1977). As the legislation's primary sponsor, his remarks are entitled to substantial weight. *See Federal Energy Administration v. Algonquin SNG, Inc.,* 426 U.S. 548, 564, 49 L.Ed. 2d 49, 96 S.Ct. 2295 (1976); *Environmental Defense Fund, Inc. v. Costle,* 636 F.2d 1229, 1243 & n.48 (D.C.Cir. 1980).

To be exempt from the permit requirements, one must demonstrate that proposed activities both *satisfy* the requirements of §(f)(1) and *avoid* the exception to the exemptions (referred to as the "recapture" provision) of §(f)(2). *Avoyelles,* 715 F.2d at 926 ((f)(2) takes away some of the exemptions provided in (f)(1)). Akers must establish that his activities are exempt.

ANALYSIS

(1) The "Normal Farming" Exemption: §1344(f)(1)(A)

The court rejected this exemption because the wetlands portion of Akers' farm "has never been subjected to any established upland farming operation," relying on 33 C.F.R. §323.4(a)(1)(ii) (1985). That regulation provides in pertinent part:

> To fall under this exemption, the activities ... must be part of an established (*i.e.,* ongoing) farming, silviculture, or ranching operation. Activities on areas lying fallow as part of a conventional rotational cycle are part of an established operation. Activities which

> bring an area into farming, silviculture, or ranching use are not part of an established operation. An operation ceases to be established when the area on which it was conducted has been converted to another use or has lain idle so long that modifications to the hydrological regime are necessary to resume operations....

Akers bases his entitlement to the exemption on the fact that all of his land, including the wetlands, has been farmed since 1897. He contends that discing and seeding have been part of the farming operation traditionally undertaken on his land.

He ignores the consequences of the new projects, however. We cannot view Akers' plowing, discing, and seeding in isolation. The record amply supports the court's finding that upland crop production has not occurred on these wetlands on a regular basis. Upland farming represents a new operation in the wetlands.

Moreover, Akers argued below that unless he were allowed to complete the work he had started, the effect of which is to drain the wetlands, he would be unable to engage in the farming activities he had planned. By his own admission, his activities require substantial hydrological alteration to Big Swamp, and run afoul of the regulations.

At oral argument, counsel for the government advocated a position of complete authority to prohibit all changes in wetland use which involve discharges of pollutants without prior Corps approval. Discing of soil is a point source of pollutants, according to the Corps.

Responding to our inquiries, government counsel asserted that the Corps would require Akers, and other farmers like him, to obtain a §404 permit before switching from one *type* of wetland crop to another, if the new crop had not been farmed previously. For example, if Akers desired to plant wild rice, a wetland crop, the Corps would require a permit since rice has not been farmed in Big Swamp in the past.

Although we affirm the injunction as a reasonable response to the peculiar facts before us, we do not endorse the government's authoritative position. We do not believe that Congress intended to place the burden of Corps permit regulation on farmers who desire merely to change from one wetland crop to another.

(2) The "Irrigation" Exemption: §1344(f)(1)(C)

The court rejected Akers' attempt to characterize the three-mile long dike bisecting the wetlands as an exempt irrigation facility. He argues that non-exempt dikes hold water on their lowland sides while exempt structures, such as his dike, hold water on their upland sides.

It is irrelevant how he characterizes the dike. Provided the structure has the effect of keeping water from the southern wetlands, its construction requires a permit. *See Huebner,* 752 F.2d at 1242. The regulation defining "minor drainage," as that term is used in the "normal farming" exemption, supports the government's position:

> Minor drainage in waters of the U.S. is limited to drainage within areas that are part of an established farming or silviculture operation. It does not include drainage associated with the immediate or gradual conversion of a wetland to a non-wetland (*e.g.,* wetland species to upland species not typically adapted to life in saturated soil conditions), or conversion from one wetland use to another (for example, silviculture to farming). In addition, minor

> drainage does not include the construction of any canal, ditch, dike or other waterway or structure which drains or otherwise significantly modifies a stream, lake, swamp, bog or any other wetland or aquatic area constituting waters of the United States. Any discharge of dredged or fill material into the waters of the United States incidental to the construction of any such structure or waterway requires a permit.

33 C.F.R. §323.4(a)(1)(iii)(C)(2) (1985).

Akers also argues that the dike is physically connected and functionally related to an irrigation ditch and, therefore, is exempt under 33 C.F.R. §323.4(a)(3) (1985):

> Discharges associated with siphons, pumps, headgates, wingwalls, weirs, diversion structures, and such other facilities as are appurtenant and functionally related to irrigation ditches are included in this exemption.

The court concluded that the dike was not one of the types of structures specified in the regulation and was not subsidiary to an irrigation ditch. Akers has not demonstrated that these factual findings are clearly erroneous.

(3) The State Water Rights Proviso: 33 U.S.C. §1251(g)

Akers asserts that the court construed 33 U.S.C. §1251(g) (1982) (also known as the "Wallop Amendment") too narrowly by rendering his state-allocated water rights "virtually meaningless." He urges us to apply the irrigation exemption "so as to not impair or abrogate state allocated water rights."

Section 1251(g) provides:

> It is the policy of Congress that the authority of each State to allocate quantities of water within its jurisdiction shall not be superseded, abrogated or otherwise impaired by this chapter. It is the further policy of Congress that nothing in this chapter shall be construed to supersede or abrogate rights to quantities of water which have been established by any State. Federal agencies shall co-operate with State and local agencies to develop comprehensive solutions to prevent, reduce and eliminate pollution in concert with programs for managing water resources.

Akers attacks the "ambiguous" references to legislative history relied on by the district court when it refused to apply §1251(g). Senator Wallop, who sponsored the amendment, described its purpose during Senate debate:

> The requirements of section 402 and 404 permits may incidentally affect individual water rights.... It is not the purpose of this amendment to prohibit those incidental effects. It is the purpose of this amendment to insure that State allocation systems are not subverted, and that effects on individual rights, if any, are prompted by legitimate and necessary water quality considerations. This amendment is an attempt to recognize the historic allocation rights contained in State constitutions. It is designed to protect historic rights from mischievous abrogation by those who would use an act, designed solely to protect water quality and wetlands, for other purposes. It does not interfere with the legitimate purposes for which the act was designed.

3 Leg. Hist. 532 (Senate Debate, Dec. 15, 1977).

As intervenor Audubon points out, any incidental effect on Akers' rights to state-allocated water from the Pit River is justified because protection of Big Swamp is the type of legitimate purpose for which the Act was intended.

In *Riverside Irrigation District v. Andrews,* 758 F.2d 508, 513 (10th Cir. 1985), the Tenth Circuit construed the Wallop Amendment as an indication

> 'that Congress did not want to interfere any more than necessary with state water management.' *National Wildlife Federation v. Gorsuch,* 224 U.S. App. D.C. 41, 693 F.2d 156, 178 (D.C. Cir. 1982). A fair reading of the statute as a whole makes clear that, where both the state's interest in allocating water and the federal government's interest in protecting the environment are implicated, Congress intended an accommodation. Such accommodations are best reached in the individual permit process.

Akers staunchly has resisted the permit process. The injunction properly compels him to participate in it.

(4) The "Roadbuilding" Exemption: § 1344(f)(1)(E)

Akers disagrees with the court's findings that he constructed a road across overflow channels of the Pit River and failed to comply with best management practices. Rather than challenging these findings as clearly erroneous, he asserts that the injunction is overbroad. He contends that instead of enjoining all roadbuilding, the appropriate remedy "was simply to notify him as to what actions were necessary to bring the road into conformity with best management practices, and require compliance therewith in future activities." We disagree.

The roadbuilding regulations set forth in 33 C.F.R. §323.4(a)(6) (1985) describe with sufficient clarity what Akers had to do to comply with §1344(f)(1)(E). As explained in the overbreadth section below, the court properly considered Akers' misunderstanding and disregard of the Act in fashioning appropriate relief.

(5) The "Recapture" Provision: §1344(f)(2)

Judge Ramirez concluded that Akers was unlikely to avoid the recapture provision even if he established an applicable exemption. Over Akers' argument that upland crops *could* have been grown in the wetlands, the court wrote:

> The proper inquiry is not what could have been done but what *was* done in the past and its relationship to what Mr. Akers is attempting to do now. Furthermore, Mr. Aker's [sic] argument ignores the question of whether there will be a change in Big Swamp from wetlands (*i.e.,* waters of the United States) to dry land (no longer waters of the United States). Whether or not there have been isolated incidents of attempted farming of upland crops in the swamp during dryer periods, there is little doubt that the area is still a wetland within the meaning of the Clean Water Act. Mr. Akers' activities taken as a whole appear to this Court to be incidental to an effort to convert the area so that it may be farmed in a way which is inconsistent with its remaining a wetland.

United States v. Akers, No. CIV-84-1276 RAR, Conclusion of Law XIV (E.D. Cal. Jan. 15, 1985). The court did not abuse its discretion in reaching this conclusion.

Additionally, Akers asserts that "use" denotes a major type of use, *e.g.*, farming, silviculture or ranching. Because the land has been used for farming since 1897, he claims there is no major change of use within the meaning of §(f)(2).

He attempts to distinguish *Huebner* and *Avoyelles,* where the recapture provision was applied. He asserts that those cases involved major changes *to* agricultural use, whereas his actions represent "a change within the farming use." However, he cannot escape the impact of these opinions, which classify as non-exempt those activities which change a wetland's hydrological regime. *See Huebner,* 752 F.2d at 1242; *Avoyelles,* 715 F.2d at 926.

While the exemptions and regulations do not distinguish major and minor changes, the intent of Congress in enacting the Act was to prevent conversion of wetlands to dry lands. For example, Representative Harsha, a member of the conference committee, stated during House debate:

> To assure that the extent of these exempted activities will not be misconstrued,... (f)(2) provides common sense limitations to protect the chemical, biological, and physical integrity of the Nation's waters. While it is understood that some of these activities may necessarily result in incidental filling and insignificant harm to aquatic resources, the exemptions do not apply to discharges that convert more extensive areas of water into dry land or impede circulation or reduce the reach or size of the water body.

3 Leg. Hist. 420 (House Debate, Dec. 15, 1977).

It is thus the substantiality of the impact on the wetland that must be considered in evaluating the reach of §(f)(2). *Cf. Huebner,* 752 F.2d at 1242 (district court properly considered results of dredging as it affected surrounding wetlands). The court's findings on wetland conversion, not clearly erroneous, establish:

> It appears likely that if this work is allowed to remain in place, or allowed to be expanded, an extensive area of the Big Swamp wetlands will be converted to non-wetland, thereby significantly reducing the reach of Big Swamp. In addition, the flow and circulation in Ash Creek and the overflow channels of the Pit River may be impaired. Furthermore, many highly significant aquatic functions now performed by the Big Swamp wetlands area will be lost or impaired.

United States v. Akers, Finding of Fact X.

Giving the recapture provision the appropriate common sense reading, it appears that Akers' activities are not exempt from permit requirements due to the likely drying effect. As discussed earlier, this is not to say that he could not change from one wetland crop to another without running afoul of the recapture provision.

(6) Is the Injunction Overbroad?

Finally, he argues that the injunction is overbroad because it requires Corps approval for all his dredge and fill activities, including those clearly exempt. The government responds by stating that the conditions are necessary to preserve the *status quo*. The government stresses the non-onerous nature of this injunction, considering the requirement that the Corps respond to a permit application within 15 days.

The district court has considerable discretion to fashion appropriate injunctive relief, particularly where the public interest is involved. *See Virginian Railway Co. v. System Federation No. 40 etc.,* 300 U.S. 515, 552, 57 S.Ct. 592, 81 L.Ed. 789 (1937); *State of California v. Tahoe Regional Planning Agency,* 766 F.2d 1319, 1324 (9th Cir.) (district court has greater power to fashion equitable relief in defense of the public interest than it has when only private interests are involved), *amended,* 775 F.2d 998 (9th Cir. 1985). The Supreme Court has recognized that the Act gives the district court discretion "to order that relief it considers necessary to secure prompt compliance with the Act." *Weinberger v. Romero-Barcelo,* 456 U.S. at 320.

In enjoining the filling of wetlands without a permit, courts have noted that the public interest requires strict enforcement of the Act to effectuate its purpose of protecting sensitive aquatic environments. *See United States v. Ciampitti,* 583 F.Supp. 483, 499 (D.N.J. 1984); *United States v. Lofgren,* 13 Envtl.L.Rep. (Envtl. L. Inst.) 20,164 at 20,166 (E.D. Mich. 1982) (presumption in favor of preliminary injunction in light of Act's objectives which include maintaining Corps's regulatory scheme) (discussed in W. Want, *Federal Wetlands Law: The Cases and the Problems,* 8 Harv. Envtl. L. Rev. 1, 52 (1984)).

Judge Ramirez did not abuse his discretion in issuing this injunction. He considered extensive testimony regarding past and present uses of Big Swamp, ecological disruption caused by the ongoing and proposed activities, Akers' avoidance of the Corps's permit process, harm incurred by Akers, and the legislative history of the exemptions. The findings and conclusions supporting the injunction are comprehensive and reflect a well-balanced consideration of the competing interests.

CONCLUSION

Akers has failed to demonstrate that the injunction was based on erroneous legal standards or clearly erroneous findings of fact. Nor does he demonstrate that Judge Ramirez abused his discretion.

We are mindful of the plight of today's farmers. So was Congress when it enacted the wetlands legislation at issue here. It did not intend to prohibit all changes of wetlands, however minor, without prior Corps approval.

The changes proposed by Akers are far from minor, however. They contemplate a major conversion from wetlands to dry lands, thereby necessitating a Corps permit. Judicial review of Corps permit approval or denial provides the necessary check against arbitrary government action. We assume that the Corps will not act arbitrarily when it rules on Akers' future permit applications.

This litigation resulted from an inability to work cooperatively. Both parties bear some fault for the breakdown in communications. Reasonableness and cooperation are indicated. The preliminary injunction is AFFIRMED. [Footnotes omitted.]

See also *Borden Ranch Partnership v. U.S. Army Corps of Engineers*, 261 F.3d 810 (9th Cir. 2001).

UNITED STATES v. LARKINS

852 F.2d 189 (6th Cir. 1988), *cert. denied* 489 U.S. 1016, 109 S.Ct. 1131, 103 L.Ed.2d 193 (1989)

Defendants-appellants Thomas R. Larkins and Herbert M. Larkins (defendants) appealed from the district court's order permanently enjoining them from modifying "wetlands" adjacent to the Obion Creek in Carlisle County, Kentucky, ordering them to restore wetlands they had earlier destroyed, and imposing a penalty of $40,000. The record disclosed the following facts.

This action arose out of alleged violations of Section 301(a) of the Clean Water Act (CWA), 33 U.S.C. §1311(a), which prohibits the discharge of pollutants, including fill dirt, into navigable waters of the United States and the fresh water wetlands adjacent thereto without first obtaining a permit from the Secretary of the Army, Army Corps of Engineers. 33 U.S.C. §1344(a). The defendants, brothers, acquired 550 acres of land in the flood plain of Obion Creek, a tributary of the Mississippi River in Carlisle County, Kentucky in 1976. When they purchased the land, Thomas Larkins noted that 10–12 acres were covered with knee-deep water. After acquisition of the land, the defendants dug drainage ditches, cut timber, blasted beaver dams, and began filling low spots. In 1980, the defendants began constructing dikes and levees on the land. On February 1, 1982, the Corps notified the defendants that its aerial inspection disclosed that the defendants had been discharging materials into approximately 110 acres of the land which the Corps believed were classified as wetlands subject to the CWA. The defendants nevertheless completed the dikes and levees. The levees formed an 18-acre impoundment or pond, which collected much of the water that previously saturated the land.

On February 10, 1984, the United States commenced the present action in the United States District Court for the Western District of Kentucky alleging CWA violations as a result of the construction of the dikes and levees. At trial, the government introduced a number of aerial photographs showing standing water on the land where the impoundment was eventually constructed and the land northeast thereof. The defendants acknowledged that much of this land was covered by standing water, but attributed that condition to beaver activity. Photographs taken in 1972 and 1979 also revealed that this area was forested and contained numerous sloughs and depressions which collected standing water.

The government presented three expert witnesses to identify the vegetation depicted in the various aerial photographs. These experts had been trained in identifying vegetation from aerial photographs by its "signature," *i.e.,* the color, shade, tint, and texture of the vegetation. Martin Keller (Keller) testified that the area was "an area of black willow, buttonbush and several different species of herbaceous aquatic and semi-aquatic plants." Keller further testified that a 1980 photograph was "typical of the many thousands of similar sites that we have seen over the last 10 years of areas such as this, and in every case these areas have been classified as wetlands."

Thomas Welborn (Welborn) of the U.S. Environmental Protection Agency, testified that he had inspected the land in 1984 and discovered an undisturbed area of vegetation consisting of spike rush, wild millet, and nut sedge, all vegetation indicative of wetland conditions. Welborn testified that in a 1980 aerial photograph the signature of this area was the same as the area where the impoundment is now located and the land northeast thereof. Welborn therefore concluded that the entire area was wetlands in 1980.

In 1980, a forested area was located due east of what is now the impoundment which forest was subsequently cleared by the defendants. Expert David Parsons (Parsons) examined aerial photographs of this area and concluded that it was "palustrum forested broadleaf deciduous seasonally inundated wetlands."

Another government expert witness, Charles Newling (Newling), dug soil samples in 1984 in the northeast area and concluded from the reduced amount of oxygen in the soil that in the past 2,000 years the soil had developed under wetland conditions. Parsons acknowledged that this oxygen test was incapable of disclosing whether the area had been wetlands for the last 200 years. Welborn took a soil sample east of the impoundment and reached a similar conclusion. An official Carlisle County Soil Survey compiled by the U.S. Department of Agriculture in 1937 indicated that the entire area north and east of the impoundment was composed of Waverly and Falaya soils which are "hydric" or wetland soil types.

With regard to the land southwest of the impoundment, Newling testified that during a court ordered inspection of the land in May 1985 he observed water marks or silt marks on the trees approximately 30 inches above ground level. Keller, Welborn, and Parsons all conducted a vegetation survey of this area and discovered that the predominant vegetation in this area was that which thrived in saturated soil ("group 1 vegetation") and that which could tolerate saturated soil ("group 2 vegetation").

Newling conducted soil tests on this area of land and concluded that this soil also developed under wetlands conditions. Newling also observed that water filled the sample holes while he was taking samples in this area.

The defendants introduced the testimony of two local farmers who stated that flood waters on the property tended to drain away quickly. On cross-examination, both witnesses agreed that, before being purchased by the defendants, the land tended to be covered by standing water.

Following a bench trial, the district court found that the 110 acres in dispute were indeed wetlands subject to regulation under the CWA. The court further concluded that the defendants' construction activities were not entitled to the "farm exception" under 33 U.S.C. §1344(f) which exempts normal farming activity from the permit requirement so long as no "discharge of dredged or fill material into the navigable waters incidental to any activity [has] as its purpose bringing an area of the navigable waters into a use to which it was not previously subject...." 33 U.S.C. §1344(f)(2). The court determined that the defendants "constructed the dikes and levees for the purpose of bringing the wetlands adjacent to Obion Creek under cultivation, a use to which the site was not previously subject," and that they were not therefore entitled to the exemption. Their failure to obtain a permit before constructing the dikes and levees was, therefore, in violation of the CWA. *United States v. Larkins,* 657 F. Supp. 76 (W.D. Ky. 1987). The defendants thereafter commenced this timely appeal.

On appeal, defendants first asserted that the district court erred in concluding that the land in question was "wetlands" as defined in 33 C.F.R. §328.3(b) prior to 1980 because the court failed to examine the amount and frequency of the soil's saturation, *i.e.,* its "hydrology," in making its determination. This assignment of error is without merit. In *United States v. Riverside Bayview*

Homes, Inc., 474 U.S. 121, 106 S.Ct. 455, 88 L.Ed. 2d 419 (1985), the Supreme Court rejected the notion that 33 C.F.R. §328.3(b) required that land be frequently inundated to be considered wetlands and concluded that the regulation's only requirement was that "the saturation is sufficient to and does support wetland vegetation." 474 U.S. at 130, 106 S.Ct. at 461. The presence of vegetation that requires saturated soil conditions for growth and reproduction on land adjacent to a body of navigable water is sufficient to bring the land under the regulation's definition of "wetlands." 474 U.S. at 130-31, 106 S.Ct. at 461. *See also United States v. Cumberland Farms of Conn., Inc.,* 826 F.2d 1151, 1154 (1st Cir. 1987) ("The Corps further extended its jurisdiction over wetlands by eliminating the requirement that the wetland be periodically inundated, requiring only that it be inundated or saturated by surface or groundwater at a sufficient frequency to support vegetation adapted for life in saturated soils."), *cert. denied,* 484 U.S. 1061, 108 S.Ct. 1016, 98 L.Ed.2d 981 (1988). Accordingly, the district court properly found that the land adjacent to the Obion Creek was "wetlands" under 33 C.F.R. §328.3(b) because it was sufficiently saturated to and did support wetland vegetation. Furthermore, given the evidence summarized above, the finding that the land was sufficiently saturated to and did support wetland vegetation was not clearly erroneous. Fed.R.Civ.P. 52(a).

The defendants also argued that the district court erroneously concluded that they were not entitled to the "farm exception" under 33 U.S.C. §1344(f), which provides, in part:

> (1) Except as provided in paragraph (2) of this subsection, the discharge of dredged or fill material—
>
> > (A) from normal farming, silviculture, and ranching activities such as plowing, seeding, cultivating, minor drainage, harvesting for the production of food, fiber, and forest products, or upland soil and water conservation practices;...
>
> is not prohibited by or otherwise subject to regulation under this Section....
>
> (2) Any discharge of dredged or fill material into the navigable waters incidental to any activity having as *its purpose bringing an area of the navigable waters into a use to which it was not previously subject,* where the flow or circulation of navigable waters may be impaired or the reach of such waters be reduced, shall be required to have a permit under this section.

(Emphasis added.) The district court concluded that because the land had not previously been used as farmland, the defendants were not entitled to the farm exception. Aerial photographs taken before the dikes and levees were constructed showed pooled water and inundated areas and that much of the land was covered by trees. There was no evidence that the land in question had been cultivated for farming.

Defendants nevertheless asserted the land was used for "silviculture," *i.e.,* tree farming, and that when they cleared the land, they were merely harvesting trees. Trees were not replanted, they asserted, because they merely made an economic decision to plant more profitable crops, *i.e.,* soybeans, after the trees had been removed. This argument is without merit. The silviculture exception contained in 33 U.S.C. §1344(f)(1)(A) applies to the *normal* harvesting of timber, not to the activity of clearing timber "to permanently change the area from wetlands into nonwetland agricultural tract for row crop cultivation." *Avoyelles Sportsmen's League, Inc. v. Marsh,* 715 F.2d 897, 926 n.46 (5th Cir. 1983)(citations omitted). *See also* 33 C.F.R. §323.4(c) ("[A] permit will be required for ... the conversion of a wetland from silviculture to agricultural use when there is a discharge of dredged or fill materials into waters of the United States in conjunction with the construction of dikes, drainage ditches, or other works or structures used to effect such conversion"). Consequently, the district court did not err in determining that the defendants were not entitled to the farming exception.

This court has considered defendants' remaining assignments of error and concludes that they are without merit. Accordingly, the judgment of the district court is hereby AFFIRMED.

MERRITT, Circuit Judge, concurring.

I want to make an issue clear that the landowner at oral argument expressly declined to raise. I mention it simply to make it clear that we do not reach the issue.

The Clean Water Act does not mention "wetlands," nor does it use any language which explicitly includes "wetlands." Instead, it defines the pollution jurisdiction of the Corps of Engineers as limited to "navigable waters," *see* §404 of the Clean Water Act, 33 U.S.C. §1344.

In *United States v. Riverside Bayview Homes, Inc.,* 474 U.S. 121, 106 S.Ct. 455, 88 L.Ed. 2d 419 (1985), the Supreme Court defined the "navigable waters" jurisdiction of the Corps to include "wetlands" adjacent to "navigable" or "open waters," even though the wet area is not caused by flooding or ground water flowing from the adjacent waters. 106 S. Ct. at 462. The Supreme Court arrived at this expansive interpretation by pointing to the legislative history of §404, which indicates, in a general way, a desire to adopt legislation for the "protection of aquatic ecosystems." *Id.*

The Supreme Court's actual holding in *Riverside Bayview Homes* is limited, however, by the important fact that the "wetlands" in question in that case were "*located adjacent to a body of navigable water,* since the area characterized by saturated soil conditions and wetland vegetation extended beyond the boundary of respondent's property to Black Creek, *a navigable waterway.*" *Id.* at 461 (emphasis added). In footnote 8 of its opinion, the Supreme Court reserved the question of the jurisdiction of the Corps of Engineers under §404 over "wetlands that are not adjacent to bodies of open water." *Id.* at 461 ("we do not express any opinion on that question").

Had the landowners at oral argument not said that they do not raise the issue, this case would present the issue the Supreme Court reserved in *Riverside Bayview Homes.* Obion Creek, so far as we can tell from the record before us, is a small nonnavigable creek or stream that empties into the Mississippi River many miles away. The land at issue in this case is adjacent to Obion Creek. The Corps of Engineers, as plaintiff, had the burden in this case of proving that the land in question is adjacent to a "body of open water," the phrase used by the Supreme Court in footnote 8 of *Riverside Bayview Homes.*

If this is true, then the Corps has now expanded the definition of "navigable waters" to include any creek or stream or moist area. It has arrived at the precise point predicted in our earlier opinion in the *Riverside Bayview Homes* case, which the Supreme Court reversed. There we said: "Under such a construction [as proposed by the Corps of Engineers] low lying backyards miles from a navigable waterway would become wetlands." *United States v. Riverside Bayview Homes, Inc.,* 729 F.2d 391, 401 (6th Cir. 1984), *rev'd,* 474 U.S. 121, 106 S.Ct. 455, 88 L.Ed.2d 419 (1985). The Corps' definition has apparently detached and untied the "wetlands" jurisdiction of the Corps from any concept of "open waters" or navigable waters. A farmer's low lying farmland or a homeowner's low lying backyard—adjacent to a small stream or creek but many miles from any navigable waterway—has apparently been converted into government property no longer subject to control or improvement by the owner without government permission. A statute that does not mention "wetlands" has apparently been read to include simply "moist land adjacent to a creek."

The framers of the Constitution were solicitous of the rights of landowners—especially small farmers struggling for survival—not to have land appropriated by the government. They therefore adopted the provision of the Fifth Amendment of the Constitution prohibiting the taking of private property for public use without just compensation. Although the Supreme Court has stated that "[a] requirement that a person obtain a permit before engaging in a certain use of his or her property does not itself 'take' the property in any sense," 106 S.Ct. at 459, the injunction the Corps has been granted in this case will force the Larkins to destroy the terracing work they have done on their land and to restore the land to its original nonagricultural use. Because farming appears to be the only economically viable use of the land in question, *see Agins v. Tiburon,* 447 U.S. 255, 260, 65 L.Ed. 2d 106, 100 S.Ct. 2138 (1980), it is arguable that the Larkins could successfully assert a takings claim if they are not allowed to keep the work they have already done. *See Riverside Bayview Homes,* 106 S. Ct. at 460 n.6 ("Because the Corps has now denied respondent a permit to fill its property, respondent may well have a ripe claim that a taking has occurred.") It is arguable that the injunction issued in this case constitutes a taking without compensation. Since the landowner has not raised this issue and at oral argument expressly declined to raise any question about whether Obion Creek is navigable, or constitutes "open waters," the Court's opinion should not be read to decide this issue. [Footnotes omitted.]

See also *U.S. v. Sargent County Water Resource Dist.*, 876 F.Supp. 1090 (D.N.D. 1994).

Part 3
Permitting procedures

The regulations concerning the Corps' permitting procedures are set forth in great detail at 33 C.F.R. §325.1. As stated previously, the Corps is also required to follow certain Guidelines promulgated by the Environmental Protection Agency in deciding whether to issue or deny a permit.

In addition to these national regulations, because the Corps has traditionally been "a highly decentralized organization," much of the permitting authority has been delegated to the 36 District Engineers and 11 Division Engineers. Thus, if a district or Division Engineer makes a permit decision, if it was made in accordance with the regulations, the decision is final. Another manifestation of the Corps' traditional decentralization is that each District Engineer should have established local procedures and policies to allow potential applicants to contact the office for pre-application consultation for major projects. The District Engineer should "endeavor, at this stage, to provide the potential applicant with all helpful information necessary in pursuing the application, including factors which the Corps must consider in its permit decision making process."

Particularly in the case of potential permit applications which "may involve the preparation of an environmental document," the District Engineer should advise the potential permit applicants of the requirements for the permit(s) and the attendant public interest review." Once the applicant indicates his or her intention to apply for a permit, the District Engineer will assign a single point of contact to coordinate the regulatory process.

Potential applicants should be aware that even the basic permit application form may have regional variations, thus the potential applicant should obtain an application form from the office of the district in which the wetland lies. In general, however, the application must include a complete description of the proposed activity including necessary drawings, sketches, or plans sufficient for public notice (detailed engineering plans and specifications are not required); the location, purpose, and need for the proposed activity; scheduling of the activity; the names and addresses of adjoining property owners; the location and dimensions of adjacent structures; and a list of authorizations required by other federal, interstate, state, or local agencies for the work, including all approvals received or denials already made. The description of the activities must include all activities which are reasonably related to the same project and for which a permit would be required. If the activity would involve the discharge of dredged or fill material in waters of the United States, the application must also include the source of the material; the purpose of the discharge; a description of the type, composition, and quantity of the material; the method of transportation and disposal of the material; and the location of the disposal site. The Corps may require additional information on compliance with the EPA's Guidelines, other environmental data, and information on alternate methods and sites.

The Corps is subject to some fairly stringent time requirements in its processing of permit applications. For example, if the Corps determines that an application is incomplete, it has 15 days from receipt of the application to request additional information. If, on the other hand, the Corps determines that the application is complete, it must issue the public notice, seeking comments from the public for no more than 30 nor less than 15 days (plus one 30-day extension if warranted). After considering any comments received from the public, the Corps prepares a

Statement of Findings (or, if an Environmental Impact Statement has been included in the permit application, a Record of Decision) of the Corps views on the probable effect of the project on the public interest including the project's conformity with the Guidelines. The Statement of Decision will also include any special conditions if a permit is to be issued. If the permit is to be denied, the Corps must advise the applicant in writing of the reasons for denial. The Corps must also consult with the relevant other federal or state agencies whenever endangered species, historic properties, or coastal zones are involved.

Ordinarily the Corps will decide permit applications within 60 days after receipt of a complete application. Time extensions and the time requirements for authorizations under other statutes, may prevent decisions within this time period but, if the period is suspended, it will restart as soon as the other suspension is lifted.

There is a $100 application fee for each permit application when the planned or ultimate purpose of the project is commercial or industrial in nature, and is in support of operations that charge for the production, distribution, or sale of goods or services. The application fee for non-commercial projects is $10.00. Either fee is not payable until the Corps has determined that the proposed activity is not contrary to the public interest.

Chapter 15

PUBLIC NOTICE AND COMMENT

This regulation requires that the information be included in the public notice be sufficient "to give a clear understanding of the magnitude of the activity to generate meaningful comment." The "meaningful comment" contemplated by the regulation is an evaluation of the "probable impact on the public interest." The Corps is required to state in the public notice 16 separate items of information as they apply to a §404 permit application:

(1) A statement of the applicable statutory authority(ies);

(2) The name and address of the applicant;

(3) The name or title, address and telephone number of the Corps contact person from whom additional information concerning the application may be obtained;

(4) The location of the proposed activity;

(5) A brief description of the proposed activity, its purpose and intended use, including a description of the type of structures, if any, to be erected on fills or pile or float-supported platforms;

(6) A plan and elevation drawing showing the general and specific site location and character of all proposed activities, including the size relationship of the proposed structures to the size of the impacted waterway and depth of water in the area;

(7) If the proposed activity would occur in the territorial seas or ocean waters, a description of the activity's relationship to the baseline from which the territorial sea is measured;

(8) A list of other government authorizations obtained or requested by the applicant, including required certifications relative to water quality, coastal zone management, or marine sanctuaries;

(9) If appropriate, a statement that the activity is a categorical exclusion for purposes of the National Environmental Policy Act;

(10) A statement of the District Engineer's current knowledge on historic properties;

(11) A statement of the District Engineer's current knowledge on endangered species (if the District Engineer finds that a proposed activity may affect an endangered or threatened species, he will initiate formal consultation procedures with the U.S. Fish and Wildlife Service or National Marine Fisheries Services);

(12) A statement on evaluation factors. The exact wording of this statement, which is repeated in the regulations at 33 C.F.R. §320.4(a), must be included verbatim: "The decision whether to issue a permit will be based on an evaluation of the probable impact including cumulative impacts of the proposed activity on the public interest. That decision will reflect the national concern both for protection and utilization of important resources. The benefit which reasonably may be expected to accrue from the proposal

must be balanced against its reasonably foreseeable detriments. All factors which may be relevant to the proposal will be considered including the cumulative effects thereof; among those are conservation, economics, aesthetics, general environmental concerns, wetlands, historic properties, fish and wildlife values, flood hazards, floodplain values, land use, navigation, shoreline erosion and accretion, recreation, water supply and conservation, water quality, energy needs, safety, food and fiber production, mineral needs, considerations of property ownership and, in general, the needs and welfare of the people." 33 C.F.R. §325.3(c)(1). Further, if the activity is to occur in a wetland, the statement must also include an application of the Environmental Protection Agency's Guidelines;

(13) Any other available information which may assist interested parties in evaluating the likely impact of the proposed activity, if any, on factors affecting the public interest;

(14) The comment period;

(15) A statement that any person may request, in writing, within the comment period specified in the notice, that a public hearing be held to consider the application provided that the request shall "state, with particularity, the reasons for holding a public hearing"; and

(16) For private applications in states with an approved Coastal Zone Management Plan, a statement on compliance with the approved Plan.

The public notice must be distributed in appropriate public places in the vicinity of the proposed work as well as sent to the applicant, appropriate city and county officials, adjoining property owners, appropriate state agencies, concerned federal agencies and Indian tribes, concerned businesses and conservation organizations, local news media, and any other interested party. The Corps presumes that interested parties will wish to respond consequently a lack of response will be interpreted as meaning there is no objection to the proposed project. The list of names and addresses to whom the public notice was sent is included in the administrative record of the permit application.

CHAPTER 16

CONFLICT RESOLUTION

Having received a complete application and issued a public notice, the applicant then enters the "conflict resolution" stage of the permit procedure which lasts for 15 to 30 days but may be extended. The Corps is required to acknowledge receipt of all comments and to "consider all comments received in response to the public notice." The Corps must seek the advice and special expertise of other federal agencies if the comments received render such advice and expertise relevant. Most importantly, the Corps is required to inform the applicant of any comments and to receive "the views of the applicant on a particular issue to make a public interest determination." This step in the process is mandatory and a permit denial may be remanded to the Corps if a court finds that the Corps engaged in secret meetings with objectors to the proposed activity. *Mall Properties v. Marsh*, 672 F.Supp. 561 (D.Mass. 1987). The applicant is given the option to contact the commentators directly to resolve their objections, however, since the Corps is solely responsible to make a permit decision, it may convene a Corps-staffed mediation session between the applicant and the commentators. This part of the permit procedure must be followed diligently by the Corps with delays not to exceed 30 days allowed only upon the request of the applicant.

CHAPTER 17

PUBLIC HEARINGS

Upon receipt of any such request for a public hearing, assuming the request states with particularity the reasons for holding a public hearing, the Corps may expeditiously attempt to resolve the issues informally. Otherwise, it shall promptly set a time and place for the public hearing, and give due notice thereof. Requests for a public hearing shall be granted, unless the Corps determines that the issues raised are insubstantial or there is otherwise no valid interest to be served by a hearing. The Corps will make such a determination in writing, and communicate the reasons therefore to all requesting parties. In case of doubt, a public hearing shall be held. In fixing the time and place for a hearing, the convenience and necessity of the interested public will be duly considered. The Corps is not required to hold a public hearing nor does due process require one.

AJA ASSOCIATES v. ARMY CORPS OF ENGINEERS

817 F.2d 1070 (3d Cir. 1987)

The Army Corps of Engineers ("the Corps") appeals from the district court's remand order concerning an application for a dredge-and-fill permit by AJA Associates ("AJA"). Because the applicant has already been given the meaningful opportunity to be heard that due process requires, we conclude that the district court erred in remanding to the Corps for "an informal oral hearing." Accordingly, we will instruct the district court to vacate its remand order and consider AJA's remaining assertions of impropriety in the processing of its application.

I

AJA owns property on a canal in Key Colony Beach, Florida. On September 21, 1983, the prior owner of AJA's lot, Glen Cafferty, filed an application with the Corps for a permit to construct a seawall (or "bulkhead"), to backfill behind the seawall, and to dredge the base of the seawall. These activities require a permit under §404 of the Clean Water Act, 33 U.S.C. §1344 (1986), and §10 of the Rivers and Harbors Act of 1899, 33 U.S.C. §403 (1986). The Jacksonville District of the Corps published a notice describing the application on November 2, 1984. Consideration of the application, number 84R-4588, had been delayed by the Corps until that time because it was negotiating with the City of Key Colony Beach to secure modification of a city ordinance that required seawall construction in the manner presented in the application.

On November 27, 1984, a Corps Area Engineer submitted a report that considered this permit application along with 15 other similar proposals for the construction of bulkheads. The report concluded with respect to application 84R-4588: "Recommend bulkhead be placed at landward edge of wetland zone and a pile supported pier for boat access. Recommend no dredging waterward of bulkhead line." Record at 51. Thus the report did not support construction of the seawall as proposed.

In response to the public notice, the Environmental Protection Agency, the Fish and Wildlife Service of the Department of the Interior, and the National Marine Fisheries Service of the National Oceanic and Atmospheric Administration submitted comments. Each agency recommended denial of the AJA permit application as well as denial of permits for the 15 other similar projects under consideration. The EPA comment, for example, describes the wetlands at issue in the permit applications as "a valuable public resource." Wetlands provide "fish and wildlife habitat, hydrological buffering, shoreline stabilization, water purification, pollution and erosion traps, and food chain production." According to the EPA, "although the proposed projects would impact only a relatively small area of wetlands, the cumulative effects of many such projects would have a devastating impact on the wetland resources of the Florida Keys." Record at 67.

Albert Ciardi, a principal in the AJA partnership, then received a letter from an official in the Corps Permit Section dated February 5, 1985, and addressed to Glen Boe, the manager who had actually submitted the permit application for the AJA lot. The letter requested a written response from the applicant addressing the three agency reports that had recommended denial of the application; copies of the three reports were sent along with the letter. In addition to addressing the agency reports, the Corps letter directed the applicant to provide a discussion of (1) the public and private need for the project, (2) why the proposed fill must be located in the wetland resource, and (3) alternative plans that have been considered and why the alternatives are not feasible.

Ciardi's response states that the private need "is so that I can construct a home." The public need "is that the project be constructed safely and that a monstrous pier not jut out in the middle of the waterway which can be dangerous to boat traffic." Ciardi wrote that the seawall must be located in the wetland resource "because that is where it is." He stated that he had not considered an alternative site "because I have spent good money for this site; ergo, it would not be feasible to spend money for another site." Record at 86. Ciardi also wrote:

> Having this information in your possession, why don't you deny the permit so that we can take the matter before the courts and let a Judge make a decision that will determine once and for all the wisdom of your denial of a permit on a lot which is totally enclosed by two (2) built-up lots with bulkheads on a lagoon which has been in existence for many years without any significant environmental impact whatsoever.

Record at 87. Glen Boe submitted a five-page response to the agency reports, but began with the statement:

> The issues surrounding the applications in question, as you well know, have been discussed at great and tedious length for at least a decade. It is difficult to believe that you really want to rehash the hours of discussions, letters, arguments, contentions, inspections, claims, counterclaims, allegations, opinions, suggestions, demands and lamentations that have spewed forth for lo these many years.

Record at 88. A July 30, 1985, letter from Ciardi to the Corps of Engineers complained about the length of time the application process was taking. Ciardi stated, "I am commencing with the construction of my seawall. See you in court!" Record at 119. In all, Ciardi wrote four threatening letters to the Corps. See Record at 86-87, 101-02, 104, 118-19.

On August 5, 1985, the Corps completed its evaluation of the permit application and notified Ciardi that it would not grant a permit. The Corps had prepared a seven-page "Statement of Findings on 84R-4588" for the administrative record. Ciardi apparently received a copy of this statement, which summarized all the information before the Corps and the basis for its decision, along with his notice of permit denial. The Corps found Ciardi's proposed project "not in compliance with the Corps wetland policy since the area to be filled is considered a vital wetland that constitutes a valuable and productive public resource." The Corps also concluded that the project was "not in accordance with the 404(b)(1) guidelines since practical alternatives are available for shoreline protection." The permit was denied because the proposed work "would have an unacceptable adverse impact on an important public resource by destroying wetland vegetation and productive seagrasses." Record at 127. The notice to Ciardi, signed by Colonel Charles Myers of the Corps, stated, "I have evaluated your application and the cumulative impacts of permitting many other such applications in the city of Key Colony Beach and have determined there would be an adverse cumulative impact on the environment if these permits were issued." Record at 128.

On September 4, 1985, AJA filed suit in district court, seeking to set aside the permit denial. AJA asserted that the Corps' action was arbitrary and thus not in accordance with law, and that the Corps unlawfully delayed evaluation of the permit application. Nowhere in the complaint did AJA assert that the Corps should have held a hearing as a part of its decision-making process.

The Corps on January 13, 1986, filed a motion for summary judgment and a motion for a protective order to prevent the deposition of Colonel Myers. In opposition to the motion for summary judgment, AJA argued for the first time that procedural due process required an adjudicatory hearing during the Corps' review of AJA's application. AJA also argued, as asserted in the complaint, that the Corps had erred in taking an unreasonable amount of time to process the application and in considering the environmental impact of AJA's application together with the 15 other similar proposals before the Corps. In a memorandum opinion dated June 12, 1986, Judge Weiner denied the Corps' motions and remanded the case for an administrative hearing. The district court held that "plaintiff is entitled to appear at an informal oral hearing before a proper agency officer so that plaintiff can hear and respond to reasons why its individual permit application (84R-4588) was denied by the Army Corps of Engineers." Judge Weiner stressed, "We do not hold, however, that due process requires an informal oral hearing in every application before defendant." Mem. Op. at 5.

II

Before considering the merits of this appeal, we must determine whether the court has appellate jurisdiction under 28 U.S.C. §1291 to review the remand order presented here. "Remands to administrative agencies are not ordinarily appealable under section 1291." *United Steelworkers of America, Local 1913 v. Union Railroad Co.,* 648 F.2d 905, 909 (3d Cir. 1981). Nevertheless, *Union Railroad and Horizons International, Inc. v. Baldrige,* 811 F.2d 154 (3d Cir. 1987), recognize that when a district court finally resolves an important legal issue in reviewing an administrative agency action and denial of appellate review before remand to the agency would foreclose appellate review as a practical matter, the remand order is immediately appealable.

The present appeal challenges a remand order based on the district court's analysis of due process requirements in a dredge-and-fill permit proceeding. The district court has resolved an issue of wide-reaching impact, even though the lower court carefully confined its decision to the facts of this case. The decision opens up for all applicants the argument, raised after permit denial, that due process requires a hearing in their particular cases. This important decision cannot receive later appellate review. If on remand the Corps grants AJA a permit, the case will never return to the courts. If the Corps again denies the permit after a hearing, judicial review sought by AJA will not allow consideration of the right-to-hearing issue, because the issue will have become moot. We conclude that the appeal presents a final order within the meaning of 28 U.S.C. §1291 as it has been interpreted in this circuit.

III

"The fundamental requirement of due process is the *opportunity* to be heard 'at a meaningful time and in a meaningful manner.' *Armstrong v. Manzo,* 380 U.S. 545, 552, 14 L.Ed. 2d 62, 85 S.Ct. 1187 (1965)." *Mathews v. Eldridge,* 424 U.S. 319, 333, 47 L.Ed. 2d 18, 96 S.Ct. 893 (1976) (emphasis added). In this case, AJA took advantage of its opportunity to advance arguments in support of its permit application through written submissions to the Corps. The issue now, after the permit has been denied, is whether due process requires remand for an informal oral hearing even though AJA did not take advantage of its opportunity during the comment period to request an oral hearing. Due process does not so require; a permit applicant cannot lay blame on an agency for the applicant's own failure to pursue every available channel of advocacy.

The regulation governing hearings to consider dredge-and-fill permit applications states:

> Unless the public notice specifies that a public hearing will be held, [which in this case the notice did not], any person may request, in writing, within the comment period specified in the public notice on a Department of the Army permit application or on a Federal project, that a public hearing be held to consider the material matters in issue in the permit application or Federal project. Upon receipt of any such request, stating with particularity the reasons for holding a public hearing, the District Engineer may expeditiously attempt to resolve the issues informally. Otherwise, he shall promptly set a time and place for the public hearing and give due notice thereof.... Requests for a public hearing under this paragraph shall be granted, unless the District Engineer determines that the issues raised are insubstantial or there is otherwise no valid interest to be served by a hearing. The District Engineer will make such a determination in writing, and communicate his reasons therefore to all requesting parties.

33 C.F.R. §327.4(b). AJA did not submit a request for a hearing during the comment period. Indeed, throughout the period prior to the Corps' decision to deny the permit, AJA pressured the Corps for a speedy resolution of its application. Only after it had filed the complaint in this case did AJA first advance the claim that it needed a face-to-face meeting with Corps officials.

It has long been routine for administrative agencies to require a request for a hearing before holding a hearing on an application under consideration by the agency. Such a request requirement has survived numerous due process challenges. For example, in *Goldsmith v. Board of Tax Appeals,* 270 U.S. 117, 70 L.Ed. 494, 46 S.Ct. 215 (1926), the Supreme Court rejected Goldsmith's argument, after he was denied admission to practice before the Board, that due process "entitled petitioner to be heard before an opportunity to make a living in his profession was taken away from him." 270 U.S. at 118 (summary of Goldsmith's argument before the Court). Goldsmith had not demanded from the Board the right to be heard on the charges against him that eventually resulted in denial of admission to practice. The Court concluded that "until he had sought a hearing from the Board, and been denied it, he could not appeal to the courts for any remedy and certainly not for mandamus to compel enrollment." 270 U.S. at 123.

Moreover, the Supreme Court has upheld agencies' requirements, prior to providing a hearing, that an applicant not only request a hearing, but also present reasons why a hearing would be useful. *See, e.g., Costle v. Pacific Legal Foundation,* 445 U.S. 198, 63 L.Ed. 2d 329, 100 S.Ct. 1095 (1980); *Weinberger v. Hynson, Westcott & Dunning,* 412 U.S. 609, 37 L.Ed. 2d 207, 93 S.Ct. 2469 (1973). In *Hynson, Westcott & Dunning,* the Court held that the FDA's decision, articulated in its regulations, "that it will not provide a formal hearing where it is apparent at the threshold that the applicant has not tendered *any* evidence which *on its face* meets the statutory standards [for a new drug application]" did not violate due process protections. 412 U.S. at 620-21.

AJA acknowledges that 33 C.F.R. §327 governs the processing of its permit application. *See* Appellee's Brief at 4. Despite obfuscation in the brief submitted to this court, AJA's counsel at oral argument admitted that no hearing had been requested, either in writing or orally, prior to the Corps' decision to deny the dredge-and-fill permit. AJA offers no extenuating circumstance as a possible basis for ignoring the regulation's requirement of a request before a hearing will be held. AJA can cite no case granting a permit applicant an administrative hearing on due process grounds where the applicant gave no indication it desired or needed a hearing during the time when the agency was considering its application. As numerous prior decisions have held, we hold that the administrative agency here may, in keeping with due process, condition a hearing upon a request for one. The Corps gave AJA several meaningful opportunities to be heard. The applicant chose to submit its application for decision based upon a detailed "paper hearing" and cannot now complain that this process was inadequate.

IV

For reasons of institutional integrity, we will, in addition to instructing the district court to vacate its remand order, return the case to the lower court for consideration of AJA's other assertions of error by the Corps. We note, however, that the papers submitted to this court indicate that AJA's remaining arguments may also be meritless, and resolution of the case on a motion for summary judgment may be appropriate.

See also *Buttry v. United States*, 690 F.2d 1170 (5th Cir. 1982), *cert. denied*, 461 U.S. 927, 77 L.Ed.2d 298, 103 S.Ct. 2087 (1983); *Kreider Dairy Farms, Inc. v. Glickman*, 190 F.3d 113 (3d Cir. 1999); *Water Works & Sewer Bd. Of the City of Birmingham v. U.S. Dept. of Army, Corps of Engineers*, 983 F.Supp. 1052 (N.D.Ala. 1997); *Shoreline Assoc. v. Marsh*, 555 F.Supp. 169 (D.Md. 1983), *aff'd. without op.*, 725 F.2d 677 (4th Cir. Md. 1984); *Nofelco Realty Corp. v. United States*, 521 F.Supp. 458 (S.D.N.Y. 1981).

NATIONAL WILDLIFE FEDERATION v. MARSH

568 F. Supp. 985 (D.C.D.C. 1983)

This environmental law proceeding involves the validity of a permit issued by the defendant, the Secretary of the Army, (Secretary or Army), to the Hampton Roads Energy Company, a company seeking to build an oil refinery on Chesapeake Bay at Portsmouth, Virginia. Plaintiffs, National Wildlife Federation and other environmental groups, seek a judicial declaration that the permit was wrongfully issued and an injunction prohibiting the Secretary from authorizing any activities under the permit pending compliance with the Administrative Procedure Act (APA), 5 U.S.C. §§551 *et seq.*; section 404 of the Federal Water Pollution Control Act, as amended by the Clean Water Act of 1977 (CWA), 33 U.S.C. §1344; and the National Environmental Policy Act of 1969 (NEPA), 42 U.S.C. §§4321 *et seq.*

For the reasons stated below, the Court finds merit in a number of the plaintiffs' claims and consequently enjoins the Army from authorizing any activities under the permit until certain significant procedural defects associated with the granting of the permit are rectified.

BACKGROUND

Chesapeake Bay is the largest estuary in the United States, with 19 major rivers and hundreds of smaller rivers as tributaries. It serves as a habitat for numerous species of birds and fish, and as a valuable resource for tourism and recreation.

In March 1975, defendant-intervenor Hampton Roads Energy Company submitted an application to the Army Corps of Engineers, Norfolk District, for a permit to undertake work in the Chesapeake Bay in conjunction with its construction of an oil refinery along the west bank of the Elizabeth River in Portsmouth, Virginia. The application called for the construction of a marine terminal, the dredging of an access channel and anchorage basin, and the disposal of the dredged fill. The undertaking required a permit from the Army Corps of Engineers under section 10 of the Rivers and Harbors Appropriation Act of 1899 (RHA), 33 U.S.C. §403, and section 404 of the CWA. The Army Corps' District Engineer for the Norfolk District issued a public notice and invited comment on the permit application. *See* 33 C.F.R. §§325.1(a); 325.2(2)(3); 325.3. In addition, pursuant to section 102(2)(C) of NEPA, 42 U.S.C. §4332(2)(C), and 33 C.F.R. §325.4(b)(3), the District Engineer released a draft Environmental Impact Statement for public review and comment.

Numerous comments on the proposal were received from federal, state, and local agencies as well as from private groups and citizens. A public hearing was then held in the spring of 1976. *See* 33 C.F.R. §§325.2(a)(5); 325.3(b)(3); 327. Illustrating the deep public interest in the project, more than 1,000 persons attended the hearing, where the plaintiffs and other organizations offered testimony, statements, and recommendations. These were then utilized by the District Engineer in the preparation of a Final Environmental Impact Statement (FEIS), which was released to the public for review and comment. *See* 33 C.F.R. §325.4(c). Again, intense public comment was generated, with 535 letters of comment received from various governmental agencies, citizens groups (including plaintiffs) and the general public.

In January 1978, the District Engineer recommended denial of the permit application finding that the risks to human health, water quality, and marine life outweighed the benefits accruing from the refinery's contribution to the nation's energy requirements. He concluded that the project was not in the public interest. However, because this recommendation was contrary to the stated position of the Governor of Virginia, the matter was referred from the District Engineer to the North Atlantic Division Engineer of the Army Corps. *See* 33 C.F.R. §§325.8(b); 325.8(d)(2). Following the District Engineer's recommendation, some 83 additional comments were received into the administrative record.

Relying on the earlier documentation of the record, but drawing a contrary conclusion, the Division Engineer reversed the District Engineer's decision and recommended granting the permit subject to a number of conditions. But because of objections to the issuance of the permit raised by a number of federal agencies—the National Marine Fisheries Service, the Fish and Wildlife Service and the Environmental Protection Agency—on environmental grounds, the Division Engineer's decision was not final, and the matter was referred to the Chief Engineer of the Army Corps. *See* 33 C.F.R. §§325.8(c); 325.8(d)(1).

After a review of the proceedings at the District and Division levels, the Chief Engineer determined that a more extensive analysis of alternative refinery sites was required before he could pass on the merits of the permit. To review the alternatives, he formed a Federal Interagency Task Force consisting of representatives from the Environmental Protection Agency, Department of Energy, the Coast Guard, the National Marine Fisheries Service, and the Fish and Wildlife Service. Based on the Task Force report and on additional information the Army Corps prepared and circulated for review a draft Supplemental Environmental Impact Statement (SEIS). *See* 33 C.F.R. §230.11(b). Later, a final SEIS was prepared and released, and it too was subject to public comment.

The final SEIS was considerably expanded and incorporated the findings of the Task Force on alternative sites. Sixty-seven alternatives were discussed, 48 of which were summarily dismissed as inappropriate. The remaining 19—including the Hampton Roads site—were discussed in narrative form and the narrative was then summarized in a tabular matrix with letter-grade ratings. The Hampton Roads site fared poorly in the matrix, generally receiving one of the worst, if not the worst, set of ratings of the various sites.

Plaintiffs submitted comments on both the draft and the final SEIS. On the basis of the entire record, including the expanded analysis of alternative sites, the Chief Engineer made a preliminary decision to issue the permit to the Hampton Roads Energy Company, finding that the need for additional refinery capacity on the east coast outweighed the environmental costs.

However, this decision of the Chief Engineer, even though the third determination made by the Army Corps, was not final. An earlier 1967 Memorandum of Understanding between the Secretary of the Army and the Secretary of the Interior required "full coordination and cooperation between their respective Departments" in permit decision-making. 33 C.F.R. §325, App. B. Therefore, in November 1978, the Chief Engineer notified Interior and several other agencies of his tentative decision. The Departments of Defense, Energy, and the Treasury expressed support for the permit application. However, the Environmental Protection Agency, the National Oceanic and Atmospheric Administration, and, most importantly, Interior, expressed their opposition. Because of Interior's opposition, the permit proposal was referred to the Secretary of the Army for yet another determination, this time to be made in consultation with the Secretary of the Interior in accordance with the Memorandum of Understanding.

The staff of the Secretary of the Army began an extensive review of the proposal. The Assistant Secretary of the Army (Civil Works) then reopened the comment period in response to various requests; conferred with representatives of the Departments of Commerce, Defense, Energy, Interior, Labor, Transportation, Treasury, and the Environmental Protection Agency, and had a member of the Secretary's staff meet with one of the plaintiffs and other environmental groups. The Assistant Secretary also further explored oil spill recovery possibilities.

To assist the Secretary of the Army, the staff of the Assistant Secretary also prepared a 100-page Staff Evaluation. In two respects, the environmental focus of the Evaluation differed to some extent from the focus in any of the earlier environmental impact statements and in the decisions of the various engineers. First, the Evaluation did not measure the benefits of the refinery in terms of the east coast's need for additional refinery capacity. Rather, it measured the benefits in terms of Net Economic Development (NED), that is, the reduction in the cost of transporting the refined oil products to the metropolitan centers of the east coast from the Hampton Roads refinery, as compared to the cost of transporting the oil products from Gulf Coast refineries. Second, the evaluation differed in its rating of the various site alternatives. When compared with the 18 other alternatives that were previously examined at length in the SEIS, the Hampton Roads site was rated by the Staff Evaluation as one of the five best, while in the SEIS's matrix the site was rated one of the worst. In explaining that seeming inconsistency, the Staff Evaluation said of the SEIS's matrix that

> we find gross inconsistencies in the way narrative data were translated into the tabular matrix.... Because this information is very misleading on the comparability of [Hampton Roads] to other alternatives, we find the matrix invalid as a decisional guide. The evaluation of alternatives requires a more thorough analysis than the matrix offers. Our analysis follows:....

The Staff Evaluation was then placed in the administrative record *after the close of the final comment period. The plaintiffs were thus unable to comment on the Evaluation.*

The decision-making process closed in early December 1979, despite the objections of the Secretary of the Interior to the Staff Evaluation and to the issuance of the permit. The Secretary of the Army announced his decision in favor of the permit and, like the Chief and Division Engineers, he decided that the potential benefits outweighed the environmental costs of the project. However, in basing his decision on the 100-page Staff Evaluation, he departed from the analyses of the Chief and Division Engineers by measuring the benefits of the refinery in terms of savings in transportation costs, rather than in terms of the east coast's need for increased energy supplies. In addition, he relied on the analysis of alternatives in the Staff Evaluation, rather than on the analysis of alternatives in the SEIS. His decision closed the four-and-a-half year period of review. The permit was issued to the Hampton Roads Energy Company on December 28, 1979. Plaintiffs filed suit on September 16, 1980. Because of this lawsuit and another lawsuit currently pending before the Supreme Court of Virginia, Hampton Roads Energy Company has not begun construction of the refinery.

ANALYSIS

National Wildlife contends that the permit is defective for two procedural reasons: first, because National Wildlife was denied the opportunity to comment on the 100-page Staff Evaluation, in contravention of the APA, section 404 of the CWA, and the Army Corps' regulation, 33 C.F.R. §325.3(a); second, because the underlying data employed in the Staff Evaluation concerning the reduction in transportation costs and the re-analysis of alternatives were never incorporated into the FEIS or SEIS, in contravention of NEPA. National Wildlife also contends that the permit is substantively defective in that the Secretary's decision was arbitrary and capricious on the merits. The Court considers each contention in turn.

I PROCEDURAL REVIEW

A. Comment and Hearing Under the APA, the CWA and the Army Corps' Regulation.

The Secretary and Hampton Roads Energy Company concede that the procedure adopted by the Army Corps in passing on the permit amounted to only an informal adjudication, but they argue that nothing more than an informal adjudication was required by the relevant statutes. National Wildlife, however, contends that section 404 of the CWA, by requiring "notice and opportunity for public hearings," confers a right to a formal, trial-type adjudication. According to National Wildlife, the most flagrant violation of its purported right to a formal adjudication occurred with the placing of the Assistant Secretary's Staff Evaluation in the record without a public hearing and an opportunity for comment. National Wildlife claims that it was neither able to comment upon nor submit evidence regarding the new analysis of the refinery's benefits in terms of the reduced transportation costs.

The procedures for a formal adjudication are provided in sections 7 and 8 of the APA, 5 U.S.C. §§556-57. Under section 5(a), 5 U.S.C. §554(a), the formal procedures of sections 7 and 8 are applicable to any "adjudication required by statute to be determined on the record after an opportunity for agency hearing." Thus, the determination of whether section 404 of the CWA mandates a formal, trial-type hearing, hinges on the question of whether its language, "after notice and opportunity for public hearing," constitutes a statute requiring an "adjudication to be determined on the record after an opportunity for agency hearing" under section 5(a) of the APA.

The Court is empowered to make this determination by virtue of section 10(e)(2)(D) of the APA, 5 U.S.C. §706(2)(D), which states that a reviewing court shall set aside agency findings found to be "without observance of procedure required by law."

In support of its argument that section 404 requires a formal hearing, National Wildlife analogizes section 404 to section 402 of the CWA, 42 U.S.C. §1342, which governs the issuance of permits by the Environmental Protection Agency for the discharge of pollutants. Three circuit courts have held that the language in section 402, "opportunity for public hearing,"—language virtually identical to that of section 404—requires a formal adjudicatory hearing. *See Seacoast Anti-Pollution League v. Costle,* 572 F.2d 872 (1st Cir.), *cert. denied,* 439 U.S. 824, 58 L.Ed. 2d 117, 99 S.Ct. 94 (1978); *Marathon Oil Co. v. Environmental Protection Agency*, 564 F.2d 1253 (9th Cir. 1977); *United States Steel Corp. v. Train,* 556 F.2d 822 (7th Cir. 1977). The plaintiffs want the same sort of adjudicatory hearing to apply to the permit sought under section 404.

The Court, however, agrees with the Secretary, that the plaintiffs are entitled to no more than an informal adjudicatory hearing. Recently the Fifth Circuit in *Buttrey v. United States,* 690 F.2d 1170 (5th Cir. 1982), *cert. denied,* 461 U.S. 927, 103 S.Ct. 2087, 77 L.Ed.2d 298 (1983), decided that section 404 requires nothing more. Though aware of the similarity in language between sections 402 and 404, the court pointed out that it is "very possible 'for a term to have different meanings even in the same statute.'" *Id.* at 1175, *quoting Environmental Defense Fund, Inc., v. Costle,* 203 U.S. App. D.C. 340, 631 F.2d 922, 927 (D.C. Cir. 1980), *cert. denied,* 449 U.S. 1112, 66 L.Ed. 2d 841, 101 S.Ct. 923 (1981). After examining the CWA's legislative history, which stressed the need for simplified permit procedures, *Buttrey* concluded that whatever procedures section 402 may mandate, section 404 requires only an informal hearing. *Id.* at 1175-76. That informal hearing is only a "speech-making hearing" at which "proponents and opponents of the project are allowed to be heard." *Id.* at 1176, *quoting Taylor v. District Engineer,* 567 F.2d 1332, 1338 (5th Cir. 1978). The scope of such a hearing is suggested by the Army's regulations:

> Public hearing means a public proceeding conducted for the purpose of acquiring information or evidence which will be considered in evaluating a proposed Department of the Army permit action, or Federal project, and which affords to the public the opportunity to present their views, opinions, and information on such permit actions or Federal projects.

Buttrey, 690 F.2d at 1176, *quoting* 33 C.F.R. §327.3(a).

In sum, the plaintiffs had no right under section 404 of the CWA to a formal adjudicatory hearing on the merits of the permit application.

However, this Court's determination that section 404 in conjunction with the APA requires only an informal, rather than a formal or trial-type, adjudicatory proceeding does not completely dispose of National Wildlife's claim. Section 404 provides for "public hearings"; the Army's regulations provide that there be an opportunity for "meaningful comments." 33 C.F.R. §325.3(a). Even in an informal adjudicatory setting, if the public is not apprised of the rationale behind a proposed decision, or if the public is informed of the rationale only after the close of the comment and hearing period, then the agency cannot be said to have provided a realistic opportunity for public hearings or meaningful comments. The requirements that

> an agency ... provide initial notices of proposed action, disclose internal reports, and state its reasons for acting as it did, all rest on the fundamental proposition that the right to comment or the opportunity to be heard on questions relating to the public interest is of little or no significance when one is not apprised of the issues and positions to which argument is relevant. Only when the public is adequately informed can there be any exchange of views and any real dialogue as to the final decision. And without such dialogue any notion of real public participation is necessarily an illusion.

U.S. Lines v. Federal Maritime Commission, 189 U.S. App. D.C. 361, 584 F.2d 519, 540 (D.C.Cir. 1978) (footnotes omitted). In *U.S. Lines,* because the rationale for the agency's decision in an informal adjudicatory process was not disclosed to the public prior to the close of the comment and hearing period, the proceeding was remanded to the agency. *See Portland Cement Association v. Ruckelshaus,* 158 U.S. App. D.C. 308, 486 F.2d 375, 392-93, 393 n.67 (D.C.Cir. 1973), *cert. denied,* 417 U.S. 921, 41 L. Ed. 2d 226, 94 S. Ct. 2628 (1974).

Based on *U.S. Lines,* this Court holds that even in the informal adjudicatory process under section 404 of the CWA, the opportunity to comment and the right to a hearing both necessarily require that the Army present for public scrutiny the rationale and pivotal data underlying its proposed action before the close of the comment and hearing period. Unfortunately, that requirement was not satisfied in the administrative proceeding here. After a careful examination of the administrative record, the Court finds that the inclusion of the Staff Evaluation in the administrative record *after* the close of the comment and hearing period had the effect of shielding the essential data and the agency's rationale from public hearing and comment. Plaintiffs are correct that the pivotal analysis of the refinery's benefits in terms of reductions of transportation costs was absent from the administrative record as initially amassed; that it was the Staff Evaluation which first introduced the rather extensive array of data which formed the basis of the Secretary's decision; and that because this information was first introduced by the

Staff Evaluation, the information improperly eluded the public comment and hearing requirements....

Lastly, by now it should be abundantly clear that this new data introduced by the Staff Evaluation was not simply a "bit of background information" that may permissibly avoid the procedures for comment and hearing because of its inconsequence. *B.F. Goodrich Co. v. Department of Transportation,* 541 F.2d 1178, 1184 (6th Cir. 1976), *cert. denied,* 430 U.S. 930, 97 S. Ct. 1549, 51 L. Ed. 2d 773 (1977). *Cf. Sierra Club v. Costle,* 211 U.S. App. D.C. 336, 657 F.2d 298, 387, 396-400 (D.C.Cir. 1981) (no improper denial of right to comment on informal rulemaking when some 300 submissions reviewed after the close of the comment period were not crucial to the rules validity). The Secretary relied upon the Staff Evaluation's analysis of the benefits derived from reduced transportation costs in concluding that the permit be issued. The Evaluation was perhaps the most important document influencing the Secretary's decision. In the Army's own words, it was the Staff Evaluation "which led to [Secretary of the Army Clifford] Alexander's preliminary finding." Until the introduction of the Staff Evaluation, the import of the record was that the refinery's *raison d'etre* was its fulfillment of the nation's energy needs and its increase of the nation's refinery capacity. Only after the close of the administrative record, with the introduction of the Staff Evaluation, did the true rationale and its supporting data become apparent: The refinery was to be built because of savings in transportation costs, not because of any materially beneficial contribution to the nation's energy supply.

Because of the sudden shift in rationale from energy need and refinery capacity to savings in transportation costs, and because of the introduction of new data relating to transportation costs, this Court finds that the public was denied its opportunity to comment and its right to a public hearing....

CONCLUSION

Despite the extensive, often admirable effort made by the Army, the Court finds that a number of flaws afflicted the administrative processing of the permit. First, the introduction of the transportation-cost data in the Staff Evaluation violated the APA, section 404 of the CWA, and 33 C.F.R. §325.3(a). Second, the Staff Evaluation's introduction of the transportation-cost data and its re-analysis of alternatives violated section 102(2)(B) and (C) of NEPA. However, the Court finds no merit in the other challenges presented by National Wildlife to the issuance of the permit. [Footnotes omitted.]

See also *Shoreline Assoc. v. Marsh*, 555 F.Supp. 169 (D.Md. 1983), *aff'd.*, 725 F.2d 677 (4th Cir. Md. 1984); *Friends of the Earth v. Hall*, 693 F.Supp. 904 W.D.Wa. 1988); *Nofelco Realty Corp. v. United States*, 521 F.Supp. 458 (S.D.N.Y. 1981).

Public notice shall be given of any hearing to be held. The notice shall contain time, place, and nature of hearing; the legal authority and jurisdiction under which the hearing is held; and location of and availability of the draft environmental impact statement or environmental assessment.

Such notice should normally provide for a period of not less than 30 days following the date of public notice during which time interested parties may prepare themselves for the hearing. Notice shall also be given to all Federal agencies affected by the proposed action, and to state and local agencies and other parties having an interest in the subject matter of the hearing.

Notice shall be sent to all persons requesting a hearing and shall be posted in appropriate government buildings and provided to newspapers of general circulation for publication.

The District Engineer, in whose district a matter arises, shall normally serve as the presiding officer. When the District Engineer is unable to serve, he may designate the deputy District Engineer or other qualified person as presiding officer. In cases of unusual interest, the Chief of Engineers or the Division Engineer may appoint such person as he deems appropriate to serve as the presiding officer. The presiding officer shall include in the administrative record of the permit action the request or requests for the hearing and any data or material submitted in justification thereof, materials submitted in opposition to or in support of the proposed action, the hearing transcript, and such other material as may be relevant or pertinent to the subject matter of the hearing. The administrative record shall be available for public inspection with the exception of material exempt from disclosure under the Freedom of Information Act.

Hearings shall be conducted by the presiding officer in an orderly but expeditious manner. The presiding officer shall make an opening statement outlining the purpose of the hearing and prescribing the general procedures to be followed. Any person may appear on his own behalf, or may be represented by counsel, or by other representatives and shall be permitted to submit oral or written statements concerning the subject matter of the hearing, to call witnesses who may present oral or written statements, and to present recommendations as to an appropriate decision. Any person may present written statements for the hearing record prior to the time the hearing record is closed to public submissions, and may present proposed findings and recommendations. The presiding officer shall afford participants a reasonable opportunity for rebuttal. The presiding officer shall have discretion to establish reasonable limits upon the time allowed for statements of witnesses, for arguments of parties or their counsel or representatives, and upon the number of rebuttals. Cross-examination of witnesses shall not be permitted.

All public hearings shall be reported verbatim. Copies of the transcripts of proceedings may be purchased by any person from the Corps or the reporter of such hearing. A copy will be available for public inspection at the office of the appropriate District Engineer. All written statements, charts, tabulations, and similar data offered in evidence at the hearing shall, subject to exclusion by the presiding officer for reasons of redundancy, be received in evidence and shall constitute a part of the record. The presiding officer shall allow a period of not less than ten days after the close of the public hearing for submission of written comments.

The transcript of the public hearing, together with all evidence introduced at the hearing, shall be made a part of the administrative record. The Corps shall fully consider the matters discussed at the public hearing in arriving at its initial decision or recommendation and shall address, in its decision or recommendation, all substantial and valid issues presented at the hearing. Where a person other than the Corps serves as presiding officer, such person shall forward the transcript of the public hearing and all evidence received in connection therewith to the Corps together with a report summarizing the issues covered at the hearing. The report of the presiding officer and the transcript of the public hearing and evidence submitted thereat shall in such cases be fully considered by the Corps in making his decision or recommendation to higher authority as to such permit action.

The Corps can override state and local government zoning or land use decisions but must document the override as well as other agencies' views.

SIERRA CLUB v. ALEXANDER

484 F. Supp. 455 (N.D.N.Y. 1980)

This matter was originally before the Court on motion for a temporary restraining order and a preliminary injunction brought by plaintiff to halt construction by defendant Pyramid of a shopping center mall in the Town of New Hartford, New York. Pursuant to Rule 65(a)(2) of the Fed.R.Civ.Pro. the Court ordered the trial of the action on the merits advanced and consolidated with the evidentiary hearing on the preliminary injunction application with the consent of the parties herein, during the course of the evidentiary hearing which commenced on December 3, 1979, and continued through December 14, 1979. ...

The complaint in this action was filed November 27, 1979. In it plaintiff seeks declaratory and injunctive relief halting construction of the shopping center mall until such time as the Court is satisfied that the Army Corps of Engineers has complied with all of the requirements set forth in the National Environmental Policy Act (NEPA), 42 U.S.C. §§4321 et seq.; The Fish and Wildlife Coordination Act, 16 U.S.C. §§661 et seq.; The Federal Water Pollution Control Act, as amended, 33 U.S.C. §1344; The Rivers and Harbors Act of 1899, as amended, 33 U.S.C. §§401 & 403; certain regulations promulgated pursuant to the above Acts and Executive Orders Nos. 11988 and 11990.

By virtue of an amendment to its complaint, allowed by the Court during trial, plaintiff also requests issuance of an order directing defendants to remove any fill material which has been placed on the project site and requiring restoration of the site to its preconstruction condition.

In addition to plaintiff's request for a preliminary injunction, all parties have moved for summary judgment. Jurisdiction is predicated upon 28 U.S.C. §1331(a) and 28 U.S.C. §§2201 and 2202.

BACKGROUND

1979 PROJECT PROPOSAL

The regional shopping mall proposed by defendant Pyramid in 1979, is currently under construction on a 115-acre site near the southeast corner of the intersection of Routes 5 and 5A in the Town of New Hartford, approximately two miles west of the City of Utica, New York. The fully enclosed one story mall will upon completion occupy nearly sixty acres of the total site and will contain three major department stores (Sears, J.C. Penney, and Hess). The gross building area will be 850,000 square feet with 770,000 square feet of leasable space. Parking is planned for 3,960 cars.

Prior to the commencement of work on the project, the site consisted of uplands and approximately 55 acres of wetlands, including streamside and cattail wetlands and swamp areas. A predominant feature of the site is Mud Creek and its low lying flood plain. Mud Creek, a moderately sized tributary to Saquoit Creek, meanders through the site in a northeasterly direction. The Creek bank, prior to construction, was stabilized with vegetation, trees and shrubs. Its flood plain, described as a one-hundred year flood contour, slowed the effect of downstream flooding.

The mall site is generally agreed to have been a productive area for diverse fish and wildlife species, including such fish species as shiners and suckers and wildlife species as skunks, rabbits, song birds, black ducks, woodcock, pheasants and marsh hawks. Wildlife presence is due in part to the high ratio of "edges" on the site.

Construction of the mall will involve filling in approximately thirty-eight acres of wetlands on the site with a resulting loss of the area as a wildlife habitat. This is due in part to the destruction of the vegetative cover. The flood control function of the site's open space drainage area will also be lost. In addition, construction involves the rechannelization of around 2,000 linear feet of Mud Creek.

In order to lessen the environmental impact of the project, certain mitigation measures have been proposed by defendant Pyramid. On-site measures include the construction of three detention basins, designated A, B, and C, which will provide 150% of the preconstruction storm capacity of the site. An additional four acres of cattail wetlands will be created in the detention basin area. The new bed constructed for Mud Creek will contain meanders and riffles along with shore line plantings. The old Creek bed will be filled in with on-site materials.

Off-site mitigation measures have also been included in the proposal. Defendant Pyramid has agreed to purchase nearly 159 acres of land approximately one and a half miles upstream from the project site in an area known as the "Limberlost" property. This property was described by one witness as a mono-type wet meadow.

The off-site mitigation plan calls for the creation of new wetlands in the uplands area of Limberlost, and the construction of four small ponds on that site. Wetland plantings are to be made on the property by Pyramid. This property is then to be deeded over to the Town of New Hartford for public use. Work by Pyramid with regard to both on-site and off-site mitigation measures is to be closely monitored by the New York State Department of Environmental Conservation (DEC).

1977 PROJECT PROPOSAL

The project previously described was not the first proposal by a Pyramid related company for the construction of a regional shopping center mall in the Utica-New Hartford area.

In 1977, Pyramid Systems, Inc., proposed the construction of a shopping center mall in the same general areas as the one now under attack. However, the permits necessary under New York State Law were denied on March 12, 1978, after a public hearing, in a decision by then Commissioner of the State DEC, Peter A. Berle. The permits were denied based upon the failure of the applicant to demonstrate need for the project and the unavailability of alternatives, in a clear enough manner, to allow balancing of the socio-economic benefits of wetlands with that of the socio-economic development of the State of New York through construction of the mall. A request for reconsideration was denied on July 18, 1978, on the same general basis.

Plaintiff contends that the 1977 proposal and the 1979 proposal are virtually identical. However, the hearing officer at the State DEC public hearings on the 1979 proposal made a finding that the project was an entirely new proposal and not a resubmission of the 1977 plan. In fact, according to defendant Pyramid, new applications for permits were submitted at the suggestion of State DEC officials.

STATE DEC INVOLVEMENT WITH THE 1979 PROPOSAL

Under New York State law, defendant Pyramid was required to obtain a freshwater wetlands permit, an indirect source permit and an impoundment permit from the New York State DEC. Approval of the project was also required under the State Environmental Quality Review Act (SEQRA). New York State ECL §§8-0101 et seq.

Although it is the issuance of a permit pursuant to Section 404 of the Federal Water Pollution Control Act, 33 U.S.C. §1344, which is the focus of this action, a review of the actions of the New York State DEC with regard to State requirements is both helpful and necessary in deciding this lawsuit.

Defendant Pyramid, in accordance with the requirements set forth in the N.Y. ECL at §8-0109(2), caused to be prepared and submitted to the State DEC a draft environmental impact statement ("DEIS") and a document entitled "Storm Water Management Report."

The DEIS contained analyses of the socio-economic impact of the project (retail-analysis), air and water quality, traffic, energy use and conservation, impact on soil and geological resources, and impact on the vegetation and wildlife on the site. It also included discussion of the unavoidable impacts, the proposed mitigation measures, and alternatives, including both the no build alternative and alternative sites.

Beginning on March 6, 1979, and concluding April 6, 1979, the State DEC conducted nineteen days of public hearings on the applications. Plaintiff, along with several other environmental organizations, was a party to the hearings. The Club was represented by one of its members who resided in New Hartford.

The June 22, 1979, decision of Robert F. Flacke, Commissioner of the State DEC, based upon the findings in the 55-page hearing report (also designated as the final environmental impact statement) submitted by the hearing officer, Robert S. Drew, directed issuance of the requested permits. In issuing the permits, the State DEC determined that the project was consistent with local land use plans, that it would fulfill a need in the area for a full-line department store, and that the loss of the wetlands would be adequately compensated by the proposed mitigation measures.

Pursuant to recommendations in the hearing report, issuance of the permits was conditioned upon submission to the DEC of construction plans, a schedule for completion of the detention basins, the new channel for Mud Creek, erosion control measures, proposed on-site plantings, and the work to be done on the Limberlost property. Pyramid was also required to post a $100,000 bond to insure successful completion of the work on both sites.

SECTION 404 PERMIT

On January 23, 1979, defendant Pyramid submitted an application for a Section 404 permit to the New York District Office of the Army Corps of Engineers. The application contained a description of the activity for which the permit was sought, stating that it:

> ... consists of realigning 2,000 l. f. of Mud Creek, construction of two entrance roads with culverted stream crossings, construction of 1,400 feet of dikes and construction of storm water detention areas to accommodate a regional Mall Shopping Facility. After completion of the new channel and crossings, the existing creek bed and adjacent lands will be filled with on-site material.

Included with the application were site drawings, a site photo, and three copies of the "Storm Water Management Report."

After making a preliminary determination that an Environmental Impact Statement (EIS) was not required, Corps officials prepared and sent out a public notice regarding the application. The Environmental Protection Agency (EPA), upon receipt of the notice, expressed concern over issuance of the permit and requested that a meeting be held with interested Federal officials and a Pyramid representative. The meeting was held on May 30, 1979, at the Corps offices in New York City and was followed by a site visit on June 14, 1979.

Although subsequent to the meeting and site visit, the EPA dropped its objection to the issuance of the permit, United States Fish and Wildlife Services (FWS) continued in its objection to the issuance of the permit. Modifications to the project proposed by FWS were, however, rejected by both defendant Pyramid and future tenant J.C. Penney.

On August 22, 1979, an Environmental Assessment of the impact of the project was issued by Corps officials. A Supplemental Assessment dealing with the comments received in response to the public notice and Pyramid's response to those comments was issued on September 13, 1979.

A Section 404 permit was issued to defendant Pyramid on September 24, 1979, over the still unresolved objection of the Fish and Wildlife Service. A special condition contained in the permit required Pyramid to submit to the Corps office all of the construction plans and schedules which are to be submitted to the State DEC, after DEC approval has been obtained....

Pursuant to the Fish and Wildlife Coordination Act, §§661 et seq., the Army Corps of Engineers is obligated to consult with the Fish and Wildlife Service concerning the impact on fish and wildlife resources of issuance of a Section 404 permit. *See Zabel v. Tabb,* 430 F.2d 199, 209 (5th Cir. 1970). Plaintiff contends that the Corps failed to comply with the Act in issuance of the permit to Pyramid.

There is no question but that Fish and Wildlife Service officials were opposed to issuance of the permit to Pyramid, without certain modification of the project proposed by the Service. The proposed modifications involved changes which would dispense with the need for the rechannelization of Mud Creek. Pyramid, given the opportunity to respond to the Fish and Wildlife Service position as required under 33 C.F.R. §325.2(a)(3), found the proposed modifications economically unfeasible.

The Fish and Wildlife Service did not change its position prior to the Corps decision to issue the permit but did refuse the opportunity to seek higher review of the decision to issue the permit. Plaintiff argues that issuance of the permit over the unresolved objection of the Fish and Wildlife Service violated the Fish and Wildlife Coordination Act, as well as the Corps' own Regulation which required it to give "great weight" to the views of the Fish and Wildlife Service concerning fish and wildlife conservation.

Plaintiff fails to recognize, however, that the final decision rested with the Corps, which had to base its determination not only on the impact of the project on fish and wildlife but on a "careful weighing of all those factors which become relevant in each particular case.... The benefit which reasonably may be expected to accrue from the proposal must be balanced against its reasonably foreseeable detriments." 33 C.F.R. §320.4(a)(1).

The Fish and Wildlife Coordination Act does not require that the Corps decision always correspond to the views of the Fish and Wildlife Service. Rather the Act requires that the views be given serious consideration, and there is nothing in the Corps record which shows that the Corps failed to do so.... [Footnotes omitted.]

HART AND MILLER ISLANDS AREA ENVIRONMENTAL GROUP, INC. v. CORPS OF ENGINEERS OF THE UNITED STATES ARMY

505 F. Supp. 732 (D.Md. 1980)

This lawsuit involves the planned construction of a diked dredged spoil disposal facility at the Hart and Miller Islands in Baltimore County, Maryland. On June 30, 1977, a number of environmental groups and concerned individuals filed suit against the United States Army Corps of Engineers, challenging the Corps' decision to issue a permit to the State of Maryland for the Hart and Miller Islands disposal structure. This court granted the motions of the State of Maryland and the Steamship Trade Association of Baltimore, Inc. to intervene as defendants in this action on October 10, 1977....

On February 23, 1972, the State of Maryland, through its Department of General Services, filed an application with the Army Corps of Engineers for a permit pursuant to the Rivers and Harbors Act of 1899, 33 U.S.C. §401 et seq., and section 404 of the Federal Water Pollution Control Act Amendments of 1972, as amended, 33 U.S.C. §1344, to construct a diked dredged spoil disposal facility at the Hart and Miller Islands in the Chesapeake Bay....

The Hart and Miller Islands are located within the Chesapeake Bay approximately 13 miles east of Baltimore, Maryland. The dike and containment area is to be constructed on the bayward (eastern) side of the Hart and Miller Islands about one mile from the mainland and will occupy an area of 1,100 acres or approximately two square miles. The stated purpose of the diked disposal area is to contain approximately 52 million cubic yards of dredged spoil to be removed from the Baltimore Harbor and its approach channels.

When the dike is completed, its walls will stand 18 feet above mean low water, somewhat higher than the current maximum elevations of the Hart and Miller Islands, which are 5.5 feet and 2.3 feet, respectively. However, only 12 percent of Hart Island and 52 percent of Miller Island will be covered by the disposal area. Basically, the disposal area will be rectangular in shape with the islands fitting into the northwestern, longer side of the area and the structure occupying principally an area to the southeast of the islands. Dredged spoil will be transported to the disposal area by pumping the material through hydraulic pipelines either from the dredging sites in the Baltimore Harbor or from barges which will carry the dredged spoil from the dredging site to the disposal area. The dredged material will be pumped into the diked containment area and the sand walls of the dike will allow the water to percolate out of the containment area, leaving only the dredged material inside. Once the area has been completely filled with dredged spoil, the entire structure will be at the height of eighteen feet above mean low water. As a means of protection against erosion on the bayward side of the structure, this side will be rip-rapped with stone, all other sides consisting of the sand-constructed walls of the dike.

The Corps of Engineers held a public hearing on August 29, 1972 to consider the State of Maryland's permit application (A.R. 57). On February 22, 1973, the Corps completed its draft Environmental Impact Statement (A.R. 177). At least in part to address objections raised to the proposed Hart and Miller Islands project, the State of Maryland arranged to have a private consultant, Roy Mann Associates, Inc., evaluate certain aspects of the plans for the structure. The Mann Report was completed in July 1975, and is entitled, "Peer Review of the Evaluation of Hart and Miller Islands and Alternatives for Dredged Materials Disposal" (A.R. 634). A second public hearing was held on May 10, 1975 (A.R. 527), and in February 1976, the Corps of Engineers, as required by the National Environmental Policy Act, 42 U.S.C. §4321 et seq., issued its Final Environmental Impact Statement (E.I.S.) (A.R. 745). Upon completion of the Impact Statement, the District Engineer for the Baltimore District prepared a report on the application recommending issuance of the permit with the inclusion of certain conditions in the permit (A.R. 744). This recommendation was concurred in by the Corps' North Atlantic Division on March 8, 1976 (A.R. 755), and the final report was sent to the Corps' headquarters in Washington for final approval. Final approval was given in November 1976, and the State of Maryland was issued a permit for the diked disposal facility under 33 U.S.C. §§403 and 1344 (A.R. 815, 816, 817)....

Finally, plaintiffs stress the objections of other federal agencies involved with environmental issues to the Hart and Miller Islands project. The Environmental Protection Agency (EPA), in a letter dated September 23, 1976, expressed concern over many issues, including whether or not additional wetlands will be created to compensate for those lost due to dike construction, whether or not the Hart and Miller Islands complex will ultimately be used as a recreational facility, and whether or not alternatives to diked disposal areas will be considered in the future (A.R. 795). Although expressing reservations, the EPA did lend its support to the Hart and Miller Islands project in this letter. By letter dated October 13, 1976, however, the EPA reversed its position and withdrew its approval of the project as a result of its continuing concern over the structural integrity of the proposed dike (A.R. 799).

The National Marine Fisheries Service asserted its objections to the Hart and Miller Islands project in a letter to the Corps of Engineers dated September 17, 1976 (A.R. 790):

> In summation, we do not believe that the applicant has convincingly demonstrated that the Hart and Miller Islands disposal site is necessarily the best available, based on our assessment of the potential impacts on living marine resources and their environments. Our doubts regarding the proposed project stem from the paucity of biological and engineering data that have been made available, and the fact that biological and other information presented in the FEIS was often inconsistent. Therefore, in our opinion, a sufficient data base does not exist from which we can recommend a site which would result in the least environmental impact.

In a similar vein, the Department of the Interior informed the Corps of its conclusion that the Final Environmental Impact Statement on the Hart and Miller Islands project was deficient in a letter dated September 21, 1976 (A.R. 793):

> A June 30, 1976 letter from Under Secretary Frizzell to General Gribble, pursuant to the Memorandum of Understanding, identified areas of concern to this Department. We have reviewed the final environmental impact statement (FEIS) with these concerns in mind. We have concluded that it is deficient in at least three areas: (1) its recognition and discussion of the total spoil disposal problem in the Chesapeake Bay system, of which Hart-Miller is only a partial answer, and the cumulative environmental impacts which will result; (2) treatment of alternative disposal sites in sufficient depth so that an informed comparison and judgment can be made on the best location or locations for spoil disposal; and (3) identification of the final use to be made of the Hart-Miller complex following completion of the spoil disposal project in terms of recreational and fish and wildlife values.

Although the Department softened its position in a subsequent letter, it continued to express reservations about the wisdom of the Hart and Miller Islands project and the adequacy of the Corps' Environmental Impact Statement (A.R. 807).

Plaintiffs do not argue that the views expressed by the Environmental Protection Agency, the Department of the Interior and the National Marine Fisheries Service, standing alone, have any particular legal significance. Rather, they offer the statements made by these agencies to buttress the allegations of their complaint. The court is impressed by the weight of the evidence presented by plaintiffs and the light it sheds on the possible consequences of the Hart and Miller dike. These agency comments do not, however, persuade the court that plaintiffs' claims merit further discussion than they have already received. The requirement of NEPA is that Federal agencies with special expertise be consulted and allowed to comment upon the proposed action; that the comments of the agency consulted are negative does not give rise to a NEPA violation.

V. CONCLUSION

By its holding in this case, the court does not lend its imprimatur to the Corps' approval of the State of Maryland's permit application. To the contrary, this court has found some of plaintiffs' substantive arguments to have considerable merit. However, as the court has reiterated throughout this opinion, the Supreme Court has clearly held that the mandates of the National Environmental Policy Act are essentially procedural, and that the court's role in cases like the one at bar is limited and narrow. This court has neither the expertise, the power nor the responsibility to review the merits of the Corps' conclusions, but only the sufficiency under NEPA of the procedures followed in reaching them.

In National Center for Preservation Law, supra, 496 F.Supp. at 737, the court summarized the standard of review to be applied to summary judgment motions in cases brought pursuant to NEPA:

> The NEPA requires an EIS to discuss certain factors.... The legal test for determining the adequacy of a discussion of the necessary factors is one which examines whether or not the subject EIS is one which will provide the decision-makers with sufficient information of the environmental consequences of their action so that they can make a reasoned decision. See *Vermont Yankee Nuclear Power Corp. v. NRDC*, 435 U.S. 519, 98 S. Ct. 1197, 55 L. Ed. 2d 460 (1978); *Sierra Club v. Morton*, 510 F.2d 813 (5th Cir. 1975). Those opposing the agency action on NEPA grounds must advance evidence which is substantial and

> dependable to prove that an EIS is fatally flawed or a NEPA complaint will not withstand a motion for summary judgment. *Upper Westfork River Watershed Ass'n v. Corps of Engineers*, 414 F.Supp. at 922. This burden is not met by merely establishing a prima facie showing of deficiencies. *Conservation Council of North Carolina v. Froehlke*, 435 F.Supp. 775, 791 (M.D.N.C.1977). In reviewing the adequacy of an EIS as part of the record before the decision-makers in a NEPA case, the district court's sole role is to insure that the sponsoring agencies have considered the environmental consequences of the proposed action. *Strycker's Bay Neighborhood Council, Inc. v. Karlen*, 444 U.S. 223, 227, 100 S. Ct. 497, 500, 62 L. Ed. 2d 433 (1980).

For the reasons discussed throughout this opinion, the court believes that plaintiffs have failed to advance substantial and dependable evidence which proves that the Environmental Impact Statement in this case is fatally flawed. Consequently, this court will enter an order denying plaintiffs' summary judgment motion and granting summary judgment to defendants.

[Footnotes omitted.]

CHAPTER 18

ENVIRONMENTAL PROTECTION AGENCY GUIDELINES

As the Corps is proceeding in its permit decision, gathering all the information necessary, receiving comments after the public notice, and conducting any public hearing it considers necessary, the Corps is required to determine "the probable effect of the proposed work on the public interest" in conformity with the Guidelines established by the Environmental Protection Agency.

Wetlands present a special case of permit decision for the Corps because of the multitude of expressions of policy against their alteration or destruction. *See e.g.,* 33 C.F.R. §320.4(b)(1): "Most wetlands constitute a productive and valuable public resource, the unnecessary alteration or destruction of which should be discouraged as contrary to the public interest"; 33 C.F.R. §320.4(b)(4): "No permit will be granted which involves the alteration of wetlands ... unless the (Corps) concludes ... that the benefits of the proposed alteration outweigh the damage to the wetlands resource." The Guidelines themselves contain similar admonitions to the Corps and the permit applicant: "Fundamental to the Guidelines is the precept that dredged or fill material should not be discharged into the aquatic ecosystem, unless it can be demonstrated that such a discharge will not have an unacceptable adverse impact either individually or in combination with known and/or probable impacts of other activities affecting the ecosystems of concern" (40 C.F.R. §230.1(c)) and "From a national perspective, the degradation or destruction of special aquatic sites, such as filling operations in wetlands, is considered to be among the most severe environmental impacts covered by these Guidelines. The guiding principle should be that degradation or destruction of special sites may represent an irreversible loss of valuable aquatic resources."(40 C.F.R. §230.1(d)). In fact, the Corps's regulations require that a §404 permit be denied if the discharge would not comply with the EPA's Guidelines.

BERSANI v. UNITED STATES ENVIRONMENTAL PROTECTION AGENCY

850 F.2d 36 (2d Cir. 1988), *cert. denied* 489 U.S. 1089, 109 S.Ct. 1556, 103 L.Ed.2d 859 (1989)

This case arises out of Pyramid's attempt to build a shopping mall on certain wetlands in Massachusetts known as Sweedens Swamp. Acting under the Clean Water Act, 33 U.S.C. §1251 *et seq.* (1982), EPA vetoed the approval by the Corps of a permit to build the mall because EPA found that an alternative site had been available to Pyramid at the time it entered the market to search for a site for the mall. The alternative site was purchased later by another developer and arguably became unavailable by the time Pyramid applied for a permit to build the mall.

On appeal, the thrust of Pyramid's argument is a challenge to what it calls EPA's "market entry" theory, *i.e.,* the interpretation by EPA of the relevant regulation, which led EPA to consider the availability of alternative sites at the time Pyramid entered the market for a site, instead of at the time it applied for a permit. Pyramid argues principally (1) that the market entry approach is contrary to the regulatory language and past practice; and (2) that since the Corps, another agency which was jointly responsible with EPA for administering the program in question, interpreted the pertinent regulation in a different way than EPA had, and since the market entry issue does not involve environmental expertise, this Court should not defer to EPA's interpretation of the regulation. Other subordinate claims are raised by appellants as well as by two intervenors and the amicus curiae.

We hold (1) that the market entry theory is consistent with both the regulatory language and past practice; (2) that EPA's interpretation, while not necessarily entitled to deference, is reasonable; and (3) that EPA's application of the regulation is supported by the administrative record. We agree with the district court's conclusion that EPA's findings were not arbitrary and capricious. We also hold that Pyramid's other arguments, and the arguments of one intervenor and the amicus, lack merit.

We AFFIRM.

I

We shall summarize only those facts and prior proceedings believed necessary to an understanding of the issues raised on appeal.

A. Statutory and Regulatory Framework

One of the sections of the Clean Water Act (the "Act") relevant to the instant case is §301(a), 33 U.S.C. §1311(a) (1982), which prohibits the discharge of any pollutant, including dredged or fill materials, into the nation's navigable waters, except in compliance with the Act's provisions, including §404. It is undisputed that Sweedens Swamp is a "navigable water," as defined in 33 U.S.C. §1362 (1982), and that Pyramid's shopping center proposal will involve the discharge of dredged or fill materials.

Section 404 of the Act, 33 U.S.C. §1344 (1982 & Supp. III 1985), focusing on dredged or fill materials, provides that the United States Army and EPA will share responsibility for implementation of its provisions. EPA and the Corps also share responsibility for enforcing the Act. 33 U.S.C. §§1311 (1982), 1319 (1982), 1344(n) and (s) (1982). Section 404(a) authorizes the Secretary of the Army, acting through the Corps, to issue permits for the discharge of dredged or fill materials at particular sites. 33 U.S.C. §1344(a) (1982). Section 404(b) provides that, subject to §404(c), the Corps must base its decisions regarding permits on guidelines (the "404(b)(1) guidelines") developed by EPA in conjunction with the Secretary of the Army. 33 U.S.C. §1344(b) (Supp. III 1985).

The 404(b)(1) guidelines, published at 40 C.F.R. Part 230 (1987), are regulations containing the requirements for issuing a permit for discharge of dredged or fill materials. 40 C.F.R. §230.10(a) covers "non-water dependent activities" (*i.e.,* activities that could be performed on non-wetland sites, such as building a mall) and provides essentially that the Corps must determine whether an alternative site is available that would cause less harm to the wetlands. Specifically, it provides that "no discharge of dredged or fill material shall be permitted if there is a practicable alternative" to the proposal that would have a "less adverse impact" on the "aquatic ecosystem." It also provides that a practicable alternative may include "an area not presently owned by the applicant which could reasonably be obtained, utilized, expanded or managed in order to fulfill the basic purpose of the proposed activity." 40 C.F.R. 230.10(a)(2). It further provides that, "unless clearly demonstrated otherwise," practicable alternatives are (1) "presumed to be available" and (2) "presumed to have less adverse impact on the aquatic ecosystem." 40 C.F.R. 230.10(a)(3). Thus, an applicant such as Pyramid must rebut both of these presumptions in order to obtain a permit. Sections 230.10(c) and (d) require that the Corps not permit any discharge that would contribute to significant degradation of the nation's wetlands and that any adverse impacts must be mitigated through practicable measures....

In short, both EPA and the Corps are responsible for administering the program for granting permits for discharges of pollutants into wetlands under §404. The Corps has the authority to issue permits following the 404(b)(1) guidelines developed by it and EPA; EPA has the authority under §404(c) to veto any permit granted by the Corps. The Corps processes about 11,000 permit applications each year. EPA has vetoed five decisions by the Corps to grant permits.

B. FACTUAL BACKGROUND OF THE SWEEDENS SWAMP PROJECT

Sweedens Swamp is a 49.5 acre wetland which is part of an 80-acre site near Interstate 95 in South Attleboro, Massachusetts. Although some illegal dumping and motorbike intrusions have occurred, these activities have been found to have had little impact on the site which remains a "high-quality red maple swamp" providing wildlife habitat and protecting the area from flooding and pollution.

The effort to build a mall on Sweedens Swamp was initiated by Pyramid's predecessor, the Edward J. DeBartolo Corporation ("DeBartolo"). DeBartolo purchased the Swamp some time before April 1982. At the time of this purchase an alternative site was available in North Attleboro (the "North Attleboro site"). Since Massachusetts requires state approval (in addition to federal approval) for projects that would fill wetlands, DeBartolo applied to the Massachusetts Department of Environmental Quality Engineering ("DEQE") for permission to build on Sweedens Swamp. DEQE denied the application in April 1982.

Pyramid took over the project in 1983 while the appeal of the DEQE denial was pending. In April 1983, Massachusetts adopted more rigorous standards for approval of permits. The new standards added wildlife habitat as a value of wetlands to be protected and required the absence of a "practicable alternative." In March 1985, DEQE granted approval under the old, less stringent, regulations. The Massachusetts District Court reversed on the ground that DEQE should have applied the new regulations, but the Massachusetts Supreme Judicial Court ultimately upheld DEQE's approval. *Citizens for Responsible Environmental Management v. Attleboro Mall, Inc.*, 400 Mass. 658, 511 N.E.2d 562 (1987).

One of the key issues in dispute in the instant case is just when did Pyramid begin searching for a suitable site for its mall. EPA asserts that Pyramid began to search in the Spring of 1983. Pyramid asserts that it began to search several months later, in September 1983. The difference is crucial because on July 1, 1983—a date between the starting dates claimed by EPA and Pyramid—a competitor of Pyramid, the New England Development Co. ("NED"), purchased options to buy the North Attleboro site. This site was located upland and could have served as a "practicable alternative" to Sweedens Swamp, *if* it had been "available" at the relevant time. Thus, if the relevant time to determine whether an alternative is "available" is the time the applicant is searching for a site (an issue that is hotly disputed), and if Pyramid began to search at a time *before* NED acquired options on the North Attleboro site, there definitely would have been a "practicable alternative" to Sweedens Swamp, and Pyramid's application should have been denied. On the other hand, if Pyramid did not begin its search until *after* NED acquired options on the North Attleboro site, then the site arguably was not "available" and the permit should have been granted. Of course it also is possible that the North Attleboro site remained "available" after NED's acquisition of the options, since Pyramid arguably could have purchased the options from NED. Moreover, since the North Attleboro site indisputably was "available" when Pyramid's predecessor, DeBartolo, purchased Sweedens Swamp, one might argue, as EPA does, that Pyramid should be held to stand in its predecessor's shoes. The district court apparently agreed with Pyramid on the issue of when Pyramid entered the market, stating that "Pyramid initially became interested in developing a shopping mall in the Attleboro area in September 1983". *Bersani v. EPA,* 674 F. Supp. 405, 409 (N.D.N.Y. 1987).

In December 1983, Pyramid purchased Sweedens Swamp from DeBartolo. In August 1984, Pyramid applied under §404(a) to the New England regional division of the Corps (the "NE Corps") for a permit. It sought to fill or alter 32 of the 49.6 acres of the Swamp; to excavate nine acres of uplands to create artificial wetlands; and to alter 13.3 acres of existing wetlands to improve its environmental quality. Later Pyramid proposed to mitigate the adverse impact on the wetlands by creating 36 acres of replacement wetlands in an off-site gravel pit.

During the review of Pyramid's application by EPA, by the Fish and Wildlife Service ("FWS") and by the Corps, Pyramid submitted information on "practicable alternatives," especially the North Attleboro site. In rejecting that site as an alternative, Pyramid asserted that building a mall there was not *feasible,* not that the site was *unavailable.* In the words of the district court, Pyramid claimed that

> the site lacked sufficient traffic volume and sufficient access from local roads, potential department store tenants had expressed strong doubts about the *feasibility* of the site and previous attempts to develop the site had met with strong resistance from the surrounding community.

Bersani, supra, 674 F. Supp. at 410 (emphasis added).

In November 1984, EPA and FWS submitted official comments to the NE Corps recommending denial of the application because Pyramid's proposal was inconsistent with the 404(b)(1) guidelines. Pyramid had failed (1) to overcome the presumption of the availability of alternatives and (2) to mitigate adequately the adverse impact on wildlife. EPA threatened a §404(c) review. Pyramid then proposed to create additional artificial wetlands at a nearby upland site, a proposal it eventually abandoned.

In January 1985, the NE Corps hired a consultant to investigate the feasibility of Sweedens Swamp and the North Attleboro site. The consultant reported that either site was feasible but that from a commercial standpoint only one mall could survive in the area. On February 19, 1985, the NE Corps advised Pyramid that denial of its permit was imminent. On May 2, 1985, the NE Corps sent its recommendation to deny the permit to the national headquarters of the Corps. Although the NE Corps ordinarily makes the final decision on whether to grant a permit, *see* 33 C.F.R. §325.8 (1982), in the instant case, because of widespread publicity, General John F. Wall, the Director of Civil Works at the national headquarters of the Corps, decided to review the NE Corps' decision. Wall reached a different conclusion. He decided to grant the permit after finding that Pyramid's offsite mitigation proposal would reduce the adverse impacts sufficiently to allow the "practicable alternative" test to be deemed satisfied. He stated:

> In a proper case, mitigation measures can be said to reduce adverse impacts of a proposed activity to the point where there is no 'easily identifiable difference in impact' between the proposed activity (including mitigation) versus the alternatives to that activity.

Although he did not explicitly address the issue, Wall apparently assumed that the relevant time to determine whether there was a practicable alternative was the time of the application, not the time the applicant entered the market. In other words, Wall appears to have assumed that the market entry theory was not the correct approach. For example, while addressing the traditional "practicable alternatives" analysis as an alternative ground for his decision, Wall found that the North Attleboro site was unavailable "because it has been optioned by another developer." Since the site was *not* optioned at the time EPA argues Pyramid entered the market, this language suggests (to Pyramid at least) that Wall could not have been employing the market entry approach.

On May 31, 1985, Wall ordered the NE Corps to send Pyramid, EPA and FWS a notice of its intent to grant the permit. The NE Corps complied on June 28, 1985.

On July 23, 1985, EPA's RA initiated a §404(c) review of the Corps' decision. Following the procedure set forth in 40 C.F.R. Part 231 (discussed above), EPA published notice of its intent to prohibit the project in the *Federal Register*; held a public hearing on September 26, 1985; and permitted a period for public comment which closed on October 4, 1985. A second hearing was held on November 18, 1985.

On March 4, 1986, the RA recommended that EPA veto the permit because of adverse impacts on wildlife and available "practicable alternatives." In particular, the RA found that Pyramid had not overcome the presumption that an alternative existed, in part because Pyramid had failed to provide information on the availability of the North Attleboro site. After first refusing to provide the information, Pyramid later had claimed "there is no further or more detailed information. It simply does not exist." The RA alternatively reasoned that the North Attleboro site had been available to DeBartolo, and that EPA should attribute this availability to Pyramid because Pyramid had benefitted from DeBartolo's application for state approval.

On May 13, 1986, EPA issued its final determination, which prohibited Pyramid from using Sweedens Swamp. It found (1) that the filling of the Swamp would adversely affect wildlife; (2) that the North Attleboro site could have been available to Pyramid at the time Pyramid investigated the area to search for a site; (3) that considering Pyramid's failure or unwillingness to provide further materials about its investigation of alternative sites, it was uncontested that, at best, Pyramid never checked the availability of the North Attleboro site as an alternative; (4) that the North Attleboro site was feasible and would have a less adverse impact on the wetland environment; and (5) that the mitigation proposal did not make the project preferable to other alternatives because of scientific uncertainty of success. In the second of these findings, EPA used what Pyramid calls the "market entry" approach.

On July 1, 1986, Pyramid commenced the instant action in the district court to vacate EPA's final determination as arbitrary and capricious. After the parties filed cross-motions for summary judgment, the newspapers reported that Pyramid intended to enter a joint venture with NED to build a mall at the North Attleboro site. Affidavits submitted concerning this development did not indicate whether Pyramid planned to continue the Sweedens Swamp project. Since the joint venture agreement was still in draft form, EPA did not take the position that the case was moot.

On October 6, 1987, the court granted EPA's motion for summary judgment. The court stated that, with regard to the market entry theory, EPA's interpretation of its regulations was entitled to deference. This appeal followed.

For the reasons which follow, we AFFIRM.

II

One of Pyramid's principal contentions is that the market entry approach is inconsistent with both the language of the 404(b)(1) guidelines and the past practice of the Corps and EPA.

A

With regard to the language of the regulations, Pyramid reasons that the 404(b)(1) guidelines are framed in the present tense, while the market entry approach focuses on the *past by considering whether a practicable alternative was* available at the time the applicant entered the market to search for a site. To support its argument that the 404(b)(1) guidelines are framed in the present tense, Pyramid quotes the following language:

> An alternative is practicable if it *is* available.... If it is otherwise a practicable alternative, an area not *presently* owned by the applicant which *could* reasonably *be* obtained, utilized, expanded or managed in order to fulfill the basic purpose of the proposed activity *may be* considered.

40 C.F.R. §230.10(a)(2) (emphasis added). It then argues that EPA says "is" means "was." It cites *Gwaltney of Smithfield v. Chesapeake Bay Foundation,* 484 U.S. 49, 108 S.Ct. 376, 381, 98 L.Ed.2d 306 (1987), to indicate that the Supreme Court believes that the "most natural" reading of present tense language in §505(a) of the Act refers only to the present and future.

While this argument has a certain surface appeal, we are persuaded that it is contrary to a common sense reading of the regulations; that it entails an overly literal and narrow interpretation of the language; and that it creates requirements not intended by Congress.

First, while it is true that the language is in the present tense, it does not follow that the "most natural" reading of the regulations would create a time-of-application rule. As EPA points out, "the regulations do not indicate *when* it is to be determined whether an alternative 'is' available," (emphasis in original) *i.e.,* the "present" of the regulations might be the time the application is submitted; the time it is reviewed; or any number of other times. Based upon a reading of the language in the context of the controlling statute and the regulations as a whole, moreover, we conclude that when the agencies drafted the language in question they simply were not thinking of the specific issues raised by the instant case, in which an applicant had available alternatives at the time it was selecting its site but these alternatives had evaporated by the time it applied for a permit. We therefore agree with the district court that the regulations are essentially silent on the issue of timing and that it would be appropriate to consider the objectives of the Act and the intent underlying the promulgation of the regulations. *Bersani, supra,* 674 F. Supp. at 412.

Second, as EPA has pointed out, the preamble to the 404(b)(1) guidelines states that the purpose of the "practicable alternatives" analysis is "to recognize the special value of wetlands and to avoid their unnecessary destruction, particularly where practicable alternatives were available in non-aquatic areas to achieve the basic purpose of the proposal." 45 *Fed. Reg.* 85,338 (1980) (emphasis added). In other words, the purpose is to create an incentive for developers to avoid choosing wetlands when they could choose an alternative upland site. Pyramid's reading of the regulations would thwart this purpose because it would remove the incentive for a developer to search for an alternative site at the time such an incentive is needed, *i.e.,* at the time it is making the decision to select a particular site. If the practicable alternatives analysis were applied to the time of the application for a permit, the developer would have little incentive to search for alternatives, especially if it were confident that alternatives soon would disappear. Conversely, in a case in which alternatives were not available at the time the developer made its selection, but became available by the time of application, the developer's application would be denied even though it could not have explored the alternative site at the time of its decision.

Pyramid attacks this reasoning by arguing that few developers would take the risk that an available alternative site would become unavailable and that EPA's reading improperly considers the motives and subjective state of mind of the applicant. These arguments are wide of the mark. Whether most real-life developers would take such a risk is irrelevant. The point is that Pyramid's time-of-application theory is completely at odds with the expressed intent of the regulations to provide an incentive to avoid choosing wetlands. Similarly, EPA's interpretation does not require courts to investigate the subjective state of mind of a developer. EPA discusses state-of-mind issues only because it is discussing the *purpose* behind the regulations, which is concerned with incentives, and thus in fact is indirectly concerned with the developer's state of mind.

In short, we conclude that a common-sense reading of the statute can lead only to the use of the market entry approach used by EPA....

We turn next to the issue of whether EPA's interpretation of the 404(b)(1) guidelines is entitled to the deference usually accorded an agency with regard to its interpretation of regulations it is charged with administering, *see EPA v. National Crushed Stone Ass'n,* 449 U.S. 64, 83, 66 L.Ed.2d 268, 101 S.Ct. 295 (1980), and participated in formulating. See also *United States v. Hescorp, Heavy Equip. Sales Corp.,* 801 F.2d 70, 76 (2 Cir.), *cert. denied,* 479 U.S. 1018, 107 S.Ct. 672, 93 L.Ed. 2d 723 (1986). The district court implied in its decision that it was according EPA such deference in examining its market entry approach.

Pyramid contends that such deference was unwarranted because two agencies—EPA and the Corps—developed and administered the regulations, and the Corps reached a different conclusion from that of EPA on the market entry issue. It asserts that, contrary to EPA's market entry approach, the "Corps' position is that the availability should be determined as of the time an application is under review." Pyramid points out that under §404(b) the regulations are to be developed by EPA "in conjunction with" the Secretary of the Army (who acts through the Corps). It cites *General Elec. Co. v. Gilbert,* 429 U.S. 125, 144-45, 97 S.Ct. 401, 50 L.Ed. 2d 343 (1976), for the proposition that a court must use its own judgment in construing a regulation when two agencies with responsibility for administering it reach divergent conclusions. It also contends that the Corps has greater experience with and expertise in assessing the "availability" of alternatives than EPA, because it is the Corps that makes the initial decision on thousands of applications while EPA reviews under §404(c) only rarely. Furthermore, Pyramid claims that the availability analysis implicates zoning, economic and financial issues, not environmental ones.

In response, EPA asserts that the Corps did not take a developed opposing policy position on the issue of what time is relevant in the "practicable alternatives" analysis. The reason for this is that the Corps, acting through General Wall, based its decision primarily on its finding that Pyramid's mitigation proposal was workable. EPA also asserts, on the issue of its expertise, that its "selective and most infrequent invocation" of its veto power underscores EPA's "seriousness" about using the veto. Finally EPA asserts that the Act's legislative history indicates that Congress intended EPA to have the "final word" on any disputes with the Corps.

While none of EPA's assertions is entirely persuasive, there also are difficulties with Pyramid's position. It is undeniable, for example, that Wall in fact did find that the North Attleboro site was "unavailable" and thus it appears that the Corps tacitly was applying a time-of-application test. On the other hand, it is possible that Wall believed that Pyramid did not enter the market until after NED had purchased the North Attleboro site. Accordingly, Wall may have found the alternative site "unavailable" under the market entry approach. Pyramid's and EPA's other arguments similarly cut both ways or are inconclusive.

Even if we are not thoroughly persuaded that EPA's interpretation was entitled to deference, however, we nevertheless conclude that the district court's decision in its favor must be upheld. As Pyramid itself points out (to the detriment of its argument), the issue of deference is separate from the issue of the standards of review of the district court and of our Court.

On appeal, we must subject the district court's judgment to plenary review, *Potenze v. New York Shipping Ass'n,* 804 F.2d 235, 239 (2 Cir. 1986), *cert. denied,* 481 U.S. 1029, 107 S.Ct. 1955, 95 L.Ed. 2d 528 (1987), and apply the same summary judgment test as applied by the district court. *See T. W. Elec. Serv., Inc. v. Pacific Elec. Contractors Ass'n,* 809 F.2d 626, 630 (9 Cir. 1987). An agency's interpretation of its own regulations raises a question of law, *White Indus. v. FAA,* 692 F.2d 532, 534 (8 Cir. 1982), and thus is freely reviewable by our Court. *Pennzoil Co. v. FERC,* 789 F.2d 1128, 1135 (5 Cir. 1986).

The standard of review for the district court in this case is that the court shall set aside EPA's findings, conclusions or actions only if they are "arbitrary, capricious, an abuse of discretion, or otherwise not in accordance with law." Administrative Procedure Act §10(e), 5 U.S.C. §706(2)(A) (1982). As stated by the Supreme Court in *Motor Vehicle Mfrs. Ass'n v. State Farm Mut. Auto. Ins. Co.,* 463 U.S. 29, 77 L.Ed. 2d 443, 103 S.Ct. 2856 (1983),

> A reviewing court may not set aside an agency rule that is rational, based on consideration of the relevant factors, and within the scope of the authority delegated to the agency by the statute.... The scope of review under the 'arbitrary and capricious' standard is narrow and a court is not to substitute its judgment for that of the agency. Nevertheless, the agency must examine the relevant data and articulate a satisfactory explanation for its action including a 'rational connection between the facts found and the choice made.'"

Id. at 42-43 (quoting *Burlington Truck Lines, Inc. v. United States,* 371 U.S. 156, 168, 9 L.Ed.2d 207, 83 S.Ct. 239 (1962)).

Applying these standards, we are convinced that EPA's market entry interpretation was reasonable, and therefore was neither "arbitrary and capricious" nor "not in accordance with law." We therefore hold that the district court correctly found that EPA's interpretation of the regulations was reasonable.

We AFFIRM the district court's decision in all respects.

V

To summarize:

We hold (1) that the market entry theory is consistent with both the regulatory language and past practice; (2) that EPA's interpretation, while not necessarily entitled to deference, is reasonable and its application of its rule is supported by the record; and (3) that Pyramid's other arguments lack merit.

AFFIRMED.

[Dissenting Opinion and Footnotes omitted.]

See also *U.S. v. Mango*, 199 F.3d 85 (2d Cir. 1999); *Town of Norfolk v. U.S. Army Corps of Engineers*, 968 F.2d 1438 (1st Cir. 1992); *Smerka v. Glass*, 945 F.2d 405 (6th Cir. 1991); *Sylvester v. U.S. Army Corps of Engineers*, 882 F.2d 407 (9th Cir. 1989); *Louisiana Wildlife Federation, Inc. v. York*, 603 F.Supp. 518 (W.D.La. 1985), *aff'd. in part and vacated in part*, 761 F.2d 1044 (5th Cir. 1985).

The *Guidelines* are divided into eight subparts, two of which will be considered in this text: Subpart A, 40 C.F.R. §§230.1-230.7, which outlines general policy, definitions, and procedures to be followed; and, Subpart B, 40 C.F.R. §§230.10-230.12, which outlines restrictions on discharge, factual determinations to be made, and findings of compliance or non-compliance with the general restrictions on discharge.

In applying the Guidelines to determine whether a potential discharge may be permitted, the Corps must follow a specific procedure. First, it reviews the restrictions on discharge set forth in 40 C.F.R. §§230.10(a) through (d), then the minimization actions in 40 C.F.R. §§230.70 through 230.77, and then the factual determinations required to be made in 40 C.F.R. §230.11.

Next the Corps must determine whether any general permits apply. 40 C.F.R. §230.5(b). This regulation refers the Corps to 40 C.F.R. §230.7, "General Permits," which restates the familiar conditions for issuance of general permits, *i.e.*, (1) that the Corps determine that the activities in the category of activities to be generally permitted are similar in nature and similar in their impact upon water quality and the aquatic environment; (2) that the activities in such category will have only minimal adverse effects when performed separately; and (3) that the activities will have only minimal cumulative adverse effects on water quality and the aquatic environment. Further the Corps, in its evaluation of a potential general permit, must consider the four prohibitions listed in 40 C.F.R. §230.10(b), namely (1) that the discharge may not cause or contribute to violations of any applicable state water quality standard; (2) that the discharge may not violate any applicable toxic effluent standard or prohibition; (3) that the discharge may not jeopardize the continued existence of endangered or threatened species or result in the likelihood of destruction or adverse modification of a critical habitat unless an exemption has been granted; and (4) that the discharge may not violate any requirement imposed to protect any designated marine sanctuary, and to 40 C.F.R. §230.10(c), which states the factors to be considered by the Corps in issuing a general permit, namely that there be no discharge which cause or contribute to significant degradation of waters of the United States.

If no general permits apply, the Corps then must examine "practicable alternatives" to the proposed discharge which are either to not allow the discharge at all, or to permit the discharge but into an alternative aquatic site with potentially less damaging consequences after determining proposed alternative sites by applying certain specific factors listed in 40 C.F.R. §230.10(a). If the Corps decides to permit the discharge, it must then "delineate the candidate disposal site" following the criteria and evaluations set forth in 40 C.F.R. §230.11(f). 40 C.F.R. §230.5(d). Generally the "mixing zone" between the discharge and the aquatic environment "shall be confined to the smallest practicable zone within each specified disposal site" taking into consideration the type of dispersion determined to be appropriate unless, under "unique environmental conditions" in which widespread dispersion by natural means will not result in significant adverse environmental effects, the discharge may be spread in a very thin layer over a large area. 40 C.F.R. §230.11(f)(1). To make the foregoing determination, the Corps must consider ten factors including the depth of the water at the disposal site; the current velocity, direction, and variability; the degree of turbulence; any stratification attributable to causes such as obstructions, salinity or density profiles; discharge vessel speed and direction if appropriate; the rate of discharge; any ambient concentration of constituents of interest; the dredged material characteristics particularly concentrations of constituents, amount of material, type of material, and settling velocities; the number of discharge actions per unit of time; and any other factors that affect rates and patterns of mixing. 40 C.F.R. §230.11(f)(2).

Next, following Subpart C, the Corps must determine the potential impacts on the physical and chemical characteristics of the aquatic ecosystem by considering the effects on the substrate, the suspended particulates, the chemistry and physical characteristics of the receiving water, current patterns and water circulation, normal water fluctuations such as daily, seasonal, and annual tidal and flood fluctuations, and existing salinity gradients. The Corps then must evaluate any special or critical characteristics of the candidate disposal site and any surrounding areas which may be affected related to their living communities or human uses following the factors listed in Subparts D, E, and F: potential impacts upon biological characteristics including threatened and endangered species, fish, crustaceans, mollusks, and other aquatic organisms in the food web, and other wildlife; potential impacts upon special aquatic sites including sanctuaries and refuges, wetlands, mud flats, vegetated shallows, coral reefs, and riffle and pool complexes; and potential impacts upon human use characteristics including municipal and private water supplies, recreational and commercial fisheries, water-related recreation, aesthetics, and parks, national and historical monuments, national seashores, wilderness areas, research sites, and other similar preserves.

Next the Corps will review its factual determinations to ensure that the information meets the requirements of 40 C.F.R. §230.11. The Corps must also evaluate the material to be discharged to determine the possibility of chemical contamination or physical incompatibility using the procedures outlined in 40 C.F.R. §§230.60 and 230.61. The Corps must also consider appropriate and practicable changes to the project plan to minimize the environmental impact of the discharge by changing the location of the discharge, changing the material to be discharged, controlling the material after its discharge, changing the method of dispersion, use of appropriate technology, design, and equipment, minimizing the adverse effects of plant and animal populations, minimizing adverse effects on human uses, and other miscellaneous actions in special kinds of projects.

All of these Corps factual determinations, findings of compliance, and minimization actions must be made in writing. Even so, the regulations recognize that some projects may be so minor or routine that a full-blown determination with written findings is not necessary, that "different levels of effort ... should be associated with varying degrees of impact and require or prepare commensurate documentation."

Chapter 19

WATER DEPENDENCY

In the short history of the Clean Water Act, a few of the *Guidelines* have been applied more frequently and/or with more sweeping effect than others. One of the more notable *Guidelines* is a regulatory presumption that practicable alternatives which do not involve discharges into wetlands are available when the project "does not require access or proximity to or siting within" a wetland to fulfill the project's basic purpose, *i.e.*, is not "water dependent", unless the applicant can clearly demonstrate otherwise. Lack of water-dependency may be very broad. Proposed houses with their own boat slips are not water-dependent. *Korteweg v. U.S. Army Corps of Engineers*, 650 F.Supp. 603 (D.Conn. 1986). On the other hand, a county water supply reservoir was held to be "water-dependent" perhaps on the basis that the "alternatives" proposed by the EPA did not persuade the Court as "practicable." *James City County, Virginia v. EPA*, 955 F.2d 254 (4th Cir. Va. 1992), *cert. denied*, 130 L.Ed.2d 39, 115 S.Ct. 87 (1994).

CHAPTER 20

SIGNIFICANT DEGRADATION OF WATER

Similar to the "recapture provision" applicable to Nationwide Permits, the regulations provide that even if the applicant can pass all of the factual determinations and minimization requirements, if the Corps still finds that the project's discharge would cause a "significant degradation of waters of the United States," the Corps may deny a permit. The finding of a significant degradation must be based upon the factual determinations, evaluations, and tests described above but it must also pay special heed to the "persistence and permanence" of the adverse effects and may be considered individually or collectively. 40 C.F.R. §230.10(c).

Some of these catch-all adverse effects are the discharge of pollutants which affects human health or welfare (including municipal water supplies, plankton, fish, shellfish, wildlife, and special aquatic sites); on the life stages of aquatic life and other wildlife dependent on aquatic ecosystems (including the transfer, concentration, and spread of pollutants or their by products outside of the disposal site through biological, physical, and chemical processes); on aquatic ecosystem diversity, productivity, and stability (including loss of fish and wildlife habitat or the loss of the capacity of a wetland to assimilate nutrients, purify water, or reduce wave energy); and, on recreational, aesthetic, and economic values.

Chapter 21
OTHER CONSIDERATIONS

Non-Wetlands Environmental Effects

The Corps may consider other factors than simply the direct effect of a discharge of dredged or fill material in a wetland when making its permit decision. As has been discussed above, there are many opportunities in the regulations for the Corps to accept advice and comments from other agencies particularly the U.S. Fish and Wildlife Service. State and local land use and zoning decisions will not be considered.

Socio-Economic Effects

The Corps is permitted to consider to a limited extent socio-economic effects of permit applications under §10 of the Rivers and Harbors Act but not under §404 of the Clean Water Act. However, the Corps insists that it will continue to consider socio-economic effects although District Engineers are cautioned to "give less weight to impacts that are, at best, weakly related to the purpose of our permit action and statutory authority, and not let such impacts be the sole or most important basis for a permit denial." *See also Mall Properties v. Marsh*, 672 F.Supp. 561 (D.Mass. 1987), *appeal dismissed*, 841 F.2d 440 (1st Cir. 1988), *cert. denied*, 488 U.S. 848, 102 L.Ed.2d 101, 109 S.Ct. 129 (1988); Regulatory Guidance Letter No. 88-11, *Mall Properties v. Marsh, Inc.*, August 22, 1988.

Indirect Effects

The Corps has attempted to distinguish between attenuated and non-attenuated indirect impacts and tries to consider the attenuated indirect impacts less heavily. Some examples of indirect impacts are water withdrawals for hydroelectric power generation on downstream aquatic communities and spin-off development from a major project. The Corps considers the spin-off development to be attenuated and thus not entitled to "heavy" consideration. On the other hand, the effect on downstream aquatic communities, while also indirect, is not attenuated and thus must be considered "heavily."

RIVERSIDE IRRIGATION DISTRICT v. ANDREWS

758 F.2d 508 (10th Cir. 1985)

The issue in this case is whether the Corps of Engineers exceeded its authority when it denied plaintiffs a nationwide permit for deposit of dredge material for construction of Wildcat Dam and Reservoir. The Corps based its decision on the potential downstream impact on an endangered species due to the resulting increased consumptive use of water.

Plaintiffs seek to build a dam and reservoir on Wildcat Creek, a tributary of the South Platte River. Because construction of the dam involves depositing dredge and fill material in a navigable waterway, the plaintiffs are required to obtain a permit from the Corps of Engineers under Section 404 of the Clean Water Act, 33 U.S.C. §1344. The regulations under the Clean Water Act create categories of nationwide permits that provide automatic authority to place fill material if certain conditions are met. 33 C.F.R. §330.4. If the conditions are not met, the party must seek an individual permit through a public notice and hearing process. The Corps determined that the proposed deposit did not meet the required conditions because the increased use of water that the resulting reservoir would facilitate would deplete the stream flow and endanger a critical habitat of the whooping crane, an endangered species. The Corps therefore informed the plaintiffs that they would be required to obtain an individual permit before the project could proceed.

Plaintiffs filed this suit seeking declaratory and injunctive relief and review of the agency action, claiming that the project is entitled to proceed under a nationwide permit and that the Corps exceeded its authority when it considered the effect of depletions caused by consumptive use of the water to be stored in the reservoir. An interlocutory appeal was taken from the district court's decision denying the government's motion to dismiss for lack of jurisdiction. This court affirmed the trial court, and remanded "for a determination whether the Engineer acted within his authority and to resolve whatever issues may remain." *Riverside Irrigation District v. Stipo,* 658 F.2d 762, 768 (10th Cir.1981). On remand, the district court held that the engineer had acted within his authority and that he was required, under the Clean Water Act and the Endangered Species Act, to deny the nationwide permit. Plaintiffs appeal.

A nationwide permit is one covering a category of activities occurring throughout the country that involve discharges of dredge or fill material that will cause only minimal adverse effects on the environment when performed separately and that will have only minimal cumulative effects. *See* 33 U.S.C. §1344(e)(1). Such a permit is automatic in that if one qualifies, no application is needed before beginning the discharge activity. *Riverside Irrigation District v. Andrews,* 568 F. Supp. 583, 585 (D.Colo.1983). The Corps has the authority and duty, however, to ensure that parties seeking to proceed under a nationwide permit meet the requirements for such action. One condition of a nationwide permit is that the discharge not destroy a threatened or endangered species as identified under the Endangered Species Act, or destroy or adversely modify the critical habitat of such species. 33 C.F.R. §330.4(b)(2). The regulations thus are consistent with the Corps' obligation, under the Endangered Species Act, to ensure that "any action authorized, funded, or carried out by such agency ... is not likely to jeopardize the continued existence of any endangered species or threatened species or result in the destruction or adverse modification of habitat of such species which is determined by the Secretary ... to be critical." 16 U.S.C. §1536(a)(2).

No one claims that the fill itself will endanger or destroy the habitat of an endangered species or adversely affect the aquatic environment. However, the fill that the Corps is authorizing is required to build the earthen dam. The dam will result in the impoundment of water in a reservoir, facilitating the use of the water in Wildcat Creek. The increased consumptive use will allegedly deplete the stream flow, and it is this depletion that the Corps found would adversely affect the habitat of the whooping crane.

The Endangered Species Act does not, by its terms, enlarge the jurisdiction of the Corps of Engineers under the Clean Water Act. *Riverside Irrigation District,* 568 F.2d at 588; *cf. United States v. Stoeco Homes, Inc.,* 498 F.2d 597, 607 (3d Cir. 1974) (federal environmental statutes do not enlarge the Corps' jurisdiction under the Rivers and Harbors Appropriations Act). However, it imposes on agencies a mandatory obligation to consider the environmental impacts of the projects that they authorize or fund. As the Supreme Court stated in *TVA v. Hill,* 437 U.S. 153, 173, 98 S. Ct. 2279, 2291, 57 L. Ed. 2d 117 (1978):

> One would be hard pressed to find a statutory provision whose terms were any plainer than those of §7 of the Endangered Species Act. Its very words affirmatively command all federal agencies "to *insure* that actions *authorized, funded or carried out* by them do not jeopardize the continued existence" of an endangered species or "result in the destruction or adverse modification of habitat of such species." 16 U.S.C. §1536. This language admits of no exception.

(emphasis in original). The question in this case is how broadly the Corps is authorized to look under the Clean Water Act in determining the environmental impact of the discharge that it is authorizing.

Plaintiffs claim that the Corps is authorized to consider only the direct, onsite effects of the discharge, particularly the effects on water quality, and that the Corps exceeded its authority by considering downstream effects of changes in water quantity. However, both the statute and the regulations authorize the Corps to consider downstream effects of changes in water quantity as well as on-site changes in water quality in determining whether a proposed discharge qualifies for a nationwide permit. The statute explicitly requires that a permit be obtained for any discharge "incidental to any activity having as its purpose bringing an area of navigable waters into a use to which it was not previously subject, where the flow or circulation of navigable waters may be impaired or the reach of such waters reduced." 33 U.S.C. §1344(f)(2). The guidelines for determining compliance with section 404(b)(1), developed by the Secretary of the Army and the Environmental Protection Agency, require the permitting authority to consider factors related to water quantity, including the effects of the discharge on water velocity, current patterns, water circulation, and normal water fluctuations. 40 C.F.R. §§230.23, 230.24. Thus, the statute focuses not merely on water quality, but rather on all of the effects on the "aquatic environment" caused by replacing water with fill material. 33 U.S.C. §1344(f)(1)(E). *Minnehaha Creek Watershed District v. Hoffman,* 597 F.2d 617, 627 (8th Cir.1979).

Plaintiffs argue that, even if the Corps can consider effects of changes in water quantity, it can do so only when the change is a direct effect of the discharge. In the present case, the depletion of water is an indirect effect of the discharge, in that it results from the increased consumptive use of water facilitated by the discharge. However, the Corps is required, under both the Clean Water Act and the Endangered Species Act, to consider the environmental impact of the discharge that it is authorizing. To require it to ignore the indirect effects that result from its actions would be to require it to wear blinders that Congress has not chosen to impose. The fact that the reduction in water does not result "from direct federal action does not lessen the appellee's duty under §7 [of the Endangered Species Act]." *National Wildlife Federation v. Coleman,* 529 F.2d 359, 374 (5th Cir.1976). The relevant consideration is the total impact of the discharge on the crane. *Id.* at 373. In *National Wildlife Federation,* the Fifth Circuit held that the federal agency was required to consider both the direct and the indirect impacts of proposed highway construction, including the residential and commercial development that would develop around the highway interchanges. Similarly, in this case, the Corps was required to consider all effects, direct and indirect, of the discharge for which authorization was sought.

The cases cited by the plaintiffs to the contrary are not controlling. Each involves the National Environmental Protection Act (NEPA), which authorizes the government to look at environmental concerns only when there is "major federal action." 42 U.S.C. §4332(2)(C) (1976). Thus, in each, the question is whether the project is sufficiently federal to require an environmental impact statement at all. The Clean Water Act does not require major federal action before the

Corps must consider environmental impacts. Rather, the Corps must consider the environmental impact of each act that it authorizes, both major and minor. In creating categories of nationwide permits, the Corps has "acted" to authorize discharges. Thus, simply allowing a party to proceed under the nationwide permit is an action by the Corps triggering its obligation to consider environmental impacts.

There is no authority for the proposition that, once it is required to consider the environmental impact of the discharge that it is authorizing, the Corps is limited to consideration of the direct effects of the discharge. The reduction of water flows resulting from the increased consumptive use *is* an effect, albeit indirect, of the discharge to be authorized by the Corps. The discharge thus may "destroy or adversely modify" the critical habitat of an endangered species, and the Corps correctly found that the proposed project did not meet the requirements for a nationwide permit.

Plaintiffs claim that the Corps cannot deny them a nationwide permit because the denial impairs the state's right to allocate water within its jurisdiction, in violation of section 101(g) of the Act (the "Wallop Amendment"). Even if denial of a nationwide permit is considered an impairment of the state's authority to allocate water, a question that we do not decide, the Corps acted within its authority. As discussed above, the statute and regulations expressly require the Corps to consider changes in water quantity in granting nationwide permits. Section 101(g), which is only a general policy statement, "cannot nullify a clear and specific grant of jurisdiction, even if the particular grant seems inconsistent with the broadly stated purpose." *Connecticut Light and Power Co. v. Federal Power Commission,* 324 U.S. 515, 527, 65 S. Ct. 749, 754, 89 L. Ed. 1150 (1945). Thus, the Corps did not exceed its authority in denying a nationwide permit based on its determination that the depletion in water flow resulting from increased consumptive use of water would adversely affect the critical habitat of the whooping crane.

The Wallop Amendment does, however, indicate "that Congress did not want to interfere any more than necessary with state water management." *National Wildlife Federation v. Gorsuch,* 224 U.S. App. D.C. 41, 693 F.2d 156, 178 (D.C.Cir.1982). A fair reading of the statute as a whole makes clear that, where both the state's interest in allocating water and the federal government's interest in protecting the environment are implicated, Congress intended an accommodation. Such accommodations are best reached in the individual permit process.

We need not reach the question raised by plaintiffs of whether Congress can unilaterally abrogate an interstate compact. The action by the Corps has not denied Colorado its right to water use under the South Platte River Compact. All that has been done is to deny them the ability to proceed under a nationwide permit and to require them to apply for an individual permit under public notice and hearing procedures. As plaintiffs may receive an individual permit and be able to proceed with the project, a decision on the question of the impact of the interstate compact would be premature.

We also need not decide whether the project will, in fact, have an adverse impact on the habitat of the whooping crane. Plaintiffs are entitled to proceed under a nationwide permit only if they can show that they meet the conditions for such a permit. Thus, plaintiffs must show "that the discharge will not destroy a threatened or endangered species as identified in the Endangered Species Act or destroy or adversely modify the critical habitat of such species." 33 C.F.R. §330.4(b)(2). The record supports the Corps' finding that the discharge may adversely modify the critical habitat of the whooping crane. Thus, plaintiffs did not meet their burden of showing, as a matter of fact, that the discharge will not have such an adverse impact. The Corps acted within its authority in requiring the plaintiffs to proceed under the individual permit procedure.

AFFIRMED.

CHAPTER 22

MITIGATION

Mitigation differs from the previously-discussed "minimization" in the permit-issuing regulations. "Minimization" requires that the impacts of the proposed activity on a wetland be held to a minimum from the outset of the project design. "Mitigation" comes into play only after the amount of wetland damage has been reduced to its barest minimum but there will still be some damage which must be mitigated. The Environmental Protection Agency defines mitigation in terms of a process: "Mitigation" includes:

- Avoiding the impact altogether by not taking a certain action or parts of an action.
- Minimizing impacts by limiting the degree or magnitude of the action and its implementation.
- Rectifying the impact by repairing, rehabilitating, or restoring the affected environment.
- Reducing or eliminating the impact over time by preservation and maintenance operations during the life of the action.
- Compensating for the impact by replacing or providing substitute resources or environments. 40 CFR §1508.20.

Effective February 7, 1990, the Corps and the Environmental Protection Agency entered into a *Memorandum Of Agreement Between the U.S. Environmental Protection Agency and U.S. Department of the Army Concerning the Determination of Mitigation Under The Clean Water Act Section 404(b)(1) Guidelines*, (February 7, 1990) (hereinafter the *Mitigation MOA*). This *Mitigation MOA* contains a detailed exposition of the mandatory sequence of analysis when considering applications for individual permits which involve issues of compliance with the *Guidelines*. The *Mitigation MOA* recognizes that the national goal of no net loss of wetlands functions and values may not be achieved in every individual permit action because individual mitigation measures are "not feasible, not practicable, or would accomplish only inconsequential reductions in impacts."

In considering whether to allow mitigation, the Corps is required to follow a specific sequence: first it must determine that potential impacts have been avoided to the maximum extent possible, then it must determine that remaining unavoidable impacts will be mitigated "to the extent appropriate and practicable by requiring steps to minimize impacts, and then to compensate for aquatic resource values." The Corps may "deviate" from this sequence when the Corps and the Environmental Protection Agency "agree that the proposed discharge is necessary to avoid environmental harm (*e.g.*, to protect a natural aquatic community from saltwater intrusion, chemical contamination, or other deleterious physical or chemical impacts), or the Environmental Protection Agency and the Corps agree that the proposed discharge can reasonably be expected to result in environmental gain or insignificant environmental losses." Further, the *Mitigation MOA* allows a flexible determination of "appropriate and practicable", *i.e.*, one which is "appropriate to the scope and degree of those impacts and practicable in terms of cost, existing technology, and logistics in light of overall project purposes."

The overriding principle of permit issuance is the avoidance of impacts such that no discharge will be permitted if there is a practicable alternative to the proposed discharge which would have a less adverse impact on the aquatic ecosystem, so long as the alternative does not have other significant adverse environmental consequences. Therefore, the first step for the Corps is to determine the least environmentally damaging practicable alternative. Compensatory mitigation is forbidden in this early determination as a method to reduce environmental impacts.

The second step is for the Corps to require appropriate and practicable project modifications and permit conditions in order to minimize the adverse impacts. The *Mitigation MOA* refers the Corps to Subpart H of the *Guidelines* (40 C.F.R. §§230.70-230.77) for the means of minimizing impacts.

Finally, appropriate and practicable compensatory mitigation is required for those impacts remaining after the foregoing avoidance and minimization steps have been satisfied, for the so called "unavoidable" impacts. Compensatory mitigation contemplates the restoration of existing degraded wetlands or the creation of man-made wetlands first of all on-site, or in areas adjacent or contiguous to the discharge site, and only secondarily off-site in the same geographic area (defined as close physical proximity and, to the extent possible, the same watershed) if practicable. In addition to the preference for on-site compensatory mitigation over off-site, the Corps must consider the functional values lost by the resource impacted with particular attention to be paid to the likelihood of success of the effort. Since wetland creation is an uncertain endeavor, restoration is the preferred method of compensatory mitigation.

The *Mitigation MOA* mentions a concept called "mitigation banking." Under this concept, existing wetlands may be purchased and used as compensatory mitigation only if the Corps and the Environmental Protection Agency approve the use of the bank for specified identified projects regardless of the practicability of other forms of compensatory mitigation. The Environmental Protection Agency has developed further specific guidance on this subject.

In considering the amount of required compensatory mitigation in the case of unavoidably impacted wetlands, the *Mitigation MOA* requires a one-to-one acreage replacement of functions and values as a "reasonable surrogate" with "an adequate margin of safety to reflect the expected degree of success associated with the mitigation plan, recognizing that this minimum requirement may not be appropriate and practicable, and thus may not be relevant in all cases." The one-to-one requirement may be modified if the functional values of the impacted wetland are high and the likelihood of success of the mitigation project is low, or, inversely, if the functional value is low and the likelihood of success is high.

The *Mitigation MOA* also requires that mitigators engage in monitoring the compensatory mitigation especially in areas of "scientific uncertainty." If the Corps determines that the mitigation effort is failing, it is authorized to follow the procedures outlined for enforcement in 33 C.F.R. §326 to "ensure those waters (of the United States) are not misused and to maintain the integrity of the program." A permissible permit condition is to require long-term monitoring in mitigation efforts involving "higher levels of scientific uncertainty," however, if the mitigation plan is neither "reasonably implementable or enforceable, the permit shall be denied."

Chapter 23

OTHER APPROVALS

In addition to obtaining a §404 permit, applicants must always obtain a state water quality certificate, and frequently must obtain other approvals as well. The Corps, too, is required to consult with other agencies with respect to permit review. *Memorandum of Agreement Between the Environmental Protection Agency and the Department of the Army Concerning Clean Water Act Section 404(q)*, (August 11, 1992); *Memorandum of Agreement Between the Department of Commerce and the Department of the Army Concerning Clean Water Act Section 404(q)*, (August 11, 1992); *Memorandum of Agreement between the Department of the Interior and the Department of the Army, Concerning Clean water Act Section 404(q)*, (December 21, 1992). If there is a dispute between the Corps and these agencies, these *Memoranda* require that the dispute be "elevated" to a higher level within the agency so as to avoid delay in individual permit decisions when there is policy dispute.

State Water Quality Certification

The Clean Water Act and the regulations require that any applicant for a §404 permit "that may result in a discharge of a pollutant into waters of the United States" also obtain a certification from the discharge-originating state or the interstate water pollution control agency which has jurisdiction over the point source of the pollution that the discharge will comply with the "applicable effluent limitations and water quality standards." Although technically no permit will be granted until the certification has been obtained, a waiver by the certifying agency may be deemed to have occurred if the agency fails to act within 60 days of the request. The Corps has the authority to notify the agency that a shorter period of time than 60 days may be required, and, conversely, the Corps may determine that a longer period will be necessary based on information provided by the agency. In no event will this time enlargement last longer than one year.

Once the certification has been issued prior to the permit decision, any subsequent denial or modification of the certification will not affect ordinarily a §404 permit but the Corps may consider the subsequent denial or modification as part of the public interest review and may respond accordingly. However, if the Corps finds that there has been a "sufficient change" in the project such then the Corps may require that a new water quality certification be applied for. An exception to this process is when a state court voids a certification prior to the §404 permit issuance. In that case, the Corps cannot issue the §404 permit until the certification is "legally revived," *i.e.*, by the appellate process, re-issuance, or waiver.

After the §404 permit has been issued, a subsequent denial or modification of a certification or the certification is voided by a court, will not necessarily affect the terms of the §404 permit but the Corps may consider modification, suspension, or revocation of the §404 permit. *See also* Regulatory Guidance Letter no. 90-4, *Water Quality Considerations*, March 13, 1990.

Coastal Zone Management Program

Obviously not all states have a coastal zone management program but among those that do, the Coastal Zone Management Act, 16 U.S.C. §1456(c), requires the applicant to furnish another certification that the proposed activity will comply with the state's coastal zone management program. The procedure for obtaining the certificate is a little different from the water quality certification. The applicant submits his "certification" directly to the Corps which then sends a copy of the public notice, including the applicant's certification, to the National Oceanic and Atmospheric Administration (which administers the federal Coastal Zone Management Act, and to the relevant state coastal zone management agency requesting its concurrence or objection. If the state agency objects, the Corps cannot issue the §404 permit until the state agency concurs or is overruled by the Secretary of Commerce on the grounds that the proposed activity is consistent with the federal coastal zone management program or is "necessary in the interest of national security." The state agency has only six months to concur or object after which concurrence is conclusively presumed. *See also* Regulatory Guidance Letter No. 92-4, *Section 401 Water Quality Certification and Coastal Zone Management Act Conditions for Nationwide Permits*, September 14, 1992.

Marine Protection, Research, and Sanctuaries Act

The applicant should determine whether his proposed activities will take place in an area which has been designated as a marine sanctuary by the Secretary of Commerce under the Marine Protection, Research, and Sanctuaries Act, 16 U.S.C. §1432. If so, then the proposed activities must also be certified by the Secretary as consistent with the purposes of the Act and consistent with the regulations under the Act. Generally these areas are in coastal areas.

Environmental Impact Statement

The regulations require that the provisions of the National Environmental Policy Act apply to the §404 permit process although generally only for small portions of larger federal projects. For most §404 permit applications, the Corps will require only an Environmental Assessment, reserving the requirement of a full Environmental Impact Statement for large projects with considerable federal involvement.

National Historic Preservation Act

Under the National Historic Preservation Act, the Advisory Council on Historic Preservation is authorized to review and comment upon federally-licensed activities which will have an effect upon properties listed (or eligible for listing) in the National Register of Historic Places. Whenever a project "alters any terrain such that significant historical or archaeological data is threatened, the Secretary of the Interior may take action necessary to recover and preserve the data prior to the commencement of the project." The Corps' regulations state that §404 permit application actions "should, insofar as possible, be consistent with, and avoid significant adverse effects on the values or purposes for which" a classification such as the National Register of Historic Places was established. The Corps should attempt to reach an agreement with the Federal Advisory Council on Historic Preservation on how the project will be carried out but, if no agreement is possible, the Corps may proceed to permit issuance without it.

Interstate Land Sales Full Disclosure Act

The Interstate Land Sales Full Disclosure Act (15 U.S.C. §1701 *et seq.*) requires a developer, prior to selling or leasing any lot in a subdivision (defined in 15 U.S.C. §1701(3)), to provide a written report which states whether or not a §404 permit has been applied for, issued, or denied; and/or whether any enforcement action has been taken as a consequence of any non-application for or denial of a permit.

Endangered Species Act

The Endangered Species Act declares a dual intent to conserve threatened and endangered species as well as the ecosystems on which those species depend. In conserving ecosystems, even those beyond the geographic area of the project in question if the Corps finds that the activity will have a physical effect on off-site endangered species or if the project can be redesigned to avoid the effect on endangered species, the Corps must consult with the U.S. Fish and Wildlife Service and the National Marine Fisheries Service to take any action necessary to insure that a §404 licensed project "is not likely to jeopardize the continued existence of such endangered or threatened species or result in the destruction or adverse modification of habitat of such species" which the Secretaries of Commerce or Interior have determined to be critical.

SAVE THE BAY, INC. v. UNITED STATES CORPS OF ENGINEERS

610 F.2d 322 (5th Cir. 1980), *cert. denied* 449 U.S. 900, 101 S.Ct. 269, 66 L.Ed.2d 130 (1980)

Appellant appeals from the District Court's adoption and entry of judgment in conformity with the refusal of the United States Magistrate, acting on behalf of the District Court by consent of the parties, to require the United States Corps of Engineers to prepare an Environmental Impact Statement (EIS) as provided for under the National Environmental Policy Act of 1969 (NEPA), 42 U.S.C. §4321 *et seq*. Appellants argue the Court below erred in concluding that the environmental assessment by the District Engineer was reasonable and based on substantial evidence, that the activity involved was not a major federal action significantly affecting the quality of the human environment, and that the Corps of Engineers was not required to consider the environmental consequences of the entire project but only the effects of the installation and maintenance of a 24-inch outfall pipeline. Appellees argue on appeal that Appellants have no standing to challenge the actions of the Corps of Engineers. For the reasons stated below, we affirm the ruling of the United States Magistrate.

FACTS

At the time this litigation began, the defendant, E.I. Du Pont De Nemours & Co., Inc., proposed to construct and operate a massive titanium dioxide manufacturing facility in Delisle, Mississippi. Pursuant to this plan, Du Pont sought necessary authorization and permits from appropriate state and federal agencies.

On November 21, 1974, Du Pont sought authorization from the defendant, Army Corps of Engineers, to install a 24-inch diameter effluent line into the marshlands and Bay of St. Louis. The effluent line would carry approximately two million gallons per day of industrial wastewater and discharge it into the Bay of St. Louis. The line would be approximately 2,200 feet in length extending into the Bay and construction would require removal of 610 cubic yards of dredged material from the Bay.

On February 3, 1975, the Mississippi Air and Water Pollution Control Commission, acting pursuant to authority delegated to it by the Environmental Protection Agency, issued a National

Pollutant Discharge Elimination System (NPDES) permit to Du Pont allowing discharge of the wastewater in accordance with the conditions of the permit.

Following solicitation of comments from federal, state and local agencies concerning the proposed pipeline construction permit, the Corps of Engineers announced a public hearing would be held on June 19, 1975, to answer any questions concerning issuing of the pipeline construction permit. In keeping with the Corps' prior determination that only the construction of the pipeline was subject to their regulation, the public notice for the hearing was limited to the installation of the 24-inch diameter pipeline and made no mention of consideration of other aspects of the Du Pont plant in the issuance of its permit. On June 19, 1975 the hearing was held and all proponents and opponents were allowed to express their views. The proponents consisted mostly of governmental or business organizations and generally testified as to the favorable economic impact the plant would have. The opponents, consisting mostly of ecological and recreational organizations, testified generally that a potential danger to marine life existed and that an Environmental Impact Statement was necessary.

On July 17, 1975, Colonel Drake Wilson, District Engineer for the Mobile Corps of Engineers, issued a Statement of Findings assessing the impact the proposed activity would have on the environment. The Corps determined there would be no adverse effect on air quality and that water quality would be only temporarily affected. The findings also noted the issuance of the NPDES permit and that the Environmental Protection Agency had no objection to the issuance of the Corps' permit. The statement, also taking into consideration the determinations of the Mississippi Marine Resources Council and the Gulf Coast Research Laboratory, found there would be no significant adverse effect on land use, visual aesthetics, wildlife, sealife, vegetation, or historical interests. Based on the administrative record, Colonel Wilson directed that the permit be issued. The permit only authorized building the pipeline and was subject to several conditions, one of which required that Du Pont have a proper NPDES permit governing the effluent discharge.

The Plaintiff, Save the Bay, Inc., brought suit pursuant to the National Environmental Policy Act (NEPA) against the United States Army Corps of Engineers, the United States Army, Colonel Drake Wilson, Mobile District Office of the Corps of Engineers, and Du Pont seeking declaratory and injunctive relief and monetary damages. The case was referred to the United States Magistrate by the District Judge and thereafter the defendant's Motions for Summary Judgment were granted and judgment was entered December 16, 1977 dismissing the complaint with prejudice.

STANDING

Save the Bay's complaint alleges that it is a nonprofit corporation organized under the laws of the State of Mississippi; that its membership is primarily composed of numerous full-time and part-time residents of Harrison and Hancock Counties in the State of Mississippi; and that its members will be adversely affected economically, aesthetically and environmentally.

Appellee Du Pont urges on appeal that Save the Bay has failed to establish standing under §10 of the Administrative Procedures Act, 5 U.S.C. §702. Specifically, Du Pont argues that under *Sierra Club v. Morton,* 405 U.S. 727, 92 S.Ct. 1361, 31 L.Ed. 2d 636 (1972) *and United States v. SCRAP,* 412 U.S. 669, 93 S.Ct. 2405, 37 L.Ed. 2d 254 (1973), Save the Bay must allege that its members "use" the area and that the proposed federal action will significantly affect their "use." Du Pont's reliance on *Sierra Club v. Morton, supra,* is misplaced. Here, the Plaintiff has alleged economic, aesthetic and environmental injury to its members and clearly has gone beyond mere general allegations of grievance on behalf of the public interest. Du Pont's argument, that failure to specifically allege "usage" of the geographic area is fatal to Plaintiff's standing, is without merit. An obvious inference of the English language is that residents of a geographical area "use" that geographical area. An allegation of residence coupled with an allegation of injury caused by federal action affecting the area of that residence clearly demonstrates that the party seeking review is among those injured. We fail to see how the acts of camping, hiking, fishing or sightseeing, in a particular geographic location, held sufficient for standing in *United States v. SCRAP, supra,* can be considered more relevant for purposes of standing than can the act of residing in a particular geographic location.

REASONABLENESS OF THE CORPS DECISION

The Court below noted that the standard for review of an agency determination that an Environmental Impact Statement need not be prepared is whether such determination is reasonable. This standard was set forth by this Court in *Save Our Ten Acres v. Kreger,* 472 F.2d 463 (5th Cir. 1973). If the determination is reasonable and made objectively and in good faith on a reviewable environmental record, the determination must be upheld. The Court below found that the environmental assessment prepared by the Corps completely and fully addressed the possible environmental consequences, that the assessment was based on substantial evidence, and that Corps complied with appropriate federal statutes and regulations. Appellants contend that the Corps' determination was unreasonable. They argue that the testimony and evidence offered in opposition to the building of the pipeline and plant should compel the conclusion that an EIS is required. The Appellants further argue that the Corps abdicated its responsibilities by failing to conduct independent studies and by considering the evaluations of other governmental agencies concerning the pipeline's potential adverse effects.

We do not agree with Appellant's contentions. Without detailing every point and counter-point of evidence before the Corps, it is clear that the Corps had testimony, evidence and comments from individuals and governmental agencies which could lead it to reasonably conclude that an EIS would not be necessary. The Corps received and reviewed comments from several governmental agencies as well as from quasi-governmental and business organizations. With little exception, all comments from governmental agencies indicated there would be no significant adverse impact on the environment. We cannot agree with Appellant that consulting with these agencies was improper. The National Environmental Policy Act, 42 U.S.C. §4332(2)(C) requires that federal agencies consult with other agencies whose area of expertise is superior to their own. Of course, this should not be understood as allowing the Corps to base their determination solely on the comments of other agencies. Perhaps the most basic requirement of NEPA is that all federal agencies make an Independent environmental assessment of the proposed action. The Court below correctly recognized this in distinguishing this case from *Mahelona v. Hawaiian Electric Company,* 418 F. Supp. 1328 (D.Hawaii 1976) wherein the Corps of Engineers erroneously considered the advisements of the EPA as determinative and consequently failed to independently determine whether or not the proposed action would have a significant impact on the human environment. For these reasons we hold the Corps' decision was not unreasonable.

A. MAJOR FEDERAL ACTION?

Appellants contend the court below erred in not finding the grant of the pipeline construction permit was a "major Federal action significantly affecting the quality of the human environment," under 42 U.S.C. §4332(2)(C), and therefore requiring preparation of an EIS. In furtherance of this contention they argue that granting almost any Federal permit to this massive multi-million dollar manufacturing plant should trigger the obligations of NEPA.

The Court below held that the provisions of NEPA must be read in context of other language in the Federal Water Pollution Control Act (FWPCA), 33 U.S.C. §1251 *et seq.,* which places control of water pollution caused by discharges of effluents in the hands of the states and the EPA. *United States v. SCRAP, supra.* The court went on to hold, *citing Sierra Club v. Hodel,* 544 F.2d 1036 (9th Cir. 1979) and *Port of Astoria v. Hodel,* 8 ERC 1156, aff'd 595 F.2d 467 (9th Cir. 1979), that the issuance of the Corps' permit was not a sufficient nexus between the Corps and construction of the Du Pont plant to make the Corps a partner in such construction and thereby "federalize" the construction of the Du Pont plant. In other words, the granting of the pipeline permit by the Corps was not a "major Federal action" within the meaning of NEPA.

In addition to the Court's holding, it should also be noted that FWPCA, 33 U.S.C. §1371(c)(1), ordinarily prohibits the issuance of a NPDES permit from being deemed a major Federal action significantly affecting the quality of the human environment within the meaning of NEPA. Furthermore, §(c)(2) prohibits Federal agencies, under guidance of NEPA, from reviewing any effluent limitation under a NPDES permit or from imposing any effluent limitation as a condition precedent to issuance of a license.

The decision of the Court below in no way held that the Corps was precluded from preparing an EIS because of FWPCA, but instead held that the Corps' determination, of whether or not issuance of the construction permit was a "major Federal action," was limited to construction and operation of the pipeline itself and correctly held that the environmental consequences of the effluent was a factor to be excluded from their consideration.

In reaching our conclusion on this point we are not unmindful of the impact that building of this massive manufacturing plant will have on the people of Harrison and Hancock Counties, but the requirements of NEPA do not reach private acts only "major Federal actions." We fail to see how granting of the pipeline construction permit, after issuance of a valid NPDES permit, can be considered a Major Federal action. An examination of the guidelines issued by the Council on Environmental Quality, 40 C.F.R. 1500.6(c), indicates that a private project does not become a "major Federal action" merely because of some incidental federal involvement. In this case, the pipeline itself was not a necessity for operation of the plant. At least one alternative method of discharge, not requiring any Corps permit, was available to Du Pont. We are not saying that the requisite Federal action must be a condition precedent to private action in order for preparation of an EIS to be required. But we do hold that in order for there to exist "major Federal action" some greater involvement, than is present in the case at hand, must exist.

THE PIPELINE OR THE WHOLE PLANT?

Appellant's most vigorously argued point on appeal and perhaps the point which would control the outcome of this case contests the Corps looking only to the environmental consequences of the pipeline construction and maintenance instead of considering the entire Du Pont project in its decision on whether or not to prepare an EIS. Appellants assert that narrowing the scope of inquiry to the pipeline construction alone is the "blinder" approach which should be rejected by this Court. By analogy they compare the Du Pont facility to a living organism which at one end eats chlorine gas and at the other end excretes hydrochloric acid, iron, chromium, zinc, and other nastiness to the tune of 2,000,000 gallons per day. Their argument is that but for the permit there would be no pipeline; without the pipeline there would be no excretion; without the ability to excrete the plant would suffocate in its own waste. They argue that the permit "enables" the plant to exist and therefore the entire plant should be taken into consideration in whether or not the pipeline construction permit should be issued. In support of this "Enablement Theory," appellants *cite Port of Astoria v. Hodel, supra, Mahelona v. Hawaiian Electric Company, Inc., supra, and Citizens for Clean Air, Inc. et al. v. United States Army Corps of Engineers et al.,* 349 F. Supp. 696 (S.D.N.Y.1972).

Upon review of these cases, this Court does not disagree with their reasoning but the circumstances of those cases are clearly distinguishable from those before us. The case of Citizens for Clean Air preceded the FWPCA Amendments of 1972 and therefore is no longer supportive of the proposition advanced here. In *Port of Astoria* there existed a long-term contractual relationship between a Federal agency and a private corporation in which the proposed private manufacturing plant was entirely dependent upon electrical power to be supplied by the Federal agency. In *Mahelona* the problem was not that the Corps failed to examine the effects of the electrical generating plant, but rather failed to review the consequences of its own construction permit allowing a wastewater discharge facility. In short, the results of these cases do not compel the conclusion which the Appellants desire. Absent facts or circumstances which are not present here, we decline to hold that NEPA required the Corps as a matter of law to consider the entire Du Pont facility in determining whether or not an EIS was necessary.

AFFIRMED.

WINNEBAGO TRIBE OF NEBRASKA v. UNITED STATES ARMY CORPS OF ENGINEERS

621 F.2d 269 (8th Cir. 1980), *cert. denied* 449 U.S. 836, 101 S.Ct. 110, 66 L.Ed.2d 43 (1980)

Winnebago Tribe of Nebraska (the Tribe) appeals an order of the district court denying its request for a permanent injunction to bar construction of a proposed power line running from Raun, Iowa, to Hoskins, Nebraska. The Tribe claims the district court erred in holding that the issuance of a permit to cross the Missouri River by the Army Corps of Engineers (Corps) was not a "major federal action" within the meaning of the National Environmental Policy Act of 1969 (NEPA), 42 U.S.C. §§4321-47 (1976). The Tribe also maintains that, contrary to the district court's holding, it sustained its burden of proof by raising substantial environmental issues. Finally, the Tribe argues that the Corps' determination not to prepare an environmental impact statement (EIS) was unreasonable. For reasons set forth below, we reject these contentions and affirm the holding of the district court.

I. BACKGROUND

Appellee Nebraska Public Power District (NPPD) began planning construction of a 345 KV transmission line from Raun, Iowa, to Hoskins, Nebraska, in 1975. The proposed line would cross the Missouri River 150 feet south of an Omaha Public Power District (OPPD) line and run through the Winnebago Indian Reservation. In the fall of 1977, NPPD informed the Tribe and the Bureau of Indian Affairs of its intent.

On July 13, 1978, appellee Iowa Public Service Company (IPS), a joint venturer with NPPD in this project, applied to the Corps for a permit to cross the Missouri River, as required by 33 U.S.C. §403 (1976) (originally enacted as Rivers and Harbors Appropriation Act of March 3, 1899, ch. 425, §10, 30 Stat. 1151) (hereinafter section 10). Before granting the permit, the Corps prepared an environmental effect assessment on the impact of the river-crossing portion of the line (approximately 1.25 miles out of 67 miles). The assessment concluded that an environmental impact statement was not required because "[t]here are no significant environmental impacts associated with this project." The assessment did not mention any possible adverse effect on bald eagles, a protected species. The Corps granted the section 10 permit on January 10, 1979.

On April 30, 1979, the Tribe filed the present suit alleging noncompliance with NEPA and seeking to enjoin construction pending compliance. On May 1, 1979, the district court granted a temporary restraining order. In the course of a three-day trial in May, the court heard testimony on the potential harm to the American bald eagle, a protected species, as well as arguments on the sufficiency and scope of the Corps' assessment. The trial court ruled that the assessment properly considered only the river-crossing portion of the line, because the scope of the federal permit was limited to this area and the federal government was not funding the project. After weighing the evidence on danger to the American bald eagle, the district court concluded that the Tribe had failed to raise a substantial environmental issue. Accordingly, the trial court denied the requested injunctive relief.

II. ANALYSIS

Section 102(2)(C) of NEPA, 42 U.S.C. §4332(2)(C) (1976), requires that the relevant federal agency prepare an EIS for "major federal actions significantly affecting the quality of the human environment." Initially, the agency determines whether the proposed action triggers the EIS requirement. *See Minnesota Public Interest Research Group v. Butz,* 498 F.2d 1314, 1319-20 (8th Cir. 1974) (*en banc*) (MPIRG I). In MPIRG I, supra, this court set forth the standard for judicial review of an agency's threshold determination not to prepare an EIS:

> To upset an agency determination not to prepare an impact statement, it still must be shown that the agency's determination was not reasonable under the circumstances. This will require a showing that the project could significantly affect the quality of the human environment. *Save Our Ten Acres v. Kreger,* (472 F.2d 463, 466 (5th Cir. 1973)). We therefore hold that review of an agency's determination not to prepare an impact statement should be measured by its reasonableness in the circumstances, not as to whether it was arbitrary, capricious, an abuse of discretion, or otherwise not in accordance with law. (*MPIRG I, supra,* 498 F.2d at 1320 (footnote omitted); accord, *Monarch Chemical Works, Inc. v. Thone,* 604 F.2d 1083, 1087-88 (8th Cir. 1979).)

MPIRG I, in requiring that the plaintiff must show "that the project could significantly affect the quality of the human environment," relied upon *Save Our Ten Acres v. Kreger,* 472 F.2d 463, 466 (5th Cir. 1973) (*SOTA*). In *SOTA* and subsequent cases, the Fifth Circuit elaborated upon the required showing by allocating burdens of proof: the plaintiff must raise a substantial environmental issue concerning the proposed project, and then the burden shifts to the defendant to support the reasonableness of the negative determination. *See SOTA, supra,* 472 F.2d at 467; *Hiram Clarke Civic Club, Inc. v. Lynn,* 476 F.2d 421, 425 (5th Cir. 1973); *Image of Greater San Antonio, Texas v. Brown,* 570 F.2d 517, 522 (5th Cir. 1978).

In the present suit, the district court assigned appellant the burden of raising a substantial environmental issue. The parties to the present appeal do not take issue with the district court's use of this approach, nor do we find the method inappropriate. A number of district courts throughout the country have employed this analysis. See *Pokorny v. Costle,* 464 F.Supp. 1273 (D.Neb.1979); *Hiatt Grain & Feed, Inc. v. Bergland,* 446 F.Supp. 457 (D.Kan.1978), *aff'd* 602 F.2d 929 (10th Cir. 1979); *Mid-Shiawassee County Concerned Citizens v. Train,* 408 F.Supp. 650 (E.D.Mich.1976), *aff'd mem.*, 559 F.2d 1220 (6th Cir. 1977); *Jones v. HUD*, 390 F.Supp. 579 (E.D.La.1974). Indeed, without commenting on the district court's characterization of the burden of proof, this court has affirmed an opinion that concluded that many of the plaintiff's claims failed to raise a substantial environmental issue. *Monarch Chemical Works, Inc. v. Exon,* 466 F.Supp. 639 (D.Neb.*), aff'd sub nom. Monarch Chemical Works, Inc. v. Thone,* 604 F.2d 1083 (8th Cir. 1979). Accordingly, we must determine whether the district court erred in holding that the Tribe failed to meet its burden.

To establish a substantial environmental issue, the "(plaintiff) must allege facts (omitted from consideration in the administrative record) which, if true, would constitute a 'substantial' impact upon the environment." *Hiatt Grain & Feed, Inc. v. Bergland, supra,* 446 F.Supp. at 490 (citations omitted). The alleged deficiency must be of sufficient significance to warrant shifting the burden of proof. See *Monarch Chemical Works, Inc. v. Exon, supra,* 466 F.Supp. at 647-48; *Pokorny v. Costle, supra,* 464 F.Supp. at 1275-77.

The Tribe claims that the administrative record is deficient in three respects: (1) it ignores 65 miles of the 67-mile transmission line; (2) it does not consider certain viable alternatives; and (3) it does not contemplate potential harm to bald eagles. We deal with these claims in the order presented.

A. FAILURE TO CONSIDER THE ENTIRE PROJECT

The Tribe alleges that the administrative record should have considered environmental impacts posed by the entire transmission line, rather than just the river-crossing portion. Appellant's claim presents two related issues: (a) whether the Corps wields such control and responsibility over the entire project that nonfederal segments must be included in the assessment; and (b) assuming limited federal involvement, whether the Corps nevertheless must consider the impacts of nonfederal segments as secondary effects of the proposed action.

The Tribe notes initially that the power line will not be constructed without the section 10 permit. In light of "but for" veto power, the Tribe argues, the Corps wields sufficient control over the entire project to require project-wide environmental analysis. Factual or veto control, however, must be distinguished from legal control or "enablement." *See NAACP v. Medical Center,*

Inc., 584 F.2d 619 (3d Cir. 1978) (*Medical Center); Atlanta Coalition on the Transportation Crisis, Inc. v. Atlanta Regional Commission,* 599 F.2d 1333 (5th Cir. 1979) (*Atlanta Coalition*).

In "enablement" cases federal action is a legal condition precedent to accomplishment of an entire nonfederal project. *Medical Center, supra,* 584 F.2d at 632-33; *Atlanta Coalition, supra,* 599 F.2d at 1345-47. Thus, for example, the federal statute at issue in *Greene County Planning Board v. FPC,* 455 F.2d 412 (2d Cir.), *cert. denied,* 409 U.S. 849, 93 S.Ct. 56, 34 L.Ed.2d 90 (1972), required the Federal Power Commission to ensure that the entire project was "best adapted" to a comprehensive environmental plan before licensing construction of a power line. See also *Cady v. Morton,* 527 F.2d 786 (9th Cir. 1975) (the federal grant of Indian coal leases was the legal condition precedent for the strip mining project); *Davis v. Morton,* 469 F.2d 593 (10th Cir. 1972) (99 year lease of Indian lands was legal condition precedent to entire development project). The statute at issue in this case is far narrower and cannot be construed as a grant of legal control over the entire project.

The court in *Medical Center*, supra, identified three factors helpful in determining whether "but for" or factual control requires project-wide analysis: (1) the degree of discretion exercised by the agency over the federal portion of the project; (2) whether the federal government has given any direct financial aid to the project; and (3) whether "the overall federal involvement with the project (is) sufficient to turn essentially private action into federal action." *Id.* at 629 (citation omitted). In *Medical Center*, the agency had little or no discretion, there was no direct federal aid, and the court found the federal involvement insufficient.

In the present suit, while the Corps has broad discretion to consider environmental impacts (*see Zabel v. Tabb*, 430 F.2d 199 (5th Cir. 1970), *cert. denied*, 401 U.S. 910, 91 S.Ct. 873, 27 L.Ed. 2d 808 (1971)), that discretion must be exercised within the scope of the agency's authority. As noted above, the Corps' jurisdiction under section 10 extends only to areas in and affecting navigable waters. See *United States v. Sexton Cove Estates, Inc.*, 526 F.2d 1293, 1299 (5th Cir. 1976); *Weiszmann v. District Engineer, United States Army Corps of Engineers,* 526 F.2d 1302, 1304 (5th Cir. 1976); *United States v. Joseph G. Moretti, Inc.*, 526 F.2d 1306 (5th Cir. 1976). As the Third Circuit observed in *United States v. Stoeco Homes, Inc.*, 498 F.2d 597, 607 (3d Cir. 1974):

> The federal environmental protection statutes did not ... by their terms enlarge the jurisdiction of the Army Corps of Engineers under the Rivers and Harbors Appropriation Act of 1899. If there is no such jurisdiction environmental protection is still a matter primarily of state concern.

Thus, the Corps' discretion under section 10 does not dictate project-wide review.

The factors remaining for consideration under Medical Center are the presence of direct federal funding and the degree of federal involvement. There has been no direct or even indirect federal funding for this project. *Cf. Ely v. Velde,* 451 F.2d 1130 (4th Cir. 1971) (Law Enforcement Assistance Administration involvement in and funding for a state prison amounts to major federal action). As for federal involvement, the fact that part of the line will cross the Winnebago Reservation does not suffice to turn this essentially private action into federal action. Federal law allows the state to condemn this land for any public purpose in the same manner as land owned in fee. 25 U.S.C. §357 (1976). Thus, we conclude that the Corps did not have sufficient control and responsibility to require it to study the entire project.

The Tribe also notes that an agency must consider secondary or indirect impacts in determining whether there are any significant impacts upon the environment. See 40 C.F.R. §1500.6(b)(1978). Appellant argues that the administrative record does not reflect consideration of a secondary effect of granting the permit namely, building the remainder of the line. If, however, appellant's position were correct, then an EIS for a properly segmented portion of highway would have to consider impacts of subsequent segments as well. A careful reading of the Council on Environmental Quality Guidelines, 40 C.F.R. §1500.8(a)(3)(ii)(1978), leads us to reject appellant's contention as erroneous. Completion of the nonfederal aspects of this single project does not constitute a secondary or indirect effect of the federal action.

B. ALTERNATIVES

Appellant's second alleged deficiency in the administrative record is the absence of certain alternatives; however, the Tribe did not allege this failure in its complaint, nor did the district court consider the claim in its memorandum opinion. Because appellant failed to raise this issue to the trial court, we will not consider it as a basis for reversal. *See Morrow v. Greyhound Lines, Inc.,* 541 F.2d 713, 724 (8th Cir. 1976), and cases cited therein. Furthermore, we conclude that our refusal to consider the issue would not result in "a plain miscarriage of justice," nor is it "inconsistent with substantial justice." *Id.*

C. POTENTIAL HARM TO EAGLES

Finally, the Tribe claims it raised a substantial environmental issue concerning possible harm to bald eagles. The trial court summarized the evidence regarding eagles as follows:

> (First), the Corps considered several different varieties of birds in evaluating the area and concluded that there would be only short-term impacts resulting from the actual construction of the project, though some terrestrial habitats would be disturbed. Second, the Corps did not specifically consider the American bald eagle in its evaluation. Third, some eagles have been sighted in the area but there is no evidence that they nest in the area. Fourth, a small number of eagles are electrocuted each year throughout the United States.

The trial court noted that there was no evidence establishing either that high power lines affect eagles differently than the species of birds considered in the assessment, or that the existing OPPD power line has detrimentally affected the bald eagles in the area. We hold that on the basis of this evidence the trial court did not err in concluding that the Tribe failed to establish a significant environmental impact on eagles.

III. CONCLUSION

The Tribe has failed to meet its burden of raising a substantial environmental issue omitted from consideration in the administrative record. Accordingly, we affirm the order of the trial court denying a permanent injunction.

ON STAY OF MANDATE

Appellant Winnebago Tribe requests a stay of mandate pending its application for writ of certiorari before the Supreme Court. Nongovernmental appellees resist the application for stay, asserting that the effect of the stay would serve to continue an order of this court dated October 15,

1979, which enjoined construction of the power line and condemnation procedures pending disposition of the appeal.

Initially, we observe that in a civil case appellants may apply for certiorari to the Supreme Court within 90 days after entry of the judgment in this court. 28 U.S.C. §2101(c) (1976). The same is true where our mandate is issued, except the record would be obtained from the clerk of the court possessed of that record. Sup.Ct. R. 12(2).

The filing of a record in the Supreme Court is not a prerequisite for docketing an appeal. Sup.Ct. R. 12(1). In the ordinary civil case the stay of mandate may facilitate procedures because the clerk of this court on request will forward the record from this court to the Supreme Court. Sup.Ct. R. 12(2).

Here, however, a stay of mandate would also serve to extend the injunction issued pending appeal. In light of our disposition on the merits, we do not think it appropriate to continue the injunction issued pending appeal.

Accordingly, the stay of mandate is granted, subject to the following conditions:

> 1) The injunction pending appeal issued by this court on October 15, 1979, is dissolved herewith.
>
> 2) The appellant's motion to stay the mandate is granted for a period of thirty days from the date of this order, pending application for a writ of certiorari before the Supreme Court. If said petition is filed within 30 days, the stay shall continue until disposition of the case by the Supreme Court.

It is so ORDERED. [Footnotes omitted.]

See also Riverside Irrigation District v. U.S. Army Corps of Engineers, 758 F.2d 508 (10th Cir. 1985).

CHAPTER 24

ADMINISTRATIVE APPEALS

Prior to the establishment of an administrative appeal procedure, property owners who were unhappy with their permit decisions were forced to violate the permit, draw an enforcement penalty, and then seek judicial review of the enforcement penalty. *Southern Pines Associates v. United States*, 912 F.2d 713 (4th Cir. Va. 1990); *Hampton Venture No. One v. United States*, 768 F.Supp. 174 (E.D.Va. 1991); *Route 26 Land Development Association v. United States*, 753 F.Supp. 532 (D.Del. 1990), *aff'd.* 961 F.2d 1568 (3d Cir. Del. 1992); *Fercom Aquaculture Corp. v. United States*, 740 F.Supp. 736 (E.D.Mo. 1990); *USI Properties Corp. v. U.S. Environmental Protection Agency*, 517 F.Supp. 1235 (D.P.R. 1981).

In 1999, the Corps established policies and procedures to be used for the administrative appeal of permit applications denied with prejudice, and for the administrative appeals of declined individual permits. Affected parties may appeal permit denials or declined individual permits where the permit denial or the proffered individual permit occurs after March 9, 1999, but may not appeal permit denials or declined permits where the Corps took that action before March 9, 1999. The appeal process will allow the affected party to pursue an administrative appeal of certain final Corps of Engineers decisions with which they disagree. It is the announced policy of the Corps "to promote and maintain an administrative appeal process that is independent, objective, fair, prompt, and efficient." No affected party, however, may file a legal action in the Federal courts based on a permit denial or declined individual permit until after a final Corps decision has been made and the appellant has exhausted all applicable administrative remedies. The appellant is considered to have exhausted all administrative remedies when a final Corps decision is made in accordance with the administrative appeal procedures.

Under this new procedure, permit decisions made by a Division Engineer or higher authority may be appealed to an Army official at least one level higher than the decision-maker. Affected parties will be notified in writing of a Corps decision on an appealable action. For permit denials, the notification must include a copy of the decision document for the permit application, a special "fact sheet" and a Request For Appeal or "RFA" form. For proffered individual permits, when the initial proffered permit is sent to the applicant, the notification must include a fact sheet. For declined permits (*i.e.*, proffered individual permits that the applicant refuses to accept and sends back to the Corps), the notification must include a fact sheet and a Request For Appeal form. Additionally, an affected party has the right to obtain a copy of the administrative record.

"Declined permit" means a proffered individual permit, including a letter of permission, that an applicant has refused to accept, because he has objections to the terms and conditions therein. A declined permit can also be an individual permit that the applicant originally accepted, but where such permit was subsequently modified by the District Engineer in such a manner that the resulting permit contains terms and conditions that lead the applicant to decline the modified permit, provided that the applicant has not started work in waters of the United States authorized by such permit. Where an applicant declines a permit (either initial or modified), the applicant does not have a valid permit to conduct regulated activities in waters of the United States, and must not begin construction of the work requiring a Corps permit unless and until the applicant receives and accepts a valid Corps permit. *"Permit denial"* means a written denial with prejudice of an individual permit application

The Reviewing Officer will conduct an independent review of the administrative record to address the reasons for the appeal cited by the applicant in the Request For Appeal. In addition, to the extent that it is practicable and feasible, the Reviewing Officer will also conduct an independent review of the administrative record to verify that the record provides an adequate and reasonable basis supporting the District Engineer's decision, that facts or analysis essential to the District Engineer's decision have not been omitted from the administrative record, and that all relevant requirements of law, regulations, and officially-promulgated Corps policy guidance have been satisfied. Should the Reviewing Officer require expert advice regarding any subject, he may seek such advice from any employee of the Corps or of another Federal or state agency, or from any recognized expert, so long as that person had not been previously involved in the action under review.

The reason(s) for requesting an appeal of a permit denial, or a declined individual permit, must be specifically stated in the Request For Appeal, and must be more than a simple request for appeal because the affected party did not like the permit decision, or the permit conditions. Examples of reasons for appeals include, but are not limited to, the following: a procedural error, an incorrect application of law, regulation or officially-promulgated policy, omission of material fact, incorrect application of the Section 404(b)(1) Guidelines, or use of incorrect data.

An affected party appealing a permit denial or declined permit must submit an Request For Appeal that is received by the Division Engineer within 60 days of the date of the permit denial or permit rejection. In the case where an applicant objects to a proffered individual permit, the appeal process proceeds as follows: To initiate the appeal process regarding the terms and conditions of the permit, the applicant must write a letter to the District Engineer explaining his objections to the permit. The District Engineer, upon evaluation of the applicant's objections, may: modify the permit to address all of the applicant's objections, or modify the permit to address some, but not all, of the applicant's objections, or not modify the permit, having determined that the permit should be issued as previously written. In the event that the District Engineer agrees to modify the proffered individual permit to address all of the applicant's objections, the District Engineer will issue such modified permit. Should the District Engineer modify the proffered individual permit to address some, but not all, of the applicant's objections, the District Engineer will send the applicant such modified permit and the decision document for the project. If the District Engineer does not modify the proffered individual permit, the District Engineer will offer the unmodified permit to the applicant a second time, enclosing a copy of the decision document. If the applicant still has objections, the applicant may decline such modified or unmodified permit; this declined individual permit may be appealed to the Division Engineer upon submittal of a complete Request For Appeal form. The completed Request For Appeal must be received by the Division Engineer within 60 days of the notice from the Corps District Engineer.

Upon receipt of a Request For Appeal, the Corps shall review the Request and the administrative record to determine whether the Request meets the criteria for appeal. If the Request meets the criteria for appeal, the Reviewing Officer will so notify the appellant in writing within 30 days of the receipt of the Request. If the Reviewing Officer believes that the Request does not meet the criteria for appeal, the Reviewing Officer will make a recommendation on the Request to the Division Engineer. If the Division Engineer determines that the Request is not acceptable, the Division Engineer will notify the appellant of this determination by a certified letter detailing the reason(s) why the appeal failed to meet the criteria for appeal. No further administrative appeal is available, unless the appellant revises the Request to correct the deficiencies noted in the

Division Engineer's letter. The revised Request must be received by the Division Engineer within 30 days of the date of the certified letter refusing the initial Request. If the Corps determines that the revised Request still fails to meet the criteria for appeal, the Division Engineer will notify the appellant of this determination by a certified letter within 30 days of the date of the receipt of the revised Request, and will advise the appellant that the matter is not eligible for appeal. No further Requests will be accepted after this point.

Within 30 days of receipt of a complete Request For Appeal, the Reviewing Officer should determine if a site investigation is needed to clarify the administrative record. The Reviewing Officer should conduct any such site investigation within 60 days of receipt of a complete Request. The Reviewing Officer may also conduct a site investigation at the request of the appellant, provided he or she has determined that such an investigation would be of benefit in interpreting the administrative record. The appellant and the appellant's authorized agent(s) must be provided an opportunity to participate in any site investigation, and will be given 15 days notice of any site investigation. The Reviewing Officer, the appellant, the appellant's agent(s) and the Corps district staff are authorized participants at the site investigation. The Reviewing Officer may also invite any other party the Reviewing Officer has determined to be appropriate, such as any technical experts consulted by the Corps.

Conferences held in accordance with the appeal process will be informal, and will be chaired by the Reviewing Officer. The purpose of the appeal conference is to provide a forum that allows the participants to discuss freely all relevant issues and material facts associated with the appeal. An appeal conference will be held for every appeal of a permit denial or a declined individual permit, unless the Reviewing Officer and the appellant mutually agree to forego a conference. The conference will take place within 60 days of receipt of an acceptable Request For Appeal, unless the Reviewing Officer determines that unforeseen or unusual circumstances require scheduling the conference for a later date. Presentations by the appellant and the Corps district representatives may include interpretation, clarification, or explanation of the legal, policy, and factual bases for their positions.

The conference will be governed by the following guidelines: The Reviewing Officer will set a date, time, and location for the conference. The Reviewing Officer will notify the appellant and the Corps district office in writing within 30 days of receipt of the Request For Appeal, and not less than 15 days before the date of the conference.

The purpose of the appeal conference will be to discuss the reasons for appeal contained in the RFA. Any material in the administrative record may be discussed during the conference, but the discussion should be focused on relevant issues needed to address the reasons for appeal contained in the RFA. Issues not identified in the administrative record by the date of the permit decision for the application may not be raised or discussed, because substantive new information or project modifications would be treated as a new permit application.

The appeal conference is an informal proceeding, intended to provide clarifications and explanations of the administrative record for the Reviewing Officer and the Division Engineer; it is not intended to supplement the administrative record. Consequently, the proceedings of the conference will not be recorded verbatim by the Corps or any other party attending the conference, and no verbatim transcripts of the conference will be made. However, after the conference, the Reviewing Officer will write a memorandum for the record (MFR) summarizing the presentations made at the conference, and will provide a copy of that MFR to the Division Engineer, the appellant, and the District Engineer.

Because a decision to deny or condition a permit depends on the facts, circumstances, and physical conditions particular to the specific project and site being evaluated, appeal decisions would be of little or no precedential utility. Therefore, an appeal decision of the Division Engineer is applicable only to the instant appeal, and has no other precedential effect. Such a decision may not be cited in any other administrative appeal, and may not be used as precedent for the evaluation of any other permit application. While administrative appeal decisions lack precedential value and may not be cited by an appellant or a District Engineer in any other appeal proceeding, the Corps goal is to have the Corps regulatory program operate as consistently as possible, particularly with respect to interpretations of law, regulation, an Executive Order, and officially promulgated policy. Therefore, a copy of each appeal decision will be forwarded to Corps Headquarters; those decisions will be periodically reviewed at the headquarters level for consistency with law, Executive Orders and policy. Additional official guidance will be issued as necessary to maintain or improve the consistency of the Corps' appellate and permit decisions.

The Division Engineer will disapprove the entirety of or any part of the District Engineer's decision only if he determines that the decision on some relevant matter was arbitrary, capricious, an abuse of discretion, not supported by substantial evidence in the administrative record, or plainly contrary to a requirement of law, regulation, an Executive Order, or officially-promulgated Corps policy guidance. The Division Engineer will not attempt to substitute his judgment for that of the District Engineer regarding a matter of fact, so long as the District Engineer's determination was supported by substantial evidence in the administrative record, or regarding any other matter if the District Engineer's determination was reasonable and within the zone of discretion delegated to the District Engineer by Corps regulations. The Division Engineer may instruct the District Engineer on how to correct any procedural error that was prejudicial to the appellant (*i.e.*, that was not a "harmless" procedural error), or to reconsider the decision where any essential part of the District Engineer's decision was not supported by accurate or sufficient information, or analysis, in the administrative record. The Division Engineer will document his decision on the merits of the appeal in writing, and provide a copy of this decision to the applicant (using certified mail) and the District Engineer. The final decision of the Division Engineer on the merits of the appeal will conclude the administrative appeal process, and this decision will be filed in the administrative record for the project.

After-the-fact permit denials and declined individual after the fact are appealable actions for the purposes of these regulations. If the Corps accepts an after-the-fact permit application, an administrative appeal of a permit denial or declined individual permit may be filed and processed in accordance with these regulations subject to the following special procedures: If the District Engineer determines that initial corrective measures are necessary, a Request For Appeal for an appealable action will not be accepted by the Corps, until the initial corrective measures have been completed to the satisfaction of the District Engineer.

If an affected party requests an administrative appeal of an appealable action prior to the resolution of the unauthorized activity, and the Division Engineer determines that the appeal has no merit, the responsible party remains subject to any civil, criminal, and administrative penalties as provided by law.

Any person who applies for an after-the-fact permit, where the application is accepted and processed by the Corps, thereby agrees that the statute of limitations regarding any violation associated with that application is tolled until one year after the final Corps decision. Moreover, the applicant for an after-the-fact permit must also memorialize that agreement to toll the statute of limitations, by signing an agreement to that effect, in exchange for the Corps acceptance of the after-the-fact permit application, and/or any administrative appeal. No after-the-fact permit application or administrative appeal will be accepted until such written tolling agreement is furnished to the District Engineer.

Part 4
Enforcement

The power to penalize the discharge of dredged or fill material into a wetland without a permit, or a violation of a condition or limitation in an existing permit, stems from three statutory sources: the Environmental Protection Agency's power under §404(C) to prohibit the use of any defined area as a disposal site when the discharge would have an unacceptable adverse effect, 33 U.S.C. §1344(c); the EPA's power to issue administrative orders against unpermitted discharges and/or permit violations under §309 of the Clean Water Act, 33 U.S.C. §1319; and the Corps's power to punish permit violators under §404(S), 33 U.S.C. §1344(S), and the regulations under both sections.

Chapter 25
EPA CIVIL ORDERS AND ACTIONS

Section 309(a) of the Clean Water Act, 33 U.S.C. §1319(a), states in relevant part that:

> (1) Whenever, on the basis of any information available to him, the Administrator finds that any person is in violation of any condition or limitation … in a permit issued by a State under an approved permit program under section … 404 of this title he shall proceed under his authority in paragraph (3) of this subsection or he shall notify the person in alleged violation and such State of such finding. If beyond the thirtieth day after the Administrator's notification the State has not commenced appropriate enforcement action, the Administrator shall issue an order requiring such person to comply with such condition or limitation or shall bring a civil action in accordance with subsection (b) of this section....
>
> (3) Whenever on the basis of any information available to him the Administrator finds that any person … is in violation of any permit condition or limitation … in a permit issued under section 404 of this title by a State, he shall issue an order requiring such person to comply with such section or requirement, or he shall bring a civil action in accordance with subsection (b) of this section.
>
> (4) A copy of any order issued under this subsection shall be sent immediately by the Administrator to the State in which the violation occurs and other affected States. In any case in which an order under this subsection (or notice to a violator under paragraph (1) of this subsection) is issued to a corporation, a copy of such order (or notice) shall be served on any appropriate corporate officers....
>
> (5) (A) Any order issued under this subsection shall be by personal service, shall state with reasonable specificity the nature of the violation, and shall specify a time for compliance not to exceed 30 days in the case of a violation of an interim compliance schedule or operation and maintenance requirement and not to exceed a time the Administrator determines to be reasonable in the case of a violation of a final deadline, taking into account the seriousness of the violation and any good faith efforts to comply with applicable requirements.

The EPA is also authorized to commence a civil action for appropriate relief, including a permanent or temporary injunction, for any violation for which he is authorized to issue a compliance order under §309(a). Any action under §309(a) may be brought in the district court of the United States for the district in which the defendant is located or resides or is doing business, and such court shall have jurisdiction to restrain such violation and to require compliance. Notice of the commencement of such action shall be given immediately to the appropriate State. §309(b).

CHAPTER 26

EPA CIVIL PENALTIES

Whenever on the basis of any information available the EPA finds that any person has violated any permit condition or limitation in a permit issued under §404 by a State, or the Secretary of the Army finds that any person has violated any permit condition or limitation in a permit issued under §404 by the Corps, the EPA or Corps, as the case may be, may, after consultation with the State in which the violation occurs, assess a class I civil penalty or a class II civil penalty under §309(g)(1).

There are two classes of penalties: The amount of a Class I civil penalty may not exceed $10,000 per violation, except that the maximum amount of any Class I civil penalty under this subparagraph shall not exceed $25,000. Before issuing an order assessing a civil penalty under §309(g)(1), the EPA or the Secretary, as the case may be, shall give to the person to be assessed such penalty written notice of the EPA's or Secretary's proposal to issue such order and the opportunity to request, within 30 days of the date the notice is received by such person, a hearing on the proposed order. Such hearing shall not be subject to section 554 or 556 of title 5 (the Administrative Procedure Act), but shall provide a reasonable opportunity to be heard and to present evidence. §309(g)(2)(A).

The amount of a Class II civil penalty may not exceed $10,000 per day for each day during which the violation continues; except that the maximum amount of any Class II civil penalty under this subparagraph shall not exceed $125,000. Except as otherwise provided in§309(g)(2)(B), a Class II civil penalty shall be assessed and collected in the same manner, and subject to the same provisions, as in the case of civil penalties assessed and collected after notice and opportunity for a hearing on the record in accordance with section 554 of title 5. The EPA and the Secretary may issue rules for discovery procedures for hearings under §309(g)(2)(B).

The procedures under §309 for assessing a Class I penalty are similar to the Corps' procedures under 33 C.F.R. §326. There are a handful of special procedures for Class II penalty assessments under 40 C.F.R. §22.38.

In determining the amount of any penalty assessed under §309(g), the EPA shall take into account the nature, circumstances, extent and gravity of the violation, or violations, and, with respect to the violator, ability to pay, any prior history of such violations, the degree of culpability, economic benefit or savings (if any) resulting from the violation, and such other matters as justice may require. §309(g)(3).

Before issuing an order assessing a civil penalty under §309(g) the EPA shall provide public notice of and reasonable opportunity to comment on the proposed issuance of such order. §309(g)(4)(A).

Any person who comments on a proposed assessment of a penalty shall be given notice of any hearing to be held and of the order assessing such penalty. In any hearing held under §309(g), such person shall have a reasonable opportunity to be heard and to present evidence. §309(g)(4)(B).

If no hearing is held before issuance of an order assessing a penalty under §309(g), any person who commented on the proposed assessment may petition, within 30 days after the issuance of such order, the EPA to set aside such order and to provide a hearing on the penalty. If the evidence presented by the petitioner in support of the petition is material and was not considered in the issuance of the order, the EPA shall immediately set aside such order and provide a hearing in accordance with §309(g)(2)(A) in the case of a Class I civil penalty and §309(g)(2)(B) in the case of a Class II civil penalty. If the EPA denies a hearing under §309(g)(4), the EPA shall provide to the petitioner, and publish in the Federal Register, notice of and the reasons for such denial. §309(g)(4)(C).

An order issued under §309(g) shall become final 30 days after its issuance unless a petition for judicial review is filed or a hearing is requested. If such a hearing is denied, such order shall become final 30 days after such denial. §309(g)(5).

Any action taken by the EPA under §309(g) shall not affect or limit the EPA's authority to enforce any provision of §309; except that any violation with respect to which the EPA has commenced and is diligently prosecuting an action under this subsection, or with respect to which a State has commenced and is diligently prosecuting an action under a State law comparable to §309(g), or for which the EPA or the State has issued a final order not subject to further judicial review and the violator has paid a penalty assessed under §309, or such comparable State law, as the case may be, shall not be the subject of a civil penalty action under §309(d) or 33 U.S.C. §1321(b) or 33 U.S.C. §1365. §309(g)(6)(A).

The limitations contained in §309(g)(6)(A) on civil penalty actions under 33 U.S.C. §1365 (the citizen's suit provision) of this title shall not apply with respect to any violation for which a citizen's suit has been filed prior to commencement of an action under§309(g), or notice of an alleged violation has been given in accordance with 33 U.S.C. §505(b)(1)(A) prior to commencement of an action under §309(g) and an action under 33 U.S.C. §505(a)(1) with respect to such alleged violation is filed before the 120th day after the date on which such notice is given. §309(g)(6)(B).

If any person fails to pay an assessment of a civil penalty after the order making the assessment has become final, or after a court in an action brought under §309(g)(8) has entered a final judgment in favor of the EPA, the EPA shall request the Attorney General to bring a civil action in an appropriate district court to recover the amount assessed (plus interest at currently prevailing rates from the date of the final order or the date of the final judgment, as the case may be). In such an action, the validity, amount, and appropriateness of such penalty shall not be subject to review. Any person who fails to pay on a timely basis the amount of an assessment of a civil penalty as described in the first sentence of this paragraph shall be required to pay, in addition to such amount and interest, attorneys fees and costs for collection proceedings and a quarterly nonpayment penalty for each quarter during which such failure to pay persists. Such nonpayment penalty shall be in an amount equal to 20 percent of the aggregate amount of such person's penalties and nonpayment penalties which are unpaid as of the beginning of such quarter. §309(g)(9).

The EPA may issue subpoenas for the attendance and testimony of witnesses and the production of relevant papers, books, or documents in connection with hearings under this subsection. If a witness refuses to obey a subpoena, the district court of the United States for any district in which the witness is found, resides, or transacts business shall have jurisdiction to issue an order requiring the witness to appear and give testimony before the administrative law judge, or to appear and produce documents before the administrative law judge, or both, and any failure to obey such order of the court may be punished by such court as a contempt thereof. §309(g)(10).

In the case of the assessment of a Class II penalty, there are a few special procedures in 40 C.F.R. §22.38:

> (b) *Consultation with states.* The Administrator will consult with the state in which the alleged violation occurs before issuing a final order assessing a Class II civil penalty.
>
> (c) *Public notice.* Before issuing a final order assessing a Class II civil penalty, the Administrator will provide public notice of the complaint.
>
> (d) *Comment by a person who is not a party.* A person not a party to the Class II proceeding who wishes to comment upon a complaint must file written comments with the Regional Hearing Clerk within 30 days after public notice of the complaint and serve a copy of the comments upon each party. For good cause shown the Administrator, the Regional Administrator, or the Presiding Officer, as appropriate, may accept late comments. The Administrator will give any person who comments on a complaint notice of any hearing and notice of the final order assessing a penalty. Although commenters may be heard and present evidence at any hearing held under section 309(g) of the Act, commenters shall not be accorded party status with right of cross examination unless they formally move to intervene and are granted party status under section 22.11.
>
> (e) *Administrative procedure and judicial review.* Action of the Administrator for which review could have been obtained under section 509(b)(1) of the Act shall not be subject to review in an administrative proceeding for the assessment of Class II civil penalty under section 309(g).
>
> (f) *Petitions to set aside an order and to provide a hearing.* If no hearing on the complaint is held before issuance of an order assessing a Class II civil penalty, any person who commented on the complaint may petition the Administrator, within 30 days after issuance of the order, to set aside the order and to provide a hearing on the complaint. If the evidence presented by the petitioner in support of the petition is material and was not considered in the issuance of the order, the Administrator will immediately set aside the order and provide a hearing in accordance with the Consolidated Rules of Practice and these supplemental rules of practice. If the Administrator denies a hearing under section 309(g)(4)(C) of the Act, the Administrator will provide to the petitioner, and publish in the Federal Register, notice of and the reasons for the denial.

Whenever a municipality is a party to a civil action brought by the United States under §309, the State in which such municipality is located shall be joined as a party. Such State shall be liable for payment of any judgment, or any expenses incurred as a result of complying with any judgment, entered against the municipality in such action to the extent that the laws of that State prevent the municipality from raising revenues needed to comply with such judgment. §309(e).

Chapter 27

CORPS CLASS I ADMINISTRATIVE PENALTIES

Under 33 C.F.R. §326.6, the Corps has authority to issue administrative penalties for permit violations although they are different in amount and procedure from the Environmental Protection Agency's penalty regulations. The Corps can assess "Class I" penalties of up to $10,000 for each permit violation up to a total maximum penalty of $25,000 but do not have to follow the federal Administrative Procedure Act. If the Corps elects to proceed under 33 C.F.R. §326.6, it cannot later pursue any judicial action, such as a referral to the U.S. Attorney for criminal or civil penalties for willful, repeated, flagrant or violations of substantial impact.

Corps Class I penalty proceedings for violation of any permit condition or limitation contained in a permit are initiated by the Corps District Engineer preparing and processing a proposed order, specifying the amount of the penalty, and stating with reasonable specificity the nature of the violation. The proposed order is to be served on the permittee giving him or her 30 days to request a hearing. The Corps must also give public notice of the proposed order, provide a reasonable opportunity for public comment on the proposed order, and notify the appropriate state agency of the proposed order. If the permittee does not request a hearing, those members of the public who submitted written comments will be given notice of the final order and have 30 days to petition to have the order set aside and provide a hearing. The Corps does not have to hold a hearing if the evidence presented by the public commentator is either immaterial or was already considered when the order was issued.

At any time after the public notice of a proposed penalty order is given under 33 C.F.R. §326.6(c), the Corps shall make available the administrative record at reasonable times for inspection and copying by any interested person, subject to provisions of law restricting the public disclosure of confidential information. Any person requesting copies of the administrative record or portions of the administrative record may be required by the Corps to pay reasonable charges for reproducing the information requested.

The administrative record includes the following: documentation relied on by the Corps to support the violations alleged in the proposed penalty order with a summary of violations, if a summary has been prepared; proposed penalty order or assessment notice; public notice of the proposed order with evidence of notice to the permittee and to the public; comments by the permittee and/or the public on the proposed penalty order, including any requests for a hearing; all orders or notices of the Presiding Officer; subpoenas issued, if any, for the attendance and testimony of witnesses and the production of relevant papers, books, or documents in connection with any hearings; all submittals or responses of any persons or comments to the proceeding, including exhibits, if any; a complete and accurate record or transcription of any hearing; the recommended decision of the Presiding Officer and final decision and/or order of the Corps issued by the Corps; and any other appropriate documents related to the administrative proceeding.

A permittee may be represented at all stages of the proceeding by counsel. After receiving notification that a permittee or any other party or commenter is represented by counsel, the Presiding Officer and Corps shall direct all further communications to that counsel.

If the permittee desires that a hearing be held, he or she must request the hearing in writing within the 30-day period, specifying in summary form the factual and legal issues which are in dispute and the specific factual and legal grounds for the permittee's defense. The permittee waives the right to a hearing if the permittee does not submit the request for the hearing within 30 calendar days of receipt of the notice. The Corps determines the date of receipt of notice by permittee's signed and dated return receipt or such other evidence that constitutes proof of actual notice on a certain date.

The Corps will schedule requested hearings and provide reasonable notice of the hearing schedule to all participants, except that no hearing shall be scheduled prior to the end of the 30-day public comment period provided in §326.6(c)(2). The Corps may grant any delays or continuances necessary or desirable to resolve the case fairly. The hearing shall be held at the district office or a location chosen by the Corps, except the permittee may request in writing upon a showing of good cause that the hearing be held at an alternative location. Action on such request is at the discretion of the Corps.

Hearings will be informal, adjudicatory hearings and are not subject to §§554 or 556 of the Administrative Procedure Act. Permittees may present evidence either orally or in written form in accordance with the hearing procedures specified in §326.6(i).

The Corps will give written notice of any hearing to any person who commented on the proposed administrative penalty order under §326.6(c). This notice shall specify a reasonable time prior to the hearing within which the commenter may request an opportunity to be heard and to present oral evidence or to make comments in writing in any such hearing. The notice shall require that any such request specify the facts or issues which the commenter wishes to address. Any commenter who files comments pursuant to §326.6(c) (2) shall have a right to be heard and to present evidence at the hearing.

The Corps will select a member of the Corps counsel staff or other qualified person to serve as Presiding Officer of the hearing. The Presiding Officer shall exercise no other responsibility, direct or supervisory, for the investigation or prosecution of any case before him. The Presiding Officer shall conduct hearings as specified by these rules and make a recommended decision to the Corps. The Presiding Officer will consider each case on the basis of the evidence presented, and must have no prior connection with the case. The Presiding Officer is solely responsible for the recommended decision in each case.

No interested person outside the Corps or member of the interested Corps staff shall make, or knowingly cause to be made, any *ex parte* communication on the merits of the proceeding. The Presiding Officer shall not make, or knowingly cause to be made, any *ex parte* communication on the proceeding to any interested person outside the Corps or to any member of the interested Corps staff. The Corps may replace the Presiding Officer in any proceeding in which it is demonstrated to the Corps's satisfaction that the Presiding Officer has engaged in prohibited *ex parte* communications to the prejudice of any participant.

The rules applicable to Presiding Officers under §326.6(h)(5) regarding *ex parte* communications are also applicable to the Corps and to any person who advises the Corps on the decision or the order, except that communications between the Corps and the Presiding Officer do not constitute *ex parte* communications, nor do communications between the Corps District Engineer and his staff prior to issuance of the proposed order. The Corps may request additional information on specified issues from the participants, in whatever form the Corps designates, giving all participants a fair opportunity to be heard on such additional matters. The Corps shall include this additional information in the administrative record.

Whenever an *ex parte* communication in violation of this section is received by the Presiding Officer or made known to the Presiding Officer, the Presiding Officer shall immediately notify all participants in the proceeding of the circumstances and substance of the communication and may require the person who made the communication or caused it to be made, or the party whose representative made the communication or caused it to be made, to the extent consistent with justice and the policies of the Clean Water Act, to show cause why that person or party's claim or interest in the proceedings should not be dismissed, denied, disregarded, or otherwise adversely affected on account of such violation.

The Presiding Officer may issue subpoenas for documents and witnesses. The Presiding Officer shall provide any person who filed a request to participate under §326.6(c), and any other person attending the hearing a reasonable opportunity to be heard and to present evidence The Presiding Officer may establish reasonable time limits for oral testimony. Prior to the commencement of the hearing, the Corps shall provide to the Presiding Officer the complete administrative record as of that date. During the hearing, the Corps may summarize the basis for the proposed administrative order. Thereafter, the administrative record will be admitted into evidence and the Presiding Officer shall maintain the administrative record of the proceedings and shall include in that record all documentary evidence, written statements, correspondence, the record of hearing, and any other relevant matter.

The Presiding Officer will cause a tape recording, written transcript or other permanent, verbatim record of the hearing to be made, which will be included in the administrative record, and will, upon written request, be made available, for inspection or copying, to the permittee or any person, subject to provisions of law restricting the public disclosure of confidential information. The Presiding Officer is not bound by strict rules of evidence and may determine the weight to be accorded the evidence. The permittee has the right to examine, to respond to the administrative record, and to offer into evidence, in written form or through oral testimony, a response to the administrative record including, any facts, statements, explanations, documents, testimony, or other exculpatory items which bear on any appropriate issues. The Presiding Officer may question the permittee and require the authentication of any written exhibit or statement. The Presiding Officer may exclude any repetitive or irrelevant matter.

At the close of the permittee's presentation of evidence, the Presiding Officer should allow the introduction of rebuttal evidence. The Presiding Officer may allow the permittee to respond to any such rebuttal evidence submitted and to cross-examine any witness. The Presiding Officer may take official notice of matters that are not reasonably in dispute and are commonly known in the community or are ascertainable from readily available sources of known accuracy. Prior to taking official notice of a matter, the Presiding Officer shall give the Corps and the permittee an opportunity to show why such notice should not be taken. In any case in which official notice is taken, the Presiding Officer shall place a written statement of the matters as to which such notice was taken in the record, including the basis for such notice and a statement that the Corps or permittee consented to such notice being taken or a summary of the objections of the Corps or the permittee.

After all evidence has been presented, any participant may present argument on any relevant issue, subject to reasonable time limitations set at the discretion of the Presiding Officer. The hearing record shall remain open for a period of ten business days from the date of the hearing so that the permittee or any person who has submitted comments on the proposed order may examine and submit responses for the record. At the close of this ten business day period, the Presiding Officer may allow the introduction of rebuttal evidence. The Presiding Officer may hold the record open for an additional ten business days to allow the presentation of such rebuttal evidence.

Within a reasonable time following the close of the hearing and receipt of any statements following the hearing and after consultation with the state pursuant to §326.6(d), the Presiding Officer shall forward a recommended decision accompanied by a written statement of reasons to the Corps. The decision shall recommend that the Corps withdraw, issue, or modify and issue the proposed order as a final order. The recommended decision shall be based on a preponderance of the evidence in the administrative record. If the Presiding Officer finds that there is not a preponderance of evidence in the record to support the penalty or the amount of the penalty in a proposed order, the Presiding Officer may recommend that the order be withdrawn or modified and then issued on terms that are supported by a preponderance of evidence on the record. The Presiding Officer also shall make the complete administrative record available to the Corps for review.

The Presiding Officer's recommended decision to the Corps shall become part of the administrative record and shall be made available to the parties to the proceeding at the time the Corps's decision is released pursuant to §326.6 (j) (5). The Presiding Officer's recommended decision shall not become part of the administrative record until the Corps's final decision is issued, and shall not be made available to the permittee or public prior to that time.

Within a reasonable time following receipt of the Presiding Officer's recommended decision, the Corps shall withdraw, issue, or modify and issue the proposed order as a final order. The Corps's decision shall be based on a preponderance of the evidence in the administrative record, shall consider the penalty factors set out in §309(g)(3) of the Clean Water Act, shall be in writing, shall include a clear and concise statement of reasons for the decision, and shall include any final order assessing a penalty. The Corps's decision, once issued, shall constitute final Corps action for purposes of judicial review. The Corps shall issue the final order by sending the order, or written notice of its withdrawal, to the permittee by certified mail. Issuance of the order under this subparagraph constitutes final Corps action for purposes of judicial review. The Corps shall provide written notice of the issuance, modification and issuance, or withdrawal of the proposed order to every person who submitted written comments on the proposed order. The notice shall include a statement of the right to judicial review and of the procedures and deadlines for obtaining judicial review. The notice shall also note the right of a commenter to petition for a hearing pursuant to §326.6(c)(3) if no hearing was previously held.

Any final order issued under this subpart shall become effective 30 calendar days following its issuance unless an appeal is taken pursuant to §309(g)(8) of the Clean Water Act, or in the case where no hearing was held prior to the final order, and a petition for hearing is filed by a prior commenter.

If a petition for hearing is received within 30 days after the final order is issued, the Corps shall review the evidence presented by the petitioner; if the evidence is material and was not considered in the issuance of the order, the Corps shall immediately set aside the final order and schedule a hearing. In that case, a hearing will be held, a new recommendation will be made by the Presiding Officer to the Corps and a new final decision issued by the Corps; if the Corps denies a hearing, the Corps shall provide to the petitioner, and publish in the Federal Register, notice of, and the reasons for, such denial.

Any permittee against whom a final order assessing a civil penalty under these regulations or any person who provided written comments on a proposed order may obtain judicial review of the final order. In order to obtain judicial review, the permittee or commenter must file a notice of appeal in the United States District Court for either the District of Columbia, or the district in which the violation was alleged to have occurred, within 30 calendar days after the date of issuance of the final order. Simultaneously with the filing of the notice of appeal, the permittee or commenter must send a copy of such notice by certified mail to the Corps District Engineer and the Attorney General.

CHAPTER 28

CRIMINAL PENALTIES

In assessing criminal penalties, the EPA makes the following distinctions in §309(c): negligent violations; knowing violations; and knowing endangerment in which a person knows at that time that, by virtue of the violation, he thereby places another person in imminent danger of death or serious bodily injury, shall, upon conviction, be subject to a fine of not more than $250,000 or imprisonment of not more than 15 years, or both. A person which is an organization shall, upon conviction of violating this subparagraph, be subject to a fine of not more than $1,000,000. If a conviction of a person is for a violation committed after a first conviction of such person under this paragraph, the maximum punishment shall be doubled with respect to both fine and imprisonment. §309(c).

In determining whether a defendant who is an individual knew that his conduct placed another person in imminent danger of death or serious bodily injury, the person is responsible only for actual awareness or actual belief that he possessed; and knowledge possessed by a person other than the defendant but not by the defendant himself may not be attributed to the defendant; except that in proving the defendant's possession of actual knowledge, circumstantial evidence may be used, including evidence that the defendant took affirmative steps to shield himself from relevant information. §309(c)(3)(B)(i).

It is an affirmative defense to prosecution that the conduct charged was consented to by the person endangered and that the danger and conduct charged were reasonably foreseeable hazards of an occupation, a business, or a profession; or medical treatment or medical or scientific experimentation conducted by professionally approved methods and such other person had been made aware of the risks involved prior to giving consent; and such defense may be established under this subparagraph by a preponderance of the evidence. §309(c)(3)(B)(ii).

Any person who knowingly makes any false material statement, representation, or certification in any application, record, report, plan, or other document filed or required to be maintained under this chapter or who knowingly falsifies, tampers with, or renders inaccurate any monitoring device or method required to be maintained under this chapter, shall upon conviction, be punished by a fine of not more than $10,000, or by imprisonment for not more than two years, or by both. If a conviction of a person is for a violation committed after a first conviction of such person under this paragraph, punishment shall be by a fine of not more than $20,000 per day of violation, or by imprisonment of not more than four years, or by both. §309(c)(4).

UNITED STATES OF AMERICA v. WILSON

133 F.3d 251 (4th Cir. 1997)

The defendants in this case were convicted of felony violations of the Clean Water Act for knowingly discharging fill and excavated material into wetlands of the United States without a permit. On this appeal they challenge: (1) the validity of federal regulations purporting to regulate activities that "could affect" interstate commerce; (2) the district court's application of the Clean Water Act to wetlands that do not have a "direct or indirect surface connection to other waters of the United States"; (3) the district court's application of the Clean Water Act to a practice known as "sidecasting" (depositing excavated material from wetland drainage ditches next to the ditch); (4) the district court's interpretation of the *mens rea* required for a felony conviction under the Act; (5) evidentiary rulings of the district court; and (6) aspects of their sentences.

Because we conclude that 33 C.F.R. §328.3(a)(3) (1993) (defining waters of the United States to include those waters whose degradation "could affect" interstate commerce) is unauthorized by the Clean Water Act as limited by the Commerce Clause and therefore is invalid, and that the district court erred in failing to require *mens rea* with respect to each element of an offense defined by the Act, we reverse and remand for a new trial....

The defendants also contend that the district court erred in instructing the jury about the criminal intent, the "*mens rea*," required to prove a felony violation of the Clean Water Act. They argue (1) that the statute requires a showing that they were aware of the *illegality* of their conduct, and (2) that the required *mens rea*, however it is defined, must accompany each element of the offense. They note that the district court's jury instructions comported with neither requirement.

The district court charged the jury that the government must prove each of four elements of the offense beyond a reasonable doubt:

- First, that is the defendant knowingly ... discharged or caused to be discharged a pollutant.
- Second, that the pollutant was discharged from a point source.
- Third, that the pollutant entered a water of the United States; and fourth, that the discharge was unpermitted.

The court defined an act as "knowingly" done "if it is done voluntarily and intentionally and not because of ignorance, mistake, accident or other innocent reason." For each felony count, the court stated,

> the government must prove that the defendants knew, one, that the areas which are the subject of these discharges had the general characteristics of wetland; and, two, the general nature of their acts. *The government does not have to prove that the defendants knew the actual legal status of wetlands or the actual legal status of the materials discharged into the wetlands. The government does not have to prove that the defendants knew that they were violating the law when they committed their acts.*

(Emphasis added). Finally, the court instructed on willful blindness, which it stated could stand in the place of actual knowledge. Determining the *mens rea* requirement of a felony violation of the Clean Water Act requires us to make an interpretation based on "construction of the statute and ... inference of the intent of Congress." *United States v. Balint*, 258 U.S. 250, 253, 66 L.Ed. 604, 42 S.Ct. 301 (1922), *quoted in Staples v. United States*, 511 U.S. 600, 605, 128 L. Ed. 2d 608, 114 S. Ct. 1793 (1994). We thus begin our analysis by looking at the language of 33 U.S.C. §1319, as well as its place in the larger statutory structure.

Section 1319(c)(2)(A), making an illegal discharge of a pollutant a felony if accompanied by the defined *mens rea*, provides: "Any person who *knowingly violates* section 1311 ... shall be punished." (Emphasis added). Section 1311 makes unlawful "the discharge of any pollutant" without a permit. And finally, §1362 defines "discharge of a pollutant" to include "any addition of any pollutant to navigable waters from any point source" and defines "navigable waters" as "waters of the United States." 33 U.S.C. §§1362(7) & (12). Within that statutory structure, we must determine the nature of intent that the statute requires for each element of the offense.

On a first reading of the clause, "any person who *knowingly violates section 1311 shall be punished," the order of words suggests that "knowingly" modifies "violates" so that the clause imposes punishment only when one violates the statute with knowledge that he is violating it, i.e.* with knowledge of the illegality of his conduct. But the statute's structure, the architecture of which includes a series of sections incorporating other sections, its legislative history, and the body of Supreme Court jurisprudence addressing *mens rea* of federal criminal statutes caution that our first reading may not so simply lead us to the proper interpretation.

Our first concern is a pragmatic one engendered by the overall structure of the Clean Water Act. The conduct that is made criminal with the "knowingly violates" language encompasses numerous elements from other substantive statutory sections. *See* 33 U.S.C. §1319(c)(2)(A). Each of those substantive sections may also be enforced with other civil and criminal penalties if the actions proscribed therein are performed with different scienter. *See generally* 33 U.S.C. §1319. If Congress intended that the "knowing" *mens rea* accompany each element of the offense, as we have previously assumed is the case, *see United States v. Ellen* , 961 F.2d 462, 466 n.2 (4th Cir. 1992), the task of inserting the alternative *mens rea* requirements for the multiple civil and criminal enforcement provisions within each substantive prohibition would require confusingly repetitious drafting. A shorthand method of accomplishing the same purpose thus would be to insert "knowingly" in a single place where the conduct is made criminal, in this case, §1319(c)(2)(A). *See United States v. International Minerals & Chemical Corp.*, 402 U.S. 558, 562, 29 L. Ed. 2d 178, 91 S. Ct. 1697 (1971) (the phrase "knowingly violates [applicable regulations]" was "a shorthand designation for specific acts or omissions which violate the act").

Our second and more profound problem with our first-blush interpretative proposal arises from a recognition of two general common law principles regarding *mens rea*. First, in Anglo-American jurisprudence, criminal offenses are ordinarily required to have a *mens rea*. *Staples*, 511 U.S. at 605. This supposition is based on "the contention that an injury can amount to a crime only when inflicted by intention." *Id.* (quoting *Morissette v. United States*, 342 U.S. 246, 250, 96 L. Ed. 288, 72 S. Ct. 240 (1952)). Indeed, statutes requiring no *mens rea* are generally disfavored. *See Staples*, 511 U.S. at 606. But a second and deeply-rooted common law principle is that ignorance of the law provides no defense to its violation. *See Cheek v. United States*, 498 U.S. 192, 199, 112 L.Ed. 2d 617, 111 S.Ct. 604 (1991); *Barlow v. United States*, 32 U.S. (7 Pet.) 404, 411, 8 L.Ed. 728 (1833) (Story, J.). Thus, while some level of deliberateness is usually required to impose criminal punishment, it is also usually true that the defendant need not appreciate the illegality of his conduct. Applying those principles to a statute similar to the one before us, the Supreme Court in *International Minerals* declined "to attribute to Congress the inaccurate view that [the] Act requires proof of knowledge of the law, as well as the facts." *International Minerals*, 402 U.S. at 563. In that case, the statute—which provided that whoever "knowingly violates any such regulation" shall be fined or imprisoned—was held to be a "shorthand designation" for knowledge of the specific acts or omissions which violate the Act. *Id.* at 559, 562. When so viewed, the Court noted, "the Act ... does not signal an exception to the rule that ignorance of the law is no excuse." *Id.* at 562. *Compare Liparota v. United States*, 471 U.S. 419, 423 & 425 n.9, 85 L.Ed. 2d 434, 105 S.Ct. 2084 (1995) (holding that a statute providing "who[ ]ever knowingly uses, transfers, acquires, alters or possesses [food stamps] in a manner not authorized by [the law]" was subject to a fine and imprisonment requires knowledge that the defendant know possession of food stamps was "unauthorized," but stating that this interpretation creates no mistake-of-law defense). In light of these background rules of common law, we may conclude that *mens rea* requires not that a defendant know that his conduct was illegal, but only that he "know the *facts that make his conduct illegal,*" *Staples*, 511 U.S. at 605, unless Congress clearly specifies otherwise. And this knowledge must generally be proven with respect to each element of the offense. *See, e.g., United States v. X-citement Video, Inc.*, 513 U.S. 64, 78, 130 L.Ed.2d 372, 115 S.Ct. 464 (1994) (construing a statute prohibiting knowingly shipping a visual depiction which involved "the use of a minor engaging in sexually explicit conduct" to require the defendant's knowledge that the person depicted was in fact a minor); *Ellen*, 961 F.2d at 466 n.2.

Finally, our first-blush reading of the phrase "knowingly violates" is cast into doubt by the legislative history, which suggests that Congress, by amending the statute in 1987, intended to facilitate enforcement of the Clean Water Act and increase the impact of sanctions by creating a separate felony provision for deliberate, as distinct from negligent, activity. Before the amendment, the Act imposed a single set of criminal penalties for "willful or negligent" violations. *See* 33 U.S.C. §1319(d)(1) (1986). The 1987 amendments, however, segregated the penalties for negligent violations, making them misdemeanors, and added felony provisions for knowing violations. *See* 33 U.S.C. §1319(c)(1)(A) ("negligent" violation) and §1319(c)(2)(A) ("knowing" violation). Thus, before 1987, the statute proscribed "willful or negligent" violations and after 1987 it proscribed separate "knowing" and "negligent" violations. In changing from "willful" to "knowing," we should assume that Congress intended to effect a change in meaning. *See United States v. Hopkins* , 53 F.3d 533, 539 (2d Cir. 1995); *United States v. Sinskey*, 119 F.3d 712, 716 (8th Cir. 1997). Because "willful" generally connotes a conscious performance of bad acts *with an appreciation of their illegality, see Ratzlaf v. United States*, 510 U.S. 135, 141, 126 L. Ed. 2d 615, 114 S. Ct. 655 (1994), we can conclude that Congress intended to provide a different and lesser standard when it used the word "knowingly." If we construe the word "knowingly" as requiring that the defendant must appreciate the illegality of his acts, we obliterate its distinction from the willfulness.

Based upon these interpretative guides, then, we cannot conclude that Congress intended to require the defendant to know that his conduct was illegal when it stated that "Any person who *knowingly* violates [incorporated statutory sections] ... shall be punished." The ready alternative interpretation is that Congress intended that the defendant have knowledge of each of the elements constituting the proscribed conduct even if he were unaware of their legal significance. This interpretation would not carry with it the corollary that the defendant's ignorance of his conduct's illegality provides him a defense, but would afford a defense for a mistake of fact. Thus, if a defendant thought he was discharging water when he was in fact discharging gasoline, he would not be guilty of knowingly violating the act which prohibits the discharge of pollutants. *See Ahmad v. United States*, 101 F.3d 386, 393 (5th Cir. 1996); *see also International Minerals*, 402 U.S. at 563-64.

Accordingly, we hold that the Clean Water Act, 33 U.S.C. §1319(c)(1)(A), requires the government to prove the defendant's knowledge of *facts* meeting each essential element of the substantive offense, *see Ellen*, 961 F.2d at 466 n.2, but need not prove that the defendant knew his conduct to be illegal, *see International Minerals*, 402 U.S. at 563.

Urging us to reach a different conclusion, the defendants argue that we should be governed by the decision in *Liparota v. United States*, 471 U.S. 419, 85 L. Ed. 2d 434, 105 S. Ct. 2084 (1985), where the Court concluded that in proving a violation of a food stamp statute, the government had to prove that the defendant *knew that his action or his possession of food stamps was unauthorized.* The Court reached the conclusion there largely because, if it were not to require such a *mens rea*, the result would be to outlaw a number of acts which a reasonable person would very likely believe were entirely unregulated, including actions that were wholly accidental. The statute provided that "whoever knowingly uses, transfers, acquires, alters, or possesses [food stamps] in any manner not authorized by [the statute] or the regulations" was subject to a fine and imprisonment. 7 U.S.C. §2024(b)(1). If the court did not apply a requirement that the defendant appreciate that his conduct was unauthorized, the result would render criminal "a nonrecipient of food stamps who 'possessed' stamps because he was mistakenly sent them through the mail due to an administrative error, 'altered' them by tearing them up, and 'transferred' them by throwing them away." *Id.* at 426-27. The Court concluded that the evidence of Congress' intent to create such a harsh regime was too meager to justify the interpretation. At the same time, however, the Court reiterated its conclusion that even then it did not provide a mistake-of-law defense, stating that no defendant could escape culpability by demonstrating that it did not know it to be illegal to use food stamps in an authorized way. *Id.* at 425 n.9.

In our case, we believe the several factors we have already discussed indicate a different congressional intent than that found by the Court in *Liparota*, as we too resist the temptation to create a mistake-of-law defense. As we noted, interpreting the phrase "knowingly violate" to mean violation with knowledge of an act's illegality would require us to ignore the distinction between a knowing and a willful violation, a distinction that Congress recognized in amending the law in 1987. We also note that at the time the penalty provisions of the Clean Water Act were first written, the Supreme Court had already held in *International Minerals* that the use of the same construction at issue here—"knowingly violates [applicable regulations]"—was "a shorthand designation for specific acts or omissions which violate the Act." 402 U.S. at 562. Thus, it is logical to conclude that Congress would have used a similar shorthand designation to incorporate the *mens rea* requirement against each of the substantive requirements found in the incorporated sections of the Clean Water Act without also intending to create a defense of ignorance of the law.

The defendants argue, however, that *International Minerals* has no bearing on this case because it was a case involving a "public welfare" offense. Under this somewhat amorphous exception to general common law scienter requirements, a threat to public health and safety posed by an object or activity and the inherent dangerousness or deleterious nature of the prohibited item are considered sufficient in themselves to place the defendant on notice of the likelihood of regulation and thus to excuse the need to prove *mens rea* with respect to one or more elements of the offense. Even under this public welfare doctrine, however, true or rigid strict liability does not generally follow, as ignorance of the facts usually remains a defense. *See Staples*, 511 U.S. at 607 n.3. Thus, *International Minerals* held that prosecution for transporting sulfuric acid without following proper regulatory procedures under a statute prohibiting one from "knowingly violating any such regulation" did not establish an ignorance of-the-law defense by requiring the government to prove the defendant knew of the regulation and appreciated that his conduct violated it. 402 U.S. at 563-64. Rather, the government would have to prove that the defendant knew of the operative facts which themselves were the essential elements of the regulatory violation. *Id.* The Court thus preserved mistake-of-fact defenses and did not, at the same time, create true strict liability. Later cases which did not involve "public welfare" offenses have required no more than knowledge of the facts. *See, e.g., Staples*, 511 U.S. at 606.

The fact that *International Minerals* involved regulations of an inherently deleterious substance of a type not involved in the present prosecution does not undercut our belief that Congress did not here intend to create a mistake-of-law defense. Even though the materials involved in this case, fill and native soil from a wetland, may not be inherently deleterious, the Clean Water Act is, as a general matter, largely concerned with pollutants that are inherently deleterious. The legislative history of the Act records Congress' explicit concern with public health. See S. Rep. No. 92-414 (1972), reprinted in 1972 U.S.C.C.A.N. 3668, 3670-71. And the Act specifically authorized research to determine the harmful effects of pollutants on the health or welfare of persons. *See* 33 U.S.C. §1254(c). To date, three other circuits have concluded that the Clean Water Act involves public welfare offenses, recognizing that in each of those cases the pollutants were inherently deleterious. *See Sinskey*, 119 F.3d at 716 (meat packing plant waste water containing large amounts of ammonia nitrate); *Hopkins*, 53 F.3d at 534 (waste water containing zinc and other toxic chemicals); *United States v. Weitzenhoff*, 35 F.3d 1275, 1284 (9th Cir. 1994) (sewage).

While a statute which in some applications is a public welfare statute may in other applications be held to require a different *mens rea*, *see Staples*, 511 U.S. at 605, even in the latter situation, the government need prove only that the defendant knew the operative facts which make his action illegal. The government need not prove that the defendants understood the legal consequences of those facts or were even aware of the existence of the law granting them significance. *Compare United States v. Freed*, 401 U.S. 601, 609, 28 L.Ed.2d 356, 91 S.Ct. 1112 (1971) (holding that violation for possession of unregistered hand grenade under 26 U.S.C. §5861(d) was public welfare offense and the government was not required to prove that defendant knew grenade to be unregistered) with *Staples*, 511 U.S. at 619 (holding that violation for possession of unregistered machine gun under 26 U.S.C. §5861(d) was not a public welfare offense and the government thus was required to prove defendant's knowledge of the specific characteristics which qualify the weapon as a statutory machine gun); *see also Hamling v. United States*, 418 U.S. 87, 119-121, 41 L.Ed.2d 590, 94 S.Ct. 2887 (1974) (requiring government to prove that a defendant knew the contents of a mailed package, but not their legal status as obscene materials); *accord Rosen v. United States*, 161 U.S. 29, 32-33, 40 L.Ed. 606, 16 S.Ct. 434 (1896).

In light of our conclusion that the government need only prove the defendant's knowledge of the facts meeting each essential element of the substantive offense and not the fact that defendant knew his conduct to be illegal, in order to establish a felony violation of the Clean Water Act, we hold that it must prove: (1) that the defendant knew that he was discharging a substance, eliminating a prosecution for accidental discharges; (2) that the defendant correctly identified the substance he was discharging, not mistaking it for a different, unprohibited substance; (3) that the defendant knew the method or instrumentality used to discharge the pollutants; (4) that the defendant knew the physical characteristics of the property into which the pollutant was discharged that identify it as a wetland, such as the presence of water and water-loving vegetation; (5) that the defendant was aware of the facts establishing the required link between the wetland and waters of the United States; and (6) that the defendant knew he did not have a permit. This last requirement does not require the government to show that the defendant knew that permits were available or required. Rather, it, like the other requirements, preserves the availability of a mistake of fact offense if the defendant has something he mistakenly believed to be a permit to make the discharges for which he is being prosecuted.

While we thus reject the defendants' challenge to the district court's instructions based on the contention that the government must prove awareness of the illegality of their conduct, we agree that the instructions did not adequately impose on the government the burden of proving knowledge *with regard to each statutory element.* For this reason, a new trial is required.

See also *United States v. Deaton*, 209 F.3d 331 (4th Cir. 2000); *United States v. Sartori*, 62 F.Supp.2d 1362 (S.D.Fla. 1999); *National Ass'n. of Home Builders v. United States Army Corps of Engineers*, 2000 WL 433072 (E.D.Va. 2000).

UNITED STATES v. POZSGAI

999 F.2d 719 (3d Cir. 1993)

In this civil enforcement action, John and Gizella Pozsgai appeal the district court's judgment finding them strictly liable for discharging fill material into wetlands on their property in violation of the Clean Water Act. Defendants also appeal various orders granting the government injunctive relief, finding John Pozsgai in contempt of the injunction, and denying the Pozsgais' motion for relief from judgment. We will affirm.

I

In April 1987, the U.S. Army Corps of Engineers received information that fill material was being dumped into wetlands on a 14-acre site in Morrisville, Pennsylvania. The Corps investigated the site, determined that nearly the entire property constituted wetlands, and found that concrete rubble, earth, and building scraps had been dumped onto one-half to three-quarters of an acre of the wetlands portion of the property. Corps biologist and field investigator Martin Miller described the site as "a forested wetland dominated by arrowwood" and noted "areas of standing water were scattered throughout the site," and "a stream flows along the east border of the property and wetland and is a tributary to the Pennsylvania Canal." Miller also observed several species of vegetation on the site which require a saturated environment to survive, including skunk cabbage, sensitive fern, red maple, sweet gum, ash, and aspen. Soil borings taken by Miller and other Corps biologists confirmed the initial determination of wetlands, revealing water either at or within one inch of the surface of the soil. This so-called hydric soil takes 100 years or more to develop.

Unpermitted discharge of dredged or fill materials into certain wetlands violates a regulation promulgated under the Clean Water Act, 33 U.S.C. §1251 *et seq.* (1988). Miller's field report stated that "the violation consists of the placement of fill (concrete rubble, earth, and building scraps) in three portions of the wetland for the purpose of raising the elevation for construction of a garage." The report identified the violator as John Pozsgai.

At the time of the Corps investigation, John and Gizella Pozsgai were considering purchasing the property to expand their truck repair business. John Pozsgai planned to build a garage on the property, a project which would require filling a significant amount of the area. In preparation for this purchase, Pozsgai hired the engineering firm of J.G. Park Associates to examine the suitability of the property for building. On December 12, 1986, J.G. Park President Nicholas Moran advised Pozsgai by letter of the results of its site investigation of the property. The letter stated:

> Based upon this investigation, it is my professional opinion that the entire site meets the criteria set forth by the Army Corps of Engineers as "wetlands." This is based upon soils, hydrology, and vegetation.
>
> Please be advised that any further development that might be considered on this site would have to be approved and reviewed by the Army Corps of Engineers, and it has been our experience in the past that the Corps is most reluctant to issue permits for sites that have conditions such as this.

This advice turned out to be accurate. Corps biologist Miller spoke to Pozsgai by telephone and advised him not to place fill in the wetlands until he had obtained a permit. Pozsgai told Miller a previous prospective buyer was responsible for at least some of the filling but that Pozsgai planned to fill enough area to build a garage. Pozsgai also agreed to stop his filling activities until he had complied with the permit requirements and said his engineer would call Miller to discuss these requirements.

Pozsgai continued his efforts to purchase the property. Apparently dissatisfied with J.G. Park's opinion, Pozsgai hired a second engineer, Ezra Golub, to evaluate the property. Golub, too, advised Pozsgai the property was wetlands and the Corps would have to approve any building. Seeking yet a third opinion, Pozsgai hired Majors Engineers, who concurred in the views expressed by the previous two engineers.

After receiving the engineers' reports, Pozsgai renegotiated the sale contract for the property. The original sale contract, for a purchase price of $175,000, made the sale contingent on Pozsgai obtaining building permits for his proposed garage. The revised contract replaced the contingency provision with an "as is" clause and included a $32,000 reduction in the purchase price, from $175,000 to $143,000. Under this revised sale contract, Pozsgai purchased the property on June 19, 1987.

In the meantime, Corps investigator Miller continued to monitor activities at the property. Following his April 1987 visit, Miller had several telephone conversations with Pozsgai. Each time, Miller told Pozsgai to stop his filling activities and explained the permit requirements. Additionally, the Corps issued a cease and desist letter to the Cassalias, the prior owners of the property. The Cassalias responded by letter, stating they had sold the property to Pozsgai but had never given him permission to place fill on the property. Miller returned to the site in August 1987 and observed that fill had been placed on an additional two acres of the property. He reiterated to Pozsgai that he would need a permit to discharge the fill and indicated the Corps would issue a cease and desist order if Pozsgai did not stop filling the wetlands. Pozsgai told Miller that township officials and the police had visited him and shown him the cease and desist letter sent to the Cassalias. He also told Miller he had stopped work on the property.

On September 3, 1987, the Corps sent John and Gizella Pozsgai a cease and desist letter. The letter stated fill was being placed on the Pozsgais' property in federally regulated wetlands without a permit in violation of the Clean Water Act and directed the Pozsgais to stop "conducting, contracting, or permitting any further work of this nature." In response, the Pozsgais' counsel wrote the Corps on September 24, reporting that John Pozsgai had conferred with engineers regarding the cease and desist letter and expressing Pozsgai's opinion that the site did not "naturally" contain wetlands but had only become saturated as a result of construction of an overpass near the property.

Miller visited the site again on October 6 and observed additional fill. On this visit, Miller determined almost the entire property constituted wetlands. He ordered Pozsgai not to do any more filling on the property. Pozsgai said he believed the area was not wetlands because he had excavated the stream on the property. Miller returned to the site in November, again observing new fill since his last visit. Miller reiterated the need for Pozsgai to obtain a permit. On December 17, the Corps sent the Pozsgais a second cease and desist letter, directing them to stop filling, and offering them two options to resolve the violation—removing all fill material and restoring the site to its former condition, or obtaining a Water Quality Certification from the Pennsylvania Department of Environmental Resources.

In May 1988, the Corps again discovered that John Pozsgai was continuing to fill the wetlands. Subsequent investigation revealed Pozsgai had received several hundred truckloads of fill from at least five different hauling companies. On August 18, 1988, following a complaint from a neighbor about the dumping, the U.S. Environmental Protection Agency installed a video camera in the neighbor's house. The video camera recorded dumping on the property.

On August 24, 1988, the United States filed a civil complaint in federal district court, alleging that John and Gizella Pozsgai, and two of the hauling companies hired by the Pozsgais, had violated the Clean Water Act by filling the wetlands on the Pozsgais' property without a permit. The government sought an order to restore the property to its original state, as well as civil penalties. It simultaneously moved for a temporary restraining order and a preliminary injunction to stop further discharge. The district court entered the TRO. Two days later, on August 26, the video camera recorded 25 truckloads of dirt dumped on the site, and a man, identified by witnesses as John Pozsgai, operating a bulldozer leveling the fill.

On September 2, the government obtained an Order to Show Cause why Pozsgai should not be held in contempt for violating the TRO. The district court held a hearing on the contempt proceeding and the preliminary injunction on September 9 and September 16. After the hearing, the court granted the preliminary injunction and held Pozsgai in contempt, ordering him to pay $5,000 within 48 hours.

In the meantime, the government initiated a parallel federal criminal proceeding against John Pozsgai. On December 30, 1988, a jury convicted Pozsgai of 40 counts of unpermitted discharge. The district judge sentenced him to three years for the pre-Sentencing Guideline counts and twenty-seven months for post-Guideline counts, to run concurrently, placed him on five years probation, and fined him $200,000. We affirmed the conviction. *United States v. Pozsgai*, 897 F.2d 524 (3d Cir.), *cert. denied*, 498 U.S. 812, 111 S.Ct. 48, 112 L.Ed.2d 24 (1990).

On January 8, 1990, the district court granted a permanent injunction in the government's civil action. The court found the property contained wetlands subject to the Corps' jurisdiction and held the Pozsgais and the haulers strictly liable for the unpermitted discharge. It further ordered defendants to implement the plan developed by the Corps to restore the property. The Pozsgais filed a motion to reconsider which the district court denied.

On June 18, the court implemented its restoration order and directed the defendant haulers to restore the property by removing fill from the wetland areas and depositing it in other non-wetland areas of the property. The Pozsgais filed a Fed.R.Civ.P. 60(b) motion for relief from this order, objecting to the locations where the haulers placed the fill and requesting the court to order the haulers to remove the fill from the Pozsgais' property altogether. The court denied the motion, ruling that the Pozsgais had no "veto power" over the restoration process and that it would be inequitable to require the haulers to move the fill a second time when the Pozsgais had improperly disposed of it in the first place. The court entered final judgment on April 1, 1992. The Pozsgais appealed.

II

In furtherance of its purpose to "restore and maintain the chemical, physical, and biological integrity of the Nation's waters," 33 U.S.C. §1251(a), the Clean Water Act prohibits the discharge of pollutants into navigable waters without a permit. 33 U.S.C. § 1311; *United States v. Riverside Bayview Homes*, 474 U.S. 121, 123, 88 L.Ed. 2d 419, 106 S.Ct. 455 (1985). The Act defines the operative terms of this prohibition broadly. The term "pollutants" includes fill material such as "dredged spoil,... rock, sand, [and] cellar dirt," 33 U.S.C. §1362(6), and "navigable waters" means "the waters of the United States," *id.* §1362(7). In so defining the term "navigable waters," Congress expressed a clear intent "to repudiate limits that had been placed on federal regulations by earlier water pollution control statutes and to exercise its powers under the Commerce Clause to regulate at least some waters that would not be deemed 'navigable' under the classical understanding of that term." *Riverside Bayview Homes*, 474 U.S. at 133 (citing S. Conf. Rep. No. 92-1236, p. 144 (1972); 118 Cong. Rec. 33756-57 (1972) (statement of Rep. Dingell)).

The Corps of Engineers has by regulation interpreted the term "waters of the United States" to include "wetlands," defined as "areas that are inundated or saturated by surface or ground water at a frequency or duration sufficient to support, and that under normal circumstances do support, a prevalence of vegetation typically adapted for life in saturated soil conditions, [and] generally includes swamps, marshes, bogs, and similar areas." 33 C.F.R. §328.3(b) (1992). The regulation extends the Corps' authority to wetlands "adjacent" to tributaries of waters presently or formerly used, or susceptible to use, in interstate commerce. *Id.* The Supreme Court has upheld this regulation as a reasonable interpretation of the Clean Water Act. *Riverside Bayview Homes*, 474 U.S. at 135.

Section 404 of the Act authorizes the Corps of Engineers to issue permits for "the discharge of dredged or fill material into the navigable waters...." 33 U.S.C. §1344(a). The permit program is the central enforcement tool of the Clean Water Act. The program reflects the Act's strategic shift in water pollution policy, which previously had employed only water quality standards. These standards proved unsuccessful in controlling pollution because the Corps had difficulty linking the quality of the water to discharges from a particular source. The Act sought to avoid this problem by focusing pollution control efforts at the point of discharge. See *EPA v. California ex rel. State Water Resources Control Board*, 426 U.S. 200, 204, 48 L.Ed. 2d 578, 96 S.Ct. 2022 (1976). The Environmental Protection Agency implemented that strategy in part by establishing national effluent standards. The permit system translates these standards into site-specific limitations to accommodate individual circumstances and ease enforcement. *Id.* at 205. Unpermitted discharge is the archetypal Clean Water Act violation, and subjects the discharger to strict liability. 33 U.S.C. §1311(a) ("except as in compliance with [a permit], the discharge of any pollutant by any person shall be unlawful").

III

On appeal, the Pozsgais do not dispute they discharged fill onto wetlands without a permit. They urge instead that this conduct did not violate the Clean Water Act. The Pozsgais contend that filling wetlands does not constitute discharge of pollutants "into water" within the meaning of the Clean Water Act, that their wetlands fall outside the Corps' regulation and permit requirements, and that the regulation as applied to them violates the Commerce Clause.

A

We first address the Pozsgais' argument that they did not discharge pollutants "into water" within the meaning of the Clean Water Act. 33 U.S.C. §1362(6). They contend that the fill materials deposited on their property were not "pollutants," and that they discharged only into "wetlands," which are not equivalent to "water."

To assess these contentions, we look to the statute. The operative section of the Clean Water Act is §301, which provides that absent a permit, "the discharge of any pollutant by any person shall be unlawful." 33 U.S.C. §1311(a). The Act defines "pollutant" to mean "dredged spoil, rock, sand" and other materials "discharged into water," *id.* §1362(6), and defines "discharge of a pollutant" to mean "any addition of any pollutant to navigable waters from any point source," *id.* §1362(12). The Act defines "navigable waters" to mean "the waters of the United States." *Id.* §1362(7). The Corps' regulation upheld in *Riverside Bayview* defines "waters of the United States" to include certain wetlands.

(1)

In ruling the Pozsgais' fill material constituted "pollutants," the district court cited evidence that they placed "concrete rubble" and "cinder block" on their property and cleared and redeposited vegetation there. The court held each of these qualified as "pollutants," defined to include "dredged spoil, solid waste,... rock, sand,... municipal, and agricultural waste...." 33 U.S.C. §1362(6). On appeal, the Pozsgais stress the absence of the words "fill material" in the definition of "pollutant." They point to Congress' use of the term "fill material" in the Act's permitting provision, *id.* §1344, as evidence Congress was aware of this phrase and chose not to include it in the definition of "pollutant." This argument is unconvincing. Because the term "pollutant" includes "dredged spoil, rock, [and] sand," *id.* §1362(6), which are the constituents of the fill material used here, the materials discharged by the Pozsgais constituted "pollutants."

(2)

The Pozsgais' second contention is more sweeping. They argue that the phrase "into water" in the definition of "pollutant" forecloses application of the Clean Water Act to their activities, which consisted only of depositing fill material into "wetlands." Again, the district court disagreed, citing the Corps regulation that defines "waters of the United States" to include "wetlands" adjacent to waters used in interstate commerce, 33 C.F.R. §328.3(a)(7), and to the Supreme Court's *Riverside Bayview Homes* decision upholding this regulation as a reasonable interpretation of the Act, 474 U.S. at 135.

The Pozsgais contend the district court misconstrued the Act. In their view, the phrase "into water" in the definition of "pollutant" is the critical limiting feature of the Act because this phrase determines application of the Act's permit requirement. They base this argument on the Act's liability section, which provides that without a permit, "the discharge of any pollutant by any person shall be unlawful." 33 U.S.C. §1311 (a). By contrast, they contend, the phrase "waters of the United States"—and the Corps' regulation interpreting that phrase to include adjacent wetlands—only define the Act's geographic jurisdiction and cannot alone support a finding of liability. Thus, the Pozsgais maintain, the district court's reliance on these provisions, and on *Riverside Bayview*'s interpretation of them, was misplaced. They conclude that because neither *Riverside Bayview* nor the Corps regulation address the definition of "pollutant," these authorities do not obviate the statutory obstacle to liability created by the requirement that materials only constitute "pollutants" if they are discharged "into water."

The interpretive problem raised by the Pozsgais' argument lies in knitting together the various statutory provisions. Incorporating the definition of "pollutant" in §1362(6) into the definition of "discharge of a pollutant" in §1362(12) creates an apparent redundancy, as the term "discharge of a pollutant" then reads: "any addition of any 'dredged spoil ... discharged into water' to navigable waters from any point source." The question then becomes how the phrase "into water" and the phrase "to navigable waters" co-exist in this definition. The Pozsgais avoid this problem by ignoring the definition of "discharge of a pollutant," and focusing instead exclusively on the definition of "pollutant" and the use of the word "pollutant" in the Act's liability section, §1311. This reading is untenable because although §1311 contains the word "pollutant," it does so in the context of expressly prohibiting "discharge of any pollutant." We read this as a clear cross-reference to the definition of "discharge of a pollutant" in §1362(12).

At oral argument, the Pozsgais argued §§1362(6) and (12) are not in conflict. They asserted that because the term "discharge of a pollutant" itself includes the term "pollutant," the former definition, including its use of "navigable waters," is necessarily limited by the phrase "into water" in the definition of "pollutant." The more natural reading of the definition of "discharge of a pollutant" is that the phrase "navigable waters" modifies the phrase "into water," and accordingly, that the critical definition is that given the term "navigable waters." As a textual matter, the word "navigable" is an adjective modifying the word "water." Moreover, the statute contains numerous references to the phrase "navigable waters," revealing that this phrase, rather than "into water," is the focus of the Act's coverage. The Act's "Congressional declaration of goals and policy" states: "it is the national goal that the discharge of pollutants into the *navigable waters* be eliminated by 1985." 33 U.S.C. §1251(a)(1). Section 404 provides that "the Secretary [of the Army] may issue permits ... for the discharge of dredged or fill material into the *navigable waters* at specified disposal sites." *Id.* §1344(a). Additionally, the Act defines "navigable waters" to mean "waters of the United States." *Id.* §1362(7).[6]

The legislative history also demonstrates the significance and breadth of the term "navigable waters." The Conference Report states: "the conferees fully intend that the term 'navigable waters' be given the broadest possible constitutional interpretation...." S. Rep. No. 1236, 92d Cong., 2d Sess. 144, reprinted in 1 A Legislative History of the Water Pollution Control Act Amendments of 1972 327 (1973); *see also* H.R. Rep. No. 911, 92d Cong., 2d Sess. 131 (containing identical language), in 1 Legislative History 818.

Moreover, the Senate Report makes clear it is the discharge of materials constituting "pollutants" into "navigable waters" that triggers the Act's permit requirement. The Report provides:

> For the first time the Committee would add to the law a definition of the term pollutant. In order to trigger the control requirements over addition of materials to the navigable water, waters of the contiguous zone and the ocean, it is necessary to define such materials so that litigable issues are avoided over the question of whether the addition of a particular material is subject to the control requirements.... The control strategy of the Act extends to navigable waters....

S.Rep.No. 414, 92d Cong., 1st Sess. 77-78, in 2 Legislative History 1494-95. This legislative history supports our view that the phrase "navigable waters" rather than "into water" is the critical statutory language. It also demonstrates the definition of "pollutant" establishes the types of materials whose discharge violates the Act rather than the locus of their discharge, further undermining the significance of the "into water" phrase.

Our emphasis on "navigable waters" also comports with the interpretation of the Clean Water Act by other courts, who have reached the same conclusion without expressly considering the "into water" portion of the definition of "pollutant." In upholding the Corps' wetlands regulation in *Riverside Bayview*, the Supreme Court stated simply: "the act prohibits discharges into 'navigable waters,' see Clean Water Act §§301(a), 404(a), 502(12), 33 U.S.C. §§1311(a), 1344(a), 1362(12)." 474 U.S. at 133. We find significant both the Court's summary treatment of this question and its citation only to the "discharge of a pollutant" definition, §1362(12), not to the "pollutant" definition, §1362(6).

The Pozsgais maintain the phrase "navigable waters," which they note is defined as "waters of the United States," refers only to the geographic jurisdiction of the Act. Therefore, they contend, that definition does not modify the phrase "into water," which they read only to describe the conduct regulated by the Act. This distinction is illusory. The purpose of extending the Corps' geographic jurisdiction to "waters of the United States," including adjacent wetlands, is precisely so the Corps can control conduct occurring on these wetlands, *i.e.*, the discharge of pollutants. Indeed, such conduct has given rise to this action.

For the reasons we have outlined, we believe Congress intended "navigable waters" to be the controlling phrase in defining the scope of the Clean Water Act, and we believe this phrase modifies the more general term "into water" appearing in the definition of "pollutant." Accordingly, the Pozsgais' wetlands filling activities constituted "discharge into water" and fall within the statute. Our conclusion that the Act's permit requirement applies to pollutants discharged into "navigable waters" does not, however, dispose of the Pozsgais' second statutory argument—that the Corps' wetlands regulation represents an impermissible construction of the unambiguous statutory term "water."

B

In asserting the term "water" as used in the Clean Water Act is unambiguous, the Pozsgais seek to bring this case within the exception to the rule of deference to an agency's statutory interpretation established by *Chevron U.S.A., Inc. v. Natural Resources Defense Council*, 467 U.S. 837, 81 L.Ed.2d 694, 104 S.Ct. 2778 (1984). Under *Chevron*, courts should not defer to an agency regulation where legislative language is unambiguous because Congress has chosen to define precisely the statutory meaning and has left no implicit or explicit gap in statutory coverage for the agency to fill. 467 U.S. at 843-44. Where, on the other hand, a statute is "silent or ambiguous with respect to the specific issue, the question for the court is whether the agency's [regulation addressing the issue] is based on a permissible construction of the statute." *Id.* at 843. Thus, *Chevron* commands a two-step approach. The court first determines whether the statute is clear, and if it is unclear, the court decides whether the agency's construction is reasonable. *N.L.R.B. v. New Jersey Bell Telephone Co.*, 936 F.2d 144, 147 (3d Cir. 1991).

Applying *Chevron* in *Riverside Bayview*, the Supreme Court squarely rejected the contention that "water" cannot mean "wetlands." Like the Pozsgais, the defendant in *Riverside Bayview* sought to place fill materials on its property without a Clean Water Act permit in preparation for a construction project, and the Corps of Engineers obtained an injunction against the filling. The defendant contended the Corps' regulation extending the permit requirement to adjacent wetlands exceeded the bounds of the Clean Water Act. Rejecting this contention, the Court determined not only that the phrase "water" lacked a fixed meaning, 474 U.S. at 132, but also that the Corps "acted reasonably in interpreting the Act to require permits for the discharge of fill material into wetlands adjacent to the 'waters of the United States,'" *id.* at 139.

In urging Congress' use of the term "water" forecloses application of the Act to their activities, the Pozsgais insist the word "water" means "the liquid state of H20," not "wetlands" or "moist soil" or "dry land that the Corps determines to be water." In *Riverside Bayview*, the Supreme Court took a different view, stating:

> On a purely linguistic level, it may appear unreasonable to classify "lands," wet or otherwise, as "waters." Such a simplistic response, however, does justice neither to the problem faced by the Corps in defining the scope of its authority under §404(a) nor to the realities of the problem of water pollution that the Clean Water Act was intended to combat. In determining the limits of its power to regulate discharges under the Act, the Corps must necessarily choose some point at which water ends and land begins. Our common experience tells us that this is often no easy task: the transition from water to solid ground is not necessarily or even typically an abrupt one. Rather, between open waters and dry land may lie shallows, marshes, mudflats, swamps, bogs—in short, a huge array of areas that are not wholly aquatic but nevertheless fall far short of being dry land. Where on this continuum to find the limit of "waters" is far from obvious.

474 U.S. at 132.

Having determined the term "water" was ambiguous, the Court then moved to *Chevron*'s second step and considered whether the Corps' interpretation of the term to include adjacent wetlands was reasonable. The Court noted that, in determining "the landward limit of Federal jurisdiction under Section 404 [of the Clean Water Act] must include any adjacent wetlands that form the border of or are in reasonable proximity to other waters of the United States," the Corps concluded that "water moves in hydrologic cycles, and the pollution of [adjacent wetlands] ... will affect the water quality of the other waters within that aquatic system." *Riverside Bayview*, 474 U.S. at 121 (quoting 42 Fed. Reg. 37128, 88 L. Ed. 2d 419, 106 S. Ct. 455 (1977)). Upholding this interpretation, the Court recognized "the evident breadth of congressional concern for protection of water quality and aquatic ecosystems" embodied in the Act, 474 U.S. at 133, and determined: "we cannot say that the Corps' conclusion that adjacent wetlands are inseparably bound up with the 'waters' of the United States—based as it is on the Corps' and EPA's technical expertise—is unreasonable," *id.* at 134.

The Pozsgais attempt to distinguish *Riverside Bayview* on the ground that the Court based its ruling on the "navigable waters" definition rather than the "into water" phrase. But as we have shown, "navigable waters" is the operative phrase. Moreover, as the quoted passage indicates, the Supreme Court's analysis dealt with a question common to both statutory phrases—whether the Corps reasonably interpreted the term "water" to include adjacent wetlands.

The rationales underlying *Chevron* apply with particular force to the Corps' application of the Clean Water Act to wetlands. In *Chevron*, the Court defended deference to agency interpretations on the grounds that unlike a court, an agency has specialized knowledge of the relevant statutory area and is a politically accountable body. 467 U.S. at 865 ("judges are not experts in the field, and are not part of either political branch of the Government"); *see* Cass R. Sunstein, *Law and Administration after Chevron*, 90 Colum. L. Rev. 2071, 2086-87 (1990).

The *Chevron* Court indicated these rationales are particularly powerful where "the regulatory scheme is technical and complex." 467 U.S. at 865. Like the Clean Air Act in *Chevron*, the Clean Water Act addresses a scientifically complicated subject, and has an intricate regulatory structure. Thus, the Supreme Court recognized in *Riverside Bayview*:

> In view of the breadth of federal regulatory authority contemplated by the Act itself and the inherent difficulties of defining precise bounds to regulable waters, the Corps' ecological judgment about the relationship between waters and their adjacent wetlands provides an adequate basis for a legal judgment that adjacent wetlands may be defined as waters under the Act.

474 U.S. at 134; *see also Arkansas v. Oklahoma*, 117 L.Ed. 2d 239, 112 S.Ct. 1046, 1061 (1992) (reversing Court of Appeals decision to invalidate Clean Water Act permit issued by EPA because that court failed to defer to EPA's interpretation of its water quality regulation and therefore "made a policy choice that it was not authorized to make"); *Chemical Manufacturers Ass'n v. Natural Resources Defense Council*, 470 U.S. 116, 125, 84 L.Ed. 2d 90, 105 S.Ct. 1102 (1985) (deferring to EPA interpretation of Clean Water Act because "EPA's understanding of this very 'complex statute' is a sufficiently rational one to preclude a court from substituting its judgment for that of EPA," and citing *Chevron*).

The *Chevron* Court's concern that agencies have political accountability, which courts lack, also supports deference to the Corps' wetlands regulation. In articulating this rationale, the Court reasoned:

> the arguments over policy that are advanced in the parties' briefs create the impression that respondents are now waging in a judicial forum a specific policy battle which they ultimately lost in the agency and in the 32 jurisdictions opting for the "bubble concept," but one which was never waged in the Congress. Such policy arguments are more properly addressed to legislators or administrators, not to judges.... In such a case, federal judges—who have no constituency—have a duty to respect legitimate policy choices made by those who do.

467 U.S. at 864-66.

The regulation the Pozsgais challenge here represents the product of a nearly 20-year policy battle over the scope of federal wetlands protection. The Corps initially interpreted the term "navigable waters" to apply only to those waters "subject to the ebb and flow of the tide," the regulatory definition used by the Corps under the River and Harbor Act of 1899. The Environmental Protection Agency, which shared administrative authority under the Clean Water Act with the Corps, believed the Act should be construed to cover wetlands because of their significance to water pollution control. This fight culminated in a 1975 court decision ordering the Corps to revise and broaden its regulation. *Natural Resources Defense Council v. Callaway*, 392 F. Supp. 685 (D.D.C. 1975). Following this decision, the Corps revised its regulation, a process which lasted two years, engendered more than 4,500 comments, and resulted in a final rule defining the term "navigable waters" to include wetlands. 42 Fed. Reg. 37122 (1977).

Nonetheless, during the debate on the Clean Water Act of 1977, "because of the pressure of many farm, forestry and land development groups, there were continued efforts to amend the Act to redefine the term 'navigable waters' in a more traditional and restrictive sense.... None passed." *Avoyelles Sportsmen's League, Inc. v. Alexander*, 511 F.Supp. 278, 288 (W.D.La. 1981), *aff'd*, 715 F.2d 897 (5th Cir. 1983). Thus, the *Avoyelles* court concluded, "wetlands is a jurisdictional term, the product of the legislative process, of political pressure groups." 511 F.Supp. at 288; *see also Riverside Bayview*, 474 U.S. at 138 (citing Congress' refusal to limit the definition of "navigable waters" in the 1977 Act as "additional support for a conclusion that Congress in 1977 acquiesced in the Corps' definition of waters as including adjacent wetlands").

The Pozsgais acknowledge the Corps' wetlands jurisdiction continues to be the subject of heated political debate. They note "numerous Congressional hearings have been held," and 52 bills introduced in Congress, to address the regulation of wetlands. Indeed, the dispute over the scope of federal wetlands regulation has been at least as dominant a feature of the political landscape as the debate over the "bubble concept" at issue in *Chevron*. And like the plaintiffs opposed to EPA's "bubble" regulation in *Chevron*, the Pozsgais seek here to "wage in a judicial forum a specific policy battle which [was] ultimately lost in the agency." 467 U.S. at 864. But as the Supreme Court stated last term, "it is not our role ... to decide which policy choice is the better one, for it is clear that Congress has entrusted such decisions" to the Corps of Engineers. *Arkansas v. Oklahoma*, 112 S.Ct. at 1061. Therefore, we hold that the Clean Water Act's use of the word "water," both as part of the "into water" phrase in the definition of "pollutant" and in the phrase "navigable waters," pose no statutory obstacle to the Corps regulation under which the district court found the Pozsgais liable.

IV

The Pozsgais also contend the wetlands on their property fell outside the scope of the Corps regulation prohibiting unpermitted discharge on adjacent wetlands. In disputing application of the regulation to their activities, the Pozsgais make two arguments, one based on the evidence, the other based on the terms of the regulation. In the evidentiary argument, the Pozsgais maintain the government failed to prove their wetlands are "adjacent" within the meaning of the regulation.

A

The regulation grants the Corps jurisdiction over "waters of the United States," defined in 33 C.F.R. §328.3(a) to include: "all waters which are currently used, or were used in the past, or may be susceptible to use in interstate or foreign commerce," §328.3(a)(1); "tributaries of [these] waters," §328.3(a)(5); and "wetlands adjacent to [these] waters [or their tributaries]," §328.3(a)(7). Applying this regulation, the district court found the Pozsgais discharged into wetlands (§(a)(7)), which were "adjacent" to a stream on the Pozsgais' property which was a "tributary of the Pennsylvania Canal" (§(a)(5)). The Canal, in turn, flowed into the Delaware River, which, the court ruled, satisfied the requirement that the Pennsylvania Canal is, was, or could be used in interstate commerce (§(a)(1)). We review these factual findings under the clearly erroneous standard. *Sheet Metal Workers Int'l Assn. Local 19 v. 2300 Group, Inc.*, 949 F.2d at 1278.

The Pozsgais dispute the stream is a tributary of the Pennsylvania Canal. In making this finding, the district court relied on aerial photographs and testimony from Corps biologist Miller. The government has since conceded the photographs are inaccurate. But the government also introduced other evidence which the Pozsgais have not contested. The eyewitness accounts of two Corps biologists, Martin Miller and Michael Claffey, recorded in Miller's report of his investigation of the property in April 1987, and in Claffey's affidavit, confirm the stream is a tributary of the Pennsylvania Canal. Given this uncontradicted evidence, we believe the district court's finding was not clearly erroneous.

The Pozsgais also dispute that the Pennsylvania Canal is, was, or could be used in interstate commerce. The district court reached this conclusion by noting the Canal flowed into the Delaware River, which it believed was enough to satisfy the broad reach of the Clean Water Act. The Pozsgais argue that this fact, without more, does not establish the Canal itself was, is, or could be used in interstate commerce. Even if true, this argument is unavailing, because the government has pointed to other evidence supporting the conclusion the Canal in the past was used in interstate commerce, which satisfies the terms of §328.3(a)(1).

The government requests that we take judicial notice of the Canal's historic significance as an interstate commerce route. It cites Robert McCullough & Walter Leuba, *The Pennsylvania Main Line Canal* (1960), and C.P. Yoder, *Delaware Canal Journal* (1972), two history books which discuss the Canal's nearly 100-year history as a shipping route for coal and other commodities.

Under Fed.R.Evid. 201, we may take judicial notice of any fact "not subject to reasonable dispute in that it is ... capable of accurate and ready determination by resort to sources whose accuracy cannot be reasonably questioned." Fed.R.Evid. 201(a). Furthermore, because "judicial notice may be taken at any stage of the proceeding," Fed.R.Evid. 201(f), we may take judicial notice of a fact although the district court did not.

The Pozsgais dispute neither that an appellate court may take judicial notice nor that the history books cited by the government are suitable sources for judicial notice. Instead, they contend only that the books do not prove that the Pennsylvania Canal was ever used in interstate commerce. We disagree.

A cursory review of *The Pennsylvania Main Line Canal* and *Delaware Canal Journal* reveals the Canal's important role as a shipping route carrying coal in interstate commerce. In the middle of the century, the Canal consistently carried more than half a million tons of coal per year, reaching its peak volume with 792,000 tons of coal in 1866. Many of the coal barges served the Philadelphia market. Others continued on to New York City, after being towed by steam boats across the Delaware River to Bordentown, New Jersey, where they reached the Delaware and Raritan Canal. In 1939, the Delaware Division Canal Company donated the entire canal property to the Commonwealth of Pennsylvania, which established Roosevelt State Park. In recognition of its vital role in "providing a convenient and economic means of transporting coal to Philadelphia, New York and the eastern seaboard," the Canal was designated a National Historic Landmark in 1976. United States Army Corps of Engineers, Preliminary Case Report for Neshaminy Water Resources Authority, Point Pleasant Diversion Project, Point Pleasant, Bucks County, Pennsylvania §2.1 at 7 (1982).

This is at least as much evidence of an effect on interstate commerce as that found to satisfy this jurisdictional requirement in prior similar cases. *See Quivira Mining Co. v. United States E.P.A.*, 765 F.2d 126, 130 (10th Cir. 1985) (non-navigable creeks and "arroyos" affect interstate commerce because during times of "intense rainfall" there could be a surface connection between these waterways and navigable streams), *cert. denied,* 474 U.S. 1055, 88 L.Ed. 2d 769, 106 S.Ct. 791 (1986); *United States v. Ashland Oil and Transportation Co.*, 504 F.2d 1317, 1329 (6th Cir.

1974) (Act constitutionally applies to discharge of oil into non-navigable tributary three waterways removed from navigable river). In so holding, these courts recognized Congress' intent to give the term "navigable waters" the "broadest possible constitutional interpretation." *Ashland Oil*, 504 F.2d at 1317 (citing 118 Cong. Rec. 33756-57 (1972) (statement of Representative Dingell)); *Quivira Mining*, 765 F.2d at 129. The Pozsgais maintain these cases are distinguishable as both involved discharge into waterways rather than wetlands. But this is a distinction without a difference in light of the Corps' regulation, which equates adjacent wetlands with waterways.

B

The Pozsgais also contend the regulation does not apply because the government failed to establish their discharge affected interstate commerce. The regulations require proof of an effect on interstate commerce, they argue, because their wetlands are "essentially isolated." In coining the term "essentially isolated," the Pozsgais seek to take this case outside *Riverside Bayview*, where the Supreme Court expressly reserved the question whether the Act authorized the Corps to regulate wetlands not "adjacent to open bodies of water." *Id.* at 131 n.8. They also use the term "essentially isolated" in an effort to bring their wetlands within the section of the regulation governing "isolated" wetlands. That section conditions application of the permit requirement to "isolated" wetlands on a showing of a site-specific impact on interstate commerce. 33 C.F.R. §328.3(a)(3).

The Pozsgais assert their wetlands are "essentially isolated" because they are "above the headwaters," the term "headwaters" being defined as "the point on a non-tidal stream above which the average annual flow is less than five cubic feet per second." 33 C.F.R. §330.2(b). They note the regulation contains Nationwide Permit 26, which exempts the "discharge of dredged or fill materials" into wetlands above the headwaters from the individual permit requirement provided the discharger meets certain conditions. 33 C.F.R. §330.5(a)(26). Establishment of this nationwide permit, the Pozsgais claim, reflects the Corps' policy judgment that these "essentially isolated" wetlands are the functional equivalent of isolated wetlands. Therefore, they conclude, an individualized showing of an interstate commerce effect is required to subject their "essentially isolated" wetlands to the Clean Water Act.

The Corps' decision to establish a nationwide permit for discharge of fill material into wetlands above the headwaters apparently reflects the agency's expert judgment that these wetlands pose less of a water pollution concern than do certain other wetlands. *See* 33 C.F.R. §320.1(a)(3) (justifying the nationwide permit program as "the primary method of eliminating unnecessary federal control over activities which do not justify individual control or which are adequately regulated by another agency"). But Nationwide Permit 26 hardly suggests wetlands above the headwaters are environmentally insignificant, as it conditions discharge on a water quality certification from the state in which the wetlands are located, 33 U.S.C. §1341(a)(1) and 33 C.F.R. §§330.5(b)(11), 330.9(b)(3), and requires written notification to the Corps prior to discharge, 33 C.F.R. §§330.5(a)(26), 330.7(b).

Moreover, the Pozsgais' contention that discharge into wetlands above the headwaters may only be regulated upon the showing of a specific effect on interstate commerce is foreclosed by §328.3, in which the Corps distinguished for interstate commerce purposes between adjacent and isolated wetlands, and did not treat separately wetlands above the headwaters. Where, as here, the Pozsgais' wetlands are both above the headwaters and adjacent, only the latter characteristic matters for interstate commerce purposes. An explanatory statement issued by the Corps upon promulgation of the final regulation supports this conclusion: "we emphasize that the 'headwaters' concept used in this new regulation ... is not to be construed as the point beyond which a stream ceases to be a water of the United States...." 47 *Fed. Reg.* 37129 (1977).

The Pozsgais' claim that their wetlands are "essentially isolated" thus reduces to an attack on the "adjacency" regulation upheld in *Riverside Bayview*. But the use of the adjective "essentially" cannot convert the Pozsgais' "adjacent" wetland to an "isolated" wetland. This transparent effort to rewrite the regulation, like the Pozsgais' argument that the term "water" cannot mean "wetlands," is a policy question properly put to Congress or the Corps. *See Riverside Bayview*, 474 U.S. at 134 ("we cannot say that the Corps' conclusion that adjacent wetlands are inseparably bound up with the 'waters' of the United States—based as it is on the Corps' and the EPA's technical expertise—is unreasonable"); *Chevron*, 467 U.S. at 866.

Accordingly, because the wetlands here qualify as "adjacent" within the meaning of the regulation, the government was not required to prove that "the use, degradation or destruction of [the Pozsgais' wetlands] could affect interstate commerce," 33 C.F.R. §328.3(a)(3), in order to subject the Pozsgais to liability under the Clean Water Act. Under the regulation, the requisite interstate commerce nexus was established because the wetlands were adjacent to a tributary of a waterway formerly used in interstate commerce. 33 C.F.R. §328.3(a)(1), (7).

V

We now consider the Pozsgais' argument that the Corps' adjacent wetlands regulation as applied to them violates the Commerce Clause because the regulation does not require proof of a specific effect on interstate commerce from the Pozsgais' filling, and because wetlands above the headwaters, as a class of wetlands, do not significantly affect interstate commerce. We review challenges to Congress' exercise of its Commerce Clause power under a deferential standard. We will uphold application of the law if there is a "rational basis" for the congressional determination that the regulated activity "affects interstate commerce," and if the means chosen to regulate the activity are reasonable. *Hodel v. Virginia Surface Mining & Reclamation Ass'n*, 452 U.S. 264, 276, 69 L.Ed. 2d 1, 101 S.Ct. 2352 (1981); *United States v. Frame*, 885 F.2d 1119, 1126 (3d Cir. 1989), *cert. denied*, 493 U.S. 1094, 107 L. Ed. 2d 1070, 110 S. Ct. 1168 (1990).

In contending the Constitution requires an individualized effect on interstate commerce, the Pozsgais rely on cases construing other federal statutes—the Sherman Act, the Hobbs Act, the federal arson statute, and two federal labor statutes—which do require an individualized showing. But these cases demonstrate only that in those statutes, Congress chose to satisfy the Commerce Clause by requiring an individualized interstate commerce effect in each application of the law. The Clean Water Act, by contrast, handles the interstate commerce nexus differently. Under the Act, the Corps, acting under its statutorily delegated authority to establish the permit program, 33 U.S.C. §1344, has determined that wetlands which are adjacent to tributaries of waters usable or formerly used in interstate commerce themselves affect interstate commerce. Several other Courts of Appeal have upheld this regulation against constitutional attack on the ground that congressional regulation of water pollution is permissible under the Commerce Clause, *United States v. Byrd*, 609 F.2d 1204, 1209 (7th Cir. 1979), *United States v. Tull*, 769 F.2d at 185, *United States v. Ashland Oil*, 504 F.2d at 1325, and the Supreme Court has upheld this reasoning. *Hodel*, 452 U.S. at 282 ("we agree with the lower federal courts that have uniformly found the power conferred by the Commerce Clause broad enough to permit congressional regulation of activities causing air or water pollution").

The Pozsgais seek to distinguish these cases, contending the challenged activities in each of them involved "substantial effects" on interstate commerce, and arguing the government established no such effects here. But even assuming Congress' Commerce Power is circumscribed by a "substantiality" requirement, the Pozsgais misapply this standard. In contending their discharge activities did not have substantial effects on interstate commerce, the Pozsgais ignore the well-settled principle that "where the class of activities is regulated and that class is within the reach of the federal [commerce] power, the courts have no power 'to excise, as trivial, individual instances' of the class." *Perez v. United States*, 402 U.S. 146, 154, 28 L.Ed. 2d 686, 91 S.Ct. 1357 (1971) (quoting *Maryland v. Wirtz,* 392 U.S. 183, 193, 20 L.Ed. 2d 1020, 88 S.Ct. 2017 (1968)). The Pozsgais claim this so-called "cumulative effect" principle is inapplicable because wetlands above the headwaters, as a "class of activities," do not substantially affect interstate commerce. But the only evidence they offer in support of this argument is the Corps' decision to regulate these wetlands under Nationwide Permit 26. As discussed above, however, by the regulation's terms, this classification has no significance for interstate commerce purposes.

The Pozsgais also argue the cumulative effect principle has no application to wetlands generally. In announcing this principle to hold that federal production quotas could constitutionally be applied to a farmer who grew wheat for his own consumption in *Wickard v. Filburn*, 317 U.S. 111, 87 L.Ed. 122, 63 S.Ct. 82 (1942), the Supreme Court stressed that in the aggregate, home consumption of wheat competed with wheat grown for sale and therefore affected interstate commerce. The Pozsgais contend that discharge into wetlands cannot be similarly aggregated because their filling activities cannot be added to filling activities in California or Texas which involve other aquatic systems.

This reasoning is factually and legally flawed. In factual terms, it ignores that discharge by other property owners into wetlands above the headwaters within the same aquatic system as the Pozsgais clearly should be aggregated with the Pozsgais' discharge to determine the amount of pollution in that system. As a legal matter, we find no language in *Wickard* or its progeny requiring a showing of local or regional aggregation. Indeed, it would be illogical to impose such a requirement on the Corps of Engineers in the course of making national water pollution policy. The regulation reflects the Corps' expert determination that, in the aggregate, discharge into wetlands above the headwaters which are adjacent to tributaries of waters used or usable in interstate commerce, increases water pollution. It matters not whether the increase is substantial in a particular region, or just in the nation as a whole. *Compare Perez v. United States*, 402 U.S. at 155 (finding *Wickard* applies to loan sharking, a $350 million per year national business, without discussing cumulation of particular transactions in regional or local credit markets). For these reasons, we hold that application of the Corps' wetlands regulation to the Pozsgais' discharge activities did not violate the Commerce Clause.

VI

We now turn to the Pozsgais' appeal from various orders entered by the district court during the course of this litigation. The Pozsgais contend the district court's contempt order was defective because, although labeled as "civil" contempt, the order was in fact "criminal" contempt. The two types of contempt differ in important respects. Civil contempt is remedial in nature, serving to coerce compliance with a court order or to compensate the other party for losses sustained due to noncompliance. By complying with the order, a civil contemnor can purge the contempt. Criminal contempt, by contrast, is a punitive sanction, designed to vindicate the court's authority for the contemnor's past non-compliance with a court order, and therefore cannot be cured by the contemnor. *Hicks on Behalf of Feiock v. Feiock*, 485 U.S. 624, 631-32, 99 L.Ed. 2d 721, 108 S.Ct. 1423 (1988); 11 Charles A. Wright and Arthur R. Miller, *Federal Practice and Procedure* §2960 at 583-85 (1973).

The purpose and nature of the sanction, rather than the label attached to it, determine whether it is civil or criminal. *Hicks*, 485 U.S. at 631. The two types of contempt also have different burdens of proof. Civil contempt must be proved by "clear and convincing" evidence, *Quinter v. Volkswagen of America*, 676 F.2d 969, 974 (3d Cir. 1982), while criminal contempt must be proved beyond a reasonable doubt, *Hicks*, 485 U.S. at 632. To be valid, a criminal contempt proceeding must comport with Federal Rule of Criminal Procedure 42(b), which requires such proceedings to be "prosecuted on notice ... stating the time and place of hearing, allowing a reasonable time for the preparation of the defense,... stating the essential facts constituting the criminal contempt, and describing it as such."

Here, the district court found Pozsgai in contempt for his past violations of the TRO against filling on the property, and ordered him to pay $5,000 within 48 hours or be put in jail. Although the order contains aspects of civil contempt, two significant features convince us it qualifies as criminal contempt. First, it was retroactive in nature, seeking to penalize previous violations. Second, it was punitive rather than remedial, because it did not compensate the government, but rather sought to vindicate the authority of the Court to enjoin Pozsgai from continuing his filling activities.

We believe the court afforded Pozsgai the protections necessary for a valid finding of criminal contempt. The Pozsgais contend the district court's failure to label the contempt as criminal in the hearing notice violated Rule 42(b), that this error was compounded by the government's request for "civil" contempt in its petition for an order to show cause, and that these errors render the proceeding invalid. We disagree. The government's petition for an order to show cause specifically enumerated past violations for which it sought contempt sanctions. Additionally, the government expressly requested not only that Pozsgai be incarcerated until he complied with the TRO, a civil contempt sanction, but also requested that he be incarcerated five days for each prior violation and fined $25,000 for each continued violation. Because the government sought a retroactive sanction, we believe its petition put Pozsgai on notice of the criminal nature of the contempt proceeding.

Additionally, we do not believe Pozsgai was prejudiced by the timing of the notice. The Supreme Court has held a district court's failure to label a contempt proceeding as criminal in the hearing notice is grounds for reversal only when the failure causes "substantial prejudice" to the defendant resulting from his lack of awareness that the proceeding is criminal. *United States v. United Mine Workers of America*, 330 U.S. 258, 297-98, 91 L.Ed. 884, 67 S.Ct. 677 (1946). Pozsgai has not argued, nor presented any evidence, that "a more explicit motion ... would have aided him in the preparation of his defense." *United States v. Partin*, 524 F.2d 992, 999 (5th Cir. 1975), *cert. denied*, 425 U.S. 904, 47 L.Ed.2d 753, 96 S.Ct. 1493 (1976). His defense consisted entirely of testimony denying he had violated the TRO. The court chose not to believe him, expressly finding "beyond any doubt whatsoever" not only that Pozsgai knew of the post-TRO dumping but also that it occurred with his approval. The videotape recording this activity provided overwhelming support for this conclusion. Accordingly, we will affirm the district court's order of contempt.

The Pozsgais' final claims concern the district court's restoration order, which directed removal of fill material from the wetlands portion of the Pozsgais' property and redeposit of the material on the non-wetlands portion of the property. The Pozsgais object to the order on three grounds: (1) that it violates Fed.R.Civ.P. 65(d)'s standards for injunctive remedies because it fails to describe specifically the area of the property to be restored; (2) that the order itself was an abuse of discretion given the small degree of harm caused by the discharge and his financial inability to comply with it; and (3) that the court was wrong to deny the Pozsgais' Fed.R.Civ.P. 60(b) motion for relief from the restoration order seeking control over where on their property the restoration of the fill would take place.

With respect to the particularity of the restoration order, we note the injunction anticipated further negotiation between the Pozsgais and the government regarding the restoration plan, and that such negotiation has taken place, most recently in the parties' August 15, 1991, stipulation to a new map detailing the wetland areas to be restored. We reject the Pozsgais' contention that the restoration order was inequitable because of the small degree of harm caused by their discharge and their financial inability to comply with the order. The undisputed facts demonstrating the Pozsgais' repeated noncompliance with the Act and with the Corps' directives to stop filling foreclose any such equitable argument.

Finally, we consider the Pozsgais' motion for relief from judgment, in which they seek control to determine the location on the property where the material is redeposited. Denying the motion, the district court found it would be inequitable to give the Pozsgais such veto power—particularly now that the haulers have completed their work—because the Pozsgais caused the improper filling and refused to remedy the condition. We agree fully with this reasoning. Accordingly, we believe the district court did not abuse its discretion in fashioning the restoration order.

VII

For the foregoing reasons, we will affirm the judgment of the district court. [Footnotes omitted.]

UNITED STATES v. ELLEN

961 F.2d 462 (4th Cir. 1992), *cert. denied* 506 U.S. 875, 113 S.Ct. 217, 121 L.Ed.2d 155 (1992)

This case presents several issues pertaining to defendant's conviction for illegally discharging pollutants into wetlands in violation of the Clean Water Act, 33 U.S.C. §1251 *et seq.* Defendant appeals his conviction, and both defendant and the United States appeal the district court's application of the Sentencing Guidelines. We affirm both the conviction and the sentence.

I

Defendant William B. Ellen received a degree of Bachelor of Science in Engineering from Old Dominion University in 1972. For the following four years, he was a staff environmental engineer with the Virginia Marine Resources Commission and was responsible for reviewing the regulation of certain wetlands projects. In 1976, Ellen formed William B. Ellen, Inc., which specialized in the design of, and acquisition of permits for, construction projects in tidal wetlands and subaqueous areas.

In August 1987, Ellen was hired by Paul T. Jones II to assist in the development of property on the Eastern Shore of Maryland into a personal and corporate retreat that would serve as a hunting preserve and wildlife sanctuary. Ellen advised Jones as to the acquisition of the property—named Tudor Farms—and, after the purchase, became the project manager responsible for land clearing, road construction, and pond excavation. Tudor Farms is low, wet land. It is surrounded on three sides by tidal waters and marshes, and the property itself contains large areas of wooded wetlands and tidal marshes and some upland fields and roads. Prior to the construction on the property, Tudor Farms served as habitat for an endangered species, the Delmarva fox squirrel, as well as an American bald eagle, various migratory birds, and wood ducks.

Ellen supervised extensive excavation and construction at the Tudor Farms site. Ellen admits that he was responsible for acquiring environmental permits and complying with the various state and federal environmental regulations. Indeed, throughout construction at Tudor Farms, Ellen made clear—to officials of the Maryland Department of Natural Resources, to the Dorchester County Highway Department, and to Army Corps of Engineers (Corps) enforcement officials, among others—that he assumed the responsibility for acquiring all needed environmental permits.

In February 1988, a Corps enforcement official visited the site, indicated to Ellen what could and could not be done without a Corps permit, and issued a cease and desist letter that ordered Tudor Farms to stop filling wetlands. When Corps officials returned to the site in January 1989, they found several wetlands sites where work had progressed without the necessary permits. They instructed the site manager that all work in wetlands cease, but construction continued nonetheless. The Corps issued a second cease and desist letter on February 15. Upon visiting the site on March 3, Corps officials noticed additional violations. When Ellen refused to comply with their order to stop work, the Corps officials contacted the subcontractors directly, and only then did work cease. Upon learning that Ellen had not obtained all necessary environmental permits, Jones fired Ellen.

Ellen was tried on six counts of knowingly filling in wetlands without a permit in violation of the Clean Water Act, 33 U.S.C. §§1311(a) and 1319(c)(2)(A). He did not controvert the United States' allegations as to the construction activity that occurred at Tudor Farms. Instead, Ellen disputed two elements of the offenses alleged: that the areas where work occurred were wetlands and, if they were wetlands, that Ellen knew they were wetlands and that permits were required. The jury convicted Ellen on five of the six counts. The district court imposed a sentence of six months' imprisonment and one year of supervised release, with the latter conditioned upon four months' home detention and 60 hours of community service.

Both Ellen and the United States have appealed.

II

We pause briefly at the outset to describe the relevant statutory provisions. Congress enacted the Clean Water Act (CWA), 33 U.S.C. §1251 *et seq.*, "to restore and maintain the chemical, physical, and biological integrity of the Nation's waters." Id. §1251(a). To this end, the CWA prohibits the discharge "of any pollutant to navigable waters from any point source" without a permit. 33 U.S.C. §§1311(a), 1362(12)(A). The CWA defines navigable waters as "the waters of the United States," *id.* §1362(7), though it does not define the latter phrase. Both the Environmental Protection Agency (EPA), *see* 40 C.F.R. §230.3(s)(2), (7) (1991), and the Army Corps of Engineers, *see* 33 C.F.R. §328.3(a)(2), (7) (1991), define "waters of the United States" to include wetlands, and both define wetlands as follows:

> Those areas that are inundated or saturated by surface or ground water at a frequency and duration sufficient to support, and that under normal circumstances do support, a prevalence of vegetation typically adapted for life in saturated soil conditions. Wetlands generally include swamps, marshes, bogs and similar areas.

40 C.F.R. §230.3(t) (1991); 33 C.F.R. §328.3(b) (1991). This regulatory definition has remained unchanged since 1977. *See* Proposed Revisions to 1989 Wetlands Manual, 56 Fed. Reg. 40,446, 40,446 (1991) [hereinafter Proposed Revisions].

Four federal agencies—EPA, the Corps, the Fish and Wildlife Service, and the Soil Conservation Service—are principally involved in the identification and delineation of wetlands. *See* Federal Interagency Committee for Wetland Delineation, *Federal Manual for Identifying and Delineating Jurisdictional Wetlands 1* (1989) [hereinafter *1989 Manual*]. The Corps is authorized by CWA §404 to issue permits for the discharge of dredged and fill materials into wetlands, *see* 33 U.S.C. §1344(a), though both EPA and the Corps are responsible for making wetlands determinations under §404. *See 1989 Manual, supra*, at 1. Prior to 1989, EPA and the Corps each developed its own procedures for identifying and delineating wetlands, which were set forth in technical manuals. *See* Environmental Protection Agency, (*Wetland Identification and Delineation Manual* 1988); *Environmental Laboratory, Dep't of the Army, Corps of Engineers Wetlands Delineation Manual* (1987).

The absence of a uniform federal methodology resulted in inconsistent wetlands determinations for similar areas. *See* Proposed Revisions, *supra,* at 40,449. As a result of these inconsistencies, in 1989 the four federal agencies merged their methods and issued a single wetlands delineation manual, which provides a uniform national procedure for wetland determinations. *See 1989 Manual, supra.* Application of the *1989 Manual* resulted in a significant increase in lands identified as wetlands as compared with the EPA and Corps manuals. *See* Proposed Revisions, *supra,* at 40,450; S. Rep. No. 80, 102d Cong., 1st Sess. 54 (1991). In August 1991, the four agencies proposed a revised manual, application of which would result in fewer lands classified as wetlands than under the *1989 Manual. See* Proposed Revisions, *supra.*

III

Ellen argues that his conviction violated the Due Process Clause and the Ex Post Facto Clause. His argument under both clauses is essentially the same. The five counts for which he was convicted involved discharging pollutants from a point source in areas alleged to be wetlands. The United States was required to prove at trial that the areas in which the conduct occurred were, in fact, wetlands. Ellen concedes that the regulatory definition of "wetlands" promulgated by EPA and the Corps remained unchanged since the commencement of the charged conduct and was the definition included in the district court's instructions to the jury. The constitutional problems arise, according to Ellen, because some government witnesses at trial based their conclusions that the areas were wetlands on the more inclusive *1989 Manual,* while the conduct for which he was charged occurred in 1987 and 1988, before its promulgation. Ellen asserts that the district court's admission of such testimony permitted the jury to convict him on the basis of subsequently developed standards—which assertedly violates the non-retroactivity principle of the Ex Post Facto and Due Process Clauses.

For the reasons set forth below, we reject Ellen's ex post facto and due process arguments and therefore affirm his conviction.

A

The Ex Post Facto Clause provides: "No ... ex post facto Law shall be passed." U.S. Const., art. I, §9. As the text of the Clause makes clear, the ex post facto prohibition applies only to "laws." Accordingly, "the constitutional prohibition against ex post facto laws ... is directed to the legislative branch of government rather than to the other branches." *Prater v. U.S. Parole Comm'n,* 802 F.2d 948, 951 (7th Cir. 1986) (*en banc*). This is not to say, however, that all actions of administrative agencies are exempt from Ex Post Facto Clause scrutiny. "When Congress has delegated to an agency the authority to make a rule instead of making the rule itself, the resulting administrative rule is an extension of the statute for purposes of the Clause." *Rodriguez v. United States Parole Comm'n,* 594 F.2d 170, 173 (7th Cir. 1979). The reason for applying the Clause to such legislative rules is straightforward: Congress "should not be allowed to do indirectly what it is forbidden to do directly." *Prater,* 802 F.2d at 954. But when an agency promulgates an interpretive rule, the Ex Post Facto Clause is inapplicable. "Interpretive rules simply state what the administrative agency thinks the statute means, and only 'remind' affected parties of existing duties." *Jerri's Ceramic Arts, Inc. v. Consumer Product Safety Comm'n,* 874 F.2d 205, 207 (4th Cir. 1989). Unlike legislative rules, which "have the force of law," *id.,* interpretive rules "are statements of enforcement policy. They are ... 'merely guides, and not laws: guides may be discarded where circumstances require; laws may not.' " *Prater,* 802 F.2d at 954 (quoting *Inglese v. United States Parole Comm'n,* 768 F.2d 932, 936 (7th Cir. 1985)). Whether the Ex Post Facto Clause applies in this case, therefore, depends on whether the *1989 Manual* is a legislative rule or merely an interpretive guide.

Ellen has presented no reasons why the *1989 Manual* is legislative rather than interpretive in nature, and we find no indication that promulgation of the *1989 Manual* was an exercise of the agencies' delegated legislative function. Rather, it seems clear that the four agencies that promulgated the *1989 Manual* intended it to be only an interpretive guide to the regulatory definition of wetlands, primarily for the use of agency personnel. The agencies have described the manual as "a technical guidance document" that "provides internal procedures for agency field staff for identifying and delineating wetlands." *Proposed Revisions, supra,* at 40,446. The manual does not purport to "create new law or impose new rights or duties," *Jerri's Ceramic Arts,* 874 F.2d at 207, and it was not promulgated through the notice and comment rulemaking procedures of the Administrative Procedure Act, 5 U.S.C. §551 *et seq.,* through which all legislative rules must pass. *See Jerri's Ceramic Arts,* 874 F.2d at 208. We conclude, therefore, that the *1989 Manual* is interpretive rather than legislative in nature and, as a result, it is not a "law" within the meaning of the Ex Post Facto Clause. Accordingly, Ellen's ex post facto argument is without merit.

B

Ellen bases his due process argument on *Marks v. United States,* 430 U.S. 188, 51 L.Ed.2d 260, 97 S.Ct. 990 (1977). In *Marks,* the defendants were convicted of the interstate transportation of obscene material. The convictions were based on the definition of obscenity announced in *Miller v. California,* 413 U.S. 15, 37 L.Ed. 2d 419, 93 S.Ct. 2607 (1973), even though the conduct on which the convictions rested occurred while the narrower definition of obscenity in *Memoirs v. Massachusetts,* 383 U.S. 413, 16 L.Ed. 2d 1, 86 S.Ct. 975 (1966), governed. The Supreme Court held that application of the *Miller* definition violated the Due Process Clause because the defendants lacked "fair warning of that conduct which will give rise to criminal penalties." *Marks,* 430 U.S. at 191. Ellen argues that this case is analogous to *Marks*: there the Court invalidated the use of a subsequently developed judicial interpretation of the statutory term "obscenity," whereas here the court should invalidate the use of subsequently developed administrative criteria for determining what property falls within the regulatory definition of "wetlands."

We believe that Ellen overreads the *Marks* decision. The essence of the due process argument in *Marks* was that the new interpretation of obscenity was unforeseeable. *See id.* at 192. As the Court recently noted, *Marks* turned on the fact that, at the time of the conduct for which they were charged, "the defendants could not suspect that [their] actions would later become criminal." *Osborne v. Ohio,* 495 U.S. 103, 117, 109 L.Ed. 2d 98, 110 S.Ct. 1691 (1990). Viewed in this light, Ellen's due process contention is without merit, for Ellen's argument that he lacked fair warning that the areas in question were wetlands is foreclosed by the jury's verdict. Ellen was convicted of five counts of "knowingly" filling wetlands without a permit. *See* 33 U.S.C. §1319(c)(2)(A). Thus, the jury found, beyond a reasonable doubt, that Ellen *knew* that the areas named in the indictment were wetlands at the time that the work there was undertaken. If Ellen knew that these areas were wetlands, then he cannot claim that the criminal nature of his conduct was unforseeable.

The jury verdict is clearly supported by substantial evidence, for the record is replete with indications that Ellen possessed actual knowledge that he was working in wetlands. As early as October 1987, for example, a civil engineer hired by Ellen to provide surveying assistance at Tudor Farms told Ellen that environmental maps indicated that Ellen was working or planning to work in wetlands and, as a result, a Corps permit was required. And in February and March 1988, Corps enforcement officials toured Tudor Farms with Ellen and indicated to him areas that were wetlands. On their March visit, the Corps officials actually tied survey ribbons on trees and bushes to indicate to Ellen how to minimize the impact of proposed construction upon wetlands. These and other warnings to Ellen involved core wetlands—areas that would qualify as wetlands under any definition of that term. His disregard of those warnings—and of subsequent cease and desist letters—undercuts any argument that he was unaware of the nature of the land under development.

In sum, because the jury's conclusion that Ellen possessed actual knowledge that he was filling wetlands is supported by substantial evidence, we must conclude that Ellen had fair warning that he was subject to the CWA's criminal penalties and that his due process argument is without merit....

AFFIRMED [Footnotes omitted.]

See also *United States v. Kelley Technical Coatings, Inc.*, 157 F.3d 432 (6th Cir. 1998); *United States v. Jarrell*, 103 F.3d 121 (4th Cir. 1996); *U.S. v. Strandquist*, 993 F.2d 395 (4th Cir. 1993); *United States v. Mills*, 817 F.Supp. 1546 (N.D.Fla. 1993); *United States v. Bayshore Associates, Inc.*, 934 F.2d 1391 (6th Cir. Mich. 1991); *United States v. Rivera Torres*, 656 F.Supp. 251 (D.P.R. 1986), *aff'd,* 826 F.2d 151 (1st Cir. 1987); *United States v. Tilton*, 705 F.2d 429 (11th Cir. Fla. 1983); *United States v. Sexton Cove Estates, inc.*, 526 F.2d 1293 (5th Cir. 1976); *United States v. Leuzen*, 816 F.Supp. 1171 (S.D.Tex. 1993); *United States v. Malibu Beach, Inc.*, 711 F.Supp. 1301 (D.N.J. 1989); *United States v. Lambert*, 589 F.Supp. 366 (M.D.Fla. 1984); *United States v. Robinson*, 570 F.Supp. 1157 (M.D.Fla. 1983); *United States v. Bradshaw*, 541 F.Supp. 884 (D.Md. 1982); *United States v. Weisman*, 489 F.Supp. 1331 (M.D.Fla. 1980); *United States v. D'Annolfo*, 474 F.Supp. 220 (D.Mass. 1979).

CHAPTER 29

COURT-IMPOSED PENALTIES

Courts are permitted to assess civil penalties of their own. 33 U.S.C. §1319(d). The court's maximum penalty is $25,000 per day for each violation. Each day a violation is in place has been held to be a separate violation. Defendants have a right to a jury trial on the issue of liability, although the court will decide the amount of civil penalty and the terms of an injunction.

TULL v. UNITED STATES

481 U.S. 412, 95 L.Ed.2d 365, 107 S.Ct. 1831 (1987)

The question for decision is whether the Seventh Amendment guaranteed petitioner a right to a jury trial on both liability and amount of penalty in an action instituted by the Federal Government seeking civil penalties and injunctive relief under the Clean Water Act, 62 Stat. 1155, as amended, 33 U.S.C. 1251 *et seq.*

I

The Clean Water Act prohibits discharging, without a permit, dredged or fill material into "navigable waters," including the wetlands adjacent to the waters. 33 U.S.C. 1311, 1344, and 1362(7); 33 CFR 323.2(a)(1)-(7) (1986). "Wetlands" are "swamps, marshes, bogs and similar areas." 33 CFR 323.2(c) (1986). The Government sued petitioner, a real estate developer, for dumping fill on wetlands on the island of Chincoteague, Virginia. The Government alleged in the original complaint that petitioner dumped fill on three sites: Ocean Breeze Mobile Homes Sites, Mire Pond Properties, and Eel Creek. The Government later amended the complaint to allege that petitioner also placed fill in a manmade waterway, named Fowling Gut Extended, on the Ocean Breeze property. Section 1319 enumerates the remedies available under the Clean Water Act. Subsection (b) authorizes relief in the form of temporary or permanent injunctions. Subsection (d) provides that violators of certain sections of the Act "shall be subject to a civil penalty not to exceed $10,000 per day" during the period of the violation. The Government sought in this case both injunctive relief and civil penalties. When the complaint was filed, however, almost all of the property at issue had been sold by petitioner to third parties. Injunctive relief was therefore impractical except with regard to a small portion of the land. 2 App. 110, 119. The Government's complaint demanded the imposition of the maximum civil penalty of $22,890,000 under subsection (d). App. 31-34.

Petitioner's timely demand for a trial by jury was denied by the District Court. During the 15-day bench trial, petitioner did not dispute that he had placed fill at the locations alleged and did not deny his failure to obtain a permit. Petitioner contended, however, that the property in question did not constitute "wetlands." 615 F. Supp. 610, 615-618 (ED Va. 1983). The Government concedes that triable issues of fact were presented by disputes between experts involving the composition and nature of the fillings. Tr. of Oral Arg. 44.

The District Court concluded that petitioner had illegally filled in wetland areas on all properties in question, but drastically reduced the amount of civil penalties sought by the Government. With respect to the Ocean Breeze Mobile Homes Sites, the court imposed a civil fine of $35,000, noting that petitioner had sold seven lots at a profit of $5,000 per lot. 615 F. Supp., at 626. The court fined petitioner another $35,000 for illegal fillings on the Mire Pond Properties, *ibid.*, and $5,000 for filling that affected a single lot in Eel Creek, *ibid.*, although petitioner had realized no profit from filling in these properties. In addition, the court imposed on petitioner a $250,000 fine to be suspended, however, "on the specific condition that he restore the extension of Fowling Gut to its former navigable condition...." *Id.*, at 627. Although petitioner argued that such restoration required purchasing the land from third parties at a cost of over $700,000, thus leaving him no choice but to pay the fine, the court refused to alter this order. App. 107a-108a. The court also granted separate injunctive relief: it ordered the restoration of wetlands on the portions of Mire Pond and Eel Creek still owned by petitioner, 615 F. Supp., at 627, and further ordered the removal of fillings on five lots of the Ocean Breeze Mobile Home Sites unless petitioner were granted an "after-the-fact permit" validating the fillings. *Id.*, at 626.

The Court of Appeals affirmed over a dissent, rejecting petitioner's argument that, under the Seventh Amendment, he was entitled to a jury trial. 769 F.2d 182 (CA4 1985). The court expressly declined to follow the decision of the Court of Appeals for the Second Circuit in *United States v. J. B. Williams Co.,* 498 F.2d 414 (1974), which held that there was a Seventh Amendment "right of jury trial when the United States sues ... to collect a [statutory civil] penalty, even though the statute is silent on the right of jury trial." 498 F.2d, at 422-423 (quoting 5 J. Moore, Federal Practice §38.-311., pp. 232-233 (2d ed. 1971)).

The Court of Appeals in this case also found unpersuasive the dictum in *Hepner v. United States*, 213 U.S. 103, 115 (1909), and in *United States v. Regan*, 232 U.S. 37, 46-47 (1914), that the Seventh Amendment's guarantee applies to civil actions to collect a civil penalty. The court concluded that, while in *Hepner* and *Regan* the civil penalties were statutorily prescribed fixed amounts, the District Court in the present case exercised "statutorily conferred equitable power in determining the amount of the fine." 769 F.2d, at 187. The Court of Appeals also noted that the District Court fashioned a "package of remedies" containing both equitable and legal relief with "one part of the package affecting assessment of the others." *Ibid.*

In *Atlas Roofing Co. v. Occupational Safety and Health Review Comm'n*, 430 U.S. 442, 449, n. 6 (1977), we explicitly declined to decide whether the dictum of *Hepner* and *Regan* "correctly divines the intent of the Seventh Amendment." To resolve this question and the conflict between Circuits, we granted certiorari. 476 U.S. 1139 (1986). We reverse.

II

The Seventh Amendment provides that, "[i]n Suits at common law, where the value in controversy shall exceed 20 dollars, the right of trial by jury shall be preserved...." The Court has construed this language to require a jury trial on the merits in those actions that are analogous to "suits at common law." Prior to the Amendment's adoption, a jury trial was customary in suits brought in the English law courts. In contrast, those actions that are analogous to 18th-century cases tried in courts of equity or admiralty do not require a jury trial. See *Parsons v. Bedford*, 3 Pet. 433 (1830). This analysis applies not only to common-law forms of action, but also to causes of action created by congressional enactment. See *Curtis v. Loether*, 415 U.S. 189, 193 (1974).

To determine whether a statutory action is more similar to cases that were tried in courts of law than to suits tried in courts of equity or admiralty, the Court must examine both the nature of the action and of the remedy sought. First, we compare the statutory action to 18th-century actions brought in the courts of England prior to the merger of the courts of law and equity. See, *e.g.*, *Pernell v. Southall Realty*, 416 U.S. 363, 378 (1974); *Dairy Queen, Inc. v. Wood*, 369 U.S. 469, 477 (1962). Second, we examine the remedy sought and determine whether it is legal or equitable in nature. See, *e.g.*, *Curtis v. Loether, supra*, at 196; *Ross v. Bernhard*, 396 U.S. 531, 542 (1970).

A

Petitioner analogizes this Government suit under 1319(d) to an action in debt within the jurisdiction of English courts of law. Prior to the enactment of the Seventh Amendment, English courts had held that a civil penalty suit was a particular species of an action in debt that was within the jurisdiction of the courts of law. See, *e.g.*, *Atcheson v. Everitt*, 1 Cowper 382, 98 Eng. Rep. 1142 (K. B. 1776) (characterizing civil penalty suit as a type of action in debt); *Calcraft v. Gibbs*, 5 T. R. 19, 101 Eng. Rep. 11 (K. B. 1792) (granting new jury trial in an action in debt for a civil penalty). After the adoption of the Seventh Amendment, federal courts followed this English common law in treating the civil penalty suit as a particular type of an action in debt, requiring a jury trial. See, *e.g.*, *United States v. Mundell*, 27 F. Cas. 23 (No. 15,834) (CC Va. 1795) (bail not required in a civil penalty case tried by a jury because it was an action in debt); *Jacob v. United States*, 13 F. Cas. 267 (No. 7,157) (CC Va. 1821) (action in debt by United States to recover civil penalty of $500 and costs of violation of an Act of Congress); *Lees v. United States*, 150 U.S. 476, 479 (1893) ("[A]lthough the recovery of a penalty is a proceeding criminal in nature, yet in this class of cases it may be enforced in a civil action, and in the same manner that debts are recovered in the ordinary civil courts"). Actions by the Government to recover civil penalties under statutory provisions therefore historically have been viewed as one type of action in debt requiring trial by jury.

It was against this historical background that the Court in *Hepner v. United States*, 213 U.S. 103 (1909), considered the propriety of a directed verdict by a District Court Judge in favor of the Government where there was undisputed evidence that a defendant had committed an offense under 8 of the Alien Immigration Act of 1903, which provided for a $1,000 civil penalty. The Court held that a directed verdict was permissible and did not violate the defendant's right to a jury trial under the Seventh Amendment. The Court said:

> The objection made in behalf of the defendant, that an affirmative answer to the question certified could be used so as to destroy the constitutional right of trial by jury, is without merit and need not be discussed. The defendant was, of course, entitled to have a jury summoned in this case, but that right was subject to the condition, fundamental in the conduct of civil actions, that the court may withdraw a case from the jury and direct a verdict, according to the law if the evidence is uncontradicted and raises only a question of law. 213 U.S., at 115 (emphasis added).

In *United States v. Regan,* 232 U.S. 37 (1914), the Court assumed that a jury trial was required in civil penalty actions. In that case, the Court upheld the validity of a jury instruction in an action brought by the Government under the Alien Immigration Act of 1907. The Court stated that the instruction requiring proof beyond a reasonable doubt was incorrect because:

> While the defendant was entitled to have the issues tried before a jury, this right did not arise from Article III of the Constitution or from the Sixth Amendment, for both relate to prosecutions which are strictly criminal in their nature, but it derives out of the fact that in a civil action of debt involving more than twenty dollars a jury trial is demandable. 232 U.S., at 47 (citation omitted).

In the instant case, the Government sought penalties of over $22 million for violation of the Clean Water Act and obtained a judgment in the sum of $325,000. This action is clearly analogous to the 18th-century action in debt, and federal courts have rightly assumed that the Seventh Amendment required a jury trial. The Government argues, however, that—rather than an action in debt—the closer historical analog is an action to abate a public nuisance. In 18th-century English law, a public nuisance was "an act or omission 'which obstructs or causes inconvenience or damage to the public in the exercise of rights common to all Her Majesty's subjects.'" W. Prosser, *Law of Torts* 583 (4th ed. 1971) (hereinafter Prosser) (footnote omitted). The Government argues that the present suit is analogous to two species of public nuisances. One is the suit of the sovereign in the English courts of equity for a "purpresture" to enjoin or order the repair of an enclosure or obstruction of public waterways; the other is the suit of the sovereign to enjoin "offensive trades and manufactures" that polluted the environment. 4 W. Blackstone, Commentaries 167.

It is true that the subject matter of this Clean Water Act suit—the placement of fill into navigable waters—resembles these two species of public nuisance. Whether, as the Government argues, a public nuisance action is a better analogy than an action in debt is debatable. But we need not decide the question. As *Pernell v. Southall Realty*, 416 U.S., at 375, cautioned, the fact that the subject matter of a modern statutory action and an 18th-century English action are close equivalents "is irrelevant for Seventh Amendment purposes," because "that Amendment requires trial by jury in actions unheard of at common law." It suffices that we conclude that both the public nuisance action and the action in debt are appropriate analogies to the instant statutory action.

The essential function of an action to abate a public nuisance was to provide a civil means to redress "a miscellaneous and diversified group of minor criminal offenses, based on some interference with the interests of the community, or the comfort or convenience of the general public." Prosser 583. 5 Similarly, the essential function of an action in debt was to recover money owed under a variety of statutes or under the common law. Both of these 18th-century actions, then, could be asserted by the sovereign to seek relief for an injury to the public in numerous contexts.

We need not rest our conclusion on what has been called an "abstruse historical" search for the nearest 18th-century analog. See *Ross v. Bernhard*, 396 U.S., at 538, n. 10. We reiterate our previously expressed view that characterizing the relief sought is "[m]ore important" than finding a precisely analogous common-law cause of action in determining whether the Seventh Amendment guarantees a jury trial. *Curtis v. Loether*, 415 U.S., at 196.

B

A civil penalty was a type of remedy at common law that could only be enforced in courts of law. Remedies intended to punish culpable individuals, as opposed to those intended simply to extract compensation or restore the status quo, were issued by courts of law, not courts of equity. *See, e.g., Curtis v. Loether, supra*, at 197 (punitive damages remedy is legal, not equitable, relief); *Ross v. Bernhard, supra,* at 536 (treble-damages remedy for securities violation is a penalty, which constitutes legal relief). The action authorized by 1319(d) is of this character. Subsection (d) does not direct that the "civil penalty" imposed be calculated solely on the basis of equitable determinations, such as the profits gained from violations of the statute, but simply imposes a maximum penalty of $10,000 per day of violation. The legislative history of the Act reveals that Congress wanted the district court to consider the need for retribution and deterrence, in addition to restitution, when it imposed civil penalties. 123 Cong. Rec. 39191 (1977) (remarks of Sen. Muskie citing Environmental Protection Agency (EPA) memorandum outlining enforcement policy). A court can require retribution for wrongful conduct based on the seriousness of the violations, the number of prior violations, and the lack of good-faith efforts to comply with the relevant requirements. *Ibid.*

It may also seek to deter future violations by basing the penalty on its economic impact. *Ibid.* Subsection 1319(d)'s authorization of punishment to further retribution and deterrence clearly evidences that this subsection reflects more than a concern to provide equitable relief. In the present case, for instance, the District Court acknowledged that petitioner received no profits from filling in properties in Mire Pond and Eel Creek, but still imposed a $35,000 fine. App. to Pet. for Cert. 60a. Thus, the District Court intended not simply to disgorge profits but also to impose punishment. Because the nature of the relief authorized by 1319(d) was traditionally available only in a court of law, petitioner in this present action is entitled to a jury trial on demand.

The punitive nature of the relief sought in this present case is made apparent by a comparison with the relief sought in an action to abate a public nuisance. A public nuisance action was a classic example of the kind of suit that relied on the injunctive relief provided by courts in equity. Prosser 603. "Injunctive relief [for enjoining a public nuisance at the request of the Government] is traditionally given by equity upon a showing of [peril to health and safety]." *Steelworkers v. United States,* 361 U.S. 39, 61 (1959) (Frankfurter, J., concurring). The Government, in fact, concedes that public nuisance cases brought in equity sought injunctive relief, not monetary penalties. Brief for United States 24, n. 17. Indeed, courts in equity refused to enforce such penalties. See James, *Right to a Jury Trial in Civil Actions,* 72 Yale L. J. 655, 672 (1963).

The Government contends, however, that a suit enforcing civil penalties under the Clean Water Act is similar to an action for disgorgement of improper profits, traditionally considered an equitable remedy. It bases this characterization upon evidence that the District Court determined the amount of the penalties by multiplying the number of lots sold by petitioner by the profit earned per lot. Tr. of Oral Arg. 27. An action for disgorgement of improper profits is, however, a poor analogy. Such an action is a remedy only for restitution—a more limited form of penalty than a civil fine. Restitution is limited to "restoring the status quo and ordering the return of that which rightfully belongs to the purchaser or tenant." *Porter v. Warner Holding Co.,* 328 U.S. 395, 402 (1946). As the above discussion indicates, however, 1319(d)'s concerns are by no means limited to restoration of the status quo.

The Government next contends that, even if the civil penalties under 1319(d) are deemed legal in character, a jury trial is not required. A court in equity was empowered to provide monetary awards that were incidental to or intertwined with injunctive relief. The Government therefore argues that its claim under 1319(b), which authorizes injunctive relief, provides jurisdiction for monetary relief in equity. Brief for United States 38. This argument has at least three flaws. First, while a court in equity may award monetary restitution as an adjunct to injunctive relief, it may not enforce civil penalties. *See Porter v. Warner Holding Co., supra*, at 399. Second, the Government was aware when it filed suit that relief would be limited primarily to civil penalties, since petitioner had already sold most of the properties at issue. App. 110, 119. A potential penalty of $22 million hardly can be considered incidental to the modest equitable relief sought in this case.

Finally, the Government was free to seek an equitable remedy in addition to, or independent of, legal relief. Section 1319 does not intertwine equitable relief with the imposition of civil penalties. Instead each kind of relief is separably authorized in a separate and distinct statutory provision. Subsection (b), providing injunctive relief, is independent of subsection (d), which provides only for civil penalties. In such a situation, if a "legal claim is joined with an equitable claim, the right to jury trial on the legal claim, including all issues common to both claims, remains intact. The right cannot be abridged by characterizing the legal claim as 'incidental' to the equitable relief sought." *Curtis v. Loether*, 415 U.S., at 196 , n. 11. Thus, petitioner has a constitutional right to a jury trial to determine his liability on the legal claims.

III

The remaining issue is whether petitioner additionally has a Seventh Amendment right to a jury assessment of the civil penalties. At the time this case was tried, 1319(d) did not explicitly state whether juries or trial judges were to fix the civil penalties. The legislative history of the 1977 Amendments to the Clean Water Act shows, however, that Congress intended that trial judges perform the highly discretionary calculations necessary to award civil penalties after liability is found. 123 Cong. Rec. 39190-39191 (1977) (remarks of Sen. Muskie citing letter from EPA Assistant Administrators of Enforcement of Dec. 14, 1977) ("[P]enalties assessed by judges should be sufficiently higher than penalties to which the Agency would have agreed in settlement to encourage violators to settle"). We must decide therefore whether Congress can, consistent with the Seventh Amendment, authorize judges to assess civil penalties.

The Seventh Amendment is silent on the question whether a jury must determine the remedy in a trial in which it must determine liability. The answer must depend on whether the jury must shoulder this responsibility as necessary to preserve the "substance of the common-law right of trial by jury." *Colgrove v. Battin*, 413 U.S. 149, 157 (1973). Is a jury role necessary for that purpose? We do not think so. "'Only those incidents which are regarded as fundamental, as inherent in and of the essence of the system of trial by jury, are placed beyond the reach of the legislature.'" *Id.*, at 156, n. 11 (quoting Scott, *Trial by Jury and the Reform of Civil Procedure*, 31 Harv.L.Rev. 669, 671 (1918)). See also *Galloway v. United States*, 319 U.S. 372, 392 (1943) ("[T]he Amendment was designed to preserve the basic institution of jury trial in only its most fundamental elements"). The assessment of a civil penalty is not one of the "most fundamental elements." Congress' authority to fix the penalty by statute has not been questioned, and it was also the British practice, *see, e.g., Atcheson v. Everitt*, 1 Cowper 382, 98 Eng. Rep. 1142 (K.B. 1776). In the United States, the action to recover civil penalties usually seeks the amount fixed by Congress. *See, e.g., United States v. Regan*, 232 U.S., at 40; *Hepner v. United States*, 213 U.S., at 109. The assessment of civil penalties thus cannot be said to involve the "substance of a common-law right to a trial by jury," nor a "fundamental element of a jury trial."

Congress' assignment of the determination of the amount of civil penalties to trial judges therefore does not infringe on the constitutional right to a jury trial. Since Congress itself may fix the civil penalties, it may delegate that determination to trial judges. In this case, highly discretionary calculations that take into account multiple factors are necessary in order to set civil penalties under the Clean Water Act. These are the kinds of calculations traditionally performed by judges. See *Albemarle Paper Co. v. Moody*, 422 U.S. 405, 442-443 (1975) (REHNQUIST, J., concurring). We therefore hold that a determination of a civil penalty is not an essential function of a jury trial, and that the Seventh Amendment does not require a jury trial for that purpose in a civil action.

IV

We conclude that the Seventh Amendment required that petitioner's demand for a jury trial be granted to determine his liability, but that the trial court and not the jury should determine the amount of penalty, if any. The judgment of the Court of Appeals is therefore reversed, and the case is remanded for further proceedings consistent with this opinion.

It is so ordered. [Footnotes Omitted.]

JUSTICE SCALIA, with whom JUSTICE STEVENS joins, concurring in part and dissenting in part.

I join the Court's disposition, and Parts I and II of its opinion. I do not join Part III because in my view the right to trial by jury on whether a civil penalty of unspecified amount is assessable also involves a right to trial by jury on what the amount should be. The fact that the Legislature could elect to fix the amount of penalty has nothing to do with whether, if it chooses not to do so, that element comes within the jury-trial guarantee. Congress could, I suppose, create a private cause of action by one individual against another for a fixed amount of damages, but it surely does not follow that if it creates such a cause of action without prescribing the amount of damages, that issue could be taken from the jury.

While purporting to base its determination (quite correctly) upon historical practice, the Court creates a form of civil adjudication I have never encountered. I can recall no precedent for judgment of civil liability by jury but assessment of amount by the court. Even punitive damages are assessed by the jury when liability is determined in that fashion. One is of course tempted to make an exception in a case like this, where the Government is imposing a noncompensatory remedy to enforce direct exercise of its regulatory authority, because there comes immediately to mind the role of the sentencing judge in a criminal proceeding. If criminal trials are to be the model, however, determination of liability by the jury should be on a standard of proof requiring guilt beyond a reasonable doubt. Having chosen to proceed in civil fashion, with the advantages which that mode entails, it seems to me the Government must take the bitter with the sweet. Since, as the Court correctly reasons, the proper analogue to a civil-fine action is the common-law action for debt, the Government need only prove liability by a preponderance of the evidence; but must, as in any action for debt, accept the amount of award determined not by its own officials but by 12 private citizens. If that tends to discourage the Government from proceeding in this fashion, I doubt that the Founding Fathers would be upset.

I would REVERSE and REMAND for jury determination of both issues.

See also *Friends of the Earth, Inc. v. Laidlaw Environmental Services (TOC), Inc.*, 528 U.S. 167, 120 S.Ct. 693, 145 L.Ed.2d 610 (2000); *City of Monterey v. Del Monte Dunes of Monterey, Ltd.*, 526 U.S. 687, 119 S.Ct. 1624, 143 L.Ed.2d 882 (1999).

UNITED STATES v. M.C.C. OF FLORIDA, INC.

967 F.2d 1559 (11TH Cir. 1992)

The facts pertinent to this appeal are set out generally at *United States v. M.C.C. of Florida, Inc.*, 772 F.2d 1501 (11th Cir.1985) (*M.C.C. I*). We refer here only to the events which essentially bear on the issues now before us.

This controversy arises out of a civil action brought by the United States of America and the Florida Department of Environmental Regulation for injunctive relief to prohibit dredging activities by M.C.C. of Florida, Inc. and Michael Construction Company (hereafter collectively referred to as M.C.C.) for restoration of the areas dredged by M.C.C. and for civil penalties. The case was tried without a jury over the objection of M.C.C. The district court found that M.C.C. had violated the Rivers and Harbors Act, 33 U.S.C. §403, *et seq.,* the Clean Water Act, 33 U.S.C. §1251, *et seq.*, and various state statutes. The court ordered M.C.C. to pay a $20,000 civil penalty under the Clean Water Act and a $200,000 equitable judgment under the Rivers and Harbors Act for use in restoration projects. *United States v. M.C.C. of Florida, Inc.,* 81-2373-CIV (S.D.Fla. March 12, 1984).

On appeal to this court, M.C.C. argued that it had a right to a jury trial, and that its conduct was not prohibited by the Rivers and Harbors Act or by the Clean Water Act. This court held that M.C.C. had no right to a jury trial, that its conduct violated federal law, and that, while an equitable remedy such as that ordered by the district court was appropriate, M.C.C. should have been required to prepare and submit for court approval a proposed environmental plan for implementation of the remedy. *M.C.C. I,* 772 F.2d at 1504-07 .

M.C.C. then petitioned the United States Supreme Court for a writ of certiorari. The writ was granted and the Supreme Court issued a mandate vacating this court's judgment in *M.C.C. I,* directing this court to reconsider its opinion in light of *Tull v. United States,* 481 U.S. 412, 107 S. Ct. 1831, 95 L. Ed. 2d 365 (1987). *M.C.C. of Florida, Inc. v. United States,* 481 U.S. 1034, 107 S.Ct. 1968, 95 L.Ed. 2d 809 (1987). In *Tull,* the Supreme Court held that a defendant is entitled to a jury trial for the determination of its liability for civil penalties under the Clean Water Act. On remand, this court interpreted the Supreme Court's mandate to affect only that part of the *M.C.C. I* opinion entitled "Jury Trial," and found the remaining portions of the prior opinion to be the "law of the case." *United States v. M.C.C. of Florida, Inc.*, 848 F.2d 1133, 1134 (11th Cir.1988) (*M.C.C. II*). The panel thus remanded to the district court for a jury trial on the issue of liability only and stated: "If the jury returns a verdict for the United States, the district court will be guided by that part of our opinion captioned 'Remedy.'" *Id.*

M.C.C. petitioned for rehearing, contending that this court had misinterpreted the *Tull* decision and that M.C.C. was entitled to a retrial on *all* issues presented by the case. In an opinion denying M.C.C.'s petition, the panel held that M.C.C. was not entitled to retrial on all issues, and further noted that no jury trial would be necessary if the Government were to abandon its claim for civil penalties and simply accept the equitable restitution of $200,000. *United States v. M.C.C. of Florida, Inc.,* 863 F.2d 802, 803-04 (11th Cir.1989) (*M.C.C. III*).

Following remand to the district court, the Government waived its claim for civil penalties. The district court approved the waiver and entered an order dismissing the Government's claim for civil penalties, and requiring M.C.C. to prepare and submit an environmental plan for implementation of the remedy. *United States v. M.C.C. of Florida, Inc.*, 81-2373-CIV (S.D.Fla. Feb. 12, 1991). This appeal followed.

M.C.C. argues on this appeal that the Supreme Court's order vacating *M.C.C. I* set aside all prior proceedings and entitled M.C.C. to a retrial on all issues. We disagree.

The order of the Supreme Court stated as follows:

Certiorari granted, judgment vacated, and case remanded for further consideration in light of *Tull v. United States,* [481 U.S. 412, 107 S.Ct. 1831, 95 L.Ed.2d 365 (1987)].

M.C.C. of Florida, Inc. v. United States, 481 U.S. 1034, 107 S.Ct. 1968, 95 L.Ed.2d 809 (1987).

M.C.C. is correct in asserting that a general vacation by an appellate court of the lower court's judgment vacates the entire judgment below, divesting the lower court's earlier judgment of its binding effect. *Johnson v. Board of Educ.*, 457 U.S. 52, 102 S.Ct. 2223, 72 L.Ed.2d 668 (1982); *Dorsey v. Continental Casualty Co.,* 730 F.2d 675 (11th Cir.1984). A vacation which merely requires further consideration in light of a new Supreme Court decision, however, is of a much more limited nature. The effect of a vacation such as the one at issue was not to nullify all prior proceedings. On the contrary, it merely required the court to reconsider its opinion in *M.C.C. I* in light of the law set forth in *Tull.* The Supreme Court did not take a position on whether *Tull* actually affected the outcome of *M.C.C. I,* but was instructing this court to make that determination. Thus, although the panel was not bound by its prior decision, it was free to adopt any or all of *M.C.C. I* that, upon reconsideration, it determined to be unaffected by *Tull. See, e.g., Jones v. American Broadcasting Co.,* 961 F.2d 1546 (11th Cir.1992). *Cf. Moore v. Zant,* 885 F.2d 1497, 1502-03 (11th Cir.1989) (plurality opinion of *en banc* court) (consideration of issues beyond Supreme Court's specific mandate is "permitted by" the remand order), *cert. denied,* ___ U.S. ___, 110 S.Ct. 3255, 111 L.Ed.2d 765 (1990).

This is precisely what the court did in *M.C.C. II* and *III.* After concluding that the jury trial right recognized in *Tull* applied only to the issue of liability for civil penalties under the Clean Water Act, the court reaffirmed the rest of the district court's opinion, and issued directions to the district court for its treatment of the remedy issue:

We interpret the Supreme Court's remand to affect only that portion of our prior opinion captioned "Jury Trial," 772 F.2d 1506 at 1506-07. Thus, the remaining portions of our opinion are the law of the case. We remand to the district court for a jury trial on the issue of liability. If the jury returns a verdict for the United States, the district court will be guided by that part of our opinion captioned "Remedy," 772 F.2d at 1507-08.

M.C.C. II, 848 F.2d at 1134.

Upon M.C.C.'s petition for rehearing, the court further noted that on remand the government could dismiss its claim for the $20,000 fine assessed by the district court under the Clean Water Act and accept the equitable remedy of $200,000 under the Rivers and Harbors Act.... Thus if the government waives the $20,000 civil penalty, it being the civil penalty which entitles M.C.C. to a jury trial, then this case is taken outside the ambit of *Tull.* Any waiver by the government is subject to the approval of the district court.

M.C.C. III, 863 F.2d at 803-04.

The statement in *M.C.C. II* that the remaining portions of *M.C.C. I* were the "law of the case" may not have been technically correct in light of the Supreme Court's vacation of *M.C.C. I.* It is clear, however, that the court did not feel bound by its earlier decision. Instead, the panel simply believed that the Supreme Court's holding in *Tull* had no bearing on any portion of *M.C.C. I* beyond its treatment of the jury trial issue. Thus, the effect of the court's statement in *M.C.C. II* essentially was to reinstate by reference those portions of *M.C.C. I* that were considered to be unaffected by *Tull,* and from which the court saw no reason to depart.

Upon remand, the district court's authority was limited by the scope of the mandate issued by this court. We have previously held that

> [a] district court when acting under an appellate court's mandate, "cannot vary it, or examine it for any other purpose than execution; or give any other or further relief; or review it, even for apparent error, upon a matter decided on appeal; or intermeddle with it, further than to settle so much as has been remanded." *In re Sanford Fork & Tool Co.,* 160 U.S. 247, 255, 16 S. Ct. 291, 293, 40 L. Ed. 414 (1895).

Litman v. Massachusetts Mutual Life Ins. Co., 825 F.2d 1506, 1510-11 (11th Cir.1987) (*en banc*). Upon remand, therefore, the trial court was required to comply with the mandate and statement of the law as contained in *M.C.C. II* and *M.C.C. III.* Accordingly, the district court ordered M.C.C. to submit an environmental plan as required by *M.C.C. II,* and dismissed the Government's claim for civil penalties under the Clean Water Act as suggested by *M.C.C. III.* The district court clearly has complied with this court's mandate.

In sum, M.C.C. is not entitled to a new trial. The Supreme Court's vacation of *M.C.C. I* did not entitle M.C.C. to retrial on all issues. Further, the district court decision from which M.C.C. appeals was in full compliance with the mandate issued by *M.C.C. II* and *M.C.C. III* upon remand.

Both of the other assertions presented by M.C.C. are without merit. First, we reject M.C.C.'s contention that the United States lacks standing to seek relief in this matter. *See Zabel v. Tabb,* 430 F.2d 199 (5th Cir.1970), *cert.denied,* 401 U.S. 910, 91 S. Ct. 873, 27 L. Ed. 2d 808 (1971). Second, M.C.C. argues once again that the navigational servitude doctrine insulates M.C.C.'s activities from the dictates of both the Rivers and Harbors Act and the Clean Water Act. In *M.C.C. I,* this court rejected that argument and affirmed the district court's conclusion that M.C.C.'s activities were covered by both the Clean Water Act and the Rivers and Harbors Act. In *M.C.C. II,* the court adopted that portion of *M.C.C. I,* finding that it was not affected by the *Tull* decision. Because this issue has been previously ruled upon by a prior panel, we cannot consider it anew.

AFFIRMED.

CHAPTER 30

JUDICIAL REVIEW

Any person against whom a civil penalty is assessed under §309(g), or who commented on the proposed assessment of such penalty in accordance with §309(g)(4), may obtain review of such assessment in the case of assessment of a Class I civil penalty, in the United States District Court for the District of Columbia or in the District in which the violation is alleged to have occurred. §309(g)(8)(A). In the case of assessment of a Class II civil penalty, review is available in United States Court of Appeals for the District of Columbia Circuit or for any other Circuit in which such person resides or transacts business. §309(g)(8)(A). Review is initiated by filing a notice of appeal in such court within the 30-day period beginning on the date the civil penalty order is issued and by simultaneously sending a copy of such notice by certified mail to the EPA or the Corps, as the case may be, and the Attorney General. The EPA shall promptly file in such court a certified copy of the record on which the order was issued. Such court shall not set aside or remand such order unless there is not substantial evidence in the record, taken as a whole, to support the finding of a violation or unless the EPA's assessment of the penalty constitutes an abuse of discretion and shall not impose additional civil penalties for the same violation unless the EPA's or Corps's assessment of the penalty constitutes an abuse of discretion. §309(g)(8)(B).

UNITED STATES v. KEY WEST TOWERS, INC.

720 F. Supp. 963 (W.D.Fla. 1989)

The defendants own property in Key West, Florida, that contains wetlands, including a pond, mangroves, and transitional wetlands. A 1.9-acre pond makes up part of the 4.42 acres of total wetlands. Key West Towers partially filled the wetlands in 1984, before it received a cease and desist order from the Army Corps of Engineers ("Corps"). Despite the subsequent order and repeated requests from the Corps, Key West Towers continued filling the wetlands in 1985, 1986, and 1987. On August 7, 1985, Key West Towers submitted an Army Corps of Engineers permit application requesting after-the-fact authorization for 2.1 acres of wetlands already filled and 2.4 acres of proposed wetlands filling. The application, however, was inaccurate and over-estimated the amount of wetlands that had been previously filled, and the permit application was ultimately deactivated in 1987.

The United States, in an effort to maintain and save these beautiful wetlands in Key West, filed a civil enforcement action pursuant to the Clean Water Act, 33 U.S.C. §§1311 and 1319. On July 20, 1988, the lawsuit culminated in a jury verdict that found the pond and wetlands at Key West Towers were adjacent to waters of the United States, the specific area in dispute was wetlands as defined in the regulations of the Army Corps of Engineers, and that fill had been placed in those wetlands in 1984, 1985, 1986, and 1987.

After the jury verdict, the defendants moved for a hearing on penalty and restoration. On May 22, 1989, in open court, the parties agreed to a restoration plan, which is memorialized in this order. The court then held a hearing on the remaining issue, the civil penalty, on May 24, 1989. Although the Clean Water Act provides for a penalty of up to $10,000 per day for each violation of 33 U.S.C. §1311 prior to February 4, 1987, and up to $25,000 per day for each violation subsequent to that date, the plaintiff only seeks a penalty of $250,000. After careful consideration, the court agrees that this penalty is appropriate, but will provide the defendant with an option to satisfy this penalty. Specifically, the defendants can either pay the penalty in full or deed the two-acre pond to a charitable organization in fee simple absolute.

RESTORATION

On May 22, 1989, the parties agreed upon a restoration plan to return the Key West Towers site to its natural state prior to the defendants' activities in 1984. The defendants agree to scrape fill to natural historic elevations within the 1984 jurisdictional line as determined by the jury. The parties agree that if the defendants need to leave the paved road and a minimally necessary shoulder in place in the wetlands, they may scrape down equal square footage on the southeast side of the wetlands contiguous with the jurisdictional line.

The defendants, in terms of actual restoration, agree to replant 24 mangroves or buttonwood trees, 18 inches to 24 inches in height, around the end of the restored pond. In lieu of replanting grasses in the transitional wetlands, the defendants will remove and replace all exotic species from the restored area for three years. The parties also agree that the fill in the southeast corner will be accessed for removal directly from the south. Finally, the defendants agree to deepen a portion of the preexisting pond in the northwest corner to minus four feet below the natural grade in an area of approximately 100 square feet, to be established by the government's expert. The completion of this project will be reflected in the time zero report.

To adequately monitor the defendants' activities, the defendants will provide a time zero report at the completion of the fill removal that will include color photographs of the fill removal site taken before and after fill removal. Moreover, the defendants will provide a signed and sealed survey confirming the removal of at least .76 acres of fill in the wetlands. Similarly, the defendants will provide progress reports at time zero plus 12 months, time zero plus 24 months, and time zero plus 36 months. These reports will include color photographs and a narrative description of the natural recovery of plants and the hand removal of invasive exotics observed in the fill removal areas. Upon completion of the time zero report, the government agrees to perform an inspection. After inspection and upon the government's satisfaction of compliance of the provisions of the consent decree and compliance of all other remedies ordered by the court, including penalty, the government will provide a satisfaction of judgment. The foregoing provisions, agreed to by all parties, are approved by the court and the court retains jurisdiction to enforce the terms of the agreement.

PENALTY

While the parties were able to resolve the issues surrounding the restoration plan, they were not able to agree upon an appropriate civil penalty. The government seeks $250,000. Conversely, the defendants state that they have already been sufficiently penalized, so a further penalty is unwarranted. After considering the six factors enumerated in 33 U.S.C. §1319(d), the court agrees with the plaintiff that $250,000 is appropriate. However, because of the parties' concern with protecting the wildlife in the area, the court will allow the penalty to be lifted if the defendants deed the pond to a charitable organization.

The first consideration under 33 U.S.C. §1319(d), the seriousness of the violation, strongly favors imposing a substantial penalty. The fresh water ponds in the lower Keys are a rare and necessary habitat for certain migratory bird species. Moreover, the transitional wetlands are a critical habitat for various wading birds. Any destruction to these rare and fragile natural resources requires a substantial penalty.

The economic benefit (if any) resulting from the violation does not necessarily justify imposing a harsh penalty. Arguably, deep fill in the corner of the pond allowed easier access to the defendants' development, and perhaps this enhanced accessibility financially benefitted the defendants. This argument, however, is speculative and is not supported by the evidence in the record. Likewise, the third factor, the history of violations, does not strongly favor a severe penalty. The evidence indicates that the defendants may have filled 2.7 acres of wetlands prior to 1984. This previous violation again allows the court to increase the civil penalty, but does not significantly aid the court in determining the appropriate amount.

Unlike the previous two considerations, the fourth factor, any good-faith efforts to comply with the applicable requirements, strongly compels the court to impose a substantial civil penalty. First, the jury specifically found that the defendants filled wetlands on the Key West Towers site from 1984 through 1987. Second, the defendants' filling activities after June 1984 are especially bothersome because the filling directly violated the Corps' cease and desist order. The defendants repeatedly filled the wetlands despite being fully informed of the law. Third, the defendants had their after-the-fact permit application deactivated because of the inaccuracies contained within the application. These three factors strongly indicate the defendants did not make good-faith efforts to comply with the applicable requirements, and thus the court should impose a substantial penalty.

The fifth factor, the economic impact of the penalty on the violator, also does not provide strong guidance concerning the amount of the penalty. Specifically, the government only produced the defendants' tax returns at trial, and the production of the returns is certainly not the best method to decide whether the defendants' income justifies a $250,000 fine. On the other hand, the defendants did not present evidence that a $250,000 fine would devastate them or the corporation.

On balance, these five factors indicate that a $250,000 fine would promote the specific and general deterrence theories behind a civil penalty. *See Tull v. United States*, 481 U.S. 412, 107 S.Ct. 1831, 1838, 95 L.Ed.2d 365 (1987). However, the final consideration in determining the amount of the penalty, "such other matters as justice may require," leads the court to provide the defendants with an option. Specifically, because of the parties and the court's primary concern of protecting the pond and providing a pollution-free habitat for the migratory birds and wildlife, the court will allow the defendants the option of paying the $250,000 fine or deeding to a charitable group, such as the Florida Land Trust, the 1.9-acre pond and a 50-foot buffer zone around that pond. See *United States v. Larkins*, 657 F. Supp. 76, 87 (W.D.Ky. 1987) (penalty of $40,000 lifted if the defendants complete the ordered restoration plan). Based on the foregoing, the court

ORDERS AND ADJUDGES that the parties abide by the restoration plan announced in court on May 22, 1989. The court further

ORDERS AND ADJUDGES that the defendants are fined the sum of $250,000 payable on or before November 20, 1989. If the defendants deed the 1.9-acre pond and the 50-foot buffer zone to a charitable organization that will appropriately maintain these valued wetlands in perpetuity, the fine imposed herein will be set aside and cancelled.

DONE AND ORDERED in chambers at the United States Courthouse, Federal Courthouse Square, Miami, Florida, this 10th day of August 1989. [Footnotes omitted.]

See also United States v. Bayshore Associates, Inc., 934 F.2d 1391 (6th Cir. Mich. 1991; *United States v. Rivera Torres*, 656 F.Supp. 251 (D.P.R. 1986), *aff'd*, 826 F.2d 151 (1st Cir. P.R. 1987); *United States v. Tilton*, 705 F.2d 429 (11th Cir. Fla. 1983); *United States v. Krilich*, 948 F.Supp. 719 (N.D.Ill. 1996); *United States v. Leuzen*, 816 F.Supp. 1171 (S.D.Tex. 1993); *Tahoe Regional Planning Agency v. Terrace Land Co., Inc.*, 772 F.Supp. 506 (D.Nev. 1991); *United States v. Malibu Beach, Inc.*, 711 F.Supp. 1301 (D.N.J. 1989); *United States v. Larkins*, 657 F.Supp. 76 (W.D.Ky. 1987), *aff'd.*, 852 F.2d 189 (6th Cir. Ky. 1988), *cert. denied*, 489 U.S. 1016, 101 L.Ed.2d 193, 109 S.Ct. 1131 (1989); *United States v. Lambert*, 589 F.Supp. 366 (M.D.Fla. 1984); *United States v. Robinson*, 570 F.Supp. 1157 (M.D.Fla. 1983); *United States v. Bradshaw*, 541 F.Supp. 884 (D.Md. 1982); *United States v. Weisman*, 489 F.Supp. 1331 (M.D.Fla. 1980); *United States v. D'Annolfo*, 474 F.Supp. 220 (D.Mass. 1979). But see *United States v. Huebner*, 752 F.2d 1235 (7th Cir.), *cert. denied*, 474 U.S. 817, 88 L.Ed.2d 50, 106 S.Ct. 62 (1985); *United States v. Sexton Cove Estates, Inc.*, 526 F.2d 1293 (5th Cir. 1976).

Chapter 31
CITIZEN SUITS

Private citizens cannot sue for damages under either the Rivers and Harbors Act of 1899 or the Clean Water Act because there is no general private right of action, but citizens may sue to enforce both Acts.

STATE OF CALIFORNIA v. SIERRA CLUB

451 U.S. 287, 101 S.Ct. 1775, 68 L.Ed.2d 101 (1981)

Under review here is a decision of the Court of Appeals for the Ninth Circuit holding that private parties may sue under the Rivers and Harbors Appropriations Act of 1899 to enforce §10 of that Act. An environmental organization and two private citizens (hereafter respondents), seek to enjoin the construction and operation of water diversion facilities which are part of the California Water Project (CWP). They rely upon §10 of the Act, which prohibits "[t]he creation of any obstruction not affirmatively authorized by Congress, to the navigable capacity of any of the waters of the United States...." Since the Act does not explicitly create a private enforcement mechanism, the initial question presented by these consolidated cases is whether such a private right of action can be implied on behalf of those allegedly injured by a claimed violation of §10. Petitioner State of California also asks us to decide whether the Act requires permits for the state water allocation projects involved in these cases.

I

The California Water Project consists of a series of water storage and transportation facilities designed primarily to transport water from the relatively moist climate of northern California to the more arid central and southern portions of the State. The water which will be used by the CWP is initially stored behind dams on the Sacramento River and, as needed, released into the Sacramento-San Joaquin Delta. The CWP then diverts a quantity of this water from the Delta and directs it into canals and aqueducts which will carry it south. The project has both federal and state components. The federal component, the Central Valley Project, is designed in part to provide a constant source of water for irrigation to the Central Valley of California. Water for this project is diverted from the Delta by the Tracy Pumping Plant into the 115-mile Delta-Mendota Canal which transports the water to the Mendota Pool in California's Central Valley. The State Water Project supplies water to both central and southern California by way of the California Aqueduct. Water for this project is drawn from the Delta by the Delta Pumping Plant and deposited in the northern terminus of the California Aqueduct, through which it flows to its destinations in central and southern California

Under the present system the quality of water captured in the north and released into the Delta may be degraded by intruding salt waters from the Pacific Ocean. As a consequence the water which is diverted from the Delta to the Delta-Mendota Canal or the California Aqueduct is potentially of a lesser quality than is the water which is transported to the Delta from storage facilities in the north and from there deposited in the Delta. The State of California has proposed the construction of a 42-mile Peripheral Canal along the eastern edge of the Delta area, which would avoid any mixing of the water from the north with the saline water of the Delta. Instead of depositing water in the Delta, the canal would carry high quality water directly to the Tracy and Delta Pumping Plants.

Respondents commenced the present action in 1971 in the United States District Court for the Northern District of California. *Sierra Club v. Morton*, 400 F Supp 610 (1975). Named as defendants were the various federal and state officials who administer the agencies responsible for overseeing the operation, construction, and regulation of the CWP facilities in question. Petitioner water agencies, which had contracted with the State for water from the Delta and which had incurred extensive financial obligations in reliance thereon, were permitted to intervene. The respondents alleged that present and proposed diversions of water from the Delta degraded the quality of Delta water, and that such diversion violated §10 of the Rivers and Harbors Appropriation Act of 1899. They sought to enjoin further operation or construction of water diversion facilities until the consent of the Army Corps of Engineers was obtained as required by the Act.

The District Court concluded that respondents could avail themselves of a "private cause of action" to enforce §10 of the Act, and ruled on the merits that approval of the Corps of Engineers was required by §10 for the Tracy and Delta Pumping Plants and the Peripheral Canal. *Sierra Club v. Morton, supra.* The Court of Appeals for the Ninth Circuit agreed that a private cause of action to enforce the Act existed. *Sierra Club v. Andrus*, 610 F.2d 581 (1979). It reversed the District Court as to the Tracy Pumping Plant, however, ruling that Congress has consented to its construction and operation. We granted petitions for certiorari filed by the water agencies and the State of California. 449 U.S. 818, 66 L.Ed 2d 19, 101 S.Ct 68 (1980).

II

Cort v. Ash, 422 US 66, 45 L.Ed 2d 26, 95 S.Ct 2080 (1975), outlined a "preferred approach for determining whether a private right of action should be implied from a federal statute...." *Transamerica Mortgage Advisors, Inc. v. Lewis*, 444 US 11, 26, 62 L Ed 2d 146, 100 S Ct 242 (1979) (White, J., dissenting); see *Cannon v. University of Chicago*, 441 US 677, 60 L Ed 2d 560, 99 S Ct 1946 (1979). This approach listed four factors thought to be relevant to the inquiry:

> First, is the plaintiff 'one of the class for whose *especial* benefit the statute was enacted,'... —that is, does the statute create a federal right in favor of the plaintiff? Second, is there any indication of legislative intent, explicit or implicit, either to create such a remedy or to deny one? ... Third, is it consistent with the underlying purposes of the legislative scheme to imply such a remedy for the plaintiff? ... And finally, is the cause of action one traditionally relegated to state law, in an area basically the concern of the States, so that it would be inappropriate to infer a cause of action based solely on federal law? 422 US, at 78, 45 LEd 2d 26, 95 S.Ct 2080.

Combined, these four factors present the relevant inquiries to pursue in answering the recurring question of implied causes of action. Cases subsequent to *Cort* have explained that the ultimate issue is whether Congress intended to create a private right of action, see *Universities Research Assn. Inc. v. Coutu*, 450 US 754, 771-772, 67 L.Ed 2d 662, 101 S.Ct 1451 (1981); *Transamerica Mortgage Advisors, Inc. v. Lewis*, supra, at 23-24, 62 L Ed 2d 146, 100 S Ct 242; *Touche Ross & Co. v. Redington*, 442 US 560, 568, 575-576, 61 L.Ed 2d 82, 99 S.Ct 2479 (1979); but the four factors specified in *Cort* remain the "criteria through which this intent could be discerned." *Davis v.*

Passman, 442 U.S. 228, 241, 60 L.Ed 2d 846, 99 S.Ct 2264 (1979); *Transamerica Mortgage Advisors, Inc. v. Lewis, supra*, at 27, 62 L.Ed 2d 146, 100 S.Ct 242 (White, J., dissenting).

Under *Cort*, the initial consideration is whether the plaintiff is a member of a class for "'whose *especial* benefit the statute was enacted.'" *Cort v. Ash, supra*, at 78, 80-82, 45 L.Ed 2d 26, 95 S.Ct 2080; see *Touche Ross & Co. v. Redington, supra,* at 569-570, 61 L.Ed 2d 82, 99 S.Ct 2479; *Cannon v. University of Chicago, supra*, at 689-694, 60 L.Ed 2d 560, 99 S.Ct 1946. Without analyzing either the language or legislative history of the Act, the Court of Appeals here concluded that the Act was designed for the especial benefit of private parties who may suffer "special injury" caused by an unauthorized obstruction to a navigable waterway. It was apparently reasoned that since Congress enacted a statute that forbids such obstructions in navigable waters, any person who would be "especially harmed" by an unauthorized obstruction was an especial beneficiary of the Act. But such a definition of "especial" beneficiary makes this factor meaningless. Under this view, a victim of any crime would be deemed an especial beneficiary of the criminal statute's proscription. *Cort* did not adopt such a broad-gauge approach. *Cort v. Ash, supra*, at 80-82, 45 L.Ed 2d 26, 95 S.Ct 2080. The question is not simply who would benefit from the Act, but whether Congress intended to confer federal rights upon those beneficiaries. See *Cannon, supra*, at 690-693, n 13, 60 L.Ed 2d 560, 99 S.Ct 1946.

In ascertaining this intent, the first consideration is the language of the Act. Here, the statute states no more than a general proscription of certain activities; it does not unmistakably focus on any particular class of beneficiaries whose welfare Congress intended to further. Such language does not indicate an intent to provide for private rights of action. "There would be far less reason to infer a private remedy in favor of individual persons if Congress, instead of drafting Title IX [of the Education amendments of 1972] with an unmistakable focus on the benefited class, had written it simply as a ban on discriminatory conduct by recipients of federal funds or as a prohibition against the disbursement of public funds to educational institutions engaged in discriminatory practices." *Cannon v. University of Chicago, supra*, at 690-693, 60 L.Ed 2d 560, 99 S.Ct 1946; see also *Touche Ross & Co. v. Redington, supra*, at 569; *Cort v. Ash, supra*, at 80-82, 61 L.Ed 2d 82, 99 S.Ct 2479. Section 10 of the Rivers and Harbors Appropriation Act is the kind of general ban which carries with it no implication of an intent to confer rights on a particular class of persons.

Neither the Court of Appeals nor respondents have identified anything in the legislative history suggesting that §10 was created for the especial benefit of a particular class. On the contrary, the legislative history supports the view that the Act was designed to benefit the public at large by empowering the Federal Government to exercise its authority over interstate commerce with respect to obstructions on navigable rivers caused by bridges and similar structures. In part, the Act was passed in response to this Court's decision in *Willamette Iron Bridge Co. v. Hatch*, 125 US 1, 31 L.Ed 629, 8 S.Ct 811 (1888). There the Court held that there was no federal common law "which prohibits obstructions and nuisances in navigable rivers." *Id.,* at 8, 31 L.Ed 629, 8 S.Ct 811. Although Willamette involved private parties, the clear implication of the Court's opinion was that in the absence of specific legislation no party, including the Federal Government, would be empowered to take any action under federal law with respect to such obstructions. The Act was intended to enable the Secretary of War to take such action. See 21 Cong Rec 8603, 8605, and 8607 (1890); see also *United States v. Pennsylvania Industrial Chemical Corp.*, 411 U.S. 655, 663-664, 36 L.Ed2d 567, 93 S.Ct 1804 (1973); *United States v. Standard Oil Co.*, 384 U.S. 224, 227-229, 16 L.Ed2d 492, 86 S.Ct 1427 (1966); *United States v. Republic Steel Corp.*, 362 U.S.

482, 485-488, 499-500, 4 L.Ed2d 903, 80 S.Ct 884 (1960). Congress was not concerned with the rights of individuals.

It is not surprising, therefore, that there is no "indication of legislative intent, explicit or implicit, either to create such a remedy or to deny one." *Cort v. Ash*, 422 US, at 78, 82-84, 45 L.Ed 2d 26, 95 S.Ct 2080; *Touche Ross & Co. v Redington*, 442 US, at 571, 61 L.Ed 2d 82, 99 S.Ct 2479; *Cannon v. University of Chicago*, 441 US, at 694-703, 60 L.Ed2d 560, 99 S.Ct 1946. The Court of Appeals recognized as much: "The legislative history of the Rivers and Harbors Act of 1899 does not reflect a congressional intent either to afford a private remedy or to deny one." 610 F.2d, at 588. This silence on the remedy question serves to confirm that in enacting the Act, Congress was concerned not with private rights but with the Federal Government's ability to respond to obstructions on navigable waterways.

As recently emphasized, the focus of the inquiry is on whether Congress intended to create a remedy. *Universities Research Assn. Inc. v. Coutu*, 450 US, at 771-772 67 L.Ed2d 662, 101 S.Ct 1451 (1981); *Transamerica Mortgage Advisors, Inc. v. Lewis*, 444 US, at 23-24, 62 L.Ed2d 146, 100 S.Ct 242; *Touche Ross & Co. v. Redington, supra,* at 575-576, 61 L.Ed2d 82, 99 S.Ct 2479. The federal judiciary will not engraft a remedy on a statute, no matter how salutary, that Congress did not intend to provide. Here consideration of the first two Cort factors is dispositive. The language of the statute and its legislative history do not suggest that the Act was intended to create federal rights for the especial benefit of a class of persons but rather that it was intended to benefit the public at large through a general regulatory scheme to be administered by the then Secretary of War. Nor is there any evidence that Congress anticipated that there would be a private remedy. This being the case, it is unnecessary to inquire further to determine whether the purpose of the statute would be advanced by the judicial implication of a private action or whether such a remedy is within the federal domain of interest. These factors are only of relevance if the first two factors give indication of congressional intent to create the remedy. *Touche Ross & Co. v. Redington, supra*, at 574-576, 61 L.Ed2d 82, 99 S.Ct 2479. There being no such indication, the judgment of the Court of Appeals must be reversed.

III

Petitioner the State of California urges that we reach the merits of these cases-whether permits are required for the state water allocation projects-regardless of our disposition of the private-cause-of-action issue. This we decline to do. Our ruling that there is no private cause of action permitting respondents to commence this action disposes of the cases: we cannot consider the merits of a claim which Congress has not authorized respondents to raise.

The judgment of the Court of Appeals is accordingly reversed, and the cases are remanded for proceedings consistent with this opinion.

It is so ORDERED.

Justice *Stevens,* CONCURRING.

In 1888 this Court reversed a decree enjoining the construction of a bridge over a navigable river. *Willamette Iron Bridge Co. v. Hatch*, 125 US 1, 31 L.Ed 629, 8 S.Ct 811. The Court's opinion in that case did not question the right of the private parties to seek relief in a federal court; rather, the Court held that no federal rule of law prohibited the obstruction of the navigable waterway.

Congress responded to the Willamette case in the Rivers and Harbors Act of 1890 by creating a federal prohibition of such obstructions absent a permit from the Secretary of War. 26 Stat 426, 454. At the time the statute was enacted, I believe the lawyers in Congress simply assumed that private parties in a position comparable to that of the litigants in the Willamette case would have a remedy for any injury suffered by reason of a violation of the new federal statute. For at that time the implication of private causes of action was a well-known practice at common law and in American courts. Therefore, in my view, the Members of Congress merely assumed that the federal courts would follow the ancient maxim "*ubi jus ibi remedium*" and imply a private right of action. *See Texas & Pacific R. Co. v. Rigsby*, 241 US 33, 39-40, 60 L.Ed 874, 36 S.Ct 482.

Accordingly, if I were writing on a clean slate, I would hold that an implied remedy is available to respondents under this statute.

The slate, however, is not clean. Because the problem of ascertaining legislative intent that is not expressed in legislation is often so difficult, the Court has wisely developed rules to guide judges in deciding whether a federal remedy is implicitly a part of a federal statute. In *Cort v. Ash*, 422 U.S. 66, 45 L.Ed.2d 26, 95 S.Ct 2080, all of my present colleagues subscribed to a unanimous formulation of those rules, and in *Cannon v. University of Chicago*, 441 U.S. 677, 60 L.Ed2d 560, 99 S.Ct 1946, a majority of the Court joined my attempt to explain the application of those rules in that case. The *Cort v. Ash* analysis is therefore a part of our law.

In these cases, I believe the Court correctly concludes that application of the *Cort v. Ash* analysis indicates that no private cause of action is available. I think it is more important to adhere to the analytical approach the Court has adopted than to base my vote on my own opinion about what Congress probably assumed in 1890. *Cf. Florida Dept. of Health & Rehabilitative Services v. Florida Nursing Home Assn.*, 450 U.S. 147, 151, 67 L.Ed.2d 132, 101 S.Ct 1032 (Stevens, J., concurring). I therefore join Justice White's opinion for the Court.

Justice Rehnquist, with whom The Chief Justice, Justice Stewart, and Justice Powell join, concurring in the judgment.

I agree completely with the conclusion of the Court that in these cases "Congress was not concerned with the rights of individuals" and that it is not surprising, therefore, that there is no "indication of legislative intent, explicit or implicit, either to create ... a [private] remedy or to deny one." *Ante*, at 295, 68 L.Ed.2d, at 109.

I also agree with the Court's analysis, *ante*, at 297, 68 L.Ed.2d, at 110, where it says:

> As recently emphasized, the focus of the inquiry is on whether Congress intended to create a remedy. *Universities Research Assn., Inc. v. Coutu*, 450 U.S. at 297, [67 L.Ed.2d 662, 101 S.Ct. 1451]. *Transamerica Mortgage Advisors, Inc. v. Lewis*, 444 U.S. at 23-24, [62 L.Ed.2d 146, 100 S.Ct. 242]; *Touche Ross & Co. v. Redington*, 442 U.S. at 575-576, [61 L.Ed2d 82, 99 S.Ct. 2479]. The federal judiciary will not engraft a remedy on a statute, no matter how salutary, that Congress did not intend to provide.

My only difference, and the difference which leads me to write this separate concurrence in the judgment, is that I think the Court's opinion places somewhat more emphasis on *Cort v. Ash*, 422 U.S. 66, 45 L.Ed.2d 26, 95 S.Ct. 2080 (1975), than is warranted in light of several more recent "implied right of action" decisions which limit it. These decisions make clear that the so-called *Cort* factors are merely guides in the central task of ascertaining legislative intent, *see Transamerica*

Mortgage Advisors, Inc. v. Lewis, 444 U.S. 11, 15, 62 L.Ed.2d 146, 100 S.Ct. 242 (1979); *Touche Ross & Co. v. Redington*, 442 U.S. 560, 575-576, 61 L.Ed.2d 82, 99 S.Ct. 2479 (1979); *Cannon v. University of Chicago*, 441 U.S. 677, 739-740, 60 L.Ed.2d 560, 99 S.Ct. 1946 (1979) (Powell, J., dissenting), that they are not of equal weight, *Transamerica, supra*, at 15, 23-24, 62 L.Ed.2d 146, 100 S.Ct 242; *Touche Ross, supra*, at 575-576, 61 L.Ed.2d 82, 99 S.Ct. 2479; and that in deciding an implied-right-of-action case courts need not mechanically trudge through all four of the factors when the dispositive question of legislative intent has been resolved, *Transamerica, supra*, at 24, 62 L.Ed.2d 146, 100 S.Ct. 242; *Touche Ross, supra*, at 575-576, 61 L.Ed.2d 82, 99 S.Ct. 2479; *Kissinger v. Reporters Committee for Freedom of the Press*, 445 U.S. 136, 148-149, 63 L.Ed.2d 267, 100 S.Ct. 960 (1980). Surely it cannot be seriously argued that a mechanical application of the *Cort* analysis lends "predictability" to implied-right-of-action jurisprudence: including today's decision, five of the last six statutory implied-right-of-action cases in which we have reviewed analysis by the Courts of Appeals after Cort have resulted in reversal of erroneous Court of Appeals decisions. *See Universities Research Assn., Inc. v. Coutu*, 450 US 754, 67 L.Ed.2d 662, 101 S.Ct. 1451 (1981); *Transamerica, supra; Touche Ross, supra; Cannon, supra. Cf. Northwest Airlines, Inc. v. Transport Workers, ante*, p.77, 67 L.Ed.2d 750, 101 S.Ct. 1571. While this may be predictability of a sort, it is not the sort which the Court in *Cort v. Ash, supra,* or in any other case seeking to afford guidance to statutory construction intended.

But in these cases, I am happy to agree with the Court that there is no implied right of action because "[t]he language of the statute and its legislative history do not suggest that the Act was intended to create federal rights for the especial benefit of a class of persons," *ante,* at 297-298, 68 L.Ed.2d, at 110-111, and because there is no "evidence that Congress anticipated that there would be a private remedy." *Ante*, at 298, 68 L.Ed.2d, at 110. [Footnotes omitted.]

MIDDLESEX COUNTY SEWERAGE AUTHORITY v. NATIONAL SEA CLAMMERS ASSOCIATION

453 US 1, 101 S Ct 2615, 69 L Ed 2d 435 (1981)

In these cases, involving alleged damage to fishing grounds caused by discharges and ocean dumping of sewage and other waste, we are faced with questions concerning the availability of a damages remedy, based either on federal common law or on the provisions of two Acts-the Federal Water Pollution Control Act (FWPCA), 86 Stat 816, as amended, 33 U.S.C. §1251 *et seq.* (1976 ed and Supp III) [33 U.S.C.A. §§1251 et seq.], and the Marine Protection, Research, and Sanctuaries Act of 1972 (MPRSA), 86 Stat 1052, as amended, 33 U.S.C. §1401 *et seq.* (1976 ed. and Supp III). [33 U.S.C.A. §§1401 et seq.].

Respondents are an organization whose members harvest fish and shellfish off the coast of New York and New Jersey, and one individual member of that organization. In 1977, they brought suit in the United States District Court for the District of New Jersey against petitioners—various governmental entities and officials from New York, New Jersey, and the Federal Government. Their complaint alleged that sewage, sewage "sludge," and other waste materials were being discharged into New York Harbor and the Hudson River by some of the petitioners. In addition it complained of the dumping of such materials directly into the ocean from maritime vessels. The complaint alleged that, as a result of these activities, the Atlantic Ocean was becoming polluted, and it made special reference to a massive growth of algae said to have appeared offshore in 1976. It then stated that this pollution was causing the "collapse of the fishing, clamming and lobster industries which operate in the waters of the Atlantic Ocean."

Invoking a wide variety of legal theories, respondents sought injunctive and declaratory relief, $250 million in compensatory damages, and $250 million in punitive damages. The District Court granted summary judgment to petitioners on all counts of the complaint.

In holdings relevant here, the District Court rejected respondents' nuisance claim under federal common law, *see Illinois v. Milwaukee*, 406 U.S. 91, 31 L.Ed.2d 712, 92 S.Ct. 1385 (1972), on the ground that such a cause of action is not available to private parties. With respect to the claims based on alleged violations of the FWPCA, the court noted that respondents had failed to comply with the 60-day notice requirement of the "citizen suit" provision in §505(b)(1)(A) of the Act, 86 Stat 888, 33 U.S.C. §1365(b)(1)(A) [33 U.S.C.A. §1365(b)(1)(A)]. This provision allows suits under the Act by private citizens, but authorizes only prospective relief, and the citizen plaintiffs first must give notice to the EPA, the State, and any alleged violator. *Ibid.* Because respondents did not give the requisite notice, the court refused to allow them to proceed with a claim under the Act independent of the citizen-suit provision and based on the general jurisdictional grant in 28 U.S.C. §1331 [28 U.S.C.A. §1331]. The court applied the same analysis to respondents' claims under the MPRSA, which contains similar citizen-suit and notice provisions. 33 U.S.C. §1415(g) [33 U.S.C.A. §1415(g)]. Finally, the court rejected a possible claim of maritime tort, both because respondents had failed to plead such claim explicitly and because they had failed to comply with the procedural requirements of the federal and state Tort Claims Acts.

The United States Court of Appeals for the Third Circuit reversed as to the claims based on the FWPCA, the MPRSA, the federal common law of nuisance, and maritime tort. *National Sea Clammers Assn. v. City of New York*, 616 F.2d 1222 (1980). With respect to the FWPCA, the court held that failure to comply with the 60-day notice provision in §505(b)(1)(A), 33 U.S.C. §1365(b)(1)(A) [33 U.S.C.A. §1365(b)(1)(A)], does not preclude suits under the Act in addition to the specific "citizen suits" authorized in §505. It based this conclusion on the saving clause in §505(e), 33 U.S.C. §1365(e) [33 U.S.C.A. §1365(e)], preserving "any right which any person (or class of persons) may have under any statute or common law to seek enforcement of any effluent standard or limitation or to seek any other relief." 616 F.2d, at 1226-1228; see n.10; *supra*. The Court of Appeals then went on to apply our precedents in the area of implied statutory rights of action, and concluded that "Congress intended to permit the federal courts to entertain a private cause of action implied from the terms of the [FWPCA], preserved by the savings clause of the Act, on behalf of individuals or groups of individuals who have been or will be injured by pollution in violation of its terms." 616 F.2d, at 1230-1231.

The court then applied this same analysis to the MPRSA, concluding again that the District Court had erred in dismissing respondents' claims under this Act. Although the court was not explicit on this question, it apparently concluded that suits for *damages*, as well as for injunctive relief, could be brought under the FWPCA and the MPRSA.

With respect to the federal common-law nuisance claims, the Court of Appeals rejected the District Court's conclusion that private parties may not bring such claims. It also held, applying common-law principles, that respondents "alleged sufficient individual damage to permit them to recover damages for this essentially public nuisance." *Id.*, at 1234. It thus went considerably beyond *Illinois v. Milwaukee*, 406 U.S. 91, 31 L.Ed.2d 712, 92 S.Ct. 1385 (1972), which involved purely prospective relief sought by a state plaintiff.

Petitions for a writ of certiorari raising a variety of arguments were filed in this Court by a group of New Jersey sewerage authorities (No. 79-1711), by the Joint Meeting of Essex and Union Counties in New Jersey (No. 79-1754), by the City and Mayor of New York (No. 79-1760), and by all of the federal defendants named in this suit (No. 80-12). We granted these petitions, limiting review to three questions: (i) whether FWPCA and MPRSA imply a private right of action independent of their citizen-suit provisions, (ii) whether all federal common-law nuisance actions concerning ocean pollution now are pre-empted by the legislative scheme contained in the FWPCA and the MPRSA, and (iii) if not, whether a private citizen has standing to sue for damages under the federal common law of nuisance. We hold that there is no implied right of action under these statutes and that the federal common law of nuisance has been fully pre-empted in the area of ocean pollution.

II

The Federal Water Pollution Control Act was first enacted in 1948. Act of June 30, 1948, 62 Stat 1155. It emphasized state enforcement of water quality standards. When this legislation proved ineffective, Congress passed the Federal Water Pollution Control Act Amendments of 1972. Pub.L. 92-500, 86 Stat 816, 33 U.S.C. §1251 et seq. [33 U.S.C.A. §§1251 et seq.]. The Amendments shifted the emphasis to "direct restrictions on discharges," *EPA v. California ex rel. State Water Resources Control Board*, 426 U.S. 200, 204, 48 L.Ed.2d 578, 96 S.Ct. 2022 (1976), and made it "unlawful for any person to discharge a pollutant without obtaining a permit and complying with its terms," *id.* at 205, 48 L.Ed.2d 578, 96 S.Ct. 2022. While still allowing for state administration and enforcement under federally approved state plans, §§402(b), (c), 33 U.S.C. §§1342(b), (c) [33 U.S.C.A. §1342(b), (c)], the Amendments created various federal minimum effluent standards, §§301-307, 33 U.S.C. §§1311-1317 [33 U.S.C.A. §§1311-1317].

The Marine Protection, Research, and Sanctuaries Act of 1972, Pub.L. 92-532, 86 Stat 1052, sought to create comprehensive federal regulation of the dumping of materials into ocean waters near the United States coastline. Section 101(a) of the Act requires a permit for any dumping into ocean waters, when the material is transported from the United States or on an American vessel or aircraft. 33 U.S.C. §1411(a) [33 U.S.C.A. §1411(a)]. In addition, it requires a permit for the dumping of material transported from outside the United States into the territorial seas or in the zone extending 12 miles from the coastline, "to the extent that it may affect the territorial sea or the territory of the United States." §1411(b).

The exact nature of respondents' claims under these two Acts is not clear, but the claims appear to fall into two categories. The main contention is that the EPA and the Army Corps of Engineers have permitted the New Jersey and New York defendants to discharge and dump pollutants in amounts that are not permitted by the Acts. In addition, they seem to allege that the New York and New Jersey defendants have violated the terms of their permits. The question before us is whether respondents may raise either of these claims in a private suit for injunctive and monetary relief, where such a suit is not expressly authorized by either of these Acts.

A

It is unnecessary to discuss at length the principles set out in recent decisions concerning the recurring question whether Congress intended to create a private right of action under a federal statute without saying so explicitly. The key to the inquiry is the intent of the Legislature. *Texas Industries, Inc. v. Radcliff Materials, Inc.*, 451 U.S. 630, 639, 68 L.Ed.2d 500, 101 S.Ct. 2061

(1981); *California v. Sierra Club*, 451 U.S. 287, 293, 68 L.Ed.2d 101, 101 S Ct. 1775 (1981); *Universities Research Assn. v. Coutu*, 450 U.S. 754, 770, 67 L.Ed.2d 662, 101 S.Ct. 1451 (1981); *Transamerica Mortgage Advisors, Inc. v. Lewis*, 444 U.S. 11, 15, 62 L.Ed.2d 146, 100 S.Ct. 242 (1979); *Touche Ross & Co. v. Redington*, 442 U.S. 560, 568, 61 L.Ed.2d 82, 99 S.Ct. 2479 (1979). We look first, of course, to the statutory language, particularly to the provisions made therein for enforcement and relief. Then we review the legislative history and other traditional aids of statutory interpretation to determine congressional intent.

These Acts contain unusually elaborate enforcement provisions, conferring authority to sue for this purpose both on government officials and private citizens. The FWPCA, for example, authorizes the EPA Administrator to respond to violations of the Act with compliance orders and civil suits. §309, 33 U.S.C. §1319 [33 U.S.C.A. §1319]. He may seek a civil penalty of up to $10,000 per day, §309(d), 33 U.S.C. §1319(d) [33 U.S.C.A. §1319(d)] and criminal penalties also are available, §309(c), 33 U.S.C. §1319(c) [33 U.S.C.A. §1319(c)]. States desiring to administer their own permit programs must demonstrate that state officials possess adequate authority to abate violations through civil or criminal penalties or other means of enforcement. §402(b)(7), 33 U.S.C. §1342(b)(7) [33 U.S.C.A. §1342(b)(7)]. In addition, under §509(b), 33 U.S.C. §1369(b) [33 U.S.C.A. §1369(b)], "any interested person" may seek judicial review in the United States courts of appeals of various particular actions by the Administrator, including establishment of effluent standards and issuance of permits for discharge of pollutants. Where review could have been obtained under this provision, the action at issue may not be challenged in any subsequent civil or criminal proceeding for enforcement. §1369(b)(2).

These enforcement mechanisms, most of which have their counterpart under the MPRSA, are supplemented by the express citizen-suit provisions in §505(a) of the FWPCA, 33 U.S.C. §1365(a) [33 U.S.C.A. §1365(a)], and §105(g) of the MPRSA, 33 U.S.C. §1415(g) [33 U.S.C.A. §1415(g)]. *See* nn.9, 11, supra. These citizen-suit provisions authorize private persons to sue for injunctions to enforce these statutes. Plaintiffs invoking these provisions first must comply with specified procedures-which respondents here ignored-including in most cases 60 days prior notice to potential defendants.

In view of these elaborate enforcement provisions it cannot be assumed that Congress intended to authorize by implication additional judicial remedies for private citizens suing under MPRSA and FWPCA. As we stated in *Transamerica Mortgage Advisors, supra*, "it is an elemental canon of statutory construction that where a statute expressly provides a particular remedy or remedies, a court must be chary of reading others into it." 444 U.S., at 19, 62 L.Ed.2d 146, 100 S.Ct. 242. See also *Touche Ross & Co. v. Redington, supra,* at 571-574, 61 L.Ed.2d 82, 99 S.Ct. 2479. In the absence of strong indicia of a contrary congressional intent, we are compelled to conclude that Congress provided precisely the remedies it considered appropriate.

As noted above, the Court of Appeals avoided this inference. Discussing the FWPCA, it held that the existence of a citizen-suit provision in §505(a) does not rule out implied forms of private enforcement of the Act. It arrived at this conclusion by asserting that Congress intended in §505(a) to create a limited cause of action for "private attorneys general"—"non-injured member[s] of the public" suing to promote the general welfare rather than to redress an injury to their own welfare. 616 F.2d at 1227. It went on to conclude:

> A private party who is *injured* by the alleged violation, as these plaintiffs allege they were, has an alternate basis for suit under section 505(e), 33 U.S.C. §1365(e) [33 U.S.C.A. §1365(e)], and the general federal question jurisdiction of the Judicial Code, 28 U.S.C.

> §1331 (1976) [28 U.S.C.A. §1331]. Section 505(e) is a savings clause that preserves all rights to enforce the Act or seek relief against the Administrator. Coupled with the general federal question jurisdiction it permits this suit to be brought by these parties. *Ibid.* (footnotes omitted) (emphasis added).

There are at least three problems with this reasoning. First, the language of the saving clause on which the Court of Appeals relied, *see* n.10, *supra*, is quite ambiguous concerning the intent of Congress to "preserve" remedies under the FWPCA itself. It merely states that nothing in the citizen-suit provision "shall restrict any right which any person ... may have under any statute or common law to seek enforcement of any effluent standard or limitation or to seek any other relief." It is doubtful that the phrase "any statute" includes the very statute in which this statement was contained.

Moreover, the reasoning on which the Court of Appeals relied is flawed for another reason. It draws a distinction between "non-injured" plaintiffs who may bring citizen suits to enforce provisions of these Acts, and the "injured" plaintiffs in this litigation who claim a right to sue under the Acts, not by virtue of the citizen-suit provisions, but rather under the language of the saving clauses. In fact, it is clear that the citizen-suit provisions apply only to persons who can claim some sort of injury and there is, therefore, no reason to infer the existence of a separate right of action for "injured" plaintiffs. "Citizen" is defined in the citizen-suit section of the FWPCA as "a person or persons having an interest which is or may be adversely affected." §505(g), 33 U.S.C. §1365(g) [33 U.S.C.A. §1365(g)]. It is clear from the Senate Conference Report that this phrase was intended by Congress to allow suits by all persons possessing standing under this Court's decision in *Sierra Club v. Morton*, 405 U.S. 727, 31 L.Ed.2d 636, 92 S.Ct. 1361 (1972). See S.Conf.Rep. No. 92-1236, p 146 (1972). This broad category of potential plaintiffs necessarily includes both plaintiffs seeking to enforce these statutes as private attorneys general, whose injuries are "noneconomic" and probably noncompensable, and persons like respondents who assert that they have suffered tangible economic injuries because of statutory violations.

Finally, the Court of Appeals failed to take account of the rest of the enforcement scheme expressly provided by Congress—including the opportunity for "any interested person" to seek judicial review of a number of EPA actions within 90 days, §509(b), 33 U.S.C. § 1369(b) [33 U.S.C.A. §1369(b)]. *See supra*, at 13-14, 69 L Ed 2d, at 446-447.

The Court of Appeals also applied its reasoning to the MPRSA. But here again we are persuaded that Congress evidenced no intent to authorize by implication private remedies under these Acts apart from the expressly authorized citizen suits. The relevant provisions in the MPRSA are in many respects almost identical to those of the FWPCA. 33 U.S.C. §1415(g) [33 U.S.C.A. §1415(g)]. Although they do not expressly limit citizen suits to those who have suffered some injury from a violation of the Act, we are not persuaded by this fact alone that Congress affirmatively intended to imply the existence of a parallel private remedy, after setting out expressly the manner in which private citizens can seek to enjoin violations.

In *Cort v. Ash*, 422 U.S. 66, 78, 45 L.Ed.2d 26, 95 S.Ct. 2080 (1975), the Court identified several factors that are relevant to the question of implied private remedies. These include the legislative history. *See ibid.* ("Second, is there any indication of legislative intent, explicit or implicit, either to create such a remedy or to deny one?"). This history does not lead to a contrary conclusion with respect to implied remedies under either Act. Indeed, the Reports and debates provide affirmative support for the view that Congress intended the limitations imposed on citizen suits to apply to all private suits under these Acts.

Thus, both the structure of the Acts and their legislative history lead us to conclude that Congress intended that private remedies in addition to those expressly provided should not be implied. Where, as here, Congress has made clear that implied private actions are not contemplated, the courts are not authorized to ignore this legislative judgment.

B

Although the parties have not suggested it, there remains a possible alternative source of *express* congressional authorization of private suits under these Acts. Last Term, in *Maine v. Thiboutot*, 448 U.S. 1, 65 L.Ed.2d 555, 100 S.Ct. 2502 (1980), the Court construed 42 U.S.C. §1983 [42 U.S.C.A. §1983], as authorizing suits to redress violations by state officials of rights created by federal statutes. Accordingly, it could be argued that respondents may sue the municipalities and sewerage boards among the petitioners under the FWPCA and MPRSA by virtue of a right of action created by §1983.

It is appropriate to reach the question of the applicability of *Maine v. Thiboutot* to this setting, despite the failure of respondents to raise it here or below. This litigation began long before that decision. Moreover, if controlling, this argument would obviate the need to consider whether Congress intended to authorize private suits to enforce these particular federal statutes. The claim brought here arguably falls within the scope of *Maine v. Thiboutot* because it involves a suit by a private party claiming that a federal statute has been violated under color of state law, causing an injury. The Court, however, has recognized two exceptions to the application of §1983 to statutory violations. In *Pennhurst State School and Hospital v. Halderman*, 451 U.S. 1, 67 L.Ed.2d 694, 101 S.Ct. 1531 (1981), we remanded certain claims for a determination (i) whether Congress had foreclosed private enforcement of that statute in the enactment itself, and (ii) whether the statute at issue there was the kind that created enforceable "rights" under §1983. *Id.*, at 28, 67 L.Ed.2d 694, 101 S.Ct. 1531. In the present cases because we find that Congress foreclosed a §1983 remedy under these Acts, we need not reach the second question whether these Acts created "rights, privileges, or immunities" within the meaning of §1983.

When the remedial devices provided in a particular Act are sufficiently comprehensive, they may suffice to demonstrate congressional intent to preclude the remedy of suits under §1983. As Justice Stewart, who later joined the majority in *Maine v. Thiboutot*, stated in *Chapman v. Houston Welfare Rights Organization*, 441 U.S. 600, 673, n. 2, 60 L.Ed.2d 508, 99 S.Ct. 1905 (1979) (dissenting opinion), when "a state official is alleged to have violated a federal statute which provides its own comprehensive enforcement scheme, the requirements of that enforcement procedure may not be bypassed by bringing suit directly under §1983." As discussed above, the FWPCA and MPRSA do provide quite comprehensive enforcement mechanisms. It is hard to believe that Congress intended to preserve the §1983 right of action when it created so many specific statutory remedies, including the two citizen-suit provisions. See *Chesapeake Bay Foundation v. Virginia State Water Control Board*, 501 F.Supp. 821 (E.D.Va. 1980) (rejecting a §1983 action under the FWPCA against the Chairman of a State Water Board, with reasoning based on the comprehensiveness of the remedies provided and the federalism concerns raised). We therefore conclude that the existence of these express remedies demonstrates not only that Congress intended to foreclose implied private actions but also that it intended to supplant any remedy that otherwise would be available under §1983. *Cf. Carlson v. Green*, 446 U.S. 14, 23, 64 L.Ed.2d 15, 100 S.Ct. 1468 (1980).

III

The remaining two issues on which we granted certiorari relate to respondents' federal claims based on the federal common law of nuisance. The principal precedent on which these claims were based is *Illinois v. Milwaukee*, 406 U.S. 91, 31 L.Ed.2d 712, 92 S.Ct. 1385 (1972), where the Court found that the federal courts have jurisdiction to consider the federal common-law issues raised by a suit for injunctive relief by the State of Illinois against various Wisconsin municipalities and public sewerage commissions, involving the discharge of sewage into Lake Michigan. In these cases, we need not decide whether a cause of action may be brought under federal common law by a private plaintiff, seeking damages. The Court has now held that the federal common law of nuisance in the area of water pollution is entirely pre-empted by the more comprehensive scope of the FWPCA, which was completely revised soon after the decision in *Illinois v. Milwaukee. See Milwaukee v. Illinois*, 451 U.S. 304, 68 L.Ed.2d 114, 101 S.Ct. 1784 (1981).

This decision disposes entirely of respondents' federal common-law claims, since there is no reason to suppose that the pre-emptive effect of the FWPCA is any less when pollution of coastal waters is at issue. To the extent that this litigation involves ocean waters not covered by the FWPCA, and regulated under the MPRSA, we see no cause for different treatment of the pre-emption question. The regulatory scheme of the MPRSA is no less comprehensive, with respect to ocean dumping, than are analogous provisions of the FWPCA.

We therefore must dismiss the federal common-law claims because their underlying legal basis is now pre-empted by statute. As discussed above, we also dismiss the claims under the MPRSA and the FWPCA because respondents lack a right of action under those statutes. We vacate the judgment below with respect to these two claims, and remand for further proceedings.

It is so ORDERED. [DISSENT, CONCURRENCE, and Footnotes omitted.]

But *see In Re Exxon Valdez*, 270 F.3d 1215 (9th Cir. 2001).

Private citizens can, however, sue the United States, the Environmental Protection Agency, and/or the Corps for an unpermitted discharge of fill material in a wetland, a wrongful permit issuance, and erroneous determinations of wetlands jurisdiction, and can seek equitable relief in the form of an injunction directly against violators. Jurisdiction in the federal courts is authorized by the general federal question statute, 28 U.S.C. §1331, and, under the Clean Water Act only, a special citizens' suit provision, 33 U.S.C. 1365. Venue is proper only in the district in which the "source is located," *i.e.*, usually but not necessarily where the wetland is located. If the citizen suit seeks monetary penalties, the statute of limitations is five years from the date on which knowledge of the violation was first obtained, rather than the date of the violation itself.

HOUGH v. MARSH

557 F Supp. 74 (D.Mass. 1982)

This case involves an attempt by two individuals, defendants Carroll and Jones, to construct for their private use two residences and a tennis court on a three-acre tract of land abutting Edgartown Harbor on Martha's Vineyard. A necessary step in this undertaking is the deposit of 6,500 cubic yards of landfill on approximately one-quarter acre of wetlands—an action requiring approval by the Army Corps of Engineers (the Corps) under section 404 of the Clean Water Act (CWA), 33 U.S.C. §1344. At issue here is the propriety of the Corps' decision granting a permit for such fill. The plaintiffs, ten residents of Edgartown, allege that the Corps' action contravenes the provisions of, and regulations accompanying, three federal statutes—the CWA, the National Environmental Policy Act (NEPA), 42 U.S.C. §4321 *et seq.*, and the National Historic Preservation Act (NHPA), 16 U.S.C. §470 *et seq.*—along with those of certain state and local laws. The defendants, who in addition to the private developers include the Secretary of the Army, the Corps engineer who issued the §404 permit here and the Edgartown building inspector, contend that all statutory directives have been satisfied. Both sides have moved for summary judgment.

BACKGROUND

The following facts are undisputed. The parcel of land in question is in a scenic area known as "Starbuck's Neck," between North Water Street and the harbor shoreline. Directly across the street is the Harbor View Hotel, also owned by defendants Carroll and Jones. The parcel is separated from the harbor and a connecting salt-water pond only by a narrow barrier beach and a gravel roadway curving out to the Edgartown lighthouse some 270 yards away.

In May 1976, the private defendants commenced the arduous task of obtaining all necessary governmental authorizations by applying to the Edgartown Board of Selectmen for building permits. These permits were signed but remained undelivered pending compliance with other local requirements. Second, the defendants applied to the Edgartown Planning Board for endorsement of a plan subdividing the project site into two lots. Construing the application as a proposed "Development of Regional Impact" under Mass. St. 1974, c. 637, the Planning Board referred it to the Martha's Vineyard Commission (MVC), a regional commission created to ensure that "land usages" do not "unduly" impair the "unique natural, historical, ecological, scientific and cultural values of Martha's Vineyard." *Id.* §1. Following a public hearing, the MVC on September 16, 1976, disapproved of the proposed subdivision, stating that the plan would "be detrimental to the public welfare," that it would "cause irreversible environmental damage," and that "no benefits [existed] to offset these detrimental impacts." Although the defendants never appealed this ruling, the residents of Edgartown subsequently voted, in a referendum on April 13, 1978, and pursuant to Mass. St. 1977, c. 836, to withdraw from the MVC. Third, on December 2, 1976, the defendants provided the Edgartown Conservation Commission with notice of its project as required by the Wetlands Protection Act, Mass. G.L. c. 131, §40. Following two preliminary stages of administrative hearings examining the propriety of the proposed fill and construction, an adjudicatory hearing was held before the Massachusetts Department of Environmental Quality Engineering (DEQE). On December 20, 1979, the DEQE Commissioner ruled that the contemplated development would impinge upon none of the environmental concerns embraced by the Wetlands Protection Act and thus could proceed without condition.

As the local regulatory processes were winding down, the federal process commenced. Immediately following the DEQE decision, the private defendants, apparently unaware of the applicability of the Clean Water Act, initiated filling operations. Upon receipt of a cease and desist order from the Corps, they applied under section 404 of the CWA for approval to retain the fill unlawfully discharged and to deposit additional fill on the site. The Corps disseminated public notice of the permit application and, in response to its invitation for public comment, received 259 written objections to the project, including a petition bearing over 200 signatures and letters from the Vineyard Open Land Foundation and the 1,000-member Vineyard Conservation Society, Inc. A single letter was received in support of the project. The views of three interested federal agencies, also solicited by the Corps, were less one-sided. The Environmental Protection Agency urged that the permit be issued, concluding that the development would have insignificant effects on marine fisheries, shell fisheries, waterfowl and wildlife and would cause no "permanent unacceptable disruption to the aquatic ecosystem of the salt pond or Edgartown Harbor." The National Marine Fisheries Service and the Fish and Wildlife Service, by contrast, recommended denial of the permit. The former, while acknowledging the parcel to be "of marginal value to fishery resources," cited the loss of "nutrients and habitat to the surrounding ecosystem." The latter characterized the area as a "valuable" habitat for wildlife, a "storage area for storm and flood water," and a "buffer zone acting to filter and trap runoff and pollutants."

Armed with these sundry submissions, the transcript of the DEQE hearing and its own field reports, the Corps determined that a public hearing on the section 404 permit application was unnecessary for an informed agency decision. That decision was announced on May 6, 1981, in favor of the applicants. In his Findings of Fact and an accompanying Environmental Assessment, the Division Engineer—after canvassing an array of environmental, aesthetic, economic, historic and other considerations—concluded that the applicants' "right to reasonable use of [their] property for reasonable residential purposes" overrode the minimal impact of the development on these values and that it was therefore "in the public interest to issue this permit." The plaintiffs now seek to overturn the Corps' determination for its alleged failure to have considered sufficiently, or at all, several factors highly germane to the section 404 inquiry.

JURISDICTION AND CAUSE OF ACTION

Plaintiffs seek review under the Administrative Procedure Act (APA), 5 U.S.C. §§701-06. Except when a statute specifically precludes judicial review or when agency action is committed to agency discretion by law, *id.* §701(a), the APA authorizes review of all "final agency action for which there is no other adequate remedy in a court," *id.* §704, at the behest of any person "suffering legal wrong because of agency action, or adversely affected or aggrieved by agency action within the meaning of a relevant statute." *Id.* §702. It is now settled that, although the APA provides no independent source of subject-matter jurisdiction, *Califano v. Sanders,* 430 U.S. 99, 104-07, 51 L.Ed.2d 192, 97 S.Ct. 980 (1977), APA review can properly rest on the grant of federal-question jurisdiction in 28 U.S.C. §1331(a). *E.g., id.* at 105; *CETA Workers' Org. Comm. v. New York,* 617 F.2d 926, 935 (2d Cir. 1980). The defendants contend, however, that APA review of Corps decisions under the Clean Water Act is unavailable because an "adequate remedy" already exists. They point to the citizen-suit provision in section 505, 33 U.S.C. §1365, which authorizes private actions against (1) any person alleged to be in violation of an "effluent standard or limitation under this chapter" or of an EPA or state order "with respect to such a standard or limitation," and (2) the EPA Administrator for failure to perform "any act or duty under this chapter which is not discretionary." *Id.* §1365(a). Relying on *Middlesex County Sewerage Auth. v. National Sea Clammers Assoc.,* 453 U.S. 1, 69 L.Ed.2d 435, 101 S.Ct. 2615 (1980), in which the Court rejected the suggestion that the CWA authorized by implication additional private rights of action, the defendants argue that section 505 provided plaintiffs with their only available remedy. As plaintiffs admittedly have failed to comply with the notice requirement prescribed by section 505(b), it is contended that the action must be dismissed.

This argument misconstrues the CWA's enforcement mechanism. Section 505 by its express language is inapplicable to the present suit, even if it otherwise encompasses the section 404 permit process. Plaintiffs are not seeking to enjoin private conduct allegedly violative of the statute, nor to compel an agency official to perform a nondiscretionary duty. Quite to the contrary, they are alleging an abuse of discretion in the issuance of a permit. That such an administratively oriented complaint differs from those contemplated by the citizen-suit provision is suggested by section 509, which states that review of specified actions of the EPA Administrator—including the issuance or denial of a National Pollutant Discharge Elimination System permit under 33 U.S.C. §1342—may be had at the Court of Appeals level. *Id.* §1369(b)(1). This provision makes no reference to section 404 permits. However, contrary to the alternative implication in defendants' argument, it is apparent that nothing in the CWA was intended to foreclose judicial review of the section 404 process at the behest of an interested, private party. First, even if the Corps' decisions in this context could be considered "actions" of the EPA Administrator within the meaning of section 509, the lack of reference there to section 404 permits is of no import: "The mere fact that some acts are made reviewable should not suffice to support an implication of exclusion as to others." *Abbott Laboratories v. Gardner,* 387 U.S. 136, 141, 18 L.Ed.2d 681, 87 S.Ct. 1507 (1967); *e.g., State of Washington v. EPA,* 573 F.2d 583, 587-88 (9th Cir. 1978) (the designation of "a specific mode of judicial review for those actions of the Administrator enumerated in §509(b) (1) of the Act does not alone suffice to preclude an alternative form of judicial review of final administrative action not encompassed [therein]"). More important, the citizen-suit provision contains a saving clause which states in part: "Nothing in this section shall restrict any right which any person ... may have under any statute ... to seek any other relief...." 33 U.S.C. §1365(e). The Court in *Middlesex* held that, notwithstanding this provision, the CWA conferred no private right of action for damages stemming from alleged statutory violations, remarking: "It is doubtful that the phrase 'any statute' includes the very statute in which this statement was contained." 453 U.S. at 15-16 (footnote omitted). The plaintiffs here, however, base their cause of action not on the CWA itself but on the APA. Defendants' reliance on the *Middlesex* case is thus misplaced.

For the foregoing reasons, the court concludes that, pursuant to 28 U.S.C. §1331(a) and the APA, the plaintiffs may seek review of the Corps' decision to grant a section 404 permit. *See, e.g., Hart & Miller Islands Area Envir. Group, Inc. v. Corps of Engineers,* 505 F. Supp. 732, 735 n.1 (D.Md. 1980); *Sierra Club v. Alexander,* 484 F.Supp. 455, 459-64 (N.D.N.Y.), *aff'd mem.,* 633 F.2d 206 (2d Cir. 1980); *Sierra Club v. Bergland,* 451 F. Supp. 120, 123 (N.D.Miss. 1978); *see also Boles v. Onton Dock, Inc.,* 659 F.2d 74 (6th Cir. 1981); *Action for Rational Transit v. West Side Highway Project,* 536 F.Supp. 1225 (S.D.N.Y. 1982). The applicable scope of review calls for a determination of whether the Corps' action was "arbitrary, capricious, an abuse of discretion, or otherwise not in accordance with law" or "without observance of procedure required by law." 5 U.S.C. §706(2) (A), (D).

REQUIREMENT FOR A PUBLIC HEARING

Preliminarily, the plaintiffs contend that the Corps' failure to conduct a public hearing constituted an abuse of discretion under the CWA and accompanying regulations. The statute contains only an oblique reference to this issue, stating that the Secretary of the Army, acting through the Chief of Engineers, may issue permits "after notice and opportunity for public hearings." 33 U.S.C. §1344(a). The Corps' implementing regulations, however, provide greater detail:

> Any person may request, in writing,... that a public hearing be held.... Upon receipt of any such request, stating with particularity the reasons for holding a public hearing, the District Engineer shall promptly set a time and place for the public hearing.... Requests for a public hearing under this paragraph shall be granted, unless the District Engineer determines that the issues raised are insubstantial or there is otherwise no valid interest to be served by a hearing.

33 C.F.R. §327.4(b). Of the 259 letters received by the Corps in opposition to the permit application, eight requested a hearing. Five of these proffered no reasons, and in two others the authors simply expressed a belief that other persons might wish to be heard. The eighth letter, however, written by an attorney on behalf of plaintiff Mary Wakeman, did attempt to justify the request, contending that a hearing was necessary for thorough evaluation of the Corps' section 404 criteria, the project's impact on the public view of the Edgartown lighthouse and the relevance of local land use and planning schemes. In subsequently rejecting these requests, the Corps stated that a hearing would contribute no "new information of value" to the already "substantial administrative record" and would otherwise serve no "valid interest." It added that the record would remain open for additional written comments until final action was taken.

There is no dispute concerning the validity of the Corps regulations; the Supreme Court has recently upheld EPA regulations under section 402 of the CWA that similarly condition the right to a hearing on an applicant's ability "to meet a threshold burden of tendering evidence suggesting the need for a hearing." *Costle v. Pacific Legal Foundation,* 445 U.S. 198, 214, 63 L.Ed.2d 329, 100 S.Ct. 1095 (1980); *accord, Georgia-Pacific Corp. v. EPA,* 671 F.2d 1235, 1241 (9th Cir. 1982). But unlike the petitioning party in *Costle,* whose request "raised legal, rather than factual, issues," 445 U.S. at 219-20, Plaintiff Wakeman arguably has satisfied this threshold burden here. Although her references to the permit criteria and local land use plans might be disregarded as insufficiently concrete, her expressed concern for preserving a view of the lighthouse seemingly raised a specific factual issue. More generally, the Corps' determination that a hearing would serve no "valid interest" is not entirely convincing under the circumstances. That the project was controversial had been evidenced, not only by the considerable public opposition, but by the opinions of two federal agencies recommending rejection of the permit application. And although the state DEQE had earlier conducted a full-scale adjudicatory hearing, the transcript of which had been included in the administrative record, even the Corps recognized that such was of limited applicability. The Chief of the Corps' Enforcement Section reported:

> The DEQE review is limited by Mass. law to only a few issues and is not as broad as our review. A great deal of available evidence was not admitted at the State hearing because it was not relevant to those limited issues. Much of the omitted evidence, however, would be relevant to our permit decision.

It is also worth noting that "the legislative history of the [CWA] indicates a strong congressional desire that the public have input in decisions concerning the elimination of water pollution," *Costle v. Pacific Legal Foundation*, 445 U.S. at 215, and that "an opportunity to submit documents [does not] constitute ... a public hearing." *Seacoast Anti-Pollution League v. Costle,* 572 F.2d 872, 879 (1st Cir.) (footnote omitted), *cert. denied,* 439 U.S. 824, 58 L.Ed.2d 117, 99 S.Ct. 94 (1978).

To be sure, these several factors, particularly when balanced against the agency's considerable discretion in this area and the need for streamlined administration of permit programs, do not free the issue of all doubt. Yet this court need not decide whether the Corps' refusal to conduct a hearing would by itself necessitate reversal. Since, as explained below, a remand is otherwise necessary, it suffices to conclude that a public hearing should be conducted in conjunction with these further proceedings.

THE CLEAN WATER ACT CRITERIA

The Clean Water Act, for all its myriad provisions, offers little guidance in the present inquiry; all of the governing criteria appear in agency regulations. The statute's general mandate is contained in section 301: "Except as in compliance with this section and sections 1312, 1316, 1317, 1328, 1342, and 1344 of this title, the discharge of any pollutant by any person shall be unlawful." 33 U.S.C. §1311(a). Section 404 states in part: "The Secretary [of the Army] may issue permits, after notice and opportunity for public hearings[,] for the discharge of dredged or fill material into the navigable waters at specified disposal sites." *Id.* §1344(a). It also provides that the consideration of permit applications shall occur "through the application of guidelines developed by the Administrator [of EPA], in conjunction with the Secretary [of the Army]," *id.* §404(b), "acting through the Chief of Engineers." *Id.* §404(d).

The section 404 permit process is governed simultaneously by Corps regulations, 33 C.F.R. Parts 320-329, and by EPA guidelines, 40 C.F.R. Part 230. Both sets of rules must be observed. *See* 33 C.F.R. §323.5(a); 40 C.F.R. §230.2(a). The Corps regulations prescribe 12 "general policies" for evaluating permit applications, five of which are here relevant. Four of these pertain to all permit applications. First, the Corps must conduct a "public interest review," balancing the "benefit which reasonably may be expected to accrue from the proposal" against "its reasonably foreseeable detriments." 33 C.F.R. §320.4(a). This provision recites a non-exhaustive list of some 16 factors—quoted by the Division Engineer, *see* note 3 *supra*—that are germane to this inquiry, and then declares: "No permit will be granted unless its issuance is found to be in the public interest." 33 C.F.R. §320.4(a). Second, the Corps is instructed to consult with the Fish and Wildlife Service and the National Marine Fisheries Service and to accord "great weight" to their views on "fish and wildlife considerations." *Id.* §320.4(c). A third provision mandates that "due consideration" be given to the proposal's effect on the "enhancement, preservation, or development" of "historic, cultural, scenic, conservation, recreational or similar values." *Id.* §320.4(e) (1). "Particular attention," moreover, "should be directed toward any ... building, structure, or object listed or eligible for listing in the National Register of Historic Places." *Id.* §320.4(e)(2)(ii). Fourth, the Division Engineer must inquire into other federal, state, or local requirements: "Permits will not be issued where certification or authorization of the proposed work is required by Federal, State and/or local law and that certification or authorization has been denied." *Id.* § 320.4(j) (6).

The final Corps "policy" pertains specifically to wetlands. It declares that wetlands "are vital areas that constitute a productive and valuable public resource, the unnecessary alteration or destruction of which should be discouraged as contrary to the public interest." *Id.* §320.4(b)(1). This provision then identifies seven types of functions performed by wetlands that are "important to the public interest," *id.* §320.4(b) (2), and states that "no permit will be granted to work in wetlands identified as important" under any of these criteria unless the Corps makes the following two findings: (1) that, under the public interest review analysis, "the benefits of the proposed alteration outweigh the damage to the wetlands resource," and (2) that "the proposed alteration is necessary to realize those benefits." *Id.* §320.4(b)(4). In making this latter determination, the District Engineer "shall consider whether the proposed activity is primarily dependent on being located in, or in close proximity to, the aquatic environment and whether feasible alternative sites are available." *Id.* The applicant has the burden of providing information as to the project's water-dependency and also data "on the basis of which the availability of feasible alternative sites can be evaluated." *Id.*

The pertinent EPA guidelines can be described more briefly. At the outset, they announce a general presumption against discharge:

> Fundamental to these Guidelines is the precept that dredged or fill material should not be discharged into the aquatic ecosystem, unless it can be demonstrated that such a discharge will not have an unacceptable adverse impact either individually or in combination with known and/or probable impacts of other activities affecting the ecosystems of concern.

40 C.F.R. §230.1(c). The guidelines parallel the Corps regulations in deeming wetlands worthy of special protection. Wetlands are included in the category of "special aquatic sites," defined as "geographic areas, large or small, possessing special ecological characteristics of productivity, habitat, wildlife protection, or other important and easily disrupted ecological values." *Id.* §230.3(q-1). With respect to such sites, the guidelines state:

> From a national perspective, the degradation or destruction of special aquatic sites, such as filling operations in wetlands, is considered to be among the most severe environmental impacts covered by these Guidelines. The guiding principle should be that degradation or destruction of special sites may represent an irreversible loss of valuable aquatic resources.

Id. §230.1(d). Such heightened solicitude for wetlands is specifically manifested in the treatment of alternatives. For all proposed projects, the guidelines prohibit issuance of a permit if there is a "practicable alternative"—defined as one that "is available and capable of being done after taking into consideration cost, existing technology, and logistics in light of overall project purposes"—that would have "less adverse impact on the aquatic ecosystem." *Id.* §230.10(a). With respect to wetlands and other "special" sites, however, "where the activity associated with a discharge which is proposed ... does not require access or proximity to or siting within the special aquatic site (*i.e.*, is not 'water dependent'), practicable alternatives that do not involve special aquatic sites are presumed to be available, unless clearly demonstrated otherwise." *Id.* §230.10(a)(3). Thus, the guidelines couple a general presumption against all discharges into aquatic ecosystems with a specific presumption that practicable alternatives to the fill of wetlands exist.

The District Engineer found that the private defendants had successfully shouldered the formidable evidentiary burden imposed by this regulatory scheme. He determined first that the wetland in question performed functions that satisfied—barely—one of the seven indicia of "importance" in 33 C.F.R. §320.4(b)(2), thereby triggering the two-pronged requirement of "net benefit" and "necessity" delineated in section 320.4(b)(4). Regarding the former component, he concluded that the likely benefits—particularly an expanded tax base, additional jobs and the owners' "right to reasonable use" of their property—outweighed the "insignificant loss of wetland." And with respect to the latter, he determined that the project, although not "water-dependent," was nonetheless necessary because of the absence of feasible alternatives. This last finding hinged on a certified statement of an Edgartown real estate broker, dated February 22, 1980 and submitted by the defendants, that "the only lot available in the prime residential and central area of Edgartown" was a parcel "measuring 120 X 215 feet and having a selling price of $90,000.00." The Engineer agreed this site was impractical because it would not "fulfill the basic purpose" of providing two homes and a tennis court and because acquiring it would subject the defendants to "extraordinary expense." Turning to the "public interest review," he determined that the project's impact, both singly and cumulatively, on wildlife, aesthetic, economic and the other specified concerns was insufficient to override the anticipated benefits. Finally, the Engineer concluded that the development would not unduly impinge on historic and scenic values and that all requisite state and local authorizations had been met.

This court's function in reviewing the Corps' decision is not to "substitute its judgment for that of the agency" but rather to ascertain "whether the decision was based on a consideration of the relevant factors and whether there has been a clear error of judgment." *Citizens to Preserve Overton Park, Inc. v. Volpe*, 401 U.S. 402, 416, 28 L.Ed.2d 136, 91 S.Ct. 814 (1971); *accord, e.g., Strycke's Bay Neighborhood Council, Inc. v. Karlen*, 444 U.S. 223, 227-28, 62 L.Ed.2d 433, 100 S.Ct. 497 (1980) (per curiam); *Roosevelt Campobello Int'l Park Comm'n v. EPA,* 684 F.2d 1041, slip op. at 5-6 (1st Cir. 1982); *Grazing Fields Farm v. Goldschmidt,* 626 F.2d 1068, 1071-72 (1st Cir. 1980). The plaintiffs initially assert that the Corps "could not find" that the public benefit stemming from the construction of two private dwellings outweighed the loss of wetlands and open space and that it was "required to deny the permit without further review." This contention invites precisely the sort of substituted judgment that this court is precluded from exercising. They next maintain that, under the Corps rules, "water dependency" is a prerequisite to the issuance of any permit, the conceded absence of which here compels disapproval of the project. This interpretation misconstrues the applicable regulation. The provision states only that, in evaluating the necessity of any project impinging upon "important" wetlands, the Engineer "shall consider" the water-dependency and feasible-alternative factors. 33 C.F.R. §320.4(b) (4). Had mandatory compliance with both criteria been contemplated by the drafters, that intent easily could have been evinced.

At the same time, the fact that the project is not water-dependent should necessitate a more persuasive showing than otherwise concerning the lack of alternatives. Indeed, the EPA guidelines specifically require in such a case that an applicant "clearly demonstrate" that practicable alternatives to the proposed fill of wetlands do not exist. 40 C.F.R. §230.10(a) (3). It is in this regard that the Engineer's determination appears troublesome. The private defendants' entire effort to satisfy this burden consisted, as noted above, of the production of a certified letter from a single realtor written more than fourteen months prior to the Engineer's decision. There was no showing that this letter, citing the availability of only one parcel "in the prime residential and central area of Edgartown," remained an accurate depiction of the local real estate market during these 14 months. And even if there had been, problems would still persist. No inquiry was conducted into the availability of suitable lots outside this "prime residential" area, and no explanation was offered for limiting the search in such manner. Moreover, although the one reported parcel was too small to support two houses, the private defendants never explained the need to construct their respective dwellings side-by-side. The "exorbitant cost" of that parcel, furthermore, by itself carries little weight; although cost is relevant to an assessment of an alternative's "practicability," the Corps conducted no examination of whether the price was unreasonably high, whether the defendants could afford it, and whether the wetlands parcel could be sold for a comparable or greater amount. Given these unexplored avenues, the court cannot agree that defendants have "clearly demonstrated" that no feasible alternatives to the proposed fill exist.

Plaintiffs advance a separate challenge to the Corps' treatment of the provision in 33 C.F.R. §320.4(j) addressing "other federal, state, or local requirements." As noted above, this subsection prohibits the issuance of any permit "where certification or authorization of the proposed work is required by Federal, State and/or local law and that certification or authorization has been denied." *Id.* §320.4(j)(6). The Corps determined that, notwithstanding this provision, the disapproval of the proposed subdivision by the Martha's Vineyard Commission (MVC) did not require denial of the permit since Edgartown subsequently withdrew from the MVC. Plaintiffs now argue to the contrary and point to *McCarthy v. Planning Board of Edgartown*, 381 Mass. 86, 407 N.E.2d 348 (1980) in which the Supreme Judicial Court ruled that an MVC regulation remained in force in Edgartown following its withdrawal. Under the governing statute, the regulation there was to be incorporated into the ordinances and by-laws of each participating municipality and thereafter administered as if it were a part thereof. The Court thus reasoned that the regulation remained in effect following a town's withdrawal, until repealed "by action in the usual manner to amend its zoning by-laws," *id.* at 89—when action Edgartown had not taken. An examination of the governing statute, Mass. St. 1974, c. 637, however, reveals that the *McCarthy* case, despite its factual similarity, is inapposite. Chapter 637 in brief entrusted the MVC with supervision over two distinct concerns: specified geographic areas entitled "districts of critical planning concern," *id.* §§9-12, and proposed development projects called "developments of regional impact." *Id.* §§13-17. With respect to the former, the MVC was empowered to issue guidelines governing the development of such districts and to ensure that all regulations promulgated by each member town accorded with these guidelines. For any town that failed to adopt such complementary regulations, moreover, the MVC itself could issue regulations "applicable to such municipality's portion of the district" that were to be "incorporated" into its by-laws. *Id.* §11. An MVC regulation adopted under this provision was at issue in *McCarthy.* The MVC's responsibilities concerning "developments of regional impact" were different; rather than approve or issue regulations, it was empowered to review all applications for requisite permits, licenses, or authorizations submitted to local planning boards and to grant or withhold approval based on specified criteria. *Id.* §15. The MVC's review of the subdivision application in the present case was pursuant to this latter section. It is therefore apparent that MVC approval of the proposed subdivision was not mandated by any regulation that had been "incorporated" into Edgartown's by-laws, and thus under *McCarthy* remained in effect following the town's withdrawal until repealed, but rather was required by a statutory provision that, upon withdrawal, ceased to apply. Consequently, the MVC's disapproval of the application does not bar issuance of a permit under 33 C.F.R. §320.4(j)(6).

A problem remains, however. Section 13.2 of Edgartown's zoning by-laws prohibits the filling of any "tidal marsh"—defined in part as any "marsh area in which action of the oceanic tide causes a change in the water level from time to time"—without a "special permit" form the planning board, which the private defendants have not obtained. Section 13.4 of the by-laws, moreover, imposes a flat ban on filling for the purpose of constructing private residences within any "beach area," defined as that area "extending from the mean low water line to the inland edge of land covered by sand dunes or by beach grass." In addition, the MVC has incorporated these restrictions in a "district of critical planning concern" regulation placing the project site within the "shore zone" of the "coastal district"—a regulation which under *McCarthy* remains in effect until repealed. Since no "certification or authorization has been denied" with respect to these laws, 33 C.F.R. §320.4(j) (6) is seemingly unimplicated. However, section 320.4(j)(2) states:

> Where officially adopted State, regional, or local land-use classifications, determinations, or policies are applicable to the land or water areas under consideration, they shall be presumed to reflect local factors of the public interest and shall be considered in addition with the other national factors of the public interest identified in §320.4(a).

The Corps' failure to consider these potentially applicable local requirements necessitates remand on this issue also.

To complete the discussion of the Clean Water Act, the court notes two additional factors that the Corps failed to address properly in connection with the public interest review mandated by 33 C.F.R. §320.4(a). These issues, although not raised by plaintiffs specifically, merit attention since a remand is otherwise necessary. The "public interest" provision includes among the factors that "must be considered" those dealing with "economics" and "cumulative effects." With respect to the former, the Corps did mention the positive anticipated impact of the proposal on jobs and municipal taxes. But it sidestepped any consideration of adverse economic effects—particularly, in its words, the "elimination of an attraction [the Edgartown lighthouse] on the itinerary of sightseeing buses"—with the comment: "This is a local issue and the proposed use of the land is consistent with local land use regulations." This conclusion, aside from arguably misconstruing the local laws, ignores the directive in the Corps regulations to consider all economic factors. Second, the Corps' finding of no adverse cumulative effects rested upon the observation that "future applications for similar work will be evaluated in light of the public interest on their own merit." This constitutes only half of the requisite inquiry in this regard; the Corps regulations specifically require consideration of the "probable impact of each proposal in relation to the cumulative effect created by other *existing* and anticipated structures or work in the general area." *Id.* §320.4(a)(2)(iv) (emphasis added). Consequently, remand appears appropriate to enable the Corps to address these issues.

THE NATIONAL HISTORIC PRESERVATION ACT

Plaintiffs' final challenge centers upon the Corps' alleged disregard of the historic values associated with the Edgartown lighthouse, which as noted above lies at the end of a gravel walkway adjacent to the project site. Aside from the reference in his economic-factors evaluation just mentioned, the District Engineer considered the lighthouse only in his assessment of the proposal's impact on scenic and aesthetic values, stating that "the private homes will interrupt the view of the harbor and the lighthouse from many points on North Water Street but the view will not be completely shut off and other viewing sites are available." In evaluating the effect on historic values, as mandated both by 33 C.F.R. §320.4(a) in connection with the public interest review and independently by section 320.4(e), the Engineer limited his inquiry to the buildings along North Water Street. Plaintiffs allege that the failure to include the lighthouse in this assessment violated the Corps regulations and, more importantly, the provisions of the National Historic Preservation Act (NHPA). This statute provides in relevant part:

> The head of any Federal department or independent agency having authority to license any undertaking shall, prior to ... the issuance of any license,... take into account the effect of the undertaking on any ... building, structure, or object that is included in or eligible for inclusion in the National Register [of Historic Places]. The head of any such Federal agency shall afford the Advisory Council on Historic Preservation ... a reasonable opportunity to comment with regard to such undertaking.

16 U.S.C. §470f. The Advisory Council on Historic Preservation has promulgated regulations implementing this directive. 36 C.F.R. Part 800. In capsule form, they require an agency, in conjunction with the appropriate state office, to determine whether the undertaking will have an adverse effect on any property listed in or eligible for inclusion in the National Register of Historic Places lying within the "area of the undertaking's potential environmental impact" and then to forward that determination to the Advisory Council for comment.

Were these procedures applicable in the present case, the Corps unquestionably deviated from them. Its sole communication with the Massachusetts Historical Commission consisted of a telephone call in October 1980 to ascertain whether the lighthouse had been nominated for listing in the Register. And its only contact with the Advisory Council, again a telephone call to determine whether the lighthouse had been nominated, occurred on August 14, 1981—over three months after its decision. The defendants respond that NHPA was inapplicable since the lighthouse was at no time "eligible" for listing in the Register, and that in any event the Corps' consideration of the proposal's impact on the view of the lighthouse adequately addressed all NHPA concerns.

The latter contention is plainly without merit. It is true that the Advisory Council's directives impose only a procedural obligation with no direct bearing on the Corps' substantive decision. As the Department of the Interior, which decides which properties gain a listing in the Register, has indicated in its regulations:

> Having complied with this procedural requirement the Federal agency may adopt any course of action it may feel appropriate. While the Advisory Council comments must be taken into account and integrated into the decision-making process, the program decision rests with the agency implementing the undertaking.

36 C.F.R. §60.2(c). Nonetheless, to suggest that the Corps necessarily would have reached the same decision had it determined or learned that the lighthouse was eligible for Register listing is entirely speculative. Its brief consideration of the view of the lighthouse cannot fill this void, particularly since the Corps failed to mention the lighthouse at all in its discussion of historic values. Thus, any noncompliance with NHPA's requirements cannot be dismissed as unimportant.

In contending that the lighthouse was not "eligible" for listing within the meaning of the statute and thus did not trigger the Advisory Council's regulations, the defendants point to the absence of any official determination of eligibility by the Interior Department, the Advisory council or the Massachusetts Historical Commission. The Advisory Council regulations, however, belie any suggestion that the Corps can passively rely on other agencies to satisfy its responsibilities under NHPA. "Eligible property" is defined as "any district, site, building, structure, or object that *meets the National Register Criteria*," 36 C.F.R. §800.2(f) (emphasis added)—not any structure that has been determined to meet such criteria. More specifically, the regulations speak of an agency's "affirmative responsibilities to locate and identify eligible properties that are within the area of the undertaking's potential environmental impact and that may be affected by the undertaking." *Id.* §800.4(a)(2). And although the Interior regulations provide for the issuance of "Determinations of Eligibility" by the Secretary, 36 C.F.R. Part 63, this procedure is invoked only upon request by a federal agency, *id.* §63.2, and indeed must be invoked whenever the federal or consulting state agency determines that the criteria have been met or that a question exists with respect thereto. 36 C.F.R. §800.4(a) (3*); see Stop H-3 Assoc. v. Coleman,* 533 F.2d 434, 441 n.13 (9th Cir.), *cert. denied,* 429 U.S. 999, 97 S.Ct. 526, 50 L.Ed.2d 610 (1976). It is thus apparent that the absence of any official determination of eligibility here did not render the statute inapplicable.

Since it cannot be said on the present record that the lighthouse is clearly ineligible for inclusion in the Register, the court will remand to enable the Corps also to address this issue in accordance with the applicable regulations. The court of course wishes to be understood as expressing no view on the outcome of this specific issue or on the Corps' ultimate decision whether to grant or deny a section 404 permit to the private defendants.

Plaintiffs' motion for summary judgment is ALLOWED. Defendants' motion for summary judgment is DENIED. Case is remanded for further proceedings in accordance with this opinion.

SO ORDERED.

See also *Conservation Law Foundation v. Busey*, 79 F.3d 1250 (1st Cir. 1996); *Conservation Law Foundation v. Federal Highway Admin.*, 827 F.Supp. 871 (D.R.I. 1993); *American Littoral Soc. v. Herndon*, 720 F.Supp. 942 (S.D.Fla. 1988).

UNITED STATES v. HOBBS

736 F. Supp. 1406 (E.D.Va. 1990), *cert. denied* 504 U.S. 940, 112 S.Ct. 2274, 119 L.Ed.2d 200 (1992)

This action was brought by the United States seeking injunctive relief and the imposition of civil penalties against the defendants for placing fill materials into waters of the United States without first seeking a permit from the United States Army Corps of Engineers (hereinafter referred to as "Corps"). The court conducted a twelve (12) day jury trial in January, 1990, to determine liability of each defendant. On January 26, 1990, the jury determined that the property owned by Phillip Ray Hobbs and his wife, Dorothy V. Hobbs, and the property owned by S. Paul Hobbs and his wife, Donna M. Hobbs, all located on Ware Neck in Gloucester, Virginia, are wetlands adjacent to waters of the United States. The jury found that defendants Phillip Ray Hobbs and Dorothy V. Hobbs discharged pollutants onto their wetlands property in 1980, 1984, and 1985. The jury further found that defendants S. Paul Hobbs and Donna M. Hobbs discharged pollutants onto their wetlands property in 1986, 1987, and 1988. On January 24, 1990, the court conducted an extensive hearing on numerous motions presented by both parties in this case. At that time, the court determined that this action against the defendants was not time-barred and submitted the case to the jury. Both parties articulated their positions at the hearing and have since filed briefs with respect to the statute of limitations issues. This opinion sets forth the court's reasoning on these issues in further detail.

APPLICABLE STATUTE OF LIMITATIONS

No specific statute of limitations exists for actions commenced pursuant to the CWA. Ordinarily, when a federal statute does not contain a limitations period, federal courts apply the "most appropriate" statute of limitations under state law, if there is no "relevant" federal statute of limitations. *Johnson v. Railway Express Agency, Inc.*, 421 U.S. 454, 462, 44 L.Ed.2d 295, 95 S.Ct. 1716 (1975). This general rule is qualified by an exception, namely that an otherwise applicable state limitations period should not be applied where its application would undermine federal policy. *Occidental Life Ins. Co. v. EEOC*, 432 U.S. 355, 367, 53 L.Ed.2d 402, 97 S.Ct. 2447 (1977). The Supreme Court in *Occidental* stated:

> When Congress has created a cause of action and has not specified the period of time within which it may be asserted, the Court has frequently inferred that Congress intended that a local time limitation should apply....
>
> But the Court has not mechanically applied a state statute of limitations simply because a limitations period is absent from the federal statute. State legislatures do not devise their limitations periods with national interests in mind, and it is the duty of the federal courts to assure that the importation of state law will not frustrate or interfere with the implementation of national policies.

Id.

The court must first consider whether a relevant federal statute of limitation exists. *See, e.g., Sierra Club v. Chevron U.S.A., Inc.*, 834 F.2d 1517, 1521 (9th Cir. 1987). Both parties have identified 28 U.S.C. §2462 as a relevant federal statute of limitations. That section provides:

> Except as otherwise provided by Act of Congress, an action, suit or proceeding for the enforcement of any civil fine, penalty, or forfeiture, pecuniary or otherwise, shall not be entertained unless commenced within five years from the date when the claim first accrued....

And, in the context of a citizen enforcement suit, the Court of Appeals for the Ninth Circuit in *Chevron* stated that "section [2462] clearly applies to enforcement actions brought by the EPA; such actions are by the government and 'for the enforcement of [a] civil fine.'" Chevron, 834 F.2d at 1521 (citing 28 U.S.C. §2462).

Defendants agree that 28 U.S.C. §2462 is applicable to the instant case. They argue, however, that it applies *only if* the court determines that Virginia's one-year statute of limitations is inapplicable. *See* Defendants' Trial Memorandum on Statute of Limitations at 1-3 (Feb. 9, 1990) (hereinafter referred to as "Defendants' Brief"). Defendants state: "If this Court determines that no Virginia statute of limitations applies to Clean Water Act enforcement actions, the federal statute of limitations at 28 U.S.C. §2462 clearly applies." *Id.* at 1 (emphasis added). Defendants' argument is inconsistent with the requirement in *Johnson* to use a relevant federal statute of limitations, if available. *See supra*, 421 U.S. at 462. Implicit in defendants' recognition that Section 2462 is an applicable federal limitations period is an acknowledgment that the instant case falls within the contours of *Johnson*. The requirement as stated in *Johnson* is to use a state statute of limitations only if no federal one applies; it is not to use an applicable federal statute of limitations only if no state limitations statute applies. *See* 421 U.S. at 462. Moreover, even if Virginia's one-year statute of limitations was applicable here, its application would interfere with the implementation of national policy underlying the CWA.

Congress designed the CWA to recapture and preserve the "integrity of the Nation's waters." 33 U.S.C. §1251(a); *see P.F.Z. Properties, Inc. v. Train,* 393 F.Supp. 1370 (D.D.C. 1975); *United States v. Holland,* 373 F.Supp. 665 (M.D.Fla. 1974). Indeed, a primary objective of the CWA is the "national goal" of eliminating the discharge of pollutants into navigable waters. 33 U.S.C. §1251(a)(1). Application of diverse state limitations periods would produce not only non-uniform enforcement from state to state, but it would also diminish the effective enforcement of the CWA. *Chesapeake Bay Found. v. Bethlehem Steel Corp.*, 608 F.Supp. 440, 447 (D. Md. 1985). Each state potentially could manipulate its statute of limitations depending on its concerns with respect to the environment. *Id.* States hostile to polluters could adopt a lengthier statute of limitations while others, more accommodating to violators of the CWA, could provide for a brief limitations period. *Id.* Clearly, "in the context of the Clean Water Act, it could not have been the intent of Congress to have federal courts borrow state statutes of limitations and certainly not statutes as short as one year." *Id.* Therefore, because a relevant federal statute of limitations exists and because applying Virginia's one-year statute of limitations would frustrate national policy, this court finds that 28 U.S.C. §2462 is the most appropriate limitations period to be applied to this action for civil penalties.

ACCRUAL

Title 28 U.S.C. §2462 requires commencement of suit for civil penalties within five years from the date when the claim *first accrued*. Defendants maintain that the claims against them first accrued when they actually physically ditched and drained their property. Defendants' Brief at 4. However, it has been held that accrual, for statute of limitations purposes under the CWA, occurs *not* "when the violations actually occurred, but when the reports that document[] those violations [are] filed with the EPA." *Atlantic States Legal Found. v. Al Tech Specialty Steel Corp.,* 635 F. Supp. 284, 287 (N.D.N.Y. 1986); *see National Wildlife Fed'n v. Army Dep't,* 1989 U.S. Dist. Decision, 29 Env't.Rep.Cas. 1941, 1944 (E.D.N.C. 1989). In *Atlantic States*, the court indicated that:

> It would have been practically impossible for the plaintiff to have discovered the alleged violations of the defendant on its own. It is only when reports are filed with the EPA that the public becomes aware that violations have occurred. To hold that the statute begins to run when violations actually occur, as opposed to when they are discovered, would impede, if not foreclose, the remedial benefits of the statute.

Id. at 287-88.

The evidence established at trial indicates that on December 12, 1988, Mr. Gary Frazer, a biologist with the United States Fish and Wildlife Service, submitted his report on the defendants' property to EPA Region III. In his report, Mr. Frazer analyzed field data collected from the defendants' property and recommended that the Corps issue a cease and desist order. While the evidence presented at the jury trial indicates that the EPA may have been alerted to possible violations involving the defendants shortly before receiving Mr. Frazer's report, the report nevertheless is the first piece of information to formally detail and document the results of any field studies conducted on defendants' property. Therefore, consistent with the holding in *Atlantic States,* this court finds that the plaintiff's cause of action accrued on December 12, 1988, when EPA Region III received the Frazer report. The plaintiff filed a counterclaim which is the basis for the instant action on June 23, 1989, well within the five year period contemplated by 28 U.S.C. §2462. Accordingly, the plaintiff's action for civil penalties is not time-barred.

INJUNCTIVE RELIEF

The limitations period set forth in 28 U.S.C. §2462 applies only to suits for civil penalties. This section, by its own terms, has no bearing on suits in equity. Plaintiff in this case seeks both civil penalties pursuant to 33 U.S.C. §1319(d) and injunctive relief pursuant to 33 U.S.C. §1319(b). While this court finds that 28 U.S.C. §2462 applies to enforcement actions under the CWA, *see supra* at 2-6, that holding does not govern this court's actions with respect to the equitable relief sought by plaintiff. *See Holmberg v. Armbrecht,* 327 U.S. 392, 396, 90 L.Ed. 743, 66 S.Ct. 582 (1946) ("Traditionally ... statutes of limitation are not controlling measures of equitable relief"); *North Carolina Wildlife Fed'n v. Army Dep't,* 1989 U.S. Dist. Decision, 29 Env't Rep. Cas. 1941, 1944 (E.D.N.C. 1989) (plaintiffs' citizen enforcement suit is governed by the doctrine of laches since 28 U.S.C. §2462 does not apply to a suit seeking only equitable relief). Instead, the doctrine of laches governs the availability of equitable relief. Statutes of limitations serve the purpose of protecting litigants against claims made stale by the passage of time. Laches, on the other hand, has as its chief concern not the issue of time but the inequity of allowing a claim to be enforced. *Holmberg,* 327 U.S. 392 at 396, 90 L.Ed. 743, 66 S.Ct. 582 (quoting *Galliher v. Cadwell,* 145 U.S. 368, 373, 36 L.Ed. 738, 12 S.Ct. 873 (1892)). Laches will justify dismissal of a suit in equity if a plaintiff has not diligently pursued the case and "where the plaintiff[s] 'lack of diligence is wholly unexcused; and both the nature of the claim and the situation of the parties was such as to call for diligence.'" *Id.* (quoting *Benedict v. City of New York,* 250 U.S. 321, 328, 63 L.Ed. 1005, 39 S.Ct. 476 (1919)). Nothing in the record of this case shows any lack of diligence by the plaintiff in commencing this action. Therefore, plaintiff's claim for injunctive relief is not barred by the doctrine of laches.

The Clerk shall forward a copy of the Memorandum Opinion to all counsel of record. [Footnotes omitted.]

See also *U.S. v. Banks*, 115 F.3d 916 (11th Cir. 1997); *Sasser v. EPA*, 990 F.2d 127 (4th Cir. 1993); *United States v. Windward Properties, Inc.*, 821 F.Supp. 690 (N.D.Ga.1993); *Public Interest Research Group of New Jersey v. Powell Duffryn Terminals, Inc.*, 913 F.2d 64 (3d Cir. N.J. 1990), *cert. denied*, 498 U.S. 1109, 112 L.Ed.2d 1100, 111 S.Ct. 1018 (1991); *Atlantic States Legal Foundation, Inc. v. Al Tech Specialty Steel Corp.*, 635 F.Supp. 284 (N.D.N.Y. 1986).

CHESAPEAKE BAY FOUNDATION, INC. v. GWALTNEY OF SMITHFIELD, LTD.

890 F.2d 690 (4th Cir. 1989)

This case, a frequent visitor in this court, continues to present serious issues concerning the interpretation of §505 of the Clean Water Act (the Act). Gwaltney of Smithfield, Ltd. (Gwaltney), appeals the finding of the district court that plaintiffs-appellees Chesapeake Bay Foundation, Inc. (CBF), and Natural Resources Defense Council, Inc. (NRDC), proved ongoing violations by Gwaltney at the time suit was brought. Gwaltney also raises standing and mootness objections to this action. We affirm in part and reverse in part.

FACTS AND PROCEDURAL HISTORY

The original action was brought by CBF under the citizen suit provisions of 33 U.S.C. §1365 (§505 of the Act). CBF based its claims on violations by Gwaltney of its National Pollutant Discharge Elimination System (NPDES) permit, and requested both injunctive relief and civil penalties under 33 U.S.C. §§1365(a) and 1319(d) (§§505(a) and 309(d) of the Act). The district court found that CBF had standing to bring the suit, that the court had subject matter jurisdiction, and that Gwaltney was liable for its violations. *Chesapeake Bay Foundation v. Gwaltney of Smithfield, Ltd.,* 611 F.Supp. 1542 (E.D.Va. 1985). Using the Environmental Protection Agency Civil Penalty Policy as a guideline, the court imposed upon Gwaltney a civil penalty of $1,285,322, with interest, of which $289,822 was for violations of Gwaltney's total Kjeldahl nitrogen (TKN) limit, and $995,500 was for violations of the chlorine limit. *Id.* at 1565.

Gwaltney appealed to this court, challenging the district court's subject matter jurisdiction and its method of calculating penalties. The facts affecting the first issue were largely undisputed, but the parties disagreed on the application of the statute to the facts. Gwaltney reported more than 150 violations of its NPDES permit between 1981 and 1984, the last violation occurring on May 15, 1984. The two environmental groups had sent notice of intent to sue in February 1984, and filed suit on June 15, 1984, one month after Gwaltney's last recorded violation. The Act permits citizen suits against any person "who is alleged to be in violation" of NPDES permit limitations, 33 U.S.C. §1365(a); Gwaltney contended this meant there must be continuing violations at the time of suit in order for the court to have jurisdiction. We found that the statute, although ambiguous, also conferred jurisdiction for citizen suits based on wholly past violations, and so affirmed the district court without reaching the question of whether CBF had made a good-faith allegation of ongoing violations. *Chesapeake Bay Foundation, Inc. v. Gwaltney of Smithfield, Ltd.,* 791 F.2d 304, 308 n. 9, 316-17 (4th Cir. 1986). We also affirmed the district court with regard to its methodology for assessing penalties.

The United States Supreme Court granted certiorari on the issue of jurisdiction in order to resolve a split among the circuits and subsequently held that §1365(a) does not permit citizen suits for wholly past violations. It remanded the case to us to consider whether CBF's complaint had made a good-faith allegation of ongoing violations, holding that such allegation would be sufficient to establish subject matter jurisdiction. *Gwaltney of Smithfield v. Chesapeake Bay Foundation,* 484 U.S. 49, 108 S.Ct. 376, 384-85, 98 L.Ed.2d 306 (1987). The district court, in its initial consideration, had suggested as an alternative holding that CBF had made sufficient good faith allegations of continuing violations to establish jurisdiction. 611 F.2d at 1549 n. 8. On remand from the Supreme Court, we held that this finding was not clearly erroneous, and remanded the case to the district court "for further findings as to whether, on the merits, plaintiffs proved at trial an ongoing violation." *Chesapeake Bay Foundation, Inc. v. Gwaltney of Smithfield Ltd.,* 844 F.2d 170, 171 (4th Cir. 1988).

After remand to the district court, Gwaltney again challenged the subject matter jurisdiction of the court, moving to dismiss the case as moot and, alternatively, to dismiss because the plaintiffs did not have standing. Gwaltney also asserted that even if the court did have jurisdiction to hear the case, it did not have jurisdiction as to Gwaltney's chlorine violations, because no reasonable person could in good faith allege that the chlorine violations were ongoing at the time of trial. Finally, Gwaltney asserted that CBF had failed to meet its burden of proving that there were ongoing violations, even of TKN, at the time of trial.

The district court interpreted our mandate to foreclose any consideration of mootness, standing, or severability of the chlorine and TKN violations, instructing it only to determine whether CBF had proved ongoing violations. Finding that CBF had done so, the court reinstated its original judgment of $1,285,322 in civil penalties. *Chesapeake Bay Foundation, Inc. v. Gwaltney of Smithfield, Ltd.*, 688 F. Supp. 1078, 1080 (E.D.Va. 1988).

Gwaltney now appeals to this court, claiming there was insufficient evidence to support the district court's finding of ongoing violations. Gwaltney claims that even if there was sufficient evidence the district court erred in reinstating penalties for chlorine as well as TKN violations. Gwaltney also appeals on the standing and mootness issues. Normally, because they are jurisdictional, we would consider the standing and mootness questions first. In this case, however, the jurisdictional issues are intertwined with the finding of ongoing violations; therefore, we address the substantive dispute first.

II. WHETHER THERE WAS AN ONGOING VIOLATION

Gwaltney asserts that the district court erred in finding that there was an ongoing violation at the time suit was brought. As we now know, essentially the last violation occurred on May 15, 1984. Gwaltney claims that at the remand hearing the district court should have considered the evidence of its compliance since that time. Gwaltney also asserts that there was not sufficient evidence adduced at the time of trial to permit a finding of ongoing violation.

In its opinion in this case, the Supreme Court stated that, at trial, the citizen-plaintiff must prove its allegations of ongoing violation in order to prevail. *Id.* at 386. The Court defined a §1365 ongoing violation to be "a reasonable likelihood that a past polluter will continue to pollute in the future." 484 U.S. 49, 108 S.Ct. 376, 98 L.Ed.2d 306. In our remand to the district court, we instructed that the citizen-plaintiffs could prove an ongoing violation

> either (1) by proving violations that continue on or after the date the complaint is filed, or (2) by adducing evidence from which a reasonable trier of fact could find a continuing likelihood of a recurrence in intermittent or sporadic violations. Intermittent or sporadic violations do not cease to be ongoing until the date when there is no real likelihood of repetition....
>
> The district court may wish to consider whether remedial actions were taken to cure violations, the *ex ante* probability that such remedial measures would be effective, and any other evidence presented during the proceedings that bears on whether the risk of defendant's continued violation had been completely eradicated when citizen-plaintiffs filed suit.

844 F.2d at 171-72.

There is no doubt that Gwaltney was a past polluter. Its discharge monitoring reports revealed violations in almost every month from the time Gwaltney purchased the plant in 1981 until one month before suit was filed. The question is whether, at the time suit was brought, there was a reasonable likelihood that this past polluter would continue to pollute in the future.

Gwaltney points to its record of near-perfect compliance after May 15, 1984 as conclusive evidence that there was no ongoing violation at the time of trial. However, the proper point from which to assess the likelihood of continuing violations is not the present, with its advantage of hindsight, but the time of the original suit. That is, did CBF carry its burden at trial of proving ongoing violations, either by proving actual violations after the date of filing suit, or by proving a reasonable likelihood that intermittent or sporadic violations would recur at Gwaltney?

The testimony at trial showed the following. Gwaltney purchased the meat processing plant in October of 1981. In June of 1982, it hired a consulting engineer to design modifications so the wastewater treatment facility would adequately treat the plant waste. After various delays, a final plan was approved, and the modifications were completed in October of 1983. Nevertheless, violations of Gwaltney's TKN permit limitation occurred during the winter of 1983-84.

CBF sent notice of intention to sue in February 1984. The last violation of Gwaltney's permit occurred on May 15, 1984. CBF filed suit on June 15, 1984. Trial was held on December 19, 1984. CBF put on as its only witness Dr. Bruce A. Bell. Gwaltney put on, *inter alia,* the testimony of Mr. J. Willis Sneed. Both Dr. Bell and Mr. Sneed testified that a major factor leading to TKN violations is low water temperatures. Dr. Bell's testimony included the following:

> Q. Do you have an opinion based upon your review of the records in this case and your visit to the Gwaltney facility, with regard to whether the Gwaltney facility will meet T.K.N. limits this winter?
>
> A. Assuming we have a normally cold winter, I think it is unlikely that they will.
>
> Q. What is the basis for those doubts?
>
> A. Primarily the question of waste water temperature. They are still using surface aerators, which tend to act to cool the system. And the larger of the two anaerobic lagoons being used has not at this time, or as of a week ago, formed a grease cover over most of the lagoon. And that grease cover is needed to act as an insulating blanket during the cold temperatures.

Mr. Sneed testified that the primary cause of the TKN violations the previous winter had been the lack of an adequate grease cover on the anaerobic lagoon. At another point he testified as follows:

> Q. Mr. Sneed, is adequate grease cover important to proper winter TKN treatment of the plant?
>
> A. On the anaerobic lagoon, yes.
>
> Q. You were with us last week when we toured the facility, were you not?
>
> A. Yes.
>
> Q. Isn't it in fact true at that point in time, in December, the lower anaerobic lagoon did not have adequate grease cover?

A. Yes. Earlier in the summer time that lagoon was covered with grease. And that was what we expected would happen. Quite frankly we were very surprised that that grease cover has deteriorated to this point, and we have since taken steps to accelerate the formation of that grease cover.

Q. Given the importance, as you mentioned before, of maintaining adequate grease cover, isn't there some doubt in your mind as to whether the Gwaltney facility would be in compliance with TKN limits this winter?

A. Yes, we have.

Q. Isn't there some doubt? That is all I am asking.

A. Yes, Sir. I think there is some doubt every year that you would expect the plant to go out of compliance at some time.

Thus, at the time of trial, there had been no violations at Gwaltney during the previous summer months, but there had been TKN violations during the previous winter due to an inadequate grease cover. The trial was held on the threshold of another winter, the parties' witnesses agreed that TKN violations were more likely to occur in the winter, there was testimony from both parties' witnesses that the grease cover on the anaerobic lagoon was at the time inadequate to protect against normal winter temperatures, and both witnesses expressed doubt whether Gwaltney could stay in compliance with its TKN limitation through the winter.

There was other evidence adduced at the trial that would indicate recurring violations of the TKN limitation were likely. Dr. Bell expressed concerns about the configuration of the anaerobic lagoon, the use of surface aerators, and the unknown effect of storm water on the system. Dr. Bell and a Gwaltney witness, Mr. Terry L. Rettig, testified that there were problems with the laboratory procedures used at Gwaltney, which would have an adverse effect on Gwaltney's ability to properly assess the operational needs of its treatment facility. There also was evidence that proper wastewater treatment did not receive a high priority at Gwaltney.

Given all of the above, we think that "a reasonable trier of fact could find a continuing likelihood of a recurrence in intermittent or sporadic violations." We therefore affirm the district court in so finding.

III. STANDING

The Supreme Court set forth the elements of Article III standing in *Allen v. Wright,* 468 U.S. 737, 751, 82 L.Ed.2d 556, 104 S.Ct. 3315 (1984): "A plaintiff must allege personal injury fairly traceable to the defendant's allegedly unlawful conduct and likely to be redressed by the requested relief." Gwaltney urges that CBF cannot demonstrate that its injury is "likely to be redressed by the requested relief." It argues that, since its permit violations had ceased at the time suit was filed, the only remedy available to CBF was an assessment of civil penalties against Gwaltney. Since civil penalties are paid into the United States Treasury, Gwaltney urges that such payments could not redress any injury to CBF. However, we already have held that such payments are causally related to a citizen-plaintiff's injury and are therefore likely to redress that injury. *Sierra Club v. Simkins Indus., Inc.,* 847 F.2d 1109, *reh'g & reh'g en banc denied* (4th Cir. 1988), *cert. denied,* 491 U.S. 904, 109 S.Ct. 3185, 105 L.Ed.2d 694 (1989). *Simkins* involved a citizen suit against a polluter for failing to sample its discharge and file quarterly reports as required by its NPDES permit. In the appeal from judgment for the citizens, we said:

> The judicial relief of civil penalties, even if payable only to the United States Department of the Treasury, is causally connected to a citizen-plaintiff's injury. Such penalties can be an important deterrence against future violations. [Plaintiffs] must show actual or threatened injury traceable to the wrong and a particularized interest in deterring violations of the Act, but once they have done so, the imposition of civil penalties is causally connected to the injury.

Id. at 1113 (footnote omitted).

Gwaltney argues that the case *sub judice* is factually distinguishable from *Simkins* because here the pollution occurred in the past while in *Simkins* the violation was an ongoing one. The attempted distinction fails, however, because the district court here on remand found, and we affirm, that Gwaltney's violations were ongoing. Gwaltney argues alternatively that *Simkins* was wrongly decided and urges us to depart from its holding. This panel, of course, is not at liberty to casually deviate from our established precedent. *See, e.g., Caldwell v. Ogden Sea Transp., Inc.,* 618 F.2d 1037, 1041 (4th Cir. 1980); *Doe v. Charleston Area Medical Center, Inc.,* 529 F.2d 638, 642 (4th Cir. 1975). Furthermore, the cases Gwaltney cites as support for its position do not deal with statutes analogous to the Clean Water Act, in which Congress essentially has deputized citizens to represent the public interest as private attorneys general. *See Gwaltney,* 791 F.2d at 308.

IV. MOOTNESS

Although this jurisdictional issue was not raised in the original trial or on appeal from that judgment and therefore was not specifically included in our order of remand, mootness may be raised at any stage of the proceedings. *See United States v. Munsingwear, Inc.,* 340 U.S. 36, 39, 95 L.Ed. 36, 71 S.Ct. 104 (1950); *Southern Pac. Terminal Co. v. Interstate Commerce Comm'n,* 219 U.S. 498, 514, 55 L.Ed. 310, 31 S.Ct. 279 (1911). Moreover, since the record in this respect is fully developed, nothing would be gained by another remand for an initial decision by the district court on this issue. We therefore consider Gwaltney's mootness contention and conclude that the case is not moot.

The Supreme Court's mootness doctrine is well summarized in *Cedar Coal Co. v. United Mine Workers,* 560 F.2d 1153 (4th Cir. 1977), *cert. denied,* 434 U.S. 1047, 54 L.Ed.2d 798, 98 S.Ct. 893 (1978).

> Courts are not empowered to decide moot questions or abstract propositions, but the exercise of judicial power depends upon the existence of a case or controversy. The suit must be definite and concrete, touching the legal relations of parties having adverse legal interests and be a real and substantial controversy admitting of specific relief through a decree of conclusive character as distinguished from an opinion of what the law would be upon a hypothetical statement of facts.

Id. at 1162 (paraphrasing *North Carolina v. Rice,* 404 U.S. 244, 30 L.Ed.2d 413, 92 S.Ct. 402 (1971)).

The question here is whether litigation over penalties imposed for past violations which are linked with ongoing violations presents a live case or controversy, even though primary subject matter jurisdiction is based on alleged continuing violations. In our view, the penalty factor keeps the controversy alive between plaintiffs and defendants in a citizen suit, even though the defendant has come into compliance and even though the ultimate judicial remedy is the imposition of civil penalties assessed for past acts of pollution. This conclusion follows from the structure of both §1319—authorizing actions by the government against polluters—and §1365—permitting citizen suits.

It is well established that the simple cessation of illegal activity upon the filing of a complaint does not moot a case. *See, e.g., City of Mesquite v. Aladdin's Castle, Inc.,* 455 U.S. 283, 289, 71 L.Ed.2d 152, 102 S.Ct. 1070 (1982); *United States v. W.T. Grant Co.,* 345 U.S. 629, 632, 97 L.Ed. 1303, 73 S.Ct. 894 (1953). Under the Clean Water Act, civil penalties attach as of the date a permit violation occurs. Liability is fixed by the happening of an event (discharge of effluent with an excessive burden of pollution) that occurred in the past. Thus, the initiation of §1319 actions by the government can be based on wholly past violations, so that a suit seeking penalties is intrinsically incapable of being rendered moot by the polluter's corrective actions. See, for example, *United States v. ITT Rayonier, Inc.,* 627 F.2d 996, 1000 (9th Cir. 1980), where the Ninth Circuit held that when the Environmental Protection Agency brings suit for injunctive relief and civil penalties under the Act, an appeal is not mooted even if injunctive relief becomes inappropriate.

A similar rationale governs our consideration of putative mootness arguably brought on by corrective action after a §1365 citizen suit has been initiated. When the Supreme Court concluded in its *Gwaltney* decision that §1365 permits citizens' actions against polluters while there are ongoing violations, the Court effectively approved the assessment of penalties based on past violations (the only possible basis for assessing a penalty). Assuming, then, proof of an ongoing violation, a citizen action, like a government action, cannot become moot once there is assessment of civil penalties, so long as the penalties are for past violations that were part of or which contiguously preceded the ongoing violations.

The Court in *Gwaltney* instructed that citizen suits are unavailable for violations "wholly unconnected with any present ... wrongdoing." 108 S.Ct. at 386. However, if the plaintiffs prove an ongoing violation at trial, the violations are related to present wrongdoing. Section 1319(d) of the Act states that any person who violates a permit condition shall be subject to a civil penalty. This language coupled with §1365(a) indicates that, once an ongoing violation is shown, the court is virtually obligated to assess penalties. *Stoddard v. Western Carolina Regional Sewer Auth.,* 784 F.2d 1200, 1208 (4th Cir. 1986).

We think the Supreme Court's dicta on mootness in its *Gwaltney* opinion supports our view. There the Court indicated that the issue of a permit violation may become moot if a defendant

> demonstrate[s] that it is *absolutely clear* that the allegedly wrongful behavior could not reasonably be expected to recur. Mootness doctrine thus protects defendants from the maintenance of suit under the Clean [Water] Act based solely on violations wholly unconnected to any present or future wrongdoing, while it also protects plaintiffs from defendants who seek to evade sanction by predictable protestations of repentance and reform.

108 S. Ct. at 386 (emphasis in original; quotation marks and citations omitted). The burden on the defendant—to prove that the issue has become moot because of corrective action it has

taken—is a heavy one. Under the rationale of the *Gwaltney* dicta, whether corrective action moots the issue of an ongoing violation *vel non* is a factual question. Conceptually, a myriad of factual questions could be posed in this context. *See* Note, *Clean Water Citizen Suits after Gwaltney: Applying Mootness Principles in Private Enforcement Actions,* 4 Fla. St.U.L.Rev. 143, 158-59 (1988) (authored by Reed Benson). Here, however, we need not speculate—the district court has found as a matter of fact that Gwaltney's violations were ongoing as that term is explained in the Supreme Court's *Gwaltney* decision. As we have explained, that finding is not clearly erroneous, and it shapes the dimensions of this case on appeal. The district court's judgment was based on its conclusion that Gwaltney was guilty of an ongoing violation at the time suit was filed, and the penalty levied against it was based, as it necessarily must be, on past violations. It is both the ongoing nature of the violation and CBF's interest as a private attorney general seeking a remedy for that violation that presents a live controversy in the Article III context.

V. BIFURCATION OF THE TKN AND CHLORINE VIOLATIONS

Our remand instructed the district court to determine whether there had been an ongoing violation at Gwaltney at the time of trial. At the remand hearing, Gwaltney urged that the court should make separate determinations for the TKN and chlorine violations. The court, interpreting our remand quite strictly, deemed it was permitted only to determine whether there was an ongoing violation; finding that there was, the court then reinstated the original judgment, which was based on both TKN and chlorine violations. We reverse.

It is "absolutely clear" that there were no ongoing chlorine violations at the time this suit was brought. Gwaltney had installed new chlorination equipment in March of 1982, had made further modifications over the summer, and had experienced no violations of its chlorine limitations since October of 1982. Clearly Gwaltney had abated its chlorine problems by the time CBF filed suit in June of 1984. Had Gwaltney violated no other permit parameters, the court would have had no subject matter jurisdiction over this suit. *Gwaltney,* 108 S.Ct. at 384-85.

However, Gwaltney did violate other parameters, including the TKN violations which were ongoing at the time suit was filed, and CBF seeks to use that fact to justify imposition of penalties for the chlorine violations. CBF contends that the jurisdictional requirement of §1365 refers to finding an ongoing violation of the *permit*; having done so, the court may then impose penalties for any past violation of any permit parameter. We do not think the statutory language can support that position. Section 1365(a) permits citizen suits against persons alleged to be in violation of "an effluent standard or limitation." Penalties under §1319(d) may be assessed for violations of "any permit condition or limitation." The entire structure of the Clean Water Act and regulations involves identifying specific pollutants and setting a permit limit for each pollutant of concern. It thus makes sense within this scheme to view each parameter separately for purposes both of determining ongoing violation and of assessing penalties.

CBF's theory also runs against the reasoning of the Supreme Court in finding that there must be an ongoing violation to create subject-matter jurisdiction. If Congress wished to permit citizen suits only when a discharger fails to abate a problem and the government fails to take enforcement action, *see* 108 S.Ct. at 382-83, then it would make little sense to permit penalties for wholly past violations of one parameter simply because there are ongoing violations of another parameter. The chlorine and TKN problems were due to distinct equipment and operational failures, and were corrected by distinct engineering solutions. While it was questionable at the time of suit whether Gwaltney had corrected its TKN violations, it was clear the company had abated its chlorine violations.

We therefore hold that the district court had no jurisdiction to impose penalties for Gwaltney's wholly past chlorine violations. We vacate the judgment for $1,285,322 and remand for the court to enter judgment against Gwaltney in the amount of $289,822—the amount attributable to TKN violations—with interest.

AFFIRMED in part, REVERSED in part, and REMANDED with instructions. [Footnotes omitted.]

See also *Natural Resources Defense Council v. Southwest Marine, Inc.*, 39 F.Supp.2d 1235 (S.D.Cal. 1999); *Public Interest Research Group of New Jersey v. Star Enterprise*, 771 F.Supp. 655 (D.N.J. 1991).

Of course, the citizen suit must be an actual case or controversy under Article III of the U.S. Constitution meaning that plaintiff must have standing to bring the action by showing individualized harm.

CANE CREEK CONSERVATION AUTHORITY v. ORANGE WATER AND SEWER AUTHORITY

590 F. Supp. 1123 (M.D.N.C. 1984)

These cases come before the Court on numerous motions by the opposing parties. Inasmuch as these two actions involve common questions of law and fact, and parties with identical interests, the actions have been consolidated for the purpose of considering these motions.

I. INTRODUCTION

A. CANE CREEK I

In this action, plaintiffs seek a declaratory judgment and an injunction prohibiting the defendant Orange Water and Sewer Authority (OWASA) from proceeding under an allegedly expired Section 404 permit to pursue the construction of a water supply dam and reservoir on Cane Creek. In response, defendant OWASA seeks a declaratory judgment upholding the validity of the Section 404 permit, declaring it in full force and effect. By Order filed on November 16, 1983, this Court granted the defendants' motion to join additional parties Marsh (Secretary of the Army), Bratton (Chief Engineer of the Army) and Hughes (District Engineer of the Army) as party defendants. In addition, the Court denied the plaintiffs' motion for summary judgment since material factual issues still remained in dispute. As a result of the joinder of the additional parties defendant, an amended Complaint was filed on December 20, 1983, with defendant OWASA filing an answer on January 17, 1984. On the federal defendants' own initiative, the administrative record was filed with the Clerk of Court on April 9 and April 30, 1984. A hearing on all pending motions was held in Greensboro on July 20, 1984, where stipulations of dismissal were entered for plaintiffs Edward Johnson, Cecil Crawford, and Forrest Young. Thus, Cane Creek Conservation Authority (CCCA) and Teer Farms, Inc. remain as the only plaintiffs.

B. CANE CREEK II

In this related action, plaintiffs seek a declaratory judgment and an injunction prohibiting OWASA from proceeding under an allegedly invalid Section 404 permit to pursue the construction of the same dam. Specifically, plaintiffs contend that the aforementioned Section 404 permit was issued by the District Engineer in reliance upon the North Carolina Environmental Management Commission's certification of the Cane Creek Project (*See* N.C.Gen.Stat. §162A-7), which certification had been reversed and declared invalid by the North Carolina Court of Appeals on the same date that the District Engineer issued the Section 404 permit. *See In re Environmental Management Commission Final Order,* 53 N.C.App. 135, 280 S.E.2d 520 (1981). Moreover, plaintiffs contend that the District Engineer's decision to issue the Section 404 permit was deficient as a matter of law for failure properly to evaluate the various public interests involved in the issuance of a permit, in direct violation of the Administrative Procedure Act, 5 U.S.C. §§551 *et seq.,* the National Environmental Policy Act, 42 U.S.C. §§4321, *et seq.,* and the Federal Water Pollution Control Act, 33 U.S.C. §§1251, *et seq.*

The defendants counter that, among other things, the first claim is moot and meritless; the North Carolina Court of Appeals in overturning the initial certification clearly made no decision on the merits of the certification; and in any event, 33 C.F.R. §320.4(j)(5) (1981) provided authority for the defendants to process the application if there was delay at the state level. Furthermore, defendants assert that the plaintiffs' second claim should be estopped for failure to raise this claim in Cane Creek I. Hence, defendants seek a declaratory judgment upholding the validity of the Section 404 permit, and declaring it in full force and effect. The administrative record for Cane Creek II was also filed with the Clerk of Court on April 9 and 30, 1984. A hearing on all pending motions was held in Greensboro on July 20, 1984, and this case was consolidated with Cane Creek I for purposes of oral argument. Stipulations of dismissal were entered in this action as well for plaintiffs Edward Johnson, Cecil Crawford, and Forrest Young, leaving CCCA and Teer Farms, Inc. as the only remaining plaintiffs.

II. DISCUSSION

The plaintiffs have apparently brought these actions against OWASA and the federal defendants under Section 10 of the Administrative Procedure Act ("APA"), 5 U.S.C. §702, which gives any person "adversely affected or aggrieved by agency action within the meaning of a relevant statute" the right to seek federal court review. These suits seek to prevent construction of the reservoir dam by challenging (1) the continued validity of the Section 404 permit, because no construction work was started within the time limits of the permit, and (2) the administrative procedure followed by the District Engineer in issuing the Section 404 permit for the project. The threshold issue, however, is whether the plaintiffs have alleged particularized actual or threatened injuries sufficient to give this Article III Court jurisdiction to hear their claims. While the APA has broadened "the categories of injury that may be alleged in support of Article III standing," it has not displaced the analytical framework under which that determination is made. *Simon v. Eastern Kentucky Welfare Rights Organization*, 426 U.S. 26, 39, 96 S.Ct. 1917, 1924, 48 L.Ed.2d 450 (1976).

Article III of the United States Constitution confines the federal courts to adjudicating "cases" or "controversies". An individual seeking judicial relief from an Article III court must demonstrate that there is an actual case or controversy which has caused him some judicially cognizable injury. At a minimum, such an individual must show "'that he personally has suffered some actual or threatened injury as a result of the putatively illegal conduct of the defendant,' ... and that the injury 'fairly can be traced to the challenged action' and 'is likely to be redressed by a favorable decision.'" *Valley Forge Christian College v. Americans United for Separation of Church and State, Inc.*, 454 U.S. 464, 472, 102 S.Ct. 752, 758, 70 L.Ed.2d 700 (1982); *quoting Gladstone v. Village of Bellwood,* 441 U.S. 91, 99, 99 S.Ct. 1601, 1607, 60 L.Ed.2d 66 (1979); *Simon v. Eastern Kentucky Welfare Rights Organization,* 426 U.S. 26, 38, 41, 96 S.Ct. 1917, 1924, 1925, 48 L.Ed. 2d 450 (1976). *See also Havens Realty Corp. v. Coleman,* 455 U.S. 363, 376, 102 S.Ct. 1114, 1122, 71 L.Ed.2d 214 (1982); *Duke Power Co. v. Carolina Environmental Study Group, Inc.*, 438 U.S. 59, 72, 98 S.Ct. 2620, 2629, 57 L.Ed.2d 595 (1978); *Warth v. Seldin,* 422 U.S. 490, 499, 95 S.Ct. 2197, 2205, 45 L.Ed.2d 343 (1975*); Association of Data Processing Service Organizations v. Camp,* 397 U.S. 150, 90 S.Ct. 827, 25 L.Ed.2d 184 (1970). These cases demonstrate that the focus of the standing inquiry must always be the party's "injury in fact"—whether he has suffered a sufficiently concrete injury to justify the invocation of the judiciary's remedial powers. *Accord, Motor Coach Industries, Inc. v. Dole,* 725 F.2d 958, 963 (4th Cir.1984).

While constitutional analysis of standing requires evaluation of concepts not easily susceptible of precise definition, *see Valley Forge Christian College,* 454 U.S. at 471-476, 102 S. Ct. at 757-60, the Supreme Court has noted that many standing questions can be answered by comparing the allegations of the particular complaint to those made in prior standing cases. *See, e.g., City of Los Angeles v. Lyons,* 461 U.S. 95, 103 S.Ct. 1660, 75 L.Ed.2d 675 (1983). As the Supreme Court recently instructed in *Allen v. Wright,* 468 U.S. 737, 82 L.Ed.2d 556, 104 S.Ct. 3315, 3324-26 (1984):

> The standing inquiry requires careful judicial examination of a complaint's allegations to ascertain whether the particular plaintiff is entitled to an adjudication of the particular claims asserted. Is the injury too abstract, or otherwise not appropriate, to be considered judicially cognizable? Is the line of causation between the illegal conduct and injury too attenuated? Is the prospect of obtaining relief from the injury as a result of a favorable ruling too speculative? These questions and any others relevant to the standing inquiry must be answered by reference to the Article III notion that federal courts may exercise power only "in the last resort, and as a necessity," *Chicago & Grand Trunk R. Co. v. Wellman,* 143 U.S. 339, 345 [12 S.Ct. 400, 402, 36 L.Ed. 176] (1892), and only when adjudication is consistent with a system of separated powers and the [dispute is one] traditionally thought to be capable of resolution through the judicial process, *Flast v. Cohen,* 392 U.S. 83, 97 [88 S.Ct. 1942, 1951, 20 L.Ed.2d 947] (1968).

Defendants assert that the plaintiffs fail to satisfy a critical element for standing because the complaint has not identified any injury within the zone of interests protected by the APA, the National Environmental Policy Act, or the Federal Water Pollution Control Act. For instance, in Cane Creek I, the defendants note that the allegations contained in the plaintiffs' complaint only contend that OWASA is attempting to proceed under an expired Section 404 permit. Yet the plaintiffs allege no injury from the federal defendants' claim that the permit has not expired. Further, in Cane Creek II, the defendants note that the plaintiffs allege no statutory or equitable source of injury from the original issuance of the permit under federal guidelines, and consequently, have not identified any injury to any protected interest.

This Court is in agreement that actual injuries within the zone of interests protected by the relevant federal statutes have not been alleged sufficiently, if at all. Normally, a person has standing to seek judicial review under the APA only if he can show that he has suffered or will suffer actual injury, whether economic or otherwise. *Data Processing, supra; Barlow v. Collins,* 397 U.S. 159, 90 S.Ct. 832, 25 L.Ed.2d 192 (1970). This constitutional standard has not been confined to those who show economic harm, as "aesthetic and environmental well-being, like economic well-being, are important ingredients of the quality of life in our society." *Sierra Club v. Morton,* 405 U.S. 727, 734, 92 S.Ct. 1361, 1365, 31 L.Ed. 2d 636 (1972); *see also, Duke Power Co. v. Carolina Environmental Study Group, Inc.*, 438 U.S. 59, 98 S.Ct. 2620, 57 L.Ed.2d 595 (1978); *United States v. SCRAP,* 412 U.S. 669, 93 S.Ct. 2405, 37 L.Ed.2d 254 (1972). In *Sierra Club,* however, the Supreme Court stressed the importance of demonstrating that the party seeking review be himself among the injured, for it is this requirement that gives a litigant a direct stake in the controversy. In that case, "the Sierra Club failed to allege that it or its members would be affected in any of their activities or pastimes ... by the development." 405 U.S. at 735, 92 S.Ct. at 1366. Here, as in *Sierra Club,* "nowhere in the pleadings or affidavits did the [plaintiffs] state that its members use [the Cane Creek area] for any purpose, much less that they use it in any way that would be significantly affected by the proposed action of the [defendants]." 405 U.S. at 735, 92 S.Ct. at 1366. *See generally, Sierra Club v. Froehlke,* 486 F.2d 946 (7th Cir.1973). When a plaintiff asserts no individualized harm to itself or its members, such a party lacks standing to maintain the action. *Sierra Club,* 405 U.S. at 731-41, 92 S.Ct. at 1364-69. Mere allegations of administrative irregularity without allegations of substantive injury will not support a claim. *Codd v. Velger,* 429 U.S. 624, 626-28, 97 S.Ct. 882, 883-84, 51 L.Ed.2d 92 (1977); *NRDC v. EPA,* 481 F.2d 116, 120-21 (10th Cir.1973).

Hence, the plaintiffs in the subject cases have failed to allege the kind of direct harm required under Article III; rather, plaintiffs allege only a generalized fear of the loss of the natural environment currently found in the Cane Creek area. Such a generalized grievance, shared in substantially equal measure by all members of the public, is insufficient to give plaintiffs standing to challenge the administrative determinations made in this matter. *See Gladstone v. Village of Bellwood,* 441 U.S. 91, 99 S.Ct. 1601, 60 L.Ed.2d 66 (1979); *Warth v. Seldin, supra; Schlesinger v. Reservists to Stop the War,* 418 U.S. 208, 94 S.Ct. 2925, 41 L.Ed.2d 706 (1974); *Matthews v. United States,* 526 F. Supp. 993 (M.D.Ga.1981), *aff'd* 713 F.2d 677 (11th Cir.1983). As a result, plaintiffs' claims in both actions merely serve as an attempt to compel this Court to usurp the defendants' administrative function without demonstrating the violation of a specific legal obligation that has caused plaintiffs direct harm. *See Allen v. Wright,* ___U.S. ___, 104 S.Ct. at 3330-31; *Minnesota State Board v. Knight,* 465 U.S. 271, 79 L.Ed.2d 299, 104 S.Ct. 1058, 1065-67, (1984); *Vermont Yankee Nuclear Power Corp. v. NRDC,* 435 U.S. 519, 556-558, 98 S.Ct. 1197, 1218-19, 55 L.Ed.2d 460 (1978).

III. CONCLUSION

Accordingly, the plaintiffs' unopposed motion to consolidate these actions is granted for purposes of this ruling, and the defendants' motions to dismiss in Cane Creek I and II are hereby granted. In so ruling, the Court notes that the following motions are hereby rendered moot because of this ruling, and are denied: plaintiffs' motion to intervene, plaintiffs' motion for summary judgment, plaintiffs' motion for preliminary injunction, and plaintiffs' motion to vacate and remand to supplement the administrative record. In addition, plaintiffs' motion to amend the complaint is also moot since it only pertains to the plaintiffs who entered Stipulations of Dismissal. Consequently, this action is hereby dismissed and each party shall bear its own costs. [Footnotes omitted.]

Prior to actually filing a citizen suit, plaintiff is required under 33 U.S.C. §1365(b) to give a notice of intent to sue to the violator, the Environmental Protection Agency (and, although not specifically mentioned, to the Secretary of the Army as well), and to the state in which the wetland is located. This notice is mandatory and, therefore, jurisdictional. 40 C.F.R. §§135.1, 135.2, and 135.3 for service and content requirements of the notice.

NATIONAL ENVIRONMENTAL FOUNDATION v. ABC RAIL CORPORATION

926 F.2d 1096 (11th Cir. 1991)

The issue presented is whether a citizen action brought against an industrial polluter is an action pursuant to 33 U.S.C. §1317(a)(§307(a) of the Clean Water Act) for the purposes of waiving the 60-day notice requirement found in 33 U.S.C. §1365 (§505 of that act). We must, however, first decide whether the 60-day notice requirement is mandatory. Because we hold that it is mandatory and that appellant's suit is not an action respecting 33 U.S.C. §1317(a), we affirm the district court's dismissal of appellant's complaint.

I

Appellee ABC Rail Corporation (ABC) operates a plant in Calera, Alabama. This plant, as part of its operation, discharges chemicals into Buxahatchee Creek under the authorization of the Alabama Department of Environmental Management (ADEM) in accordance with and subject to the provisions of the Clean Water Act (Act), 33 U.S.C. §§1251 *et seq.* and relevant state statutes. On January 22, 1989, appellant the National Environmental Foundation (NEF) sent notice to the appellee, the Environmental Protection Administration (EPA) and ADEM advising them that it would file a citizens suit against ABC. NEF filed a complaint in the federal district court for the Northern District of Alabama the next day. The complaint alleged that ABC's Calera plant was discharging pollutants, including the toxic chemicals of copper, lead, and zinc, in violation of the Act. It specifically alleged violations of 33 U.S.C. §§1311(a) and 1317 and the plant's National Pollution Discharge Elimination Systems Permit issued pursuant to the Act.

ABC moved to dismiss the complaint on the grounds that NEF had failed to give 60 day's notice as required by 33 U.S.C. §1365(b). The district court granted ABC's motion. It held that appellant's action against ABC for violations of toxic effluent limitations is an action respecting 33 U.S.C. §1317(d). Since only suits respecting 33 U.S.C. §1317(a) (§1317(a)) were exempt from the notice requirement, the appellant was required to give 60 day's notice before filing its complaint under 33 U.S.C. §1365(b) (§1365(b)). Appellant, however, had given only one day's notice. The district court dismissed appellant's complaint without prejudice, noting that it could refile after complying with the Act's notice provision. NEF now appeals the dismissal of its complaint.

II

Before we address appellant's argument, we must first establish whether the 60-day notice requirement in 33 U.S.C. §1365(b) is mandatory. This section allows citizens to bring suits against EPA, state environmental agencies, and alleged polluters for violations of the Clean Water Act. It does, however, impose some restrictions on citizen suits. It provides:

> No action may be commenced—
>
> (1) under subsection (a)(1) of this section—
>
> > (A) prior to 60 days after the plaintiff has given notice of the alleged violation (i) to the Administrator, (ii) to the State in which the alleged violation occurs, and (iii) to any alleged violator of the standard, limitation, or order, ... except that such action may be brought immediately after such notification in the case of an action under this section respecting a violation of sections 1316 and 1317(a) of this title....

33 U.S.C. §1365(b).

In *Hallstrom v. Tillamook County,* 493 U.S. 20, 110 S.Ct. 304, 107 L.Ed.2d 237 (1989), the United States Supreme Court held that the 60-day notice requirement of the Resource Conservation and Recovery Act (RCRA) found in 42 U.S.C. §6972 was mandatory: when a plaintiff does not comply with its provisions, the complaint must be dismissed. Section 6972 of Title 42 states that "no action may be commenced ... prior to 60 days after the plaintiff has given notice of the violation." The Court, looking at the plain language of the statute, concluded "compliance with the 60-day notice provision is a mandatory, not optional, condition precedent for suit." *Id.* 110 S.Ct. at 309.

Section 1365(b) of Title 33 is a direct analogue of the RCRA 60-day notice provision examined in *Hallstrom. Id.,* at 307 n.1. We also find the language of 33 U.S.C. §1365 equally clear: like 42 U.S.C. §6972, Section 1365(b) states that except in certain enumerated instances "no action may be commenced ... prior to 60 days after the plaintiff has given notice." Consequently, we hold that the 60-day notice requirement of 33 U.S.C. §1365(b) is a mandatory condition precedent to the filing of a citizen suit under the Clean Water Act. If a plaintiff fails to comply with this notice requirement where it is applicable, the district court is required to dismiss the action.

III

While the notice requirement contained in 33 U.S.C. §1365(b) is mandatory, there are two exemptions recognized in the statute: citizen suits brought "respecting a violation of §1316 or § 1317(a)" of Title 33. 33 U.S.C. §1365(b). Appellant argues that its complaint alleging ABC's violations of toxic effluent limitations is a complaint alleging violations of 33 U.S.C. §1317(a), and therefore it is not required to give 60 day's notice. The district court rejected this argument. It held that §1317(a) is directed solely at the Administrator of EPA. Therefore, any suit brought for violations of this subsection would have to brought against the Administrator. It held that appellant's suit had been brought under §1317(d)—the subsection directed at private parties and proscribing violations of standards created in the other portions of §1317. Appellant now argues that the district court erred in its construction of §1317(a) and (d). We agree with the district court.

The starting point in every case involving construction of a statute is the language of the statute itself. *Consumer Product Safety Comm'n v. GTE Sylvania*, Inc., 447 U.S. 102, 108, 100 S.Ct. 2051, 2056, 64 L.Ed.2d 766 (1980). The language of Section 1317(a) clearly addresses the Administrator only. It directs him or her to establish a list of toxic pollutants. It also directs the Administrator to establish effluent limitations, and gives the Administrator the authority to create national effluent standards. Since §1317(a) prescribes duties only upon the Administrator, it follows that only the Administrator can be sued for violating it.

Subsection 1317(d) is the first and only subsection of §1317 to impose duties upon or proscribe conduct by private parties. It follows, therefore, from the plain language of the statute, that any suit against a private entity for a violation of a limitation set forth under any of the provisions of §1317(a) is an action for a violation of §1317(d). Appellant's suit is just such an action.

The appellant admits that at first glance the plain language of §1317(a) would indicate that it applies only to the Administrator. It argues, however, that if this literal reading of §1317(a) is applied to the statutory exemptions in §1365(b), it will produce a result demonstrably at odds with the intentions of Congress.

Appellant argues that the legislative history of §1365(b) shows that Congress intended to allow immediate citizen's suits for violations of toxic effluent limitations, citing Senate Report (Public Works Comm.) No. 92-414 Oct. 28, 1971, reprinted at 1972 U.S. Code Cong. and Admin. News, p.3668. The portions of the report cited by appellant show that the committee emphasized that there should be no waiting period for citizen's suits where the alleged violation "is a failure to comply with an administrative enforcement order, a violation of a standard of performance, or a prohibition, or effluent standard or limitation in the act...." Senate Report, *supra* at 3746.

We do not find this portion of the legislative history to be illuminating. For, as appellant admits, the committee's language does not reflect the restrictive language ultimately adopted in the statute. We find no clearly expressed intent contrary to the plain language of the statute. Therefore the plain language of the statute controls. *Product Safety Comm'n,* 447 U.S. at 108, 100 S.Ct. at 2056.

Appellant finally argues that a strict reading of §1317(a) in conjunction with the requirements of §1365(b) would frustrate the primary objective in §1317 of preventing toxic effluents. We disagree. The Supreme Court has explained that the purpose of §1365(b) is to give the alleged violator an opportunity to bring itself into compliance with the Act, and thus make the citizen suit unnecessary. *Gwaltney of Smithfield v. Chesapeake Bay Foundation, Inc.,* 484 U.S. 49, 60, 108 S.Ct. 376, 382, 98 L.Ed.2d 306 (1987); *see also Atlantic States Legal Foundation v. Tyson Foods,* 897 F.2d 1128, 1131 (11th Cir.1990). Section 1365(b)(1)(B) allows either federal or state authorities to bring an enforcement action within the 60 day period. A government enforcement action brought during the notice period bars the citizen suit. *Gwaltney,* 484 U.S. at 59, 108 S.Ct. at 382. We believe that another purpose behind the notice requirement of §1365 is to effectuate Congress's preference that the Act be enforced by governmental prosecution. *See Gwaltney,* 484 U.S. at 60, 108 S.Ct. at 382; *Atlantic,* 897 F.2d 1128 at 1131 n.4. A literal interpretation of §1317(a) in conjunction with the 60-day notice requirement does not conflict with the general goal of reducing toxic emissions. This application simply gives other methods of enforcement—compliance under the threat of litigation and government enforcement actions—priority over citizen law suits.

The appellant has failed to show any reason why we should not follow the plain language of 33 U.S.C. §1317(a) and (d) in the application of the notice requirement of 33 U.S.C. §1365(b). We hold that the appellant's suit brought against ABC for alleged violations of toxic limitations is an action respecting a violation of 33 U.S.C. §1317(d). As a result, the appellant is required under 33 U.S.C. §1365(b) to give EPA, ADEM and the appellee 60 days notice before filing its complaint.

The appellant failed to comply with this notice requirement. As a result, the district court properly dismissed the complaint.

IV

The ORDER of the district court dismissing appellant's complaint with out prejudice is—

AFFIRMED.

ANDERSON, Circuit Judge, concurring specially.

I concur, but my concurrence is based upon a different rational. The opinion for the court assumes that an action under subsection 1317(d) cannot be an action "respecting a violation of section ... 1317(a)." Respectfully, it seems to me that there may be some doubt about that proposition and since the case is easily resolved on the basis of another rationale, I prefer not to decide that issue.

Section 1365 provides for the mandatory 60-day notice except in actions "respecting a violation of sections 1316 and 1317(a)." There is at least a colorable argument that an action against a private party pursuant to subsection 1317(d) is an action "respecting" a violation of subsection 1317(a) when the action seeks to enforce an effluent standard which was promulgated under subsection 1317(a).

It is not necessary in the instant case to resolve the foregoing potential ambiguity in the statute, because the instant suit does not seek to enforce an effluent standard promulgated under subsection 1317(a). Rather, the instant suit relates to pollutants with respect to which the Administrator has promulgated no effluent standards pursuant to subsection 1317(a). For that reason, it is clear that the instant action is not an action "respecting" a violation of subsection 1317(a). [Footnotes omitted.]

See also *Atwell v. KW Plastics Recycling Div.*, 173 F.Supp.2d 1213 (M.D.Ala. 2001); *Cromer c. U.S.E.P.A.*, 143 F.Supp.2d 1376 (M.D.Ga. 2001).

CANADA COMMUNITY IMPROVEMENT SOCIETY, INC. v. CITY OF MICHIGAN CITY, INDIANA

742 F. Supp. 1025 (N.D.Ind. 1990)

This is a citizens' suit under the Clean Water Act, 33 U.S.C. §1365, and the National Environmental Policy Act ("NEPA"), 42 U.S.C. §§4321-4347, against the Secretary of the Army, the City of Michigan City, Indiana, and the Michigan City Port Authority concerning the dredging of Trail Creek and the storage of the dredged material in a contained disposal facility in Michigan City. Four dispositive motions pend in this case: (1) the Secretary's motion for partial dismissal and for summary judgment; (2) the Michigan City defendants' motion for summary judgment; (3) the plaintiffs' cross motion for partial summary judgment; and (4) the Secretary's recent motion to dismiss for lack of subject matter jurisdiction, filed July 12, 1990.

Plaintiffs Canada Community Improvement Society, Inc. and the LaPorte County Environmental Association jointly challenge the decision of the Secretary, acting through the Corps of Engineers, to engage in a dredging project at Trail Creek in Michigan City, Indiana. The plaintiffs charge Michigan City and its Port Authority with violation of the "no discharge" prohibitions contained in the Clean Water Act ("CWA"), 33 U.S.C. §1311(a), for the discharge of pollutants into United States waters without permits issued under 33 U.S.C. §§1342 and 1344. The plaintiffs' amended complaint further charges the Secretary with violation of NEPA and the Corps' regulations implementing NEPA, 33 C.F.R. §230.11(b), in failing to prepare a Supplemental Environmental Impact Statement ("SEIS") for the dredging of Trail Creek before the second dredging. The plaintiffs seek declaratory and injunctive relief along with civil penalties against the defendants.

A party seeking summary judgment must demonstrate that no genuine issue of fact exists for trial and that the movant is entitled to judgment as a matter of law. Fed.R.Civ.P. 56(e); *Hannon v. Turnage*, 892 F.2d 653, 656 (7th Cir. 1990). If that showing is made and the motion's opponent would bear the burden at trial on the matter that forms the basis of the motion, the opponent must come forth with evidence to show what facts are in actual dispute. *Celotex Corp. v. Catrett*, 477 U.S. 317, 91 L.Ed.2d 265, 106 S.Ct. 2548 (1986); *Whetstine v. Gates Rubber Co.*, 895 F.2d 388, 392 (7th Cir. 1990). If he fails to do so, summary judgment is proper. *National Diamond Syndicate, Inc. v. UPS*, 897 F.2d 253, 260 (7th Cir. 1990). A genuine factual issue exists only when there is sufficient evidence for a jury to return a verdict for the motion's opponent. *Santiago v. Lane*, 894 F.2d 218, 221 (7th Cir. 1990). Summary judgment should be granted if no reasonable jury could return a verdict for the motion's opponent. *Anderson v. Liberty Lobby, Inc.*, 477 U.S. 242, 91 L.Ed.2d 202, 106 S.Ct. 2505 (1986); *Sims v. Mulcahy*, 902 F.2d 524, 540 (7th Cir. 1990).

The parties cannot rest on mere allegations in the pleadings, *Koclanakis v. Merrimack Mut. Fire Ins. Co.*, 899 F.2d 673, 675 (7th Cir. 1990); *Puckett v. Soo Line R.R. Co.*, 897 F.2d 1423, 1425-1426 (7th Cir. 1990), or upon conclusory allegations in affidavits. *Palucki v. Sears, Roebuck & Co.*, 879 F.2d 1568, 1572 (7th Cir. 1989). The court must draw any permissible inferences from the materials before it in favor of the non-moving party, *Matsushita Electric Industrial Co. v. Zenith Radio Corp.*, 475 U.S. 574, 89 L.Ed.2d 538, 106 S. Ct. 1348 (1986); *Johnson v. Pelker*, 891 F.2d 136, 138 (7th Cir. 1989), as long as the inferences are reasonable. *Spring v. Sheboygan Area School District*, 865 F.2d 883, 886 (7th Cir. 1989); *Mays v. Chicago Sun-Times*, 865 F.2d 134, 136 (7th Cir. 1989). The non-moving party must show that the disputed fact is material, or outcome-determinative, under applicable law. *Johnson v. Pelker*, 891 F.2d 136, 138 (7th Cir. 1989).

For the reasons that follow, the court concludes that under these standards, the defendants have demonstrated the absence of any material factual issue and entitlement to judgment as a matter of law on each of the plaintiffs' claims. Accordingly, the court grants the defendants' summary judgment motions.

I

In 1976 and 1977, the Chicago District of the U.S. Army Corps of Engineers began planning for a ten-year harbor dredging project at the Michigan City harbor. Plans were made to dredge the harbor and to dredge Trail Creek to allow commercial and recreational craft further access upstream and to prevent the continued silting of Trail Creek. The EPA classified the material that was to be taken from Trail Creek as unsuitable for unrestricted or open-lake disposal. Accordingly, in January, 1978, the city and the Corps entered into a local cooperation agreement, 33

U.S.C. §1293(a), for the construction of a contained disposal facility ("CDF") into which the dredged material would be deposited. The EPA found that applicable water standards would not be violated.

Also in 1978, the Corps issued its Final Environmental Impact Statement ("FEIS") after circulating a draft environmental impact statement among interested federal and state agencies, including the Environmental Protection Agency and the U.S. Fish and Wildlife Service, and soliciting public comment. The FEIS estimated that the dredging project would involve ten years (with two maintenance dredgings at approximately five year intervals) and the removal of approximately 50,000 cubic yards of sediment. The FEIS predicted that the removal of pollutants from Trail Creek would enhance water quality. The Corps, which is responsible for issuing permits for discharge of dredged or fill material into United States waters, did not issue a permit either to itself or to the city, but complied with its own regulations concerning Corps dredging projects.

The Corps completed the project's first phase, involving the removal of about 25,000 cubic yards of sediment, in July, 1979. From July, 1978 through March, 1979, the Corps monitored the Trail Creek soil sediments. "Dredged spoil" from Trail Creek was placed in the CDF by means of an hydraulic dredge connected by a pipeline to the CDF. A sand filter contained in a dike adjacent to Trail Creek was to filter the sediment so that only water and a small amount of suspended solids containing sediments were to be discharged from the CDF into Trail Creek. During disposal operations, however, the sand filter and discharge pipes clogged, producing a "bathtub" effect.

The city did not actively involve itself in the dredging, although it assisted the Corps in coordinating the removal of the dredged material to the CDF. The city furnished the land, easements, and rights-of-way necessary for the CDF's construction, operation, and maintenance, and agreed to operate the facility in a manner satisfactory to the Corps after the CDF's completion.

In December, 1985, in anticipation of completing the project, the Corps procured further sediment sampling tests of Trail Creek by a Peoria, Illinois, engineering firm. Those tests disclosed some polluted and heavily polluted sediment, but indicated that Trail Creek was cleaner in 1985 than it had been in 1978. The Corps modified its dredging operation for the completion of the project: a mechanical dredge with a closed-bucket clamshell was selected to remove the dredged material, which then was to be transported by barge to a rehandling site, where the material was to be placed in watertight trucks for transport to the CDF. A small de-watering structure at the CDF was designed to collect any water contained in the sediment and send it by pipe to the Michigan City sanitary district. Water monitoring was expanded in the second phase.

The Corps prepared no supplemental environment impact statement before embarking on the 1987 phase of the project.

II

The Secretary has moved for dismissal under 12(b)(1) or in the alternative for summary judgment on the CWA claims brought by the plaintiffs and for summary judgment, alleging no issue of material fact on the NEPA claim. The Secretary argues, last but jurisdictionally, that all claims against him are moot because the project has been completed (rendering moot the demand for a SEIS) and because the CDF will be turned over to Michigan City in the near future. Because the Secretary retains control over the CDF, the court declines to find the CWA claims moot; the mootness issue with respect to the NEPA claim will be discussed below.

A

As to the CWA claims, the Secretary argues (1) the plaintiffs failed to comply with the notice requirements of the CWA, barring suit; (2) §402 of the CWA does not apply to this "dredge and fill" project; and (3) §404 the Army Corps of Engineers need not issue itself a permit under §404 of the CWA, but need only comply with its own regulations, which provide a substantial equivalent of the permitting procedure, and that the Corps complied with those regulations concerning the Trail Creek project. The court finds the first argument persuasive, and so need not reach the next two points to resolve the CWA claims against the Secretary.

The Secretary contends that the court lacks subject matter jurisdiction over the CWA claims since the plaintiffs failed to give the government the required notice of their intent to sue as required under statutory law. Section 505 of the CWA, 33 U.S.C. §1365, requires at least 60 days notice to the administrator, the state, and the alleged violator before a citizens' suit may be filed. That provision allows the administrator to determine the manner in which such notice shall be given. EPA regulations require such notice to be given by either certified mail or by personal service on the head of the agency.

Notice of this action was made by certified mail to the municipal defendants (addressed to the city clerk of Michigan City and the president of the board of directors of the Michigan City Port Authority) and copies were sent to various officials of the State of Indiana, the Regional Administrator of the EPA, and the Chicago District of the U.S. Corps of Army Engineers, among many others. The Secretary claims not only that the Corps did not receive notice in the prescribed manner, but that the notices provided failed to set forth each violation alleged, notably excluding those under §§402 and 404 of the CWA. Claiming that the courts have strictly applied these notice requirements to citizens' actions, *Hallstrom v. Tillamook County*, 493 U.S. 20, 107 L.Ed.2d 237, 110 S.Ct. 304 (1989), the Secretary asserts that dismissal of the CWA action is warranted.

The plaintiffs concede that their notice failed to satisfy the regulation's precise requirements, but contend that the notice was timely and sufficed to give "notice in fact." The Secretary responds that the Supreme Court's decision in *Hallstrom* sounded the death knell for the "notice in fact" theory upon which many courts (including this one) have relied. The plaintiffs, in turn, argue that *Hallstrom* addressed only the requisite timing of notice, rather than the requisite form or content of notice.

The court need not determine whether, as the Secretary argues, the "notice in fact" doctrine has been laid to rest by *Hallstrom*. The notice sent to the Secretary, although sent in a timely manner, did not suffice to provide the Secretary with the sort of notice that would constitute "notice in fact." While the Secretary's (or, more accurately, the Corps' Chicago district's) copy of the notice to Michigan City contained some reference to the Clean Water Act, it cannot be viewed as informing anyone that the plaintiffs believed the Corps was violating §§402 or 404 of the Clean Water Act.

In *Fishel v. Westinghouse Electric Corp.*, 617 F.Supp. 1531 (M.D.Pa. 1985), the court found sufficient notice in fact despite the notice's failure to specify the regulations allegedly violated, the persons responsible for the violation or the dates of the violations. The notice in the case at bar suffered from the first two defects, as well. The *Fishel* plaintiffs were able to show, however, that the EPA and the state agency had been investigating the alleged violations for several months before notice was given, however. No similar showing has been made here.

The court recognizes that the notice in this case was prepared by members of a citizens group, rather than by a trained lawyer, and knowledge that one must serve the Secretary of the Army to complain about a local dredging project is not intuitive. Nonetheless, the *Hallstrom* Court rejected the argument that environmental claims (or at least claims under the Resource Conservation and Recovery Act) should be viewed with the solicitude afforded to *pro se* employment discrimination plaintiffs. No principled distinction can be found between the RCRA claimant and the CWA claimant: both types of environmental plaintiffs face, not a race that may be lost before counsel is found, but the task of waiting for possible post-notice, pre-filing administrative resolution. For lack of sufficient notice then, plaintiffs' CWA claims against the Corps must fail at the summary judgment stage.

B

In response to the NEPA claim, the Secretary argues first that the case is moot, because he is about to turn the CDF over to Michigan City. The court cannot agree. The Secretary operates the CDF today; after the turnover, the Secretary will continue to monitor the city's operation of the CDF. It is not absolutely clear that the allegedly wrongful conduct could not recur. *Gwaltney of Smithfield, Ltd. v. Chesapeake Bay Foundation, Inc.*, 484 U.S. 49, 66, 98 L.Ed.2d 306, 108 S.Ct. 376 (1987). The case is not moot.

On the merits of the plaintiffs' NEPA claim, the Secretary contends that the facts in this case did not evidence a "seriously different picture" from the time of filing of the Final Environmental Impact Statement in January 1978 warranting the preparation of a Supplemental Environmental Impact Statement. He contends essentially that the decision whether to prepare a SEIS is left to the administrative agency (here, the Corps), that courts owe great deference to such agency decisions, *Robertson v. Methow Valley Citizens Council,* 490 U.S. 332, 109 S.Ct. 1835, 104 L.Ed.2d 351 (1989), and that such decisions are not to be overturned by a court unless shown to be arbitrary and capricious, an abuse of discretion, or otherwise not in accordance with law. *Marsh v. Oregon Natural Resources Council,* 490 U.S. 360, 109 S.Ct. 1851, 104 L.Ed.2d 377 (1989).

The Secretary maintains that the changes in the dredging activity at Trail Creek since the FEIS were all designed to mitigate adverse environmental effects; as such, the changes did not warrant a new assessment of environmental impact since that impact undoubtedly would fall below that previously determined. Evaluations by both the Corps and the EPA regional office indicated that there was no need to prepare a SEIS between the first and second dredging activities.

In response, the plaintiffs contend that the appropriate inquiry is whether "the agency took a hard look at the environmental factors implicated and based its decision on a rational consideration of the relevant factors." *Van Abbema v. Fornell,* 807 F.2d 633, 636 (7th Cir. 1986). The plaintiffs argue that an SEIS was warranted in light of various events, in addition to the Corps' own changes to the project, particularly the "bathtub effect" noted within the CDF and the designation of the nearby Waste, Inc. land as a Superfund site. The plaintiffs deny that the post-FEIS changes in the dredging project at Trail Creek were all mitigating, but further argue that a SEIS was necessary nonetheless. The plaintiffs also ask for the preparation of such a supplemental report as part of their relief in this action.

The record before the court discloses that between the first dredging and second dredging, the Corps made plans to modify the dredging method so as to employ a mechanical dredge with a closed-bucket clamshell, contracted for a bottom sediment sampling of Trail Creek, modified the method of transporting the dredged material, designed a small de-watering structure at the CDF to collect water contained in the sediment and transport it to the Michigan City sanitary district, and undertook a water monitoring plan that involved reports to local, state, and federal agencies. Indeed, the EPA considered whether a supplemental statement should be prepared and decided that no SEIS was needed.

In light of the foregoing, no reasonable trier of fact could fail to find that this constituted the "hard look" of which the Seventh Circuit spoke in *Van Abbema v. Fornell,* 807 F.2d at 636, or that the Secretary's decision to proceed without an SEIS was not arbitrary and capricious, *Marsh v. Oregon Natural Resources Council,* 490 U.S. 360, 109 S.Ct. 1851, 104 L.Ed.2d 377, giving appropriate deference to the Secretary. *Robertson v. Methow Valley Citizens Council,* 490 U.S. 332, 109 S.Ct. 1835, 104 L.Ed.2d 351. Summary judgment in favor of the Corps on the NEPA is, therefore, appropriate.

III

The plaintiffs contend that the Michigan City defendants are violating §§402 and 404 of the CWA.

A

Section 402 of the Act, 33 U.S.C. §1342, has no application to the events involved here, for §404 alone applies to "dredge and fill" operations. The plaintiffs argue that adequate environmental safeguards are absent unless §§402 and 404 each apply, but that argument must be directed to Congress. "The starting point for interpreting a statute is the language of the statute itself." *Consumer Product Safety Com'n v. GTE Sylvania, Inc.,* 447 U.S. 102, 108, 64 L.Ed.2d 766, 100 S.Ct. 2051 (1980). Section 402(a)(1) provides for the issuance of permits under that section, "Except as provided in sections 1328 and 1344 of this title..." Further,

> ... considerable weight should be accorded to an executive department's construction of a statutory scheme it is entrusted to administer, and the principle of deference to administrative interpretations has been consistently followed by this Court whenever decision as to the meaning or reach of a statute has involved reconciling policies, and a full understanding of the force of the statutory policy in the given situation has depended upon more than ordinary knowledge respecting the matters subjected to agency regulations.

Chevron, U.S.A. v. Natural Resources Defense Council, Inc., 467 U.S. 837, 844-845, 81 L.Ed.2d 694, 104 S.Ct. 2778 (1984). With this principle in mind, the court notes that the Environmental Protection Agency's regulations, 33 C.F.R. §122.3(b), provide:

> The following discharges do not require NPDES [§402] permits:...
>
> (b) Discharges of dredged or fill material into waters of the United States which are regulated under Section 404 of CWA.

Both the statute and the regulations explicitly differentiate between activities subject to §402 and §404. Regardless of the persuasiveness of the plaintiffs' arguments that dual permits should be required in this instance, the plain language of federal regulations and statutes, and not such policy choices, must govern this court and its determinations. Accordingly, the court concludes that the Michigan City defendants are entitled to judgment as a matter of law on the plaintiffs' claims under §402 of the CWA.

B

The plaintiffs have come forth with no evidence establishing a violation of §404 by the Michigan City defendants. The record contains no evidence that these defendants have dredged Trail Creek, placed the dredged materials into the CDF, transported the dredged materials in leaking trucks through residential areas, or operated the CDF. These things, if done at all, have been done by the Corps. The hour of municipal control over the CDF may be near, and it may be true that the city must acquire a §404 permit before it may maintain the CDF. The record before the court does not, however, allow an inference that the Michigan City defendants will take over the maintenance of the CDF without a §404 permit or will allow discharges that would bring §404 into play.

C

Accordingly, the Michigan City defendants are entitled to judgment as a matter of law on the §404 claim against them.

IV

Based on the foregoing, the court concludes that, although the action is not moot and the Secretary's dismissal motion of July 16 accordingly must be DENIED, the defendants' summary judgment motions should be, and the motions hereby are, GRANTED. Because the defendants are entitled to judgment as a matter of law, the plaintiffs' motion for partial summary judgment must be, and hereby is, DENIED.

SO ORDERED. [Footnotes omitted.]

The purpose of the notice is to provide the government an opportunity to bring its own enforcement action because citizen suits were never intended to take the place of government enforcement actions, but only as an aid in the protection of the environment.

ATLANTIC STATES LEGAL FOUNDATIONS, INC. v. UNIVERSAL TOOL & STAMPING CO., INC.

735 F.Supp. 1404 (N.D.Ind. 1990)

This matter is before the court on defendant's motion for summary judgment filed on September 15, 1988, and plaintiff's motion for partial summary judgment filed on September 23, 1988. On November 10, 1988, the defendant responded to the plaintiff's motion for partial summary judgment and on November 14, 1988, the plaintiff responded to defendant's motion for summary judgment. A hearing was held on the motions on August 23, 1989. On January 29, 1990, plaintiff filed a supplemental submission in support of motion for partial summary judgment and in opposition to defendant's motion for summary judgment. Also on January 29, 1990, the defendant filed a supplemental affidavit in support of motion for summary judgment. On February 27, 1990, the defendant responded to plaintiff's supplemental submission and on March 2, 1990, the plaintiff responded to defendant's supplemental submission.

SUMMARY JUDGMENT

Summary judgment is proper "if the pleadings, depositions, answers to interrogatories, and admissions on file, together with the affidavits, if any, show that there is no genuine issue as to any material fact and that the moving party is entitled to a judgment as a matter of law." Fed.R.Civ.P. 56(c). Rule 56(c) mandates the entry of summary judgment, after adequate time for discovery, against a party "who fails to make a showing sufficient to establish the existence of an element essential to that party's case, and in which that party will bear the burden of proof at trial." *Celotex Corp. v. Catrett,* 477 U.S. 317, 106 S.Ct. 2548, 2552-53, 91 L.Ed.2d 265 (1986). The standard for granting summary judgment mirrors the directed verdict standard under Rule 50(a), which requires the court to grant a directed verdict where there can be but one reasonable conclusion. *Anderson v. Liberty Lobby, Inc.*, 477 U.S. 242, 106 S.Ct. 2505, 2511, 91 L.Ed.2d 202 (1986). A scintilla of evidence in support of the non-moving party's position is not sufficient to successfully oppose summary judgment; "there must be evidence on which the jury could reasonably find for the plaintiff." *Id.* 106 S.Ct. at 2512; *In re Matter of Wildman,* 859 F.2d 553, 557 (7th Cir. 1988); *Klein v. Ryan,* 847 F.2d 368, 374 (7th Cir. 1988); *Valentine v. Joliet Tp. High School Dist. No. 204,* 802 F.2d 981, 986 (7th Cir. 1986).

Initially, Rule 56 requires the moving party to inform the court of the basis for the motion, and to identify those portions of the pleadings, depositions, answers to interrogatories, and admission on file, together with the affidavits, if any, which demonstrate the absence of a genuine issue of material fact, *Celotex,* 106 S.Ct. at 2553. The non-moving party may oppose the motion with any of the evidentiary materials listed in Rule 56(c), but reliance on the pleadings alone is not sufficient to withstand summary judgment. *Goka v. Bobbitt,* 862 F.2d 646, 649 (7th Cir. 1988); *Guenin v. Sendra Corp.*, 700 F.Supp. 973, 974 (N.D.Ind. 1988); *Posey v. Skyline Corp.,* 702 F.2d 102, 105 (7th Cir.), *cert. denied,* 464 U.S. 960, 78 L.Ed.2d 336, 104 S.Ct. 392 (1983). In ruling on a summary judgment motion the court accepts as true the non-moving party's evidence, draws all legitimate inferences in favor of the non-moving party, and does not weigh the evidence or the credibility of witnesses. *Anderson,* 106 S.Ct. at 2511.

Substantive law determines which facts are material; that is, which facts might affect the outcome of the suit under the governing law. *Id.* at 2510. Irrelevant or unnecessary facts do not preclude summary judgment even when they are in dispute. *Id.* The issue of fact must be genuine. Fed.R.Civ.P. 56(c), (e). To establish a genuine issue of fact, the non-moving party "must do more than simply show that there is some metaphysical doubt as to the material facts." *Matsushita Elec. Indus. Co. v. Zenith Radio,* 475 U.S. 574, 106 S.Ct. 1348, 1356, 89 L.Ed.2d 538 (1986); *First National Bank of Cicero v. Lewco Securities Corp.*, 860 F.2d 1407, 1411 (7th Cir. 1988). The non-moving party must come forward with specific facts showing that there is a genuine issue for trial. *Id.* A summary judgment determination is essentially an inquiry as to "whether the evidence presents a sufficient disagreement to require submission to a jury or whether it is so one-sided that one party must prevail as a matter of law." *Anderson,* 106 S.Ct. at 2512.

FACTUAL BACKGROUND

Plaintiff, Atlantic States Legal Foundation, Inc. (Atlantic), has brought a citizen's suit under §505 of the Clean Water Act, 33 U.S.C. §1365, against Universal Tool & Stamping Co., Inc. (Universal) alleging that Universal has repeatedly violated the terms and conditions of its National Pollutant Discharge Elimination System (NPDES) permit under circumstances warranting the imposition of civil penalties and the award of attorney fees and costs.

Universal operates a manufacturing plant which is located on U.S. Route 6 just west of the municipal limits of the City of Butler in DeKalb County, Indiana. Universal manufactures jacks for the automobile industry. The manufacturing process involves machining bar and flat stock steel which is then protected from corrosion by a process of phosphating and painting and by zinc plating with a decorative chrome chemical coating.

Universal received its first NPDES permit in 1975 and has had several since that time. The permit which is the basis of this lawsuit became effective on April 28, 1984 and was to expire on February 28, 1989. This permit authorized Universal to discharge wastewater containing limited quantities of pollutants from outfalls 001 and 101 into the Teutsch Ditch. At outfall 101 the wastewaters that Universal discharged into Teutsch Ditch from its phosphating, painting, zinc plating and chrome coating manufacturing procedures were monitored after the wastewaters had passed through Universal's wastewater treatment facility. These waters then combined with wastewaters which had moved through the manufacturing system as non-contact cooling waters. Just before entry of these combined waters into Teutsch Ditch, the wastewater was monitored at outfall 001. Under its permit, defendant was required to establish and maintain records, install, use and maintain monitoring equipment, sample effluents, and report on a monthly basis to the state of Indiana regarding defendant's discharge of pollutants.

From the inception of its April 1984 permit, Universal had difficulty achieving continuous compliance with its permit. In January 1985, Universal received a Notice of Violation from the State of Indiana for violations of its NPDES permit requiring that Universal's processes for wastewater treatment be reviewed. Universal submitted a proposal to the State involving a series of tasks which it was believed would bring Universal back into compliance with its NPDES permit by June 30, 1985. However, continuous compliance with the NPDES permit was not achieved; and, on September 20, 1985, the State of Indiana issued an Order of Compliance issued for violations of Indiana Stream Pollution Control Board Rule 330 IAC 5 (since amended), which provided for a penalty of up to $25,000.00 per day per violation. On May 15, 1986, the State advised Universal of the results of a compliance sampling survey which the State had conducted on January 21-22, 1986. The results showed that the revisions made by Universal to its system had failed to bring about full compliance and a different approach was needed.

Having failed to achieve full compliance with its NPDES permit utilizing the recommendations of its Certified Waste Treatment Operator, Universal sought the help of an environmental engineer, Scott O. Lougheed, in June of 1986. Mr. Lougheed was hired to undertake an extensive study of Universal's manufacturing processes and wastewater treatment system so as to plan whatever was needed to obtain continuous, uninterrupted compliance with the 1984 NPDES permit. This effort, referred to as a Plant Assessment, was already underway when, on or about

September 15, 1986, Atlantic gave notice to Universal of violations of its NPDES permit and of plaintiff's intent to file suit. Atlantic commenced this action on or about April 9, 1987.

As part of Universal's response to the State's initial enforcement action, an Interlocutory Consent Decree was entered into between Universal and the State on November 14, 1986. Following an exchange of information, continued negotiation and agreements as to further compliance schedule dates, Universal and the State entered into a Final Consent Order which was adopted on July 13, 1987. The Final Consent Order provided, among other things, that it was subject to being set aside upon successful petition by interested persons. Notice of publication was given in Marion County and DeKalb County, and a copy was given to Atlantic's counsel. The Final Consent Order, which provides for $40,000.00 in fines, with $30,000.00 thereof being waived upon successful and timely completion of designated tasks, established a sequence of tasks which were to culminate with Universal's new wastewater treatment system achieving effective, continuous and uninterrupted compliance with its NPDES permit on or before September 1, 1988.

UNIVERSAL'S MOTION FOR SUMMARY JUDGMENT

Universal claims that the compliance specified by the Final Consent Order has been achieved and that no violations of the interim permit limits established by the Final Consent Order have occurred since November 6, 1987. Universal further states that, since July 1, 1987, it has exceeded interim permit limits only on three days in September 1987 when an electrode sensor became inoperative, and one day in November 1987 when a tank developed a leak.

In its motion for summary judgment, Universal advances four grounds for the barring of any relief to Atlantic: (1) lack of standing; (2) diligent prosecution of an administrative action by the Indiana Department of Environmental Management; (3) mootness; and (4) the unconstitutionality of the statute authorizing a citizen's suit.

I. STANDING

The doctrine of standing is based upon Article III of the United States Constitution, which limits the judicial power of the federal courts to resolution of actual cases and controversies. *Flast v. Cohen*, 392 U.S. 83, 88 S.Ct. 1942, 20 L.Ed.2d 947 (1968). In terms of its Article III requirement, "the standing question is whether the plaintiff has 'alleged such a personal stake in the outcome of the controversy' as to warrant his invocation of federal court jurisdiction and to justify exercise of the court's remedial powers on his behalf." *Warth v. Seldin*, 422 U.S. 490, 95 S.Ct. 2197, 45 L.Ed.2d 343 (1975). The constitutional requirements for standing, injury in fact, causation, and redressability, were clearly summarized in *Valley Forge Christian College v. Americans United*, 454 U.S. 464, 102 S.Ct. 752, 70 L.Ed.2d 700 (1982). The Court stated:

> At an irreducible minimum, Art. III requires the party who invokes the court's authority to 'show that he personally has suffered some actual or threatened injury as a result of the putatively illegal conduct of the defendant,' *Gladstone Realtors v. Village of Bellwood*, 441 U.S. 91, 99, 99 S.Ct. 1601, 1608, 60 L.Ed.2d 66 (1979), and that the injury 'fairly can be traced to the challenged action' and 'is likely to be redressed by a favorable decision.' *Simon v. Eastern Kentucky Welfare Rights Org.*, 426 U.S. 26, 38, 41, 96 S.Ct. 1917, 1924, 1925, 48 L.Ed.2d 450 (1976).

Id. 102 S. Ct. at 758.

As noted above, Atlantic brought this action pursuant to §505 of the Clean Water Act, 33 U.S.C. §1365, which authorizes any "citizen" to commence a civil action on his own behalf against a person who is alleged to be in violation of the Act. "Citizen" is defined as "a person or persons having an interest which is or may be adversely affected." 33 U.S.C. §1365(g). In interpreting this section of the Clean Water Act, the United States Supreme Court has stated that:

> It is clear from the Senate Conference Report that this phrase was intended by Congress to allow suits by all persons possessing standing under this Court's decision in *Sierra Club v. Morton,* 405 U.S. 727, 92 S.Ct. 1361, 31 L.Ed.2d 636 (1972). See S.Conf.Rep. No. 92-1236, p. 146 (1972). This broad category of potential plaintiffs necessarily includes both plaintiffs seeking to enforce these statutes as private attorneys general, whose injuries are "noneconomic" and probably noncompensable, and persons like respondents who assert that they have suffered tangible economic injuries because of statutory violations.

Middlesex County Sewerage Auth. v. National Sea Clammers Ass'n, 453 U.S. 1, 101 S.Ct. 2615, 2624, 69 L.Ed.2d 435 (1981).

Universal contends that none of Atlantic's members have suffered a redressable harm as a result of Atlantic's allegedly illegal discharges and, therefore, Atlantic fails to meet the requirements for standing set forth in *Sierra Club v. Morton*, 405 U.S. 727, 92 S.Ct. 1361, 31 L.Ed.2d 636 (1972). In Sierra Club, a conservation organization brought an action to enjoin development of a national game refuge. The Sierra Club asserted that it had standing to maintain that action based upon its special interest and expertise in environmental matters. The Supreme Court, while recognizing that injuries to environmental or aesthetic interests could suffice to establish standing, held that the Sierra Club lacked standing. The Court stated that "the injury in fact test requires more than an injury to a cognizable interest. It requires that the party seeking review to be himself among the injured." *Id.* 92 S.Ct. at 1366. Because the Sierra Club failed to show that any of its members suffered an injury as a result of the development, there was no standing. As the Supreme Court stated:

> The Sierra Club failed to allege that it or its members would be affected in any of their activities or pastimes by the Disney development. Nowhere in the pleadings or affidavits did the Club state that its members use Mineral King for any purpose, much less that they use it in any way that would be significantly affected by the proposed actions of the respondents.

Id.

Defendant argues that Atlantic, like the Sierra Club, has failed to demonstrate that its members have personally suffered distinct and palpable injuries from defendant's allegedly illegal discharges. Defendant further argues that Atlantic's members are, at best, merely concerned about pollution of the local waters and that their alleged injuries are neither traceable to Universal's discharge nor redressable by the relief sought in this case. Due to these alleged deficiencies, defendant asserts that Atlantic's suit should be dismissed.

In response, Atlantic claims that the defendant does not understand the proper application of the standing requirements to persons attempting to establish standing under the Clean Water Act. Atlantic claims that to satisfy the first requirement for standing, injury in fact, a plaintiff suing under the Clean Water Act need only show that defendant violated its NPDES permit limitations and that plaintiff, through its members, used the affected waterways in some manner.

Thus, Atlantic is asserting that, under the Clean Water Act, a plaintiff need not show that its members were physically or economically harmed by defendant's violations. The case law clearly supports Atlantic's position that "injury" for standing purposes can be injury to aesthetic, recreational, or environmental values. In *Natural Resources Defense Council, Inc. v. Outboard Marine Corp.,* 692 F.Supp. 801 (N.D.Ill. 1988), the district court held that:

> It is enough for NRDC to show its members use the water into which OMC's allegedly illegal discharges flow.... Such standing is not undermined because NRDC's members have not explicitly said they are harmed by OMC's permit violations. It is enough that they identify harm to their aesthetic or environmental interests from the overall pollution of the waterways. If OMC is proved to be violating the terms of its permit, that alone constitutes injury to those using the affected waters.

Id. at 807-08. *See also Student Public Interest Research Group v. P.D. Oil & Chemical Storage,* 627 F. Supp. 1074 (D.N.J. 1986); *Student Public Interest Research Group v. AT & T Bell Laboratories,* 617 F.Supp. 1190 (D.N.J. 1985). In the present case, Atlantic has submitted deposition testimony of two of its members who live in the region of Tuetsch Ditch, Big Run Creek, and the St. Joseph River. These individuals describe various actual and potential detrimental impacts on their aesthetic, recreational, and conservational interests due to pollution to these waters. Therefore, under the Clean Water Act, Atlantic, through its members, has alleged sufficient injury to satisfy the first requirement of standing.

Atlantic further claims that its members also satisfy the second and third requirements for standing. That is, the defendant's violations of its NPDES permit caused the injuries alleged by Atlantic's members and a favorable decision by this court would redress those injuries. As noted above, defendant has argued that Atlantic lacks standing because defendant's violations of its NPDES permit were so minimal that they did not harm plaintiff's members and therefore, the members' injuries were not caused by the defendant and would not be redressed by a favorable decision. In support of its motion for summary judgment, defendant offers the testimony of a professional engineer, Fred G. Krikau. Krikau states that his research indicates that for the period from January 1, 1980 through August 31, 1988, no aquatic life, plant life or wildlife in or adjacent to the waters of Teutsch Ditch, Big Run Creek or the St. Joseph River in the stretch from defendant's outfall 001 to the Filtration Plant at Fort Wayne, Indiana was harmed by any effluent discharge from defendant governed by its NPDES permit.

Atlantic asserts that the Clean Water Act presumes unlawful discharges to reduce water quality because definite proof of the proposition is often nearly impossible. Atlantic claims that, under the Clean Water Act, the focus is on the *quantity of pollutants discharged by each* polluter and not the quality of the waters and thus defendant's assertions that its permit violations did not cause the water to become discolored, unsafe to drink, or unfit for animal life, even if true, are irrelevant in determining Atlantic's standing to sue based on its members' injuries. Again, the case law clearly supports Atlantic's contentions. In *Student Public Interest Research Group v. Georgia-Pacific,* 615 F.Supp. 1419 (D.N.J. 1985), the district court held that:

> Plaintiffs need not show that this lawsuit will restore the Delaware to a pristine state, only that defendant's role in polluting the river may be lessened thereby. For purposes of establishing standing to sue, the size of the injury is not a valid criterion for determining whether an injury has occurred at all. In *United States v. SCRAP,* 412 U.S. 669, 93 S.Ct. 2405, 37 L.Ed.2d 254 (1973), the Court rejected an invitation to limit standing to those "significantly" affected by an alleged wrong. Instead, the Court held that plaintiffs may sue

> so long as they can demonstrate an "identifiable trifle" constituting actual or threatened injury, because such harm is sufficient to guarantee that plaintiffs have a concrete interest in the outcome of the litigation. 412 U.S. at 689 n. 14, 93 S.Ct at 2417, n.14. *See Baker v. Carr,* 369 U.S. 186, 204, 82 S.Ct. 691, 703, 7 L.Ed.2d 663 (1962). Congress has identified NPDES violations, however trifling, as injurious to persons such as plaintiffs' members, who use bodies of waters into which a permittee's effluents flow.

Id. at 1424.

Applying these principles to the present case, Atlantic clearly has satisfied the second requirement of standing. Universal, by violating its NPDES permit, has polluted the water which Atlantic's members use thereby causing them injury. The court further finds that Atlantic has satisfied the third requirement of standing in that a favorable decision, requiring defendant to come into compliance with its NPDES permit and/or imposing civil penalties, will redress the injuries alleged by the plaintiff's members. Consequently, the court finds that Atlantic has proper standing to initiate and pursue this lawsuit.

II. IDEM PROSECUTION

Universal's second argument in support of its motion for summary judgment is that Atlantic is barred from any relief because the Indiana Department of Environmental Management (IDEM) was diligently prosecuting a pending administrative action against Universal at the time Atlantic filed suit. Universal admits that Atlantic has a right to file citizen suits under the Clean Water Act. However, Universal points out that Atlantic's right to file a citizen's suit pursuant to 33 U.S.C. §365(b) is not unfettered because Atlantic's complaint could only be filed after giving Universal at least 60 days notice of its intention to file the action. Then, if the EPA Administrator or the IDEM had filed a court action that was being diligently prosecuted at the time of Atlantic's proposed filing, Atlantic's action would be barred. Universal further points out that 33 U.S.C. §1319(g)(6)(A), a 1987 amendment to the Clean Water Act, imposes yet another potential bar to the filing of Atlantic's action. The 1987 amendment provides that if an administrative action had been filed by the EPA administrator, or by the IDEM under comparable state law, and such administrative action was being diligently prosecuted, or if a final order in such an action had been issued and a penalty paid, then Atlantic's action would be barred. Universal submits that Atlantic is barred from pursuing the present citizen's suit under both §1365(b) and §1319(g)(6)(A).

Universal argues that at the time Atlantic filed its complaint on April 17, 1987, an administrative action had been filed and was being duly prosecuted by the IDEM. Universal claims that this administrative action qualifies as a "court action" and, as such, results in the preclusion of Atlantic's claim under §1365(b). Moreover, Universal argues, the IDEM's administrative action was being diligently prosecuted under Indiana law which was comparable to the administrative penalty provisions of §1319(g) and, consequently, Atlantic's action is also precluded by §1319(g)(6)(A). Finally, Universal argues that Atlantic's citizen's suit does not fall within one of the recognized exceptions to 33 U.S.C. §1319(g)(6)(B), so as to avoid preclusion by the IDEM's administrative action.

A. SECTION 1365(B)

Universal claims that an IDEM administrative proceeding, which was commenced on September 24, 1985, constitutes the equivalent of an "action in court" under §1319(b). Universal argues that, under certain circumstances, an administrative proceeding may be the functional equivalent of a court action sufficient under the Clean Water Act to preclude a citizen suit. Universal relies on *Baughman v. Bradford Coal Co.*, 592 F.2d 215 (3d Cir. 1979) to support its argument. *Baughman* set forth the requirements which an administrative proceeding must meet in order to be deemed an "action in court." The *Baughman* test requires that (1) the state agency have coercive powers to compel compliance with effluent limitations and (2) there be procedural similarities to a suit in federal court with citizens having the right to intervene. Universal submits that the IDEM's administrative action against it satisfies the requirements of the *Baughman* test.

In *Baughman,* the Third Circuit decided in what was then a case of first impression, that "an administrative board may be a 'court' if its powers and characteristics make such a classification necessary to achieve statutory goals." 592 F.2d at 217. A primary factor in making this determination was stated by the court as follows:

> [A] tribunal must have the power to accord relief which is the substantial equivalent to that available to the EPA in federal courts under the Clean Air Act.

Id. at 219. Accordingly, the *Baughman* court found that an administrative proceeding was not the functional equivalent of a court action if the administrative agency could not assess the same penalty as could be obtained in a court action, or if it lacked statutory authority to enjoin violations without obtaining a court order. Applying this test, the *Baughman* court found that the administrative proceeding at issue there was *not* the equivalent of a court action.

Atlantic argues that, contrary to Universal's assertions, the IDEM administrative action could not be a functional equivalent to an action in a court for the simple reason that IDEM lacks power to enforce its civil penalty and cease and desist provisions without bringing an action in court. IC 13-7-13-1(a), which governs the imposition of civil penalties for violations of IDEM orders, provides:

> Any person who violates any ... determination, permit, or order made or issued by the commissioner ... is liable for a civil penalty not to exceed twenty-five thousand dollars ($25,000) per day of any violation, *which may be recovered in a civil action commenced in any court of competent jurisdiction* by the department, and a request may be made in any such action that the person be enjoined from continuing the violation. (emphasis supplied).

Consequently, since the IDEM lacks power to accord relief which is the substantial equivalent to that available in an action in court, the IDEM cannot be considered the functional equivalent of a court and §1365(b) does not bar Atlantic from maintaining this suit.

B. SECTION 1319(G)(6)(A)

Universal also argues that this action is barred under §1319(g)(6)(A) of the Act because an administrative penalties action has been brought under state law which is comparable to §1319(g). Section 1319(g) was added to the Clean Water Act in 1987 and created a totally new procedure for the imposition of administrative penalties. One provision of that statute, §1319(g)(6)(A), imposes limitations on the bringing of citizen suits for violations which are the subject of such administrative proceedings. That provision precludes a civil penalty action under §1365 of the Clean Water Act as to any violation with respect to which a State has commenced and is diligently prosecuting an action under a state law comparable to §1319(g), or which the state has issued a final order not subject to further judicial review and the violator has paid a penalty assessed under §1319(g) or such comparable state law. Thus, in order to find that §1319(g)(6)(A) bars this lawsuit, this court must determine whether the Indiana statutes, as written, are "comparable" to §1319(g) of the Clean Water Act.

Universal argues that as of the time Atlantic filed its complaint initiating the present action, the IDEM had been continuously taking action to bring Universal into compliance with its permit limitations for some time. According to defendant, the IDEM's action against Universal began with its Order of Compliance issued in September, 1985, which lead to the issuance of the Complaint on November 14, 1986 in IDEM Case No. B-1039, and the entry of an interlocutory consent decree on November 14, 1986 requiring Universal's compliance with a number of deadlines. The IDEM's enforcement action culminated in the approval of the Final Consent Order on July 14, 1987, which provided for civil penalties and allowed for public comments and objections prior to becoming effective. Universal states that it has paid a $10,000.00 fine pursuant to the Final Consent Order.

Universal concludes that for both of the reasons specified in §1319(g)(6)(A) Atlantic's action is barred: (1) the IDEM, pursuant to comparable state law, had commenced and was diligently prosecuting an action against Universal and (2) the IDEM, pursuant to comparable state law, has issued a final order not subject to further judicial review under which Universal has paid a penalty. Universal steadfastly maintains that a comparison of the enforcement provisions of §1319(g) to those under Indiana law clearly demonstrates that the respective provisions are not only comparable, but virtually identical.

In determining whether the Indiana statutes are "comparable" to §1319(g) the court notes the remarks by Senator John Chaffee, the principal author and sponsor of the 1987 amendments to the Clean Water Act:

> The limitation of 309(g) applies only where a State is proceeding under a State law that is comparable to section 309(g). For example, in order to be comparable, a State law *must* provide for a right to a hearing and for public notice and participation procedures similar to those set forth in section 309(g); it *must* include analogous penalty assessment factors and judicial review standards; and it *must* include provisions that are analogous to the other elements of section 309(g). (emphasis supplied).

133 Cong. Rec. S737 (daily ed., Jan. 14, 1987).

Thus, for a state law to be considered "comparable" within the meaning of §1319(g)(6)(A), the state law must include provisions as to public notice and participation, penalty assessment, judicial review, and other matters comparable to those in §1319(g). While the defendant asserts that the Indiana law is nearly identical to the federal law, Atlantic points out several deficiencies in the Indiana law as compared to the federal law. The federal law, §1319(g)(4), provides that before issuing an order assessing a penalty, the Administrator must provide "public notice of and reasonable opportunity to comment on the proposed issuance of such order." 33 U.S.C. §1319(g)(4)(A). It also provides that, if a hearing is held, the members of the public who have commented on the proposed penalty shall have the opportunity to be heard and to present evidence at the hearing. 33 U.S.C. §1319(g)(4)(B). If no hearing is held, members of the public who commented on the proposed order have the right to petition the Administrator to set aside the order and hold a hearing. If the Administrator denies the request for the hearing, he must publish the reasons for the denial in the Federal Register within 30 days of the denial. 33 U.S.C. §1319(g)(4)(C). Section 1319(g)(8) provides that persons against whom penalties are assessed and persons who have commented on the proposed assessment of a penalty have the right to obtain judicial review of the assessment of the administrative penalty. 33 U.S.C. §1319(g)(8).

In contrast to these provisions of §1319(g), IC 13-7-11-2(e) now requires public notice of "hearings," but not of matters concluded by consent decree. Prior to July 1, 1987, when most of the administrative proceedings against Universal occurred, IC 13-7-11-2 did not even require mandatory public notice of "hearings." Rather, notice was merely permissible. Atlantic also points out that there is no Indiana counterpart to §1319(g)'s provision that members of the public be given a reasonable opportunity to comment upon the penalty assessment. In addition, citizens may not obtain judicial review of administrative orders under conditions similar to those under §1319(g)(8).

In addition, the Indiana statutes have no comparable provision to §1319(g)(3) regarding the factors to be considered in assessing a penalty. Section 1319(g)(3) requires that, in imposing a civil administrative penalty, the decision maker must consider

> the nature, circumstances, extent and gravity of the violation or violations and, with respect to the violator, ability to pay, any prior history of such violations, the degree of culpability, economic benefit or savings (if any) resulting from the violation and such other matters as justice may require.

33 U.S.C. §1319(g)(3). In contrast, the pertinent Indiana statutes do not contain any provision which specifies any factors to be considered in assessing a penalty.

It is clear from the foregoing that the statutes under which IDEM brought its administrative proceeding against Universal are not "comparable" to §1319(g), and therefore that proceeding does not bar the present case. Even if the court would find that the Indiana statutes are comparable to §1319(g), Atlantic argues that the IDEM did not diligently prosecute Universal's violations, and therefore, §1319(g)(6)(A) could not bar Atlantic's suit.

In contesting Universal's claims of diligent prosecution by the IDEM, Atlantic points out that Norman Ritenour, Universal's president, informed the IDEM that their administrative proceeding had little effect upon Universal's efforts to comply with its permit and that it was Atlantic's threat of a lawsuit that spurred Universal to action. Atlantic further notes that counsel for Universal "walked through" the Interlocutory Consent Decree for approval in the offices of the IDEM in a single day. This procedure was highly unusual as the approval and signing of such decrees often takes four to six weeks to accomplish. Atlantic concludes that, in light of IDEM's apparent willingness to bend its procedures on Universal's behalf, the fact that Universal continued to violate its permit limitations long after the administrative proceeding was commenced, the lenient penalty assessment of only $10,000 for the hundreds of reported violations, despite statutory authority for penalties of $25,000 per violation, and Mr. Ritenour's acknowledgment that it was plaintiff's notice of intent to sue, and not the IDEM administrative proceeding, that had moved Universal to take steps to comply with its permit, it is clear that the IDEM proceeding was not "diligent prosecution" under the Clean Water Act. The court agrees with Atlantic and finds that the IDEM did not diligently prosecute Universal for its violations of the Clean Water Act.

C. SECTION 1319(G)(6)(B)

As noted above, Universal's position is that §1319(g)(6)(A) bars Atlantic's action, because the Indiana law is comparable to the federal law, unless one of the two exceptions specified in §1319(g)(6)(B) apply. However, the court has determined that §1319(g)(6)(A) is not applicable to Atlantic's action for the reason that the Indiana statutes under which the IDEM brought its administrative proceeding against Universal are not "comparable" to §1319(g). Consequently, the court need not discuss Universal's argument that Atlantic fails to fit within the exceptions to §1319(g)(6)(A).

III. MOOTNESS

Universal argues in its motion for summary judgment that Atlantic's action should be dismissed on the ground of mootness due to Universal's purported current compliance with the effluent limitations of its NPDES permit.

The concept of mootness can be traced back to the "case or controversy" requirement under Article III of the United States Constitution. *DeFunis v. Odegaard,* 416 U.S. 312, 316, 40 L.Ed.2d 164, 94 S.Ct. 1704 (1974). For Article III purposes, "a case is moot when the issues presented are no longer 'live' or the parties lack a legally cognizable interest in the outcome." *County of Los Angeles v. Davis,* 440 U.S. 625, 631, 59 L.Ed.2d 642, 99 S.Ct. 1379 (1979), *quoting Powell v. McCormack,* 395 U.S. 486, 23 L.Ed.2d 491, 89 S.Ct. 1944 (1969). These principles of mootness prevent the maintenance of suit when "'there is no reasonable expectation that the wrong will be repeated.'" *United States v. W.T. Grant Co.*, 345 U.S. 629, 73 S. Ct. 894, 897, 97 L. Ed. 1303 (1953) (quoting *United States v. Aluminum Co. of America,* 148 F.2d 416, 448 (2d Cir. 1945)). In seeking to have a case dismissed as moot, however, the defendant's burden is a "heavy one." 73 S.Ct. at 897. The defendant must demonstrate that it is "absolutely clear that the allegedly wrongful behavior could not reasonably be expected to recur." *United States v. Phosphate Export Ass'n, Inc.*, 393 U.S. 199, 89 S.Ct. 361, 364, 21 L.Ed.2d 344 (1968). It is well established that the simple cessation of illegal activity upon the filing of a complaint does not moot a case. *See, e.g., City of Mesquite v. Aladdin's Castle, Inc.,* 455 U.S. 283, 102 S.Ct. 1070, 1074, 71 L.Ed.2d 152 (1982); *United States v. W.T. Grant Co.*, 345 U.S. 629, 73 S.Ct. 894, 897, 97 L.Ed. 1303 (1953).

Universal claims that, because of the success of its new wastewater treatment system, it has been in compliance with its NPDES permit limitations since November 1987, and thus Atlantic's action is moot. However, Atlantic contends that Universal's assertion is untrue and that Universal continuously violated its permit throughout the first seven months of 1988. Atlantic insists that Universal has not met its heavy burden of guaranteeing that no future permit violations would occur and further argues that even if Universal could convince the court that no future permit violations will occur, thereby rendering Atlantic's claim for injunctive relief moot, Atlantic's claim for civil penalties would still be "alive."

Both parties cite *Gwaltney of Smithfield, Ltd. v. Chesapeake Bay Foundation, Inc.,* 484 U.S. 49, 108 S.Ct. 376, 98 L.Ed.2d 306 (1987), in support of their respective positions. In *Gwaltney* the Supreme Court indicated that the issue of a permit violation may become moot if a defendant

> demonstrate[s] that it is *absolutely clear* that the allegedly wrongful behavior could not reasonably be expected to recur. Mootness doctrine thus protects defendants from the maintenance of suit under the Clean [Water] Act based solely on violations wholly uncon-

> nected to any present or future wrongdoing, while it also protects plaintiffs from defendants who seek to evade sanction by predictable protestations of repentance and reform.

108 S. Ct. at 386 (emphasis in original; quotation marks and citations omitted). As Universal notes, *Gwaltney* clearly stands for the proposition that citizen suits cannot be maintained for wholly past violations of the Act. Fortunately, *Gwaltney's* subsequent history provides guidance for determining when citizen suits are not mooted by a defendant's post-complaint compliance with permit limitations.

Following the Supreme Court's decision and remand to the Fourth Circuit, the Fourth Circuit remanded *Gwaltney* to the district court for further proceedings. 844 F.2d 170 (4th Cir. 1988). Upon remand, the district court found that plaintiffs had established ongoing violations of defendant's permit sufficient to invoke subject matter jurisdiction, and reinstated the penalty which had originally been imposed. 688 F.Supp. 1078 (E.D.Va. 1988). Defendant then appealed to the Fourth Circuit and argued that the action was moot because defendant had not violated its permit after the litigation had commenced. The Fourth Circuit rejected this argument and stated:

> In our view, the penalty factor keeps the controversy alive between plaintiffs and defendants in a citizen's suit, even though the defendant has come into compliance and even though the ultimate judicial remedy is imposition of civil penalties assessed for past acts of pollution....
>
> A similar rationale governs our consideration of putative mootness arguably brought on by corrective action after a §1365 citizen suit has been initiated. When the Supreme Court concluded in its *Gwaltney* decision that §1365 permits citizens' actions against polluters while there are ongoing violations, the court effectively approved the assessment of penalties based on past violations (the only possible basis for assessing a penalty). Assuming, then, proof of an ongoing violation, a citizen action, like a government action, cannot become moot once there is assessment of civil penalties, so long as the penalties are for past violations that were part of or which contiguously preceded the ongoing violations.

Chesapeake Bay Foundation, Inc. v. Gwaltney of Smithfield, Ltd., 890 F.2d 690 at 696-97 (4th Cir. 1989).

The Fourth Circuit found that, to the extent plaintiff had established that there were ongoing violations at the time the litigation was commenced, the case was not moot even though a defendant had subsequently come into compliance with its permit limitations.

A similar holding was made by the Eleventh Circuit in *Atlantic States Legal Foundation, Inc. v. Tyson Foods, Inc.*, 897 F.2d 1128, 1990 U.S. App. Decision (11th Cir. 1990). In *Tyson* the district court had held that the Supreme Court's decision in *Gwaltney* required it to dismiss as moot a citizen suit seeking relief for violations which, although occurring before and after filing of suit, had ceased at the time of defendant's motion for summary judgment. The Eleventh Circuit, however, reversed and remanded, holding that for purposes of assessing a plaintiff's allegations of ongoing violations, the court must always look to the date the complaint was filed. As Atlantic had shown the existence of ongoing violations, by way of DMR's filed by Tyson, the court further held that Atlantic had established liability under the Clean Water Act and was entitled to seek civil penalties for Tyson's non-compliance with its NPDES permit.

Atlantic argues that in the instant case the *Gwaltney* mootness analysis, insofar as it held that citizen suits cannot be maintained for past violations, is factually inapplicable because Universal has continued to be out of compliance over an extended period of time after suit had been commenced. Atlantic points out that Universal's DMRs show that, at the time suit was commenced, and continuing thereafter, there were and continued to be violations of Universal's permit limitations for various pollutants. Therefore, Atlantic concludes, Universal has not met its burden of showing to an *absolute certainty that it will not violate its NPDES permit in the future.*

In ruling on a summary judgment motion the court accepts as true the non-moving party's evidence, draws all legitimate inferences in favor of the non-moving party, and does not weigh the evidence or the credibility of witnesses. *Anderson v. Liberty Lobby, Inc.,* 477 U.S. 242, 106 S.Ct. 2505, 2511, 91 L.Ed.2d 202 (1986). In support of its motion for summary judgment Universal has submitted an affidavit of Edward P. Guindon, a chemical engineer who was employed as Universal's certified wastewater treatment operator. In his affidavit Mr. Guindon states that Universal's DMRs reflect that there were no permit exceedences in December of 1987, but there were four incidents of mass loading exceedences in January of 1988, and there were two incidents of mass loading exceedences in February of 1988. The Guindon Affidavit further states that from March of 1988 through August of 1988 Universal was in complete compliance with its NPDES permit. In its brief in opposition of Universal's motion for summary judgment, Atlantic contends that the Guindon Affidavit is inaccurate in several respects. In Exhibit D of its brief Atlantic sets forth these inaccuracies showing that Universal has exceeded the limitations of its NPDES permit numerous times during the time period of July 1987 to July 1988. At oral arguments held on August 23, 1989, Universal argued that prior to September 1, 1988, the date the Final Consent Order specified that Universal was to be in compliance with its NPDES permit, Universal was not subject to any mass loading requirements and therefore could not be in violation of any mass loading requirements. In response to Universal's argument, Atlantic noted that Universal has reported violations of its NPDES permit in March and April of 1989, as well as in September, October and November of 1988.

In light of the foregoing evidence it is abundantly clear that Universal has not met its "heavy burden" of showing that it will not violate its permit in the future. Considering Universal's DMRs for 1988 and 1989 it is questionable that Universal will ever be in compliance with its permit. Consequently, the court finds that Atlantic's action is not moot.

CONSTITUTIONALITY OF SECTION 505 OF THE CLEAN WATER ACT

Universal's last argument in support of its motion for summary judgment is that §505 of the Clean Water Act, 33 U.S.C. §1365, which authorizes civil penalty enforcement by private citizens, is unconstitutional. Universal contends that this provision violates both the separation of powers doctrine and the appointments clause of the United States Constitution. Universal cites *Buckley v. Valeo,* 424 U.S. 1, 96 S.Ct. 612, 46 L.Ed.2d 659 (1976), and *Bowsher v. Synar,* 478 U.S. 714, 106 S.Ct. 3181, 92 L.Ed.2d 583 (1986), in support of its argument that institution of a lawsuit to enforce federal law is an executive function, and since the citizen suit provisions allow persons who are not officers of the United States to enforce the Clean Water Act through private litigation, the provisions contravene established separation of powers principles. Universal's reasoning is flawed for two reasons. First, *Buckley* and *Bowsher* both address separation of powers *vis-a-vis* Congress and the Executive, not private persons and the Executive. Second, Universal ignores the principal that Congress creates statutory rights and obligations, and it determines who may enforce them and in what manner.

Buckley involved, *inter alia,* a constitutional challenge to the composition of the Federal Election Commission. The Commission was established to administer and enforce the Federal Election Campaign Act. That act granted the Commission broad investigatory, rulemaking, and enforcement powers. Two members of the Commission were also members of Congress, four Commission members were appointed by Congress, and the remaining two were appointed by the President. Because four of the six voting members were appointed by and obligated to Congress, the Supreme Court ruled that certain provisions of the Act violated the separation of powers doctrine:

> We hold that these provisions of the Act, vesting in the Commission primary responsibility for conducting civil litigation in the courts of the United States for vindicating public rights, violate Art. II, §2, cl.2, of the Constitution. Such functions may be discharged only by persons who are "Officers of the United States" within the language of that section.

Buckley v. Valeo, 96 S. Ct. at 692.

Throughout its opinion, the Supreme Court stressed the fact that the separation of powers doctrine prohibited one branch from intruding into the sphere of another and struck down certain provisions of the Federal Election Campaign Act because the provisions allowed Congress to exercise executive authority by appointing persons who would enforce the laws. Congress may not "vest in itself ... the authority to appoint officers of the United States when the Appointments Clause by clear implication prohibits it from doing so." *Id.* at 690.

Clearly *Buckley v. Valeo* was concerned with Congress expanding its powers at the expense of the Executive Branch. The opinion does not stand for the proposition, as Universal would have the court believe, that private persons may not enforce any federal laws simply because they are not "Officers of the United States" appointed in accordance with Article II of the Constitution.

Similarly, *Bowsher v. Synar* does not support Universal's argument. In *Bowsher,* the Supreme court struck down a provision of the Gramm-Rudmann-Hollings Act which provided that the Comptroller General would exercise necessary budget reductions:

> By placing the responsibility for execution of the Balanced Budget and Emergency Deficit Control Act in the hands of an officer who is subject to removal only by itself, Congress in effect has retained control over the execution of the Act and has intruded into the executive function. The Constitution does not permit such intrusion.

Bowsher v. Synar, 106 S. Ct. at 3192.

The Supreme Court has made it clear that executive powers may not be entrusted to an officer who is subservient to or may be controlled by Congress, as was the Comptroller General. Private litigants, however, are not controlled by Congress. Consequently, *Bowsher* does not support Universal's contentions. Because §505 of the Clean Water Act, 33 U.S.C. §1365, does not expand Congress' power at the expense of the Executive Branch, and because Congress may determine who will enforce the statutory rights and obligations that it creates, the citizen suit provision of the Clean Water Act does not violate the constitutional principle of separation of powers. Accordingly, Universal's motion for summary judgment must be denied.

Atlantic's Motion for Partial Summary Judgment

Atlantic argues that it is entitled to partial summary judgment on the issue of liability of Universal for numerous violations of the Clean Water Act. Atlantic asserts that the uncontroverted facts demonstrate that defendant, by its own admission, has operated its facility in violation of the terms and conditions of its NPDES permit. Atlantic concludes that there is no genuine issue of material fact concerning defendant's liability for violation of its NPDES permit and thus of the Clean Water Act.

As noted earlier, the Clean Water Act requires any permit issued under the NPDES program to: (a) include effluent limitations based on the effluent limitations established pursuant to §1311(b) for the permit holder's industrial category, upon such limitations as the Administrator deems necessary if he has not promulgated effluent limitations for the permit holder's industrial category, or upon the State's requirements or any applicable water quality standards promulgated pursuant to §§1312 and 1313 of the Clean Water Act; (b) require the permit holder to be in compliance with the effluent limitations in the permit by a specified date; and (c) require the permit holder to monitor its discharges and report the results to the EPA or the State in DMRs. If the permit holder complies with all of the permit provisions, it is deemed to be in compliance with §1311 for purposes of both the EPA and citizen enforcement actions. If it fails to comply with its permit, it is deemed to be in violation.

Atlantic notes that Universal has admitted in official reports that its discharges have exceeded the effluent limitations in its NPDES permit. Universal, in fact, does not deny that it has violated its NPDES permit or that it has violated the Clean Water Act. At oral arguments held on August 23, 1989, Universal conceded that, but for the arguments raised in its motion for summary judgment, Atlantic is entitled to summary judgment on the issue of liability. Consequently, as the court has already determined that Atlantic has properly brought this action against Universal and Universal's motion for summary judgment must therefore be denied, Atlantic's motion for partial summary judgment must be granted.

Conclusion

For the foregoing reasons defendant's motion for summary judgment is hereby DENIED and plaintiff's motion for partial summary judgment is hereby GRANTED. [Footnotes omitted.]

NEW YORK PUBLIC INTEREST RESEARCH GROUP, INC. v. LIMCO MANUFACTURING CORP.

697 F. Supp. 608 (E.D.N.Y. 1987)

New York Public Interest Research Group, Inc. ("NYPIRG"), a not-for-profit corporation, The Coalition to Save Hempstead Harbor, Inc. ("Coalition"), a membership corporation, and Paul Thurman, Patti Conti, Elizabeth Weinstein, Patti Ringrose and Louise Tripoli, members of the Coalition, instituted this action against Limco Manufacturing Corporation ("Limco") claiming that Limco has, since April 27, 1984, violated regulations promulgated by the Administrator of the United States Environmental Protection Agency ("EPA") pursuant to Section 307(b) of the Federal Water Pollution Control Act ("the Act"), as amended, 33 U.S.C. §1317(b).

Limco is engaged in the business of electroplating various metals onto a base material. In its electroplating operations it discharges more than 10,000 gallons of wastewater into a Publicly Owned Treatment Works ("POTW") which is owned and operated by the City of Glen Cove. The claim alleges that Limco failed to comply with the pretreatment standards established by the regulations in the Act. The complaint seeks an injunction, civil penalties, attorney's fees and costs.

Limco moves to dismiss the complaint, on the following grounds:

> 1. The instant action is barred by §1365(b) (1) of the Act, in that on or about August 7, 1987, the City of Glen Cove commenced an action in the New York State Supreme Court which seeks compliance with the standards established in the Act. On or about July 21, 1987, the City of Glen Cove commenced a criminal proceeding in the City Court of the City of Glen Cove charging "Violation of Sewer Use Ordinance—Pretreatment Permit Requirements." The instant action was started on August 13, 1987 with the filing of a complaint.
>
> 2. Limco as a "metal finisher" must comply with the standard set forth in 40 C.F.R. §433 and not 40 C.F.R. §413 as charged in paragraph 26 of the complaint.
>
> 3. Plaintiffs lack standing. The argument is based on the manner in which the waters are discharged, first into the POTW. Plaintiffs cannot show that the water Limco discharges enters Hempstead Harbor or Long Island Sound and therefore cannot show injury.

Alternatively, Limco moves to stay this action until final determination of the civil action and criminal proceeding in the state courts. Limco also moves to stay pre-trial discovery pending the outcome of its motion to dismiss.

THE PENDENCY OF A CIVIL ACTION AND CROMINAL PROCEEDING

Limco does not challenge the allegation that plaintiffs gave notice of the alleged violation to the Administrator for New York State and to Limco as a prerequisite to instituting suit as required under §1365(b)(1)(A). Limco's position is that the EPA approved the City's Industrial Pretreatment Program (Exhibit B appended to motion) and recognized the City's authority to enforce "national pretreatment standards for certain industries which discharge into [the City's] municipal sewerage system." (Exhibit C). Limco claims support for its position in that the New York State Department of Environmental Conservation stated that it "finds that primary enforcement responsibility rests with the City of Glen Cove.... Hence, in this matter, the City of Glen Cove should be taking appropriate enforcement action for alleged pretreatment violations within its sewage treatment system." (Exhibit O). Limco argues that the institution of a civil action and criminal proceeding was an exercise of the City of Glen Cove's "authority, as delegated by the Federal and State governments...." (Memo p.9).

We note that §1362 defines the terms "State water pollution control agency," "State" and "municipality," when those terms are "used in this Act." As defined, "State" does not include "municipality." Congress designated the Administrator and the State to be the central enforcement arm under the Act. *See Hamker v. Diamond Shamrock Chemical Co.,* 756 F.2d 392, 395 (5th Cir. 1985). "The private enforcement action, on the other hand, is supplementary to the scheme of the statute overall." *Sierra Club v. Shell Oil Co.,* 817 F.2d 1169, 1175 (5th Cir. 1987). The Second

Circuit Court of Appeals in *Friends of the Earth v. Consolidated Rail Corp.,* 768 F.2d 57, 63 (2d Cir. 1985) defined the right of a private citizen to enforce the requirements of the Act and his or her subordination of that right to the Administrator and State. While recognizing the disruptive effect of unlimited public actions it also saw such citizens as "welcomed participants."

To permit a municipality or any state agency not specifically authorized to bring an action to enforce the Act's standards to substitute for the Administrator and the State would seriously impair the role that Congress designed for citizens.

We hold that the actions commenced by the City do not bar the instant citizens' action....

STANDING

The complaint alleges that members of NYPIRG reside or own property in or near portions of Hempstead Harbor and Long Island Sound and that Limco's discharge into those waters "directly affects the health, economic, recreational, aesthetic and environmental interests and well-being of NYPIRG's members." (Complaint at para. 7). The complaint alleges that "Plaintiffs Paul Thurman and Patty Conti each live within one mile of the Glen Cove Treatment Plant and Hempstead Harbor. Both are avid boaters and use Hempstead Harbor for this purpose." (Complaint at para. 8).

The authorization of citizens' suits under §1365 is limited to "a person or persons having an interest which is or may be adversely affected." §1365(g).

The Court in *Sierra Club v. Morton,* 405 U.S. 727, 734-35, 92 S.Ct. 1361, 1366, 31 L.Ed.2d 636 (1972) held:

> Aesthetic and environmental well-being, like economic well-being, are important ingredients of the quality of life in our society, and the fact that particular environmental interests are shared by the many rather than the few does not make them less deserving of legal protection through the judicial process. But the "injury in fact" test requires more than an injury to a cognizable interest. It requires that the party seeking review be himself among the injured.

See also Friends of the Earth, 768 F.2d at 60-61.

Some of the plaintiffs are property owners. The depreciation in property values resulting from the inability to use Hempstead Harbor and the Long Island Sound, because of the discharge, to the same extent as if the waters were clear, is "injury to a cognizable interest." Plaintiffs allege more. They claim damage to aesthetic, conservational and recreational values.

The further argument for lack of standing is that "Plaintiffs have not and cannot allege that Limco discharged into Hempstead Harbor or Long Island Sound, which are presumably the real areas of their interest." (Memo at p.12). "Plaintiffs have not and cannot establish a connection between defendant's alleged violations and the pollution in Hempstead Harbor or Long Island Sound." (Reply Memo at p. 13-14).

The simple answer to the challenge is that the complaint (at paras. 7 & 9) alleges that "Hempstead Harbor and the Long Island Sound ... are affected by defendant's discharge of pollutants" and that the discharge "affects the health, economic, recreational, aesthetic and environmental interests and well-being" of plaintiffs.

Assuming as we must the truth of the allegations of the complaint in a Rule 12(b) motion, Limco's challenge to standing is rejected.

REQUEST FOR A STAY

We reject Limco's application to stay the instant action pending the outcome of the state court proceedings. Congress conferred jurisdiction on the U.S. district courts to enforce effluent standards and limitations established under the Act, §1365(a). We have the obligation to exercise the jurisdiction conferred. *See Moses H. Cone Memorial Hosp. v. Mercury Construction Corp.*, 460 U.S. 1, 14, 103 S.Ct. 927, 936, 74 L.Ed.2d 765 (1983). We recognize that the prior institution of suit in the state court is a factor favoring abstention. But the issue should not be resolved by that factor alone—particularly in view of the fact that statutory notice given by plaintiffs to the Administrator, State and Limco predated the commencement of the state court proceedings. The plaintiffs' claim in the instant action goes back further in time and charges more violations than the state civil action or state criminal charge.

ORDER

The motion of the defendant Limco Manufacturing Corp. to dismiss the complaint pursuant to Rule 12(b) or alternatively stay the action is in all respects denied.

The motion of the defendant Limco Manufacturing Corp. to stay discovery is in all respects denied.

SO ORDERED. [Footnotes omitted.]

See also *Ohio Public Interest Research Group v. Laidlaw Environmental Services, Inc.*, 963 F.Supp. 635 (S.D.Ohio 1996).

CONNECTICUT FUND FOR THE ENVIRONMENT v. THE JOB PLATING COMPANY, INC.

623 F. Supp. 207 (D.Conn. 1985)

This is a citizen suit under the federal Clean Water Act against the operator of an electroplating plant that concededly discharges pollutants into the Quinnipiac River. The suit was brought against the Job Plating Company of Plainville, Connecticut, by the Connecticut Fund for the Environment and the Natural Resources Defense Council.

The environmental organizations contend that Job Plating violated the Clean Water Act on 174 occasions by discharging effluents in excess of the amount permitted by its National Pollutant Discharge Elimination System permit. The plaintiffs seek a declaratory judgment that Job Plating has violated the Clean Water Act, an injunction to prevent further violations, and civil penalties of up to $10,000 per violation payable to the United States Treasury. They also seek costs and attorneys' fees.

Job Plating does not deny that it has exceeded the discharge levels authorized by its NPDES permit. However, the company asserts that this action should nonetheless be dismissed for any of five reasons. The court finds none of these arguments to be persuasive.

First, Job Plating contends that the suit was not brought within the applicable statute of limitations. The court finds, however, that the action is governed by the five-year statute of limitations applicable to government suits under the Clean Water Act rather than by the shorter statute of limitations that would be provided by state law. Accordingly, the action is timely.

Second, Job Plating asserts that penalties for past violations cannot be recovered in citizen suits under the Clean Water Act. The court finds that, while private damages may not be recoverable under the Act, civil penalties (including fines) may be obtained on behalf of the United States.

Third, Job Plating argues that the court, in an exercise of its discretion, should defer in this matter to the Connecticut Department of Environmental Protection. However, the court finds that no such deference is called for where, as here, the suit does not raise complex issues of fact that are peculiarly within the agency's expertise.

Fourth, Job Plating contends that the action should be dismissed because, under the Clean Water Act, a citizen suit is precluded by a state's "diligent prosecution" of the same matter. The court finds that there was no "diligent prosecution" in this case, however, because the state's suit against Job Plating was initiated only after the citizen suit.

Finally, Job Plating argues that its NPDES permit is unenforceable because it was not properly promulgated. The court, noting that Job Plating failed to take advantage of earlier opportunities to challenge its permit, holds that the validity of the permit cannot be raised in this action.

Accordingly, the court finds that Job Plating is liable to the plaintiffs for violation of the Clean Water Act. The court defers a decision with respect to the relief that ought to be granted as a result of this ruling.

This action, a citizen suit brought pursuant to Section 505 of the Clean Water Act ("Act"), 33 U.S.C. §1365, was commenced on November 17, 1983. The plaintiffs are environmental organizations some of whose members meet the standing requirements established for citizen suits pursuant to Article III of the United States Constitution and 33 U.S.C. §1365. *See* Endorsement Ruling (entered Mar. 28, 1985) on Defendant's Motion for Judgment on the Pleadings (filed Dec. 28, 1984); Certified Official Transcript of Oral Ruling delivered at a Hearing Held on November 19, 1984 (filed Nov. 26, 1984) (discussion of standing requirements in the context of this case); *Sierra Club v. SCM Corporation*, 747 F.2d 99, 103-107 (2d Cir. 1984) (standard for standing for citizen suits brought under 33 U.S.C. §1365); *Friends of the Earth v. Consolidated Rail Corp.*, 768 F.2d 57, slip op. 5201, 5209-5210 (2d Cir. 1985) (recent case applying *Sierra Club v. SCM Corporation* standard for standing and upholding standing in conditions similar to this case). The defendant is a Connecticut corporation that operates an electroplating plant in Plainville, Connecticut, and concededly discharges effluents into the Quinnipiac River.

The plaintiffs allege that the defendant violated its National Pollutant Discharge Elimination System ("NPDES") permit, *see* 33 U.S.C. §1342(a), (b) (authorizing state issuance of NPDES permits pursuant to approval of the state's program by the Administrator of the federal Environmental Protection Agency ["EPA"]). Specifically, the plaintiffs contend, based on the Discharge Monitoring Reports ("DMRs") that the defendant is required to file by law, that the defendant exceeded the permissible discharge allowed under its NDPES permit on 174 occasions. See 33 U.S.C. §1318; 40 C.F.R. §122.41(j); Plaintiffs' Statement Pursuant to [Local] Rule 9[c] in Support of Their Motion for Summary Judgment ("Plaintiffs' Statement"), para. 4, Exhibit D attached to Notice of Motion (filed Mar. 2, 1984). The plaintiffs seek declaratory relief with respect to the defendant's alleged past violations of its NPDES permit, injunctive relief preventing future violations, civil penalties of up to $10,000 per violation payable to the United States pursuant to 33 U.S.C. §§1319(d), 1365(a), and costs and attorney's fees pursuant to 33 U.S.C. §1365(d).

On March 2, 1984, the plaintiffs filed a motion for partial summary judgment accompanied by a statement of undisputed facts, exhibits, an affidavit and a memorandum of law. On May 11, 1984, the defendant filed a memorandum in opposition to plaintiffs' motion. The defendant filed a motion to dismiss accompanied by exhibits, an affidavit and a memorandum of law. Each of the parties thereafter filed several additional papers concerning the outstanding motions. On November 19, 1984 (after the transfer of this case to me), oral argument was held on the pending motions. The motion for partial summary judgment and motion to dismiss became ripe for decision as of March 28, 1985, the date on which the plaintiffs' standing was upheld.

II

The following material facts are undisputed:

1. On February 23, 1976, the Connecticut Department of Environmental Protection (DEP) issued NPDES permit number CT0022284 to the defendant. The permit was reissued on March 23, 1978. *See* Plaintiffs' Statement, para. 3 and Exhibit A (NPDES permits).

2. The defendant is required by its NDPES permit to file monthly DMRs. These reports indicate whether the defendant, on the basis of the results of specific tests, is in compliance with its permit. *See* Plaintiffs' Statement, para. 4; Exhibit D *attached to* Plaintiffs' Statement (copies of DMRs).

3. The defendant reported in its DMRs that, between May 1978 and November 17, 1983, it had on 174 occasions discharged substances in excess of the amounts allowed by its permit. *See* Plaintiffs' Statement, para. 5.

4. On September 9, 1983, the plaintiffs sent a Notice of Intent to Sue to the Administrator of EPA, DEP and the defendant pursuant to 33 U.S.C. §1365(b)(1)(A). *See* Affidavit of Alfred J. Mastriani (executed May 8, 1984) ("Mastriani Aff."), para. 7, Ex. B.

5. Neither the EPA nor the DEP had filed any action against the defendant as of November 17, 1983, the date this action was filed. *See* Mastriani Aff., paras. 8-10.

6. On December 9, 1983, the Commissioner of DEP issued an Order to Abate Pollution, No. 3639 to the defendant. Mastriani Aff. para. 9, Ex. C.

7. On February 9, 1984, Mike Harder, Senior Sanitary Engineer for the Water Compliance Unit, DEP, sent a letter to the defendant that stated that the defendant was in violation of DEP's Abatement Order and that the matter had been referred to the Attorney General's Office for further action. *See* Mastriani Aff. para. 10, Ex. D.

8. The plaintiffs have never contacted the defendant and requested that they be permitted to join in negotiations with the DEP and the defendant, nor have they been denied the opportunity to so join in. *See* Mastriani Aff., para. 11.

9. On March 19, 1984 the State of Connecticut, through DEP, instituted a civil action in the Connecticut Superior Court against the defendant to enforce Abatement Order No. 3639. *See* Mastriani Aff., Ex. E (copy of complaint). The defendant was served with the Summons and Complaint on March 23, 1984, and counsel filed an appearance on April 3, 1984 on behalf of the defendant. On April 6, 1984, the plaintiffs' counsel was informed by the defendant's attorney of the suit by DEP. *See* Mastriani Aff., para. 13.

10. The state's suit in the Connecticut Superior Court seeks enforcement of Order No. 3639, issued on December 9, 1983, requiring submission of an engineering report and subsequent placement of approved waste water treatment facilities in operation by May 31, 1984; the instant citizen suit seeks penalties for violation of effluent limitations set forth in NPDES Permit No. CT0022284, and an injunction against future violations of the permit limits. *See* Affidavit of Richard F. Webb (executed June 19, 1985) ("Webb Aff."), para. 2(c).

11. The state's suit has been resolved, with no penalties assessed against the defendant and the filing of a Stipulated Judgment in the Superior Court on June 6, 1984. *See* Webb Aff., para. 2(c), Attachment (Stipulated Judgment).

III

The defendant raises five arguments in favor of its motion to dismiss and in opposition to the plaintiffs' motion for summary judgment: (1) that this action is barred by the applicable statute of limitations; (2) that 33 U.S.C. §1365 precludes retrospective relief in citizen suits; (3) that the DEP has primary jurisdiction over this lawsuit; (4) that the court does not have jurisdiction over this lawsuit because the state has diligently prosecuted an action against the defendant within the meaning of Section 1365(b)(1)(B), which makes the lack of such prosecution a prerequisite for a citizen suit; and (5) that the defendant's NPDES permit is invalid because it was not properly promulgated and therefore cannot be enforced against the defendant. If the defendant fails to prevail on at least one of these arguments, partial summary judgment on the issue of liability must enter in favor of the plaintiffs. *See* Section IV, *infra*. Each of these arguments shall be addressed *seriatim*.

A. STATUTE OF LIMITATIONS

The Act provides no statute of limitations for actions brought under it. The defendant argues that state law should supply the applicable statute of limitations for state-promulgated NPDES permits. *See* Memorandum of Law in Support of Motion to Dismiss (filed May 11, 1984) ("Defendant's Memorandum I") at 21-23; Defendant's Job Plating Company, Inc. Supplemental Memorandum of Law in Support of Motion to Dismiss (filed Sept. 19, 1984) ("Defendant's Memorandum III") at 1-3. In this case, the defendant contends that the applicable statute of limitations is one year pursuant to Conn. Gen. Stat. §52-585 (civil penalty actions), or three years under the statute governing nuisance actions. *See* Defendant's Memorandum I at 22-23; Defendant's Memorandum III at 3. The defendant maintains that the federal five-year statute of limitations applicable to civil penalty actions, 28 U.S.C. §2462, does not apply to citizen suits under the Act because that statute covers only actions brought on behalf of the United States; Section 1365(a) refers to "citizen actions" as brought on the "[citizen's] behalf[.]" Defendant's Memorandum I at 21-22; Defendant's Memorandum III at 1-2.

The plaintiffs, citing cases on point, claim either that the five-year limitations period of 28 U.S.C. §2462 uniformly should apply to citizen (and government) suits under the Act or that no statute of limitations is applicable to citizen suits. *See* Plaintiffs' Memorandum in Opposition to Defendant's Motion to Dismiss and Response to Defendant's Opposition to Plaintiffs' Motion for Summary Judgment (filed June 21, 1984) ("Plaintiffs' Memorandum II") at 11-13; Plaintiffs' Supplemental Memorandum on Statutes of Limitations (filed Oct. 12, 1984) ("Plaintiffs' Memorandum III") at 1-6; Memorandum of Law and Index of Cases (filed June 19, 1985) ("Plaintiffs' Memorandum IV") at 2.

Our Court of Appeals recently has held that

> when Congress creates a federal cause of action but does not expressly provide an applicable statute of limitations, [it is to be] assume[d] that Congress intended the courts to adopt the limitation period of an analogous cause of action ... and "resort to state law remains the norm for borrowing of limitations periods." ... But where the application of a state statute of limitations would "frustrate or interfere with the implementation of national policies" or "be inconsistent with the underlying policies of the federal statute," courts should borrow a timeliness rule from federal law.

Monarch Long Beach Corp. v. Soft Drink Workers, Local 812, International Brotherhood of Teamsters, 762 F.2d 228, 230 (2d Cir. 1985) ("*Soft Drink Workers*") (emphasis supplied) (citations omitted).

The defendant has not drawn to the court's attention any case in which a court has applied a state statute of limitations to a citizen suit under the Act. In contrast, several courts specifically have refused to apply state limitations periods because to do so would frustrate the federal policy of uniform enforcement of the Act. *See Chesapeake Bay Foundation v. Bethlehem Steel Corporation,* 608 F. Supp. 440, 446-450 (D. Md. 1985) ("*Chesapeake Bay I*"); *Student Public Interest Research Group of New Jersey, Inc. ("NJSPIRG") v. Tenneco Polymers,* 602 F. Supp. 1394, 1398-1399 (D.N.J. 1985) ("*NJSPIRG I*"); *NJSPIRG v. Monsanto Co.,* 600 F. Supp. 1474, 1477 (D.N.J. 1985) ("*NJSPIRG II*"); *Sierra Club v. Simkins Industries, Inc.,* 617 F. Supp. 1120, slip op. at 6-8 (D. Md. 1985).

The court concludes that application of the state statute of limitations to citizen suits under the Act is inappropriate, precisely for the reason noted by the Court of Appeals in *Soft Drink Workers. See Chesapeake Bay I, supra,* 608 F.Supp. at 446-450 (noting that application of a state statute of limitations to citizen suits would be inconsistent with the five-year statute of limitations available for similar suits seeking identical relief initiated by the federal government pursuant to the Act); *NJSPIRG I, supra* 602 F.Supp. at 1398-1399 (same).

Three of the cases that have dealt with the appropriate statute of limitations for citizen suits under the Act, including one in this Circuit, have applied the five-year limitations period of 28 U.S.C. §2462. *See Friends of the Earth v. Facet Enterprises, Inc.,* 618 F. Supp. 532, 22 Env't Rep. Cas. (BNA) 1143, 1145-1146 (W.D.N.Y. 1984) ("*Friends of the Earth*") (defendant argued for five-year limitations period under federal law or, in the alternative, a three-year period under state law; plaintiff argued for no statute of limitations); *Chesapeake Bay I, supra,* 608 F. Supp. at 449-

450; *Sierra Club v. Simkins Industries, Inc., supra,* slip op. at 6-8. Two others, *NJSPIRG I* and *NJSPIRG II,* found both state statutes of limitations and Section 2462 to be inapplicable and concluded that there is no statute of limitations for actions brought pursuant to the Act.

This court assumes without deciding that 28 U.S.C. §2462 is not directly applicable to citizen suits brought under the Act. *See Bertha Building Corp. v. National Theatres Corp.*, 269 F.2d 785, 788-789 (2d Cir. 1959) (Section 2462 applies only to actions brought on behalf of the United States and *qui tam* actions), *cert. denied,* 361 U.S. 960, 4 L.Ed.2d 542, 80 S.Ct. 585 (1960); *but cf. Friends of the Earth, supra,* 618 F.Supp. 532, 22 Env't.Rep.Cas. (BNA) at 1145-1146 (holding Section 2462 to be directly applicable to citizen suits under the Act). However, a citizen suit brought under the Act is closely analogous to an action brought under the same Act on behalf of the United States. *See Chesapeake Bay I, supra,* 608 F. Supp. at 449-450; *Soft Drink Workers, supra,* 762 F.2d at 230-232. Accordingly, the five-year statute of limitations period of Section 2462 ought to be applied in citizen suits brought pursuant to Section 1365.

B. PENALTIES FOR PAST VIOLATIONS

The defendant contends that 33 U.S.C. §1365(a) only permits prospective relief in citizen suits and, therefore, no remedy is available for past violations of an NPDES permit. Defendant's Memorandum I at 20-21. To support its position that only prospective (injunctive) relief for ongoing violations is appropriate, the defendant points to the language of Section 1365(a) that authorizes citizen suits against "any person ... who *is* alleged to be in violation [of an NPDES permit,]" *id.* (emphasis added), and invokes cases holding that *damages* are not available in citizen actions under Section 1365. *See Middlesex County Sewerage Authority v. National Sea Clammers,* 453 U.S. 1, 14, 17-18, 69 L.Ed.2d 435, 101 S.Ct. 2615 (1981); *City of Evansville, Indiana v. Kentucky Liquid Recycling,* 604 F.2d 1008, 1014 (7th Cir. 1979), *cert. denied,* 444 U.S. 1025, 100 S.Ct. 689, 62 L.Ed.2d 659 (1980). The plaintiffs, on the other hand, contend that, although damages may not be recoverable in citizen suits brought under Section 1365, liability and remedies (including fines) may be imposed on the defendant for past violations of NPDES permits. Plaintiffs' Memorandum II at 13-14; Plaintiffs' Memorandum IV at 5-7.

Every court but two that has considered this issue has ruled in favor of the plaintiffs' position for the reason that Section 1365 explicitly authorizes district courts "to apply any appropriate civil penalties under [33 U.S.C.] section 1319(d)" and because the remedies obtainable in citizen suits should be coextensive with those available in suits initiated by the federal government. *See Sierra Club v. Aluminum Company of America,* 585 F.Supp. 842, 853-854 (N.D.N.Y. 1984) (Miner, J.); *NJSPIRG II, supra,* 600 F.Supp. 1476-1477; *Sierra Club v. C.G. Manufacturing, Inc.*, 638 F.Supp. 492, slip op. at 3-6 (D.Mass. 1985) (Zobel, J.); *Chesapeake Bay Foundation, Inc. v. Gwaltney of Smithfield, Ltd.*, 611 F.Supp. 1542 (E.D.Va. 1985) (Merhige, J.) ("*Chesapeake Bay II*") slip op. at 3-6; *NJSPIRG v. Anchor Thread Company,* 22 Env't.Rep.Cas. (BNA) 1150, 1154 (D.N.J. 1984) ("*NJSPIRG III*"); *Sierra Club v. Raytheon Company*, 22 Env't.Rep.Cas. (BNA) 1050, 1053-1055 (D.Mass. 1984). *See also Friends of the Earth, supra,* 22 Env't Rep. Cas. (BNA) at 1146; *NJSPIRG v. Fritzsche, Dodge & Olcott, Inc.*, 759 F.2d 1131, 1138 (3d Cir. 1985) ("*NJSPIRG IV*"); *NJSPIRG I, supra,* 602 F. Supp. at 1399. *Accord, Illinois v. Outboard Marine, Inc.*, 680 F.2d 473, 480-481 (7th Cir. 1982) (Wisdom, J., sitting by designation).

The cases relied upon by the defendant only state the undisputed proposition that private damages are not recoverable by plaintiffs in citizen suits brought under Section 1365; in fact, those very cases refer to the availability of civil penalties for past violations in such suits. *See*

Middlesex County Sewerage Authority v. National Sea Clammers Association, supra, 453 U.S. at 14, n.25, 17-18, n.27; *City of Evansville, Indiana v. Kentucky Liquid Recycling, supra,* 604 F.2d at 1014, n.16. *See also NJSPIRG II, supra,* 600 F.Supp. at 1474 (noting distinction of cases cited by defendant); *Chesapeake Bay II, supra,* slip op. at 18-19 (same); *Sierra Club v. C.G. Manufacturing, Inc., supra,* at 3-6 (same).

Two cases contrary to the plaintiffs' position, *Hamker v. Diamond Shamrock Chemical Co.*, 756 F.2d 392, 395-399 (5th Cir. 1985) (*dicta* in case involving one-time discharge not subject to any permit); *Pawtuxet Cove Marina, Inc. v. Ciba-Geigy Corp.,* 21 Env't.Rep.Cas. (BNA) 1393 (D.R.I. 1984), are inapposite and unpersuasive. *See Chesapeake Bay II, supra,* slip op. at 15-18 (criticizing and distinguishing *Hamker v. Diamond Shamrock Chemical Co.* and *Pawtuxet Cove Marina, Inc. v. Ciba-Geigy Corp.*); *Sierra Club v. Simkins Industries, Inc., supra* slip op. at 22-23 (distinguishing *Hamker v. Diamond Shamrock Chemical Co.* on its facts).

Accordingly, the court finds that the plaintiffs in this action may obtain relief for the defendant's past violations of its NPDES permit.

C. PRIMARY JURISDICTION

The defendant contends that the doctrine of primary jurisdiction should cause the court, in an exercise of its discretion, to defer to DEP's abatement proceeding. *See* Defendant's Memorandum I at 17-19. The plaintiffs, on the other hand, argue that the doctrine of primary jurisdiction has no application to this case because of the absence of complex issues of fact with which the court is unfamiliar and with respect to which the agency arguably is expert. *See Far East Conference v. United States,* 342 U.S. 570, 574-575, 96 L.Ed. 576, 72 S.Ct. 492 (1952); *Skoller v. Blue Cross-Blue Shield of Greater New York,* 584 F.Supp. 288, 290 (S.D.N.Y. 1984) (Lasker, J.).

Assuming *arguendo* that the doctrine of primary jurisdiction may be applied to require a deference of some kind to state administrative agencies in matters treated by federal law, the factors that would lead the court to invoke that doctrine are not present in this case. The court is not faced with complex issues of fact, but rather with a straightforward enforcement action in which legal issues are presented. In fact, the drafters of Section 1365 unequivocally asserted that "enforcement of pollution regulations is not a technical matter beyond the competence of the courts." Senate Comm. on Public Works, Federal Water Pollution Control Act Amendments of 1972, S. Rep. No. 92-414, 92d Cong., 2d Sess., reprinted in 1972 U.S. Code Cong. & Ad. News 3668, 3747 (1972). *See Board of Education of the City School District of the City of New York v. Harris,* 622 F.2d 599, 606-607 (2d Cir. 1979) ("It is well established that the courts need not defer to an agency where the issue involved is a strictly legal one, involving neither the agency's particular expertise nor its fact finding prowess."), *cert. denied sub nom., Hufstedler v. Board of Education of the City School District of the City of New York,* 449 U.S. 1124, 67 L.Ed.2d 110, 101 S.Ct. 940 (1981).

A case relied upon by the defendant, *Montgomery Environmental Coalition Citizens Coordinating Committee on Friendship Heights v. Washington Suburban Sanitary Commission,* 197 U.S. App. D.C. 64, 607 F.2d 378, 381-382 (D.C. Cir. 1979), is clearly distinguishable on its facts. In that case, the relevant NPDES permit had yet to be promulgated by the administrative agency, and administrative proceedings were pending on technical issues concerning the permit. In contrast, in this case, the NPDES permit already has been issued by DEP and the plaintiffs seek only its enforcement in this action. To the extent that any proceedings before DEP are relevant to this case, they involve the issue of diligent prosecution discussed in Section III.D., *infra*.

The court concludes that the doctrine of primary jurisdiction does not prevent it from exercising jurisdiction over this action to enforce an NPDES permit.

D. DILIGENT POSECUTION

The defendant contends that the state, by bringing an abatement action against it in state court, was "diligently prosecuting" an action within the meaning of 33 U.S.C. §1365(b)(1)(B), and such purported diligent prosecution precludes a citizen suit pursuant to Section 1365(a). *See* Section 1365(b)(1)(B); Defendant's Memorandum I at 9-17. The plaintiffs maintain that a state proceeding brought several months after the commencement of this action and since concluded does not constitute "diligent prosecution" that would bar this action. Furthermore, the plaintiffs maintain that the state's action differed from this suit in important respects and that the state suit was intended to supplement, not preclude, this action. *See* Plaintiffs' Memorandum II at 3-5; Webb Aff.; Plaintiffs' Memorandum IV at 3-5.

On its face, the diligent prosecution provision of Section 1365(b)(1)(B) does not apply to a case in which the state did not take any enforcement action until *after* the citizen suit was filed. The language of Section 1365(b)(1)(B) (captioned "Notice"), to the effect that "no action *may be commenced* ... if the ... State *has commenced*" an action, clearly contemplates action *prior* to the filing of a citizen suit. Only where there has been such prior action is it possible to consider whether that action is "diligent prosecution" that would preclude the filing of the citizen suit. *See Sierra Club v. Simkins Industries, Inc., supra,* slip op. at 9 (state administrative action initiated *after* the filing of a citizen suit does not fall within the ambit of Section 1365(b)(1)(B)). *See also Friends of the Earth v. Consolidated Rail Corp., supra,* slip op. at 5213-5216 (Section 1365(b)(1)(B)'s language should be strictly construed).

Apart from *Sierra Club v. Simkins Industries, Inc., supra,* in which the state agency acted after the citizen suit had been filed in federal court, all the cases that have considered Section 1365(b)(1)(B)'s diligent prosecution provision (and the analogous provision of the Clean Air Act, 42 U.S.C §7604(b)(1)(B)) deal with enforcement actions that commenced (and usually culminated) *prior* to the institution of the citizen suit. *See Hudson River Sloop Clearwater, Inc. v. Consolidated Rail Corporation,* 591 F.Supp. 345, 346-353 (N.D.N.Y. 1984), *rev'd sub. nom, Friends of the Earth v. Consolidated Rail Corp., supra* (state administrative action is not "diligent prosecution" under Section 1365(b)(1)(B)); *Sierra Club v. SCM Corporation,* 572 F. Supp. 828, 829-831 (W.D.N.Y. 1983); *Love v. New York State Department of Environmental Conservation,* 529 F.Supp. 832, 843-844 (S.D.N.Y. 1981); *Gardeski v. Colonial Sand & Stone Company, Inc.,* 501 F.Supp. 1159, 1161-1168 (S.D.N.Y. 1980); *NJSPIRG IV, supra,* 759 F.2d at 1132-1139; *Baughman v. Bradford Coal Co.,* 592 F.2d 215, 216-219 (3d Cir.), *cert. denied,* 441 U.S. 961, 60 L.Ed.2d 1066, 99 S.Ct. 2406 (1979).

The court concludes that, in accordance with the unambiguous language of Section 1365(b)(1)(B), actions taken by the state after the filing of a citizen suit may not be considered as constituting "diligent prosecution" pursuant to that section.

E. VALIDITY OF NPDES PERMITS ISSUED BY DEP

The defendant's final argument goes to the very validity and enforceability of the NPDES permits issued by DEP. Specifically, the defendant contends that because certain "guidelines" that DEP used to set the effluent standards in the NPDES permit allegedly were not properly promulgated under the Uniform Administrative Procedure Act, Conn. Gen. Stat. §§ 4-177 to 4-182, the standards are not enforceable in this action. *See* Memorandum of Law in Support of Defendant's Motion in Opposition to Plaintiffs' Motion for Summary Judgment (filed May 11, 1984) ("Defendant's Memorandum II") at 5-12. The plaintiffs counter that an attack on the defendant's NPDES permit is inappropriate in this proceeding and that, in any case, the provisions of the NPDES permit are valid and enforceable. *See* Plaintiffs' Memorandum III at 5-11.

The defendant has failed to avail itself of two different fora in which it might have challenged its NPDES permit. First, the defendant did not commence an administrative challenge to the NPDES permit within 30 days of its issuance by DEP, as permitted by statute. *See* Conn. Gen. Stat. §§22a-430, 22a-436; *Water Resources Commissioner v. Connecticut Sand and Stone Corporation,* 170 Conn. 27, 31-32, 364 A.2d 208 (1975) (failure to pursue a timely administrative challenge to DEP order under predecessor statute precluded a subsequent challenge); *Costle v. Meadow Haven, Inc.,* 32 Conn.Supp. 121, 342 A.2d 373, 373-374 (Conn. Super. 1975) (same).

By failing to challenge its NPDES permit under state law at a time when its purported legal deficiency should have been as apparent to the defendant as it is now, the defendant is precluded from doing so in this action.

Second, the defendant could have filed an application for review (in the United States Court of Appeals), challenging EPA's approval of the state's allegedly invalid NPDES permit program. *See* 33 U.S.C. §1369(b)(1); *Peabody Coal Company v. Train,* 518 F.2d 940, 941-943 (6th Cir. 1975) (dismissal of challenge to state plan under Section 1369(b)(1) as untimely); *Sun Enterprises, Ltd. v. Train,* 532 F.2d 280, 290-291 (2d Cir. 1976) (same with respect to a federal permit, *see* note 8, *infra*).

This case is clearly distinguishable from *Sierra Club v. Indiana-Kentucky Electric Corporation,* 716 F.2d 1145, 1148-1151 (7th Cir. 1983), in which state environmental standards under the different procedures of the Clean Air Act were held to be unenforceable in a federal action because a state court had found that the standards had not been properly promulgated pursuant to state law. In contrast, in this case, there is no ruling by a state court that any NPDES permits issued by the DEP are invalid for procedural reasons. Furthermore, *Sierra Club v. Indiana-Kentucky Electric Corporation, supra,* 716 F.2d at 1150-1151, stands for the proposition that state courts are the preferred, if not the mandatory, forum in which to challenge a state's promulgation of environmental standards.

For the reasons stated above, the defendant may not raise the issue of the validity of its NPDES permit in this enforcement proceeding. *Cf. Adamo Wrecking Co. v. United States,* 434 U.S. 275, 287, 54 L. Ed. 2d 538, 98 S. Ct. 566 (1978) ("narrow inquiry" in criminal enforcement proceeding concerning violation of environmental standard does not include examination of the validity of the procedures used to promulgate that standard).

IV. SUMMARY JUDGMENT FOR PLAINTIFFS

Courts have granted summary judgment for plaintiffs in numerous citizen suits brought pursuant to Section 1365 on the issue of liability. The decisions in these cases were based on findings of strict liability derived from discharge data reported in defendants' DMRs that exceeded levels allowed by NPDES permits. *See, e.g., NJSPIRG I, supra,* 602 F. Supp. at 1399-1400, *NJSPIRG v. Fritzsche, Dodge & Olcott,* 579 F.Supp. 1528, 1528-1539 (D.N.J.), *aff'd, NJSPIRG IV, supra,* 759 F.2d at 1139; *NJSPIRG III, supra,* 22 Env't.Rep.Cas. (BNA) at 1151-1154; *Sierra Club v. Raytheon Co., supra,* 22 Env't Rep. Cas. (BNA) at 1051-1052, 1055; *Chesapeake Bay Foundation v. Gwaltney of Smithfield, Ltd.,* 611 F.Supp. 1542 (E.D.Va. 1984) (Merhige, J.); *Chesapeake Bay I, supra,* at 28-36; *Sierra Club v. Simkins Industries, Inc., supra,* at 12-15. It is undisputed that the defendant's DMRs show that the defendant violated the terms of its NPDES permit on at least 174 occasions. In these circumstances, the plaintiffs' Motion for Summary Judgment should be granted.

CONCLUSION

For the reasons stated above, the plaintiffs' Motion for Partial Summary Judgment is granted and the defendant's Motion to Dismiss is denied.

If the parties are unable to reach agreement by October 15, 1985 on the relief that ought to be granted as a result of this ruling, the parties shall file by that date proposed orders and memoranda with respect to the relief that would be appropriate in these circumstances. In preparing their papers on the issue of relief, the parties shall acquaint themselves with decisions by other district courts on the subject. *See, e.g., Chesapeake Bay II, supra,* slip op. at 19-48.

It is so ORDERED. [Footnotes omitted.]

See also *Long Island Soundkeeper Fund, Inc. v. New York City Dept. of Environmental Protection*, 27 F.Supp.2d 380 (E.D.N.Y. 1998).

SAVE OUR SOUND FISHERIES ASSOCIATION v. CALLAWAY

429 F. Supp. 1136 (D.R.I. 1977)

Plaintiff moves for an award of attorneys' fees and costs pursuant to the Federal Water Pollution Control Act of 1972 (FWPCA), 33 U.S.C. §1365(d) (Supp. 1976), and the Marine Protection, Research, and Sanctuaries Act of 1972 (MPRSA) 33 U.S.C. §1415(g)(4) (Supp. 1976).

The action giving rise to the motion was brought to enjoin defendants, the Secretary of the Army and the Chief of the Corps of Engineers of the United States Army, as well as a private corporation retained under government contract, from dumping dredged spoil at an ocean site off Rhode Island coastal waters without proper permits. An order issued enjoining further dumping in certain areas of those waters until such time as public hearings were held, and permits were issued and complied with. *See Save Our Sound Fisheries Association v. Callaway* (hereinafter *SOSF I*), 387 F.Supp. 292 (D.R.I. 1974). It is undisputed now that the said injunction prohibited defendants from dumping about 50,000 cubic yards of dredge material at a location where eight million cubic yards from the same project had already been dumped in previous years. The government has now complied with the court order. A hearing has been held, a new location adopted, and the dumping of material dredged from the Providence River project has continued without further objection from plaintiff.

JURISDICTION TO AWARD ATTORNEYS' FEES

Without specific authorization federal courts are not free to award attorneys' fees to prevailing parties except in certain narrow circumstances not relevant here. *See Alyeska Pipeline Service Co. v. Wilderness Society,* 421 U.S. 240, 44 L.Ed.2d 141, 95 S.Ct. 1612 (1975). However, Congress has passed an increasing number of remedial statutes which specifically provide for the award of attorneys' fees to litigants. *See e.g., id.,* at 260 n. 33. The possibility of such fees serves as an incentive for private parties to enforce provisions of various statutes deemed too important to be left to the limited enforcement resources of the Justice Department.

Both the FWPCA and the MPRSA grant federal courts jurisdiction over such "citizen suits," and provide in almost identical language for awards of attorneys' fees and costs. Defendants argue that since this Court has previously based jurisdiction over this matter on the Administrative Procedure Act, 5 U.S.C. §§701–706 (1967), and on 28 U.S.C. §1331 (1966), the citizen suit jurisdictional provisions, which authorize attorneys' fees, are inapplicable. In *SOSF I,* the Court stated:

> Jurisdiction having been properly premised on the APA, 5 U.S.C. §702, and on 28 U.S.C. §1331(a), this Court need not reach the question of the applicability of the "citizen suit" provisions of both the FWPCA, 33 U.S.C. §1365, and the MPRSA, 33 U.S.C. §1415(g).

387 F. Supp. at 298. *See also id.,* at 300 n.9.

The Court passed the question of jurisdiction grounded directly on FWPCA and MPRSA, although it was properly presented and fully briefed, because jurisdiction for the purposes of injunctive relief was properly grounded otherwise. The Court thus avoided the difficult jurisdictional questions posed in applying the requirements of 33 U.S.C. §1365 and §1415(g) to the facts of this case. Other courts have since followed this Court's lead. *See, e.g., Natural Resources Defense Council v. Callaway,* 524 F.2d 79, 83 (2nd Cir. 1975); *Natural Resources Defense Council v. Train,* 166 U.S. App. D.C. 312, 510 F.2d 692, 702 (1974); *State of Minnesota, Spannaus v. Callaway,* 401 F. Supp. 524 (D. Minn. 1975). None of these opinions, finding jurisdiction over FWPCA and MPRSA claims under 28 U.S.C. §1331, discussed the problems of awarding attorneys' fees, as provided by the FWPCA and MPRSA, when jurisdiction is thus acquired.

One possible approach, reading attorneys' fees provisions as applying to all suits brought to enforce the statutes, whether premised on the citizen suit provisions, §1365 and §1415(g), or otherwise, *i.e.*, §1331, is firmly foreclosed by the language of citizen suit provisions and their legislative history. Section 1365(d), for example, authorizes courts to award fees and costs "in issuing any final order in any action *brought pursuant to this section* [1365]" (emphasis added.) Had Congress wished to induce private enforcement of all of the FWPCA's provisions, it could easily have done so by changing "pursuant to this section [1365]" to "pursuant to this Act." The legislative history shows without doubt that Congress sought to induce citizen suits with awards of attorneys' fees to remedy only specified acts of polluters and the Administrator of the Environmental Protection Agency (hereinafter, the Administrator). Jurisdiction over suits challenging other actions, illegal under the statutes, is not available under the citizen suit provisions. *See* 33

U.S.C. §1365(a)(1)(A)–(B)(2); S. Rep. 92-414, 92nd Cong., 2nd Sess., reprinted in 1972 U.S. Code Cong. and Adm. News 3747. A savings clause makes possible suits under the Administrative Procedure Act and 28 U.S.C. §1331 to remedy a broad range of illegal actions under the FWPCA and MPRSA; but the normal American rule on attorneys' fees applies to such suits. *See* 33 U.S.C. § 1365(e); 33 U.S.C. §1415(g)(5). *See also Natural Resources Defense Council v. Train, supra,* at 699-701. *Cf. Citizens Ass'n of Georgetown v. Washington,* 175 U.S.App.D.C. 356, 535 F.2d 1318, 1320 (district court may not award fees where jurisdiction over claims arising under the Clean Air Act is based on 28 U.S.C. §1331 rather than on citizen suit provisions).

Plaintiffs contend that *SOSF I* did not dispositively reject jurisdiction premised on the citizen suit provisions of the FWPCA and MPRSA. The Court agrees. In *SOSF I,* there was no need to reach the difficult question of whether the formal notice requirements of §§1365 and 1415(g) are a strict jurisdictional bar on the maintenance of this suit under those provisions. *SOSF I, supra,* 387 F. Supp. at 298, 300 n.9. Because plaintiff's request for attorneys' fees can be granted only if such jurisdiction exists, such an inquiry is now necessary.

Both §§1365 and 1415(g) authorize citizen suits against limited categories of violations. Sixty-day notice of the alleged violation to the Administrator, the alleged violator, and the State in which the violation occurs (FWPCA), or the Secretary of the Army and the violator (MPRSA) is a prerequisite to the maintenance of such suits, with certain exceptions described *infra.* The suit at bar challenged violations of the FWPCA and MPRSA for which citizen suits are authorized. Therefore, an award of attorneys' fees is authorized only if the notice requirements were met or were inapplicable. Two basic theories have been advanced to justify the Court's holding that it has jurisdiction to award attorneys' fees in this case.

A. The 60-day notice requirement in §1365(b) does not apply to actions respecting violations of §§1316 or 1317(a). 33 U.S.C. §1365(b). Pointing to paragraph 8 of their amended complaint, plaintiffs argue that they have sought to remedy a violation of §1317(a). The Court rejects this argument. Paragraph 8 challenges illegal dumping; but section 1317(a)(5) does not prohibit illegal dumping. It merely directs the Administrator to designate categories of sources (including dumping of dredged material) to which effluent standards will apply. Violations of §1317(a) consist solely of the failure of the Administrator to issue and publish lists, categories, and standards. Substantive violation of those standards by polluters is not covered by § 1317(a), but rather by §1317(d). Thus, paragraph 8 does not allege a violation of §1317(a) justifying this Court's jurisdiction in the absence of 60 days notice of the violation to the necessary parties. Indeed, as of August 1973, there were as yet no relevant standards issued pursuant to §1317(a) for which paragraph 8 could have alleged a violation. *See NRDC v. Train,* __ F. Supp.__, 8 E.R.C. 2120 (D.D.C. Nos. 73-2153 *et seq.*, June 8, 1976).

B. Nor does paragraph 8 of plaintiff's amended complaint, *supra,* properly allege a violation of any portion of §1316 so as to fall within §1365(b)'s waiver of the 60-day notice requirement. Section 1316(e), the only arguably relevant subsection, provides:

After the effective date of standards of performance promulgated under this section, it shall be unlawful for any owner or operator of any new source to operate such source in violation of any standard of performance applicable to such source.

However, the only standards of performance to which the Court has been directed are those published at 38 *Fed. Reg.* 8725 and 12871 (April 5, 1973 and May 16, 1973). These regulations are entitled "Ocean Dumping," and are explicitly issued pursuant to title I of the MPRSA and §403(c) of the FWPCA (33 U.S.C. §1343(c)). Since these regulations are not promulgated under §1316, allegations that they have been violated cannot serve to authorize suit absent 60 days notice.

Because plaintiff's complaint does not properly allege violations of either §1316 or §1317(a), the Court concludes that plaintiff has not brought itself within the narrow exceptions to the 60-day notice requirement set forth in §1365(b).

B. Plaintiff also contends that the 60-day notice provision of §§1365(b) and 1415(g)(2) should be deemed either satisfied, or not jurisdictional, in the narrow circumstances presented here. For the reasons stated below, the Court agrees that the notice requirement must be considered satisfied. This finding serves to ground jurisdiction under citizen suit provisions of both the MPRSA, 33 U.S.C. §1415(g), and the FWPCA, 33 U.S.C. §1365.

The Court will refer interchangeably to the citizen suit provisions of the FWPCA and MPRSA, since the relevant provisions and the legislative history regarding these provisions are virtually identical.

Two major Congressional concerns regarding citizen suits stand out from the legislative history of §§1365 and 1415(g). First, Congress thought it vital to supplement administrative enforcement of the statutes with enforcement by citizen suits. Second, Congress put strong reliance on administrative enforcement, generally allowing citizen enforcement only after the Administrator had an opportunity to bring his powers of enforcement to bear on the polluter. *See e.g.,* S.Rep.No. 92-414, *supra,* 1972 U.S. Code Cong. and Adm. News 3747. *Cf. Natural Resources Defense Council v. Train, supra,* 510 F.2d at 723-730.

It is a necessary inference from the 60-day waiting period itself, and the legislative history, that Congress chose to foreclose the possibility of judicial relief to remedy some actions, wrongful under the Acts, which the Administrator could not or would not remedy himself within the 60-day period. It was for Congress, after weighing the competing advantages of immediate citizen enforcement, and enforcement by the orderly processes of the Administrator, to decide how the Acts were to be enforced. The choice Congress made was at least permissible. Certainly it is not the province of this Court to disregard that Congressional decision.

However, in requiring citizens to notify the Administrator (in the case of the FWPCA violations alleged here) and the Secretary of the Army (in the case of the MPRSA violations alleged here) of any violation 60 days prior to bringing suit, Congress was also aware that the requirements of these and other Acts made it virtually certain that alert citizens would always be given more than 60 days' notice of actions that might violate FWPCA or MPRSA, so that the statutory waiting period could be satisfied and court action commenced if necessary before the allegedly wrongful act would take place. Provisions of the National Environmental Policy Act of 1969 [NEPA], 42 U.S.C. §4321-47 (1973), and the permit systems required by FWPCA and MPRSA comprehensively insured that citizens would always be given advance warning of major federal actions which might damage the marine environment.

Specifically, the guidelines of the Council on Environmental Quality, implementing NEPA, provide that a draft Environmental Impact Statement (EIS), which must be prepared for each major federal action, must be available for public evaluation for a full ninety days before the contemplated action can proceed. Guidelines, Council on Environmental Quality, 36 Fed. Reg. 7724029 (April 23, 1971). The MPRSA requires notice and public hearing before the Corps of Engineers may transport and dump dredged material. 33 U.S.C. §1413. *See SOSF I, supra,* at 300-303. The FWPCA requires notice and public hearing before the Secretary of the Army, acting through the Chief of the Corps of Engineers, may issue permits for the discharge of dredged material into navigable waters. 33 U.S.C. §1344. *See SOSF I, supra,* at 304-307.

Had defendants complied with even one of these statutes, plaintiff would clearly have been able to satisfy the requirements of 40 CFR §135.3 (1973), §1365(b), and §1415(g) to the letter. It is undisputed that plaintiff had a long-standing concern in the project at issue, notifying the Corps of that concern as early as January 26, 1972, and requesting hearings on the proposed dredging and dumping. *See generally SOSF I, supra.*

Even leaving aside, for the moment, the permit requirements of the FWPCA and MPRSA, deliberately bypassed here, the CEQ guidelines gave plaintiff a clear expectation that the dredging contract could not be awarded by the Corps until at least a month after August 25, 1973, 90 days after filing of the *draft* EIS on May 25. And plaintiffs could reasonably expect further delay, since the Corps generally proceeded by issuing a separate notice-to-proceed letter some time after the awarding of the contract, contemplating commencement of the work within 30 days.

Nevertheless, as the Court found in *SOSF I*, defendants violated NEPA, FWPCA, and MPRSA, and awarded the contract on June 24, 1973. A notice-to-proceed letter followed on July 24. Plaintiff's counsel, unaware that the contract had been awarded, wrote on July 12 to the Corps, requesting information on the status of the project, and was notified by a letter dated July 23 (the day before the Corps issued the notice-to-proceed letter) that the contract had been awarded. Plaintiff thereupon on August 1 filed formal notice with the necessary parties, as required by §§1365(b) and 1415(g), and commenced this action on August 7.

In the face of these facts, the government contends that there is no jurisdiction under the citizen suit provisions because plaintiff failed to comply with the 60-day waiting period. Under the government's view of the case, although plaintiff would have been able to comply with the requisite notice precedent to filing a citizen suit had the Corps complied with NEPA, FWPCA, and MPRSA, the Corps' violation of these three important statutes effectively removed plaintiff's opportunity to maintain a citizen suit under the Acts, until the damage sought to be avoided would have been largely accomplished. This Court cannot sanction such a transparent attempt to undermine Congressional policies and intention. The government's view turns all three Acts on their heads. The Court does not believe that Congress wished the courts to interpret the jurisdictional provisions of §§1365(a) and 1415(g) in such a crabbed manner. The Court finds, in the narrow circumstances here presented, that plaintiff's expressed interest and concern about the dredging project, presented to the Corps as early as January 26, 1972, constructively satisfied the requirements of §§1365(a) and 1415(g).

The government contended vigorously at oral argument that *Commonwealth of Massachusetts v. United States Veterans Administration,* 541 F.2d 119 (1st Cir. 1976) (Coffin, C.J.) controls this case, citing it for the proposition that failure strictly to comply with the 60-day notice requirement defeats jurisdiction. However, far from supporting defendant's position, the First Circuit in that case expressly agreed that there could be "constructive compliance" with the notice requirement in certain circumstances. *Id.,* at 121-122. The Court believes that the instant case presents precisely the situation of constructive compliance adverted to by Chief Judge Coffin. The Court notes that at no time after suit commenced did the Secretary or the Administrator attempt to effect voluntary compliance in the spirit of the 60-day notice provision. Indeed, defendants' position throughout the case was not that it disagreed with a particular standard, or needed time to meet a particular standard—the classic situations where the 60-day administrative period may be efficacious—but rather that it did not need to comply with either Act at all. Both the Corps and the Administrator had far longer than 60 days to reach such an important (and mistaken) policy judgment.

Far from bypassing administrative procedures itself, plaintiff's complaint is precisely that the government agency-defendants had bypassed those procedures. Based on its knowledge of defendant's contentions during this lawsuit, the Court concludes that an attempt by plaintiff to seek administrative enforcement when it uncovered the fact that dredging was about to begin would indeed have been futile. This futility was guaranteed by defendant's own prior statements and actions making clear that, in their opinion, they were not bound by NEPA, FWPCA, or MPRSA.

For these reasons, plaintiff's suit is maintainable under the citizen suit provisions of §§1365 and 1415(g). The Court must next determine whether an award of fees is appropriate. *See* 33 U.S.C. §1365(d); 33 U.S.C. §1415(g)(4).

APPROPRIATENESS OF A FEE

Defendants contend that the direction of §§1365(d) and 1415(g)(4) to award attorneys' fees "whenever the Court determines such award is appropriate" imposes on the courts a duty to balance a number of factors to determine whether a fee should be awarded or not, including, *inter alia,* whether the suit implements a strong public policy, the number of persons benefitting from the suit, and the relative economic position of the parties. This position is without merit.

As plaintiff correctly observes, all of the authority cited by defendants in support of their position relates to the propriety of awarding fees in the absence of an authorizing statute. *See, e.g., Harrisburg Coalition Against Ruining the Environment v. Volpe,* 381 F.Supp. 893 (M.D. Penn. 1974). Such authority is inapposite to the case at hand. Although Congress has directed the Courts to award fees "as appropriate," the courts do not have the unfettered equitable discretion which courts drew upon under the now rejected equitable private attorney general theory. As the Supreme Court observed in *Alyeska, supra,*

> Under this scheme of things, it is apparent that the circumstances under which attorneys' fees are to be awarded and the range of discretion of the courts in making those awards are matters for Congress to determine.

421 U.S. at 262.

In a similar situation, where Congress passed a remedial program and provided for enforcement in large measure through citizen enforcement, without the possibility of damages, the Supreme Court has ruled that the Congressional intention was that fees were to be awarded unless plaintiffs acted in bad faith, or litigated vexatiously. *Newman v. Piggie Park Enterprises,* 390 U.S. 400, 19 L.Ed.2d 1263, 88 S.Ct. 964 (1968) (per curiam). *Newman* is strong authority for this Court's holding that both the FWPCA and MPRSA contemplate the award of fees absent exceptional circumstances as detailed in *Newman, supra.* As the Supreme Court said in *Newman*:

> When the Civil Rights Act of 1964 was passed, it was evident that enforcement would prove difficult and that the Nation would have to rely in part upon private litigation as a

> means of securing broad compliance with the law. A Title II suit is thus private in form only. When a plaintiff brings an action under that Title, he cannot recover damages. If he obtains an injunction, he does so not for himself alone but also as a "private attorney general," vindicating a policy that Congress considered of the highest priority. If successful plaintiffs were routinely forced to bear their own attorneys' fees, few aggrieved parties would be in a position to advance the public interest by invoking the injunctive powers of the federal courts. Congress therefore enacted the provision for counsel fees—not simply to penalize litigants who deliberately advance arguments they know to be untenable but, more broadly, to encourage individuals injured by racial discrimination to seek judicial relief under Title II.
>
> It follows that one who succeeds in obtaining an injunction under that Title should ordinarily recover an attorney's fee unless special circumstances would render such an award unjust.

Id. at 402 (footnotes omitted.)

The legislative history of both the FWPCA and MPRSA also amply support this holding. *See* S. Rep. No. 92-411, *supra,* 1972 U.S. Code Cong. and Adm. News 3747 (FWPCA); S. Rep. No. 92-451, 92nd Cong., 2nd Sess., 1972 U.S. Code Cong. and Adm. News 4249-50 (MPRSA). *Cf. Natural Resources Defense Council v. Train, supra,* 524 F.2d at 723-730 (extracts of the congressional debate regarding attorneys' fees awards under the Clean Air Act.) The Court therefore holds, for the above reasons, that a fee award is appropriate. *Cf. Natural Resources Defense Council v. Environmental Protection Agency,* 484 F.2d 1331 (1st Cir. 1973) (hereinafter *NRDC v. EPA*).

THE SIZE OF THE FEE

In *Natural Resources Defense Council v. Environmental Protection Agency, supra,* the First Circuit granted an award of attorneys' fees to the NRDC pursuant to statutory authorization of the Clean Air Act. The court seemed to hold that the fee should be set at less than the prevailing rate:

> As the government has not addressed in detail the question of the reasonableness of petitioners' requested sum, we now ask the parties to submit memoranda on that question. We will scrutinize carefully the requested costs and fees. Petitioners are not a public agency and are legally responsible to no one but themselves; we must satisfy ourselves that the taxpayers' money will not be used to support needless or excessive legal items. We must also recognize that petitioners, as surrogate attorneys for the interests of the public and the EPA, have volunteered and 'imposed' their services on 'clients' that never contracted for them. As attorneys for involuntary clients, their fees may properly be less than those they could have received by entering the marketplace and selling their services to the private client who would make the highest bid for them. 484 F.2d at 1339.

Although defendant has not suggested that this Court is bound by that holding, the Court believes it is appropriate to set forth the reasons why it does not consider this First Circuit decision controlling in the present case.

On October 19, 1976, President Ford signed into law S. 2278, providing for the award of attorneys' fees in the court's discretion, in certain civil rights actions. 42 U.S.C. §1988, reprinted in 20

Crim.L.Rep. 2092 (October 27, 1976). The legislative history of the new provision details the Congressional concern with citizen enforcement of the civil rights statutes, and specifies four cases which it felt adequately found and applied the standards Congress wished to govern the award of attorneys' fees. These cases reject the position taken by the First Circuit in the attorneys' fees cases it has decided, *e.g., Souza v. Travisono*, 512 F.2d 1137 (1st Cir. 1975); *NRDC v. EPA, supra,* and rely instead on the decision of the Fifth Circuit in *Johnson v. Georgia Highway Express,* 488 F.2d 714 (5th Cir. 1974). Under the Fifth Circuit's approach, now approved by the Congress, fees are to be competitive with the prevailing rates in a community. As the Senate Report states,

> It is intended that the amount of fees awarded under S. 2278 be governed by the same standards which prevail in other types of equally complex Federal litigation, such as antitrust cases and not be reduced because the rights involved may be nonpecuniary in nature. The appropriate standards, see *Johnson v. Georgia Highway Express,* 488 F.2d 714 (5th Cir. 1974), are correctly applied in such cases as *Stanford Daily v. Zurcher,* 64 F.R.D. 680 (N.D. Cal. 1974); *Davis v. County of Los Angeles,* 8 E.P.D. P 9444 (C.D. Cal. 1974); and *Swann v. Charlotte-Mecklenburg Board of Education,* 66 F.R.D. 483 (W.D.N.C. 1975). These cases have resulted in fees which are adequate to attract competent counsel, but which do not produce windfalls to attorneys. In computing the fee, counsel for prevailing parties should be paid, as is traditional with attorneys compensated by a fee-paying client, "for all time reasonably expended on a matter." *Davis, supra; Stanford Daily, supra,* at 684.

S. Rep. No. 94-1011, 94th Cong., 2d Sess. (1976), at 6.

Careful study of Senate Report No. 94-1011, *supra, Newman, Alyeska,* and the legislative history of the FWPCA and MPRSA convinces this Court that there is no principled distinction which would justify attributing to Congress an intention that fees be reduced in environmental cases, but not in civil rights cases. The Congressional interest in enforcement, exemplified by provision for citizen suits, is strong in both cases. The Supreme Court has agreed that the standards for fees are to be governed by seeking out Congressional intention, not by the unbridled equitable discretion of the courts. Therefore, the Court is convinced that it should adopt a rule in line with congressional intention as specified in the legislative history of 42 U.S.C. §1988. The standards which govern the award of attorneys' fees in this case, under the FWPCA and MPRSA are those stated in *Johnson, supra,* and applied in the cases cited *supra.*

Should the parties be unable to agree as to either the correct fee per hour, or the number of hours for which plaintiff is entitled to be paid, the Court will hold a hearing at which plaintiff shall show, by competent evidence, the total fee to which it is entitled.

Plaintiff's motion for an award of attorneys' fees and costs is granted. [Footnotes omitted.]

PENNSYLVANIA ENVIRONMENTAL DEFENSE FOUNDATION v. BELLEFONTE BOROUGH

718 F. Supp. 431 (M.D.Pa. 1989)

I. INTRODUCTION

Pennsylvania Environmental Defense Foundation (the Foundation) commenced this citizen suit pursuant to 33 U.S.C. §1365 (which is §505 of the Clean Water Act, also known as the Federal Water Pollution Control Act, *see Gwaltney of Smithfield v. Chesapeake Bay Foundation, Inc.*, 484 U.S. 49, 108 S. Ct. 376, 378, 98 L. Ed. 2d 306 (1987)) by filing a complaint on June 27, 1988, in which it named as the sole Defendant Bellefonte Borough Sewage Authority. By order of July 5, 1988, we granted the Foundation's motion filed the same day to amend its complaint by changing the name of the Defendant from Bellefonte Borough Sewage Authority to Bellefonte Borough. The primary allegation made by the Foundation in its complaint is that Bellefonte Borough (Bellefonte) operates a sewage treatment plant in Centre County, Pennsylvania, that this plant discharges waste water into Spring Creek, and that the discharge from the plant has repeatedly violated the terms and provisions of its National Pollutant Discharge Elimination System permit by emptying more pollutants into Spring Creek than it was authorized so to do by its National Pollutant Discharge Elimination System permit.

On January 31, 1989, Bellefonte filed a motion to enter consent decree. The Foundation concurred in this motion. Bellefonte filed along with its motion to enter consent decree a copy of a proposed consent decree between the Foundation and Bellefonte and served a copy upon the Attorney General of the United States and the Administrator of the Environmental Protection Agency as required by 33 U.S.C. §1365(c)(3). On March 20, 1989, the United States filed "comments" with regard to the Foundation's and Bellefonte's proposed consent decree. We issued an order on March 24, 1989, setting forth a briefing schedule concerning (1) whether we should consider the comments filed by the United States regarding the proposed consent decree and (2) whether we should grant Bellefonte's motion to enter consent decree. On March 27, 1989, the Foundation filed a motion to preclude the comments of the United States to the proposed consent decree and a brief in support thereof. Bellefonte concurred in the Foundation's motion to preclude the comments of the United States to the proposed consent decree. On March 31, 1989, we issued an order setting forth a briefing schedule on the Foundation's motion to preclude the comments of the United States to the proposed consent decree. Briefing has been completed with regard to both Bellefonte's motion to enter consent decree and the Foundation's motion to preclude the comments of the United States to the proposed consent decree and both motions are ripe for disposition.

II. DISCUSSION

A. The Foundation's Motion to Preclude the Comments of the United States to the Proposed Consent Decree.

1. May we Consider the Comments Filed by the United States Regarding the Proposed Consent Decree in this Case.

The first issue we must resolve in ruling upon the Foundation's motion to preclude the comments of the United States to the proposed consent decree is whether we may consider the United States' comments. Section 1365(c) of 33 U.S.C. provides in pertinent part as follows:

> (2) In such action under this section, the Administrator [of the Environmental Protection Agency], if not a party, may intervene as a matter of right.
>
> (3) Protection of Interests of United States
>
> Whenever any action is brought under this section in a court of the United States, the plaintiff shall serve a copy of the complaint on the Attorney General and the Administrator. No consent judgment shall be entered in an action in which the United States is not a party prior to 45 days following the receipt of a copy of the proposed consent judgment by the Attorney General and the Administrator.

The Foundation argues that the above-quoted portions of 33 U.S.C. §1365(c) do not specifically authorize the United States to file comments regarding a proposed consent decree in a case in which the United States is not a party without first becoming a party to the action. The Foundation further asserts that the purpose of the 45-day notice provision in 33 U.S.C. §1365(c)(3) is to give the Administrator of the Environmental Protection Agency an opportunity to intervene in the action pursuant to 33 U.S.C. §1365(c)(2). Based upon (1) its view of the purpose of 33 U.S.C. §1365(c)(2) and (3), (2) its assertion that there is no indication that Congress intended to give the United States or any of its officials or agencies the "extra-judicial authority" to affect the outcome of citizen suits brought pursuant to the Clean Water Act without first becoming a party thereto, and (3) its claim that permitting the United States to comment on a judicial proceeding without it first becoming a party thereto deprives the parties of "their rights under the Federal Procedural Law," the Foundation maintains that we may not consider the United States' comments to the proposed consent decree in this case because neither the United States nor the Administrator of the Environmental Protection Agency has intervened.

The United States counters the Foundation's arguments by making the following assertions which demonstrate, it contends, that we may consider its comments: (1) Congress has charged the United States with primary responsibility for insuring that the Clean Water Act is properly enforced; (2) individuals or groups which bring citizen suits pursuant to the Clean Water Act are acting as private attorneys general and such citizen suits are meant to vindicate the public's health and welfare rather than private interests; (3) the United States could not possibly intervene in every citizen's suit brought pursuant to the Clean Water Act in order to insure that any consent decree was consistent with its interpretation of the relevant statutes; (4) filing comments regarding proposed consent decrees in citizen suits brought pursuant to the Clean Water Act is fully consistent with Congress' intent that the United States have primary responsibility for insuring that the Clean Water Act is properly enforced; and (5) its comments are in the nature of an *amicus curiae* brief.

The United States has the primary responsibility for insuring that the Clean Water Act is properly enforced. *See Gwaltney of Smithfield v. Chesapeake Bay Foundation, Inc.*, __U.S. at__, 108 S.Ct. at 383. Further, individuals or groups which bring citizen suits pursuant to the Clean Water Act are acting as private attorneys general and, accordingly, the purpose of such a suit is to protect and advance the public's interest in pollution-free waterways rather than to promote private interests. *See Middlesex County Sewerage Authority v. National Sea Clammers Association,* 453 U.S. 1, 16-17, 17 n.27, and 21, 69 L.Ed.2d 435, 101 S.Ct. 2615 (1981).

We are of the view that the United States' comments are in the nature of an *amicus* brief. District courts have broad discretion to appoint *amici curiae*. *Hoptowit v. Ray,* 682 F.2d 1237, 1260 (9th Cir. 1982). When an appeal is taken from a district court order and no party to the appeal supports the decision under review, the court of appeals may appoint an attorney as *amicus curiae* to defend the district court's decision, the purpose being to give the court of appeals the benefit of an adversarial presentation of the issue. See *United States v. Haldeman,* 181 U.S.App.D.C. 254, 559 F.2d 31, 138-139 (D.C.Cir. 1976), *cert. denied,* 431 U.S. 933, 53 L.Ed.2d 250, 97 S.Ct. 2641 (1977), *rehearing denied,* 433 U.S. 916, 97 S.Ct. 2992, 53 L.Ed.2d 1103 (1977). Were we not permitted to consider the United States' comments to the proposed consent decree in this case, we would be deprived of an adversarial presentation as to the propriety of approving the proposed consent decree. Because of the United States' role in enforcing the Clean Water Act, because of the proper goal of a citizen suit pursuant to the Clean Water Act and because of the absence of any statutory language which prohibits us from considering comments by the United States even though the United States is not a party to the action, we are of the view that, construing the United States' comments to be an *amicus* brief, we may consider such comments in ruling upon Bellefonte's motion to enter consent decree. Interestingly enough, in a case to which the Foundation refers for another proposition, that court considered the United States' comments to the proposed consent decree in deciding whether to approve the consent decree. *See Natural Resources Defense Council v. Interstate Paper Corp.,* 1988 U.S. Dist. Decision, No. 487-169 (S.D.Ga. 1988) (appended to the parties' response filed April 17, 1989, to the United States' comments).

2. Should We Consider the Comments Filed by the United States Regarding the Proposed Consent Decree.

Having decided that we may consider the comments filed by the United States concerning the proposed consent decree in this case, we must next decide whether we should exercise our discretion and in fact consider the United States' comments. As stated above, were we to not consider the United States' comments, there would be no adversarial presentation to the Court as to the propriety or wisdom of approving the proposed consent decree. Our judicial system is designed to function best when a Court is presented with opposing viewpoints concerning an issue which is before it for decision. Such an adversarial presentation is particularly helpful in a case such as this when the proposed consent decree at issue is meant to vindicate the interest of the public but when no real representative of the public is a party to the litigation. Whether to grant or deny a person leave to participate in a case as *amicus curiae* rests within our discretion. We consider whether the proffered information is timely and useful in making our decision. *See Leigh v. Engle,* 535 F.Supp. 418, 420 (N.D.Ill. 1982). We are of the view that the United States' comments are both timely and useful. We will consider the United States' comments in ruling upon Bellefonte's motion to enter consent decree.

BELLEFONTE'S MOTION TO ENTER THE CONSENT DECREE

The United States opposes our approving the proposed consent decree because the United States objects to the following two aspects of it: (1) the proposed consent decree does not require Bellefonte to pay any civil penalties to the United States and (2) the proposed consent decree requires Bellefonte to place $35,000.00 into an escrow account to be used by Trout Unlimited but there is, allegedly, no requirement that this money be used to mitigate the environmental harm caused or threatened by Bellefonte's alleged violations of the applicable federal pollution statute. Bellefonte responds to the United States' two concerns by stating the following: (1) the proposed consent decree filed for approval proposes to put money in escrow to be used by Trout Unlimited, an organization well acquainted with the needs of Bellefonte and Centre County, to better Spring Creek, the creek allegedly polluted by Bellefonte's sewage treatment plant; (2) early in Bellefonte's discussions with the Environmental Protection Agency, Bellefonte agreed to pay to the United States treasury a civil penalty of $60,000.00; (3) Bellefonte has never argued that it should not be subject to this penalty; and (4) the proposed consent decree now before the Court does not include a civil penalty to be paid to the United States because Bellefonte is concerned that any money paid to the United States pursuant to this decree might not be credited to Bellefonte when it enters into an expected consent decree with the Environmental Protection Agency which Bellefonte and the Environmental Protection Agency are in the process of working out. The Foundation responds as follows to the United States' two concerns with the proposed consent decree:

> Under the Consent Decree between P.E.D.F. and Bellefonte, money is being contributed by agreement to a reputable organization and is not being diverted from the U.S. Treasury. The money is going to the Spring Creek Chapter of Trout Unlimited with the requirement that the funds be spent on projects on Spring Creek that meet the goals of the Federal Clean Water Act.

The Foundation's and Bellefonte's response filed April 17, 1989, to the United States' comments at 15.

The United States Supreme Court in *Local No. 93, International Association of Firefighters v. City of Cleveland,* 478 U.S. 501, 106 S.Ct. 3063, 92 L.Ed.2d 405 (1986), discussed the role of a federal court in approving a consent decree:

> [A] federal court is more than "a recorder of contracts" from whom parties can purchase injunctions; it is "an organ of government constituted to make judicial decisions...." 1B J. Moore, J. Lucas & T., Currier, Moore's Federal Practice para. 0.409[5], p. 331 (1984).... Accordingly, a consent decree must spring from and serve to resolve a dispute within the court's subject-matter jurisdiction. Furthermore, consistent with this requirement, the consent decree must "com[e] within the general scope of the case made by the pleadings," *Pacific R. Co. v. Ketchum,* 11 Otto 289, 297, 101 U.S. 289, 297, 25 L.Ed. 932 (1880), and must further the objectives of the law upon which the complaint was based, [citations omitted]....
>
> This is not to say that the parties may agree to take action that conflicts with or violates the statute upon which the complaint was based.
>
> U.S. at ___ , 106 S. Ct. at 3077.

Had this case gone to trial and had the Foundation prevailed at trial, we would only be able to (1) enter an injunction to enforce the Clean Water Act against Bellefonte, (2) order Bellefonte to pay a civil penalty to the United States, and (3) award litigation costs, including reasonable attorney and expert witness fees, to the Foundation, 33 U.S.C. §1365(a), (d); *Middlesex County Sewerage Authority v. National Sea Clammers Association,* 453 U.S. at 14-15. An individual or entity may not maintain a citizen suit pursuant to 33 U.S.C. §1365 for wholly past violations of the Clean Water Act. *Gwaltney of Smithfield v. Chesapeake Bay Foundation, Inc.,* 484 U.S. 49, 108 S.Ct. 376, 98 L.Ed.2d 306. Although Bellefonte has admitted that in the past its sewage treatment plant violated the pollutant discharge limits of Bellefonte's National Pollutant Discharge Elimination System permit (*see* Bellefonte's statement filed July 29, 1988, of material facts to which there is no genuine issue, paragraph 11; Bellefonte's brief filed July 29, 1988, in support of its motion for summary judgment at 14-15, 18), there is no unequivocal evidence before the Court that Bellefonte's sewage treatment plant is presently violating or will in the future violate the pollutant discharge limits of Bellefonte's National Pollutant Discharge Elimination System permit. Because of the absence of proof that Bellefonte's sewage treatment plant is violating or will violate the applicable pollutant discharge limits, we are of the view that the Supreme Court's decision in *Gwaltney of Smithfield v. Chesapeake Bay Foundation* makes it impermissible in a citizen suit brought pursuant to 33 U.S.C. §1365 to disapprove a proposed consent decree solely for the reason because it does not contain a provision requiring the Defendant to pay a civil penalty to the United States.

The Environmental Protection Agency has developed guidelines which set forth conditions under which it will enter into a consent decree to settle a case in which it is a party that is brought for a violation or violations of the Clean Water Act. These guidelines, set forth in a document entitled "Clean Water Act—Penalty Policy for Civil Settlement Negotiations," which is appended to the United States' comments filed in this case, authorizes the Environmental Protection Agency to consent to settlements in cases brought under the Clean Water Act even though the settlement may require the Defendant to expend money for a "mitigation project" rather than require the Defendant's entire financial obligation as a result of the action to consist of a civil penalty paid to the United States. However, the "mitigation projects" which are authorized under the Environmental Protection Agency's Penalty Policy are, in general, only those which "closely address the environmental effects of the defendant's violation." Environmental Protection Agency's Clean Water Act—Penalty Policy for Civil Settlement Negotiations, V(2) at p.7. (This rule will hereafter be referred to as the "mitigation project rule.") The United States recognizes in its comments regarding the proposed consent decree that the Environmental Protection Agency's Penalty Policy is not binding on this Court. United States' comments at 6 n.5. The stated objective of the Clean Water Act is "to restore and maintain the chemical, physical, and biological integrity of the Nation's waters." 33 U.S.C. §1251(a). The Environmental Protection Agency's mitigation project rule clearly furthers the objective of the Clean Water Act specified in 33 U.S.C. §1251(a). Because the mitigation project rule seems wise to us, because the Environmental Protection Agency has been given primary responsibility for enforcing the Clean Water Act on behalf of the United States (*see* 33 U.S.C. §1319), and because the United States Supreme Court has long recognized that considerable weight should be given to an executive department's construction of a statutory scheme it is entrusted to administer (*Chevron U.S.A., Inc. v. Natural Resources Defense Council, Inc.,* 467 U.S. 837, 844, 81 L.Ed.2d 694, 104 S.Ct. 2778 (1984)), we will require that the mitigation project rule be met before approving the proposed consent decree in this case. The issue, therefore, is whether the proposed consent decree in this case meets the mitigation project rule.

The pertinent portion of the proposed consent decree reads as follows:

> ix. civil penalties and payment of attorney's fees
>
> 12. In full satisfaction of PEDF's claims for violatins as alleged in the Complaint and Amended Complaint filed herein through the date of lodging of this Decree, defendant Bellefonte shall, within thirty (30) days after the entry of this Consent Decree, tender:
>
> (a) Into an escrow account $ 35,000, and hold and maintain such funds with principal and interest to be used by Trout Unlimited, Spring Creek Chapter, for the

> purposes of fulfilling the goals of the CWA [Clean Water Act]. Trout Unlimited shall select and submit projects to Bellefonte and request disbursement of the funds necessary to effectuate such projects. Bellefonte shall disburse the funds necessary for the projects within forty-five (45) days of submission by Trout Unlimited unless Bellefonte believes said projects are beyond the terms of the CWA. If so, Bellefonte must submit the matter to dispute resolution within the same forty-five (45) day period.

We are of the view that the above-quoted portion of the proposed consent decree does not comply with the mitigation project rule. In fact, a careful reading of the above-quoted provision from the proposed consent decree reveals that there is no requirement that the $35,000.00 be used for projects in, next to, or close to Spring Creek and there is no explicit requirement that the $35,000.00 be used for a project which "closely addresses the environmental effects of the defendant's violation[s]." We decline to approve the proposed consent decree because the provision setting forth the use of the aforementioned $35,000.00 does not require that this money be used in conformity with the mitigation project rule.

If the parties wish to redraft paragraph 12(a) and resubmit the proposed consent decree as amended within the time specified in the dispositive portion of this order, and if the parties are unable in that time to devise a suitable mitigation project which is in conformity with the mitigation project rule, the parties may consider specifying certain parameters for the mitigation project and also inserting a provision that the precise project will be determined in the first instance by an independent person or entity, such as an academician at the Pennsylvania State University, and the project submitted to the Court for final approval.

Still pending in this case are Bellefonte's motion filed July 29, 1988, for summary judgment and the Foundation's motion filed October 5, 1988, for partial summary judgment. We shall stay all action on these two motions for a reasonable time in order to give the parties time to submit a proposed amended consent decree if they so desire.

NOW, THEREFORE, IT IS ORDERED THAT:

1. The Foundation's motion filed March 27, 1989, to preclude the comments of the United States to the proposed consent decree is denied.

2. Bellefonte's motion filed January 31, 1989, to enter consent decree is denied.

3. All action on Bellefonte's motion filed July 29, 1988, for summary judgment and on the Foundation's motion filed October 5, 1988, for partial summary judgment is stayed for 45 days from the date of this order. If the parties choose to file a proposed amended consent decree within 45 days from the date of this order, the aforementioned stay shall automatically be extended until we make a ruling whether to enter the proposed amended consent decree.

4. If the parties choose to file a proposed amended consent decree, they shall append to the proposed amended consent decree a certificate stating which paragraphs have been amended.

5. The Clerk of Court shall send a copy of this order to Amelia S. Salzman, Esq., Land & Natural Resources Division, 10th and Pennsylvania Avenue, N.W., Washington, D.C., 20530.

See also Friends of the Earth v. Archer Daniels Midland Co., 780 F.Supp. 95 (N.D.N.Y. 1992)

If, however, the government declines to take action within the 60-day notice period, then the citizen must also serve a copy of his or her complaint on the government to allow it to monitor the citizen suit for potential abuse. 40 C.F.R. §135.4. Another limitation on the availability of citizen suits is that they cannot be used to force the government to take enforcement action, which has been held repeatedly to be a "discretionary," as opposed to a "mandatory," duty of the government. *See* 5 U.S.C. §500, *et seq.* For the distinction between the maintenance of citizen's suits to compel the government's performance of mandatory as opposed to discretionary duties.

HARMON COVE CONDOMINIUM ASSOCIATES, INC. v. MARSH

815 F.2d 949 (3d Cir. 1987)

Appellant Harmon Cove I Condominium Association, Inc. (the Association) appeals from the final order of the district court dismissing its action against John O. Marsh, Secretary of the Army (the Secretary), Hartz Mountain Industries, Inc. (HMI), and Hartz Mountain Associates (HMA). We have jurisdiction under 28 U.S.C. §1291 (1982).

I.

In April 1974, HMI requested a permit to dredge and fill portions of the Hackensack River, in order to build the Harmon Cove condominium complex in Secaucus, New Jersey. The Secretary, acting through the U.S. Army Corps of Engineers (Corps), is authorized to grant such permission under Section 10 of the Rivers and Harbors Act of 1899 (RHA), 33 U.S.C. §403 (1982), and Section 404 of the Federal Water Pollution Control Act (FWPCA), 33 U.S.C. §1344 (1982).

On September 30, 1975 the Secretary issued Permit No. 9444, authorizing HMI to dredge and fill portions of the River in accordance with certain stipulated terms. The permit requires HMI to "maintain the structure or work authorized herein in good condition and in accordance with the plans and drawings attached." A Special Condition of the permit provides that HMI is not relieved "from taking all proper steps to insure the integrity of the structure permitted herein and the safety of boats moored thereto from damage by wave wash [from passing vessels]." In addition, a Special Condition provides that "when the work authorized herein includes periodic maintenance dredging, it may be performed under the permit for ten years from the date of issuance of the permit." The permit was effective until September 30, 1985. HMI proceeded to build the condominium complex.

On September 30, 1985, the Association filed this action. The complaint alleges HMI has delegated some of its duties under the permit to HMA. It then alleges that, despite the conditions of the permit, both HMI and HMA failed to maintain the marina area in good condition and in accordance with the plans approved by the Corps. It also alleges that HMI and HMA failed to prevent damage to the piers and embankments from wave wash and failed to perform periodic maintenance dredging. The failures of HMI and HMA are alleged to have resulted in damage to the marina and other structures comprising the condominium complex and to have created a potential for danger to condominium residents and other persons. Finally, the complaint alleges that the Association on several occasions had requested the Secretary to require HMA and HMI to comply with the conditions of the permit, but that the Secretary had taken no action.

At a hearing on the defendants' motions to dismiss, the district court stated that "there is no jurisdiction under the FWPCA for mandamus," and that, even "assuming there [is] subject matter jurisdiction, it is inappropriate to grant [mandamus] here because what we have here is not a ministerial act, but a discretionary act in the nature of a decision of whether ... to prosecute." By order entered on June 5, 1986 the district court dismissed the Association's claims. This appeal followed.

II.

The first count of the complaint requested the issuance of a writ of mandamus under 28 U.S.C. §1361 (1982) to compel the Secretary to enforce the conditions of the permit. The Association contends that the district court erred in dismissing its request. Our review of this issue is plenary.

The Secretary makes two basic arguments in support of the district court's order dismissing the Association's mandamus petition: (1) the FWPCA precludes actions against him under Section 1361, and (2) in any event, mandamus is not available because the Secretary owes no nondiscretionary duty to the Association. We shall assume without deciding that the FWPCA does not bar the Association's claim under Section 1361, and turn to the Association's contention that it is entitled to relief under that Section.

The Supreme Court has stated that relief is available to a plaintiff under Section 1361 "only if he has exhausted all other avenues of relief and only if the defendant owes him a clear, nondiscretionary duty." *Heckler v. Ringer*, 466 U.S. 602, 616, 80 L.Ed.2d 622, 104 S.Ct. 2013 (1984). This court has explained further that

> in order for mandamus to issue, a plaintiff must allege that an officer of the Government owes him a legal duty which is a specific, plain ministerial act "devoid of the exercise of judgment or discretion." An act is ministerial only when its performance is positively commanded and so plainly prescribed as to be free from doubt.

Richardson v. United States, 465 F.2d 844, 849 (3rd Cir. 1972) (en banc) (citations omitted), rev. on other grounds, 418 U.S. 166, 41 L. Ed. 2d 678, 94 S. Ct. 2940 (1974); *See also Naporano Metal and Iron Co. v. Secretary of Labor,* 529 F.2d 537, 542 (3rd Cir. 1976).

In *Heckler v. Chaney,* 470 U.S. 821, 84 L.Ed.2d 714, 105 S.Ct. 1649 (1985) the Supreme Court stated that agency decisions whether to take enforcement action are generally committed to agency discretion. *Id.* at 831-32. For this reason, the court concluded such decisions are presumptively immune from judicial review under the Administrative Procedure Act. *Id.* at 832. The court noted that the presumption "may be rebutted where the substantive statute has provided guidelines for the agency to follow in exercising its enforcement powers." *Id.* at 833 (footnote omitted).

The Association argues that the *Chaney* principle that enforcement decisions are committed to agency discretion does not apply in this case. It contends that enforcement decisions of the type discussed in *Chaney* "were already made when the Secretary issued Permit No. 9444," that "the types of assessments discussed in [*Chaney*] ... are not implicated in the present case at this stage," and that "the Secretary now has an obligation to act consistently with [the previously made enforcement] determinations...." We must reject the Association's argument. There is no support for the Association's contention that enforcement decisions regarding Permit No. 9444 were made when the Secretary issued it. In addition, the Secretary's decision whether to compel compliance with the conditions of the permit is a classic example of the enforcement decisions described in *Chaney*.

In evaluating the Association's claim that it is entitled to mandamus relief, following *Chaney*, we commence with the proposition that the Secretary's decision whether to enforce compliance with the conditions of Permit No. 9444 is presumptively unreviewable. The Association can rebut that presumption only by showing that pertinent sections of RHA or FWPCA provide guidelines for the Corps to follow in exercising its enforcement powers.

The Association first contends that the permit itself imposes a duty on the Secretary to enforce compliance with its conditions. Even if a permit such as Permit No. 9444 could impose such a duty on the Secretary, nothing in the language of Permit No. 9444 limits the Secretary's discretion. Accordingly, Permit No. 9444 does not by its terms impose a duty on the Secretary to enforce compliance with its conditions, much less provide guidelines.

The Association next argues that Section 10 of the RHA, 33 U.S.C. §403, imposes a duty on the Secretary to enforce compliance with the conditions of the permit. This provision, however, does not restrict the Secretary's enforcement discretion in any way. For this reason, we conclude that Section 10 of the RHA does not impose a duty on the Secretary to enforce compliance with the provisions of the permit.

The Association then contends that Section 404 of the FWPCA imposes a duty on the Secretary to enforce compliance with the conditions of the permit. Section 404 provides, in relevant part:

> Whenever on the basis of any information available to him the Secretary finds that any person is in violation of any condition or limitation set forth in a permit issued by the Secretary under this section, the Secretary shall issue an order requiring such person to comply with such condition or limitation, or the Secretary shall bring a civil action in accordance with paragraph (3) of this subsection.

This section does not limit the Secretary's discretion to enforce compliance with the conditions of the permit in the instant circumstances. The statute imposes no duty on the Secretary to make a finding of violation, because it contains no guidelines for the Secretary to follow in choosing to initiate enforcement activity. Thus, no mandamus remedy is available to the Association. *Cf. City of Seabrook v. Costle*, 659 F.2d 1371, 1375 (5th Cir. 1981) (construing virtually identical language of Section 113(a) of the Clean Air Act, 42 U.S.C. §7413, and concluding that EPA Administrator does not have a nondiscretionary duty to make a finding regarding every alleged violation of a state implementation plan).

The Association also asserts that the Secretary did not have unlimited discretion in determining the content of the permit issued to HMI. Therefore the Association argues, "the limitations on the Secretary's discretion that guide the content of the permit when it is issued must logically extend to the Secretary's duty to enforce the specifications and conditions of the permit once it has been issued." Assuming the soundness of the premise, the Association fails to explain how its conclusion inexorably follows. Because the Association offers no support for its argument, and because the argument ignores the teachings of *Chaney,* and the statutory language, we must reject it.

The Association argues finally that "it would be anomalous to suggest that the Secretary has no duty to ensure that [permit] guidelines are complied with after a permit has been issued." The short answer is that in the absence of some guidelines binding the Secretary's enforcement decisions, this court is bound by the Supreme Court's ruling that such determinations are left to the Secretary's discretion.

Because we discern no guidelines for the Secretary to follow in deciding whether to find violations of permits, we conclude the Secretary's decision is committed exclusively to his discretion. Consequently, the Secretary owed no duty to the Association. For this reason, the Association is not entitled to mandamus relief under Section 1361, and the district court properly dismissed count one of the complaint.

III.

The Association also contends the district court erred in dismissing its claims against HMI and HMA seeking to compel them to comply with the permit requirements and to pay for damages. The Association invoked jurisdiction of the district court under 28 U.S.C. §1331 (1982). Our review of this issue is also plenary.

The Association argues that it has stated claims against HMI and HMA under the RHA and FWPCA. It is well settled, however, that RHA does not explicitly provide a private cause of action, *California v. Sierra Club,* 451 U.S. 287, 289-90, 68 L.Ed.2d 101, 101 S.Ct. 1775 (1981), and that there are no implied private causes of action under Section 10 of RHA. *Id.* at 298. Similarly, the citizens' suit provision of FWPCA, 33 U.S.C. §1365 (1982), does not authorize an action against HMA or HMI on the facts alleged in this case, and the Supreme Court has held that there are no implied private causes of action under FWPCA. *Middlesex County Sewerage Authority v. National Sea Clammers Association,* 453 U.S. 1, 18, 69 L.Ed.2d 435, 101 S.Ct. 2615 (1981). While the Association contends that *Sierra Club* and *Sea Clammers* do not govern here because those cases did not involve alleged violations of permit conditions, the distinction is not a principled reason for declining to follow the clear teachings of those cases. Accordingly, we conclude that the Association's claims against HMA and HMI were properly dismissed.

IV.

For the foregoing reasons, the order of the district court will be AFFIRMED. [Footnotes omitted.]

A final problem in maintaining a citizen suit is what to do with the monetary penalties once the suit has been successful. Obviously it would do little to advance the cause of protecting the environment if private citizens could keep the penalty award. Generally, the funds should be used for environmental improvement projects, either directly or indirectly related to the violation. *See also Loggerhead Turtle v. County Council of Volusia County, Fla.*, 120 F.Supp.2d 1005 (M.D.Fla. 2000); *Missouri Coalition for Environment v. Corps of Engineers of U.S. Army*, 678 F.Supp. 790 (E.D.Mo. 1988); *Sierra Club v. Train*, 557 F.2d 485 (5th Cir. Ala. 1977); *National Wildlife Federation v. Laubscher*, 662 F.Supp. 548 (S.D.Tex. 1987). *But see Hurst v. United States*, 882 F.2d 306 (8th Cir. S.D. 1989).

SIERRA CLUB, INC. v. ELECTRONIC CONTROLS DESIGN, INC.

909 F.2d 1350 (9th Cir. 1990)

Sierra Club, Inc. appeals the refusal to enter a proposed consent judgment in its citizens' suit against Electronic Controls Design (ECD) for alleged violations of the Federal Water Pollution Control Act ("Clean Water Act" or "the Act"), 33 U.S.C. §1365 (1988). We reverse.

On February 23, 1987, the Sierra Club filed a citizens' suit against ECD under section 505 of the Clean Water Act, 33 U.S.C. §1365. *See Sierra Club, Inc. v. Electronic Controls Design,* 703 F. Supp. 875, 875-76 (D.Or. 1989). The complaint alleged that ECD violated section 301(a) of the Act, 33 U.S.C. §1311(a), by discharging pollutants from its printed circuit board manufacturing plant into the Molalla River via Milk Creek, in violation of the terms of ECD's National Pollutant Discharge Elimination System (NPDES) permit.

On September 30, 1988, the parties filed a Stipulation for Entry of Consent Judgment. In the proposed judgment, ECD agreed to: (1) comply with the terms of its NPDES permit and to terminate all discharges if it violates its permit after June 1, 1989; (2) pay $45,000 to various identified private environmental organizations for their efforts to maintain and protect water quality in Oregon; (3) pay additional sums to these organizations if ECD violates its permit between September 1, 1988, and June 1, 1989; and (4) pay $5,000 to the Sierra Club for attorney and expert witness fees. In the consent judgment ECD did not admit any violation, and none was established.

The United States filed an objection to the proposed consent judgment, arguing that the proposed judgment was illegal because it contained no requirement that ECD make payments to the U.S. treasury. The Clean Water Act authorizes the imposition of civil penalties only if paid to the federal treasury. The district court concluded that the payments to be made under the proposed consent judgment were civil penalties within the meaning of the Act and therefore refused to enter the order. *Sierra Club,* 703 F. Supp. at 876-77.

Recognizing "that Congress encourages settlements that put money directly to use in protecting the environment," the court also reasoned that a settlement could dictate that money be "channeled towards environmental projects, but perhaps not through private entities [such as those in this proposed consent judgment]." *Id.* at 877-78. Accordingly, the court indicated that it would approve a consent judgment designating the Oregon Water Quality Program as the "civil penalty recipient." *Id.* at 879.

JURISDICTION

As a threshold issue we must determine whether we have jurisdiction to hear this timely appeal. As a general rule, the courts of appeals have jurisdiction only over final decisions of the district court which "end the litigation on the merits." *See Van Cauwenberghe v. Biard,* 486 U.S. 517, 521-22, 100 L.Ed.2d 517, 108 S.Ct. 1945 (1988) (quoting *Catlin v. United States,* 324 U.S. 229, 233, 89 L. Ed. 911, 65 S. Ct. 631 (1945)). Congress has created certain exceptions. *See Carson v. American Brands, Inc.,* 450 U.S. 79, 83, 67 L.Ed.2d 59, 101 S.Ct. 993 (1981). Pursuant to 28 U.S.C. §1292(a) (1), the courts may hear appeals from "interlocutory orders of the district courts ...

granting, continuing, modifying, refusing or dissolving injunctions...." In 1981, the Supreme Court held that an interlocutory order denying a motion to enter a consent decree providing injunctive relief may be appealable under 28 U.S.C. §1292(a) as an order refusing an injunction. *See Carson,* 450 U.S. 79, 67 L.Ed.2d 59, 101 S.Ct. 993. *See also EEOC v. Pan American World Airways, Inc.*, 796 F.2d 314 (9th Cir. 1986) (adopting the *Carson* analysis), *cert. denied,* 479 U.S. 1030, 93 L. Ed. 2d 829, 107 S. Ct. 874 (1987).

In *Carson* the Court effectively set forth a tripartite test to determine when an order denying a motion to enter a consent judgment may be appealable pursuant to 28 U.S.C. §1292(a) (1). First, the interlocutory order must have the practical effect of denying an injunction. *Id.* at 83-84. Second, the order must have "serious, perhaps irreparable consequences." *Id.* at 84. Finally, the order must be one that can be "effectually challenged" only by immediate appeal. *Id.*

The United States does not contest that the proposed consent judgment contained injunctive relief. It argues instead that injunctive relief was not denied because the district court stated its willingness to accept the judgment's injunctive aspects. According to *Carson,* however, an order need only have the "practical effect" of denying an injunction to be appealable. *Carson,* 450 U.S. at 83. Because the court refused to enter the entire consent judgment, its denial had the practical effect of denying an out-of-court settlement containing injunctive relief.

We also find that the district court's refusal to enter the proposed consent judgment may result in serious and perhaps irreparable harm that can be challenged effectively only by immediate appeal. *Carson,* 450 U.S. at 84. Like the appellant in *Carson,* the Sierra Club was denied the injunctive relief settled upon until the case is finally resolved. *See also Durrett v. Housing Authority of the City of Providence,* 896 F.2d 600, 602 (1st Cir. 1990) (serious consequences found where denial of consent decree would delay improvement of substandard housing). Moreover, if the district court were correct in characterizing the payments required by the proposed consent judgment as civil penalties, unlawful under the Clean Water Act, further settlement negotiations between the parties could not continue unless the ECD agreed to pay penalties to the U.S. treasury. If we were to deny review of the rejection of the proposed consent judgment at this juncture and allow the case to continue to trial, the validity of the consent judgment could be moot and unreviewable following a final judgment on the merits. The loss of an opportunity to effectively challenge an order that denies the parties injunctive relief "plainly has 'serious, perhaps irreparable consequences.'" *Carson,* 450 U.S. at 86. We therefore conclude that jurisdiction exists under 28 U.S.C. §1292(a)(1).

THE MERITS

Section 505 of the Clean Water Act authorizes any citizen to commence an action against any person who is alleged to be in violation of the Act. 33 U.S.C. §1365(a). A citizen can seek injunctive relief and civil penalties. *Id. See generally* J. Miller, *Citizens Suits: Private Enforcement of Federal Pollution Control Laws,* §8.4, 89 (1987); 18 Env't.Rep. (BNA) No. 19, Special Report at 51-59 (Sept. 4, 1987). The district court held that the monetary payments agreed to in the settlement were civil penalties within the meaning of the Act and that all civil penalties must be paid to the federal treasury. The court therefore concluded that the settlement was illegal.

We agree with the district court that if the payments required under the proposed consent decree are civil penalties within the meaning of the Clean Water Act, they may be paid only to the U.S. treasury. We disagree, however, that the payments are civil penalties. No violation of the Act was found or determined by the proposed settlement judgment. When a defendant agrees before trial to make payments to environmental organizations without admitting liability, the agreement is simply part of an out-of-court settlement which the parties are free to make.

The Supreme Court has stated on two occasions that civil penalties imposed by a court in a citizens' suit under the Clean Water Act must be made payable to the U.S. treasury. *Gwaltney,* 484 U.S. at 53 ("If the citizen prevails in such an action, the court may order injunctive relief and/or impose civil penalties payable to the United States Treasury"); *Middlesex County Sewerage Authority v. National Sea Clammers Ass'n,* 453 U.S. 1, 14, 69 L.Ed.2d 435, 101 S.Ct. 2615 n.25 (1981) ("Under the [Federal Water Pollution Control Act], civil penalties, payable to the Government, also may be ordered by the court. §505(a), 33 U.S.C. §1365(a).") *See also Sierra Club v. Chevron, USA, Inc.,* 834 F.2d 1517, 1522 (9th Cir. 1987) ("any penalties recovered from [a citizens' suit] are paid into the United States Treasury") (quoting *Chesapeake Bay Foundation v. Bethlehem Steel Corp.,* 608 F. Supp. 440, 449 (D.Md. 1985)). Because the monetary payments required under the proposed consent judgment will not go to the U.S. treasury, the district court was correct in concluding that if they are "civil penalties" they violate the Clean Water Act.

While it is clear that a court cannot order a defendant in a citizens' suit to make payments to an organization other than the U.S. treasury, this prohibition does not extend to a settlement agreement whereby the defendant does not admit liability and the court is not ordering non-consensual monetary relief. "Consent decrees bear some of the earmarks of judgments entered after litigation. At the same time, because their terms are arrived at through mutual agreement of the parties, consent decrees also closely resemble contracts." *Local No. 93, International Ass'n of Firefighters, AFL-CIO v. City of Cleveland,* 478 U.S. 501, 519, 92 L. Ed. 2d 405, 106 S. Ct. 3063 (1986).

Because of the unique aspects of settlements, a district court should enter a proposed consent judgment if the court decides that it is fair, reasonable and equitable and does not violate the law or public policy. *See Citizens for a Better Environment v. Gorsuch,* 231 U.S. App. D.C. 79, 718 F.2d 1117, 1125-26 (D.C.Cir. 1983), *cert. denied,* 467 U.S. 1219, 104 S. Ct. 2668, 81 L. Ed. 2d 373 (1984); *cf. Davis v. City and County of San Francisco,* 890 F.2d 1438, 1444-45 (9th Cir. 1989) (district court reviews proposed consent decree in a class action suit brought under Fed.R.Civ.P. 23(c) to determine whether the settlement is "fundamentally fair, adequate and reasonable") (quoting *Officers for Justice v. Civil Serv. Comm'n of the City and County of San Francisco,* 688 F.2d 615, 625 (9th Cir. 1982), *cert. denied,* 459 U.S. 1217, 103 S. Ct. 1219, 75 L. Ed. 2d 456 (1983)).

In *Local No. 93,* the Supreme Court upheld a district court's order entering a consent decree that went beyond the type of relief provided by the civil rights statute under which the suit had been brought. 478 U.S. 501, 106 S.Ct. 3063, 92 L.Ed.2d 405. The Court stated that "a federal court is not necessarily barred from entering a consent decree merely because the decree provides broader relief than the court could have awarded after a trial." 478 U.S. at 525. As long as the consent decree comes "'within the general scope of the case made by the pleadings,'" furthers "the objectives upon which the law is based," and does not "violate the statute upon which the complaint was based," the parties' agreement may be entered by the court. *Id.* at 525-26 (*quoting Pacific R. Co. v. Ketchum,* 101 U.S. 289, 297, 25 L. Ed. 932 (1880) (citations omitted)).

The consent decree agreed to by the Sierra Club and ECD comes within the scope of the pleadings, furthers the broad objectives upon which the complaint was based and does not violate the Clean Water Act. The Sierra Club's complaint was based upon the allegation that ECD was not in compliance with the Clean Water Act and was polluting the Oregon waters. The district court found that compelling ECD to comply with the terms of its permit or cease all discharges is "in the public interest." *Sierra Club,* 703 F.Supp. at 878. It also acknowledged that the environmental organizations that will receive funds under the proposed consent judgment "will apply the money in ways that will help further the goals of the Act." *Id.* Moreover, as the court noted, "Congress 'encourages' settlements of this type 'which preserve the punitive nature of enforcement actions while putting the funds collected to use on behalf of environmental protection.'" *Id.* at 877 (quoting H.R.Conf. Rep. No. 1004, 99th Cong., 2d Sess. 139 (1986)).

The Clean Water Act also does not render the proposed consent judgment unlawful. The provisions of the Act provide no limitation on the type of payments to which parties to citizens' suits can agree in a settlement. There is no indication that where a defendant agrees to a settlement it must also agree to pay penalties to the treasury. Likewise, the Act's legislative history reveals no Congressional intent that private parties be precluded from entering into settlements which do not require the defendant to tender civil penalties to the United States.

In 1987, Congress amended the Act to give the government more power to oversee and monitor the entry of consent judgments in citizens' suits. *See* 33 U.S.C. §1365(c) (3). The new provision prohibits a court from entering proposed consent judgments in citizens' suit where the United States is not a party until 45 days after the Attorney General and the administrator of the EPA receive copies of the proposed consent. Congress did not take this opportunity to comment on the type of relief permitted in citizens' suit settlements and did not indicate that the settlements must include payment of civil penalties to the U.S. treasury. See 33 U.S.C. §1365(c) (3); Pub. L. No. 100-4, Title V §505(c), 101 Stat. 76 (Feb. 4, 1987).

We therefore find that the proposed consent decree furthers the purpose of the statute upon which the complaint was based and does not violate its terms or policy. The payments to the environmental organizations are not in recognition of liability under the Clean Water Act and are not civil penalties. No liability was ever judicially established. The district court abused its discretion in failing to enter the proposed consent judgment. *See Citizens for a Better Environment,* 718 F.2d at 1125-26 (district court should enter proposed consent decree if it is fair, reasonable and equitable and does not violate the law or public policy). Upon remand, the district court should enter the consent decree proposed by the Sierra Club and ECD and award costs and attorney fees pursuant to the decree....

REVERSED AND REMANDED. [Footnotes omitted.]

See also *Sierra Club v. Whitman*, 268 F.3d 898 (9th Cir. 2001); *Vieux Carre Property Owners, Residents & Assocs. v. Brown*, 875 F.2d 453 (5th Cir. La. 1989), *cert. denied*, 493 U.S. 1020, 107 L.Ed.2d 739, 110 S.Ct. 720 (1990); *Orleans Audubon Society v. Lee*, 742 F.2d 901 (5th Cir. 1984), *reh'g. denied*, 750 F.2d 69 (5th Cir. 1984).

PART 5

REGULATORY TAKINGS

The Fifth Amendment to the United States Constitution provides in relevant part "... nor shall private property be taken for public use, without just compensation." As a response to a permit action, the Fifth Amendment is not precisely a defense since its successful outcome against the government does not alter the Corps's wetland determination or permit denial or conditioning. Instead, the plaintiff will receive money but will still lose his or her property through a forced sale to the government. It may be fairly said that liability under the Clean Water Act is truly strict liability, with only a Fifth Amendment claim available to ameliorate the effects of what the Corps intended to do in the first place—make a wetlands determination and/or deny a permit.

Before we examine the wetlands regulatory cases, however, we must first discover two things that will always prevent the plaintiff/landowner from asserting a takings claim against the government: the public trust doctrine and the doctrine of nuisance. At their simplest interpretation, these doctrines both prevent the takings claim by denying the plaintiff a property right in the first place. In short, there is nothing for the government to have taken.

CHAPTER 32

THE PUBLIC TRUST DOCTRINE

An ancient concept of sovereignty allows a government to limit the uses to which certain land may be put in the public interest by controlling the natural resources found on the land. This concept is now called the "public trust doctrine." Under this concept of sovereignty, which may have its roots as far back in time as the first organized society, there is recognized the notion that some natural resources are so important to all of society that no individual private citizen should be able to exclude others from their use. Even though one of the essential elements of private property ownership is the right to exclude others, nonetheless, some "things common to mankind by the law of nature" (the Roman law definition, from the Institutes of Justinian, which included air, running water, the sea, and the seashore below high tide line) are so universally important to the survival and prosperity of all that they should remain in common usage and there should be no exclusion of anyone. There is even a modern argument that there is no right of property ownership in the orthodox sense in these natural resources; that they simply cannot be owned by human beings.

Under Roman law, these natural resources were held in trust for the public by the sovereign. The English went further saying that the crown actually owned, as opposed to held in trust, tidal navigable waterways. In the United States the doctrine was adopted by the thirteen colonies with each colony holding its individual navigable waterways in trust. With the westward expansion away from the coast line, as the new states were added to the Union, they, too, acquired control over navigable waterways in trust for the public. However, since not all of the navigable waterways in the interior portions of the United States are tidal, the United States included nontidal navigable waterways in its public trust doctrine.

MARTIN v. LESSEE OF WADDELL

41 U.S. 367, 16 Pet. 367, 10 L.Ed. 997 (1842)

This case is brought here by writ of error from the circuit court of the United States for the district of New Jersey. It was fully argued at the last term. But it was not then decided; because the important principles involved in it, made it proper that the case should be heard and determined by a full court, and as some of the justices were not present at the former hearing, a re-argument was ordered. In pursuance of this order, it has been again elaborately discussed by counsel; and having been carefully considered by the court, I am instructed to deliver their opinion.

The questions before us arise upon an action of ejectment, instituted by the defendant in error, who was the plaintiff in the court below, to recover one hundred acres of land, covered with water, situated in the township of Perth Amboy, in the state of New Jersey. At the trial in the circuit court, the jury found a special verdict, setting forth, among other things, that the land claimed lies beneath the navigable waters of the Raritan river and bay, where the tide ebbs and flows. And it appears, that the principal matter in dispute, is the right to the oyster fishery in the public rivers and bays of East New Jersey.

The plaintiff makes title under the charters granted by Charles II to his brother, the Duke of York, in 1664 and 1674, for the purpose of enabling him to plant a colony on this continent. The last-mentioned grant is precisely similar to the former in every respect, and was made for the purpose of removing doubts which had then arisen as to the validity of the first. The boundaries in the two charters are the same, and they embrace the territory which now forms the state of New Jersey. The part of this territory known as East New Jersey, afterwards, by sundry deeds and conveyances, which it is not necessary to enumerate, was transferred to 24 persons, who were called the proprietors of East New Jersey; who, by the terms of the grants, were invested, within the portion of the territory conveyed to them, with all the rights of property and government which had been originally conferred on the Duke of York by the letters-patent of the king. Some serious difficulties, however, took place, in a short time, between these proprietors and the British authorities; and after some negotiations upon the subject, they, in 1702, surrendered to the crown all the powers of government, retaining their rights of private property.

The defendant in error claims the land covered with water, mentioned in the declaration, by virtue of a survey made in 1834, under the authority of the proprietors, and duly recorded in the proper office. And if they were authorized to make this grant, he is entitled to the premises, as owner of the soil, and has an exclusive right to the fishery in question. The plaintiff in error also claims an exclusive right to take oysters in the same place; and derives his title under a law of the state of New Jersey, passed in 1824, and a supplement thereto, passed in the same year. The point in dispute between the parties, therefore, depends upon the construction and legal effect of the letters-patent to the Duke of York, and of the deed of surrender subsequently made by the proprietors.

The letters-patent to the duke included a very large territory, extending along the Atlantic coast from the river St. Croix to the Delaware bay, and containing within it many navigable rivers, bays and arms of the sea; and after granting the tract of country and islands therein described, 'together with all the lands, islands, soils, rivers, harbors, mines, minerals, quarries, woods, marshes, waters, lakes, fishings, hawkings, huntings and fowlings, and all other royalties, profits, commodities and hereditaments to the said several islands, lands and premises belonging and appertaining, with their and every of their appurtenances, and all the estate, right, title, interest, benefit and advantage, claim and demand of the king, in the said land and premises'; the letters-patent proceed to confer upon him, his heirs, deputies, agents, commissioners and assigns, the powers of government; with a proviso, that the statutes, ordinances, and proceedings established by his authority, should 'not be contrary to, but as nearly as might be agreeable to, the laws, statutes and government of the realm of England; saving also an appeal to the king, in all cases, from any judgment or sentence which might be given in the colony, and authorizing the duke, his heirs and assigns, to lead and transport out of any of the realms of the king to the country granted, all such and so many of his subjects, or strangers not prohibited, or under restraint, who would become the 'loving subjects' of the king, and live under his allegiance, and who should willingly accompany the duke, his heirs and assigns.'

The right of the king to make this grant, with all of its prerogatives and powers of government, cannot, at this day, be questioned. But in order to enable us to determine the nature and extent of the interest which it conveyed to the duke, it is proper to inquire into the character of the right claimed by the British crown, in the country discovered by its subjects, on this continent; and the principles upon which it was parcelled out and granted.

The English possessions in America were not claimed by right of conquest, but by right of discovery. For, according to the principles of international law, as understood by the then civilized powers of Europe, the Indian tribes in the new world were regarded as mere temporary occupants of the soil, and the absolute rights of property and dominion were held to belong to the European nation by which any particular portion of the country was first discovered. Whatever forbearance may have been sometimes practiced towards the unfortunate aborigines, either from humanity or policy, yet the territory they occupied was disposed of by the governments of Europe, at their pleasure, as if it had been found without inhabitants. The grant to the Duke of York, therefore, was not of lands won by the sword; nor were the government or laws he was authorized to establish intended for a conquered people.

The country mentioned in the letters-patent was held by the king in his public and regal character, as the representative of the nation, and in trust for them. The discoveries made by persons acting under the authority of the government were for the benefit of the nation; and the crown, according to the principles of the British constitution, was the proper organ to dispose of the public domains; and upon these principles rest the various charters and grants of territory made on this continent. The doctrine upon this subject is clearly stated in the case of *Johnson* v. *McIntosh*, 8 Wheat. 595. In that case, the court, after stating it to be a principle of universal law, that an uninhabited country, if discovered by a number of individuals who owe no allegiance to any government, becomes the property of the discoverers, proceed to say, that, 'if the discovery be made and possession taken under the authority of an existing government, which is acknowledged by the emigrants, it that the discovery is made for the benefit of the whole nation; and the vacant soil is to be disposed of by that organ of the government which has the constitutional power to dispose of the national domains; by that organ, in which all territory is vested by law. According to the theory of the British constitution, all vacant lands are vested in the crown, as representing the nation, and the exclusive power to grant them is admitted to reside in the crown, as a branch of the royal prerogative. It has been already shown, that this principle was as fully recognised in America as in the island of Great Britain.'

This being the principle upon which the charter in question was founded, by what rules ought it to be construed? We do not propose to meddle with the point which was very much discussed at the bar, as to the power of the king, since Magna Charta, to grant to a subject a portion of the soil covered by the navigable waters of the kingdom, so as to give him an immediate and exclusive right of fishery, either for shell-fish or floating fish, within the limits of his grant. The question is not free from doubt, and the authorities referred to in the English books cannot, perhaps, be altogether reconciled. But from the opinions expressed by the justices of the court of king's bench, in the case of *Blundell* v. *Catterall*, 5 Barn. & Ald. 287, 294, 304, 309; and in the case of the *Duke of Somerset* v. *Fogwell*, 5 Barn. & Cres. 883-4, the question must be regarded as settled in England, against the right of the king, since Magna Charta, to make such a grant. The point does not, however, arise in this case, unless it shall first be decided, that in the grant to the Duke of York, the king intended to sever the bottoms of the navigable waters from the prerogative powers of government conferred by the same charter; and to convert them into mere franchises in the hands of a subject, to be held and used as his private property. And we the more willingly forbear to express an opinion on this subject, because it has ceased to be a matter of much interest in the United States. For when the revolution took place, the people of each state became themselves sovereign; and in that character hold the absolute right to all their navigable waters, and the soils under them, for their own common use, subject only to the rights since surrendered by the constitution to the general government. A grant made by their authority must, therefore, manifestly be tried and determined by different principles from those which apply to grants of the British crown, when the title is held by a single individual, in trust for the whole nation.

Neither is it necessary to examine the many cases which have been cited in the argument on both sides, to show the degree of strictness with which grants of the king are to be construed. The decisions and authorities referred to apply more properly to a grant of some prerogative right to an individual, to be held by him as a franchise, and which is intended to become private property in his hands. The dominion and property in navigable waters, and in the lands under them, being held by the king as a public trust, the grant to an individual of an exclusive fishery in any portion of it, is so much taken from the common fund entrusted to his care for the common benefit. In such cases, whatever does not pass by the grant, still remains in the crown, for the benefit and advantage of the whole community. Grants of that description are, therefore, construed strictly; and it will not be presumed, that he intended to part from any portion of the public domain, unless clear and especial words are used to denote it. But in the case before us, the rivers, bays and arms of the sea, and all prerogative rights, within the limits of the charter, undoubtedly passed to the Duke of York, and were intended to pass, except those saved in the letters-patent. The words used evidently show this intention; and there is no room, therefore, for the application of the rule above mentioned.

The questions upon this charter are very different ones; they are—Whether the dominion and propriety in the navigable waters, and in the soils under them, passed, as a part of the prerogative rights annexed to the political powers conferred on the duke? Whether, in his hands, they were intended to be a trust for the common use of the new community about to be established; or private property to be parcelled out and sold to individuals, for his own benefit? And in deciding a question like this, we must not look merely to the strict technical meaning of the words of the letters-patent. The laws and institutions of England, the history of the times, the object of the charter, the contemporaneous construction given to it, and the usages under it, for the century and more which has since elapsed, are all entitled to consideration and weight. It is not a deed conveying private property, to be interpreted by the rules applicable to cases of that description. It was an instrument upon which was to be founded the institutions of a great political community; and in that light it should be regarded and construed.

Taking this rule for our guide, we can entertain no doubt as to the true construction of these letters-patent. The object in view appears upon the face of them. They were made for the purpose of enabling the Duke of York to establish a colony upon the newly discovered continent, to be governed, as nearly as circumstances would permit, according to the laws and usages of England; and in which the duke, his heirs and assigns, were to stand in the place of the king, and administer the government according to the principles of the British constitution. And the people who were to plant this colony, and to form the political body over which he was to rule, were subjects of Great Britain, accustomed to be governed according to its usages and laws.

It is said by HALE, in his treatise *de Jure Maris*, Harg. Law Tracts 11, when speaking of the navigable waters, and the sea on the coasts within the jurisdiction of the British crown, 'that although the king is the owner of this great, coast, and as a consequent of his propriety, hath the primary right of fishing in the sea, and creeks and arms thereof, yet the common people of England have, regularly, a liberty of fishing in the sea, or creeks or arms thereof, as a public common of piscary, and may not, without injury to their right, be restrained of it, unless in such places, creeks or navigable rivers, where either the king or some particular subject hath gained a propriety exclusive of that common liberty.'

The principle here stated by HALE, as to 'the public common of piscary' belonging to the common people of England, is not questioned by any English writer upon that subject. The point upon which different opinions have been expressed, is whether, since Magna Charta, 'either the king or any particular subject can gain a propriety exclusive of the common liberty.' For, undoubtedly, rights of fishery, exclusive of the common liberty, are, at this day, held and enjoyed by private individuals under ancient grants. But the existence of a doubt as to the right of the king to make such a grant, after Magna Charta, would, of itself, show how fixed has been the policy of that government on this subject, for the last six hundred years; and how carefully it has preserved this common right for the benefit of the public. And there is nothing in the charter before us, indicating that a different and opposite line of policy was designed to be adopted in that colony. On the contrary, after enumerating in the clause herein before quoted, some of the prerogative rights annexed to the crown, but not all of them, general words are used, conveying 'all the estate, right, title, interest, benefit, advantage, claim and demand' of the king, in the lands and premises before granted. The estate and rights of the king passed to the duke, in the same condition in which they had been held by the crown, and upon the same trusts. Whatever was held by the king, as a prerogative right, passed to the duke in the same character. And if the word 'soils' be an appropriate word to pass lands covered with navigable water, as contended for on the part of the defendant in error, it is associated in the letters-patent with 'other royalties,' and conveyed as such. No words are used for the purpose of separating them from the *jura regalia*, and converting them into private property, to be held and enjoyed by the duke, apart from and independent of the political character with which he was clothed by the same instrument. Upon a different construction, it would have been impossible for him to have complied with the conditions of the grant. For it was expressly enjoined upon him, as a duty in the government he was about to establish, to make it, as near as might be, agreeable, in their new circumstances, to the laws and statutes of England; and how could this be done, if in the charter itself, this high prerogative trust was severed from the regal authority? If the shores, and rivers and bays and arms of the sea, and the land under them, instead of being held as a public trust for the benefit of the whole community, to be freely used by all for navigation and fishery, as well for shell-fish as floating fish, had been converted by the charter itself into private property, to be parcelled out and sold by the duke, for his own individual emolument? There is nothing, we think, in the terms of the letters-patent, nor in the purposes for which it was granted, that would justify this construction. And in the judgment of the court, the lands under the navigable waters passed to the grantee, as one of the royalties incident to the powers of government; and were to be held by him, in the same manner, and for the same purposes, that the navigable waters of England, and the soils under them, are held by the crown.

This opinion is confirmed, by referring to similar grants for other tracts of country upon this continent, made about the same period of time. Various other charters for large territories on the Atlantic cost, were granted, by different monarchs of the Stuart dynasty, to different persons, for the purposes of settlement and colonization, in which the powers of government were united with the grant of territory. Some of these charters very nearly resembled in every respect the one now in controversy; and none of them, it is believed, differed materially from it, in the terms in which the bays, rivers and arms of the sea, and the soils under them, were conveyed to the grantees. Yet, in no one of these colonies, has the soil under its navigable waters, and the rights of fishery for shell-fish or floating fish, been severed by the letters-patent from the powers of government. In all of them, from the time of the settlement to the present day, the previous habits and usages of the colonists have been respected, and they have been accustomed to enjoy in common, the benefits and advantages of the navigable waters, for the same purposes, and to the same extent, that they have been used and enjoyed, for centuries, in England. Indeed, it could not well have been otherwise; for the men who first formed the English settlements, could not have been expected to encounter the many hardships that unavoidably attended their emigration to the new world, and to people the banks of its bays and rivers, if the land under the water at their very doors was liable to immediate appropriation by another, as private property; and the settler upon the fast land thereby excluded from its enjoyment, and unable to take a shell-fish from its bottom, or fasten there a stake, or even bathe in its waters, without becoming a trespasser upon the rights of another. The usage in New Jersey has, in this respect, from its original settlement, conformed to the practice of the other chartered colonies. And it would require very plain language in these letters-patent, to persuade us that the public and common right of fishery in navigable waters, which has been so long and so carefully guarded in England, and which was preserved in every other colony founded on the Atlantic borders, was intended, in this one instance, to be taken away. But we see nothing in the charter to require this conclusion.

The same principles upon which the court have decided upon the construction of the letters-patent to the Duke of York, apply with equal force to the surrender afterwards made by the 24 proprietors. It appears by the special verdict, that all the interest of the duke in East New Jersey, including the royalties and powers of government, were conveyed to these proprietors, as fully and amply, and in the same condition, as they had been granted to him; and they had the same dominion and propriety in the bays, and rivers and arms of the sea, and the soil under them, and in the rights of fishery, that had belonged to him under the original charter. In their hands, therefore, as well as in those of the duke, this dominion and propriety was an incident to the regal authority, and was held by them as a prerogative right, associated with the powers of government. And being thus entitled, they, in 1702, surrendered and yielded up to Anne, Queen of England, and to her heirs and successors, 'all the powers and authorities in the said letters-patent granted, to correct, punish, pardon, govern and rule all or any of her majesty's subjects or others, who then were inhabitants, or thereafter might adventure into or inhabit within the said province of East New Jersey; and also to nominate, make, constitute, ordain and confirm any laws, orders, ordinances, directions and instruments for those purposes, or any of them; and to nominate, constitute or appoint, revoke, discharge, change or alter any government or governors, officers or ministers, which were or should be appointed within the said province; and to make, ordain and establish any orders, laws, directions, instruments, forms or ceremonies of government and magistracy, for or concerning the same, or on the sea, in going to or coming from the same; or to put in execution, or abrogate, revoke or change such as were already made, for or concerning such government, or any of them; and also all the powers and authorities by the said letters-patent to use and exercise martial law in the said province of East New Jersey; and to admit any person or persons to trade or traffic there; and of encountering, repelling and resisting by force of arms, any person or persons attempting to inhabit there without the license of them, the said proprietors, their heirs and assigns: and all other the powers, authorities and privileges of and concerning the province last aforesaid, or the inhabitants thereof, which were granted, or mentioned to be granted, by the said several above-recited letters-patent, or either of them;' which said surrender was afterwards accepted by the queen.

We give the words of the surrender, as found by the special verdict, and they are broad enough to cover the *jura regalia* which belonged to the proprietors. They yield up 'all the powers, authorities and privileges of and concerning the government of the province;' and the right in dispute was one of these authorities and privileges. No words are used, for the purpose of withholding from the crown any of its ordinary and well-known prerogatives. The surrender, according to its evident object and meaning, restored them in the same plight and condition in which they originally came to the hands of the Duke of York. Whatever he held as a royal or prerogative right, was restored, with the political power to which it was incident. And if the great right of dominion and ownership in the rivers, bays and arms of the sea, and the soils under them, were to have been severed from the sovereignty, and withheld from the crown; if the right of common fishery for the common people, stated by HALE in the passage before quoted, was intended to be withdrawn, the design to make this important change in this particular territory would have been clearly indicated by appropriate terms; and would not have been left for inference from ambiguous language.

The negotiations previous to the surrender have been referred to, in order to influence the construction of the deed. But whatever propositions may have been made, or opinions expressed, before the execution of that instrument, the deed itself must be regarded as the final agreement between the parties; and that deed, by its plain words, re-established the authority of the crown, with all of its customary powers and privileges. And when the people of New Jersey took possession of the reins of government, and took into their own hands the powers of sovereignty, the prerogatives and regalities which before belonged either to the crown or the parliament, became immediately and rightfully vested in the state.

This construction of the surrender is evidently the same with that which it received from all the parties interested, at the time it was executed. For it appears, by the history of New Jersey, as gathered from the acts, documents and proceedings of the public authorities, that the crown, and the provincial government established by its authority, always afterwards, in this territory, exercised the same prerogative powers that the king was accustomed to exercise in his English dominions. And as concerns the particular dominion and propriety now in question, the colonial government, from time to time, authorized the construction of bridges with abutments on the soil covered by navigable waters; established forts; authorized the erection of wharves; and as early as 1719, passed a law for the preservation of the oyster fishery in its waters. The public usages, also, in relation to the fisheries, continued to be the same. And from 1702, when the surrender was made, until a very recent date, the people of New Jersey have exercised and enjoyed the rights of fishery for shell-fish and floating fish, as a common and undoubted right, without opposition or remonstrance from the proprietors. The few unimportant grants made by them, at different times, running into the navigable waters, which were produced in the argument, do not appear to have been recognised as valid, by the provincial or state authorities, nor to have been sanctioned by the courts. And the right now claimed was not seriously asserted on their part, before the case of *Arnold v. Mundy*, reported in 1 Halst. 1; which suit was not instituted until the year 1818; and upon that occasion, the supreme court of the state held, that the claim made by the proprietors was without foundation.

The effect of this decision by the state court, has been a good deal discussed at the bar. It is insisted by the plaintiffs in error, that as the matter in dispute is local in its character, and the controversy concerns only fixed property, within the limits of New Jersey, the decision of her tribunals ought to settle the construction of the charter; and that the courts of the United States are bound to follow it. It may, however, be doubted, whether this case falls within the rule, in relation to the judgments of state courts when expounding their own constitution and laws.

The question here depends, not upon the meaning of instruments framed by the people of New Jersey, or by their authority, but upon charters granted by the British crown; under which certain rights are claimed by the state, on the one hand, and by private individuals on the other. And if this court had been of opinion, that upon the face of these letters-patent, the question was clearly against the state, and that the proprietors had been derived at their just rights, by the erroneous judgment of the state court; it would, perhaps, be difficult to maintain, that this decision, of itself, bound the conscience of this court. It is, however, unquestionably, entitled to great weight. It confirms the construction uniformly placed on these charters and instruments, by the other public authorities; and in which the proprietors had so long acquiesced. Public acts and laws, both of the colonial and state governments, have been founded upon this interpretation; and extensive and valuable improvements made under it. In the case referred to, the sanction of the judicial authority of the state is given to it. And if the words of the letters-patent had been far more doubtful than they are, this decision, made upon such a question, with great deliberation and research, ought, in our judgment, to be regarded as conclusive.

Independently, however, of this decision of the supreme court of New Jersey, we are of opinion, that the proprietors are not entitled to the rights in question; and the judgment of the circuit court must, therefore, be reversed.

THOMPSON, Justice. (*Dissenting.*)

The premises in question in this case are a mud-flat covered by the waters of the bay of Amboy, in the state of New Jersey. The cause comes up on facts found by a special verdict in the court below; by which it appears, that the lessors of the plaintiff produced upon the trial, a regular deduction of title from Charles II down to themselves, and the premises in question are admitted to be within the grant. And the general question in the case is, whether this mud-flat passed under the grant, and in virtue of the several conveyances set out in the special verdict, became vested in the proprietors of New Jersey, as private property. The opinion of a majority of the court is against this right, in which opinion, however, I cannot concur, and shall briefly assign the reasons upon which my opinion rests.

Some objections have been made to the right of maintaining an action of ejectment, growing out of the nature of the subject-matter in controversy. There can be no grounds for such an objection. The subject in question is the right to land, and not to water. It is the ordinary case of an ejectment for land covered with water, and the premises are so set out and described in the declaration; and the special verdict finds, that the lessors of the plaintiff, under the title by them shown, entered into the tenements, with the appurtenances, in the declaration mentioned, and were thereof possessed, until the defendant afterwards entered upon, and ejected, expelled and removed the plaintiff from such possession. So that the subject-matter in controversy is found not only to be subsceptible of actual possession, but to have been so possessed and enjoyed.

A majority of the court seem to have and coasts of the sea, including both the waters and the land under the water, are common to the people of New Jersey; and that, under the grant of Charles II to the Duke of York, all the rights, which they call royalties, passed to the duke, as governor of the province, exercising the royal authority, and not as the proprietor of the soil; but that he held them as trustee for the benefit of all settlers in the province, and that the proprietors did not acquire any such right to the soil, that they would grant a several fishery; and that no person who plants a bed of oysters in a navigable river, has such property in the oysters as to enable him to maintain an action of trespass against any one who encroaches upon it. And this rests on the broad proposition, that the title to the land under the water did not, and could not, pass to the Duke of York, as private property. To maintain this proposition, it must rest on the ground, that the land under the water of a navigable river, is not the subject of a private right; for if it can be conveyed by words, the grant in the present case is broad enough to pass the title to the land in question.

It is worthy of observation, that the course of New Jersey in relation to this claim is hardly consistent with her pretensions. In the case of *Arnold v. Mundy*, the chief justice says, upon the revolution, all these rights became vested in the people of New Jersey, as the sovereign of the country, and are now in their hands; and the legislature may regulate them, &c. But the power which may be exercised by the sovereignty of the state is nothing more than what is called the *jus regium;* the right of regulating, improving and securing the same, for the benefit of every individual citizen. The sovereign power itself, therefore, cannot, consistently with the principles of the law of nature, and the constitution of a well-ordered society, make a direct and absolute grant of the waters of the state, divesting all the citizens of a common right. It would be a grievance which never could be long borne by a free people.

If this be the received doctrine in New Jersey, in relation to the navigable waters of that state, and the oyster fisheries, they remain common to all the citizens of New Jersey, and never can be appropriated to any private or individual use, and all laws having such object in view must be utterly null and void; and it is difficult to perceive, how the law of New Jersey, found by the special verdict, can be sustained. This act declares, that the shore and land covered with water may be set apart and laid out by commissioners, for the purpose of growing and planting oysters thereon, reserving such parts as might be judged necessary for public accommodation; provided, that nothing in the said act contained should authorize the commissioners to present any obstruction, or cause any injury to the navigation of the said sound and river, or to any fishery or fisheries therein. Here, the legislature treat these flats in all respects as land, to be used for planting and growing oysters; and for the use of which a revenue is derived to the state, by the payment of a rent reserved. It is not the use of the water for any public purpose, that this law contemplates; but an exclusive right to the use of the land under the water, in contradistinction to the use of the water for purposes of navigation; and that this law is so to be considered, is manifest, from the proviso, that no obstruction should be made to the fishery or fisheries therein; and here is a manifest distinction made between a fishery and an oyster-bed. For if it had been understood, that the fisheries included oysteries, the enacting clause and the proviso would present a glaring inconsistency. The enacting clause authorizes the setting apart the oystery to exclusive private use, when, by the proviso, no obstruction is to be made to the fisheries. So that, if an oystery is a fishery, the owner is deprived of the exclusive use of it. The act seems to be founded upon a distinction clearly held up, in many cases to be found in the books, between an oystery and a fishery, in the common use of the term. The one applying to the use of land under the water, which is peculiarly adapted to the growing of oysters, and to be used for that purpose, in the cultivation of oysters, as other lands are used for the purpose to which they are particularly adapted; whereas, a fishery, in common acceptation, has reference to the use of the water for floating fish; and this is a very obvious and natural distinction.

That the title to land under a navigable stream of water must be held subject to certain public rights, cannot be denied. But the question still remains, what are such public rights? Navigation, passing and repassing, are certainly among those public rights. And should it be admitted, that the right to fish for floating fish was included in this public right, it would not decide the present question. The premises in dispute are a mud-flat; and the use to which it has been and is claimed to be applied, is the growing and planting of oysters. It is the use of land, and not of water, that is in question. For the purpose of navigation, the water is considered as a public highway, common to all; like a public highway on land. If land over which a public highway passes, is conveyed, the soil passes, subject to that use; and the purchaser may maintain an action for an injury to this soil, not connected with the use; and whenever it ceases to be used as a public highway, the exclusive right of the owner attaches; so with respect to the land under water, the public use for passing and repassing, and all the purposes for which a public way may be used, are open to the public; the owner, nevertheless, retaining all the rights and benefits of the soil, that may not impede or interfere with the use as a public highway. Should a coal-mine, for instance, be discovered under such highway, it would belong to the owner of the soil, and might be used for his benefit; preserving, unimpaired, the public highway. So, with respect to an oyster-bed, which is local, and is attached to the soil. It is not the water that is over the beds that is claimed; that is common, and may be used by the public; but the use of the soil by the owner which is consistent with the use of the water by the public, is reserved to the owner. Suppose, this mud-flat should, by the wash from the shore, or the receding of the water, or in any other manner, be filled up and become solid ground (which is by no means an extravagant supposition); would not the proprietors be considered the owners of this land, and have the exclusive right to the use and enjoyment of it, if they had in no way parted with such right? This cannot be denied, if the soil passed to and became vested in the proprietors, under the grant to them. It surely would not be claimed by the state, it being no longer susceptible of public use.

The case of *Brown v. Kennedy*, 5 Har. & Johns. 195, is fully to this point. The question there related to the right to the soil in the bed of a navigable river, which had been diverted to a canal; and it was held, that the property in the soil covered by the water was vested in the lord proprietary, by the charter of Maryland; that by the common law, the right was in the king, and he might dispose of it *sub modo;* that the property in the soil may be granted, subject to the *jus publicum;* that by the terms of the charter to Lord Baltimore, they clearly passed the property in the soil covered by any waters, within the limits of the charter; and if the bed of the river had not been conveyed away, it would have remained in the proprietary; and if an island had sprung up, it would have been his; or if the bed of the river had been left bare, it would be his, as the *jus publicum* would be destroyed.

The rules and principles laid down by Lord HALE, as we find them in Hargrave's Law Tracts, are admitted as containing the correct common-law doctrine as to the rights and power of the king over the arms of the sea and navigable streams of water. We there find it laid down, that the king of England hath a double right in the sea, viz., a right of jurisdiction, which he ordinarily exercises by his admiral, and a right of propriety or ownership. Harg. 10. The king's right of propriety or ownership in the sea and soil thereof, is evinced principally in these things that follow. The right of fishing in the sea, and the creeks and arms thereof, is originally lodged in the crown; as the right of depasturing is originally lodged in the owner of the coast whereof he is lord, or as the right of fishing belongs to him that is the owner of a private or inland river. But though the king is the owner of this great coast, and as a consequence of his propriety, hath the primary right of fishing in the sea, and the creeks and arms thereof; yet the common people of England have regularly a liberty of fishing in the sea, or creeks or arms thereof, as a public common of piscary, and may not, without injury to their right, be restrained of it, unless in such places, creeks or navigable rivers, where either the king or some particular subject hath gained a propriety exclusive of that common liberty (p. 11). In many ports and arms of the sea, there is an exclusion of public fishing by prescription or custom (p. 12), although the king hath *primâ facie* this right in the arms and creeks of the sea, *communi jure*, and in common presumption; yet a subject may have such a right in two ways. 1. By the king's charter or grant; and this is without question. The king may grant fishing within some known bounds, though within the main sea, and may grant the water and soil of a navigable river (p. 17); and such a grant (when apt words are used) will pass the soil itself; and if there shall be a recess of the sea, leaving a quantity of land, it will belong to the grantee. 2. The second mode is by custom or prescription. There may be the right of fishing, without having the soil, or by reason of owning the soil, or a local fishery that arises from ownership of the soil (p. 18). That, *de communi jure*, the right of the arms of the sea belongs to the king; yet a subject may have a separate right of fishing, exclusive of the king and of the common right of the subject (p. 20). But this interest or right of the subject must be so used as not to occasion a common annoyance to the passage of the ships or boats; for that is prohibited by the common law, as well as by several statutes. For the *jus privatum* that is acquired to the subject, either by patent or prescription, must not prejudice the *jus publicum*, wherewith public rivers or arms of the sea are affected for public use (p. 22)—as the soil of a highway, in which, though in point of property, may be a private man's freehold, yet it is charged with a public interest of the people, which may not be prejudiced or damnified (p. 36).

These rules, as laid down by Lord HALE, have always been considered as settling the law upon the subjects so which they apply, and have been understood by all elementary writers, as governing rules, and have been recognized by the courts of justice as controlling doctrines. They establish, that by the common law, the king is the owner of all navigable rivers, bays and shores. That he owns them in full dominion and propriety, and has full power and authority to convey the same; that he may grant a several fishery in a navigable stream, and the common law has annexed only two limitations upon this power: that these waters shall remain highways for passage and navigation, and that whilst they remain ungranted, there is a common right of fishery in them; but subject to these limitations, the king has as full power to convey as an individual has to convey the land of which he is the owner.

I see nothing to countenance the distinctions set up, that the king holds these subjects as trustee, any more than does the dry land; or that he cannot convey them, discharged of the right of common fishery. There is no reason for such distinction with respect to land under water. The true rule on the subject is, that *primâ facie* a fishery in a navigable river is common, and he who sets up an exclusive right, must show title, either by grant or prescription. This is the doctrine of the king's bench, in England, in the case in 4 Burr. 2163. It was an action of trespass for breaking and entering the plaintiff's close, called the river Severn; and the defence set up was, that it was a navigable river, and an arm of the sea, wherein every subject has a right to fish; and that an exclusive right cannot be maintained by a subject, in a river that is an arm of the sea, but that the general right of fishing is common to all. But this doctrine was not recognised by the court. Lord MANSFIELD said, the rule of law is uniform. In rivers not navigable, the proprietors of the land have the right of fishing on their respective sides, and it generally extends *ad filum medium aquoe*. But in navigable rivers, the proprietors of the land on each side have it not; the fishery is common; it is *primâ facie* in the king, and is public. If any one claims it exclusively, he must show a right. If he can show a right by prescription, he may then exercise an exclusive right; though the presumption is against him, unless he can prove such a prescriptive right. Here, it is claimed and found. It is, therefore, consistent with all the cases, that he may have an exclusive privilege of fishing, although it is an arm of the sea; such a right shall not be presumed, but the contrary, *primâ facie;* but it is capable of being proved, and must have been so in the present case. And YATES, Justice, says, he was concerned in such a case, but the right was not proved, and so found common; but such a right may be proved. It may be appropriated by prescription; and he refers to the royal salmon fishery in the river Banne, in Sir John Davies's reports, and says, it is agreeable to this, and that it is a very good case. That it appears by it, that the crown may grant a several fishery in a navigable river, where the sea flows and reflows, or in the arm of the sea. And he refers to the case in 1 Mod. 105, where, he observes, Lord HALE says truly, if any one will appropriate a privilege to himself, the proof lieth on his side. Now, if it may be granted, it may be prescribed for; for a prescription implies a grant.

In the argument of this case, the counsel on the part of the defendant referred to the case of *Warren v. Matthews*, as reported in 6 Mod. 73, where it is said, every subject, of common right, may fish with lawful nets, &c., in a navigable river, as well as in the sea, and the king's grant cannot bar them thereof; and this case has been much relied on, in the argument of the case now before the court. But this report of the case in 6 Mod. 73, is clearly a mistake. It is the only case to be found, in which the broad proposition here stated is recognised, that the king's grant cannot bar the subject of the common right of fishing. And in the report of the same case, 1 Salk. 357, the case as stated is, that one claimed *solam piscariam*, in the river Ex, by a grant from the crown. And NOTT, Chief Justice, said, the subject has a right to fish in all navigable rivers, as he has to fish in the sea; and a *quo warranto* ought to be granted to try the title of this grantee, and the validity of his grant. Lord NOTT, here, no doubt, meant to speak of the *primâ facie* right of the subject. For if he intended to say, that no such exclusive right could be given by grant from the king, it would be absurd to issue a *quo warranto* to try the title and validity of the grant, if, by no possibility, a valid grant could be made. At all events, it is very certain, that the king's bench, in the case of *Carter v. Murcot*, did not recognise the doctrine of *Warren v. Matthews*, as reported in 6 Mod. 73. And under these circumstances, it is entitled to no weight in the decision of the case now before the court.

It is unnecessary to refer to the numerous cases in the English books on this subject; the doctrine as laid down in the case of *Carter v. Murcot* is universally recognised as the settled law on the subject, and is fully adopted and sanctioned by the courts of this country. Numerous cases of this description have come before the courts in the state of New York, and the principles and rules as laid down in the case of *Carter v. Murcot* fully recognised and adopted. In the case of *James v. Gould*, 6 Cow. 376, the court in referring to that case, place the decision upon it, and say, 'this is the acknowledged law of Great Britain and of this state'; and cases are referred to showing such to be the settled law.

In the case of *Johnson v. McIntosh*, 8 Wheat. 595, this court say, that according to the theory of the British constitution, all vacant lands are vested in the crown, as representing the nation, and the exclusive power to grant them is admitted to reside in the crown as a branch of the royal prerogative. And this principle is as fully recognised in America as in Great Britain; all the lands we hold were originally granted by the crown; our whole country has been granted; and the grants purport to convey the soil as well as the right of dominion to the grantee. Here, the absolute ownership is recognised as being in the crown, and to be granted by the crown, as the source of all title; and this extends as well to land covered by water as to the dry land; otherwise, no title could be acquired to land under water. There is, in this case, no intimation that any of the lands are vested in the crown, as trustee, but as absolute owner. If lands under water can be granted, and are actually granted, the grantees must, of course, acquire all the right to the use and enjoyment of such lands of which they are susceptible, as private property, as much so as the dry land; and there can be no grounds for any implied reservation of ungranted rights, in the one case, more than in the other; and the grant of the soil carries with it, of course, all the uses to which it may be applied, among which is an exclusive or several fishery. All grants of land, whether dry land or covered with water, are for great public purposes, subject to the control of the sovereign power of the country. So, the grant of the soil under water, which carries with it a several fishery, is subject to the use of the water for the public purposes of navigation, and passing and repassing; but it is nowhere laid down as the law of the land, that a several fishery is a part of the *jus publicum*, and open to the use of the public. So long as the fishery remains ungranted, it is common, and may be used by the public; but when granted to individuals, it becomes private property as much as any other subject whatever; and I think the law is too well settled, that a fishery may be the subject of a private grant, to be at this day drawn in question.

If, then, according to the principles of the common law, the king had the power to grant the soil under the waters of a navigable stream, where the tide ebbs and flows; and if such grant of soil carries with it the right of a several fishery, to the exclusion of a public use, the remaining inquiries are, whether the grant of Charles II to the Duke of York, in the year 1994, did convey the premises in question? and if so, then, whether this right was surrendered by the proprietors of New Jersey to Queen Anne, in the year 1702?

This charter to the Duke of York is one containing not only a grant of the soil, but of the powers of government. This court, in the case of *Johnson v. McIntosh*, in noticing the various charters from the crown, observe, that they purport to convey the soil and right of dominion to the grantees. In those governments which were denominated royal, where the right to the soil was not vested in individuals, but remained in the crown, or was vested in the colonial government, the king claimed and exercised the right of granting the lands. Some of these charters purport to convey the soil alone, and in those cases in which the powers of government as well as the soil are conveyed to individuals, the crown has always acknowledged itself to be bound by the grant; and in some instances, even after the powers of government were revested in the crown, the title of the proprietors of the soil was respected. The Carolinas were originally proprietary governments; but in 1721, a revolution was effected by the people, who shook off their obedience to the proprietors, and declared their dependence immediately on the crown, and the king purchased the title of those proprietors who were disposed to sell. Lord Carteret, however, who was one of the proprietors, surrendered his interest in the government, but retained his title to the soil; and that title was respected till the revolution, when it was forfeited by the laws of war.

This shows the light in which these charters, granting the soil, were considered by this court. That they conveyed an absolute interest in the soil, and passed everything susceptible of private and individual ownership, of which a fishery is certainly one, according to the settled law, by the authorities I have referred to. Subject always, as before mentioned, to the *jus publicum*, or rights of navigation and trade; but of which the right of a common fishery forms no part, after the soil has been conveyed as private property.

It is unnecessary to notice particularly the various charters and mesne conveyances set out in the special verdict. It was admitted, on the argument, that the premises in question fall within these conveyances; and vested in the proprietors of New Jersey all the right and title, both of soil and the powers of government, which passed to the Duke of York under the charter of Charles II. The terms employed in the description of the rights conveyed, are of the most comprehensive character, embracing the land, soil and waters. After a general description and designation of the territory embraced within the charter, and comprehending the premises in question, it adds, 'together with all the lands, islands, soils, rivers, harbors, mines, minerals, quarries, woods, marshes, waters, lakes, fishings, hawkings, huntings and fowlings, and all other royalties, profits, commodities and hereditaments, to the said several islands, lands and premises belonging and appertaining, with all and every of their appurtenances, and all our estate, right, title, interest, benefit, advantage, claim and demand of, in or to the said lands and premises, or any part or parcel thereof, and the reversion and reversions, remainder and remainders thereof; to have and to hold, all and singular the premises hereby granted, or herein mentioned, unto our brother James, Duke of York, his heirs and assigns for ever; to be holden of us, our heirs and successors, in free and common socage.' If these terms are not broad enough to include everything susceptible of being conveyed, it is difficult to conceive, what others could be employed for that purpose. The special verdict, after setting out the mesne conveyances by which the title is deduced down to the proprietors of New Jersey, sets out a confirmation of the title in the proprietors by Charles II, as follows: 'And the jurors, on their oath aforesaid, further say, that the said Charles II, afterwards, to wit, on the 23d day of November, in the year of our Lord 1683, by a certain instrument in writing, duly executed, bearing date on the same day and year last aforesaid, and reciting the said last-mentioned indenture from the said Duke of York to the said 24 proprietors, did recognise their right to the soil and government of the said province of East New Jersey, whereof the tenements aforesaid, with the appurtenances, in the declaration aforesaid, are parcel, and did strictly charge and command the planters and inhabitants, and all other persons concerned in the same, to submit and yield all due obedience to the laws and government of the said 24 proprietors, their heirs and assigns, as absolute proprietors and governors thereof, who, in the words of the said instrument in writing, had the sole power and right, derived under the said Duke of York, from him, the said Charles II., to settle and dispose of the said province of East New Jersey, upon such terms and conditions, as to the 24 proprietors, their heirs and assigns, should deem meet.' Here is the most full recognition and confirmation of the right and title of the proprietors to the soil, with the absolute power to dispose of the same, in such manner as they should think proper. The absolute ownership could not be expressed in a more full and unqualified a manner. In the case of *Fairfax v. Hunter's Lessee*, 7 Cranch 618, the question was as to the legal effect and operation of certain descriptive words in a charter of Charles II; and Mr. Justice STORY, in giving the opinion of the court, said, 'The first question is, whether Lord Fairfax was proprietor of, and seised of, the soil of the waste and unappropriated lands in the Northern Neck, by virtue of the royal grants of Charles II, and James II; or whether he had mere seignoral rights therein, as lord paramount, disconnected with all interest in the land, except of sale and alienation. The royal charter expressly conveys all that entire tract, territory and parcel of land, situate, &c., together with all the rivers, islands, woods, timber, &c., mines, quarries of stone, and coal, &c., to the grantees and their heirs and assigns, to their only use and behoof, and to no other use, intent and purpose whatsoever.' 'It is difficult,' say the court, 'to conceive terms more explicit than these to vest a title and interest in the soil itself. The land is given, and the exclusive use thereof; and if the union of the title, and the exclusive use, do not constitute the complete and absolute dominion in the property, it will not be easy to fix any which shall constitute such dominion.' The terms here used are certainly not more broad and comprehensive than those used in the charter under consideration; and if they will pass the right to the soil, in the one case, they certainly must, in the other. The land in the one case, being covered with water, and in the other not, can make no difference as to the passing of the title, if land under water can be conveyed at all; and whatever the public right to the use of the water may be, it can give no right to the use of the land under the water, which has, by the grant, become private property. And if, as I think, the authorities clearly show, a grant of the soil carries with it the right to every private use to which it can be applied, including the cultivation of oysters, there can be no ground upon which this can be claimed as a common right. A several fishery and a common fishery are utterly incompatible with each other. The former is founded upon and annexed to the right of soil; and when that right of soil is acquired by an individual, the several fishery begins, and the common fishery ends.

Did the proprietors, then, by the surrender of Queen Anne, in the year 1702, relinquish any rights of private property in the soil, derived under the charter of Charles II? I think it very clear, that they surrendered nothing but the mere powers of government granted by the charter, retaining, unaffected in any manner whatever, the right of private property.

The special verdict states the surrender as follows: 'That on the 15th day of April, in the year 1702, the said 24 proprietors, and the other persons in whom, by sundry means conveyances and assurances in the law, the whole estate, right, title and interest in the said province of East New Jersey, were vested, at the said last-mentioned date, as proprietors thereof, by an instrument in writing, under their hands and seals, bearing date the same day and year last aforesaid, did, for themselves and their heirs, surrender and yield up unto Anne, Queen of England, &c., and to her heirs and successors, all the powers and authorities in the said letters-patent granted, to correct, punish, pardon, govern and rule all or any of her said majesty's subjects, or others who then were, as inhabitants, or thereafter might adventure into, or inhabit, within the said province of East New Jersey. And also to nominate, make, constitute, ordain and confirm any laws, orders, ordinances, directions and instruments, for those purposes, or any of them; and to nominate, constitute or appoint, revoke, discharge, change or alter any governor or governors, officers or ministers, which were or should be appointed within the said province; and to make, ordain and establish any orders, laws, directions, instruments, forms or ceremonies of government and magistracy, for or concerning the same, or on the sea, in going to or coming from the same, or to put in execution or abrogate, revoke or change such as were already made, for or concerning such government, or any of them. And also the powers and authorities by the said letters-patent granted, to use and exercise martial law in the said province of East New Jersey. And to admit any persons to trade or traffic there. And of encountering, repelling and resisting by force of arms, any person or persons attempting to inhabit there, without the license of them, the said proprietors, their heirs and assigns. And all other the powers, authorities and privileges of and concerning the government of the province last aforesaid, or the inhabitants thereof, which were granted, or mentioned to be granted, by the said several above-recited letters-patent, or either of them. And that the said Queen Anne, afterwards, to wit, on the 17th day of the same month of April, in the year last aforesaid, did accept of the said surrender of the said powers of government, so made by the said proprietors, in and over the premises last aforesaid.'

I do not perceive, in this surrender, a single term or expression that can, in the remotest degree, have any reference to the private property conveyed by the grant, or to any matter except that which related to the powers of government; all the enumerated subjects manifestly have relation only to such powers. And after this specification of particulars, comes the special clause, 'and all other the powers, authorities and privileges of and concerning the government'; necessarily implying that the specified subjects related to the powers of government; and the acceptance by the queen manifestly limits the surrender to such powers; she accepts the said surrender of the said powers of government so made by the proprietors in and over the premises.

If there was anything in the language here used, which could in the least degree render doubtful the object and purpose of this surrender, the memorials of the proprietors, and the correspondence which took place on the subject, referred to on the argument, as contained in the collection of Leaming & Spicer, must remove all doubt, and show that the surrender was confined exclusively to the powers of government, and intended to operate, nor only as a surrender of such powers, but as a confirmation of all right and title to the soil and private property of the proprietors. And if so, the proprietors' right must depend upon the power of the king to grant the right claimed in the premises, and the construction of the charter, as to what it does embrace. And I have endeavored to show, that by the settled and uncontradicted principles of the common law, the king had the power to grant the land under the water of a navigable river; and that such grant carries with it to the grantee, all rights of private property of which the susceptible, subject to the *jus publicum;* that the grant of the soil necessarily carries with it a several and exclusive fishery, which is utterly incompatible with the rights of a common fishery, and which, of course, can form no part of the *jus publicum;* and that the grant in question of Charles II. to the Duke of York, conveyed all private right in the soil which could be conveyed by the king; all which rights, by sundry mesne conveyances, became vested in the proprietors of East New Jersey, and from them to the lessor of the plaintiff. And I can discover nothing in the authorities, giving countenance to the idea, that the king held the land covered by the waters of a navigable river, as trustee, or by a tenure different from that by which he held the dry land. And I must again repeat, if the king held such lands as trustee, for the common benefit of all his subjects, and inalienable as private property, I am unable to discover, on what ground the state of New Jersey can hold the land discharged of such trust, and can assume to dispose of it to the private and exclusive use of individuals. If it was a trust estate in the king, for the benefit of his subjects, and upon the revolution, the government of New Jersey became the trustee, in the place of the king, and the trust devolved upon such government, and the land became as inalienable in the government of New Jersey as in the hands of the king, and the state must be bound to hold all such lands subject to the trust, which, as contended, embraces a common right of fishery in the waters, and the dredging for oysters in the land covered by the waters; and if this be so, there certainly can be no power in the state, without a breach of trust, to deprive the citizens of New Jersey of such common right, and convert these oyster grounds to the private and exclusive use of individuals.

There is nothing in the case, in my judgment, showing a usage in the state, by which the proprietors have, either directly or by implication, relinquished or abandoned any right of property which they derived under the charter of Charles II. All the authority exercised by the state in granting ferries, bridges, turnpikes and railroads, &c., are the exercise of powers vested in the government over private property, for public uses, and formed a part of the powers of government surrendered by the proprietors to Queen Anne; and it is only since the decision in *Arnold v. Mundy*, that the private right of the proprietors to the lands under the waters in New Jersey has been denied, and assumed by the state to grant the same to individuals; and even in such cases, it has been done cautiously, and apparently with hesitation as to the right of the state. In the two cases referred to on the argument, of a grant to N. Burden, on the 8th of November 1836, and to Aaron Ogden, on the 25th of January 1837, of land under the water, the grant is a mere release or quit-claim of the state; but the proprietors have been in the habit of making grants for land under the water, from the time of the surrender to Queen Anne down to the year 1820, and numerous instances of such grants were referred to on the argument.

With respect, however, to the right of fishery, there is, in my judgment, a marked distinction, both in reason and authority, between the right in relation to floating fish, and the right of dredging for oysters. The latter is entirely local and connected with the soil. There are natural beds of oysters, but in other places, there is a peculiar soil, adapted to the growing of oysters. They are planted and cultivated by the hand of man, like other productions of the earth; and the books in many cases clearly hold up such a distinction, and speak of the oyster fishery as distinct from that of floating fish (5 Burr. 2814); and in the case of *Rogers v. Allen*, 1 Camp. 309, this distinction is expressly taken. It was an action of trespass for breaking and entering the several oyster fishery of the plaintiffs, in Burnham river, and fishing and dredging for oysters. The defence set up was, that the *locus in quo* was a navigable river, in which all the king's subjects had a right to fish and dredge for oysters; and evidence was introduced, showing that all who chose, had been accustomed to fish in Burnham river, for all sorts of floating fish, without interruption; and it was contended, that a fishery was entire, and that as it had been proved, that it was lawful for all the king's subjects to catch floating fish, so they might lawfully dredge for oysters. But HEATH, Justice, ruled otherwise, and said, a fishery was divisible; a part may be abandoned, and another part of more value may be preserved. The public may be entitled to catch floating fish, in the river Burnham, but it by no means follows, that they are justified in dredging for oysters, which may still remain private property; and although a new trial was granted upon another point in the case, the doctrine as above stated was not at all impugned by the court of king's bench.

Upon the whole, I am of opinion, that the judgment of the circuit court ought to be affirmed.

POLLARD v. HAGAN

44 U.S. 212, 3 How. 212, 11 L.Ed. 565 (1845)

This case comes before this court upon a writ of error to the Supreme Court of Alabama.

An action of ejectment was brought by the plaintiffs against the defendants, in the Circuit Court of Mobile county, in said state; and upon the trial, to support their action, 'the plaintiffs read in evidence a patent from the United States for the premises in question, and an act of Congress passed the 6th day of July, 1836, confirming to them the premises in the patent mentioned, together with an act of Congress passed the 20th of May, 1824. The premises in question were admitted by the defendants to be comprehended within the patent; and there was likewise an admission by both parties that the land lay between Church street and North Boundary street, in the city of Mobile; and there the plaintiffs rested their case.'

'The defendants, to maintain the issue on their part, introduced a witness to prove that the premises in question, between the years 1819 and 1823, were covered by water of the Mobile river at common high tide'; to which evidence the plaintiffs by their counsel objected; but the court overruled the objection, and permitted the evidence to go to the jury. 'It was also in proof, on the part of the defendant, that ruled the objection, and permitted grant to Panton, Leslie & Co., under which they claim, the waters of the Mobile bay, at high tide, flowed over what is now Water street, and over about one-third of the lot west of Water street, conveyed by the Spanish grant to Panton, Leslie & Co.; and that the waters continued to overflow Water street, and the premises sued for, during all the time up to 1822 or 1823; to all which admissions of evidence, on part of the defendants, the plaintiffs excepted.' 'The court charged the jury, that if they believed the premises sued for were below usual high water-mark, at the time Alabama was admitted into the union, then the act of Congress, and the patent in pursuance thereof, could give the plaintiffs no title, whether the waters had receded by the labor of man only, or by alluvion; to which the plaintiffs excepted. Whereupon a verdict and judgment were rendered in favor of the defendants, and which judgment was afterwards affirmed by the Supreme Court of the state.'

This question has been heretofore raised, before this court, in cases from the same state, but they went off upon other points. As now presented, it is the only question necessary to the decision of the case before us, and must, therefore, be decided. And we now enter into its examination with a just sense of its great importance to all the states of the union, and particularly to the new ones. Although this is the first time we have been called upon to draw the line that separates the sovereignty and jurisdiction of the government of the union, and the state governments, over the subject in controversy, many of the principles which enter into and form the elements of the question have been settled by previous, well considered, decisions of this court, to which we shall have occasion to refer in the course of this investigation.

The counsel for the plaintiffs insisted, in argument, that the United States derived title to that part of Alabama, in which the land in controversy lies, from the King of Spain; and that they succeeded to all his rights, powers, and jurisdiction, over the territory ceded, and therefore hold the land and soil, under navigable waters, according to the laws and usages of Spain; and by those laws and usages the rights of a subject to land derived from the crown could not extend beyond high water-mark, on navigable waters, without an express grant; and that all alluvion belonged to the crown, and might be granted by this king, together with all land between high water and the channel of such navigable waters; and by the compact between the United States and Alabama, on her admission into the union, it was agreed, that the people of Alabama for ever disclaimed all right or title to the waste or unappropriated lands lying within the state, and that the same should remain at the sole disposal of the United States; and that all the navigable waters within the state should for ever remain public highways, and free to the citizens of that state and the United States, without any tax, duty, or impost, or toll therefor, imposed by that state. That by these articles of the compact, the land under the navigable waters, and the public domain above high water, were alike reserved to the United States, and alike subject to be sold by them; and to give any other construction to these compacts, would be to yield up to Alabama, and the other new states, all the public lands within their limits.

We think a proper examination of this subject will show, that the United States never held any municipal sovereignty, jurisdiction, or right of soil in and to the territory, of which Alabama, or any of the new states were formed; except for temporary purposes, and to execute the trusts created by the acts of the Virginia and Georgia legislatures, and the deeds of cession executed by them to the United States, and the trust created by the treaty with the French republic, of the 30th of April, 1803, ceding Louisiana.

All that part of Alabama which lies between the thirty-first and thirty-fifth degree of north latitude, was ceded by the state of Georgia to the United States, by deed bearing date the 24th day of April, 1802, which is substantially, in all its principles and stipulations, like the deed of cession executed by Virginia to the United States, on the 1st day of March, 1784, by which she ceded to the United States the territory north-west of the river Ohio. Both of these deeds of cession stipulated, that all the lands within the territory ceded, and not reserved or appropriated to other purposes, should be considered as a common fund for the use and benefit of all the United States, to be faithfully and *bona fide* disposed of for that purpose, and for no other use or purpose whatever. And the statute passed by Virginia authorizing her delegates to execute this deed, and which is recited in it, authorizes them, in behalf of the state, by a proper deed to convey to the United States, for the benefit of said states, all the right, title, and claim, as well of soil as jurisdiction, 'upon condition that the territory so ceded shall be laid out and formed into states, containing a suitable extent of territory, not less than 100, nor more than 150 miles square, or as near thereto as circumstances will admit: and that the states so formed shall be republican states and admitted members of the federal union, having the same rights of sovereignty, freedom, and independence, as the other states.' And the delegates conclude the deed thus: 'Now know ye, that we, the said Thomas Jefferson, Samuel Hardy, Arthur Lee, and James Monroe, by virtue of the power and authority committed to us by the act of the said general assembly of Virginia before recited, and in the name and for and on behalf of the said commonwealth, do by these presents convey, transfer, assign, and make over unto the United States in Congress assembled, for the benefit of said states, Virginia inclusive, all right, title, and claim, as well of soil as of jurisdiction, which the said commonwealth hath to the territory or tract of country within the limits of the Virginia charter, situate, lying, and being to the north-west of the river Ohio, to and for the uses and purposes, and on the conditions of the said recited act.'

And in the deed of cession by Georgia it is expressly stipulated, 'That the territory thus ceded shall form a state and be admitted as such into the union as soon as it shall contain sixty thousand free inhabitants, or at an earlier period if Congress shall think it expedient, on the same conditions and restrictions, with the same privileges, and in the same manner, as is provided in the ordinance of Congress of the 13th day of July, 1787, for the government of the north-western territory of the United States, which ordinance shall in all its parts extend to the territory contained in the present act of cession, that article only excepted which forbids slavery.' The manner in which the new states were to be admitted into the union, according to the ordinance of 1787, as expressed therein, is as follows: 'And whenever any of the said states shall have sixty thousand free inhabitants therein, such state shall be admitted by its delegates into the Congress of the United States, on an equal footing with the original states in all respects whatever.' Thus it appears that the stipulations, trusts, and conditions, are substantially the same in both of these deeds of cession; and the acts of Congress, and of the state legislatures in relation thereto, are founded in the same reasons of policy and interest, with this exception, however—the cession made by Virginia was before the adoption of the Constitution of the United States, and that of Georgia afterwards. Taking the legislative acts of the United States, and the states of Virginia and Georgia, and their deeds of cession to the United States, and giving to each, separately, and to all jointly, a fair interpretation, we must come to the conclusion that it was the intention of the parties to invest the United States with the eminent domain of the country ceded, both national and municipal, for the purposes of temporary government, and to hold it in trust for the performance of the stipulations and conditions expressed in the deeds of cession and the legislative acts connected with them. To a correct understanding of the rights, powers, and duties of the parties to these contracts, it is necessary to enter into a more minute examination of the rights of eminent domain, and the right to the public lands. When the United States accepted the cession of the territory, they took upon themselves the trust to hold the municipal eminent domain for the new states, and to invest them with it, to the same extent, in all respects, that it was held by the states ceding the territories.

The right which belongs to the society, or to the sovereign, of disposing, in case of necessity, and for the public safety, of all the wealth contained in the state, is called the *eminent domain*. It is evidence that this right is, in certain cases, necessary to him who governs, and is, consequently, a part of the empire, or sovereign power. Vat. Law of Nations, section 244. This definition shows, that the eminent domain, although a sovereign power, does not include all sovereign power, and this explains the sense in which it is used in this opinion. The compact made between the United States and the state of Georgia, was sanctioned by the Constitution of the United States; but the 3d section of the 4th article of which it is declared, that 'New states may be admitted by the Congress into this union; but no new state shall be formed or erected within the jurisdiction of any other state, nor any state be formed by the junction of two or more states or parts of states, without the consent of the legislatures of the states concerned, as well as of Congress.'

When Alabama was admitted into the union, on an equal footing with the original states, she succeeded to all the rights of sovereignty, jurisdiction, and eminent domain which Georgia possessed at the date of the cession, except so far as this right was diminished by the public lands remaining in the possession and under the control of the United States, for the temporary purposes provided for in the deed of cession and the legislative acts connected with it. Nothing remained to the United States, according to the terms of the agreement, but the public lands. And, if an express stipulation had been inserted in the agreement, granting the municipal right of sovereignty and eminent domain to the United States, such stipulation would have been void and inoperative: because the United States have no constitutional capacity to exercise municipal jurisdiction, sovereignty, or eminent domain, within the limits of a state or elsewhere, except in the cases in which it is expressly granted. [footnote omitted.]

By the 16th clause of the 8th section of the 1st article of the Constitution, power is given to Congress 'to exercise exclusive legislation in all cases whatsoever, over such district (not exceeding ten miles square) as may by cession of particular states, and the acceptance of Congress, become the seat of government of the United States,' and to exercise like authority over all places purchased, by the consent of the legislature of the state in which the same may be, for the erection of forts, magazines, arsenals, dock-yards, and other needful buildings. Within the District of Columbia, and the other places purchased and used for the purposes above mentioned, the national and municipal powers of government, of every description, are united in the government of the union. And these are the only cases, within the United States, in which all the powers of government are united in a single government, except in the cases already mentioned of the temporary territorial governments, and there a local government exists. The right of Alabama and every other new state to exercise all the powers of government, which belong to and may be exercised by the original states of the union, must be admitted, and remain unquestioned, except so far as they are, temporarily, deprived of control over the public lands.

We will now inquire into the nature and extent of the right of the United States to these lands, and whether that right can in any manner affect or control the decision of the case before us. This right originated in voluntary surrenders, made by several of the old states, of their waste and unappropriated lands, to the United States, under a resolution of the old Congress, of the 6th of September, 1780, recommending such surrender and cession, to aid in paying the public debt, incurred by the war of the Revolution. The object of all the parties to these contracts of cession, was to convert the land into money for the payment of the debt, and to erect new states over the territory thus ceded; and as soon as these purposes could be accomplished, the power of the United States over these lands, as property, was to cease.

Whenever the United States shall have fully executed these trusts, the municipal sovereignty of the new states will be complete, throughout their respective borders, and they, and the original states, will be upon an equal footing, in all respects whatever. We, therefore, think the United States hold the public lands within the new states by force of the deeds of cession, and the statutes connected with them, and not by any municipal sovereignty which it may be supposed they possess, or have reserved by compact with the new states, for that particular purpose. The provision of the Constitution above referred to shows that no such power can be exercised by the United States within a state. Such a power is not only repugnant to the Constitution, but it is inconsistent with the spirit and intention of the deeds of cession. The argument so much relied on by the counsel for the plaintiffs, that the agreement of the people inhabiting the new states, 'that they for ever disclaim all right and title to the waste or unappropriated lands lying within the said territory; and that the same shall be and remain at the sole and entire disposition of the United States,' cannot operate as a contract between the parties, but is binding as a law. Full power is given to Congress 'to make all needful rules and regulations respecting the territory or other property of the United States.' This authorized the passage of all laws necessary to secure the rights of the United States to the public lands, and to provide for their sale, and to protect them from taxation.

And all constitutional laws are binding on the people, in the new states and the old ones, whether they consent to be bound by them or not. Every constitutional act of Congress is passed by the will of the people of the United States, expressed through their representatives, on the subject- matter of the enactment; and when so passed it becomes the supreme law of the land, and operates by its own force on the subject-matter, in whatever state or territory it may happen to be. The proposition, therefore, that such a law cannot operate upon the subject-matter of its enactment, without the express consent of the people of the new state where it may happen to be, contains its own refutation, and requires no farther examination. The propositions submitted to the people of the Alabama territory, for their acceptance or rejection, by the act of Congress authorizing them to form a constitution and state government for themselves, so far as they related to the public lands within that territory, amounted to nothing more nor less than rules and regulations respecting the sales and disposition of the public lands. The supposed compact relied on by the counsel for the plaintiffs, conferred no authority, therefore, on Congress to pass the act granting to the plaintiffs the land in controversy.

And this brings us to the examination of the question, whether Alabama is entitled to the shores of the navigable waters, and the soils under them, within her limits. The principal argument relied on against this right, is, that the United States acquired the land in controversy from the

King of Spain. Although there was no direct reference to any particular treaty, we presume the treaty of the 22d of February, 1819, signed at Washington, was the one relied on, and shall so consider the argument. It was insisted that the United States had, under the treaty, succeeded to all the rights and powers of the King of Spain; and as by the laws and usages of Spain, the king had the right to grant to a subject the soil under navigable waters, that, therefore, the United States had the right to grant the land in controversy, and thereby the plaintiffs acquired a complete title.

If it were true that the United States acquired the whole of Alabama from Spain, no such consequences would result as those contended for. It cannot be admitted that the King of Spain could, by treaty or otherwise, impart to the United States any of his royal prerogatives; and much less can it be admitted that they have capacity to receive or power to exercise them. Every nation acquiring territory, by treaty or otherwise, must hold it subject to the constitution and laws of its own government, and not according to those of the government ceding it. Vat. Law of Nations, b. 1, c. 19, s. 210, 244, 245, and b. 2, c. 7, s. 80.

The United States have never claimed any part of the territory included in the states of Mississippi or Alabama, under any treaty with Spain, although she claimed at different periods a considerable portion of the territory in both of those states. By the treaty between the United States and Spain, signed at San Lorenzo el Real, on the 27th of October, 1795, 'The high contracting parties declare and agree, that the line between the United States and East and West Florida, shall be designated by a line, beginning on the river Mississippi, at the northernmost part of the thirty-first degree of north latitude, which from thence shall be drawn due east to the middle of the Chatahouchee river,' &c. This treaty declares and agrees, that the line which was described in the treaty of peace between Great Britain and the United States, as their southern boundary, shall be the line which divides their territory from East and West Florida. The article does not import to be a cession of territory, but the adjustment of a controversy between the two nations. It is understood as an admission that the right was originally in the United States.

Had Spain considered herself as ceding territory, she could not have neglected to stipulate for the property of the inhabitants, a stipulation which every sentiment of justice and of national honor would have demanded, and which the United States would not have refused. But, instead of requiring an article to this effect, she expressly stipulated to withdraw the settlements then within what the treaty admits to be the territory of the United States, and for permission to the settlers to take their property with them. 'We think this an unequivocal acknowledgment that the occupation of the territory by Spain was wrongful, and we think the opinion thus clearly indicated was supported by the state of facts. It follows, that Spanish grants made after the treaty of peace can have no intrinsic validity.' *Henderson v. Poindexter*, 12 Wheat., 535.

Previous to the cession made by Georgia, the United States, by the act of Congress of the 7th of April, 1798, had established the Mississippi territory including the territory west of the Chatahouchee river, to the Mississippi river, above the 31st degree of north latitude, and below the Yazous river, subject to the claim of Georgia to any portion of the territory. And the territory thus erected was subjected to the ordinance of the 13th of July, 1787, for its government, that part of it excepted which prohibited slavery: 1 Story's Laws, 494. And by the act of the 1st of March, 1817, having first obtained consent of Georgia to make two states instead of one within the ceded territory, Congress authorized the inhabitants of the western part of the Mississippi territory to form for themselves a constitution and state government, 'to consist of all the territory included within the following boundaries, to wit: Beginning on the river Mississippi at the point where the southern boundary line of the state of Tennessee strikes the same; thence east along the said boundary line to the Tennessee river; thence up the same to the mouth of Bear creek: thence by a direct line, to the north-west corner of Washington county; thence due south to the Gulf of Mexico; thence westwardly, including all the islands within six leagues of the shore, to the junction of Pearl river with Lake Borgne; thence up said river to the thirty-first degree of north latitude; thence west along said degree of latitude to the Mississippi river; thence up the same to the beginning.' 3 Story's Laws, 1620. And on the 3d of March, 1817, Congress passed an act declaring, 'That all that part of the Mississippi territory which lies within the following boundaries, to wit: Beginning at the point where the line of the thirty-first degree of north latitude intersects the Perdido river; thence east to the western boundary line of the state of Georgia; thence along said line to the southern boundary line of the state of Tennessee; thence west, along said boundary line, to the Tennessee river; thence up the same to the mouth of Bear creek; thence by a direct line to the north-west corner of Washington county; thence due south to the Gulf of Mexico; thence eastwardly, including all the islands within six leagues of the shore to the Perdido river; thence up the same to the beginning; shall, for the purposes of temporary government, constitute a separate territory, and be called Alabama.'

And by the 2d section of the same act it is enacted, 'That all offices which exist, and all laws which may be in force when this act shall go into effect, shall continue to exist and be in force until otherwise provided by law.' 3 Story's Laws, 1634, 1635. And by the 2d article of the compact contained in the ordinance of 1787, which was then in force in the Mississippi territory, among other things, it was provided, that 'The inhabitants of the said territory shall always be entitled to the benefits of the writ of habeas corpus, and of the trial by jury, and of judicial proceedings according to the course of the common law.' And by the proviso to the 5th section of the act of the 2d of March, 1819, authorizing the people of the Alabama territory to form a constitution and state government, it is enacted, 'That the constitution, when formed, shall be republican, and not repugnant to the ordinance of the 13th of July, 1787, between the states and the people of the territory north-west of the Ohio river, so far as the same has been extended to the said territory [of Alabama] by the articles of agreement between the United States and the state of Georgia.' By these successive acts on part of the United States, the common law has been extended to all the territory within the limits of the state of Alabama, and therefore excluded all other law, Spanish or French.

It was after the date of the treaty of the 22d of February, 1819, between the United States and Spain, but before its ratification, the people of the Alabama territory were authorized to form a constitution; and the state was admitted into the union, according to the boundaries established when the country was erected into a territorial government. But the United States have never admitted that they derived title from the Spanish government to any portion of the territory included within the limits of Alabama. Whatever claim Spain may have asserted to the territory above the thirty-first degree of north latitude, prior to the treaty of the 27th of October, 1795, was abandoned by that treaty, as has been already shown. We will now inquire whether she had any right to territory below the thirty-first degree of north latitude, after the treaty between France and the United States, signed at Paris on the 30th of April, 1803, by which Louisiana was ceded to the United States. The legislative and executive departments of the government have constantly asserted the right of the United States to this portion of the territory under the 1st article of this treaty; and a series of measures intended to maintain the right have been adopted. Mobile was taken possession of, and erected into a collection district, by act of the 24th of February, 1804, chap. 13, (2 Story's Laws, 914.) In the year 1810, the President issued his proclamation, directing the governor of the Orleans territory to take possession of the country, as far as the Perdido, and hold it for the United States. It April, 1812, Congress passed an act to enlarge the limits of Louisiana. This act includes part of the country claimed by Spain, as West Florida. And in February, 1813, the President was authorized to occupy and hold all that tract of country called West Florida, which lies west of the river Perdido, not then in the possession of the United States. And these measures having been followed by the erection of Mississippi territory into a state, and the erection of Alabama into a territory, and afterwards into a state, in the year 1819, and extending them both over this territory: could it be doubted that these measures were intended as an assertion of the title of the United States to this country?

In the case of *Foster* and *Elam v. Neilson*, 2 Pet., 253, the right of the United States to this country underwent a very able and thorough investigation. And Chief Justice Marshall, in delivering the opinion of the court, said: 'After these acts of sovereign power over the territory in dispute, asserting the American construction of the treaty, by which the government claims it, to maintain the opposite construction in its own courts would certainly be an anomaly in the history and practice of nations. If those departments, which are entrusted with the foreign intercourse of the nation, which assert and maintain its interests against foreign powers, have unequivocally asserted its rights of dominion over a country of which it is in possession, and which it claims under a treaty; if the legislature has acted on the construction thus asserted, it is not in its own courts that this construction is to be denied.' The chief justice then discusses the validity of the grant made by the Spanish government, after the ratification of the treaty between the United States and France, and it is finally rejected on the ground that the country belonged to the United States, and not to Spain, when the grant was made. The same doctrine was maintained by this court in the case of *Garcia v. Lee*, 12 Pet., 511. These cases establish, beyond controversy, the right of the United States to the whole of this territory, under the treaty with France.

Alabama is therefore entitled to the sovereignty and jurisdiction over all the territory within her limits, subject to the common law, to the same extent that Georgia possessed it before she ceded it to the United States. To maintain any other doctrine, is to deny that Alabama has been admitted into the union on an equal footing with the original states, the constitution, laws, and compact, to the contrary notwithstanding. But her rights of sovereignty and jurisdiction are not governed by the common law of England as it prevailed in the colonies before the Revolution, but as modified by our own institutions. In the case of *Martin and others v. Waddell*, 16 Pet., 410, the present chief justice, in delivering the opinion of the court, said: 'When the Revolution took place, the people of each state became themselves sovereign; and in that character hold the absolute right to all their navigable waters, and the soils under them for their own common use, subject only to the rights since surrendered by the Constitution.' Then to Alabama belong the navigable waters, and soils under them, in controversy in this case, subject to the rights surrendered by the Constitution to the United States; and no compact that might be made between her and the United States could diminish or enlarge these rights.

The declaration, therefore, contained in the compact entered into between them when Alabama was admitted into the union, 'that all navigable waters within the said state shall for ever remain public highways, free to the citizens of said state, and of the United States, without any tax, duty, impost, or toll therefor, imposed by the said state,' would be void if inconsistent with the Constitution of the United States. But is this provision repugnant to the Constitution? By the 8th section of the 1st article of the Constitution, power is granted to Congress 'to regulate commerce with foreign nations, and among the several states.' If, in the exercise of this power, Congress can impose the same restrictions upon the original states, in relation to their navigable waters, as are imposed, by this article of the compact, on the state of Alabama, then this article is a mere regulation of commerce among the several states, according to the Constitution, and, therefore, as binding on the other states as Alabama.

In the case of *Gibbons v. Ogden*, 9 Wheat., 196, after examining the preliminary questions respecting the regulation of commerce with foreign nations, and among the states, as connected with the subject-matter there in controversy, Chief Justice Marshall said: 'We are now arrived at the inquiry: What is this power?

'It is the power to regulate, that is, to prescribe the rule by which commerce is to be governed. This power, like all others vested in Congress, is complete in itself, may be exercised to its utmost extent, and acknowledges no limitations other than are prescribed in the Constitution. These are expressed in plain terms, and do not affect the questions which arise in this case. If, as has been always understood, the sovereignty of Congress, though limited to specified objects, is plenary as to those objects, the power over commerce with foreign nations, and among the several states, is vested in Congress as absolutely as it would be in a single government having in its constitution the same restrictions on the exercise of the power as are found in the Constitution of the United States.' As the provision of what is called the compact between the United States and the state of Alabama does not, by the above reasoning, exceed the power thereby conceded to Congress over the original states on the same subject, no power or right was, by the compact, intended to be reserved by the United States, nor to be granted to them by Alabama.

This supposed compact is, therefore, nothing more than a regulation of commerce, to that extent, among the several states, and can have no controlling influence in the decision of the case before us. This right of eminent domain over the shores and the soils under the navigable waters, for all municipal purposes, belongs exclusively to the states within their respective territorial jurisdictions, and they, and they only, have the constitutional power to exercise it. To give to the United States the right to transfer to a citizen the title to the shores and the soils under the navigable waters, would be placing in their hands a weapon which might be wielded greatly to the injury of state sovereignty, and deprive the states of the power to exercise a numerous and important class of police powers. But in the hands of the states this power can never be used so as to affect the exercise of any national right of eminent domain or jurisdiction with which the United States have been invested by the Constitution. For, although the territorial limits of Alabama have extended all her sovereign power into the sea, it is there, as on the shore, but municipal power, subject to the Constitution of the United States, 'and the laws which shall be made in pursuance thereof.'

By the preceding course of reasoning we have arrived at these general conclusions: First, The shores of navigable waters, and the soils under them, were not granted by the Constitution to the United States, but were reserved to the states respectively. Secondly, The new states have the same rights, sovereignty, and jurisdiction over this subject as the original states. Thirdly, The right of the United States to the public lands, and the power of Congress to make all needful rules and regulations for the sale and disposition thereof, conferred no power to grant to the plaintiffs the land in controversy in this case. The judgment of the Supreme Court of the state of Alabama is, therefore, affirmed.

In the case of inland, non-tidal navigable waterways, the upper reach of the waterway held in public trust was the ordinary high water line.

BARNEY v. KEOKUK

94 U.S. 324, 4 Otto 324, 24 L.Ed. 224 (1876)

We agree with the court below that the dedication of the streets of Keokuk was a dedication at common law, and not under the statute; and that, in making this dedication, the original proprietors of the tract reserved the title to the soil in the street, particularly in Water Street; and that this title went with the several lots fronting on the street, and extended to the Mississippi River. Whether, under the laws of Iowa, it also attached to the new ground formed by filling in upon the bed of the river is not so clear. It appears to be the settled law of that State that the title of the riparian proprietors on the banks of the Mississippi extends only to ordinary high-water mark, and that the shore between high and low water mark, as well as the bed of the river, belongs to the State. This is also the common law with regard to navigable waters; although, in England, no waters are deemed navigable except those in which the tide ebbs and flows. In this country, as a general thing, all waters are deemed navigable which are really so; and especially it is true with regard to the Mississippi and its principal branches. The question as to the extent of the riparian title was elaborately discussed in the case of *McManus v. Carmichael*, 3 Iowa, 1. The above conclusion was reached, and has always been adhered to in that State. *Haight v. The City of Keokuk*, 4 Iowa, 199; *Tomlin v. Dubuque, & c. Railroad Co.*, 32 id. 106.

The peculiar origin of the title to the 'Half-breed Sac and Fox reservation,' in the peninsula lying between the rivers Mississippi and Des Moines, did not take it out of the general rule. This was so held in *Haight v. The City of Keokuk, supra*. That case was nearly identical with the present as respects the claim of the adjoining proprietor to the title of the land in Water Street and on the river bank. Haight contested the right of the city to control the wharf along said street, claiming, by virtue of his fee-simple title, the right to erect a private wharf and to receive the emoluments thereof. His claim was overruled, and on the question of title the court said:—

'According to the case of *McManus v. Carmichael*, then, Haight owns the soil to high water only. But here is interposed the argument, that this land is not held under the United States by the usual manner of grants, that is, by patent, after a survey, and described by section, town, and range. This is true; but yet it will not affect the extent of the complainant's right. The grant to the half-breeds was to them as persons and not as a political body. The political jurisdiction remained in the United States. Had the grant been to them as a political society, it would have been a question of boundary between nations or States, and then the line would have been the *medium filum aquae*, as it is now between Iowa and Illinois.... The grant was to them as individuals,—as tenants in common,—and is to be construed as any other grant or sale to individuals.'

The court then goes on to refer to various cases to show that the government cannot convey the land between high and low water on the public or navigable rivers, but that this space belongs to the State; citing *Mayor of Mobile v. Eslava*, 9 Port. 578; 16 Pet. 234; *Pollard's Lessee v. Hagan*, 3 How. 212.

It is generally conceded that the riparian title attaches to subsequent accretions to the land effected by the gradual and imperceptible operation of natural causes. But whether it attaches to land reclaimed by artificial means from the bed of the river, or to sudden accretions produced by unusual floods, is a question which each State decides for itself. By the common law, as before remarked, such additions to the land on navigable waters belong to the crown; but as the only waters recognized in England as navigable were tide-waters, the rule was often expressed as applicable to tide-waters only, although the reason of the rule would equally apply to navigable waters above the flow of the tide; that reason being, that the public authorities ought to have entire control of the great passageways of commerce and navigation, to be exercised for the public advantage and convenience. The confusion of navigable with tide water, found in the monuments of the common law, long prevailed in this country, notwithstanding the broad differences existing between the extent and topography of the British island and that of the American continent. It had the influence for two generations of excluding the admiralty jurisdiction from our great rivers and inland seas; and under the like influence it laid the foundation in many States of doctrines with regard to the ownership of the soil in navigable waters above tide-water at variance with sound principles of public policy. Whether, as rules of property, it would now be safe to change these doctrines where they have been applied, as before remarked, is for the several States themselves to determine. If they choose to resign to the riparian proprietor rights which properly belong to them in their sovereign capacity, it is not for others to raise objections. In our view of the subject the correct principles were laid down in *Martin v. Waddell*, 16 Pet. 367, *Pollard's Lessee v. Hagan*, 3 How. 212, and *Goodtitle v. Kibbe*, 9 id. 471. These cases related to tide-water, it is true; but they enunciate principles which are equally applicable to all navigable waters. And since this court, in the case of *The Genesee Chief*, 12 id. 443, has declared that the Great Lakes and other navigable waters of the country, above as well as below the flow of the tide, are, in the strictest sense, entitled to the denomination of navigable waters, and amenable to the admiralty jurisdiction, there seems to be no sound reason for adhering to the old rule as to the proprietorship of the beds and shores of such waters. It properly belongs to the States by their inherent sovereignty, and the United States has wisely abstained from extending (if it could extend) its survey and grants beyond the limits of high water. The cases in which this court has seemed to hold a contrary view depended, as most cases must depend, on the local laws of the States in which the lands were situated. In Iowa, as before stated, the more correct rule seems to have been adopted after a most elaborate investigation of the subject.

The exhaustive examination of this question by the Supreme Court of Iowa in 1856, in the case of *McManus v. Carmichael*, 3 Iowa, 1, really leaves nothing to be said. The precise point was directly before the court,—namely, whether the title of the riparian proprietor extends below high water, in the Mississippi River; and it was decided that it does not. This decision has been followed by subsequent cases, especially the cases of *Haight v. The City of Keokuk*, 4 id. 199; and *Tomlin v. Dubuque Railroad Co.*, 32 id. 106.

But whatever may be the true rule on this vexed question, and whether we rightly comprehend the Iowa decisions or not, we have no doubt that the city authorities of Keokuk, representing the public, had the right to widen and improve Water Street to any extent on the river side, by filling in below high water, and building wharves and levees for the public accommodation. By the charter of the city, passed Dec. 13, 1848, it was provided,—

> 'SECT. 14. That the city council shall have power ... to establish and constitute landing-places, wharves, docks, and basins in said city, at or on any of the city property, and fix the rates of landing, wharfage, and dockage of all steamboats, boats, rafts, and other water-crafts, and of all goods, wares, merchandise, produce, and other articles that may be moored at, landed on, or taken from any landing, wharf, dock, or basin belonging to said city.'

> 'SECT. 16. That the city council shall have power ... to license and establish ferries across the Mississippi River from said city to the opposite shore, to fix the rates of the same.' ...

> 'SECT. 22. The city council shall have exclusive power to establish and regulate the grade of wharves, streets, and banks along the Mississippi River, within the corporate limits of said city.'

And by a supplement, passed Jan. 22, 1853, it was provided,—

> 'SECT. 7. The said city of Keokuk shall have the power to establish and regulate wharf or wharves in said city, and more particularly to use the whole of Water Street for said purpose.' ...

Although it should be conceded that the title of the plaintiff attached to the ground reclaimed and filled in by the city outside of the original high water, it was a bare legal title, subject to the public easement and use, not only for street purposes, but for the purposes of wharves, landings, and levees. A street bordering on the river, as this did, according to the plan of the town adopted by the decree of partition, must be regarded as intended to be used for the purposes of access to the river, and the usual accommodations of navigation in such a connection. This subject is discussed in Haight's case, where the court said,—

> 'One further thought, presented by the petitioner, should be noticed. It is, that if this ground is dedicated to the public, it is as a street only; and that if his rights are subject to the public uses, they are so subject to the use of it only as a street or highway, and not as a wharf, and that it is named and called a street and not a wharf. He claims that the object of a street is for passage, for travelling over, and not to land or deposit goods upon. This is taking a very narrow and close view. The streets of a town are fairly subject to many purposes to which a highway in the country would not be. More regard should be paid to the object and purpose than to the name. The ways of a town would be of comparatively little use if the citizens and traders could not deposit their goods in them temporarily, in their transit to the storehouse; and so of other things, and so it is of the wharf. If goods cannot be deposited upon it in preparation for shipping them, or unladen upon it from boats and vessels, why is a town located near the river upon land which, in other respects, is inconvenient, and is expensive to grade, to bring into form and order, and to keep in repair, instead of upon an even prairie, requiring no such trouble and outlay?'

On the general question as to the rights of the public in a city street, we cannot see any material difference in principle with regard to the extent of those rights, whether the fee is in the public or in the adjacent land-owner, or in some third person. In either case, the street is legally open and free for the public passage, and for such other public uses as are necessary in a city, and do not prevent its use as a thoroughfare, such as the laying of water-pipes, gas-pipes, and the like; and, according to the laws of Iowa (which must be taken to govern the case), it may be occupied by those improved iron ways for public passage which modern skill has devised, and which the advance of general improvement requires. It cannot be denied that horse-railroads have contributed immensely to the public convenience in furnishing a rapid, cheap, and convenient means of communication between different parts of large towns, and have greatly promoted their increase and growth in wealth and population. By the accommodation which they afford, the citizen can reside miles from his shop or place of business. Though attended with some inconveniences, they have greatly added to the efficiency of the public thoroughfares, and have more than doubled their capacity for travel and transportation.

So other railways coming to cities add greatly to their population and wealth, and furnish greatly increased facilities of communication with other portions of the country.

In Iowa, by the act called the 'Right of Way Act,' found in the Code of 1851, sect. 735, it is declared that,—

> 'The county court may also grant licenses for the construction of any canal or railroad, or any macadamized or plank-road, or any other improvement of a similar character, or any telegraph line, to keep the same up for a period not exceeding fifty years, and to use for this purpose any portion of the public highway or other property, public or private, if necessary: *Provided*, such use shall not obstruct the highway.' Iowa Revision of 1860, p. 206.

By the construction given to this act by the Supreme Court of the State, railroads, especially when located and constructed under municipal regulation and control, are not regarded as obstructions to a highway in the legal sense, nor as creating, when laid thereon, any injury to the proprietors of the adjacent lands, for which they are entitled to compensation. The cases referred to by the Circuit Court (which are given below) abundantly demonstrate this conclusion, and no elaborate discussion of the subject is required from us. See *Milburn v. Cedar Rapids*, 12 Iowa, 249-260; *Clinton v. Cedar Rapids & Mo. Railroad Co.*, 24 id. 455; *Tomlin v. Dubuque Railroad Co.*, 32 id. 106; *Chicago, Newton, & S. W. Railroad Co.*, 36 id. 299; *Cook v. City of Burlington*, id. 357; *Clinton v. Clinton & Lyon Railroad Co.*, 37 id. 61; *Ingraham et al. v. Chicago, Dubuque, & Minn. Railroad Co.*, 38 id. 669.

The cases cited, it is true, are generally those in which the fee of the streets was in the cities respectively, as is commonly the case in Iowa. But in Haight's case, in 4 Iowa, the very street now in question was under consideration, and the plaintiff had the same title as that of the plaintiff in the present case; and the principles laid down in all the later cases apply as well where the title of the soil is in the adjacent proprietor as where it is in the city or a third party. And, as before remarked, we can perceive no well-founded difference in principle between the one and the other as to the rights of the public.

The Circuit Court is clearly correct, however, in holding that the construction of a permanent freight depot in Water Street was an unauthorized and improper occupation of that street. It was a total obstruction of the passage; and this, as we have said, cannot be created or allowed. It is subversive of, and totally repugnant to, the dedication of the street, as well as to the rights of the public.

We also concur in the view taken by the Circuit Court as to the reasonableness of the erection of the packet depot in the place where it is located. It is a necessary adjunct to the steamboat landing, and the use of the wharf and levee for the purposes of navigation, and does not occupy any portion of the original street. It is a public use of the river bank, which is absolutely necessary to the use of the river as a navigable water. The erection of levees, wharves, and other accommodations on the very ground appropriated to such purposes by the original plot of the town, or, stronger still, on ground made and reclaimed from the bed of the river adjoining the street thus appropriated, and in enlargement thereof, is clearly within the powers of the city authorities as laid down in the cases referred to.

Judgment AFFIRMED.

In some cases, lands held in public trust have included non-navigable tributaries of navigable waterways if the activity in the tributary affects the public trust value in the navigable portion. *National Audubon Society v. Superior Court*, 33 Cal.3d 419, 189 Cal.Rptr. 346, 658 P.2d 709, *cert. denied*, 464 U.S. 977, 78 L.Ed.2d 351, 104 S.Ct. 413 (1983).

Under Roman and English law, the public trust doctrine protected commercial shipping and fishing. In the United States these activities as well as recreational activities, fowling, and drinking and irrigation water needs have been included. *See, e.g., Lamprey v. Metcalf*, 52 Minn. 181, 53 N.W. 1139 (1893). As the uses to which water is put have increased, the courts have similarly expanded the interest protected under the public trust doctrine. For example, California now includes lands in their natural state that may serve as ecological study areas, provide food and habitat for birds and marine life, or simply serve to favorably affect the scenery and climate of the area. Perhaps the most modern expression of the public trust doctrine is that whereas in the past the sovereign held certain lands in trust for certain uses, now there is some discussion that the resources themselves, independent of their human use, may be entitled to protection in their own right. See Stone, Christopher D., *Should Trees Have Standing? Toward Legal Rights For Natural Objects*, Palo Alto: William Kaufmann, Inc. (1974), p. 9. Stone's essay proposes "... that we give legal rights to forests, oceans, rivers and other so-called 'natural objects' in the environment—indeed, to the natural environment as a whole." See also Leopold, Aldo, *A Sand County Almanac And Sketches Here and There*, New York: Oxford University Press (American Museum of Natural History, 1968 ed.).

The public trust doctrine would appear to grant authority to the government to take almost any action with respect to private property so long as it could be justified as a measure to protect an essential public resource. Governmental limitations on the use of property under the authority of the Clean Water Act would seem to be a particularly appropriate application of the public trust doctrine in light of the special purpose of the statute, to restore and maintain clean water. Apart from the discussion of whether water itself would have a right to protection, certainly the public's interest in a continued supply of clean water should outweigh an individual's use that fouls it. Indeed some conservationists have taken this middle position, between the water having its own right to protection and the individual's right to do anything he or she chooses with the water present on private property. To some extent the argument was successful until a constitutional principle, the Fifth Amendment Taking Clause, was applied to limit the unfettered application of the public trust doctrine.

NOLLAN v. CALIFORNIA COASTAL COMMISSION

483 U.S. 825, 107 S.Ct. 3141, 97 L.Ed.2d 677 (1987)

James and Marilyn Nollan appeal from a decision of the California Court of Appeal ruling that the California Coastal Commission could condition its grant of permission to rebuild their house on their transfer to the public of an easement across their beachfront property. 177 Cal.App.3d 719, 223 Cal.Rptr. 28 (1986). The California court rejected their claim that imposition of that condition violates the Takings Clause of the Fifth Amendment, as incorporated against the States by the Fourteenth Amendment. Ibid. We noted probable jurisdiction. 479 U.S. 913, 107 S.Ct. 312, 93 L.Ed.2d 286 (1986).

I

The Nollans own a beachfront lot in Ventura County, California. A quarter-mile north of their property is Faria County Park, an oceanside public park with a public beach and recreation area. Another public beach area, known locally as "the Cove," lies 1,800 feet south of their lot. A concrete seawall approximately eight feet high separates the beach portion of the Nollans' property from the rest of the lot. The historic mean high tide line determines the lot's oceanside boundary.

The Nollans originally leased their property with an option to buy. The building on the lot was a small bungalow, totaling 504 square feet, which for a time they rented to summer vacationers. After years of rental use, however, the building had fallen into disrepair, and could no longer be rented out.

The Nollans' option to purchase was conditioned on their promise to demolish the bungalow and replace it. In order to do so, under Cal.Pub.Res. Code Ann. §§30106, 30212, and 30600 (West 1986), they were required to obtain a coastal development permit from the California Coastal Commission. On February 25, 1982, they submitted a permit application to the Commission in which they proposed to demolish the existing structure and replace it with a three-bedroom house in keeping with the rest of the neighborhood.

The Nollans were informed that their application had been placed on the administrative calendar, and that the Commission staff had recommended that the permit be granted subject to the condition that they allow the public an easement to pass across a portion of their property bounded by the mean high tide line on one side, and their seawall on the other side. This would make it easier for the public to get to Faria County Park and the Cove. The Nollans protested imposition of the condition, but the Commission overruled their objections and granted the permit subject to their recordation of a deed restriction granting the easement. App. 31, 34.

On June 3, 1982, the Nollans filed a petition for writ of administrative mandamus asking the Ventura County Superior Court to invalidate the access condition. They argued that the condition could not be imposed absent evidence that their proposed development would have a direct adverse impact on public access to the beach. The court agreed, and remanded the case to the Commission for a full evidentiary hearing on that issue. *Id.*, at 36.

On remand, the Commission held a public hearing, after which it made further factual findings and reaffirmed its imposition of the condition. It found that the new house would increase blockage of the view of the ocean, thus contributing to the development of "a 'wall' of residential structures" that would prevent the public "psychologically ... from realizing a stretch of coastline exists nearby that they have every right to visit." *Id.*, at 58. The new house would also increase private use of the shorefront. *Id.*, at 59. These effects of construction of the house, along with other area development, would cumulatively "burden the public's ability to traverse to and along the shorefront." *Id.*, at 65-66. Therefore the Commission could properly require the Nollans to offset that burden by providing additional lateral access to the public beaches in the form of an easement across their property. The Commission also noted that it had similarly conditioned 43 out of 60 coastal development permits along the same tract of land, and that of the 17 not so conditioned, 14 had been approved when the Commission did not have administrative regulations in place allowing imposition of the condition, and the remaining three had not involved shorefront property. *Id.*, at 47-48.

The Nollans filed a supplemental petition for a writ of administrative mandamus with the Superior Court, in which they argued that imposition of the access condition violated the Takings Clause of the Fifth Amendment, as incorporated against the States by the Fourteenth Amendment. The Superior Court ruled in their favor on statutory grounds, finding, in part to avoid "issues of constitutionality," that the California Coastal Act of 1976, Cal.Pub.Res.Code Ann. §30000 et seq. (West 1986), authorized the Commission to impose public access conditions on coastal development permits for the replacement of an existing single-family home with a new one only where the proposed development would have an adverse impact on public access to the sea. App. 419. In the court's view, the administrative record did not provide an adequate factual basis for concluding that replacement of the bungalow with the house would create a direct or cumulative burden on public access to the sea. Id., at 416-417. Accordingly, the Superior Court granted the writ of mandamus and directed that the permit condition be struck.

The Commission appealed to the California Court of Appeal. While that appeal was pending, the Nollans satisfied the condition on their option to purchase by tearing down the bungalow and building the new house, and bought the property. They did not notify the Commission that they were taking that action.

The Court of Appeal reversed the Superior Court. 177 Cal.App.3d 719, 223 Cal.Rptr. 28 (1986). It disagreed with the Superior Court's interpretation of the Coastal Act, finding that it required that a coastal permit for the construction of a new house whose floor area, height or bulk was more than ten percent larger than that of the house it was replacing be conditioned on a grant of access. *Id.*, at 723-724, 223 Cal.Rptr., at 31; see Cal.Pub.Res.Code Ann. §30212. It also ruled that the requirement did not violate the Constitution under the reasoning of an earlier case of the Court of Appeal, *Grupe v. California Coastal Comm'n,* 166 Cal.App.3d 148, 212 Cal.Rptr. 578 (1985). In that case, the court had found that so long as a project contributed to the need for public access, even if the project standing alone had not created the need for access, and even if there was only an indirect relationship between the access exacted and the need to which the project contributed, imposition of an access condition on a development permit was sufficiently related to burdens created by the project to be constitutional. 177 Cal.App.3d, at 723, 223 Cal.Rptr., at 30-31; *see Grupe, supra,* 166 Cal.App.3d, at 165-168, 212 Cal.Rptr., at 587-590; *see also Remmenga v. California Coastal Comm'n,* 163 Cal.App.3d 623, 628, 209 Cal.Rptr. 628, 631, appeal dism'd, 474 U.S. 915, 106 S.Ct. 241, 88 L.Ed.2d 250 (1985). The Court of Appeal ruled that the record established that that was the situation with respect to the Nollans' house. 177 Cal.App.3d, at 722-723, 223 Cal.Rptr., at 30-31. It ruled that the Nollans' taking claim also failed because, although the condition diminished the value of the Nollans' lot, it did not deprive them of all reasonable use of their property. Id., at 723, 223 Cal.Rptr., at 30; *see Grupe, supra,* 166 Cal.App.3d, at 175-176, 212 Cal.Rptr., at 595-596. Since, in the Court of Appeal's view, there was no statutory or constitutional obstacle to imposition of the access condition, the Superior Court erred in granting the writ of mandamus. The Nollans appealed to this Court, raising only the constitutional question.

II

Had California simply required the Nollans to make an easement across their beachfront available to the public on a permanent basis in order to increase public access to the beach, rather than conditioning their permit to rebuild their house on their agreeing to do so, we have no doubt there would have been a taking. To say that the appropriation of a public easement across a landowner's premises does not constitute the taking of a property interest but rather (as

Justice BRENNAN contends) "a mere restriction on its use," *post*, at 3154, n.3, is to use words in a manner that deprives them of all their ordinary meaning. Indeed, one of the principal uses of the eminent domain power is to assure that the government be able to require conveyance of just such interests, so long as it pays for them. J. Sackman, 1 *Nichols on Eminent Domain* §2.1[1] (Rev. 3d ed. 1985), 2 id., §5.01[5]; *see* 1 *id.*, §1.42 [9], 2 *id.*, §6.14. Perhaps because the point is so obvious, we have never been confronted with a controversy that required us to rule upon it, but our cases' analysis of the effect of other governmental action leads to the same conclusion. We have repeatedly held that, as to property reserved by its owner for private use, "the right to exclude [others is] 'one of the most essential sticks in the bundle of rights that are commonly characterized as property.'" *Loretto v. Teleprompter Manhattan CATV Corp.*, 458 U.S. 419, 433, 102 S.Ct. 3164, 3175, 73 L.Ed.2d 868 (1982), quoting *Kaiser Aetna v. United States,* 444 U.S. 164, 176, 100 S.Ct. 383, 391, 62 L.Ed.2d 332 (1979). In *Loretto* we observed that where governmental action results in "[a] permanent physical occupation" of the property, by the government itself or by others, see 458 U.S., at 432-433, n. 9, 102 S.Ct., at 3174-3175, n.9, "our cases uniformly have found a taking to the extent of the occupation, without regard to whether the action achieves an important public benefit or has only minimal economic impact on the owner," *id.*, at 434-435, 102 S.Ct., at 3175-3176. We think a "permanent physical occupation" has occurred, for purposes of that rule, where individuals are given a permanent and continuous right to pass to and fro, so that the real property may continuously be traversed, even though no particular individual is permitted to station himself permanently upon the premises. [Footnote omitted.]

Justice BRENNAN argues that while this might ordinarily be the case, the California Constitution's prohibition on any individual's "exclu[ding] the right of way to [any navigable] water whenever it is required for any public purpose," Art. X, §4, produces a different result here. Post, at 3153-3154; see also post, at 3157, 3158-3159. There are a number of difficulties with that argument. Most obviously, the right of way sought here is not naturally described as one to navigable water (from the street to the sea) but along it; it is at least highly questionable whether the text of the California Constitution has any prima facie application to the situation before us. Even if it does, however, several California cases suggest that Justice BRENNAN's interpretation of the effect of the clause is erroneous, and that to obtain easements of access across private property the State must proceed through its eminent domain power. *See Bolsa Land Co. v. Burdick,* 151 Cal. 254, 260, 90 P. 532, 534-535 (1907); *Oakland v. Oakland Water Front Co.,* 118 Cal. 160, 185, 50 P. 277, 286 (1897); *Heist v. County of Colusa,* 163 Cal.App.3d 841, 851, 213 Cal.Rptr. 278, 285 (1984); *Aptos Seascape Corp. v. Santa Cruz,* 138 Cal.App.3d 484, 505-506, 188 Cal.Rptr. 191, 204-205 (1982). (None of these cases specifically addressed the argument that Art. X, §4 allowed the public to cross private property to get to navigable water, but if that provision meant what Justice BRENNAN believes, it is hard to see why it was not invoked.) *See* also 41 Op.Cal.Atty.Gen. 39, 41 (1963) ("In spite of the sweeping provisions of [Art. X, §4], and the injunction therein to the Legislature to give its provisions the most liberal interpretation, the few reported cases in California have adopted the general rule that one may not trespass on private land to get to navigable tidewaters for the purpose of commerce, navigation or fishing"). In light of these uncertainties, and given the fact that, as Justice BLACKMUN notes, the Court of Appeal did not rest its decision on Art. X, §4, post, at 3162, we should assuredly not take it upon ourselves to resolve this question of California constitutional law in the first instance. *See, e.g., Jenkins v. Anderson,* 447 U.S. 231, 234, n.1, 100 S.Ct. 2124, 2127, n.1, 65 L.Ed.2d 86 (1980). That would be doubly inappropriate since the Commission did not advance this argument in the Court of Appeal, and the Nollans argued in the Superior Court that any claim that there was a pre-existing public right of access had to be asserted through a quiet title action, *see* Points and Authorities in Support of Motion for Writ of Administrative Mandamus, No. SP50805 (Super.Ct.Cal.),

p. 20, which the Commission, possessing no claim to the easement itself, probably would not have had standing under California law to bring. See Cal.Code Civ.Proc.Ann. §738 (West 1980). [Footnote omitted.]

Given, then, that requiring uncompensated conveyance of the easement outright would violate the Fourteenth Amendment, the question becomes whether requiring it to be conveyed as a condition for issuing a land-use permit alters the outcome. We have long recognized that land-use regulation does not effect a taking if it "substantially advance[s] legitimate state interests" and does not "den[y] an owner economically viable use of his land," *Agins v. Tiburon,* 447 U.S. 255, 260, 100 S.Ct. 2138, 2141, 65 L.Ed.2d 106 (1980). See also *Penn Central Transportation Co. v. New York City,* 438 U.S. 104, 127, 98 S.Ct. 2646, 2660, 57 L.Ed.2d 631 (1978)("[A] use restriction may constitute a 'taking' if not reasonably necessary to the effectuation of a substantial government purpose"). Our cases have not elaborated on the standards for determining what constitutes a "legitimate state interest" or what type of connection between the regulation and the state interest satisfies the requirement that the former "substantially advance" the latter. [Footnote omitted.] They have made clear, however, that a broad range of governmental purposes and regulations satisfies these requirements. *See Agins v. Tiburon, supra,* 447 U.S., at 260-262, 100 S.Ct., at 2141-2142 (scenic zoning); *Penn Central Transportation Co. v. New York City, supra* (landmark preservation); *Euclid v. Ambler Realty Co.,* 272 U.S. 365, 47 S.Ct. 114, 71 L.Ed. 303 (1926) (residential zoning); Laitos & Westfall, *Government Interference with Private Interests in Public Resources,* 11 Harv.Envtl.L.Rev. 1, 66 (1987). The Commission argues that among these permissible purposes are protecting the public's ability to see the beach, assisting the public in overcoming the "psychological barrier" to using the beach created by a developed shorefront, and preventing congestion on the public beaches. We assume, without deciding, that this is so—in which case the Commission unquestionably would be able to deny the Nollans their permit outright if their new house (alone, or by reason of the cumulative impact produced in conjunction with other construction) [Footnote omitted.] would substantially impede these purposes, unless the denial would interfere so drastically with the Nollans' use of their property as to constitute a taking. *See Penn Central Transportation Co. v. New York City, supra.*

The Commission argues that a permit condition that serves the same legitimate police-power purpose as a refusal to issue the permit should not be found to be a taking if the refusal to issue the permit would not constitute a taking. We agree. Thus, if the Commission attached to the permit some condition that would have protected the public's ability to see the beach notwithstanding construction of the new house—for example, a height limitation, a width restriction, or a ban on fences—so long as the Commission could have exercised its police power (as we have assumed it could) to forbid construction of the house altogether, imposition of the condition would also be constitutional. Moreover (and here we come closer to the facts of the present case), the condition would be constitutional even if it consisted of the requirement that the Nollans provide a viewing spot on their property for passersby with whose sighting of the ocean their new house would interfere. Although such a requirement, constituting a permanent grant of continuous access to the property, would have to be considered a taking if it were not attached to a development permit, the Commission's assumed power to forbid construction of the house in order to protect the public's view of the beach must surely include the power to condition construction upon some concession by the owner, even a concession of property rights, that serves the same end. If a prohibition designed to accomplish that purpose would be a legitimate exercise of the police power rather than a taking, it would be strange to conclude that providing the owner an alternative to that prohibition which accomplishes the same purpose is not.

The evident constitutional propriety disappears, however, if the condition substituted for the prohibition utterly fails to further the end advanced as the justification for the prohibition. When that essential nexus is eliminated, the situation becomes the same as if California law forbade shouting fire in a crowded theater, but granted dispensations to those willing to contribute $100 to the state treasury. While a ban on shouting fire can be a core exercise of the State's police power to protect the public safety, and can thus meet even our stringent standards for regulation of speech, adding the unrelated condition alters the purpose to one which, while it may be legitimate, is inadequate to sustain the ban. Therefore, even though, in a sense, requiring a $100 tax contribution in order to shout fire is a lesser restriction on speech than an outright ban, it would not pass constitutional muster. Similarly here, the lack of nexus between the condition and the original purpose of the building restriction converts that purpose to something other than what it was. The purpose then becomes, quite simply, the obtaining of an easement to serve some valid governmental purpose, but without payment of compensation. Whatever may be the outer limits of "legitimate state interests" in the takings and land-use context, this is not one of them. In short, unless the permit condition serves the same governmental purpose as the development ban, the building restriction is not a valid regulation of land use but "an out-and-out plan of extortion." *J.E.D. Associates, Inc. v. Atkinson,* 121 N.H. 581, 584, 432 A.2d 12, 14-15 (1981); *see* Brief for United States as *Amicus Curiae* 22, and n.20. *See* also *Loretto v. Teleprompter Manhattan CATV Corp.,* 458 U.S., at 439, n.17, 102 S.Ct., at 3178, n.17. [Footnote omitted.]

III

The Commission claims that it concedes as much, and that we may sustain the condition at issue here by finding that it is reasonably related to the public need or burden that the Nollans' new house creates or to which it contributes. We can accept, for purposes of discussion, the Commission's proposed test as to how close a "fit" between the condition and the burden is required, because we find that this case does not meet even the most untailored standards. The Commission's principal contention to the contrary essentially turns on a play on the word "access." The Nollans' new house, the Commission found, will interfere with "visual access" to the beach. That in turn (along with other shorefront development) will interfere with the desire of people who drive past the Nollans' house to use the beach, thus creating a "psychological barrier" to "access." The Nollans' new house will also, by a process not altogether clear from the Commission's opinion but presumably potent enough to more than offset the effects of the psychological barrier, increase the use of the public beaches, thus creating the need for more "access." These burdens on "access" would be alleviated by a requirement that the Nollans provide "lateral access" to the beach.

Rewriting the argument to eliminate the play on words makes clear that there is nothing to it. It is quite impossible to understand how a requirement that people already on the public beaches be able to walk across the Nollans' property reduces any obstacles to viewing the beach created by the new house. It is also impossible to understand how it lowers any "psychological barrier" to using the public beaches, or how it helps to remedy any additional congestion on them caused by construction of the Nollans' new house. We therefore find that the Commission's imposition of the permit condition cannot be treated as an exercise of its land-use power for any of these purposes. [Footnote omitted.] Our conclusion on this point is consistent with the approach taken by every other court that has considered the question, with the exception of the California state courts. *See Parks v. Watson,* 716 F.2d 646, 651-653 (CA9 1983); *Bethlehem Evangelical Lutheran Church v. Lakewood,* 626 P.2d 668, 671-674 (Colo.1981); *Aunt Hack Ridge Estates, Inc. v. Planning Comm'n,* 160 Conn. 109, 117-120, 273 A.2d 880, 885 (1970); *Longboat*

Key v. Lands End, Ltd., 433 So.2d 574 (Fla.App.1983); *Pioneer Trust & Savings Bank v. Mount Prospect,* 22 Ill.2d 375, 380, 176 N.E.2d 799, 802 (1961); *Lampton v. Pinaire,* 610 S.W.2d 915, 918-919 (Ky.App.1980); *Schwing v. Baton Rouge,* 249 So.2d 304 (La.App.), *application denied,* 259 La. 770, 252 So.2d 667 (1971); *Howard County v. JJM, Inc.,* 301 Md. 256, 280-282, 482 A.2d 908, 920-921 (1984); *Collis v. Bloomington,* 310 Minn. 5, 246 N.W.2d 19 (1976); *State ex rel. Noland v. St. Louis County,* 478 S.W.2d 363 (Mo.1972); *Billings Properties, Inc. v. Yellowstone County,* 144 Mont. 25, 33-36, 394 P.2d 182, 187-188 (1964); *Simpson v. North Platte,* 206 Neb. 240, 292 N.W.2d 297 (1980); *Briar West, Inc. v. Lincoln,* 206 Neb. 172, 291 N.W.2d 730 (1980); *J.E.D. Associates v. Atkinson,* 121 N.H. 581, 432 A.2d 12 (1981); *Longridge Builders, Inc. v. Planning Bd. of Princeton,* 52 N.J. 348, 350-351, 245 A.2d 336, 337-338 (1968); *Jenad, Inc. v. Scarsdale,* 18 N.Y.2d 78, 271 N.Y.S.2d 955, 218 N.E.2d 673 (1966); *MacKall v. White,* 85 App.Div.2d 696, 445 N.Y.S.2d 486 (1981), *appeal denied,* 56 N.Y.2d 503, 450 N.Y.S.2d 1025, 435 N.E.2d 1100 (1982); *Frank Ansuini, Inc. v. Cranston,* 107 R.I. 63, 68-69, 71, 264 A.2d 910, 913, 914 (1970); *College Station v. Turtle Rock Corp.,* 680 S.W.2d 802, 807 (Tex.1984); *Call v. West Jordan,* 614 P.2d 1257, 1258-1259 (Utah 1980); *Board of Supervisors of James City County v. Rowe,* 216 Va. 128, 136-139, 216 S.E.2d 199, 207-209 (1975); *Jordan v. Menomonee Falls,* 28 Wis.2d 608, 617-618, 137 N.W.2d 442, 447-449 (1965), *appeal dism'd,* 385 U.S. 4, 87 S.Ct. 36, 17 L.Ed.2d 3 (1966). *See also Littlefield v. Afton,* 785 F.2d 596, 607 (CA8 1986); Brief for National Association of Home Builders et al. as Amici Curiae 9-16.

Justice BRENNAN argues that imposition of the access requirement is not irrational. In his version of the Commission's argument, the reason for the requirement is that in its absence, a person looking toward the beach from the road will see a street of residential structures including the Nollans' new home and conclude that there is no public beach nearby. If, however, that person sees people passing and repassing along the dry sand behind the Nollans' home, he will realize that there is a public beach somewhere in the vicinity. *Post,* at 3154-3155. The Commission's action, however, was based on the opposite factual finding that the wall of houses completely blocked the view of the beach and that a person looking from the road would not be able to see it at all. App. 57-59.

Even if the Commission had made the finding that Justice BRENNAN proposes, however, it is not certain that it would suffice. We do not share Justice BRENNAN's confidence that the Commission "should have little difficulty in the future in utilizing its expertise to demonstrate a specific connection between provisions for access and burdens on access," *post,* at 3161, that will avoid the effect of today's decision. We view the Fifth Amendment's Property Clause to be more than a pleading requirement, and compliance with it to be more than an exercise in cleverness and imagination. As indicated earlier, our cases describe the condition for abridgement of property rights through the police power as a "substantial advanc[ing]" of a legitimate state interest. We are inclined to be particularly careful about the adjective where the actual conveyance of property is made a condition to the lifting of a land-use restriction, since in that context there is heightened risk that the purpose is avoidance of the compensation requirement, rather than the stated police-power objective.

We are left, then, with the Commission's justification for the access requirement unrelated to land-use regulation:

> "Finally, the Commission notes that there are several existing provisions of pass and repass lateral access benefits already given by past Faria Beach Tract applicants as a result of prior coastal permit decisions. The access required as a condition of this permit is part

> of a comprehensive program to provide continuous public access along Faria Beach as the lots undergo development or redevelopment." App. 68.

That is simply an expression of the Commission's belief that the public interest will be served by a continuous strip of publicly accessible beach along the coast. The Commission may well be right that it is a good idea, but that does not establish that the Nollans (and other coastal residents) alone can be compelled to contribute to its realization. Rather, California is free to advance its "comprehensive program," if it wishes, by using its power of eminent domain for this "public purpose," see U.S. Const., Amdt. 5; but if it wants an easement across the Nollans' property, it must pay for it.

REVERSED.

Justice BRENNAN, with whom Justice MARSHALL joins, dissenting.

Appellants in this case sought to construct a new dwelling on their beach lot that would both diminish visual access to the beach and move private development closer to the public tidelands. The Commission reasonably concluded that such "buildout," both individually and cumulatively, threatens public access to the shore. It sought to offset this encroachment by obtaining assurance that the public may walk along the shoreline in order to gain access to the ocean. The Court finds this an illegitimate exercise of the police power, because it maintains that there is no reasonable relationship between the effect of the development and the condition imposed.

The first problem with this conclusion is that the Court imposes a standard of precision for the exercise of a State's police power that has been discredited for the better part of this century. Furthermore, even under the Court's cramped standard, the permit condition imposed in this case directly responds to the specific type of burden on access created by appellants' development. Finally, a review of those factors deemed most significant in takings analysis makes clear that the Commission's action implicates none of the concerns underlying the Takings Clause. The Court has thus struck down the Commission's reasonable effort to respond to intensified development along the California coast, on behalf of landowners who can make no claim that their reasonable expectations have been disrupted. The Court has, in short, given appellants a windfall at the expense of the public.

I

The Court's conclusion that the permit condition imposed on appellants is unreasonable cannot withstand analysis. First, the Court demands a degree of exactitude that is inconsistent with our standard for reviewing the rationality of a State's exercise of its police power for the welfare of its citizens. Second, even if the nature of the public-access condition imposed must be identical to the precise burden on access created by appellants, this requirement is plainly satisfied.

A

There can be no dispute that the police power of the States encompasses the authority to impose conditions on private development. *See, e.g., Agins v. Tiburon,* 447 U.S. 255, 100 S.Ct. 2138, 65 L.Ed.2d 106 (1980); *Penn Central Transportation Co. v. New York City,* 438 U.S. 104, 98 S.Ct. 2646, 57 L.Ed.2d 631 (1978); *Gorieb v. Fox,* 274 U.S. 603, 47 S.Ct. 675, 71 L.Ed. 1228 (1927).

It is also by now commonplace that this Court's review of the rationality of a State's exercise of its police power demands only that the State "could *rationally have decided*" that the measure adopted might achieve the State's objective. *Minnesota v. Clover Leaf Creamery Co.,* 449 U.S. 456, 466, 101 S.Ct. 715, 725, 66 L.Ed.2d 659 (1981)(emphasis in original). [Footnote omitted.] In this case, California has employed its police power in order to condition development upon preservation of public access to the ocean and tidelands. The Coastal Commission, if it had so chosen, could have denied the Nollans' request for a development permit, since the property would have remained economically viable without the requested new development. [Footnote omitted.] Instead, the State sought to accommodate the Nollans' desire for new development, on the condition that the development not diminish the overall amount of public access to the coastline. Appellants' proposed development would reduce public access by restricting visual access to the beach, by contributing to an increased need for community facilities, and by moving private development closer to public beach property. The Commission sought to offset this diminution in access, and thereby preserve the overall balance of access, by requesting a deed restriction that would ensure "lateral" access: the right of the public to pass and repass along the dry sand parallel to the shoreline in order to reach the tidelands and the ocean. In the expert opinion of the Coastal Commission, development conditioned on such a restriction would fairly attend to both public and private interests.

The Court finds fault with this measure because it regards the condition as insufficiently tailored to address the precise type of reduction in access produced by the new development. The Nollans' development blocks visual access, the Court tells us, while the Commission seeks to preserve lateral access along the coastline. Thus, it concludes, the State acted irrationally. Such a narrow conception of rationality, however, has long since been discredited as a judicial arrogation of legislative authority. "To make scientific precision a criterion of constitutional power would be to subject the State to an intolerable supervision hostile to the basic principles of our Government." *Sproles v. Binford,* 286 U.S. 374, 388, 52 S.Ct. 581, 585, 76 L.Ed. 1167 (1932). *Cf. Keystone Bituminous Coal Assn. v. DeBenedictis,* 480 U.S. 470, 491, n. 21, 107 S.Ct. 1232, 1245, n.21, 94 L.Ed.2d 472 (1987) ("The Takings Clause has never been read to require the States or the courts to calculate whether a specific individual has suffered burdens ... in excess of the benefits received"). As this Court long ago declared with regard to various forms of restriction on the use of property:

> "Each interferes in the same way, if not to the same extent, with the owner's general right of dominion over his property. All rest for their justification upon the same reasons which have arisen in recent times as a result of the great increase and concentration of population in urban communities and the vast changes in the extent and complexity of the problems of modern city life. State legislatures and city councils, who deal with the situation from a practical standpoint, are better qualified than the courts to determine the necessity, character, and degree of regulation which these new and perplexing conditions require; and their conclusions should not be disturbed by the courts unless clearly arbitrary and unreasonable." *Gorieb,* 274 U.S., at 608, 47 S.Ct., at 677 (citations omitted).

The Commission is charged by both the State Constitution and legislature to preserve overall public access to the California coastline. Furthermore, by virtue of its participation in the Coastal Zone Management Act (CZMA) program, the State must "exercise effectively [its] responsibilities in the coastal zone through the development and implementation of management programs to achieve wise use of the land and water resources of the coastal zone," 16 U.S.C. §1452(2), so as to provide for, *inter alia*, "public access to the coas[t] for recreation purposes." §1452(2)(D). The

Commission has sought to discharge its responsibilities in a flexible manner. It has sought to balance private and public interests and to accept tradeoffs: to permit development that reduces access in some ways as long as other means of access are enhanced. In this case, it has determined that the Nollans' burden on access would be offset by a deed restriction that formalizes the public's right to pass along the shore. In its informed judgment, such a tradeoff would preserve the net amount of public access to the coastline. The Court's insistence on a precise fit between the forms of burden and condition on each individual parcel along the California coast would penalize the Commission for its flexibility, hampering the ability to fulfill its public trust mandate.

The Court's demand for this precise fit is based on the assumption that private landowners in this case possess a reasonable expectation regarding the use of their land that the public has attempted to disrupt. In fact, the situation is precisely the reverse: it is private landowners who are the interlopers. The public's expectation of access considerably antedates any private development on the coast. Article X, §4, of the California Constitution, adopted in 1879, declares:

> "No individual, partnership, or corporation, claiming or possessing the frontage or tidal lands of a harbor, bay, inlet, estuary, or other navigable water in this State, shall be permitted to exclude the right of way to such water whenever it is required for any public purpose, nor to destroy or obstruct the free navigation of such water; and the Legislature shall enact such laws as will give the most liberal construction to this provision, so that access to the navigable waters of this State shall always be attainable for the people thereof."

It is therefore private landowners who threaten the disruption of settled public expectations. Where a private landowner has had a reasonable expectation that his or her property will be used for exclusively private purposes, the disruption of this expectation dictates that the government pay if it wishes the property to be used for a public purpose. In this case, however, the State has sought to protect public expectations of access from disruption by private land use. The State's exercise of its police power for this purpose deserves no less deference than any other measure designed to further the welfare of state citizens.

Congress expressly stated in passing the CZMA that "[i]n light of competing demands and the urgent need to protect and to give high priority to natural systems in the coastal zone, present state and local institutional arrangements for planning and regulating land and water uses in such areas are inadequate." 16 U.S.C. §1451(h). It is thus puzzling that the Court characterizes as a "non-land-use justification," *ante,* at ___, the exercise of the police power to "'provide continuous public access along Faria Beach as the lots undergo development or redevelopment.'" *Ibid.* (quoting App. 68). The Commission's determination that certain types of development jeopardize public access to the ocean, and that such development should be conditioned on preservation of access, is the essence of responsible land-use planning. The Court's use of an unreasonably demanding standard for determining the rationality of state regulation in this area thus could hamper innovative efforts to preserve an increasingly fragile national resource. [Footnote omitted.]

B

Even if we accept the Court's unusual demand for a precise match between the condition imposed and the specific type of burden on access created by the appellants, the State's action easily satisfies this requirement. First, the lateral access condition serves to dissipate the impression that the beach that lies behind the wall of homes along the shore is for private use only. It requires no exceptional imaginative powers to find plausible the Commission's point that the average person passing along the road in front of a phalanx of imposing permanent residences, including the appellants' new home, is likely to conclude that this particular portion of the shore is not open to the public. If, however, that person can see that numerous people are passing and repassing along the dry sand, this conveys the message that the beach is in fact open for use by the public. Furthermore, those persons who go down to the public beach a quarter-mile away will be able to look down the coastline and see that persons have continuous access to the tidelands, and will observe signs that proclaim the public's right of access over the dry sand. The burden produced by the diminution in visual access—the impression that the beach is not open to the public—is thus directly alleviated by the provision for public access over the dry sand. The Court therefore has an unrealistically limited conception of what measures could reasonably be chosen to mitigate the burden produced by a diminution of visual access.

The second flaw in the Court's analysis of the fit between burden and exaction is more fundamental. The Court assumes that the only burden with which the Coastal Commission was concerned was blockage of visual access to the beach. This is incorrect. [Footnote omitted.] The Commission specifically stated in its report in support of the permit condition that "[t]he Commission finds that the applicants' proposed development would present an increase in view blockage, an increase in private use of the shorefront, and that this impact would burden the public's ability to traverse to and along the shorefront." App. 65-66 (emphasis added). It declared that the possibility that "the public may get the impression that the beachfront is no longer available for public use" would be "due to the encroaching nature of private use immediately adjacent to the public use, as well as the visual 'block' of increased residential build-out impacting the visual quality of the beachfront." *Id.*, at 59 (emphasis added).

The record prepared by the Commission is replete with references to the threat to public access along the coastline resulting from the seaward encroachment of private development along a beach whose mean high-tide line is constantly shifting. As the Commission observed in its report: "The Faria Beach shoreline fluctuates during the year depending on the seasons and accompanying storms, and the public is not always able to traverse the shoreline below the mean high tide line." *Id.*, at 67. As a result, the boundary between publicly owned tidelands and privately owned beach is not a stable one, and "[t]he existing seawall is located very near to the mean high water line." *Id.*, at 61. When the beach is at its largest, the seawall is about ten feet from the mean high-tide mark; "[d]uring the period of the year when the beach suffers erosion, the mean high water line appears to be located either on or beyond the existing seawall." *Ibid.* Expansion of private development on appellants' lot toward the seawall would thus "increase private use immediately adjacent to public tidelands, which has the potential of causing adverse impacts on the public's ability to traverse the shoreline." *Id.*, at 62. As the Commission explained:

> "The placement of more private use adjacent to public tidelands has the potential of creating use conflicts between the applicants and the public. The results of new private use encroachment into boundary/buffer areas between private and public property can create situations in which landowners intimidate the public and seek to prevent them from using public tidelands because of disputes between the two parties over where the exact boundary between private and public ownership is located. If the applicants' project would result in further seaward encroachment of private use into an area of clouded title,

> new private use in the subject encroachment area could result in use conflict between private and public entities on the subject shorefront." *Id.*, at 61-62.

The deed restriction on which permit approval was conditioned would directly address this threat to the public's access to the tidelands. It would provide a formal declaration of the public's right of access, thereby ensuring that the shifting character of the tidelands, and the presence of private development immediately adjacent to it, would not jeopardize enjoyment of that right. [Footnote omitted.] The imposition of the permit condition was therefore directly related to the fact that appellants development would be "located along a unique stretch of coast where lateral public access is inadequate due to the construction of private residential structures and shoreline protective devices along a fluctuating shoreline." *Id.*, at 68. The deed restriction was crafted to deal with the particular character of the beach along which appellants sought to build, and with the specific problems created by expansion of development toward the public tidelands. In imposing the restriction, the State sought to ensure that such development would not disrupt the historical expectation of the public regarding access to the sea. [Footnote omitted.]

The Court is therefore simply wrong that there is no reasonable relationship between the permit condition and the specific type of burden on public access created by the appellants' proposed development. Even were the Court desirous of assuming the added responsibility of closely monitoring the regulation of development along the California coast, this record reveals rational public action by any conceivable standard.

II

The fact that the Commission's action is a legitimate exercise of the police power does not, of course, insulate it from a takings challenge, for when "regulation goes too far it will be recognized as a taking." *Pennsylvania Coal Co. v. Mahon,* 260 U.S. 393, 415, 43 S.Ct. 158, 160, 67 L.Ed. 322 (1922). Conventional takings analysis underscores the implausibility of the Court's holding, for it demonstrates that this exercise of California's police power implicates none of the concerns that underlie our takings jurisprudence.

In reviewing a Takings Clause claim, we have regarded as particularly significant the nature of the governmental action and the economic impact of regulation, especially the extent to which regulation interferes with investment-backed expectations. *Penn Central,* 438 U.S., at 124, 98 S.Ct., at 2659. The character of the government action in this case is the imposition of a condition on permit approval, which allows the public to continue to have access to the coast. The physical intrusion permitted by the deed restriction is minimal. The public is permitted the right to pass and repass along the coast in an area from the seawall to the mean high-tide mark. App. 46. This area is at its widest ten feet, *id.*, at 61, which means that even without the permit condition, the public's right of access permits it to pass on average within a few feet of the seawall. Passage closer to the eight-foot-high rocky seawall will make the appellants even less visible to the public than passage along the high-tide area farther out on the beach. The intrusiveness of such passage is even less than the intrusion resulting from the required dedication of a sidewalk in front of private residences, exactions which are commonplace conditions on approval of development. [Footnote omitted.] Furthermore, the high-tide line shifts throughout the year, moving up to and beyond the seawall, so that public passage for a portion of the year would either be impossible or would not occur on appellant's property. Finally, although the Commission had the authority to provide for either passive or active recreational use of the property, it chose the least intrusive alternative: a mere right to pass and repass. *Id.*, at 370. [Footnote omitted.] As this Court made clear in *PruneYard Shopping Center v. Robins,* 447 U.S. 74, 83, 100 S.Ct. 2035, 2042, 64 L.Ed.2d 741 (1980), physical access to private property in itself creates no takings problem if it does not "unreasonably impair the value or use of [the] property." Appellants can make no tenable claim that either their enjoyment of their property or its value is diminished by the public's ability merely to pass and repass a few feet closer to the seawall beyond which appellants' house is located.

PruneYard is also relevant in that we acknowledged in that case that public access rested upon a "state constitutional ... provision that had been construed to create rights to the use of private property by strangers." *Id.*, at 81, 100 S.Ct., at 2041. In this case, of course, the State is also acting to protect a state constitutional right. See supra, at ___ (quoting Art. X, §4, of California Constitution). The constitutional provision guaranteeing public access to the ocean states that "the Legislature shall enact such laws as will give the most liberal construction to this provision so that access to the navigable waters of this State shall be always attainable for the people thereof." Cal. Const., Art. X, §4 (emphasis added). This provision is the explicit basis for the statutory directive to provide for public access along the coast in new development projects, Cal.Pub.Res.Code Ann. §30212 (West 1986), and has been construed by the state judiciary to permit passage over private land where necessary to gain access to the tidelands. *Grupe v. California Coastal Comm'n,* 166 Cal.App.3d 148, 171- 172, 212 Cal.Rptr. 578, 592-593 (1985). The physical access to the perimeter of appellants' property at issue in this case thus results directly from the State's enforcement of the State Constitution.

Finally, the character of the regulation in this case is not unilateral government action, but a condition on approval of a development request submitted by appellants. The State has not sought to interfere with any pre-existing property interest, but has responded to appellants' proposal to intensify development on the coast. Appellants themselves chose to submit a new development application, and could claim no property interest in its approval. They were aware that approval of such development would be conditioned on preservation of adequate public access to the ocean. The State has initiated no action against appellants' property; had the Nollans' not proposed more intensive development in the coastal zone, they would never have been subject to the provision that they challenge.

Examination of the economic impact of the Commission's action reinforces the conclusion that no taking has occurred. Allowing appellants to intensify development along the coast in exchange for ensuring public access to the ocean is a classic instance of government action that produces a "reciprocity of advantage." *Pennsylvania Coal,* 260 U.S., at 415, 43 S.Ct., at 160. Appellants have been allowed to replace a one-story, 521-square-foot beach home with a two-story, 1,674-square-foot residence and an attached two-car garage, resulting in development covering 2,464 square feet of the lot. Such development obviously significantly increases the value of appellants' property; appellants make no contention that this increase is offset by any diminution in value resulting from the deed restriction, much less that the restriction made the property less valuable than it would have been without the new construction. Furthermore, appellants gain an additional benefit from the Commission's permit condition program. They are able to walk along the beach beyond the confines of their own property only because the Commission has required deed restrictions as a condition of approving other new beach developments. [Footnote omitted.] Thus, appellants benefit both as private landowners and as members of the public from the fact that new development permit requests are conditioned on preservation of public access.

Ultimately, appellants' claim of economic injury is flawed because it rests on the assumption of entitlement to the full value of their new development. Appellants submitted a proposal for more intensive development of the coast, which the Commission was under no obligation to approve, and now argue that a regulation designed to ameliorate the impact of that development deprives them of the full value of their improvements. Even if this novel claim were somehow cognizable, it is not significant. "[T]he interest in anticipated gains has traditionally been viewed as less compelling than other property-related interests." *Andrus v. Allard,* 444 U.S. 51, 66, 100 S.Ct. 318, 327, 62 L.Ed.2d 210 (1979).

With respect to appellants' investment-backed expectations, appellants can make no reasonable claim to any expectation of being able to exclude members of the public from crossing the edge of their property to gain access to the ocean. It is axiomatic, of course, that state law is the source of those strands that constitute a property owner's bundle of property rights. "[A]s a general proposition[,] the law of real property is, under our Constitution, left to the individual States to develop and administer." *Hughes v. Washington,* 389 U.S. 290, 295, 88 S.Ct. 438, 441, 19 L.Ed.2d 530 (1967) (Stewart, J., concurring). *See also Borax Consolidated, Ltd. v. Los Angeles,* 296 U.S. 10, 22, 56 S.Ct. 23, 29, 80 L.Ed. 9 (1935) ("Rights and interests in the tideland, which is subject to the sovereignty of the State, are matters of local law"). In this case, the State Constitution explicitly states that no one possessing the "frontage" of any "navigable water in this State, shall be permitted to exclude the right of way to such water whenever it is required for any public purpose." Cal. Const., Art. X, §4. The state Code expressly provides that, save for exceptions not relevant here, "[p]ublic access from the nearest public roadway to the shoreline and along the coast shall be provided in new development projects." Cal.Pub.Res.Code Ann. §30212 (West 1986). The Coastal Commission Interpretative Guidelines make clear that fulfillment of the Commission's constitutional and statutory duty requires that approval of new coastline development be conditioned upon provisions ensuring lateral public access to the ocean. App. 362. At the time of appellants' permit request, the Commission had conditioned all 43 of the proposals for coastal new development in the Faria Family Beach Tract on the provision of deed restrictions ensuring lateral access along the shore. *Id.*, at 48. Finally, the Faria family had leased the beach property since the early part of this century, and "the Faria family and their lessees [including the Nollans] had not interfered with public use of the beachfront within the Tract, so long as public use was limited to pass and re-pass lateral access along the shore." *Ibid.* California therefore has clearly established that the power of exclusion for which appellants seek compensation simply is not a strand in the bundle of appellants' property rights, and appellants have never acted as if it were. Given this state of affairs, appellants cannot claim that the deed restriction has deprived them of a reasonable expectation to exclude from their property persons desiring to gain access to the sea.

Even were we somehow to concede a pre-existing expectation of a right to exclude, appellants were clearly on notice when requesting a new development permit that a condition of approval would be a provision ensuring public lateral access to the shore. Thus, they surely could have had no expectation that they could obtain approval of their new development and exercise any right of exclusion afterward. In this respect, this case is quite similar to *Ruckelshaus v. Monsanto Co.,* 467 U.S. 986, 104 S.Ct. 2862, 81 L.Ed.2d 815 (1984). In *Monsanto*, the respondent had submitted trade data to the Environmental Protection Agency (EPA) for the purpose of obtaining registration of certain pesticides. The company claimed that the agency's disclosure of certain data in accordance with the relevant regulatory statute constituted a taking. The Court conceded that the data in question constituted property under state law. It also found, however, that certain of the data had been submitted to the agency after Congress had made clear that only limited confidentiality would be given data submitted for registration purposes. The Court observed that the statute served to inform Monsanto of the various conditions under which data might be released, and stated:

> "If, despite the data-consideration and data-disclosure provisions in the statute, Monsanto chose to submit the requisite data in order to receive a registration, it can hardly argue that its reasonable investment-backed expectations are disturbed when EPA acts to use or disclose the data in a manner that was authorized by law at the time of the submission." *Id.,* at 1006-1007, 104 S.Ct., at 2874-2875.

The Court rejected respondent's argument that the requirement that it relinquish some confidentiality imposed an unconstitutional condition on receipt of a Government benefit:

> "[A]s long as Monsanto is aware of the conditions under which the data are submitted, and the conditions are rationally related to a legitimate Government interest, a voluntary submission of data by an applicant in exchange for the economic advantages of a registration can hardly be called a taking." *Id.,* at 1007, 104 S.Ct., at 2875.

The similarity of this case to *Monsanto* is obvious. Appellants were aware that stringent regulation of development along the California coast had been in place at least since 1976. The specific deed restriction to which the Commission sought to subject them had been imposed since 1979 on all 43 shoreline new development projects in the Faria Family Beach Tract. App. 48. Such regulation to ensure public access to the ocean had been directly authorized by California citizens in 1972, and reflected their judgment that restrictions on coastal development represented "'the advantage of living and doing business in a civilized community.'" *Andrus v. Allard, supra,* 444 U.S., at 67, 100 S.Ct., at 328, quoting *Pennsylvania Coal Co. v. Mahon,* 260 U.S., at 422, 43 S.Ct., at 163 (Brandeis, J., dissenting). The deed restriction was "authorized by law at the time of [appellants' permit] submission," *Monsanto, supra,* 467 U.S., at 1007, 104 S.Ct., at 2875, and, as earlier analysis demonstrates, *supra,* at ___, was reasonably related to the objective of ensuring public access. Appellants thus were on notice that new developments would be approved only if provisions were made for lateral beach access. In requesting a new development permit from the Commission, they could have no reasonable expectation of, and had no entitlement to, approval of their permit application without any deed restriction ensuring public access to the ocean. As a result, analysis of appellants' investment-backed expectations reveals that "the force of this factor is so overwhelming ... that it disposes of the taking question." *Monsanto, supra,* at 1005, 104 S.Ct., at 2874. [Footnote omitted.]

Standard Takings Clause analysis thus indicates that the Court employs its unduly restrictive standard of police power rationality to find a taking where neither the character of governmental action nor the nature of the private interest affected raise any takings concern. The result is that the Court invalidates regulation that represents a reasonable adjustment of the burdens and benefits of development along the California coast.

III

The foregoing analysis makes clear that the State has taken no property from appellants. Imposition of the permit condition in this case represents the State's reasonable exercise of its police power. The Coastal Commission has drawn on its expertise to preserve the balance between private development and public access, by requiring that any project that intensifies development on the increasingly crowded California coast must be offset by gains in public access. Under the normal standard for review of the police power, this provision is eminently reasonable. Even accepting the Court's novel insistence on a precise quid pro quo of burdens and benefits, there is a reasonable relationship between the public benefit and the burden created by appellants' development. The movement of development closer to the ocean creates the prospect of encroachment on public tidelands, because of fluctuation in the mean high-tide line. The deed restriction ensures that disputes about the boundary between private and public property will not deter the public from exercising its right to have access to the sea.

Furthermore, consideration of the Commission's action under traditional takings analysis underscores the absence of any viable takings claim. The deed restriction permits the public only to pass and repass along a narrow strip of beach, a few feet closer to a seawall at the periphery of appellants' property. Appellants almost surely have enjoyed an increase in the value of their property even with the restriction, because they have been allowed to build a significantly larger new home with garage on their lot. Finally, appellants can claim the disruption of no expectation interest, both because they have no right to exclude the public under state law, and because, even if they did, they had full advance notice that new development along the coast is conditioned on provisions for continued public access to the ocean.

Fortunately, the Court's decision regarding this application of the Commission's permit program will probably have little ultimate impact either on this parcel in particular or the Commission program in general. A preliminary study by a Senior Lands Agent in the State Attorney General's Office indicates that the portion of the beach at issue in this case likely belongs to the public. App. 85. [Footnote omitted.] Since a full study had not been completed at the time of appellants' permit application, the deed restriction was requested "without regard to the possibility that the applicant is proposing development on public land." *Id.*, at 45. Furthermore, analysis by the same Land Agent also indicated that the public had obtained a prescriptive right to the use of Faria Beach from the seawall to the ocean. *Id.*, at 86. [Footnote omitted.] The Superior Court explicitly stated in its ruling against the Commission on the permit condition issue that "no part of this opinion is intended to foreclose the public's opportunity to adjudicate the possibility that public rights in [appellants'] beach have been acquired through prescriptive use." *Id.*, at 420.

With respect to the permit condition program in general, the Commission should have little difficulty in the future in utilizing its expertise to demonstrate a specific connection between provisions for access and burdens on access produced by new development. Neither the Commission in its report nor the State in its briefs and at argument highlighted the particular threat to lateral access created by appellants' development project. In defending its action, the State emphasized the general point that overall access to the beach had been preserved, since the diminution of access created by the project had been offset by the gain in lateral access. This approach is understandable, given that the State relied on the reasonable assumption that its action was justified under the normal standard of review for determining legitimate exercises of a State's police power. In the future, alerted to the Court's apparently more demanding requirement, it need only make clear that a provision for public access directly responds to a particular type of burden on access created by a new development. Even if I did not believe that the record in this case satisfies this requirement, I would have to acknowledge that the record's documentation of the impact of coastal development indicates that the Commission should have little problem presenting its findings in a way that avoids a takings problem.

Nonetheless it is important to point out that the Court's insistence on a precise accounting system in this case is insensitive to the fact that increasing intensity of development in many areas calls for far-sighted, comprehensive planning that takes into account both the interdependence of land uses and the cumulative impact of development. [Footnote omitted.] As one scholar has noted:

> "Property does not exist in isolation. Particular parcels are tied to one another in complex ways, and property is more accurately described as being inextricably part of a network of relationships that is neither limited to, nor usefully defined by, the property boundaries with which the legal system is accustomed to dealing. Frequently, use of any given parcel of property is at the same time effectively a use of, or a demand upon, property beyond the border of the user." Sax, *Takings, Private Property, and Public Rights*, 81 Yale L.J. 149, 152 (1971) (footnote omitted).

As Congress has declared: "The key to more effective protection and use of the land and water resources of the coastal zone [is for the states to] develo[p] land and water use programs for the coastal zone, including unified policies, criteria, standards, methods, and processes for dealing with land and water use decisions of more than local significance." 16 U.S.C. §1451(i). This is clearly a call for a focus on the overall impact of development on coastal areas. State agencies therefore require considerable flexibility in responding to private desires for development in a way that guarantees the preservation of public access to the coast. They should be encouraged to regulate development in the context of the overall balance of competing uses of the shoreline. The Court today does precisely the opposite, overruling an eminently reasonable exercise of an expert state agency's judgment, substituting its own narrow view of how this balance should be struck. Its reasoning is hardly suited to the complex reality of natural resource protection in the 20th century. I can only hope that today's decision is an aberration, and that a broader vision ultimately prevails. [Footnote omitted.]

I DISSENT.

Justice BLACKMUN, dissenting.

I do not understand the Court's opinion in this case to implicate in any way the public-trust doctrine. The Court certainly had no reason to address the issue, for the Court of Appeal of California did not rest its decision on Art. X, §4, of the California Constitution. Nor did the parties base their arguments before this Court on the doctrine.

I disagree with the Court's rigid interpretation of the necessary correlation between a burden created by development and a condition imposed pursuant to the State's police power to mitigate that burden. The land-use problems this country faces require creative solutions. These are not advanced by an "eye for an eye" mentality. The close nexus between benefits and burdens that the Court now imposes on permit conditions creates an anomaly in the ordinary requirement that a State's exercise of its police power need be no more than rationally based. *See, e.g., Minnesota v. Clover Leaf Creamery Co.,* 449 U.S. 456, 466, 101 S.Ct. 715, 725, 66 L.Ed.2d 659 (1981). In my view, the easement exacted from appellants and the problems their development created are adequately related to the governmental interest in providing public access to the beach. Coastal development by its very nature makes public access to the shore generally more difficult. Appellants' structure is part of that general development and, in particular, it diminishes the public's visual access to the ocean and decreases the public's sense that it may have physical access to the beach. These losses in access can be counteracted, at least in part, by the condition on appellants' construction permitting public passage that ensures access along the beach.

Traditional takings analysis compels the conclusion that there is no taking here. The governmental action is a valid exercise of the police power, and, so far as the record reveals, has a nonexistent economic effect on the value of appellants' property. No investment-backed expectations were diminished. It is significant that the Nollans had notice of the easement before they purchased the property and that public use of the beach had been permitted for decades.

For these reasons, I respectfully DISSENT.

Justice STEVENS, with whom Justice BLACKMUN joins, dissenting.

The debate between the Court and Justice BRENNAN illustrates an extremely important point concerning government regulation of the use of privately owned real estate. Intelligent, well-informed public officials may in good faith disagree about the validity of specific types of land-use regulation. Even the wisest lawyers would have to acknowledge great uncertainty about the scope of this Court's takings jurisprudence. Yet, because of the Court's remarkable ruling in *First English Evangelical Lutheran Church of Glendale v. Los Angeles County,* 482 U.S. 304, 107 S.Ct. 2378, 96 L.Ed.2d 250 (1987), local governments and officials must pay the price for the necessarily vague standards in this area of the law.

In his dissent in *San Diego Gas & Electric Co. v. San Diego,* 450 U.S. 621, 101 S.Ct. 1287, 67 L.Ed.2d 551 (1981), Justice BRENNAN proposed a brand new constitutional rule.[1] He argued that a mistake such as the one that a majority of the Court believes that the California Coastal Commission made in this case should automatically give rise to pecuniary liability for a "temporary taking." *Id.,* at 653-661, 101 S.Ct., at 1304-1309. Notwithstanding the unprecedented chilling effect that such a rule will obviously have on public officials charged with the responsibility for drafting and implementing regulations designed to protect the environment and the public welfare, six Members of the Court recently endorsed Justice BRENNAN's novel proposal. See *First English Evangelical Lutheran Church, supra.*

I write today to identify the severe tension between that dramatic development in the law and the view expressed by Justice BRENNAN's dissent in this case that the public interest is served by encouraging state agencies to exercise considerable flexibility in responding to private desires for development in a way that threatens the preservation of public resources. *See ante*, at 3154-3155. I like the hat that Justice BRENNAN has donned today better than the one he wore in *San Diego*, and I am persuaded that he has the better of the legal arguments here. Even if his position prevailed in this case, however, it would be of little solace to land-use planners who would still be left guessing about how the Court will react to the next case, and the one after that. As this case demonstrates, the rule of liability created by the Court in *First English* is a shortsighted one. Like Justice BRENNAN, I hope that "a broader vision ultimately prevails." *Ante*, at 3161.

I respectfully DISSENT.

---

[1] "The constitutional rule I propose requires that, once a court finds that a police power regulation has effected a 'taking,' the government entity must pay just compensation for the period commencing on the date the regulation first effected the 'taking,' and ending on the date the government entity chooses to rescind or otherwise amend the regulation." 450 U.S., at 658, 101 S.Ct., at 1307.

Chapter 33
THE DOCTRINE OF NUISANCE

Under the doctrine of nuisance, certain uses of land may be legitimately abated by government action without there being any danger of a taking if those uses impact negatively on resources and injure the public. Some environmentalists would extend this maxim to include land development in the concept of nuisance because it destroys the function of wetlands to the detriment of the public interest in this resource.

SWEET v. RECHEL

159 U.S. 380, 40 L.Ed. 188, 16 S.Ct. 43 (1895)

In Error to the Circuit Court of the United States for the District of Massachusetts.

This was a writ of entry by William A. Sweet and Maria H. Sweet, his wife, and Frank G. Tallman and Peleg. H. Tallman against Christian Rechel to recover certain lands in the city of Boston, Mass. Judgment was rendered in the circuit court for the defendant. 37 Fed. 323. Plaintiffs bring error. Affirmed.

The real estate, the title to which is involved in the present writ of entry, formerly belonged to Peleg Tallman, Sr., of Maine, who died on the 12th day of March 1840, having made a will which was duly admitted to record in that state, and a copy whereof was admitted to probate, May 10, 1841, in Suffolk county, Mass., where the premises in controversy are situated.

The parcel of land in dispute, with other real estate, was devised to Henry Tallman, to hold for life, and at his decease to descend to his son Peleg Tallman, Jr. The devisee in remainder was born April 18, 1836, and died April 15, 1863, leaving two children, Frank G. Tallman and Peleg H. Tallman; also a widow, who subsequently intermarried with William A. Sweet, one of the plaintiffs in error.

The plaintiffs in error, who were the plaintiffs below, and are citizens of New York, claim title under the will of Peleg Tallman, Sr.

The defendant, a citizen of Massachusetts, claims title under proceedings instituted by the guardian of the devisee in remainder in the probate court of Suffolk county, Mass., by the order of which court, and in full compliance therewith, as is contended, the interest of Peleg Tallman, Jr., in certain real estate, including the lot in dispute, was sold in 1884, Henry Tallman, the owner of the life estate, becoming the purchaser. In the same year the latter conveyed, with warranty, to Rober Knott, who purchased in good faith, at the price of $2,900. In 1869 Knott conveyed by warranty deed to the defendant, Rechel, for the sum of $4,800, in cash or its equivalent. Rechel bought in good faith, for full value, without actual notice of any alleged defect in the title, and erected buildings and made improvements on the premises in dispute at a cost of $8,575.

The defendant also claims that the title to the lot in controversy was taken by the city of Boston in 1867, the title being, at that time, apparently, in Knott, under a statute of Massachusetts, approved June 1, 1867, entitled 'An act to enable the city of Boston to abate a nuisance existing therein, and for the preservation of the public health in said city.' St. Mass. 1867, c. 308.

By reason of its grade being lower, and because it was incapable of being properly drained, the condition of the territory of which the lot in controversy was a part was such, during the period between the years 1860 and 1870, as to endanger the public health. Various plans having been suggested for the raising of the grade and for the proper drainage of the territory, the legislature passed the act of June 1, 1867.

By that act it was provided that the city of Boston 'may purchase or otherwise take the lands or any of them in said city, with the buildings and other fixtures thereon,' situated within a certain defined district, which included the lands here in dispute; that the 'city shall within sixty days from the time they shall take any of said lands, file in the office of the registry of deeds for the county of Suffolk, a description of the lands so taken as certain as is required in a common conveyance of lands,' with 'statement that the same are taken pursuant to the provisions of this act, which said description and statement shall be signed by the mayor of said city'; that 'the title to all land so taken shall vest in the city of Boston, and if any party whose land is taken shall agree with the said city upon the damage done to him by the said taking, the same shall be paid to him by the said city forthwith.' It was made 'the duty of the city of Boston forthwith to raise the grade of said territory so taken or purchased, laying out and filling up the same with good materials, with reference to a complete drainage thereof, so as to abate the present nuisance and to preserve the health of the city.' Section 1. Any person having an interest in the land taken was at liberty, within one year after the same was taken, as well in his own behalf as in behalf of all other persons having estates therein, to file a bill in equity in the supreme judicial court, in the county of Suffolk, setting forth the taking of the complainant's land, the condition of the same in respect to its capacity for drainage, and whether the complainant claimed any, and what, damages against the city or the Boston Water Power Company, or other corporation or person, 'by reason of any and what wrongful act or omission by their causing a diminution in the value of his land at the time of said taking, and praying an assessment of damages against such parties'; notice of such bill being given to the parties named therein as defendants, according to the course of courts of equity, and also public notice thereof to all persons in whose behalf such bill was filed to appear and become come parties thereto, if they thought fit to do so. It was made the duty of the court to prescribe how such public notice should be given, and what length of time should be allowed for appearing and becoming a party to the suit. Any one interested who failed to appear and become a party within the time prescribed by the court was forever barred from recovering any damages on account of such taking. Each person appearing and becoming a party, having filed a written description of the land in which he claimed an estate, together with a plan thereof, so as clearly to distinguish the same from all other lands, was required to declare what estate he claimed therein. If he claimed that the value of said lands at the time of the taking was lessened by any unlawful act or omission of the city of Boston, or of the Boston Water Power Company, or of any other corporation or person, 'so that the value of the land in its condition when taken would not be a just compensation for all the estate and rights of the party in and in reference to the same,' he was also to state 'what such injury is, and how and by whom the same had been, or is, caused, and what right or title of the party is violated, and what amount of damages in gross is claimed by him, as compensation therefor, from each of the parties defendant.' St. Mass. 1867, c. 308.

Other sections of the act provided for the appointment of commissioners to hear the parties, after due notice, to assess the value of the land taken, and to make report to the court of their doings. Any party aggrieved by the report might except thereto, and have his exception heard as in a suit in equity, or might apply for the framing of proper issues to be tried by a jury.

The seventh section provides: 'When it shall be finally determined what amount of damages any party is entitled to recover against the city of Boston, or the Boston Water Power Company, or any other party defendant, a separate decree shall be entered accordingly and execution therefor shall be issued, without regard to the pendency of the claims of any other party or parties, or of other claims of such complainant.'

The city council approved and spread upon its records an instrument reciting the act of 1867, and stating that, pursuant to its provisions, the city 'has taken, and by these presents does take,' a certain parcel of land 'belonging to Robert Knott,—in whose name, as we have seen, that title then stood of record,—'to have and to hold the same to the said city of Boston, its successors and assigns, to its and their sole use and behoof, forever, agreeably to the provisions of the said act.' This instrument was approved by the mayor, who certified that 'the lands described in said instrument were and are taken pursuant to the provisions of the said act.' Within 60 days of the taking of the land, to wit, on May 22, 1868, that instrument was filed in the Suffolk registry of deeds, and was fully recorded.

It was admitted at the trial that the city followed the provisions of the statute, and that the premises were held by the defendant under Knott and the city; also that the city forthwith performed the duty imposed on it by the statute at an immense outlay; that 'the grade of the land was raised, and the buildings thereon, the territory was laid out and filled, a complete and effective system of drainage was provided, the nuisance abated, and the value of the land was greatly enhanced. The lot in suit was filled in to a depth of several feet, the buildings were raised and underpinned, and the value increased.'

Subsequently, a settlement was had with the assignee of Knott, in relation to the taking of the land, and, Knott having executed a release, the city conveyed, by deed of March 14, 1870, to the defendant, Rechel, the deed reciting that the property had been previously taken by the city under the above act of 1867.

It was also admitted that no compensation was ever paid to the plaintiffs by reason or on account of any proceedings by the city under the act of June, 1867. And it was agreed that 'in 1869 a bill in equity was brought under the statute, reported in 109 Mass. 438, the case being *Cobb v. Boston*, on behalf of Cobb and all others entitled to have damages assessed for this taking; that this case was pending in the supreme court until the April term, 1882; that it was ordered by the court in this case that the time from December 23, 1869, to first Tuesday of April, 1870, be allowed to parties to bill; that notice was published in papers on said order; and that such persons as came in had their damages assessed under said bill.'

Mr. Justice HARLAN, after stating the facts in the foregoing language, delivered the opinion of the court.

The grounds upon which the plaintiffs impeach the validity of the sale of 1844 are: That the notice required to be given of the proceedings in the Suffolk probate court was not shown to have been published as often as required, and, therefore, such jurisdiction of the ward was not acquired as authorized an order for the sale of his property; that the notice of the sale did not specify both the time and place of sale; that the guardian could only sell for money in hand, and was without authority to sell and convey, and immediately take, as was done, a mortgage back for the purchase money; that no return of the proceeds of sale was ever made by the guardian; and that an affidavit setting forth the time and place of the sale was not filed by the guardian within the time prescribed by the statute.

But, obviously, the question to be first considered is whether an absolute title passed to the City of Boston. If the title passed in virtue of what was done under the act of 1867, it will become unnecessary to determine whether the sale made by the guardian of Peleg Tallman, Jr., in 1844, was invalid upon any of the grounds assigned by the plaintiffs. For, if that sale was, in itself, ineffectual to divest the title of the devisee in remainder, and if, at the time the city proceeded under the statute of 1867, the title was not, in law, in Knott or in the defendant, Rechel, but in the children and widow of the devisee in remainder upon his death in 1863, the title nevertheless passed to the city, if the provisions of that statute were followed, and unless, as plaintiffs contend, the statute was unconstitutional and void.

The constitution of Massachusetts recognizes the right of each individual to be protected in his life, liberty, and property, according to standing laws, declares his obligation to contribute his share to the expense of such protection, and provides that 'no part of the property of any individual can, with justice, be taken from him, or applied to public uses, without his own consent, or that of the representative body of the people,' and 'whenever the public exigencies require, that the property of any individual should be appropriated to public uses, he shall receive a reasonable compensation therefor.' Const. Mass. pt. 1, art. 10. The legislative department of the commonwealth has, however, full power 'from time to time to make, ordain, and establish, all manner of wholesome and reasonable orders, laws, statutes and ordinances, directions and instructions, either with penalties or without, so as the same be not repugnant or contrary to this constitution, as they shall judge to be for the good and welfare of this commonwealth, and for the government and ordering thereof.' Part 2, c.1, art. 4, §1.

The authority for the enactment of the statute of 1867 is found in these constitutional provisions. The territory of which the lot in controversy formed a part was in such condition, for many years, as to require, or at least to justify, legislative interference under the power to ordain and establish wholesome and reasonable regulations conducive to the good and welfare of the people, and not inconsistent with the fundamental law of the commonwealth. And no restrictions are imposed by the Massachusetts constitution upon the mode in which this power may be exerted, except that it is expressly required that the orders, regulations, and statutes prescribed by the legislature must not be repugnant to the constitution, and it was necessarily implied that the exercise of the power must have some real, substantial relation to the general good and welfare. But, in determining whether the legislature, in a particular enactment, has passed the limits of its constitutional authority, every reasonable presumption must be indulged in favor of the validity of such enactment. It must be regarded as valid, unless it can be clearly shown to be in conflict with the constitution. It is a well-settled rule of constitutional exposition that, if a statute may or may not be, according to circumstances, within the limits of legislative authority, the existence of the circumstances necessary to support it must be presumed. *Talbot v. Hudson*, 16 Gray, 417, 422; *Fletcher v. Peck*, 6 Cranch, 87, 128; *Sinking Fund Cases*, 99 U.S. 700, 718.

We must, therefore, assume that the act of 1867 had for its real object the protection of the public health, and not the mere acquisition of the property in question for purposes of sale and profit, after it had increased in value by reason of the grade being raised. It is not alleged in the pleadings, nor was there any evidence tending to show, that the cost of raising the grade would have been so slight, compared with the real value of the property, that a due regard to the constitution demanded that the owner should have been given opportunity to raise the grade at his own expense, and retain the property in its improved condition. On the contrary, it appears that the public health justified prompt action, and the use of such means as could be effectively supplied only by municipal authority acting under legislative sanction.

In *Dingley v. Boston*, 100 Mass. 544, 554-560, this act of 1867 was assailed upon various grounds. It was there adjudged that the statute authorized the property described in it to be taken by the city for public purposes,—that its language imported a title in fee simple. The point was pressed that the legislature had assumed the power to declare the existence of a public nuisance on the land of the plaintiff, and that this was an exercise of judicial power because it charged him with an offense, and decided the question without giving him an opportunity to be heard, and then proceeded to deprive him of his land. But this point was overruled, the court holding that the statute did not regard him as an offender in any sense, because it gave him a right to compensation, not only for all damage occasioned by the taking of his land, but for its deterioration in value before the taking; that it regarded him as an innocent person, whose land was taken, on the ground of public necessity, in order to protect the health of the city; and that, upon the facts stated, it was apparent that no indictment would lie against him, notwithstanding the nuisance, for it had been created by the acts of others which were beyond his control, and it was not in his power to remove it.

After observing that the work specified in the act was regarded by the legislature as a great public enterprise, to accomplish a highly important object, one that needed to be prosecuted by legislative authority, and which could not have been dealt with by a judicial tribunal under any known forms of proceeding, the court proceeded: 'Where the sanitary condition of a large city requires an interference with the real estate of a great number of persons, making expensive and essential changes in the condition and character of the land, a case is presented within that clause of the constitution which confers authority upon the legislature to make all manner of wholesome and reasonable laws, so as the same be not repugnant or contrary to this constitution.' Part 2, c.1, art. 4, §1. In *Hingham & Q. Bridge & Turnpike Co. v. County* of Norfolk, 6 Allen, 353, Bigelow, C.J., says one of the main purposes of this clause was to vest in the legislature a superintending and controlling authority, under and by virtue of which it might enact all laws not repugnant to the constitution of a police and municipal nature, and necessary to the due regulation of the internal affairs of the commonwealth.

In the same case it was objected that, as the act authorized the city to first take the land, and thereby transfer to itself the fee, without the consent of the owners, and as the only object of the legislature was to abate a nuisance, the act should only have granted power to occupy the land until its object was effected by raising the grade, which being done, the land should have been restored to the owners, applying the benefit received therefrom in offset to the damages. That objection was fully met. Conceding it to be true that the raising of the grade did not require an occupation of the land for a great length of time, and that when the work was completed the nuisance was abated, and the land in a condition to be occupied by private persons, the court said: 'But its condition will be greatly changed, almost as much as raising flats into upland. The former surface will be deeply buried under the earth that will have been brought upon it, and the changed condition is to be perpetual. If the old property is restored, the new property which has been annexed to it must go with it. This would be very unjust to the city, which has been compelled to incur the great expense of destroying the nuisance, unless the owner were required to make a reasonable compensation, which might be far beyond the amount of the damages to which he would be entitled. It would be difficult to adjust the matter, and in many cases it might operate harshly upon the owner to compel him to take and pay for the improvements. On the whole, therefore, the plan of compelling the city to take the land in fee simple, and the owner to part with his whole title for a just compensation, would seem to be the most simple and equitable that could be adopted, unless there is some objection on the ground that a fee simple is more sacred than an estate for life or years, or than an easement of greater or less duration. We can see no ground for regarding one of these titles as more sacred than another, or for regarding land as more sacred than personal property.' Again: 'Whether land be taken under the clause authorizing the making of wholesome and reasonable laws, or by virtue of the clause authorizing the appropriation on private property to public uses, it must in either case be left to the legislature to decide what quantity of estate ought to be taken in order to accomplish its purpose, and do the most complete justice to all parties.... The constitution provides for the protection of all private property, and it provides that, when the public exigencies require that the property of any individual shall be appropriated to public uses, he shall receive a reasonable compensation therefor. But it leaves the legislature, without any restriction, express or implied, to decide, in each case as it arises, what constitutes such exigency; and, if land is to be taken, what estate in it shall pass.'

But the validity of the act of 1867 is questioned on the ground, not suggested in *Dingley v. Boston*, that it did not provide for compensation to be made to the owners of the property in advance of its actual appropriation by the commonwealth.

Upon this point the defendant insists that the statute was enacted under the authority to ordain and establish laws and regulations reasonably adapted to secure the good and welfare of the people, and that statutes, having such objects in view which deprive individuals of the control and use of their property, need not make provision at all for compensation to such individuals.

In support of this position reference is made to *Bancroft v. Cambridge*, 126 Mass. 438, 441. That case arose under a statute empowering the city of Cambridge to require the owners of certain lands to fill them to a prescribed grade in order to abate a nuisance. If the owners failed to do so, then the city was authorized to raise the grade, the expense thereby incurred to become a lien on the land filled. If any one gave due notice of his dissatisfaction with the assessment of the expense of raising the grade, the city was thereupon required to 'take' the land, and, within a named time, file in the registry of deeds a description of it, together with a statement that it was taken under the statute. If the parties did not agree as to the amount of damage done by the taking, then the question of damage was to be determined by a jury, proper allowance being made for the improvement by reason of the grade of the land being raised.

The court said that the compensation to which the owner was entitled was the value of the land at the time of the taking, making due allowance for the improvement; that this excluded loss or inconvenience caused to the owner by proceedings prior to the taking; that the purpose of the statute was to give to each owner the right to elect whether he would pay the expenses of filling his land and retain his estate, or surrender his estate to the city for a fair compensation; and that the act gave no right, either to the owner who surrendered, or to the owner who did not surrender, to recover for previous loss or inconvenience. "Nor," the court said, "is the statute made unconstitutional by this construction. It is entitled 'An act to provide for the prevention and abatement of nuisances and the preservation of the public health.' It was not passed to delegate the right of eminent domain, but under the police power of the commonwealth. Laws passed in the legitimate exercise of this power are not obnoxious to constitutional provisions, merely because they do not provide compensation to the individual who is inconvenienced by them. He is presumed to be rewarded by the common benefits secured. Instances of its exercise are found in all quarantine and health regulations, and in all laws for the abatement of existing and the prevention of threatened nuisances.... The legislature is ordinarily the proper judge of the necessity for the exercise of the power, and there is nothing in this case which shows that this act was not required for the preservation of health and protection against a nuisance."

That case does not sustain the view advanced in behalf of the present defendant. The statement, in the opinion of the court, that laws passed in the legitimate exercise of the police power are not to be held objectionable, on constitutional grounds, merely because they do not provide for compensation to the individual inconvenienced by them, had reference only to so much of the statute then under examination as directed, in the interest of the public health, the abatement of the nuisance created by the condition of the property in question. The abatement of a nuisance, nothing more being required or done, is not of itself, and within the meaning of the constitution, an appropriation of property to public uses. The court did not say that private property, the condition of which was such as to endanger the public health, could be legally taken by the commonwealth and appropriated to public use without reasonable compensation to the owner. On the contrary, the statute there under examination contemplated that, if the owner did not himself abate the nuisance in the mode prescribed, then the property, the condition of which was the cause of the nuisance, was to be taken by the city, the owner to receive such damages as a jury awarded, allowance being made for the improvement that resulted from the raising of the grade at the expense of the city. That case, it is manifest, proceeded upon the ground that the provisions of the constitution above quoted are to be construed together, so that if private property be actually taken and appropriated for public uses, although taken or appropriated in virtue of a statute having as its main or primary object the conservation of the public health, reasonable compensation must be made to the owner. This necessarily follows from the restriction, imposed by the constitution, to the effect that statutes passed in the exercise of the police power of the commonwealth must not be repugnant or contrary to the constitution, one of the provisions of which is that the owner of private property appropriated to public uses shall receive a reasonable compensation therefor. And it was so appropriated when the city took the fee, and thereby acquired a right to sell the property after it was improved, and put the proceeds into its treasury. *Commissioners v. Armstrong*, 45 N.Y. 234, 244.

Undoubtedly, the state, without taking the title to itself, may, in some appropriate mode, and without compensation to the owner, forbid the use of specified private property, where such use would be injurious to the public health. For, as said by Chief Justice Shaw, in *Com. v. Alger*, 7 Cush. 53, 84, "it is a settled principle, growing out of the nature of well-ordered society, that every holder of property, however absolute and unqualified may be his title, holds it under the implied liability that his use of it shall not be injurious to the equal enjoyment of others having an equal right to the enjoyment of their property, nor injurious to the rights of the community." "Rights of property, like all other social and conventional rights, are subject to such reasonable limitations in their enjoyment as shall prevent them from being injurious, and to such reasonable restraints and regulations, established by law, as the legislature, under the governing and controlling power vested in them by the constitution, may think necessary and expedient." This, the court said, was not the power of eminent domain, but rather the police power,—"the power vested in the legislature by the constitution to make, ordain, and establish all manner of wholesome and reasonable laws, statutes, and ordinances, either with penalties or without, not repugnant to the constitution, as they shall judge to be for the good and welfare of the commonwealth and of the subjects of the same."

When, however, the legislature provides for the actual taking and appropriation of private property for public uses, authority to enact such a regulation rests upon its right of eminent domain,—a right vital to the existence and safety of government. But it is a condition precedent to the exercise of such power that the statute make provision for reasonable compensation to the owner.

The difference between an act passed with exclusive reference to the police power of the state, without any purpose to take and apply property to public uses, and a statute like the one here involved, which, for the general good, ordains and establishes regulations declaring the existence of a nuisance created by the condition of particular property, and, in addition, and as the best mode of accomplishing the end in view, authorizes the same property to be appropriated by the public, is illustrated by *Com. v. Tewksbury*, 11 Metc. (Mass.) 55, 59. That case related to a statute of Massachusetts which, for the protection of the harbor of Boston, forbade, under penalties, the removal of any stones, gravel, or mud from any of the beaches in the town of Chelsea. The court, observing that all property was acquired and held under the tacit condition that it should not be so used as to injure the equal rights of others, or to destroy or greatly impair the public rights and interests of the community, said that "a law prohibiting an owner from removing the soil composing a natural embankment to a valuable, navigable stream, port, or harbor, is not such a taking, such an interference with the right and title of the owner, as to give him a constitutional right to compensation, and to render an act unconstitutional which makes no such provision, but is a just restraint of an injurious use of the property, which the legislature have authority to make."

The principle is also illustrated by the case of *Turner v. Nye*, 154 Mass. 579, 581, 28 N.E. 1048. That case involved the validity of a statute authorizing the flowage of certain lands or flats, upon prescribed terms and conditions, for the purpose of creating and raising a pond for the cultivation of useful fishes. Referring to the constitutional provision giving power to enact all manner of wholesome and reasonable laws for the general good (Const. Mass. pt. 2, c.1, art. 4, §1), the court in that case said: "The provision above quoted does not authorize the legislature to take property from one person and give it to another, not to take property for public uses without compensation, nor wantonly to interfere with private rights. These are always to be carefully guarded and protected. But, of necessity, cases will arise where there will or may be a conflict of interests in the use and disposition of property, and questions may and will come up affecting the public welfare in regard to the use which shall or shall not be permitted of certain property." *City of Salem v. Eastern R.R.*, 98 Mass. 431, 437.

But must compensation be actually made or tendered in advance of such taking or appropriation? Is it not sufficient, in order to meet the requirements of the constitution, if adequate provision be made for compensation?

The constitutions of some of the states expressly require that compensation be first made to the owner before the rights of the public can attach. But neither the constitution of Massachusetts not the constitution of the United States contains any such provision. The former only requires that the owner "shall receive a reasonable compensation"; the latter, that private property shall not be taken for public use 'without just compensation.' Reasonable compensation and just compensation mean the same thing.

In *Haverhill Bridge Prop'rs. v. County Com'rs.*, 103 Mass. 120, 124, the court said: "The duty of paying an adequate compensation for private property taken is inseparable from the exercise of the right of eminent domain. The act granting the power must provide for compensation, and a ready means of ascertaining the amount. Payment need not precede the seizure, but the means for securing indemnity must be such that the owner will be put to no risk or unreasonable delay."

A leading case upon this point is *Connecticut River R.R. v. Franklin Com'rs.*, 127 Mass. 50, 52, 56. That case arose under a statute of Massachusetts authorizing the manager of a railroad owned by the commonwealth to take land for a passenger station to be used by that and other railroads, and providing no other mode of compensation to the owner than that the land should be paid for out of the earnings of the railroad. The statute was held to be void.

The court said: "It has long been settled by the decisions of this court, that a statute which undertakes to appropriate private property for a public highway of any kind, without adequate provision for the payment of compensation, is unconstitutional and void, and does not justify an entry on the land of the owner without his consent,"—citing among other cases *Boston & L.R. Corp. v. Salem & L.R. Co.*, 2 Gray 1, 37. Again: "Statutes taking private property for a public highway, and providing for the ascertaining of the damages, and for payment thereof out of the treasury of the county, town, or city, have often been held to be constitutional. But, in the cases in which it has been so held, the liability to pay the damages rested upon the whole property of the inhabitants of the municipality, and might be enforced by writ of execution or warrant of distress, or by mandamus to compel the levy of a general tax. The rule has not been extended to cases in which only a special fund was charged with the payment of the damages, and the municipality had no power to levy a general tax to pay them." "When," the court said, "private property is taken directly by the commonwealth for the public use, it is not necessary or usual that the commonwealth should be made subject to compulsory process for the collection of the money to be paid by way of compensation. It is sufficient if the statute which authorizes the taking of the property should provide for the assessment of the damages in the ordinary manner, and direct that the damages so assessed be paid out of the treasury of the commonwealth, and authorize the governor to draw his warrant therefor."

Much stress was placed by counsel in that case upon the admitted fact that the earnings of the railroad owned by the commonwealth would probably be sufficient to meet and extinguish all claims for damages for lands taken. But that, the court well said, fell short of the constitutional requirement that the owner of property shall have prompt and certain compensation, without being subjected to undue risk or unreasonable delay.

In the later case of *Brickett v. Haverhill Aqueduct Co.*, 142 Mass. 394, 396, 8 N.E. 119, the language of the court was that "a statute which attempts to authorize the appropriation of private property for public uses, without making adequate provision for compensation, is unconstitutional and void."

In view of these authorities, it is clear that, as the constitution of Massachusetts does not require compensation to be first actually made or tendered before the rights of the public in the property taken or applied become complete, the requirements of that instrument are fully met where the statute makes such provision for reasonable compensation as will be adequate and certain in its results. It is equally clear that an adequate provision is made when the statute, authorizing a public municipal corporation to take private property for public uses, directs the regular ascertainment, without improper delay and in some legal mode, of the damages sustained by the owner, and gives him an unqualified right to a judgment for the amount of such damages, which can be enforced—that is, collected—by judicial process.

Substantially the same principles have been announced by this court when interpreting the clause of the constitution of the United States that forbids the taking of private property for public use without just compensation. In *Cherokee Nation v. Southern Kansas Ry. Co.*, 135 U.S. 641, 658, 10 Sup.Ct. 965, it was suggested that the act of congress there involved violated the constitution of the United States in that it did not provide for compensation to be made to the plaintiff before the defendant entered upon lands taken for the purpose of constructing its road over them. This objection was not sustained. The court said: "The constitution declares that private property shall not be taken for public use without just compensation. It does not provide or require that compensation shall be actually paid in advance of the occupancy of the land to be taken. But the owner is entitled to reasonable, certain, and adequate provision before his occupancy is disturbed. Whether a particular provision be sufficient to secure the compensation to which, under the constitution, he is entitled, is sometimes a question of difficulty. In the present case, the requirements of the constitution have, in our judgment, been fully met. The third section provides that, before the railway shall be constructed through any lands proposed to be taken, full compensation shall be made to the owner for all property to be taken or damage done by reason of the construction of the road. In the event of an appeal from the finding of the referees, the company is required to pay into court double the amount of the award, to abide its judgment; and that being done, the company may enter upon the property sought to be condemned, and proceed with the construction of its road. We are of the opinion that this provision is sufficiently reasonable, certain, and adequate to secure the just compensation to which the owner is entitled." "The plaintiff asks, what will be its condition, as to compensation, if, upon the trial de novo of the question of damages, the amount assessed in its favor should exceed the sum which may be paid into court by the defendant? This question would be more embarrassing than it is, if, by the terms of the act of congress, the title to the property appropriated passed from the owner to the defendant, when the latter, having made the required deposit in court, is authorized to enter upon the land pending the appeal, and to proceed in the construction of its road. But clearly [under the act of congress] the title does not pass until compensation is actually made to the owner. Within the meaning of the constitution [and under that act], the property, although entered upon, pending the appeal, is not taken until the compensation is ascertained in some legal mode, and being paid the title passes from the owner."

In *Kennedy v. Indianopolis*, 103 U.S. 599, 603, cited by the plaintiffs, the controlling question was whether the owner of certain lands, taken under an Indiana statute for a public object, had been divested of his title. And that question depended upon the construction of the clause of the state constitution, providing "that no man's particular services shall be demanded, or property taken or applied to public use, without the consent of his representatives, or without just compensation being made therefor." Const. Ind. 1816, art. 1, §7. It should be here stated that the Indiana statute (Rev. St. Ind. 1838, p. 337, c. 55) contained no clause expressly declaring at what stage of the proceedings the owner's title should be divested. Necessarily, therefore, it was held that, under the Indiana constitution, the owner was not divested of title until he was compensated. After referring to adjudged cases in that and other states, this court, speaking by Chief Justice Waite, said: "Not to multiply cases further, it seems to us that, both on principle and authority, the rule is, under such a constitution as that of Indiana, that the right to enter and use the property is complete as soon as the property is actually appropriated under the authority of law for a public use, but the title does not pass from the owner without his consent until just compensation has been made to him."

But that case by no means controverts the doctrine that the legislature may authorize a municipal corporation to take, for public use, at the outset, the absolute title to specific private property, if either the statute under which that is done, or a general statute, recognizes the absolute right of the owner, upon his property being taken, to just or reasonable compensation therefor, and makes provision, in the event of the disagreement of the parties, for the ascertainment, by suit, without unreasonable delay of risk to the owner, of the compensation to which under the constitution he is entitled, and to a judgment in his favor, enforceable against such corporation in some effective mode, so that the owner can certainly obtain the amount of such compensation. The Massachusetts statute of 1867, unlike the Indiana statute, expressly declares that, from the moment the property was taken, in accordance with its provisions, the title should be vested in the city of Boston, that the city should thereupon proceed forthwith with the work of raising the grade, and that the owner should have the right, for the prompt enforcement of which adequate provision was made, to obtain reasonable compensation for his property.

Numerous authorities have been cited which, it is supposed, are in conflict with the views we have expressed. But a careful examination will show that the cases cited are distinguishable from those to which we have referred.

In *Baltimore & S.R. Co. v. Nesbitt*, 10 How. 395, 398, 399, it was said that it was the payment or tender of the value assessed by the inquisition that gave title to a railroad company that had taken private property for its road, and, consequently, without such payment or tender no title could pass. But it was so declared because, by the very terms of the statute, the company was entitled to the estate and interest of the owner in the land condemned when it paid or tendered the value so ascertained.

In *Bloodgood v. Railroad Co.*, 18 Wend. 9. 17. 18, which was a case of private property taken for a railroad company, Chancellor Walworth said that the payment of the damages awarded, or the deposit of the amount as prescribed, was in the nature of a condition precedent, not only to the acquisition of the legal title to the land, but also to the right to enter and take permanent possession of the land for the use of the corporation. But that was said with reference to a statute providing that, upon the payment of the damages awarded, with the costs of the appraisement, or upon the deposit of the amount in a bank in a named city to the credit of the owner, of which notice should be given, the railroad company should "be deemed to be seized and possessed of the fee simple of all such land or real estate as shall have been appraised." That the chancellor did not hold to the doctrine that payment or tender of payment must in every case precede the divestiture of the owner's title is clear from the preceding parts of his opinion. He said: "It certainly was not the intention of the framers of the constitution to authorize the property of a citizen to be taken and actually appropriated to the use of the public, and thus to compel him to trust to the future justice of the legislature to provide him a compensation therefor. The compensation must be either ascertained and paid to him before his property is thus appropriated, or an appropriate remedy must be provided, and upon an adequate fund, whereby he may obtain such compensation through the medium of the courts of justice, if those whose duty it is to make such compensation refuse to do so." "The public purse, or the property of the town or county upon which the assessment is to be made, may justly be considered an adequate fund. He had no such remedy, however, against the legislature, to compel the passage of the necessary laws to ascertain the amount of compensation he is to receive, or the fund out of which he is to be paid."

So, in *People v. Hayden*, 6 Hill 359, 361, Chief Justice Nelson said: "Although it may not be necessary, within the constitutional provision, that the amount of compensation should be actually ascertained and paid before property is thus taken, it is, I apprehend, the settled doctrine, even as it respects the state itself, that, at least, certain and ample provision must be first made by law, except in cases of public emergency, so that the owner can coerce payment through the judicial tribunals or otherwise without any unreasonable or unnecessary delay." See, also, *Brinckerhoff v. Wemple*, 1 Wend. 470-472; *Rogers v. Bradshaw*, 20 Johns. 735, 741; *Baker v. Johnson*, 2 Hill 342, 347.

In *Stacy v. Railroad Co.*, 27 Vt. 39, 44, the court said that the railroad company derived no title to the condemned land, nor any easement growing out of it, and acquired no right to enter upon it or exercise ownership over the same, until it paid the damages awarded to the owner, or deposited the money as prescribed by the statute. The reason given for this was that the statute expressly provided that that should be done before any right in the land accrued to the company.

The case now before us differs from all, or nearly all, of those cited by the plaintiffs in this: that in the latter the statute under which the property was taken, either expressly or by necessary implication, made the payment or tender of the compensation awarded to the owner of the property appropriated to public use a condition precedent to the acquisition of title by the party at whose instance the property was taken; whereas, in the present case, the statute vests the title in the city of Boston from at least the time it filed in the office of the registry of deeds a description of the lands taken by it, describing them with as much certainty as is required in a common conveyance of lands, and stating that the same were taken pursuant to the provisions of the statute. As soon as they were so taken, the city, invested from that time with the title, had the right forthwith to raise the grade, and could not throw the property back upon the former owner, or compel him to pay the cost of raising the grade; and the owner became, from the moment the property was taken, absolutely entitled to reasonable compensation, the amount to be ascertained without undue delay, in the mode prescribed, and its payment to be assured, if necessary, by decree against the city, which could be effectively enforced.

We are of opinion that, upon both principle and authority, it was competent for the legislature, in the exercise of the police powers of the commonwealth, and of its power to appropriate private property for public uses, to authorize the city to take the fee in the lands described in the statute, prior to making compensation, and that the provision made for compensating the owner was certain and adequate.

It results that, as the title to the lands here in question passed to the city of Boston when such lands were actually taken in the mode prescribed in the statute of 1867, the persons who were then the owners, whoever they were, had thereafter no interest in them, but were only entitled to reasonable compensation.

If the proceedings in the probate court of Suffolk county were so defective that the title of the ward was not legally divested by the sale in 1844, upon which question it has become unnecessary, in the present case, to express any opinion, nevertheless the title passed, under the act of 1867, to the city of Boston, when following the provisions of that statute, it took these lands. In this view, no action can be maintained by the plaintiffs to recover the land under the title of the owner as that title existed prior to the acquisition of the property by the city. The judgment is AFFIRMED.

MUGLER v. KANSAS

123 U.S. 623, 31 L.Ed. 205, 8 S.Ct. 273 (1887)

These cases involve an inquiry into the validity of certain statutes of Kansas relating to the manufacture and sale of intoxicating liquors. The first two are indictments, charging Mugler, the plaintiff in error, in one case, with having sold, and in the other with, having manufactured, spirituous, vinous, malt, fermented, and other intoxicating liquors, in Saline County, Kansas, without having the license or permit required by the statute. The defendant, having been found guilty, was fined, in each case, $100, and ordered to be committed to the county jail until the fine was paid. Each judgment was affirmed by the supreme court of Kansas, and thereby, it is contended, the defendant was denied rights, privileges, and immunities guarantied by the constitution of the United States. The third case (*Kansas v. Ziebold & Hagelin*) was commenced by petition filed in one of the courts of the state. The relief sought is (1) that the group of buildings in Atchison county, Kansas, constituting the brewery of the defendants, partners as Ziebold & Hagelin, be adjudged a common nuisance, and the sheriff or other proper officer directed to shut up and abate the same; (2) that the defendants be enjoined from using, or permitting to be used, the said premises as a place where intoxicating liquors may be sold, bartered, or given away, or kept for barter, sale, or gift, otherwise than by authority of law. The defendants answered, denying the allegations of the petition, and averring-First, that said buildings were erected by them prior to the adoption, by the people of Kansas, of the constitutional amendment prohibiting the manufacture and sale of intoxicating liquors for other than medicinal, scientific, and mechanical purposes, and before the passage of the prohibitory liquor statute of that state; second, that they were erected for the purpose of manufacturing beer, and cannot be put to any other use, and, if not so used, they will be of little value; third, that the statute under which said suit is brought is void under the fourteenth amendment of the constitution of the United States. Upon the petition and bond of the defendants, the cause was removed into the circuit court of the United States for the district of Kansas, upon the ground that the suit was one arising under the constitution of the United States. A motion to remand it to the state court was denied. The pleadings were recast so as to conform to the equity practice in the courts of the United States; and, the cause having been heard upon bill and answer, the suit was dismissed. From that decree the state prosecutes an appeal.

By a statute of Kansas, approved March 3, 1868, it was made a misdemeanor, punishable by fine and imprisonment, for any one, directly or indirectly, to sell spirituous, vinous, fermented, or other intoxicating liquors, without having a dram-shop, tavern, or grocery license. It was also enacted, among other things, that every place where intoxicating liquors were sold in violation of the statute should be taken, held, and deemed to be a common nuisance; and it was required that all rooms, taverns, eating-houses, bazaars, restaurants, groceries, coffee-houses, cellars, or other places of public resort where intoxicating liquors were sold, in violation of law, should be abated as public nuisances. Gen. St. Kan. 1868, c. 35. But in 1880 the people of Kansas adopted a more stringent policy. On the second of November of that year they ratified an amendment to the state constitution, which declared that the manufacture and sale of intoxicating liquors should be forever prohibited in that state, except for medical, scientific, and mechanical purposes. In order to give effect to that amendment, the legislature repealed the act of 1868, and passed an act, approved February 19, 1881, to take effect May 1, 1881, entitled "An act to prohibit the manufacture and sale of intoxicating liquors, except for medical, scientific, and mechanical purposes, and to regulate the manufacture and sale thereof for such excepted purposes." Its first section provides 'that any person or persons who shall manufacture, sell, or barter any spirituous, malt, vinous, fermented, or other intoxicating liquors shall be guilty of a misdemeanor: provided, however, that such liquors may be sold for medical, scientific, and mechanical purposes, as provided in this act.' The second section makes it unlawful for any person to sell or barter for either of such excepted purposes any malt, vinous, spirituous, fermented, or other intoxicating liquors without having procured a druggist's permit therefor, and prescribes the conditions upon which such permit may be granted. The third section relates to the giving by physicians of prescriptions for intoxicating liquors to be used by their patients, and the fourth, to the sale of such liquors by druggists. The fifth section forbids any person from manufacturing or assisting in the manufacture of intoxicating liquors in the state, except for medical, scientific, and mechanical purposes, and makes provision for the granting of licenses to engage in the business of manufacturing liquors for such excepted purposes. The seventh section declares it to be a misdemeanor for any person, not having the required permit, to sell or barter, directly or indirectly, spirituous, malt, vinous, fermented, or other intoxicating liquors; the punishment prescribed being, for the first offense, a fine of not less than 100 nor more than 500 dollars, or imprisonment in the county jail not less than 20 nor more than 90 days; for the second offense, a fine of not less than 200 nor more than 500 dollars, or imprisonment in the county jail not less than 60 days nor more than six months; and for every subsequent offense, a fine not less than 500 nor more than 1,000 dollars, or imprisonment in the county jail not less than three months nor more than one year, or both such fine and imprisonment, in the discretion of the court. The eighth section provides for similar fines and punishments against persons who manufacture, or aid, assist, or abet the manufacture of, any intoxicating liquors without having the required permit. The thirteenth section declares, among other things, all places where intoxicating liquors are manufactured, sold, bartered, or given away, or are kept for sale, barter, or use, in violation of the act, to be common nuisances, and provides that upon the judgment of any court having jurisdiction finding such place to be a nuisance, the proper officer shall be directed to shut up and abate the same.

Under that statute, the prosecutions against Mugler were instituted. It contains other sections in addition to those above referred to; but as they embody merely the details of the general scheme adopted by the state for the prohibition of the manufacture and sale of intoxicating liquors, except for the purposes specified, it is unnecessary to set them out. On the seventh of March, 1885, the legislature passed an act amendatory and supplementary to that of 1881. The thirteenth section of the former act, being the one upon which the suit against Ziebold & Hagelin is founded, will be given in full in a subsequent part of this opinion.

The facts necessary to a clear understanding of the questions, common to these cases, are the following: Mugler and Ziebold & Hagelin were engaged in manufacturing beer at their respective establishments, (constructed specially for that purpose,) for several years prior to the adoption of the constitutional amendment of 1880. They continued in such business in defiance of the statute of 1881, and without having the required permit. Nor did Mugler have a license or permit to sell beer. The single sale of which he was found guilty occurred in the state, and after May 1, 1881, that is, after the act of February 19, 1881, took effect, and was of beer manufactured before its passage. The buildings and machinery constituting these breweries are of little value if not used for the purpose of manufacturing beer; that is to say, if the statutes are enforced against the defendants the value of their property will be very materially diminished.

The general question in each case is whether the foregoing statutes of Kansas are in conflict with that clause of the fourteenth amendment, which provides that 'no state shall make or enforce any law which shall abridge the privileges or immunities of citizens of the United States; nor shall any state deprive any person of life, liberty, or property without due process of law.' That legislation by a state prohibiting the manufacture within her limits of intoxicating liquors, to be there sold or bartered for general use as a beverage, does not necessarily infringe any right, privilege, or immunity secured by the constitution of the United States, is made clear by the decisions of this court, rendered before and since the adoption of the fourteenth amendment; to some of which, in view of questions to be presently considered, it will be well to refer.

In the License Cases, 5 How. 504, the question was whether certain statutes of Massachusetts, Rhode Island, and New Hampshire, relating to the sale of spirituous liquors, were repugnant to the constitution of the United States. In determining that question, it became necessary to inquire whether there was any conflict between the exercise by Congress of its power to regulate commerce with foreign countries, or among the several states, and the exercise by a state of what are called police powers. Although the members of the court did not fully agree as to the grounds upon which the decision should be placed, they were unanimous in holding that the statutes then under examination were not inconsistent with the constitution of the United States, or with any act of congress. Chief Justice TANEY said: "If any state deems the retail and internal traffic in ardent spirits injurious to its citizens, and calculated to produce idleness, vice, or debauchery, I see nothing in the constitution of the United States to prevent it from regulating and restraining the traffic, or from prohibiting it altogether, if it thinks proper." Mr. Justice MCLEAN, among other things, said: "A state regulates its domestic commerce, contracts, the transmission of estates, real and personal, and acts upon internal matters which relate to its moral and political welfare. Over these subjects the federal government has no power.... The acknowledged police power of a state extends often to the destruction of property. A nuisance may be abated. Everything prejudicial to the health or morals of a city may be removed." Mr. Justice WOODBURY observed: "How can they [the states] be sovereign within their respective spheres, without power to regulate all their internal commerce, as well as police, and direct how, when, and where it shall be conducted in articles intimately connected either with public morals or public safety or public prosperity?" Mr. Justice GRIER, in still more empathic language, said: "The true question presented by these cases, and one which I am not disposed to evade, is whether the states have a right to prohibit the sale and consumption of an article of commerce which they believe to be pernicious in its effects, and the cause of disease, pauperism, and crime.... Without attempting to define what are the peculiar subjects or limits of this power, it may safely be affirmed that every law for the restraint or punishment of crime, for the preservation of the public peace, health, and morals must come within this category.... It is not necessary, for the sake of justifying the state legislation now under consideration, to array the appalling statistics of misery, pauperism, and crime which have their origin in the use or abuse of ardent spirits. The police power, which is exclusively in the states, is alone competent to the correction of these great evils, and all measures of restraint or prohibition necessary to effect the purpose are within the scope of that authority."

In *Bartemeyer v. Iowa*, 18 Wall. 129, it was said that, prior to the adoption of the fourteenth amendment, state enactments, regulating or prohibiting the traffic in intoxicating liquors, raised no question under the constitution of the United States; and that such legislation was left to the discretion of the respective states, subject to no other limitations than those imposed by their own constitutions, or by the general principles supposed to limit all legislative power. Referring to the contention that the right to sell intoxicating liquors was secured by the fourteenth amendment, the court said that, 'so far as such a right exists, it is not one of the rights growing out of citizenship of the United States.' In *Beer Co. v. Massachusetts*, 97 U. S. 33, it was said that, 'as a measure of police regulation, looking to the preservation of public morals, a state law prohibiting the manufacture and sale of intoxicating liquors is not repugnant to any clause of the constitution of the United States.' Finally, in *Foster v. Kansas*, 112 U. S. 206, 5 Sup. Ct. Rep. 97, the court said that the question as to the constitutional power of a state to prohibit the manufacture and sale of intoxicating liquors was no longer an open one in this court. These cases rest upon the acknowledged right of the states of the Union to control their purely internal affairs, and, in so doing, to protect the health, morals, and safety of their people by regulations that do not interfere with the execution of the powers of the general government, or violate rights secured by the constitution of the United States. The power to establish such regulations, as was said in *Gibbons v. Ogden*, 9 Wheat. 203, reaches everything within the territory of a state not surrendered to the national government.

It is, however, contended that, although the state may prohibit the manufacture of intoxicating liquors for sale or barter within her limits, for general use as a beverage, 'no convention or legislature has the right, under our form of government, to prohibit any citizen from manufacturing for his own use, or for export or storage, any article of food or drink not endangering or affecting the rights of others.' The argument made in support of the first branch of this proposition, briefly stated, is that, in the implied compact between the state and the citizen, certain rights are reserved by the latter, which are guarantied by the constitutional provision protecting persons against being deprived of life, liberty, or property, without due process of law, and with which the state cannot interfere; that among those rights is that of manufacturing for one's use either food or drink; and that while, according to the doctrines of the commune, the state may control the tastes, appetites, habits, dress, food, and drink of the people, our system of government, based upon the individuality and intelligence of the citizen, does not claim to control him, except as to his conduct to others, leaving him the sole judge as to all that only affects himself. It will be observed that the proposition, and the argument made in support of it, equally concede that the right to manufacture drink for one's personal use is subject to the condition that such manufacture does not endanger or affect the rights of others. If such manufacture does prejudicially affect the rights and interests of the community, it follows, from the very premises stated, that society has the power to protect itself, by legislation, against the injurious consequences of that business. As was said in *Munn v. Illinois*, 94 U. S. 124, while power does not exist with the whole people to control rights that are purely and exclusively private, government may require 'each citizen to so conduct himself, and so use his own property, as not unnecessarily to injure another.' But by whom, or by what authority, is it to be determined whether the manufacture of particular articles of drink, either for general use or for the personal use of the maker, will injuriously affect the public? Power to determine such questions, so as to bind all, must exist somewhere; else society will be at the mercy of the few, who, regarding only their own appetites or passions, may be willing to imperil the peace and security of the many, provided only they are permitted to do as they please. Under our system that power is lodged with the legislative branch of the government. It belongs to that department to exert what are known as the police powers of the state, and to determine, primarily, what measures are appropriate or needful for the protection of the public morals, the public health, or the public safety.

It does not at all follow that every statute enacted ostensibly for the promotion of these ends is to be accepted as a legitimate exertion of the police powers of the state. There are, of necessity, limits beyond which legislation cannot rightfully go. While every possible presumption is to be indulged in favor of the validity of a statute, (*Sinking Fund Cases*, 99 U. S. 718,) the courts must obey the constitution rather than the law-making department of government, and must, upon their own responsibility, determine whether, in any particular case, these limits have been passed. "to what purpose," it was said in *Marbury v. Madison*, 1 Cranch, 137, 167, "are powers limited, and to what purpose is that limitation committed to writing, if these limits may, at any time, be passed by those intended to be restrained? The distinction between a government with limited and unlimited powers is abolished, if those limits do not confine the persons on whom they are imposed, and if acts prohibited and acts allowed are of equal obligation." The courts are not bound by mere forms, nor are they to be misled by mere pretenses. They are at liberty, indeed, are under a solemn duty, to look at the substance of things, whenever they enter upon the inquiry whether the legislature has transcended the limits of its authority. If, therefore, a statute purporting to have been enacted to protect the public health, the public morals, or the public safety, has no real or substantial relation to those objects, or is a palpable invasion of rights secured by the fundamental law, it is the duty of the courts to so adjudge, and thereby give effect to the constitution.

Keeping in view these principles, as governing the relations of the judicial and legislative departments of government with each other, it is difficult to perceive any ground for the judiciary to declare that the prohibition by Kansas of the manufacture or sale, within her limits, of intoxicating liquors for general use there as a beverage, is not fairly adapted to the end of protecting the community against the evils which confessedly result from the excessive use of ardent spirits. There is no justification for holding that the state, under the guise merely of police regulations, is here aiming to deprive the citizen of his constitutional rights; for we cannot shut out of view the fact, within the knowledge of all, that the public health, the public morals, and the public safety, may be endangered by the general use of intoxicating drinks; nor the fact established by statistics accessible to every one, that the idleness, disorder, pauperism, and crime existing in the country, are, in some degree at least, traceable to this evil. If, therefore, a state deems the absolute prohibition of the manufacture and sale within her limits, of intoxicating liquors, for other than medical, scientific, and mechanical purposes, to be necessary to the peace and security of society, the courts cannot, without usurping legislative functions, override the will of the people as thus expressed by their chosen representatives. They have nothing to do with the mere policy of legislation. Indeed, it is a fundamental principle in our institutions, indispensable to the preservation of public liberty, that one of the separate departments of government shall not usurp powers committed by the constitution to another department. And so, if, in the judgment of the legislature, the manufacture of intoxicating liquors for the maker's own use, as a beverage, would tend to cripple, if it did not defeat, the efforts to guard the community against the evils attending the excessive use of such liquors, it is not for the courts, upon their views as to what is best and safest for the community, to disregard the legislative determination of that question. So far from such a regulation having no relation to the general end sought to be accomplished, the entire scheme of prohibition, as embodied in the constitution and laws of Kansas, might fail, if the right of each citizen to manufacture intoxicating liquors for his own use as a beverage were recognized. Such a right does not inhere in citizenship. Nor can it be said that government interferes with or impairs any one's constitutional rights of liberty or of property, when it determines that the manufacture and sale of intoxicating drinks, for general or individual use, as a beverage, are, or may become, hurtful to society, and constitute, therefore, a business in which no one may lawfully engage. Those rights are best secured, in our government, by the observance, upon the part of all, of such regulations as are established by competent authority to promote the common good. No one may rightfully do that which the law-making power, upon reasonable grounds, declares to be prejudicial to the general welfare.

This conclusion is unavoidable, unless the fourteenth amendment of the constitution takes from the states of the Union those powers of police that were reserved at the time the original constitution was adopted. But this court has declared, upon full consideration, *Barbier v. Connolly* 113 U. S. 31, that the fourteenth amendment had no such effect. After observing, among other things, that that amendment forbade the arbitrary deprivation of life or liberty, and the arbitrary spoliation of property, and secured equal protection to all under like circumstances, in respect as well to their personal and civil rights as to their acquisition and enjoyment of property, the court said: "But neither the amendment, broad and comprehensive as it is, nor any other amendment, was designed to interfere with the power of the state, sometimes termed 'its police power,' to prescribe regulations to promote the health, peace, morals, education, and good order of the people, and to legislate so as to increase the industries of the state, develop its resources, and add to its wealth and prosperity." Undoubtedly the state, when providing, by legislation, for the protection of the public health, the public morals, or the public safety, is subject to the paramount authority of the constitution of the United States, and may not violate rights secured or guarantied by that instrument, or interfere with the execution of the powers confided to the general government. *Henderson v. Mayor of New York*, 92 U.S. 259; *Railroad v. Husen*, 95 U.S. 465; *Gas-Light Co. v. Light Co.*, 115 U.S. 650, 6 Sup.Ct. Rep. 252; *Walling v. Michigan*, 116 U. S. 446, 6 Sup.Ct.Rep. 454; *Yick Wo v. Hopkins*, 118 U.S. 356, 6 Sup.Ct.Rep. 1064; *Steam-Ship Co. v. Board of Health*, 118 U.S. 455, 6 Sup.Ct.Rep. 1114.

Upon this ground, if we do not misapprehend the position of defendants, it is contended that, as the primary and principal use of beer is as a beverage; as their respective breweries were erected when it was lawful to engage in the manufacture of beer for every purpose; as such establishments will become of no value as property, or, at least, will be materially diminished in value, if not employed in the manufacture of beer for every purpose,—the prohibition upon their being so employed is, in effect, a taking of property for public use without compensation, and depriving the citizen of his property without due process of law. In other words, although the state, in the exercise of her police powers, may lawfully prohibit the manufacture and sale, within her limits, of intoxicating liquors to be used as a beverage, legislation having that object in view cannot be enforced against those who, at the time, happen to own property, the chief value of which consists in its fitness for such manufacturing purposes, unless compensation is first made for the diminution in the value of their property, resulting from such prohibitory enactments.

This interpretation of the fourteenth amendment is inadmissible. It cannot be supposed that the states intended, by adopting that amendment, to impose restraints upon the exercise of their powers for the protection of the safety, health, or morals of the community. In respect to contracts, the obligations of which are protected against hostile state legislation, this court in *Union Co. v. Landing Co.*, 111 U.S. 751, 4 Sup.Ct.Rep. 652, said that the state could not, by any contract, limit the exercise of her power to the prejudice of the public health and the public morals. So, in *Stone v. Mississippi*, 101 U.S. 816, where the constitution was invoked against the repeal by the state of a charter, granted to a private corporation, to conduct a lottery, and for which that corporation paid to the state a valuable consideration in money, the court said: 'No legislature can bargain away the public health or the public morals. The people themselves cannot do it, much less their servants.... Government is organized with a view to their preservation, and cannot divest itself of the power to provide for them.' Again, in *Gas-Light Co. v. Light Co.*, 115 U.S. 650, 672, 6 Sup.Ct.Rep. 252: "The constitutional prohibition upon state laws impairing the obligation of contracts does not restrict the power of the state to protect the public health, the public morals, or the public safety, as the one or the other may be involved in the execution of such contracts. Rights and privileges arising from contracts with a state are subject to regulations for the protection of the public health, the public morals, and the public safety, in the same sense, and to the same extent, as are all contracts and all property, whether owned by natural persons or corporations."

The principal that no person shall be deprived of life, liberty, or property without due process of law, was embodied, in substance, in the constitutions of nearly all, if not all, of the states at the time of the adoption of the fourteenth amendment; and it has never been regarded as incompatible with the principle, equally vital, because essential to the peace and safety of society, that all property in this country is held under the implied obligation that the owner's use of it shall not be injurious to the community. *Beer Co. v. Massachusetts*, 97 U.S. 32; *Com. v. Alger, 7 Cush.* 53. An illustration of this doctrine is afforded by *Patterson v. Kentucky*, 97 U.S. 501. The question there was as to the validity of a statute of Kentucky, enacted in 1874, imposing a penalty upon any one selling or offering for sale oils and fluids, the product of coal, petroleum, or other bituminous substances, which would burn or ignite at a temperature below 1300 Fahrenheit. Patterson having sold within that commonwealth, a certain oil, for which letters patent were issued in 1867, but which did not come up to the standard required by said statute, and having been indicted therefor, disputed the state's authority to prevent or obstruct the exercise of that right. This court upheld the legislation of Kentucky, upon the ground that, while the state could not impair the exclusive right of the patentee, or of his assignee, in the discovery described in the letters patent, the tangible property, the fruit of the discovery, was not beyond control in the exercise of her police powers. It was said: "By the settled doctrines of this court, the police power extends, at least, to the protection of the lives, the health, and the property of the community against the injurious exercise by any citizen of his own rights. State legislation, strictly and legitimately for police purposes, does not, in the sense of the constitution, necessarily intrench upon any authority which has been confided, expressly or by implication, to the national government. The Kentucky statute under examination manifestly belongs to that class of legislation. It is, in the best sense, a mere policy regulation, deemed essential to the protection of the lives and property of citizens." Referring to the numerous decisions of this court guarding the power of congress to regulate commerce against encroachment, under the guise of state regulations, established for the purpose and with the effect of destroying or impairing rights secured by the constitution, it was further said: "It has, nevertheless, with marked distinctness and uniformity, recognized the necessity, growing out of the fundamental conditions of civil society, of upholding state police regulations which were enacted in good faith, and had appropriate and direct connection with that protection to life, health, and property which each state owes to her citizens." See, also, *U.S. v. Dewitt*, 9 Wall. 41; *License Tax Cases*, 5 Wall. 462; *Pervear v. Com.*, Id. 475.

Another decision very much in point upon this branch of the case, is *Fertilizing Co. v. Hyde Park*, 97 U. S. 659, 667, also decided after the adoption of the fourteenth amendment. The court there sustained the validity of an ordinance of the village of Hyde Park, in Cook County, Illinois, passed under legislative authority, forbidding any person from transporting through that village offal or other offensive or unwholesome matter, or from maintaining or carrying on an offensive or unwholesome business or establishment within its limits. The fertilizing company, had, at large expense, and under authority expressly conferred by its charter, located its works at a particular point in the county. Besides, the charter of the village, at that time, provided that it should not interfere with parties engaged in transporting animal matter from Chicago, or from manufacturing it into a fertilizer or other chemical product. The enforcement of the ordinance in question operated to destroy the business of the company, and seriously to impair the value of its property. As, however, its business had become a nuisance to the community in which it was conducted, producing discomfort, and often sickness, among large masses of people, the court maintained the authority of the village, acting under legislative sanction, to protect the public health against such nuisance. It said: "We cannot doubt that the police power of the state was applicable and adequate to give an effectual remedy. That power belonged to the states when the federal constitution was adopted. They did not surrender it, and they all have it now. It extends to the entire property and business within their local jurisdiction. Both are subject to it in all proper cases. It rests upon the fundamental principle that every one shall so use his own as not to wrong and injure another. To regulate and abate nuisances is one of its ordinary functions."

It is supposed by the defendants that the doctrine for which they contend is sustained by *Pumpelly v. Green Bay Co.*, 13 Wall. 168. But in that view we do not concur. This was an action for the recovery of damages for the overflowing of the plaintiff's land by water, resulting from the construction of a dam across a river. The defense was that the dam constituted a part of the system adopted by the state for improving the navigation of Fox and Wisconsin rivers; and it was contended that, as the damages of which the plaintiff complained were only the result of the improvement, under legislative sanction, of a navigable stream, he was not entitled to compensation from the state or its agents. The case, therefore, involved the question whether the overflowing of the plaintiff's land, to such an extent that it became practically unfit to be used, was a taking of property, within the meaning of the constitution of Wisconsin, providing that "the property of no person shall be taken for public use without just compensation therefor." This court said it would be a very curious and unsatisfactory result, were it held that, "if the government refrains from the absolute conversion of real property to the uses of the public, it can destroy its value entirely, can inflict irreparable and permanent injury to any extent, can, in effect, subject it to total destruction, without making any compensation, because, in the narrowest sense of that word, it is not taken for the public use. Such a construction would pervert the constitutional provision into a restriction upon the rights of the citizen, as those rights stood at the common law, instead of the government, and make it an authority for the invasion of private rights under the pretext of the public good, which had no warrant in the laws or practices of our ancestors."

These principles have no application to the case under consideration. The question in *Pumpelly v. Green Bay Co.*, arose under the state's power of eminent domain; while the question now before us arises under what are, strictly, the police powers of the state, exerted for the protection of the health, morals, and safety of the people. That case, as this court said in *Transportation Co. v. Chicago*, 99 U.S. 642, was an extreme qualification of the doctrine, universally held, that "acts done in the proper exercise of governmental powers, and not directly encroaching upon private property, though these consequences may impair its use," do not constitute a taking within the meaning of the constitutional provision, or entitle the owner of such property to compensation from the state or its agents, or give him any right of action. It was a case in which there was a "permanent flooding of private property," a "physical invasion of the real estate of the private owner, and a practical ouster of his possession." His property was, in effect, required to be devoted to the use of the public, and, consequently, he was entitled to compensation.

As already stated, the present case must be governed by principles that do not involve the power of eminent domain, in the exercise of which property may not be taken for public use without compensation. A prohibition simply upon the use of property for purposes that are declared, by valid legislation, to be injurious to the health, morals, or safety of the community, cannot, in any just sense, be deemed a taking or an appropriation of property for the public benefit. Such legislation does not disturb the owner in the control or use of his property for lawful purposes, nor restrict his right to dispose of it, but is only a declaration by the state that its use by any one, for certain forbidden purposes, is prejudicial to the public interests. Nor can legislation of that character come within the fourteenth amendment, in any case, unless it is apparent that its real object is not to protect the community, or to promote the general well-being, but, under the guise of police regulation, to deprive the owner of his liberty and property, without due process of law. The power which the states have of prohibiting such use by individuals of their property, as will be prejudicial to the health, the morals, or the safety of the public, is not, and, consistently with the existence and safety of organized society, cannot be, burdened with the condition that the state must compensate such individual owners for pecuniary losses they may sustain, by reason of their not being permitted, by a noxious use of their property, to inflict injury upon the community. The exercise of the police power by the destruction of property which is itself a public nuisance, or the prohibition of its use in a particular way, whereby its value becomes depreciated, is very different from taking property for public use, or from depriving a person of his property without due process of law. In the one case, a nuisance only is abated; in the other, unoffending property is taken away from an innocent owner. It is true, when the defendants in these cases purchased or erected their breweries, the laws of the state did not forbid the manufacture of intoxicating liquors. But the state did not thereby give any assurance, or come under an obligation, that its legislation upon that subject would remain unchanged. Indeed, as was said in *Stone v. Mississippi*, 101 U. S. 814, the supervision of the public health and the public morals is a governmental power, 'continuing in its nature,' and 'to be dealt with as the special exigencies of the moment may require;' and that, 'for this purpose, the largest legislative discretion is allowed, and the discretion cannot be parted with any more than the power itself." So in *Beer Co. v. Massachusetts*, 97 U. S. 32: "If the public safety or the public morals require the discontinuance of any manufacture or traffic, the hand of the legislature cannot be stayed from providing for its discontinuance by any incidental inconvenience which individuals or corporations may suffer."

It now remains to consider certain questions relating particularly to the thirteenth section of the act of 1885. That section, which takes the place of section 13 of the act of 1881, is as follows:

> "Sec. 13. All places where intoxicating liquors are manufactured, sold, bartered, or given away in violation of any of the provisions of this act, or where intoxicating liquors are kept for sale, barter, or delivery in violation of this act, are hereby declared to be common nuisances, and upon the judgment of any court having jurisdiction finding such place to be a nuisance under this section, the sheriff, his deputy, or under-sheriff, or any constable of the proper county, or marshal of any city where the same is located, shall be directed to shut up and abate such place by taking possession thereof and destroying all intoxicating liquors found therein, together with all signs, screens, bars, bottles, glasses, and other property used in keeping and maintaining said nuisance, and the owner or keeper thereof shall, upon conviction, be adjudged guilty of maintaining a common nuisance, and shall

> be punished by a fine of not less than one hundred dollars nor more than five hundred dollars, and by imprisonment in the county jail not less than thirty days nor more than ninety days. The attorney general, county attorney, or any citizen of the county where such nuisance exists, or is kept, or is maintained, may maintain an action in the name of the state to abate and perpetually enjoin the same. The injunction shall be granted at the commencement of the action, and no bond shall be required. Any person violating the terms of any injunction granted in such proceeding, shall be punished as for contempt, by a fine of not less than 100 nor more than 500 dollars, or by imprisonment in the county jail not less than 30 days nor more than six months, or by both such fine and imprisonment, in the discretion of the court."

It is contended by counsel in the case of *Kansas v. Ziebold & Hagelin* that the entire scheme of this section is an attempt to deprive persons who come within its provisions of their property and of their liberty without due process of law; especially when taken in connection with that clause of section 14, (amendatory of section 21 of the act of 1881,) which provides that, "in prosecutions under this act, by indictment or otherwise,... it shall not be necessary in the first instance for the state to prove that the party charged did not have a permit to sell intoxicating liquors for the excepted purposes." We are unable to perceive anything in these regulations inconsistent with the constitutional guaranties of liberty and property. The state having authority to prohibit the manufacture and sale of intoxicating liquors for other than medical, scientific, and mechanical purposes, we do not doubt her power to declare that any place, kept and maintained for the illegal manufacture and sale of such liquors, shall be deemed a common nuisance, and be abated, and, at the same time, to provide for the indictment and trial of the offender. One is a proceeding against the property used for forbidden purposes, while the other is for the punishment of the offender.

It is said that by the thirteenth section of the act of 1885, the legislature, finding a brewery within the state in actual operation, without notice, trial, or hearing, by the mere exercise of its arbitrary caprice, declares it to be a common nuisance, and then prescribes the consequences which are to follow inevitably by judicial mandate required by the statute, and involving and permitting the exercise of no judicial discretion or judgment; that the brewery being found in operation, the court is not to determine whether it is a common nuisance, but, under the command of the statute, is to find it to be one; that it is not the liquor made, or the making of it, which is thus enacted to be a common nuisance, but the place itself, including all the property used in keeping and maintaining the common nuisance; that the judge having thus signed without inquiry, and, it may be, contrary to the fact and against his own judgment, the edict of the legislature, the court is commanded to take possession by its officers of the peace and shut it up; nor is all this destruction of property, by legislative edict, to be made as a forfeiture consequent upon conviction of any offense, but merely because the legislature so commands; and it is done by a court of equity, without any previous conviction first had, or any trial known to the law. This, certainly, is a formidable arraignment of the legislation of Kansas, and if it were founded upon a just interpretation of her statutes, the court would have no difficulty in declaring that they could not be enforced without infringing the constitutional rights of the citizen. But those statutes have no such scope, and are attended with no such results as the defendants suppose. The court is not required to give effect to a legislative "decree" or "edict," unless every enactment by the lawmaking power of a state is to be so characterized. It is not declared that every establishment is to be deemed a common nuisance because it may have been maintained prior to the passage of the statute as a place for manufacturing intoxicating liquors. The statute is prospective in its operation; that is, it does not put the brand of a common nuisance upon any place, unless, after its passage, that place is kept and maintained for purposes declared by the legislature to be injurious to the community. Nor is the court required to adjudge any place to be a common nuisance simply because it is charged by the state to be such. It must first find it to be of that character; that is, must ascertain, in some legal mode, whether, since the statute was passed, the place in question has been, or is being, so used as to make it a common nuisance.

Equally untenable is the proposition that proceedings in equity for the purposes indicated in the thirteenth section of the statute are inconsistent with due process of law. "In regard to public nuisances," Mr. Justice Story says, "the jurisdiction of courts of equity seems to be of a very ancient date, and has been distinctly traced back to the reign of Queen Elizabeth. The jurisdiction is applicable, not only to public nuisances, strictly so called, but also to purprestures upon public rights and property.... In case of public nuisances, properly so called, an indictment lies to abate them, and to punish the offenders. But an information also lies in equity to redress the grievance by way of injunction." 2 Stroy, Eq.Jur. §§921, 922. The ground of this jurisdiction in cases of purpresture, as well as of public nuisances, is the ability of courts of equity to give a more speedy, effectual, and permanent remedy than can be had at law. They cannot only prevent nuisances that are threatened, and before irreparable mischief ensues, but arrest or abate those in progress, and, by perpetual injunction, protect the public against them in the future; whereas courts of law can only reach existing nuisances, leaving future acts to be the subject of new prosecutions or proceedings. This is a salutary jurisdiction, especially where a nuisance affects the health, morals, or safety of the community. Though not frequently exercised, the power undoubtedly exists in courts of equity thus to protect the public against injury. *District Atty. v. Railroad Co.*, 16 Gray, 245; *Attorney Gen. v. Railroad*, 3 N. J. Eq. 139; *Attorney Gen. v. Ice Co.*, 104 Mass. 244; *State v. Mayor*, 5 Port. (Ala.) 279, 294; *Hoole v. Attorney Gen.*, 22 Ala. 194; *Attorney Gen. v. Hunter*, 1 Dev.Eq. 13; *Attorney Gen. v. Forbes*, 2 Mylne & C. 123, 129, 133; *Attorney Gen. v. Railway Co.*, 1 Drew. & S. 161; Eden, Inj. 259; Kerr, Inj. (2d Ed.) 168.

As to the objection that the statute makes no provision for a jury trial in cases like this one, it is sufficient to say that such a mode of trial is not required in suits in equity brought to abate a public nuisance. The statutory direction that an injunction issue at the commencement of the action is not to be construed as dispensing with such preliminary proof as is necessary to authorize an injunction pending the suit.

The court is not to issue an injunction simply because one is asked, or because the charge is made that a common nuisance is maintained in violation of law. The statute leaves the court at liberty to give effect to the principle that an injunction will not be granted to restrain a nuisance, except upon clear and satisfactory evidence that one exists. Here the fact to be ascertained was not whether a place, kept and maintained for purposes forbidden by the statute, was per se a nuisance, that fact being conclusively determined by the statute itself, but whether the place in question was so kept and maintained. If the proof upon that point is not full or sufficient, the court can refuse an injunction, or postpone action until the state first obtains the verdict of a jury in her favor. In this case, it cannot be denied that the defendants kept and maintained a place that is within the statutory definition of a common nuisance. Their petition for the removal of the cause from the state court, and their answer to the bill, admitted every fact necessary to maintain this suit, if the statute, under which it was brought, was constitutional.

Touching the provision that in prosecutions, by indictment or otherwise, the state need not, in the first instance, prove that the defendant has not the permit required by the statute, we may remark that, if it has any application to a proceeding like this, it does not deprive him of the presumption that he is innocent of any violation of law. It is only a declaration that when the state has proven that the place described is kept and maintained for the manufacture or sale of intoxicating liquors, such manufacture or sale being unlawful except for specified purposes, and then only under a permit, the prosecution need not prove a negative, namely, that the defendant has not the required license or permit. If the defendant has such license or permit, he can easily produce it, and thus overthrow the prima facie case established by the state.

A portion of the argument in behalf of the defendants is to the effect that the statutes of Kansas forbid the manufacture of intoxicating liquors to be exported, or to be carried to other states, and, upon that ground, are repugnant to the clause of the constitution of the United States, giving congress power to regulate commerce with foreign nations and among the several states. We need only say, upon this point, that there is no intimation in the record that the beer which the respective defendants manufactured was intended to be carried out of the state or to foreign countries. And, without expressing an opinion as to whether such facts would have constituted a good defense, we observe that it will be time enough to decide a case of that character when it shall come before us.

For the reasons stated, we are of opinion that the judgments of the supreme court of Kansas have not denied to Mugler, the plaintiff in error, any right, privilege, or immunity secured to him by the constitution of the United States, and its judgment, in each case, is accordingly affirmed. We are also of opinion that the circuit court of the United States erred in dismissing the bill of the state against Ziebold & Hagelin. The decree in that case is reversed, and the cause remanded, with directions to enter a decree granting to the state such relief as the act of March 7, 1885, authorizes. It is so ORDERED. (Dissent omitted.)

MILLER v. SCHOENE

48 S.Ct. 246, 276 U.S. 272, 72 L.Ed. 568 (1928)

Acting under the Cedar Rust Act of Virginia, Acts Va. 1914, c. 36, as amended by Acts Va. 1920, c. 260, now embodied in Va. Code (1924) as sections 885 to 893, defendant in error, the state entomologist, ordered the plaintiffs in error to cut down a large number of ornamental red cedar trees growing on their property, as a means of preventing the communication of a rust or plant disease with which they were infected to the apple orchards in the vicinity. The plaintiffs in error appealed from the order to the circuit court of Shenandoah County which, after a hearing and a consideration of evidence, affirmed the order and allowed to plaintiffs in error $100 to cover the expense of removal of the cedars. Neither the judgment of the court nor the statute as interpreted allows compensation for the value of the standing cedars or the decrease in the market value of the realty caused by their destruction whether considered as ornamental trees or otherwise. But they save to plaintiffs in error the privilege of using the trees when felled. On appeal the Supreme Court of Appeals of Virginia affirmed the judgment. *Miller v. State Entomologist*, 146 Va. 175, 135 S.E. 813. Both in the circuit court and the Supreme Court of Appeals plaintiffs in error challenged the constitutionality of the statute under the due process clause of the Fourteenth Amendment and the case is properly here on writ of error. Judicial Code, §237a (28 USCA §344).

The Virginia statute presents a comprehensive scheme for the condemnation and destruction of red cedar trees infected by cedar rust. By section 1 it is declared to be unlawful for any person to "own, plant or keep alive and standing" on his premises any red cedar tree which is or may be the source or "host plant" of the communicable plant disease known as cedar rust, and any such tree growing within a certain radius of any apple orchard is declared to be a public nuisance, subject to destruction. Section 2 makes it the duty of the state entomologist, "upon the request in writing of ten or more reputable freeholders of any county or magisterial district, to make a preliminary investigation of the locality … to ascertain if any cedar tree or trees … are the source of, harbor or constitute the host plant for the said disease … and constitute a menace to the health of any apple orchard in said locality, and that said cedar tree or trees exist within a radius of two miles of any apple orchard in said locality." If affirmative findings are so made, he is required to direct the owner in writing to destroy the trees and, in his notice, to furnish a statement of the "fact found to exist whereby it is deemed necessary or proper to destroy" the trees and to call attention to the law under which it is proposed to destroy them. Section 5 authorizes the state entomologist to destroy the trees if the owner, after being notified, fails to do so. Section 7 furnishes a mode of appealing from the order of the entomologist to the circuit court of the county, which is authorized to "hear the objections" and "pass upon all questions involved," the procedure followed in the present case.

As shown by the evidence and as recognized in other cases involving the validity of this statute, *Bowman v. Virginia State Entomologist*, 128 Va. 351, 105 S.E. 141, 12 A.L.R. 1121; *Kelleher v. Schoene*, (D.C.) 14 F.2d 341, cedar rust is an infectious plant disease in the form of a fungoid organism which is destructive of the fruit and foliage of the apple, but without effect on the value of the cedar. Its life cycle has two phases which are passed alternately as a growth on red cedar and on apple trees. It is communicated by spores from one to the other over a radius of at least two miles. It appears not to be communicable between trees of the same species, but only from one species to the other, and other plants seem not to be appreciably affected by it. The only practicable method of controlling the disease and protecting apple trees from its ravages is the destruction of all red cedar trees, subject to the infection, located within two miles of apple orchards.

The red cedar, aside from its ornamental use, has occasional use and value as lumber. It is indigenous to Virginia, is not cultivated or dealt in commercially on any substantial scale, and its value throughout the state is shown to be small as compared with that of the apple orchards of the state. Apple growing is one of the principal agricultural pursuits in Virginia. The apple is used there and exported in large quantities. Many millions of dollars are invested in the orchards, which furnish employment for a large portion of the population, and have induced the development of attendant railroad and cold storage facilities.

On the evidence we may accept the conclusion of the Supreme Court of Appeals that the state was under the necessity of making a choice between the preservation of one class of property and that of the other wherever both existed in dangerous proximity. It would have been none the less a choice if, instead of enacting the present statute, the state, by doing nothing, had permitted serious injury to the apple orchards within its borders to go on unchecked. When forced to such a choice the state does not exceed its constitutional powers by deciding upon the destruction of one class of property in order to save another which, in the judgment of the legislature, is of greater value to the public. It will not do to say that the case is merely one of a conflict of two private interests and that the misfortune of apple growers may not be shifted to cedar owners by ordering the destruction of their property; for it is obvious that there may be, and that here there is, a preponderant public concern in the preservation of the one interest over the other. Compare *Bacon v. Walker*, 204 U.S. 311, 27 S.Ct. 289, 51 L.Ed. 499; *Missouri, Kansas & Texas R. Co. v. May*, 194 U.S. 267, 24 S.Ct. 638, 48 L.Ed. 971; *Chicago, Terre Haute & Southeastern R. Co. v. Anderson*, 242 U.S. 283, 37 S.Ct. 124, 61 L.Ed. 302; *Perley v. North Carolina*, 249 U.S. 510, 39 S.Ct. 357, 63 L.Ed. 735. And where the public interest is involved preferment of that interest over the property interest of the individual, to the extent even of its destruction, is one of the distinguishing characteristics of every exercise of the police power which affects property. *Mugler v. Kansas*, 123 U.S. 623, 8 S.Ct. 273, 31 L.Ed. 205; *Hadacheck v. Los Angeles*, 239 U.S. 394, 36 S.Ct. 143, 60 L.Ed. 348, Ann.Cas. 1917B, 927; *Village of Euclid v. Ambler Realty Co.*, 272 U.S. 365, 47 S.Ct. 114, 71 L.Ed. 303; *Northwestern Fertilizer Co. v. Hyde Park*, 97 U.S. 659, 24 L.Ed. 1036; *Northwestern Laundry v. Des Moines*, 239 U.S. 486, 36 S.Ct. 206, 60 L.Ed. 396; *Lawton v. Steele*, 152 U.S. 133, 14 S.Ct. 499, 38 L.Ed. 385; *Sligh v. Kirkwood*, 237 U.S. 52, 35 S.Ct. 501, 59 L.Ed. 835; *Reinman v. Little Rock*, 237 U.S. 171, 35 S.Ct. 511, 59 L.Ed. 900.

We need not weigh with nicety the question whether the infected cedars constitute a nuisance according to the common law; or whether they may be so declared by statute. See *Hadacheck v. Los Angeles, supra*, 411 (36 S.Ct, 143). For where, as here, the choice is unavoidable, we cannot say that its exercise, controlled by considerations of social policy which are not unreasonable, involves any denial of due process. The injury to property here is no more serious, nor the public interest less, than in *Hadacheck v. Los Angeles, supra, Northwestern Laundry v. Des Moines, supra, Reinman v. Little Rock, supra*, or *Sligh v. Kirkwood, supra*.

The statute is not, as plaintiffs in error argue, subject to the vice which invalidated the ordinance considered by this court in *Eubank v. Richmond*, 226 U.S. 137, 33 S.Ct. 76, 57 L.Ed. 146, 42 L.R.A.N.S. 1123, Ann. Cas. 1914B, 192. That ordinance directed the committee on streets of the city of Richmond to establish a building line, not less than five nor more than 30 feet from the street line whenever requested to do so by the owners of two-thirds of the property abutting on the street in question. No property owner might build beyond the line so established. Of this the court said (page 143 (33 S.Ct. 77)):

> 'It (the ordinance) leaves no discretion in the committee on streets as to whether the street (building, semble) line shall or shall not be established in a given case. The action of the committee is determined by two-thirds of the property owners. In other words, part of the property owners fronting on the block determine the extent of use that other owners shall make of their lots, and against the restriction they are impotent.'

The function of the property owners there is in no way comparable to that of the 'ten or more reputable freeholders' in the Cedar Rust Act. They do not determine the action of the state entomologist. They merely request him to conduct an investigation. In him is vested the discretion to decide, after investigation, whether or not conditions are such that the other provisions of the statute shall be brought into action; and his determination is subject to judicial review. The property of plaintiffs in error is not subjected to the possibly arbitrary and irresponsible action of a group of private citizens.

The objection of plaintiffs in error to the vagueness of the statute is without weight. The state court has held it to be applicable and that is enough when, by the statute, no penalty can be incurred or disadvantage suffered in advance of the judicial ascertainment of its applicability. Compare *Connally v. General Construction Co.*, 269 U.S. 385, 46 S.Ct. 126, 70 L.Ed. 322.

AFFIRMED.

Chapter 34

THE FIFTH AMENDMENT TAKING CLAUSE

As a written legal principle the Taking Clause is nearly 800 years old. Chapter 28 of the Magna Carta contains a similar limitation on the unfettered application of sovereignty, perhaps in reaction to King John's abuse of the public trust doctrine to take for himself all the best hunting grounds. Chapter 28 says, directly enough, "... no constable or other bailiff of ours shall take anyone's corn or other chattels unless he pays on the spot in cash for them or can delay payment by arrangement with the seller." Two other chapters also require the "agreement" of the property owner before the crown could take property: Chapter 30 promised that "... (n)o sheriff, or bailiff of ours, or anyone else shall take the horses or carts of any free man for transport work save with the agreement of that free man," and Chapter 31 promises "... (n)either we nor our bailiffs will take, for castles or other works of ours, timber which is not ours, except with the agreement of him whose timber it is." Obviously the "agreement" contemplated in Chapters 30 and 31 would be forthcoming upon the payment of compensation.

Chapters 28, 30, and 31 of the Magna Carta did not forbid the crown from ever taking property—the ancient concept of the public trust was preserved—they only require the payment of money or the consent of the owner. Similarly it is important to remember that the Taking Clause does not forbid the government from taking property for public use; it, too, only requires that just compensation be paid.

The Taking Clause applies to the states as well as the federal government by operation of the Due Process Clause in the Fourteenth Amendment. *Palazzolo v. Rhode Island*, 533 U.S. 606, 121 S.Ct. 2448, 150 L.Ed.2d 592 (2001). Further, many state constitutions contain provisions similar to the Taking Clause thus those states' interpretations of their constitutions may also be instructive.

The character of the governmental action inquiry distinguishes actual physical invasions from regulations on uses, and weighs the private burden against the public benefit or prevention of nuisances as previously discussed. Where there is a physical invasion, the diminution in value or interference with investment-backed expectations are irrelevant no matter how minor is the invasion nor how great the public benefit obtained thereby.

LORETTO v. TELEPROMPTER MANHATTAN CATV CORP.

102 S.Ct. 3164, 458 U.S. 419, 73 L.Ed.2d 868 (1982)

This case presents the question whether a minor but permanent physical occupation of an owner's property authorized by government constitutes a "taking" of property for which just compensation is due under the Fifth and Fourteenth Amendments of the Constitution. New York law provides that a landlord must permit a cable television company to install its cable facilities upon his property. N.Y.Exec.Law §828(1) (McKinney Supp. 1981-1982). In this case, the cable installation occupied portions of appellant's roof and the side of her building. The New York Court of Appeals ruled that this appropriation does not amount to a taking. 53 N.Y.2d 124, 440 N.Y.S.2d 843, 423 N.E.2d 320 (1981). Because we conclude that such a physical occupation of property is a taking, we reverse.

I

Appellant Jean Loretto purchased a five-story apartment building located at 303 West 105th Street, New York City, in 1971. The previous owner had granted appellees Teleprompter Corp. and Teleprompter Manhattan CATV (collectively Teleprompter) [footnote omitted] permission to install a cable on the building and the exclusive privilege of furnishing cable television (CATV) services to the tenants. The New York Court of Appeals described the installation as follows:

> "On June 1, 1970 TelePrompter installed a cable slightly less than one-half inch in diameter and of approximately 30 feet in length along the length of the building about 18 inches above the roof top, and directional taps, approximately 4 inches by 4 inches by 4 inches, on the front and rear of the roof. By June 8, 1970 the cable had been extended another 4 to 6 feet and cable had been run from the directional taps to the adjoining building at 305 West 105th Street." *Id.*, at 135, 440 N.Y.S.2d, at 847, 423 N.E.2d, at 324.

Teleprompter also installed two large silver boxes along the roof cables. The cables are attached by screws or nails penetrating the masonry at approximately two-foot intervals, and other equipment is installed by bolts.

Initially, Teleprompter's roof cables did not service appellant's building. They were part of what could be described as a cable "highway" circumnavigating the city block, with service cables periodically dropped over the front or back of a building in which a tenant desired service. Crucial to such a network is the use of so-called "crossovers"—cable lines extending from one building to another in order to reach a new group of tenants. [Footnote omitted.] Two years after appellant purchased the building, Teleprompter connected a "noncrossover" line— *i.e.*, one that provided CATV service to appellant's own tenants—by dropping a line to the first floor down the front of appellant's building.

Prior to 1973, Teleprompter routinely obtained authorization for its installations from property owners along the cable's route, compensating the owners at the standard rate of five percent of the gross revenues that Teleprompter realized from the particular property. To facilitate tenant access to CATV, the State of New York enacted §828 of the Executive Law, effective January 1, 1973. Section 828 provides that a landlord may not "interfere with the installation of cable television facilities upon his property or premises," and may not demand payment from any tenant for permitting CATV, or demand payment from any CATV company "in excess of any amount which the [State Commission on Cable Television] shall, by regulation, determine to be reasonable." [Footnote omitted.] The landlord may, however, require the CATV company or the tenant to bear the cost of installation and to indemnify for any damage caused by the installation. Pursuant to §828(1)(b), the State Commission has ruled that a one-time $1 payment is the normal fee to which a landlord is entitled. *In the Matter of Implementation of Section 828 of the Executive Law*, No. 90004, Statement of General Policy (New York State Commission on Cable Television, Jan. 15, 1976) (Statement of General Policy), App. 51-52; Clarification of General Policy (Aug. 27, 1976), App. 68-69. The Commission ruled that this nominal fee, which the Commission concluded was equivalent to what the landlord would receive if the property were condemned pursuant to New York's Transportation Corporations Law, satisfied constitutional requirements "in the absence of a special showing of greater damages attributable to the taking." Statement of General Policy, App. 52.

Appellant did not discover the existence of the cable until after she had purchased the building. She brought a class action against Teleprompter in 1976 on behalf of all owners of real property in the State on which Teleprompter has placed CATV components, alleging that Teleprompter's installation was a trespass and, insofar as it relied on §828, a taking without just compensation. She requested damages and injunctive relief. [Footnote omitted.] Appellee City of New York, which has granted Teleprompter an exclusive franchise to provide CATV within certain areas of Manhattan, intervened. The Supreme Court, Special Term, granted summary judgment to Teleprompter and the city, upholding the constitutionality of §828 in both crossover and non-crossover situations. 98 Misc.2d 944, 415 N.Y.S.2d 180 (1979). The Appellate Division affirmed without opinion. 73 A.D.2d 849, 422 N.Y.S.2d 550 (1979)....

The Court of Appeals determined that §828 serves the legitimate public purpose of "rapid development of and maximum penetration by a means of communication which has important educational and community aspects," 53 N.Y.2d, at 143-144, 440 N.Y.S.2d, at 852, 423 N.E.2d, at 329, and thus is within the State's police power. We have no reason to question that determination. It is a separate question, however, whether an otherwise valid regulation so frustrates property rights that compensation must be paid. *See Penn Central Transportation Co. v. New York City*, 438 U.S. 104, 127-128, 98 S.Ct. 2646, 2660-2661, 57 L.Ed.2d 631 (1978); *Delaware, L. & W. R. Co. v. Morristown*, 276 U.S. 182, 193, 48 S.Ct. 276, 278, 72 L.Ed. 523 (1928). We conclude that a permanent physical occupation authorized by government is a taking without regard to the public interests that it may serve. Our constitutional history confirms the rule, recent cases do not question it, and the purposes of the Takings Clause compel its retention.

A

In *Penn Central Transportation Co. v. New York City, supra*, the Court surveyed some of the general principles governing the Takings Clause. The Court noted that no "set formula" existed to determine, in all cases, whether compensation is constitutionally due for a government restriction of property. Ordinarily, the Court must engage in "essentially ad hoc, factual inquiries." *Id.*, at 124, 98 S.Ct., at 2659. But the inquiry is not standardless. The economic impact of the regulation, especially the degree of interference with investment-backed expectations, is of particular significance. "So, too, is the character of the governmental action. A 'taking' may more readily be found when the interference with property can be characterized as a physical invasion by government, than when interference arises from some public program adjusting the benefits and burdens of economic life to promote the common good." *Ibid.* (Citation omitted.)

As *Penn Central* affirms, the Court has often upheld substantial regulation of an owner's use of his own property where deemed necessary to promote the public interest. At the same time, we have long considered a physical intrusion by government to be a property restriction of an unusually serious character for purposes of the Takings Clause. Our cases further establish that when the physical intrusion reaches the extreme form of a permanent physical occupation, a taking has occurred. In such a case, "the character of the government action" not only is an important factor in resolving whether the action works a taking but also is determinative.

When faced with a constitutional challenge to a permanent physical occupation of real property, this Court has invariably found a taking. [Footnote omitted.] As early as 1872, in *Pumpelly v. Green Bay Co.*, 13 Wall. (80 U.S.) 166, 20 L.Ed. 557, this Court held that the defendant's construction, pursuant to state authority, of a dam which permanently flooded plaintiff's property constituted a taking. A unanimous Court stated, without qualification, that "where real estate is actually invaded by superinduced additions of water, earth, sand, or other material, or by having any artificial structure placed on it, so as to effectually destroy or impair its usefulness, it is a taking, within the meaning of the Constitution." *Id.*, 13 Wall. (80 U.S.) at 181. Seven years later, the Court reemphasized the importance of a physical occupation by distinguishing a regulation that merely restricted the use of private property. In *Northern Transportation Co. v. Chicago*, 99 U.S. 635, 25 L.Ed. 336 (1879), the Court held that the city's construction of a temporary dam in a river to permit construction of a tunnel was not a taking, even though the plaintiffs were thereby denied access to their premises, because the obstruction only impaired the use of plaintiffs' property. The Court distinguished earlier cases in which permanent flooding of private property was regarded as a taking, *e.g., Pumpelly, supra*, as involving "a physical invasion of the real estate of the private owner, and a practical ouster of his possession." In this case, by contrast, "[n]o entry was made upon the plaintiffs' lot." 99 U.S., at 642.

Since these early cases, this Court has consistently distinguished between flooding cases involving a permanent physical occupation, on the one hand, and cases involving a more temporary invasion, or government action outside the owner's property that causes consequential damages within, on the other. A taking has always been found only in the former situation. *See United States v. Lynah*, 188 U.S. 445, 468-470, 23 S.Ct. 349, 356-357, 47 L.Ed. 539 (1903); *Bedford v. United States*, 192 U.S. 217, 225, 24 S.Ct. 238, 240, 48 L.Ed. 414 (1904); *United States v. Cress*, 243 U.S. 316, 327-328, 37 S.Ct. 380, 384-385, 61 L.Ed. 746 (1917); *Sanguinetti v. United States*, 264 U.S. 146, 149, 44 S.Ct. 264, 265, 68 L.Ed. 608 (1924) (to be a taking, flooding must "constitute an actual, permanent invasion of the land, amounting to an appropriation of, and not merely an injury to, the property"); *United States v. Kansas City Life Ins. Co.*, 339 U.S. 799, 809-810, 70 S.Ct. 885, 890-891, 94 L.Ed. 1277 (1950).

In *St. Louis v. Western Union Telegraph Co.*, 148 U.S. 92, 13 S.Ct. 485, 37 L.Ed. 380 (1893), the Court applied the principles enunciated in *Pumpelly* to a situation closely analogous to the one presented today. In that case, the Court held that the city of St. Louis could exact reasonable compensation for a telegraph company's placement of telegraph poles on the city's public streets. The Court reasoned:

> "The use which the [company] makes of the streets is an exclusive and permanent one, and not one temporary, shifting and in common with the general public. The ordinary traveler, whether on foot or in a vehicle, passes to and fro along the streets, and his use and occupation thereof are temporary and shifting. The space he occupies one moment he abandons the next to be occupied by any other traveler.... *But the use made by the telegraph company is, in respect to so much of the space as it occupies with its poles, permanent and exclusive.* It as effectually and permanently dispossesses the general public as if it had destroyed that amount of ground. Whatever benefit the public may receive in the way of transportation of messages, that space is, so far as respects its actual use for purposes of highway and personal travel, wholly lost to the public....
>
> "... It matters not for what that exclusive appropriation is taken, whether for steam railroads or street railroads, telegraphs or telephones, the state may if it chooses exact from the party or corporation given such exclusive use pecuniary compensation to the general public for being deprived of the common use of the portion thus appropriated." *Id.*, at 98-99, 101-102, 13 S.Ct., at 488-489 (emphasis added). [Footnote omitted.]

Similarly, in *Western Union Telegraph Co. v. Pennsylvania R. Co.*, 195 U.S. 540, 25 S.Ct. 133, 49 L.Ed. 312 (1904), a telegraph company constructed and operated telegraph lines over a railroad's right of way. In holding that federal law did not grant the company the right of eminent domain or the right to operate the lines absent the railroad's consent, the Court assumed that the invasion of the telephone lines would be a compensable taking. *Id.*, at 570, 25 S.Ct., at 141 (the right-of-way "cannot be appropriated in whole or in part except upon the payment of compensation"). Later cases, relying on the character of a physical occupation, clearly establish that permanent occupations of land by such installations as telegraph and telephone lines, rails, and underground pipes or wires are takings even if they occupy only relatively insubstantial amounts of space and do not seriously interfere with the landowner's use of the rest of his land. *See, e.g., Lovett v. West Va. Central Gas Co.*, 65 W.Va. 739, 65 S.E. 196 (1909); *Southwestern Bell Telephone Co. v. Webb*, 393 S.W.2d 117, 121 (Mo.App.1965). *Cf. Portsmouth Harbor Land & Hotel Co. v. United States*, 260 U.S. 327, 43 S.Ct. 135, 67 L.Ed. 287 (1922). *See* generally 2 J. Sackman, Nichols' Law of Eminent Domain §6.21 (rev. 3d ed. 1980). [Footnote omitted.]

More recent cases confirm the distinction between a permanent physical occupation, a physical invasion short of an occupation, and a regulation that merely restricts the use of property. In *United States v. Causby*, 328 U.S. 256, 66 S.Ct. 1062, 90 L.Ed. 1206 (1946), the Court ruled that frequent flights immediately above a landowner's property constituted a taking, comparing such overflights to the quintessential form of a taking:

> "If, by reason of the frequency and altitude of the flights, respondents could not use this land for any purpose, their loss would be complete. It would be as complete as if the United States had entered upon the surface of the land and taken exclusive possession of it." *Id.*, at 261, 66 S.Ct., at 1065. [Footnote omitted.]

As the Court further explained,

> "We would not doubt that, if the United States erected an elevated railway over respondents' land at the precise altitude where its planes now fly, there would be a partial taking, even though none of the supports of the structure rested on the land. The reason is that there would be an intrusion so immediate and direct as to subtract from the owner's full enjoyment of the property and to limit his exploitation of it." *Id.*, at 264-265, 66 S.Ct., at 1067.

The Court concluded that the damages to the respondents "were not merely consequential. They were the product of a direct invasion of respondents' domain." *Id.*, at 265-266, 66 S.Ct., at 1067-1068. *See* also *Griggs v. Allegheny County*, 369 U.S. 84, 82 S.Ct. 531, 7 L.Ed.2d 585 (1962).

Two wartime takings cases are also instructive. In *United States v. Pewee Coal Co.*, 341 U.S. 114, 71 S.Ct. 670, 95 L.Ed. 809 (1951), the Court unanimously held that the Government's seizure and direction of operation of a coal mine to prevent a national strike of coal miners constituted a taking, though members of the Court differed over which losses suffered during the period of Government control were compensable. The plurality had little difficulty concluding that because there had been an "actual taking of possession and control," the taking was as clear as if the Government held full title and ownership. *Id.*, at 116, 71 S.Ct., at 671 (plurality opinion of Black, J., with whom Frankfurter, Douglas, and Jackson, JJ., joined; no other Justice challenged this portion of the opinion). In *United States v. Central Eureka Mining Co.*, 357 U.S. 155, 78 S.Ct. 1097, 2 L.Ed.2d 1228 (1958), by contrast, the Court found no taking where the Government had issued a wartime order requiring nonessential gold mines to cease operations for the purpose of conserving equipment and manpower for use in mines more essential to the war effort. Over dissenting Justice Harlan's complaint that "as a practical matter the Order led to consequences no different from those that would have followed the temporary acquisition of physical possession of these mines by the United States," *id.*, at 181, 78 S.Ct., at 1110; the Court reasoned that "the Government did not occupy, use, or in any manner take physical possession of the gold mines or of the equipment connected with them." *Id.*, at 165-166, 78 S.Ct., at 1102-1103. The Court concluded that the temporary though severe restriction on *use* of the mines was justified by the exigency of war. [Footnote omitted.] *Cf. YMCA v. United States*, 395 U.S. 85, 92, 89 S.Ct. 1511, 1515, 23 L.Ed.2d 117 (1969) ("Ordinarily, of course, government occupation of private property deprives the private owner of his use of the property, and it is this deprivation for which the Constitution requires compensation").

Although this Court's most recent cases have not addressed the precise issue before us, they have emphasized that physical *invasion* cases are special and have not repudiated the rule that any permanent physical *occupation* is a taking. The cases state or imply that a physical invasion is subject to a balancing process, but they do not suggest that a permanent physical occupation would ever be exempt from the Takings Clause.

Penn Central Transportation Co. v. New York City, as noted above, contains one of the most complete discussions of the Takings Clause. The Court explained that resolving whether public action works a taking is ordinarily an ad hoc inquiry in which several factors are particularly significant—the economic impact of the regulation, the extent to which it interferes with investment-backed expectations, and the character of the governmental action. 438 U.S., at 124, 98 S.Ct., at 2659. The opinion does not repudiate the rule that a permanent physical occupation is a government action of such a unique character that it is a taking without regard to other factors that a court might ordinarily examine. [Footnote omitted.]

In *Kaiser Aetna v. United States*, 444 U.S. 164, 100 S.Ct. 383, 62 L.Ed.2d 332 (1979), the Court held that the Government's imposition of a navigational servitude requiring public access to a pond was a taking where the landowner had reasonably relied on Government consent in connecting the pond to navigable water. The Court emphasized that the servitude took the landowner's right to exclude, "one of the most essential sticks in the bundle of rights that are commonly characterized as property." *Id.*, at 176, 100 S.Ct., at 391. The Court explained:

> "This is not a case in which the Government is exercising its regulatory power in a manner that will cause an insubstantial devaluation of petitioner's private property; rather, the imposition of the navigational servitude in this context will result in an *actual physical invasion* of the privately owned marina.... And even if the Government physically invades only an easement in property, it must nonetheless pay compensation." *See United States v. Causby*, 328 U.S. 256, 265 [66 S.Ct. 1062, 1067, 90 L.Ed. 1206] (1946); *Portsmouth Co. v. United States*, 260 U.S. 327 [43 S.Ct. 135, 67 L.Ed. 287] (1922)." *Id.*, at 180, 100 S.Ct., at 393 (emphasis added).

Although the easement of passage, not being a permanent occupation of land, was not considered a taking *per se, Kaiser Aetna* reemphasizes that a physical invasion is a government intrusion of an unusually serious character. [Footnote omitted.]

Another recent case underscores the constitutional distinction between a permanent occupation and a temporary physical invasion. In *PruneYard Shopping Center v. Robins*, 447 U.S. 74, 100 S.Ct. 2035, 64 L.Ed.2d 741 (1980), the Court upheld a state constitutional requirement that shopping center owners permit individuals to exercise free speech and petition rights on their property, to which they had already invited the general public. The Court emphasized that the

State Constitution does not prevent the owner from restricting expressive activities by imposing reasonable time, place, and manner restrictions to minimize interference with the owner's commercial functions. Since the invasion was temporary and limited in nature, and since the owner had not exhibited an interest in excluding all persons from his property, "the fact that [the solicitors] may have 'physically invaded' [the owners'] property cannot be viewed as determinative." *Id.*, at 84, 100 S.Ct., at 338. [Footnote omitted.]

In short, when the "character of the governmental action," *Penn Central*, 438 U.S., at 124, 98 S.Ct., at 2659, is a permanent physical occupation of property, our cases uniformly have found a taking to the extent of the occupation, without regard to whether the action achieves an important public benefit or has only minimal economic impact on the owner.

B

The historical rule that a permanent physical occupation of another's property is a taking has more than tradition to commend it. Such an appropriation is perhaps the most serious form of invasion of an owner's property interests. To borrow a metaphor, *cf. Andrus v. Allard*, 444 U.S. 51, 65-66, 100 S.Ct. 318, 326-327, 62 L.Ed.2d 210 (1979), the government does not simply take a single "strand" from the "bundle" of property rights: it chops through the bundle, taking a slice of every strand.

Property rights in a physical thing have been described as the rights "to possess, use and dispose of it." *United States v. General Motors Corp.*, 323 U.S. 373, 378, 65 S.Ct. 357, 359, 89 L.Ed. 311 (1945). To the extent that the government permanently occupies physical property, it effectively destroys *each* of these rights. First, the owner has no right to possess the occupied space himself, and also has no power to exclude the occupier from possession and use of the space. The power to exclude has traditionally been considered one of the most treasured strands in an owner's bundle of property rights. [Footnote omitted.] *See Kaiser Aetna*, 444 U.S., at 179-180, 100 S.Ct., at 392-393; *see* also Restatement of Property §7 (1936). Second, the permanent physical occupation of property forever denies the owner any power to control the use of the property; he not only cannot exclude others, but can make no nonpossessory use of the property. Although deprivation of the right to use and obtain a profit from property is not, in every case, independently sufficient to establish a taking, *see Andrus v. Allard, supra*, at 66, 100 S.Ct., at 327, it is clearly relevant. Finally, even though the owner may retain the bare legal right to dispose of the occupied space by transfer or sale, the permanent occupation of that space by a stranger will ordinarily empty the right of any value, since the purchaser will also be unable to make any use of the property.

Moreover, an owner suffers a special kind of injury when a *stranger* directly invades and occupies the owner's property. As Part II-A, *supra*, indicates, property law has long protected an owner's expectation that he will be relatively undisturbed at least in the possession of his property. To require, as well, that the owner permit another to exercise complete dominion literally adds insult to injury. *See* Michelman, *Property, Utility, and Fairness: Comments on the Ethical Foundations of "Just Compensation" Law*, 80 Harv.L.Rev. 1165, 1228, and n.110 (1967). Furthermore, such an occupation is qualitatively more severe than a regulation of the *use* of property, even a regulation that imposes affirmative duties on the owner, since the owner may have no control over the timing, extent, or nature of the invasion. *See* n.19, *infra*.

The traditional rule also avoids otherwise difficult line-drawing problems. Few would disagree that if the State required landlords to permit third parties to install swimming pools on the landlords' rooftops for the convenience of the tenants, the requirement would be a taking. If the cable installation here occupied as much space, again, few would disagree that the occupation would be a taking. But constitutional protection for the rights of private property cannot be made to depend on the size of the area permanently occupied. [Footnote omitted.] Indeed, it is possible that in the future, additional cable installations that more significantly restrict a landlord's use of the roof of his building will be made. Section 828 requires a landlord to permit such multiple installations. [Footnote omitted.]

Finally, whether a permanent physical occupation has occurred presents relatively few problems of proof. The placement of a fixed structure on land or real property is an obvious fact that will rarely be subject to dispute. Once the fact of occupation is shown, of course, a court should consider the *extent* of the occupation as one relevant factor in determining the compensation due. [Footnote omitted.] For that reason, moreover, there is less need to consider the extent of the occupation in determining whether there is a taking in the first instance.

C

Teleprompter's cable installation on appellant's building constitutes a taking under the traditional test. The installation involved a direct physical attachment of plates, boxes, wires, bolts, and screws to the building, completely occupying space immediately above and upon the roof and along the building's exterior wall. [Footnote omitted.]

In light of our analysis, we find no constitutional difference between a crossover and a noncrossover installation. The portions of the installation necessary for both crossovers and noncrossovers permanently appropriate appellant's property. Accordingly, each type of installation is a taking.

Appellees raise a series of objections to application of the traditional rule here. Teleprompter notes that the law applies only to buildings used as rental property, and draws the conclusion that the law is simply a permissible regulation of the use of real property. We fail to see, however, why a physical occupation of one type of property but not another type is any less a physical occupation. Insofar as Teleprompter means to suggest that this is not a permanent physical invasion, we must differ. So long as the property remains residential and a CATV company wishes to retain the installation, the landlord must permit it. [Footnote omitted.]

Teleprompter also asserts the related argument that the State has effectively granted a tenant the property right to have a CATV installation placed on the roof of his building, as an appurtenance to the tenant's leasehold. The short answer is that §828(1)(a) does not purport to give the *tenant* any enforceable property rights with respect to CATV installation, and the lower courts did not rest their decisions on this ground. [Footnote omitted.] Of course, Teleprompter, not appellant's tenants, actually owns the installation. Moreover, the government does not have unlimited power to redefine property rights. *See Webb's Fabulous Pharmacies, Inc. v. Beckwith*, 449 U.S. 155, 164, 101 S.Ct. 446, 452, 66 L.Ed.2d 358 (1980) ("a State, by *ipse dixit*, may not transform private property into public property without compensation").

Finally, we do not agree with appellees that application of the physical occupation rule will have dire consequences for the government's power to adjust landlord-tenant relationships.

This Court has consistently affirmed that States have broad power to regulate housing conditions in general and the landlord-tenant relationship in particular without paying compensation for all economic injuries that such regulation entails. *See, e.g., Heart of Atlanta Motel, Inc. v. United States*, 379 U.S. 241, 85 S.Ct. 348, 13 L.Ed.2d 258 (1964) (discrimination in places of public accommodation); *Queenside Hills Realty Co. v. Saxl*, 328 U.S. 80, 66 S.Ct. 850, 90 L.Ed. 1096 (1946) (fire regulation); *Bowles v. Willingham*, 321 U.S. 503, 64 S.Ct. 641, 88 L.Ed. 892 (1944) (rent control); *Home Building & Loan Assn. v. Blaisdell*, 290 U.S. 398, 54 S.Ct. 231, 78 L.Ed. 413 (1934) (mortgage moratorium); *Edgar A. Levy Leasing Co. v. Siegel*, 258 U.S. 242, 42 S.Ct. 289, 66 L.Ed. 595 (1922) (emergency housing law); *Block v. Hirsh*, 256 U.S. 135, 41 S.Ct. 458, 65 L.Ed. 865 (1921) (rent control). In none of these cases, however, did the government authorize the permanent occupation of the landlord's property by a third party. Consequently, our holding today in no way alters the analysis governing the State's power to require landlords to comply with building codes and provide utility connections, mailboxes, smoke detectors, fire extinguishers, and the like in the common area of a building. So long as these regulations do not require the landlord to suffer the physical occupation of a portion of his building by a third party, they will be analyzed under the multifactor inquiry generally applicable to nonpossessory governmental activity. *See Penn Central Transportation Co. v. New York City*, 438 U.S. 104, 98 S.Ct. 2646, 57 L.Ed.2d 631 (1978). [Footnote omitted.]

III

Our holding today is very narrow. We affirm the traditional rule that a permanent physical occupation of property is a taking. In such a case, the property owner entertains a historically rooted expectation of compensation, and the character of the invasion is qualitatively more intrusive than perhaps any other category of property regulation. We do not, however, question the equally substantial authority upholding a State's broad power to impose appropriate restrictions upon an owner's *use* of his property.

Furthermore, our conclusion that §828 works a taking of a portion of appellant's property does not presuppose that the fee which many landlords had obtained from Teleprompter prior to the law's enactment is a proper measure of the value of the property taken. The issue of the amount of compensation that is due, on which we express no opinion, is a matter for the state courts to consider on remand. [Footnote omitted.]

The judgment of the New York Court of Appeals is reversed, and the case is remanded for further proceedings not inconsistent with this opinion.

It is so ordered.

Justice BLACKMUN, with whom Justice BRENNAN and Justice WHITE join, dissenting. [Omitted.]

Not so obvious are cases in which takings have been found when there was less than a physical invasion. These cases are called "regulatory takings" or "inverse condemnations." The allegation is that the governmental regulation has gone "too far" and so limited the use to which private property may be put that the government might as well have condemned the property outright and taken all the badges of ownership including fee simple title. These cases are called "inverse condemnations" because the plaintiff is the landowner, whereas, in ordinary condemnation cases, the plaintiff is the government. In the first case to discuss regulatory takings, the Supreme

Court could not even agree on what type of property was being taken nor for what governmental purpose. In this case the dissent is as instructive as the majority opinion.

PENNSYLVANIA COAL CO. v. MAHON

260 U.S. 393, 67 L.Ed. 322, 43 S.Ct. 158 (1922)

This is a bill in equity brought by the defendants in error to prevent the Pennsylvania Coal Company from mining under their property in such way as to remove the supports and cause a subsidence of the surface and of their house. The bill sets out a deed executed by the Coal Company in 1878, under which the plaintiffs claim. The deed conveys the surface but in express terms reserves the right to remove all the coal under the same and the grantee takes the premises with the risk and waives all claim for damages that may arise from mining out the coal. But the plaintiffs say that whatever may have been the Coal Company's rights, they were taken away by an Act of Pennsylvania, approved May 27, 1921 (P. L. 1198), commonly known there as the Kohler Act. The Court of Common Pleas found that if not restrained the defendant would cause the damage to prevent which the bill was brought but denied an injunction, holding that the statute if applied to this case would be unconstitutional. On appeal the Supreme Court of the State agreed that the defendant had contract and property rights protected by the Constitution of the United States, but held that the statute was a legitimate exercise of the police power and directed a decree for the plaintiffs, A writ of error was granted bringing the case to this Court.

The statute forbids the mining of anthracite coal in such way as to cause the subsidence of, among other things, any structure used as a human habitation, with certain exceptions, including among them land where the surface is owned by the owner of the underlying coal and is distant more than one hundred and fifty feet from any improved property belonging to any other person. As applied to this case the statute is admitted to destroy previously existing rights of property and contract. The question is whether the police power can be stretched so far.

Government hardly could go on if to some extent values incident to property could not be diminished without paying for every such change in the general law. As long recognized some values are enjoyed under an implied limitation and must yield to the police power. But obviously the implied limitation must have its limits or the contract and due process clauses are gone. One fact for consideration in determining such limits is the extent of the diminution. When it reaches a certain magnitude, in most if not in all cases there must be an exercise of eminent domain and compensation to sustain the act. So the question depends upon the particular facts. The greatest weight is given to the judgment of the legislature but it always is open to interested parties to contend that the legislature has gone beyond its constitutional power.

This is the case of a single private house. No doubt there is a public interest even in this, as there is in every purchase and sale and in all that happens within the commonwealth. Some existing rights may be modified even in such a case. *Rideout v. Knox,* 2 L.R.A. 81, 12 Am.St. Rep. 560. But usually in ordinary private affairs the public interest does not warrant much of this kind of interference. A source of damage to such a house is not a public nuisance even if similar damage is inflicted on others in different places. The damage is not common or public. *Wesson v. Washburn Iron Co.,* 13 Allen (Mass.) 96, 103, 90 Am.Dec. 181. The extent of the public interest is shown by the statute to be limited, since the statute ordinarily does not apply to land when the surface is owned by the owner of the coal. Furthermore, it is not justified as a protection of personal safety. That could be provided for by notice. Indeed the very foundation of this bill is that the defendant gave timely notice of its intent to mine under the house. On the other hand the extent of the taking is great. It purports to abolish what is recognized in Pennsylvania as an estate in land—a very valuable estate—and what is declared by the Court below to be a contract hitherto binding the plaintiffs. If we were called upon to deal with the plaintiffs' position alone we should think it clear that the statute does not disclose a public interest sufficient to warrant so extensive a destruction of the defendant's constitutionally protected rights.

But the case has been treated as one in which the general validity of the act should be discussed. The Attorney General of the State, the City of Scranton and the representatives of other extensive interests were allowed to take part in the argument below and have submitted their contentions here. It seems, therefore, to be our duty to go farther in the statement of our opinion, in order that it may be known at once, and that further suits should not be brought in vain.

It is our opinion that the act cannot be sustained as an exercise of the police power, so far as it affects the mining of coal under streets or cities in places where the right to mine such coal has been reserved. As said in a Pennsylvania case, 'For practical purposes, the right to coal consists in the right to mine it. *Commonwealth v. Clearview Coal Co.,* 256 Pa. 328, 331, 100 Atl. 820, L.R.A. 1917E, 672. What makes the right to mine coal valuable is that it can be exercised with profit. To make it commercially impracticable to mine certain coal has very nearly the same effect for constitutional purposes as appropriating or destroying it. This we think that we are warranted in assuming that the statute does.

It is true that in *Plymouth Coal Co. v. Pennsylvania*, 232 U.S. 531, 34 Sup.Ct. 359, 58 L.Ed. 713, it was held competent for the legislature to require a pillar of coal to the left along the line of adjoining property, that with the pillar on the other side of the line would be a barrier sufficient for the safety of the employees of either mine in case the other should be abandoned and allowed to fill with water. But that was a requirement for the safety of employees invited into the mine, and secured an average reciprocity of advantage that has been recognized as a justification of various laws.

The rights of the public in a street purchased or laid out by eminent domain are those that it has paid for. If in any case its representatives have been so short sighted as to acquire only surface rights without the right of support we see no more authority for supplying the latter without compensation than there was for taking the right of way in the first place and refusing to pay for it because the public wanted it very much. The protection of private property in the Fifth Amendment presupposes that it is wanted for public use, but provides that it shall not be taken for such use without compensation. A similar assumption is made in the decisions upon the Fourteenth Amendment. *Hairston v. Danville & Western Ry. Co.*, 208 U.S. 598, 605, 28 Sup.Ct. 331, 52 L.Ed. 637, 13 Ann.Cas. 1008. When this seemingly absolute protection is found to be qualified by the police power, the natural tendency of human nature is to extend the qualification more and more until at last private property disappears. But that cannot be accomplished in this way under the Constitution of the United States.

The general rule at least is that while property may be regulated to a certain extent, if regulation goes too far it will be recognized as a taking. It may be doubted how far exceptional cases, like the blowing up of a house to stop a conflagration, go—and if they go beyond the general rule, whether they do not stand as much upon tradition as upon principle. *Bowdith v. Boston*, 101 U.S. 16, 25 L.Ed. 980. In general it is not plain that a man's misfortunes or necessities will justify his shifting the damages to his neighbor's shoulders. *Spade v. Lynn & Boston Ry. Co.*, 172 Mass. 488, 489, 52 N.\E. 747, 43 L.R.A. 832, 70 Am.St. Rep. 298. We are in danger of forgetting that a strong public desire to improve the public condition is not enough to warrant achieving the desire by a shorter cut than the constitutional way of paying for the change. As we already have said this is a question of degree—and therefore cannot be disposed of by general propositions. But we regard this as going beyond any of the cases decided by this Court. The late decisions upon laws dealing with the congestion of Washington and New York, caused by the war, dealt with laws intended to meet a temporary emergency and providing for compensation determined to be reasonable by an impartial board. They were to the verge of the law but fell far short of the present act. *Block & Hirsh*, 256 U.S. 135, 41 Sup.Ct. 458, 65 L.Ed. 865, 16 A.L.R. 165; *Marcus Brown Holding Co. v. Feldman*, 256 U.S. 170, 41 Sup.Ct. 465, 65 L.Ed. 877; *Levy Leasing Co. v. Siegel*, 258 U.S. 242, 42 Sup.Ct. 289, 66 L.Ed. 595, March 20, 1922.

We assume, of course, that the statute was passed upon the conviction that an exigency existed that would warrant it, and we assume that an exigency exists that would warrant the exercise of eminent domain. But the question at bottom is upon whom the loss of the changes desired should fall. So far as private persons or communities have seen fit to take the risk of acquiring only surface rights, we cannot see that the fact that their risk has become a danger warrants the giving to them greater rights than they bought.

Mr. Justice BRANDEIS dissenting.

The Kohler Act prohibits, under certain conditions, the mining of anthracite coal within the limits of a city in such a manner or to such an extent 'as to cause the ... subsidence of ... any dwelling or other structure used as a human habitation, or any factory, store, or other industrial or mercantile establishment in which human labor is employed.' Act Pa. May 27, 1921, §1 (P.L. 1198). Coal in place is land, and the right of the owner to use his land is not absolute. He may not so use it as to create a public nuisance, and uses, once harmless, may, owing to changed conditions, seriously threaten the public welfare. Whenever they do, the Legislature has power to prohibit such uses without paying compensation; and the power to prohibit extends alike to the manner, the character and the purpose of the use. Are we justified in declaring that the Legislature of Pennsylvania has, in restricting the right to mine anthracite, exercised this power so arbitrarily as to violate the Fourteenth Amendment?

Every restriction upon the use of property imposed in the exercise of the police power deprives the owner of some right theretofore enjoyed, and is, in that sense, an abridgment by the state of rights in property without making compensation. But restriction imposed to protect the public health, safety or morals from dangers threatened is not a taking. The restriction here in question is merely the prohibition of a noxious use. The property so restricted remains in the possession of its owner. The state does not appropriate it or make any use of it. The state merely prevents the owner from making a use which interferes with paramount rights of the public. Whenever the use prohibited ceases to be noxious—as it may because of further change in local or social conditions—the restriction will have to be removed and the owner will again be free to enjoy his property as heretofore.

The restriction upon the use of this property cannot, of course, be lawfully imposed, unless its purpose is to protect the public. But the purpose of a restriction does not cease to be public, because incidentally some private persons may thereby receive gratuitously valuable special benefits. Thus, owners of low buildings may obtain, through statutory restrictions upon the height of neighboring structures, benefits equivalent to an easement of light and air. *Welch v. Swasey*, 214 U.S. 91, 29 Sup.Ct. 567, 53 L.Ed. 923. Compare *Lindsley v. Natural Carbonic Gas Co.*, 220 U.S. 61, 31 Sup.Ct. 337, 55 L.Ed. 369, Ann.Cas. 1912C, 160; *Walls v. Midland Carbon Co.*, 254 U.S. 300, 41 Sup.Ct. 118, 65 L.Ed. 276. Furthermore, a restriction, though imposed for a public purpose, will not be lawful, unless the restriction is an appropriate means to the public end. But to keep coal in place is surely an appropriate means of preventing subsidence of the surface; and ordinarily it is the only available means. Restriction upon use does not become inappropriate as a means, merely because it deprives the owner of the only use to which the property can then be profitably put. The liquor and the oleomargine cases settled that. *Mugler v. Kansas*, 123 U.S. 623, 668, 669, 8 Sup.Ct. 273, 31 L.Ed. 205; *Powell v. Pennsylvania*, 127 U.S. 678, 682, 8 Sup.Ct. 992, 1257, 32 L.Ed. 253. *See* also *Hadacheck v. Los Angeles*, 239 U.S. 394, 36 Sup.Ct. 143, 60 L.Ed. 348, Ann.Cas. 1917B, 927; *Pierce Oil Corporation v. City of Hope*, 248 U.S. 498, 39 Sup.Ct. 172, 63 L.Ed. 381. Nor is a restriction imposed through exercise of the police power inappropriate as a means, merely because the same end might be effected through exercise of the power of eminent domain, or otherwise at public expense. Every restriction upon the height of buildings might be secured through acquiring by eminent domain the right of each owner to build above the limiting height; but it is settled that the state need not resort to that power. Compare *Laurel Hill Cemetary v. San Francisco*, 216 U.S. 358, 30 Sup.Ct. 301, 54 L.Ed. 515; *Missouri Pacific Railway Co. v. Omaha*, 235 U.S. 121, 35 Sup.Ct. 82, 59 L.Ed. 157. If by mining anthracite coal the owner would necessarily unloose poisonous gases, I suppose no one would doubt the power of the state to prevent the mining, without buying his coal fields. And why may not the state, likewise, without paying compensation, prohibit one from digging so deep or excavating so near the surface, as to expose the community to like dangers? In the latter case, as in the former, carrying on the business would be a public nuisance.

It is said that one fact for consideration in determining whether the limits of the police power have been exceeded is the extent of the resulting diminution in value, and that here the restriction destroys existing rights of property and contract. But values are relative. If we are to consider the value of the coal kept in place by the restriction, we should compare it with the value of all other parts of the land. That is, with the value not of the coal alone, but with the value of the whole property. The rights of an owner as against the public are not increased by dividing the interests in his property into surface and subsoil. The sum of the rights in the parts can not be greater than the rights in the whole. The estate of an owner in land is grandiloquently described as extending *ab orco usque ad coelum*. But I suppose no one would contend that by selling his interest above 100 feet from the surface he could prevent the state from limiting, by the police power, the height of structures in a city. And why should a sale of underground rights bar the state's power? For aught that appears the value of the coal kept in place by the restriction may be negligible as compared with the value of the whole property, or even as compared with that part of it which is represented by the coal remaining in place and which may be extracted despite the statute. Ordinarily a police regulation, general in operation, will not be held void as to a particular property, although proof is offered that owing to conditions peculiar to it the restriction could not reasonably be applied. *See Powell v. Pennsylvania*, 127 U.S. 678, 681, 684, 8 Sup.Ct. 992, 1257, 32 L.Ed. 253; *Murphy v. California*, 225 U.S. 623, 629, 32 Sup.Ct. 697, 56 L. Ed. 1229, 41 L.R.A. (N.S.) 153. But even if the particular facts are to govern, the statute should, in my opinion be upheld in this case. For the defendant has failed to adduce any evidence from which it appears that to restrict its mining operations was an unreasonable exercise of the police power. Compare *Reinman v. Little Rock*, 237 U.S. 171, 177, 180, 35 Sup.Ct. 511, 59 L.Ed. 900; *Pierce Oil Corporation v. City of Hope*, 248 U.S. 498, 500, 39 Sup.Ct. 172, 63

L.Ed. 381. Where the surface and the coal belong to the same person, self-interest would ordinarily prevent mining to such an extent as to cause a subsidence. It was, doubtless, for this reason that the Legislature, estimating the degrees of danger, deemed statutory restriction unnecessary for the public safety under such conditions.

It is said that this is a case of a single dwelling house, that the restriction upon mining abolishes a valuable estate hitherto secured by a contract with the plaintiffs, and that the restriction upon mining cannot be justified as a protection of personal safety, since that could be provided for by notice. The propriety of deferring a good deal to tribunals on the spot has been repeatedly recognized. *Welch v. Swasey*, 214 U.S. 91, 106, 29 Sup.Ct. 567, 53 L.Ed. 923; *Laurel Hill Cemetary v. San Francisco*, 216 U.S. 358, 365, 30 Sup.Ct. 301, 54 L.Ed. 515; *Patsone v. Pennsylvania*, 232 U.S. 138, 144, 34 Sup.Ct. 281, 58 L.Ed. 539. May we say that notice would afford adequate protection of the public safety where the Legislature and the highest court of the state, with greater knowledge of local conditions, have declared, in effect, that it would not? If the public safety is imperiled, surely neither grant, nor contract, can prevail against the exercise of the police power. *Fertilizing Co. v. Hyde Park*, 97 U.S. 659, 24 L.Ed. 1036; *Atlantic Coast Line RR Co. v. North Carolina*, 232 U.S. 548, 34 Sup.Ct. 364, 58 L.Ed. 721; *Union Dry Goods Co. v. Georgia Public Service Corporation*, 248 U.S. 372, 39 Sup.Ct. 117, 63 L.Ed. 309, 9 A.L.R. 1420; *St. Louis Poster Advertising Co. v. St. Louis*, 249 U.S. 269, 39 Sup.Ct. 274, 63 L.Ed. 599. The rule that the state's power to take appropriate measures to guard the safety of all who may be within its jurisdiction may not be bargained away was applied to compel carriers to establish grade crossings at their own expense, despite contracts to the contrary (*Chicago, Burlington & Quincy RR Co. v. Nebraska*, 170 U.S. 57, 18 Sup.Ct. 513, 42 L.Ed. 948); and, likewise, to supersede, by an Employers' Liability Act, the provision of a charter exempting a railroad from liability for death of employees, since the civil liability was deemed a matter of public concern, and not a mere private right. *Texas & New Orleans RR Co. v. Miller*, 221 U. S. 408, 31 Sup. Ct. 534, 55 L. Ed. 789. Compare *Boyd v. Alabama*, 94 U. S. 645, 24 L. Ed. 302; *Stone v. Mississippi*, 101 U. S. 814, 25 L. Ed. 1079; *Butchers' Union Co. v. Crescent City Co.*, 111 U.S. 746, 4 Sup. Ct. 652, 28 L.Ed. 585; *Douglas v. Kentucky*, 168 U.S. 488, 18 Sup.Ct. 199, 42 L.Ed. 553; *Pennsylvania Hospital v. Philadelphia*, 245 U.S. 20, 23, 38 Sup.Ct. 35, 62 L.Ed. 124. Nor can existing contracts between private individuals preclude exercise of the police power. 'One whose rights, such as they are, are subject to state restriction cannot remove them from the power of the state by making a contract about them.' *Hudson Water Co. v. McCarter*, 209 U.S. 349, 357, 28 Sup.Ct. 529, 52 L.Ed. 828, 14 Ann. Cas. 560; *Knoxville Water Co. v. Knoxville*, 189 U.S. 434, 438, 23 Sup.Ct. 531, 47 L.Ed. 887; *Rast v. Van Deman & Lewis Co.*, 240 U.S. 342, 36 Sup.Ct. 370, 60 L.Ed. 679, L.R.A. 1917A, 421, Ann.Cas. 1917B, 455. The fact that this suit is brought by a private person is, of course, immaterial. To protect the community through invoking the aid, as litigant, of interested private citizens is not a novelty in our law. That it may be done in Pennsylvania was decided by its Supreme Court in this case. And it is for a state to say how its public policy shall be enforced.

This case involves only mining which causes subsidence of a dwelling house. But the Kohler Act contains provisions in addition to that quoted above; and as to these, also, an opinion is expressed. These provisions deal with mining under cities to such an extent as to cause subsidence of—

> (a) Any public building or any structure customarily used by the public as a place of resort, assemblage, or amusement, including, but not limited to, churches, schools, hospitals, theaters, hotels, and railroad stations.

(b) Any street, road, bridge, or other public passageway, dedicated to public use or habitually used by the public.

(c) Any track, roadbed, right of way, pipe, conduit, wire, or other facility, used in the service of the public by any municipal corporation or public service company as defined by the Public Service Law, section 1.

A prohibition of mining which causes subsidence of such structures and facilities is obviously enacted for a public purpose; and it seems, likewise, clear that mere notice of intention to mine would not in this connection secure the public safety. Yet it is said that these provisions of the act cannot be sustained as an exercise of the police power where the right to mine such coal has been reserved. The conclusion seems to rest upon the assumption that in order to justify such exercise of the police power there must be 'average reciprocity of advantage' as between the owner of the property restricted and the rest of the community; and that here such reciprocity is absent. Reciprocity of advantage is an important consideration, and may even be an essential, where the state's power is exercised for the purpose of conferring benefits upon the property of a neighborhood, as in drainage projects (*Wurts v. Hoagland*, 114 U.S. 606, 5 Sup.Ct. 1086, 29 L.Ed. 229; *Fallbrook Irrigation District v. Bradley*, 164 U.S. 112, 17 Sup.Ct. 56, 41 L.Ed. 369); or upon adjoining owners, as by party wall provisions (*Jackman v. Rosenbaum Co.*, 260 U.S. 22, 43 Sup.Ct. 9, 67 L.Ed. 107, decided October 23, 1922). But where the police power is exercised, not to confer benefits upon property owners but to protect the public from detriment and danger, there is in my opinion, no room for considering reciprocity of advantage. There was no reciprocal advantage to the owner prohibited from using his oil tanks in 248 U.S. 498, 39 Sup.Ct. 172, 63 L.Ed. 381; his brickyard, in 239 U. S. 394, 36 Sup.Ct. 143, 60 L.Ed. 348, Ann.Cas, 1917B, 927; his livery stable, in 237 U.S. 171, 35 Sup.Ct. 511, 59 L.Ed. 900; his billiard hall, in 225 U.S. 623, 32 Sup.Ct. 697, 56 L.Ed. 1229, 41 L.R.A. (N.S.) 153; his oleomargarine factory, in 127 U. S. 678, 8 Sup. Ct. 992, 1257, 32 L. Ed. 253; his brewery, in 123 U.S. 623, 8 Sup.Ct. 273, 31 L.Ed. 205; unless it be the advantage of living and doing business in a civilized community. That reciprocal advantage is given by the act to the coal operators.

In spite of the disagreement in *Pennsylvania Coal Co. v. Mahon*, under the Taking Clause, "property" means more than fee simple ownership of real estate. "Property" as the term is used in Taking Clause cases means "the group of rights inhering in the citizen's relation to the physical thing, as the right to possess, use, and dispose of it." *See, e.g., Ruckleshaus v. Monsanto Co.*, 467 U.S. 986, 81 L.Ed.2d 815 (1984). In *Ruckelshaus* the property interests alleged to have been taken were trade secrets that the plaintiff was required to disclose to the Environmental Protection Agency in support of an application for a pesticide registration. For a period of time while the application was pending, the Environmental Protection Agency had a duty to keep the information confidential. Instead, it revealed the information. The court found that during the confidentiality-guaranteed period, the government had taken the trade secret. *See also Philip Morris, Inc. v. Reilly*, 267 F.3d 45 (1st Cir. 2001).

"Property" will almost always be an interest in real property, such as fee simple ownership, but it can also include possessory interests such as easements (*United States v. Welch*, 217 U.S. 1256 (1910); *United States v. 8.41 Acres of Land*, 783 F.2d 388 (5th Cir. Tex. 1982), *cert. denied*, 479 U.S. 820, 93 L.Ed.2d 38, 107 S.Ct. 85 (1986)) leaseholds (*Alamo Land & Cattle Co. v. Arizona*, 424 U.S. 295 (1976); *Almota Farmers Elevator & Warehouse Co. v. United States*, 409 U.S. 470, 35 L.Ed.2d 1, 93 S.Ct. 791 (1973); *United States v. Pewee Coal Co.*, 341 U.S. 114, 95 L.Ed.2d 809, 71 S.Ct. 670 (1951); *United States v. Westinghouse Electric & Mfg. Co.*, 339 U.S. 261, 94 L.Ed.2d 816,

70 S.Ct. 644 (1950); *United States v. Petty Motor Co.*, 327 U.S. 372, 90 L.Ed.2d 729, 66 S.Ct. 596 (1946), *reh'g. denied*, 327 U.S. 818, 90 L.Ed. 1040, 66 S.Ct. 813 (1946); *United States v. General Motors*, 323 U.S. 373, 89 L.Ed. 311, 65 S.Ct. 357 (1945); *United States v. Right To Use And Occupy 3.38 Acres Of Land*, 484 F.2d 1140 (4th Cir. 1973); *Sun Oil Co. v. United States*, 572 F.2d 786 (Ct.Cl. 1978)), liens (*Louisville Joint Stock Land Bank v. Radford*, 295 U.S. 555 (1935)), mineral estates (*Keystone Bituminous Coal Association v. De Benedictis*, 480 U.S. 470 (1987); *Pennsylvania Coal Co. v. Mahon*, 260 U.S. 393, 67 L.Ed. 322, 43 S.Ct. 158 (1922)), air space *Griggs v. Allegheny County*, 369 U.S. 84, 7 L.Ed.2d 585, 82 S.Ct. 531, *reh'g. denied*, 369 U.S. 857, 8 L.Ed.2d 16, 82 S.Ct. 931 (1962); *United States v. Causby*, 328 U.S. 256, 90 L.Ed. 1206, 66 S.Ct. 1062 (1946) (which holds that a landowner, in this case a chicken farmer, "owns at least as much of the space above the ground as he can occupy or use in connection with the land," thus when government aircraft flew over the chicken barn, causing the chickens to panic and fly against the inside of the barn killing themselves, the court found that the government had taken the air space (and presumably the chickens as well) by its direct and immediate interference with the use and enjoyment of the land). *See also* W. Blackstone, 2 Commentaries, §18, for the Latin legal maxim *Cujus est solum, ejus est usque ad coelum et ad infernos*, or "To whomsoever the soil belongs, he owns also to the sky and to the depths"), and water rights (*United States v. Gerlach Livestock Co.*, 339 U.S. 725, 94 L.Ed. 1231, 70 S.Ct. 955 (1950); *Ball v. United States*, 1 Cl.Ct. 180 (1982)). In addition to these traditional ownership or possessory interests in land, it is at least logically possible that some aspects of personal property might be taken in a wetland case, such as the interest of a limited partner in a real estate development partnership that was denied a permit by the Corps.

Assuming there is a property right which the law recognizes as protectable, the next step is to focus on the character of the governmental activity to determine whether a regulatory taking has occurred. The first and most obvious is when the government actually invades the land, such as by building new roads, widening streets, erecting utility poles, and the like. The government will institute an action to force the landowner to sell his land for "just compensation." A middle type of case is when the governmental invasion is intermittent or less than continuous. In these cases the issue is the proper measure of damages. The third and last type of governmental activity is when there is no physical invasion but a regulation is applied to limit the uses to which the property may be put. The essential inquiry in these "regulatory taking" cases will be whether it is fair to force a few private individuals to bear a burden alone (by not receiving any compensation for the limitation on the use of their property) or whether it is fair than the burden should be spread over all of society (by requiring the government to pay compensation out of the public fisc).

The complaining landowner cannot stop a regulatory taking because the Taking Clause only prohibits uncompensated takings, not the taking of property for public use. There is no action available for injunction or declaratory relief when plaintiff alleges a taking. Instead, the landowner can only sue the government for compensation.

In making a plaintiff's case, landowners should be aware that "there is no set formula to determine where a regulation ends and taking begins." Concepts of fairness, justice, and judgment rule the day. The Supreme Court has struggled to devise a system of analysis by which regulatory takings could be distinguished from abatements of nuisances (which have always been permissible under the police power of the government), minor intrusions on property ownership rights (without which government could not function), and major intrusions that amount to takings, although not in all instances.

HADACHECK v. SEBASTIAN

239 U.S. 394, 36 S.Ct. 143, 60 L.Ed. 348 (1915)

Habeas corpus prosecuted in the Supreme Court of the State of California for the discharge of plaintiff in error from the custody of defendant in error, chief of police of the city of Los Angeles.

Plaintiff in error, to whom we shall refer as petitioner, was convicted of a misdemeanor for the violation of an ordinance of the city of Los Angeles which makes it unlawful for any person to establish or operate a brickyard or brickkiln, or any establishment, factory, or place for the manufacture or burning of brick within described limits in the city. Sentence was pronounced against him and he was committed to the custody of defendant in error as chief of police of the city of Los Angeles.

Being so in custody he filed a petition in the supreme court of the state for a writ of habeas corpus. The writ was issued. Subsequently defendant in error made a return thereto, supported by affidavits, to which petitioner made sworn reply. The court rendered judgment discharging the writ and remanding petitioner to custody. The chief justice of the court then granted this writ of error.

The petition sets forth the reason for resorting to habeas corpus and that petitioner is the owner of a tract of land within the limits described in the ordinance, upon which tract of land there is a very valuable bed of clay, of great value for the manufacture of brick of a fine quality, worth to him not less than $100,000 per acre, or about $800,000 for the entire tract for brickmaking purposes, and not exceeding $60,000 for residential purposes, or for any purpose other than the manufacture of brick. That he has made excavations of considerable depth and covering a very large area of the property, and that on account thereof the land cannot be utilized for residential purposes or any purpose other than that for which it is now used. That he purchased the land because of such bed of clay and for the purpose of manufacturing brick; that it was, at the time of purchase, outside of the limits of the city, and distant from dwellings and other habitations, and that he did not expect or believe, nor did other owners of property in the vicinity expect or believe, that the territory would be annexed to the city. That he has erected expensive machinery for the manufacture of bricks of fine quality which have been and are being used for building purposes in and about the city.

That if the ordinance be declared valid, he will be compelled to entirely abandon his business and will be deprived of the use of his property.

That the manufacture of brick must necessarily be carried on where suitable clay is found, and the clay cannot be transported to some other location; and, besides, the clay upon his property is particularly fine, and clay of as good quality cannot be found in any other place within the city where the same can be utilized for the manufacture of brick. That within the prohibited district there is one other brickyard besides that of plaintiff in error.

That there is no reason for the prohibition of the business; that its maintenance cannot be and is not in the nature of a nuisance as defined in §3479 of the Civil Code of the state, and cannot be dangerous or detrimental to health or the morals or safety or peace or welfare or convenience of the people of the district or city.

That the business is so conducted as not to be in any way or degree a nuisance; no noises arise therefrom, and no noxious odors, and that by the use of certain means (which are described) provided and the situation of the brickyard an extremely small amount of smoke is emitted from any kiln, and what is emitted is so dissipated that it is not a nuisance nor in any manner detrimental to health or comfort. That during the seven years which the brickyard has been conducted no complaint has been made of it, and no attempt has ever been made to regulate it.

That the city embraces 107.62 square miles in area and 75 percent of it is devoted to residential purposes; that the district described in the ordinance includes only about three square miles, is sparsely settled, and contains large tracts of unsubdivided and unoccupied land; and that the boundaries of the district were determined for the sole and specific purpose of prohibiting and suppressing the business of petitioner and that of the other brickyard.

That there are and were, at the time of the adoption of the ordinance, in other districts of the city thickly built up with residences brickyards maintained more detrimental to the inhabitants of the city. That a petition was filed, signed by several hundred persons, representing such brickyards to be a nuisance, and no ordinance or regulation was passed in regard to such petition, and the brickyards are operated without hindrance or molestation. That other brickyards are permitted to be maintained without prohibition or regulation.

That no ordinance or regulation of any kind has been passed at any time regulating or attempting to regulate brickyards, or inquiry made whether they could be maintained without being a nuisance or detrimental to health.

That the ordinance does not state a public offense, and is in violation of the Constitution of the state and the 14th Amendment to the Constitution of the United States.

That the business of petitioner is a lawful one, none of the materials used in it are combustible, the machinery is of the most approved pattern, and its conduct will not create a nuisance.

There is an allegation that the ordinance, if enforced, fosters and will foster a monopoly, and protects and will protect other persons engaged in the manufacture of brick in the city, and discriminates and will discriminate against petitioner in favor of such other persons, who are his competitors, and will prevent him from entering into competition with them.

The petition, after almost every paragraph, charges a deprivation of property, the taking of property without compensation, and that the ordinance is in consequence invalid.

We have given this outline of the petition, as it presents petitioner's contentions, with the circumstances (which we deem most material) that give color and emphasis to them.

But there are substantial traverses made by the return to the writ, among others, a denial of the charge that the ordinance was arbitrarily directed against the business of petitioner, and it is alleged that there is another district in which brickyards are prohibited.

There was a denial of the allegations that the brickyard was conducted or could be conducted sanitarily, or was not offensive to health. And there were affidavits supporting the denials. In these it was alleged that the fumes, gases, smoke, soot, steam, and dust arising from petitioner's brickmaking plant have from time to time caused sickness and serious discomfort to those living in the vicinity.

There was no specific denial of the value of the property, or that it contained deposits of clay, or that the latter could not be removed and manufactured into brick elsewhere. There was, however, a general denial that the enforcement of the ordinance would "entirely deprive petitioner of his property and the use thereof."

How the supreme court dealt with the allegations, denials, and affidavits we can gather from its opinion. The court said, through Mr. Justice Sloss: "The district to which the prohibition was applied contains about three square miles. The petitioner is the owner of a tract of land, containing eight acres, more or less, within the district described in the ordinance. He acquired his land in 1902, before the territory to which the ordinance was directed had been annexed to the city of Los Angeles. His land contains valuable deposits of clay suitable for the manufacture of brick, and he has, during the entire period of his ownership, used the land for brickmaking, and has erected thereon kilns, machinery, and buildings necessary for such manufacture. The land, as he alleges, is far more valuable for brickmaking than for any other purpose." [165 Cal. 418, L. R. A. 1916B, 1248, 132 Pac. 584.]

The court considered the business one which could be regulated, and that regulation was not precluded by the fact "that the value of investments made in the business prior to any legislative action will be greatly diminished," and that no complaint could be based upon the fact that petitioner had been carrying on the trade in that locality for a long period.

And, considering the allegations of the petition, the denials of the return, and the evidence of the affidavits, the court said that the latter tended to show that the district created has become primarily a residential section, and that the occupants of the neighboring dwellings are seriously incommoded by the operations of petitioner; and that such evidence, "when taken in connection with the presumptions in favor of the propriety of the legislative determination, is certainly sufficient to overcome any contention that the prohibition [of the ordinance] was a mere arbitrary invasion of private right, not supported by any tenable belief that the continuance of the business ... was so detrimental to the interests of others as to require suppression."

The court, on the evidence, rejected the contention that the ordinance was not in good faith enacted as a police measure, and that it was intended to discriminate against petitioner, or that it was actuated by any motive of injuring him as an individual.

The charge of discrimination between localities was not sustained. The court expressed the view that the determination of prohibition was for the legislature, and that the court, without regard to the fact shown in the return that there was another district in which brickmaking was prohibited, could not sustain the claim that the ordinance was not enacted in good faith, but was designed to discriminate against petitioner and the other brickyard within the district. "The facts before us," the court finally said, "would certainly not justify the conclusion that the ordinance here in question was designed, in either its adoption or its enforcement, to be anything but what it purported to be; viz., a legitimate regulation, operating alike upon all who come within its terms."

We think the conclusion of the court is justified by the evidence and makes it unnecessary to review the main cases cited by petitioner in which it is decided that the police power of a state cannot be arbitrarily exercised. The principle is familiar, but in any given case it must plainly appear to apply. It is to be remembered that we are dealing with one of the most essential powers of government,—one that is the least limitable. It may, indeed, seem harsh in its exercise, usually is on some individual, but the imperative necessity for its existence precludes any limitation upon it when not exerted arbitrarily. A vested interest cannot be asserted against it because of conditions once obtaining. *Chicago & A. R. Co. v. Tranbarger*, 238 U. S. 67, 78, 59 L. ed. 1204, 1211, 35 Sup. Ct. Rep. 678. To so hold would preclude development and fix a city forever in its primitive conditions. there must be progress, and if in its march private interests are in the way, they must yield to the good of the community. The logical result of petitioner's contention would seem to be that a city could not be formed or enlarged against the resistance of an occupant of the ground, and that if it grows at all it can only grow as the environment of the occupations that are usually banished to the purlieus.

The police power and to what extent it may be exerted we have recently illustrated in *Reinman v. Little Rock*, 237 U.S. 171, 59 L.Ed. 900, 35 Sup.Ct.Rep. 511. The circumstances of the case were very much like those of the case at bar, and give reply to the contentions of petitioner, especially that which asserts that a necessary and lawful occupation that is not a nuisance per se cannot be made so by legislative declaration. There was a like investment in property, encouraged by the then conditions; a like reduction of value and deprivation of property was asserted against the validity of the ordinance there considered; a like assertion of an arbitrary exercise of the power of prohibition. Against all of these contentions, and causing the rejection of them all, was adduced the police power. There was a prohibition of a business, lawful in itself, there as here. It was a livery stable there; a brickyard here. They differ in particulars, but they are alike in that which cause and justify prohibition in defined localities,—that is, the effect upon the health and comfort of the community.

The ordinance passed upon prohibited the conduct of the business within a certain defined area in Little Rock, Arkansas. This court said of it: granting that the business was not a nuisance per se, it was clearly within the police power of the state to regulate it, "and to that end to declare that in particular circumstances and in particular localities a livery stable shall be deemed a nuisance in fact and in law." And the only limitation upon the power was stated to be that the power could not be exerted arbitrarily or with unjust discrimination. There was a citation of cases. We think the present case is within the ruling thus declared.

There is a distinction between *Reinman v. Little Rock* and the case at bar. There a particular business was prohibited which was not affixed to or dependent upon its locality; it could be conducted elsewhere. Here, it is contended, the latter condition does not exist, and it is alleged that the manufacture of brick must necessarily be carried on where suitable clay is found, and that the clay on petitioner's property cannot be transported to some other locality. This is not urged as a physical impossibility, but only, counsel say, that such transportation and the transportation of the bricks to places where they could be used in construction work would be prohibitive "from a financial standpoint." But upon the evidence the supreme court considered the case, as we understand its opinion, from the standpoint of the offensive effects of the operation of a brickyard, and not from the deprivation of the deposits of clay, and distinguished *Ex parte Kelso*, 147 Cal. 609, 2 L.R.A. (N.S.) 796, 109 Am.St.Rep. 178, 82 Pac. 241, wherein the court declared invalid an ordinance absolutely prohibiting the maintenance or operation of a rock or stone quarry within a certain portion of the city and county of San Francisco. The court there said that the effect of the ordinance was "to absolutely deprive the owners of real property within such limits of a valuable right incident to their ownership, viz., the right to extract therefrom such rock and stone as they may find it to their advantage to dispose of." The court expressed the view that the removal could be regulated, but that "an absolute prohibition of such removal under the circumstances" could not be upheld.

In the present case there is no prohibition of the removal of the brick clay; only a prohibition within the designated locality of its manufacture into bricks. And to this feature of the ordinance our opinion is addressed. Whether other questions would arise if the ordinance were broader, and opinion on such questions, we reserve.

Petitioner invokes the equal protection clause of the Constitution and charges that it is violated in that the ordinance (1) "prohibits him from manufacturing brick upon his property while his competitors are permitted, without regulation of any kind, to manufacture brick upon property situated in all respects similarly to that of plaintiff in error;" and (2) that it "prohibits the conduct of his business while it permits the maintenance within the same district of any other kind of business, no matter how objectionable the same may be, either in its nature or in the manner in which it is conducted."

If we should grant that the first specification shows a violation of classification, that is, a distinction between businesses which was not within the legislative power, petitioner's contention encounters the objection that it depends upon an inquiry of fact which the record does not enable us to determine. It is alleged in the return to the petition that brickmaking is prohibited in one other district, and an ordnance is referred to regulating business in other districts. To this plaintiff in error replied that the ordinance attempts to prohibit the operation of certain businesses having mechanical power, and does not prohibit the maintenance of any business or the operation of any machine that is operated by animal power. In other words, petitioner makes his contention depend upon disputable considerations of classification and upon a comparison of conditions of which there is no means of judicial determination, and upon which, nevertheless, we are expected to reverse legislative action exercised upon matters of which the city has control.

To a certain extent the latter comment may be applied to other contentions; and, besides, there is no allegation or proof of other objectionable businesses being permitted within the district, and a speculation of their establishment or conduct at some future time is too remote.

In his petition and argument something is made of the ordinance as fostering a monopoly and suppressing his competition with other brickmakers. The charge and argument are too illusive. It is part of the charge that the ordinance was directed against him. The charge, we have seen, was rejected by the supreme court, and we find nothing to justify it.

It may be that brickyards in other localities within the city where the same conditions exist are not regulated or prohibited, but it does not follow that they will not be. That petitioner's business was first in time to be prohibited does not make its prohibition unlawful. And it may be, as said by the supreme court of the state, that the conditions justify a distinction. However, the inquiries thus suggested are outside of our province.

There are other and subsidiary contentions which, we think, do not require discussion. They are disposed of by what we have said. It may be that something else than prohibition would have satisfied the conditions. Of this, however, we have no means of determining, and besides, we cannot declare invalid the exertion of a power which the city undoubtedly has because of a charge that it does not exactly accommodate the conditions, or that some other exercise would have been better or less harsh. We must accord good faith to the city in the absence of a clear showing to the contrary and an honest exercise of judgment upon the circumstances which induced its action.

We do not notice the contention that the ordinance is not within the city's charter powers, nor that it is in violation of the state Constitution, such contentions raising only local questions which must be deemed to have been decided adversely to petitioner by the supreme court of the state.

Judgment AFFIRMED.

ANDRUS v. ALLARD

444 U.S. 51100 S.Ct. 318, 62 L.Ed.2d 210 (1979)

The Eagle Protection Act and the Migratory Bird Treaty Act are conservation statutes designed to prevent the destruction of certain species of birds. Challenged in this case is the validity of regulations promulgated by appellant Secretary of the Interior that prohibit commercial transactions in parts of birds legally killed before the birds came under the protection of the statutes. The regulations provide in pertinent part:

50 CFR §21.2(a) (1978):

> "Migratory birds, their parts, nests, or eggs, lawfully acquired prior to the effective date of Federal protection under the Migratory Bird Treaty Act ... may be possessed or transported without a Federal permit, but may not be imported, exported, purchased, sold, bartered, or offered for purchase, sale, trade, or barter...."

50 CFR §22.2(a) (1978):

> "Bald eagles, alive or dead, or their parts, nests, or eggs lawfully acquired prior to June 8, 1940, and golden eagles, alive or dead, or their parts, nests, or eggs lawfully acquired prior to October 24, 1962, may be possessed, or transported without a Federal permit, but may not be imported, exported, purchased, sold, traded, bartered, or offered for purchase, sale, trade or barter...."

Appellees are engaged in the trade of Indian artifacts: several own commercial enterprises, one is employed by such an enterprise, and one is a professional appraiser. A number of the artifacts are partly composed of the feathers of currently protected birds, but these artifacts existed before the statutory protections came into force. After two of the appellees who had sold "pre-existing" artifacts were prosecuted for violations of the Eagle Protection Act and the Migratory Bird Treaty Act, appellees brought this suit for declaratory and injunctive relief in the District Court for the District of Colorado. The complaint alleged that the statutes do not forbid the sale of appellees' artifacts insofar as the constituent birds' parts were obtained prior to the effective dates of the statutes. It further alleged that if the statutes and regulations do apply to such property, they violate the Fifth Amendment.

A three-judge court, convened pursuant to 28 U.S.C. §2282 (1970 ed.), held that because of "grave doubts whether these two acts would be constitutional if they were construed to apply to pre-act bird products," the Acts were to be interpreted as "not applicable to preexisting, legally-obtained bird parts or products therefrom...." App. to Juris. Statement 13a-14a. Accordingly, the court ruled that "the interpretive regulations, 50 C.F.R. §§21.2(a) and 22.2(a), [are] void as unauthorized extensions of the Migratory Bird Treaty Act and the Eagle Protection Act and [are] violative of the [appellees'] Fifth Amendment property rights." *Id.*, at 14a. Judgment was entered declaring "the subject regulations to be invalid and unenforceable as against the [appellees'] property rights in feathers and artifacts owned before the effective date of the subject statute," and enjoining appellants "from any interference with the exercise of such rights, including the rights of sale, barter or exchange." *Id.,* at 16a-17a. We noted probable jurisdiction. 440 U.S. 905, 99 S.Ct. 1210, 59 L.Ed.2d 452 (1979). We reverse.

I

Appellant Secretary of the Interior contends that both the Eagle Protection and Migratory Bird Treaty Acts contemplate regulatory prohibition of commerce in the parts of protected birds, without regard to when those birds were originally taken. Appellees respond that such a prohibition serves no purpose, arguing that statutory protection of wildlife is not furthered by am embargo upon traffic in avian artifacts that existed before the statutory safeguards came into effect.

A

Our point of departure in statutory analysis is the language of the enactment. *See Southeastern Community College v. Davis,* 442 U.S. 397, 405, 99 S.Ct. 2361, 2366, 60 L.Ed.2d 980 (1979). "Though we may not end with the words in construing a disputed statute, one certainly begins there." F. Frankfurter, Some Reflections on the Reading of Statutes 16 (1947).

The terms of the Eagle Protection Act plainly must be read as appellant Secretary argues. The sweepingly framed prohibition in §668(a) makes it unlawful to "take, possess, sell, purchase, barter, offer to sell, purchase or barter, transport, export or import" protected birds. Congress expressly dealt with the problem of pre-existing bird products by qualifying that general prohibition with the proviso that "nothing herein shall be construed to prohibit *possession or transportation*" of bald or golden eagle parts taken prior to the effective date of coverage under the Act. (Emphasis supplied.)

In view of the exhaustive and careful enumeration of forbidden acts in §668(a), the narrow limitation of the proviso to "possession or transportation" compels the conclusion that, with respect to pre-existing artifacts, Congress specifically declined to except any activities other than *possession* and *transportation* from the general statutory ban. To read a further exemption for pre-existing artifacts into the Eagle Protection Act, "we would be forced to ignore the ordinary meaning of plain language." *TVA v. Hill,* 437 U.S. 153, 173, 98 S.Ct. 2279, 2291, 57 L.Ed.2d 117 (1978). Nor can there be any question of oversight or drafting error. Throughout the statute the distinct concepts of possession, transportation, taking, and sale or purchase are treated with precision. The broad proscriptive provisions of the Eagle Protection Act were consistently framed to encompass a full catalog of prohibited acts, always including sale or purchase. *See* §§668(a), 668(b), 668b(b). In contrast, the exemptions created were specifically limited to possession or transportation, §668(a), taking, §668a, or taking, possession, or transportation, *ibid.*

That this precise use of terminology was intentional is clear from the legislative history. An explanatory letter from the Department of Agriculture that was adopted in the Senate Report on the bill defines the reach of the Eagle Protection Act to make it unlawful to

> "take, possess, sell, purchase, transport, or otherwise deal with the bald eagle ... with the proviso to the effect that it will not apply to the *possession* or *transportation* of any such eagle ... taken prior to the effective date of the bill." S.Rep. No. 1589, 76th Cong., 3d Sess., 1 (1940). (Emphasis added.)

Further when Congress amended the Eagle Protection Act in 1962 to cover golden eagles, it once again excepted only possession and transportation of pre-existing artifacts from the general ban. 76 Stat. 1246. And it is particularly relevant that Congress has twice reviewed and amended the statute without rejecting the Department's view that it is authorized to bar the sale of pre-existing artifacts. [Footnote omitted] *Cf. NLRB v. Bell Aerospace Co.,* 416 U.S. 267, 275, 94 S.Ct. 1757, 1762, 40 L.Ed.2d 134 (1974).

The prohibition against the sale of bird parts lawfully taken before the effective date of federal protection is fully consonant with the purposes of the Eagle Protection Act. It was reasonable for Congress to conclude that the possibility of commercial gain presents a special threat to the preservation of the eagles because that prospect creates a powerful incentive both to evade statutory prohibitions against taking birds and to take a large volume of birds. The legislative draftsmen might well view evasion as a serious danger because there is no sure means by which to determine the age of bird feathers; feathers recently taken can easily be passed off as having been obtained long ago.

Appellees argue that even if the age of feathers cannot be ascertained, it is still possible to date the Indian artifacts of which the feathers are a constituent. Thus, they contend that the goal of preventing evasion of the statute could have been achieved by means less onerous than a general sales ban: for example, by requiring documentation and appraisal of feathered artifacts. The short answer is that this legislation is not limited to the sale of feathers as part of artifacts; it broadly addresses sale or purchase of feathers and other bird parts in any shape or form. The prohibitions of the statute were devised to resist any evasion, whether in the sale of feathers as part of datable artifacts or in the sale of separate undatable bird products. Moreover, even if there were alternative ways to insure statutory evasion, Congress was free to choose the method it found most efficacious and convenient. "[T]he legislature ... is authorized to pass measures for the protection of the people ... in the exercise of the police power, and is itself the judge of the necessity or expediency of the means adopted." *New York ex rel. Silz v. Hesterberg,* 211 U.S. 31, 40, 29 S.Ct. 10, 12, 53 L.Ed. 75 (1908).

B

The fundamental prohibition in the Migratory Bird Treaty Act is couched in language as expansive as that employed in the Eagle Protection Act. Title 16 U.S.C. §703 provides that

> "[u]nless and except as permitted by regulations made as hereinafter provided in this subchapter, it shall be unlawful ... to pursue, hunt, take, capture, kill, attempt to take, capture, or kill, possess, offer for sale, sell, offer to barter, barter, offer to purchase, purchase, deliver for shipment, ship, export, import, cause to be shipped, exported, or

> imported, deliver for transportation, transport or cause to be transported, carry or cause to be carried, or receive for shipment, transportation, carriage, or export ..."

protected birds. But the Migratory Bird Treaty Act contains no explicit exception for the possession or transportation of bird parts obtained before the federal protection became effective: that exception is created by the Secretary's regulation. 50 CFR §21.2 (1978). Unlike our analysis under the Eagle Protection Act, therefore, reliance upon the negative inference from a narrow statutory exemption for the transportation or possession of pre-existing artifacts is precluded. Nevertheless, the text, context, and purpose of the Migratory Bird Treaty Act support the Secretary's interpretative regulations of that enactment.

On its face, the comprehensive statutory prohibition is naturally read as forbidding transactions in all bird parts, including those that compose pre-existing artifacts. While there is no doubt that regulations may exempt transactions from the general ban, nothing in the statute *requires* an exception for the sale of pre-existing artifacts. And no such statutory exception can be implied. When Congress wanted an exemption from the statutory prohibition, it provided so in unmistakable terms. *Cf.* 16 U.S.C. §711.

The structure and context of this enactment—to the extent that they enlighten—also suggest congressional understanding that regulatory authorities could ban the sale of lawfully taken birds, except where otherwise expressly instructed by the statute. If Congress had assumed that lawfully taken birds could automatically be sold under the Act, it would have been unnecessary to specify in §711 that it is permissible under certain circumstances to sell game birds lawfully bred on farms and preserves. Furthermore, Congress could not have been unaware that a traditional legislative tool for enforcing conservation policy was a flat proscription on the sale of wildlife, without regard to the legality of the taking. At the time, a number of States, for example, simply prohibited or restricted possession or sale of wildlife during seasons closed to hunting. *See New York ex rel. Silz v. Hesterberg, supra,* at 40, 29 S.Ct., at 12. Also before Congress was the Canadian law implementing the Migratory Bird Treaty, and that law itself contained a provision barring the purchase, sale, or possession of protected bird parts "*during the time* when the capturing, killing, or taking of such bird, nest, or egg is prohibited by law," 55 Cong.Rec. 5412 (1917). (Emphasis added.) The Canadian sale ban—of which Congress was aware—thus applied not to illegally taken birds, but rather to all protected birds during the season in which hunting was prohibited. Against this background, the absence of a statutory exemption for pre-existing avian artifacts implies that the Migratory Bird Treaty Act was intended to embrace the traditional conservation technique of banning transactions in protected birds, whenever taken.

Related statutes may sometimes shed light upon a previous enactment. *Cf. United States v. Aluminum Co. of America,* 148 F.2d 416, 429 (CA2 1945) (L. Hand, J.). Other conservation legislation enacted by Congress has employed the enforcement technique of forbidding the sale of protected wildlife without respect to the lawfulness of the taking. The Eagle Protection Act is a notable example. The more recent Endangered Species Act of 1973, as originally framed, prohibited the sale of products or parts of endangered species, without an exception for those products legally held for commercial purposes at the time of the Act's passage. *See* 16 U.S.C. §1538; *United States v. Kepler,* 531 F.2d 796 (CA6 1976); *Delbay Pharmaceuticals, Inc. v. Department of Commerce,* 409 F.Supp. 637, 641-642, 644 (D.C.D.C.1976); *see* also H.R.Rep. No. 94-823, pp. 3-4 (1976) (discussing an amendment to the Endangered Species Act). And when Congress has meant to exempt lawfully taken items from the retroactive application of statutory prohibitions, it has taken care to do so explicitly, *see* 16 U.S.C. §1372 (Marine Mammal Protection Act of 1972); 16 U.S.C. §1538(b) (Endangered Species Act of 1973), or it has specifically amended the statute for that purpose, *see* 90 Stat. 911, amending 16 U.S.C. §1539 (Endangered Species Act); 92 Stat. 3760, amending 16 U.S.C. §§1538 and 1539 (Endangered Species Act). In contrast, Congress has never established a pre-existing artifacts exception to the Migratory Bird Treaty Act, even though it has amended the statute on several occasions.

We are therefore persuaded that the Migratory Bird Treaty Act empowers the Secretary of the Interior to bar commercial transactions in covered bird parts in spite of the fact that the parts were lawfully taken before the onset of federal protection. We see no indication to the contrary. It follows that the Secretary could properly permit the possession or transportation, and not the sale or purchase, of pre-existing bird artifacts. Accordingly, we disagree with the District Court's interpretation of the Act as inapplicable to pre-existing legally obtained bird parts.

II

We also disagree with the District Court's holding that, as construed to authorize the prohibition of commercial transactions in pre-existing avian artifacts, the Eagle Protection and Migratory Bird Treaty Acts violate appellees' Fifth Amendment property rights because the prohibition wholly deprives them of the opportunity to earn a profit from those relics.

Penn Central Transportation Co. v. New York City, 438 U.S. 104, 123-128, 98 S.Ct. 2646, 2659-2662, 57 L.Ed.2d 631 (1978), is our most recent exposition on the Takings Clause. That exposition need not be repeated at length here. Suffice it to say that government regulation—by definition—involves the adjustment of rights for the public good. Often this adjustment curtails some potential for the use or economic exploitation of private property. To require compensation in all such circumstances would effectively compel the government to regulate by *purchase*. "Government hardly could go on if to some extent values incident to property could not be diminished without paying for every such change in the general law." *Pennsylvania Coal Co. v. Mahon,* 260 U.S. 393, 413, 43 S.Ct. 158, 159, 67 L.Ed. 322 (1922); *see Penn Central, supra,* 438 U.S., at 124, 98 S.Ct., at 2659.

The Takings Clause, therefore, preserves governmental power to regulate, subject only to the dictates of "'justice and fairness.'" *Ibid.*; 98 S.Ct., at 2659; *see Goldblatt v. Hempstead,* 369 U.S. 590, 594, 82 S.Ct. 987, 990, 8 L.Ed.2d 130 (1962). There is no abstract or fixed point at which judicial intervention under the Takings Clause becomes appropriate. Formulas and factors have been developed in a variety of settings. *See Penn Central, supra,* 438 U.S., at 123-128, 98 S.Ct., at 2659-2662. Resolution of each case, however, ultimately calls as much for the exercise of judgment as for the application of logic.

The regulations challenged here do not compel the surrender of the artifacts, and there is no physical invasion or restraint upon them. Rather, a significant restriction has been imposed on one means of disposing of the artifacts. But the denial of one traditional property right does not always amount to a taking. At least where an owner possesses a full "bundle" of property rights, the destruction of one "strand" of the bundle is not a taking, because the aggregate must be viewed in its entirety. Compare *Penn Central, supra,* at 130-131, 98 S.Ct., at 2662-2663 and *United States v. Twin City Power Co.,* 350 U.S. 222, 76 S.Ct. 259, 100 L.Ed. 240 (1956), with *Pennsylvania Coal Co. v. Mahon, supra,* and *United States v. Virginia Electric & Power Co.,* 365 U.S. 624, 81 S.Ct. 784, 5 L.Ed.2d 838 (1961). *See* also Michelman, Property, Utility, and Fairness:

Comments on the Ethical Foundations of "Just Compensation" Law, 80 Harv.L.Rev. 1165, 1230-1233 (1967). In this case, it is crucial that appellees retain the rights to possess and transport their property, and to donate or devise the protected birds.

It is, to be sure, undeniable that the regulations here prevent the most profitable use of appellees' property. Again, however, that is not dispositive. When we review regulation, a reduction in the value of property is not necessarily equated with a taking. Compare *Goldblatt v. Hempstead, supra,* 369 U.S., at 594, 82 S.Ct., at 990, and *Hadacheck v. Sebastian,* 239 U.S. 394, 36 S.Ct. 143, 60 L.Ed. 348 (1915), with *Pennsylvania Coal Co. v. Mahon, supra.* In the instant case, it is not clear that appellees will be unable to derive economic benefit from the artifacts; for example, they might exhibit the artifacts for an admissions charge. At any rate, loss of future profits—unaccompanied by any physical property restriction—provides a slender reed upon which to rest a takings claim. Prediction of profitability is essentially a matter of reasoned speculation that courts are not especially competent to perform. Further, perhaps because of its very uncertainty, the interest in anticipated gains has traditionally been viewed as less compelling than other property-related interests. *Cf., e.g.,* Fuller & Perdue, *The Reliance Interest in Contract Damages* (pt. 1), 46 Yale L.J. 52 (1936).

Regulations that bar trade in certain goods have been upheld against claims of unconstitutional taking. For example, the Court has sustained regulations prohibiting the sale of alcoholic beverages despite the fact that individuals were left with previously acquired stocks. *Everard's Breweries v. Day,* 265 U.S. 545, 44 S.Ct. 628, 68 L.Ed. 1174 (1924), involved a federal statute that forbade the sale of liquors manufactured before passage of the statute. The claim of a taking in violation of the Fifth Amendment was tersely rejected. *Id.*, at 563, 44 S.Ct., at 633. Similarly, in *Jacob Ruppert, Inc. v. Caffey,* 251 U.S. 264, 40 S.Ct. 141, 64 L.Ed. 260 (1920), a federal law that extended a domestic sales ban from intoxicating to nonintoxicating alcoholic beverages "on hand at the time of the passage of the act," *id.,* at 302, 40 S.Ct., at 150, was upheld. Mr. Justice Brandeis dismissed the takings challenge, stating that "there was no appropriation of private property, but merely a lessening of value due to a permissible restriction imposed upon its use." *Id.,* at 303, 40 S.Ct., at 151. *See Mugler v. Kansas,* 123 U.S. 623, 8 S.Ct. 273, 31 L.Ed. 205 (1887).

It is true that appellees must bear the costs of these regulations. But, within limits, that is a burden borne to secure "the advantage of living and doing business in a civilized community." *Pennsylvania Coal Co. v. Mahon, supra,* 260 U.S., at 422, 43 S.Ct., at 163 (Brandeis, J., dissenting). We hold that the simple prohibition of the sale of lawfully acquired property in this case does not effect a taking in violation of the Fifth Amendment.

[Footnotes omitted.]

REVERSED.

THE CHIEF JUSTICE concurs in the judgment of the Court.

After *Pennsylvania Coal* there was a 50-year hiatus in major taking cases until *Penn Central Transportation* and *Agins*. *Penn Central* refined taking case analysis beyond the diminution in value test to include an examination of three factors: (1) the economic impact of the government action; (2) the extent to which there is interference with the distinct investment-backed expectations; and, (3) the character of the government action.

PENN CENTRAL TRANSPORTATION COMPANY v. CITY OF NEW YORK

438 U.S. 104, 57 L.Ed.2d 631, 98 S.Ct. 2646 (1978), *reh'g denied*, 439 U.S. 883, 58 L.Ed.2d, 198, 99 S.Ct. 226 (1978)

The question presented is whether a city may, as part of a comprehensive program to preserve historic landmarks and historic districts, place restrictions on the development of individual historic landmarks—in addition to those imposed by applicable zoning ordinances—without effecting a "taking" requiring the payment of "just compensation." Specifically, we must decide whether the application of New York City's Landmarks Preservation Law to the parcel of land occupied by Grand Central Terminal has "taken" its owners' property in violation of the Fifth and Fourteenth Amendments.

I

A

Over the past 50 years, all 50 States and over 500 municipalities have enacted laws to encourage or require the preservation of buildings and areas with historic or aesthetic importance. These nationwide legislative efforts have been precipitated by two concerns. The first is recognition that, in recent years, large numbers of historic structures, landmarks, and areas have been destroyed without adequate consideration of either the values represented therein or the possibility of preserving the destroyed properties for use in economically productive ways. The second is a widely shared belief that structures with special historic, cultural, or architectural significance enhance the quality of life for all. Not only do these buildings and their workmanship represent the lessons of the past and embody precious features of our heritage, they serve as examples of quality for today. "[H]istoric conservation is but one aspect of the much larger problem, basically an environmental one, of enhancing—or perhaps developing for the first time—the quality of life for people."

New York City, responding to similar concerns and acting pursuant to a New York State enabling Act, adopted its Landmarks Preservation Law in 1965. *See* N.Y.C. Admin. Code, ch. 8-A, §205-1.0 *et seq.* (1976). The city acted from the conviction that "the standing of [New York City] as a world-wide tourist center and world capital of business, culture and government" would be threatened if legislation were not enacted to protect historic landmarks and neighborhoods from precipitate decisions to destroy or fundamentally alter their character. §205-1.0(a). The city believed that comprehensive measures to safeguard desirable features of the existing urban fabric would benefit its citizens in a variety of ways: *e.g.*, fostering "civic pride in the beauty and noble accomplishments of the past"; protecting and enhancing "the city's attractions to tourists and visitors"; "support[ing] and stimul[ating] business and industry"; "strengthen[ing] the economy of the city"; and promoting "the use of historic districts, landmarks, interior landmarks and scenic landmarks for the education, pleasure and welfare of the people of the city." §205-1.0(b).

The New York City law is typical of many urban landmark laws in that its primary method of achieving its goals is not by acquisitions of historic properties, but rather by involving public entities in land-use decisions affecting these properties and providing services, standards, controls, and incentives that will encourage preservation by private owners and users. While the law does place special restrictions on landmark properties as a necessary feature to the attainment of its larger objectives, the major theme of the law is to ensure the owners of any such properties both a "reasonable return" on their investments and maximum latitude to use their parcels for purposes not inconsistent with the preservation goals.

The operation of the law can be briefly summarized. The primary responsibility for administering the law is vested in the Landmarks Preservation Commission (Commission), a broad based, 11-member agency assisted by a technical staff. The Commission first performs the function, critical to any landmark preservation effort, of identifying properties and areas that have "a special character or special historical or aesthetic interest or value as part of the development, heritage or cultural characteristics of the city, state or nation." §207-1.0(n); *see* §207- 1.0(h). If the Commission determines, after giving all interested parties an opportunity to be heard, that a building or area satisfies the ordinance's criteria, it will designate a building to be a "landmark," §207-1.0(n), situated on a particular "landmark site," §207-1.0(o), or will designate an area to be a "historic district," §207-1.0(h). After the Commission makes a designation, New York City's Board of Estimate, after considering the relationship of the designated property "to the master plan, the zoning resolution, projected public improvements and any plans for the renewal of the area involved," §207-2.0(g)(1), may modify or disapprove the designation, and the owner may seek judicial review of the final designation decision. Thus far, 31 historic districts and over 400 individual landmarks have been finally designated, and the process is a continuing one.

Final designation as a landmark results in restrictions upon the property owner's options concerning use of the landmark site. First, the law imposes a duty upon the owner to keep the exterior features of the building "in good repair" to assure that the law's objectives not be defeated by the landmark's falling into a state of irremediable disrepair. *See* §207-10.0(a). Second, the Commission must approve in advance any proposal to alter the exterior architectural features of the landmark or to construct any exterior improvement on the landmark site, thus ensuring that decisions concerning construction on the landmark site are made with due consideration of both the public interest in the maintenance of the structure and the landowner's interest in use of the property. *See* §§207-4.0 to 207-9.0.

In the event an owner wishes to alter a landmark site, three separate procedures are available through which administrative approval may be obtained. First, the owner may apply to the Commission for a "certificate of no effect on protected architectural features": that is, for an order approving the improvement or alteration on the ground that it will not change or affect any architectural feature of the landmark and will be in harmony therewith. *See* §207-5.0. Denial of the certificate is subject to judicial review.

Second, the owner may apply to the Commission for a certificate of "appropriateness." *See* §207-6.0. Such certificates will be granted if the Commission concludes—focusing upon aesthetic, historical, and architectural values—that the proposed construction on the landmark site would not unduly hinder the protection, enhancement, perpetuation, and use of the landmark. Again, denial of the certificate is subject to judicial review. Moreover, the owner who is denied either a certificate of no exterior effect or a certificate of appropriateness may submit an alternative or modified plan for approval. The final procedure—seeking a certificate of appropriateness on the ground of "insufficient return," *see* §207-8.0—provides special mechanisms, which vary depending on whether or not the landmark enjoys a tax exemption, to ensure that designation does not cause economic hardship.

Although the designation of a landmark and landmark site restricts the owner's control over the parcel, designation also enhances the economic position of the landmark owner in one significant respect. Under New York City's zoning laws, owners of real property who have not developed their property to the full extent permitted by the applicable zoning laws are allowed to transfer development rights to contiguous parcels on the same city block. *See* New York City, Zoning Resolution Art. I, ch. 2, §12-10 (1978) (definition of "zoning lot"). A 1968 ordinance gave the owners of landmark sites additional opportunities to transfer development rights to other parcels. Subject to a restriction that the floor area of the transferee lot may not be increased by more than 20 percent above its authorized level, the ordinance permitted transfers from a landmark parcel to property across the street or across a street intersection. In 1969, the law governing the conditions under which transfers from landmark parcels could occur was liberalized, *see* New York City Zoning Resolutions 74-79 to 74-793, apparently to ensure that the Landmarks Law would not unduly restrict the development options of the owners of Grand Central Terminal. *See* Marcus, "Air Rights Transfers in New York City," 36 *Law & Contemp. Prob.* 372, 375 (1971). The class of recipient lots was expanded to include lots "across a street and opposite to another lot or lots which except for the intervention of streets or street intersections f[or]m a series extending to the lot occupied by the landmark building [, provided that] all lots [are] in the same ownership." New York City Zoning Resolution 74-79 (emphasis deleted). In addition, the 1969 amendment permits, in highly commercialized areas like midtown Manhattan, the transfer of all unused development rights to a single parcel. *Ibid.*

B

This case involves the application of New York City's Landmarks Preservation Law to Grand Central Terminal (Terminal). The Terminal, which is owned by the Penn Central Transportation Co. and its affiliates (Penn Central), is one of New York City's most famous buildings. Opened in 1913, it is regarded not only as providing an ingenious engineering solution to the problems presented by urban railroad stations, but also as a magnificent example of the French beaux-arts style.

The Terminal is located in midtown Manhattan. Its south facade faces 42d Street and that street's intersection with Park Avenue. At street level, the Terminal is bounded on the west by Vanderbilt Avenue, on the east by the Commodore Hotel, and on the north by the Pan-American Building. Although a 20-story office tower, to have been located above the Terminal, was part of the original design, the planned tower was never constructed. The Terminal itself is an eight-story structure which Penn Central uses as a railroad station and in which it rents space not needed for railroad purposes to a variety of commercial interests. The Terminal is one of a number of properties owned by appellant Penn Central in this area of midtown Manhattan. The others include the Barclay, Biltmore, Commodore, Roosevelt, and Waldorf-Astoria Hotels, the Pan-American Building and other office buildings along Park Avenue, and the Yale Club. At least eight of these are eligible to be recipients of development rights afforded the Terminal by virtue of landmark designation.

On August 2, 1967, following a public hearing, the Commission designated the Terminal a "landmark" and designated the "city tax block" it occupies a "landmark site." The Board of Estimate confirmed this action on September 21, 1967. Although appellant Penn Central had opposed the designation before the Commission, it did not seek judicial review of the final designation decision.

On January 22, 1968, appellant Penn Central, to increase its income, entered into a renewable 50-year lease and sublease agreement with appellant UGP Properties, Inc. (UGP), a wholly owned subsidiary of Union General Properties, Ltd., a United Kingdom corporation. Under the terms of the agreement, UGP was to construct a multistory office building above the Terminal. UGP promised to pay Penn Central $1 million annually during construction and at least $3 million annually thereafter. The rentals would be offset in part by a loss of some $700,000 to $1 million in net rentals presently received from concessionaires displaced by the new building.

Appellants UGP and Penn Central then applied to the Commission for permission to construct an office building atop the Terminal. Two separate plans, both designed by architect Marcel Breuer and both apparently satisfying the terms of the applicable zoning ordinance, were submitted to the Commission for approval. The first, Breuer I, provided for the construction of a 55-story office building, to be cantilevered above the existing facade and to rest on the roof of the Terminal. The second, Breuer II Revised, called for tearing down a portion of the Terminal that included the 42d Street facade, stripping off some of the remaining features of the Terminal's facade, and constructing a 53-story office building. The Commission denied a certificate of no exterior effect on September 20, 1968. Appellants then applied for a certificate of "appropriateness" as to both proposals. After four days of hearings at which over 80 witnesses testified, the Commission denied this application as to both proposals.

The Commission's reasons for rejecting certificates respecting Breuer II Revised are summarized in the following statement: "To protect a Landmark, one does not tear it down. To perpetuate its architectural features, one does not strip them off." Record 2255. Breuer I, which would have preserved the existing vertical facades of the present structure, received more sympathetic consideration. The Commission first focused on the effect that the proposed tower would have on one desirable feature created by the present structure and its surroundings: the dramatic view of the Terminal from Park Avenue South. Although appellants had contended that the Pan-American Building had already destroyed the silhouette of the south facade and that one additional tower could do no further damage and might even provide a better background for the facade, the Commission disagreed, stating that it found the majestic approach from the south to be still unique in the city and that a 55-story tower atop the Terminal would be far more detrimental to its south facade than the Pan-American Building 375 feet away. Moreover, the Commission found that from closer vantage points the Pan Am Building and the other towers were largely cut off from view, which would not be the case of the mass on top of the Terminal planned under Breuer I. In conclusion, the Commission stated:

> "[We have] no fixed rule against making additions to designated buildings—it all depends on how they are done ... But to balance a 55-story office tower above a flamboyant Beaux-Arts facade seems nothing more than an aesthetic joke. Quite simply, the tower would overwhelm the Terminal by its sheer mass. The 'addition' would be four times as high as the existing structure and would reduce the Landmark itself to the status of a curiosity.
>
> "Landmarks cannot be divorced from their settings—particularly when the setting is a dramatic and integral part of the original concept. The Terminal, in its setting, is a great example of urban design. Such examples are not so plentiful in New York City that we can afford to lose any of the few we have. And we must preserve them in a meaningful

> way—with alterations and additions of such character, scale, materials and mass as will protect, enhance and perpetuate the original design rather than overwhelm it." *Id.*, at 2251.

Appellants did not seek judicial review of the denial of either certificate. Because the Terminal site enjoyed a tax exemption, remained suitable for its present and future uses, and was not the subject of a contract of sale, there were no further administrative remedies available to appellants as to the Breuer I and Breuer II Revised plans.... Further, appellants did not avail themselves of the opportunity to develop and submit other plans for the Commission's consideration and approval. Instead, appellants filed suit in New York Supreme Court, Trial Term, claiming, *inter alia*, that the application of the Landmarks Preservation Law had "taken" their property without just compensation in violation of the Fifth and Fourteenth Amendments and arbitrarily deprived them of their property without due process of law in violation of the Fourteenth Amendment. Appellants sought a declaratory judgment, injunctive relief barring the city from using the Landmarks Law to impede the construction of any structure that might otherwise lawfully be constructed on the Terminal site, and damages for the "temporary taking" that occurred between August 2, 1967, the designation date, and the date when the restrictions arising from the Landmarks Law would be lifted. The trial court granted the injunctive and declaratory relief, but severed the question of damages for a "temporary taking."

Appellees appealed, and the New York Supreme Court, Appellate Division, reversed. [citation omitted]. The Appellate Division held that the restrictions on the development of the Terminal site were necessary to promote the legitimate public purpose of protecting landmarks and therefore that appellants could sustain their constitutional claims only by proof that the regulation deprived them of all reasonable beneficial use of the property. The Appellate Division held that the evidence appellants introduced at trial—"Statements of Revenues and Costs," purporting to show a net operating loss for the years 1969 and 1971, which were prepared for the instant litigation—had not satisfied their burden. First, the court rejected the claim that these statements showed that the Terminal was operating at a loss, for in the court's view, appellants had improperly attributed some railroad operating expenses and taxes to their real estate operations and compounded that error by failing to impute any rental value to the vast space in the Terminal devoted to railroad purposes. Further, the Appellate Division concluded that appellants had failed to establish either that they were unable to increase the Terminal's commercial income by transforming vacant or underutilized space to revenue-producing use, or that the unused development rights over the Terminal could not have been profitably transferred to one or more nearby sites. The Appellate Division concluded that all appellants had succeeded in showing was that they had been deprived of the property's most profitable use, and that this showing did not establish that appellants had been unconstitutionally deprived of their property.

The New York Court of Appeals affirmed. [citation omitted]. That court summarily rejected any claim that the Landmarks Law had "taken" property without "just compensation," [citation omitted] indicating that there could be no "taking" since the law had not transferred control of the property to the city, but only restricted appellants' exploitation of it. In that circumstance, the Court of Appeals held that appellants' attack on the law could prevail only if the law deprived appellants of their property in violation of the Due Process Clause of the Fourteenth Amendment. Whether or not there was a denial of substantive due process turned on whether the restrictions deprived Penn Central of a "reasonable return" on the "privately created and privately managed ingredient" of the Terminal. [citation omitted] The Court of Appeals concluded that the Landmarks Law had not effected a denial of due process because: (1) the landmark regulation permitted the same use as had been made of the Terminal for more than half a century; (2) the appellants had failed to show that they could not earn a reasonable return on their investment in the Terminal itself; 3) even if the Terminal proper could never operate at a reasonable profit some of the income from Penn Central's extensive real estate holdings in the area, which include hotels and office buildings, must realistically be imputed to the Terminal; and (4) the development rights above the Terminal, which had been made transferable to numerous sites in the vicinity of the Terminal, one or two of which were suitable for the construction of office buildings, were valuable to appellants and provided "significant, perhaps 'fair,' compensation for the loss of rights above the terminal itself." [citation omitted].

Observing that its affirmance was "[o]n the present record," and that its analysis had not been fully developed by counsel at any level of the New York judicial system, the Court of Appeals directed that counsel "should be entitled to present ... any additional submissions which, in the light of [the court's] opinion, may usefully develop further the factors discussed." [citation omitted] Appellants chose not to avail themselves of this opportunity and filed a notice of appeal in this Court. We noted probable jurisdiction. [citation omitted]. We affirm.

II

The issues presented by appellants are (1) whether the restrictions imposed by New York City's law upon appellants' exploitation of the Terminal site effect a "taking" of appellants' property for a public use within the meaning of the Fifth Amendment, which of course is made applicable to the States through the Fourteenth Amendment, *see Chicago, B. & Q. R. Co. v. Chicago*, 166 U.S. 226, 239, 17 S.Ct. 581, 585, 41 L.Ed. 979 (1897), and, (2), if so, whether the transferable development rights afforded appellants constitute "just compensation" within the meaning of the Fifth Amendment. We need only address the question whether a "taking" has occurred.

A

Before considering appellants' specific contentions, it will be useful to review the factors that have shaped the jurisprudence of the Fifth Amendment injunction "nor shall private property be taken for public use, without just compensation." The question of what constitutes a "taking" for purposes of the Fifth Amendment has proved to be a problem of considerable difficulty. While this Court has recognized that the "Fifth Amendment's guarantee ... [is] designed to bar Government from forcing some people alone to bear public burdens which, in all fairness and justice, should be borne by the public as a whole," *Armstrong v. United States*, 364 U.S. 40, 49, 80 S.Ct. 1563, 1569, 4 L.Ed.2d 1554 (1960), this Court, quite simply, has been unable to develop any "set formula" for determining when "justice and fairness" require that economic injuries caused by public action be compensated by the government, rather than remain disproportionately concentrated on a few persons. *See Goldblatt v. Hempstead*, 369 U.S. 590, 594, 82 S.Ct. 987, 990, 8 L.Ed.2d 130 (1962). Indeed, we have frequently observed that whether a particular restriction will be rendered invalid by the government's failure to pay for any losses proximately caused by it depends largely "upon the particular circumstances [in that] case." *United States v. Central Eureka Mining Co.*, 357 U.S. 155, 168, 78 S.Ct. 1097, 1104, 2 L.Ed.2d 1228 (1958); *see United States v. Caltex, Inc.*, 344 U.S. 149, 156, 73 S.Ct. 200, 203, 97 L.Ed. 157 (1952).

In engaging in these essentially ad hoc, factual inquiries, the Court's decisions have identified several factors that have particular significance. The economic impact of the regulation on the claimant and, particularly, the extent to which the regulation has interfered with distinct investment-backed expectations are, of course, relevant considerations. *See Goldblatt v. Hempstead, supra,* 369 U.S., at 594, 82 S.Ct., at 990. So, too, is the character of the governmental action. A "taking" may more readily be found when the interference with property can be characterized as a physical invasion by government, *see, e.g., United States v. Causby,* 328 U.S. 256, 66 S.Ct. 1062, 90 L.Ed. 1206 (1946), than when interference arises from some public program adjusting the benefits and burdens of economic life to promote the common good.

"Government hardly could go on if to some extent values incident to property could not be diminished without paying for every such change in the general law," *Pennsylvania Coal Co. v. Mahon,* 260 U.S. 393, 413, 43 S.Ct. 158, 159, 67 L.Ed. 322 (1922), and this Court has accordingly recognized, in a wide variety of contexts, that government may execute laws or programs that adversely affect recognized economic values. Exercises of the taxing power are one obvious example. A second are the decisions in which this Court has dismissed "taking" challenges on the ground that, while the challenged government action caused economic harm, it did not interfere with interests that were sufficiently bound up with the reasonable expectations of the claimant to constitute "property" for Fifth Amendment purposes. *See, e.g., United States v. Willow River Power Co.,* 324 U.S. 499, 65 S.Ct. 761, 89 L.Ed. 1101 (1945) (interest in high-water level of river for runoff for tailwaters to maintain power head is not property); *United States v. Chandler-Dunbar Water Power Co.,* 229 U.S. 53, 33 S.Ct. 667, 57 L.Ed. 1063 (1913) (no property interest can exist in navigable waters); *see* also *Demorest v. City Bank Co.,* 321 U.S. 36, 64 S.Ct. 384, 88 L.Ed. 526 (1944); *Muhlker v. Harlem R. Co.,* 197 U.S. 544, 25 S.Ct. 522, 49 L.Ed. 872 (1905); Sax, Takings and the Police Power, 74 Yale L.J. 36, 61-62 (1964).

More importantly for the present case, in instances in which a state tribunal reasonably concluded that "the health, safety, morals, or general welfare" would be promoted by prohibiting particular contemplated uses of land, this Court has upheld land-use regulations that destroyed or adversely affected recognized real property interests. *See Nectow v. Cambridge,* 277 U.S. 183, 188, 48 S.Ct. 447, 448, 72 L.Ed. 842 (1928). Zoning laws are, of course, the classic example, *see Euclid v. Ambler Realty Co.,* 272 U.S. 365, 47 S.Ct. 114, 71 L.Ed. 303 (1926) (prohibition of industrial use); *Gorieb v. Fox,* 274 U.S. 603, 608, 47 S.Ct. 675, 677, 71 L.Ed. 1228 (1927) (requirement that portions of parcels be left unbuilt); *Welch v. Swasey,* 214 U.S. 91, 29 S.Ct. 567, 53 L.Ed. 923 (1909) (height restriction), which have been viewed as permissible governmental action even when prohibiting the most beneficial use of the property. *See Goldblatt v. Hempstead, supra,* 369 U.S., at 592-593, 82 S.Ct., at 988-989, and cases cited; *see* also *Eastlake v. Forest City Enterprises, Inc.,* 426 U.S. 668, 674, n. 8, 96 S.Ct. 2358, 2362 n. 8, 49 L.Ed.2d 132 (1976).

Zoning laws generally do not affect existing uses of real property, but "taking" challenges have also been held to be without merit in a wide variety of situations when the challenged governmental actions prohibited a beneficial use to which individual parcels had previously been devoted and thus caused substantial individualized harm. *Miller v. Schoene,* 276 U.S. 272, 48 S.Ct. 246, 72 L.Ed. 568 (1928), is illustrative. In that case, a state entomologist, acting pursuant to a state statute, ordered the claimants to cut down a large number of ornamental red cedar trees because they produced cedar rust fatal to apple trees cultivated nearby. Although the statute provided for recovery of any expense incurred in removing the cedars, and permitted claimants to use the felled trees, it did not provide compensation for the value of the standing trees or for the resulting decrease in market value of the properties as a whole. A unanimous Court held that this latter omission did not render the statute invalid. The Court held that the State might properly make "a choice between the preservation of one class of property and that of the other" and since the apple industry was important in the State involved, concluded that the State had not exceeded "its constitutional powers by deciding upon the destruction of one class of property [without compensation] in order to save another which, in the judgment of the legislature, is of greater value to the public." *Id.*, at 279, 48 S.Ct., at 247.

Again, *Hadacheck v. Sebastian,* 239 U.S. 394, 36 S.Ct. 143, 60 L.Ed. 348 (1915), upheld a law prohibiting the claimant from continuing his otherwise lawful business of operating a brickyard in a particular physical community on the ground that the legislature had reasonably concluded that the presence of the brickyard was inconsistent with neighboring uses. *See* also *United States v. Central Eureka Mining Co., supra* (Government order closing gold mines so that skilled miners would be available for other mining work held not a taking); *Atchison, T. & S. F. R. Co. v. Public Utilities Comm'n,* 346 U.S. 346, 74 S.Ct. 92, 98 L.Ed. 51 (1953) (railroad may be required to share cost of constructing railroad grade improvement); *Walls v. Midland Carbon Co.,* 254 U.S. 300, 41 S.Ct. 118, 65 L.Ed. 276 (1920) (law prohibiting manufacture of carbon black upheld); *Reinman v. Little Rock,* 237 U.S. 171, 35 S.Ct. 511, 59 L.Ed. 900 (1915) (law prohibiting livery stable upheld); *Mugler v. Kansas,* 123 U.S. 623, 8 S.Ct. 273, 31 L.Ed. 205 (1887) (law prohibiting liquor business upheld).

Goldblatt v. Hempstead, supra, is a recent example. There, a 1958 city safety ordinance banned any excavations below the water table and effectively prohibited the claimant from continuing a sand and gravel mining business that had been operated on the particular parcel since 1927. The Court upheld the ordinance against a "taking" challenge, although the ordinance prohibited the present and presumably most beneficial use of the property and had, like the regulations in *Miller* and *Hadacheck,* severely affected a particular owner. The Court assumed that the ordinance did not prevent the owner's reasonable use of the property since the owner made no showing of an adverse effect on the value of the land. Because the restriction served a substantial public purpose, the Court thus held no taking had occurred. It is, of course, implicit in *Goldblatt* that a use restriction on real property may constitute a "taking" if not reasonably necessary to the effectuation of a substantial public purpose, *see Nectow v. Cambridge, supra; cf. Moore v. East Cleveland,* 431 U.S. 494, 513-514, 97 S.Ct. 1932, 1943, 52 L.Ed.2d 531 (1977) (STEVENS, J., concurring), or perhaps if it has an unduly harsh impact upon the owner's use of the property.

Pennsylvania Coal Co. v. Mahon, 260 U.S. 393, 43 S.Ct. 158, 67 L.Ed. 322 (1922), is the leading case for the proposition that a state statute that substantially furthers important public policies may so frustrate distinct investment-backed expectations as to amount to a "taking." There the claimant had sold the surface rights to particular parcels of property, but expressly reserved the right to remove the coal thereunder. A Pennsylvania statute, enacted after the transactions, forbade any mining of coal that caused the subsidence of any house, unless the house was the property of the owner of the underlying coal and was more than 150 feet from the improved property of another. Because the statute made it commercially impracticable to mine the coal, *id.*, at 414, 43 S.Ct., at 159, and thus had nearly the same effect as the complete destruction of rights claimant had reserved from the owners of the surface land, *see id.*, at 414-415, 43 S.Ct., at 159-160, the Court held that the statute was invalid as effecting a "taking" without just compensation. *See* also *Armstrong v. United States,* 364 U.S. 40, 80 S.Ct. 1563, 4 L.Ed.2d 1554 (1960) (Government's complete destruction of a materialman's lien in certain property held a "taking"); *Hudson Water Co. v. McCarter,* 209 U.S. 349, 355, 28 S.Ct. 529, 531, 52 L.Ed. 828 (1908) (if height restriction makes property wholly useless "the rights of property ... prevail over the other public interest" and compensation is required). *See* generally Michelman, *Property, Utility, and Fair-*

ness: Comments on the Ethical Foundations of "Just Compensation" Law, 80 Harv.L.Rev. 1165, 1229-1234 (1967).

Finally, government actions that may be characterized as acquisitions of resources to permit or facilitate uniquely public functions have often been held to constitute "takings." *United States v. Causby,* 328 U.S. 256, 66 S.Ct. 1062, 90 L.Ed. 1206 (1946), is illustrative. In holding that direct overflights above the claimant's land, that destroyed the present use of the land as a chicken farm, constituted a "taking," *Causby* emphasized that Government had not "merely destroyed property [but was] using a part of it for the flight of its planes." *Id.,* 328 U.S., at 262-263, n. 7, 66 S.Ct., at 1066. *See* also *Griggs v. Allegheny County,* 369 U.S. 84, 82 S.Ct. 531, 7 L.Ed.2d 585 (1962) (overflights held a taking); *Portsmouth Co. v. United States,* 260 U.S. 327, 43 S.Ct. 135, 67 L.Ed. 287 (1922) (United States military installations' repeated firing of guns over claimant's land is a taking); *United States v. Cress,* 243 U.S. 316, 37 S.Ct. 380, 61 L.Ed. 746 (1917) (repeated floodings of land caused by water project is taking); but *see YMCA v. United States,* 395 U.S. 85, 89 S.Ct. 1511, 23 L.Ed.2d 117 (1969) (damage caused to a building when federal officers who were seeking to protect the building were attacked by rioters held not a taking). *See* generally Michelman, *supra,* at 1226-1229; Sax, *Takings and the Police Power,* 74 Yale L.J. 36 (1964).

B

In contending that the New York City law has "taken" their property in violation of the Fifth and Fourteenth Amendments, appellants make a series of arguments, which, while tailored to the facts of this case, essentially urge that any substantial restriction imposed pursuant to a landmark law must be accompanied by just compensation if it is to be constitutional. Before considering these, we emphasize what is not in dispute. Because this Court has recognized, in a number of settings, that States and cities may enact land-use restrictions or controls to enhance the quality of life by preserving the character and desirable aesthetic features of a city, *see New Orleans v. Dukes,* 427 U.S. 297, 96 S.Ct. 2513, 49 L.Ed.2d 511 (1976); *Young v. American Mini Theatres, Inc.,* 427 U.S. 50, 96 S.Ct. 2440, 49 L.Ed.2d 310 (1976); *Village of Belle Terre v. Boraas,* 416 U.S. 1, 9-10, 94 S.Ct. 1536, 39 L.Ed.2d 797 (1974); *Berman v. Parker,* 348 U.S. 26, 33, 75 S.Ct. 98, 102, 99 L.Ed. 27 (1954); *Welch v. Swasey,* 214 U.S., at 108, 29 S.Ct., at 571, appellants do not contest that New York City's objective of preserving structures and areas with special historic, architectural, or cultural significance is an entirely permissible governmental goal. They also do not dispute that the restrictions imposed on its parcel are appropriate means of securing the purposes of the New York City law. Finally, appellants do not challenge any of the specific factual premises of the decision below. They accept for present purposes both that the parcel of land occupied by Grand Central Terminal must, in its present state, be regarded as capable of earning a reasonable return, and that the transferable development rights afforded appellants by virtue of the Terminal's designation as a landmark are valuable, even if not as valuable as the rights to construct above the Terminal. In appellants' view none of these factors derogate from their claim that New York City's law has effected a "taking."

They first observe that the airspace above the Terminal is a valuable property interest, citing *United States v. Causby, supra.* They urge that the Landmarks Law has deprived them of any gainful use of their "air rights" above the Terminal and that, irrespective of the value of the remainder of their parcel, the city has "taken" their right to this superadjacent airspace, thus entitling them to "just compensation" measured by the fair market value of these air rights.

Apart from our own disagreement with appellants' characterization of the effect of the New York City law, *see infra*, at 2665, the submission that appellants may establish a "taking" simply by showing that they have been denied the ability to exploit a property interest that they heretofore had believed was available for development is quite simply untenable. Were this the rule, this Court would have erred not only in upholding laws restricting the development of air rights, *see Welch v. Swasey, supra,* but also in approving those prohibiting both the subjacent, *see Goldblatt v. Hempstead,* 369 U.S. 590, 82 S.Ct. 987, 8 L.Ed.2d 130 (1962), and the lateral, *see Gorieb v. Fox,* 274 U.S. 603, 47 S.Ct. 675, 71 L.Ed. 1228 (1927), development of particular parcels. "Taking" jurisprudence does not divide a single parcel into discrete segments and attempt to determine whether rights in a particular segment have been entirely abrogated. In deciding whether a particular governmental action has effected a taking, this Court focuses rather both on the character of the action and on the nature and extent of the interference with rights in the parcel as a whole—here, the city tax block designated as the "landmark site."

Secondly, appellants, focusing on the character and impact of the New York City law, argue that it effects a "taking because its operation has significantly diminished the value of the Terminal site. Appellants concede that the decisions sustaining other land-use regulations, which like the New York City law, are reasonably related to the promotion of the general welfare, uniformly reject the proposition that diminution in property value, standing alone, can establish a "taking," *see Euclid v. Ambler Realty Co.,* 272 U.S. 365, 47 S.Ct. 114, 71 L.Ed. 303 (1926) (75% diminution in value caused by zoning law); *Hadacheck v. Sebastian*, 239 U.S. 394, 36 S.Ct. 143, 60 L.Ed. 348 (1915) (87 1/2 % diminution in value); *cf. Eastlake v. Forest City Enterprises, Inc.,* 426 U.S., at 674 n. 8, 96 S.Ct., at 2362 n. 8, and that the taking issue in these contexts is resolved by focusing on the uses the regulations permit. *See* also *Goldblatt v. Hempstead, supra*. Appellants, moreover, also do not dispute that a showing of diminution in property value would not establish a taking if the restriction had been imposed as a result of historic-district legislation, *see* generally *Maher v. New Orleans,* 516 F.2d 1051 (CA5 1975), but appellants argue that New York City's regulation of individual landmarks is fundamentally different from zoning or from historic-district legislation because the controls imposed by New York City's law apply only to individuals who own selected properties.

Stated baldly, appellants' position appears to be that the only means of ensuring that selected owners are not singled out to endure financial hardship for no reason is to hold that any restriction imposed on individual landmarks pursuant to the New York City scheme is a "taking" requiring the payment of "just compensation." Agreement with this argument would, of course, invalidate not just New York City's law, but all comparable landmark legislation in the Nation. We find no merit in it.

It is true, as appellants emphasize, that both historic-district legislation and zoning laws regulate all properties within given physical communities whereas landmark laws apply only to selected parcels. But, contrary to appellants' suggestions, landmark laws are not like discriminatory, or "reverse spot," zoning: that is, a land-use decision which arbitrarily singles out a particular parcel for different, less favorable treatment than the neighboring ones. *See* 2 A. Rathkopf, The Law of Zoning and Planning 26-4, and n. 6 (4th ed. 1978). In contrast to discriminatory zoning, which is the antithesis of land-use control as part of some comprehensive plan, the New York City law embodies a comprehensive plan to preserve structures of historic or aesthetic interest wherever they might be found in the city, and as noted, over 400 landmarks and 31 historic districts have been designated pursuant to this plan.

Equally without merit is the related argument that the decision to designate a structure as a landmark "is inevitably arbitrary or at least subjective, because it is basically a matter of taste," Reply Brief for Appellants 22, thus unavoidably singling out individual landowners for disparate and unfair treatment. The argument has a particularly hollow ring in this case. For appellants not only did not seek judicial review of either the designation or of the denials of the certificates of appropriateness and of no exterior effect, but do not even now suggest that the Commission's decisions concerning the Terminal were in any sense arbitrary or unprincipled. But, in any event, a landmark owner has a right to judicial review of any Commission decision, and, quite simply, there is no basis whatsoever for a conclusion that courts will have any greater difficulty identifying arbitrary or discriminatory action in the context of landmark regulation than in the context of classic zoning or indeed in any other context.

Next, appellants observe that New York City's law differs from zoning laws and historic-district ordinances in that the Landmarks Law does not impose identical or similar restrictions on all structures located in particular physical communities. It follows, they argue, that New York City's law is inherently incapable of producing the fair and equitable distribution of benefits and burdens of governmental action which is characteristic of zoning laws and historic-district legislation and which they maintain is a constitutional requirement if "just compensation" is not to be afforded. It is, of course, true that the Landmarks Law has a more severe impact on some landowners than on others, but that in itself does not mean that the law effects a "taking." Legislation designed to promote the general welfare commonly burdens some more than others. The owners of the brickyard in *Hadacheck*, of the cedar trees in *Miller v. Schoene*, and of the gravel and sand mine in *Goldblatt v. Hempstead*, were uniquely burdened by the legislation sustained in those cases. Similarly, zoning laws often affect some property owners more severely than others but have not been held to be invalid on that account. For example, the property owner in *Euclid* who wished to use its property for industrial purposes was affected far more severely by the ordinance than its neighbors who wished to use their land for residences.

In any event, appellants' repeated suggestions that they are solely burdened and unbenefited is factually inaccurate. This contention overlooks the fact that the New York City law applies to vast numbers of structures in the city in addition to the Terminal—all the structures contained in the 31 historic districts and over 400 individual landmarks, many of which are close to the Terminal. Unless we are to reject the judgment of the New York City Council that the preservation of landmarks benefits all New York citizens and all structures, both economically and by improving the quality of life in the city as a whole—which we are unwilling to do—we cannot conclude that the owners of the Terminal have in no sense been benefited by the Landmarks Law. Doubtless appellants believe they are more burdened than benefited by the law, but that must have been true, too, of the property owners in *Miller, Hadacheck, Euclid*, and *Goldblatt*.

Appellants' final broad-based attack would have us treat the law as an instance, like that in *United States v. Causby*, in which government, acting in an enterprise capacity, has appropriated part of their property for some strictly governmental purpose. Apart from the fact that *Causby* was a case of invasion of airspace that destroyed the use of the farm beneath and this New York City law has in nowise impaired the present use of the Terminal, the Landmarks Law neither exploits appellants' parcel for city purposes nor facilitates nor arises from any entrepreneurial operations of the city. The situation is not remotely like that in *Causby* where the airspace above the property was in the flight pattern for military aircraft. The Landmarks Law's effect is simply to prohibit appellants or anyone else from occupying portions of the airspace above the Terminal, while permitting appellants to use the remainder of the parcel in a gainful fashion. This is no more an appropriation of property by government for its own uses than is a zoning law prohibiting, for "aesthetic" reasons, two or more adult theaters within a specified area, *see Young v. American Mini Theatres, Inc.*, 427 U.S. 50, 96 S.Ct. 2440, 49 L.Ed.2d 310 (1976), or a safety regulation prohibiting excavations below a certain level. *See Goldblatt v. Hempstead.*

C

Rejection of appellants' broad arguments is not, however, the end of our inquiry, for all we thus far have established is that the New York City law is not rendered invalid by its failure to provide "just compensation" whenever a landmark owner is restricted in the exploitation of property interests, such as air rights, to a greater extent than provided for under applicable zoning laws. We now must consider whether the interference with appellants' property is of such a magnitude that "there must be an exercise of eminent domain and compensation to sustain [it]." *Pennsylvania Coal Co. v. Mahon*, 260 U.S., at 413, 43 S.Ct., at 159. That inquiry may be narrowed to the question of the severity of the impact of the law on appellants' parcel, and its resolution in turn requires a careful assessment of the impact of the regulation on the Terminal site.

Unlike the governmental acts in *Goldblatt, Miller, Causby, Griggs*, and *Hadacheck*, the New York City law does not interfere in any way with the present uses of the Terminal. Its designation as a landmark not only permits but contemplates that appellants may continue to use the property precisely as it has been used for the past 65 years: as a railroad terminal containing office space and concessions. So the law does not interfere with what must be regarded as Penn Central's primary expectation concerning the use of the parcel. More importantly, on this record, we must regard the New York City law as permitting Penn Central not only to profit from the Terminal but also to obtain a "reasonable return" on its investment.

Appellants, moreover, exaggerate the effect of the law on their ability to make use of the air rights above the Terminal in two respects. First, it simply cannot be maintained, on this record, that appellants have been prohibited from occupying *any* portion of the airspace above the Terminal. While the Commission's actions in denying applications to construct an office building in excess of 50 stories above the Terminal may indicate that it will refuse to issue a certificate of appropriateness for any comparably sized structure, nothing the Commission has said or done suggests an intention to prohibit *any* construction above the Terminal. The Commission's report emphasized that whether any construction would be allowed depended upon whether the proposed addition "would harmonize in scale, material and character with [the Terminal]." Record 2251. Since appellants have not sought approval for the construction of a smaller structure, we do not know that appellants will be denied any use of any portion of the airspace above the Terminal.

Second, to the extent appellants have been denied the right to build above the Terminal, it is not literally accurate to say that they have been denied *all* use of even those pre-existing air rights. Their ability to use these rights has not been abrogated; they are made transferable to at least eight parcels in the vicinity of the Terminal, one or two of which have been found suitable for the construction of new office buildings. Although appellants and others have argued that New York City's transferable development-rights program is far from ideal, the New York courts here supportably found that, at least in the case of the Terminal, the rights afforded are valuable. While these rights may well not have constituted "just compensation" if a "taking" had occurred, the rights nevertheless undoubtedly mitigate whatever financial burdens the law has imposed on appellants and, for that reason, are to be taken into account in considering the impact of regulation. *Cf. Goldblatt v. Hempstead*, 369 U.S., at 594 n. 3, 82 S.Ct., at 990 n. 3.

On this record, we conclude that the application of New York City's Landmarks Law has not effected a "taking" of appellants' property. The restrictions imposed are substantially related to the promotion of the general welfare and not only permit reasonable beneficial use of the landmark site but also afford appellants opportunities further to enhance not only the Terminal site proper but also other properties.

[Footnotes omitted.]

AFFIRMED. [Dissent omitted.]

Two years later another refinement came in *Agins v. City of Tiburon,* 447 U.S. 255, 260, 100 S.Ct. 2138, 65 L.Ed.2d 106 (1980), which was to be applied in land use cases: (1) does the regulation deny all economically viable use; and (2) does the regulation substantially advance a legitimate government interest? Wetland regulation is considered a land use question thus the *Agins* two-part analysis has been applied but the *Penn Central* three-part test is subsumed into the economic viability inquiry in the *Agins* test.

AGINS v. CITY OF TIBURON

447 U.S. 255, 260, 100 S.Ct. 2138, 2141, 65 L.Ed.2d 106 (1980)

The question in this case is whether municipal zoning ordinances took appellants' property without just compensation in violation of the Fifth and Fourteenth Amendments.

I

After the appellants acquired five acres of unimproved land in the city of Tiburon, Cal., for residential development, the city was required by state law to prepare a general plan governing both land use and the development of open-space land. Cal.Govt.Code Ann. §§65302(a) and (e) (West Supp.1979); *see* §65563. In response, the city adopted two ordinances that modified existing zoning requirements. Tiburon, Cal., Ordinances Nos. 123 N.S. and 124 N.S. (June 28, 1973). The zoning ordinances placed the appellants' property in "RPD-1," a Residential Planned Development and Open Space Zone. RPD-1 property may be devoted to one-family dwellings, accessory buildings, and open-space uses. Density restrictions permit the appellants to build between one and five single-family residences on their 5-acre tract. The appellants never have sought approval for development of their land under the zoning ordinances.

The appellants filed a two-part complaint against the city in State Superior Court. The first cause of action sought $2 million in damages for inverse condemnation. The second cause of action requested a declaration that the zoning ordinances were facially unconstitutional. The gravamen of both claims was the appellants' assertion that the city had taken their property without just compensation in violation of the Fifth and Fourteenth Amendments. The complaint alleged that land in Tiburon has greater value than any other suburban property in the State of California. App. 3. The ridgelands that appellants own "possess magnificent views of San Francisco Bay and the scenic surrounding areas [and] have the highest market values of all lands" in Tiburon. *Id.*, at 4. Rezoning of the land "forever prevented [its] development for residential use...." *Id.*, at 5. Therefore, the appellants contended, the city had "completely destroyed the value of [appellants'] property for any purpose or use whatsoever...." *Id.*, at 7.

The city demurred, claiming that the complaint failed to state a cause of action. The Superior Court sustained the demurrer, and the California Supreme Court affirmed. 24 Cal.3d 266, 157 Cal.Rptr. 372, 598 P.2d 25 (1979). The State Supreme Court first considered the inverse condemnation claim. It held that a landowner who challenges the constitutionality of a zoning ordinance may not "sue in inverse condemnation and thereby transmute an excessive use of the police power into a lawful taking for which compensation in eminent domain must be paid." *Id.*, at 273, 157 Cal.Rptr. at 375, 598 P.2d, at 28. The sole remedies for such a taking, the court concluded, are mandamus and declaratory judgment. Turning therefore to the appellants' claim for declaratory relief, the California Supreme Court held that the zoning ordinances had not deprived the appellants of their property without compensation in violation of the Fifth Amendment.

We noted probable jurisdiction. 444 U.S. 1011, 100 S.Ct. 658, 62 L.Ed.2d 639 (1980). We now affirm the holding that the zoning ordinances on their face does not take the appellants' property without just compensation.

II

The Fifth Amendment guarantees that private property shall not "be taken for public use, without just compensation." The appellants' complaint framed the question as whether a zoning ordinance that prohibits all development of their land effects a taking under the Fifth and Fourteenth Amendments. The California Supreme Court rejected the appellants' characterization of the issue by holding, as a matter of state law, that the terms of the challenged ordinances allow the appellants to construct between one and five residences on their property. The court did not consider whether the zoning ordinances would be unconstitutional if applied to prevent appellants from building five homes. Because the appellants have not submitted a plan for development of their property as the ordinances permit, there is as yet no concrete controversy regarding the application of the specific zoning provisions. *See Socialist Labor Party v. Gilligan*, 406 U.S. 583, 588, 92 S.Ct. 1716, 1719, 32 L.Ed.2d 317 (1972). *See* also *Goldwater v. Carter*, 444 U.S. 996, 997, 100 S.Ct. 533, 534, 62 L.Ed.2d 428 (1979) (POWELL, J., concurring). Thus, the only question properly before us is whether the mere enactment of the zoning ordinances constitutes a taking.

The application of a general zoning law to particular property effects a taking if the ordinance does not substantially advance legitimate state interests, *see Nectow v. Cambridge*, 277 U.S. 183, 188, 48 S.Ct. 447, 448, 72 L.Ed. 842 (1928), or denies an owner economically viable use of his land, *see Penn Central Transp. Co. v. New York City*, 438 U.S. 104, 138, n. 36, 98 S.Ct. 2646, 2666, 57 L.Ed.2d 631 (1978). The determination that governmental action constitutes a taking is, in essence, a determination that the public at large, rather than a single owner, must bear the burden of an exercise of state power in the public interest. Although no precise rule determines when property has been taken, *see Kaiser Aetna v. United States*, 444 U.S. 164, 100 S.Ct. 383, 62 S.Ct. 332 (1979), the question necessarily requires a weighing of private and public interests. The seminal decision in *Euclid v. Ambler Co.*, 272 U.S. 365, 47 S.Ct. 114, 71 L.Ed. 303 (1926), is illustrative. In that case, the landowner challenged the constitutionality of a municipal ordinance that restricted commercial development of his property. Despite alleged diminution in value of the owner's land, the Court held that the zoning laws were facially constitutional. They bore a substantial relationship to the public welfare, and their enactment inflicted no irreparable injury upon the landowner. *Id.*, at 395-397, 47 S.Ct., at 121.

In this case, the zoning ordinances substantially advance legitimate governmental goals. The State of California has determined that the development of local open-space plans will discourage the "premature and unnecessary conversion of open-space land to urban uses." Cal.Govt.Code Ann. §65561(b) (West Supp.1979). Regulations at issue are exercises of the city's police power to protect the residents of Tiburon from the ill effects of urbanization. Such governmental purposes long have been recognized as legitimate. *See Penn Central Transp. Co. v. New York City, supra*, 438 U.S., at 129, 98 S.Ct., at 2662; *Village of Belle Terre v. Boraas*, 416 U.S. 1, 9, 94 S.Ct. 1536, 1541, 39 L.Ed.2d 797 (1974); *Euclid v. Ambler Co., supra*, 272 U.S., at 394-395, 47 S.Ct., at 120-121.

The ordinances place appellants' land in a zone limited to single-family dwellings, accessory buildings, and open-space uses. Construction is not permitted until the builder submits a plan compatible with "adjoining patterns of development and open space." Tiburon, Cal., Ordinance No. 123 N.S. §2(F). In passing upon a plan, the city also will consider how well the proposed development would preserve the surrounding environment and whether the density of new construction will be offset by adjoining open spaces. *Ibid.* The zoning ordinances benefit the appellants as well as the public by serving the city's interest in assuring careful and orderly development of residential property with provision for open-space areas. There is no indication that the appellants' 5-acre tract is the only property affected by the ordinances. Appellants therefore will share with other owners the benefits and burdens of the city's exercise of its police power. In assessing the fairness of the zoning ordinances, these benefits must be considered along with any diminution in market value that the appellants might suffer.

Although the ordinances limit development, they neither prevent the best use of appellants' land, *see United States v. Causby*, 328 U.S. 256, 262, and n.7, 66 S.Ct. 1062, 1066, 90 L.Ed. 1206 (1946), nor extinguish a fundamental attribute of ownership, *see Kaiser Aetna v. United States, supra*, at 179-180, 100 S.Ct., at 393. The appellants have alleged that they wish to develop the land for residential purposes, that the land is the most expensive suburban property in the State, and that the best possible use of the land is residential. App. 3-4. The California Supreme Court has decided, as a matter of state law, that appellants may be permitted to build as many as five houses on their five acres of prime residential property. At this juncture, the appellants are free to pursue their reasonable investment expectations by submitting a development plan to local officials. Thus, it cannot be said that the impact of general land-use regulations has denied appellants the "justice and fairness" guaranteed by the Fifth and Fourteenth Amendments. *SeePenn Central Transp. Co. v. New York City*, 438 U.S., at 124, 98 S.Ct., at 2659.[9]

---

[9] Appellants also claim that the city's precondemnation activities constitute a taking. *See* nn.1, 3, and 5, *supra*. The State Supreme Court correctly rejected the contention that the municipality's good-faith planning activities, which did not result in successful prosecution of an eminent domain claim, so burdened the appellants' enjoyment of their property as to constitute a taking. *See* also *City of Walnut Creek v. Leadership Housing Systems, Inc.*, 73 Cal.App.3d 611, 620-624, 140 Cal.Rptr. 690, 695-697 (1977). Even if the appellants' ability to sell their property was limited during the pendency of the condemnation proceeding, the appellants were free to sell or develop their property when the proceedings ended. Mere fluctuations in value during the process of governmental

continued on next page

III

The State Supreme Court determined that the appellants could not recover damages for inverse condemnation even if the zoning ordinances constituted a taking. The court stated that only mandamus and declaratory judgment are remedies available to such a landowner. Because no taking has occurred, we need not consider whether a State may limit the remedies available to a person whose land has been taken without just compensation.

The judgment of the Supreme Court of California is AFFIRMED.

Under the substantial advancement test, the old concept of abating a nuisance arises as the court first looks to see whether the intended but now regulated use was a nuisance. If the court finds a nuisance, the case ends and there is no taking. But if the court cannot find a nuisance, it must find some public benefit (a legitimate government interest) and then weigh the benefit against the burden to the landowner.

LUCAS v. SOUTH CAROLINA COASTAL COUNCIL

505 U.S. 1003, 112 S.Ct. 2886, 120 L.Ed.2d 798 (1992)

In 1986, petitioner David H. Lucas paid $975,000 for two residential lots on the Isle of Palms in Charleston County, South Carolina, on which he intended to build single-family homes. In 1988, however, the South Carolina Legislature enacted the Beachfront Management Act, S.C.Code Ann. §48-39-250 et seq. (Supp.1990), which had the direct effect of barring petitioner from erecting any permanent habitable structures on his two parcels. *See* §48-39-290(A). A state trial court found that this prohibition rendered Lucas's parcels "valueless." App. to Pet. for Cert. 37. This case requires us to decide whether the Act's dramatic effect on the economic value of Lucas's lots accomplished a taking of private property under the Fifth and Fourteenth Amendments requiring the payment of "just compensation." U.S. Const., Amdt. 5.

I

A

South Carolina's expressed interest in intensively managing development activities in the so-called "coastal zone" dates from 1977 when, in the aftermath of Congress's passage of the federal Coastal Zone Management Act of 1972, 86 Stat. 1280, as amended, 16 U.S.C. §1451 et seq., the legislature enacted a Coastal Zone Management Act of its own. *See* S.C.Code Ann. §48-39-10 et seq. (1987). In its original form, the South Carolina Act required owners of coastal zone

---

decisionmaking, absent extraordinary delay, are "incidents of ownership. They cannot be considered as a 'taking' in the constitutional sense." *Danforth v. United States*, 308 U.S. 271, 285, 60 S.Ct. 231, 236, 84 L.Ed. 240 (1939). *See Thomas W. Garland, Inc. v. City of St. Louis*, 596 F.2d 784, 787 (CA8), cert. denied, 444 U.S. 899, 100 S.Ct. 208, 62 L.Ed.2d 135 (1979); *Reservation Eleven Associates v. District of Columbia*, 136 U.S.App.D.C. 311, 315-316, 420 F.2d 153, 157-158 (1969); *Virgin Islands v. 50.05 Acres of Land*, 185 F.Supp. 495, 498 (V.I.1960); 2 J. Sackman & P. Rohan, Nichols' Law of Eminent Domain §6.13[3] (3d ed. 1979).

land that qualified as a "critical area" (defined in the legislation to include beaches and immediately adjacent sand dunes, §48-39-10(J)) to obtain a permit from the newly created South Carolina Coastal Council (Council) (respondent here) prior to committing the land to a "use other than the use the critical area was devoted to on [September 28, 1977]." §48-39-130(A).

In the late 1970's, Lucas and others began extensive residential development of the Isle of Palms, a barrier island situated eastward of the city of Charleston. Toward the close of the development cycle for one residential subdivision known as "Beachwood East," Lucas in 1986 purchased the two lots at issue in this litigation for his own account. No portion of the lots, which were located approximately 300 feet from the beach, qualified as a "critical area" under the 1977 Act; accordingly, at the time Lucas acquired these parcels, he was not legally obliged to obtain a permit from the Council in advance of any development activity. His intention with respect to the lots was to do what the owners of the immediately adjacent parcels had already done: erect single-family residences. He commissioned architectural drawings for this purpose.

The Beachfront Management Act brought Lucas's plans to an abrupt end. Under that 1988 legislation, the Council was directed to establish a "baseline" connecting the landward-most "point[s] of erosion ... during the past 40 years" in the region of the Isle of Palms that includes Lucas's lots. S.C.Code Ann. §48-39-280(A)(2) (Supp.1988). [Footnote omitted.] In action not challenged here, the Council fixed this baseline landward of Lucas's parcels. That was significant, for under the Act construction of occupiable improvements [footnote omitted] was flatly prohibited seaward of a line drawn 20 feet landward of, and parallel to, the baseline. §48-39-290(A). The Act provided no exceptions.

B

Lucas promptly filed suit in the South Carolina Court of Common Pleas, contending that the Beachfront Management Act's construction bar effected a taking of his property without just compensation. Lucas did not take issue with the validity of the Act as a lawful exercise of South Carolina's police power, but contended that the Act's complete extinguishment of his property's value entitled him to compensation regardless of whether the legislature had acted in furtherance of legitimate police power objectives. Following a bench trial, the court agreed. Among its factual determinations was the finding that "at the time Lucas purchased the two lots, both were zoned for single-family residential construction and ... there were no restrictions imposed upon such use of the property by either the State of South Carolina, the County of Charleston, or the Town of the Isle of Palms." App. to Pet. for Cert. 36. The trial court further found that the Beachfront Management Act decreed a permanent ban on construction insofar as Lucas's lots were concerned, and that this prohibition "deprive[d] Lucas of any reasonable economic use of the lots,... eliminated the unrestricted right of use, and render[ed] them valueless." *Id.*, at 37. The court thus concluded that Lucas's properties had been "taken" by operation of the Act, and it ordered respondent to pay "just compensation" in the amount of $1,232,387.50. *Id.*, at 40.

The Supreme Court of South Carolina reversed. It found dispositive what it described as Lucas's concession "that the Beachfront Management Act [was] properly and validly designed to preserve ... South Carolina's beaches." 304 S.C. 376, 379, 404 S.E.2d 895, 896 (1991). Failing an attack on the validity of the statute as such, the court believed itself bound to accept the "uncontested ... findings" of the South Carolina Legislature that new construction in the coastal zone—such as petitioner intended—threatened this public resource. *Id.*, at 383, 404 S.E.2d, at 898. The court ruled that when a regulation respecting the use of property is designed "to prevent serious public harm," *id.*, at 383, 404 S.E.2d, at 899 (citing, inter alia, *Mugler v. Kansas*, 123 U.S. 623, 8 S.Ct. 273, 31 L.Ed. 205 (1887)), no compensation is owing under the Takings Clause regardless of the regulation's effect on the property's value.

Two justices dissented. They acknowledged that our *Mugler* line of cases recognizes governmental power to prohibit "noxious" uses of property—*i.e.*, uses of property akin to "public nuisances"—without having to pay compensation. But they would not have characterized the Beachfront Management Act's "primary purpose [as] the prevention of a nuisance." 304 S.C., at 395, 404 S.E.2d, at 906 (Harwell, J., dissenting). To the dissenters, the chief purposes of the legislation, among them the promotion of tourism and the creation of a "habitat for indigenous flora and fauna," could not fairly be compared to nuisance abatement. *Id.*, at 396, 404 S.E.2d, at 906. As a consequence, they would have affirmed the trial court's conclusion that the Act's obliteration of the value of petitioner's lots accomplished a taking.

We granted certiorari. 502 U.S. 966, 112 S.Ct. 436, 116 L.Ed.2d 455 (1991).

II

As a threshold matter, we must briefly address the Council's suggestion that this case is inappropriate for plenary review. After briefing and argument before the South Carolina Supreme Court, but prior to issuance of that court's opinion, the Beachfront Management Act was amended to authorize the Council, in certain circumstances, to issue "special permits" for the construction or reconstruction of habitable structures seaward of the baseline. *See* S.C.Code Ann. §48-39- 290(D)(1) (Supp.1991). According to the Council, this amendment renders Lucas's claim of a permanent deprivation unripe, as Lucas may yet be able to secure permission to build on his property. "[The Court's] cases," we are reminded, "uniformly reflect an insistence on knowing the nature and extent of permitted development before adjudicating the constitutionality of the regulations that purport to limit it." *MacDonald, Sommer & Frates v. Yolo County*, 477 U.S. 340, 351, 106 S.Ct. 2561, 2567, 91 L.Ed.2d285 (1986). *See* also *Agins v. City of Tiburon*, 447 U.S. 255, 260, 100 S.Ct. 2138, 2141, 65 L.Ed.2d 106 (1980). Because petitioner "has not yet obtained a final decision regarding how [he] will be allowed to develop [his] property," *Williamson County Regional Planning Comm'n v. Hamilton Bank of Johnson City*, 473 U.S. 172, 190, 105 S.Ct. 3108, 3118, 87 L.Ed.2d 126 (1985), the Council argues that he is not yet entitled to definitive adjudication of his takings claim in this Court.

We think these considerations would preclude review had the South Carolina Supreme Court rested its judgment on ripeness grounds, as it was (essentially) invited to do by the Council. *See* Brief for Respondent 9, n.3. The South Carolina Supreme Court shrugged off the possibility of further administrative and trial proceedings, however, preferring to dispose of Lucas's takings claim on the merits. *Cf., e.g., San Diego Gas & Electric Co. v. San Diego*, 450 U.S. 621, 631-632, 101 S.Ct. 1287, 1293-1294, 67 L.Ed.2d 551 (1981). This unusual disposition does not preclude Lucas from applying for a permit under the 1990 amendment for future construction, and challenging, on takings grounds, any denial. But it does preclude, both practically and legally, any takings claim with respect to Lucas's past deprivation, *i.e.*, for his having been denied construction rights during the period before the 1990 amendment. *See* generally *First English Evangelical Lutheran Church of Glendale v. County of Los Angeles*, 482 U.S. 304, 107 S.Ct. 2378, 96 L.Ed.2d 250 (1987) (holding that temporary deprivations of use are compensable under the Takings Clause). Without even so much as commenting upon the consequences of the South Carolina Supreme Court's judgment in this respect, the Council insists that permitting Lucas to press his claim of a past deprivation on this appeal would be improper, since "the issues of whether and to what extent [Lucas] has incurred a temporary taking ... have simply never been addressed." Brief for Respondent 11. Yet Lucas had no reason to proceed on a "temporary taking" theory at trial, or even to seek remand for that purpose prior to submission of the case to the South Carolina Supreme Court, since as the Act then read, the taking was unconditional and permanent. Moreover, given the breadth of the South Carolina Supreme Court's holding and judgment, Lucas would plainly be unable (absent our intervention now) to obtain further state-court adjudication with respect to the 1988-1990 period.

In these circumstances, we think it would not accord with sound process to insist that Lucas pursue the late-created "special permit" procedure before his takings claim can be considered ripe. Lucas has properly alleged Article III injury in fact in this case, with respect to both the pre-1990 and post-1990 constraints placed on the use of his parcels by the Beachfront Management Act.[3] That there is a discretionary "special permit" procedure by which he may regain—for the future, at least—beneficial use of his land goes only to the prudential "ripeness" of Lucas's challenge, and for the reasons discussed we do not think it prudent to apply that prudential requirement here. *See Esposito v. South Carolina Coastal Council*, 939 F.2d 165, 168 (CA4 1991), cert. denied, 505 U.S. 1219, 112 S.Ct. 3027, 120 L.Ed.2d 898 (1992).[4] We leave for decision on remand, of course, the questions left unaddressed by the South Carolina Supreme Court as a consequence of its categorical disposition.[5]

---

[3] Justice BLACKMUN insists that this aspect of Lucas's claim is "not justiciable," post, at 2907, because Lucas never fulfilled his obligation under *Williamson County Regional Planning Comm'n v. Hamilton Bank of Johnson City*, 473 U.S. 172, 105 S.Ct. 3108, 87 L.Ed.2d 126 (1985), to "submi[t] a plan for development of [his] property" to the proper state authorities, *id.*, at 187, 105 S.Ct., at 3117. *See* post, at 2907. But such a submission would have been pointless, as the Council stipulated below that no building permit would have been issued under the 1988 Act, application or no application. Record 14 (stipulations). Nor does the peculiar posture of this case mean that we are without Article III jurisdiction, as Justice BLACKMUN apparently believes. *See* post, at 2907, and n.5. Given the South Carolina Supreme Court's dismissive foreclosure of further pleading and adjudication with respect to the pre-1990 component of Lucas's takings claim, it is appropriate for us to address that component as if the case were here on the pleadings alone. Lucas properly alleged injury in fact in his complaint. *See* App. to Pet. for Cert. 154 (complaint); *id.*, at 156 (asking "damages for the temporary taking of his property" from the date of the 1988 Act's passage to "such time as this matter is finally resolved"). No more can reasonably be demanded. *Cf. First English Evangelical Lutheran Church of Glendale v. County of Los Angeles*, 482 U.S. 304, 312-313, 107 S.Ct. 2378, 2384, 96 L.Ed.2d 250 (1987). Justice BLACKMUN finds it "baffling," post, at 2908, n.5, that we grant standing here, whereas "just a few days ago, in *Lujan v. Defenders of Wildlife*, 504 U.S. 555, 112 S.Ct. 2130, 119 L.Ed.2d 351 (1992)," we denied standing. He sees in that strong evidence to support his repeated imputations that the Court "presses" to take this case, post, at 2904, is "eager to decide" it, post, at 2909, and is unwilling to "be denied," post, at 2907. He has a point: The decisions are indeed very close in time, yet one grants standing and the other denies it. The distinction, however, rests in law rather than chronology. Lujan, since it involved the establishment of injury in fact at the summary judgment stage, required specific facts to be adduced by sworn testimony; had the same challenge to a generalized allegation of injury in fact been made at the pleading stage, it would have been unsuccessful.

[4] In that case, the Court of Appeals for the Fourth Circuit reached the merits of a takings challenge to the 1988 Beachfront Management Act identical to the one Lucas brings here even though the Act was amended, and the special permit procedure established, while the case was under submission. The court observed:

> "The enactment of the 1990 Act during the pendency of this appeal, with its provisions for special permits and other changes that may affect the plaintiffs, does not relieve us of the need to address the plaintiffs' claims under the provisions of the 1988 Act. Even if the amended Act cured all of the plaintiffs' concerns, the amendments would not foreclose the possibility that a taking had occurred during the years when the 1988 Act was in effect." *Esposito v. South Carolina Coastal Council*, 939 F.2d 165, 168 (1991).

[5] Justice BLACKMUN states that our "intense interest in Lucas' plight ... would have been more prudently expressed by vacating the judgment below and remanding for further consideration in light of the 1990 amendments" to the

continued on next page

III

A

Prior to Justice Holmes's exposition in *Pennsylvania Coal Co. v. Mahon*, 260 U.S. 393, 43 S.Ct. 158, 67 L.Ed. 322 (1922), it was generally thought that the Takings Clause reached only a "direct appropriation" of property, Legal Tender Cases, 12 Wall. 457, 551, 20 L.Ed. 287 (1871), or the functional equivalent of a "practical ouster of [the owner's] possession," *Transportation Co. v. Chicago*, 99 U.S. 635, 642, 25 L.Ed. 336 (1879). *See* also *Gibson v. United States*, 166 U.S. 269, 275-276, 17 S.Ct. 578, 580, 41 L.Ed. 996 (1897). Justice Holmes recognized in *Mahon*, however, that if the protection against physical appropriations of private property was to be meaningfully enforced, the government's power to redefine the range of interests included in the ownership of property was necessarily constrained by constitutional limits. 260 U.S., at 414-415, 43 S.Ct., at 160. If, instead, the uses of private property were subject to unbridled, uncompensated qualification under the police power, "the natural tendency of human nature [would be] to extend the qualification more and more until at last private property disappear[ed]." *Id.*, at 415, 43 S.Ct., at 160. These considerations gave birth in that case to the oft-cited maxim that, "while property may be regulated to a certain extent, if regulation goes too far it will be recognized as a taking." *Ibid.*

Nevertheless, our decision in *Mahon* offered little insight into when, and under what circumstances, a given regulation would be seen as going "too far" for purposes of the Fifth Amendment. In 70-odd years of succeeding "regulatory takings" jurisprudence, we have generally eschewed any "set formula" for determining how far is too far, preferring to "engag[e] in ... essentially ad hoc, factual inquiries." *Penn Central Transportation Co. v. New York City*, 438 U.S. 104, 124, 98 S.Ct. 2646, 2659, 57 L.Ed.2d 631 (1978) (quoting *Goldblatt v. Hempstead*, 369 U.S. 590, 594, 82 S.Ct. 987, 990, 8 L.Ed.2d 130 (1962)). *See* Epstein, *Takings: Descent and Resurrection*, 1987 S.Ct. Rev. 1, 4. We have, however, described at least two discrete categories of regulatory action as compensable without case-specific inquiry into the public interest advanced in support of the restraint. The first encompasses regulations that compel the property owner to suffer a physical "invasion" of his property. In general (at least with regard to permanent invasions), no matter how minute the intrusion, and no matter how weighty the public purpose behind it, we have required compensation. For example, in *Loretto v. Teleprompter Manhattan CATV Corp.*, 458 U.S. 419, 102 S.Ct. 3164, 73 L.Ed.2d 868 (1982), we determined that New York's law requiring landlords to allow television cable companies to emplace cable facilities in their apartment buildings constituted a taking, *id.*, at 435-440, 102 S.Ct., at 3175-3178, even though the facilities occupied at most only 1 1/2 cubic feet of the landlords' property, *See id.*, at 438, n. 16, 102 S.Ct., at 3177. *See* also *United States v. Causby*, 328 U.S. 256, 265, and n. 10, 66 S.Ct. 1062, 1067, and n. 10, 90 L.Ed. 1206 (1946) (physical invasions of airspace); *cf. Kaiser Aetna v. United States*, 444 U.S. 164, 100 S.Ct. 383, 62 L.Ed.2d 332 (1979) (imposition of navigational servitude upon private marina).

Beachfront Management Act. Post, at 2909, n.7. That is a strange suggestion, given that the South Carolina Supreme Court rendered its categorical disposition in this case after the Act had been amended, and after it had been invited to consider the effect of those amendments on Lucas's case. We have no reason to believe that the justices of the South Carolina Supreme Court are any more desirous of using a narrower ground now than they were then; and neither "prudence" nor any other principle of judicial restraint requires that we remand to find out whether they have changed their mind.

The second situation in which we have found categorical treatment appropriate is where regulation denies all economically beneficial or productive use of land. *See Agins*, 447 U.S., at 260, 100 S.Ct., at 2141; *See* also *Nollan v. California Coastal Comm'n*, 483 U.S. 825, 834, 107 S.Ct. 3141, 3147, 97 L.Ed.2d 677 (1987); *Keystone Bituminous Coal Assn. v. DeBenedictis*, 480 U.S. 470, 495, 107 S.Ct. 1232, 1247, 94 L.Ed.2d 472 (1987); *Hodel v. Virginia Surface Mining & Reclamation Assn., Inc.*, 452 U.S. 264, 295- 296, 101 S.Ct. 2352, 2370, 69 L.Ed.2d 1 (1981).[6] As we have said on numerous occasions, the Fifth Amendment is violated when land-use regulation "does not substantially advance legitimate state interests or denies an owner economically viable use of his land." *Agins*, *supra*, 447 U.S., at 260, 100 S.Ct., at 2141 (citations omitted) (emphasis added).[7]

---

[6] We will not attempt to respond to all of Justice BLACKMUN's mistaken citation of case precedent. Characteristic of its nature is his assertion that the cases we discuss here stand merely for the proposition "that proof that a regulation does not deny an owner economic use of his property is sufficient to defeat a facial takings challenge" and not for the point that "denial of such use is sufficient to establish a takings claim regardless of any other consideration." Post, at 2911, n.11. The cases say, repeatedly and unmistakably, that "'[t]he test to be applied in considering [a] facial [takings] challenge is fairly straightforward. A statute regulating the uses that can be made of property effects a taking if it 'denies an owner economically viable use of his land.'" *Keystone*, 480 U.S., at 495, 107 S.Ct., at 1247 (quoting *Hodel*, 452 U.S., at 295-296, 101 S.Ct., at 2370 (quoting *Agins*, 447 U.S., at 260, 100 S.Ct., at 2141)) (emphasis added).

Justice BLACKMUN describes that rule (which we do not invent but merely apply today) as "alter[ing] the long-settled rules of review" by foisting on the State "the burden of showing [its] regulation is not a taking." Post, at 2909. This is of course wrong. Lucas had to do more than simply file a lawsuit to establish his constitutional entitlement; he had to show that the Beachfront Management Act denied him economically beneficial use of his land. Our analysis presumes the unconstitutionality of state land-use regulation only in the sense that any rule with exceptions presumes the invalidity of a law that violates it—for example, the rule generally prohibiting content-based restrictions on speech. *See, e.g., Simon & Schuster, Inc. v. N.Y. Members of State Crime Victims Bd.*, 502 U.S. 105, 115, 112 S.Ct. 501, 508, 116 L.Ed.2d 476 (1991) ("A statute is presumptively inconsistent with the First Amendment if it imposes a financial burden on speakers because of the content of their speech"). Justice BLACKMUN's real quarrel is with the substantive standard of liability we apply in this case, a long-established standard we see no need to repudiate.

[7] Regrettably, the rhetorical force of our "deprivation of all economically feasible use" rule is greater than its precision, since the rule does not make clear the "property interest" against which the loss of value is to be measured. When, for example, a regulation requires a developer to leave 90 percent of a rural tract in its natural state, it is unclear whether we would analyze the situation as one in which the owner has been deprived of all economically beneficial use of the burdened portion of the tract, or as one in which the owner has suffered a mere diminution in value of the tract as a whole. (For an extreme—and, we think, unsupportable—view of the relevant calculus, *see Penn Central Transportation Co. v. New York City*, 42 N.Y.2d 324, 333-334, 397 N.Y.S.2d 914, 920, 366 N.E.2d 1271, 1276-1277 (1977), aff'd, 438 U.S. 104, 98 S.Ct. 2646, 57 L.Ed.2d 631 (1978), where the state court examined the diminution in a particular parcel's value produced by a municipal ordinance in light of total value of the takings claimant's other holdings in the vicinity.) Unsurprisingly, this uncertainty regarding the composition of the denominator in our "deprivation" fraction has produced inconsistent pronouncements by the Court. Compare *Pennsylvania Coal Co. v. Mahon*, 260 U.S. 393, 414, 43 S.Ct. 158, 160, 67 L.Ed. 322 (1922) (law restricting subsurface extraction of coal held to effect a taking), with *Keystone Bituminous Coal Assn. v. DeBenedictis*, 480 U.S. 470, 497-502, 107 S.Ct. 1232, 1248-1251, 94 L.Ed.2d 472 (1987) (nearly identical law held not to effect a taking); *see* also id., at 515-520, 107 S.Ct., at 1257-1260 (REHNQUIST, C.J., dissenting); Rose, *Mahon Reconstructed: Why the Takings Issue is Still a Muddle,* 57 S.Cal.L.Rev. 561, 566-569 (1984). The answer to this difficult question may lie in how the owner's reasonable expectations have been shaped by the State's law of property—*i.e.*, whether and to what degree the State's law has accorded legal recognition and protection to the particular interest in land with respect to which the takings claimant alleges a diminution in (or elimination of) value. In any event, we avoid this difficulty in the present case, since the "interest in land" that Lucas has pleaded (a fee simple interest) is an estate with a rich tradition of protection at common law, and since the South Carolina Court of Common Pleas found that the Beachfront Management Act left each of Lucas's beachfront lots without economic value.

We have never set forth the justification for this rule. Perhaps it is simply, as Justice Brennan suggested, that total deprivation of beneficial use is, from the landowner's point of view, the equivalent of a physical appropriation. *See San Diego Gas & Electric Co. v. San Diego*, 450 U.S., at 652, 101 S.Ct., at 1304 (dissenting opinion). "[F]or what is the land but the profits thereof[?]" 1 E. Coke, Institutes, ch. 1, §1 (1st Am. ed. 1812). Surely, at least, in the extraordinary circumstance when no productive or economically beneficial use of land is permitted, it is less realistic to indulge our usual assumption that the legislature is simply "adjusting the benefits and burdens of economic life," *Penn Central Transportation Co.*, 438 U.S., at 124, 98 S.Ct., at 2659, in a manner that secures an "average reciprocity of advantage" to everyone concerned, *Pennsylvania Coal Co. v. Mahon*, 260 U.S., at 415, 43 S.Ct., at 160. And the functional basis for permitting the government, by regulation, to affect property values without compensation—that "Government hardly could go on if to some extent values incident to property could not be diminished without paying for every such change in the general law," *id.*, at 413, 43 S.Ct., at 159—does not apply to the relatively rare situations where the government has deprived a landowner of all economically beneficial uses.

On the other side of the balance, affirmatively supporting a compensation requirement, is the fact that regulations that leave the owner of land without economically beneficial or productive options for its use—typically, as here, by requiring land to be left substantially in its natural state—carry with them a heightened risk that private property is being pressed into some form of public service under the guise of mitigating serious public harm. *See, e.g., Annicelli v. South Kingstown*, 463 A.2d 133, 140- 141 (R.I.1983) (prohibition on construction adjacent to beach justified on twin grounds of safety and "conservation of open space"); *Morris County Land Improvement Co. v. Parsippany-Troy Hills Township*, 40 N.J. 539, 552-553, 193 A.2d 232, 240 (1963) (prohibition on filling marshlands imposed in order to preserve region as water detention basin and create wildlife refuge). As Justice Brennan explained: "From the government's point of view, the benefits flowing to the public from preservation of open space through regulation may be equally great as from creating a wildlife refuge through formal condemnation or increasing electricity production through a dam project that floods private property." *San Diego Gas & Elec. Co., supra*, 450 U.S., at 652, 101 S.Ct., at 1304 (dissenting opinion). The many statutes on the books, both state and federal, that provide for the use of eminent domain to impose servitudes on private scenic lands preventing developmental uses, or to acquire such lands altogether, suggest the practical equivalence in this setting of negative regulation and appropriation. *See, e.g.*, 16 U.S.C. §410ff-1(a) (authorizing acquisition of "lands, waters, or interests [within Channel Islands National Park] (including but not limited to scenic easements)"); §460aa-2(a) (authorizing acquisition of "any lands, or lesser interests therein, including mineral interests and scenic easements" within Sawtooth National Recreation Area); §§3921-3923 (authorizing acquisition of wetlands); N.C. Gen.Stat. §113A-38 (1990) (authorizing acquisition of, inter alia, "'scenic easements'" within the North Carolina natural and scenic rivers system); Tenn.Code Ann. §§11-15-101 to 11-15-108 (1987) (authorizing acquisition of "protective easements" and other rights in real property adjacent to State's historic, architectural, archaeological, or cultural resources).

We think, in short, that there are good reasons for our frequently expressed belief that when the owner of real property has been called upon to sacrifice all economically beneficial uses in the name of the common good, that is, to leave his property economically idle, he has suffered a taking.[8]

B

The trial court found Lucas's two beachfront lots to have been rendered valueless by respondent's enforcement of the coastal-zone construction ban.[9] Under Lucas's theory of the case, which rested upon our "no economically viable use" statements, that finding entitled him to compensation. Lucas believed it unnecessary to take issue with either the purposes behind the Beachfront Management Act, or the means chosen by the South Carolina Legislature to effectuate those purposes. The South Carolina Supreme Court, however, thought otherwise. In its view, the Beachfront Management Act was no ordinary enactment, but involved an exercise of South Carolina's "police powers" to mitigate the harm to the public interest that petitioner's use of his land might occasion. 304 S.C., at 384, 404 S.E.2d, at 899. By neglecting to dispute the findings enumerated in the Act[10] or otherwise to challenge the legislature's purposes, petitioner "concede[d] that the beach/dune area of South Carolina's shores is an extremely valuable public resource; that the erection of new construction, inter alia, contributes to the erosion and destruction of

---

[8] Justice STEVENS criticizes the "deprivation of all economically beneficial use" rule as "wholly arbitrary," in that "[the] landowner whose property is diminished in value 95 percent recovers nothing," while the landowner who suffers a complete elimination of value "recovers the land's full value." Post, at 2919. This analysis errs in its assumption that the landowner whose deprivation is one step short of complete is not entitled to compensation. Such an owner might not be able to claim the benefit of our categorical formulation, but, as we have acknowledged time and again, "[t]he economic impact of the regulation on the claimant and ... the extent to which the regulation has interfered with distinct investment-backed expectations" are keenly relevant to takings analysis generally. *Penn Central Transportation Co. v. New York City*, 438 U.S. 104, 124, 98 S.Ct. 2646, 2659, 57 L.Ed.2d 631 (1978). It is true that in at least some cases the landowner with 95 percent loss will get nothing, while the landowner with total loss will recover in full. But that occasional result is no more strange than the gross disparity between the landowner whose premises are taken for a highway (who recovers in full) and the landowner whose property is reduced to 5 percent of its former value by the highway (who recovers nothing). Takings law is full of these "all-or-nothing" situations.

Justice STEVENS similarly misinterprets our focus on "developmental" uses of property (the uses proscribed by the Beachfront Management Act) as betraying an "assumption that the only uses of property cognizable under the Constitution are developmental uses." Post, at 2919, n.3. We make no such assumption. Though our prior takings cases evince an abiding concern for the productive use of, and economic investment in, land, there are plainly a number of noneconomic interests in land whose impairment will invite exceedingly close scrutiny under the Takings Clause. *See, e.g., Loretto v. Teleprompter Manhattan CATV Corp.*, 458 U.S. 419, 436, 102 S.Ct. 3164, 3176, 73 L.Ed.2d 868 (1982) (interest in excluding strangers from one's land).

[9] This finding was the premise of the petition for certiorari, and since it was not challenged in the brief in opposition we decline to entertain the argument in respondent's brief on the merits, *see* Brief for Respondent 45-50, that the finding was erroneous. Instead, we decide the question presented under the same factual assumptions as did the Supreme Court of South Carolina. *See Oklahoma City v. Tuttle*, 471 U.S. 808, 816, 105 S.Ct. 2427, 2432, 85 L.Ed.2d 791 (1985).

[10] The legislature's express findings include the following:
"The General Assembly finds that:
"(1) The beach/dune system along the coast of South Carolina is extremely important to the people of this State and serves the following functions:
"(a) protects life and property by serving as a storm barrier which dissipates wave energy and contributes to shoreline stability in an economical and effective manner;

continued on next page

this public resource; and that discouraging new construction in close proximity to the beach/dune area is necessary to prevent a great public harm." *Id.*, at 382- 383, 404 S.E.2d, at 898. In the court's view, these concessions brought petitioner's challenge within a long line of this Court's cases sustaining against Due Process and Takings Clause challenges the State's use of its "police powers" to enjoin a property owner from activities akin to public nuisances. *See Mugler v. Kansas*, 123 U.S. 623, 8 S.Ct. 273, 31 L.Ed. 205 (1887) (law prohibiting manufacture of alcoholic beverages); *Hadacheck v. Sebastian*, 239 U.S. 394, 36 S.Ct. 143, 60 L.Ed. 348 (1915) (law barring operation of brick mill in residential area); *Miller v. Schoene*, 276 U.S. 272, 48 S.Ct. 246, 72 L.Ed. 568 (1928) (order to destroy diseased cedar trees to prevent infection of nearby orchards); *Goldblatt v. Hempstead*, 369 U.S. 590, 82 S.Ct. 987, 8 L.Ed.2d 130 (1962) (law effectively preventing continued operation of quarry in residential area).

It is correct that many of our prior opinions have suggested that "harmful or noxious uses" of property may be proscribed by government regulation without the requirement of compensation. For a number of reasons, however, we think the South Carolina Supreme Court was too quick to conclude that that principle decides the present case. The "harmful or noxious uses" principle was the Court's early attempt to describe in theoretical terms why government may, consistent with the Takings Clause, affect property values by regulation without incurring an obligation to compensate—a reality we nowadays acknowledge explicitly with respect to the full scope of the State's police power. *See, e.g., Penn Central Transportation Co.*, 438 U.S., at 125, 98 S.Ct., at 2659 (where State "reasonably conclude[s] that 'the health, safety, morals, or general welfare' would be promoted by prohibiting particular contemplated uses of land," compensation need not accompany prohibition); *See* also *Nollan v. California Coastal Comm'n*, 483 U.S., at 834-835, 107 S.Ct., at 3147 ("Our cases have not elaborated on the standards for determining what constitutes a 'legitimate state interest[,]' [but] [t]hey have made clear ... that a broad range of governmental purposes and regulations satisfy these requirements"). We made this

---

"(b) provides the basis for a tourism industry that generates approximately two-thirds of South Carolina's annual tourism industry revenue which constitutes a significant portion of the state's economy. The tourists who come to the South Carolina coast to enjoy the ocean and dry sand beach contribute significantly to state and local tax revenues;

"(c) provides habitat for numerous species of plants and animals, several of which are threatened or endangered. Waters adjacent to the beach/dune system also provide habitat for many other marine species;

"(d) provides a natural health environment for the citizens of South Carolina to spend leisure time which serves their physical and mental well-being.

"(2) Beach/dune system vegetation is unique and extremely important to the vitality and preservation of the system.

"(3) Many miles of South Carolina's beaches have been identified as critically eroding.

"(4) ... [D]evelopment unwisely has been sited too close to the [beach/dune] system. This type of development has jeopardized the stability of the beach/dune system, accelerated erosion, and endangered adjacent property. It is in both the public and private interests to protect the system from this unwise development.

"(5) The use of armoring in the form of hard erosion control devices such as seawalls, bulkheads, and rip-rap to protect erosion-threatened structures adjacent to the beach has not proven effective. These armoring devices have given a false sense of security to beachfront property owners. In reality, these hard structures, in many instances, have increased the vulnerability of beachfront property to damage from wind and waves while contributing to the deterioration and loss of the dry sand beach which is so important to the tourism industry.

"(6) Erosion is a natural process which becomes a significant problem for man only when structures are erected in close proximity to the beach/dune system. It is in both the public and private interests to afford the beach/dune system space to accrete and erode in its natural cycle. This space can be provided only by discouraging new construction in close proximity to the beach/dune system and encouraging those who have erected structures too close to the system to retreat from it....

"(8) It is in the state's best interest to protect and to promote increased public access to South Carolina's beaches for out-of-state tourists and South Carolina residents alike." S.C. Code Ann. §48-39-250 (Supp.1991).

very point in *Penn Central Transportation Co.*, where, in the course of sustaining New York City's landmarks preservation program against a takings challenge, we rejected the petitioner's suggestion that Mugler and the cases following it were premised on, and thus limited by, some objective conception of "noxiousness":

> "[T]he uses in issue in *Hadacheck*, *Miller*, and *Goldblatt* were perfectly lawful in themselves. They involved no 'blameworthiness, ... moral wrongdoing or conscious act of dangerous risk-taking which induce[d society] to shift the cost to a pa[rt]icular individual.' Sax, *Takings and the Police Power*, 74 Yale L.J. 36, 50 (1964). These cases are better understood as resting not on any supposed 'noxious' quality of the prohibited uses but rather on the ground that the restrictions were reasonably related to the implementation of a policy—not unlike historic preservation—expected to produce a widespread public benefit and applicable to all similarly situated property." 438 U.S., at 133-134, n. 30, 98 S.Ct., at 2664, n. 30.

"Harmful or noxious use" analysis was, in other words, simply the progenitor of our more contemporary statements that "land-use regulation does not effect a taking if it 'substantially advance[s] legitimate state interests'...." *Nollan*, *supra*, 483 U.S., at 834, 107 S.Ct., at 3147 (quoting *Agins v. Tiburon*, 447 U.S., at 260, 100 S.Ct., at 2141); *see* also *Penn Central Transportation Co.*, *supra*, 438 U.S., at 127, 98 S.Ct., at 2660; *Euclid v. Ambler Realty Co.*, 272 U.S. 365, 387-388, 47 S.Ct. 114, 118, 71 L.Ed. 303 (1926).

The transition from our early focus on control of "noxious" uses to our contemporary understanding of the broad realm within which government may regulate without compensation was an easy one, since the distinction between "harm-preventing" and "benefit-conferring" regulation is often in the eye of the beholder. It is quite possible, for example, to describe in either fashion the ecological, economic, and esthetic concerns that inspired the South Carolina Legislature in the present case. One could say that imposing a servitude on Lucas's land is necessary in order to prevent his use of it from "harming" South Carolina's ecological resources; or, instead, in order to achieve the "benefits" of an ecological preserve.[11] Compare, *e.g.*, *Claridge v. New Hampshire Wetlands Board*, 125 N.H. 745, 752, 485 A.2d 287, 292 (1984) (owner may, without compensation, be barred from filling wetlands because landfilling would deprive adjacent coastal habitats and marine fisheries of ecological support), with, *e.g.*, *Bartlett v. Zoning Comm'n of Old Lyme*, 161 Conn. 24, 30, 282 A.2d 907, 910 (1971) (owner barred from filling tidal

---

[11] In the present case, in fact, some of the "[South Carolina] legislature's 'findings'" to which the South Carolina Supreme Court purported to defer in characterizing the purpose of the Act as "harm-preventing," 304 S.C. 376, 385, 404 S.E.2d 895, 900 (1991), seem to us phrased in "benefit-conferring" language instead. For example, they describe the importance of a construction ban in enhancing "South Carolina's annual tourism industry revenue," S.C. Code Ann. §48-39- 250(1)(b) (Supp.1991), in "provid[ing] habitat for numerous species of plants and animals, several of which are threatened or endangered," §48-39-250(1)(c), and in "provid[ing] a natural healthy environment for the citizens of South Carolina to spend leisure time which serves their physical and mental well-being," §48-39-250(1)(d). It would be pointless to make the outcome of this case hang upon this terminology, since the same interests could readily be described in "harm-preventing" fashion.

Justice BLACKMUN, however, apparently insists that we must make the outcome hinge (exclusively) upon the South Carolina Legislature's other, "harm-preventing" characterizations, focusing on the declaration that "prohibitions on building in front of the setback line are necessary to protect people and property from storms, high tides, and beach erosion." Post, at 2906. He says "[n]othing in the record undermines [this] assessment," *ibid.*, apparently seeing no significance in the fact that the statute permits owners of existing structures to remain (and even to rebuild if their structures are not "destroyed beyond repair," S.C. Code Ann. §48-39-290(B) (Supp.1988)), and in the fact that the 1990 amendment authorizes the Council to issue permits for new construction in violation of the uniform prohibition, *see* S.C. Code Ann. §48-39-290(D)(1) (Supp.1991).

marshland must be compensated, despite municipality's "laudable" goal of "preserv[ing] marshlands from encroachment or destruction"). Whether one or the other of the competing characterizations will come to one's lips in a particular case depends primarily upon one's evaluation of the worth of competing uses of real estate. *See* Restatement (Second) of Torts §822, Comment g, p. 112 (1979) ("Practically all human activities unless carried on in a wilderness interfere to some extent with others or involve some risk of interference"). A given restraint will be seen as mitigating "harm" to the adjacent parcels or securing a "benefit" for them, depending upon the observer's evaluation of the relative importance of the use that the restraint favors. *See* Sax, *Takings and the Police Power*, 74 Yale L.J. 36, 49 (1964) ("[T]he problem [in this area] is not one of noxiousness or harm-creating activity at all; rather it is a problem of inconsistency between perfectly innocent and independently desirable uses"). Whether Lucas's construction of single-family residences on his parcels should be described as bringing "harm" to South Carolina's adjacent ecological resources thus depends principally upon whether the describer believes that the State's use interest in nurturing those resources is so important that any competing adjacent use must yield.[12]

When it is understood that "prevention of harmful use" was merely our early formulation of the police power justification necessary to sustain (without compensation) any regulatory diminution in value; and that the distinction between regulation that "prevents harmful use" and that which "confers benefits" is difficult, if not impossible, to discern on an objective, value-free basis; it becomes self-evident that noxious-use logic cannot serve as a touchstone to distinguish regulatory "takings"—which require compensation—from regulatory deprivations that do not require compensation. A fortiori the legislature's recitation of a noxious-use justification cannot be the basis for departing from our categorical rule that total regulatory takings must be compensated. If it were, departure would virtually always be allowed. The South Carolina Supreme Court's approach would essentially nullify *Mahon*'s affirmation of limits to the noncompensable exercise of the police power. Our cases provide no support for this: None of them that employed the logic of "harmful use" prevention to sustain a regulation involved an allegation that the regulation wholly eliminated the value of the claimant's land. *See Keystone Bituminous Coal Assn.*, 480 U.S., at 513-514, 107 S.Ct., at 1257 (REHNQUIST, C.J., dissenting). [Footnote omitted]

Where the State seeks to sustain regulation that deprives land of all economically beneficial use, we think it may resist compensation only if the logically antecedent inquiry into the nature of the owner's estate shows that the proscribed use interests were not part of his title to begin with. [Footnote omitted] This accords, we think, with our "takings" jurisprudence, which has traditionally been guided by the understandings of our citizens regarding the content of, and the State's power over, the "bundle of rights" that they acquire when they obtain title to property. It seems to us that the property owner necessarily expects the uses of his property to be restricted, from time to time, by various measures newly enacted by the State in legitimate exercise of its police powers; "[a]s long recognized, some values are enjoyed under an implied limitation and must yield to the police power." *Pennsylvania Coal Co. v. Mahon*, 260 U.S., at 413, 43 S.Ct., at 159. And in the case of personal property, by reason of the State's traditionally high degree of control over commercial dealings, he ought to be aware of the possibility that new regulation

---

[12] In Justice BLACKMUN's view, even with respect to regulations that deprive an owner of all developmental or economically beneficial land uses, the test for required compensation is whether the legislature has recited a harm-preventing justification for its action. *See* post, at 2906, 2910-2912. Since such a justification can be formulated in practically every case, this amounts to a test of whether the legislature has a stupid staff. We think the Takings Clause requires courts to do more than insist upon artful harm-preventing characterizations.

might even render his property economically worthless (at least if the property's only economically productive use is sale or manufacture for sale). *See Andrus v. Allard*, 444 U.S. 51, 66-67, 100 S.Ct. 318, 327, 62 L.Ed.2d 210 (1979) (prohibition on sale of eagle feathers). In the case of land, however, we think the notion pressed by the Council that title is somehow held subject to the "implied limitation" that the State may subsequently eliminate all economically valuable use is inconsistent with the historical compact recorded in the Takings Clause that has become part of our constitutional culture. [Footnote omitted.]

Where "permanent physical occupation" of land is concerned, we have refused to allow the government to decree it anew (without compensation), no matter how weighty the asserted "public interests" involved, *Loretto v. Teleprompter Manhattan CATV Corp.*, 458 U.S., at 426, 102 S.Ct., at 3171—though we assuredly would permit the government to assert a permanent easement that was a pre-existing limitation upon the landowner's title. Compare *Scranton v. Wheeler*, 179 U.S. 141, 163, 21 S.Ct. 48, 57, 45 L.Ed. 126 (1900) (interests of "riparian owner in the submerged lands ... bordering on a public navigable water" held subject to Government's navigational servitude), with *Kaiser Aetna v. United States*, 444 U.S., at 178-180, 100 S.Ct., at 392-393 (imposition of navigational servitude on marina created and rendered navigable at private expense held to constitute a taking). We believe similar treatment must be accorded confiscatory regulations, *i.e.*, regulations that prohibit all economically beneficial use of land: Any limitation so severe cannot be newly legislated or decreed (without compensation), but must inhere in the title itself, in the restrictions that background principles of the State's law of property and nuisance already place upon land ownership. A law or decree with such an effect must, in other words, do no more than duplicate the result that could have been achieved in the courts—by adjacent landowners (or other uniquely affected persons) under the State's law of private nuisance, or by the State under its complementary power to abate nuisances that affect the public generally, or otherwise. [Footnote omitted.]

On this analysis, the owner of a lake-bed, for example, would not be entitled to compensation when he is denied the requisite permit to engage in a landfilling operation that would have the effect of flooding others' land. Nor the corporate owner of a nuclear generating plant, when it is directed to remove all improvements from its land upon discovery that the plant sits astride an earthquake fault. Such regulatory action may well have the effect of eliminating the land's only economically productive use, but it does not proscribe a productive use that was previously permissible under relevant property and nuisance principles. The use of these properties for what are now expressly prohibited purposes was always unlawful, and (subject to other constitutional limitations) it was open to the State at any point to make the implication of those background principles of nuisance and property law explicit. *See* Michelman, *Property, Utility, and Fairness, Comments on the Ethical Foundations of "Just Compensation" Law*, 80 Harv.L.Rev. 1165, 1239-1241 (1967). In light of our traditional resort to "existing rules or understandings that stem from an independent source such as state law" to define the range of interests that qualify for protection as "property" under the Fifth and Fourteenth Amendments, *Board of Regents of State Colleges v. Roth*, 408 U.S. 564, 577, 92 S.Ct. 2701, 2709, 33 L.Ed.2d 548 (1972); *See, e.g., Ruckelshaus v. Monsanto Co.*, 467 U.S. 986, 1011-1012, 104 S.Ct. 2862, 2877, 81 L.Ed.2d 815 (1984); *Hughes v. Washington*, 389 U.S. 290, 295, 88 S.Ct. 438, 441, 19 L.Ed.2d 530 (1967) (Stewart, J., concurring), this recognition that the Takings Clause does not require compensation when an owner is barred from putting land to a use that is proscribed by those "existing rules or understandings" is surely unexceptional. When, however, a regulation that declares "off-limits" all economically productive or beneficial uses of land goes beyond what the relevant background principles would dictate, compensation must be paid to sustain it.[17]

The "total taking" inquiry we require today will ordinarily entail (as the application of state nuisance law ordinarily entails) analysis of, among other things, the degree of harm to public lands and resources, or adjacent private property, posed by the claimant's proposed activities, *see, e.g.*, Restatement (Second) of Torts §§826, 827, the social value of the claimant's activities and their suitability to the locality in question, *see, e.g.*, *id.*, §§828(a) and (b), 831, and the relative ease with which the alleged harm can be avoided through measures taken by the claimant and the government (or adjacent private landowners) alike, *see, e.g.*, *id.*, §§827(e), 828(c), 830. The fact that a particular use has long been engaged in by similarly situated owners ordinarily imports a lack of any common-law prohibition (though changed circumstances or new knowledge may make what was previously permissible no longer so, *see id.*, §827, Comment g. So also does the fact that other landowners, similarly situated, are permitted to continue the use denied to the claimant.

It seems unlikely that common-law principles would have prevented the erection of any habitable or productive improvements on petitioner's land; they rarely support prohibition of the "essential use" of land, *Curtin v. Benson*, 222 U.S. 78, 86, 32 S.Ct. 31, 33, 56 L.Ed. 102 (1911). The question, however, is one of state law to be dealt with on remand. We emphasize that to win its case South Carolina must do more than proffer the legislature's declaration that the uses Lucas desires are inconsistent with the public interest, or the conclusory assertion that they violate a common-law maxim such as sic utere tuo ut alienum non laedas. As we have said, a "State, by *ipse dixit*, may not transform private property into public property without compensation...." *Webb's Fabulous Pharmacies, Inc. v. Beckwith*, 449 U.S. 155, 164, 101 S.Ct. 446, 452, 66 L.Ed.2d 358 (1980). Instead, as it would be required to do if it sought to restrain Lucas in a common-law action for public nuisance, South Carolina must identify background principles of nuisance and property law that prohibit the uses he now intends in the circumstances in which the property is presently found. Only on this showing can the State fairly claim that, in proscribing all such beneficial uses, the Beachfront Management Act is taking nothing. [Footnote omitted.]

The judgment is reversed, and the case is remanded for proceedings not inconsistent with this opinion.

SO ORDERED.

Justice KENNEDY, concurring in the judgment.

The case comes to the Court in an unusual posture, as all my colleagues observe. *Ante*, at 2890; post, at 2906 (BLACKMUN, J., dissenting); post, at 2917 (STEVENS, J., dissenting); post, at 2925 (statement of SOUTER, J.). After the suit was initiated but before it reached us, South Carolina amended its Beachfront Management Act to authorize the issuance of special permits at variance with the Act's general limitations. *See* S.C.Code Ann. §48-39-290(D)(1) (Supp.1991). Petitioner has not applied for a special permit but may still do so. The availability of this alternative, if it

---

[17] Of course, the State may elect to rescind its regulation and thereby avoid having to pay compensation for a permanent deprivation. *See First English Evangelical Lutheran Church*, 482 U.S., at 321, 107 S.Ct., at 2389. But "where the [regulation has] already worked a taking of all use of property, no subsequent action by the government can relieve it of the duty to provide compensation for the period during which the taking was effective." *Ibid.*

can be invoked, may dispose of petitioner's claim of a permanent taking. As I read the Court's opinion, it does not decide the permanent taking claim, but neither does it foreclose the Supreme Court of South Carolina from considering the claim or requiring petitioner to pursue an administrative alternative not previously available.

The potential for future relief does not control our disposition, because whatever may occur in the future cannot undo what has occurred in the past. The Beachfront Management Act was enacted in 1988. S.C.Code Ann. §48-39-250 et seq. (Supp.1990). It may have deprived petitioner of the use of his land in an interim period. §48-39-290(A). If this deprivation amounts to a taking, its limited duration will not bar constitutional relief. It is well established that temporary takings are as protected by the Constitution as are permanent ones. *First English Evangelical Lutheran Church of Glendale v. County of Los Angeles*, 482 U.S. 304, 318, 107 S.Ct. 2378, 2387, 96 L.Ed.2d 250 (1987).

The issues presented in the case are ready for our decision. The Supreme Court of South Carolina decided the case on constitutional grounds, and its rulings are now before us. There exists no jurisdictional bar to our disposition, and prudential considerations ought not to militate against it. The State cannot complain of the manner in which the issues arose. Any uncertainty in this regard is attributable to the State, as a consequence of its amendment to the Beachfront Management Act. If the Takings Clause is to protect against temporary deprivations, as well as permanent ones, its enforcement must not be frustrated by a shifting background of state law.

Although we establish a framework for remand, moreover, we do not decide the ultimate question whether a temporary taking has occurred in this case. The facts necessary to the determination have not been developed in the record. Among the matters to be considered on remand must be whether petitioner had the intent and capacity to develop the property and failed to do so in the interim period because the State prevented him. Any failure by petitioner to comply with relevant administrative requirements will be part of that analysis.

The South Carolina Court of Common Pleas found that petitioner's real property has been rendered valueless by the State's regulation. App. to Pet. for Cert. 37. The finding appears to presume that the property has no significant market value or resale potential. This is a curious finding, and I share the reservations of some of my colleagues about a finding that a beach-front lot loses all value because of a development restriction. Post, at 2908 (BLACKMUN, J., dissenting); post, at 2919, n. 3 (STEVENS, J., dissenting); post, at 2925 (statement of SOUTER, J.). While the Supreme Court of South Carolina on remand need not consider the case subject to this constraint, we must accept the finding as entered below. *See Oklahoma City v. Tuttle*, 471 U.S. 808, 816, 105 S.Ct. 2427, 2432, 85 L.Ed.2d 791 (1985). Accepting the finding as entered, it follows that petitioner is entitled to invoke the line of cases discussing regulations that deprive real property of all economic value. *See Agins v. City of Tiburon*, 447 U.S. 255, 260, 100 S.Ct. 2138, 2141, 65 L.Ed.2d 106 (1980).

The finding of no value must be considered under the Takings Clause by reference to the owner's reasonable, investment-backed expectations. *Kaiser Aetna v. United States*, 444 U.S. 164, 175, 100 S.Ct. 383, 390, 62 L.Ed.2d 332 (1979); *Penn Central Transportation Co. v. New York City*, 438 U.S. 104, 124, 98 S.Ct. 2646, 2659, 57 L.Ed.2d 631 (1978); *see* also *W.B. Worthen Co. v. Kavanaugh*, 295 U.S. 56, 55 S.Ct. 555, 79 L.Ed. 1298 (1935). The Takings Clause, while conferring substantial protection on property owners, does not eliminate the police power of the State to enact limitations on the use of their property. *Mugler v. Kansas*, 123 U.S. 623, 669, 8 S.Ct. 273,

301, 31 L.Ed. 205 (1887). The rights conferred by the Takings Clause and the police power of the State may coexist without conflict. Property is bought and sold, investments are made, subject to the State's power to regulate. Where a taking is alleged from regulations which deprive the property of all value, the test must be whether the deprivation is contrary to reasonable, investment-backed expectations.

There is an inherent tendency towards circularity in this synthesis, of course; for if the owner's reasonable expectations are shaped by what courts allow as a proper exercise of governmental authority, property tends to become what courts say it is. Some circularity must be tolerated in these matters, however, as it is in other spheres. *E.g., Katz v. United States*, 389 U.S. 347, 88 S.Ct. 507, 19 L.Ed.2d 576 (1967) (Fourth Amendment protections defined by reasonable expectations of privacy). The definition, moreover, is not circular in its entirety. The expectations protected by the Constitution are based on objective rules and customs that can be understood as reasonable by all parties involved.

In my view, reasonable expectations must be understood in light of the whole of our legal tradition. The common law of nuisance is too narrow a confine for the exercise of regulatory power in a complex and interdependent society. *Goldblatt v. Hempstead*, 369 U.S. 590, 593, 82 S.Ct. 987, 989, 8 L.Ed.2d 130 (1962). The State should not be prevented from enacting new regulatory initiatives in response to changing conditions, and courts must consider all reasonable expectations whatever their source. The Takings Clause does not require a static body of state property law; it protects private expectations to ensure private investment. I agree with the Court that nuisance prevention accords with the most common expectations of property owners who face regulation, but I do not believe this can be the sole source of state authority to impose severe restrictions. Coastal property may present such unique concerns for a fragile land system that the State can go further in regulating its development and use than the common law of nuisance might otherwise permit.

The Supreme Court of South Carolina erred, in my view, by reciting the general purposes for which the state regulations were enacted without a determination that they were in accord with the owner's reasonable expectations and therefore sufficient to support a severe restriction on specific parcels of property. *See* 304 S.C. 376, 383, 404 S.E.2d 895, 899 (1991). The promotion of tourism, for instance, ought not to suffice to deprive specific property of all value without a corresponding duty to compensate. Furthermore, the means, as well as the ends, of regulation must accord with the owner's reasonable expectations. Here, the State did not act until after the property had been zoned for individual lot development and most other parcels had been improved, throwing the whole burden of the regulation on the remaining lots. This too must be measured in the balance. *See Pennsylvania Coal Co. v. Mahon*, 260 U.S. 393, 416, 43 S.Ct. 158, 160, 67 L.Ed. 322 (1922).

With these observations, I CONCUR in the judgment of the Court.

Justice BLACKMUN, dissenting.

Today the Court launches a missile to kill a mouse.

The State of South Carolina prohibited petitioner Lucas from building a permanent structure on his property from 1988 to 1990. Relying on an unreviewed (and implausible) state trial court finding that this restriction left Lucas' property valueless, this Court granted review to determine whether compensation must be paid in cases where the State prohibits all economic use of real estate. According to the Court, such an occasion never has arisen in any of our prior cases, and the Court imagines that it will arise "relatively rarely" or only in "extraordinary circumstances." Almost certainly it did not happen in this case.

Nonetheless, the Court presses on to decide the issue, and as it does, it ignores its jurisdictional limits, remakes its traditional rules of review, and creates simultaneously a new categorical rule and an exception (neither of which is rooted in our prior case law, common law, or common sense). I protest not only the Court's decision, but each step taken to reach it. More fundamentally, I question the Court's wisdom in issuing sweeping new rules to decide such a narrow case. Surely, as Justice KENNEDY demonstrates, the Court could have reached the result it wanted without inflicting this damage upon our Takings Clause jurisprudence.

My fear is that the Court's new policies will spread beyond the narrow confines of the present case. For that reason, I, like the Court, will give far greater attention to this case than its narrow scope suggests—not because I can intercept the Court's missile, or save the targeted mouse, but because I hope perhaps to limit the collateral damage.

I

A

In 1972 Congress passed the Coastal Zone Management Act. 16 U.S.C. §1451 et seq. The Act was designed to provide States with money and incentives to carry out Congress' goal of protecting the public from shoreline erosion and coastal hazards. In the 1980 amendments to the Act, Congress directed States to enhance their coastal programs by "[p]reventing or significantly reducing threats to life and the destruction of property by eliminating development and redevelopment in high-hazard areas." [Footnote omitted.] 16 U.S.C. § 1456b(a)(2) (1988 ed., Supp. II).

South Carolina began implementing the congressional directive by enacting the South Carolina Coastal Zone Management Act of 1977. Under the 1977 Act, any construction activity in what was designated the "critical area" required a permit from the South Carolina Coastal Council (Council), and the construction of any habitable structure was prohibited. The 1977 critical area was relatively narrow.

This effort did not stop the loss of shoreline. In October 1986, the Council appointed a "Blue Ribbon Committee on Beachfront Management" to investigate beach erosion and propose possible solutions. In March 1987, the Committee found that South Carolina's beaches were "critically eroding," and proposed land-use restrictions. Report of the South Carolina Blue Ribbon Committee on Beachfront Management i, 6-10 (Mar. 1987). In response, South Carolina enacted the Beachfront Management Act on July 1, 1988. S.C.Code Ann. §48-39-250 et seq. (Supp.1990). The 1988 Act did not change the uses permitted within the designated critical areas. Rather, it enlarged those areas to encompass the distance from the mean high watermark to a setback line established on the basis of "the best scientific and historical data" available. [Footnote omitted.] S.C.Code Ann. §48-39-280 (Supp.1991).

B

Petitioner Lucas is a contractor, manager, and part owner of the Wild Dune development on the Isle of Palms. He has lived there since 1978. In December 1986, he purchased two of the last four pieces of vacant property in the development. [Footnote omitted.] The area is notoriously unstable. In roughly half of the last 40 years, all or part of petitioner's property was part of the beach or flooded twice daily by the ebb and flow of the tide. Tr. 84. Between 1957 and 1963, petitioner's property was under water. *Id.*, at 79, 81-82. Between 1963 and 1973 the shoreline was 100 to 150 feet onto petitioner's property. *Ibid.* In 1973 the first line of stable vegetation was about halfway through the property. *Id.*, at 80. Between 1981 and 1983, the Isle of Palms issued 12 emergency orders for sandbagging to protect property in the Wild Dune development. *Id.*, at 99. Determining that local habitable structures were in imminent danger of collapse, the Council issued permits for two rock revetments to protect condominium developments near petitioner's property from erosion; one of the revetments extends more than halfway onto one of his lots. *Id.*, at 102.

C

The South Carolina Supreme Court found that the Beachfront Management Act did not take petitioner's property without compensation. The decision rested on two premises that until today were unassailable—that the State has the power to prevent any use of property it finds to be harmful to its citizens, and that a state statute is entitled to a presumption of constitutionality.

The Beachfront Management Act includes a finding by the South Carolina General Assembly that the beach/dune system serves the purpose of "protect[ing] life and property by serving as a storm barrier which dissipates wave energy and contributes to shoreline stability in an economical and effective manner." S.C.Code Ann. §48-39-250(1)(a) (Supp.1990). The General Assembly also found that "development unwisely has been sited too close to the [beach/dune] system. This type of development has jeopardized the stability of the beach/dune system, accelerated erosion, and endangered adjacent property." §48-39-250(4); *see* also §48-39-250(6) (discussing the need to "afford the beach/dune system space to accrete and erode").

If the state legislature is correct that the prohibition on building in front of the setback line prevents serious harm, then, under this Court's prior cases, the Act is constitutional. "Long ago it was recognized that all property in this country is held under the implied obligation that the owner's use of it shall not be injurious to the community, and the Takings Clause did not transform that principle to one that requires compensation whenever the State asserts its power to enforce it." *Keystone Bituminous Coal Assn. v. DeBenedictis*, 480 U.S. 470, 491-492, 107 S.Ct. 1232, 1245, 94 L.Ed.2d 472 (1987) (internal quotation marks omitted); *see* also *id.*, at 488-489, and n. 18, 107 S.Ct., at 1244, n. 18. The Court consistently has upheld regulations imposed to arrest a significant threat to the common welfare, whatever their economic effect on the owner. *See, e.g., Goldblatt v. Hempstead*, 369 U.S. 590, 592-593, 82 S.Ct. 987, 989, 8 L.Ed.2d 130 (1962); *Euclid v. Ambler Realty Co.*, 272 U.S. 365, 47 S.Ct. 114, 71 L.Ed. 303 (1926); *Gorieb v. Fox*, 274 U.S. 603, 608, 47 S.Ct. 675, 677, 71 L.Ed. 1228 (1927); *Mugler v. Kansas*, 123 U.S. 623, 8 S.Ct. 273, 31 L.Ed. 205 (1887).

Petitioner never challenged the legislature's findings that a building ban was necessary to protect property and life. Nor did he contend that the threatened harm was not sufficiently serious to make building a house in a particular location a "harmful" use, that the legislature had not made sufficient findings, or that the legislature was motivated by anything other than a desire to minimize damage to coastal areas. Indeed, petitioner objected at trial that evidence as to the purposes of the setback requirement was irrelevant. Tr. 68. The South Carolina Supreme Court accordingly understood petitioner not to contest the State's position that "discouraging new construction in close proximity to the beach/dune area is necessary to prevent a great public harm," 304 S.C. 376, 383, 404 S.E.2d 895, 898 (1991), and "to prevent serious injury to the community." *Id.*, at 387, 404 S.E.2d, at 901. The court considered itself "bound by these uncontested legislative findings ... [in the absence of] any attack whatsoever on the statutory scheme." *Id.*, at 383, 404 S.E.2d, at 898.

Nothing in the record undermines the General Assembly's assessment that prohibitions on building in front of the setback line are necessary to protect people and property from storms, high tides, and beach erosion. Because that legislative determination cannot be disregarded in the absence of such evidence, *see, e.g., Euclid*, 272 U.S., at 388, 47 S.Ct., at 118; *O'Gorman & Young, Inc. v. Hartford Fire Ins. Co.*, 282 U.S. 251, 257-258, 51 S.Ct. 130, 132, 75 L.Ed. 324 (1931) (Brandeis, J.), and because its determination of harm to life and property from building is sufficient to prohibit that use under this Court's cases, the South Carolina Supreme Court correctly found no taking.

II

My disagreement with the Court begins with its decision to review this case. This Court has held consistently that a land-use challenge is not ripe for review until there is a final decision about what uses of the property will be permitted. The ripeness requirement is not simply a gesture of good will to land-use planners. In the absence of "a final and authoritative determination of the type and intensity of development legally permitted on the subject property," *MacDonald, Sommer & Frates v. Yolo County*, 477 U.S. 340, 348, 106 S.Ct. 2561, 2566, 91 L.Ed.2d 285 (1986), and the utilization of state procedures for just compensation, there is no final judgment, and in the absence of a final judgment there is no jurisdiction, *see San Diego Gas & Electric Co. v. San Diego*, 450 U.S. 621, 633, 101 S.Ct. 1287, 1294, 67 L.Ed.2d 551 (1981); *Agins v. City of Tiburon*, 447 U.S. 255, 260, 100 S.Ct. 2138, 2141, 65 L.Ed.2d 106 (1980).

This rule is "compelled by the very nature of the inquiry required by the Just Compensation Clause," because the factors applied in deciding a takings claim "simply cannot be evaluated until the administrative agency has arrived at a final, definitive position regarding how it will apply the regulations at issue to the particular land in question." *Williamson County Regional Planning Comm'n v. Hamilton Bank of Johnson City*, 473 U.S. 172, 190, 191, 105 S.Ct. 3108, 3118, 3119, 87 L.Ed.2d 126 (1985). *See* also *MacDonald, Sommer & Frates*, 477 U.S., at 348, 106 S.Ct., at 2566 ("A court cannot determine whether a regulation has gone 'too far' unless it knows how far the regulation goes") (citation omitted).

The Court admits that the 1990 amendments to the Beachfront Management Act allowing special permits preclude Lucas from asserting that his property has been permanently taken. *See ante*, at 2890-2891. The Court agrees that such a claim would not be ripe because there has been no final decision by respondent on what uses will be permitted. The Court, however, will not be denied: It determines that petitioner's "temporary takings" claim for the period from July 1, 1988, to June 25, 1990, is ripe. But this claim also is not justiciable.[4]

From the very beginning of this litigation, respondent has argued that the courts

> "lac[k] jurisdiction in this matter because the Plaintiff has sought no authorization from Council for use of his property, has not challenged the location of the baseline or setback line as alleged in the Complaint and because no final agency decision has been rendered concerning use of his property or location of said baseline or setback line." Tr. 10 (answer, as amended).

Although the Council's plea has been ignored by every court, it is undoubtedly correct.

Under the Beachfront Management Act, petitioner was entitled to challenge the setback line or the baseline or erosion rate applied to his property in formal administrative, followed by judicial, proceedings. S.C.Code Ann. §48-39- 280(E) (Supp.1991). Because Lucas failed to pursue this administrative remedy, the Council never finally decided whether Lucas' particular piece of property was correctly categorized as a critical area in which building would not be permitted. This is all the more crucial because Lucas argued strenuously in the trial court that his land was perfectly safe to build on, and that his company had studies to prove it. Tr. 20, 25, 36. If he was correct, the Council's final decision would have been to alter the setback line, eliminating the construction ban on Lucas' property.

That petitioner's property fell within the critical area as initially interpreted by the Council does not excuse petitioner's failure to challenge the Act's application to his property in the administrative process. The claim is not ripe until petitioner seeks a variance from that status. "[W]e have made it quite clear that the mere assertion of regulatory jurisdiction by a governmental body does not constitute a regulatory taking." *United States v. Riverside Bayview Homes, Inc.*, 474 U.S. 121, 126, 106 S.Ct. 455, 459, 88 L.Ed.2d 419 (1985). *See* also *Williamson County*, 473 U.S., at 188, 105 S.Ct., at 3117 (claim not ripe because respondent did not seek variances that would have allowed it to develop the property, notwithstanding the commission's finding that the plan did not comply with the zoning ordinance and subdivision regulations).[5]

---

[4] The Court's reliance, *ante*, at 2892, on *Esposito v. South Carolina Coastal Council*, 939 F.2d 165, 168 (CA4 1991), cert. denied, 505 U.S. 1219, 112 S.Ct. 3027, 120 L.Ed.2d 898 (1992), in support of its decision to consider Lucas' temporary takings claim ripe is misplaced. In Esposito the plaintiffs brought a facial challenge to the mere enactment of the Act. Here, of course, Lucas has brought an as-applied challenge. *See* Brief for Petitioner 16. Facial challenges are ripe when the Act is passed; applied challenges require a final decision on the Act's application to the property in question.

[5] Even more baffling, given its decision, just a few days ago, in *Lujan v. Defenders of Wildlife*, 504 U.S. 555, 112 S.Ct. 2130, 119 L.Ed.2d 351 (1992), the Court decides petitioner has demonstrated injury in fact. In his complaint, petitioner made no allegations that he had any definite plans for using his property. App. to Pet. for Cert. 153-156. At trial, Lucas testified that he had house plans drawn up, but that he was "in no hurry" to build "because the lot was appreciating in value." Tr. 28-29. The trial court made no findings of fact that Lucas had any plans to use the property from 1988 to 1990. "'[S]ome day' intentions—without any description of concrete plans, or indeed even any specification of when the some day will be—do not support a finding of the 'actual or imminent' injury that our cases require." 504 U.S., at 564, 112 S.Ct., at 2138. The Court circumvents Defenders of Wildlife by deciding to resolve this case as if it arrived on the pleadings alone. But it did not. Lucas had a full trial on his claim for "'damages for the temporary taking of his property' from the date of the 1988 Act's 'passage to such time as this matter is finally resolved,'" *ante*, at 2892, n.3, quoting the complaint, and failed to demonstrate any immediate concrete plans to build or sell.

Even if I agreed with the Court that there were no jurisdictional barriers to deciding this case, I still would not try to decide it. The Court creates its new takings jurisprudence based on the trial court's finding that the property had lost all economic value. [Footnote omitted.] This finding is almost certainly erroneous. Petitioner still can enjoy other attributes of ownership, such as the right to exclude others, "one of the most essential sticks in the bundle of rights that are commonly characterized as property." *Kaiser Aetna v. United States*, 444 U.S. 164, 176, 100 S.Ct. 383, 391, 62 L.Ed.2d 332 (1979). Petitioner can picnic, swim, camp in a tent, or live on the property in a movable trailer. State courts frequently have recognized that land has economic value where the only residual economic uses are recreation or camping. *See, e.g., Turnpike Realty Co. v. Dedham*, 362 Mass. 221, 284 N.E.2d 891 (1972) cert. denied, 409 U.S. 1108, 93 S.Ct. 908, 34 L.Ed.2d 689 (1973); *Turner v. County of Del Norte*, 24 Cal.App.3d 311, 101 Cal.Rptr. 93 (1972); *Hall v. Board of Environmental Protection*, 528 A.2d 453 (Me.1987). Petitioner also retains the right to alienate the land, which would have value for neighbors and for those prepared to enjoy proximity to the ocean without a house.

Yet the trial court, apparently believing that "less value" and "valueless" could be used interchangeably, found the property "valueless." The court accepted no evidence from the State on the property's value without a home, and petitioner's appraiser testified that he never had considered what the value would be absent a residence. Tr. 54-55. The appraiser's value was based on the fact that the "highest and best use of these lots ... [is] luxury single family detached dwellings." *Id.*, at 48. The trial court appeared to believe that the property could be considered "valueless" if it was not available for its most profitable use. Absent that erroneous assumption, *see Goldblatt*, 369 U.S., at 592, 82 S.Ct., at 989, I find no evidence in the record supporting the trial court's conclusion that the damage to the lots by virtue of the restrictions was "total." Record 128 (findings of fact). I agree with the Court, *ante*, at 2896, n.9, that it has the power to decide a case that turns on an erroneous finding, but I question the wisdom of deciding an issue based on a factual premise that does not exist in this case, and in the judgment of the Court will exist in the future only in "extraordinary circumstance[s]," *ante*, at 2894.

Clearly, the Court was eager to decide this case.[7] But eagerness, in the absence of proper jurisdiction, must—and in this case should have been—met with restraint.

III

The Court's willingness to dispense with precedent in its haste to reach a result is not limited to its initial jurisdictional decision. The Court also alters the long-settled rules of review.

The South Carolina Supreme Court's decision to defer to legislative judgments in the absence of a challenge from petitioner comports with one of this Court's oldest maxims: "[T]he existence of facts supporting the legislative judgment is to be presumed." *United States v. Carolene Products*

[7] The Court overlooks the lack of a ripe and justiciable claim apparently out of concern that in the absence of its intervention Lucas will be unable to obtain further adjudication of his temporary takings claim. The Court chastises respondent for arguing that Lucas' temporary takings claim is premature because it failed "so much as [to] commen[t]" upon the effect of the South Carolina Supreme Court's decision on petitioner's ability to obtain relief for the two-year period, and it frets that Lucas would "be unable (absent our intervention now) to obtain further state-court adjudication with respect to the 1988-1990 period." *Ante*, at 2891. Whatever the explanation for the Court's intense interest in Lucas' plight when ordinarily we are more cautious in granting discretionary review, the concern would have been more prudently expressed by vacating the judgment below and remanding for further consideration in light of the 1990 amendments. At that point, petitioner could have brought a temporary takings claim in the state courts.

Co., 304 U.S. 144, 152, 58 S.Ct. 778, 783, 82 L.Ed. 1234 (1938). Indeed, we have said the legislature's judgment is "well-nigh conclusive." *Berman v. Parker*, 348 U.S. 26, 32, 75 S.Ct. 98, 102, 99 L.Ed. 27 (1954). *See* also *Sweet v. Rechel*, 159 U.S. 380, 392, 16 S.Ct. 43, 45-46, 40 L.Ed. 188 (1895); *Euclid*, 272 U.S., at 388, 47 S.Ct., at 118 (If the validity of the legislative classification for zoning purposes be fairly debatable, the legislative judgment must be allowed to control).

Accordingly, this Court always has required plaintiffs challenging the constitutionality of an ordinance to provide "some factual foundation of record" that contravenes the legislative findings. *O'Gorman & Young*, 282 U.S., at 258, 51 S.Ct., at 132. In the absence of such proof, "the presumption of constitutionality must prevail." *Id.*, at 257, 51 S.Ct., at 132. We only recently have reaffirmed that claimants have the burden of showing a state law constitutes a taking. *See Keystone Bituminous Coal*, 480 U.S., at 485, 107 S.Ct., at 1242. *See* also *Goldblatt*, 369 U.S., at 594, 82 S.Ct., at 990 (citing "the usual presumption of constitutionality" that applies to statutes attacked as takings).

Rather than invoking these traditional rules, the Court decides the State has the burden to convince the courts that its legislative judgments are correct. Despite Lucas' complete failure to contest the legislature's findings of serious harm to life and property if a permanent structure is built, the Court decides that the legislative findings are not sufficient to justify the use prohibition. Instead, the Court "emphasize[s]" the State must do more than merely proffer its legislative judgments to avoid invalidating its law. *Ante*, at 2901. In this case, apparently, the State now has the burden of showing the regulation is not a taking. The Court offers no justification for its sudden hostility toward state legislators, and I doubt that it could.

IV

The Court does not reject the South Carolina Supreme Court's decision simply on the basis of its disbelief and distrust of the legislature's findings. It also takes the opportunity to create a new scheme for regulations that eliminate all economic value. From now on, there is a categorical rule finding these regulations to be a taking unless the use they prohibit is a background common-law nuisance or property principle. *See ante*, at 2899-2901.

A

I first question the Court's rationale in creating a category that obviates a "case-specific inquiry into the public interest advanced," *ante*, at 2893, if all economic value has been lost. If one fact about the Court's takings jurisprudence can be stated without contradiction, it is that "the particular circumstances of each case" determine whether a specific restriction will be rendered invalid by the government's failure to pay compensation. *United States v. Central Eureka Mining Co.*, 357 U.S. 155, 168, 78 S.Ct. 1097, 1104, 2 L.Ed.2d 1228 (1958). This is so because although we have articulated certain factors to be considered, including the economic impact on the property owner, the ultimate conclusion "necessarily requires a weighing of private and public interests." *Agins*, 447 U.S., at 261, 100 S.Ct., at 2141. When the government regulation prevents the owner from any economically valuable use of his property, the private interest is unquestionably substantial, but we have never before held that no public interest can outweigh it. Instead the Court's prior decisions "uniformly reject the proposition that diminution in property value, standing alone, can establish a 'taking.'" *Penn Central Transp. Co. v. New York City*, 438 U.S. 104, 131, 98 S.Ct. 2646, 2663, 57 L.Ed.2d 631 (1978).

This Court repeatedly has recognized the ability of government, in certain circumstances, to regulate property without compensation no matter how adverse the financial effect on the owner may be. More than a century ago, the Court explicitly upheld the right of States to prohibit uses of property injurious to public health, safety, or welfare without paying compensation: "A prohibition simply upon the use of property for purposes that are declared, by valid legislation, to be injurious to the health, morals, or safety of the community, cannot, in any just sense, be deemed a taking or an appropriation of property." *Mugler v. Kansas*, 123 U.S., at 668-669, 8 S.Ct., at 301. On this basis, the Court upheld an ordinance effectively prohibiting operation of a previously lawful brewery, although the "establishments will become of no value as property." *Id.*, at 664, 8 S.Ct., at 298; *see* also *id.*, at 668, 8 S.Ct., at 300.

Mugler was only the beginning in a long line of cases. [Footnote omitted.] In *Powell v. Pennsylvania*, 127 U.S. 678, 8 S.Ct. 992, 32 L.Ed. 253 (1888), the Court upheld legislation prohibiting the manufacture of oleomargarine, despite the owner's allegation that "if prevented from continuing it, the value of his property employed therein would be entirely lost and he be deprived of the means of livelihood." *Id.*, at 682, 8 S.Ct., at 994. In *Hadacheck v. Sebastian*, 239 U.S. 394, 36 S.Ct. 143, 60 L.Ed. 348 (1915), the Court upheld an ordinance prohibiting a brickyard, although the owner had made excavations on the land that prevented it from being utilized for any purpose but a brickyard. *Id.*, at 405, 36 S.Ct., at 143. In *Miller v. Schoene*, 276 U.S. 272, 48 S.Ct. 246, 72 L.Ed. 568 (1928), the Court held that the Fifth Amendment did not require Virginia to pay compensation to the owner of cedar trees ordered destroyed to prevent a disease from spreading to nearby apple orchards. The "preferment of [the public interest] over the property interest of the individual, to the extent even of its destruction, is one of the distinguishing characteristics of every exercise of the police power which affects property." *Id.*, at 280, 48 S.Ct., at 247. Again, in *Omnia Commercial Co. v. United States*, 261 U.S. 502, 43 S.Ct. 437, 67 L.Ed. 773 (1923), the Court stated that "destruction of, or injury to, property is frequently accomplished without a 'taking' in the constitutional sense." *Id.*, at 508, 43 S.Ct., at 437.

More recently, in Goldblatt, the Court upheld a town regulation that barred continued operation of an existing sand and gravel operation in order to protect public safety. 369 U.S., at 596, 82 S.Ct., at 991. "Although a comparison of values before and after is relevant," the Court stated, "it is by no means conclusive." [Footnote omitted.] *Id.*, at 594, 82 S.Ct., at 990. In 1978, the Court declared that "in instances in which a state tribunal reasonably concluded that 'the health, safety, morals, or general welfare' would be promoted by prohibiting particular contemplated uses of land, this Court has upheld land-use regulation that destroyed ... recognized real property interests." Penn Central Transp. Co., 438 U.S., at 125, 98 S.Ct., at 2659. In *First English Evangelical Lutheran Church of Glendale v. County of Los Angeles*, 482 U.S. 304, 107 S.Ct. 2378, 96 L.Ed.2d 250 (1987), the owner alleged that a floodplain ordinance had deprived it of "all use" of the property. *Id.*, at 312, 107 S.Ct., at 2384. The Court remanded the case for consideration whether, even if the ordinance denied the owner all use, it could be justified as a safety measure. [Footnote omitted.] *Id.*, at 313, 107 S.Ct., at 2385. And in *Keystone Bituminous Coal*, the Court summarized over 100 years of precedent: "[T]he Court has repeatedly upheld regulations that destroy or adversely affect real property interests."[11] 480 U.S., at 489, n. 18, 107 S.Ct., at 1244, n. 18.

---

[11] The Court's suggestion that *Agins v. City of Tiburon*, 447 U.S. 255, 100 S.Ct. 2138, 65 L.Ed.2d 106 (1980), a unanimous opinion, created a new per se rule, only now discovered, is unpersuasive. In *Agins*, the Court stated that "no precise rule determines when property has been taken" but instead that "the question necessarily requires a weighing of public and private interest." *Id.*, at 260-262, 100 S.Ct., at 2141-2142. The other cases cited by the

continued on the next page

The Court recognizes that "our prior opinions have suggested that 'harmful or noxious uses' of property may be proscribed by government regulation without the requirement of compensation," *ante*, at 2897, but seeks to reconcile them with its categorical rule by claiming that the Court never has upheld a regulation when the owner alleged the loss of all economic value. Even if the Court's factual premise were correct, its understanding of the Court's cases is distorted. In none of the cases did the Court suggest that the right of a State to prohibit certain activities without paying compensation turned on the availability of some residual valuable use.[12] Instead, the cases depended on whether the government interest was sufficient to prohibit the activity, given the significant private cost.[13]

These cases rest on the principle that the State has full power to prohibit an owner's use of property if it is harmful to the public. "[S]ince no individual has a right to use his property so as to create a nuisance or otherwise harm others, the State has not 'taken' anything when it asserts its power to enjoin the nuisance-like activity." Keystone Bituminous Coal, 480 U.S., at 491, n. 20, 107 S.Ct., at 1245, n. 20. It would make no sense under this theory to suggest that an owner has a constitutionally protected right to harm others, if only he makes the proper showing of economic loss. [Footnote omitted.] *See* Pennsylvania Coal Co. v. Mahon, 260 U.S. 393, 418, 43 S.Ct. 158, 161, 67 L.Ed. 322 (1922) (Brandeis, J., dissenting) ("Restriction upon [harmful] use does not

---

Court, *ante*, at 2893, repeat the *Agins* sentence, but in no way suggest that the public interest is irrelevant if total value has been taken. The Court has indicated that proof that a regulation does not deny an owner economic use of his property is sufficient to defeat a facial takings challenge. *See Hodel v. Virginia Surface Mining & Reclamation Assn., Inc.*, 452 U.S. 264, 295-297, 101 S.Ct. 2352, 2370-2371, 69 L.Ed.2d 1 (1981). But the conclusion that a regulation is not on its face a taking because it allows the landowner some economic use of property is a far cry from the proposition that denial of such use is sufficient to establish a takings claim regardless of any other consideration. The Court never has accepted the latter proposition.

The Court relies today on dicta in *Agins, Hodel, Nollan v. California Coastal Comm'n*, 483 U.S. 825, 107 S.Ct. 3141, 97 L.Ed.2d 677 (1987), and *Keystone Bituminous Coal Ass'n. v. DeBenedictis*, 480 U.S. 470, 107 S.Ct. 1232, 94 L.Ed.2d 472 (1987), for its new categorical rule. *Ante*, at 2893. I prefer to rely on the directly contrary holdings in cases such as *Mugler v. Sebastian*, 239 U.S. 394, 36 S.Ct. 143, 60 L.Ed. 348 (1915), and *Hadacheck v. Kansas*, 123 U.S. 623, 8 S.Ct. 273, 31 L.Ed. 205 (1887), not to mention contrary statements in the very cases on which the Court relies. *See Agins*, 447 U.S., at 260-262, 100 S.Ct., at 2141- 2142; *Keystone Bituminous Coal*, 480 U.S., at 489, n. 18, 491-492, 107 S.Ct., at 1243-1244, n. 18, 1245-1246.

[12] *Miller v. Schoene*, 276 U.S. 272, 48 S.Ct. 246, 72 L.Ed. 568 (1928), is an example. In the course of demonstrating that apple trees are more valuable than red cedar trees, the Court noted that red cedar has "occasional use and value as lumber." *Id.*, at 279, 48 S.Ct., at 247. But the Court did not discuss whether the timber owned by the petitioner in that case was commercially salable, and nothing in the opinion suggests that the State's right to require uncompensated felling of the trees depended on any such salvage value. To the contrary, it is clear from its unanimous opinion that the *Schoene* Court would have sustained a law requiring the burning of cedar trees if that had been necessary to protect apple trees in which there was a public interest: The Court spoke of preferment of the public interest over the property interest of the individual, "to the extent even of its destruction." *Id.*, at 280, 48 S.Ct., at 247.

[13] The Court seeks to disavow the holdings and reasoning of *Mugler* and subsequent cases by explaining that they were the Court's early efforts to define the scope of the police power. There is language in the earliest takings cases suggesting that the police power was considered to be the power simply to prevent harms. Subsequently, the Court expanded its understanding of what were government's legitimate interests. But it does not follow that the holding of those early cases—that harmful and noxious uses of property can be forbidden whatever the harm to the property owner and without the payment of compensation—was repudiated. To the contrary, as the Court consciously expanded the scope of the police power beyond preventing harm, it clarified that there was a core of public interests that overrode any private interest. *See Keystone Bituminous Coal*, 480 U.S., at 491, n. 20, 107 S.Ct., at 1245, n. 20.

become inappropriate as a means, merely because it deprives the owner of the only use to which the property can then be profitably put").

B

Ultimately even the Court cannot embrace the full implications of its per se rule: It eventually agrees that there cannot be a categorical rule for a taking based on economic value that wholly disregards the public need asserted. Instead, the Court decides that it will permit a State to regulate all economic value only if the State prohibits uses that would not be permitted under "background principles of nuisance and property law." [Footnote omitted.] *Ante*, at 2901.

Until today, the Court explicitly had rejected the contention that the government's power to act without paying compensation turns on whether the prohibited activity is a common-law nuisance.[16] The brewery closed in *Mugler* itself was not a common-law nuisance, and the Court specifically stated that it was the role of the legislature to determine what measures would be appropriate for the protection of public health and safety. *See* 123 U.S., at 661, 8 S.Ct., at 297. In upholding the state action in *Miller*, the Court found it unnecessary to "weigh with nicety the question whether the infected cedars constitute a nuisance according to common law; or whether they may be so declared by statute." 276 U.S., at 280, 48 S.Ct., at 248. *See* also *Goldblatt*, 369 U.S., at 593, 82 S.Ct., at 989; *Hadacheck*, 239 U.S., at 411, 36 S.Ct., at 146. Instead the Court has relied in the past, as the South Carolina court has done here, on legislative judgments of what constitutes a harm.[17]

The Court rejects the notion that the State always can prohibit uses it deems a harm to the public without granting compensation because "the distinction between 'harm-preventing' and 'benefit-conferring' regulation is often in the eye of the beholder." *Ante*, at 2897. Since the characterization will depend "primarily upon one's evaluation of the worth of competing uses of real estate," *ante*, at 2898, the Court decides a legislative judgment of this kind no longer can provide the desired "objective, value-free basis" for upholding a regulation, *ante*, at 2899. The Court, however, fails to explain how its proposed common-law alternative escapes the same trap.

---

[16] Also, until today the fact that the regulation prohibited uses that were lawful at the time the owner purchased did not determine the constitutional question. The brewery, the brickyard, the cedar trees, and the gravel pit were all perfectly legitimate uses prior to the passage of the regulation. *See Mugler v. Kansas*, 123 U.S., at 654, 8 S.Ct., at 293; *Hadacheck v. Sebastian*, 239 U.S. 394, 36 S.Ct. 143, 60 L.Ed. 348 (1915); *Miller*, 276 U.S., at 272, 48 S.Ct., at 246; *Goldblatt v. Hempstead*, 369 U.S. 590, 82 S.Ct. 987, 8 L.Ed.2d 130 (1962). This Court explicitly acknowledged in *Hadacheck* that "[a] vested interest cannot be asserted against [the police power] because of conditions once obtaining. To so hold would preclude development and fix a city forever in its primitive conditions." 239 U.S., at 410, 36 S.Ct., at 145 (citation omitted).

[17] The Court argues that finding no taking when the legislature prohibits a harmful use, such as the Court did in *Mugler* and the South Carolina Supreme Court did in the instant case, would nullify Pennsylvania Coal. *See ante*, at 2897. Justice Holmes, the author of *Pennsylvania Coal*, joined *Miller v. Schoene*, 276 U.S. 272, 48 S.Ct. 246, 72 L.Ed. 568 (1928), six years later. In *Miller*, the Court adopted the exact approach of the South Carolina court: It found the cedar trees harmful, and their destruction not a taking, whether or not they were a nuisance. Justice Holmes apparently believed that such an approach did not repudiate his earlier opinion. Moreover, this Court already has been over this ground five years ago, and at that point rejected the assertion that *Pennsylvania Coal* was inconsistent with *Mugler, Hadacheck, Miller,* or the others in the string of "noxious use" cases, recognizing instead that the nature of the State's action is critical in takings analysis. *Keystone Bituminous Coal*, 480 U.S., at 490, 107 S.Ct., at 1244.

The threshold inquiry for imposition of the Court's new rule, "deprivation of all economically valuable use," itself cannot be determined objectively. As the Court admits, whether the owner has been deprived of all economic value of his property will depend on how "property" is defined. The "composition of the denominator in our 'deprivation' fraction," *ante*, at 2894, n.7, is the dispositive inquiry. Yet there is no "objective" way to define what that denominator should be. "We have long understood that any land-use regulation can be characterized as the 'total' deprivation of an aptly defined entitlement.... Alternatively, the same regulation can always be characterized as a mere 'partial' withdrawal from full, unencumbered ownership of the landholding affected by the regulation...." [Footnote omitted.] Michelman, *Takings*, 1987, 88 Colum.L.Rev. 1600, 1614 (1988).

The Court's decision in *Keystone Bituminous Coal* illustrates this principle perfectly. In *Keystone*, the Court determined that the "support estate" was "merely a part of the entire bundle of rights possessed by the owner." 480 U.S., at 501, 107 S.Ct., at 1250. Thus, the Court concluded that the support estate's destruction merely eliminated one segment of the total property. *Ibid.* The dissent, however, characterized the support estate as a distinct property interest that was wholly destroyed. *Id.*, at 519, 107 S.Ct., at 1260. The Court could agree on no "value-free basis" to resolve this dispute.

Even more perplexing, however, is the Court's reliance on common-law principles of nuisance in its quest for a value-free takings jurisprudence. In determining what is a nuisance at common law, state courts make exactly the decision that the Court finds so troubling when made by the South Carolina General Assembly today: They determine whether the use is harmful. Common-law public and private nuisance law is simply a determination whether a particular use causes harm. *See* Prosser, Private Action for Public Nuisance, 52 Va.L.Rev. 997 (1966) ("Nuisance is a French word which means nothing more than harm"). There is nothing magical in the reasoning of judges long dead. They determined a harm in the same way as state judges and legislatures do today. If judges in the 18th and 19th centuries can distinguish a harm from a benefit, why not judges in the 20th century, and if judges can, why not legislators? There simply is no reason to believe that new interpretations of the hoary common-law nuisance doctrine will be particularly "objective" or "value free."[19] Once one abandons the level of generality of sic utere tuo ut alienum non laedas, *ante*, at 2901, one searches in vain, I think, for anything resembling a principle in the common law of nuisance.

C

Finally, the Court justifies its new rule that the legislature may not deprive a property owner of the only economically valuable use of his land, even if the legislature finds it to be a harmful use, because such action is not part of the "long recognized" "understandings of our citizens." *Ante*, at 2899. These "understandings" permit such regulation only if the use is a nuisance under the common law. Any other course is "inconsistent with the historical compact recorded in the

---

[19] "There is perhaps no more impenetrable jungle in the entire law than that which surrounds the word 'nuisance.' It has meant all things to all people, and has been applied indiscriminately to everything from an alarming advertisement to a cockroach baked in a pie." W. Keeton, D. Dobbs, R. Keeton & D. Owen, *Prosser and Keeton on The Law of Torts* 616 (5th ed. 1984) (footnotes omitted). It is an area of law that "straddles the legal universe, virtually defies synthesis, and generates case law to suit every taste." W. Rodgers, *Environmental Law* §2.4, p. 48 (1986) (footnotes omitted). The Court itself has noted that "nuisance concepts" are "often vague and indeterminate." *Milwaukee v. Illinois*, 451 U.S. 304, 317, 101 S.Ct. 1784, 1792, 68 L.Ed.2d 114 (1981).

Takings Clause." *Ante*, at 2900. It is not clear from the Court's opinion where our "historical compact" or "citizens' understanding" comes from, but it does not appear to be history.

The principle that the State should compensate individuals for property taken for public use was not widely established in America at the time of the Revolution.

"The colonists ... inherited ... a concept of property which permitted extensive regulation of the use of that property for the public benefit—regulation that could even go so far as to deny all productive use of the property to the owner if, as Coke himself stated, the regulation 'extends to the public benefit ... for this is for the public, and every one hath benefit by it.'" F. Bosselman, D. Callies, & J. Banta, *The Taking Issue* 80-81 (1973), quoting *The Case of the King's Prerogative in Saltpetre*, 12 Co.Rep. 12-13 (1606) (hereinafter Bosselman). *See* also Treanor, *The Origins and Original Significance of the Just Compensation Clause of the Fifth Amendment*, 94 Yale L.J. 694, 697, n. 9 (1985). [Footnote omitted.]

Even into the 19th century, state governments often felt free to take property for roads and other public projects without paying compensation to the owners. [Footnote omitted.] *See* M. Horwitz, *The Transformation of American Law*, 1780-1860, pp. 63-64 (1977) (hereinafter Horwitz); Treanor, 94 Yale L.J., at 695. As one court declared in 1802, citizens "were bound to contribute as much of [land], as by the laws of the country, were deemed necessary for the public convenience." *McClenachan v. Curwin*, 3 Yeates 362, 373 (Pa.1802). There was an obvious movement toward establishing the just compensation principle during the 19th century, but "there continued to be a strong current in American legal thought that regarded compensation simply as a 'bounty given ... by the State' out of 'kindness' and not out of justice." Horwitz 65, quoting *Commonwealth v. Fisher*, 1 Pen. & W. 462, 465 (Pa.1830). *See* also *State v. Dawson*, 3 Hill 100, 103 (S.C.1836)). [Footnote omitted.]

Although, prior to the adoption of the Bill of Rights, America was replete with land-use regulations describing which activities were considered noxious and forbidden, *see* Bender, *The Takings Clause: Principles or Politics?*, 34 Buffalo L.Rev. 735, 751 (1985); L. Friedman, *A History of American Law* 66-68 (1973), the Fifth Amendment's Takings Clause originally did not extend to regulations of property, whatever the effect. [Footnote omitted.] *See ante*, at 2892. Most state courts agreed with this narrow interpretation of a taking. "Until the end of the nineteenth century ... jurists held that the constitution protected possession only, and not value." Siegel, *Understanding the Nineteenth Century Contract Clause: The Role of the Property-Privilege Distinction and "Takings" Clause Jurisprudence*, 60 S.Cal.L.Rev. 1, 76 (1986); Bosselman 106. Even indirect and consequential injuries to property resulting from regulations were excluded from the definition of a taking. *See ibid.*; *Callender v. Marsh*, 1 Pick. 418, 430 (Mass.1823).

Even when courts began to consider that regulation in some situations could constitute a taking, they continued to uphold bans on particular uses without paying compensation, notwithstanding the economic impact, under the rationale that no one can obtain a vested right to injure or endanger the public.[24] In the Coates cases, for example, the Supreme Court of New York found

[24] For this reason, the retroactive application of the regulation to formerly lawful uses was not a controlling distinction in the past. "Nor can it make any difference that the right is purchased previous to the passage of the by-law," for "[e]very right, from an absolute ownership in property, down to a mere easement, is purchased and holden subject to the restriction, that it shall be so exercised as not to injure others. Though, at the time, it be remote and inoffensive, the purchaser is bound to know, at his peril, that it may become otherwise." *Coates v. City of New York*, 7 Cow. 585, 605 (N.Y.1827). *See* also *Brick Presbyterian Church v. City of New York*, 5 Cow. 538, 542 (N.Y.1826); *Commonwealth v. Tewksbury*, 11 Metc. 55 (Mass.1846); *State v. Paul*, 5 R.I. 185 (1858).

no taking in New York's ban on the interment of the dead within the city, although "no other use can be made of these lands." *Coates v. City of New York*, 7 Cow. 585, 592 (N.Y.1827). *See* also *Brick Presbyterian Church v. City of New York*, 5 Cow. 538 (N.Y.1826); *Commonwealth v. Alger*, 7 Cush. 53, 59, 104 (Mass.1851); *St. Louis Gunning Advertisement Co. v. St. Louis*, 235 Mo. 99, 146, 137 S.W. 929, 942 (1911), appeal dism'd, 231 U.S. 761, 34 S.Ct. 325, 58 L.Ed. 470 (1913). More recent cases reach the same result. *See Consolidated Rock Products Co. v. Los Angeles*, 57 Cal.2d 515, 20 Cal.Rptr. 638, 370 P.2d 342, appeal dism'd, 371 U.S. 36, 83 S.Ct. 145, 9 L.Ed.2d 112 (1962); *Nassr v. Commonwealth*, 394 Mass. 767, 477 N.E.2d 987 (1985); *Eno v. Burlington*, 125 Vt. 8, 209 A.2d 499 (1965); *Turner v. County of Del Norte*, 24 Cal.App.3d 311, 101 Cal.Rptr. 93 (1972).

In addition, state courts historically have been less likely to find that a government action constitutes a taking when the affected land is undeveloped. According to the South Carolina court, the power of the legislature to take unimproved land without providing compensation was sanctioned by "ancient rights and principles." *Lindsay v. Commissioners*, 2 S.C.L. 38, 57 (1796). "Except for Massachusetts, no colony appears to have paid compensation when it built a state-owned road across unimproved land. Legislatures provided compensation only for enclosed or improved land." Treanor, 94 Yale L.J., at 695. [Footnotes omitted.] This rule was followed by some States into the 1800s. *See* Horwitz 63-65.

With similar result, the common agrarian conception of property limited owners to "natural" uses of their land prior to and during much of the 18th century. *See id.*, at 32. Thus, for example, the owner could build nothing on his land that would alter the natural flow of water. *See id.*, at 44; *see* also, *e.g.*, *Merritt v. Parker*, 1 Coxe 460, 463 (N.J.1795). Some more recent state courts still follow this reasoning. *See, e.g.*, *Just v. Marinette County*, 56 Wis.2d 7, 201 N.W.2d 761, 768 (1972).

Nor does history indicate any common-law limit on the State's power to regulate harmful uses even to the point of destroying all economic value. Nothing in the discussions in Congress concerning the Takings Clause indicates that the Clause was limited by the common-law nuisance doctrine. Common-law courts themselves rejected such an understanding. They regularly recognized that it is "for the legislature to interpose, and by positive enactment to prohibit a use of property which would be injurious to the public." *Tewksbury*, 11 Metc., at 57. [Footnote omitted.] Chief Justice Shaw explained in upholding a regulation prohibiting construction of wharves, the existence of a taking did not depend on "whether a certain erection in tide water is a nuisance at common law or not." *Alger*, 7 Cush., at 104; *see* also *State v. Paul*, 5 R.I. 185, 193 (1858); Commonwealth v. Parks, 155 Mass. 531, 532, 30 N.E. 174 (1892) (Holmes, J.) ("[T]he legislature may change the common law as to nuisances, and may move the line either way, so as to make things nuisances which were not so, or to make things lawful which were nuisances").

In short, I find no clear and accepted "historical compact" or "understanding of our citizens" justifying the Court's new takings doctrine. Instead, the Court seems to treat history as a grab bag of principles, to be adopted where they support the Court's theory, and ignored where they do not. If the Court decided that the early common law provides the background principles for interpreting the Takings Clause, then regulation, as opposed to physical confiscation, would not be compensable. If the Court decided that the law of a later period provides the background principles, then regulation might be compensable, but the Court would have to confront the fact that legislatures regularly determined which uses were prohibited, independent of the common law, and independent of whether the uses were lawful when the owner purchased. What makes the Court's analysis unworkable is its attempt to package the law of two incompatible eras and peddle it as historical fact. [Footnote omitted.]

V

The Court makes sweeping and, in my view, misguided and unsupported changes in our takings doctrine. While it limits these changes to the most narrow subset of government regulation—those that eliminate all economic value from land—these changes go far beyond what is necessary to secure petitioner Lucas' private benefit. One hopes they do not go beyond the narrow confines the Court assigns them to today.

I DISSENT.

Justice STEVENS, dissenting.

Today the Court restricts one judge-made rule and expands another. In my opinion it errs on both counts. Proper application of the doctrine of judicial restraint would avoid the premature adjudication of an important constitutional question. Proper respect for our precedents would avoid an illogical expansion of the concept of "regulatory takings."

I

As the Court notes, *ante*, at 2890-2891, South Carolina's Beachfront Management Act has been amended to permit some construction of residences seaward of the line that frustrated petitioner's proposed use of his property. Until he exhausts his right to apply for a special permit under that amendment, petitioner is not entitled to an adjudication by this Court of the merits of his permanent takings claim. *MacDonald, Sommer & Frates v. Yolo County*, 477 U.S. 340, 351, 106 S.Ct. 2561, 2567, 91 L.Ed.2d 285 (1986).

It is also not clear that he has a viable "temporary takings" claim. If we assume that petitioner is now able to build on the lot, the only injury that he may have suffered is the delay caused by the temporary existence of the absolute statutory ban on construction. We cannot be sure, however, that that delay caused petitioner any harm because the record does not tell us whether his building plans were even temporarily frustrated by the enactment of the statute. [Footnote omitted.] Thus, on the present record it is entirely possible that petitioner has suffered no injury in fact even if the state statute was unconstitutional when he filed this lawsuit.

It is true, as the Court notes, that the argument against deciding the constitutional issue in this case rests on prudential considerations rather than a want of jurisdiction. I think it equally clear, however, that a Court less eager to decide the merits would follow the wise counsel of Justice Brandeis in his deservedly famous concurring opinion in *Ashwander v. TVA*, 297 U.S. 288, 341, 56 S.Ct. 466, 480, 80 L.Ed. 688 (1936). As he explained, the Court has developed "for its own governance in the cases confessedly within its jurisdiction, a series of rules under which it has avoided passing upon a large part of all the constitutional questions pressed upon it for decision." *Id.*, at 346, 56 S.Ct., at 482. The second of those rules applies directly to this case.

> "2. The Court will not 'anticipate a question of constitutional law in advance of the necessity of deciding it.' *Liverpool, N.Y. & P.S.S. Co. v. Emigration Commissioners*, 113 U.S. 33, 39

> [5 S.Ct. 352, 355, 28 L.Ed. 899]; [citing five additional cases]. 'It is not the habit of the Court to decide questions of a constitutional nature unless absolutely necessary to a decision of the case.' *Burton v. United States*, 196 U.S. 283, 295 [25 S.Ct. 243, 245, 49 L.Ed. 482]." *Id.*, at 346-347, 56 S.Ct., at 483.

Cavalierly dismissing the doctrine of judicial restraint, the Court today tersely announces that "we do not think it prudent to apply that prudential requirement here." *Ante*, at 2892. I respectfully disagree and would save consideration of the merits for another day. Since, however, the Court has reached the merits, I shall do so as well.

II

In its analysis of the merits, the Court starts from the premise that this Court has adopted a "categorical rule that total regulatory takings must be compensated," *ante*, at 2899, and then sets itself to the task of identifying the exceptional cases in which a State may be relieved of this categorical obligation, *ante*, at 2899-2900. The test the Court announces is that the regulation must do no more than duplicate the result that could have been achieved under a State's nuisance law. *Ante*, at 2900. Under this test the categorical rule will apply unless the regulation merely makes explicit what was otherwise an implicit limitation on the owner's property rights.

In my opinion, the Court is doubly in error. The categorical rule the Court establishes is an unsound and unwise addition to the law and the Court's formulation of the exception to that rule is too rigid and too narrow.

THE CATEGORICAL RULE

As the Court recognizes, *ante*, at 2892-2893, *Pennsylvania Coal Co. v. Mahon*, 260 U.S. 393, 43 S.Ct. 158, 67 L.Ed. 322 (1922), provides no support for its—or, indeed, any—categorical rule. To the contrary, Justice Holmes recognized that such absolute rules ill fit the inquiry into "regulatory takings." Thus, in the paragraph that contains his famous observation that a regulation may go "too far" and thereby constitute a taking, the Justice wrote: "As we already have said, this is a question of degree—and therefore cannot be disposed of by general propositions." *Id.*, at 416, 43 S.Ct., at 160. What he had "already ... said" made perfectly clear that Justice Holmes regarded economic injury to be merely one factor to be weighed: "One fact for consideration in determining such limits is the extent of the diminution [of value.] So the question depends upon the particular facts." *Id.*, at 413, 43 S.Ct., at 159.

Nor does the Court's new categorical rule find support in decisions following *Mahon*. Although in dicta we have sometimes recited that a law "effects a taking if [it] ... denies an owner economically viable use of his land," *Agins v. City of Tiburon*, 447 U.S. 255, 260, 100 S.Ct. 2138, 2141, 65 L.Ed.2d 106 (1980), our rulings have rejected such an absolute position. We have frequently—and recently—held that, in some circumstances, a law that renders property valueless may nonetheless not constitute a taking. *See, e.g., First English Evangelical Lutheran Church of Glendale v. County of Los Angeles*, 482 U.S. 304, 313, 107 S.Ct. 2378, 2385, 96 L.Ed.2d 250 (1987); *Goldblatt v. Hempstead*, 369 U.S. 590, 596, 82 S.Ct. 987, 991, 8 L.Ed.2d 130 (1962); *United States v. Caltex*, 344 U.S. 149, 155, 73 S.Ct. 200, 203, 97 L.Ed. 157 (1952); *Miller v. Schoene*, 276 U.S. 272, 48 S.Ct. 246, 72 L.Ed. 568 (1928); *Hadacheck v. Sebastian*, 239 U.S. 394, 405, 36 S.Ct. 143, 143, 60 L.Ed. 348 (1915); *Mugler v. Kansas*, 123 U.S. 623, 657, 8 S.Ct. 273, 294, 31 L.Ed. 205 (1887); *cf. Ruckelshaus v. Monsanto Co.*, 467 U.S. 986, 1011, 104 S.Ct. 2862, 2877, 81 L.Ed.2d 815

(1984); *Connolly v. Pension Benefit Guaranty Corporation*, 475 U.S. 211, 225, 106 S.Ct. 1018, 1026, 89 L.Ed.2d 166 (1986). In short, as we stated in *Keystone Bituminous Coal Assn. v. DeBenedictis*, 480 U.S. 470, 490, 107 S.Ct. 1232, 1244, 94 L.Ed.2d 472 (1987), "'Although a comparison of values before and after' a regulatory action 'is relevant,... it is by no means conclusive.'"

In addition to lacking support in past decisions, the Court's new rule is wholly arbitrary. A landowner whose property is diminished in value 95 percent recovers nothing, while an owner whose property is diminished 100 percent recovers the land's full value. The case at hand illustrates this arbitrariness well. The Beachfront Management Act not only prohibited the building of new dwellings in certain areas, it also prohibited the rebuilding of houses that were "destroyed beyond repair by natural causes or by fire." 1988 S.C. Acts 634, §3; *see* also *Esposito v. South Carolina Coastal Council*, 939 F.2d 165, 167 (CA4 1991). [Footnote omitted.] Thus, if the homes adjacent to Lucas' lot were destroyed by a hurricane one day after the Act took effect, the owners would not be able to rebuild, nor would they be assured recovery. Under the Court's categorical approach, Lucas (who has lost the opportunity to build) recovers, while his neighbors (who have lost both the opportunity to build and their homes) do not recover. The arbitrariness of such a rule is palpable.

Moreover, because of the elastic nature of property rights, the Court's new rule will also prove unsound in practice. In response to the rule, courts may define "property" broadly and only rarely find regulations to effect total takings. This is the approach the Court itself adopts in its revisionist reading of venerable precedents. We are told that—notwithstanding the Court's findings to the contrary in each case—the brewery in *Mugler*, the brickyard in *Hadacheck*, and the gravel pit in *Goldblatt* all could be put to "other uses" and that, therefore, those cases did not involve total regulatory takings.[3] *Ante*, at 2899, n. 13.

On the other hand, developers and investors may market specialized estates to take advantage of the Court's new rule. The smaller the estate, the more likely that a regulatory change will effect a total taking. Thus, an investor may, for example, purchase the right to build a multifamily home on a specific lot, with the result that a zoning regulation that allows only single-family homes would render the investor's property interest "valueless."[4] In short, the categorical rule will likely have one of two effects: Either courts will alter the definition of the "denominator" in the takings "fraction," rendering the Court's categorical rule meaningless, or investors will manipulate the relevant property interests, giving the Court's rule sweeping effect. To my mind,

---

[3] Of course, the same could easily be said in this case: Lucas may put his land to "other uses"—fishing or camping, for example—or may sell his land to his neighbors as a buffer. In either event, his land is far from "valueless."

This highlights a fundamental weakness in the Court's analysis: its failure to explain why only the impairment of "economically beneficial or productive use," *ante*, at 2893 (emphasis added), of property is relevant in takings analysis. I should think that a regulation arbitrarily prohibiting an owner from continuing to use her property for bird watching or sunbathing might constitute a taking under some circumstances; and, conversely, that such uses are of value to the owner. Yet the Court offers no basis for its assumption that the only uses of property cognizable under the Constitution are developmental uses.

[4] This unfortunate possibility is created by the Court's subtle revision of the "total regulatory takings" dicta. In past decisions, we have stated that a regulation effects a taking if it "denies an owner economically viable use of his land," *Agins v. City of Tiburon*, 447 U.S. 255, 260, 100 S.Ct. 2138, 2141, 65 L.Ed.2d 106 (1980) (emphasis added), indicating that this "total takings" test did not apply to other estates. Today, however, the Court suggests that a regulation may effect a total taking of any real property interest. *See ante*, at 2894, n. 7.

neither of these results is desirable or appropriate, and both are distortions of our takings jurisprudence.

Finally, the Court's justification for its new categorical rule is remarkably thin. The Court mentions in passing three arguments in support of its rule; none is convincing. First, the Court suggests that "total deprivation of feasible use is, from the landowner's point of view, the equivalent of a physical appropriation." *Ante*, at 2894. This argument proves too much. From the "landowner's point of view," a regulation that diminishes a lot's value by 50 percent is as well "the equivalent" of the condemnation of half of the lot. Yet, it is well established that a 50 percent diminution in value does not by itself constitute a taking. *See Euclid v. Ambler Realty Co.*, 272 U.S. 365, 384, 47 S.Ct. 114, 117, 71 L.Ed. 303 (1926) (75 percent diminution in value). Thus, the landowner's perception of the regulation cannot justify the Court's new rule.

Second, the Court emphasizes that because total takings are "relatively rare" its new rule will not adversely affect the government's ability to "go on." *Ante*, at 2894. This argument proves too little. Certainly it is true that defining a small class of regulations that are per se takings will not greatly hinder important governmental functions—but this is true of any small class of regulations. The Court's suggestion only begs the question of why regulations of this particular class should always be found to effect takings.

Finally, the Court suggests that "regulations that leave the owner ... without economically beneficial ... use ... carry with them a heightened risk that private property is being pressed into some form of public service." *Ibid.* As discussed more fully below, *see* Part III, infra, I agree that the risks of such singling out are of central concern in takings law. However, such risks do not justify a *per se* rule for total regulatory takings. There is no necessary correlation between "singling out" and total takings: A regulation may single out a property owner without depriving him of all of his property, *see, e.g., Nollan v. California Coastal Comm'n*, 483 U.S. 825, 837, 107 S.Ct. 3141, 3149, 97 L.Ed.2d 677 (1987); *J.E.D. Associates, Inc. v. Atkinson*, 121 N.H. 581, 432 A.2d 12 (1981); and it may deprive him of all of his property without singling him out, *see, e.g., Mugler v. Kansas*, 123 U.S. 623, 8 S.Ct. 273, 31 L.Ed. 205 (1887); *Hadacheck v. Sebastian*, 239 U.S. 394, 36 S.Ct. 143, 60 L.Ed. 348 (1915). What matters in such cases is not the degree of diminution of value, but rather the specificity of the expropriating act. For this reason, the Court's third justification for its new rule also fails.

In short, the Court's new rule is unsupported by prior decisions, arbitrary and unsound in practice, and theoretically unjustified. In my opinion, a categorical rule as important as the one established by the Court today should be supported by more history or more reason than has yet been provided.

THE NUISANCE EXCEPTION

Like many bright-line rules, the categorical rule established in this case is only "categorical" for a page or two in the U.S. Reports. No sooner does the Court state that "total regulatory takings must be compensated," *ante*, at 2899, than it quickly establishes an exception to that rule.

The exception provides that a regulation that renders property valueless is not a taking if it prohibits uses of property that were not "previously permissible under relevant property and nuisance principles." *Ante*, at 2901. The Court thus rejects the basic holding in *Mugler v. Kansas*, 123 U.S. 623, 8 S.Ct. 273, 31 L.Ed. 205 (1887). There we held that a state-wide statute that prohibited the owner of a brewery from making alcoholic beverages did not effect a taking, even though the use of the property had been perfectly lawful and caused no public harm before the statute was enacted. We squarely rejected the rule the Court adopts today:

> "It is true, that, when the defendants ... erected their breweries, the laws of the State did not forbid the manufacture of intoxicating liquors. But the State did not thereby give any assurance, or come under an obligation, that its legislation upon that subject would remain unchanged. [T]he supervision of the public health and the public morals is a governmental power, 'continuing in its nature,' and 'to be dealt with as the special exigencies of the moment may require;' ... 'for this purpose, the largest legislative discretion is allowed, and the discretion cannot be parted with any more than the power itself.'" *Id.*, at 669, 8 S.Ct., at 301.

Under our reasoning in *Mugler*, a State's decision to prohibit or to regulate certain uses of property is not a compensable taking just because the particular uses were previously lawful. Under the Court's opinion today, however, if a State should decide to prohibit the manufacture of asbestos, cigarettes, or concealable firearms, for example, it must be prepared to pay for the adverse economic consequences of its decision. One must wonder if government will be able to "go on" effectively if it must risk compensation "for every such change in the general law." *Mahon*, 260 U.S., at 413, 43 S.Ct., at 159.

The Court's holding today effectively freezes the State's common law, denying the legislature much of its traditional power to revise the law governing the rights and uses of property. Until today, I had thought that we had long abandoned this approach to constitutional law. More than a century ago we recognized that "the great office of statutes is to remedy defects in the common law as they are developed, and to adapt it to the changes of time and circumstances." *Munn v. Illinois*, 94 U.S. 113, 134, 24 L.Ed. 77 (1877). As Justice Marshall observed about a position similar to that adopted by the Court today:

"If accepted, that claim would represent a return to the era of *Lochner v. New York*, 198 U.S. 45 [25 S.Ct. 539, 49 L.Ed. 937] (1905), when common-law rights were also found immune from revision by State or Federal Government. Such an approach would freeze the common law as it has been constructed by the courts, perhaps at its 19th-century state of development. It would allow no room for change in response to changes in circumstance. The Due Process Clause does not require such a result." *PruneYard Shopping Center v. Robins*, 447 U.S. 74, 93, 100 S.Ct. 2035, 2047, 64 L.Ed.2d 741 (1980) (concurring opinion).

Arresting the development of the common law is not only a departure from our prior decisions; it is also profoundly unwise. The human condition is one of constant learning and evolution—both moral and practical. Legislatures implement that new learning; in doing so they must often revise the definition of property and the rights of property owners. Thus, when the Nation came to understand that slavery was morally wrong and mandated the emancipation of all slaves, it, in effect, redefined "property." On a lesser scale, our ongoing self-education produces similar changes in the rights of property owners: New appreciation of the significance of endangered species, *see, e.g.*, *Andrus v. Allard*, 444 U.S. 51, 100 S.Ct. 318, 62 L.Ed.2d 210 (1979); the importance of wetlands, *see, e.g.*, 16 U.S.C. § 3801 et seq.; and the vulnerability of coastal lands, *see, e.g.*, 16 U.S.C. §1451 et seq., shapes our evolving understandings of property rights.

Of course, some legislative redefinitions of property will effect a taking and must be compensated—but it certainly cannot be the case that every movement away from common law does so. There is no reason, and less sense, in such an absolute rule. We live in a world in which changes in the economy and the environment occur with increasing frequency and importance. If it was wise a century ago to allow government "'the largest legislative discretion'" to deal with "'the special exigencies of the moment,'" *Mugler*, 123 U.S., at 669, 8 S.Ct., at 301, it is imperative to do so today. The rule that should govern a decision in a case of this kind should focus on the future, not the past. [Footnote omitted.]

The Court's categorical approach rule will, I fear, greatly hamper the efforts of local officials and planners who must deal with increasingly complex problems in land-use and environmental regulation. As this case—in which the claims of an individual property owner exceed $1 million—well demonstrates, these officials face both substantial uncertainty because of the ad hoc nature of takings law and unacceptable penalties if they guess incorrectly about that law.[6]

Viewed more broadly, the Court's new rule and exception conflict with the very character of our takings jurisprudence. We have frequently and consistently recognized that the definition of a taking cannot be reduced to a "set formula" and that determining whether a regulation is a taking is "essentially [an] ad hoc, factual inquir[y]." *Penn Central Transportation Co. v. New York City*, 438 U.S. 104, 124, 98 S.Ct. 2646, 2659, 57 L.Ed.2d 631 (1978) (quoting *Goldblatt v. Hempstead*, 369 U.S., at 594, 82 S.Ct., at 990. This is unavoidable, for the determination whether a law effects a taking is ultimately a matter of "fairness and justice," *Armstrong v. United States*, 364 U.S. 40, 49, 80 S.Ct. 1563, 1569, 4 L.Ed.2d 1554 (1960), and "necessarily requires a weighing of private and public interests," *Agins*, 447 U.S., at 261, 100 S.Ct., at 2141. The rigid rules fixed by the Court today clash with this enterprise: "fairness and justice" are often disserved by categorical rules.

III

It is well established that a takings case "entails inquiry into [several factors:] the character of the governmental action, its economic impact, and its interference with reasonable investment-backed expectations." *PruneYard*, 447 U.S., at 83, 100 S.Ct., at 2042. The Court's analysis today focuses on the last two of these three factors: The categorical rule addresses a regulation's "economic impact," while the nuisance exception recognizes that ownership brings with it only certain "expectations." Neglected by the Court today is the first and, in some ways, the most important factor in takings analysis: the character of the regulatory action.

The Just Compensation Clause "was designed to bar Government from forcing some people alone to bear public burdens which, in all fairness and justice, should be borne by the public as a whole." *Armstrong*, 364 U.S., at 49, 80 S.Ct., at 1569. Accordingly, one of the central concerns of our takings jurisprudence is "prevent[ing] the public from loading upon one individual more than his just share of the burdens of government." *Monongahela Navigation Co. v. United States*, 148 U.S. 312, 325, 13 S.Ct. 622, 626, 37 L.Ed. 463 (1893). We have, therefore, in our takings law frequently looked to the generality of a regulation of property. [Footnote omitted]

---

[6] As the Court correctly notes, in regulatory takings, unlike physical takings, courts have a choice of remedies. *See* ante, at 2901, n. 17. They may "invalidat[e the] excessive regulation" or they may "allo[w] the regulation to stand and orde[r] the government to afford compensation for the permanent taking." *First English Evangelical Lutheran Church of Glendale v. County of Los Angeles*, 482 U.S. 304, 335, 107 S.Ct. 2378, 2396, 96 L.Ed.2d 250 (1987) (STEVENS, J., dissenting); *see* also id., at 319-321, 107 S.Ct., at 2388-2389. In either event, however, the costs to the government are likely to be substantial and are therefore likely to impede the development of sound land-use policy.

For example, in the case of so-called "developmental exactions," we have paid special attention to the risk that particular landowners might "b[e] singled out to bear the burden" of a broader problem not of his own making. *Nollan*, 483 U.S., at 835, n. 4, 107 S.Ct., at 3148, n. 4; *see* also *Pennell v. San Jose*, 485 U.S. 1, 23, 108 S.Ct. 849, 863, 99 L.Ed.2d 1 (1988). Similarly, in distinguishing between the Kohler Act (at issue in *Mahon*) and the Subsidence Act (at issue in *Keystone*), we found significant that the regulatory function of the latter was substantially broader. Unlike the Kohler Act, which simply transferred back to the surface owners certain rights that they had earlier sold to the coal companies, the Subsidence Act affected all surface owners—including the coal companies—equally. *See Keystone*, 480 U.S., at 486, 107 S.Ct., at 1242. Perhaps the most familiar application of this principle of generality arises in zoning cases. A diminution in value caused by a zoning regulation is far less likely to constitute a taking if it is part of a general and comprehensive land-use plan, *see Euclid v. Ambler Realty Co.*, 272 U.S. 365, 47 S.Ct. 114, 71 L.Ed. 303 (1926); conversely, "spot zoning" is far more likely to constitute a taking, *see Penn Central*, 438 U.S., at 132, and n.28, 98 S.Ct., at 2663, and n.28.

The presumption that a permanent physical occupation, no matter how slight, effects a taking is wholly consistent with this principle. A physical taking entails a certain amount of "singling out." [Footnote omitted.] Consistent with this principle, physical occupations by third parties are more likely to effect takings than other physical occupations. Thus, a regulation requiring the installation of a junction box owned by a third party, *Loretto v. Teleprompter Manhattan CATV Corp.*, 458 U.S. 419, 102 S.Ct. 3164, 73 L.Ed.2d 868 (1982), is more troubling than a regulation requiring the installation of sprinklers or smoke detectors; just as an order granting third parties access to a marina, *Kaiser Aetna v. United States*, 444 U.S. 164, 100 S.Ct. 383, 62 L.Ed.2d 332 (1979), is more troubling than an order requiring the placement of safety buoys in the marina.

In analyzing takings claims, courts have long recognized the difference between a regulation that targets one or two parcels of land and a regulation that enforces a statewide policy. *See, e.g.*, *A.A. Profiles, Inc. v. Ft. Lauderdale*, 850 F.2d 1483, 1488 (CA11 1988); *Wheeler v. Pleasant Grove*, 664 F.2d 99, 100 (CA5 1981); *Trustees Under Will of Pomeroy v. Westlake*, 357 So.2d 1299, 1304 (La.App.1978); *see* also *Burrows v. Keene*, 121 N.H. 590, 596, 432 A.2d 15, 21 (1981); *Herman Glick Realty Co. v. St. Louis County*, 545 S.W.2d 320, 324-325 (Mo.App.1976); *Huttig v. Richmond Heights*, 372 S.W.2d 833, 842-843 (Mo.1963). As one early court stated with regard to a waterfront regulation, "If such restraint were in fact imposed upon the estate of one proprietor only, out of several estates on the same line of shore, the objection would be much more formidable." *Commonwealth v. Alger*, 61 Mass. 53, 102 (1851).

In considering Lucas' claim, the generality of the Beachfront Management Act is significant. The Act does not target particular landowners, but rather regulates the use of the coastline of the entire State. *See* S.C. Code Ann. §48-39-10 (Supp.1990). Indeed, South Carolina's Act is best understood as part of a national effort to protect the coastline, one initiated by the federal Coastal Zone Management Act of 1972. Pub.L. 92-583, 86 Stat. 1280, codified as amended at 16 U.S.C. §1451 et seq. Pursuant to the federal Act, every coastal State has implemented coastline regulations. [Footnote omitted.] Moreover, the Act did not single out owners of undeveloped land. The Act also prohibited owners of developed land from rebuilding if their structures were destroyed, *see* 1988 S.C. Acts 634, §3, [footnote omitted] and what is equally significant, from repairing erosion control devices, such as seawalls, *see* S.C. Code Ann. §48-39-290(B)(2) (Supp.1990). In addition, in some situations, owners of developed land were required to "renouris[h] the beach ... on a yearly basis with an amount ... of sand ... not ... less than one and one-half times the yearly volume of sand lost due to erosion." 1988 S.C. Acts 634, §3, p. 5140.

[Footnote omitted.] In short, the South Carolina Act imposed substantial burdens on owners of developed and undeveloped land alike.[12] This generality indicates that the Act is not an effort to expropriate owners of undeveloped land.

Admittedly, the economic impact of this regulation is dramatic and petitioner's investment-backed expectations are substantial. Yet, if anything, the costs to and expectations of the owners of developed land are even greater: I doubt, however, that the cost to owners of developed land of renourishing the beach and allowing their seawalls to deteriorate effects a taking. The costs imposed on the owners of undeveloped land, such as petitioner, differ from these costs only in degree, not in kind.

The impact of the ban on developmental uses must also be viewed in light of the purposes of the Act. The legislature stated the purposes of the Act as "protect[ing], preserv[ing], restor[ing] and enhanc[ing] the beach/dune system" of the State not only for recreational and ecological purposes, but also to "protec[t] life and property." S.C. Code Ann. §48-39-260(1)(a) (Supp.1990). The State, with much science on its side, believes that the "beach/dune system [acts] as a buffer from high tides, storm surge, [and] hurricanes." *Ibid.* This is a traditional and important exercise of the State's police power, as demonstrated by Hurricane Hugo, which in 1989, caused 29 deaths and more than $6 billion in property damage in South Carolina alone. [Footnote omitted.]

In view of all of these factors, even assuming that petitioner's property was rendered valueless, the risk inherent in investments of the sort made by petitioner, the generality of the Act, and the compelling purpose motivating the South Carolina Legislature persuade me that the Act did not effect a taking of petitioner's property.

Accordingly, I respectfully dissent.

Statement of Justice SOUTER.

I would dismiss the writ of certiorari in this case as having been granted improvidently. After briefing and argument it is abundantly clear that an unreviewable assumption on which this case comes to us is both questionable as a conclusion of Fifth Amendment law and sufficient to frustrate the Court's ability to render certain the legal premises on which its holding rests.

The petition for review was granted on the assumption that the State by regulation had deprived the owner of his entire economic interest in the subject property. Such was the state trial court's conclusion, which the State Supreme Court did not review. It is apparent now that in light of our prior cases, *see, e.g., Keystone Bituminous Coal Assn. v. DeBenedictis*, 480 U.S. 470, 493-502, 107 S.Ct. 1232, 1246-1251, 94 L.Ed.2d 472 (1987); *Andrus v. Allard*, 444 U.S. 51, 65-66, 100 S.Ct. 318, 326-327, 62 L.Ed.2d 210 (1979); *Penn Central Transportation Corp. v. New York City*, 438 U.S. 104, 130-131, 98 S.Ct. 2646, 2662, 57 L.Ed.2d 631 (1978), the trial court's conclusion is highly questionable. While the respondent now wishes to contest the point, *see* Brief for Respondent 45-50, the Court is certainly right to refuse to take up the issue, which is not fairly included

---

[12] In this regard, the Act more closely resembles the Subsidence Act in *Keystone* than the Kohler Act in *Pennsylvania Coal Co. v. Mahon*, 260 U.S. 393, 43 S.Ct. 158, 67 L.Ed. 322 (1922), and more closely resembles the general zoning scheme in *Euclid v. Ambler Realty Co.*, 272 U.S. 365, 47 S.Ct. 114, 71 L.Ed. 303 (1926), than the specific landmark designation in *Penn Central Transportation Co. v. New York City*, 438 U.S. 104, 98 S.Ct. 2646, 57 L.Ed.2d 631 (1978).

within the question presented, and has received only the most superficial and one-sided treatment before us.

Because the questionable conclusion of total deprivation cannot be reviewed, the Court is precluded from attempting to clarify the concept of total (and, in the Court's view, categorically compensable) taking on which it rests, a concept which the Court describes, *see ante*, at 2893, n. 6, as so uncertain under existing law as to have fostered inconsistent pronouncements by the Court itself. Because that concept is left uncertain, so is the significance of the exceptions to the compensation requirement that the Court proceeds to recognize. This alone is enough to show that there is little utility in attempting to deal with this case on the merits.

The imprudence of proceeding to the merits in spite of these unpromising circumstances is underscored by the fact that, in doing so, the Court cannot help but assume something about the scope of the uncertain concept of total deprivation, even when it is barred from explicating total deprivation directly. Thus, when the Court concludes that the application of nuisance law provides an exception to the general rule that complete denial of economically beneficial use of property amounts to a compensable taking, the Court will be understood to suggest (if it does not assume) that there are in fact circumstances in which state-law nuisance abatement may amount to a denial of all beneficial land use as that concept is to be employed in our takings jurisprudence under the Fifth and Fourteenth Amendments. The nature of nuisance law, however, indicates that application of a regulation defensible on grounds of nuisance prevention or abatement will quite probably not amount to a complete deprivation in fact. The nuisance enquiry focuses on conduct, not on the character of the property on which that conduct is performed, *see* 4 Restatement (Second) of Torts §821B (1979) (public nuisance); *id.*, §822 (private nuisance), and the remedies for such conduct usually leave the property owner with other reasonable uses of his property, *see* W. Keeton, D. Dobbs, R. Keeton, & D. Owen, *Prosser and Keeton on Law of Torts* §90 (5th ed. 1984) (public nuisances usually remedied by criminal prosecution or abatement), *id.*, §89 (private nuisances usually remedied by damages, injunction, or abatement); *see* also, *e.g.*, *Mugler v. Kansas*, 123 U.S. 623, 668-669, 8 S.Ct. 273, 301, 31 L.Ed. 205 (1887)(prohibition on use of property to manufacture intoxicating beverages "does not disturb the owner in the control or use of his property for lawful purposes, nor restrict his right to dispose of it, but is only a declaration by the State that its use ... for certain forbidden purposes, is prejudicial to the public interests"); *Hadacheck v. Sebastian*, 239 U.S. 394, 412, 36 S.Ct. 143, 146, 60 L.Ed. 348 (1915) (prohibition on operation of brickyard did not prohibit extraction of clay from which bricks were produced). Indeed, it is difficult to imagine property that can be used only to create a nuisance, such that its sole economic value must presuppose the right to occupy it for such seriously noxious activity.

The upshot is that the issue of what constitutes a total deprivation is being addressed by indirection, and with uncertain results, in the Court's treatment of defenses to compensation claims. While the issue of what constitutes total deprivation deserves the Court's attention, as does the relationship between nuisance abatement and such total deprivation, the Court should confront these matters directly. Because it can neither do so in this case, nor skip over those preliminary issues and deal independently with defenses to the Court's categorical compensation rule, the Court should dismiss the instant writ and await an opportunity to face the total deprivation question squarely. Under these circumstances, I believe it proper for me to vote to dismiss the writ, despite the Court's contrary preference. *See, e.g., Welsh v. Wisconsin*, 466 U.S. 740, 755, 104 S.Ct. 2091, 2100, 80 L.Ed.2d 732 (1984) (Burger, C.J.); *United States v. Shannon*, 342 U.S. 288, 294, 72 S.Ct. 281, 285, 96 L.Ed. 321 (1952) (Frankfurter, J.).

In examining the burden to the landowner, the court moves to the three issues in *Penn Central.* A remaining economically viable use does not mean the property's highest and best use and is calculated including the value of the property as a whole.

KEYSTONE BITUMINOUS COAL ASSOCIATION v. DE BENEDICTIS

480 U.S. 470, 495, 107 S.Ct. 1232, 1247, 94 L.Ed.2d 472 (1987)

In *Pennsylvania Coal Co. v. Mahon*, 260 U.S. 393, 43 S.Ct. 158, 67 L.Ed. 322 (1922), the Court reviewed the constitutionality of a Pennsylvania statute that admittedly destroyed "previously existing rights of property and contract." *Id.*, at 413, 43 S.Ct., at 159. Writing for the Court, Justice Holmes explained:

> "Government hardly could go on if to some extent values incident to property could not be diminished without paying for every such change in the general law. As long recognized, some values are enjoyed under an implied limitation and must yield to the police power. But obviously the implied limitation must have its limits, or the contract and due process clauses are gone. One fact for consideration in determining such limits is the extent of the diminution. When it reaches a certain magnitude, in most if not in all cases there must be an exercise of eminent domain and compensation to sustain the act. So the question depends upon the particular facts." *Ibid.*

In that case the "particular facts" led the Court to hold that the Pennsylvania Legislature had gone beyond its constitutional powers when it enacted a statute prohibiting the mining of anthracite coal in a manner that would cause the subsidence of land on which certain structures were located.

Now, 65 years later, we address a different set of "particular facts," involving the Pennsylvania Legislature's 1966 conclusion that the Commonwealth's existing mine subsidence legislation had failed to protect the public interest in safety, land conservation, preservation of affected municipalities' tax bases, and land development in the Commonwealth. Based on detailed findings, the legislature enacted the Bituminous Mine Subsidence and Land Conservation Act (Subsidence Act or the Act), Pa.Stat.Ann., Tit. 52, §1406.1 et seq. (Purdon Supp.1986). Petitioners contend, relying heavily on our decision in Pennsylvania Coal, that §§4 and 6 of the Subsidence Act and certain implementing regulations violate the Takings Clause, and that §6 of the Act violates the Contracts Clause of the Federal Constitution. The District Court and the Court of Appeals concluded that Pennsylvania Coal does not control for several reasons and that our subsequent cases make it clear that neither §4 nor §6 is unconstitutional on its face. We agree.

I

Coal mine subsidence is the lowering of strata overlying a coal mine, including the land surface, caused by the extraction of underground coal. This lowering of the strata can have devastating effects. [Footnote omitted.] It often causes substantial damage to foundations, walls, other structural members, and the integrity of houses and buildings. Subsidence frequently causes sinkholes or troughs in land which make the land difficult or impossible to develop. Its effect on farming has been well documented—many subsided areas cannot be plowed or properly prepared. Subsidence can also cause the loss of groundwater and surface ponds. [Footnote omitted.] In short, it presents the type of environmental concern that has been the focus of so much federal, state, and local regulation in recent decades. [Footnote omitted.]

Despite what their name may suggest, neither of the "full extraction" mining methods currently used in western Pennsylvania [footnote omitted] enables miners to extract all subsurface coal; considerable amounts need to be left in the ground to provide access, support, and ventilation to the mines. Additionally, mining companies have long been required by various Pennsylvania laws and regulations, the legitimacy of which is not challenged here, to leave coal in certain areas for public safety reasons. [Footnote omitted.] Since 1966, Pennsylvania has placed an additional set of restrictions on the amount of coal that may be extracted; these restrictions are designed to diminish subsidence and subsidence damage in the vicinity of certain structures and areas.

Pennsylvania's Subsidence Act authorizes the Pennsylvania Department of Environmental Resources (DER) to implement and enforce a comprehensive program to prevent or minimize subsidence and to regulate its consequences. Section 4 of the Subsidence Act, Pa.Stat.Ann., Tit. 52, §1406.4 (Purdon Supp.1986), prohibits mining that causes subsidence damage to three categories of structures that were in place on April 17, 1966: public buildings and noncommercial buildings generally used by the public; dwellings used for human habitation; and cemeteries. [Footnote omitted.] Since 1966 the DER has applied a formula that generally requires 50 percent of the coal beneath structures protected by §4 to be kept in place as a means of providing surface support. [Footnote omitted.] Section 6 of the Subsidence Act, Pa.Stat.Ann., Tit. 52, §1406.6 (Purdon Supp.1986), authorizes the DER to revoke a mining permit if the removal of coal causes damage to a structure or area protected by §4 and the operator has not within six months either repaired the damage, satisfied any claim arising therefrom, or deposited a sum equal to the reasonable cost of repair with the DER as security. [Footnote omitted.]

II

In 1982, petitioners filed a civil rights action in the United States District Court for the Western District of Pennsylvania seeking to enjoin officials of the DER from enforcing the Subsidence Act and its implementing regulations. Petitioners are an association of coal mine operators, and four corporations that are engaged, either directly or through affiliates, in underground mining of bituminous coal in western Pennsylvania. The members of the association and the corporate petitioners own, lease, or otherwise control substantial coal reserves beneath the surface of property affected by the Subsidence Act. The defendants in the action, respondents here, are the Secretary of the DER, the Chief of the DER's Division of Mine Subsidence, and the Chief of the DER's Section on Mine Subsidence Regulation.

The complaint alleges that Pennsylvania recognizes three separate estates in land: The mineral estate; the surface estate; and the "support estate." Beginning well over 100 years ago, landowners began severing title to underground coal and the right of surface support while retaining or conveying away ownership of the surface estate. It is stipulated that approximately 90 percent of the coal that is or will be mined by petitioners in western Pennsylvania was severed from the surface in the period between 1890 and 1920. When acquiring or retaining the mineral estate, petitioners or their predecessors typically acquired or retained certain additional rights that would enable them to extract and remove the coal. Thus, they acquired the right to deposit wastes, to provide for drainage and ventilation, and to erect facilities such as tipples, roads, or railroads, on the surface. Additionally, they typically acquired a waiver of any claims for damages that might result from the removal of the coal.

In the portions of the complaint that are relevant to us, petitioners alleged that both §4 of the Subsidence Act, as implemented by the 50 percent rule, and §6 of the Subsidence Act, constitute a taking of their private property without compensation in violation of the Fifth and Fourteenth Amendments. They also alleged that §6 impairs their contractual agreements in violation of Article I, §10, of the Constitution. [Footnote omitted.] The parties entered into a stipulation of facts pertaining to petitioners' facial challenge, and filed cross-motions for summary judgment on the facial challenge. The District Court granted respondents' motion.

In rejecting petitioners' Takings Clause claim, the District Court first distinguished Pennsylvania Coal, primarily on the ground that the Subsidence Act served valid public purposes that the Court had found lacking in the earlier case. 581 F.Supp. 511, 516 (W.D.Pa.1984). The District Court found that the restriction on the use of petitioners' property was an exercise of the Commonwealth's police power, justified by Pennsylvania's interest in the health, safety, and general welfare of the public. In answer to petitioners' argument that the Subsidence Act effectuated a taking because a separate, recognized interest in realty—the support estate—had been entirely destroyed, the District Court concluded that under Pennsylvania law the support estate consists of a bundle of rights, including some that were not affected by the Act. That the right to cause damage to the surface may constitute the most valuable "strand" in the bundle of rights possessed by the owner of a support estate was not considered controlling under our decision in Andrus v. Allard, 444 U.S. 51, 100 S.Ct. 318, 62 L.Ed.2d 210 (1979).

In rejecting petitioners' Contracts Clause claim, the District Court noted that there was no contention that the Subsidence Act or the DER regulations had impaired any contract to which the Commonwealth was a party. Since only private contractual obligations had been impaired, the court considered it appropriate to defer to the legislature's determinations concerning the public purposes served by the legislation. The court found that the adjustment of the rights of the contracting parties was tailored to those "significant and legitimate" public purposes. 581 F.Supp., at 514. At the parties'request, the District Court certified the facial challenge for appeal.

The Court of Appeals affirmed, agreeing that Pennsylvania Coal does not control because the Subsidence Act is a legitimate means of "protect[ing] the environment of the Commonwealth, its economic future, and its well-being." 771 F.2d 707, 715 (1985). The Court of Appeals' analysis of the Subsidence Act's effect on petitioners' property differed somewhat from the District Court's, however. In rejecting the argument that the support estate had been entirely destroyed, the Court of Appeals did not rely on the fact that the support estate itself constitutes a bundle of many rights, but rather considered the support estate as just one segment of a larger bundle of rights that invariably includes either the surface estate or the mineral estate. As Judge Adams explained:

> "To focus upon the support estate separately when assessing the diminution of the value of plaintiffs' property caused by the Subsidence Act therefore would serve little purpose. The support estate is more properly viewed as only one 'strand' in the plaintiff's 'bundle' of property rights, which also includes the mineral estate. As the Court stated in Andrus, "[t]he destruction of one 'strand' of the bundle is not a taking because the aggregate must be viewed in its entirety." 444 U.S. at 65 [100 S.Ct. at 326].... The use to which the mine operators wish to put the support estate is forbidden. However, because the plaintiffs still

> possess valuable mineral rights that enable them profitably to mine coal, subject only to the Subsidence Act's requirement that they prevent subsidence, their entire 'bundle' of property rights has not been destroyed." *Id.*, at 716.

With respect to the Contracts Clause claim, the Court of Appeals agreed with the District Court that a higher degree of deference should be afforded to legislative determinations respecting economic and social legislation affecting wholly private contracts than when the State impairs its own agreements. The court held that the impairment of private agreements effectuated by the Subsidence Act was justified by the legislative finding "that subsidence damage devastated many surface structures and thus endangered the health, safety, and economic welfare of the Commonwealth and its people." *Id.*, at 718. We granted certiorari, 475 U.S. 1080, 106 S.Ct. 1456, 89 L.Ed.2d 714 (1986), and now affirm.

III

Petitioners assert that disposition of their takings claim [footnote omitted] calls for no more than a straightforward application of the Court's decision in *Pennsylvania Coal Co. v. Mahon*. Although there are some obvious similarities between the cases, we agree with the Court of Appeals and the District Court that the similarities are far less significant than the differences, and that Pennsylvania Coal does not control this case.

In Pennsylvania Coal, the Pennsylvania Coal Company had served notice on Mr. and Mrs. Mahon that the company's mining operations beneath their premises would soon reach a point that would cause subsidence to the surface. The Mahons filed a bill in equity seeking to enjoin the coal company from removing any coal that would cause "the caving in, collapse or subsidence" of their dwelling. The bill acknowledged that the Mahons owned only "the surface or right of soil" in the lot, and that the coal company had reserved the right to remove the coal without any liability to the owner of the surface estate. Nonetheless, the Mahons asserted that Pennsylvania's then recently enacted Kohler Act of 1921, P.L. 1198, Pa.Stat.Ann., Tit. 52, §661 et seq. (Purdon 1966), which prohibited mining that caused subsidence under certain structures, entitled them to an injunction.

After initially having entered a preliminary injunction pending a hearing on the merits, the Chancellor soon dissolved it, observing:

> "[T]he plaintiffs' bill contains no averment on which to base by implication or otherwise any finding of fact that any interest public or private is involved in the defendant's proposal to mine the coal except the private interest of the plaintiffs in the prevention of private injury." Tr. of *Record in Pennsylvania Coal v. Mahon*, O.T. 1922, No. 549, p. 23.

The Pennsylvania Supreme Court reversed, concluding that the Kohler Act was a proper exercise of the police power. 274 Pa. 489, 118 A. 491 (1922). One Justice dissented. He concluded that the Kohler Act was not actually intended to protect lives and safety, but rather was special legislation enacted for the sole benefit of the surface owners who had released their right to support. *Id.*, at 512-518, 118 A., at 499-501.

The company promptly appealed to this Court, asserting that the impact of the statute was so severe that "a serious shortage of domestic fuel is threatened." Motion to Advance for Argument in *Pennsylvania Coal v. Mahon*, O.T. 1922, No. 549, p. 3. The company explained that until the

Court ruled, "no anthracite coal which is likely to cause surface subsidence can be mined," and that strikes were threatened throughout the anthracite coal fields. [Footnote omitted.] In its argument in this Court, the company contended that the Kohler Act was not a bona fide exercise of the police power, but in reality was nothing more than "robbery under the forms of law" because its purpose was "not to protect the lives or safety of the public generally but merely to augment the property rights of a favored few." *See* 260 U.S., at 396-398, 43 S.Ct., at 159, quoting *Loan Assn. v. Topeka*, 20 Wall. 655, 664, 22 L.Ed. 455 (1874).

Over Justice Brandeis' dissent, this Court accepted the company's argument. In his opinion for the Court, Justice Holmes first characteristically decided the specific case at hand in a single, terse paragraph:

> "This is the case of a single private house. No doubt there is a public interest even in this, as there is in every purchase and sale and in all that happens within the commonwealth. Some existing rights may be modified even in such a case. *Rideout v. Knox*, 148 Mass. 368 [19 N.E. 390]. But usually in ordinary private affairs the public interest does not warrant much of this kind of interference. A source of damage to such a house is not a public nuisance even if similar damage is inflicted on others in different places. The damage is not common or public. *Wesson v. Washburn Iron Co.*, 13 Allen, 95, 103. The extent of the public interest is shown by the statute to be limited, since the statute ordinarily does not apply to land when the surface is owned by the owner of the coal. Furthermore, it is not justified as a protection of personal safety. That could be provided for by notice. Indeed the very foundation of this bill is that the defendant gave timely notice of its intent to mine under the house. On the other hand the extent of the taking is great. It purports to abolish what is recognized in Pennsylvania as an estate in land—a very valuable estate—and what is declared by the Court below to be a contract hitherto binding the plaintiffs. If we were called upon to deal with the plaintiffs' position alone, we should think it clear that the statute does not disclose a public interest sufficient to warrant so extensive a destruction of the defendant's constitutionally protected rights. 260 U.S., at 413-414, 43 S.Ct., at 159.

Then—uncharacteristically—Justice Holmes provided the parties with an advisory opinion discussing "the general validity of the Act." [Footnote omitted.] In the advisory portion of the Court's opinion, Justice Holmes rested on two propositions, both critical to the Court's decision. First, because it served only private interests, not health or safety, the Kohler Act could not be "sustained as an exercise of the police power." *Id.*, at 414, 43 S.Ct., at 159. Second, the statute made it "commercially impracticable" to mine "certain coal" in the areas affected by the Kohler Act. [Footnote omitted.]

The holdings and assumptions of the Court in Pennsylvania Coal provide obvious and necessary reasons for distinguishing Pennsylvania Coal from the case before us today. The two factors that the Court considered relevant, have become integral parts of our takings analysis. We have held that land use regulation can effect a taking if it "does not substantially advance legitimate state interests,... or denies an owner economically viable use of his land." *Agins v. Tiburon*, 447 U.S. 255, 260, 100 S.Ct. 2138, 2141, 65 L.Ed.2d 106 (1980) (citations omitted); *see* also *Penn Central Transportation Co. v. New York City*, 438 U.S. 104, 124, 98 S.Ct. 2646, 2659, 57 L.Ed.2d 631 (1978). Application of these tests to petitioners' challenge demonstrates that they have not satisfied their burden of showing that the Subsidence Act constitutes a taking. First, unlike the Kohler Act, the character of the governmental action involved here leans heavily against finding a taking; the Commonwealth of Pennsylvania has acted to arrest what it perceives to be a significant threat to the common welfare. Second, there is no record in this case to support a finding, similar to the one the Court made in Pennsylvania Coal, that the Subsidence Act makes it impossible for petitioners to profitably engage in their business, or that there has been undue interference with their investment-backed expectations.

THE PUBLIC PURPOSE

Unlike the Kohler Act, which was passed upon in Pennsylvania Coal, the Subsidence Act does not merely involve a balancing of the private economic interests of coal companies against the private interests of the surface owners. The Pennsylvania Legislature specifically found that important public interests are served by enforcing a policy that is designed to minimize subsidence in certain areas. Section 2 of the Subsidence Act provides:

> "This act shall be deemed to be an exercise of the police powers of the Commonwealth for the protection of the health, safety and general welfare of the people of the Commonwealth, by providing for the conservation of surface land areas which may be affected in the mining of bituminous coal by methods other than 'open pit' or 'strip' mining, to aid in the protection of the safety of the public, to enhance the value of such lands for taxation, to aid in the preservation of surface water drainage and public water supplies and generally to improve the use and enjoyment of such lands and to maintain primary jurisdiction over surface coal mining in Pennsylvania." Pa.Stat.Ann., Tit. 52, §1406.2 (Purdon Supp.1986).

The District Court and the Court of Appeals were both convinced that the legislative purposes [Footnote omitted.] set forth in the statute were genuine, substantial, and legitimate, and we have no reason to conclude otherwise. [Footnote omitted.]

None of the indicia of a statute enacted solely for the benefit of private parties identified in Justice Holmes' opinion are present here. First, Justice Holmes explained that the Kohler Act was a "private benefit" statute since it "ordinarily does not apply to land when the surface is owned by the owner of the coal." 260 U.S., at 414, 43 S.Ct. at 159. The Subsidence Act, by contrast, has no such exception. The current surface owner may only waive the protection of the Act if the DER consents. *See* 25 Pa. Code §89.145(b) (1983). Moreover, the Court was forced to reject the Commonwealth's safety justification for the Kohler Act because it found that the Commonwealth's interest in safety could as easily have been accomplished through a notice requirement to landowners. The Subsidence Act, by contrast, is designed to accomplish a number of widely varying interests, with reference to which petitioners have not suggested alternative methods through which the Commonwealth could proceed.

Petitioners argue that at least §6, which requires coal companies to repair subsidence damage or pay damages to those who suffer subsidence damage, is unnecessary because the Commonwealth administers an insurance program that adequately reimburses surface owners for the cost of repairing their property. But this argument rests on the mistaken premise that the statute was motivated by a desire to protect private parties. In fact, however, the public purpose that motivated the enactment of the legislation is served by preventing the damage from occurring in the first place—in the words of the statute—"by providing for the conservation of surface land areas." Pa.Stat.Ann., Tit. 52, §1406.2 (Purdon Supp.1986). The requirement that the mine operator assume the financial responsibility for the repair of damaged structures deters the operator from causing the damage at all—the Commonwealth's main goal—whereas an insurance program would merely reimburse the surface owner after the damage occurs. [Footnote omitted.]

Thus, the Subsidence Act differs from the Kohler Act in critical and dispositive respects. With regard to the Kohler Act, the Court believed that the Commonwealth had acted only to ensure against damage to some private landowners' homes. Justice Holmes stated that if the private individuals needed support for their structures, they should not have "take[n] the risk of acquiring only surface rights." 260 U.S., at 416, 43 S.Ct., at 160. Here, by contrast, the Commonwealth is acting to protect the public interest in health, the environment, and the fiscal integrity of the area. That private individuals erred in taking a risk cannot estop the Commonwealth from exercising its police power to abate activity akin to a public nuisance. The Subsidence Act is a prime example that "circumstances may so change in time ... as to clothe with such a [public] interest what at other times ... would be a matter of purely private concern." Block v. Hirsh, 256 U.S. 135, 155, 41 S.Ct. 458, 459, 65 L.Ed. 865 (1921).

In Pennsylvania Coal the Court recognized that the nature of the State's interest in the regulation is a critical factor in determining whether a taking has occurred, and thus whether compensation is required. [Footnote omitted.] The Court distinguished the case before it from a case it had decided eight years earlier, *Plymouth Coal Co. v. Pennsylvania*, 232 U.S. 531, 34 S.Ct. 359, 58 L.Ed. 713 (1914). There, "it was held competent for the legislature to require a pillar of coal to be left along the line of adjoining property." *Pennsylvania Coal*, 260 U.S., at 415, 43 S.Ct., at 160. Justice Holmes explained that unlike the Kohler Act, the statute challenged in *Plymouth Coal* dealt with "a requirement for the safety of employees invited into the mine, and secured an average reciprocity of advantage that has been recognized as a justification of various laws." 260 U.S., at 415, 43 S.Ct., at 160.

Many cases before and since Pennsylvania Coal have recognized that the nature of the State's action is critical in takings analysis.[18] In *Mugler v. Kansas*, 123 U.S. 623, 8 S.Ct. 273, 31 L.Ed. 205 (1887), for example, a Kansas distiller who had built a brewery while it was legal to do so challenged a Kansas constitutional amendment which prohibited the manufacture and sale of intoxicating liquors. Although the Court recognized that the "buildings and machinery constituting these breweries are of little value" because of the Amendment, *id.*, at 657, 8 S.Ct., at 294, Justice Harlan explained that a

> "prohibition simply upon the use of property for purposes that are declared, by valid legislation, to be injurious to the health, morals, or safety of the community, cannot, in any just sense, be deemed a taking or appropriation of property.... The power which the States have of prohibiting such use by individuals of their property as will be prejudicial

[18] Of course, the type of taking alleged is also an often critical factor. It is well settled that a "'taking'" may more readily be found when the interference with property can be characterized as a physical invasion by government, *see, e.g., United States v. Causby*, 328 U.S. 256, 66 S.Ct. 1062, 90 L.Ed. 1206 (1946), than when interference arises from some public program adjusting the benefits and burdens of economic life to promote the common good." *Penn Central Transportation Co. v. New York City*, 438 U.S. 104, 124, 98 S.Ct. 2646, 2659, 57 L.Ed.2d 631 (1978). While the Court has almost invariably found that the permanent physical occupation of property constitutes a taking, *see Loretto v. Teleprompter Manhattan CATV Corp.*, 458 U.S. 419, 435-438, 102 S.Ct. 3164, 3175-3177, 73 L.Ed.2d 868 (1982), the Court has repeatedly upheld regulations that destroy or adversely affect real property interests. *See, e.g., Connolly v. Pension Benefit Guaranty Corporation*, 475 U.S. 211, 106 S.Ct. 1018, 89 L.Ed.2d 166 (1986); *Penn Central Transportation Co. v. New York City*, 438 U.S., at 125, 98 S.Ct., at 2659; *Eastlake v. Forest City Enterprises, Inc.*, 426 U.S. 668, 674, n. 8, 96 S.Ct. 2358, 2362, n. 8, 49 L.Ed.2d 132 (1976); *Goldblatt v. Hempstead*, 369 U.S. 590, 592-593, 82 S.Ct. 987, 988-989, 8 L.Ed.2d 130 (1962); *Euclid v. Ambler Realty Co.*, 272 U.S. 365, 47 S.Ct. 114, 71 L.Ed. 303 (1926); *Gorieb v. Fox*, 274 U.S. 603, 608, 47 S.Ct. 675, 677, 71 L.Ed. 1228 (1927); *Welch v. Swasey*, 214 U.S. 91, 29 S.Ct. 567, 53 L.Ed. 923 (1909). This case, of course, involves land use regulation, not a physical appropriation of petitioners' property.

> to the health, the morals, or the safety of the public, is not—and, consistently with the existence and safety of organized society cannot be—burdened with the condition that the State must compensate such individual owners for pecuniary losses they may sustain, by reason of their not being permitted, by a noxious use of their property, to inflict injury upon the community." *Id.*, at 668-669, 8 S.Ct., at 300-301.

See also *Plymouth Coal Co., supra*; *Hadacheck v. Sebastian*, 239 U.S. 394, 36 S.Ct. 143, 60 L.Ed. 348 (1915); *Reinman v. Little Rock*, 237 U.S. 171, 35 S.Ct. 511, 59 L.Ed. 900 (1915); *Powell v. Pennsylvania*, 127 U.S. 678, 8 S.Ct. 992, 32 L.Ed. 253 (1888).

We reject petitioners' implicit assertion that Pennsylvania Coal overruled these cases which focused so heavily on the nature of the State's interest in the regulation. Just five years after the *Pennsylvania Coal* decision, Justice Holmes joined the Court's unanimous decision in *Miller v. Schoene*, 276 U.S. 272, 48 S.Ct. 246, 72 L.Ed. 568 (1928), holding that the Takings Clause did not require the State of Virginia to compensate the owners of cedar trees for the value of the trees that the State had ordered destroyed. The trees needed to be destroyed to prevent a disease from spreading to nearby apple orchards, which represented a far more valuable resource. In upholding the state action, the Court did not consider it necessary to "weigh with nicety the question whether the infected cedars constitute a nuisance according to common law; or whether they may be so declared by statute." *Id.*, at 280, 48 S.Ct., at 247. Rather, it was clear that the State's exercise of its police power to prevent the impending danger was justified, and did not require compensation. *See* also *Euclid v. Ambler Realty Co.*, 272 U.S. 365, 47 S.Ct. 114, 71 L.Ed. 303 (1926); *Omnia Commercial Co. v. United States*, 261 U.S. 502, 509, 43 S.Ct. 437, 438, 67 L.Ed. 773 (1923). Other subsequent cases reaffirm the important role that the nature of the state action plays in our takings analysis. *See Goldblatt v. Hempstead*, 369 U.S. 590, 82 S.Ct. 987, 8 L.Ed.2d 130 (1962); *Consolidated Rock Products Co. v. Los Angeles*, 57 Cal.2d 515, 20 Cal.Rptr. 638, 370 P.2d 342, appeal dism'd, 371 U.S. 36, 83 S.Ct. 145, 9 L.Ed.2d 112 (1962). As the Court explained in *Goldblatt* : "Although a comparison of values before and after" a regulatory action "is relevant, ... it is by no means conclusive...." 369 U.S., at 594, 82 S.Ct., at 990. [Footnote omitted.]

The Court's hesitance to find a taking when the State merely restrains uses of property that are tantamount to public nuisances is consistent with the notion of "reciprocity of advantage" that Justice Holmes referred to in *Pennsylvania Coal.*[20] Under our system of government, one of the State's primary ways of preserving the public weal is restricting the uses individuals can make of their property. While each of us is burdened somewhat by such restrictions, we, in turn, benefit

---

[20] The special status of this type of state action can also be understood on the simple theory that since no individual has a right to use his property so as to create a nuisance or otherwise harm others, the State has not "taken" anything when it asserts its power to enjoin the nuisance-like activity. *Cf.* Sax, *Takings, Private Property and Public Rights*, 81 Yale L.J. 149, 155-161 (1971); Michelman, *Property, Utility, and Fairness: Comments on the Ethical Foundations of 'Just Compensation' Law*, 80 Harv.L.Rev. 1165, 1235-1237 (1967).

However, as the current CHIEF JUSTICE has explained: "The nuisance exception to the taking guarantee is not coterminous with the police power itself." *Penn Central Transportation Co.*, 438 U.S., at 145, 98 S.Ct., at 2669 (REHNQUIST, J., dissenting). This is certainly the case in light of our recent decisions holding that the "scope of the 'public use' requirement of the Takings Clause is 'coterminous with the scope of a sovereign's police powers.'" *See Ruckelshaus v. Monsanto Co.*, 467 U.S. 986, 1014, 104 S.Ct. 2862, 2879, 81 L.Ed.2d 815 (1984) (quoting *Hawaii Housing Authority v. Midkiff*, 467 U.S. 229, 240, 104 S.Ct. 2321, 2329, 81 L.Ed.2d 186 (1984)). *See* generally R. Epstein, *Takings* 108-112 (1985).

greatly from the restrictions that are placed on others.[21] *See Penn Central Transportation Co. v. New York City*, 438 U.S., at 144-150, 98 S.Ct., at 2669-2672 (REHNQUIST, J., dissenting); *cf. California Reduction Co. v. Sanitary Reduction Works*, 199 U.S. 306, 322, 26 S.Ct. 100, 104, 50 L.Ed. 204 (1905). These restrictions are "properly treated as part of the burden of common citizenship." *Kimball Laundry Co. v. United States*, 338 U.S. 1, 5, 69 S.Ct. 1434, 1437, 93 L.Ed. 1765 (1949). Long ago it was recognized that "all property in this country is held under the implied obligation that the owner's use of it shall not be injurious to the community," *Mugler v. Kansas*, 123 U.S., at 665, 8 S.Ct., at 299; *see* also *Beer Co. v. Massachusetts*, 97 U.S. (7 Otto) 25, 32, 24 L.Ed. 989 (1877), and the Takings Clause did not transform that principle to one that requires compensation whenever the State asserts its power to enforce it.[22] *See Mugler*, 123 U.S., at 664, 8 S.Ct., at 298.

In *Agins v. Tiburon*, we explained that the "determination that governmental action constitutes a taking, is, in essence, a determination that the public at large, rather than a single owner, must bear the burden of an exercise of state power in the public interest," and we recognized that this question "necessarily requires a weighing of private and public interests." 447 U.S., at 260-261, 100 S.Ct., at 2141. As the cases discussed above demonstrate, the public interest in preventing activities similar to public nuisances is a substantial one, which in many instances has not required compensation. The Subsidence Act, unlike the Kohler Act, plainly seeks to further such an interest. Nonetheless, we need not rest our decision on this factor alone, because petitioners have also failed to make a showing of diminution of value sufficient to satisfy the test set forth in *Pennsylvania Coal* and our other regulatory takings cases.

DIMINUTION OF VALUE AND INVESTMENT-BACKED EXPECTATIONS

The second factor that distinguishes this case from *Pennsylvania Coal* is the finding in that case that the Kohler Act made mining of "certain coal" commercially impracticable. In this case, by contrast, petitioners have not shown any deprivation significant enough to satisfy the heavy burden placed upon one alleging a regulatory taking. For this reason, their takings claim must fail.

In addressing petitioners' claim we must not disregard the posture in which this case comes before us. The District Court granted summary judgment to respondents only on the facial challenge to the Subsidence Act. The court explained that "[b]ecause plaintiffs have not alleged any injury due to the enforcement of the statute, there is as yet no concrete controversy regard-

---

21 The Takings Clause has never been read to require the States or the courts to calculate whether a specific individual has suffered burdens under this generic rule in excess of the benefits received. Not every individual gets a full dollar return in benefits for the taxes he or she pays; yet, no one suggests that an individual has a right to compensation for the difference between taxes paid and the dollar value of benefits received.

22 Courts have consistently held that a State need not provide compensation when it diminishes or destroys the value of property by stopping illegal activity or abating a public nuisance. *See Nassr v. Commonwealth*, 394 Mass. 767, 477 N.E.2d 987 (1985) (hazardous waste operation); *Kuban v. McGimsey*, 96 Nev. 105, 605 P.2d 623 (1980) (brothel); *MacLeod v. Takoma Park*, 257 Md. 477, 263 A.2d 581 (1970) (unsafe building); *Eno v. Burlington*, 125 Vt. 8, 209 A.2d 499 (1965) (fire and health hazard); *Pompano Horse Club, Inc. v. State ex rel. Bryan*, 93 Fla. 415, 111 So. 801 (1927) (gambling facility); *People ex rel. Thrasher v. Smith*, 275 Ill. 256, 114 N.E. 31 (1916)("bawdyhouse"). It is hard to imagine a different rule that would be consistent with the maxim "sic utere tuo ut alienum non laedas" (use your own property in such manner as not to injure that of another.) *See* generally *Empire State Insurance Co. v. Chafetz*, 278 F.2d 41 (CA5 1960). As Professor Epstein has recently commented: "The issue of compensation cannot arise until the question of justification has been disposed of. In the typical nuisance prevention case, this question is resolved against the claimant." Epstein, *supra*, at 199.

ing the application of the specific provisions and regulations. Thus, the only question before this court is whether the mere enactment of the statutes and regulations constitutes a taking." 581 F.Supp., at 513 (emphasis added). The next phase of the case was to be petitioners' presentation of evidence about the actual effects the Subsidence Act had and would have on them. Instead of proceeding in this manner, however, the parties filed a joint motion asking the court to certify the facial challenge for appeal. The parties explained that an assessment of the actual impact that the Act has on petitioners' operations "will involve complex and voluminous proofs," which neither party was currently in a position to present, App. 15-17, and stressed that if an appellate court were to reverse the District Court on the facial challenge, then all of their expenditures in adjudicating the as-applied challenge would be wasted. Based on these considerations, the District Court certified three questions relating to the facial challenge.[23]

The posture of the case is critical because we have recognized an important distinction between a claim that the mere enactment of a statute constitutes a taking and a claim that the particular impact of government action on a specific piece of property requires the payment of just compensation. This point is illustrated by our decision in *Hodel v. Virginia Surface Mining & Reclamation Assn.*, Inc., 452 U.S. 264, 101 S.Ct. 2352, 69 L.Ed.2d 1 (1981), in which we rejected a preenforcement challenge to the constitutionality of the Surface Mining Control and Reclamation Act of 1977. We concluded that the District Court had been mistaken in its reliance on Pennsylvania Coal as support for a holding that two statutory provisions were unconstitutional because they deprived coal mine operators of the use of their land. The Court explained:

> "[T]he court below ignored this Court's oft-repeated admonition that the constitutionality of statutes ought not be decided except in an actual factual setting that makes such a decision necessary. *See Socialist Labor Party v. Gilligan*, 406 U.S. 583, 588 [92 S.Ct. 1716, 1719, 32 L.Ed.2d 317] (1972); *Rescue Army v. Municipal Court*, 331 U.S. 549, 568-575, 584 [67 S.Ct. 1409, 1419-1423, 1427, 91 L.Ed. 1666] (1947); *Alabama State Federation of Labor v. McAdory*, 325 U.S. 450, 461 [65 S.Ct. 1384, 1389, 89 L.Ed. 1725] (1945). Adherence to this rule is particularly important in cases raising allegations of an unconstitutional taking of private property. Just last Term, we reaffirmed:
>
> "'[T]his Court has generally' been unable to develop any 'set formula' for determining when 'justice and fairness' require that economic injuries caused by public action be compensated by the government, rather than remain disproportionately concentrated on a few persons." Rather, it has examined the "taking" question by engaging in essentially ad hoc, factual inquiries that have identified several factors—such as the economic impact of the regulation, its interference with reasonable investment backed expectations, and the character of the government action—that have particular significance." *Kaiser Aetna v. United States*, 444 U.S. 164, 175 [100 S.Ct. 383, 390, 62 L.Ed.2d 332] (1979) (citations omitted).

---

[23] The certified questions asked whether §§4, 5, or 6 of the Subsidence Act, and various regulations:

"1. Violate the Rule of the Mahon Decision[,]

"2. Constitute Per Se Takings,

"3. Violate Article I, §10 of the Constitution of the United States." App. 12.

The Court of Appeals recognized the limited nature of its inquiry, pointing out that it was passing only on the facial challenge, and that the "as-applied challenge remains for disposition in the district court." 771 F.2d, at 710, n. 3.

> "These 'ad hoc, factual inquiries' must be conducted with respect to specific property, and the particular estimates of economic impact and ultimate valuation relevant in the unique circumstances.
>
> "Because appellees' taking claim arose in the context of a facial challenge, it presented no concrete controversy concerning either application of the Act to particular surface mining operations or its effect on specific parcels of land. Thus, the only issue properly before the District Court and, in turn, this Court, is whether the 'mere enactment' of the Surface Mining Act constitutes a taking. *See Agins v. Tiburon*, 447 U.S. 255, 260 [100 S.Ct. 2138, 2141, 65 L.Ed.2d 106] (1980). The test to be applied in considering this facial challenge is fairly straightforward. A statute regulating the uses that can be made of property effects a taking if it 'denies an owner economically viable use of his land....' *Agins v. Tiburon, supra*, at 260 [100 S.Ct., at 2141]; *see* also *Penn Central Transp. Co. v. New York City*, 438 U.S. 104 [98 S.Ct. 2646, 57 L.Ed.2d 631] (1978)." 452 U.S., at 295-296, 101 S.Ct., at 2370.

Petitioners thus face an uphill battle in making a facial attack on the Act as a taking.

The hill is made especially steep because petitioners have not claimed, at this stage, that the Act makes it commercially impracticable for them to continue mining their bituminous coal interests in western Pennsylvania. Indeed, petitioners have not even pointed to a single mine that can no longer be mined for profit. The only evidence available on the effect that the Subsidence Act has had on petitioners' mining operations comes from petitioners' answers to respondents' interrogatories. Petitioners described the effect that the Subsidence Act had from 1966-1982 on 13 mines that the various companies operate, and claimed that they have been required to leave a bit less than 27 million tons of coal in place to support §4 areas. The total coal in those 13 mines amounts to over 1.46 billion tons. *See* App. 284. Thus §4 requires them to leave less than two percent of their coal in place. [Footnote omitted.] But, as we have indicated, nowhere near all of the underground coal is extractable even aside from the Subsidence Act. The categories of coal that must be left for §4 purposes and other purposes are not necessarily distinct sets, and there is no information in the record as to how much coal is actually left in the ground solely because of §4. We do know, however, that petitioners have never claimed that their mining operations, or even any specific mines, have been unprofitable since the Subsidence Act was passed. Nor is there evidence that mining in any specific location affected by the 50 percent rule has been unprofitable.

Instead, petitioners have sought to narrowly define certain segments of their property and assert that, when so defined, the Subsidence Act denies them economically viable use. They advance two alternative ways of carving their property in order to reach this conclusion. First, they focus on the specific tons of coal that they must leave in the ground under the Subsidence Act, and argue that the Commonwealth has effectively appropriated this coal since it has no other useful purpose if not mined. Second, they contend that the Commonwealth has taken their separate legal interest in property—the "support estate."

Because our test for regulatory taking requires us to compare the value that has been taken from the property with the value that remains in the property, one of the critical questions is determining how to define the unit of property "whose value is to furnish the denominator of the fraction." Michelman, *Property, Utility, and Fairness: Comments on the Ethical Foundations of "Just Compensation" Law*, 80 Harv.L.Rev. 1165, 1192 (1967). [Footnote omitted.] In *Penn Central* the Court explained:

> "'Taking' jurisprudence does not divide a single parcel into discrete segments and attempt to determine whether rights in a particular segment have been entirely abrogated. In deciding whether a particular governmental action has effected a taking, this Court focuses rather both on the character of the action and on the nature of the interference with rights in the parcel as a whole—here the city tax block designated as the 'landmark site.'" 438 U.S., at 130-131, 98 S.Ct., at 2662.

Similarly, in *Andrus v. Allard*, 444 U.S. 51, 100 S.Ct. 318, 62 L.Ed.2d 210 (1979), we held that "where an owner possesses a full 'bundle' of property rights, the destruction of one 'strand' of the bundle is not a taking because the aggregate must be viewed in its entirety." *Id.*, at 65-66, 100 S.Ct., at 326-327. Although these verbal formulizations do not solve all of the definitional issues that may arise in defining the relevant mass of property, they do provide sufficient guidance to compel us to reject petitioners' arguments.

THE COAL IN PLACE

The parties have stipulated that enforcement of the DER's 50 percent rule will require petitioners to leave approximately 27 million tons of coal in place. Because they own that coal but cannot mine it, they contend that Pennsylvania has appropriated it for the public purposes described in the Subsidence Act.

This argument fails for the reason explained in *Penn Central* and *Andrus*. The 27 million tons of coal do not constitute a separate segment of property for takings law purposes. Many zoning ordinances place limits on the property owner's right to make profitable use of some segments of his property. A requirement that a building occupy no more than a specified percentage of the lot on which it is located could be characterized as a taking of the vacant area as readily as the requirement that coal pillars be left in place. Similarly, under petitioners' theory one could always argue that a setback ordinance requiring that no structure be built within a certain distance from the property line constitutes a taking because the footage represents a distinct segment of property for takings law purposes. *Cf. Gorieb v. Fox*, 274 U.S. 603, 47 S.Ct. 675, 71 L.Ed. 1228 (1927) (upholding validity of setback ordinance) (Sutherland, J.). There is no basis for treating the less than two percent of petitioners' coal as a separate parcel of property.

We do not consider Justice Holmes' statement that the Kohler Act made mining of "certain coal" commercially impracticable as requiring us to focus on the individual pillars of coal that must be left in place. That statement is best understood as referring to the Pennsylvania Coal Company's assertion that it could not undertake profitable anthracite coal mining in light of the Kohler Act. There were strong assertions in the record to support that conclusion. For example, the coal company claimed that one company was "unable to operate six large collieries in the city of Scranton, employing more than five thousand men." Motion to Advance for Argument in *Pennsylvania Coal Co. v. Mahon*, O.T. 1922, No. 549, p. 2. [Footnote omitted.] As Judge Adams explained:

> "At first blush, this language seems to suggest that the Court would have found a taking no matter how little of the defendants' coal was rendered unmineable—that because 'certain' coal was no longer accessible, there had been a taking of that coal. However, when one reads the sentence in context, it becomes clear that the Court's concern was with whether the defendants' 'right to mine coal ... [could] be exercised with profit.' 260 U.S. at 414 [43 S.Ct., at 159] (emphasis added).... Thus, the Court's holding in Mahon must

> be assumed to have been based on its understanding that the Kohler Act rendered the business of mining coal unprofitable." 771 F.2d, at 716, n. 6.

When the coal that must remain beneath the ground is viewed in the context of any reasonable unit of petitioners' coal mining operations and financial-backed expectations, it is plain that petitioners have not come close to satisfying their burden of proving that they have been denied the economically viable use of that property. The record indicates that only about 75 percent of petitioners' underground coal can be profitably mined in any event, and there is no showing that petitioners' reasonable "investment-backed expectations" have been materially affected by the additional duty to retain the small percentage that must be used to support the structures protected by §4. [Footnote omitted.]

THE SUPPORT ESTATE

Pennsylvania property law is apparently unique in regarding the support estate as a separate interest in land that can be conveyed apart from either the mineral estate or the surface estate. [Footnote omitted.] Petitioners therefore argue that even if comparable legislation in another State would not constitute a taking, the Subsidence Act has that consequence because it entirely destroys the value of their unique support estate. It is clear, however, that our takings jurisprudence forecloses reliance on such legalistic distinctions within a bundle of property rights. For example, in *Penn Central*, the Court rejected the argument that the "air rights" above the terminal constituted a separate segment of property for Takings Clause purposes. 438 U.S., at 130, 98 S.Ct., at 2662. Likewise, in *Andrus v. Allard*, we viewed the right to sell property as just one element of the owner's property interest. 444 U.S., at 65-66, 100 S.Ct., at 326-327. In neither case did the result turn on whether state law allowed the separate sale of the segment of property.

The Court of Appeals, which is more familiar with Pennsylvania law than we are, concluded that as a practical matter the support estate is always owned by either the owner of the surface or the owner of the minerals. It stated:

> "The support estate consists of the right to remove the strata of coal and earth that undergird the surface or to leave those layers intact to support the surface and prevent subsidence. These two uses cannot co-exist and, depending upon the purposes of the owner of the support estate, one use or the other must be chosen. If the owner is a mine operator, the support estate is used to exploit the mineral estate. When the right of support is held by the surface owner, its use is to support that surface and prevent subsidence. Thus, although Pennsylvania law does recognize the support estate as a 'separate' property interest, *id.*, it cannot be used profitably by one who does not also possess either the mineral estate or the surface estate. *See* Montgomery, The Development of the Right of Subjacent Support and the 'Third Estate in Pennsylvania,' 25 Temple L.Q. 1, 21 (1951)." 771 F.2d, at 715- 716.

Thus, in practical terms, the support estate has value only insofar as it protects or enhances the value of the estate with which it is associated. Its value is merely a part of the entire bundle of rights possessed by the owner of either the coal or the surface. Because petitioners retain the right to mine virtually all of the coal in their mineral estates, the burden the Act places on the support estate does not constitute a taking. Petitioners may continue to mine coal profitably even if they may not destroy or damage surface structures at will in the process.

But even if we were to accept petitioners' invitation to view the support estate as a distinct segment of property for "takings" purposes, they have not satisfied their heavy burden of sustaining a facial challenge to the Act. Petitioners have acquired or retained the support estate for a great deal of land, only part of which is protected under the Subsidence Act, which, of course, deals with subsidence in the immediate vicinity of certain structures, bodies of water, and cemeteries. *See* n.6, *supra*. The record is devoid of any evidence on what percentage of the purchased support estates, either in the aggregate or with respect to any individual estate, has been affected by the Act. Under these circumstances, petitioners' facial attack under the Takings Clause must surely fail. [Footnote omitted.]

IV

In addition to their challenge under the Takings Clause, petitioners assert that §6 of the Subsid ence Act violates the Contracts Clause by not allowing them to hold the surface owners to their contractual waiver of liability for surface damage. Here too, we agree with the Court of Appeals and the District Court that the Commonwealth's strong public interests in the legislation are more than adequate to justify the impact of the statute on petitioners' contractual agreements.

Prior to the ratification of the Fourteenth Amendment, it was Article I, §10, that provided the primary constitutional check on state legislative power. The first sentence of that section provides:

> "No State shall enter into any Treaty, Alliance, or Confederation; grant Letters of Marque and Reprisal; coin Money; emit Bills of Credit; make any Thing but gold or silver Coin a Tender in Payment of Debts; pass any Bill of Attainder, ex post facto Law, or Law impairing the Obligation of Contracts, or grant any Title of Nobility." U.S. Const., Art. I, §10.

Unlike other provisions in the section, it is well settled that the prohibition against impairing the obligation of contracts is not to be read literally. *W.B. Worthen Co. v. Thomas*, 292 U.S. 426, 433, 54 S.Ct. 816, 818, 78 L.Ed. 1344 (1934). The context in which the Contracts Clause is found, the historical setting in which it was adopted, [Footnote omitted] and our cases construing the Clause, indicate that its primary focus was upon legislation that was designed to repudiate or adjust pre-existing debtor-creditor relationships that obligors were unable to satisfy. *See e.g., ibid.*; *Home Building & Loan Assn. v. Blaisdell*, 290 U.S. 398, 54 S.Ct. 231, 78 L.Ed. 413 (1934). Even in such cases, the Court has refused to give the Clause a literal reading. Thus, in the landmark case of *Home Building & Loan Assn. v. Blaisdell*, the Court upheld Minnesota's statutory moratorium against home foreclosures, in part, because the legislation was addressed to the "legitimate end" of protecting "a basic interest of society," and not just for the advantage of some favored group. *Id.*, at 445, 54 S.Ct., at 242.

As Justice Stewart explained:

> "[I]t is to be accepted as a commonplace that the Contract Clause does not operate to obliterate the police power of the States. 'It is the settled law of this court that the interdiction of statutes impairing the obligation of contracts does not prevent the State from exercising such powers as are vested in it for the promotion of the common weal, or are necessary for the general good of the public, though contracts previously entered into between individuals may thereby be affected. This power, which in its various ramifications is known as the police power, is an exercise of the sovereign right of the Govern-

> ment to protect the lives, health, morals, comfort and general welfare of the people, and is paramount to any rights under contracts between individuals.' *Manigault v. Springs*, 199 U.S. 473, 480 [26 S.Ct. 127, 130, 50 L.Ed. 274 (1905)]. As Mr. Justice Holmes succinctly put the matter in his opinion for the Court in *Hudson Water Co. v. McCarter*, 209 U.S. 349, 357 [28 S.Ct. 529, 531, 52 L.Ed. 828 (1908)]: 'One whose rights, such as they are, are subject to state restriction, cannot remove them from the power of the State by making a contract about them. The contract will carry with it the infirmity of the subject matter.'" *Allied Structural Steel Co. v. Spannaus*, 438 U.S. 234, 241-242, 98 S.Ct. 2716, 2720-2721, 57 L.Ed.2d 727 (1978).

In assessing the validity of petitioners' Contracts Clause claim in this case, we begin by identifying the precise contractual right that has been impaired and the nature of the statutory impairment. Petitioners claim that they obtained damages waivers for a large percentage of the land surface protected by the Subsidence Act, but that the Act removes the surface owners' contractual obligations to waive damages. We agree that the statute operates as "a substantial impairment of a contractual relationship," *id.*, at 244, 98 S.Ct., at 2722, and therefore proceed to the asserted justifications for the impairment.[31]

The record indicates that since 1966 petitioners have conducted mining operations under approximately 14,000 structures protected by the Subsidence Act. It is not clear whether that number includes the cemeteries and water courses under which mining has been conducted. In any event, it is petitioners' position that, because they contracted with some previous owners of property generations ago, [footnote omitted] they have a constitutionally protected legal right to conduct their mining operations in a way that would make a shambles of all those buildings and cemeteries. As we have discussed, the Commonwealth has a strong public interest in preventing this type of harm, the environmental effect of which transcends any private agreement between contracting parties.

Of course, the finding of a significant and legitimate public purpose is not, by itself, enough to justify the impairment of contractual obligations. A court must also satisfy itself that the legislature's "adjustment of 'the rights and responsibilities of contracting parties [is based] upon reasonable conditions and [is] of a character appropriate to the public purpose justifying [the legislation's] adoption.'" *Energy Reserves Group, Inc. v. Kansas Power & Light Co.*, 459 U.S. 400, 412, 103 S.Ct. 697, 704, 74 L.Ed.2d 569 (1983) (quoting *United States Trust Co. v. New Jersey*, 431 U.S. 1, 22, 97 S.Ct. 1505, 1517, 52 L.Ed.2d 92 (1977)). But, we have repeatedly held that unless the State is itself a contracting party, courts should "'properly defer to legislative judgment as to the necessity and reasonableness of a particular measure.'" *Energy Reserves Group, Inc.*, 459 U.S., at 413, 103 S.Ct., at 705 (quoting *United States Trust Co.*, 431 U.S., at 23, 97 S.Ct., at 1518).

As we explained more fully above, the Subsidence Act plainly survives scrutiny under our standards for evaluating impairments of private contracts. [Footnote omitted.] The Common-

---

[31] As we have mentioned above, we do not know what percentage of petitioners' acquired support estate is in fact restricted under the Subsidence Act. *See supra*, at 1250. Moreover, we have no basis on which to conclude just how substantial a part of the support estate the waiver of liability is. *See id.*, at n. 29. These inquiries are both essential to determine the "severity of the impairment," which in turn affects "the level of scrutiny to which the legislation will be affected." *Energy Reserves Group, Inc. v. Kansas Power & Light Co.*, 459 U.S. 400, 411, 103 S.Ct. 697, 704, 74 L.Ed.2d 569 (1983). While these dearths in the record might be critical in some cases, they are not essential to our discussion here because the Subsidence Act withstands scrutiny even if it is assumed that it constitutes a total impairment.

wealth has determined that in order to deter mining practices that could have severe effects on the surface, it is not enough to set out guidelines and impose restrictions, but that imposition of liability is necessary. By requiring the coal companies either to repair the damage or to give the surface owner funds to repair the damage, the Commonwealth accomplishes both deterrence and restoration of the environment to its previous condition. We refuse to second-guess the Commonwealth's determinations that these are the most appropriate ways of dealing with the problem. We conclude, therefore, that the impairment of petitioners' right to enforce the damages waivers is amply justified by the public purposes served by the Subsidence Act.

The judgment of the Court of Appeals is

AFFIRMED.

Chief Justice REHNQUIST, with whom Justice POWELL, Justice O'CONNOR, and Justice SCALIA join, dissenting.

More than 50 years ago, this Court determined the constitutionality of Pennsylvania's Kohler Act as it affected the property interests of coal mine operators. *Pennsylvania Coal Co. v. Mahon*, 260 U.S. 393, 43 S.Ct. 158, 67 L.Ed. 322 (1922). The Bituminous Mine Subsidence and Land Conservation Act approved today effects an interference with such interests in a strikingly similar manner. The Court finds at least two reasons why this case is different. First, we are told, "the character of the governmental action involved here leans heavily against finding a taking." *Ante*, at 1242. Second, the Court concludes that the Subsidence Act neither "makes it impossible for petitioners to profitably engage in their business," nor involves "undue interference with [petitioners'] investment-backed expectations." *Ibid.* Neither of these conclusions persuades me that this case is different, and I believe that the Subsidence Act works a taking of petitioners' property interests. I therefore dissent.

I

In apparent recognition of the obstacles presented by *Pennsylvania Coal* to the decision it reaches, the Court attempts to undermine the authority of Justice Holmes' opinion as to the validity of the Kohler Act, labeling it "uncharacteristically ... advisory." *Ante*, at 1241. I would not so readily dismiss the precedential value of this opinion. There is, to be sure, some language in the case suggesting that it could have been decided simply by addressing the particular application of the Kohler Act at issue in the case. *See, e.g.*, *Pennsylvania Coal*, *supra*, at 414, 43 S.Ct., at 159 ("If we were called upon to deal with the plaintiffs' position alone, we should think it clear that the statute does not disclose a public interest sufficient to warrant so extensive a destruction of the defendant's constitutionally protected rights"). The Court, however, found that the validity of the Act itself was properly drawn into question: "[T]he case has been treated as one in which the general validity of the [Kohler] act should be discussed." *Ibid.* [Footnote omitted.] The coal company clearly had an interest in obtaining a determination that the Kohler Act was unenforceable if it worked a taking without providing for compensation. For these reasons, I would not find the opinion of the Court in *Pennsylvania Coal* advisory in any respect.

The Court's implication to the contrary is particularly disturbing in this context, because the holding in *Pennsylvania Coal* today discounted by the Court has for 65 years been the foundation of our "regulatory takings" jurisprudence. *See Penn Central Transportation Co. v. New York City*, 438 U.S. 104, 127, 98 S.Ct. 2646, 2660, 57 L.Ed.2d 631 (1978); D. Hagman & J. Juergensmeyer,

Urban Planning and Land Development Control Law 319 (2d ed. 1986) ("*Pennsylvania Coal* was a monumental decision which remains a vital element in contemporary taking law"). We have, for example, frequently relied on the admonition that "if regulation goes too far it will be recognized as a taking." *Pennsylvania Coal, supra*, 260 U.S., at 415, 43 S.Ct., at 160. *See, e.g., MacDonald, Sommer & Frates v. Yolo County*, 477 U.S. 340, 348, 106 S.Ct. 2561, 2566, 91 L.Ed.2d 285 (1986); *Ruckelshaus v. Monsanto Co.*, 467 U.S. 986, 1003, 104 S.Ct. 2862, 81 L.Ed.2d 815 (1984); *PruneYard Shopping Center v. Robins*, 447 U.S. 74, 83, 100 S.Ct. 2035, 2041, 64 L.Ed.2d 741 (1980); *Goldblatt v. Hempstead*, 369 U.S. 590, 594, 82 S.Ct. 987, 990, 8 L.Ed.2d 130 (1962); *United States v. Central Eureka Mining Co.*, 357 U.S. 155, 168, 78 S.Ct. 1097, 1104, 2 L.Ed.2d 1228 (1958). Thus, even were I willing to assume that the opinion in *Pennsylvania Coal* standing alone is reasonably subject to an interpretation that renders more than half the discussion "advisory," I would have no doubt that our repeated reliance on that opinion establishes it as a cornerstone of the jurisprudence of the Fifth Amendment's Just Compensation Clause.

I accordingly approach this case with greater deference to the language as well as the holding of *Pennsylvania Coal* than does the Court. Admittedly, questions arising under the Just Compensation Clause rest on ad hoc factual inquiries, and must be decided on the facts and circumstances in each case. *See Penn Central Transportation Co. v. New York City, supra*, 438 U.S., at 124, 98 S.Ct., at 2659; *United States v. Central Eureka Mining Co., supra*, 357 U.S., at 168, 78 S.Ct., at 1104. Examination of the relevant factors presented here convinces me that the differences between them and those in Pennsylvania Coal verge on the trivial.

II

The Court first determines that this case is different from Pennsylvania Coal because "the Commonwealth of Pennsylvania has acted to arrest what it perceives to be a significant threat to the common welfare." *Ante*, at 1242. In my view, reliance on this factor represents both a misreading of *Pennsylvania Coal* and a misunderstanding of our precedents.

A

The Court opines that the decision in *Pennsylvania Coal* rested on the fact that the Kohler Act was "enacted solely for the benefit of private parties," *ante*, at 1242, and "served only private interests." *Ante*, at 1242. A review of the Kohler Act shows that these statements are incorrect. The Pennsylvania Legislature passed the statute "as remedial legislation, designed to cure existing evils and abuses." *Mahon v. Pennsylvania Coal Co.*, 274 Pa. 489, 495, 118 A. 491, 492 (1922) (quoting the Act). These were public "evils and abuses," identified in the preamble as "wrecked and dangerous streets and highways, collapsed public buildings, churches, schools, factories, streets, and private dwellings, broken gas, water and sewer systems, the loss of human life...." *Id.*, at 496, 118 A., at 493. [Footnote omitted.] The Pennsylvania Supreme Court recognized that these concerns were "such as to create an emergency, properly warranting the exercise of the police power ...." *Id.*, at 497, 118 A., at 493. There can be no doubt that the Kohler Act was intended to serve public interests.

Though several aspects of the Kohler Act limited its protection of these interests, *see Pennsylvania Coal*, 260 U.S., at 414, 43 S.Ct., at 159, this Court did not ignore the public interests served by the Act. When considering the protection of the "single private house" owned by the Mahons, the Court noted that "[n]o doubt there is a public interest even in this." *Id.*, at 413, 43 S.Ct., at 159 (emphasis added). It recognized that the Act "affects the mining of coal under streets or cities in places where the right to mine such coal has been reserved." *Id.*, at 414, 43 S.Ct., at 159. *See* also *id.*, at 416, 43 S.Ct., at 160 ("We assume ... that the statute was passed upon the conviction that an exigency existed that would warrant it, and we assume that an exigency exists that would warrant the exercise of eminent domain"). The strong public interest in the stability of streets and cities, however, was insufficient "to warrant achieving the desire by a shorter cut than the constitutional way of paying for the change." *Ibid.* Thus, the Court made clear that the mere existence of a public purpose was insufficient to release the government from the compensation requirement: "The protection of private property in the Fifth Amendment presupposes that it is wanted for public use, but provides that it shall not be taken for such use without compensation." *Id.*, at 415, 43 S.Ct., at 160.

The Subsidence Act rests on similar public purposes. These purposes were clearly stated by the legislature: "[T]o aid in the protection of the safety of the public, to enhance the value of [surface area] lands for taxation, to aid in the preservation of surface water drainage and public water supplies and generally to improve the use and enjoyment of such lands...." Pa.Stat.Ann., Title 52, §1406.2 (Purdon Supp.1986). The Act's declaration of policy states that mine subsidence "has seriously impeded land development ... has caused a very clear and present danger to the health, safety and welfare of the people of Pennsylvania [and] erodes the tax base of the affected municipalities." §§1406.3(2), (3), (4). The legislature determined that the prevention of subsidence would protect surface structures, advance the economic future and well-being of Pennsylvania, and ensure the safety and welfare of the Commonwealth's residents. *Ibid.* Thus, it is clear that the Court has severely understated the similarity of purpose between the Subsidence Act and the Kohler Act. The public purposes in this case are not sufficient to distinguish it from *Pennsylvania Coal.*[3]

B

The similarity of the public purpose of the present Act to that in *Pennsylvania Coal* does not resolve the question whether a taking has occurred; the existence of such a public purpose is merely a necessary prerequisite to the government's exercise of its taking power. *See Hawaii Housing Authority v. Midkiff*, 467 U.S. 229, 239-243, 245, 104 S.Ct. 2321, 2328- 2331, 2331-2332, 81 L.Ed.2d 186 (1984); *Berman v. Parker*, 348 U.S. 26, 32- 33, 75 S.Ct. 98, 102, 99 L.Ed. 27 (1954). The nature of these purposes may be relevant, for we have recognized that a taking does not occur where the government exercises its unquestioned authority to prevent a property owner from using his property to injure others without having to compensate the value of the forbidden use. *See Goldblatt v. Hempstead*; *Hadacheck v. Sebastian*, 239 U.S. 394, 36 S.Ct. 143, 60 L.Ed. 348 (1915); *Mugler v. Kansas*, 123 U.S. 623, 8 S.Ct. 273, 31 L.Ed. 205 (1887). *See* generally *Penn Central Transportation Co. v. New York City*, 438 U.S., at 144-146, 98 S.Ct., at 2669-2670 (REHNQUIST, J., dissenting). The Court today indicates that this "nuisance exception" alone

[3] The Court notes that the particulars of the Subsidence Act better serve these public purposes than did the Kohler Act. Ante, at 1242. This may well be true, but our inquiry into legislative purpose is not intended as a license to judge the effectiveness of legislation. When considering the Fifth Amendment issues presented by Hawaii's Land Reform Act, we noted that the Act, "like any other, may not be successful in achieving its intended goals. But 'whether in fact the provisions will accomplish the objectives is not the question: the [constitutional requirement] is satisfied if ... the ... [State] Legislature rationally could have believed that the [Act] would promote its objective.'" *Hawaii Housing Authority v. Midkiff*, 467 U.S. 229, 242, 104 S.Ct. 2321, 2330, 81 L.Ed.2d 186 (1984), quoting *Western & Southern Life Insurance Co. v. State Bd. of Equalization*, 451 U.S. 648, 671-672, 101 S.Ct. 2070, 2084-2085, 68 L.Ed.2d 514 (1981). Conversely, our cases have never found it sufficient that legislation efficiently achieves its desired objectives to hold that the compensation required by the Fifth Amendment is unavailable.

might support its conclusion that no taking has occurred. Despite the Court's implication to the contrary, *see ante*, at 1242, and n.15, the legitimacy of this purpose is a question of federal, rather than state, law, subject to independent scrutiny by this Court. This statute is not the type of regulation that our precedents have held to be within the "nuisance exception" to takings analysis.

The ease with which the Court moves from the recognition of public interests to the assertion that the activity here regulated is "akin to a public nuisance" suggests an exception far wider than recognized in our previous cases. "The nuisance exception to the taking guarantee," however, "is not coterminous with the police power itself," *Penn Central Transportation*, *supra*, at 145, 98 S.Ct., at 2669 (REHNQUIST, J., dissenting), but is a narrow exception allowing the government to prevent "a misuse or illegal use." *Curtin v. Benson*, 222 U.S. 78, 86, 32 S.Ct. 31, 32, 56 L.Ed. 102 (1911). It is not intended to allow "the prevention of a legal and essential use, an attribute of its ownership." *Ibid.*

The narrow nature of this exception is compelled by the concerns underlying the Fifth Amendment. Though, as the Court recognizes, *ante*, at 1245, the Fifth Amendment does not prevent actions that secure a "reciprocity of advantage," *Pennsylvania Coal*, *supra*, 260 U.S., at 415, 43 S.Ct., at 160, it is designed to prevent "the public from loading upon one individual more than his just share of the burdens of government, and says that when he surrenders to the public something more and different from that which is exacted from other members of the public, a full and just equivalent shall be returned to him." *Monongahela Navigation Co. v. United States*, 148 U.S. 312, 325, 13 S.Ct. 622, 625, 37 L.Ed. 463 (1893). *See* also *Penn Central Transportation Co. v. New York City*, *supra*, 438 U.S., at 123-125, 98 S.Ct., at 2658-2659; *Armstrong v.United States*,364 U.S. 40, 49, 80 S.Ct. 1563, 1569, 4 L.Ed.2d 1554 (1960). A broad exception to the operation of the Just Compensation Clause based on the exercise of multifaceted health, welfare, and safety regulations would surely allow government much greater authority than we have recognized to impose societal burdens on individual landowners, for nearly every action the government takes is intended to secure for the public an extra measure of "health, safety, and welfare."

Thus, our cases applying the "nuisance" rationale have involved at least two narrowing principles. First, nuisance regulations exempted from the Fifth Amendment have rested on discrete and narrow purposes. *See Goldblatt v. Hempstead*, *supra*; *Hadacheck v. Sebastian*, *supra*; *Mugler v. Kansas*, *supra*. The Subsidence Act, however, is much more than a nuisance statute. The central purposes of the Act, though including public safety, reflect a concern for preservation of buildings, economic development, and maintenance of property values to sustain the Commonwealth's tax base. We should hesitate to allow a regulation based on essentially economic concerns to be insulated from the dictates of the Fifth Amendment by labeling it nuisance regulation.

Second, and more significantly, our cases have never applied the nuisance exception to allow complete extinction of the value of a parcel of property. Though nuisance regulations have been sustained despite a substantial reduction in value, we have not accepted the proposition that the State may completely extinguish a property interest or prohibit all use without providing compensation. Thus, in *Mugler v. Kansas*, *supra*, the prohibition on manufacture and sale of intoxicating liquors made the distiller's brewery "of little value" but did not completely extinguish the value of the building. Similarly, in *Miller v. Schoene*, 276 U.S. 272, 48 S.Ct. 246, 72 L.Ed. 568 (1928), the individual forced to cut down his cedar trees nevertheless was able "to use the felled trees." *Penn Central Transportation Co. v. New York City, supra*, 438 U.S., at 126, 98 S.Ct., at 2660. The restriction on surface mining upheld in *Goldblatt v. Hempstead, supra*, may have prohibited "a beneficial use" of the property, but did not reduce the value of the lot in question. 369 U.S., at 593, 594, 82 S.Ct., at 990. In none of these cases did the regulation "destroy essential uses of private property." *Curtin v. Benson, supra*, 222 U.S., at 86, 32 S.Ct., at 32.

Here, petitioners' interests in particular coal deposits have been completely destroyed. By requiring that defined seams of coal remain in the ground, *see ante*, at 1237-1238, and n.7, §4 of the Subsidence Act has extinguished any interest one might want to acquire in this property, for "'the right to coal consists in the right to mine it.'" *Pennsylvania Coal*, 260 U.S., at 414, 43 S.Ct., at 159, quoting *Commonwealth ex rel. Keator v. Clearview Coal Co.*, 256 Pa. 328, 331, 100 A. 820 (1917). Application of the nuisance exception in these circumstances would allow the State not merely to forbid one "particular use" of property with many uses but to extinguish all beneficial use of petitioners' property. [Footnote omitted.]

Though suggesting that the purposes alone are sufficient to uphold the Act, the Court avoids reliance on the nuisance exception by finding that the Subsidence Act does not impair petitioners' investment-backed expectations or ability to profitably operate their businesses. This conclusion follows mainly from the Court's broad definition of the "relevant mass of property," *ante*, at 1248, which allows it to ascribe to the Subsidence Act a less pernicious effect on the interests of the property owner. The need to consider the effect of regulation on some identifiable segment of property makes all important the admittedly difficult task of defining the relevant parcel. *See Penn Central Transportation Co. v. New York City*, 438 U.S., at 149, n.13, 98 S.Ct., at 2672, n.13 (REHNQUIST, J., dissenting). For the reasons explained below, I do not believe that the Court's opinion adequately performs this task.

III

The *Pennsylvania Coal* Court found it sufficient that the Kohler Act rendered it "commercially impracticable to mine certain coal." 260 U.S., at 414, 43 S.Ct., at 159. The Court, *ante*, at 1249, observes that this language is best understood as a conclusion that certain coal mines could not be operated at a profit. Petitioners have not at this stage of the litigation rested their claim on similar proof; they have not "claimed that their mining operations, or even any specific mines, have been unprofitable since the Subsidence Act was passed." *Ante*, at 1248. The parties have, however, stipulated for purposes of this facial challenge that the Subsidence Act requires petitioners to leave in the ground 27 million tons of coal, without compensation therefor. Petitioners also claim that the Act extinguishes their purchased interests in support estates which allow them to mine the coal without liability for subsidence. We are thus asked to consider whether these restrictions are such as to constitute a taking.

A

The Court's conclusion that the restriction on particular coal does not work a taking is primarily the result of its view that the 27 million tons of coal in the ground "do not constitute a separate segment of property for takings law purposes." *Ante*, at 1248. This conclusion cannot be based on the view that the interests are too insignificant to warrant protection by the Fifth Amendment, for it is beyond cavil that government appropriation of "relatively small amounts of private property for its own use" requires just compensation. *Ante*, at 1249, n.27. Instead, the Court's refusal to recognize the coal in the ground as a separate segment of property for takings purposes is based on the fact that the alleged taking is "regulatory," rather than a physical intrusion. *See ante*, at 1244, n. 18. On the facts of this case, I cannot see how the label placed on the government's action is relevant to consideration of its impact on property rights.

Our decisions establish that governmental action short of physical invasion may constitute a taking because such regulatory action might result in "as complete [a loss] as if the [government] had entered upon the surface of the land and taken exclusive possession of it." *United States v. Causby*, 328 U.S. 256, 261, 66 S.Ct. 1062, 1065, 90 L.Ed. 1206 (1946). Though the government's direct benefit may vary depending upon the nature of its action, the question is evaluated from the perspective of the property holder's loss rather than the government's gain. *See ibid.*; *United States v. General Motors Corp.*, 323 U.S. 373, 378, 65 S.Ct. 357, 359, 89 L.Ed. 311 (1945); *Boston Chamber of Commerce v. Boston*, 217 U.S. 189, 195, 30 S.Ct. 459, 460, 54 L.Ed. 725 (1910). Our observation that "[a] 'taking' may more readily be found when the interference with property can be characterized as a physical invasion by government," *Penn Central Transportation Co. v. New York City, supra*, 438 U.S., at 124, 98 S.Ct., at 2659, was not intended to alter this perspective merely because the claimed taking is by regulation. Instead, we have recognized that regulations—unlike physical invasions—do not typically extinguish the "full bundle" of rights in a particular piece of property. In *Andrus v. Allard*, 444 U.S. 51, 66, 100 S.Ct. 318, 327, 62 L.Ed.2d 210 (1979), for example, we found it crucial that a prohibition on the sale of avian artifacts destroyed only "one 'strand' of the bundle" of property rights, "because the aggregate must be viewed in its entirety." This characteristic of regulations frequently makes unclear the breadth of their impact on identifiable segments of property, and has required that we evaluate the effects in light of the "several factors" enumerated in *Penn Central Transportation Co.*: "The economic impact of the regulation on the claimant,... the extent to which the regulation has interfered with investment-backed expectations, [and] the character of the governmental action." 438 U.S., at 124, 98 S.Ct., at 2659.

No one, however, would find any need to employ these analytical tools where the government has physically taken an identifiable segment of property. Physical appropriation by the government leaves no doubt that it has in fact deprived the owner of all uses of the land. Similarly, there is no need for further analysis where the government by regulation extinguishes the whole bundle of rights in an identifiable segment of property, for the effect of this action on the holder of the property is indistinguishable from the effect of a physical taking.[5] Thus, it is clear our decision in *Andrus v. Allard, supra*, would have been different if the Government had confiscated the avian artifacts. In my view, a different result would also follow if the Government simply prohibited every use of that property, for the owner would still have been "deprive[d] of all or most of his interest in the subject matter." *United States v. General Motors Corp. supra*, 323 U.S., at 378, 65 S.Ct., at 359.

---

[5] There is admittedly some language in *Penn Central Transportation Co. v. New York City*, 438 U.S. 104, 130-131, 98 S.Ct. 2646, 2662, 57 L.Ed.2d 631 (1978), that suggests a contrary analysis: "'Taking' jurisprudence does not divide a single parcel into discrete segments and attempt to determine whether rights in a particular segment have been entirely abrogated. In deciding whether a particular governmental action has effected a taking, this Court focuses rather both on the character of the action and on the nature and extent of the interference with rights in the parcel as a whole." The Court gave no guidance on how one is to distinguish a "discrete segment" from a "single parcel." It was not clear, moreover, that the air rights at issue in *Penn Central* were entirely eliminated by the operation of New York City's Landmark Preservation Law, for, as the Court noted, "it simply cannot be maintained, on this record, that appellants have been prohibited from occupying any portion of the airspace above the Terminal." Id., at 136, 98 S.Ct., at 2665.

In this case, enforcement of the Subsidence Act and its regulations will require petitioners to leave approximately 27 million tons of coal in place. There is no question that this coal is an identifiable and separable property interest. Unlike many property interests, the "bundle" of rights in this coal is sparse. "'For practical purposes, the right to coal consists in the right to mine it.'" *Pennsylvania Coal*, 260 U.S., at 414, 43 S.Ct., at 159, quoting *Commonwealth ex rel. Keater v. Clearview Coal Co.*, 256 Pa., at 331, 100 A., at 820. From the relevant perspective—that of the property owners—this interest has been destroyed every bit as much as if the government had proceeded to mine the coal for its own use. The regulation, then, does not merely inhibit one strand in the bundle, *cf. Andrus v. Allard, supra*, but instead destroys completely any interest in a segment of property. In these circumstances, I think it unnecessary to consider whether petitioners may operate individual mines or their overall mining operations profitably, for they have been denied all use of 27 million tons of coal. I would hold that §4 of the Subsidence Act works a taking of these property interests.

B

Petitioners also claim that the Subsidence Act effects a taking of their support estate. Under Pennsylvania law, the support estate, the surface estate, and the mineral estate are "three distinct estates in land which can be held in fee simple separate and distinct from each other...." *Captline v. County of Allegheny*, 74 Pa.Commw. 85, 91, 459 A.2d 1298, 1301 (1983), cert. denied, 466 U.S. 904, 104 S.Ct. 1679, 80 L.Ed.2d 154 (1984). In refusing to consider the effect of the Subsidence Act on this property interest alone, the Court dismisses this feature of Pennsylvania property law as simply a "legalistic distinctio[n] within a bundle of property rights." *Ante*, at 1250. "Its value," the Court informs us, "is merely a part of the entire bundle of rights possessed by the owner of either the coal or the surface." *Ante*, at 1250. *See* also 771 F.2d 707, 716 (1985) ("To focus upon the support estate separately ... would serve little purpose"). This view of the support estate allows the Court to conclude that its destruction is merely the destruction of one "strand" in petitioners' bundle of property rights, not significant enough in the overall bundle to work a taking.

Contrary to the Court's approach today, we have evaluated takings claims by reference to the units of property defined by state law. In *Ruckleshaus v. Monsanto, Co.*, for example, we determined that certain "health, safety, and environmental data" was "cognizable as a trade-secret property right under Missouri law," 467 U.S., at 1003, 104 S.Ct., at 2873, and proceeded to evaluate the effects of governmental action on this state-defined property right. [Footnote omitted] Reliance on state law is necessitated by the fact that "'[p]roperty interests ... are not created by the Constitution. Rather, they are created and their dimensions are defined by existing rules or understandings that stem from an independent source such as state law.'" *Webb's Fabulous Pharmacies, Inc. v. Beckwith*, 449 U.S. 155, 161, 101 S.Ct. 446, 450, 66 L.Ed.2d 358 (1980), quoting *Board of Regents v. Roth*, 408 U.S. 564, 577, 92 S.Ct. 2701, 2709, 33 L.Ed.2d 548 (1972). In reality, the Court's decision today cannot reject this necessary reliance on state law. Rather, it simply rejects the support estate as the relevant segment of property and evaluates the impact of the Subsidence Act by reference to some broader, yet undefined, segment of property presumably recognized by state law.

I see no reason for refusing to evaluate the impact of the Subsidence Act on the support estate alone, for Pennsylvania has clearly defined it as a separate estate in property. The Court suggests that the practical significance of this estate is limited, because its value "is merely part of the bundle of rights possessed by the owner of either the coal or the surface." *Ante*, at 1250.

Though this may accurately describe the usual state of affairs, I do not understand the Court to mean that one holding the support estate alone would find it worthless, for surely the owners of the mineral or surface estates would be willing buyers of this interest. [Footnote omitted.] Nor does the Court suggest that the owner of both the mineral and support estates finds his separate interest in support to be without value. In these circumstances, where the estate defined by state law is both severable and of value in its own right, it is appropriate to consider the effect of regulation on that particular property interest.

When held by owners of the mineral estate, the support estate "consists of the right to remove the strata of coal and earth that undergird the surface...." 771 F.2d, at 715. Purchase of this right, therefore, shifts the risk of subsidence to the surface owner. Section 6 of the Subsidence Act, by making the coal mine operator strictly liable for any damage to surface structures caused by subsidence, purports to place this risk on the holder of the mineral estate regardless of whether the holder also owns the support estate. Operation of this provision extinguishes petitioners' interests in their support estates, making worthless what they purchased as a separate right under Pennsylvania law. Like the restriction on mining particular coal, this complete interference with a property right extinguishes its value, and must be accompanied by just compensation. [Footnote omitted.]

IV

In sum, I would hold that Pennsylvania's Bituminous Mine Subsidence and Land Conservation Act effects a taking of petitioners' property without providing just compensation. Specifically, the Act works to extinguish petitioners' interest in at least 27 million tons of coal by requiring that coal to be left in the ground, and destroys their purchased support estates by returning to them financial liability for subsidence. I respectfully dissent from the Court's decision to the contrary.[9]

FLORIDA ROCK INDUSTRIES, INC. v. UNITED STATES

45 Fed.Cl. 21, 38 (1999)

This case is before the court on remand from the Court of Appeals for the Federal Circuit. The court is to determine what use, if any, remained after the United States Army Corps of Engineers (Army Corps or Corps), pursuant to the Clean Water Act, denied plaintiff's application for a permit to mine limestone. The court must then determine if the permit denial requires just compensation under the Fifth Amendment to the Constitution.

If all economically viable use of plaintiff's property was destroyed, then a total taking of plaintiff's property occurred, and compensation is due. If the court finds that some economically viable use remains, it must apply a three-factor test to determine whether a compensable partial regulatory taking occurred. A partial regulatory taking requires that the government pay for the property rights taken, but not for the rights remaining in plaintiff's possession. The court must

---

[9] Because I would find §6 of the Subsidence Act unconstitutional under the Fifth Amendment, I would not reach the Contracts Clause issue addressed by the Court, *ante*, at 1250-1253.

consider the economic impact of the regulation, plaintiff's reasonable investment-backed expectations, and the character of the government action to make its determination. Compensation is due when this test indicates that plaintiff was singled out to bear a burden which ought to be paid for by society as a whole.

The court finds that the permit denial resulted in a severe, but not total, loss of the economically viable use of plaintiff's property. The court also finds that plaintiff's reasonable investment-backed expectations were frustrated. Finally, the court finds that the government action was a legitimate exercise of governmental power designed to enhance the public stock of wetlands. The court does not inquire into whether the government action was justified. Under the Tucker Act it is enough that the officials had statutory authority and acted within the scope of their duties for there to be jurisdiction and a valid taking claim. In some circumstances, such as acts of war, emergency measures, or the abatement of a nuisance, the character of the government action might prevent a taking from being found. That is not the case here.

After analyzing economic impact, reasonable investment-backed expectations, and the character of the governmental action, the court finds that the Army Corps has engaged in a compensable partial regulatory taking of plaintiff's property under the Fifth Amendment. Florida Rock is entitled to just compensation for the taking of its common law right to mine the underlying limestone on its land. The court hereby awards plaintiff $752,444 plus interest from the date of taking and attorney fees under the Uniform Relocation Assistance and Real Property Acquisition Policies Act of 1970(URA), 42 U.S.C. §4654(c).

INTRODUCTION

The text of the Takings Clause appears simple enough: "nor shall private property be taken for public use without just compensation" U.S. Const. Amend. V. Defining its key terms, however, has proved a difficult goal. In 1922 Justice Holmes wrote, "[g]overnment hardly could go on if to some extent values incident to property could not be diminished without paying for every such change in the general law. As long recognized some values are enjoyed under an implied limitation and must yield to the police power." *Pennsylvania Coal Co. v. Mahon*, 260 U.S. 393, 413, 43 S.Ct. 158, 67 L.Ed. 322 (1922). But this pragmatic concern must also take into account the protection of property enshrined in the Fifth Amendment: "The general rule at least is that while property may be regulated to a certain extent, if regulation goes too far it will be recognized as a taking." *Id.* at 415, 43 S.Ct. 158; but *see Hage v. United States*, 35 Fed.Cl. 147, 150-52 (1996) (judicial role in takings claims is not that of "super legislator or executive, intent on preventing regulation that 'goes too far'").

More recent cases in the various courts have begun to define what the less-than-objective "goes too far" means in terms of economic impact, compensable property interests, and types of government action. These cases have used the traditional common law tools of analogous reasoning, statutory construction, and precedent to sort out protected property interests. While this process has sometimes been called balancing, it is more analogous to building a stable structure. It is using evidence, like an architect uses beams and timbers to support a floor, a wall, or a roof. It is the creation of a logical framework based upon well-established rules and principles. It is not an act of judicial will, but an exercise of judicial reasoning. While the landscape of taking law might seem littered with partial theories and broken concepts, a stable framework is beginning to crystallize.

The notion that the government can take two thirds of your property and not compensate you but must compensate you if it takes 100 percent has a ring of irrationality, if not unfairness, about it. If the law said that those injured by tortious conduct could only have their estates compensated if they were killed, but not themselves if they could still breathe, no matter how seriously injured, we would certainly think it odd, if not barbaric. Yet in takings trials, we have the government trying to prove that the patient has a few breaths left, while the plaintiffs seek to prove, often at great expense, that the patient is dead. This all-or-nothing approach seems to ignore the point of the Takings Clause.

As the Supreme Court explained in *Armstrong v. United States*, 364 U.S. 40, 49, 80 S.Ct. 1563, 4 L.Ed.2d 1554 (1960), the Takings Clause is triggered by regulation which forces "some people alone to bear public burdens which, in all fairness and justice, should be borne by the public as a whole." The present case puts the Armstrong principle to the test and goes to the heart of Justice Holmes' formulation of regulatory takings.

Florida Rock has suffered a severe, but only partial, destruction of its property value when its parcel is viewed as a whole. It suffered a deprivation of all of its traditional common law right to its subsurface estate, as well as all economically viable use of the surface of its property. Its reasonable investment-backed expectations have been severely frustrated. Nevertheless, Florida Rock still has property rights in the encumbered parcel, albeit far fewer than it originally possessed.

Thus, the question before the court is whether Florida Rock may be singled out to bear a public burden merely because the regulation of its property does not take its fee simple. The answer, based on the facts of this particular case, is no. The balancing test announced in *Penn Central v. City of New York*, 438 U.S. 104, 124-128, 98 S.Ct. 2646, 57 L.Ed.2d 631 (1978), weighing the economic impact, reasonable investment-backed expectations, and character of the government action to determine whether compensation is mandated, shows that valuable property rights have been taken from Florida Rock.

While the outcome of the *Penn Central* test is determined by the facts of each case, it is not an entirely ad hoc inquiry. Certain legal principles and rules apply to the significance of the various facts. The government, in this case, has acted to achieve legitimate and important goal. Our role, however, is not to make policy choices about the best ratio of regulation to individual rights, but to answer the question whether the public must pay for its regulations in this case. If those regulations take property the Constitution gives a simple answer: yes it must. The Founders chose to provide for just compensation, and this court must determine whether the Takings Clause is triggered by the facts before us today.

Considering the facts of this case and applying the law to them, it is clear that part of Florida Rock's property was taken. Inasmuch as property is taken at all, there must be compensation. This principle can be traced to William Blackstone, who noted: "So great moreover is the regard for private property, that it will not authorize the least violation of it; no, not even for the general good of the whole community." W. Blackstone, 1 Commentaries 135 (1765). To deny compensation in this case would create a doctrine under which property could not, by its very nature, be divided. Such a law of property is foreign to the state of Florida, and, for that matter, to the English common law tradition. As the Supreme Court noted in *United States v. General Motors Corp.*, 323 U.S. 373, 377-78, 65 S.Ct. 357, 89 L.Ed. 311 (1945), the word "property" in the Takings Clause "may have been employed in a more accurate sense to denote the group of rights inhering in the citizen's relation to the particular thing, as the right to possess, use and dispose of it." To hold that property cannot be partially taken by a regulation, on these facts, would be to hold that the need for government regulation trumps the Takings Clause. Yet, the need for government regulation is why the Takings Clause was enacted as a vital protection. Any other reading would make that clause a virtual nullity. Rather, in a free society, property rights and regulation must exist together. Their ends are not inconsistent. In fact, the Takings Clause implies that property may be taken but that property owners must be compensated.

BACKGROUND

The facts involved in this case have been concisely set forth in the appellate decision. *Florida Rock Indus., Inc. v. United States*, 18 F.3d 1560 (Fed.Cir.1994), cert. denied, 513 U.S. 1109, 115 S.Ct. 898, 130 L.Ed.2d 783 (1995)(*Florida Rock IV*). Previous decisions also recount the factual issues of the case. *Florida Rock Indus., Inc. v. United States*, 8 Cl.Ct. 160 (1985) (*Florida Rock I*), rev'd and remanded, *Florida Rock Indus., Inc. v. United States*, 791 F.2d 893 (Fed.Cir.1986), cert. denied, 479 U.S. 1053, 107 S.Ct. 926, 93 L.Ed.2d 978 (1987) (*Florida Rock II*), on remand, *Florida Rock Indus., Inc. v. United States*, 21 Cl.Ct. 161 (1990) (*Florida Rock III*). Key relevant facts are repeated here for convenience.

In September 1972, plaintiff, Florida Rock Industries, Inc. (Florida Rock), purchased a 1,560 acre parcel located west of Miami in Dade County, Florida known as the Andrus site. The purchase price of the property was $2,964,000 ($1,900 per acre), and the tract was largely composed of wetlands. Plaintiff, a corporation engaged primarily in large-scale limestone mining, purchased the tract specifically for the subsurface limestone, for extraction and conversion into aggregates used in the construction industry. Plaintiff began preliminary mining operations between 1972 and 1974 but, because of a slump in the construction industry, temporarily delayed mining the property until 1978. Plaintiff had complied with state and local permit requirements to mine limestone. *See Florida Rock II*, 791 F.2d at 897; Florida Rock I, 8 Cl.Ct. at 164.

After plaintiff purchased the tract, Congress passed, and the President signed into law, the Clean Water Act Amendments of 1972 (the Clean Water Act or CWA). Under section 404 of the Act, the Corps was given the authority to issue permits to discharge dredge or fill material into waters under their jurisdiction. *See* 33 U.S.C. §1344. The Corps asserted a gradually expanding jurisdiction until, with phase three of the program on July 1, 1977, section 404 permits were required to dredge or fill in all waters of the United States, including wetlands such as Florida Rock's which were not adjacent to navigable waters or their primary tributaries. 33 C.F.R. §§323.2(a)(5), 323.3(a)(4), 323.4-4 (1978). In 1978, plaintiff proceeded with mining the parcel. Plaintiff performed additional road construction, constructed a dragline tower, and completed the initial "key cut." In September 1978, the Corps issued a cease and desist order directing Florida Rock to halt immediately any further activity on the site because it believed a section 404 permit to be necessary. Plaintiff complied with the order.

Plaintiff began negotiating with the Corps for a permit to mine the parcel, initially applying for a permit under section 404 to mine the entire 1,560 acres. Because the Corps indicated it would only consider applications covering mining needs sufficient to satisfy a three-year period, plaintiff submitted an application for 98 acres—the amount sufficient to fulfill its three-year needs. The Corps denied this application on October 2, 1980.

Plaintiff's property, like that surrounding it, is considered "wetlands" in that it is regularly inundated with surface or ground water so as to constitute a swamp, marsh, bog, or similar area. *See*

40 C.F.R. §230.3(t). Wetlands are included as "waters of the United States" and therefore subject to the Clean Water Act. The Corps classifies rock, sand, and other fill materials as pollutants and prohibits their discharge onto wetlands. *See* 40 C.F.R. §§230.3(o), 230.10(c), 230.11(c)(3). Under such constraints, the remaining uses for Florida Rock's land are severely limited. Residential or commercial development are precluded by the need to deposit fill upon the wetlands sufficient to support a structure and a road or pathway to reach it.

After denial of the permit, plaintiff filed suit in the Claims Court seeking just compensation for a regulatory taking under the Fifth Amendment. Then Chief Judge Kozinski bifurcated the suit and held separate trials on liability and damages. In the first trial, determining liability, the court found the permit denial on October 2, 1980 to be a compensable regulatory taking. *See Florida Rock I*, 8 Cl.Ct. at 165. After a subsequent trial on damages, the court, in a verbal ruling, set the damages at $1,029,000 ($10,500 per acre) for the regulatory taking of the 98 acres at issue. [Footnote omitted.]

On appeal, the Federal Circuit affirmed the trial court's refusal to determine that land was taken in excess of the 98-acre parcel, vacated in part, and remanded the case to the Claims Court for further proceedings. *Florida Rock II*, 791 F.2d at 905-06. The Federal Circuit found error in the court's focus on "immediate use" and its exclusion of evidence of a potential investment market for the property in determining post-permit denial value. The court noted that the proper focus should instead have been on determination of a "solid and adequate fair market value (for the 98 acres)." *Id.* at 903.

Florida Rock, interpreting the appellate court's instructions on remand to require that a post-permit denial of fair market value be established using only investors knowledgeable of the regulatory restrictions, presented evidence to show that no market existed among such knowledgeable investors. *See Florida Rock III*, 21 Cl.Ct. at 172. The court concluded that only a nominal residual value of $500 per acre remained after permit denial, the value which the property would have to a government entity. *Id.* at 175. Finding the evidence provided by Florida Rock was persuasive, the Claims Court decided in *Florida Rock III* that a taking of 98 acres had occurred and again awarded $1,029,000 ($10,500 per acre), plus interest from the date of taking, October 2, 1980. *Id.* at 176.

The court of appeals, remanding in *Florida Rock IV*, 18 F.3d at 1566, 1567, found uncontroverted evidence of an "active though speculative investment market for Florida Rock's land." The Federal Circuit indicated that long-term speculative investment was a viable economic use of Florida Rock's land which the trial court must consider along with other uses such as immediate mining and development. The court remanded for a determination of "what economic use as measured by market value, if any, remained after the permit denial, and for consideration of whether, in light of the properly assessed value of the land, Florida Rock has a valid takings claim." *Id.* at 1564.

DISCUSSION

In 1922, the Supreme Court expressly recognized that regulation that "goes too far" in interfering with the rights of property owners can work a taking.[5] *Pennsylvania Coal Co.*, 260 U.S. at 415, 43 S.Ct. 158. After *Pennsylvania Coal* little elaboration on the concept of regulatory takings occurred until, in *Penn Central Transportation Co. v. City of New York*, 438 U.S. 104, 124-26, 98 S.Ct. 2646, 57 L.Ed.2d 631 (1978), the Court announced an ad hoc inquiry, taking into account three factors when deciding whether a regulation has caused a taking:

1) the regulation's economic impact on the claimant;

2) the regulation's interference with distinct investment-backed expectations; and,

3) the character of the government action.

These legal concepts work to ensure that the Takings Clause operates "to bar Government from forcing some people alone to bear public burdens which, in all fairness and justice, should be borne by the public as a whole." *Armstrong v. United States*, 364 U.S. at 49, 80 S.Ct. 1563.

In *Agins v. City of Tiburon*, 447 U.S. 255, 260, 100 S.Ct. 2138, 65 L.Ed.2d 106 (1980), the Court established that a regulatory taking is effected where a zoning law "denies an owner economically viable use of his land." Recently, the Court held that the deprivation of all economically beneficial or productive use of property constitutes a categorical taking regardless of the importance of the governmental interest being served. *See Lucas v. South Carolina Coastal Council*, 505 U.S. 1003, 1015, 112 S.Ct. 2886, 120 L.Ed.2d 798 (1992).

In contrast to the ad hoc inquiry which applies to the regulation of land when all economic value is not destroyed, the permanent physical invasion of real property is always a categorical taking. *See id.* In *Loretto v. Teleprompter Manhattan CATV Corp.*, 458 U.S. 419, 102 S.Ct. 3164, 73 L.Ed.2d 868 (1982), the Court compensated a minute but permanent partial taking of real estate where New York required a landlord to permit installation of cable facilities on her roof. *See* also *Hendler v. United States*, 952 F.2d 1364, 1376 (Fed.Cir.1991) (periodic physical intrusion by EPA on plaintiff's property to install and inspect groundwater monitoring wells).

"The fact that the source of any particular taking is a regulation rather than a physical entry should make no difference—the nature of legal interests defining the property affected remains unchanged." *Florida Rock IV*, 18 F.3d at 1572; *see* also *San Diego Gas & Electric Co. v. San Diego*, 450 U.S. 621, 652, 101 S.Ct. 1287, 67 L.Ed.2d 551 (1981) (Brennan, J., dissenting) ("Police power regulations such as zoning ordinances and other land-use restrictions can destroy the use and enjoyment of property in order to promote the public good just as effectively as formal condemnation or physical invasion of property"). Accordingly, a regulation which is sufficiently similar

---

[5] Compensation for the indirect or regulatory destruction of property rights was not a new idea in 1922, however. State courts required just compensation for such takings from the early days of the republic. *See* Kris Kobach, *The Origins of Regulatory Takings: Setting the Record Straight*, 1996 Utah L. Rev. 1211 (providing history of early state decisions compensating indirect or regulatory takings). Most famously, in 1816, Chancellor Kent held that government diversion of a stream constituted a compensable taking of water rights although there was no physical invasion of theland itself. *See Gardner v. Village of Newburgh*, 2 Johns.Ch. 162 (N.Y.1816). Also, in 1870 the Supreme Court compensated a regulatory taking claim based on the taking of property rights. *See Yates v. Milwaukee*, 77 U.S. (10 Wall.) 497, 19 L.Ed. 984 (1870) (City of Milwaukee must compensate property owner for removal of his wharf pursuant to state legislation).

to a permanent physical taking of property should require just compensation. When there is a complete destruction of property value it is easy to see that the property owner is in the same position she would be in if the government had permanently occupied the land. But when is a partial diminution in value not merely a diminution, but equivalent to a permanent physical occupation of the land?

I. COMPENSABLE PROPERTY INTEREST

The initial step in our takings inquiry is to determine whether plaintiff has a compensable property interest. "If plaintiff establishes ownership of its property rights under state law, the second step of the process would then go to liability, or whether government action has actually taken those rights." *Store Safe Redlands Assocs. v. United States*, 35 Fed.Cl. 726, 730 (1996). In this case, it is not disputed that plaintiff owns the 98 acres at issue. The government contends, however, that Florida Rock never had a right to mine limestone on its property, and therefore cannot be compensated for the loss of this use.

Plaintiff responds that the law of the case has already resolved this issue. The court is inclined to agree. This court held that all necessary state and local permits to mine limestone on Florida Rock's property were granted at the time of application to the Army Corps of Engineers. The court found that, "at the time, had an application been made for the full 1,560 acres and considered on the merits, that [Florida Rock] did have all of the permits necessary from Dade County." Tr. 1-39, June 12, 1984 Hearing. The court confirmed this ruling in its later opinion, concluding, "[a]t the time the Corps issued its cease and desist order, plaintiff had all the necessary state permits or waivers...." *Florida Rock I*, 8 Cl.Ct. at 164. This finding as to state and local permits was not disturbed by the Federal Circuit on appeal. *Florida Rock II*, 791 F.2d at 897. The court hereby reaffirms its earlier ruling.

Moreover, there were no federal laws like the Clean Water Act in place at the time of plaintiff's purchase of the land. The evidence is clear that plaintiff could have mined limestone on its property but for the Corps' permit denial. It is also the law of the case that mining of limestone on Florida Rock's property did not constitute a nuisance. The Federal Circuit noted that Florida Rock's use of the property "does no harm," *Florida Rock II*, 791 F.2d at 904, and this court held that "even if the Federal Circuit's statements were not binding on this court, the court on its own is not persuaded that plaintiff's proposed activities would have constituted a nuisance so as to deny plaintiff its rights to just compensation." *Florida Rock III*, 21 Cl.Ct. at 166.

The government argues, however, that Florida Rock's rights must be reconsidered in light of the Supreme Court decision in Lucas, a holding which came after the court's findings in *Florida Rock III*. The court addresses the government's arguments below.

A. NUISANCE

"The government argues that there is no right to compensation because, [o]n the record developed herein, the United States has clearly established that Florida Rock's proposed property use would have been injurious to the public health and safety, as defined by Congress. Def. Post-trial Br. at 71. The government appears to hold the view that Congress' definitions of public health and safety, and a valid finding that these definitions were met, are sufficient to preclude a compensable property interest in land use which conflicts with these definitions. It follows that since this court must take as given that the revisions in the regulations of the Army Corps of

Engineers, and the entire body of federal navigational and environmental laws to which they give effect, advance legitimate and important federal interests," *Deltona v. United States*, 228 Ct.Cl. 476, 657 F.2d 1184, 1192, a legitimate permit denial would therefore preclude a taking. *See* Def. Post-trial Br. at 71-73.

This argument would make sense if legitimate use of the government's regulatory power precluded any takings liability. *See Forest Properties, Inc. v. United States*, 39 Fed.Cl. 56, 69 (1997) (discussing evolution of "nuisance exception" to takings liability). "[H]owever, the Supreme Court narrowed the concept of uses that may be considered injurious to the community to a much more limited concept of uses that would be prohibited by background principles of the state's law of property and nuisance." *Id.*

Nuisance law for purposes of the Takings Clause is not simply defined by Congress, whenever it declares that a use should not occur. The government's argument would enable Congress to pass laws which eliminate property rights retroactively as if those rights never existed in the first place. Where there is a confiscatory regulation, the *Lucas* Court declared: "Any limitation so severe cannot be newly legislated or decreed (without compensation), but must inhere in the title itself, in the restrictions that background principles of the State's law of property and nuisance already place upon land ownership." 505 U.S. at 1029, 112 S.Ct. 2886; *see* also *Keystone*, 480 U.S. 470, 519, 107 S.Ct. 1232, 94 L.Ed.2d 472 (1987) (Rehnquist, J., dissenting) ("Reliance on state law is necessitated by the fact that '[p]roperty interests ... are not created by the Constitution. Rather, they are created and their dimensions are defined by existing rules or understandings that stem from an independent source such as state law.'") (quoting *Webb's Fabulous Pharmacies, Inc. v. Beckwith*, 449 U.S. 155, 161, 101 S.Ct. 446, 66 L.Ed.2d 358 (1980)). The government must show a limit on plaintiff's property rights which inhered in the title when it was purchased by its owner. The federal government, "by *ipse dixit*, may not transform private property into public property without compensation." *Beckwith*, 449 U.S. at 164, 101 S.Ct. 446. Congress or regulators cannot simply bypass the Fifth Amendment's just compensation provision by declaring long-settled property rights illegal or not permitted. Nor can the artful recitation of a harm-preventing or benefit conferring justification transform compensable government action into that which is not compensable. *Lucas*, 505 U.S. at 1027, n. 12, 112 S.Ct. 2886.

Where a federal statute was already in place at the time the property was bought, the expectations of the property owner may be different. In *M & J Coal Company v. United States*, 47 F.3d 1148 (1995), the Federal Circuit emphasized that "at the time M & J [the property owner] acquired its mining rights, whatever they were, it knew or should have known that it could not mine in such a way as to endanger public health or safety and that any state authorization it may have received was subordinate to the national standards that were established by [federal statute]." *Id.* at 1154.

In this case, the Clean Water Act was not enacted until after Florida Rock's property was acquired. Similarly, in *Loveladies Harbor*, 28 F.3d at 1183, the Federal Circuit explained, "It is important to note that Loveladies purchased the property with the intent to develop it long before these particular state and federal regulatory programs came into effect." In *Loveladies*, unlike *M & J*, it was relevant that the state had granted a permit to develop the property. *See id.* ("[N]othing in the state's conduct reflected a considered determination that certain defined activities would violate the state's understanding of its nuisance powers"). As in *Loveladies*, the court finds it relevant here that plaintiff had secured all necessary state and local permits or waivers to use the land for limestone mining. *See Florida Rock I*, 8 Cl.Ct. at 164; *Florida Rock II*, 791 F.2d at 897.

It remains then to determine whether Florida law understood this type of property use to be a nuisance at the time of the taking. *See Lucas*, 505 U.S. at 1029, 112 S.Ct. 2886. The Supreme Court of Florida has stated that

> An owner or occupant of property must use it in a way that will not be a nuisance to other owners and occupants in the same community. Anything which annoys or disturbs one in the free use, possession, or enjoyment of his property, or which renders its ordinary use or occupation physically uncomfortable, is a "nuisance" and may be restrained.

Mercer v. Keynton, 121 Fla. 87, 163 So. 411 (1935) (quoted in *Knowles v. Central Allapattae Properties, Inc.*, 145 Fla. 123, 198 So. 819 (1940); *City of Miami v. City of Coral Gables*, 233 So.2d 7 (Fla.Dist.Ct.App.1970)). Florida also has a public nuisance statute which stated in relevant part:

> Whoever shall erect, establish, continue, or maintain, own or lease any ... place which tends to annoy the community or injure the health of the community ... or any place where any law of the state is violated, shall be deemed guilty of maintaining a nuisance and the ... place ... [is] declared a nuisance.

Fl. Stat. § 823.05 (1979).

Here, the only disturbance or activity injurious to the health of the community alleged by the government is that plaintiff's limestone mining would result in "pollution" of the wetlands as defined by Clean Water Act regulations. The authority of the Army Corps to prevent such pollution by denying plaintiff's section 404 permit is undisputed. Florida state nuisance law, however, does not appear to preclude such "pollution." Nor is plaintiff's proposed activity alleged to violate any other Florida laws. Thus, the court finds that plaintiff's activity was, except for the Corps' denial, permissible under relevant property and nuisance principles. *See Lucas*, 505 U.S. at 1029, 1030, 112 S.Ct. 2886.

The court follows the Federal Circuit's pronouncement in *Florida Rock II* that the Army Corps district engineer's decision established that any pollution of water by Florida Rock for its proposed activity was not very serious. *Florida Rock II*, 791 F.2d at 904; *see* also *Florida Rock III*, 21 Cl.Ct. at 166 (not a nuisance). As noted in *Florida Rock II*, "[W]hen appellant characterizes the regulatory action as one to prevent pollution, it is really elevating form over substance." 791 F.2d at 904. Moreover, the district engineer's decision declared that "'[w]ater pollution does not appear to be a problem' at (water supply) wells adjacent to similar pits." *Id.* Indeed, "a moderate and pro forma polluter such as Florida Rock does no harm." *Id.*

Nevertheless, the placing of fill upon wetlands technically amounts to "pollution" under the Clean Water Act. Mining or development of plaintiff's land unavoidably requires the placement of fill. Plaintiff's placement of fill on wetlands, however, would be a violation of federal, not state law. In fact, the Florida Department of Transportation told Florida Rock that it was their recommendation and that of the Dade County Planning Department that new rock plants be located within the Pennsuco area, where plaintiff's property is located. The Clean Water Act concerns do not show the existence of a nuisance under state law. As the Federal Circuit observed in *Florida Rock II*, "The concern of the district engineer is almost exclusively the continued existence of the wetland, not the temporary and moderate pollution incident to the occurrence of actual mining." 791 F.2d at 904.

As the Lucas court noted:

> The fact that a particular use has long been engaged in by similarly situated owners ordinarily imports a lack of any common-law prohibition (though changed circumstances or new knowledge may make what was previously permissible no longer so....) So also does the fact that other landowners, similarly situated, are permitted to continue the use denied to the claimant.

505 U.S. at 1031, 112 S.Ct. 2886 (emphasis added).

In this case, other landowners in the vicinity have been allowed to operate rock quarries. These other limestone mining operations carry on apparently without official concern about their effect on ground water. Dade County and the City of Miami draw ground water from the Northwest Wellfields which lie to the east of the subject property quite close to these other quarries. Rock quarries were still in operation within the Pennsuco area at least eight years after plaintiff's application to engage in the same activity was denied. *See Florida Rock III*, 21 Cl.Ct. at 166-167.

The court finds that plaintiff's limestone mining operation would, like similar operations in the vicinity, result in only moderate, superficial pollution that does no harm, and would not be considered a nuisance under the relevant Florida laws. Indeed, plaintiff's operation was suitably located in the community and designed to help meet the community's need for aggregates to be used in construction. *See* French, Tr. 1-204 to 206.

In light of these facts, the court finds that plaintiff's proposed mining operation was not a public or private nuisance under Florida law. Florida Rock's use of its property was not a nuisance for purposes of the court's taking inquiry. Accordingly, Florida Rock had a compensable property interest in its right to mine limestone.

II. WHETHER A TAKING OCCURRED

A. CATEGORICAL TAKINGS

The first instance in which categorical takings have been found, where there is physical invasion of the property, does not apply in this case. *See Lucas*, 505 U.S. at 1015, 112 S.Ct. 2886. The second instance where categorical treatment is appropriate is "where regulation denies all economically beneficial or productive use of land." *Id.* Both parties now agree, pursuant to the Federal Circuit decision in *Florida Rock IV*, that all economically beneficial use of the land was not denied. The court finds, as further explained herein, persuasive evidence of a speculative market for property comparable to Florida Rock's land. Accordingly, the court holds that economically beneficial use of the land remained after permit denial. This is probably the case in most regulatory takings circumstances as people are usually willing to speculate that the future may bring beneficial change to the value of property. There was thus no categorical taking of Florida Rock's land.

B. PENN CENTRAL AND PARTIAL REGULATORY TAKINGS

On remand, this court is directed to:

> reconsider the assessments proffered by the parties and the other evidence in the record, and determine a fair market value accordingly. Should that determination establish, as the evidence in the record suggests, that there was some (but not total) reduction in the overall market value of plaintiff's property as a result of the regulatory imposition, the question will then be posed: does that reduction constitute a taking of property compensable under the Fifth Amendment?

Florida Rock IV, 18 F.3d at 1567, 1568. Ultimately, the question before the court is does "a partial deprivation resulting from a regulatory imposition, that is, a situation in which a regulation deprives the owner of a substantial part but not essentially all of the economic use or value of the property, constitute a partial taking, and is it compensable as such?" *Florida Rock IV*, 18 F.3d at 1568. In sum:

> By taking some portion of Florida Rock's economic use of the property—its power to disturb the overlying wetlands, and with it the common law property right to mine its subsurface minerals—the Government appears to have destroyed part of the value of Florida Rock's holdings. If that proves to be the case, and if the application of the [Penn Central] *ad hoc* tests previously described so warrant, the property interest taken belongs to the Government, and the right to just compensation for the interest taken belongs to Florida Rock.

Id. at 1572.

The *Penn Central* inquiry entails an analysis of the economic impact, effect on reasonable investment-backed expectations, and character of the government action. Using these factors, a partial regulatory taking may be found where a regulation results in a deprivation of "a substantial part but not essentially all of the economic use or value of the property," *Florida Rock IV*, 18 F.3d at 1568; *see* also *id.* at 1569, 1570 (line drawn between partial regulatory taking and mere diminution). When such a regulation "allocate[es] to some number of individuals, less than all, a burden that should be borne by all," *Florida Rock IV*, 18 F.3d at 1571, there is a taking. In the case of a partial taking the government should not be forced to buy the entire parcel, nor should the property owner be forced to relinquish the entire parcel. *See id.* at 1571-72. Justice requires, and the text of the Takings Clause mandates, "just" compensation for the property taken, no more and no less.

The *Penn Central* test the court applies today is sensitive to the facts of each case. For example, compensation has previously been required where the rights taken are of singular importance, *see, e.g., Hodel v. Irving*, 481 U.S. 704, 705, 107 S.Ct. 2076, 95 L.Ed.2d 668 (1987) (right of tribe members to pass on property to heirs); *Babbitt v. Youpee*, 519 U.S. 234, 243, 117 S.Ct. 727, 136 L.Ed.2d 696 (1997) (same), or the interference with investment-backed expectations is overwhelming, *see Kaiser Aetna*, 444 U.S. at 179, 100 S.Ct. 383 (compensation due where government consented to dredging of private marina, but then destroyed plaintiff's right to exclude others). Compensation has been denied where the economic impact was not proven, *see, e.g., Keystone*, 480 U.S. 470, 107 S.Ct. 1232, 94 L.Ed.2d 472 (plaintiffs retained right to mine almost all of their coal). In the end, however, "the question depends upon the particular facts." *Pennsylva-*

nia Coal, 260 U.S. at 413, 43 S.Ct. 158. "There simply is no bright line dividing compensable from noncompensable exercises of the Government's power when a regulatory imposition causes a partial loss to the property owner." *Florida Rock IV*, 18 F.3d at 1570. However, this does not lead to a standardless judicial exercise of will. Rather, the court must analyze the property interests, where and to what degree the alleged diminution caused by the regulation occurred, and the economic effect on the total property. This is the same analytical approach used by the common law over the last millennium to define property rights and decide disputes over them.

II. THE THREE FACTOR PENN CENTRAL TEST

A. ECONOMIC IMPACT

The first *Penn Central* factor the court considers is the economic impact of the government action on plaintiff's property. The Federal Circuit directed that on remand, the Court of Federal Claims must determine the "loss of economic use to the property owner as a result of the regulatory imposition." *Florida Rock IV*, 18 F.3d at 1571. Underlying that determination is a calculation of fair market value as it was outlined in *Florida Rock II*:

> [T]he court should consider, along with other relevant matters, the relationship of the owner's basis or investment, and the fair market value before the alleged taking, to the fair market value after the alleged taking. In determining the severity of the economic impact, the owner's opportunity to recoup its investment or better, subject to the regulation, cannot be ignored. *Id.* at 1567 (quoting *Florida Rock II*, 791 F.2d at 905). Fair market value is:
>
> [T]he price at which the property would change hands between a willing buyer and a willing seller, neither being under any compulsion to buy or to sell and both having reasonable knowledge of relevant facts.

United States v. Cartwright, 411 U.S. 546, 551, 93 S.Ct. 1713, 36 L.Ed.2d 528 (1973).

A determination of economic impact must focus on a relevant parcel of plaintiff's property. In determining the relevant parcel, the court follows the teachings of *Penn Central*, 438 U.S. at 130-31, 98 S.Ct. 2646, as recently restated in *Concrete Pipe & Prod. v. Const. Laborers Pension Trust*, 508 U.S. 602, 644, 113 S.Ct. 2264, 124 L.Ed.2d 539 (1993):

> a claimant's parcel of property could not first be divided into what was taken and what was left for the purpose of demonstrating the taking of the former to be complete and hence compensable. To the extent that any portion of property is taken, that portion is always taken in its entirety; the relevant question, however, is whether the property taken is all, or only a portion of, the parcel in question.

See also *Lucas*, 505 U.S. at 1016 n. 7, 112 S.Ct. 2886 (denominator of "deprivation" fraction); *Loveladies*, 21 Cl.Ct. 153, 160 n. 9 (1990) (citing *Loveladies Harbor Inc. v. United States*, 15 Cl.Ct. 381, 391- 393 (1988)) aff'd 28 F.3d 1171 (Fed.Cir.1994) (discussing parcel as a whole); *Keystone*, 480 U.S. at 497, 107 S.Ct. 1232 (describing the "denominator" issue).

In *Concrete Pipe*, the Supreme Court rejected plaintiff's contention that its property rights in a pension plan had been taken in their entirety and, therefore, that it had suffered a compensable taking pursuant to a *Lucas* analysis (permanent physical occupation or destruction of all economically beneficial use). The Court in *Concrete Pipe* declined to treat an interest in a pension plan as the entire parcel and instead found no taking where the regulation allegedly resulted in a 46 percent diminution in shareholder equity overall. "[M]ere diminution in the value of property, however serious, is insufficient to demonstrate a taking." *Concrete Pipe*, 508 U.S. at 645, 113 S.Ct. 2264. This principle does not preclude the partial takings analysis discussed in *Florida Rock IV*, however. *Concrete Pipe* merely says that partial destruction in the value of the parcel is inadequate to prove a compensable taking occurred. Here, the court must apply all three parts of the *Penn Central* test, recognizing that diminution in value is but one element of the calculation. In the case at bar, the relevant parcel is the 98 acres of land owned by Florida Rock, and not merely their right to mine or develop it.

1. DIMINUTION IN VALUE

A. VALUE BEFORE PERMIT DENIAL

The court conducted a separate valuation trial in 1985 after which then Chief Judge Kozinski gave an oral ruling from the bench. He established a pre-denial value of $7,500 per acre for 1,240 acres in two one-section tracts (including the 98 acres at issue) fronting on Krome Avenue and $4,000 per acre for 320 acres (1/2 section) not fronting on Krome Avenue. The 98 acres at issue, pursuant to the government's argument, was considered in light of the value taken from plaintiff's total holdings of 1,560 acres in the three large tracts rather than standing alone. Valuing the 98 acres standing alone would have led to a higher pre-denial price per acre.

Plaintiff's valuation expert, Mr. Sewell, testified that, because in his opinion there were no comparable sales, alternative approaches must be relied on. The court, however, characterized plaintiff's alternatives, the discounted present value and royalty models, as "too uncertain, ... too indefinite, ... and too speculative." Tr. 2-2521 Still, the court considered and adopted the models as indications of a high limit on value. It should be noted, however, that while comparable sales are generally the least speculative method of valuation, the Federal Circuit affirmed the discounted cash flow method in another mining case, *Whitney Benefits, Inc. v. United States*, 926 F.2d 1169 (Fed.Cir.1991).

The court, in its 1985 valuation, relied instead on comparable sales, a more traditional and orthodox method of valuing property. Beginning with the comparable sales covered in the report of Mr. Slack, the government's appraiser, the court took into account the fact that those sales were tainted by bankruptcy proceedings, that permits were not in place for one property, and that some were distress sales, not really arm's length transactions, or otherwise did not properly reflect the market. The court found that these sales took place somewhere near Florida Rock's property and somewhere near in time to when the taking was deemed to have occurred.

The court made upward adjustments from Mr. Slack's comparable sales with respect to plaintiff's property based on access to Krome Avenue and the fact that plaintiff's property was further south, and closer to the fastest growth and development. The court found Krome Avenue to be a major artery, a substantial road capable of carrying truck traffic, and that it leads directly south, providing ready access to the fastest growing area of the county. Mr. Slack's comparables were further north and not fronted on the major road. Based on these adjustments, the court established the market value of $7,500 per acre for plaintiff's 1,240 acres fronting on Krome Avenue.

The court then made additional upward adjustments, with respect to the 98 acres at issue, for three factors: frontage on Krome Avenue, presence of a road on the property, and the presence of state and local permits. The 98 acres fronts on Krome Avenue and does not extend all the way back to plaintiff's rear property line, making it relatively more valuable. A road to Krome Avenue had already been constructed on the 98 acre parcel, again making that parcel relatively more valuable than the remainder. The larger parcel, which would only be developed or mined over a longer time, was more at risk for that reason of being later limited in its use by changing local, state, or even federal restrictions. The court found that there was a state waiver and a county permit to mine Florida Rock's entire 1,560 acre property. It noted however that "one never knows how the law will change in the future." Tr. 2-2545. It determined that this uncertainty was less as to the 98 acres. The $7,500 per acre was increased by $1,000 per acre for each of these three factors. Accordingly, the court found that $10,500 per acre, or $1,029,000, was the amount by which the 1,560 acres would have been diminished by the taking of the 98 acres at issue. Tr. 2-2545-46; *see* also 5/17/85 order on valuation as of 10/2/80. The court also noted that $10,500 per acre was well within the range of what such mineable properties sold for in the area.

In *Florida Rock III* the court let stand the methodology used in determining the pre-permit denial valuation of the property because it was not clearly erroneous under the standards set forth in RUSCC 52(a). *Florida Rock III*, 21 Cl.Ct. at 165 n. 4. RUSCC 52(a) provides in part that "[f]indings of fact, whether based on oral or documentary evidence, shall not be set aside unless clearly erroneous, and due regard shall be given to the opportunity of the trial court to judge the credibility of the witnesses." *See* also *Florida Rock II*, 791 F.2d at 897, 905, 906 (court let stand Judge Kozinski's $10,500 pre-denial valuation); *Florida Rock IV*, 18 F.3d at 1563 (trial court erred in determining after-taking value, not pre-taking value). For the same reasons that its determination of pre-denial value was let stand in prior proceedings, the court now finds that the pre-denial value of the property at issue was $10,500 per acre or $1,029,000.

B. VALUE AFTER PERMIT DENIAL

The market for land in the vicinity of the subject property was based upon two ultimate uses—rock mining and development. Of the two, rock mining represented an immediate use because of existing demand for aggregates used in the construction of roads and buildings on the expanding fringe of Miami, several miles away. The demand for land for residential or commercial development had not yet reached as far as plaintiff's property at the time of permit denial. Outside of speculative investment, therefore, mining was the only economically viable use of the property at the time of the taking. *See Florida Rock I*, 8 Cl.Ct. at 166. Anticipation of possible future developmental demand and of continued aggregate demand both contributed to the purchase of land in the area.

The value of real property is in its utility. Even those who purchased land in the vicinity for resale did so based on the perception of present or future utility. Once plaintiff's dredge and fill permit had been denied the property could no longer be used for mining for the foreseeable future. At that point its only remaining value was as a speculative investment vehicle. The remaining value after permit denial was based on the possibility that wetlands regulations would someday be eased so that mining or development could then proceed.

The court views plaintiff's discounted cash flow and royalty models as indicators of high limits on value for the same reasons those valuation methods were so treated in earlier proceedings.

While those methods may be the only suitable indication of value under some circumstances, they are not appropriate for our purposes at this time on this record. Because an active market for real estate existed in the vicinity of the subject property near the time of permit denial, the court finds the market comparison or comparable sales method to be the better indicator of fair market value.

In considering the testimony of the parties' appraisers and other indications of fair market value, the court has accounted, as it did when establishing pre-denial value, for various factors that affect market value. For example, sales of smaller tracts typically occurred at higher prices per acre than larger "wholesale" transactions. Tracts with road frontage tend to be more valuable than those without. Property near the Sweetwater area outside Miami also commanded a premium for its proximity to that rapidly developing fringe. Florida Rock's was the only property in the vicinity to be denied a dredge and fill permit for rock mining by the Army Corps. None of the comparable sales used by the parties' appraisers displayed this feature.

Here, the court adopts the theory espoused by the government in *Florida Rock I* that the most appropriate valuation is reached by valuing the 98 acre parcel at issue in terms of its contribution to the larger 1,560 acre tract. When making its pre-denial determination in *Florida Rock I*, the court established a value per acre for the larger parcel and then made adjustments for features that distinguished the smaller tract from it. The court follows the same procedure now.

The government's valuation expert, Stephen Cantwell, valued the entire 1,560 acres, part of which lacked frontage on Krone Avenue, at $2,451 per acre after permit denial. Adjusting for frontage, Mr. Cantwell assigned a value of approximately $2,600 per acre to the 98 acres at issue as a part of the whole. Mr. Larry Sewell, valuation expert, assigned a value of $2,200 per acre to the entire 1,560 acre tract. Unlike Mr. Cantwell, however, Mr. Sewell did not distinguish between the acreage with frontage and that without. He valued the entire 1,560 acres and prorated the 98 acres. The court, therefore, must make an initial adjustment in Mr. Sewell's $2,200 figure to reflect the fact that 1,240 acres fronts on Krome Avenue and 320 acres does not. The court and Mr. Cantwell allotted an average of 86 percent of the entire property's value to the 1,240 acres with Krome Avenue frontage. Applying that percentage to Mr. Sewell's $3,432,000 appraisal of the entire 1,560 acres results in a price of $2,380 per acre for the 1,240 acres with frontage, of which the 98 acres is apart.

The court will utilize Mr. Cantwell's $2,600 per acre and Mr. Sewell's $2,380 per acre adjusted figure, which average $2,490 per acre for the 98 acre parcel at issue as a part of the larger 1,560 acres. This is done because both appraisers gave credible evidence and their average is well within both appraisers' error margin. Theodore Slack also testified for the government at the 1996 evidentiary hearing as to the value of plaintiff's 98 acres standing alone, but not as a part of the entire 1,560 acres. His $3,979 per acre figure cannot be fairly compared with the prices per acre from Messrs. Cantwell and Sewell which were based on larger, wholesale transactions. Because Mr. Slack's appraisal was not for the 98 acres as a part of the larger tract, the court has not included his figures in the takings analysis.

The court now turns to the adjustments for features that distinguish the 98 acre subject property from the larger 1,560 acre tract. One upward adjustment made in *Florida Rock I*, is questioned by this court, but in any event, no longer applies. At that time the court raised the value of the subject property to reflect the fact that permits and waivers had been secured from state and local authorities. This upward adjustment for the subject property reflected the uncertainty as to whether those permits would remain in effect for the remainder of the 1,560 acres, land that would not have been mined for at least three years. After permit denial, the relatively greater certainty of having permits in place for the first three years was really too speculative to be taken into consideration if it was not totally lost. Dredging and filling is now definitely forbidden on the 98 acre parcel. Accordingly, the court makes no upward adjustment for permit certainty.

The next adjustment was for road frontage on Krome Avenue. The premium previously attached to that road frontage is reduced for post-denial valuation, however, by the fact that no immediate use of the property, beyond holding for speculation, is allowed for the foreseeable future. If and when, at some unknown date in the future, wetlands regulations are eased, the owner of the property at that time will undoubtedly find that it is worth more by virtue of its road frontage. A buyer today would pay more for the possibility of realizing that future benefit. The adjustment for road frontage at the pre-taking stage was $1,000, added to the $7,500 base price. The court finds it reasonable to make a lesser adjustment at this time in proportion to the diminished price of the property post-denial. Accordingly, the court adds $332 per acre as an upward adjustment to the 98 acres based on its road frontage which increases the preliminary amount calculated above from $2,490 to $2,822 per acre for the 98 acre parcel at issue.

The last adjustment made by *Florida Rock I* was for the presence of a gravel access road on the property itself. That road is still in place on the property although the premium attached to its existence is largely eliminated in the aftermath of permit denial. If and when wetlands regulations are eased the road may have some utility. However, the road will tend to deteriorate over the years and it is unclear whether the property owner would be allowed to perform road maintenance under the terms of the CWA regulations. It also produces some liability concern. Thus, its value, if any, becomes highly speculative and will not provide a basis for an upward adjustment. Thus, the court finds that the value of plaintiff's 98 acre parcel after permit denial was $2,822 per acre.

Additional evidence of purchase offers and an appraisal done for tax assessment purposes provide strong support for the accuracy of the court's $2,822 per acre post denial valuation. Mr. Baker, Florida Rock's president, rejected post-denial offers averaging $2,869 per acre. *See* Florida Rock III, 21 Cl.Ct. at 170 n. 7. He testified that Florida Rock had intended to mine the property, not sell it, and that the offers were made under "a cloud of uncertainty" while the company was "right in the middle of a court case" involving the very property now at issue. The court does not rely on unaccepted offers to establish fair market value. *See United States v. Smith*, 355 F.2d 807, 811 (5th Cir.1966) (citing *Sharp v. United States*, 191 U.S. 341, 24 S.Ct. 114, 48 L.Ed. 211 (1903)); *Missouri Baptist Hospital v. United States*, 213 Ct.Cl. 505, 555 F.2d 290, 303 (1977); 4 Nichols, Eminent Domain 12B.04[2] (3d ed.). The court nevertheless finds the evidence of these offers a confirmation of its separate calculation of fair market value based on comparable sales.

In addition, when Florida Rock disputed its property tax assessment in state court following permit denial by the Army Corps, the court affirmed a fair market value based on comparable sales for tax purposes of $2,621 per acre. *See Florida Rock Industries v. Bystrom*, 485 So.2d 442, 447-48 (Fla.Dist.Ct.App.1986). Although this court is not bound by the findings of the Florida state court in Bystrom, the court nevertheless finds in those proceedings a further confirmation of its separate calculation of fair market value based on comparable sales. *See Florida Rock IV*, 18 F.3d at 1563 n. 6; *Florida Rock III*, 21 Cl.Ct. at 174.

C. DIMINUTION

As explained above, before the Army Corps of Engineers denied Florida Rock's section 404 permit, plaintiff's land in south Florida was worth $10,500 per acre. After permit denial the same property was worth only $2,822 per acre. For the 98 acres, this amount is a 73.1 percent diminution in value. The court does not rely on the magnitude of this diminution in value alone, however, to determine the severity of the economic impact to plaintiff resulting from permit denial.

2. RECIPROCITY OF ADVANTAGE

The economic impact of certain land use controls, when shared by other members of the community, has been held to be non-compensable. *Florida Rock IV*, 18 F.3d at 1570 (citing *Agins v. Tiburon*, 447 U.S. 255, 262-63, 100 S.Ct. 2138, 65 L.Ed.2d 106 (1980)) (shared "benefits and burdens" of a zoning ordinance); *Penn Central*, 438 U.S. at 131, 98 S.Ct. 2646 (same). "When there is reciprocity of advantage, paradigmatically in a zoning case ... then the claim that the Government has taken private property has little force: the claimant has in a sense been compensated by the public program 'adjusting the benefits and burdens of economic life to promote the common good.'" *Florida Rock IV*, 18 F.3d at 1570 (quoting *Penn Central*, 438 U.S. at 124, 98 S.Ct. 2646); *see* also *Creppel v. United States*, 41 F.3d 627, 631 (Fed.Cir.1994) (quoting *Lucas*, 505 U.S. at 1018, 112 S.Ct. 2886) ("'Mere diminution' occurs when the property owner has received the benefits of a challenged regulation, such that an 'average reciprocity of advantage' results from it."). Accordingly, when the court assesses economic impact, it must determine whether Florida Rock has been compensated through the regulation itself. *Cf. Belk v. United States*, 12 Cl.Ct. 732, 734 (1987) (American hostages of Iran were principal beneficiaries of Algerian accords by which they were freed although thereby losing their cause of action against Iran).

A "partial taking occurs when a regulation singles out a few property owners to bear burdens, while benefits are spread widely across the community." *Creppel*, 41 F.3d at 631 (citing *Florida Rock IV*, 18 F.3d at 1571). Here, the surrounding community benefits from the wetland's filtering action, stabilizing effect, and provision of habitat for flora and fauna. Florida Rock benefits from being a member of a community which has the potential for a better environment. But there can be no question that Florida Rock has been singled out to bear a much heavier burden than its neighbors, without reciprocal advantages. Limestone mines that are still allowed to operate nearby, to the east of the Dade-Broward Levee, are among those who enjoy Florida Rock's beneficence without sharing its burden.

In *Florida Rock II*, the Federal Circuit determined that

> This appears to be a situation where the balancing of public and private interests reveals a private interest much more deserving of compensation for any loss actually incurred. The private interest, unless relieved by a Tucker Act award, sustains what may well be a permanent obligation to maintain property for public benefit, to carry the taxes and other expenses, and not to receive business income from the property in return.

791 F.2d at 904. Florida Rock has paid, and continues to pay, a much higher price for its benefit than have other members of the community. The court finds that Florida Rock's disproportionately heavy burden was not offset by any reciprocity of advantage.

3. ALTERNATIVE PERMITTED ACTIVITIES

Although plaintiff can no longer mine or develop its property, the court must assess the economic impact of that restraint in terms of any other activities that are still permitted under the regulations and which are economically realistic. *See Florida Rock IV*, 18 F.3d at 1568 n. 21, 1571. The one valuable post-regulation use of Florida Rock's land, as evidenced by the court's valuation of the parcel, *supra*, is to sell the property on the speculative market. Florida Rock could also use its land for the observation of wildlife or maybe even for hunting. However, these are not commercially valuable uses. As noted in *Florida Rock II*, defendant's expert witness conceded that a "'willing buyer' subject to the regulation would have to be, and would be, one who expected to put the property to no immediate use." 791 F.2d at 901. In *Florida Rock III*, the court found "no persuasive evidence that there is a market for the property for purposes of hunting, recreation, or scientific study, other than among government entities which might be interested in acquiring the wetlands at the nominal price of [$500 per acre]." 21 Cl.Ct. at 170, n. 7 and at 171. The subject property, as well as most of the land located between U.S. 27 and the Dade-Broward Levee, has very little near-term development potential.

4. RECOUPMENT OF INVESTMENT

In determining the severity of the economic impact of permit denial, the court must also take into account whether Florida Rock was able to recoup its investment subject to the regulation. *See Florida Rock IV*, 18 F.3d at 1567 (quoting *Florida Rock II*, 791 F.2d at 905). Dr. James Nicholas, an economist, evaluated Florida Rock's economic basis in the property as of October 2, 1980. He concluded that plaintiff's economic basis in the 98 acres at issue was $597,000 as of that date, or $6,000 per acre. He arrived at this figure by combining actual expenditures for purchase price, acquisition interest, and property taxes adjusted for inflation using the consumer price index. He did not include any other provision for a return on investment, nor did he include the cost of other capital expenditures like test borings, the feasibility study, or the cost of preparing the site for mining and restoring the property as required by the Army Corps. Having considered Dr. Nicholas' credible testimony on this point and in light of the post-denial valuation otherwise established, the court finds that plaintiff could have recovered barely half of its inflation adjusted investment in the subject property through the only remaining means, resale as a speculative investment.

5. SEVERE ECONOMIC IMPACT

It is clear that Florida Rock suffered a severe economic impact when the Corps denied plaintiff's application for a dredge and fill permit. The value of its 98 acre parcel of land, for which the permit was denied, was diminished by almost three fourths. That diminution in value was not offset by any reciprocity of advantage. Furthermore, plaintiff was unable to recoup its investment in the property by selling it, the only means still available under the regulations.

B. INTERFERENCE WITH REASONABLE INVESTMENT-BACKED EXPECTATIONS.

The second prong of the Penn Central test looks to whether or not the regulation of plaintiff's property interfered with plaintiff's "distinct investment-backed expectations." 438 U.S. at 124, 98 S.Ct. 2646. Plaintiff must show that the regulation of its property frustrated reasonable expectations, however, if it is to show a taking. "A 'reasonable investment-backed expectation' must be more than a 'unilateral expectation or an abstract need.'" *See Ruckelshaus v. Monsanto*, 467 U.S. 986, 1004-1006, 104 S.Ct. 2862, 81 L.Ed.2d 815 (1984) (quoting *Webb's Fabulous Pharmacies, Inc. v. Beckwith*, 449 U.S. 155, 161, 101 S.Ct. 446, 66 L.Ed.2d 358 (1980)). In this case, plaintiff contends its reasonable investment-backed expectation to mine limestone was frustrated.

1. STATE AND LOCAL PERMITS

The government asserts that state and local regulations prohibited rock mining on the subject property, thus precluding a taking of this right. This claim is not supported by the evidence, and conflicts with the law of the case, as discussed earlier in this opinion. The mere presence of such regulatory programs does not affect our analysis. *See Forest Properties Inc. v. United States*, 39 Fed.Cl. 56, 71 (1997). Accordingly, state and local regulations did not diminish plaintiff's reasonable investment-backed expectations.

The *Penn Central* opinion suggested it is important whether or not the expected use of the property was the primary expectation for the property. *See Penn Central*, 438 U.S. at 136, 98 S.Ct. 2646 ("So the law does not interfere with what must be regarded as Penn Central's primary expectation concerning the use of the parcel."); *see* also Mandelker, *Investment-Backed Expectations in Takings Law*, 27 Urb. Law. 215, 217 (1995) (*Penn Central* "implies a landowner can claim his investment-backed expectations are frustrated if a land-use regulation does interfere with his primary expectations concerning his property.").

Florida Rock bought 1,560 acres in south Florida for limestone mining in 1972, having identified a layer of limestone approximately 50 feet deep underlying the entire property, over 100 million tons of mineable rock. All state and local permits or waivers necessary to mining were in place. Plaintiff's contract to purchase the site at issue here was revocable in the event the limestone reserves proved insufficient in quantity or quality to warrant mining. Florida Rock purchased the property for $2,964,000, and made additional expenditures to prove its reserves including test borings in April 1972. It conducted a feasibility study in 1974 which indicated that Florida Rock could proceed with its mining plan and soon be profitable. In 1974 plaintiff "commenced mining operations on the property at issue, which consisted, *inter alia*, of filling a road into the property, stripping the three to four feet of overburden from the limestone, and wet mining the limestone by dragline." Petition at 6; *see* also Pappas Tr. 1-215-17. All these steps had been completed prior to the extension of the Corps' jurisdiction to Florida Rock's property in 1977. Although extensive mining did not begin until after the regulations were passed, the court finds from the clear evidence that the property had been devoted to mining prior to the regulations.

Florida Rock had evaluated the market for aggregates near Miami, assessed the reliability of that market during the entire useful life of the mine, and made the business decision, as an experienced limestone mining company, to supply that market. It intended to profitably mine and sell limestone aggregates from the subject property for many years as Miami continued to build and expand. Florida Rock was a corporation devoted to mining. It bought the instant property with the primary expectation that it would use its land for mining limestone. Accordingly, the court holds that the "primary expectation concerning the use of the parcel," *Penn Central*, 438 U.S. at 136, 98 S.Ct. 2646, was frustrated.

Furthermore, the *Penn Central* Court emphasized the importance of obtaining a "reasonable return" on the property owner's investment in determining the presence of a taking. *Id.* ("More importantly, on this record, we must regard the New York City law as permitting *Penn Central* not only to profit from the Terminal but also to obtain a 'reasonable return' on its investment."); *id.* at 149, 98 S.Ct. 2646 (Rehnquist, J., dissenting) ("The Court has frequently held that, even where a destruction of property rights would not otherwise constitute a taking, the inability of the owner to make a reasonable return on his property requires compensation under the Fifth Amendment.") (citing *United States v. Lynah*, 188 U.S. 445, 470, 23 S.Ct. 349, 47 L.Ed. 539 (1903)). As the Court held above, in it discussion of economic impact, plaintiff was not able to recoup its investment due to the regulation of its property. Although there is no right to recoup one's investment, the inability to do so weighs in plaintiff's favor, since the regulation consequently places a greater burden on plaintiff.

An additional fact in our investment-backed expectation analysis relates to how much of the parcel of property, the 98 acres, has been burdened by the regulation. In *Keystone*, the Supreme Court held that a regulation which only impacted two percent of the coal owned by petitioners did not materially affect investment-backed expectations. *See* 480 U.S. at 499, 107 S.Ct. 1232. The Court noted that such a small percentage of the relevant parcel would not support a taking argument. *See id.*, n. 27. Accordingly, this court finds it relevant, though not dispositive, that in this case limestone underlay the entire parcel, and 100 percent of the primary use of that parcel was affected. This indicates a very large interference with investment-backed expectations.

2. PLAINTIFF'S REASONABLE INVESTMENT-BACKED EXPECTATIONS WERE FRUSTRATED

In sum, the court finds that Florida Rock's reasonable investment-backed expectations were frustrated. Florida Rock had no reason when it purchased its property to expect that its rights to mine or develop the land were open to question. The Clean Water Act was passed after Florida Rock already owned the land, and the Army Corps did not have jurisdiction under the Act over wetlands like those owned by Florida Rock until July 1, 1977. Accordingly, the Clean Water Act could not have put Florida Rock on notice that its property might be taken from it so as to destroy investment-backed expectations. Compare *Andrus v. Allard*, 444 U.S. 51, 66-67, 100 S.Ct. 318, 62 L.Ed.2d 210 (1979) (regulations barring trade in certain goods did not constitute a taking), with *Lucas*, 505 U.S. at 1027-28, 112 S.Ct. 2886 (elimination of all economic use of land requires just compensation); *Creppel*, 41 F.3d at 632 (land bought in reliance on non-existence of CWA); *Forest Properties*, 39 Fed.Cl. at 71 (section 404 permit requirement does not preclude compensable property interest); *Bowles v. United States*, 31 Fed.Cl. 37, 51 (1994) (land acquired with reasonable belief that wetlands regulations did not apply); *Ciampetti v. United States*, 18 Cl.Ct. 548, 557, 558 (1989) (awareness of permit requirement only one factor of investment-backed expectation). Plaintiff had no reason at the time of purchase to believe the use of its property would be limited to speculative investment.

C. CHARACTER OF GOVERNMENT ACTION

1. REGULATORY POWER

Turning to the third prong of the *Penn Central* test—the character of the government action—the Federal Circuit instructed that "it is for the trial court as an initial matter to determine whether the Government acted within its proper role in the circumstances presented by the case of Florida Rock." *Florida Rock IV*, 18 F.3d at 1571. Justice Holmes recognized that "some values are enjoyed under an implied limitation and must yield to the police power." Pennsylvania Coal, 260 U.S. at 413, 43 S.Ct. 158. The regulation here is not under the police power, as it was in

Pennsylvania Coal, a state case involving public safety. The power involved here is the federal power over waters of the United States. There is little dispute that the purpose of the regulatory action of permit denial was to enhance the water and ecological system of the United States and south Florida in particular by preserving more wetlands. It was to benefit the public, not prevent Florida Rock from doing any harm. Rock mining is widespread in this region of Florida. The only difference between this property and various other mining operations, as the court observed on the site view, is that it was west of an arbitrary line the government decided upon as the limit of wetland protection. Unlike the traditional nuisance case where the government prevents what the citizen had no right to do under the common law, here the activity was perfectly permissible until the permit was denied. Florida Rock's activity posed no health or safety risk. The government made a permissible policy choice that this land should benefit the public's supply of wetlands. This court cannot review or scrutinize or second guess this policy choice. Plaintiff does not ask the court to do this anymore than in a condemnation proceeding a court could review or second guess a need for a road or a school. The court must, however, decide whether this action has taken the plaintiff's property as effectively as if it had been condemned.

There is no dispute between the parties as to whether preservation of the wetlands through the Corps' implementation of the Clean Water Act serves to advance legitimate state interests. Florida Rock chose not to challenge the government's permitting power as it could have done with an Administrative Procedure Act suit in district court. Instead, it sought just compensation for a taking under the Fifth Amendment. It, of course, has this right. In fact, the difficulty of an APA challenge probably counseled this course.

III. TAKING COMPUTATION

The court must consider the economic impact, reasonable investment-backed expectations, and character of the government action to determine whether a compensable taking occurred. Here, the court must consider both the severe economic impact on Florida Rock and its frustrated expectations, as well as the government's legitimate exercise of its regulatory power. The court notes that "[w]hat is not at issue is whether the Government can lawfully prevent a property owner from filling or otherwise injuring or destroying vital wetlands. The importance of preserving the environment, the authority of state and federal governments to protect and serve ecologically significant areas ... through appropriate regulatory mechanisms is not here being questioned." *Loveladies*, 28 F.3d at 1175.

The regulation in this case destroys almost three quarters of the value of the relevant property Even though this is obviously a significant destruction of the value of plaintiff's property, it is not dispositive of the issue. Destruction of the majority of a parcel's value does not always amount to a compensable taking. *See, e.g., Euclid v. Ambler Realty Co.*, 272 U.S. 365, 47 S.Ct. 114, 71 L.Ed. 303 (1926) (no taking despite 75 percent diminution); *see Hadacheck v. Sebastian*, 239 U.S. 394, 36 S.Ct. 143, 60 L.Ed. 348 (1915) (no taking despite 87 1/2 percent diminution). However, the Supreme Court has stated time and again that the regulatory taking inquiry is an ad hoc, fact specific inquiry. As the Federal Circuit has noted, "we do not read these early precedents as creating an automatic numerical barrier preventing compensation, as a matter of law, in cases involving a smaller percentage diminution in value." *Yancey v. United States*, 915 F.2d 1534, 1541.

In *Yancey*, the Federal Circuit affirmed compensation for a 77 percent reduction in value of plaintiffs' turkeys due to a USDA quarantine. *Yancey*, 915 F.2d at 1534. The turkeys, which were for breeding, had to be sold for slaughter instead. The court concluded the Yanceys "suffered severe economic impact and had no way of anticipating the interference with their investment backed interest." *Id.* at 1543. Notably, the Yancey's turkeys had been devoted to one use, breeding, and after regulation were only valuable, at a great loss, through sale. This fact pattern is very similar in some respects to the present case, in which the property was devoted to mining. After regulation Florida Rock's land had only one remaining immediate use, sale of the property for much less than its value before regulation. As in Yancey, the court finds that the economic impact of the regulation was severe. Florida Rock suffered a very substantial loss in the value of its parcel as a whole, a loss that was not offset by reciprocity of advantage. The only remaining immediate use of any value, sale of the property, would recoup barely half of Florida Rock's inflation adjusted investment. The regulation precludes any "'reasonable return' on its investment," *Penn Central*, 438 U.S. at 136, 98 S.Ct. 2646, while inflicting substantial loss on the parcel's market value.

The frustration of Florida Rock's reasonable investment-backed expectations is beyond doubt. Moreover, the frustration is also absolute. Unlike the *Keystone* case, in which the Supreme Court noted "there is no showing that petitioners' reasonable 'investment backed expectations' have been materially affected," 480 U.S. at 499, 107 S.Ct. 1232, and where "the regulatory program places a burden on the use of only a small fraction of the property that is subjected to regulation," *id.* at n. 27, the entirety of Florida Rock's limestone is unusable. Florida Rock, which relied on the regulatory regime in place to support limestone mining, has been treated to only one immediate use for the property: resale at a loss.

This is not the "extraordinary case in which a particular activity is seen as so offensive to the public sensibility as to warrant no Constitutional protection." *Loveladies*, 28 F.3d at 1183. The question, then, is the following: "has the Government acted in a responsible way, limiting the constraints on property ownership to those necessary to achieve the public purpose, and not allocating to some number of individuals, less than all, a burden that should be borne by all?" *Florida Rock IV*, 18 F.3d at 1571. The government's action was responsible, and does not appear excessive to achieve the public purpose, but it also most certainly allocates to Florida Rock a burden that should be borne by all.

The final prong of the *Penn Central* test, the character of the government action, does not here argue against a taking, but rather for one; to benefit the public. Florida Rock's bundle of property rights was severely diminished: "the government, under the guise of regulation, cannot take from a property owner the core economic value of the property, leaving the owner with a mere shell of shambled expectations." *Hendler v. United States*, 952 F.2d 1364, 1373 (1991). Although it is true that not every strand in the bundle was cut, *see Loretto*, 458 U.S. at 435, 102 S.Ct. 3164 ("the government does not simply take single 'strand' from the 'bundle' of property rights: it chops through the bundle, taking a slice of every strand"), the thin handful which remains little resembles the full sheaf once held by Florida Rock. It strains the court's sense of logic to suggest this well-pruned parcel is still whole. Florida Rock's property, post-regulation, is different in kind, not merely degree, from its pre-regulation property, and this argues for a compensable taking. The government might as well have physically occupied the property, leaving Florida Rock the option of visiting its land for recreation, or selling it.

The court finds that Florida Rock suffered a taking of property as defined by the Fifth Amendment to the Constitution. The Takings Clause was designed to protect individuals and compensate them for very legitimate exercises of government power. The due process clause of the Fifth Amendment protects individuals from illegitimate exercises of such power.

"[B]asic understanding of the Fifth Amendment makes clear that it is designed not to limit governmental interference with property rights per se, but rather to secure compensation in the event of otherwise proper interference amounting to a taking." *First English Evangelical Lutheran Church of Glendale v. County of Los Angeles*, 482 U.S. 304, 315, 107 S.Ct. 2378, 96 L.Ed.2d 250 (1987). The court's holding today does not address policy in a larger sense, but only seeks to answer the question whether Florida Rock's property was taken without just compensation. The Supreme Court explained our duty eloquently in *First English*:

> [O]ur present holding will undoubtedly lessen to some extent the freedom and flexibility of land-use planners. ... But such consequences necessarily flow from any decision upholding a constitutional right; many of the provisions of the Constitution are designed to limit the flexibility and freedom of governmental authorities, and the Just Compensation Clause of the Fifth Amendment is one of them.

482 U.S. at 321, 107 S.Ct. 2378. As that Court did, we are bound to recognize the wisdom expressed by Justice Holmes: "[A] strong public desire to improve the public condition is not enough to warrant achieving the desire by a shorter cut than the constitutional way of paying for the change." *Pennsylvania Coal*, 260 U.S. at 416, 43 S.Ct. 158.

The property taken is the right to mine limestone, effectively destroyed by the regulation of Florida Rock's power to disturb its wetlands. In this case, the loss of these rights of use, and the concomitant loss in the parcel's value, comprise the taking. [Footnote omitted] The court notes the dissent's argument in *Florida Rock IV* that "[v]alue is not a transferable interest. Thus, a claim for loss of value does not constitute a takings claim within the meaning of the Fifth Amendment." *Florida Rock IV*, 18 F.3d at 1573 (Nies, J., dissenting). That, however, is not this case. This opinion has not treated lost value as identical to property rights. This is in accord with the *Florida Rock IV* majority's statement that "[t]he dissent is concerned that what is being taken is 'value,' not property. In fact, in a regulatory context such as this it is both." *Florida Rock IV*, 18 F.3d at 1572. Here, the value lost is indeed the measure of the property taken.

In *Loretto*, a physical taking of a minute portion of a landlord's property was deemed a taking. The Federal Circuit observed with respect to *Loretto* that "the Government was not required to buy the building." *Florida Rock IV*, 18 F.3d at 1572. "The fact that the source of any particular taking is a regulation rather than a physical entry should make no difference—the nature of legal interests defining the property affected remains unchanged." *Id.* at 1572. Regulations often require courts to look at entire parcels to determine their impact, but that does not mean property only exists in the form of the entire parcel. Inasmuch as a taking occurs, it is proper that the court compensate only for those property interests actually taken by regulation. In this case, they are the strands of Florida Rock's bundle of property rights which involve use of the surface and subsurface. The right to sell, which accounts for the remaining property value, is a valuable right and was not taken, and therefore the court may not compensate for that portion of the property, despite the severe harm to plaintiff's parcel.

CONCLUSION

The Army Corps' denial of plaintiff's application for a dredge and fill permit resulted in a 73.1 percent diminution in the value of plaintiff's land. This diminution is certainly severe, although not complete. What value remained was based almost entirely on the possibility that wetlands regulations would be relaxed at some point in the future. Plaintiff was left with only the right to hold its land or sell it to another—rights vastly different both in value and in kind from the right to mine limestone and the right to develop its land, both of which plaintiff has lost.

Plaintiff has been made the unwilling custodian of the wetlands on its property for the benefit of the public at large, at plaintiff's own risk and expense. Having analyzed the economic impact of the regulation, plaintiff's reasonable, distinct investment-backed expectations, and the character of the governmental action, the court concludes that the denial of plaintiff's section 404 permit application by the Army Corps of Engineers effected a compensable partial regulatory taking of plaintiff's 98 acre property. The compensation due plaintiff for that taking, as measured by the change in value before and after permit denial, is $752,444. The parties have agreed that the date of any taking was October 2, 1980. Defendant shall pay compound interest from that date.

Pursuant to the court's finding of a partial regulatory taking with respect to the 98 acres, plaintiff is hereby awarded $752,444 plus interest from the date of taking. The entry of judgment will be stayed pending the determination of attorneys' fees and costs to which plaintiff is entitled pursuant to the Uniform Relocation Assistance and Real Property Acquisition Policies Act of 1970 (URA), 42 U.S.C. §4654 (1994). Plaintiff is to file any such claim within 60 days from the filing of this opinion. Following the determination of attorney's fees and costs, the court will then, pursuant to RCFC 54(b), direct the Clerk of the Court to enter judgment.

The court notes that when this case was first tried the court determined that only 98 acres were compensable because the permits were for only three-year periods and 98 acres comprised the amount of land that could be mined over a three-year period. A lot of time has lapsed since the 1980 denial. During the period from the permit denial to the present time another five permits would have been applied for, but for the first permit's denial. Since the first denial has never been reconsidered the court can only assume that these permits would also have been denied. *Cf. City National Bank of Miami v. United States*, 30 Fed.Cl. 715, 720 (1994) (futility of applying for other wetlands development permits). This is in addition to the fact that the first permit's denial effectively blocked the planned utilization of the other 1,462 acres. This in some ways would be analogous to the denial of a permit to construct the first floor of a ten story building. The inhibition on the upper nine stories is obvious.

In light of this court's decision it would be manifestly unfair to require the plaintiff to sue again for these subsequent permits, as well as the future permits that will be blocked until the property's limestone reserve would have been exhausted. In view of this concern the parties are asked to recommend further courses of action. One possibility is a settlement premised on the appellate future of this ruling. In other words, "if first permit denial is a taking then the total value is X, and of course if permit denial is not a taking then no value for future denials." A second possibility is a real and full settlement based on a discounting of each side's risk of litigation success. A third option is an appeal of that part of this opinion based on the 98 acres with either a stay of the question of the other acreage or a hearing to determine its value while the 98 acre issue is appealed. These general thoughts are meant to be suggestive rather than definitive. The parties are asked to respond to this issue with short briefs within 60 days at which time the court would decide on a proper procedure for resolving all issues in this case.

[Footnotes omitted.]

Since the Clean Water Act is now 30 years old, few real estate developers could reasonably hold an investment-backed expectation of profit from developing a wetland given the publicity and common knowledge attained by the §404 permit requirement. Likewise, development of wetlands is not always a nuisance given the recognition that some wetlands may be more valuable than others and the less valuable or already damaged may be developable without egregious harm to a public resource. Developers are still cautioned that all possible plans must be submitted before the courts will hear the takings case because it is not "ripe." *Williamson County Regional Planning Commission v. Hamilton Bank*, 473 U.S. 172, 87 L.Ed.2d 126, 105 S.Ct. 3108 (1985)("... a claim that the application of government regulations effects a taking of a property interest is not ripe until the government entity charged with implementing the regulations has reached a final decision regarding application of the regulations to the property at issue"). *See* also *MacDonald, Sommer & Frates v. Yolo County*, 477 U.S. 340, 91 L.Ed.2d 285, 106 S.Ct. 2561 (1986), reh'g. denied, 478 U.S. 1035, 92 L.Ed.2d 773, 107 S.Ct. 22 (1986); *Hodel v. Virginia Surface Mining Reclamation Ass'n.*, 452 U.S. 264, 69 L.Ed.2d 1, 101 S.Ct. 2352 (1981).

PALAZZOLO v. RHODE ISLAND

533 U.S. 606, 121 S.Ct. 2448, 150 L.Ed.2 592 (2001)

Petitioner Anthony Palazzolo owns a waterfront parcel of land in the town of Westerly, Rhode Island. Almost all of the property is designated as coastal wetlands under Rhode Island law. After petitioner's development proposals were rejected by respondent Rhode Island Coastal Resources Management Council (Council), he sued in state court, asserting the Council's application of its wetlands regulations took the property without compensation in violation of the Takings Clause of the Fifth Amendment, binding upon the State through the Due Process Clause of the Fourteenth Amendment. Petitioner sought review in this Court, contending the Supreme Court of Rhode Island erred in rejecting his takings claim. We granted certiorari. 531 U.S. 923, 121 S.Ct. 296, 148 L.Ed.2d 238 (2000).

I

The town of Westerly is on an edge of the Rhode Island coastline. The town's western border is the Pawcatuck River, which at that point is the boundary between Rhode Island and Connecticut. Situated on land purchased from the Narragansett Indian Tribe, the town was incorporated in 1669 and had a precarious, though colorful, early history. Both Connecticut and Massachusetts contested the boundaries—and indeed the validity—of Rhode Island's royal charter; and Westerly's proximity to Connecticut invited encroachments during these jurisdictional squabbles. *See* M. Best, *The Town that Saved a State—Westerly* 60-83 (1943); *see* also W. McLaughlin, *Rhode Island: A Bicentennial History* 39-57 (1978). When the borders of the Rhode Island Colony were settled by compact in 1728, the town's development was more orderly, and with some historical distinction. For instance, Watch Hill Point, the peninsula at the southwestern tip of the town, was of strategic importance in the Revolutionary War and the War of 1812. *See* Best, *supra*, at 190; F. Denison, *Westerly and its Witnesses* 118-119 (1878).

In later times Westerly's coastal location had a new significance: It became a popular vacation and seaside destination. One of the town's historians gave this happy account:

> "After the Civil War the rapid growth of manufacture and expansion of trade had created a spending class on pleasure bent, and Westerly had superior attractions to offer, surf bathing on ocean beaches, quieter bathing in salt and fresh water ponds, fishing, annual sail and later motor boat races. The broad beaches of clean white sand dip gently toward the sea; there are no odorous marshes at low tide, no railroad belches smoke, and the climate is unrivalled on the coast, that of Newport only excepted. In the phenomenal heat wave of 1881 ocean resorts from northern New England to southern New Jersey sweltered as the thermometer climbed to 95 and 104 degrees, while Watch Hill enjoyed a comfortable 80. When Providence to the north runs a temperature of 90, the mercury in this favored spot remains at 77." *Best*, *supra*, at 192.

Westerly today has about 20,000 year-round residents, and thousands of summer visitors come to enjoy its beaches and coastal advantages.

One of the more popular attractions is Misquamicut State Beach, a lengthy expanse of coastline facing Block Island Sound and beyond to the Atlantic Ocean. The primary point of access to the beach is Atlantic Avenue, a well-traveled three-mile stretch of road running along the coastline within the town's limits. At its western end, Atlantic Avenue is something of a commercial strip, with restaurants, hotels, arcades, and other typical seashore businesses. The pattern of development becomes more residential as the road winds eastward onto a narrow spine of land bordered to the south by the beach and the ocean, and to the north by Winnapaug Pond, an intertidal inlet often used by residents for boating, fishing, and shellfishing.

In 1959 petitioner, a lifelong Westerly resident, decided to invest in three undeveloped, adjoining parcels along this eastern stretch of Atlantic Avenue. To the north, the property faces, and borders upon, Winnapaug Pond; the south of the property faces Atlantic Avenue and the beachfront homes abutting it on the other side, and beyond that the dunes and the beach. To purchase and hold the property, petitioner and associates formed Shore Gardens, Inc. (SGI). After SGI purchased the property petitioner bought out his associates and became the sole shareholder. In the first decade of SGI's ownership of the property the corporation submitted a plat to the town subdividing the property into 80 lots; and it engaged in various transactions that left it with 74 lots, which together encompassed about 20 acres. During the same period SGI also made initial attempts to develop the property and submitted intermittent applications to state agencies to fill substantial portions of the parcel. Most of the property was then, as it is now, salt marsh subject to tidal flooding. The wet ground and permeable soil would require considerable fill—as much as six feet in some places—before significant structures could be built. SGI's proposal, submitted in 1962 to the Rhode Island Division of Harbors and Rivers (DHR), sought to dredge from Winnapaug Pond and fill the entire property. The application was denied for lack of essential information. A second, similar proposal followed a year later. A third application, submitted in 1966 while the second application was pending, proposed more limited filling of the land for use as a private beach club. These latter two applications were referred to the Rhode Island Department of Natural Resources, which indicated initial assent. The agency later withdrew approval, however, citing adverse environmental impacts. SGI did not contest the ruling.

No further attempts to develop the property were made for over a decade. Two intervening events, however, become important to the issues presented. First, in 1971, Rhode Island enacted legislation creating the Council, an agency charged with the duty of protecting the State's coastal properties. 1971 R.I. Pub. Laws ch. 279, §1 et seq. Regulations promulgated by the Council designated salt marshes like those on SGI's property as protected "coastal wetlands," Rhode Island Coastal Resources Management Program (CRMP) §210.3 (as amended, June 28, 1983) (lodged with the Clerk of this Court), on which development is limited to a great extent. Second, in 1978 SGI's corporate charter was revoked for failure to pay corporate income taxes; and title to the property passed, by operation of state law, to petitioner as the corporation's sole shareholder.

In 1983 petitioner, now the owner, renewed the efforts to develop the property. An application to the Council, resembling the 1962 submission, requested permission to construct a wooden bulkhead along the shore of Winnapaug Pond and to fill the entire marsh land area. The Council rejected the application, noting it was "vague and inadequate for a project of this size and nature." App. 16. The agency also found that "the proposed activities will have significant impacts upon the waters and wetlands of Winnapaug Pond," and concluded that "the proposed alteration ... will conflict with the Coastal Resources Management Plan presently in effect." *Id.*, at 17. Petitioner did not appeal the agency's determination.

Petitioner went back to the drawing board, this time hiring counsel and preparing a more specific and limited proposal for use of the property. The new application, submitted to the Council in 1985, echoed the 1966 request to build a private beach club. The details do not tend to inspire the reader with an idyllic coastal image, for the proposal was to fill 11 acres of the property with gravel to accommodate "50 cars with boat trailers, a dumpster, port-a-johns, picnic tables, barbecue pits of concrete, and other trash receptacles." *Id.*, at 25.

The application fared no better with the Council than previous ones. Under the agency's regulations, a landowner wishing to fill salt marsh on Winnapaug Pond needed a "special exception" from the Council. CRMP §130. In a short opinion the Council said the beach club proposal conflicted with the regulatory standard for a special exception. *See* App. 27. To secure a special exception the proposed activity must serve "a compelling public purpose which provides benefits to the public as a whole as opposed to individual or private interests." CRMP §130A(1). This time petitioner appealed the decision to the Rhode Island courts, challenging the Council's conclusion as contrary to principles of state administrative law. The Council's decision was affirmed. *See* App. 31-42.

Petitioner filed an inverse condemnation action in Rhode Island Superior Court, asserting that the State's wetlands regulations, as applied by the Council to his parcel, had taken the property without compensation in violation of the Fifth and Fourteenth Amendments. *See* App. 45. The suit alleged the Council's action deprived him of "all economically beneficial use" of his property, *ibid.*, resulting in a total taking requiring compensation under *Lucas v. South Carolina Coastal Council*, 505 U.S. 1003, 112 S.Ct. 2886, 120 L.Ed.2d 798 (1992). He sought damages in the amount of $3,150,000, a figure derived from an appraiser's estimate as to the value of a 74-lot residential subdivision. The State countered with a host of defenses. After a bench trial, a justice of the Superior Court ruled against petitioner, accepting some of the State's theories. App. to Pet. for Cert. B-1 to B-13.

The Rhode Island Supreme Court affirmed. 746 A.2d 707 (2000). Like the Superior Court, the State Supreme Court recited multiple grounds for rejecting petitioner's suit. The court held, first, that petitioner's takings claim was not ripe, *id.*, at 712-715; second, that petitioner had no right to challenge regulations predating 1978, when he succeeded to legal ownership of the property from SGI, *id.*, at 716; and third, that the claim of deprivation of all economically beneficial use was contradicted by undisputed evidence that he had $200,000 in development value remaining on an upland parcel of the property, *id.*, at 715. In addition to holding petitioner could not assert a takings claim based on the denial of all economic use the court concluded he could not recover under the more general test of *Penn Central Transp. Co. v. City New York*, 438 U.S. 104, 98 S.Ct. 2646, 57 L.Ed.2d 631 (1978). On this claim, too, the date of acquisition of the parcel was found determinative, and the court held he could have had "no reasonable investment-backed expectations that were affected by this regulation" because it predated his ownership, 746 A.2d, at 717; *see* also *Penn Central, supra*, at 124, 98 S.Ct. 2646.

We disagree with the Supreme Court of Rhode Island as to the first two of these conclusions; and, we hold, the court was correct to conclude that the owner is not deprived of all economic use of his property because the value of upland portions is substantial. We remand for further consideration of the claim under the principles set forth in *Penn Central.*

II

The Takings Clause of the Fifth Amendment, applicable to the States through the Fourteenth Amendment, Chicago, *B. & Q.R. Co. v. Chicago*, 166 U.S. 226, 17 S.Ct. 581, 41 L.Ed. 979 (1897), prohibits the government from taking private property for public use without just compensation. The clearest sort of taking occurs when the government encroaches upon or occupies private land for its own proposed use. Our cases establish that even a minimal "permanent physical occupation of real property" requires compensation under the Clause. *Loretto v. Teleprompter Manhattan CATV Corp.*, 458 U.S. 419, 427, 102 S.Ct. 3164, 73 L.Ed.2d 868 (1982). In *Pennsylvania Coal Co. v. Mahon*, 260 U.S. 393, 43 S.Ct. 158, 67 L.Ed. 322 (1922), the Court recognized that there will be instances when government actions do not encroach upon or occupy the property yet still affect and limit its use to such an extent that a taking occurs. In Justice Holmes' well-known, if less than self-defining, formulation, "while property may be regulated to a certain extent, if a regulation goes too far it will be recognized as a taking." *Id.*, at 415, 43 S.Ct. 158.

Since Mahon, we have given some, but not too specific, guidance to courts confronted with deciding whether a particular government action goes too far and effects a regulatory taking. First, we have observed, with certain qualifications, *see* infra at 2463-2464, that a regulation which "denies all economically beneficial or productive use of land" will require compensation under the Takings Clause. *Lucas*, 505 U.S., at 1015, 112 S.Ct. 2886; *see* also *id.*, at 1035, 112 S.Ct. 2886 (KENNEDY, J., concurring); *Agins v. City of Tiburon*, 447 U.S. 255, 261, 100 S.Ct. 2138, 65 L.Ed.2d 106 (1980). Where a regulation places limitations on land that fall short of eliminating all economically beneficial use, a taking nonetheless may have occurred, depending on a complex of factors including the regulation's economic effect on the landowner, the extent to which the regulation interferes with reasonable investment-backed expectations, and the character of the government action. *Penn Central, supra*, at 124, 98 S.Ct. 2646. These inquiries are informed by the purpose of the Takings Clause, which is to prevent the government from "forcing some people alone to bear public burdens which, in all fairness and justice, should be borne by the public as a whole." *Armstrong v. United States*, 364 U.S. 40, 49, 80 S.Ct. 1563, 4 L.Ed.2d 1554 (1960).

Petitioner seeks compensation under these principles. At the outset, however, we face the two threshold considerations invoked by the state court to bar the claim: ripeness, and acquisition which postdates the regulation.

A

In *Williamson County Regional Planning Comm'n v. Hamilton Bank of Johnson City*, 473 U.S. 172, 105 S.Ct. 3108, 87 L.Ed.2d 126 (1985), the Court explained the requirement that a takings claim must be ripe. The Court held that a takings claim challenging the application of land-use regulations is not ripe unless "the government entity charged with implementing the regulations has reached a final decision regarding the application of the regulations to the property at issue." *Id.*, at 186, 105 S.Ct. 3108. A final decision by the responsible state agency informs the constitutional determination whether a regulation has deprived a landowner of "all economically beneficial use" of the property, *see Lucas, supra*, at 1015, 112 S.Ct. 2886, or defeated the reasonable investment-backed expectations of the landowner to the extent that a taking has occurred, *see Penn Central, supra*, at 124, 98 S.Ct. 2646. These matters cannot be resolved in definitive terms until a court knows "the extent of permitted development" on the land in question. *MacDonald, Sommer & Frates v. Yolo County*, 477 U.S. 340, 351, 106 S.Ct. 2561, 91 L.Ed.2d 285 (1986). Drawing on these principles, the Rhode Island Supreme Court held that petitioner had not taken the necessary steps to ripen his takings claim.

The central question in resolving the ripeness issue, under *Williamson County* and other relevant decisions, is whether petitioner obtained a final decision from the Council determining the permitted use for the land. As we have noted, SGI's early applications to fill had been granted at one point, though that assent was later revoked. Petitioner then submitted two proposals: the 1983 proposal to fill the entire parcel, and the 1985 proposal to fill 11 of the property's 18 wetland acres for construction of the beach club. The court reasoned that, notwithstanding the Council's denials of the applications, doubt remained as to the extent of development the Council would allow on petitioner's parcel. We cannot agree.

The court based its holding in part upon petitioner's failure to explore "any other use for the property that would involve filling substantially less wetlands." 746 A.2d, at 714. It relied upon this Court's observations that the final decision requirement is not satisfied when a developer submits, and a land use authority denies, a grandiose development proposal, leaving open the possibility that lesser uses of the property might be permitted. *See MacDonald, supra*, at 353, n. 9, 106 S.Ct. 2561. The suggestion is that while the Council rejected petitioner's effort to fill all of the wetlands, and then rejected his proposal to fill 11 of the wetland acres, perhaps an application to fill (for instance) five acres would have been approved. Thus, the reasoning goes, we cannot know for sure the extent of permitted development on petitioner's wetlands.

This is belied by the unequivocal nature of the wetland regulations at issue and by the Council's application of the regulations to the subject property. Winnapaug Pond is classified under the CRMP as a Type 2 body of water. *See* CRMP § 200.2. A landowner, as a general rule, is prohibited from filling or building residential structures on wetlands adjacent to Type 2 waters, *see id.*, Table 1, p. 22, and §210.3(C)(4), but may seek a special exception from the Council to engage in a prohibited use, *see id.*, §130. The Council is permitted to allow the exception, however, only where a "compelling public purpose" is served. *Id.*, §130A(2). The proposal to fill the entire property was not accepted under Council regulations and did not qualify for the special exception. The Council determined the use proposed in the second application (the beach club) did not satisfy the "compelling public purpose" standard. There is no indication the Council would have accepted the application had petitioner's proposed beach club occupied a smaller surface area. To the contrary, it ruled that the proposed activity was not a "compelling public purpose." App. 27; *cf. id.*, at 17 (1983 application to fill wetlands proposed an "activity" conflicting with the CRMP).

Williamson County's final decision requirement "responds to the high degree of discretion characteristically possessed by land-use boards in softening the strictures of the general regulations they administer." *Suitum v. Tahoe Regional Planning Agency*, 520 U.S. 725, 738, 117 S.Ct. 1659, 137 L.Ed.2d 980 (1997). While a landowner must give a land-use authority an opportunity to exercise its discretion, once it becomes clear that the agency lacks the discretion to permit any development, or the permissible uses of the property are known to a reasonable degree of certainty, a takings claim is likely to have ripened. The case is quite unlike those upon which respondents place principal reliance, which arose when an owner challenged a land-use authority's denial of a substantial project, leaving doubt whether a more modest submission or an application for a variance would be accepted. *See MacDonald, supra*, at 342, 106 S.Ct. 2561 (denial of 159-home residential subdivision); *Williamson County*, 473 U.S., at 182, 105 S.Ct. 3108 (476-unit subdivision); *cf. Agins v. City of Tiburon*, 447 U.S. 255, 100 S.Ct. 2138, 65 L.Ed.2d 106 (1980) (case not ripe because no plan to develop was submitted).

These cases stand for the important principle that a landowner may not establish a taking before a land-use authority has the opportunity, using its own reasonable procedures, to decide and explain the reach of a challenged regulation. Under our ripeness rules a takings claim based on a law or regulation which is alleged to go too far in burdening property depends upon the landowner's first having followed reasonable and necessary steps to allow regulatory agencies to exercise their full discretion in considering development. As a general rule, until these ordinary processes have been followed the extent of the restriction on property is not known and a regulatory taking has not yet been established. *See Suitum, supra*, at 736, and n. 10, 117 S.Ct. 1659 (noting difficulty of demonstrating that "mere enactment" of regulations restricting land use effects a taking). Government authorities, of course, may not burden property by imposition of repetitive or unfair land-use procedures in order to avoid a final decision. *Monterey v. Del Monte Dunes at Monterey, Ltd.*, 526 U.S. 687, 698, 119 S.Ct. 1624, 143 L.Ed.2d 882 (1999).

With respect to the wetlands on petitioner's property, the Council's decisions make plain that the agency interpreted its regulations to bar petitioner from engaging in any filling or development activity on the wetlands, a fact reinforced by the Attorney General's forthright responses to our questioning during oral argument in this case. *See* Tr. of Oral Arg. 26, 31. The rulings of the Council interpreting the regulations at issue, and the briefs, arguments, and candid statements by counsel for both sides, leave no doubt on this point: On the wetlands there can be no fill for any ordinary land use. There can be no fill for its own sake; no fill for a beach club, either rustic or upscale; no fill for a subdivision; no fill for any likely or foreseeable use. And with no fill there can be no structures and no development on the wetlands. Further permit applications were not necessary to establish this point.

As noted above, however, not all of petitioner's parcel constitutes protected wetlands. The trial court accepted uncontested testimony that an upland site located at the eastern end of the property would have an estimated value of $200,000 if developed. App. to Pet. for Cert. B-5. While Council approval is required to develop upland property which lies within 200 feet of protected waters, *see* CRMP §100.1(A), the strict "compelling public purpose" test does not govern proposed land uses on property in this classification, *see id.*, §110, Table 1A, §120. Council officials testified at trial, moreover, that they would have allowed petitioner to build a residence on the upland parcel. App. to Pet. for Cert. B-5. The State Supreme Court found petitioner's claim unripe for the further reason that he "has not sought permission for any ... use of the property that would involve ... development only of the upland portion of the parcel." 746 A.2d, at 714.

In assessing the significance of petitioner's failure to submit applications to develop the upland area it is important to bear in mind the purpose that the final decision requirement serves. Our ripeness jurisprudence imposes obligations on landowners because "[a] court cannot determine whether a regulation goes 'too far' unless it knows how far the regulation goes." *MacDonald*, 477 U.S., at 348, 106 S.Ct. 2561. Ripeness doctrine does not require a landowner to submit applications for their own sake. Petitioner is required to explore development opportunities on his upland parcel only if there is uncertainty as to the land's permitted use.

The State asserts the value of the uplands is in doubt. It relies in part on a comment in the opinion of the Rhode Island Supreme Court that "it would be possible to build at least one single-family home on the upland portion of the parcel." 746 A.2d, at 714. It argues that the qualification "at least" indicates that additional development beyond the single dwelling was possible. The attempt to interject ambiguity as to the value or use of the uplands, however, comes too late in the day for purposes of litigation before this Court. It was stated in the petition for certiorari that the uplands on petitioner's property had an estimated worth of $200,000. *See* Pet. for Cert. 21. The figure not only was uncontested but also was cited as fact in the State's brief in opposition. *See* Brief in Opposition 4, 19. In this circumstance ripeness cannot be contested by saying that the value of the nonwetland parcels is unknown. *See Lucas*, 505 U.S., at 1020, and n. 9, 112 S.Ct. 2886.

The State's prior willingness to accept the $200,000 figure, furthermore, is well founded. The only reference to upland property in the trial court's opinion is to a single parcel worth an estimated $200,000. *See* App. to Pet. for Cert B-5. There was, it must be acknowledged, testimony at trial suggesting the existence of an additional upland parcel elsewhere on the property. *See* Tr. 190-191, 199-120 (testimony of Dr. Grover Fugate, Council Executive Director); *see* also *id.* at 610 (testimony of Mr. Steven Clarke). The testimony indicated, however, that the potential, second upland parcel was on an "island" which required construction of a road across wetlands, *id.*, at 610, 623-624 (testimony of Mr. Clarke)—and, as discussed above, the filling of wetlands for such a purpose would not justify a special exception under Council regulations. *See supra*, at 2459; *see* also Brief for Respondents 10 ("Residential construction is not the basis of such a 'special exception'"). Perhaps for this reason, the State did not maintain in the trial court that additional uplands could have been developed. To the contrary, its post-trial memorandum identified only the single parcel that petitioner concedes retains a development value of $200,000. *See* State's Post-Trial Memorandum in No. 88-0297 (Super.Ct. R. I.), 25, 81. The trial court accepted the figure. So there is no genuine ambiguity in the record as to the extent of permitted development on petitioner's property, either on the wetlands or the uplands.

Nonetheless, there is some suggestion that the use permitted on the uplands is not known, because the State accepted the $200,000 value for the upland parcel on the premise that only a *Lucas* claim was raised in the pleadings in the state trial court. *See* Brief of Respondents 29-30. Since a *Penn Central* argument was not pressed at trial, it is argued, the State had no reason to assert with vigor that more than a single-family residence might be placed on the uplands. We disagree; the State was aware of the applicability of *Penn Central.* The issue whether the Council's decisions amounted to a taking under *Penn Central* was discussed in the trial court, App. to Pet. for Cert. B-7, the State Supreme Court, 746 A.2d, at 717, and the State's own post-trial submissions, *see* State's Post-Trial Supplemental Memorandum 7-10. The state court opinions cannot be read as indicating that a Penn Central claim was not properly presented from the outset of this litigation.

A final ripeness issue remains. In concluding that *Williamson County*'s final decision requirement was not satisfied the State Supreme Court placed emphasis on petitioner's failure to "appl[y] for permission to develop [the] seventy-four-lot subdivision" that was the basis for the damages sought in his inverse condemnation suit. 746 A.2d, at 714. The court did not explain why it thought this fact significant, but respondents and amici defend the ruling. The Council's practice, they assert, is to consider a proposal only if the applicant has satisfied all other regulatory preconditions for the use envisioned in the application. The subdivision proposal that was the basis for petitioner's takings claim, they add, could not have proceeded before the Council without, at minimum, zoning approval from the town of Westerly and a permit from the Rhode Island Department of Environmental Management allowing the installation of individual sewage disposal systems on the property. Petitioner is accused of employing a hide the ball strategy of submitting applications for more modest uses to the Council, only to assert later a takings action predicated on the purported inability to build a much larger project. Brief for the *National Wildlife Federation et al.* as *Amici Curiae* 9.

It is difficult to see how this concern is relevant to the inquiry at issue here. Petitioner was informed by the Council that he could not fill the wetlands; it follows of necessity that he could not fill and then build 74 single-family dwellings upon it. Petitioner's submission of this proposal would not have clarified the extent of development permitted by the wetlands regulations, which is the inquiry required under our ripeness decisions. The State's concern may be that landowners could demand damages for a taking based on a project that could not have been constructed under other, valid zoning restrictions quite apart from the regulation being challenged. This, of course, is a valid concern in inverse condemnation cases alleging injury from wrongful refusal to permit development. The instant case does not require us to pass upon the authority of a state to insist in such cases that landowners follow normal planning procedures or to enact rules to control damage awards based on hypothetical uses that should have been reviewed in the normal course, and we do not intend to cast doubt upon such rules here. The mere allegation of entitlement to the value of an intensive use will not avail the landowner if the project would not have been allowed under other existing, legitimate land use limitations. When a taking has occurred, under accepted condemnation principles the owner's damages will be based upon the property's fair market value, *see, e.g., Olson v. United States*, 292 U.S. 246, 255, 54 S.Ct. 704, 78 L.Ed. 1236 (1934); 4 J. Sackman, Nichols on Eminent Domain §12.01 (rev.3d ed.2000)—an inquiry which will turn, in part, on restrictions on use imposed by legitimate zoning or other regulatory limitations, *see id.*, at §12C.03[1].

The state court, however, did not rely upon state law ripeness or exhaustion principles in holding that petitioner's takings claim was barred by virtue of his failure to apply for a 74-lot subdivision; it relied on *Williamson County.* As we have explained, *Williamson County* and our other ripeness decisions do not impose further obligations on petitioner, for the limitations the wetland regulations imposed were clear from the Council's denial of his applications, and there is no indication that any use involving any substantial structures or improvements would have been allowed. Where the state agency charged with enforcing a challenged land use regulation entertains an application from an owner and its denial of the application makes clear the extent of development permitted, and neither the agency nor a reviewing state court has cited noncompliance with reasonable state law exhaustion or pre-permit processes, *see Felder v. Casey*, 487 U.S. 131, 150-151, 108 S.Ct. 2302, 101 L.Ed.2d 123 (1988), federal ripeness rules do not require the submission of further and futile applications with other agencies.

B

We turn to the second asserted basis for declining to address petitioner's takings claim on the merits. When the Council promulgated its wetlands regulations, the disputed parcel was owned not by petitioner but by the corporation of which he was sole shareholder. When title was transferred to petitioner by operation of law, the wetlands regulations were in force. The state court held the postregulation acquisition of title was fatal to the claim for deprivation of all economic use, 746 A.2d, at 716, and to the *Penn Central* claim, *id.*, at 717. While the first holding was couched in terms of background principles of state property law, *see Lucas*, 505 U.S., at 1015, 112 S.Ct. 2886, and the second in terms of petitioner's reasonable investment-backed expectations, *see Penn Central*, 438 U.S., at 124, 98 S.Ct. 2646, the two holdings together amount to a single, sweeping, rule: A purchaser or a successive title holder like petitioner is deemed to have notice of an earlier-enacted restriction and is barred from claiming that it effects a taking.

The theory underlying the argument that post-enactment purchasers cannot challenge a regulation under the Takings Clause seems to run on these lines: Property rights are created by the State. *See, e.g., Phillips v. Washington Legal Foundation*, 524 U.S. 156, 163, 118 S.Ct. 1925, 141 L.Ed.2d 174 (1998). So, the argument goes, by prospective legislation the State can shape and define property rights and reasonable investment-backed expectations, and subsequent owners cannot claim any injury from lost value. After all, they purchased or took title with notice of the limitation.

The State may not put so potent a Hobbesian stick into the Lockean bundle. The right to improve property, of course, is subject to the reasonable exercise of state authority, including the enforcement of valid zoning and land-use restrictions. *See Pennsylvania Coal Co.*, 260 U.S., at 413, 43 S.Ct. 158 ("Government hardly could go on if to some extent values incident to property could not be diminished without paying for every such change in the general law"). The Takings Clause, however, in certain circumstances allows a landowner to assert that a particular exercise of the State's regulatory power is so unreasonable or onerous as to compel compensation. Just as a prospective enactment, such as a new zoning ordinance, can limit the value of land without effecting a taking because it can be understood as reasonable by all concerned, other enactments are unreasonable and do not become less so through passage of time or title. Were we to accept the State's rule, the postenactment transfer of title would absolve the State of its obligation to defend any action restricting land use, no matter how extreme or unreasonable. A State would be allowed, in effect, to put an expiration date on the Takings Clause. This ought not to be the rule. Future generations, too, have a right to challenge unreasonable limitations on the use and value of land.

Nor does the justification of notice take into account the effect on owners at the time of enactment, who are prejudiced as well. Should an owner attempt to challenge a new regulation, but not survive the process of ripening his or her claim (which, as this case demonstrates, will often take years), under the proposed rule the right to compensation may not by asserted by an heir or successor, and so may not be asserted at all. The State's rule would work a critical alteration to the nature of property, as the newly regulated landowner is stripped of the ability to transfer the interest which was possessed prior to the regulation. The State may not by this means secure a windfall for itself. *See Webb's Fabulous Pharmacies, Inc. v. Beckwith*, 449 U.S. 155, 164, 101 S.Ct. 446, 66 L.Ed.2d 358 (1980) ("[A] State, by ipse dixit, may not transform private property into public property without compensation"); *cf.* Ellickson, *Property in Land*, 102 Yale L.J. 1315, 1368-1369 (1993) (right to transfer interest in land is a defining characteristic of the fee simple estate). The proposed rule is, furthermore, capricious in effect. The young owner contrasted with the older owner, the owner with the resources to hold contrasted with the owner with the need to sell, would be in different positions. The Takings Clause is not so quixotic. A blanket rule that purchasers with notice have no compensation right when a claim becomes ripe is too blunt an instrument to accord with the duty to compensate for what is taken.

Direct condemnation, by invocation of the State's power of eminent domain, presents different considerations than cases alleging a taking based on a burdensome regulation. In a direct condemnation action, or when a State has physically invaded the property without filing suit, the fact and extent of the taking are known. In such an instance, it is a general rule of the law of eminent domain that any award goes to the owner at the time of the taking, and that the right to compensation is not passed to a subsequent purchaser. *See Danforth v. United States*, 308 U.S. 271, 284, 60 S.Ct. 231, 84 L.Ed. 240 (1939); 2 Sackman, *Eminent Domain*, at §5.01[5][d][i] ("It is well settled that when there is a taking of property by eminent domain in compliance with the law, it is the owner of the property at the time of the taking who is entitled to compensation"). A challenge to the application of a land-use regulation, by contrast, does not mature until ripeness requirements have been satisfied, under principles we have discussed; until this point an inverse condemnation claim alleging a regulatory taking cannot be maintained. It would be illogical, and unfair, to bar a regulatory takings claim because of the post-enactment transfer of ownership where the steps necessary to make the claim ripe were not taken, or could not have been taken, by a previous owner.

There is controlling precedent for our conclusion. *Nollan v. California Coastal Comm'n*, 483 U.S. 825, 107 S.Ct. 3141, 97 L.Ed.2d 677 (1987), presented the question whether it was consistent with the Takings Clause for a state regulatory agency to require oceanfront landowners to provide lateral beach access to the public as the condition for a development permit. The principal dissenting opinion observed it was a policy of the California Coastal Commission to require the condition, and that the Nollans, who purchased their home after the policy went into effect, were "on notice that new developments would be approved only if provisions were made for lateral beach access." *Id.*, at 860, 107 S.Ct. 3141 (Brennan, J., dissenting). A majority of the Court rejected the proposition. "So long as the Commission could not have deprived the prior owners of the easement without compensating them," the Court reasoned, "the prior owners must be understood to have transferred their full property rights in conveying the lot." *Id.*, at 834, n. 2, 107 S.Ct. 3141.

It is argued that Nollan's holding was limited by the later decision in *Lucas v. South Carolina Coastal Council*, 505 U.S. 1003, 112 S.Ct. 2886, 120 L.Ed.2d 798 (1992). In *Lucas* the Court observed that a landowner's ability to recover for a government deprivation of all economically beneficial use of property is not absolute but instead is confined by limitations on the use of land which "inhere in the title itself." *Id.*, at 1029, 112 S.Ct. 2886. This is so, the Court reasoned, because the landowner is constrained by those "restrictions that background principles of the State's law of property and nuisance already place upon land ownership." *Id.*, at 1029, 112 S.Ct.

2886. It is asserted here that *Lucas* stands for the proposition that any new regulation, once enacted, becomes a background principle of property law which cannot be challenged by those who acquire title after the enactment.

We have no occasion to consider the precise circumstances when a legislative enactment can be deemed a background principle of state law or whether those circumstances are present here. It suffices to say that a regulation that otherwise would be unconstitutional absent compensation is not transformed into a background principle of the State's law by mere virtue of the passage of title. This relative standard would be incompatible with our description of the concept in *Lucas*, which is explained in terms of those common, shared understandings of permissible limitations derived from a State's legal tradition, *see* Lucas, *supra*, at 1029-1030, 112 S.Ct. 2886. A regulation or common-law rule cannot be a background principle for some owners but not for others. The determination whether an existing, general law can limit all economic use of property must turn on objective factors, such as the nature of the land use proscribed. *See Lucas, supra*, at 1030, 112 S.Ct. 2886 ("The 'total taking' inquiry we require today will ordinarily entail ... analysis of, among other things, the degree of harm to public lands and resources, or adjacent private property, posed by the claimant's proposed activities"). A law does not become a background principle for subsequent owners by enactment itself. *Lucas* did not overrule our holding in *Nollan*, which, as we have noted, is based on essential Takings Clause principles.

For reasons we discuss next, the state court will not find it necessary to explore these matters on remand in connection with the claim that all economic use was deprived; it must address, however, the merits of petitioner's claim under *Penn Central*. That claim is not barred by the mere fact that title was acquired after the effective date of the state-imposed restriction.

III

As the case is ripe, and as the date of transfer of title does not bar petitioner's takings claim, we have before us the alternative ground relied upon by the Rhode Island Supreme Court in ruling upon the merits of the takings claims. It held that all economically beneficial use was not deprived because the uplands portion of the property can still be improved. On this point, we agree with the court's decision. Petitioner accepts the Council's contention and the state trial court's finding that his parcel retains $200,000 in development value under the State's wetlands regulations. He asserts, nonetheless, that he has suffered a total taking and contends the Council cannot sidestep the holding in *Lucas* "by the simple expedient of leaving a landowner a few crumbs of value." Brief for Petitioner 37.

Assuming a taking is otherwise established, a State may not evade the duty to compensate on the premise that the landowner is left with a token interest. This is not the situation of the landowner in this case, however. A regulation permitting a landowner to build a substantial residence on an 18-acre parcel does not leave the property "economically idle." *Lucas, supra*, at 1019, 112 S.Ct. 2886.

In his brief submitted to us petitioner attempts to revive this part of his claim by reframing it. He argues, for the first time, that the upland parcel is distinct from the wetlands portions, so he should be permitted to assert a deprivation limited to the latter. This contention asks us to examine the difficult, persisting question of what is the proper denominator in the takings fraction. *See* Michelman, *Property, Utility, and Fairness: Comments on the Ethical Foundations of "Just Compensation" Law*, 80 Harv. L.Rev. 1165, 1192 (1967). Some of our cases indicate that the extent of deprivation effected by a regulatory action is measured against the value of the parcel as a whole, *see, e.g., Keystone Bituminous Coal Assn. v. DeBenedictis*, 480 U.S. 470, 497, 107 S.Ct. 1232, 94 L.Ed.2d 472 (1987); but we have at times expressed discomfort with the logic of this rule, *see Lucas, supra*, at 1016-1017, n.7, 112 S.Ct. 2886, a sentiment echoed by some commentators, *see, e.g.*, Epstein, *Takings: Descent and Resurrection*, 1987 Sup.Ct. Rev. 1, 16-17 (1987); Fee, Unearthing the Denominator in Regulatory Takings Claims, 61 U. Chi. L.Rev. 1535 (1994). Whatever the merits of these criticisms, we will not explore the point here. Petitioner did not press the argument in the state courts, and the issue was not presented in the petition for certiorari. The case comes to us on the premise that petitioner's entire parcel serves as the basis for his takings claim, and, so framed, the total deprivation argument fails.

For the reasons we have discussed, the State Supreme Court erred in finding petitioner's claims were unripe and in ruling that acquisition of title after the effective date of the regulations barred the takings claims. The court did not err in finding that petitioner failed to establish a deprivation of all economic value, for it is undisputed that the parcel retains significant worth for construction of a residence. The claims under the *Penn Central* analysis were not examined, and for this purpose the case should be remanded.

The judgment of the Rhode Island Supreme Court is affirmed in part and reversed in part, and the case is remanded for further proceedings not inconsistent with this opinion.

It is so ORDERED.

Justice O'CONNOR, concurring.

I join the opinion of the Court but with my understanding of how the issues discussed in Part II-B of the opinion must be considered on remand.

Part II-B of the Court's opinion addresses the circumstance, present in this case, where a takings claimant has acquired title to the regulated property after the enactment of the regulation at issue. As the Court holds, the Rhode Island Supreme Court erred in effectively adopting the sweeping rule that the preacquisition enactment of the use restriction ipso facto defeats any takings claim based on that use restriction. Accordingly, the Court holds that petitioner's claim under *Penn Central Transp. Co. v. City of New York*, 438 U.S. 104, 98 S.Ct. 2646, 57 L.Ed.2d 631 (1978), "is not barred by the mere fact that title was acquired after the effective date of the state-imposed restriction." *Ante*, at 2464.

The more difficult question is what role the temporal relationship between regulatory enactment and title acquisition plays in a proper *Penn Central* analysis. Today's holding does not mean that the timing of the regulation's enactment relative to the acquisition of title is immaterial to the *Penn Central* analysis. Indeed, it would be just as much error to expunge this consideration from the takings inquiry as it would be to accord it exclusive significance. Our polestar instead remains the principles set forth in *Penn Central* itself and our other cases that govern partial regulatory takings. Under these cases, interference with investment-backed expectations is one of a number of factors that a court must examine. Further, the regulatory regime in place at the time the claimant acquires the property at issue helps to shape the reasonableness of those expectations.

The Fifth Amendment forbids the taking of private property for public use without just compensation. We have recognized that this constitutional guarantee is "'designed to bar Government from forcing some people alone to bear public burdens which, in all fairness and justice, should be borne by the public as a whole.'" *Penn Central, supra*, at 123-124, 98 S.Ct. 2646 (quoting *Armstrong v. United States*, 364 U.S. 40, 49, 80 S.Ct. 1563, 4 L.Ed.2d 1554 (1960)). The concepts of "fairness and justice" that underlie the Takings Clause, of course, are less than fully determinate. Accordingly, we have eschewed "any 'set formula' for determining when 'justice and fairness' require that economic injuries caused by public action be compensated by the government, rather than remain disproportionately concentrated on a few persons." *Penn Central, supra*, at 124, 98 S.Ct. 2646 (quoting *Goldblatt v. Hempstead*, 369 U.S. 590, 594, 82 S.Ct. 987, 8 L.Ed.2d 130 (1962)). The outcome instead "depends largely 'upon the particular circumstances [in that] case.'" *Penn Central, supra*, at 124, 98 S.Ct. 2646 (quoting *United States v. Central Eureka Mining Co.*, 357 U.S. 155, 168, 78 S.Ct. 1097, 2 L.Ed.2d 1228 (1958)).

We have "identified several factors that have particular significance" in these "essentially ad hoc, factual inquiries." *Penn Central*, 438 U.S., at 124, 98 S.Ct. 2646. Two such factors are "[t]he economic impact of the regulation on the claimant and, particularly, the extent to which the regulation has interfered with distinct investment-backed expectations." *Ibid.* Another is "the character of the governmental action." *Ibid.* The purposes served, as well as the effects produced, by a particular regulation inform the takings analysis. *Id.*, at 127, 98 S.Ct. 2646 ("[A] use restriction on real property may constitute a 'taking' if not reasonably necessary to the effectuation of a substantial public purpose, [citations omitted], or perhaps if it has an unduly harsh impact upon the owner's use of the property"); *see* also *Yee v. Escondido*, 503 U.S. 519, 523, 112 S.Ct. 1522, 118 L.Ed.2d 153 (1992) (Regulatory takings cases "necessarily entai[l] complex factual assessments of the purposes and economic effects of government actions"). *Penn Central* does not supply mathematically precise variables, but instead provides important guideposts that lead to the ultimate determination whether just compensation is required.

The Rhode Island Supreme Court concluded that, because the wetlands regulations predated petitioner's acquisition of the property at issue, petitioner lacked reasonable investment-backed expectations and hence lacked a viable takings claim. 746 A.2d 707, 717 (2000). The court erred in elevating what it believed to be "[petitioner's] lack of reasonable investment-backed expectations" to "dispositive" status. *Ibid.* Investment-backed expectations, though important, are not talismanic under *Penn Central*. Evaluation of the degree of interference with investment-backed expectations instead is one factor that points toward the answer to the question whether the application of a particular regulation to particular property "goes too far." *Pennsylvania Coal Co. v. Mahon*, 260 U.S. 393, 415, 43 S.Ct. 158, 67 L.Ed. 322 (1922).

Further, the state of regulatory affairs at the time of acquisition is not the only factor that may determine the extent of investment-backed expectations. For example, the nature and extent of permitted development under the regulatory regime vis-a-vis the development sought by the claimant may also shape legitimate expectations without vesting any kind of development right in the property owner. We also have never held that a takings claim is defeated simply on account of the lack of a personal financial investment by a postenactment acquirer of property, such as a donee, heir, or devisee. *Cf. Hodel v. Irving*, 481 U.S. 704, 714-718, 107 S.Ct. 2076, 95 L.Ed.2d 668 (1987). Courts instead must attend to those circumstances which are probative of what fairness requires in a given case.

If investment-backed expectations are given exclusive significance in the *Penn Central* analysis and existing regulations dictate the reasonableness of those expectations in every instance, then the State wields far too much power to redefine property rights upon passage of title. On the other hand, if existing regulations do nothing to inform the analysis, then some property owners may reap windfalls and an important indicium of fairness is lost.[1] As I understand it, our decision today does not remove the regulatory backdrop against which an owner takes title to property from the purview of the *Penn Central* inquiry. It simply restores balance to that inquiry. Courts properly consider the effect of existing regulations under the rubric of investment-backed expectations in determining whether a compensable taking has occurred. As before, the salience of these facts cannot be reduced to any "set formula." *Penn Central*, 438 U.S., at 124, 98 S.Ct. 2646 (internal quotation marks omitted). The temptation to adopt what amount to per se rules in either direction must be resisted. The Takings Clause requires careful examination and weighing of all the relevant circumstances in this context. The court below therefore must consider on remand the array of relevant factors under *Penn Central* before deciding whether any compensation is due.

Justice SCALIA, concurring.

I write separately to make clear that my understanding of how the issues discussed in Part II-B of the Court's opinion must be considered on remand is not Justice O'CONNOR's.

The principle that underlies her separate concurrence is that it may in some (unspecified) circumstances be "[un]fai[r]," and produce unacceptable "windfalls," to allow a subsequent purchaser to nullify an unconstitutional partial taking (though, inexplicably, not an unconstitutional total taking) by the government. *Ante*, at 2456. The polar horrible, presumably, is the situation in which a sharp real estate developer, realizing (or indeed, simply gambling on) the unconstitutional excessiveness of a development restriction that a naive landowner assumes to be valid, purchases property at what it would be worth subject to the restriction, and then develops it to its full value (or resells it at its full value) after getting the unconstitutional restriction invalidated.

This can, I suppose, be called a windfall—though it is not much different from the windfalls that occur every day at stock exchanges or antique auctions, where the knowledgeable (or the venturesome) profit at the expense of the ignorant (or the risk averse). There is something to be said (though in my view not much) for pursuing abstract "fairness" by requiring part or all of that windfall to be returned to the naive original owner, who presumably is the "rightful" owner of it. But there is nothing to be said for giving it instead to the government—which not only did not lose something it owned, but is both the cause of the miscarriage of "fairness" and the only one of the three parties involved in the miscarriage (government, naive original owner, and sharp real estate developer) which acted unlawfully—indeed unconstitutionally. Justice O'CONNOR would eliminate the windfall by giving the malefactor the benefit of its malefaction.

---

[1] (O'Connor)] Justice SCALIA's inapt "government-as-thief" simile is symptomatic of the larger failing of his opinion, which is that he appears to conflate two questions. The first question is whether the enactment or application of a regulation constitutes a valid exercise of the police power. The second question is whether the State must compensate a property owner for a diminution in value effected by the State's exercise of its police power. We have held that "[t]he 'public use' requirement [of the Takings Clause] is ... coterminous with the scope of a sovereign's police powers." *Hawaii Housing Authority v. Midkiff*, 467 U.S. 229, 240, 104 S.Ct. 2321, 81 L.Ed.2d 186 (1984). The relative timing of regulatory enactment and title acquisition, of course, does not affect the analysis of whether a State has acted within the scope of these powers in the first place. That issue appears to be the one on which Justice SCALIA focuses, but it is not the matter at hand. The relevant question instead is the second question described above. It is to this inquiry that "investment-backed expectations" and the state of regulatory affairs upon acquisition of title are relevant under *Penn Central*. Justice SCALIA's approach therefore would seem to require a revision of the *Penn Central* analysis that this Court has not undertaken.

It is rather like eliminating the windfall that accrued to a purchaser who bought property at a bargain rate from a thief clothed with the indicia of title, by making him turn over the "unjust" profit to the thief.[1]

In my view, the fact that a restriction existed at the time the purchaser took title (other than a restriction forming part of the "background principles of the State's law of property and nuisance," *Lucas v. South Carolina Coastal Council*, 505 U.S. 1003, 1029, 112 S.Ct. 2886, 120 L.Ed.2d 798 (1992)) should have no bearing upon the determination of whether the restriction is so substantial as to constitute a taking. The "investment-backed expectations" that the law will take into account do not include the assumed validity of a restriction that in fact deprives property of so much of its value as to be unconstitutional. Which is to say that a *Penn Central* taking, *see* *Penn Central Transp. Co. v. City of New York*, 438 U.S. 104, 98 S.Ct. 2646, 57 L.Ed.2d 631 (1978), no less than a total taking, is not absolved by the transfer of title.

Justice STEVENS, concurring in part and dissenting in part.

In an admirable effort to frame its inquiries in broadly significant terms, the majority offers six pages of commentary on the issue of whether an owner of property can challenge regulations adopted prior to her acquisition of that property without ever discussing the particular facts or legal claims at issue in this case. *See ante*, at 2462-2464. While I agree with some of what the Court has to say on this issue, an examination of the issue in the context of the facts of this case convinces me that the Court has over-simplified a complex calculus and conflated two separate questions. Therefore, while I join Part II-A of the opinion, I dissent from the judgment and, in particular, from Part II-B.

I

Though States and local governments have broad power to adopt regulations limiting land usage, those powers are constrained by the Constitution and by other provisions of state law. In adopting land-use restrictions, local authorities must follow legally valid and constitutionally sufficient procedures and must adhere to whatever substantive requirements are imposed by the Constitution and supervening law. If a regulating body fails to adhere to its procedural or substantive obligations in developing land-use restrictions, anyone adversely impacted by the restrictions may challenge their validity in an injunctive action. If the application of such restriction to a property owner would cause her a "direct and substantial injury," *e.g.*, *Chicago v. Atchison*, T. & S.F.R. Co., 357 U.S. 77, 83, 78 S.Ct. 1063, 2 L.Ed.2d 1174 (1958), I have no doubt that she has standing to challenge the restriction's validity whether she acquired title to the property before or after the regulation was adopted. For, as the Court correctly observes, even future generations "have a right to challenge unreasonable limitations on the use and value of land." *Ante*, at 2463.

It by no means follows, however, that, as the Court assumes, a succeeding owner may obtain compensation for a taking of property from her predecessor in interest. A taking is a discrete event, a governmental acquisition of private property for which the state is required to provide

---

[1] (Scalia) Contrary to Justice O'CONNOR's assertion, post, at 2470, n., my contention of governmental wrongdoing does not assume that the government exceeded its police powers by ignoring the "public use" requirement of the Takings Clause, *see Hawaii Housing Authority v. Midkiff*, 467 U.S. 229, 240, 104 S.Ct. 2321, 81 L.Ed.2d 186 (1984). It is wrong for the government to take property, even for public use, without tendering just compensation.

just compensation. Like other transfers of property, it occurs at a particular time, that time being the moment when the relevant property interest is alienated from its owner. [Footnote omitted.]

Precise specification of the moment a taking occurred and of the nature of the property interest taken is necessary in order to determine an appropriately compensatory remedy. For example, the amount of the award is measured by the value of the property at the time of taking, not the value at some later date. Similarly, interest on the award runs from that date. Most importantly for our purposes today, it is the person who owned the property at the time of the taking that is entitled to the recovery. *See, e.g., Danforth v. United States*, 308 U.S. 271, 284, 60 S.Ct. 231, 84 L.Ed. 240 (1939) ("For the reason that compensation is due at the time of taking, the owner at that time, not the owner at an earlier or later date, receives the payment"). The rationale behind that rule is true whether the transfer of ownership is the result of an arm's-length negotiation, an inheritance, or the dissolution of a bankrupt debtor. *Cf. United States v. Dow*, 357 U.S. 17, 20-21, 78 S.Ct. 1039, 2 L.Ed.2d 1109 (1958).[2]

II

Much of the difficulty of this case stems from genuine confusion as to when the taking Palazzolo alleges actually occurred. According to Palazzolo's theory of the case, the owners of his Westerly, Rhode Island, property possessed the right to fill the wetland portion of the property at some point in the not-too-distant past. [Footnote omitted.] In 1971, the State of Rhode Island passed a statute creating the Rhode Island Coastal Resources Management Council (Council) and delegating the Council the authority to promulgate regulations restricting the usage of coastal land. *See* 1971 R.I. Pub. Laws, ch. 279, §1 et seq. The Council promptly adopted regulations that, inter alia, effectively foreclosed petitioner from filling his wetlands. *See ante*, at 2456; *cf.* App. to Brief for Respondents 11-22 (current version of regulations). As the regulations nonetheless provided for a process through which petitioner might seek permission to fill the wetlands, he filed two applications for such permission during the 1980s, both of which were denied. *See ante*, at 2456.

The most natural reading of petitioner's complaint is that the regulations in and of themselves precluded him from filling the wetlands, and that their adoption therefore constituted the alleged taking. This reading is consistent with the Court's analysis in Part II-A of its opinion (which I join) in which the Court explains that petitioner's takings claims are ripe for decision because respondents' wetlands regulations unequivocally provide that there can be "no fill for any likely or foreseeable use." *Ante*, at 2459. [Footnote omitted.] If it is the regulations themselves of which petitioner complains, and if they did, in fact, diminish the value of his property, they did so when they were adopted.

---

[2] (Stevens) The Court argues, *ante*, at 2463, that a regulatory taking is different from a direct state appropriation of property and that the rules this Court has developed for identifying the time of the latter do not apply to the former. This is something of an odd conclusion, in that the entire rationale for allowing compensation for regulations in the first place is the somewhat dubious proposition that some regulations go so "far" as to become the functional equivalent of a direct taking. Ultimately, the Court's regulations-are-different principle rests on the confusion of two dates: the time an injury occurs and the time a claim for compensation for that injury becomes cognizable in a judicial proceeding. That we require plaintiffs making the claim that a regulation is the equivalent of a taking to go through certain prelitigation procedures to clarify the scope of the allegedly infringing regulation does not mean that the injury did not occur before those procedures were completed. To the contrary, whenever the relevant local bodies construe their regulations, their construction is assumed to reflect "what the [regulation] meant before as well as after the decision giving rise to that construction." *Rivers v. Roadway Express, Inc.*, 511 U.S. 298, 312-313, 114 S.Ct. 1510, 128 L.Ed.2d 274 (1994).

To the extent that the adoption of the regulations constitute the challenged taking, petitioner is simply the wrong party to be bringing this action. If the regulations imposed a compensable injury on anyone, it was on the owner of the property at the moment the regulations were adopted. Given the trial court's finding that petitioner did not own the property at that time, [footnote omitted] in my judgment it is pellucidly clear that he has no standing to claim that the promulgation of the regulations constituted a taking of any part of the property that he subsequently acquired.

His lack of standing does not depend, as the Court seems to assume, on whether or not petitioner "is deemed to have notice of an earlier-enacted restriction," *ante*, at 2462. If those early regulations changed the character of the owner's title to the property, thereby diminishing its value, petitioner acquired only the net value that remained after that diminishment occurred. Of course, if, as respondent contends, *see* n.3, *supra*, even the prior owner never had any right to fill wetlands, there never was a basis for the alleged takings claim in the first place. But accepting petitioner's theory of the case, he has no standing to complain that preacquisition events may have reduced the value of the property that he acquired. If the regulations are invalid, either because improper procedures were followed when they were adopted, or because they have somehow gone "too far," *Pennsylvania Coal Co. v. Mahon*, 260 U.S. 393, 415, 43 S.Ct. 158, 67 L.Ed. 322 (1922), petitioner may seek to enjoin their enforcement, but he has no right to recover compensation for the value of property taken from someone else. A new owner may maintain an ejectment action against a trespasser who has lodged himself in the owner's orchard but surely could not recover damages for fruit a trespasser spirited from the orchard before he acquired the property.

The Court's holding in *Nollan v. California Coastal Comm'n*, 483 U.S. 825, 107 S.Ct. 3141, 97 L.Ed.2d 677 (1987) is fully consistent with this analysis. In that case the taking occurred when the state agency compelled the petitioners to provide an easement of public access to the beach as a condition for a development permit. That event—a compelled transfer of an interest in property—occurred after the petitioners had become the owner of the property and unquestionably diminished the value of petitioners' property. Even though they had notice when they bought the property that such a taking might occur, they never contended that any action taken by the State before their purchase gave rise to any right to compensation. The matter of standing to assert a claim for just compensation is determined by the impact of the event that is alleged to have amounted to a taking rather than the sort of notice that a purchaser may or may not have received when the property was transferred. Petitioners in Nollan owned the property at the time of the triggering event. Therefore, they and they alone could claim a right to compensation for the injury. [Footnote omitted.] Their successors in interest, like petitioner in this case, have no standing to bring such a claim.

III

At oral argument, petitioner contended that the taking in question occurred in 1986, when the Council denied his final application to fill the land. Tr. of Oral Arg. 16. Though this theory, to the extent that it was embraced within petitioner's actual complaint, complicates the issue, it does not alter my conclusion that the prohibition on filling the wetlands does not take from Palazzolo any property right he ever possessed.

The title Palazzolo took by operation of law in 1978 was limited by the regulations then in place to the extent that such regulations represented a valid exercise of the police power. For the reasons expressed above, I think the regulations barred petitioner from filling the wetlands on his property. At the very least, however, they established a rule that such lands could not be filled unless the Council exercised its authority to make exceptions to that rule under certain circumstances. *Cf.* App. to Brief for Respondents A-13 (laying out narrow circumstances under which the Council retains the discretion to grant a "special exception"). Under the reading of the regulations most favorable to Palazzolo, he acquired no more than the right to a discretionary determination by the Council as to whether to permit him to fill the wetlands. As his two hearings before that body attest, he was given the opportunity to make a presentation and receive such a determination. Thus, the Council properly respected whatever limited rights he may have retained with regard to filling the wetlands. *Cf. Lujan v. G & G Fire Sprinklers, Inc.*, 532 U.S. 189, 121 S.Ct. 1446, 149 L.Ed.2d 391 (2001) (holding, in a different context, that, if a party's only relevant property interest is a claim of entitlement to bring an action, the provision of a forum for hearing that action is all that is required to vindicate that property interest); *Lopez v. Davis*, 531 U.S. 230, 121 S.Ct. 714, 148 L.Ed.2d 635 (2001) (involving a federal statute that created an entitlement to a discretionary hearing without creating any entitlement to relief). [Footnote omitted.]

Though the majority leaves open the possibility that the scope of today's holding may prove limited, *see ante*, at 2464 (discussing limitations implicit in "background principles" exception); *see* also *ante*, at 2465- 2467 (O'CONNOR, J., concurring) (discussing importance of the timing of regulations for the evaluation of the merits of a takings claim); *ante*, at 2477-2478 (BREYER, J., dissenting) (same), the extension of the right to compensation to individuals other than the direct victim of an illegal taking admits of no obvious limiting principle. If the existence of valid land-use regulations does not limit the title that the first postenactment purchaser of the property inherits, then there is no reason why such regulations should limit the rights of the second, the third, or the thirtieth purchaser. Perhaps my concern is unwarranted, but today's decision does raise the spectre of a tremendous—and tremendously capricious—one-time transfer of wealth from society at large to those individuals who happen to hold title to large tracts of land at the moment this legal question is permanently resolved.

IV

In the final analysis, the property interest at stake in this litigation is the right to fill the wetlands on the tract that petitioner owns. Whether either he or his predecessors in title ever owned such an interest, and if so, when it was acquired by the State, are questions of state law. If it is clear—as I think it is and as I think the Court's disposition of the ripeness issue assumes—that any such taking occurred before he became the owner of the property, he has no standing to seek compensation for that taking. On the other hand, if the only viable takings claim has a different predicate that arose later, that claim is not ripe and the discussion in Part II-B of the Court's opinion is superfluous dictum. In either event, the judgment of the Rhode Island Supreme Court should be affirmed in its entirety.

Justice GINSBURG, with whom Justice SOUTER and Justice BREYER join, dissenting.

A regulatory takings claim is not ripe for adjudication, this Court has held, until the agency administering the regulations at issue, proceeding in good faith, "has arrived at a final, definitive position regarding how it will apply [those regulations] to the particular land in question." *Williamson County Regional Planning Comm'n v. Hamilton Bank of Johnson City*, 473 U.S. 172, 191, 105 S.Ct. 3108, 87 L.Ed.2d 126 (1985). Absent such a final decision, a court cannot "kno[w] the nature and extent of permitted development" under the regulations, and therefore cannot say "how far the regulation[s] g[o]," as regulatory takings law requires. *MacDonald, Sommer & Frates v. Yolo County*, 477 U.S. 340, 348, 351, 106 S.Ct. 2561, 91 L.Ed.2d 285 (1986). Therefore, even when a landowner seeks and is denied permission to develop property, if the denial does not demonstrate the effective impact of the regulations on the land, the denial does not represent the "final decision" requisite to generate a ripe dispute. *Williamson County*, 473 U.S., at 190, 105 S.Ct. 3108.

MacDonald illustrates how a highly ambitious application may not ripen a takings claim. The landowner in that case proposed a 159-home subdivision. 477 U.S., at 342, 106 S.Ct. 2561. When that large proposal was denied, the owner complained that the State had appropriated "all beneficial use of its property." *Id.*, at 352, n. 8, 106 S.Ct. 2561; *see* also *id.*, at 344, 106 S.Ct. 2561. This Court concluded, however, that the landowner's claim was not ripe, for the denial of the massive development left "open the possibility that some development [would] be permitted." *Id.*, at 352, 106 S.Ct. 2561. "Rejection of exceedingly grandiose development plans," the Court observed, "does not logically imply that less ambitious plans will receive similarly unfavorable reviews." *Id.*, at 353, n. 9, 106 S.Ct. 2561.

As presented to the Rhode Island Supreme Court, Anthony Palazzolo's case was a close analogue to *MacDonald*. Palazzolo's land has two components. Approximately 18 acres are wetlands that sustain a rich but delicate ecosystem. *See* 746 A.2d 707, 710, and n. 1 (R.I.2000). Additional acres are less environmentally sensitive "uplands." (The number of upland acres remains in doubt, *see ibid.*, because Palazzolo has never submitted "an accurate or detailed survey" of his property, *see* Tr. 190 (June 18-19, 1997).) Rhode Island's administrative agency with ultimate permitting authority over the wetlands, the Coastal Resources Management Council (CRMC), bars residential development of the wetlands, but not the uplands.

Although Palazzolo submitted several applications to develop his property, those applications uniformly sought permission to fill most or all of the wetlands portion of the property. None aimed to develop only the uplands. Upon denial of the last of Palazzolo's applications, Palazzolo filed suit claiming that Rhode Island had taken his property by refusing "to allow any development." App. 45 (Complaint 17).

As the Rhode Island Supreme Court saw the case, Palazzolo's claim was not ripe for several reasons, among them, that Palazzolo had not sought permission for "development only of the upland portion of the parcel." 746 A.2d, at 714. The Rhode Island court emphasized the "undisputed evidence in the record that it would be possible to build at least one single-family home on the existing upland area, with no need for additional fill." *Ibid.*

Today, the Court rejects the Rhode Island court's determination that the case is unripe, finding no "uncertainty as to the [uplands'] permitted use." *Ante*, at 2460. The Court's conclusion is, in my view, both inaccurate and inequitable. It is inaccurate because the record is ambiguous. And it is inequitable because, given the claim asserted by Palazzolo in the Rhode Island courts, the State had no cause to pursue further inquiry into potential upland development. But Palazzolo presses other claims here, and at his behest, the Court not only entertains them, but also turns the State's legitimate defense against the claim Palazzolo originally stated into a weapon against the State. I would reject Palazzolo's bait-and-switch ploy and affirm the judgment of the Rhode Island Supreme Court.

Where physical occupation of land is not at issue, the Court's cases identify two basic forms of regulatory taking. *Ante*, at 2457-2458. In *Lucas v. South Carolina Coastal Council*, 505 U.S. 1003, 112 S.Ct. 2886, 120 L.Ed.2d 798 (1992), the Court held that, subject to "certain qualifications," *ante*, at 2457, 2464, denial of "all economically beneficial or productive use of land" constitutes a taking. 505 U.S., at 1015, 112 S.Ct. 2886 (emphasis added). However, if a regulation does not leave the property "economically idle," *id.*, at 1019, 112 S.Ct. 2886, to establish the alleged taking the landowner may pursue the multifactor inquiry set out in *Penn Central Transp. Co. v. New York City*, 438 U.S. 104, 123-125, 98 S.Ct. 2646, 57 L.Ed.2d 631 (1978).

Like the landowner in *MacDonald*, Palazzolo sought federal constitutional relief only under a straightforward application of *Lucas*. *See ante*, at 2457; App. 45 (Complaint 17) ("As a direct and proximate result of the Defendants' refusal to allow any development of the property, there has been a taking" (emphasis added)); Plaintiff's Post Trial Memorandum in No. 88-0297 (Super.Ct., R.I.), p. 6 ("[T]his Court need not look beyond the Lucas case as its very lucid and precise standards will determine whether a taking has occurred"); *id.*, at 9-10 ("[T]here is NO USE for the property whatsoever .... Not one scintilla of evidence was proffered by the State to prove, intimate or even suggest a theoretical possibility of any use for this property-never mind a beneficial use. Not once did the State claim that there is, in fact, some use available for the Palazzolo parcel"); Brief of Appellant in No. 98-0333, pp. 5, 7, 9-10 (hereinafter Brief of Appellant) (restating, verbatim, assertions of Post Trial Memorandum quoted above).

Responding to Palazzolo's *Lucas* claim, the State urged as a sufficient defense this now uncontested point: CRMC "would [have been] happy to have [Palazzolo] situate a home" on the uplands, "thus allowing [him] to realize 200,000 dollars." State's Post-Trial Memorandum in No. 88-0297 (Super.Ct., R. I.), p. 81; *see* also Brief of Appellees in No. 98-0333A, p. 25 (hereinafter Brief of Appellees) (Palazzolo "never even applied for the realistic alternative of using the entire parcel as a single unitary home-site"). The State did present some evidence at trial that more than one lot could be developed. *See* infra, at 8-9. And, in a supplemental post-trial memorandum addressing a then-new Rhode Island Supreme Court decision, the State briefly urged that Palazzolo's claims would fail even under *Penn Central*. *See ante*, at 2461. The evidence of additional uses and the post-trial argument directed to Penn Central, however, were underdeveloped and unnecessary, for Palazzolo himself, in his pleadings and at trial, pressed only a *Lucas*-based claim that he had been denied all economically viable use of his property. Once the State demonstrated that an "economically beneficial" development was genuinely plausible, *Lucas*, 505 U.S., at 1015, 112 S.Ct. 2886, the State had established the analogy to *MacDonald*: The record now showed "valuable use might still be made of the land." 477 U.S., at 352, n. 8, 106 S.Ct. 2561; *see* Brief of Appellees 24-25 (relying on *MacDonald*). The prospect of real development shown by the State warranted a ripeness dismissal of Palazzolo's complaint.

Addressing the State's *Lucas* defense in Lucas terms, Palazzolo insisted that his land had "no use ... as a result of CRMC's application of its regulations." Brief of Appellant 11. The Rhode Island Supreme Court rejected Palazzolo's argument, identifying in the record evidence that Palazzolo could build at least one home on the uplands. 746 A.2d, at 714. The court therefore concluded that Palazzolo's failure to seek permission for "development only of the upland portion of the parcel" meant that Palazzolo could not "maintain a claim that the CRMC ha[d] deprived him of all beneficial use of the property." *Ibid.*

It is true that the Rhode Island courts, in the courseof ruling for the State, briefly touched base with *Penn Central*. *Cf. ante*, at 2461. The critical point, however, underplayed by the Court, is that Palazzolo never raised or argued the *Penn Central* issue in the state system: not in his complaint; not in his trial court submissions; not—even after the trial court touched on the *Penn Central* issue—in his briefing on appeal. The state high court decision, raising and quickly disposing of the matter, unquestionably permits us to consider the Penn Central issue. *See Raley v. Ohio*, 360 U.S. 423, 436-437, 79 S.Ct. 1257, 3 L.Ed.2d 1344 (1959). But the ruling below does not change the reality essential here: Palazzolo litigated his takings claim, and it was incumbent on the State to defend against that claim, only under *Lucas*.

If Palazzolo's arguments in this Court had tracked his arguments in the state courts, his petition for certiorari would have argued simply that the Rhode Island courts got it wrong in failing to see that his land had "no use" at all because of CRMC's rules. Brief of Appellant 11. This Court likely would not have granted certiorari to review the application of *MacDonald* and *Lucas* to the facts of Palazzolo's case. However, aided by new counsel, Palazzolo sought—and in the exercise of this Court's discretion obtained—review of two contentions he did not advance below. The first assertion is that the state regulations take the property under *Penn Central. See* Pet. for Cert. 20; Brief for Petitioner 47-50. The second argument is that the regulations amount to a taking under an expanded rendition of *Lucas* covering cases in which a landowner is left with property retaining only a "few crumbs of value." *Ante*, at 2464 (quoting Brief for Petitioner 37); Pet. for Cert. 20-22. Again, it bears repetition, Palazzolo never claimed in the courts below that, if the State were correct that his land could be used for a residence, a taking nonetheless occurred.

In support of his new claims, Palazzolo has conceded the very point on which the State properly relied to resist the simple Lucas claim presented below: that Palazzolo can obtain approval for one house of substantial economic value. Palazzolo does not merely accept the argument that the State advanced below. He now contends that the evidence proffered by the State in the Rhode Island courts supports the claims he presents here, by demonstrating that only one house would be approved. *See* Brief for Petitioner 13 ("[T]he uncontradicted evidence was that CRMC ... would not deny [Palazzolo] permission to build one single-family home on the small upland portion of his property." (emphasis deleted)); Pet. for Cert. 15 (the extent of development permitted on the land is "perfectly clear: one single-family home and nothing more").

As a logical matter, Palazzolo's argument does not stand up. The State's submissions in the Rhode Island courts hardly establish that Palazzolo could obtain approval for only one house of value. By showing that Palazzolo could have obtained approval for a $200,000 house (rather than, say, two houses worth $400,000), the State's submissions established only a floor, not a ceiling, on the value of permissible development. For a floor value was all the State needed to defeat Palazzolo's simple Lucas claim.

Furthermore, Palazzolo's argument is unfair: The argument transforms the State's legitimate defense to the only claim Palazzolo stated below into offensive support for other claims he states for the first time here. Casting away fairness (and fairness to a State, no less), the Court indulges Palazzolo's bait-and-switch maneuver. The Court concludes that "there is no genuine ambiguity in the record as to the extent of permitted development on ... the uplands." *Ante*, at 2460-2461. Two theories are offered to support this conclusion.

First, the Court asserts, it is "too late in the day" for the State to contend the uplands give the property more than $200,000 in value; Palazzolo "stated" in his petition for certiorari that the property has "an estimated worth of $200,000," and the State cited that contention "as fact" in its Brief in Opposition. *Ante*, at 2460. But in the cited pages of its Brief in Opposition, the State simply said it "would" approve a "single home" worth $200,000. Brief in Opposition 4, 19. That statement does not foreclose the possibility that the State would also approve another home, adding further value to the property.

To be sure, the Brief in Opposition did overlook Palazzolo's change in his theory of the case, a change that, had it been asserted earlier, could have rendered insufficient the evidence the State intelligently emphasized below. But the State's failure to appreciate that Palazzolo had moved the pea to a different shell hardly merits the Court's waiver finding. The only precedent cited for the waiver, a footnote in *Lucas*, is not remotely on point. *Ante*, at 2460. The landowner in *Lucas* had invoked a "finding" of fact by the state court, and this Court deemed the State's challenge to that finding waived because the challenge was not timely raised. *Lucas*, 505 U.S., at 1020-1022, n. 9, 112 S.Ct. 2886. There is nothing extraordinary about this Court's deciding a case on the findings made by a state court. Here, however, the "fact" this Court has stopped the State from contesting—that the property has value of only $200,000—was never found by any court. That valuation was simply asserted, inaccurately, *see* infra, at 2458, in Palazzolo's petition for certiorari. This Court's waiver ruling thus amounts to an unsavory invitation to unscrupulous litigants: Change your theory and misrepresent the record in your petition for certiorari; if the respondent fails to note your machinations, you have created a different record on which this Court will review the case.

The Court bolsters its waiver finding by asserting that the $200,000 figure is "well founded" in the record. *Ante*, at 2460. But, as earlier observed, an absence of multiple valuation possibilities in the record cannot be held against the State, for proof of more than the $200,000 development was unnecessary to defend against the Lucas claim singularly pleaded below. And in any event, the record does not warrant the Court's conclusion.

The Court acknowledges "testimony at trial suggesting the existence of an additional upland parcel elsewhere on the property" on which a second house might be built. *Ante*, at 2460. The Court discounts that prospect, however, on the ground that development of the additional parcel would require a new road forbidden under CRMC's regulations. *Ibid.* Yet the one witness on whose testimony the Court relies, Steven M. Clarke, himself concluded that it would be "realistic to apply for" development at more than one location. Tr. 612 (June 25-26, 1997). Clarke added that a state official, Russell Chateauneuf, "gave [Clarke] supporting information saying that [multiple applications] made sense." *Ibid.* The conclusions of Clarke and Chateauneuf are confirmed by the testimony of CRMC's executive director, Grover Fugate, who agreed with Palazzolo's counsel during cross-examination that Palazzolo might be able to build "on two, perhaps three, perhaps four of the lots." *Id.*, at 211 (June 20-23, 1997); *see* also Tr. of Oral Arg. 27 ("[T]here is ... uncertainty as to what additional upland there is and how many other houses can be built.").

The ambiguities in the record thus are substantial. They persist in part because their resolution was not required to address the claim Palazzolo presented below, and in part because Palazzolo failed ever to submit an accurate survey of his property. Under the circumstances, I would not step into the role of supreme topographical factfinder to resolve ambiguities in Palazzolo's favor. Instead, I would look to, and rely on, the opinion of the state court whose decision we now review. That opinion states: "There was undisputed evidence in the record that it would be possible to build at least one single-family home on the existing upland area." 746 A.2d, at 714 (emphasis added). This Court cites nothing to warrant amendment of that finding.

In sum, as I see this case, we still do not know "the nature and extent of permitted development" under the regulation in question, MacDonald, 477 U.S., at 351, 106 S.Ct. 2561. I would therefore affirm the Rhode Island Supreme Court's judgment.

[Footnotes omitted.]

Justice BREYER, dissenting.

I agree with Justice GINSBURG that Palazzolo's takings claim is not ripe for adjudication, and I join her opinion in full. Ordinarily I would go no further. But because the Court holds the takings claim to be ripe and goes on to address some important issues of substantive takings law, I add that, given this Court's precedents, I would agree with Justice O'CONNOR that the simple fact that a piece of property has changed hands (for example, by inheritance) does not always and automatically bar a takings claim. Here, for example, without in any way suggesting that Palazzolo has any valid takings claim, I believe his postregulatory acquisition of the property (through automatic operation of law) by itself should not prove dispositive.

As Justice O'CONNOR explains, under *Penn Central Transp. Co. v. New York City*, 438 U.S. 104, 98 S.Ct. 2646, 57 L.Ed.2d 631 (1978), much depends upon whether, or how, the timing and circumstances of a change of ownership affect whatever reasonable investment-backed expectations might otherwise exist. Ordinarily, such expectations will diminish in force and significance—rapidly and dramatically—as property continues to change hands over time. I believe that such factors can adequately be taken into account within the *Penn Central* framework.

Several *amici* have warned that to allow complete regulatory takings claims, *see Lucas v. South Carolina Coastal Council*, 505 U.S. 1003, 112 S.Ct. 2886, 120 L.Ed.2d 798 (1992), to survive changes in land ownership could allow property owners to manufacture such claims by strategically transferring property until only a nonusable portion remains. *See, e.g.*, Brief for Daniel W. Bromley *et al.* as *Amici Curiae* 7-8. But I do not see how a constitutional provision concerned with "'fairness and justice,'" *Penn Central, supra*, at 123-124, 98 S.Ct. 2646 (quoting *Armstrong v. United States*, 364 U.S. 40, 49, 80 S.Ct. 1563, 4 L.Ed.2d 1554 (1960)), could reward any such strategic behavior.

And finally, even if the developer bought the property before enactment of the Clean Water Act, there is not an automatic taking resulting from a permit denial.

WALCEK v. UNITED STATES

49 Fed.Cl. 248 (2001)

This regulatory taking case is before the court following a trial held in Wilmington, Delaware, and Bethany Beach, Delaware. Plaintiffs seek just compensation under the Fifth Amendment because the Army Corps of Engineers (the Corps) failed to grant a requested permit to allow for the full development of Federal wetlands on plaintiffs' property. Instead, the Corps issued a limited permit allowing only for a scaled down development, one which plaintiffs claim is not economically viable. Based on the evidence presented, and for the reasons set forth below, the court concludes that plaintiffs are not entitled to recover, as no taking of their property has occurred.

I. FINDINGS OF FACTS

Plaintiffs own 14.5 acres of real property in Bethany Beach, Delaware (the Property). In 1971, shortly before the enactment of the Clean Water Act, [footnote omitted] plaintiffs (and two other individuals no longer owners) [footnote omitted] purchased the Property in two separate transactions for a total price of $117,731. As the accompanying map [omitted] indicates, the four parcels that constitute the Property are approximately 1,500 feet deep and have approximately 570 feet frontage on Maryland Route 26, as well as over 400 feet on the Bethany Beach Loop Canal that runs parallel to Route 26. The alignment of the Property provides potential access to Central Boulevard, which, in turn, allows access to Bethany Beach without having to use the often-crowded Route 26. A topographic survey indicates that the elevation of the Property decreases significantly from the front of the Property (along Route 26) to the back of the Property (along the Bethany Loop Canal). The area nearest the highway is forested land dominated by red maples; as one moves farther away from the highway and steadily downward towards the Canal, the Property shifts from being populated by marsh elder and bushes, to a high salt marsh characterized by common reed (*e.g.*, phragmites), and, ultimately, to a salt marsh vegetated primarily by salt marsh cordgrass.

Of the 14.5 acres at issue, 13.2 acres are federally regulated wetlands under Section 404 of the Clean Water Act, 33 U.S.C. §1344, thereby requiring any filling of this property to be approved in a permit issued by the Corps. The 13.2 acres of wetlands includes tidal and non-tidal wetlands. Somewhere between 4.5 and 5.2 acres of the wetlands, lying on the portion of the Property closest to the Bethany Beach Loop Canal, are mapped as state wetlands by the State of Delaware (the State) and generally consist of tidal wetlands. Any filling of this property would require approval from the State under its Wetland Act, 7 De.C. §§6601, et seq. [Footnote omitted.] Portions of the Property are interlaced with drainage ditches, called "mosquito ditches" in the local jargon, that were installed by the Corps in the latter part of the 1930s. These tidal ditches, as well as other low-lying portions of the tidal wetlands on the site, are below the mean high water mark, and as such, are subject to regulation under Section 10 of the Rivers and Harbors Act of 1899, 33 U.S.C. §403.

Mr. Stanley Walcek, owner and representative of the co-owners of the Property and a retired attorney, has been familiar with the Bethany Beach area since 1961, when he invested in property in the area. He and his family stayed in the area during summers and eventually moved there. In 1969, Mr. Walcek was approached by the prior owners of three of the four parcels at issue, regarding the potential sale of their property. Discussions with these owners and their sons eventually prompted the plaintiffs to purchase three of the four parcels in September of 1971, for a price of approximately $108,000. In October of 1971, Mr. Walcek was advised by a realtor that there was an adjoining parcel available for purchase. Within weeks, plaintiffs purchased this fourth parcel, which contains about 1.25 acres of uplands, for a price of approximately $8,000. [Footnote omitted.]

Plaintiffs purchased the entire Property with the intent of developing it, with Mr. Walcek, who invested in 12 pieces of property between 1957 and 1976, being "the motivating force" in this regard. Mr. Walcek made all the decisions regarding the development of the Property, but consulted his partners about matters involving any significant outlays of money. [Footnote omitted.] At trial, Mr. Walcek testified that the plaintiffs purchased the Property with the intent of supplementing their retirement incomes. The Property was zoned for residential purposes, with each house required to have at least 5,000 square feet, thereby permitting approximately eight houses per acre. Before purchasing the Property, neither Mr. Walcek nor any of the other plaintiffs conducted any systematic studies of the Property, regarding such things as soil type, underground springs, or other circumstances that might impact on its suitability for development. Nor, prior to the purchase, did any of the plaintiffs contact any engineering or land-use consultants regarding the Property, or attempt to secure any information regarding any existing or impending federal restrictions on the development of the Property.

Almost from the outset, the plaintiffs were interested in having the Property zoned "commercial," in hopes that such a zoning change would cause the value of the Property to skyrocket. Toward that end, in 1974, plaintiffs submitted a concept plan to the Bethany Beach Town Zoning and Planning Commission (the Planning Commission) in an effort to have the front part of the Property, from Central Boulevard to Route 26, which encompasses about six or seven acres, zoned as commercial. This plan proposed that a canal be dredged from the Bethany Beach Loop Canal through the center of the Property, with mixed commercial and residential development on either side. In the face of public opposition, plaintiffs abandoned this plan in the mid-1980s, withdrawing the rezoning application, based, in part, on their belief that it would most certainly be denied by the Planning Commission. Indeed, John Eckrich, the building inspector for the town of Bethany Beach, testified at trial that he knew of "no residential land [in Bethany Beach] that has been zoned commercially since the 70s." In approximately September of 1987, plaintiffs shifted gears and envisioned filling the entire property, to allow for a border-to-border 77-lot residential development.

Mr. Walcek testified that he first realized that the Property was subject to wetlands regulation in early March of 1984, when he and the other plaintiffs entered into a conditional contract to sell the land for $1 million to J. Kiernan and others. When Mr. Kiernan submitted the contract to plaintiffs, he proposed building on only a portion of the Property, excluding the state wetland areas. By its terms, this contract was "contingent upon [Mr. Kiernan] obtaining all necessary permits for the construction and sales [sic] of 60 or more townhouse units upon the subject property." [Footnote omitted.] Following this event, later in 1984, Mr. Walcek requested that the Corps verify the exact contours of the state and federal wetlands on the Property. Still later that year, the Corps notified plaintiffs that the Property included 13.2 acres of federally regulated wetlands, approximately four to five acres of which were also state tidal wetlands. By the time they received this information, plaintiffs had released Kiernan from the contract, at his request.

Despite receiving notification from the Corps that 13.2 of the 14.5 acres of the Property constituted wetlands, plaintiffs, between 1984 and 1987, began filling and developing the Property without the required federal and state permits. According to Mr. Walcek, these efforts were designed to clear the Property, in hopes that it would dry out and no longer be considered wetlands. Toward this end, the Plaintiffs hired an individual to install a temporary road, to cut out the underbrush and to thin the trees on the wooded portion of the Property. At the same time, plaintiffs also sought to clean, maintain and gate the drainage ditches, in an effort to promote better drainage of the Property. Once becoming aware of these developments, the Corps, on May 27, 1986, issued a cease and desist order, requiring plaintiffs to discontinue filling and clearing activities on the Property, activities, the Corps asserted, violated the Clean Water Act, 33 U.S.C. §§1251, et seq. (1982). Under this order, plaintiffs were required to remove the unauthorized fill material from the Federal wetlands within 30 days. Ultimately, although not within the original time period specified, plaintiffs complied with the order.

On February 22, 1988, plaintiffs submitted to the Corps an application under section 404 of the Clean Water Act, 33 U.S.C. §1344 (1988), for authority to fill and develop the land. Plaintiffs apparently filed this application before applying for a state permit because the state wetlands were encompassed within the federal wetlands. The Corps rejected the application as incomplete. Instead of providing the information that had been requested by the Corps, plaintiffs chose to pursue a declaratory judgment action-which ultimately was dismissed by the U.S. District Court for the District of Delaware. In 1992, plaintiffs requested that the Corps reactivate their application and then, on November 20, 1992, after their declaratory action had been dismissed, plaintiffs chose to submit an entirely new application for a 77-lot "border to border" development. On June 8, 1993, plaintiffs responded to questions raised by the Corps and supplemented their application to include more specifics regarding, *inter alia*, the proposed use of bulkheading, drainage ditches and fill material.

In order to develop the wetlands, plaintiffs also needed to acquire a Coastal Zone Management Consistency Certification and a Section 401 Water Quality Certification from the State of Delaware. On June 25, 1993, plaintiffs notified the Delaware Department of Natural Resources and Environmental Control (DNREC) that their development plans could not conform to the Delaware Coastal Zone Management Plan regulations regarding the destruction of wetlands. [Footnote omitted.] On July 23, 1993, DNREC notified plaintiffs that their development project, as planned, was inconsistent with DNREC policies, and, therefore, it could not issue a Coastal Zone Management Consistency Certification. In the letter, the DNREC suggested that alternatives were available for development of the Property, including a "scaled down" development proposal that would fill less acreage and preserve the majority of the wetlands. [Footnote omitted.]

On December 20, 1993, after receiving notice of DNREC's denial of the required consistency certificate, the Corps notified plaintiffs that because Delaware had determined that the project was inconsistent with the Delaware Coastal Zone Management Program, the Corps was denying, without prejudice, the plaintiffs' section 404 permit application pursuant to 33 C.F.R. §§320.4(j) and 325.2(b). [Footnote omitted.] On January 6, 1994, the DNREC notified plaintiffs that their Section 401 Water Quality Certification application had been inactivated because of the Corps' denial of their federal application. On May 13, 1994, plaintiffs filed this lawsuit, alleging that defendant's December 20, 1993, denial of a section 404 permit constituted a taking of plaintiffs' property.

Subsequently, in August of 1995, in what he then described as "an addendum to the application," Mr. Walcek sent the Corps a plat showing four alternatives for use of the Property that did not involve a border-to-border development. On February 1, 1996, the Corps responded to these proposals indicating that it might approve an alternative that would utilize the upland portion of the Property and two segments of the wetlands adjacent to Route 26. This letter also noted the possibility that plaintiffs might enter an agreement to mitigate the loss of wetlands by creating or enhancing wetlands elsewhere. [Footnote omitted.] On April 11, 1996, Mr. Walcek attended a meeting with state and federal officials, presenting an alternate plan for developing the Property that would have required the filling and disturbance of approximately 8 acres of federal wetlands. On April 15, 1996, plaintiffs submitted an "Alternatives Analysis of the Walcek Property Proposed Development Plans" to the Corps, which proposed a number of different options for developing the Property, including less-extensive developments than that proposed in the 1992 application.

In response, on July 3, 1996, the Corps sent plaintiffs a letter proposing three development proposals, indicating that these proposals were being made "[i]n an effort to provide you with more specific guidance concerning what would have a better chance of being permitted." The three proposals included a 28-lot single family subdivision plan, as well as alternate configurations allowing for a 26-lot subdivision and a 36-unit townhouse development. On August 7, 1996, Corps officials met with Mr. Walcek to discuss these proposals. On August 30 and September 26, 1996, the Corps informed plaintiffs that they must "demonstrate why the [three] proposals currently under consideration would not be practicable" before the Corps would consider alternative development proposals from plaintiffs. The Corps further stated that it would issue a decision shortly, after which plaintiffs would be responsible for applying for State Water Quality and Coastal Zone Consistency Certifications.

Plaintiffs responded in letters dated September 13 and October 19, 1996, asserting that the three alternative proposals were infeasible and unacceptable for various reasons (amplified at trial), among them: (i) plaintiffs were concerned the 28-lot plan would neither be approved by the Town of Bethany Beach nor the State of Delaware because it used wetlands; (ii) plaintiffs complained that the pads in the proposed development were smaller than allowed by zoning and smaller than pads on competing lots, which would make them difficult to sell profitably; (iii) plaintiffs were concerned whether the Town would permit a lot it owned adjacent to the Property to be used for access to Central Boulevard—access that was critical to the viability of the proposed development; (iv) plaintiffs complained that the proposals utilized only a small portion of the wetlands and would not result in an acceptable return on the partners' investment; and (v) the proposals utilized uplands property for which plaintiffs had not sought a permit. [Footnote omitted.] Notwithstanding these concerns, on November 4, 1996, the Corps issued a permit authorizing a 28-lot residential development, consisting of two separate cul-de-sacs, one with direct access to Route 26 and the other with proposed access to Central Boulevard. [Footnote omitted.] Under the permit, the Corps allowed for the filling of up to 2.2 acres of federally regulated wetlands on the Property, focusing that development on portions of the Property that contained what was viewed as less environmentally-significant flora (*e.g.*, the phragmites). As a condition, however, the permit required the permittee to engage in mitigation by creating or restoring 4.4 acres of other wetlands.

In their complaint, plaintiffs sought compensation for both a permanent and temporary taking of the Property. They alleged that the Corps' 1993 decision denying, without prejudice, their permit request rendered the viable economic value of the Property useless and constituted a taking. In addition, they alleged that the delay between the cease and desist letter issued by the Corps in 1986 and the 1993 decision on the permit request amounted to a temporary taking of the Property.

On November 20, 1996, defendant filed a motion for summary judgment, arguing that, as a matter of law, neither a permanent nor a temporary taking had occurred. On December 4, 1997, plaintiffs filed a "Motion for Alternative Relief," which included a partial motion for summary judgment, arguing that genuine issues of fact existed in this case. Subsequently, this case was assigned to the undersigned judge. In an opinion dated August 11, 1999, this court held that, regarding plaintiffs' temporary taking claim, there were no genuine issues of material fact and that defendant was entitled to judgment as a matter of law. The court also held that the denial, in 1993, of plaintiffs' permit request did not effectuate a taking, as such denial was without prejudice.[13] Accordingly, the court believed that the focus of the case was on whether the 1996 permit effectuated a compensable taking. Regarding this claim, the court held that there were genuine issues of material fact concerning the value of the property allegedly taken, the value of the property remaining and plaintiffs' reasonable investment-backed expectations, which issues precluded the granting of summary judgment for either party.

Based on this summary judgment order, trial in this case was limited to the issue of whether a regulatory taking took place when the Corps issued the limited 1996 permit, which did not allow plaintiffs to develop, as planned, the Property. [Footnote omitted.] As described in greater detail below, resolution of that issue requires the court to consider three factors identified in *Penn Cent. Transp. Co. v. New York City*, 438 U.S. 104, 98 S.Ct. 2646, 57 L.Ed.2d 631 (1978), focusing on: (i) the character of the government action; (ii) the extent to which the regulation interferes with reasonable investment backed expectations; and (iii) the economic impact of the regulation on plaintiffs' property. In an effort to address these factors, each side presented an appraisal report, as well as other reports and testimony by several experts. Laurence Moynihan and Joseph N. Melson, Jr., both real estate appraisers, were the primary expert witnesses for plaintiff and defendant, respectively. They each valued various development proposals, two of which are potentially relevant here—the 77-lot development proposed by the plaintiffs and the 28-lot proposal authorized by the 1996 permit.

Mr. Moynihan prepared two appraisals of the 77-lot development. In the first of these, drafted in September of 1994, Mr. Moynihan evaluated the value of the proposed subdivision as of December 1993, using both the bulk sales and discounted cash flow methods. Under the bulk sales method, Mr. Moynihan relied on five comparable sales, adjusted them to take into account characteristic differences between the land sold and the Property, and derived a value of $2,310,000. Under the discounted cash flow method, Mr. Moynihan reviewed fifteen different sales and estimated a per lot value of $65,000 for the dry lots and $85,000 for the lots considered "wet," presumably those nearest the Bethany Loop Canal. Mr. Moynihan then estimated that the cost of developing the Property was approximately $700,000, or $9,000 per lot. In addition, Mr. Moynihan added a separate category for filling the land with 24,600 cubic yards of fill to bring the Property to a uniform elevation of four feet, adding a cost (at $5.00 per cubic yard) of $130,000 for site preparation. Based on a three-year sell out period, and applying additional deductions, *inter alia*, of 1.5 percent for transfer taxes, seven percent for sales commissions and

---

[13] In its opinion, this court noted that the ripeness doctrine enunciated in cases such as *Williamson County Reg'l Planning Comm'n v. Hamilton Bank*, 473 U.S. 172, 105 S.Ct. 3108, 87 L.Ed.2d 126 (1985), has been applied to federal takings claims. The court noted that in *Cristina Inv. Corp. v. United States*, 40 Fed.Cl. 571, 574, appeal dismissed, 155 F.3d 570 (Fed.Cir.1998), this court explained "[t]hat doctrine provides that a governmental denial will be considered final, and any federal takings claim arising from that denial will therefore accrue, if the property owner made a proper application which the government denied both on the merits and in such a manner as to reveal that reapplication for a modified plan would be futile." Applying this standard, the court concluded that while the Corps' 1993 decision denying plaintiffs' permit request "without prejudice" did not appear to be reviewable, the 1996 decision by the Corp to issue a limited permit clearly was a final reviewable determination, particularly as defendant's counsel had conceded that the 1996 permit was the broadest permit that the Corps is prepared to issue. *See* also *MacDonald, Sommer & Frates v. Yolo County*, 477 U.S. 340, 348, 106 S.Ct. 2561, 91 L.Ed.2d 285 (1986) (property owners submitted only one subdivision proposal rejected by a zoning body; as alternative uses of the site existed other than the one proposed, the takings claim was unripe because the zoning body had not yet rendered "a final and authoritative determination of the type and intensity of development legally permitted on the subject property"); *Howard W. Heck and Assocs. v. United States*, 134 F.3d 1468 (Fed.Cir.1998). *Cf. Cooley v. United States*, 46 Fed.Cl. 538 (2000) (holding permit denial a final decision where it would be futile for party to submit modified application for permit).

18 percent for profit, Mr. Moynihan derived a series of cash flows to be generated by the Property, which he then discounted at a rate of 12 percent to arrive at the present value of the Property. This discounted cash flow analysis resulted in a figure of $2,342,000 for the "before" value of the Property. The appraisal indicated that the value of the Property with wetlands restrictions fully in effect, thereby allowing development only on the uplands portion of the Property, was $352,000.

Mr. Moynihan updated his earlier report in March of 2000, setting a new value for the Property as of November 4, 1996. In this later report, Mr. Moynihan used only the bulk sales method and evaluated the Property under two scenarios-a 77-lot development and a 116-unit townhouse development. In making these valuations, Mr. Moynihan used five bulk land sales comparisons to determine that each buildable townhouse unit on the Property would have a value of $22,700 and that each lot would have a value of $34,195. In making these assessments, Mr. Moynihan adjusted the figures relating to allegedly comparable sales in the area downward due to the comparatively worse size and topography of the lots on the Property. Relying on this approach, Mr. Moynihan's report concluded that the "before" value of the Property, without state or federal wetlands regulations in place, was $2,633,000.

The Government's expert, Joseph N. Melson, Jr. appraised the 77-lot development plan, as of November 4, 1996, at $1,065,000 using a bulk sales comparison approach, and at $950,000 using the discounted cash flow approach. His report differed from that of Moynihan in several major respects. First, in appraising the development, he first reduced the proposal from 77 to 71 lots, relying on the advice of Stephen Soule, a registered professional civil engineer who testified on behalf of defendant, that approximately six lots would be lost because of storm water management needs that had not been accounted for in the plans. Second, Mr. Melson believed the development costs for the 71-lot development under the discount cash flow method were closer to $1,500,000, $670,000 higher than the figure employed by Mr. Moynihan. [Footnote omitted.] Mr. Melson deducted $1,500,000 in development costs from the sum of the "before" retail value of the Property of $4,640,000 (65 dry lots at a total of $4,190,000 and six waterfront lots at $450,000). He then further reduced the value of the property by seven percent for sales commissions, 20 percent for profit and three percent for taxes and administrative costs. This process yielded a total appraised value of a 71-lot development of $950,000. [Footnote omitted.]

The two appraisers also assigned different values to the 28-lot development plan approved by the Corps. Plaintiffs' appraiser took his estimate of the value of the Property without restriction ($2,633,000) and then deducted the value of the uplands, to arrive at the value of the property subject to federal and state wetlands regulation. By dividing the remaining property by the number of remaining acres, Mr. Moynihan determined that the wetlands, if permitted, were worth $173,744 per acre. As the 28-lot permit was designed to allow plaintiff to fill 2.2 acres, this yielded a figure of $382,237. To this, Mr. Moynihan added the value of the uplands ($377,500) and the value of the remaining untouched wetlands at $1,125 per acre, and then subtracted $187,000 in mitigation costs (4.4 acres at $42,500 per acre). Plaintiffs' appraiser thus concluded that, in 1996, the total value of the 28-lot development plan was $545,000.

By comparison, Mr. Melson valued the 28-lot development plan at $650,000. Applying a discounted cash flow model, Mr. Melson first used what he believed were comparable sales to arrive at a per lot average sale price of $64,650. Based on information received from Messrs. Launay and Soule, Melson estimated the development costs at $13,807 per lot, including the cost of wetlands mitigation elsewhere, and then deducted amounts for sales commissions, administrative expenses and profit over the two years he believed would be necessary to sell the developed lots. Relying on these assumptions and then employing a 12 percent present value factor, Mr. Melson determined that the 28-lot development was worth $630,000, plus the value of the wetlands as undeveloped of $17,500 (using comparables that yielded 10 acres at $1,750 per acre), producing a total value of approximately $650,000. Applying a bulk sales approach, Mr. Melson reviewed comparable sales, made adjustments to those figures (overall increasing their value) and concluded that the value of the Property was approximately $22,500 per lot, or $630,000. From this figure, Mr. Melson deducted $62,600 for mitigation-related costs (approximately $125,000 less than the figure employed by Mr. Moynihan), [footnote omitted] leaving a value for the 28-lot development under this approach of $565,000. Comparing this value to that derived from the discounted cash flow method, Mr. Melson ultimately concluded that, as of November 4, 1996, the 28-lot development scenario should be $650,000. In making this determination, Mr. Melson assumed that "the necessary remaining permits are obtained for developing the parcel," and, unlike Mr. Moynihan did not discount his figure to take into account the possibility that such permits might not be received.

II. DISCUSSION

The Takings Clause of the Fifth Amendment provides: "[N]or shall private property be taken for public use, without just compensation." U.S. Const. Amend. V. As recently explained by the Supreme Court, "[t]he aim of the Clause is to prevent the government 'from forcing some people alone to bear public burdens which, in all fairness and justice, should be borne by the public as a whole.'" *Eastern Enterprises v. Apfel*, 524 U.S. 498, 522, 118 S.Ct. 2131, 141 L.Ed.2d 451 (1998) (quoting *Armstrong v. United States*, 364 U.S. 40, 49, 80 S.Ct. 1563, 4 L.Ed.2d 1554 (1960)). Along these lines, Justice Holmes long ago opined that, "while property may be regulated to a certain extent, if regulation goes too far it will be recognized as a taking." *Pennsylvania Coal Co. v. Mahon*, 260 U.S. 393, 415, 43 S.Ct. 158, 67 L.Ed. 322 (1922). This oft-quoted language is the genesis of the so-called regulatory takings doctrine, first invoked to challenge mining and zoning laws, but here invoked in the context of the Federal program for the management and protection of wetlands. Plaintiffs allege that the permit issued by the Corps under that program, which allows only partial development of the Property, so diminished the value of their property as to effectuate a permanent taking.

A property owner may show that the government has effectuated a "categorical taking" by demonstrating that a regulation has denied the property owner of "all economically beneficial or productive use of land." *Lucas v. South Carolina Coastal Council*, 505 U.S. 1003, 1015, 112 S.Ct. 2886, 120 L.Ed.2d 798 (1992). Such is not the case here. Even if a property owner is unable to demonstrate such a categorical taking, he or she may be able to prove that the government affected a compensable "partial taking." *Florida Rock Indus., Inc. v. United States*, 18 F.3d 1560, 1570 (Fed.Cir.1994), cert. denied, 513 U.S. 1109, 115 S.Ct. 898, 130 L.Ed.2d 783 (1995). In such cases, the court must conduct a series of "*ad hoc*, factual inquiries" into the circumstances to determine whether there is a taking. *See Kaiser Aetna v. United States*, 444 U.S. 164, 175, 100 S.Ct. 383, 62 L.Ed.2d 332 (1979). *See* also *Connolly v. Pension Benefit Guar. Corp.*, 475 U.S. 211, 224, 106 S.Ct. 1018, 89 L.Ed.2d 166 (1986) (definition of a taking not controlled by "any set formula," but is dependent on "*ad hoc*, factual inquiries into the circumstances of each particular case"). In 1978, the Supreme Court, attempting to add a skeletal framework to this inquiry, identified three factors that are particularly significant in determining whether governmental action constitutes a taking: (1) "[t]he economic impact of the regulation on the claimant;" (2) "the extent to which the regulation has interfered with distinct investment-backed expectations;" and (3) "the character of the governmental action." *Penn Central Transp. Co. v. City of New York*, 438 U.S. 104, 124, 98 S.Ct. 2646, 57 L.Ed.2d 631 (1978). [Footnote omitted.] The court will review the application of these factors, and the evidence that relates to them, seriatim.

A. ECONOMIC IMPACT

The first criterion—the economic impact of the regulation—is "intended to ensure that not every restraint imposed by government to adjust the competing demands of private owners would result in a takings claim." *Loveladies Harbor*, 28 F.3d at 1176. *See* also *Pennsylvania Coal*, 260 U.S. at 413, 43 S.Ct. 158 ("Government hardly could go on if to some extent values incident to property could not be diminished without paying for every such change in the general law"). The focus of this factor is on the change in the fair market value of the subject property caused by the regulatory imposition—in other words, the court must "compare the value that has been taken from the property with the value that remains in the property." *Keystone Bituminous Coal Ass'n v. DeBenedictis*, 480 U.S. 470, 497, 107 S.Ct. 1232, 94 L.Ed.2d 472 (1987). *See* also *Penn Central*, 438 U.S. at 130-31, 98 S.Ct. 2646; *Florida Rock*, 18 F.3d at 1567. As will be seen, this prong of the *Penn Central* inquiry actually involves several tiers of analysis.

1. THE "PARCEL AS A WHOLE"

The economic analysis under the first *Penn Central* factor is often expressed in the form of a fraction, the numerator of which is the value of the subject property encumbered by regulation and the denominator of which is the value of the same property not so encumbered. As a threshold matter, in order to derive this fraction, the court must first define the subject property to be valued, or, in the terms of the Supreme Court in *Penn Central*, ascertain the "parcel as a whole." "This issue is particularly important for wetland cases," one commentator has noted, "because permit denials or conditions are frequently directed only to the wetland portions of properties that invariably contain uplands." Mark A. Chertok, *Federal Regulation of Wetlands* (hereinafter "Chertok"), SE98 ALI-ABA 715, 779 (2000). Thus, to the extent the property captured in the denominator includes only wetlands, the impact of the regulation in diminishing the value of the corresponding numerator is predictably more pronounced, and thus more indicative of a taking, than would be the case if the same denominator were to include not only the wetlands, but also the uplands and other property unrestricted by the regulation. Given this, it should come as little surprise that defendant argues that the Property, in its entirety, constitutes this "parcel as a whole," while plaintiffs assert that only the wetlands portion of the Property, for which the permit application was actually submitted, should be considered.

The Supreme Court has provided guidance on how to identify the requisite "parcel as a whole," sometimes referring to this as the "denominator issue."[19] In *Penn Central*, where it held that air rights over Grand Central station could not be considered separately from other contiguous property in analyzing whether a landmark law effected a taking, the Court opined that takings

---

[19] In *Keystone Bituminous Coal Ass'n v. DeBenedictis*, 480 U.S. 470, 107 S.Ct. 1232, 94 L.Ed.2d 472 (1987), the Supreme Court phrased this problem in the following terms:

> Because our test for regulatory takings requires us to compare the value that has been taken from the property with the value that remains in the property, one of the critical questions is determining how to define the unit of property 'whose value is to furnish the denominator of the fraction.' *Id.* at 497, 107 S.Ct. 1232 (quoting Frank Michelman, *Property, Utility, and Fairness: Comments on the Ethical Foundations of "Just Compensation" Law*, 80 Harv. L.Rev. 1165, 1192 (1967)).

law "does not divide a single parcel into discrete segments and attempt to determine whether rights in a particular segment have been entirely abrogated." *Penn Central*, 438 U.S. at 130, 98 S.Ct. 2646. The Court doubly stressed this principle in its post-*Lucas* decision in *Concrete Pipe & Products, Inc. of California v. Construction Laborers Pension Trust*, 508 U.S. 602, 113 S.Ct. 2264, 124 L.Ed.2d 539 (1993), first stating that "[t]o the extent that any portion of property is taken, that portion is always taken in its entirety; the relevant question, however, is whether the property taken is all, or only a portion of, the parcel in question." 508 U.S. at 644, 113 S.Ct. 2264. In the same opinion, the Court went on to recollect that, in its earlier decision in *Penn Central*, it had concluded that "a claimant's parcel of property could not first be divided into what was taken and what was left for the purpose of demonstrating the taking of the former to be complete and hence compensable." *Id. See* also *Dolan v. City of Tigard*, 512 U.S. 374, 400-01, 114 S.Ct. 2309, 129 L.Ed.2d 304 (1994) (summarizing cases); *Andrus v. Allard*, 444 U.S. 51, 65-66, 100 S.Ct. 318, 62 L.Ed.2d 210 (1979) ("[W]here an owner possesses a full 'bundle' of property rights, the destruction of one 'strand' of the bundle is not a taking, because the aggregate must be viewed in its entirety"). Various decisions of this court, the Federal Circuit and the Court of Claims affirm the application of these principles in wetlands taking cases. *See Tabb Lakes, Ltd. v. United States*, 10 F.3d 796 (Fed.Cir.1993); *Jentgen v. United States*, 228 Ct.Cl. 527, 657 F.2d 1210, 1212-13 (1981); *Ciampitti v. United States*, 22 Cl.Ct. 310, 318-19 (1991).

While the "nonsegmentation" principle established in these decisions is seemingly straightforward, the Supreme Court has cautioned that applying it often presents difficult line-drawing problems. *See Lucas*, 505 U.S. at 1016-17 n.7, 112 S.Ct. 2886. Heeding this warning and employing a somewhat holistic standard, this court has observed that "[t]he effort should be to identify the parcel as realistically and fairly as possible, given the entire factual and regulatory environment." *Ciampitti*, 22 Cl.Ct. at 319. *See* also *Keystone*, 480 U.S. at 499, 107 S.Ct. 1232 (property "is viewed in the context of any reasonable unit of petitioners' coal mining operations and financial-backed expectations..."); *Loveladies Harbor*, 28 F.3d at 1181 ("Our precedent displays a flexible approach, designed to account for factual nuances"). seeking to give effect to their view of the facts, plaintiffs rely on the recently decided *Palm Beach Isles Assocs. v. United States*, 208 F.3d 1374 (Fed.Cir.2000), on reh'g, supplemented, reaf'd, 231 F.3d 1354 (Fed.Cir.2000), as evidence that, in some circumstances, the *Penn Central* economic analysis focuses only on the portion of property for which a permit is being sought, *i.e.*, the wetlands.

In *Palm Beach*, the plaintiff purchased a 311.7 acre parcel in Florida in 1956. In 1968, it sold most of this land, but retained ownership of a 50.7 acre tract, consisting of 49.3 acres of lake bottom and 1.4 acres of adjacent shoreline. The Corps denied the plaintiff's application for a permit to dredge and fill this property, and plaintiff filed suit in this court, claiming the denial constituted a regulatory taking. This court concluded that for purposes of conducting the economic analysis, the relevant parcel was the entire 311.7 acres, and found, on that basis, that there was no regulatory taking. On appeal, the Federal Circuit rejected this court's denominator analysis and held that the relevant parcel was not the entire acreage originally purchased by the plaintiff, *i.e.*, the 311.7 acres, but rather only the 50.7 acres that plaintiff retained and was seeking to develop. 208 F.3d at 1380. In reaching this conclusion, the Federal Circuit focused on the fact that the two parcels—the 50.7 acres and the remainder—were separated by a road, never part of a common development scheme and were different types of property, subject to different zoning. It also heavily relied on the fact that all but 50.7 acres had been sold by the plaintiff in 1968, long before the development in question was proposed. *Id.* at 1380-81.

Defendant strenuously asserts that *Palm Beach* was wrongly decided and is inconsistent with prior Supreme Court and Federal Circuit precedent.[20] Whether this criticism is warranted or whether that decision instead represents a novel extension of takings jurisprudence, it remains that *Palm Beach* is clearly distinguishable on its facts. Unlike *Palm Beach*, the case sub judice is neither one in which a portion of the property was sold prior to the time a permit was sought, nor one in which uplands and the wetlands were zoned differently or intended to be developed separately. Rather, here, the Property is contiguous and unsubdivided; was purchased over a matter of a month or two, with uniform ownership; has been maintained for many years as a single parcel; has the same zoning status; and, in all the plans the partners advanced, has always been intended to be developed as a whole. Accordingly, the facts in this case stand in sharp contrast to those in *Palm Beach* and lead this court to conclude that, consistent with the economic realities in this case, it may not segment into smaller parcels, property that plaintiffs continuously have viewed and treated as inextricably linked since it was first acquired in 1971.

Indeed, in its critical features, this case factually resembles *Deltona Corp. v. United States*, 228 Ct.Cl. 476, 657 F.2d 1184 (1981), cert. denied, 455 U.S. 1017, 102 S.Ct. 1712, 72 L.Ed.2d 135 (1982). In that case, the plaintiff purchased a 10,000 acre parcel, including wetlands, with the intention of developing a residential community. While Deltona's master plan envisioned building the development in five stages, it assumed that the "community would be a thoroughly integrated, unified whole." 657 F.2d at 1188. Although Deltona was granted permits to dredge several portions of this property, following the passage of the Clean Water Act, it was denied permits to perform the same task on other portions of its property, leading it to file suit, alleging a taking, in the Court of Claims. Finding that the passage of the Clean Water Act frustrated Deltona's reasonable investment-backed expectations, the court, nonetheless, concluded that there was no taking because Deltona had derived other economic benefits from its property. Indicating that it was "important to bear in mind the Supreme Court's admonition" in *Penn Central, supra*, that "'[t]aking jurisprudence does not divide a single parcel into discrete segments,'" 657 F.2d at 1192 (quoting *Penn Central, supra*), the Court of Claims refused to focus solely on the parcels for which Deltona had previously been denied a permit, and instead considered the value of contiguous uplands, as well as other portions of the property on which permits had been granted. 657 F.2d at 1192-93. Applying this definition of "the parcel as whole," the Court found that Deltona could develop 111 acres of uplands without a permit, realizing therefrom a significant profit over what it originally paid for the entire parcel. Based on this finding, the court concluded that the permit denials did not result in a taking, but rather "some dimunition in value," as the regulations did "not deprive Deltona of the economically viable use of its land" because "Deltona's remaining land uses are plentiful and its residual economic position very great." *Id.* at 1192-93.

---

[20] For authority supporting defendant's view, *see Palm Beach Isles Associates, Inc. v. United States*, 231 F.3d 1365, 1366 (Fed.Cir.2000) (Gajarsa, J., dissenting from denial of petition for rehearing en banc). *See* also Note, Federal Circuit's Holding Introduces Subjective Factors into Takings Clause 'Denominator' Analysis, 114 Harv. L.Rev. 926, 930 (2001) (criticizing *Palm Beach* as allowing property owners to recast virtually any regulatory taking case into categorical taking by parsing their property into discrete units). *See* generally, John E. Fee, *Unearthing the Denominator in Regulatory Taking Claims*, 61 U. Chi. L.Rev. 1535, 1557 (1994) (indicating that "[t]hrough reliance on the subjective criteria of ownership and actual or intended use, courts have gone astray"). *Palm Beach, supra*, however, appears consistent with *Loveladies Harbor*, 28 F.3d at 1181, in which the Federal Circuit suggested that land "developed or sold before the regulatory environment existed" should not be included in the denominator. *See* also *Chertok, supra* at 781-83 (discussing these and other cases).

The Federal Circuit has followed *Deltona* on several occasions, most appositely, for our present purposes, in *Tabb Lakes, Ltd., supra*. In *Tabb Lakes, supra*, the court also rejected a contention that wetlands should be segregated from uplands in assessing the impact of a regulation on a contiguous property, stating:

> "While in some cases it may be difficult to determine whether all economic viable use of the "property" has been destroyed, that is not a serious problem here. Clearly, the quantum of land to be considered is not each individual lot containing wetlands or even the combined area of wetlands. If that were true, the Corps' protection of wetlands via a permit system would, *ipso facto*, constitute a taking in every case where it exercises its statutory authority. *Penn Central* ... negates that view." 10 F.3d at 802 (emphasis in original).

Similarly in Jentgen, 657 F.2d at 1213, the Federal Circuit held that the "parcel as a whole" constituted not only 80 acres of wetlands, but 20 acres of contiguous uplands, emphasizing, in so concluding, that "it is important to bear in mind the Supreme Court's admonition [in *Penn Central*]." This court, in turn, has recurringly applied these principles, with similar results, in various cases factually indistinguishable from the instant case.[21] Based upon these authorities and, in particular, their application to the facts of this case, this court thus finds that the denominator of the economic value fraction must be the value of the entire Property, unencumbered by wetlands regulations. Under this scenario, the court further finds that this denominator essentially corresponds to the value of the 77-lot border-to-border development plaintiffs have proposed. [Footnote omitted.]

But before assigning a value to this denominator, the court must yet resolve questions regarding the proper numerator to be used in the economic value fraction, that is, the value of the Property subject to wetlands regulations. Defendant argues that the 28-lot proposal offered by the Corps, in granting the permit in question, is viable and represents the best use of the property consistent with the wetland regulations. Plaintiffs, for their part, contend that this proposal is not economically viable and that the numerator of the fraction should essentially be the value of the uplands, augmented slightly by the value of the contiguous undeveloped wetlands. Plaintiffs note correctly that where the government offers to allow the partial development of property and seeks to establish a value for that development, it must show a "reasonable probability that the land is both physically adaptable for such use and that there is a demand for such use in the reasonably near future." *Loveladies Harbor*, 21 Cl.Ct. 153, 158 (1990) (quoting *United States v. 341.45 Acres of Land*, 633 F.2d 108, 111 (8th Cir.1980)), aff'd, 28 F.3d 1171 (Fed.Cir.1994). *See* also *Olson v. United States*, 292 U.S. 246, 255-56, 54 S.Ct. 704, 78 L.Ed. 1236 (1934); *Formanek v. United States*, 26 Cl.Ct. 332, 339 (1992).

---

[21] *See Forest Props. v. United States*, 39 Fed.Cl. 56, 73 (1997), aff'd, 177 F.3d 1360 (Fed.Cir.1999) (lake bottom/upland treated as single parcel where treated as single income-producing unit for purposes of financing, planning and development); *Broadwater Farms Joint Venture v. United States*, 35 Fed.Cl. 232 (1996), vacated on other grounds, 121 F.3d 727 (Fed.Cir.1997) (table) (12 lots on property treated as single parcel where intended to be developed as a whole); *Formanek v. United States*, 26 Cl.Ct. 332, 339 (1992) (12 acres of uplands included in a 112-acre tract); *Ciampitti*, 22 Cl.Ct. at 318-19 ("[i]n the case of a landowner who owns both wetlands and adjacent uplands, it would clearly be unrealistic to focus exclusively on the wetlands, and ignore whatever rights might remain in the uplands" where two properties, though not contiguous, were "inextricably linked in terms of purchasing and financing"). *Cf. Bowles v. United States*, 31 Fed.Cl. 37, 41 n. 4 (1994). Summarizing these cases, one commentator has observed that "the courts have assessed the degree of contiguity, dates of acquisition, the extent to which the parcel has been treated as a single unit (by both the owner and government), and the extent to which the undeveloped or protected lands enhance the value of the remaining lands." *Chertok* at 783.

In the instant case, the court finds that the 28-lot proposal is viable. Contrary to plaintiffs' claims, the evidence presented at trial, particularly the testimony of John Eckrich, Bethany Beach's building inspector, indicated that the 28-lot proposal would be consistent with the town's zoning requirements [Footnote omitted.] and likely would be approved by the town's planning commission. Various witnesses, including Mr. Eckrich and Mr. Launay, also testified that it was likely that the town would approve connecting the development to Central Avenue, allowing a road to be built over an unoccupied piece of land owned by the town. [Footnote omitted.] These and other witnesses essentially indicated that they believed that the town would welcome a development that would minimize the impact on the wetlands contained on the Property. Other concerns raised by plaintiffs—for example, that the lots in such a development might be smaller than those in competing developments—go not to the viability of the project, but to the value thereof, and, to the extent relevant, are discussed below.

2. ASSIGNING VALUES TO THE NUMERATOR AND DENOMINATOR

Having defined the subject property whose value, in two variations, is to be captured in the economic analysis fraction, the court must next place values on the numerator and denominator of the fraction, relying, for that purpose, on the extensive expert testimony and reports introduced at trial....

While the court believes that the expert testimony offered by the defendant's expert tends more accurately to reflect the true values of the 77-lot and 28-lot development, the court declines, for the reasons described below, to adopt outright either parties' valuations. The court will review the estimates for each of the two developments in turn.

I. THE DENOMINATOR—THE VALUE OF THE 77-LOT DEVELOPMENT

In evaluating the 77-lot development, both plaintiffs' expert witness, Mr. Moynihan, and defendant's expert, Mr. Melson, relied, to varying extent, on two methods of appraisal: (i) the bulk sales method, under which the value of the Property is derived solely by comparison to other sales; and (ii) the discounted cash flow method, in which comparable sales are used to establish gross revenue for the project, from which costs of development are then deducted, resulting in a stream of revenue that is then present valued using a discount factor to derive a value for the property. Since both of these methods begin with comparable sales, it is critical that the court finds that the comparables used by Mr. Melson more accurately reflect the value of the parcel in question than those employed by Mr. Moynihan. Indeed, virtually every comparable sale offered by Mr. Moynihan in his first report was challenged and refuted, convincingly, not only by the defendant's witnesses, but, in some cases, by Mr. Moynihan's own admissions on cross-examination. [Footnote omitted.] Nor is Mr. Moynihan's amended report any better as it appears that most of the comparison sales employed there involved properties with six or fewer units on an acre or less of property—sales that other witnesses persuasively testified were not comparable to the Property because of their relatively small size. [Footnote omitted.] By comparison, the comparables employed by Mr. Melson went virtually unchallenged by plaintiffs and appear to represent properties much more similar to the Property.

The quality of their respective comparables aside, the gap between the experts' estimates of the 77-lot development may be traced primarily to two factors: First, Mr. Melson adjusted the number of lots in the proposal downward from 77 to 71, based on plaintiffs' failure to account adequately in their plans for storm water management facilities. When asked about this point at trial, Mr. Moynihan did not contest this adjustment and the court, therefore, finds Mr. Melson's testimony on this point convincing. Second, the experts greatly disagreed regarding the cost of fill and other developments (*e.g.*, curbs, sewers, roads) needed to effectuate the 77-lot plan, with Mr. Moynihan estimating those costs at $830,000 and Mr. Melson setting the same figure at $1,468,800. On this latter count, the court finds Mr. Melson's testimony and report more credible for the reasons that follow.

In estimating the fill cost at $130,000, Mr. Moynihan relied on three major assumptions—first, that the fill quantity could be reduced by recycling soil excavated from other parts of the Property; second, that elevation figures he had been given regarding the topography of the Property were accurate; and third, that the Property needed to be filled only to a uniform level of 4.0 feet. Each of these assumptions, however, proved erroneous. Defendant's experts, Mr. Soule and Mr. Launay, convincingly demonstrated, both in their reports and their testimony, that: (i) the soil excavated on the Property could not be recycled because it would be full of organic material and sodium and thus particularly unfit for a housing development; (ii) Mr. Moynihan greatly underestimated the Property's fill needs because he relied on erroneous figures that were revealed, through a careful topography survey of the Property, to place the elevation of the Property more than a foot higher than it actually is; and (iii) the Property needed to be filled to a level of at least 4.5 feet, and, in some places, five feet, in order to avoid flooding the Property on a daily basis. Relying on the topographic survey of the Property referred to above, these witnesses calculated that the true fill needs were at least three times the estimate used by Mr. Moynihan (69,000 cubic yards versus 24,600 cubic yards). Based on the foregoing evidence, the court believes that these higher figures represent the better estimate of the true fill needs associated with the 71-lot development.

Further, in estimating development costs at $700,000, Mr. Moynihan did not follow industry standards and consult with an engineer, but instead allegedly utilized figures supplied in a guide published by the Marshall and Swift Valuation Service (the M & S guide). [Footnote omitted.] When pressed, however, Mr. Moynihan was unable to explain, in even the most rudimentary of details, how he used the guide to make these calculations, leading the court to conclude that his testimony on this point was wholly incredible. At all events, Mr. Soule, a civil engineer, testified that the figures provided by the M & S guide do not provide an adequate basis for evaluating the true costs of developing property in the Bethany Beach area. This point is borne out by the guide itself, which cautions that "[c]osts for residential street improvements vary greatly due to local code requirements for different materials, street types and layouts, and utilities. The following costs are averages including ordinary charges for engineering, plans and inspection." [Footnote omitted.] Taking into account the unusually low elevation of the Bethany Beach area, Mr. Soule submitted an expert report that estimated that the true development costs, including fill costs, were on the order of $20,687 per lot, for a total of $1,468,800. And his testimony was corroborated by Mr. Melson and by a further study provided by Mr. Launay. As such, the court concludes that the true development costs for the 77-lot development are represented by Mr. Melson's figure of $1,468,800, approximately $639,000 more than the figure Mr. Moynihan employed.

Based on the foregoing, the court concludes that plaintiffs have not shown that the Property, unrestricted by wetland regulations, is worth anywhere near the $2.6 million figure plaintiffs claim. At a bare minimum, the value plaintiffs ascribed to the 77-lot plan must be adjusted downward to account for: (i) the poor quality of the "comparables" employed by Mr. Moynihan; (ii) a reduction in the number of saleable lots from 77 to 71 to account for storm water management structures; and (iii) an increase in fill and development costs from $830,000 to $1,468,800. Because the court believes that the comparables employed by Mr. Melson better reflect the value of the Property, those figures should be used as the starting point for the value calculation, yielding an average cost per lot of $65,000. [Footnote omitted.] At the same point, the court has no reason, based upon the record, to question the other basic assumptions employed by Mr. Moynihan in his discounted cash flow method (*e.g.*, a three year sale period with two principal phases of development, two percent for administration/management, 18 percent for profit, seven percent for sales expenses, 1.5 percent for transfer taxes and 12 percent discount rate). Giving effect to these various findings and using a discounted cash flow method otherwise similar to the approach employed by Mr. Moynihan, the resulting value of the Property under the 71 lot scenario would be approximately $1,485,000 (*see* Appendix A [omitted]). The court believes that this figure represents an accurate estimate of the value of the denominator in the economic analysis fraction.[30]

II. The Numerator—The Value of the 28-Lot Development

Both appraisers also ascribed values to the proposed 28-lot development—Mr. Melson set the value at $650,000, while Mr. Moynihan estimated it at $545,000. While the approaches employed by the appraisers differed dramatically, [footnote omitted] the different values they derived were driven by the differences in their respective estimates of the cost of providing the 4.4 acres of wetlands mitigation required by the Corps permit. In this regard, Mr. Melson's appraisal, which relied on a figure supplied by Mr. Launay, set the mitigation costs at $62,600 ($45,800 for the mitigation work and $16,800 for acquiring the land), or approximately $14,227 per acre. By comparison, Mr. Moynihan, assertedly relying on information provided by Mr. Charles Miller, a wetlands biologist who had supervised other mitigation efforts, estimated the cost of mitigation to be approximately $187,000, or approximately $42,500 per acre.

Based on the evidence presented, the court believes that the true cost of mitigation lies somewhere between the parties' estimates. The basis for Mr. Launay's estimate, upon which Mr. Melson relied, was not fully explained either in testimony or in defendant's expert reports. And based upon testimony provided by several witnesses, Mr. Launay's costs for acquiring the land that would be converted into wetlands appear to be unreasonably low. At the same time, it is notable that the mitigation figure employed by Mr. Moynihan exceeds the range established by Mr. Miller, who admitted, under cross examination, that he had previously determined that a reasonable range for mitigation expenses, including the cost of acquiring the land, was between $22,000 and $40,000 per acre. Moreover, at a later point in his redirect testimony, Mr. Miller candidly testified that a figure of $30,000 per acre would be a "reasonable" estimate of mitigation costs. [Footnote omitted.] That lower figure is also supported by a stipulation filed by the parties indicating that the cost of mitigation here would be reduced, inter alia, by using the fill

---

[30] Defendant argues that the denominator should be reduced further—and significantly—to reflect the fact that, even without the Federal wetlands regulations, plaintiffs would be prohibited, under Delaware law, from developing the approximately five acres of the Property that are state wetlands. In *Ciampetti v. United States*, 18 Cl.Ct. 548, 555-56 (1989), this court rejected a similar argument, finding that the interrelationship between Federal and State wetlands laws precluded the Federal government from essentially asserting the existence of the State wetlands regime as a *per se* defense to a Federal taking. In so concluding, this court reasoned that "[a]ssuming that no economically viable use remains for the property, the Constitution could not countenance a circumstance in which there was no fifth amendment remedy merely because two government entities acting jointly or severally caused a taking." *Id.* at 556. Although unnecessary to the decision reached below, this court believes that a similar rationale warrants rejection of defendant's argument in the instant case.

excavated from a mitigation site (where wetlands are being created) and placing it on the Property where fill is required for development. Accordingly, in the court's view, the evidence supports a finding that a reasonable cost of mitigation here would be $30,000 per acre, or $12,500 per acre less than the figure Mr. Moynihan employed in estimating the value of the 28-lot development.

Projecting a savings of $12,500 per acre, and relying on the other assumptions in Mr. Moynihan's report, the court concludes that his estimate for the 28-lot development should be increased by $52,800 (4.4 acres times a $12,500), yielding a final value for the 28-lot development of $597,000.

III. PROFIT

The comparative value of the Property before and after the regulatory imposition is not the sole indicia of the economic impact of the regulation. Rather, the Federal Circuit has indicated that, in assessing the severity of the economic impact of the regulations, "the owner's opportunity to recoup its investment or better, subject to the regulation, cannot be ignored," thereby requiring the court to compare "the relationship of the owner's basis or investment" in the property before the alleged taking to the fair market value of the property after the alleged taking. *Florida Rock Indus., Inc. v. United States*, 791 F.2d 893, 905 (Fed.Cir.1986), cert. denied, 479 U.S. 1053, 107 S.Ct. 926, 93 L.Ed.2d 978 (1987).

While the case law thus makes clear that profit or return of investment is a factor to be considered in assessing economic impact, there is considerably less direction on how to perform this analysis. Indeed, although both sides agree that such a calculation must be undertaken, how such an analysis should be done is in dispute. Several observations, however, seem appropriate. Certainly, in determining an owner's basis or investment in property, it appears reasonable and logical to include not only the initial purchase price, but also other capital expenditures that the owners may have incurred with respect to their property. At the same time, it would seem inappropriate to include in the basis or investment expenses that were deducted as current (and, therefore, non-capital) expenses on the owners' income tax returns. At the very least, in calculating the owners' investment in the property, such expenses should be discounted by the value of the tax savings they have already produced. Nor, in determining the plaintiffs' basis or investment in the Property, does it seem appropriate to adjust the plaintiffs' historical costs for inflation by using the Consumer Product Index (CPI). At least three reasons warrant this conclusion and require a few words of elaboration.

To begin with, an adjustment for inflation is not ordinarily included in calculating an "investment" in property, nor most certainly is it reflected in the "basis" employed by a taxpayer in calculating gain for income tax purposes. *See* 26 U.S.C. §§1001(a), 1011, 1016(a)(1) (basis equals cost adjusted by capital expenditures). There is not the slightest indication in the original *Florida Rock* opinion, supra, that the court intended to deviate from these common and traditional formulations of the concepts of "investment" or "basis." *See* also *Deltona*, 657 F.2d at 1192 (making this profit calculation without adjusting for inflation); *Ciampitti v. United States*, 22 Cl.Ct. at 320 (same). Second, factoring inflation into this economic analysis would only serve to obscure what should be its main focus: whether the application of the regulation, standing alone, prevents a reasonable return on a prior investment. Indexation necessarily blurs this distinction as it would incorporate into the calculation a measure of whether the profit realized on the hypothetical sale of the property exceeded a baseline expectation (*i.e.*, a return in excess of inflation) unrelated to the regulation. There is no assurance that any investment, let alone an investment in property, will increase in value in lock-step with inflation and, indeed, a host of reasons, wholly unrelated to regulation, why the value of a particular parcel might be less than the cash invested therein adjusted by inflation, among them the possibility that the amount initially invested in the property exceeded its true value (*i.e.*, the owner overpaid) and that capital expenditures made with respect to the property did not contribute value thereto on a dollar-for-dollar basis. Finally, as the prior discussion illustrates, indexing a property owner's investment or basis also would introduce a plethora of uncertainties and complexities into the calculation-which index, if any, of the CPI should be employed? Should the index employed include the relatively volatile food, medical and energy components? What of regional variations in inflation? [Footnote omitted.] For these and other reasons, the court concludes that plaintiffs' use of inflation adjustments in their computations suffer from what Justice Holmes, in another context, called "[t]he dangers of a delusive exactness." *Truax v. Corrigan*, 257 U.S. 312, 342, 42 S.Ct. 124, 66 L.Ed. 254 (1921) (dissenting opinion). *Cf. Florida Rock Indus., Inc. v. United States*, 45 Fed.Cl. 21, 38 (1999) (including an adjustment for CPI without explanation), judgment entered, 2000 WL 331830 (Fed.Cl. Mar. 28, 2000).

In the instant case, the parties have stipulated that, in addition to the $117,731 paid to purchase the Property, the partners, between 1971 and 1996, paid an additional $174,238 with respect to the Property, with $144,504 of that amount expended to cover maintenance of the property. Accordingly, plaintiffs' total cash outlay with respect to the property is $291,969. Because portions of these expenditures were currently deducted on the partners' income tax returns, the parties have stipulated that, for purposes of assessing profitability and return of investment, the appropriate tax basis in the Property is $169,701. [Footnote omitted.] Based on these figures, it appears that if the plaintiffs constructed the 28-lot proposal under the permit received from the Corps, they would realize $305,031 over their total cash outlays and $427,299 over their appropriate tax basis. [Footnote omitted.]

IV. REDUX

Based on the foregoing, the court finds that the values of the 77-lot and 28- lot developments are $1,485,000 and $597,000, respectively. Consequently, the court finds that the imposition of the wetlands regulations on the Property, thereby preventing its full use, resulted in a dimunition in value of approximately 59.8 percent. In addition, under this first prong of the *Penn Central* test, the court finds that plaintiffs would derive an economic profit of at least $305,000, or approximately twice their investment, were they to proceed with the proposed 28-lot development.

B. THE EXTENT TO WHICH THE REGULATION HAS INTERFERED WITH DISTINCT INVESTMENT-BACKED EXPECTATIONS

The second factor of the *Penn Central*—the interference with distinct investment-backed expectations—is a "way of limiting takings recoveries to owners who [can] demonstrate that they bought their property in reliance on a state of affairs that did not include the challenged regulatory regime." *Loveladies Harbor*, 28 F.3d at 1177. *See* also *Creppel*, 41 F.3d at 632 (the requirement of investment-backed expectations "limits recovery to owners who can demonstrate that they bought their property in reliance on the nonexistence of the challenged regulation.") This factor encompasses two related elements: first, the extent of the plaintiffs' investment in reliance on the regulatory scheme in place at the time of the purchase; and second, the extent to which the regulation of their property was foreseeable. *See, e.g., Ruckelshaus v. Monsanto Co.*, 467 U.S.

986, 1006, 1013, 104 S.Ct. 2862, 81 L.Ed.2d 815 (1984). These expectations must be reasonable—"[a] 'reasonable investment backed expectation' must be more than a 'unilateral expectation or an abstract need.'" *Ruckelshaus*, 467 U.S. at 1005-06, 104 S.Ct. 2862 (quoting *Webb'sFabulous Pharmacies v. Beckwith*, 449 U.S. 155, 161, 101 S.Ct. 446, 66 L.Ed.2d 358 (1980)). *See* also *Good*, 189 F.3d at 1360; Ciampitti, 22 Cl.Ct. at 320-22.

Individuals purchasing property who reasonably should have been aware of the existence or impending existence of a regulatory regime negatively impacting the value of the property are deemed to have assumed the economic risk associated with that regime. As noted by the Federal Circuit:

> In legal terms, the owner who bought with knowledge of the restraint could be said to have no reliance interest, or to have assumed the risk of any economic loss. In economic terms, it could be said that the market had already discounted for the restraint, so that a purchaser could not show a loss in his investment attributable to it.

Loveladies Harbor, 28 F.3d at 1177. In such a case, "the owner presumably paid a discounted price for the property," and "[c]ompensating him for a 'taking' would confer a windfall." *Creppel*, 41 F.3d at 632. Because the market can anticipate regulatory developments, it follows that reasonable expectations may extend beyond legal restrictions already in place and encompass the foreseeable creation of a new regulatory program or the expansion of an existing program. *See Good*, 189 F.3d at 1361 (focusing on the "regulatory climate" that existed at the time of the purchase). Regarding the expansion of preexisting regulatory regimes, the Supreme Court has noted that "'[t]hose who do business in [a] regulated field cannot object if the legislative scheme is buttressed by subsequent amendments to achieve the legislative end.'" *Concrete Pipe & Prods., Inc.*, 508 U.S. at 645, 113 S.Ct. 2264 (quoting *Federal Hous. Admin. v. Darlington, Inc.*, 358 U.S. 84, 91, 79 S.Ct. 141, 3 L.Ed.2d 132 (1958)). *See* also *Branch v. United States*, 69 F.3d 1571, 1579 (Fed.Cir.1995), cert. denied, 519 U.S. 810, 117 S.Ct. 55, 136 L.Ed.2d 18 (1996); *American Cont'l Corp. v. United States*, 22 Cl.Ct. 692, 697 (1991).

Here, plaintiffs argue that they invested in the Property with the expectation that they would be permitted to develop it fully. The court does not doubt this was plaintiffs' subjective intent—but to what extent was that intent reasonable under the circumstances? In this regard, it is significant that plaintiffs purchased the Property in 1971, before the passage not only of the state regulatory scheme in 1973, but also the Clean Water Act in 1972. *See* Federal Water Pollution Control Act, Pub.L. No. 92-500, 86 Stat. 816 (1972); Delaware Wetlands Act, Del.Code Ann. Tit. 7, §§6601, *et seq.* (1973). Moreover, even after the passage of the Clean Water Act, the Corps, at first, adopted a narrow definition of the "navigable waters" subject to the Act, essentially defining them as coextensive with the "navigable waters" subject to regulation under Section 10 of the Rivers and Harbors Act. *See* 39 Fed.Reg. 12,115, 12,119 (April 3, 1974). It was not until 1975, following a district court decision invalidating the earlier regulation and ordering the issuance of broader regulations, [footnote omitted] that the Corps finally issued an interim final regulation redefining "the waters of the United States" to include all freshwater wetlands that were located near navigable waters. *See* 40 Fed.Reg. 31,324 (July 25, 1975); 33 C.F.R. §209.120(d)(2)(h) (1976). And it was not until almost ten years later, in 1985, that the Supreme Court finally resolved that these more expansive regulations represented a valid and reasonable construction of the statute. *See United States v. Riverside Bayview Homes, Inc.*, 474 U.S. 121, 130-39, 106 S.Ct. 455, 88 L.Ed.2d 419 (1985). *See* also *Brace v. United States*, 48 Fed.Cl. 272, 277-78 (2000) (describing these events and subsequent regulatory developments in greater detail); Flint B. Ogle, T*he Ongoing Struggle*

Between Private Property Rights and Wetlands Regulation: Recent Developments and Proposed Solutions, 64 U. Colo. L.Rev. 573, 575-76 (1993).

One of the issues at trial was the extent to which these developments were foreseeable. Several witnesses testified that they were and that had plaintiffs, in 1971, consulted with an engineer or land use consultant they would have been apprised that their development plans for the Property would likely run into significant environmental and ecological hurdles. However, the court discounts this testimony to the extent that it assumes that plaintiffs should have foreseen not only the passage of the Clean Water Act itself, but also the regulatory developments that occurred from 1972 through 1977. Prior to 1975, the Corps employed a definition of wetlands that would not have covered all the portions of the Property that were eventually found to be wetlands under the regulations issued in 1975, as amended in 1977. It does not seem reasonable to impute to plaintiffs, at the time they purchased the Property in 1971, an interpretation of the Clean Water Act that the Corps itself initially eschewed and did not adopt until at least 1975 (and arguably 1977). While the *Penn Central* analysis anticipates reasonably foreseeable developments, it does not require a property owner to be clairvoyant. Indeed, in *Deltona*, *supra*, the Court of Claims found that the regulatory developments described above had upset the plaintiff's reasonable investment-backed expectations, noting that the regulatory regime had been "radically transformed" and had worked "an unforeseen change in the law." 657 F.2d at 1191.

This is not to say, however, that plaintiffs' reasonable investment-backed expectations extend to all the wetlands in question. In particular, the evidence shows that plaintiffs should have known, in 1971, that the portions of the Property interlaced with the drainage ditches and otherwise below the mean high water mark were subject to the regulatory requirements imposed under the Rivers and Harbors Act of 1899. While prior to 1968, the Rivers and Harbors Act was administered solely to protect navigability, in 1968, its regulatory criteria and coverage were expanded to consider the public interest, including pollution and ecology concerns. *See* 33 Fed.Reg. 18,670 (Dec. 18, 1968) (codified at 33 C.F.R. §209). By 1970, this regulatory expansion had survived judicial challenge and the Corps' authority to limit dredging and filling based solely on ecological concerns had become accepted. *See, e.g., Zabel v. Tabb*, 430 F.2d 199 (5th Cir.1970), cert. denied, 401 U.S. 910, 91 S.Ct. 873, 27 L.Ed.2d 808 (1971). Several cases have noted these events in concluding that reasonable investors in the late 1960s had to factor in the potential impact of these regulations on their investment. *See Good*, 189 F.3d at 1362; *Deltona Corp.*, 657 F.2d at 1187 ("[O]n December 18, 1968, in response to a growing national concern for environmental values and related federal legislation, the Corps [announced that it] would consider the following additional factors in reviewing permit applications: fish and wildlife, conservation, pollution, aesthetics, ecology, and the general public interest."). *See* also *Marks v. United States*, 34 Fed.Cl. 387 (1995), aff'd without op., 116 F.3d 1496 (Fed.Cir.1997), cert. denied, 522 U.S. 1075, 118 S.Ct. 852, 139 L.Ed.2d 753 (1998) (taking rejected where land subject to navigational servitude).

Approaching thus the second prong of the *Penn Central* analysis, the court finds that, in 1971, when the Property was acquired, plaintiffs had a reasonable investment-backed expectation to develop some of the wetlands unhindered by wetlands regulations, but did not have such a reasonable expectation as to the lower-lying portions of the Property subject to the Rivers and Harbors Act. *See Dodd v. Hood River County*, 136 F.3d 1219, 1230 (9th Cir.1998), cert. denied, mot. granted, 525 U.S. 923, 119 S.Ct. 278, 142 L.Ed.2d 229 (1998) (holding that plaintiffs' investment-backed expectations to build their home in a Forest Use Zone were unreasonable since the regulations were in effect when plaintiff's purchased the property). As will be discussed in greater detail below, this finding is significant, for while the permit issued by the Corps in 1996 does not allow for the development of these lower-lying portions of the Property, *i.e.*, the land that was and is subject to the Rivers and Harbors Act, it does permit development of the other wetlands on the Property, *i.e.*, the wetlands that eventually became subject to the Clean Water Act.

C. THE CHARACTER OF THE GOVERNMENTAL ACTION

The last criterion—the character of the government action-requires the court to consider the purpose and importance of the public interest underlying the regulatory imposition, focusing, in particular, on whether the challenged restraint would constitute a nuisance under state law. In analyzing this criteria, "courts must inquire into the degree of harm created by the claimant's prohibited activity, its social value and location, and the ease with which any harm stemming from it could be prevented." *Creppel*, 41 F.3d at 631. *See* also *Forest Props., Inc.*, 177 F.3d at 1366; *Loveladies Harbor*, 28 F.3d at 1179. "[W]hile most burdens consequent upon government action undertaken in the public interest must be borne by individual landowners as concomitants of the advantage of living and doing business in a civilized community," the Supreme Court has stated, "some are so substantial and unforeseeable, and can so easily be identified and redistributed, that justice and fairness require that they be borne by the public as a whole." *Kirby Forest Indus., Inc. v. United States*, 467 U.S. 1, 14, 104 S.Ct. 2187, 81 L.Ed.2d 1 (1984). Burnishing this concept, the Supreme Court, in Eastern Enterprises, suggested that in considering whether, under this factor, a regulation "implicates [the] fundamental principles of fairness underlying the Takings Clause," two other indicia are relevant: (i) the extent to which the action is retroactive; and (ii) whether the action targets a particular individual. *Eastern Enterprises*, 524 U.S. at 537, 118 S.Ct. 2131.

There is no significant evidence in this case that the plaintiffs' proposed use of the Property would formally constitute a nuisance under Delaware state law, so that the application of the Federal wetland regulations could be viewed as enforcing a limitation already inherent in the Property. *See Creppel*, 41 F.3d at 631. *See* also *M & J Coal Co. v. United States*, 47 F.3d 1148, 1153 (Fed.Cir.1995), cert. denied, 516 U.S. 808, 116 S.Ct. 53, 133 L.Ed.2d 18 (1995). At the same time, the existence of the wetland regulations in question, as well as their application to the Property, indisputably serve an important public purpose—one which benefits plaintiffs as members of the public at large. *See, e.g., United States v. Riverside Bayview Homes, Inc.*, 474 U.S. at 131-35, 106 S.Ct. 455; *Brace*, 48 Fed.Cl. at 278-79. And, it is equally true here as it was in an earlier Federal Circuit case that "[t]he importance of preserving the environment, the authority of state and federal governments to protect and preserve ecologically significant areas ... through appropriate regulatory mechanisms is not here being questioned." *Loveladies Harbor*, 28 F.3d at 1175. Yet, it is also beyond peradventure that plaintiffs here are disproportionately burdened by those policies—a fact evident to anyone who observes that the Property is surrounded on all four sides by extensive developments that apparently were approved under prior regulatory regimes.

Considering the factors more recently identified in *Eastern Enterprises, supra*, the degree of retroactivity here is not extraordinary—even assuming arguendo that plaintiffs could not have reasonably anticipated the passage of the Clean Water Act (or the promulgation of the regulations thereunder) when they purchased the Property, it remains that portions of the Property were already subject to regulation under the Rivers and Harbors Act and that the Clean Water Act passed approximately a year after the parcels were acquired. Further, the Clean Water Act and the wetlands regulations issued thereunder are generally applicable to all similarly situated property owners and can in no way be viewed as being directed at plaintiffs. Accordingly, while the absence of a nuisance certainly cuts in favor of a finding of a taking, other circumstances in this case ameliorate somewhat the impact of the third *Penn Central* factor in this regard.

D. WEIGHING THE THREE FACTORS

Summarizing the results of its analysis, the court concludes as follows:

Economic Impact. First, under the economic analysis prong, the court finds that the imposition of the wetlands regulations here diminished the value of plaintiffs' property by approximately 59.7 percent. Such a diminishment certainly does not constitute a categorical taking under *Lucas, supra*, where the Supreme Court held that a dimunition of 93.7 percent did not constitute such a taking. While the Court in *Lucas* suggested that such a dimunition might also not be indicative of a regulatory taking under the economic analysis factor under *Penn Central*, it refrained from drawing a bright line. Indeed, while courts have often struggled with the dichotomy between compensable "partial takings" and noncompensable "mere dimunitions," searching for a bright line beyond which dimunition would be indicative of a taking, several Supreme Court decisions suggest that dimunitions in value approaching 85 to 90 percent do not necessarily dictate the existence of a taking. *See Euclid v. Ambler Realty Co.*, 272 U.S. 365, 47 S.Ct. 114, 71 L.Ed. 303 (1926) (no taking despite 75 percent dimunition); *Hadacheck v. Sebastian*, 239 U.S. 394, 36 S.Ct. 143, 60 L.Ed. 348 (1915) (no taking despite 87.5 percent dimunition). With one possible exception, this court has likewise relied on dimunitions well in excess of 85 percent before finding a regulatory taking. *See Loveladies Harbor*, 21 Cl.Ct. 153, 160 (1990) (taking—99 percent), aff'd, 28 F.3d 1171 (Fed.Cir.1994); *Bowles*, 31 Fed.Cl. at 48-49 (taking—92 to 100 percent); *Formanek*, 26 Cl.Ct. 332, 340 (1992) (taking—88 percent). *See* also 1902 *Atl. Ltd. v. United States*, 26 Cl.Ct. 575, 579 (1992) (88 percent loss satisfies "economic impact" factor, although no taking found). [Footnote omitted.] Conversely, both the Supreme Court and the Federal Circuit have held that a percentage of value loss comparable to that found here is not indicative of a taking. *See Concrete Pipe*, 508 U.S. at 645, 113 S.Ct. 2264 (no taking—46 percent dimunition); *Jentgen*, 657 F.2d at 1213 (no taking—50 percent dimunition). *See* also *Ciampitti*, 22 Cl.Ct. at 320 (no taking—25 percent dimunition). *See* generally David F. Coursen, *The Takings Jurisprudence of the Court of Federal Claims and the Federal Circuit*, 29 Envtl. L. 821, 848-51 (1999) (discussing these and other cases).

While this court is no better postured than others to set a bright line dividing compensable from noncompensable exercises of government regulatory power, in the court's view, it stretches the concept of partial taking too far to say that a dimunition on the order of 60 percent or less has the effect of a taking. [Footnote omitted.] As was recognized by the Supreme Court in another case involving a wetland permit, "[o]nly when a permit is denied and the effect of the denial is to prevent 'economically viable' use of the land in question can it be said that a taking has occurred." *United States v. Riverside Bayview Homes, Inc.*, 474 U.S. at 127, 106 S.Ct. 455. Such is not the case here, particularly as plaintiffs stand to realize a significant profit if they develop the Property consistent with the permit they have received from the Corps. The fact that this profit is less than what plaintiffs would have realized in an entirely unregulated universe is not determinative, as the Supreme Court has also made amply clear that frustration of the most profitable or highest and best use of property by the government is not necessarily indicative of a taking. *Penn Central*, 438 U.S. at 130-31, 98 S.Ct. 2646. *See* also *Andrus*, 444 U.S. at 66, 100 S.Ct. 318;

United States v. Central Eureka Mining Co., 357 U.S. 155, 168, 78 S.Ct. 1097, 2 L.Ed.2d 1228 (1958); *Florida Rock Industries*, 791 F.2d at 902.

Reasonable Investment-Backed Expectations. Second, the court finds that while plaintiffs had a reasonable investment-backed expectation that they could develop the portion of the Property that became Federal wetlands under the regulations promulgated under the Clean Water Act, no such expectation existed as to the lower-lying portions of the Property which, at the time of their purchase by plaintiffs, were already subject to regulation under the 1899 Rivers and Harbors Act. Moreover, because the permit granted by the Corps allows for development of 2.2 acres of the wetlands that became subject to regulation under the Clean Water Act, the court finds that plaintiffs' reasonable investment-backed expectations as to that portion of the Property have been accommodated to a not insignificant degree.

Character of the Government Action. Third, and finally, although there is a bit of evidence to the contrary, the court finds that development of the Property would not constitute a nuisance under state law, tending to support the conclusion that a taking occurred here. The impact of this factor, however, is ameliorated by the fact that the imposition of the wetlands regulations here was not entirely retroactive or, in the case of the Clean Water Act, at least not severely retroactive, and was not targeted on the plaintiffs.

III. CONCLUSION

On this record, the court concludes that the application of the wetlands regulations has not effected a taking of plaintiffs' property. Rather, guided by the three-tiered *Penn Central* analysis, the court finds that the limitations associated with the permit granted by the Corps result only in a noncompensable dimunition in the value of plaintiffs' property and allow plaintiffs to realize to a not insignificant degree their true reasonable investment-backed expectations.[39] As such, the Clerk is directed to enter judgment dismissing the complaint. No costs.

It is SO ORDERED.

[Appendix omitted.]

Many significant issues remain unresolved in federal Takings jurisprudence, the "denominator" issue being just one. What does it mean to consider the property "as a whole?" Another unresolved issue is the date of acquisition as it relates to the owner's "investment-backed expecta-

[39] In denying the government's petition for rehearing in *Palm Beach*, the Federal Circuit suggested that the trial court, in analyzing whether a taking had occurred, might draw a distinction between the 49.3 acres of submerged land involved in that case and the 1.4 acres of other wetlands on the grounds that the submerged land was more likely to be subject to a navigational servitude defense under the Rivers and Harbors Act. 231 F.3d at 1364. The court remanded this matter to the trial court to determine, ultimately, whether there was a taking of the 1.4 acres. *Id.* In the instant case, dividing the Property into two parcels—that is, those wetlands subject to the Rivers and Harbors Act and those not—clearly would result in a ruling that neither portion was taken. Thus, if this court were to focus first on the portion of the Property subject to the Rivers and Harbors Act, it would conclude that there was no taking based upon plaintiffs' lack of reasonable investment-backed expectations. If the court then were to focus on the portion of the Property not subject to the Rivers and Harbors Act, it would conclude that, because the Corps' permit allows for partial development of that property, the dimunition in the value of that parcel, occasioned by the imposition of the wetlands regulations, would be significantly less than the 59.7 percent dimunition occasioned by the imposition of such regulations on the entire Property. As such, the court would conclude that this second parcel was also not taken by the imposition of the wetlands regulations.

tions." Mr. Walcek's property happened to abut on a shoreline area which would have been subject to regulation as far back as 1899. That case does not answer the issue of investment-backed expectations if the property had not been on a shoreline.

If one were to glean some sense from the foregoing cases it is that there is a pendulum swinging from following the analytic process in *Pennsylvania Coal*, away, and back again. *Lucas* was a swing away; it has been rendered nearly useless after the "swing back" in *Palazzolo*. Probably the truest statement one can make about regulatory takings is that they will be considered on an *ad hoc* basis.

Index of Selected Citations

D

E

L

M

N

O

P

Q

R

T

U

V

W

Y

Government Institutes Mini-Catalog

PC #	ENVIRONMENTAL TITLES	Pub Date	Price*
949	ABCs of Environmental Regulation, Second Edition	2002	$79
812	Achieving Environmental Excellence	2003	$79
898	Book of Lists for Regulated Hazardous Substances, Tenth Edition	2001	$99
846	Clean Water Handbook, Third Edition	2003	$125
822	Environmental Compliance Auditing & Management Systems (ECAMS)	2001	$1,395
897	EH&S CFR Training Requirements, Fifth Edition	2001	$125
4300	EH&S Daily Federal Register Notification Service (e-mail)	2003	$150
890	Environmental Biotreatment: Technologies for Air, Water, Soil, and Wastes	2002	$149
4045	Environmental, Health & Safety CFRs on CD-ROM, single issue	2003	$450
825	Environmental, Health and Safety Audits, 8th Edition	2001	$115
4900	Environmental Law Expert, CD-ROM	2003	$695
955	Environmental Law Handbook, Seventeenth Edition	2003	$99
688	Environmental Health & Safety Dictionary, Seventh Edition	2000	$95
956	Environmental Statutes, 2003 Edition	2003	$125
957	Fundamentals of Environmental Sampling	2003	$79
689	Fundamentals of Site Remediation	2000	$85
907	Hazardous Materials Transportation Training, Student's Manual	2002	$89
958	Information Technology Solutions for EH&S Professionals	2003	$115
823	Integrating Environmental, Health, and Safety Systems	2001	$495
588	International Environmental Auditing	1998	$179
819	ISO 14001: Positioning Your Organization for Environmental Success	2001	$115
936	Managing Your Hazardous Wastes	2002	$89
830	RCRA CFRs Made Easy	2002	$115
841	Risk Management Planning Handbook, Second Edition	2002	$115
816	Stormwater Discharge Management	2003	$89
946	Wastewater and Biosolids Treatment Technologies	2002	$129

PC #	SAFETY and HEALTH TITLES	Pub Date	Price*
697	Applied Statistics in Occupational Safety and Health	2000	$105
893	Beyond Safety Accountability	2001	$79
894	Building Successful Safety Teams	2001	$79
843	Emergency Preparedness for Facilities	2003	$125
904	Ergonomics: A Risk Manager's Guide	2002	$159
949	Excavation Safety	2003	$85
663	Forklift Safety, Second Edition	1999	$85
814	Fundamentals of Occupational Safety & Health, Third Edition	2003	$79
818	Job Hazard Analysis	2001	$79
888	Keys to Behavior Based Safety	2001	$85
662	Machine Guarding Handbook	1999	$75
838	Managing Chemical Safety	2002	$95
889	Managing Electrical Safety	2001	$69
4800	OSHA Compliance Master CD-ROM	2003	$375
668	Safety Made Easy, Second Edition	1999	$75
947	Safety Metrics	2003	$85
815	So, You're the Safety Director, Third Edition	2003	$89

Government Institutes Order Form

4 Research Place, Suite 200 • Rockville, MD 20850-3226
Tel (301) 921-2323 • Fax (301) 921-0264
Internet: http://www.govinst.com • E-mail: giinfo@govinst.com

4 EASY WAYS TO ORDER

1. Tel: **(301) 921-2323**
Have your credit card ready when you call.

2. Fax: **(301) 921-0264**
Fax this completed order form with your company purchase order or credit card information.

3. Mail: **Government Institutes Division**
ABS Group Inc.
P.O. Box 846304
Dallas, TX 75284-6304 USA
Mail this completed order form with a check, company purchase order, or credit card information.

4. Online: **Visit http://www.govinst.com**

PAYMENT OPTIONS

❏ **Check** *(payable in US dollars to **ABS Group Inc. Government Institutes Division**)*

❏ **Purchase Order** *(This order form must be attached to your company P.O. Note: All International orders must be prepaid.)*

❏ **Credit Card** ❏ VISA ❏ MasterCard ❏ American Express

Exp. ___ /___

Credit Card No. ______________________

Signature ______________________

(Government Institutes' Federal I.D.# is 13-2695912)

CUSTOMER INFORMATION

Ship To: (Please attach your purchase order)

Name ______________________
GI Account # *(7 digits on mailing label)* ______________________
Company/Institution ______________________
Address ______________________
(Please supply street address for UPS shipping)
____
City __________ State/Province __________
Zip/Postal Code __________ Country __________
Tel ( ) ______________________
Fax ( ) ______________________
E-mail Address ______________________

Bill To: (if different from ship-to address)

Name ______________________
Title/Position ______________________
Company/Institution ______________________
Address ______________________
(Please supply street address for UPS shipping)
____
City __________ State/Province __________
Zip/Postal Code __________ Country __________
Tel ( ) ______________________
Fax ( ) ______________________
E-mail Address ______________________

Qty.	Product Code	Title	Price

Subtotal __________
MD Residents add 5% Sales Tax __________
Shipping and Handling (see box below) __________
Total Payment Enclosed __________

30 DAY MONEY-BACK GUARANTEE

If you're not completely satisfied with any product, return it undamaged within 30 days for a full and immediate refund on the price of the product.

SOURCE CODE: BP03

Shipping and Handling

Within U.S:
1-4 products: $6/product
5 or more: $4/product
Outside U.S:
Add $15 for each item (Global)

Sales Tax

Maryland 5%
Texas 8.25%
Virginia 4.5%

ISBN 0-86587-968-0